Professional Linux® Ke

Professional
Linux® Kernel Architecture

Wolfgang Mauerer

WILEY

Wiley Publishing, Inc.

Professional Linux® Kernel Architecture

Published by
Wiley Publishing, Inc.
10475 Crosspoint Boulevard
Indianapolis, IN 46256
www.wiley.com

Copyright © 2008 by Wolfgang Mauerer
Published by Wiley Publishing, Inc., Indianapolis, Indiana
Published simultaneously in Canada

ISBN: 978-0-470-34343-2

Manufactured in the United States of America

10 9 8 7 6 5 4 3 2 1

Library of Congress Cataloging-in-Publication Data:

Mauerer, Wolfgang, 1978-
 Professional Linux kernel architecture / Wolfgang Mauerer.
   p. cm.
 Includes index.
 ISBN 978-0-470-34343-2 (pbk.)
 1. Linux. 2. Computer architecture. 3. Application software. I. Title.
 QA76.9.A73M38 2008
 005.4'32--dc22
                        2008028067

About the Author

Wolfgang Mauerer is a quantum physicist whose professional interests are centered around quantum cryptography, quantum electrodynamics, and compilers for — you guessed it — quantum architectures. With the confirmed capacity of being the worst experimentalist in the known universe, he sticks to the theoretical side of his profession, which is especially reassuring considering his constant fear of accidentally destroying the universe. Outside his research work, he is fascinated by operating systems, and for more than a decade — starting with an article series about the kernel in 1997 — he has found great pleasure in documenting and explaining Linux kernel internals. He is also the author of a book about typesetting with LaTeX and has written numerous articles that have been translated into seven languages in total.

When he's not submerged in vast Hilbert spaces or large quantities of source code, he tries to take the opposite direction, namely, upward — be this with model planes, a paraglider, or on foot with an ice axe in his hands: Mountains especially have the power to outrival even the Linux kernel. Consequently, he considers planning and accomplishing a first-ascent expedition to the vast arctic glaciers of east Greenland to be the really unique achievement in his life.

Being interested in everything that is fundamental, he is also the author of the first compiler for Plankalkül, the world's earliest high-level language devised in 1942–1946 by Konrad Zuse, the father of the computer. As an avid reader, he is proud that despite the two-digit number of computers present in his living room, the volume required for books still occupies a larger share.

Credits

Executive Editor
Carol Long

Senior Development Editor
Tom Dinse

Production Editor
Debra Banninger

Copy Editors
Cate Caffrey
Kathryn Duggan

Editorial Manager
Mary Beth Wakefield

Production Manager
Tim Tate

Vice President and Executive Group Publisher
Richard Swadley

Vice President and Executive Publisher
Joseph B. Wikert

Project Coordinator, Cover
Lynsey Stanford

Proofreader
Publication Services, Inc.

Indexer
Jack Lewis

Acknowledgments

First and foremost, I have to thank the thousands of programmers who have created the Linux kernel over the years — most of them commercially based, but some also just for their own private or academic joy. Without them, there would be no kernel, and I would have had nothing to write about. Please accept my apologies that I cannot list all several hundred names here, but in true UNIX style, you can easily generate the list by:

```
for file in $ALL_FILES_COVERED_IN_THIS_BOOK; do

        git log --pretty="format:%an" $file; done |

sort -u -k 2,2
```

It goes without saying that I admire your work very much — you are all the true heroes in this story!

What you are reading right now is the result of an evolution over more than seven years: After two years of writing, the first edition was published in German by Carl Hanser Verlag in 2003. It then described kernel 2.6.0. The text was used as a basis for the low-level design documentation for the EAL4+ security evaluation of Red Hat Enterprise Linux 5, requiring to update it to kernel 2.6.18 (if the EAL acronym does not mean anything to you, then Wikipedia is once more your friend). Hewlett-Packard sponsored the translation into English and has, thankfully, granted the rights to publish the result. Updates to kernel 2.6.24 were then performed specifically for this book.

Several people were involved in this evolution, and my appreciation goes to all of them: Leslie Mackay-Poulton, with support from David Jacobs, did a tremendous job at translating a huge pile of text into English. I'm also indebted to Sal La Pietra of atsec information security for pulling the strings to get the translation project rolling, and especially to Stephan Müller for close cooperation during the evaluation. My cordial thanks also go to all other HP and Red Hat people involved in this evaluation, and also to Claudio Kopper and Hans Löhr for our very enjoyable cooperation during this project. Many thanks also go to the people at Wiley — both visible and invisible to me — who helped to shape the book into its current form.

The German edition was well received by readers and reviewers, but nevertheless comments about inaccuracies and suggestions for improvements were provided. I'm glad for all of them, and would also like to mention the instructors who answered the publisher's survey for the original edition. Some of their suggestions were very valuable for improving the current publication. The same goes for the referees for this edition, especially to Dr. Xiaodong Zhang for providing numerous suggestions for Appendix F.4.

Furthermore, I express my gratitude to Dr. Christine Silberhorn for granting me the opportunity to suspend my regular research work at the Max Planck Research Group for four weeks to work on this project. I hope you enjoyed the peace during this time when nobody was trying to install Linux on your MacBook!

As with every book, I owe my deepest gratitude to my family for supporting me in every aspect of life — I more than appreciate this indispensable aid. Finally, I have to thank Hariet Fabritius for infinite

Acknowledgments

patience with an author whose work cycle not only perfectly matched the most alarming forms of sleep dyssomnias, but who was always right on the brink of confusing his native tongue with "C," and whom she consequently had to rescue from numerous situations where he seemingly had lost his mind (see below...). Now that I have more free time again, I'm not only looking forward to our well-deserved holiday, but can finally embark upon the project of giving your laptop all joys of a proper operating system! (Writing these acknowledgments, I all of a sudden realize why people always hasten to lock away their laptops when they see me approaching....)

Contents

Contents

Contents

Contents

Contents

Contents

Contents

Contents

Introduction

UNIX is simple and coherent, but it takes a genius
(or at any rate a programmer) to understand
and appreciate the simplicity.
— *Dennis Ritchie*

Note from the authors: Yes, we have lost our minds.
Be forewarned: You will lose yours too.
— *Benny Goodheart & James Cox*

UNIX is distinguished by a simple, coherent, and elegant design — truly remarkable features that have enabled the system to influence the world for more than a quarter of a century. And especially thanks to the growing presence of Linux, the idea is still picking up momentum, with no end of the growth in sight.

UNIX and Linux carry a certain fascination, and the two quotations above hopefully capture the spirit of this attraction. Consider Dennis Ritchie's quote: Is the coinventor of UNIX at Bell Labs completely right in saying that only a genius can appreciate the simplicity of UNIX? Luckily not, because he puts himself into perspective immediately by adding that programmers also qualify to value the essence of UNIX.

Understanding the meagerly documented, demanding, and complex sources of UNIX as well as of Linux is not always an easy task. But once one has started to experience the rich insights that can be gained from the kernel sources, it is hard to escape the fascination of Linux. It seems fair to warn you that it's easy to get addicted to the joy of the operating system kernel once starting to dive into it. This was already noted by Benny Goodheart and James Cox, whose preface to their book *The Magic Garden Explained* (second quotation above) explained the internals of UNIX System V. And Linux is definitely also capable of helping you to lose your mind!

This book acts as a guide and companion that takes you through the kernel sources and sharpens your awareness of the beauty, elegance, and — last but not least — esthetics of their concepts. There are, however, some prerequisites to foster an understanding of the kernel. C should not just be a letter; neither should it be a foreign language. *Operating systems* are supposed to be more than just a "Start" button, and a small amount of algorithmics can also do no harm. Finally, it is preferable if *computer architecture* is not just about how to build the most fancy case. From an academic point of view, this comes closest to the lectures "Systems Programming," "Algorithmics," and "Fundamentals of Operating Systems." The previous edition of this book has been used to teach the fundamentals of Linux to advanced undergraduate students in several universities, and I hope that the current edition will serve the same purpose.

Discussing all aforementioned topics in detail is outside the scope of this book, and when you consider the mass of paper you are holding in your hands right now (or maybe you are not holding it, for this very reason), you'll surely agree that this would not be a good idea. When a topic not directly related to the kernel, but required to understand what the kernel does, is encountered in this book, I will briefly introduce you to it. To gain a more thorough understanding, however, consult the books on computing fundamentals that I recommend. Naturally, there is a large selection of texts, but some books that I found particularly insightful and illuminating include *C Programming Language*, by Brian W. Kernighan and Denis M. Ritchie [KR88]; *Modern Operating Systems*, by Andrew S. Tanenbaum [Tan07] on the basics of operating systems in general; *Operating Systems: Design and Implementation*, by Andrew S. Tanenbaum and Albert S. Woodhull [TW06] on UNIX (Minix) in particular; *Advanced Programming in the Unix Environment*, by W. Richard Stevens and Stephen A. Rago [SR05] on userspace programming; and the two volumes *Computer Architecture* and *Computer Organization and Design*, on the foundations of computer architecture by John L. Hennessy and David A. Patterson [HP06, PH07]. All have established themselves as classics in the literature.

Additionally, Appendix C contains some information about extensions of the GNU C compiler that are used by the kernel, but do not necessarily find widespread use in general programming.

When the first edition of this book was written, a schedule for kernel releases was more or less nonexistent. This has changed drastically during the development of kernel 2.6, and as I discuss in Appendix F, kernel developers have become pretty good at issuing new releases at periodic, predictable intervals. I have focused on kernel 2.6.24, but have also included some references to 2.6.25 and 2.6.26, which were released after this book was written but before all technical publishing steps had been completed. Since a number of comprehensive changes to the whole kernel have been merged into 2.6.24, picking this release as the target seems a good choice. While a detail here or there will have changed in more recent kernel versions as compared to the code discussed in this book, the big picture will remain the same for quite some time.

In the discussion of the various components and subsystems of the kernel, I have tried to avoid overloading the text with unimportant details. Likewise, I have tried not to lose track of the connection with source code. It is a very fortunate situation that, thanks to Linux, we are able to inspect the source of a real, working, production operating system, and it would be sad to neglect this essential aspect of the kernel. To keep the book's volume below the space of a whole bookshelf, I have selected only the most crucial parts of the sources. Appendix F introduces some techniques that ease reading of and working with the real source, an indispensable step toward understanding the structure and implementation of the Linux kernel.

One particularly interesting observation about Linux (and UNIX in general) is that it is well suited to evoke emotions. Flame wars on the Internet and heated technical debates about operating systems may be one thing, but for which other operating system does there exist a handbook (*The Unix-Haters Handbook*, edited by Simson Garfinkel et al. [GWS94]) on how best to hate it? When I wrote the preface to the first edition, I noted that it is not a bad sign for the future that a certain international software company responds to Linux with a mixture of abstruse accusations and polemics. Five years later, the situation has improved, and the aforementioned vendor has more or less officially accepted the fact that Linux has become a serious competitor in the operating system world. And things are certainly going to improve even more during the next five years. . . .

Naturally (and not astonishingly), I admit that I am definitely fascinated by Linux (and, sometimes, am also sure that I have lost my mind because of this), and if this book helps to carry this excitement to the reader, the long hours (and especially nights) spent writing it were worth every minute!

Suggestions for improvements and constrictive critique can be passed to wm@linux-kernel.net, or via www.wrox.com. Naturally, I'm also happy if you tell me that you liked the book!

What This Book Covers

This book discusses the concepts, structure, and implementation of the Linux kernel. In particular, the individual chapters cover the following topics:

- ❏ **Chapter 1** provides an overview of the Linux kernel and describes the big picture that is investigated more closely in the following chapters.

- ❏ **Chapter 2** talks about the basics of multitasking, scheduling, and process management, and investigates how these fundamental techniques and abstractions are implemented.

- ❏ **Chapter 3** discusses how physical memory is managed. Both the interaction with hardware and the in-kernel distribution of RAM via the buddy system and the slab allocator are covered.

- ❏ **Chapter 4** proceeds to describe how userland processes experience virtual memory, and the comprehensive data structures and actions required from the kernel to implement this view.

- ❏ **Chapter 5** introduces the mechanisms required to ensure proper operation of the kernel on multiprocessor systems. Additionally, it covers the related question of how processes can communicate with each other.

- ❏ **Chapter 6** walks you through the means for writing device drivers that are required to add support for new hardware to the kernel.

- ❏ **Chapter 7** explains how modules allow for dynamically adding new functionality to the kernel.

- ❏ **Chapter 8** discusses the virtual filesystem, a generic layer of the kernel that allows for supporting a wide range of different filesystems, both physical and virtual.

- ❏ **Chapter 9** describes the extended filesystem family, that is, the Ext2 and Ext3 filesystems that are the standard workhorses of many Linux installations.

- ❏ **Chapter 10** goes on to discuss procfs and sysfs, two filesystems that are not designed to store information, but to present meta-information about the kernel to userland. Additionally, a number of means to ease writing filesystems are presented.

- ❏ **Chapter 11** shows how extended attributes and access control lists that can help to improve system security are implemented.

- ❏ **Chapter 12** discusses the networking implementation of the kernel, with a specific focus on IPv4, TCP, UDP, and netfilter.

- ❏ **Chapter 13** introduces how systems calls that are the standard way to request a kernel action from userland are implemented.

- ❏ **Chapter 14** analyzes how kernel activities are triggered with interrupts, and presents means of deferring work to a later point in time.

- ❏ **Chapter 15** shows how the kernel handles all time-related requirements, both with low and high resolution.

- ❏ **Chapter 16** talks about speeding up kernel operations with the help of the page and buffer caches.

- ❏ **Chapter 17** discusses how cached data in memory are synchronized with their sources on persistent storage devices.

- ❏ **Chapter 18** introduces how page reclaim and swapping work.

Introduction

- **Chapter 19** gives an introduction to the audit implementation, which allows for observing in detail what the kernel is doing.
- **Appendix A** discusses peculiarities of various architectures supported by the kernel.
- **Appendix B** walks through various tools and means of working efficiently with the kernel sources.
- **Appendix C** provides some technical notes about the programming language C, and also discusses how the GNU C compiler is structured.
- **Appendix D** describes how the kernel is booted.
- **Appendix E** gives an introduction to the ELF binary format.
- **Appendix F** discusses numerous social aspects of kernel development and the Linux kernel community.

Introduction and Overview

Operating systems are not only regarded as a fascinating part of information technology, but are also the subject of controversial discussion among a wide public.[1] Linux has played a major role in this development. Whereas just 10 years ago a strict distinction was made between relatively simple academic systems available in source code and commercial variants with varying performance capabilities whose sources were a well-guarded secret, nowadays anybody can download the sources of Linux (or of any other free systems) from the Internet in order to study them.

Linux is now installed on millions of systems and is used by home users and professionals alike for a wide range of tasks. From miniature embedded systems in wristwatches to massively parallel mainframes, there are countless ways of exploiting Linux productively. And this makes the sources so interesting. A sound, well-established concept (UNIX) melded with powerful innovations and a strong penchant for dealing with problems that do not arise in academic teaching systems — this is what makes Linux so fascinating.

This book describes the central functions of the kernel, explains its underlying structures, and examines its implementation. Because complex subjects are discussed, I assume that the reader already has some experience in operating systems and systems programming in C (it goes without saying that I assume some familiarity with *using* Linux systems). I touch briefly on several general concepts relevant to common operating system problems, but my prime focus is on the implementation of the Linux kernel. Readers unfamiliar with a particular topic will find explanations on relevant basics in one of the many general texts on operating systems; for example, in Tanenbaum's outstanding

---

[1] It is *not* the intention of this book to participate in ideological discussions such as whether Linux can be regarded as a full operating system, although it is, in fact, just a kernel that cannot function productively without relying on other components. When I speak of Linux as an operating system without explicitly mentioning the acronyms of similar projects (primarily the GNU project, which despite strong initial resistance regarding the kernel reacts extremely sensitively when *Linux* is used instead of *GNU/Linux*), this should not be taken to mean that I do not appreciate the importance of the work done by this project. Our reasons are simple and pragmatic. Where do we draw the line when citing those involved without generating such lengthy constructs as *GNU/IBM/RedHat/HP/KDE/Linux*? If this footnote makes little sense, refer to `www.gnu.org/gnu/linux-and-gnu.html`, where you will find a summary of the positions of the GNU project.
After all ideological questions have been settled, I promise to refrain from using half-page footnotes in the rest of this book.

introductions ([TW06] and [Tan07]). A solid foundation of C programming is required. Because the kernel makes use of many advanced techniques of C and, above all, of many special features of the GNU C compiler, Appendix C discusses the finer points of C with which even good programmers may not be familiar. A basic knowledge of computer structures will be useful as Linux necessarily interacts very directly with system hardware — particularly with the CPU. There are also a large number of introductory works dealing with this subject; some are listed in the reference section. When I deal with CPUs in greater depth (in most cases I take the IA-32 or AMD64 architecture as an example because Linux is used predominantly on these system architectures), I explain the relevant hardware details. When I discuss mechanisms that are not ubiquitous in daily live, I will explain the general concept behind them, but expect that readers will also consult the quoted manual pages for more advice on how a particular feature is used from userspace.

The present chapter is designed to provide an overview of the various areas of the kernel and to illustrate their fundamental relationships before moving on to lengthier descriptions of the subsystems in the following chapters.

Since the kernel evolves quickly, one question that naturally comes to mind is which version is covered in this book. I have chosen kernel 2.6.24, which was released at the end of January 2008. The dynamic nature of kernel development implies that a new kernel version will be available by the time you read this, and naturally, some details will have changed — this is unavoidable. If it were not the case, Linux would be a dead and boring system, and chances are that you would not want to read the book. While some of the details will have changed, *concepts* will not have varied essentially. This is particularly true because 2.6.24 has seen some very fundamental changes as compared to earlier versions. Developers do not rip out such things overnight, naturally.

1.1 Tasks of the Kernel

On a purely technical level, the kernel is an intermediary layer between the hardware and the software. Its purpose is to pass application requests to the hardware and to act as a low-level driver to address the devices and components of the system. Nevertheless, there are other interesting ways of viewing the kernel.

- ❏ The kernel can be regarded as an *enhanced machine* that, in the view of the application, abstracts the computer on a high level. For example, when the kernel addresses a hard disk, it must decide which path to use to copy data from disk to memory, where the data reside, which commands must be sent to the disk via which path, and so on. Applications, on the other hand, need only issue the command *that* data are to be transferred. *How* this is done is irrelevant to the application — the details are abstracted by the kernel. Application programs have no contact with the hardware itself,[2] only with the kernel, which, for them, represents the lowest level in the hierarchy they know — and is therefore an enhanced machine.

- ❏ Viewing the kernel as a *resource manager* is justified when several programs are run concurrently on a system. In this case, the kernel is an instance that shares available resources — CPU time, disk space, network connections, and so on — between the various system processes while at the same time ensuring system integrity.

---

[2] The CPU is an exception since it is obviously unavoidable that programs access it. Nevertheless, the full range of possible instructions is not available for applications.

❑ Another view of the kernel is as a *library* providing a range of system-oriented commands. As is generally known, *system calls* are used to send requests to the computer; with the help of the C standard library, these appear to the application programs as normal functions that are invoked in the same way as any other function.

1.2 Implementation Strategies

Currently, there are two main paradigms on which the implementation of operating systems is based:

1. **Microkernels** — In these, only the most elementary functions are implemented directly in a central kernel — the *micro*kernel. All other functions are delegated to autonomous processes that communicate with the central kernel via clearly defined communication interfaces — for example, various filesystems, memory management, and so on. (Of course, the most elementary level of memory management that controls communication with the system itself is in the microkernel. However, handling on the system call level is implemented in external servers.) Theoretically, this is a very elegant approach because the individual parts are clearly segregated from each other, and this forces programmers to use "clean" programming techniques. Other benefits of this approach are dynamic extensibility and the ability to swap important components at run time. However, owing to the additional CPU time needed to support complex communication between the components, microkernels have not really established themselves in practice although they have been the subject of active and varied research for some time now.

2. **Monolithic Kernels** — They are the alternative, traditional concept. Here, the entire code of the kernel — including all its subsystems such as memory management, filesystems, or device drivers — is packed into a single file. Each function has access to all other parts of the kernel; this can result in elaborately nested source code if programming is not done with great care.

Because, at the moment, the performance of monolithic kernels is still greater than that of microkernels, Linux was and still is implemented according to this paradigm. However, one major innovation has been introduced. *Modules* with kernel code that can be inserted or removed while the system is up-and-running support the dynamic addition of a whole range of functions to the kernel, thus compensating for some of the disadvantages of monolithic kernels. This is assisted by elaborate means of communication between the kernel and userland that allows for implementing hotplugging and dynamic loading of modules.

1.3 Elements of the Kernel

This section provides a brief overview of the various elements of the kernel and outlines the areas we will examine in more detail in the following chapters. Despite its monolithic approach, Linux is surprisingly well structured. Nevertheless, it is inevitable that its individual elements interact with each other; they share data structures, and (for performance reasons) cooperate with each other via more functions than would be necessary in a strictly segregated system. In the following chapters, I am obliged to make frequent reference to the other elements of the kernel and therefore to other chapters, although I have tried to keep the number of forward references to a minimum. For this reason, I introduce the individual elements briefly here so that you can form an impression of their role and their place in the overall concept. Figure 1-1 provides a rough initial overview about the layers that comprise a complete Linux system, and also about some important subsystems of the kernel as such. Notice, however, that the individual subsystems will interact in a variety of additional ways in practice that are not shown in the figure.

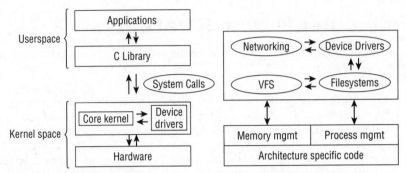

Figure 1-1: High-level overview of the structure of the Linux kernel and the layers in a complete Linux system.

1.3.1 *Processes, Task Switching, and Scheduling*

Applications, servers, and other programs running under UNIX are traditionally referred to as *processes*. Each process is assigned address space in the *virtual memory* of the CPU. The address spaces of the individual processes are totally independent so that the processes are unaware of each other — as far as each process is concerned, it has the impression of being the only process in the system. If processes want to communicate to exchange data, for example, then special kernel mechanisms must be used.

Because Linux is a multitasking system, it supports what appears to be concurrent execution of several processes. Since only as many processes as there are CPUs in the system can really run at the same time, the kernel switches (unnoticed by users) between the processes at short intervals to give them the impression of simultaneous processing. Here, there are two problem areas:

1. The kernel, with the help of the CPU, is responsible for the technical details of task switching. Each individual process must be given the illusion that the CPU is always available. This is achieved by saving all state-dependent elements of the process before CPU resources are withdrawn and the process is placed in an idle state. When the process is reactivated, the exact saved state is restored. Switching between processes is known as *task switching*.

2. The kernel must also decide *how* CPU time is shared between the existing processes. Important processes are given a larger share of CPU time, less important processes a smaller share. The decision as to which process runs for how long is known as *scheduling*.

1.3.2 UNIX *Processes*

Linux employs a hierarchical scheme in which each process depends on a parent process. The kernel starts the init program as the first process that is responsible for further system initialization actions and display of the login prompt or (in more widespread use today) display of a graphical login interface. init is therefore the root from which all processes originate, more or less directly, as shown graphically by the `pstree` program. `init` is the top of a tree structure whose branches spread further and further down.

```
wolfgang@meitner> pstree
init-+-acpid
     |-bonobo-activati
     |-cron
     |-cupsd
     |-2*[dbus-daemon]
     |-dbus-launch
     |-dcopserver
     |-dhcpcd
     |-esd
     |-eth1
     |-events/0
     |-gam_server
     |-gconfd-2
     |-gdm---gdm-+-X
     |               '-startkde-+-kwrapper
     |                          '-ssh-agent
     |-gnome-vfs-daemo
     |-gpg-agent
     |-hald-addon-acpi
     |-kaccess
     |-kded
     |-kdeinit-+-amarokapp---2*[amarokapp]
     |         |-evolution-alarm
     |         |-kinternet
     |         |-kio_file
     |         |-klauncher
     |         |-konqueror
     |         |-konsole---bash-+-pstree
     |         |                '-xemacs
     |         |-kwin
     |         |-nautilus
     |         '-netapplet
     |-kdesktop
     |-kgpg
     |-khelper
     |-kicker
     |-klogd
     |-kmix
     |-knotify
     |-kpowersave
     |-kscd
     |-ksmserver
     |-ksoftirqd/0
     |-kswapd0
     |-kthread-+-aio/0
     |         |-ata/0
     |         |-kacpid
     |         |-kblockd/0
     |         |-kgameportd
     |         |-khubd
```

```
    |          |-kseriod
    |          |-2*[pdflush]
    |          '-reiserfs/0
 ...
```

How this tree structure spreads is closely connected with how new processes are generated. For this purpose, UNIX uses two mechanisms called *fork* and *exec*.

1. **fork** — Generates an exact copy of the current process that differs from the parent process only in its PID (*process identification*). After the system call has been executed, there are two processes in the system, both performing the same actions. The memory contents of the initial process are duplicated — at least in the view of the program. Linux uses a well-known technique known as *copy on write* that allows it to make the operation much more efficient by deferring the copy operations until either parent or child writes to a page — read-only accessed can be satisfied from the same page for both.

A possible scenario for using fork is, for example, when a user opens a second browser window. If the corresponding option is selected, the browser executes a fork to duplicate its code and then starts the appropriate actions to build a new window in the child process.

2. **exec** — Loads a new program into an existing content and then executes it. The memory pages reserved by the old program are flushed, and their contents are replaced with new data. The new program then starts executing.

Threads

Processes are not the only form of program execution supported by the kernel. In addition to *heavy-weight processes* — another name for classical UNIX processes — there are also *threads*, sometimes referred to as *light-weight processes*. They have also been around for some time, and essentially, a process may consist of several threads that all share the same data and resources but take different paths through the program code. The thread concept is fully integrated into many modern languages — Java, for instance. In simple terms, a process can be seen as an executing program, whereas a thread is a program function or routine running in parallel to the main program. This is useful, for example, when Web browsers need to load several images in parallel. Usually, the browser would have to execute several fork and exec calls to generate parallel instances; these would then be responsible for loading the images and making data received available to the main program using some kind of communication mechanisms. Threads make this situation easier to handle. The browser defines a routine to load images, and the routine is started as a thread with multiple strands (each with different arguments). Because the threads and the main program share the same address space, data received automatically reside in the main program. There is therefore no need for any communication effort whatsoever, except to prevent the threads from stepping onto their feet mutually by accessing identical memory locations, for instance. Figure 1-2 illustrates the difference between a program with and without threads.

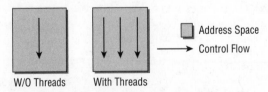

W/O Threads   With Threads

Figure 1-2: Processes with and without threads.

Linux provides the `clone` method to generate threads. This works in a similar way to `fork` but enables a precise check to be made of which resources are shared with the parent process and which are generated independently for the thread. This fine-grained distribution of resources extends the classical thread concept and allows for a more or less continuous transition between thread and processes.

Namespaces

During the development of kernel 2.6, support for namespaces was integrated into numerous subsystems. This allows different processes to have different views of the system. Traditionally, Linux (and UNIX in general) use numerous global quantities, for instance, process identifiers: Every process in the system is equipped with a unique identifier (ID), and this ID can be employed by users (or other processes) to refer to the process — by sending it a signal, for instance. With namespaces, formerly global resources are grouped differently: Every namespace can contain a specific set of PIDs, or can provide different views of the filesystem, where mounts in one namespace do not propagate into different namespaces.

Namespaces are useful; for example, they are beneficial for hosting providers: Instead of setting up one physical machine per customer, they can instead use *containers* implemented with namespaces to create multiple views of the system where each seems to be a complete Linux installation from within the container and does not interact with other containers: They are separated and segregated from each other. Every instance looks like a single machine running Linux, but in fact, many such instances can operate simultaneously on a physical machine. This helps use resources more effectively. In contrast to full virtualization solutions like KVM, only a single kernel needs to run on the machine and is responsible to manage all containers.

Not all parts of the kernel are yet fully aware of namespaces, and I will discuss to what extent support is available when we analyze the various subsystems.

1.3.3 Address Spaces and Privilege Levels

Before we start to discuss virtual address spaces, there are some notational conventions to fix. Throughout this book I use the abbreviations KiB, MiB, and GiB as units of size. The conventional units KB, MB, and GB are not really suitable in information technology because they represent decimal powers (10^3, 10^6, and 10^9) although the binary system is the basis ubiquitous in computing. Accordingly KiB stands for 2^{10}, MiB for 2^{20}, and GiB for 2^{30} bytes.

Because memory areas are addressed by means of pointers, the word length of the CPU determines the maximum size of the address space that can be managed. On 32-bit systems such as IA-32, PPC, and m68k, these are $2^{32} = 4$ GiB, whereas on more modern 64-bit processors such as Alpha, Sparc64, IA-64, and AMD64, 2^{64} bytes can be managed.

The maximal size of the address space is not related to how much physical RAM is actually available, and therefore it is known as the *virtual address space*. One more reason for this terminology is that every process in the system has the impression that it would solely live in this address space, and other processes are not present from their point of view. Applications do not need to care about other applications and can work as if they would run as the only process on the computer.

Linux divides virtual address space into two parts known as *kernel space* and *userspace* as illustrated in Figure 1-3.

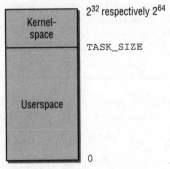

Figure 1-3: Division of virtual address space.

Every user process in the system has its own virtual address range that extends from 0 to TASK_SIZE. The area above (from TASK_SIZE to 2^{32} or 2^{64}) is reserved exclusively for the kernel — and may not be accessed by user processes. TASK_SIZE is an architecture-specific constant that divides the address space in a given ratio — in IA-32 systems, for instance, the address space is divided at 3 GiB so that the virtual address space for each process is 3 GiB; 1 GiB is available to the kernel because the total size of the virtual address space is 4 GiB. Although actual figures differ according to architecture, the general concepts do not. I therefore use these sample values in our further discussions.

This division *does not depend* on how much RAM is available. As a result of address space virtualization, *each* user process thinks it has 3 GiB of memory. The userspaces of the individual system processes are totally separate from each other. The kernel space at the top end of the virtual address space is always the same, regardless of the process currently executing.

Notice that the picture can be more complicated on 64-bit machines because these tend to use less than 64 bits to actually manage their huge principal virtual address space. Instead of 64 bits, they employ a smaller number, for instance, 42 or 47 bits. Because of this, the effectively addressable portion of the address space is smaller than the principal size. However, it is still larger than the amount of RAM that will ever be present in the machine, and is therefore completely sufficient. As an advantage, the CPU can save some effort because less bits are required to manage the effective address space than are required to address the complete virtual address space. The virtual address space will contain holes that are not addressable in principle in such cases, so the simple situation depicted in Figure 1-3 is not fully valid. We will come back to this topic in more detail in Chapter 4.

Privilege Levels

The kernel divides the virtual address space into two parts so that it is able to protect the individual system processes from each other. All modern CPUs offer several privilege levels in which processes can reside. There are various prohibitions in each level including, for example, execution of certain assembly language instructions or access to specific parts of virtual address space. The IA-32 architecture uses a system of four privilege levels that can be visualized as rings. The inner rings are able to access more functions, the outer rings less, as shown in Figure 1-4.

Whereas the Intel variant distinguishes four different levels, Linux uses only two different modes — kernel mode and user mode. The key difference between the two is that access to the memory area above TASK_SIZE — that is, kernel space — is forbidden in user mode. User processes are not able to manipulate or read the data in kernel space. Neither can they execute code stored there. This is the sole domain of the kernel. This mechanism prevents processes from interfering with each other by unintentionally influencing each other's data.

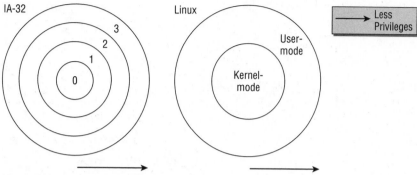

Figure 1-4: Ring system of privilege levels.

The switch from user to kernel mode is made by means of special transitions known as *system calls*; these are executed differently depending on the system. If a normal process wants to carry out any kind of action affecting the entire system (e.g., manipulating I/O devices), it can do this only by issuing a request to the kernel with the help of a system call. The kernel first checks whether the process is *permitted* to perform the desired action and then performs the action on its behalf. A return is then made to user mode.

Besides executing code on behalf of a user program, the kernel can also be activated by asynchronous hardware interrupts, and is then said to run in *interrupt context*. The main difference to running in process context is that the userspace portion of the virtual address space must not be accessed. Because interrupts occur at random times, a random userland process is active when an interrupt occurs, and since the interrupt will most likely be unconnected with the cause of the interrupt, the kernel has no business with the contents of the current userspace. When operating in interrupt context, the kernel must be more cautious than normal; for instance, it must not go to sleep. This requires extra care when writing interrupt handlers and is discussed in detail in Chapter 2. An overview of the different execution contexts is given in Figure 1-5.

Besides normal processes, there can also be *kernel threads* running on the system. Kernel threads are also not associated with any particular userspace process, so they also have no business dealing with the user portion of the address space. In many other respects, kernel threads behave much more like regular userland applications, though: In contrast to a kernel operating in interrupt context, they may go to sleep, and they are also tracked by the scheduler like every regular process in the system. The kernel uses them for various purposes that range from data synchronization of RAM and block devices to helping the scheduler distribute processes among CPUs, and we will frequently encounter them in the course of this book.

Notice that kernel threads can be easily identified in the output of ps because their names are placed inside brackets:

```
wolfgang@meitner> ps fax
  PID TTY      STAT   TIME COMMAND
    2 ?        S<     0:00 [kthreadd]
    3 ?        S<     0:00  _ [migration/0]
    4 ?        S<     0:00  _ [ksoftirqd/0]
```

```
    5 ?        S<      0:00  _ [migration/1]
    6 ?        S<      0:00  _ [ksoftirqd/1]
    7 ?        S<      0:00  _ [migration/2]
    8 ?        S<      0:00  _ [ksoftirqd/2]
    9 ?        S<      0:00  _ [migration/3]
   10 ?        S<      0:00  _ [ksoftirqd/3]
   11 ?        S<      0:00  _ [events/0]
   12 ?        S<      0:00  _ [events/1]
   13 ?        S<      0:00  _ [events/2]
   14 ?        S<      0:00  _ [events/3]
   15 ?        S<      0:00  _ [khelper]
...
15162 ?        S<      0:00  _ [jfsCommit]
15163 ?        S<      0:00  _ [jfsSync]
```

Figure 1-5: Execution in kernel and user mode. Most of the time, the CPU executes code in userspace. When the application performs a system call, a switch to kernel mode is employed, and the kernel fulfills the request. During this, it may access the user portion of the virtual address space. After the system call completes, the CPU switches back to user mode. A hardware interrupt also triggers a switch to kernel mode, but this time, the userspace portion must not be accessed by the kernel.

On multiprocessor systems, many threads are started on a per-CPU basis and are restricted to run on only one specific processor. This is represented by a slash and the number of the CPU that are appended to the name of the kernel thread.

Virtual and Physical Address Spaces

In most cases, a single virtual address space is bigger than the physical RAM available to the system. And the situation does not improve when *each* process has its own virtual address space. The kernel and CPU must therefore consider how the physical memory actually available can be mapped onto virtual address areas.

The preferred method is to use page tables to allocate *virtual* addresses to *physical* addresses. Whereas virtual addresses relate to the combined user and kernel space of a process, physical addresses are used to address the RAM actually available. This principle is illustrated in Figure 1-6.

The virtual address spaces of both processes shown in the figure are divided into portions of equal size by the kernel. These portions are known as *pages*. Physical memory is also divided into pages of the same size.

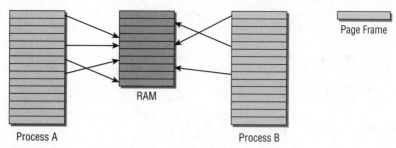

Figure 1-6: Virtual and physical addresses.

The arrows in Figure 1-6 indicate how the pages in the virtual address spaces are distributed across the physical pages. For example, virtual page 1 of process A is mapped to physical page 4, while virtual page 1 of process B is mapped to the fifth physical page. This shows that virtual addresses change their meaning from process to process.

Physical pages are often called *page frames*. In contrast, the term *page* is reserved for pages in virtual address space.

Mapping between virtual address spaces and physical memory also enables the otherwise strict separation between processes to be lifted. Our example includes a page frame explicitly shared by both processes. Page 5 of A and page 1 of B both point to the physical page frame 5. This is possible because entries in both virtual address spaces (albeit at different positions) point to the same page. Since the kernel is responsible for mapping virtual address space to physical address space, it is able to decide which memory areas are to be shared between processes and which are not.

The figure also shows that not all pages of the virtual address spaces are linked with a page frame. This may be because either the pages are not used or because data have not been loaded into memory because they are not yet needed. It may also be that the page has been swapped out onto hard disk and will be swapped back in when needed.

Finally, notice that there are two equivalent terms to address the applications that run on behalf of the user. One of them is *userland*, and this is the nomenclature typically preferred by the BSD community for all things that do not belong to the kernel. The alternative is to say that an application runs in *userspace*. It should be noted that the term *userland* will always mean applications as such, whereas the term *userspace* can additionally not only denote applications, but also the portion of the virtual address space in which they are executed, in contrast to *kernel space*.

1.3.4   Page Tables

Data structures known as *page tables* are used to map virtual address space to physical address space. The easiest way of implementing the association between both would be to use an array containing an entry for each page in virtual address space. This entry would point to the associated page frame. But there is a problem. IA-32 architecture uses, for example, 4 KiB pages — given a virtual address space of 4 GiB, this would produce an array with a million entries. On 64-bit architectures, the situation is much worse. Because each process needs its own page tables, this approach is impractical because the entire RAM of the system would be needed to hold the page tables.

As most areas of virtual address spaces are not used and are therefore not associated with page frames, a far less memory-intensive model that fulfills the same purpose can be used: multilevel paging.

To reduce the size of page tables and to allow unneeded areas to be ignored, the architectures split each virtual address into multiple parts, as shown in Figure 1-7 (the bit positions at which the address is split differ according to architecture, but this is of no relevance here). In the example, I use a split of the virtual address into four components, and this leads to a *three*-level page table. This is what most architectures offer. However, some employ four-level page tables, and Linux also adopts four levels of indirection. To simplify the picture, I stick to a three-level variant here.

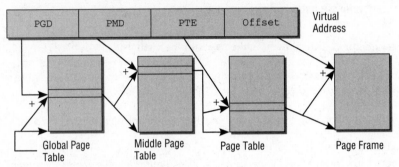

Figure 1-7: Splitting a virtual address.

The first part of the virtual address is referred to as a *page global directory* or PGD. It is used as an index in an array that exists exactly once for each process. Its entries are pointers to the start of further arrays called *page middle directories* or PMD.

Once the corresponding array has been found by reference to the PGD and its contents, the PMD is used as an index for the array. The page middle directory likewise consists of pointers to further arrays known as *page tables* or *page directories*.

The *PTE* (or *page table entry*) part of the virtual address is used as an index to the page table. Mapping between virtual pages and page frames is achieved because the page table entries point to page frames.

The last part of the virtual address is known as an *offset*. It is used to specify a byte position within the page; after all, each address points to a uniquely defined byte in address space.

A particular feature of page tables is that no page middle tables or page tables need be created for areas of virtual address space that are not needed. This saves a great deal of RAM as compared to the single-array method.

Of course, this method also has a downside. Each time memory is accessed, it is necessary to run through the entire chain to obtain the physical address from the virtual address. CPUs try to speed up this process in two ways:

1. A special part of the CPU known as a *memory management unit (MMU)* is optimized to perform referencing operations.

2. The addresses that occur most frequently in address translation are held in a fast CPU cache called a *Translation Lookaside Buffer* (*TLB*). Translation is accelerated because the address data in the cache are immediately available without needing to access the page tables and therefore the RAM.

    While caches are operated transparently on many architectures, some require special attention from the kernel, which especially implies that their contents must be invalidated whenever the contents of the page tables have been changed. Corresponding calls must be present in every part of the kernel that manipulates page tables. If the kernel is compiled for an architecture that does not require such operations, it automatically ensures that the calls are represented by do-nothing operations.

Interaction with the CPU

The IA-32 architecture uses a two-level-only method to map virtual addresses to physical addresses. The size of the address space in 64-bit architectures (Alpha, Sparc64, IA-64, etc.) mandates a three-level or four-level method, and the architecture-*independent* part of the kernel always assumes a four-level page table.

The architecture-*dependent* code of the kernel for two- and three-level CPUs must therefore emulate the missing levels by dummy page tables. Consequently, the remaining memory management code can be implemented independently of the CPU used.

Memory Mappings

Memory mappings are an important means of abstraction. They are used at many points in the kernel and are also available to user applications. Mapping is the method by which data from an arbitrary source are transferred into the virtual address space of a process. The address space areas in which mapping takes place can be processed using normal methods in the same way as regular memory. However, any changes made are transferred automatically to the original data source. This makes it possible to use identical functions to process totally different things. For example, the contents of a file can be mapped into memory. A process then need only read the contents of memory to access the contents of the file, or write changes to memory in order to modify the contents of the file. The kernel automatically ensures that any changes made are implemented in the file.

Mappings are also used directly in the kernel when implementing device drivers. The input and output areas of peripheral devices can be mapped into virtual address space; reads and writes to these areas are then redirected to the devices by the system, thus greatly simplifying driver implementation.

1.3.5   Allocation of Physical Memory

When it allocates RAM, the kernel must keep track of which pages have already been allocated and which are still free in order to prevent two processes from using the same areas in RAM. Because memory allocation and release are very frequent tasks, the kernel must also ensure that they are completed as quickly as possible. The kernel can allocate only whole page frames. Dividing memory into smaller portions is delegated to the standard library in userspace. This library splits the page frames received from the kernel into smaller areas and allocates memory to the processes.

The Buddy System

Numerous allocation requests in the kernel must be fulfilled by a continuous range of pages. To quickly detect where in memory such ranges are still available, the kernel employs an old, but proven technique: The *buddy system*.

Free memory blocks in the system are always grouped as two buddies. The buddies can be allocated independently of each other; if, however, both remain unused at the same time, the kernel merges them into a larger pair that serves as a buddy on the next level. Figure 1-8 demonstrates this using an example of a buddy pair consisting initially of two blocks of 8 pages.

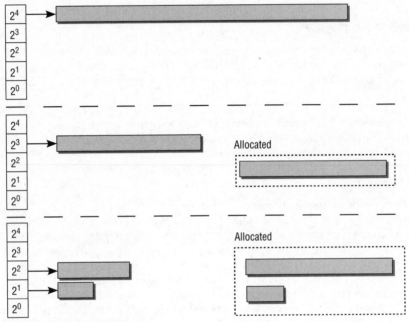

Figure 1-8: The buddy system.

All buddies of the same size (1, 2, 4, 8, 16, . . . pages) are managed by the kernel in a special list. The buddy pair with two times 8 (16) pages is also in this list.

If the system now requires 8 page frames, it splits the block consisting of 16 page frames into two buddies. While one of the blocks is passed to the application that requested memory, the remaining 8 page frames are placed in the list for 8-page memory blocks.

If the next request requires only 2 contiguous page frames, the block consisting of 8 blocks is split into 2 buddies, each comprising 4 page frames. One of the blocks is put back into the buddy lists, while the other is again split into 2 buddies consisting of 2 blocks of two pages. One is returned to the buddy system, while the other is passed to the application.

When memory is returned by the application, the kernel can easily see by reference to the addresses whether a buddy pair is reunited and can then merge it into a larger unit that is put back into the buddy list — exactly the reverse of the splitting process. This increases the likelihood that larger memory blocks are available.

When systems run for longer periods — it is not unusual for servers to run for several weeks or even months, and many desktop systems also tend to reach long uptime — a memory management problem known as *fragmentation* occurs. The frequent allocation and release of page frames may lead to a situation in which several page frames are free in the system but they are scattered throughout physical address space — in other words, there are no larger *contiguous* blocks of page frames, as would be desirable for performance reasons. This effect is reduced to some extent by the buddy system but not completely eliminated. Single reserved pages that sit in the middle of an otherwise large continuous free range can eliminate coalescing of this range very effectively. During the development of kernel 2.6.24, some effective measures were added to prevent memory fragmentation, and I discuss the underlying mechanisms in more detail in Chapter 3.

The Slab Cache

Often the kernel itself needs memory blocks much smaller than a whole page frame. Because it cannot use the functions of the standard library, it must define its own, additional layer of memory management that builds on the buddy system and divides the pages supplied by the buddy system into smaller portions. The method used not only performs allocation but also implements a generic cache for frequently used small objects; this cache is known as a *slab cache*. It can be used to allocate memory in two ways:

1. For frequently used objects, the kernel defines its own cache that contains only instances of the desired type. Each time one of the objects is required, it can be quickly removed from the cache (and returned there after use); the slab cache automatically takes care of interaction with the buddy system and requests new page frames when the existing caches are full.

2. For the general allocation of smaller memory blocks, the kernel defines a set of slab caches for various object sizes that it can access using the same functions with which we are familiar from userspace programming; a prefixed k indicates that these functions are associated with the kernel: kmalloc and kfree.

While the slab allocator provides good performance across a wide range of workloads, some scalability problems with it have arisen on really large supercomputers. On the other hand of the scale, the overhead of the slab allocator may be too much for really tiny embedded systems. The kernel comes with two drop-in replacements for the slab allocator that provide better performance in these use cases, but offer the same interface to the rest of the kernel such that it need not be concerned with which low-level allocator is actually compiled in. Since slab allocation is still the standard methods of the kernel, I will, however, not discuss these alternatives in detail. Figure 1-9 summarizes the connections between buddy system, slab allocator, and the rest of the kernel.

Swapping and Page Reclaim

Swapping enables available RAM to be enlarged virtually by using disk space as extended memory. Infrequently used pages can be written to hard disk when the kernel requires more RAM. Once the data are actually needed, the kernel swaps them back into memory. The concept of *page faults* is used to make this operation transparent to applications. Swapped-out pages are identified by a special entry in the page table. When a process attempts to access a page of this kind, the CPU initiates a page fault that is intercepted by the kernel. The kernel then has the opportunity to swap the data on disk into RAM. The user process then resumes. Because it is unaware of the page fault, swapping in and out of the page is totally invisible to the process.

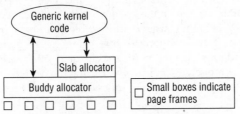

Figure 1-9: Page frame allocation is performed by the buddy system, while the slab allocator is responsible for small-sized allocations and generic kernel caches.

Page reclaim is used to synchronize modified mappings with underlying block devices — for this reason, it is sometimes referred to simply as *writing back data*. Once data have been flushed, the page frame can be used by the kernel for other purposes (as with swapping). After all, the kernel data structures contain all the information needed to find the corresponding data on the hard disk when they are again required.

1.3.6 Timing

The kernel must be capable of measuring time and time differences at various points — when scheduling processes, for example. *Jiffies* are one possible time base. A global variable named `jiffies_64` and its 32-bit counterpart `jiffies` are incremented periodically at constant time intervals. The various timer mechanisms of the underlying architectures are used to perform these updates — each computer architecture provides some means of executing periodic actions, usually in the form of timer interrupts.

Depending on architecture, `jiffies` is incremented with a frequency determined by the central constant HZ of the kernel. This is usually on the range between 1,000 and 100; in other words, the value of `jiffies` is incremented between 1,000 and 100 times per second.

Timing based on `jiffies` is relatively coarse-grained because 1,000 Hz is not an excessively large frequency nowadays. With *high-resolution timers*, the kernel provides additional means that allows for keeping time in the regime of nanosecond precision and resolution, depending on the capabilities of the underlying hardware.

It is possible to make the periodic tick *dynamic*. When there is little to do and no need for frequent periodic actions, it does not make sense to periodically generate timer interrupts that prevent the processor from powering down into deep sleep states. This is helpful in systems where power is scarce, for instance, laptops and embedded systems.

1.3.7 System Calls

System calls are the classical method of enabling user processes to interact with the kernel. The POSIX standard defines a number of system calls and their effect as implemented on all POSIX-compliant systems including Linux. Traditional system calls are grouped into various categories:

- ❑ **Process Management** — Creating new tasks, querying information, debugging

- ❑ **Signals** — Sending signals, timers, handling mechanisms

- ❑ **Files** — Creating, opening, and closing files, reading from and writing to files, querying information and status

- ❑ **Directories and Filesystem** — Creating, deleting, and renaming directories, querying information, links, changing directories

- ❑ **Protection Mechanisms** — Reading and changing UIDs/GIDs, and namespace handling

- ❑ **Timer Functions** — Timer functions and statistical information

Demands are placed on the kernel in all these functions. They cannot be implemented in a normal user library because special protection mechanisms are needed to ensure that system stability and/or security are not endangered. In addition, many calls are reliant on kernel-internal structures or functions to yield desired data or results — this also dictates against implementation in userspace. When a system call is issued, the processor must change the privilege level and switch from user mode to system mode. There is no standardized way of doing this in Linux as each hardware platform offers specific mechanisms. In some cases, different approaches are implemented on the same architecture but depend on processor type. Whereas Linux uses a special software interrupt to execute system calls on IA-32 processors, the software emulation (iBCS emulator) of other UNIX systems on IA-32 employs a different method to execute binary programs (for assembly language aficionados: the `lcall7` or `lcall27` gate). Modern variants of IA-32 also have their own assembly language statement for executing system calls; this was not available on old systems and cannot therefore be used on all machines. What all variants have in common is that system calls are the only way of enabling user processes to switch in their own incentive from user mode to kernel mode in order to delegate system-critical tasks.

1.3.8 Device Drivers, Block and Character Devices

The role of device drivers is to communicate with I/O devices attached to the system; for example, hard disks, floppies, interfaces, sound cards, and so on. In accordance with the classical UNIX maxim that *"everything is a file,"* access is performed using device files that usually reside in the /dev directory and can be processed by programs in the same way as regular files. The task of a device driver is to support application communication via device files; in other words, to enable data to be read from and written to a device in a suitable way.

Peripheral devices belong to one of the following two groups:

1. **Character Devices** — Deliver a continuous stream of data that applications read sequentially; generally, random access is not possible. Instead, such devices allow data to be read and written byte-by-byte or character-by-character. Modems are classical examples of character devices.

2. **Block Devices** — Allow applications to address their data randomly and to freely select the position at which they want to read data. Typical block devices are hard disks because applications can address any position on the disk from which to read data. Also, data can be read or written only in multiples of block units (usually 512 bytes); character-based addressing, as in character devices, is not possible.

    Programming drivers for block devices is much more complicated than for character devices because extensive caching mechanisms are used to boost system performance.

1.3.9   Networks

Network cards are also controlled by device drivers but assume a special status in the kernel because they cannot be addressed using device files. This is because data are packed into various protocol layers during network communication. When data are received, the layers must be disassembled and analyzed by the kernel before the payload data are passed to the application. When data are sent, the kernel must first pack the data into the various protocol layers prior to dispatch.

However, to support work with network connections via the file interface (in the view of applications), Linux uses *sockets* from the BSD world; these act as agents between the application, file interface, and network implementation of the kernel.

1.3.10   Filesystems

Linux systems are made up of many thousands or even millions of files whose data are stored on hard disks or other block devices (e.g., ZIP drives, floppies, CD-ROMs, etc.). Hierarchical filesystems are used; these allow stored data to be organized into directory structures and also have the job of linking other meta-information (owners, access rights, etc.) with the actual data. Many different filesystem approaches are supported by Linux — the standard filesystems Ext2 and Ext3, ReiserFS, XFS, VFAT (for reasons of compatibility with DOS), and countless more. The concepts on which they build differ drastically in part. Ext2 is based on inodes, that is, it makes a separate management structure known as an *inode* available on disk for each file. The inode contains not only all meta-information but also pointers to the associated data blocks. Hierarchical structures are set up by representing directories as regular files whose data section includes pointers to the inodes of all files contained in the directory. In contrast, ReiserFS makes extensive use of tree structures to deliver the same functionality.

The kernel must provide an additional software layer to abstract the special features of the various low-level filesystems from the application layer (and also from the kernel itself). This layer is referred to as the VFS (*virtual filesystem* or *virtual filesystem switch*). It acts as an interface downward (this interface must be implemented by all filesystems) and upward (for system calls via which user processes are ultimately able to access filesystem functions). This is illustrated in Figure 1-10.

1.3.11   Modules and Hotplugging

Modules are used to dynamically add functionality to the kernel at run time — device drivers, filesystems, network protocols, practically any subsystem[3] of the kernel can be modularized. This removes one of the significant disadvantages of monolithic kernels as compared with microkernel variants.

---

[3]With the exception of basic functions, such as memory management, which are always needed.

Modules can also be unloaded from the kernel at run time, a useful aspect when developing new kernel components.

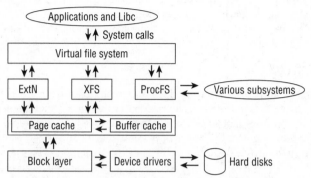

Figure 1-10: Overview of how the virtual filesystem layer, filesystem implementations, and the block layer interoperate.

Basically, modules are simply normal programs that execute in kernel space rather than in userspace. They must also provide certain sections that are executed when the module is initialized (and terminated) in order to register and de-register the module functions with the kernel. Otherwise, module code has the same rights (and obligations) as normal kernel code and can access all the same functions and data as code that is permanently compiled into the kernel.

Modules are an essential requisite to support for *hotplugging*. Some buses (e.g., USB and FireWire) allow devices to be connected while the system is running without requiring a system reboot. When the system detects a new device, the requisite driver can be automatically added to the kernel by loading the corresponding module.

Modules also enable kernels to be built to support all kinds of devices that the kernel can address without unnecessarily bloating kernel size. Once attached hardware has been detected, only the requisite modules are loaded, and the kernel remains free of superfluous drivers.

A long-standing issue in the kernel community revolves around the support of binary-only modules, that is, modules for which no source code is available. While binary-only modules are omnipresent on most proprietary operating systems, many kernel developers see them (at least!) as an incarnation of the devil: Since the kernel is developed as open-source software, they believe that modules should also be published as open source, for a variety of both legal and technical reasons. There are, indeed, strong arguments to support this reasoning (and besides, I also follow these), but they are not shared by some commercial companies that tend to think that opening up their driver sources would weaken their business position.

It is currently possible to load binary-only modules into the kernel, although numerous restrictions apply for them. Most importantly, they may not access any functions that are explicitly only made available to GPL-licensed code. Loading a binary-only module *taints* the kernel, and whenever something bad occurs, the fault is naturally attributed to the tainting module. If a kernel is tainted, this will be marked on crash dumps, for instance, and kernel developers will be very unsupportive in solving the issue that led to the crash — since the binary module could have given every part of the kernel a good shaking, it cannot be assumed that the kernel still works as intended, and support is better left to the manufacturer of the offending module.

Loading binary-only modules is not the only possibility for tainting a kernel. This happens also when, for instance, the machine has experienced certain bad exceptions, when a SMP system is built with CPUs that do not officially support multiprocessing by their specification, and other similar reasons.

1.3.12 Caching

The kernel uses *caches* to improve system performance. Data read from slow block devices are held in RAM for a while, even if they are no longer needed at the time. When an application next accesses the data, they can be read from fast RAM, thus bypassing the slow block device. Because the kernel implements access to block devices by means of page memory mappings, caches are also organized into pages, that is, whole pages are cached, thus giving rise to the name *page cache*.

The far less important *buffer cache* is used to cache data that are not organized into pages. On traditional UNIX systems, the buffer cache serves as the main system cache, and the same approach was used by Linux a long, long time ago. By now, the buffer cache has mostly been superseded by the page cache.

1.3.13 List Handling

A recurring task in C programs is the handling of doubly linked lists. The kernel too is required to handle such lists. Consequently, I will make frequent mention of the standard list implementation of the kernel in the following chapters. At this point, I give a brief introduction to the list handling API.

Standard lists as provided by the kernel can be used to link data structures of any type with each other. It is explicitly *not* type-safe. The data structures to be listed must contain an element of the list_head type; this accommodates the forward and back pointers. If a data structure is to be organized in several lists — and this is not unusual — several list_head elements are needed.

```
<list.h>
struct list_head {
        struct list_head *next, *prev;
};
```

This element could be placed in a data structure as follows:

```
struct task_struct {
...
   struct list_head run_list;
...
};
```

The starting point for linked lists is again an instance of list_head that is usually declared and initialized by the LIST_HEAD(list_name) macro. In this way, the kernel produces a cyclic list, as shown in Figure 1-11. It permits access to the first and last element of a list in $\mathbb{O}(1)$, that is, in always the same, constant time regardless of the list size.

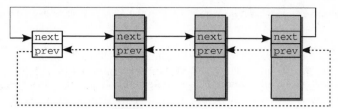

Figure 1-11: Doubly linked standard list.

`struct list_head` is called a *list element* when it is held in a data structure. An element that serves as the starting point for a list is called a *list head*.

> Pointers that connect head and tail elements of a list tend to clutter up images and often obstruct the principal intention of a figure, namely, to briefly summarize the connections of various kernel data structures. I thus usually *omit* the connection between list head and list tail in figures. The above list is in the remainder of this book therefore represented as shown in Figure 1-12. This allows for concentrating on the essential details without having to waste space for irrelevant list pointers.

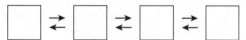

Figure 1-12: Simplified illustration of a doubly linked list. Notice that the connection between list head and list tail is *not* displayed, although it is present in kernel memory.

There are several standard functions for handling and processing lists. We will come across them again and again in the following chapters (the data type of their arguments is `struct list_head`).

❑   `list_add(new, head)` inserts `new` right after the existing `head` element.

❑   `list_add_tail(new, head)` inserts `new` right before the element specified by `head`. If the list head is specified for `head`, this causes the new element to be inserted at the end of the list because of the cyclic nature of the list (this gives the function its name).

❑   `list_del(entry)` deletes an entry from a list.

❑   `list_empty(head)` checks if a list is empty, that is, if it does not contain any elements.

❑   `list_splice(list, head)` combines two lists by inserting the list in `list` after the `head` element of an existing list.

❑   `list_entry` must be used to find a list element; at first glance, its call syntax appears to be quite complicated: `list_entry(ptr, type, member)`. `ptr` is a pointer to the `list_head` instance of the data structure, `type` is its type, and `member` is the element name used for the list element. The following sample call would be needed to find a `task_struct` instance of a list:

```
struct task_struct = list_entry(ptr, struct task_struct, run_list)
```

Explicit type specification is required because list implementation is *not* type-safe. The list element must be specified to find the correct element if there are data structures that are included in several lists.[4]

❑   `list_for_each(pos, head)` must be used to iterate through all elements of a list. `pos` indicates the current position in the list, while `head` specifies the list head.

```
struct list_head *p;

list_for_each(p, &list)
        if (condition)
                return list_entry(p, struct task_struct, run_list);
return NULL;
```

1.3.14   Object Management and Reference Counting

All over the kernel, the need to keep track of instances of C structures arises. Despite the fact that these objects will be used in the most varying forms, some operations are very similar across subsystems — just consider reference counting. This leads to code duplication. Since this is a bad thing, the kernel has adopted generic methods to manage kernel objects during the development of 2.5. The framework is, however, not just required to prevent code duplication. It also allows for providing a coherent view on objects managed by different parts of the kernel, and this information can be brought to good use in many parts of the kernel, for instance, for power management.

The generic kernel object mechanism can be used to perform the following operations on objects:

❑   Reference counting

❑   Management of lists (sets) of objects

❑   Locking of sets

❑   Exporting object properties into userspace (via the `sysfs` filesystem)

Generic Kernel Objects

The following data structure that is embedded in other data structures is used as a basis.

```
<kobject.h>
struct kobject {
        const char              * k_name;
        struct kref             kref;
        struct list_head        entry;
        struct kobject          * parent;
        struct kset             * kset;
        struct kobj_type        * ktype;
        struct sysfs_dirent     * sd;
};
```

---

[4]Even if there is only one list element in the structure, this entry is used to find the correct start address of the instance by means of pointer arithmetic; the address is translated into the required data type by means of type conversion. I deal with this in more detail in the appendix on C programming.

It is essential that **kobjects** are not linked with other data structures by means of pointers but are directly embedded. Managing the kernel object itself amounts to managing the whole containing object this way. Since **struct kobject** is embedded into many data structures of the kernel, the developers take care to keep it small. Adding a single new element to this data structure results in a size increase of many other data structures. Embedded kernel objects look as follows:

```
struct sample {
...
    struct kobject kobj;
...
};
```

The meanings of the individual elements of struct kobject are as follows:

❑   k_name is a text name exported to userspace using sysfs. Sysfs is a virtual filesystem that allows for exporting various properties of the system into userspace. Likewise sd supports this connection, and I will come back to this in Chapter 10.

❑   kref holds the general type struct kref designed to simplify reference management. I discuss this below.

❑   entry is a standard list element used to group several kobjects in a list (known as a set in this case).

❑   kset is required when an object is grouped with other objects in a set.

❑   parent is a pointer to the parent element and enables a hierarchical structure to be established between kobjects.

❑   ktype provides more detailed information on the data structure in which a kobject is embedded. Of greatest importance is the destructor function that returns the resources of the embedding data structure.

The similarity between the name kobject and the *object* concept of, well, object-oriented languages like C++ or Java is by no means coincidental: The kobject abstraction indeed allows for using object-oriented techniques in the kernel, but without requiring all the extra mechanics (and bloat, and overhead) of C++.

Table 1-1 lists the standard operations provided by the kernel to manipulate kobject instances, and therefore effectively act on the embedding structure.

The layout of the kref structure used to manage references is as follows:

<kref.h>
```
struct kref {
        atomic_t refcount;
};
```

refcount is an atomic data type to specify the number of positions in the kernel at which an object is currently being used. When the counter reaches 0, the object is no longer needed and can therefore be removed from memory.

Table 1-1: Standard Methods for Processing `kobject`**s**

Function	Meaning
`kobject_get`, `kobject_put`	Increments or decrements the reference counter of a `kobject`
`kobject_(un)register`	Registers or removes `obj` from a hierarchy (the object is added to the existing set (if any) of the parent element; a corresponding entry is created in the `sysfs` filesystem).
`kobject_init`	Initializes a `kobject`; that is, it sets the reference counter to its initial value and initializes the list elements of the object.
`kobect_add`	Initializes a kernel object and makes it visible in sysfs
`kobject_cleanup`	Releases the allocated resources when a `kobject` (and therefore the embedding object) is no longer needed

Encapsulation of the single value in a structure was chosen to prevent direct manipulation of the value. `kref_init` must always be used for initialization. If an object is in use, `kref_get` must be invoked beforehand to increment the reference counter. `kref_put` decrements the counter when the object is no longer used.

Sets of Objects

In many cases, it is necessary to group different kernel objects into a set — for instance, the set of all character devices or the set of all PCI-based devices. The data structure provided for this purpose is defined as follows:

```
<kobject.h>
struct kset {
        struct kobj_type        * ktype;
        struct list_head        list;
...
        struct kobject          kobj;
        struct kset_uevent_ops  * uevent_ops;
};
```

Interestingly, the `kset` serves as the first example for the use of kernel objects. Since the management structure for sets is nothing other than a kernel object, it can be managed via the previously discussed `struct kobj`. Indeed, an instance is embedded via `kobj`. It has nothing to do with the `kobjects` collected in the set, but only serves to manage the properties of the `kset` object itself.

The other members have the following meaning:

- ❑ `ktype` points to a further object that generalizes the behavior of the `kset`.
- ❑ `list` is used to build a list of all kernel objects that are a member of the set.
- ❑ `uevent_ops` provides several function pointers to methods that relay information about the state of the set to userland. This mechanism is used by the core of the driver model, for instance, to format messages that inform about the addition of new devices.

Another structure is provided to group common features of kernel objects. It is defined as follows:

```
<kobject.h>
struct kobj_type {
...
        struct sysfs_ops        * sysfs_ops;
        struct attribute        ** default_attrs;
};
```

Note that a `kobj_type` is *not* used to collect various kernel objects — this is already managed by `ksets`. Instead, it provides an interface to the sysfs filesystem (discussed in Section 10.3). If multiple objects export similar information via the filesystem, then this can be simplified by using a single ktype to provide the required methods.

Reference Counting

Reference counting is used to detect from how many places in the kernel an object is used. Whenever one part of the kernel needs information contained in one object, it increments the reference count, and when it does not need the information anymore, the count is decremented. Once the count has dropped to 0, the kernel knows that the object is not required anymore, and that it is safe to release it from memory. The kernel provides the following data structure to handle reference counting:

```
<kref.h>
struct kref {
        atomic_t refcount;
};
```

The data structure is really simple in that it only provides a generic, atomic reference count. "Atomic" means in this context that incrementing and decrementing the variable is also safe on multiprocessor systems, where more than one code path can access an object at the same time. Chapter 5 discusses the need for this in more detail.

The auxiliary methods `kref_init`, `kref_get`, and `kref_put` are provided to initialize, increment, or decrement the reference counter. This might seem trivial at a first glance. Nevertheless, it helps to avoid excessive code duplication because such reference counts together with the aforementioned operations are used all over the kernel.

> Although manipulating the reference counter this way is safe against concurrency issues, this does *not* imply that the surrounding data structure is safe against concurrent access! Kernel code needs to employ further means to ensure that access to data structures does not cause any problems when this can happen from multiple processors simultaneously, and I discuss these issues in Chapter 5.

Finally, notice that the kernel contains some documentation related to kernel objects in `Documentation/kobject.txt`.

1.3.15 Data Types

Some issues related to data types are handled differently in the kernel in comparison to userland programs.

Type Definitions

The kernel uses `typedef` to define various data types in order to make itself independent of architecture-specific features because of the different bit lengths for standard data types on individual processors. The definitions have names such as `sector_t` (to specify a sector number on a block device), `pid_t` (to indicate a process identifier), and so on, and are defined by the kernel in architecture-specific code in such a way as to ensure that they represent the applicable value range. Because it is not usually important to know on which fundamental data types the definitions are based, and for simplicity's sake, I do not always discuss the exact definitions of data types in the following chapters. Instead, I use them without further explanation — after all, they are simply non-compound standard data types under a different name.

> `typedef`'d variables must not be accessed directly, but only via auxiliary functions that I introduce when we encounter the type. This ensures that they are properly manipulated, although the type definition is transparent to the user.

At certain points, the kernel must make use of variables with an exact, clearly defined number of bits — for example, when data structures need to be stored on hard disk. To allow data to be exchanged between various systems (e.g., on USB sticks), the same external format must always be used, regardless of how data are represented internally in the computer.

To this end, the kernel defines several integer data types that not only indicate explicitly whether they are signed or unsigned, but also specify the *exact* number of bits they comprise. __s8 and __u8 are, for example, 8-bit integers that are either signed (__s8) or unsigned (__u8). __u16 and __s16, __u32 and __s32, and __u64 and __s64 are defined in the same way.

Byte Order

To represent numbers, modern computers use either the *big endian* or *little endian* format. The format indicates how multibyte data types are stored. With big endian ordering, the most significant byte is stored at the lowest address and the significance of the bytes decreases as the addresses increase. With little endian ordering, the least significant byte is stored at the lowest address and the significance of the bytes increases as the addresses increase (some architectures such as MIPS support both variants). Figure 1-13 illustrates the issue.

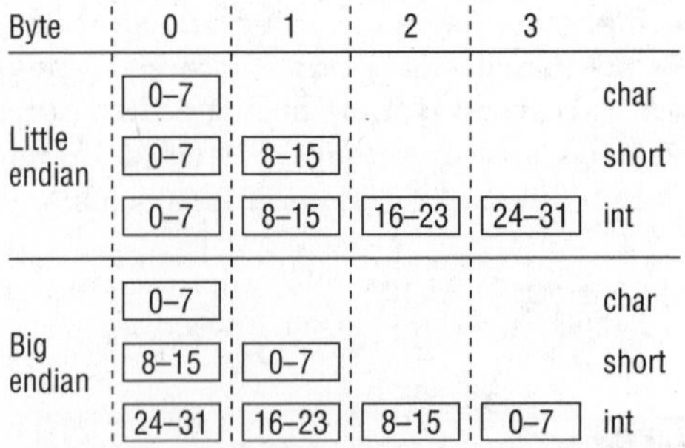

Figure 1-13: Composition of elementary data types depending on the endianness of the underlying architecture.

The kernel provides various functions and macros to convert between the format used by the CPU and specific representations: `cpu_to_le64` converts a 64-bit data type to little endian format, and `le64_to_cpu` does the reverse (if the architecture works with little endian format, the routines are, of course, no-ops; otherwise, the byte positions must be exchanged accordingly). Conversion routines are available for all combinations of 64, 32, and 16 bits for big and little endian.

Per-CPU Variables

A particularity that does not occur in normal userspace programming is per-CPU variables. They are declared with `DEFINE_PER_CPU(name, type)`, where `name` is the variable name and `type` is the data type (e.g., `int[3]`, `struct hash`, etc.). On single-processor systems, this is not different from regular variable declaration. On SMP systems with several CPUs, an instance of the variable is created for each CPU. The instance for a particular CPU is selected with `get_cpu(name, cpu)`, where `smp_processor_id()`, which returns the identifier of the active processor, is usually used as the argument for `cpu`.

Employing per-CPU variables has the advantage that the data required are more likely to be present in the cache of a processor and can therefore be accessed faster. This concept also skirts round several communication problems that would arise when using variables that can be accessed by all CPUs of a multiprocessor system.

Access to Userspace

At many points in the source code there are pointers labeled `__user`; these are also unknown in userspace programming. The kernel uses them to identify pointers to areas in user address space that may not be de-referenced without further precautions. This is because memory is mapped via page tables into the userspace portion of the virtual address space and not directly mapped by physical memory. Therefore the kernel needs to ensure that the page frame in RAM that backs the destination is actually *present* — I discuss this in further detail in Chapter 2. Explicit labeling supports the use of an automatic checker tool (`sparse`) to ensure that this requirement is observed in practice.

1.3.16 . . . and Beyond the Infinite

Although a wide range of topics are covered in this book, they inevitably just represent a portion of what Linux is capable of: It is simply impossible to discuss all aspects of the kernel in detail. I have tried to choose topics that are likely to be most interesting for a general audience and also present a representative cross-section of the whole kernel ecosystem.

Besides going through many important parts of the kernel, one of my concerns is also to equip you with the general idea of why the kernel is designed as it is, and how design decisions are made by interacting developers. Besides a discussion of numerous fields that are not directly related to the kernel (e.g., how the GNU C compiler works), but that support kernel development as such, I have also included a discussion about some nontechnical but social aspects of kernel development in Appendix F.

Finally, please note Figure 1-14, which shows the growth of the kernel sources during the last couple of years.

Kernel development is a highly dynamical process, and the speed at which the kernel acquires new features and continues to improve is sometimes nothing short of miraculous. As a study by the Linux Foundation has shown [KHCM], roughly 10,000 patches go into each kernel release, and this massive amount of code is created by nearly 1,000 developers per release. On average, 2.83 changes are integrated *every* hour, 24 hours a day, and 7 days a week! This can only be handled with mature means of source code management and communication between developers; I come back to these issues in Appendices B and F.

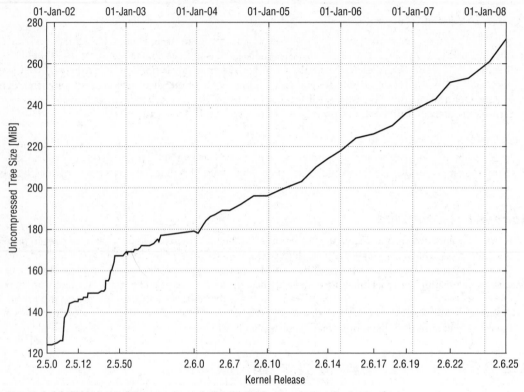

Figure 1-14: Evolution of the core kernel distribution's size during the last years.

1.4 Why the Kernel Is Special

The kernel is an amazing place — but after all, it is just a big C program with some assembler portions (and a drop or two of black magic added sometimes). So what makes the kernel so fascinating? Several factors contribute to this. First and foremost, the kernel is written by the best programmers in the world, and this shows in the code. It is well structured, written with meticulous attention for detail, and contains clever solutions all over the place. In one word: It is code as it ought to be. This, however, does not mean that the kernel is the product of a textbook-style programming methodology: While it employs cleanly designed abstractions to keep the code modular and manageable, it's the mix with the other face of the kernel that makes the code so interesting and unique: If it need be, the kernel does not back off from reusing bit positions in a context-dependent manner, overloading structure elements multiple times, squeezing yet another storage bit out of the aligned portion of pointers, using gotos freely, and numerous other things that would make any structured programmer scream miserably in agony and pain.

Techniques that would be unthinkable in many textbook solutions *can* not only be good, but are simply required for a proper real-world working kernel. It's the small path that keeps the balance between these totally opposite faces of the kernel that makes the whole thing so interesting, challenging, and fun!

Having praised the kernel sources, there are a number of more sober issues distinct from userland programs:

❏ Debugging the kernel is usually harder than debugging userland programs. While for the latter a multitude of debuggers exist, this is much harder to realize for the kernel. There *are* various mechanisms to employ debuggers in kernel development as discussed in Appendix B, but these require more effort than their userland counterparts.

❏ The kernel provides numerous auxiliary functions that resemble the standard C library found in userspace, but things are much more frugal in the kernel domain.

❏ Errors in userland applications lead to a segmentation fault or a core dump, but kernel errors will take the whole system down. Or, what is even worse: They will keep the kernel happily running, but manifest themselves in a weird system crash hours after the error occurred. Because debugging in kernel space is harder than for userland applications as mentioned above, it is essential that kernel code receives more thought and judicious consideration than userland code before it is brought into use.

❏ It must be taken into account that many architectures on which the kernel runs do not support unaligned memory access without further ado. This also affects portability of data structures across architectures because of padding that is inserted by the compiler. This issue is discussed further in Appendix C.

❏ All kernel code must be protected against concurrency. Owing to the support of multiprocessor machines, Linux kernel code must be both reentrant and thread-safe. That is, routines must allow being executed simultaneously, and data must be protected against parallel access.

❏ Kernel code must work both on machines with little and big endianness.

❏ Most architectures do not allow performing floating-point calculations in the kernel without further ado, so you need to find a way to do your calculations with integer types.

You will see how to deal with these issues in the further course of this book.

1.5   Some Notes on Presentation

Before we start to dive right into the kernel, I need to make some remarks on how I present the material, and why I have chosen my particular approach.

Notice that this book is specifically about *understanding* the kernel. Examples of how to write code have intentionally and explicitly been left out, considering that this book is already very comprehensive and voluminous. The works by Corbet et al. [CRKH05], Venkateswaran [Ven08], and Quade/Kunst [QK06] fill in this gap and discuss how to create new code, especially for drivers, by countless practical examples. While I discuss how the kernel build system, which is responsible to create a kernel that precisely suits your needs works, I won't discuss the plethora of configuration options in detail, especially because they are mostly concerned with driver configuration. However, the book by Kroah-Hartman [KH07] can be a valuable aid here.

Usually I start my discussion with a general overview about the concepts of the topic that I am going to present, and then go down to data structures and their interrelation in the kernel. Code is usually discussed last, because this requires the highest level of detail. I have chosen this *top-down* approach because it is in our opinion the most accessible and easiest way to understand the kernel. Notice that it would also be possible to discuss things from the bottom up, that is, start deep down in the kernel and then work slowly up to the C library and userspace level. Notice, however, that presenting something in inverse order does not automatically make it *better*. In my experience, more forward references are required for a bottom-up than for a top-down strategy, so I stick to the latter throughout this book.

When I directly present C source code, I sometimes take the liberty to rewrite it slightly to highlight more important elements and remove less important "due diligence" work. For example, it is very important for the kernel to check the return value of every memory allocation. While allocations *will* succeed in nearly almost all cases, it is essential to take care of cases in which not enough memory is available for a particular task. The kernel has to deal with this situation somehow, usually by returning an error return code to userspace if a task is performed as a response to a request by an application, or by omitting a warning message to the system log. However, details of this kind will in general obstruct the view of what is really important. Consider the following code, which sets up namespaces for a process:

kernel/nsproxy.c
```c
static struct nsproxy *create_new_namespaces(unsigned long flags,
                        struct task_struct *tsk, struct fs_struct *new_fs)
{
        struct nsproxy *new_nsp;
        int err;

        new_nsp = clone_nsproxy(tsk->nsproxy);
        if (!new_nsp)
                return ERR_PTR(-ENOMEM);

        new_nsp->mnt_ns = copy_mnt_ns(flags, tsk->nsproxy->mnt_ns, new_fs);
        if (IS_ERR(new_nsp->mnt_ns)) {
                err = PTR_ERR(new_nsp->mnt_ns);
                goto out_ns;
        }

        new_nsp->uts_ns = copy_utsname(flags, tsk->nsproxy->uts_ns);
        if (IS_ERR(new_nsp->uts_ns)) {
                err = PTR_ERR(new_nsp->uts_ns);
                goto out_uts;
        }

        new_nsp->ipc_ns = copy_ipcs(flags, tsk->nsproxy->ipc_ns);
        if (IS_ERR(new_nsp->ipc_ns)) {
                err = PTR_ERR(new_nsp->ipc_ns);
                goto out_ipc;
        }
...
        return new_nsp;
out_ipc:
        if (new_nsp->uts_ns)
                put_uts_ns(new_nsp->uts_ns);
out_uts:
        if (new_nsp->mnt_ns)
```

```
                    put_mnt_ns(new_nsp->mnt_ns);
out_ns:
            kmem_cache_free(nsproxy_cachep, new_nsp);
            return ERR_PTR(err);
    }
```

What the code does in detail is irrelevant right now; I come back to this in the following chapter. What is essential is that the routine tries to clone various parts of the namespace depending on some flags that control the cloning operation. Each type of namespace is handled in a separate function, for instance, in copy_mnt_ns for the filesystem namespace.

Each time the kernel copies a namespace, errors can occur, and these must be detected and passed on to the calling function. Either the error is detected directly by the return code of a function, as for clone_nsproxy, or the error is encoded in a pointer return value, which can be detected using the ERR_PTR macro, which allows for decoding the error value (I also discuss this mechanism below). In many cases, it is not sufficient to just detect an error and return this information to the caller. It is also essential that previously allocated resources that are not required anymore because of the error are released again. The standard technique of the kernel to handle this situation is as follows: Jump to a special label and free all previously allocated resources, or put down references to objects by decrementing the reference count. Handling such cases as this is one of the valid applications for the goto statement. There are various possibilities to describe what is going on in the function:

❑   Talk the reader directly through the code in huge step-by-step lists:

   1.   create_new_namespace calls clone_nsproxy. If this fails, return -ENOMEM; otherwise, continue.

   2.   create_new_namespace then calls copy_mnt_ns. If this fails, obtain the error value encoded in the return value of copy_mnt_ns and jump to the label out_ns; otherwise, proceed.

   3.   create_new_namespace then calls copy_utsname. If this fails, obtain the error value encoded in the return value of copy_utsname and jump to the label out_ns; otherwise, proceed.

   4.   ...

   While this approach is favored by a number of kernel texts, it conveys only little information in addition to what is directly visible from the source code anyway. It is appropriate to discuss some of the most complicated low-level parts of the kernel this way, but this will foster an understanding of neither the big picture in general nor the code snippet involved in particular.

❑   Summarize what the function does with words, for instance, by remarking that "create_new_namespaces is responsible to create copies or clones of the parent namespaces." We use this approach for less important tasks of the kernel that need to be done somehow, but do not provide any specific insights or use particularly interesting tricks.

❑   Use a flow diagram to illustrate what is going on in a function. With more than 150 code flow diagrams in this book, this is one of my preferred ways of dealing with code. It is important to note that these diagrams *are not supposed* to be a completely faithful representation of the operation. This would hardly simplify matters. Consider Figure 1-15, which illustrates how a faithful representation of copy_namespaces could look. It is not at all simpler to read than the source itself, so there is not much purpose in providing it.

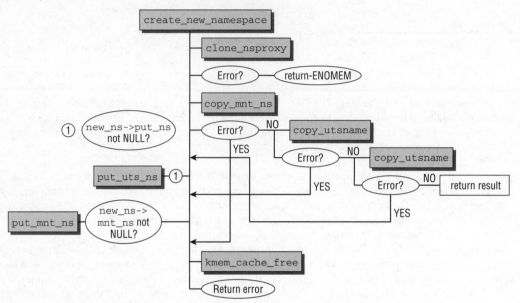

Figure 1-15: Example of a faithful, but unclear and convoluted code flow diagram.

Instead I employ code flow diagrams that illustrate the essential tasks performed by a function. Figure 1-16 shows the code flow diagram that I would have employed instead of Figure 1-15.

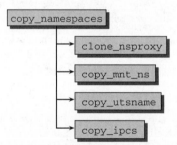

Figure 1-16: Example of the style of code flow diagrams used in this book. They allow immediately catching all essential actions without being distracted by nonessential standard tasks.

The diagram omits several things, but this is on purpose, and also essential. By looking at the figure, you will not see every detail of the function implementation, but you will instead immediately realize that the kernel uses a specific routine to create a clone of each namespace, and the function names provide a sufficient hint of which namespace is copied. This is much more important!

Handling error return codes is something that we assume goes without saying, and so we will not pay particular attention to it. This does not imply that it is not an important thing to do, and in fact it is: Linux would be a lousy kernel if it did not handle this issue properly. But handling errors also obfuscates most operations without introducing any new insights, and does not make it easier to understand the general principles of the kernel, so it's usually better to sacrifice some thoroughness for clarity. The kernel sources are always available for all the gory details!

❑ It is also often important to discuss kernel code directly if it is packed with important decisions, and I do so when I deem it necessary. However, I often take the liberty of omitting less interesting or purely mechanical parts, so don't be astonished if the code presented in the book sometimes differs slightly from the code seen in the kernel.

With respect to the source code, this book *is* self-contained, but it certainly helps if it is not read on a desolate island, but next to a computer where the Linux source code is available and can be inspected. Besides that, being on a desolate island is not much fun anyway.

Since I base many machine-specific examples on IA-32 and AMD64, some words about these terms are in order. "IA-32" includes all Intel-compatible CPUs such as Pentium, Athlon, and so on. AMD64 also includes the Intel variant EM64T. For the sake of simplicity, I use only the abbreviations IA-32 and AMD64 in this book. Since Intel undoubtedly invented IA-32 and AMD came up first with the 64-bit extensions, this seems a fair compromise. It is also interesting to note that starting with kernel 2.6.23, both architectures are unified to the generic x86 architecture within the Linux kernel. This makes the code easier to maintain for the developers because many elements can be shared between both variants, but nevertheless still distinguishes between 32- and 64-bit capabilities of the processors.

1.6 Summary

The Linux kernel is one of the most interesting and fascinating pieces of software ever written, and I hope this chapter has succeeded in whetting your appetite for the things to come in the following chapters, where I discuss many subsystems in detail. For now, I have provided a bird's eye view of the kernel to present the big picture of how responsibilities are distributed, which part of the kernel has to deal with which problems, and how the components interact with each other.

Since the kernel is a huge system, there are some issues related to the presentation of the complex material, and I have introduced you to the particular approach chosen for this book.

2

Process Management and Scheduling

All modern operating systems are able to run several processes at the same time — at least, this is the impression users get. If a system has only one processor, only one program can run on it at a given time. In multiprocessor systems, the number of processes that can truly run in parallel is determined by the number of physical CPUs.

The kernel and the processor create the illusion of *multitasking* — the ability to perform several operations in parallel — by switching repeatedly between the different applications running on the system at very rapid intervals. Because the switching intervals are so short, users do not notice the intervening brief periods of inactivity and gain the impression that the computer is actually doing several things at once.

This kind of system management gives rise to several issues that the kernel must resolve, the most important of which are listed below.

❑　Applications must not interfere with each other unless this is expressly desired. For example, an error in application A must not be propagated to application B. Because Linux is a multiuser system, it must also be ensured that programs are not able to read or modify the memory contents of other programs — otherwise, it would be extremely easy to access the private data of other users.

❑　CPU time must be shared as fairly as possible between the various applications, whereby some programs are regarded as more important than others.

I deal with the first requirement — memory protection — in Chapter 3. In the present chapter, I focus my attention on the methods employed by the kernel to share CPU time and to switch between processes. This twofold task is split into two parts that are performed relatively independently of each other.

❑ The kernel must decide how much time to devote to each process and when to switch to the next process. This begs the question as to *which* process is actually the next. Decisions of this kind are not platform-dependent.

❑ When the kernel switches from process A to process B, it must ensure that the execution environment of B is exactly the same as when it last withdrew processor resources. For example, the contents of the processor registers and the structure of virtual address space must be identical.

This latter task is extremely dependent on processor type. It cannot be implemented with C only, but requires help by pure assembler portions.

Both tasks are the responsibility of a kernel subsystem referred to as the *scheduler*. How CPU time is allocated is determined by the scheduler *policy*, which is totally separate from the *task switching* mechanism needed to switch between processes.

2.1   Process Priorities

Not all processes are of equal importance. In addition to process priority, with which most readers will be familiar, there are different criticality classes to satisfy differing demands. In a first coarse distinction, processes can be split into real-time processes and non-real-time processes.

❑ *Hard real-time processes* are subject to strict time limits during which certain tasks must be completed. If the flight control commands of an aircraft are processed by computer, they must be forwarded as quickly as possible — within a guaranteed period of time. For example, if an aircraft is on its landing approach and the pilot wants to pull up the nose, it serves little purpose if the computer forwards the command a few seconds later. By this time, the aircraft may well be buried — nose first — in the ground. The key characteristic of hard real-time processes is that they must be processed within a guaranteed time frame. Note that this does not imply that the time frame is particularly short. Instead, the system must guarantee that a certain time frame is never exceeded, even when unlikely or adverse conditions prevail.

Linux does not support hard real-time processing, at least not in the vanilla kernel. There are, however, modified versions such as RTLinux, Xenomai, or RATI that offer this feature. The Linux kernel runs as a separate "process" in these approaches and handles less important software, while real-time work is done outside the kernel. The kernel may run only if no real-time critical actions are performed.

Since Linux is optimized for throughput and tries to handle common cases as fast as possible, guaranteed response times are only very hard to achieve. Nevertheless quite a bit of progress has been made during the last years to decrease the overall kernel latency, that is, the time that elapses between making a request and its fulfillment. The efforts include the preemptible kernel mechanism, real-time mutexes, and the new completely fair scheduler discussed in this book.

❑ *Soft real-time processes* are a softer form of hard real-time processes. Although quick results are still required, it is not the end of the world if they are a little late in arriving. An example of a soft real-time process is a write operation to a CD. Data must be received by the CD writer at a certain rate because data are written to the medium in a continuous stream. If system loading is too high, the data stream may be interrupted briefly, and this may result in an unusable CD, far less drastic than a plane crash. Nevertheless, the write process should always be granted CPU time when needed — before all other normal processes.

❑ Most processes are *normal processes* that have no specific time constraints but can still be classified as more important or less important by assigning *priorities* to them.

For example, a long compiler run or numerical calculations need only very low priority because it is of little consequence if computation is interrupted occasionally for a second or two — users are unlikely to notice. In contrast, interactive applications should respond as quickly as possible to user commands because users are notoriously impatient.

The allocation of CPU time can be portrayed in much simplified form as in Figure 2-1. Processes are spread over a time slice, and the share of the slice allocated to them corresponds to their relative importance. The time flow in the system corresponds to the turning of the circle, and the CPU is represented by a "scanner" at the circumference of the circle. The net effect is that important processes are granted more CPU time than less important processes, although all eventually have their turn.

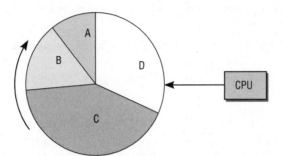

Figure 2-1: Allocation of CPU time by means of time slices.

In this scheme, known as *preemptive multitasking*, each process is allocated a certain time period during which it may execute. Once this period has expired, the kernel withdraws control from the process and lets a different process run — regardless of the last task performed by the previous process. Its runtime environment — essentially, the contents of all CPU registers and the page tables — is, of course, saved so that results are not lost and the process environment is fully reinstated when its turn comes around again. The length of the time slice varies depending on the importance of the process (and therefore on the priority assigned to it). Figure 2-1 illustrates this by allocating segments of different sizes to the individual processes.

This simplified model does not take into account several important issues. For example, processes may not be ready to execute at certain times because they have nothing to do. Because it is essential to use CPU time as profitably as possible, such processes must be prevented from executing. This is not evident in Figure 2-1 because it is assumed that all processes are always ready to run. Also ignored is the fact that Linux supports different scheduling classes (completely fair scheduling between processes, and real-time scheduling), and these must also be taken into consideration during scheduling. Neither is there an option to replace the current process with an important process that has become ready to run.

Note that process scheduling causes very fervid and excited discussion among kernel developers, especially when it comes to picking the best possible algorithm. Finding a quantitative measure for the quality of a scheduler is a very hard — if not impossible — task. It is also a very challenging task for a scheduler to fulfill the requirements imposed by the many different workloads that Linux systems have to face: Small embedded systems for automated control usually have very different requirements than large number crunchers, while these in turn differ considerably from multimedia systems. In fact, the scheduler code has seen two complete rewrites in recent years:

1. During the development series 2.5, a so-called $\mathcal{O}(1)$ scheduler replaced the previous scheduler. One particular property of this scheduler was that it could perform its work in constant time independent of the number of processes that were running on a system. The design broke quite radically with the previously employed scheduling architecture.

2. The *completely fair scheduler* was merged during the development of kernel 2.6.23. The new code again marked a complete departure from previous principles by abandoning, for instance, many heuristics that were required in previous schedulers to ensure that interactive tasks would respond quickly. The key feature of this scheduler is that it tries to resemble ideal fair scheduling as close as possible. Besides, it cannot only schedule individual tasks, but works with more general *scheduling entities*. This allows, for instance, for distribution the available time between all processes of different users, and then among the processes of each user.

    I discuss the implementation of this scheduler below in detail.

Before we concern ourselves with how scheduling is implemented in the kernel, it is useful to discuss the states that a process may have.

2.2 Process Life Cycle

A process is not always ready to run. Occasionally, it has to wait for events from external sources beyond its control — for keyboard input in a text editor, for example. Until the event occurs, the process cannot run.

The scheduler must know the status of every process in the system when switching between tasks; it obviously doesn't make sense to assign CPU time to processes that have nothing to do. Of equal importance are the transitions between individual process states. For example, if a process is waiting for data from a peripheral device, it is the responsibility of the scheduler to change the state of the process from waiting to runnable once the data have arrived.

A process may have one of the following states:

❏   **Running** — The process is executing at the moment.

❏   **Waiting** — The process is able to run but is not allowed to because the CPU is allocated to another process. The scheduler can select the process, if it wants to, at the next task switch.

❏   **Sleeping** — The process is sleeping and cannot run because it is waiting for an external event. The scheduler *cannot* select the process at the next task switch.

The system saves all processes in a process table — regardless of whether they are running, sleeping, or waiting. However, sleeping processes are specially "marked" so that the scheduler knows they are not ready to run (see how this is implemented in Section 2.3). There are also a number of queues that group sleeping processes so that they can be woken at a suitable time — when, for example, an external event that the process has been waiting for takes place.

Figure 2-2 shows several process states and transitions.

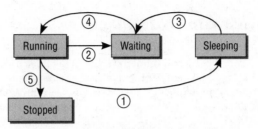

Figure 2-2: Transitions between process states.

Let's start our examination of the various transitions with a queued runnable process; the process is ready to run but is not allowed to because the CPU is allocated to a different process (its state is therefore "waiting"). It remains in this state until the scheduler grants it CPU time. Once this happens, its state changes to "running" (path 4).

When the scheduler decides to withdraw CPU resources from the process — I deal with the possible reasons why shortly — the process state changes from "running" to "waiting" (path 2), and the cycle starts anew. There are, in fact, two "sleeping" states that differ according to whether they can be interrupted by signals or not. At the moment, this difference is not important, but it is of relevance when we examine implementation more closely.

If the process has to wait for an event, its state changes (path 1) from "running" to "sleeping." However, it cannot change directly from "sleeping" to "running"; once the event it was waiting for has taken place, the process changes back to the "waiting" state (path 3) and then rejoins the normal cycle.

Once program execution terminates (e.g., the user closes the the application), the process state changes from "running" to "stopped" (path 5).

A special process state not listed above is the "zombie"state. As the name suggests, such processes are defunct but are somehow still alive. In reality, they are dead because their resources (RAM, connections to peripherals, etc.) have already been released so that they cannot and never will run again. However, they are still alive because there are still entries for them in the process table.

How do zombies come about? The reason lies in the process creation and destruction structure under UNIX. A program terminates when two events occur — first, the program must be killed by another process or by a user (this is usually done by sending a SIGTERM or SIGKILL signal, which is equivalent to terminating the process regularly); second, the parent process from which the process originates must invoke or have already invoked the wait4 (read: *wait for*) system call when the child process terminates. This confirms to the kernel that the parent process has acknowledged the death of the child. The system call enables the kernel to free resources reserved by the child process.

A zombie occurs when only the first condition (the program is terminated) applies but not the second (wait4). A process always switches briefly to the zombie state between termination and removal of its data from the process table. In some cases (if, e.g., the parent process is badly programmed and does not issue a wait call), a zombie can firmly lodge itself in the process table and remain there until the next reboot. This can be seen by reading the output of process tools such as `ps` or `top`. This is hardly a problem as the residual data take up little space in the kernel.

2.2.1 Preemptive Multitasking

The structure of Linux process management requires two further process state options — user mode and kernel mode. These reflect the fact that all modern CPUs have (at least) two different execution modes, one of which has unlimited rights while the other is subject to various restrictions — for example, access to certain memory areas can be prohibited. This distinction is an important prerequisite for creating locked "cages," which hold existing processes and prevent them from interfering with other parts of the system.

Normally the kernel is in user mode in which it may access only its own data and cannot therefore interfere with other applications in the system — it usually doesn't even notice that there are other programs besides itself.

If a process wants to access system data or functions (the latter manage the resources shared between all processes, e.g., filesystem space), it must switch to kernel mode. Obviously, this is possible only under control — otherwise all established protection mechanisms would be superfluous — and via clearly defined paths. Chapter 1 mentioned briefly that "system calls" are one way to switch between modes. Chapter 13 discusses the implementation of such calls in depth.

A second way of switching from user mode to kernel mode is by means of interrupts — switching is then triggered automatically. Unlike system calls, which are invoked intentionally by user applications, interrupts occur more or less arbitrarily. Generally, the actions needed to handle interrupts have nothing to do with the process executing when the interrupt occurred. For example, an interrupt is raised when an external block device has transferred data to RAM, although these data may be intended for any process running on the system. Similarly, incoming network packages are announced by means of an interrupt. Again, it is unlikely that the inbound package is intended for the process currently running. For this reason, Linux performs these actions in such a way that the running process is totally unaware of them.

The preemptive scheduling model of the kernel establishes a hierarchy that determines which process states may be interrupted by which other states.

❑ Normal processes may always be interrupted — even by other processes. When an important process becomes runnable — for example, an editor receives long-awaited keyboard input — the scheduler can decide whether to execute the process immediately, even if the current process is still happily running. This kind of preemption makes an important contribution to good interactive behavior and low system latency.

❑ If the system is in kernel mode and is processing a system call, no other process in the system is able to cause withdrawal of CPU time. The scheduler is forced to wait until execution of the system call has terminated before it can select another process. However, the system call can be suspended by an interrupt.[1]

❑ Interrupts can suspend processes in user mode and in kernel mode. They have the highest priority because it is essential to handle them as soon as possible after they are issued.

---

[1]It is possible to disable almost all interrupts for important kernel actions.

One option known as *kernel preemption* was added to the kernel during the development of kernel 2.5. This option supports switches to another process, if this is urgently required, even during the execution of system calls in kernel mode (but not during interrupts). Although the kernel attempts to execute system calls as quickly as possible, the time needed may be too long for some applications that are reliant on constant data streams. Kernel preemption can reduce such wait times and thus ensure "smoother" program execution. However, this is at the expense of increased kernel complexity because many data structures then need to be protected against concurrent access even on single-processor systems. This technique is discussed in Section 2.8.3.

2.3 Process Representation

All algorithms of the Linux kernel concerned with processes and programs are built around a data structure named `task_struct` and defined in `include/sched.h`. This is one of the central structures in the system. Before we move on to deal with the implementation of the scheduler, it is essential to examine how Linux manages processes.

The task structure includes a large number of elements that link the process with the kernel subsystems which I discuss below. I therefore make frequent reference to later chapters because it is difficult to explain the significance of some elements without detailed knowledge of them.

The task structure is defined as follows — in simplified form:

<sched.h>
```
struct task_struct {
        volatile long state;      /* -1 unrunnable, 0 runnable, >0 stopped */
        void *stack;
        atomic_t usage;
        unsigned long flags;      /* per process flags, defined below */
        unsigned long ptrace;
        int lock_depth;           /* BKL lock depth */

        int prio, static_prio, normal_prio;
        struct list_head run_list;
        const struct sched_class *sched_class;
        struct sched_entity se;

        unsigned short ioprio;

        unsigned long policy;
        cpumask_t cpus_allowed;
        unsigned int time_slice;

#if defined(CONFIG_SCHEDSTATS) || defined(CONFIG_TASK_DELAY_ACCT)
        struct sched_info sched_info;
#endif

        struct list_head tasks;
        /*
         * ptrace_list/ptrace_children forms the list of my children
         * that were stolen by a ptracer.
         */
        struct list_head ptrace_children;
```

```
        struct list_head ptrace_list;

        struct mm_struct *mm, *active_mm;

/* task state */
        struct linux_binfmt *binfmt;
        long exit_state;
        int exit_code, exit_signal;
        int pdeath_signal;  /*  The signal sent when the parent dies  */

        unsigned int personality;
        unsigned did_exec:1;
        pid_t pid;
        pid_t tgid;
        /*
         * pointers to (original) parent process, youngest child, younger sibling,
         * older sibling, respectively.  (p->father can be replaced with
         * p->parent->pid)
         */
        struct task_struct *real_parent; /* real parent process (when being debugged) */
        struct task_struct *parent;      /* parent process */
        /*
         * children/sibling forms the list of my children plus the
         * tasks I'm ptracing.
         */
        struct list_head children;      /* list of my children */
        struct list_head sibling;       /* linkage in my parent's children list */
        struct task_struct *group_leader;      /* threadgroup leader */

        /* PID/PID hash table linkage. */
        struct pid_link pids[PIDTYPE_MAX];
        struct list_head thread_group;

        struct completion *vfork_done;          /* for vfork() */
        int __user *set_child_tid;              /* CLONE_CHILD_SETTID */
        int __user *clear_child_tid;            /* CLONE_CHILD_CLEARTID */

        unsigned long rt_priority;
        cputime_t utime, stime, utimescaled, stimescaled;;
        unsigned long nvcsw, nivcsw; /* context switch counts */
        struct timespec start_time; /* monotonic time */
        struct timespec real_start_time; /* boot based time */
        /* mm fault and swap info: this can arguably be seen as either
           mm-specific or thread-specific */
        unsigned long min_flt, maj_flt;

        cputime_t it_prof_expires, it_virt_expires;
        unsigned long long it_sched_expires;
        struct list_head cpu_timers[3];

/* process credentials */
        uid_t uid,euid,suid,fsuid;
        gid_t gid,egid,sgid,fsgid;
        struct group_info *group_info;
        kernel_cap_t   cap_effective, cap_inheritable, cap_permitted;
```

```
        unsigned keep_capabilities:1;
        struct user_struct *user;

        char comm[TASK_COMM_LEN]; /* executable name excluding path
                                - access with [gs]et_task_comm (which lock
                                  it with task_lock())
                                - initialized normally by flush_old_exec */
/* file system info */
        int link_count, total_link_count;
/* ipc stuff */
        struct sysv_sem sysvsem;
/* CPU-specific state of this task */
        struct thread_struct thread;
/* filesystem information */
        struct fs_struct *fs;
/* open file information */
        struct files_struct *files;
/* namespace */
        struct nsproxy *nsproxy;
/* signal handlers */
        struct signal_struct *signal;
        struct sighand_struct *sighand;

        sigset_t blocked, real_blocked;
        sigset_t saved_sigmask;            /* To be restored with TIF_RESTORE_SIGMASK */
        struct sigpending pending;

        unsigned long sas_ss_sp;
        size_t sas_ss_size;
        int (*notifier)(void *priv);
        void *notifier_data;
        sigset_t *notifier_mask;

#ifdef CONFIG_SECURITY
        void *security;
#endif

/* Thread group tracking */
        u32 parent_exec_id;
        u32 self_exec_id;

/* journalling filesystem info */
        void *journal_info;

/* VM state */
        struct reclaim_state *reclaim_state;

        struct backing_dev_info *backing_dev_info;

        struct io_context *io_context;

        unsigned long ptrace_message;
        siginfo_t *last_siginfo; /* For ptrace use.   */
...
};
```

Admittedly, it is difficult to digest the amount of information in this structure. However, the structure contents can be broken down into sections, each of which represents a specific aspect of the process:

❑ State and execution information such as pending signals, binary format used (and any emulation information for binary formats of other systems), process identification number (pid), pointers to parents and other related processes, priorities, and time information on program execution (e.g., CPU time).

❑ Information on allocated virtual memory.

❑ Process credentials such as user and group ID, capabilities,[2] and so on. System calls can be used to query (or modify) these data; I deal with these in greater detail when describing the specific subsystems.

❑ Files used: Not only the binary file with the program code but also filesystem information on all files handled by the process must be saved.

❑ Thread information, which records the CPU-specific runtime data of the process (the remaining fields in the structure are not dependent on the hardware used).

❑ Information on interprocess communication required when working with other applications.

❑ Signal handlers used by the process to respond to incoming signals.

Many members of the task structure are not simple variables but pointers to other data structures examined and discussed in the following chapters. In the present chapter, I consider some elements of task_struct that are of particular significance in process management implementation.

state specifies the current state of a process and accepts the following values (these are pre-processor constants defined in <sched.h>):

❑ TASK_RUNNING means that a task is in a runnable state. It does not mean that a CPU is actually allocated. The task can wait until it is selected by the scheduler. This state guarantees that the process really is ready to run and is not waiting for an external event.

❑ TASK_INTERRUPTIBLE is set for a sleeping process that is waiting for some event or other. When the kernel signals to the process that the event has occurred, it is placed in the TASK_RUNNING state and may resume execution as soon as it is selected by the scheduler.

❑ TASK_UNINTERRUPTIBLE is used for sleeping processes disabled on the instructions of the kernel. They may not be woken by external signals, only by the kernel itself.

❑ TASK_STOPPED indicates that the process was stopped on purpose — by a debugger, for example.

❑ TASK_TRACED is not a process state per se — it is used to distinguish stopped tasks that are currently being traced (using the ptrace mechanism) from regular stopped tasks.

The following constants can be used both in the task state field of struct task_struct, but also in the field exit_state, which is specifically for exiting processes.

❑ EXIT_ZOMBIE is the zombie state described above.

❑ EXIT_DEAD is the state after an appropriate wait system call has been issued and before the task is completely removed from the system. This state is only of importance if multiple threads issue wait calls for the same task.

---

[2]Capabilities are special permissions that can be granted to a process. They allow the process to perform certain operations that normally may be performed only by root processes.

Linux provides the *resource limit* (rlimit) mechanism to impose certain system resource usage limits on processes. The mechanism makes use of the `rlim` array in `task_struct`, whose elements are of the `struct rlimit` type.

\<resource.h\>
```
struct rlimit {
        unsigned long    rlim_cur;
        unsigned long    rlim_max;
}
```

The definition is purposely kept very general so that it can accept many different resource types.

❑   `rlim_cur` is the current resource limit for the process. It is also referred to as the *soft limit*.

❑   `rlim_max` is the maximum allowed value for the limit. It is therefore also referred to as the *hard limit*.

The `setrlimit` system call is used to increase or decrease the current limit. However, the value specified in `rlim_max` may not be exceeded. `getrlimits` is used to check the current limit.

The limitable resources are identified by reference to their position in the `rlim` array, which is why the kernel defines pre-processor constants to associate resource and position. Table 2-1 lists the possible constants and their meanings. Textbooks on system programming provide detailed explanations on best use of the various limits in practice, and the manual page `setrlimit(2)` contains more detailed descriptions of all limits.

> **The numeric values differ between architectures because Linux tries to establish binary compatibility with the specific native Unix systems.**

Because the limits relate to very different parts of the kernel, the kernel must check that the limits are observed in the corresponding subsystems. This is why we encounter rlimit time and time again in later chapters of this book.

If a resource type may be used without limits (the default setting for almost all resources), `RLIM_INFINITY` is used as the value for `rlim_max`. Exceptions are, among others:

❑   The number of open files (`RLIMIT_NOFILE`, limited to 1,024 by default).

❑   The maximum number of processes per user (`RLIMIT_NPROC`), defined as `max_threads/2`. `max_threads` is a global variable whose value specifies how many threads may be generated so that an eighth of available RAM is used only for management of thread information, given a minimum possible memory usage of 20 threads.

The boot-time limits for the `init` task are defined in `INIT_RLIMITS` in `include/asm-generic-resource.h`.

Notice that kernel 2.6.25, which was still under development when this book was written, will contain one file per process in the proc filesystem, which allows for inspecting the current rlimit values:

```
wolfgang@meitner> cat /proc/self/limits
Limit                   Soft Limit        Hard Limit        Units
```

```
Max cpu time            unlimited       unlimited       ms
Max file size           unlimited       unlimited       bytes
Max data size           unlimited       unlimited       bytes
Max stack size          8388608         unlimited       bytes
Max core file size      0               unlimited       bytes
Max resident set        unlimited       unlimited       bytes
Max processes           unlimited       unlimited       processes
Max open files          1024            1024            files
Max locked memory       unlimited       unlimited       bytes
Max address space       unlimited       unlimited       bytes
Max file locks          unlimited       unlimited       locks
Max pending signals     unlimited       unlimited       signals
Max msgqueue size       unlimited       unlimited       bytes
Max nice priority       0               0
Max realtime priority   0               0
Max realtime timeout    unlimited       unlimited       us
```

Table 2-1: Process-Specific Resource Limits.

Constant	Meaning
RLIMIT_CPU	Maximum CPU time in milliseconds.
RLIMIT_FSIZE	Maximum file size allowed.
RLIMIT_DATA	Maximum size of the data segment.
RLIMIT_STACK	Maximum size of the (user mode) stack.
RLIMIT_CORE	Maximum size for core dump files.
RLIMIT_RSS	Maximum size of the *resident size set*; in other words, the maximum number of page frames that a process uses. Not used at the moment.
RLIMIT_NPROC	Maximum number of processes that the user associated with the real UID of a process may own.
RLIMIT_NOFILE	Maximum number of open files.
RLIMIT_MEMLOCK	Maximum number of non-swappable pages.
RLIMIT_AS	Maximum size of virtual address space that may be occupied by a process.
RLIMIT_LOCKS	Maximum number of file locks.
RLIMIT_SIGPENDING	Maximum number of pending signals.
RLIMIT_MSGQUEUE	Maximum number of message queues.
RLIMIT_NICE	Maximum nice level for non-real-time processes.
RLIMIT_RTPRIO	Maximum real-time priority.

Most of the code to generate the information is already present in kernel 2.6.24, but the final connection with /proc will only be made in the following kernel release.

2.3.1 Process Types

A classical UNIX process is an application that consists of binary code, a chronological thread (the computer follows a single path through the code, no other paths run at the same time), and a set of resources allocated to the application — for example, memory, files, and so on. New processes are generated using the fork and exec system calls:

❑   fork generates an identical copy of the current process; this copy is known as a *child process*. All resources of the original process are copied in a suitable way so that after the system call there are two independent instances of the original process. These instances are not linked in any way but have, for example, the same set of open files, the same working directory, the same data in memory (each with its own copy of the data), and so on.[3]

❑   exec replaces a running process with another application loaded from an executable binary file. In other words, a new program is loaded. Because exec does not create a new process, an old program must first be duplicated using fork, and then exec must be called to generate an additional application on the system.

Linux also provides the clone system call in addition to the two calls above that are available in all UNIX flavors and date back to very early days. In principle, clone works in the same way as fork, but the new process is not independent of its parent process and can share some resources with it. It is possible to specify *which* resources are to be shared and which are to be copied — for example, data in memory, open files, or the installed signal handlers of the parent process.

clone is used to implement *threads*. However, the system call alone is not enough to do this. Libraries are also needed in userspace to complete implementation. Examples of such libraries are *Linuxthreads* and *Next Generation Posix Threads*.

2.3.2 Namespaces

Namespaces provide a lightweight form of virtualization by allowing us to view the global properties of a running system under different aspects. The mechanism is similar to *zones* in Solaris or the *jail* mechanism in FreeBSD. After a general overview of the concept, I discuss the infrastructure provided by the namespace framework.

Concept

Traditionally, many resources are managed globally in Linux as well as other UNIX derivatives. For instance, all processes in the system are conventionally identified by their PID, which implies that a global list of PIDs must be managed by the kernel. Likewise, the information about the system returned by the uname system call (which includes the system name and some information about the kernel) is the same for all callers. User IDs are managed in a similar fashion: Each user is identified by a UID number that is globally unique.

---

[3]In Section 2.4.1, you will see that Linux does use the copy-on-write mechanism to not copy memory pages of the forked process until the new process performs a write access to the pages — this is more efficient than blindly copying all memory pages immediately on execution of fork. The link between the memory pages of the parent and child process needed to do this is visible to the kernel only and is transparent to the applications.

Global identifiers allow the kernel to selectively grant or deny certain privileges. While the root user with UID 0 is essentially allowed to do anything, higher user IDs are more confined. A user with PID n may, for instance, not kill processes that belong to user $m \neq n$. However, this does not prevent users from *seeing* each other: User n can see that another user m is also active on the machine. This is no problem: As long as users can only fiddle with their own processes, there is no reason why they should not be allowed to observe that other users have processes as well.

There are cases, though, where this can be undesired. Consider that a web provider wants to give full access to Linux machines to customers, including root access. Traditionally, this would require setting up one machine per customer, which is a costly business. Using virtualized environments as provided by KVM or VMWare is one way to solve the problem, but does not distribute resources very well: One separate kernel is required for each customer on the machine, and also one complete installation of the surrounding userland.

A different solution that is less demanding on resources is provided by namespaces. Instead of using virtualized systems such that one physical machine can run multiple kernels — which may well be from different operating systems — in parallel, a single kernel operates on a physical machine, and all previously global resources are abstracted in *namespaces*. This allows for putting a group of processes into a *container*, and one container is separated from other containers. The separation can be such that members of one container have no connection whatsoever with other containers. Is is, however, also possible to loosen the separation of containers by allowing them to share certain aspects of their life. For instance, containers could be set up to use their own set of PIDs, but still share portions of filesystems with each other.

Namespaces essentially create different *views* of the system. Every formerly global resource must be wrapped up in a container data structure, and only tuples of the resource and the containing namespace are globally unique. While the resource alone is enough inside a given container, it does not provide a unique identity outside the container. An overview of the situation is given in Figure 2-3.

Consider a case in which three different namespaces are present on the system. Namespaces can be hierarchically related, and I consider this case here. One namespace is the parent namespace, which has spawned two child namespaces. Assume that the containers are used in a hosting setup where each container must look like a single Linux machine. Each of them therefore has its own init task with PID 0, and the PIDs of other tasks are assigned in increasing order. Both child namespaces have an init task with PID 0, and two processes with PIDs 2 and 3, respectively. Since PIDs with identical values appear multiple times on the system, the numbers are not globally unique.

While none of the child containers has any notion about other containers in the system, the parent is well informed about the children, and consequently sees all processes they execute. They are mapped to the PID range 4 to 9 in the parent process. Although there are 9 processes on the system, 15 PIDs are required to represent them because one process can be associated with more than one PID. The "right" one depends on the context in which the process is observed.

Namespaces can also be non-hierarchical if they wrap simpler quantities, for instance, like the UTS namespace discussed below. In this case, there is no connection between parent and child namespaces.

Notice that support for namespaces in a simple form has been available in Linux for quite a long time in the form of the chroot system call. This method allows for restricting processes to a certain part of

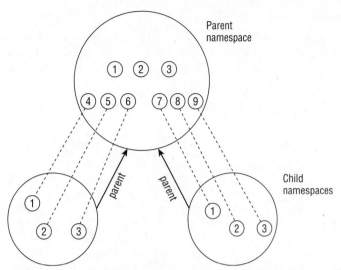

Figure 2-3: Namespaces can be related in a hierarchical order. Each namespace has a parent from which it originates, and a parent can have multiple children.

the filesystem and is thus a simple namespace mechanism. True namespaces do, however, allow for controlling much more than just the view on the filesystem.

New namespaces can be established in two ways:

1. When a new process is created with the `fork` or `clone` system call, specific options control if namespaces will be shared with the parent process, or if new namespaces are created.

2. The `unshare` system call dissociates parts of a process from the parent, and this also includes namespaces. See the manual page `unshare(2)` for more information.

Once a process has been disconnected from the parent namespace using any of the two mechanisms above, changing a — from its point of view — global property will not propagate into the parent namespace, and neither will a change on the parent side propagate into the child, at least for simple quantities. The situation is more involved for filesystems where the sharing mechanisms are very powerful and allow a plethora of possibilities, as discussed in Chapter 8.

Namespaces are currently still marked as experimental in the standard kernel, and development to make all parts of the kernel fully namespace-aware are still going on. As of kernel 2.6.24, the basic framework is, however, set up and in place.[4] The file `Documentation/namespaces/compatibility-list.txt` provides information about some problems that are still present in the current state of the implementation.

---

[4]This, however, does not imply that the approach was only recently developed. In fact, the methods have been used in production systems over many years, but were only available as external kernel patches.

Implementation

The implementation of namespaces requires two components: per-subsystem namespace structures that wrap all formerly global components on a per-namespace basis, and a mechanism that associates a given process with the individual namespaces to which it belongs. Figure 2-4 illustrates the situation.

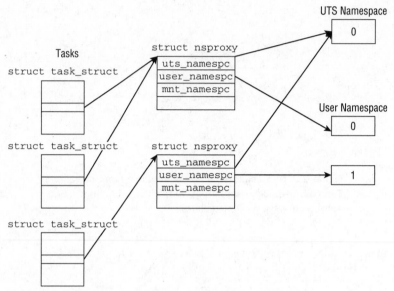

Figure 2-4: Connection between processes and namespaces.

Formerly global properties of subsystems are wrapped up in namespaces, and each process is associated with a particular selection of namespaces. Each kernel subsystem that is aware of namespaces must provide a data structure that collects all objects that must be available on a per-namespace basis. `struct nsproxy` is used to collect pointers to the subsystem-specific namespace wrappers:

<nsproxy.h>

```
struct nsproxy {
        atomic_t count;
        struct uts_namespace *uts_ns;
        struct ipc_namespace *ipc_ns;
        struct mnt_namespace *mnt_ns;
        struct pid_namespace *pid_ns;
        struct user_namespace *user_ns;
        struct net *net_ns;
};
```

Currently the following areas of the kernel are aware of namespaces:

❑ The UTS namespace contains the name of the running kernel, and its version, the underlying architecture type, and so on. UTS is a shorthand for Unix *Timesharing System*.

❑ All information related to inter-process communication (IPC) is stored in `struct ipc_namespace`.

❑ The view on the mounted filesystem is given in `struct mnt_namespace`.

❑ `struct pid_namespace` provides information about process identifiers.

❑ `struct user_namespace` is required to hold per-user information that allows for limiting resource usage for individual users.

❑ `struct net_ns` contains all networking-related namespace parameters. There is, however, still quite a lot of effort required to make this area fully aware of namespaces as you will see in Chapter 12.

I introduce the contents of the individual namespace containers when I discuss the respective subsystem. In this chapter, we will be concerned about UTS and user namespaces. Since `fork` can be instructed to open a new namespace when a new task is created, appropriate flags to control the behavior must be provided. One flag is available for each individual namespace:

<sched.h>
```
#define CLONE_NEWUTS      0x04000000    /* New utsname group? */
#define CLONE_NEWIPC      0x08000000    /* New ipcs */
#define CLONE_NEWUSER     0x10000000    /* New user namespace */
#define CLONE_NEWPID      0x20000000    /* New pid namespace */
#define CLONE_NEWNET      0x40000000    /* New network namespace */
```

Each task is associated with his own view of the namespaces:

<sched.h>
```
struct task_struct {
...
/* namespaces */
        struct nsproxy *nsproxy;
...
}
```

Because a pointer is used, a collection of sub-namespaces can be shared among multiple processes. This way, changes in a given namespace will be visible in all processes that belong to this namespace.

Notice that support for namespaces must be enabled at compile time on a per-namespace basis. Generic support for namespaces is, however, always compiled in. This allows the kernel to avoid using different code for systems with and without namespaces. By providing a default namespace that is associated with every process unless specified differently, the namespace-aware code can always be used, but the results will be identical to a situation in which all properties are global and not wrapped up in namespaces if no active support for namespaces is compiled in.

The initial global namespace is defined by `init_nsproxy`, which keeps pointers to the initial objects of the per-subsystem namespaces:

<kernel/nsproxy.c>
```
struct nsproxy init_nsproxy = INIT_NSPROXY(init_nsproxy);
```

<init_task.h>
```
#define INIT_NSPROXY(nsproxy) { \
        .pid_ns = &init_pid_ns, \
        .count = ATOMIC_INIT(1), \
```

```
            .uts_ns = &init_uts_ns, \
            .mnt_ns = NULL, \
            INIT_NET_NS(net_ns) \
            INIT_IPC_NS(ipc_ns) \
            .user_ns = &init_user_ns, \
    }
```

The UTS Namespace

The UTS namespace can be handled with particularly little effort because it only has to manage simple quantities and does not require a hierarchical organization. All relevant information is collected in an instance of the following structure:

<utsname.h>
```
struct uts_namespace {
        struct kref kref;
        struct new_utsname name;
};
```

kref is an embedded reference counter that can be used to track from how many places in the kernel an instance of struct uts_namespace is used (recall that Chapter 1 provides more information about the generic framework to handle reference counting). The information proper is contained in struct new_utsname:

<utsname.h>
```
struct new_utsname {
        char sysname[65];
        char nodename[65];
        char release[65];
        char version[65];
        char machine[65];
        char domainname[65];
};
```

The individual strings store the name of the system (Linux...), the kernel release, the machine name, and so on. The current values can be determined using the uname tool, but are also visible in /proc/sys/kernel/:

```
wolfgang@meitner> cat /proc/sys/kernel/ostype
Linux
wolfgang@meitner> cat /proc/sys/kernel/osrelease
2.6.24
```

The initial settings are stored in init_uts_ns:

init/version.c
```
struct uts_namespace init_uts_ns = {
...
        .name = {
                .sysname = UTS_SYSNAME,
                .nodename = UTS_NODENAME,
                .release = UTS_RELEASE,
                .version = UTS_VERSION,
```

```
                    .machine = UTS_MACHINE,
                    .domainname = UTS_DOMAINNAME,
            },
    };
```

The pre-processor constants are defined on various places across the kernel. UTS_RELEASE is, for instance, set in <utsrelease.h>, which is dynamically generated at build time by the top-level Makefile.

Notice that some parts of the UTS structure cannot be changed. For instance, it would not make sense to exchange sysname by anything else than Linux. It is, however, possible to change the machine name, for example.

How does the kernel go about creating a new UTS namespace? This falls under the responsibility of the function copy_utsname. The function is called when a process is forked and the flag CLONE_NEWUTS specifies that a new UTS namespace is to be established. In this case, a copy of the previous instance of uts_namespace is generated, and a corresponding pointer is installed into the nsproxy instance of the current task. Nothing more is required! Since the kernel makes sure to always operate on the task-specific uts_namespace instance whenever a UTS value is read or set, changes for the current process will not be reflected in the parent, and changes in the parent will also not propagate toward the children.

The User Namespace

The user namespace is handled similarly in terms of data structure management: When a new user namespace is requested, a copy of the current user namespace is generated and associated with the nsproxy instance of the current task. However, the representation of a user namespace itself is slightly more complex:

<user_namespace.h>
```
struct user_namespace {
        struct kref kref;
        struct hlist_head uidhash_table[UIDHASH_SZ];
        struct user_struct *root_user;
};
```

As before, kref is a reference counter that tracks in how many places a user_namespace instance is required. For each user in the namespace, an instance of struct user_struct keeps track of the individual resource consumption, and the individual instances are accessible via the hash table uidhash_table.

The exact definition of user_struct is not interesting for our purposes. It suffices to know that some statistical elements like the number of open files or processes a user has are kept in there. What is much more interesting is that each user namespace accounts resource usage for its users completely detached from other namespaces — including accounting for the root user. This is possible because a new user_struct both for the current user and the root is created when a user namespace is cloned:

kernel/user_namespace.c
```
static struct user_namespace *clone_user_ns(struct user_namespace *old_ns)
{
        struct user_namespace *ns;
        struct user_struct *new_user;
...
        ns = kmalloc(sizeof(struct user_namespace), GFP_KERNEL);
...
```

```
            ns->root_user = alloc_uid(ns, 0);

            /* Reset current->user with a new one */
            new_user = alloc_uid(ns, current->uid);

            switch_uid(new_user);
            return ns;
    }
```

alloc_uid is a helper function that allocates an instance of user_struct for a user with a given UID in the current namespace if none exists yet. Once an instance has been set up for both root and the current user, switch_uid ensures that the new user_struct will be used to account resources from now on. This essentially works by setting the user element of struct task_struct to the new user_struct instance.

Notice that if support for user namespaces is not compiled in, cloning a user namespace is a null operation: The default namespace is always used.

2.3.3 Process Identification Numbers

UNIX processes are always assigned a number to uniquely identify them in their namespace. This number is called the *process identification number* or *PID* for short. Each process generated with fork or clone is automatically assigned a new unique PID value by the kernel.

Process Identifiers

Each process is, however, not only characterized by its PID but also by other identifiers. Several types are possible:

❑ All processes in a thread group (i.e., different execution contexts of a process created by calling clone with CLONE_THREAD as we will see below) have a uniform *thread group id* (TGID). If a process does not use threads, its PID and TGID are identical.

The main process in a thread group is called the *group leader*. The group_leader element of the task structures of all cloned threads points to the task_struct instance of the group leader.

❑ Otherwise, independent processes can be combined into a *process group* (using the setpgrp system call). The pgrp elements of their task structures all have the same value, namely, the PID of the process group leader. Process groups facilitate the sending of signals to all members of the group, which is helpful for various system programming applications (see the literature on system programming, e.g., [SR05]). Notice that processes connected with pipes are contained in a process group.

❑ Several process groups can be combined in a session. All processes in a session have the same session ID which is held in the session element of the task structure. The SID can be set using the setsid system call. It is used in terminal programming but is of no particular relevance to us here.

Namespaces add some additional complexity to how PIDs are managed. Recall that PID namespaces are organized in a hierarchy. When a new namespace is created, all PIDs that are used in this namespace are visible to the parent namespace, but the child namespace does not see PIDs of the parent namespace. However this implies that some tasks are equipped with more than one PID, namely, one per namespace they are visible in. This must be reflected in the data structures. We have to distinguish between local and global IDs:

❑   *Global IDs* are identification numbers that are valid within the kernel itself and in the initial namespace to which the `init` tasks started during boot belongs. For each ID type, a given global identifier is guaranteed to be unique in the whole system.

❑   *Local IDs* belong to a specific namespace and are not globally valid. For each ID type, they are valid within the namespace to which they belong, but identifiers of identical type may appear with the same ID number in a *different* namespace.

The global PID and TGID are directly stored in the task struct, namely, in the elements `pid` and `tgid`:

<sched.h>
```
struct task_struct {
...
        pid_t pid;
        pid_t tgid;
...
}
```

Both are of type `pid_t`, which resolves to the type `__kernel_pid_t`; this, in turn, has to be defined by each architecture. Usually an `int` is used, which means that 2^{32} different IDs can be used simultaneously.

The session and process group IDs are not directly contained in the task structure itself, but in the structure used for signal handling. `task_struct->signal->__session` denotes the global SID, while the global PGID is stored in `task_struct->signal->__pgrp`. The auxiliary functions `set_task_session` and `set_task_pgrp` are provided to modify the values.

Managing PIDs

In addition to these two fields, the kernel needs to find a way to manage all local per-namespace quantities, as well as the other identifiers like TID and SID. This requires several interconnected data structures and numerous auxiliary functions that are discussed in the following.

Data Structures

Below I use the term ID to refer to *any* process identifier. I specify the identifier type explicitly (e.g., TGID for "thread group identifier") where this is necessary.

A small subsystem known as a *pid allocator* is available to speed up the allocation of new IDs. Besides, the kernel needs to provide auxiliary functions that allow for finding the task structure of a process by reference to an ID and its type, and functions that convert between the in-kernel representation of IDs and the numerical values visible to userspace.

Before I introduce the data structures required to represent IDs themselves, I need to discuss how PID namespaces are represented. The elements required for our purposes are as follows:

<pid_namespace.h>
```
struct pid_namespace {
...
        struct task_struct *child_reaper;
```

```
    ...
            int level;
            struct pid_namespace *parent;
    };
```

In reality, the structure also contains elements that are needed by the PID allocator to produce a stream of unique IDs, but these do not concern us now. What is interesting are the following elements:

❑ Every PID namespace is equipped with a task that assumes the role taken by `init` in the global picture. One of the purposes of `init` is to call `wait4` for orphaned tasks, and this must likewise be done by the namespace-specific `init` variant. A pointer to the task structure of this task is stored in `child_reaper`.

❑ `parent` is a pointer to the parent namespace, and `level` denotes the depth in the namespace hierarchy. The initial namespace has level 0, any children of this namespace are in level 1, children of children are in level 2, and so on. Counting the levels is important because IDs in higher levels must be visible in lower levels. From a given level setting, the kernel can infer how many IDs must be associated with a task.

Recall from Figure 2-3 that namespaces are hierarchically related. This clarifies the above definitions.

PID management is centered around two data structures: `struct pid` is the kernel-internal representation of a PID, and `struct upid` represents the information that is visible in a specific namespace. The definition of both structures is as follows:

```
<pid.h>
struct upid {
        int nr;
        struct pid_namespace *ns;
        struct hlist_node pid_chain;
};

struct pid
{
        atomic_t count;
        /* lists of tasks that use this pid */
        struct hlist_head tasks[PIDTYPE_MAX];
        int level;
        struct upid numbers[1];
};
```

Since these and some other data structures are comprehensively interconnected, Figure 2-5 provides an overview about the situation before I discuss the individual components.

As for `struct upid`, nr represents the numerical value of an ID, and ns is a pointer to the namespace to which the value belongs. All `upid` instances are kept on a hash table to which we will come in a moment, and `pid_chain` allows for implementing hash overflow lists with standard methods of the kernel.

The definition of `struct pid` is headed by a reference counter count. tasks is an array with a hash list head for every ID type. This is necessary because an ID can be used for several processes. All `task_struct` instances that share a given ID are linked on this list. `PIDTYPE_MAX` denotes the number of ID types:

```
<pid.h>
enum pid_type
{
        PIDTYPE_PID,
        PIDTYPE_PGID,
        PIDTYPE_SID,
        PIDTYPE_MAX
};
```

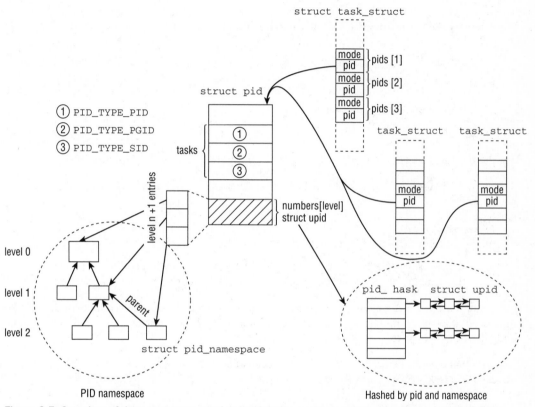

Figure 2-5: Overview of data structures used to implement a namespace-aware representation of IDs.

Notice that thread group IDs are *not* contained in this collection! This is because the thread group ID is simply given by the PID of the thread group leader, so a separate entry is not necessary.

A process can be visible in multiple namespaces, and the local ID in each namespace will be different. `level` denotes in how many namespaces the process is visible (in other words, this is the depth of the containing namespace in the namespace hierarchy), and `numbers` contains an instance of `upid` for each level. Note that the array consists formally of one element, and this is true if a process is contained only in the global namespace. Since the element is at the end of the structure, additional entries can be added to the array by simply allocating more space.

Since all task structures that share an identifier are kept on a list headed by `tasks`, a list element is required in `struct task_struct`:

<sched.h>
```
struct task_struct {
...
        /* PID/PID hash table linkage. */
        struct pid_link pids[PIDTYPE_MAX];
...
};
```

The auxiliary data structure `pid_link` permits linking of task structures on the lists headed from `struct pid`:

<pid.h>
```
struct pid_link
{
        struct hlist_node node;
        struct pid *pid;
};
```

`pid` points to a `pid` instance to which the task belongs, and `node` is used as list element.

A hash table is used to find the `pid` instance that belongs to a numeric PID value in a given namespace:

kernel/pid.c
```
static struct hlist_head *pid_hash;
```

`hlist_head` is a kernel standard data element used to create doubly linked hash lists (Appendix C describes the structure of such lists and introduces several auxiliary functions for processing them).

`pid_hash` is used as an array of `hlist_head`s. The number of elements is determined by the RAM configuration of the machine and lies between $2^4 = 16$ and $2^{12} = 4,096$. `pidhash_init` computes the apt size and allocates the required storage.

Suppose that a new instance of `struct pid` has been allocated and set up for a given ID type `type`. It is attached to a task structure as follows:

kernel/pid.c
```
int fastcall attach_pid(struct task_struct *task, enum pid_type type,
                struct pid *pid)
{
        struct pid_link *link;

        link = &task->pids[type];
        link->pid = pid;
        hlist_add_head_rcu(&link->node, &pid->tasks[type]);

        return 0;
}
```

A connection is made in both directions: The task structure can access the `pid` instance via `task_struct->pids[type]->pid`. Starting from the `pid` instance, the task can be found by iterating over the `tasks[type]` list. `hlist_add_head_rcu` is a standard function to traverse a list that additionally ensures as per the RCU mechanism (see Chapter 5) that the iteration is safe against race conditions that could arise when other kernel components manipulate the list concurrently.

Functions

The kernel provides a number of auxiliary functions to manipulate and scan the data structures described above. Essentially the kernel must be able to fulfill two different tasks:

1. Given a local numerical ID and the corresponding namespace, find the task structure that is described by this tuple.

2. Given a task structure, an ID type, and a namespace, obtain the local numerical ID.

Let us first concentrate on the case in which a `task_struct` instance must be converted into a numerical ID. This is a two-step process:

1. Obtain the `pid` instance associated with the task structure. The auxiliary functions `task_pid`, `task_tgid`, `task_pgrp`, and `task_session` are provided for the different types of IDs. This is simple for PIDs:

\<sched.h\>
```
static inline struct pid *task_pid(struct task_struct *task)
{
        return task->pids[PIDTYPE_PID].pid;
}
```

Obtaining a TGID works similarly because it is nothing other than the PID of the tread group leader. The element to grab is `task->group_leader->pids[PIDTYPE_PID].pid`.

Finding out a process group ID requires using `PIDTYPE_PGID` as array index. However, it must again be taken from the `pid` instance of the process group leader:

\<sched.h\>
```
static inline struct pid *task_pgrp(struct task_struct *task)
{
        return task->group_leader->pids[PIDTYPE_PGID].pid;
}
```

2. Once the `pid` instance is available, the numerical ID can be read off from the `uid` information available in the `numbers` array in `struct pid`:

kernel/pid.c
```
pid_t pid_nr_ns(struct pid *pid, struct pid_namespace *ns)
{
        struct upid *upid;
        pid_t nr = 0;

        if (pid && ns->level <= pid->level) {
                upid = &pid->numbers[ns->level];
                if (upid->ns == ns)
                        nr = upid->nr;
        }
        return nr;
}
```

Because a parent namespace sees PIDs in child namespaces, but not vice versa, the kernel has to ensure that the current namespace level is less than or equal to the level in which the local PID was generated.

It is also important to note that the kernel need only worry about generating global PIDs: All other ID types in the global namespace will be mapped to PIDs, so there is no need to generate, for instance, global TGIDs or SIDs.

Instead of using `pid_nr_ns` in the second step, the kernel could also employ one of these auxiliary functions:

❑   `pid_vnr` returns the local PID seen from the namespace to which the ID belongs.

❑   `pid_nr` obtains the global PID as seen from the init process.

Both rely on `pid_nr_ns` and automatically select the proper `level`: 0 for the global PID, and `pid->level` for the local one.

The kernel provides several helper functions that combine the described steps:

kernel/pid.c
```
pid_t task_pid_nr_ns(struct task_struct *tsk, struct pid_namespace *ns)
pid_t task_tgid_nr_ns(struct task_struct *tsk, struct pid_namespace *ns)
pid_t task_pgrp_nr_ns(struct task_struct *tsk, struct pid_namespace *ns)
pid_t task_session_nr_ns(struct task_struct *tsk, struct pid_namespace *ns)
```

Their meaning is obvious from the function names, so we need not add anything further.

Now let us turn our attention to how the kernel can convert a numerical PID together with the namespace into a `pid` instance. Again two steps are required:

1.   To determine the `pid` instance (the in-kernel representation of a PID) given the local numerical PID of a process and the associated namespace (the userspace representation of a PID), the kernel must employ a standard hashing scheme: First, the array index in `pid_hash` is computed from the PID and namespace pointers,[5] and then the hash list is traversed until the desired element has been found. This is handled by the auxiliary function `find_pid_ns`:

     kernel/pid.c
     ```
     struct pid * fastcall find_pid_ns(int nr, struct pid_namespace *ns)
     ```

     Instances of `struct upid` are kept on the hash, but since these are directly contained in `struct pid`, the kernel can infer the desired information using the `container_of` mechanism (see Appendix C).

2.   `pid_task` extracts the first `task_struct` instance that is queued on the list `pid->tasks[type]`.

These two steps are performed by the auxiliary function `find_task_by_pid)_type_ns`:

kernel/pid.c
```
struct task_struct *find_task_by_pid_type_ns(int type, int nr,
                struct pid_namespace *ns)
```

---

[5]For this purpose, the kernel uses multiplicative hashing with a prime number that is in a golden ratio to the largest number that can be represented in a machine word. For details, refer to [Knu97].

```
        {
                return pid_task(find_pid_ns(nr, ns), type);
        }
```

Some simpler auxiliary functions build on the most general `find_task_by_pid_type_ns`:

❑ `find_task_by_pid_ns(pid_t nr, struct pid_namespace *ns)` finds a `task_struct` instance given a numerical PID and the namespace of the task.

❑ `find_task_by_vpid(pid_t vnr)` finds a task by its local numerical PID.

❑ `find_task_by_pid(pid_t nr)` finds a task by its global numerical PID.

`find_task_by_pid` is required at many points in the kernel sources because a large number of process-specific operations (e.g., sending a signal using `kill`) identify their target process by means of its PID.

Generating Unique PIDs

In addition to managing PIDs, the kernel is also responsible for providing a mechanism to generate unique PIDs that have not yet been assigned. In this case, the differences between the various PID types can be ignored because unique numbers need only be generated for PIDs in the classical UNIX sense. All other identifiers can be derived from the PID, as we will see when discussing `fork` and `clone` below. In the sections that follow, the term PID once again refers to the classical UNIX process identifier (`PIDTYPE_PID`).

To keep track of which PIDs have been allocated and which are still free, the kernel uses a large bitmap in which each PID is identified by a bit. The value of the PID is obtained from the position of the bit in the bitmap.

Allocating a free PID is then restricted essentially to looking for the first bit in the bitmap whose value is 0; this bit is then set to 1. Conversely, freeing a PID can be implemented by "toggling" the corresponding bit from 1 to 0. These operations are implemented using

kernel/pid.c
```
static int alloc_pidmap(struct pid_namespace *pid_ns)
```

to reserve a PID, and

kernel/pid.c
```
static fastcall void free_pidmap(struct pid_namespace *pid_ns, int pid)
```

to free a PID. How they are implemented does not concern us here, but naturally, they must work on a per-namespace basis.

When a new process is created, it may be visible in multiple namespaces. For each of them a local PID must be generated. This is handled in `alloc_pid`:

kernel/pid.c
```
struct pid *alloc_pid(struct pid_namespace *ns)
{
        struct pid *pid;
        enum pid_type type;
        int i, nr;
```

```
                     struct pid_namespace *tmp;
                     struct upid *upid;
...
                     tmp = ns;
                     for (i = ns->level; i >= 0; i--) {
                            nr = alloc_pidmap(tmp);
...
                            pid->numbers[i].nr = nr;
                            pid->numbers[i].ns = tmp;
                            tmp = tmp->parent;
                     }
                     pid->level = ns->level;
...
```

Starting at the level of the namespace in which the process is created, the kernel goes down to the initial, global namespace and creates a local PID for each. All `upids` that are contained in `struct pid` are filled with the newly generated PIDs. Each `upid` instance must be placed on the PID hash:

kernel/pid.c

```
                     for (i = ns->level; i >= 0; i--) {
                            upid = &pid->numbers[i];
                            hlist_add_head_rcu(&upid->pid_chain,
                                       &pid_hash[pid_hashfn(upid->nr, upid->ns)]);
                     }
...
                     return pid;
          }
```

2.3.4 Task Relationships

In addition to the relationships resulting from ID links, the kernel is also responsible for managing the "family relationships" established on the basis of the UNIX model of process creation. The following terminology is used in this context:

❑   If process A forks to generate process B, A is known as the *parent* process and B as the *child* process.[6]

If process B forks again to create a further process C, the relationship between A and C is sometimes referred to as a *grandparent* and *grandchild* relationship.

❑   If process A forks several times therefore generating several child processes $B_1, B_2, \ldots, B_n$, the relationship between the B_i processes is known as a *siblings* relationship.

Figure 2-6 illustrates the possible family relationships graphically.

The `task_struct` task data structure provides two list heads to help implement these relationships:

<sched.h>

```
struct task_struct {
...
          struct list_head children; /* list of my children */
```

---

[6]Unlike natural families, a process has only one parent.

```
        struct list_head sibling; /* linkage in my parent's children list */
...
}
```

❑   `children` is the list head for the list of all child elements of the process.
❑   `siblings` is used to link siblings with each other.

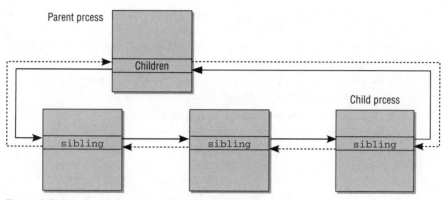

Figure 2-6: Family relationships between processes.

New children are placed at the *start* of the `siblings` list, meaning that the chronological sequence of `forks` can be reconstructed.[7]

2.4   Process Management System Calls

In this section, I discuss the implementation of the `fork` and `exec` system call families. Normally, these calls are not issued directly by applications but are invoked via an intermediate layer — the C standard library — that is responsible for communication with the kernel.

The methods used to switch from user mode to kernel mode differ from architecture to architecture. In Appendix A, I describe at length the mechanisms used to switch between these two modes and also explain how parameters are exchanged between userspace and kernel space. For the time being, it is sufficient to regard the kernel as a "program library" used by the C standard library as mentioned briefly in Chapter 1.

2.4.1   Process Duplication

The traditional UNIX system call to duplicate a process is `fork`. However, it is not the only call implemented by Linux for this purpose — in fact, there are three:

---

[7]Kernel versions before 2.6.21 had three helper functions: `younger_sibling`, `older_sibling`, and `eldest_child`, which gave some aid in accessing the described lists and their elements. They were used to produce debugging output, which had, however, not proved very useful, so it was removed. Patch author Ingo Molnar noticed that the corresponding code was among the oldest elements of the kernel and noted this accordingly. This led another well-known developer to sign off the patch as Linus `'snif' Torvalds ...`

1. `fork` is the heavy-weight call because it creates a full copy of the parent process that then executes as a child process. To reduce the effort associated with this call, Linux uses the *copy-on-write* technique, discussed below.

2. `vfork` is similar to fork but does not create a copy of the data of the parent process. Instead, it shares the data between the parent and child process. This saves a great deal of CPU time (and if one of the processes were to manipulate the shared data, the other would notice automatically).

   `vfork` is designed for the situation in which a child process just generated immediately executes an `execve` system call to load a new program. The kernel also guarantees that the parent process is blocked until the child process exits or starts a new program.

   Quoting the manual page `vfork(2)`, it is "rather unfortunate that Linux revived this specter from the past." Since `fork` uses copy-on-write, the speed argument for `vfork` does not really count anymore, and its use should therefore be avoided.

3. `clone` generates threads and enables a decision to be made as to exactly which elements are to be shared between the parent and the child process and which are to be copied.

Copy on Write

The kernel uses the *copy-on-write* technique (COW) to prevent *all* data of the parent process from being copied when `fork` is executed. This technique exploits the fact that processes normally use only a fraction of their pages in memory.[8] When `fork` is called, the kernel would usually create an identical copy of each memory page of the parent process for the child process. This has two very negative effects:

1. A large amount of RAM, a scarce resource, is used.

2. The copy operation takes a long time.

The negative impact is even greater if the application loads a new program using `exec` immediately after process duplication. This means, in effect, that the preceding copy operation was totally superfluous as the process address space is reinitialized and the data copied are no longer needed.

The kernel can get around this problem by using a trick. Not the entire address space of the process but only its page tables are copied. These establish the link between virtual address space and physical pages as described briefly in Chapter 1 and at length in Chapters 3 and 4. The address spaces of parent and child processes then point to the same physical pages.

Of course, parent and child processes must not be allowed to modify each other's pages,[9] which is why the page tables of *both* processes indicate that only read access is allowed to the pages — even though they could be written to in normal circumstances.

Providing that both processes have only read access to their pages in memory, data sharing between the two is not a problem because no changes can be made.

As soon as one of the processes attempts to write to the copied pages, the processor reports an access error to the kernel (errors of this kind are called *page faults*). The kernel then references additional memory management data structures (see Chapter 4) to check whether the page can be accessed in Read and Write mode or in Read mode only — if the latter is true, a *segmentation fault* must be reported to the

---

[8]The pages most frequently accessed by the process are called the *working set*.
[9]With the exception of pages explicitly shared by both processes.

process. As you see in Chapter 4, the actual implementation of the page fault handler is more complicated because other aspects, such as swapped-out pages, must also be taken into account.

The condition in which a page table entry indicates that a page is "Read Only" although normally it would be writable allows the kernel to recognize that the page is, in fact, a COW page. It therefore creates a copy of the page that is assigned exclusively to the process — and may therefore also be used for write operations. How the copy operation is implemented is not discussed until Chapter 4 because extensive background knowledge of memory management is required.

The COW mechanism enables the kernel to delay copying of memory pages for as long as possible and — more importantly — to make copying unnecessary in many cases. This saves a great deal of time.

Executing System Calls

The entry points for the fork, vfork, and clone system calls are the sys_fork, sys_vfork, and sys_clone functions. Their definitions are architecture-dependent because the way in which parameters are passed between userspace and kernel space differs on the various architectures (see Chapter 13 for further information). The task of the above functions is to extract the information supplied by userspace from the registers of the processors and then to invoke the architecture-*independent* do_fork function responsible for process duplication. The prototype of the function is as follows.

kernel/fork.c
```
long do_fork(unsigned long clone_flags,
             unsigned long stack_start,
             struct pt_regs *regs,
             unsigned long stack_size,
             int __user *parent_tidptr,
             int __user *child_tidptr)
```

The function requires the following arguments:

❑ A flag set (clone_flags) to specify duplication properties. The low byte specifies the signal number to be sent to the parent process when the child process terminates. The higher bytes hold various constants discussed below.

❑ The start address of the user mode stack (start_stack) to be used.

❑ A pointer to the register set holding the call parameters in raw form (regs). The data type used is the architecture-specific struct pt_regs structure, which holds all registers in the order in which they are saved on the kernel stack when a system call is executed (more information is provided in Appendix A).

❑ The size of the user mode stack (stack_size). This parameter is usually unnecessary and set to 0.

❑ Two pointers to addresses in userspace (parent_tidptr and child_tidptr) that hold the TIDs of the parent and child processes. They are needed for the thread implementation of the NPTL (*Native Posix Threads Lilbrary*) library. I discuss their meaning below.

The different fork variants are distinguished primarily by means of the flag set. On most architectures,[10] the classical fork call is implemented in the same way as on IA-32 processors.

---

[10]Exception: Sparc(64) systems that access do_fork via sparc_do_fork. IA-64 kernels only provide a single system call, sys_clone2, which is used to implement fork, vfork, and clone in userspace. Both sys_clone2 and sparc_do_fork eventually rely on do_fork.

arch/x86/kernel/process_32.c
```
asmlinkage int sys_fork(struct pt_regs regs)
{
        return do_fork(SIGCHLD, regs.esp, &regs, 0, NULL, NULL);
}
```

The only flag used is `SIGCHLD`. This means that the `SIGCHLD` signal informs the parent process once the child process has terminated. Initially, the same stack (whose start address is held in the `esp` register on IA-32 systems) is used for the parent and child processes. However, the COW mechanism creates a copy of the stack for each process if it is manipulated and therefore written to.

If `do_fork` was successful, the PID of the newly created task is returned as the result of the system call. Otherwise the (negative) error code is returned.

The implementation of `sys_vfork` differs only slightly from that of `sys_fork` in that additional flags are used (`CLONE_VFORK` and `CLONE_VM` whose meaning is discussed below).

`sys_clone` is also implemented in a similar way to the above calls with the difference that `do_fork` is invoked as follows:

arch/x86/kernel/process_32.c
```
asmlinkage int sys_clone(struct pt_regs regs)
{
        unsigned long clone_flags;
        unsigned long newsp;
        int __user *parent_tidptr, *child_tidptr;

        clone_flags = regs.ebx;
        newsp = regs.ecx;
        parent_tidptr = (int __user *)regs.edx;
        child_tidptr = (int __user *)regs.edi;
        if (!newsp)
                newsp = regs.esp;
        return do_fork(clone_flags, newsp, &regs, 0, parent_tidptr, child_tidptr);
}
```

The clone flags are no longer permanently set but can be passed to the system call as parameters in various registers. Thus, the first part of the function deals with extracting these parameters. Also, the stack of the parent process is not copied; instead, a new address (`newsp`) can be specified for it. (This is required to generate threads that share the address space with the parent process but use their own stack in this address space.) Two pointers (`parent_tidptr` and `child_tidptr`) in userspace are also specified for purposes of communication with thread libraries. Their meaning is discussed in Section 2.4.1.

Implementation of `do_fork`

All three `fork` mechanisms end up in `do_fork` in `kernel/fork.c` (an architecture-*in*dependent function), whose code flow diagram is shown in Figure 2-7.

`do_fork` begins with an invocation of `copy_process`, which performs the actual work of generating a new process and reusing the parent process data specified by the flags. Once the child process has been generated, the kernel must carry out the following concluding operations:

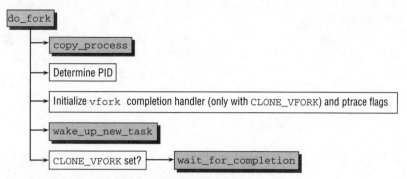

Figure 2-7: Code flow diagram for do_fork.

❑ Since fork returns the PID of the new task, it must be obtained. This is complicated because the fork operation could have opened a new PID namespace if the flag CLONE_NEWPID was set. If this is the case, then task_pid_nr_ns is required to obtain the PID that was selected for the new process in the *parent* namespace, that is, the namespace of the process that issued fork.

If the PID namespace remains unchanged, calling task_pid_vnr is enough to obtain the local PID because old and new processes will live in the same namespace.

kernel/fork.c
```
nr = (clone_flags & CLONE_NEWPID) ?
        task_pid_nr_ns(p, current->nsproxy->pid_ns) :
                task_pid_vnr(p);
```

❑ If the new process is to be monitored with Ptrace (see Chapter 13), the SIGSTOP signal is sent to the process immediately after generation to allow an attached debugger to examine its data.

❑ The child process is woken using wake_up_new_task; in other words, the task structure is added to the scheduler queue. The scheduler also gets a chance to specifically handle newly started tasks, which, for instance, allows for implementing a policy that gives new tasks a good chance to run soon, but also prevents processes that fork over and over again to consume all CPU time.

If a child process begins to run before the parent process, this can greatly reduce copying effort, especially if the child process issues an exec call after fork. However, keep in mind that enqueuing a process in the scheduler data structures does not mean that the child process begins to execute immediately but rather that it is available for selection by the scheduler.

❑ If the vfork mechanism was used (the kernel recognizes this by the fact that the CLONE_VFORK flag is set), the *completions* mechanism of the child process must be enabled. The vfork_done element of the child process task structure is used for this purpose. With the help of the wait_for_completion function, the parent process goes to sleep on this variable until the child process exits. When a process terminates (or a new application is started with execve), the kernel automatically invokes complete(vfork_done). This wakes all processes sleeping on it. In Chapter 14, I discuss the implementation of completions in greater detail.

By adopting this approach, the kernel ensures that the parent process of a child process generated using vfork remains inactive until either the child process exits or a new process is executed. The temporary inactivity of the parent process also ensures that both processes do not interfere with each other or manipulate each other's address space.

Copying Processes

In `do_fork` the bulk of the work is done by the `copy_process` function, whose code flow diagram is shown in Figure 2-8. Notice that the function has to handle the main work for the three system calls `fork`, `vfork`, and `clone`.

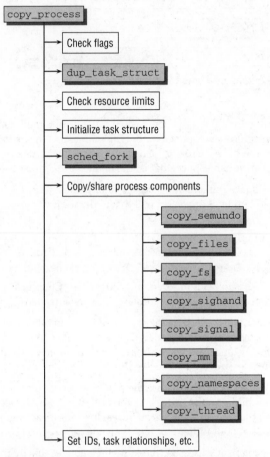

Figure 2-8: Code flow diagram for `copy_process`.

Because the kernel has to deal with a large number of special and very specific situations, let's restrict our description to a slightly simplified version of the function so as not to lose sight of the most important aspects in a myriad of details.

Quite a number of flags control the behavior of process duplication. They are all well documented in the `clone(2)` man page, and instead of repeating them here, I advise you to just take a look into it — or, for that matter, any good text on Linux systems programming. More interesting is that there are some flag combinations that do not make sense, and the kernel has to catch these. For instance, it does not make sense to request creation of a new namespace (`CLONE_NEWNS`), on the one hand, but also express the desire to share all filesystem information with the parent (CLONE_FS). It's not complicated to catch this combination and return an error code:

kernel/fork.c

```
static struct task_struct *copy_process(unsigned long clone_flags,
                                        unsigned long stack_start,
                                        struct pt_regs *regs,
                                        unsigned long stack_size,
                                        int __user *child_tidptr,
                                        struct pid *pid)
{
        int retval;
        struct task_struct *p;
        int cgroup_callbacks_done = 0;

        if ((clone_flags & (CLONE_NEWNS|CLONE_FS)) == (CLONE_NEWNS|CLONE_FS))
                return ERR_PTR(-EINVAL);
...
```

This is also a good place to recall from the introduction that Linux sometimes has to return a pointer if an operation succeeds, and an error code if something fails. Unfortunately, the C language only allows a single direct return value per function, so any information about possible errors has to be encoded into the pointer. While pointers can in general point to arbitrary locations in memory, each architecture supported by Linux has a region in virtual address space that starts from virtual address 0 and goes at least 4 KiB far where no senseful information can live. The kernel can thus reuse this pointer range to encode error codes: If the return value of fork points to an address within the aforementioned range, then the call has failed, and the reason can be determined by the numerical value of the pointer. ERR_PTR is a helper macro to perform the encoding of the numerical constant -EINVAL (invalid operation) into a pointer.

Some further flag checks are required:

❑   When a thread is created with CLONE_THREAD, signal sharing must be activated with CLONE_SIGHAND. Individual threads in a thread group cannot be addressed by a signal.

❑   Shared signal handlers can only be provided if the virtual address space is shared between parent and child (CLONE_VM). Transitive thinking reveals that threads, therefore, also have to share the address space with the parent.

Once the kernel has established that the flag set does not contradict itself, dup_task_struct is used to create an identical copy of the task structure of the parent process. The new task_struct instance for the child can be allocated at any point in kernel memory that happens to be free (see Chapter 3, in which the allocation mechanisms used for this purpose are described).

The task structures for parent and child differ only in one element: A new kernel mode stack is allocated for the new process. A pointer to it is stored in task_struct->stack. Usually the stack is stored in a union with thread_info, which holds all required processor-specific low-level information about the thread.

<sched.h>

```
union thread_union {
        struct thread_info thread_info;
        unsigned long stack[THREAD_SIZE/sizeof(long)];
};
```

In principle, individual architectures are, however, free to store whatever they like in the stack pointer if they signal this to the kernel by setting the pre-processor constant __HAVE_THREAD_FUNCTIONS. In this case, they must provide their own implementations of task_thread_info and task_stack_page, which allows for obtaining the thread information and the kernel mode stack for a given task_struct instance. Additionally, they must implement the function setup_thread_stack that is called in dup_task_struct to create a destination for stack. Currently, only IA-64 and m68k do not rely on the default methods of the kernel.

On most architectures, one or two memory pages are used to hold an instance of thread_union. On IA-32, two pages are the default setting, and thus the available kernel stack size is slightly less than 8 KiB because part is occupied by the thread_info instance. Note, though, that the configuration option 4KSTACKS decreases the stack size to 4 KiB and thus to one page. This is advantageous if a large number of processes is running on the system because one page per process is saved. On the other hand, it can lead to problems with external drivers that often tend to be "stack hogs," for example, use too much stack space. All central parts of the kernel that are part of the standard distribution have been designed to operate smoothly also with a stack size of 4 KiB, but problems can arise (and unfortunately have in the past) if binary-only drivers are required, which often have a tendency to clutter up the available stack space.

thread_info holds process data that needs to be accessed by the architecture-specific assembly language code. Although the structure is defined differently from processor to processor, its contents are similar to the following on most systems.

```
<asm-arch/thread_info.h>
struct thread_info {
        struct task_struct      *task;          /* main task structure */
        struct exec_domain      *exec_domain;   /* execution domain */
        unsigned long           flags;          /* low level flags */
        unsigned long           status;         /* thread-synchronous flags */
        __u32                   cpu;            /* current CPU */
        int                     preempt_count;  /* 0 => preemptable, <0 => BUG */

        mm_segment_t            addr_limit;     /* thread address space */
        struct restart_block    restart_block;
}
```

❑   task is a pointer to the task_struct instance of the process.

❑   exec_domain is used to implement *execution domains* with which different ABIs (*Application Binary Interfaces*) can be implemented on a machine type (e.g., to run 32-bit applications on an AMD64 system in 64-bit mode).

❑   flags can hold various process-specific flags, two of which are of particular interest to us:

   ❑   TIF_SIGPENDING is set if the process has pending signals.

   ❑   TIF_NEED_RESCHED indicates that the process should be or would like to be replaced with another process by the scheduler.

   Other possible constants — some hardware-specific — which are, however, hardly ever used, are available in <asm-*arch*/thread_info.h>.

❑   cpu specifies the number of the CPU on which a process is just executing (important on multi-processor systems — very easy to determine on single-processor systems).

❑ `preempt_count` is a counter needed to implement kernel preemption, discussed in Section 2.8.3.

❑ `addr_limit` specifies up to which address in virtual address space a process may use. As already noted, there is a limit for normal processes, but kernel threads may access the entire virtual address space, including the kernel-only portions. (This does *not* represent any kind of restriction on how much RAM a process may allocate.) Recall that I have touched on the separation between user and kernel address space in the Introduction, and will come back to the details in Section 4.

❑ `restart_block` is needed to implement the signal mechanism (see Chapter 5).

Figure 2-9 shows the relationship between `task_struct`, `thread_info` and the kernel stack. When a particular component of the kernel uses too much stack space, the kernel stack will crash into the thread information, and this will most likely lead to severe failures. Besides, this can also lead to wrong information when an emergency stack trace is printed, so the kernel provides the function `kstack_end` to decide if a given address is within the valid portion of the stack or not.

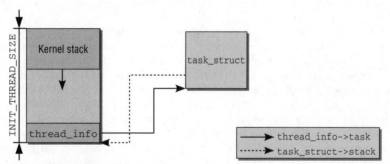

Figure 2-9: Relationship between `task_struct`, `thread_info`, and the kernel stack of a process.

`dup_task_struct` copies the contents of `task_struct` and `thread_info` instances of the parent process, but the `stack` pointer is set to the new `thread_info` instance. This means that the task structures of parent and child processes are absolutely identical at this point except for the stack pointer. The child will, however, be modified in the course of `copy_process`.

There are also two symbols named `current` and `current_thread_info` that are defined as macros or functions by all architectures. Their meanings are as follows:

❑ `current_thread_info` delivers a pointer to the `thread_info` instance of the process currently executing. The address can be determined from the kernel stack pointer because the instance is always located at the top of the stack.[11] Because a separate kernel stack is used for each process, the process to stack assignment is unique.

❑ `current` specifies the address of the `task_struct` instance of the current process. This function appears very frequently in the sources. The address can be determined using `get_thread_info`: `current = current_thread_info()->task`.

---

[11] The pointer to the kernel stack is usually held in a specially reserved register. Some architectures, especially IA-32 and AMD64, use a different solution discussed in Section A.10.3.

Let us return to `copy_process`. After `dup_task_struct` has succeeded, the kernel checks if the maximam number of processes allowed for a particular user are exceeded with the creation of the new task:

kernel/fork.c
```
        if (atomic_read(&p->user->processes) >=
                        p->signal->rlim[RLIMIT_NPROC].rlim_cur) {
            if (!capable(CAP_SYS_ADMIN) && !capable(CAP_SYS_RESOURCE) &&
                p->user != current->nsproxy->user_ns->root_user)
                    goto bad_fork_free;
        }
    ...
```

The per-user resource counters for the user owning the current process are kept in an instance of `user_struct` that is accessible via `task_struct->user`, and the number of processes currently held by a particular user is stored in `user_struct->processes`. If this value exceeds the limit set by rlimit, task creation is aborted — unless the current user is assigned special capabilities (`CAP_SYS_ADMIN` or `CAP_SYS_RESOURCE`) or is the root user. Checking for the root user is interesting: Recall from above that each PID namespace has its own root user. This must now be taken into account in the above check.

If resource limits do not prevent process creation, the interface function `sched_fork` is called to give the scheduler a chance to set up things for the new task. Before the introduction of the CFQ scheduler in kernel 2.6.23, this was more complicated because the remaining time slice of the parent had to be distributed between parent and child. Since the new scheduler does not require time slices anymore, things are a lot simpler now. Essentially, the routines initialize statistical fields and on multi-processor systems probably re-balance the available processes between the CPUs if this is necessary. Besides, the task state is set to `TASK_RUNNING` — which is not really true since the new process is, in fact, not yet running. However, this prevents any other part of the kernel from trying to change the process state from non-running to running and scheduling the new process before its setup has been completely finished.

A large number of `copy_xyz` routines are then invoked to copy or share the resources of specific kernel subsystems. The task structure contains pointers to instances of data structures that describe a sharable or cloneable resource. Because the task structure of the child starts out as an exact copy of the parent's task structure, both point to the same resource-specific instances initially. This is illustrated in Figure 2-10.

Suppose we have two resources: `res_abc` and `res_def`. Initially the corresponding pointers in the task structure of the parent and child process point to the same instance of the resource-specific data structure in memory.

If `CLONE_ABC` is set, then both processes will share `res_abc`. This is already the case, but it is additionally necessary to increment the reference counter of the instance to prevent the associated memory space from being freed too soon — memory may be relinquished to memory management only when it is no longer being used by a process. If either parent or child modifies the shared resource, the change will be visible in both processes.

If `CLONE_ABC` is not set, then a copy of `res_abc` is created for the child process, and the resource counter of the new copy is initialized to 1. Consequently, if parent or child modifies the resource, then changes will *not* propagate to the other process in this case.

As a general rule, the fewer the number of `CLONE` flags set, the less work there is to do. However, this gives parent and child processes more opportunities to mutually manipulate their data structures — and this must be taken into consideration when programming applications.

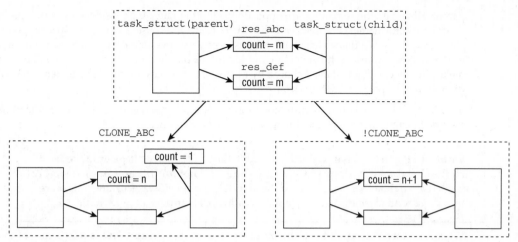

Figure 2-10: When a new thread is created, resources of the parent can either be shared or copied.

Deciding if a resource can be cloned or must be copied is done through numerous helper routines — one for each resource. It is not my intention here to discuss the (rather uninteresting) implementations of the various copy_xyz functions, but I summarize their effects below. I will introduce the data structures associated with every process component when I discuss the respective subsystem in detail in the following chapters.

- ❑ copy_semundo uses the System V semaphores of the parent process if COPY_SYSVSEM is set (see Chapter 5).

- ❑ copy_files uses the file descriptors of the parent process if CLONE_FILES is set. Otherwise, a new files structure is generated (see Chapter 8) that contains the same information as the parent process. This information can be modified independently of the original structure.

- ❑ copy_fs uses the filesystem context (task_struct->fs) of the parent process if CLONE_FS is set. This is an fs_struct type structure that holds, for example, the root directory and the current working directory of the process (see Chapter 8 for detailed information).

- ❑ copy_sighand uses the signal handlers of the parent process (task_struct->sighand) if CLONE_SIGHAND or CLONE_THREAD is set. Chapter 5 discusses the struct sighand_struct structure used in more detail.

- ❑ copy_signal uses the non-handler-specific part of signal handling (task_struct->signal, see Chapter 5) together with the parent process if CLONE_THREAD is set.

- ❑ copy_mm causes the parent process and child process to share the same address space if COPY_MM is set. In this case, both processes use the same instance of mm_struct (see Chapter 4) to which task_struct->mm points.

  If copy_mm is *not* set, it does not mean that the entire address space of the parent process is copied. The kernel does, in fact, create a copy of the page tables but does not copy the actual contents of the pages. This is done using the COW mechanism only if one of the two processes writes to one of the pages.

- ❑ copy_namespaces has special call semantics. It is used to set up namespaces for the child process. Recall that several CLONE_NEWxyz flags control which namespaces are *shared* with the parent. However, the semantics are opposite to all other flags: If `CLONE_NEWxyz` is *not* specified, then the specific namespace is shared with the parent. Otherwise, a new namespace is generated. `copy_namespace` is a dispatcher that executes a copy routine for each possible namespace. The individual copy routines, however, are not too interesting because they essentially copy data or make already existing instances shared by means of reference counter management, so I will not discuss their implementation in detail.

❑   `copy_thread` is — in contrast to all other `copy` operations discussed here — an architecture-specific function that copies the thread-specific data of a process.

> *Thread-specific* in this context does not refer to any of the **CLONE** flags or to the fact that the operation is performed for threads only and not for full processes. It simply means that all data that contribute to the architecture-specific execution context are copied (the term *thread* is used with more than one meaning in the kernel).

What is important is to fill the elements of `task_struct->thread`. This is a structure of the `thread_struct` type whose definition is architecture-dependent. It holds all registers (plus other information) needed by the kernel to save and restore process contents during low-level switching between tasks.

Intimate knowledge of the various CPUs is needed to understand the layout of the individual `thread_struct` structures. A full discussion of these structures is beyond the scope of this book. However, Appendix A includes some information relating to the contents of the structures on several systems.

Back in `copy_process`, the kernel must fill in various elements of the task structure that differ between parent and child. These include the following:

❑   The various list elements contained in `task_struct`, for instance, `sibling` and `children`.

❑   The interval timer elements `cpu_timers` (see Chapter 15).

❑   The list of pending signals (`pending`) discussed in Chapter 5.

After allocating a new `pid` instance for the task with the mechanisms described before, they are stored in the task structure. For threads, the thread group ID is the same as that of the forking process:

kernel/fork.c
```
        p->pid = pid_nr(pid);
        p->tgid = p->pid;
        if (clone_flags & CLONE_THREAD)
                p->tgid = current->tgid;
...
```

Recall that `pid_nr` computes the global numerical PID for a given `pid` instance.

For regular processes, the parent process is the forking process. This is different for threads: Since they are seen as the second (or third, or fourth,...) line of execution *within* the generating process, their parent is the parent's parent. This is easier to express in code than in words:

kernel/fork.c
```
        if (clone_flags & (CLONE_PARENT|CLONE_THREAD))
                p->real_parent = current->real_parent;
        else
```

```
            p->real_parent = current;
        p->parent = p->real_parent;
```

Regular processes that are not threads can trigger the same behavior by setting CLONE_PARENT. Another correction is required for threads: The thread group leader of a regular process is the process itself. For a thread, the group leader is the group leader of the current process:

kernel/fork.c
```
        p->group_leader = p;

        if (clone_flags & CLONE_THREAD) {
                p->group_leader = current->group_leader;
                list_add_tail_rcu(&p->thread_group, &p->group_leader->thread_group);
    ...
        }
```

The new process must then be linked with its parent process by means of the children list. This is handled by the auxiliary macro add_parent. Besides, the new process must be included in the ID data structure network as described in Section 2.3.3.

kernel/fork.c
```
        add_parent(p);

        if (thread_group_leader(p)) {
                if (clone_flags & CLONE_NEWPID)
                        p->nsproxy->pid_ns->child_reaper = p;

                set_task_pgrp(p, task_pgrp_nr(current));
                set_task_session(p, task_session_nr(current));
                attach_pid(p, PIDTYPE_PGID, task_pgrp(current));
                attach_pid(p, PIDTYPE_SID, task_session(current));
        }

        attach_pid(p, PIDTYPE_PID, pid);
    ...
        return p;
        }
```

thread_group_leader checks only whether pid and tgid of the new process are identical. If so, the process is the leader of a thread group. In this case, some more work is necessary:

❑   Recall that processes in a process namespace that is not the global namespace have their own init task. If a new PID namespace was opened by setting CLONE_NEWPID, this role must be assumed by the task that called clone.

❑   The new process must be added to the current task group and session. This allows for bringing some of the functions discussed above to good use.

Finally, the PID itself is added to the ID network. This concludes the creation of a new process!

Special Points When Generating Threads

Userspace thread libraries use the clone system call to generate new threads. This call supports flags (other than those discussed above) that produce certain special effects in the copy_process (and in the associated invoked functions). For the sake of simplicity, I omitted these flags above. However, it should be remembered that the differences between a classical process and a thread in the Linux kernel are relatively fluid and both terms are often used as synonyms (*thread* is also frequently used to mean the architecture-dependent part of a process as mentioned above). In this section, I concentrate on the flags used by user thread libraries (above all, NPTL) to implement multithreading capabilities.

❑ CLONE_PARENT_SETTID copies the PID of the generated thread to a point in userspace specified in the `clone` call (parent_tidptr, the pointer is passed to `clone`)[12]:

kernel/fork.c
```
        if (clone_flags & CLONE_PARENT_SETTID)
                put_user(nr, parent_tidptr);
```

The copy operation is performed in `do_fork` before the task structure of the new thread is initialized and before its data are created with the `copy` operations.

❑ CLONE_CHILD_SETTID first causes a further userspace pointer (child_tidptr) passed to `clone` to be stored in the task structure of the new process.

kernel/fork.c
```
p->set_child_tid = (clone_flags & CLONE_CHILD_SETTID) ? child_tidptr : NULL;
```

The `schedule_tail` function invoked when the new process is executed for the first time copies the current PID to this address.

kernel/schedule.c
```
asmlinkage void schedule_tail(struct task_struct *prev)
{
...
        if (current->set_child_tid)
                put_user(task_pid_vnr(current), current->set_child_tid);
...
}
```

❑ CLONE_CHILD_CLEARTID has the initial effect in `copy_process` that the userspace pointer child_tidptr is stored in the task structure — but this time in a different element.

kernel/fork.c
```
p->clear_child_tid = (clone_flags & CLONE_CHILD_CLEARTID) ? child_tidptr: NULL;
```

When the process terminates,[13] 0 is written to the address defined in clear_child_tid.[14]

kernel/fork.c
```
void mm_release(struct task_struct *tsk, struct mm_struct *mm)
{
        if (tsk->clear_child_tid
            && atomic_read(&mm->mm_users) > 1) {
                u32 __user * tidptr = tsk->clear_child_tid;
                tsk->clear_child_tid = NULL;

                put_user(0, tidptr);
```

---

[12]put_user is used to copy data between kernel address space and user address space as discussed in Chapter 4.

[13]Or, more accurately, when it automatically frees its memory management data structures using mm_release at process termination.

[14]The condition mm->mm_users > 1 means that the memory management data structure must be used by at least one other process in the system. The current process is therefore a thread in the classical sense — it takes its address space from another process and has just one control flow.

```
                    sys_futex(tidptr, FUTEX_WAKE, 1, NULL, NULL, 0);
        }
    ...
    }
```

In addition, `sys_futex`, a fast userspace mutex, is used to wake processes waiting for this event, namely, the end of the thread.

The above flags can be used from within userspace to check when threads are generated and destroyed in the kernel. `CLONE_CHILD_SETTID` and `CLONE_PARENT_SETTID` are used to check when a thread is generated; `CLONE_CHILD_CLEARTID` is used to pass information on the death of a thread from the kernel to userspace. These checks can genuinely be performed in parallel on multiprocessor systems.

2.4.2 Kernel Threads

Kernel threads are processes started directly by the kernel itself. They delegate a kernel function to a separate process and execute it there in ''parallel'' to the other processes in the system (and, in fact, in parallel to execution of the kernel itself).[15] Kernel threads are often referred to as *(kernel) daemons*. They are used to perform, for example, the following tasks:

❑ To periodically synchronize modified memory pages with the block device from which the pages originate (e.g., files mapped using `mmap`).

❑ To write memory pages into the swap area if they are seldom used.

❑ To manage deferred actions.

❑ To implement transaction journals for filesystems.

Basically, there are two types of kernel thread:

❑ **Type 1** — The thread is started and waits until requested by the kernel to perform a specific action.

❑ **Type 2** — Once started, the thread runs at periodic intervals, checks the utilization of a specific resource, and takes action when utilization exceeds or falls below a set limit value. The kernel uses this type of thread for continuous monitoring tasks.

The `kernel_thread` function is invoked to start a kernel thread. Its definition is architecture-specific, but it always uses the same prototype.

<asm-*arch*/processor.h>
```
int kernel_thread(int (*fn)(void *), void * arg, unsigned long flags)
```

The function passed with the `fn` pointer is executed in the generated thread, and the argument specified in `arg` is automatically passed to the function.[16] `CLONE` flags can be specified in `flags`.

The first task of `kernel_thread` is to construct a `pt_regs` instance in which the registers are supplied with suitable values, as would be the case with a regular `fork` system call. Then the familiar `do_fork` function is invoked.

```
    p = do_fork(flags | CLONE_VM | CLONE_UNTRACED, 0, &regs, 0, NULL, NULL);
```

---

[15]On multiprocessor systems, the processes genuinely execute in parallel; on single-processor systems, the scheduler simulates parallel execution.

[16]Arguments allow the function to be used for different purposes by indicating what needs to be done.

Because kernel threads are generated by the kernel itself, two special points should be noted:

1. They execute in the supervisor mode of the CPU, not in the user mode (see Chapter 1).

2. They may access only the kernel part of virtual address space (all addresses above TASK_SIZE) but not the virtual user area.

Recall from above that the two pointers to mm_structs are contained in the task structure:

```
<sched.h>
struct task_struct {
...
        struct mm_struct *mm, *active_mm;
...
}
```

The total virtual address space of a system is separated into two parts on most machines: The lower portion is accessible by userland programs, and the upper part is reserved for the kernel. When the kernel is running on behalf of a userland program to serve a system call, for instance, the userspace portion of the virtual address space is described by the mm_struct instance pointed to by mm (the exact content of this structure is irrelevant for now, but is discussed in Chapter 4). Every time the kernel performs a context switch, the userland portion of the virtual address space must be replaced to match the then-running process.

This provides some room for optimization, which goes by the name *lazy TLB handling*: Since kernel threads are not associated with any particular userland process, the kernel does not need to rearrange the userland portion of the virtual address space and can just leave the old setting in place. Since any userland process can have been running before a kernel thread, the contents of the userspace part are essentially random, and the kernel thread must not modify it. To signalize that the userspace portion must not be accessed, mm is set to a NULL pointer. However, since the kernel must know what is currently contained in the userspace, a pointer to the mm_struct describing it is preserved in active_mm.

Why are processes without an mm pointer called *lazy TLB processes*? Suppose that the process that runs after a kernel thread is the same process that has run before. In this case, the kernel does not need to modify the userspace address tables, and the information in the translation lookaside buffers is still valid. A switch (and a corresponding clearance of TLB data) is only required when a different userland process from before executes after the kernel thread.

Notice that when the kernel is operating in process context, mm and active_mm have identical values.

A kernel thread can be implemented in one of two ways. The older variant — which is still in use in some places in the kernel — is to pass a function directly to kernel_thread. The function is then responsible to assist the kernel in the transformation into a daemon by invoking daemonize. This results in the following actions:

1. The function frees all resources (e.g., memory context, file descriptors, etc.) of the user process as whose child the kernel thread was started because otherwise these would be pinned until the end of the thread — this is not desirable because daemons usually run until the system is shut down. As each daemon operates only in the address area of the kernel, it does not even need these resources.

2.   daemonize blocks the receipt of signals.

3.   init is used as the parent process of the daemon.

The more modern possibility to create a kernel thread is the auxiliary function kthread_create.

kernel/kthread.c
```
struct task_struct *kthread_create(int (*threadfn)(void *data),
                                   void *data,
                                   const char namefmt[],
                                   ...)
```

The function creates a new kernel thread with its name given by namefmt. Initially, the thread will be stopped. To start it, wake_up_process needs to be used. After this, the thread function given in threadfn will be called with data as argument.

As an alternative, the macro kthread_run (which uses the same arguments as kthread_create) will call kthread_create to create the new thread, but will wake it up immediately. A kernel thread can also be bound to a particular CPU by using kthread_create_cpu instead of kthread_create.

Kernel threads appear in the system process list but are enclosed in square brackets in the output of ps to differentiate them from normal processes.

```
wolfgang@meitner> ps fax
  PID TTY      STAT   TIME COMMAND
    2 ?        S<     0:00 [kthreadd]
    3 ?        S<     0:00  _ [migration/0]
    4 ?        S<     0:00  _ [ksoftirqd/0]
    5 ?        S<     0:00  _ [migration/1]
    6 ?        S<     0:00  _ [ksoftirqd/1]
...
   52 ?        S<     0:00  _ [kblockd/3]
   55 ?        S<     0:00  _ [kacpid]
   56 ?        S<     0:00  _ [kacpi_notify]
...
```

If a kernel thread is bound to a particular CPU, the CPU's number is noted after the slash.

2.4.3   Starting New Programs

New programs are started by replacing an existing program with new code. Linux provides the execve system call for this purpose.[17]

Implementation of execve

The entry point of the system call is the architecture-dependent sys_execve function. This function quickly delegates its work to the system-independent do_execve routine.

kernel/exec.c
```
int do_execve(char * filename,
              char __user *__user *argv,
```

---

[17]There are other exec variants with different names in the C standard library, but ultimately all are based on execve. As in the above sections, exec is often used to refer to any of these variants.

```
        char __user *__user *envp,
      struct pt_regs * regs)
```

Not only the register set with the arguments and the name of the executable file (`filename`) but also pointers to the arguments and the environment of the program are passed as in system programming.[18] The notation is slightly clumsy because `argv` and `envp` are arrays of pointers, and both the pointer to the array itself as well as all pointers in the array are located in the userspace portion of the virtual address space. Recall from the Introduction that some precautions are required when userspace memory is accessed from the kernel, and that the __user annotations allow automated tools to check if everything is handled properly.

Figure 2-11 shows the code flow diagram for `do_execve`.

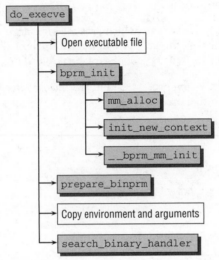

Figure 2-11: Code flow diagram for do_execve.

First, the file to be executed is opened; in other words — as described in Chapter 8 — the kernel finds the associated inode and generates a file descriptor that is used to address the file.

`bprm_init` then handles several administrative tasks: `mm_alloc` generates a new instance of `mm_struct` to manage the process address space (see Chapter 4). `init_new_context` is an architecture-specific function that initializes the instance, and `__bprm_mm_init` sets up an initial stack.

Various parameters of the new process (e.g., euid, egid, argument list, environment, filename, etc.) that are subsequently passed to other functions are, for the sake of simplicity, combined into a structure of type `linux_binprm`. `prepare_binprm` is used to supply a number of parent process values (above all, the effective UID and GID); the remaining data — the argument list — are then copied manually into the structure. Note that `prepare_binprm` also takes care of handling the SUID and SGID bits:

---

[18]`argv` includes all arguments passed to the program in the command line (for `ls -l /usr/bin` these are, e.g., `-l` and `/usr/bin`). The environment encompasses all environment variables defined at program execution time. In most shells, a list of these variables can be output using `set`.

fs/exec.c

```
int prepare_binprm(struct linux_binprm *bprm)
{
...

        bprm->e_uid = current->euid;
        bprm->e_gid = current->egid;

        if(!(bprm->file->f_vfsmnt->mnt_flags & MNT_NOSUID)) {
                /* Set-uid? */
                if (mode & S_ISUID) {
                        bprm->e_uid = inode->i_uid;
                }

                /* Set-gid? */
                /*
                 * If setgid is set but no group execute bit then this
                 * is a candidate for mandatory locking, not a setgid
                 * executable.
                 */
                if ((mode & (S_ISGID | S_IXGRP)) == (S_ISGID | S_IXGRP)) {
                        bprm->e_gid = inode->i_gid;
                }
        }
...
}
```

After making sure that MNT_NOSUID is *not* set for the mount from which the file originates, the kernel checks if the SUID or SGID bit is set. The first case is simple to handle: If S_ISUID is set, then the effective UID gets the same value as the inode (otherwise, the process's effective UID is used). The SGID case is similar, but the kernel must additionally make sure that the execute bit is also set for the group.

Linux supports various organization formats for executable files. The standard format is ELF (*Executable and Linkable Format*), which I discuss at length in Appendix E. Other alternatives are the variants shown in Table 2-2 (which lists the names of the corresponding linux_binfmt instances in the kernel).

Even though many binary formats can be used on different architectures (ELF was designed explicitly to be as system-independent as possible), this does not mean that programs in a specific binary format are able to run on multiple architectures. The assembler statements used still differ greatly from processor to processor and the binary format only indicates how the different parts of a program — data, code, and so on — are organized in the executable file and in memory.

search_binary_handler is used at the end of do_execve to find a suitable binary format for the particular file. Searching is possible because each format can be recognized by reference to special characteristics (usually a "magic number" at the beginning of the file). The binary format handler is responsible for loading the data of the new program into the old address space. Appendix E describes the steps needed to do this when the ELF format is used. Generally, a binary format handler performs the following actions:

❑   It releases all resources used by the old process.

❑   It maps the application into virtual address space. The following segments must be taken into account (the variables specified are elements of the task structure and are set to the correct values by the binary format handler):

❑ The *text segment* contains the executable code of the program. `start_code` and `end_code` specify the area in address space where the segment resides.

❑ The pre-initialized data (variables supplied with a specific value at compilation time) are located between `start_data` and `end_data` and are mapped from the corresponding segment of the executable file.

❑ The *heap* used for dynamic memory allocation is placed in virtual address space; `start_brk` and `brk` specify its boundaries.

❑ The position of the stack is defined by `start_stack`; the stack grows downward automatically on nearly all machines. The only exception is currently PA-Risc. The inverse direction of stack growth must be noted by the architecture by setting the configuration symbol `STACK_GROWSUP`.

❑ The program arguments and the environment are mapped into the virtual address space and are located between `arg_start` and `arg_end` and `env_start` and `env_end`, respectively.

❑ The instruction pointer of the process and some other architecture-specific registers are set so that the main function of the program is executed when the scheduler selects the process.

How the ELF format populates the virtual address space will be discussed in more detail in Section 4.2.1.

Table 2-2: Binary Formats Supported by Linux.

Name	Meaning
`flat_format`	The flat format is used on embedded CPUs without a memory management unit (MMU). To save space, the data in the executable can also be compressed (if zlib support is available in the kernel).
`script_format`	This is a dummy format used to run scripts using the she-bang mechanism. By looking at the first line of the file, the kernel knows which interpreter to use and starts the appropriate application (e.g., Perl for `#! /usr/bin/perl`).
`misc_format`	This is also a dummy format used to start applications requiring an external interpreter. In contrast to the `#!` mechanism, the interpreter need not be specified explicitly but is determined by reference to special file identifiers (suffix, header, etc.). This format is used, for example, to execute Java byte code or to run Windows programs with `Wine`.
`elf_format`	This is a machine- and architecture-independent format for 32 and 64 bits. It is the standard format under Linux.
`elf_fdpic_format`	ELF format with special features for systems without an MMU.
`irix_format`	ELF format with Irix-specific features.
`som_format`	HP-UX-specific format used on PA-Risc machines.
`aout_format`	a.out is the former standard format for Linux used before ELF was introduced. It is rarely used today because it is too inflexible.

Interpreting Binary Formats

Each binary format is represented in the Linux kernel by an instance of the following (simplified) data structure:

```
<binfmts.h>
struct linux_binfmt {
        struct linux_binfmt * next;
        struct module *module;
        int (*load_binary)(struct linux_binprm *, struct  pt_regs * regs);
        int (*load_shlib)(struct file *);
        int (*core_dump)(long signr, struct pt_regs * regs, struct file * file);
        unsigned long min_coredump;       /* minimal dump size */
};
```

Each binary format must provide three functions:

1. load_binary to load normal programs.

2. load_shlib to load a *shared library,* that is, a dynamic library.

3. core_dump to write a core dump if there is a program error. This dump can subsequently be analyzed using a debugger (e.g., gdb) for troubleshooting purposes. min_coredump is a lower bound on the core file size from which a coredump will be generated (usually, this is the size of a single memory page).

Each binary format must first be registered in the kernel using register_binfmt. The purpose of this function is to add a new binary format to a linked list whose list head is represented by the formats global variable from fs/exec.c. The linux_binfmt instances are linked with each other by means of their next element.

2.4.4 Exiting Processes

Processes must terminate with the exit system call. This gives the kernel the opportunity to free the resources used by the processes to the system.[19] The entry point for this call is the sys_exit function that requires an error code as its parameter in order to exit the process. Its definition is architecture-independent and is held in kernel/exit.c. Its implementation is not particularly interesting because it immediately delegates its work to do_exit.

Suffice it to say that the implementation of this function consists essentially of decrementing reference counters and returning memory areas to memory management once the reference counter has reverted to 0 and the corresponding structure is no longer being used by any process in the system.

2.5 Implementation of the Scheduler

A unique description of each process is held in memory and is linked with other processes by means of several structures. This is the situation facing the scheduler, whose task is to share CPU time between the programs to create the illusion of concurrent execution. As discussed above, this task is split into two different parts — one relating to the scheduling policy and the other to context switching.

---

[19]exit can be called explicitly by the programmer. However, the compiler automatically adds a corresponding call to the end of the main function (or to the main function used by the particular language).

2.5.1 Overview

The kernel must provide a method of sharing CPU time as fairly as possible between the individual processes while at the same time taking into account differing task priorities. There are many ways of doing this, and all have their pros and cons, which we need not discuss here (see [Tan07] for an overview of potential approaches). Our focus is on the solution adopted in the Linux kernel.

The `schedule` function is the starting point to an understanding of scheduling operations. It is defined in `kernel/sched.c` and is one of the most frequently invoked functions in the kernel code. The implementation of the scheduler is obscured a little by several factors:

❑   On multiprocessor systems, several details (some very subtle) must be noted so that the scheduler doesn't get under its own feet.

❑   Not only *priority scheduling* but also two other soft real-time policies required by the Posix standard are implemented.

❑   `gotos` are used to generate optimal assembly language code. These jump backward and forward in the C code and run counter to all principles of structured programming. However, this feature *can* be beneficial if it is used with great care, and the scheduler is one example where `gotos` make sense.

In the following overview, I consider the completely fair scheduler and neglect real-time tasks for now. I come back to them later. An outstanding feature of the Linux scheduler is that it does not require the concept of time slices, at least not in the traditional way. Classical schedulers compute time slices for each process in the system and allow them to run until their time slice is used up. When all time slices of all processes have been used up, they need to be recalculated again. The current scheduler, in contrast, considers only the wait time of a process — that is, how long it has been sitting around in the run-queue and was ready to be executed. The task with the gravest need for CPU time is scheduled.

The general principle of the scheduler is to provide maximum fairness to each task in the system in terms of the computational power it is given. Or, put differently, it tries to ensure that no task is treated unfairly. Now this clearly sounds good, but what do *fair* and *unfair* with respect to CPU time mean? Consider an ideal computer that can run an arbitrary number of tasks in parallel: If N processes are present on the system, then each one gets $\frac{1}{N}$ of the total computational power, and all tasks really execute physically parallel. Suppose that a task requires 10 minutes to complete its work. If 5 such tasks are simultaneously present on a perfect CPU, each will get 20 percent of the computational power, which means that it will be running for 50 instead of 10 minutes. However, all 5 tasks will finish their job after exactly this time span, and none of them will have ever been inactive!

This is clearly not achievable on real hardware: If a system has only a single CPU, at most one process can be run simultaneously. Multitasking is only achieved by switching back and forth between the tasks with high frequency. For users, who think considerably more slowly than the switching frequency, this creates the illusion of parallel executing, but in reality, it is not. While more CPUs in the system improve the situation and allow perfect parallel execution of a small number of tasks, there will always be situations in which fewer CPUs than processes that are to be run are available, and the problem starts anew.

If multitasking is simulated by running one process after another, then the process that is currently running is favored over those waiting to be picked by the scheduler — the poor waiting processes are being treated unfairly. The unfairness is directly proportional to the waiting time.

Every time the scheduler is called, it picks the task with the highest waiting time and gives the CPU to it. If this happens often enough, no large unfairness will accumulate for tasks, and the unfairness will be evenly distributed among all tasks in the system.

Figure 2-12 illustrates how the scheduler keeps track of which process has been waiting for how long. Since runnable processes are queued, the structure is known as the *run queue*.

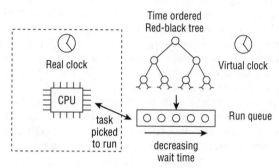

Figure 2-12: The scheduler keeps track of the waiting time of the available processes by sorting them in a red-black tree.

All runnable tasks are time-ordered in a red-black tree, essentially with respect to their waiting time. The task that has been waiting for the CPU for the largest amount of time is the leftmost entry and will be considered next by the scheduler. Tasks that have been waiting less long are sorted on the tree from left to right.

If you are not familiar with red-black trees, suffice it to know here that this data structure allows for efficient management of the entries it contains, and that the time required for lookup, insertion, and deletion operations will only moderately rise with the number of processes present in the tree.[20] Red-black trees are available as a standard data structure of the kernel, and Appendix C provides more information about them. Besides, a discussion of such trees can be found in every textbook on data structures.

Besides the red-black tree, a run queue is also equipped with a *virtual* clock.[21] Time passes slower on this clock than in real time, and the exact speed depends on the number of processes that are currently waiting to be picked by the scheduler. Suppose that four processes are on the queue: Then the virtual clock will run at one-quarter of the speed of a real clock. This is the basis to determine how much CPU time a waiting process would have gotten if computational power could be shared in a completely fair manner. Sitting on the run queue for 20 seconds in real time amounts to 5 seconds in virtual time. Four tasks executing for 5 seconds each would keep the CPU occupied for 20 seconds in real time.

---

[20]To be precise: Time complexity is $\mathcal{O}(\log n)$, where n is the number of elements in the tree. This is worse than for the old scheduler, which was famous for being an $\mathcal{O}(1)$ scheduler, that is, its run time was independent of the number of processes it had to deal with. However, the slow-down caused by the linear-logarithmic dependency of the new scheduler is negligible unless a huge number of processes is simultaneously runnable. In practice, such a situation does not occur.

[21]Notice that the kernel really used the concept of a virtual clock for the scheduling mechanism in kernel 2.6.23, but currently computes the virtual time a little differently. Since the method is easier to understand with virtual clocks, I will stick to this now and discuss how the virtual clock is emulated when I discuss the scheduler implementation.

Suppose that the virtual time of the run queue is given by `fair_clock`, while the waiting time of a process is stored in `wait_runtime`. To sort tasks on the red-black tree, the kernel uses the difference `fair_clock - wait_runtime`. While `fair_clock` is a measure for the CPU time a task would have gotten if scheduling were completely fair, `wait_runtime` is a direct measure for the unfairness caused by the imperfection of real systems.

When a task is allowed to run, the interval during which it has been running is subtracted from `wait_runtime`. This way, it will move rightward in the time-ordered tree at some point, and another process will be the leftmost one — and is consequently selected to run. Notice, however, that the virtual clock in `fair_clock` will increase when the task is running. This effectively means that the share of CPU time that the task would have received in a perfectly fair system is deducted from the time spent executing on the real CPU. This slows degradation of unfairness: Decrementing `wait_runtime` is equivalent to lowering the amount of unfairness received by the task, but the kernel must not forget that some portion of the time used to lower the unfairness would have belonged to the process in a completely fair world anyway. Suppose again that four processes sit on the run queue, and that a process has been waiting for 20 real seconds. Now it is allowed to run for 10 seconds: `wait_runtime` is afterward 10, but since the process would have gotten 10/4 = 2 seconds of this time span anyway, effectively only 8 time units account for the potentially new position on the run queue.

Unfortunately, this strategy is complicated by a number of real-world issues:

❑　Different priority levels for tasks (i.e., `nice` values) must be taken into account, and more important processes must get a higher share of CPU time than less important ones.

❑　Tasks must not be switched too often because a context switch, that is, changing from one task to another, has a certain overhead. When switching happens too often, too much time is spent with exchanging tasks that is not available for effective work anymore.

On the other hand, the time that goes by between task switches must not be too long because large unfairness values could accumulate in this case. Letting tasks run for too long can also lead to larger latencies than desired for multimedia systems.

We will see how the scheduler tackles these problems in the following discussion.

A good way to understand scheduling decisions is to activate scheduler statistics at compile time. This will generate the file `/proc/sched_debug`, which contains information on all aspects of the current state of the scheduler.

Finally, note that the `Documentation/` directory contains some files that relate to various aspects of the scheduler. Keep in mind, however, that some of them still relate to the old $\mathcal{O}(1)$ scheduler and are therefore outdated!

2.5.2　Data Structures

The scheduler uses a series of data structures to sort and manage the processes in the system. How the scheduler works is closely linked with the design of these structures. Several components interact with each other in many ways, and Figure 2-13 provides a first overview of the connections.

Scheduling can be activated in two ways: either directly if a task goes to sleep or wants to yield the CPU for other reasons, or by a periodic mechanism that is run with constant frequency and that checks from time to time if switching tasks is necessary. I denote these two components *generic scheduler* or *core scheduler* in the following. Essentially, the generic scheduler is a dispatcher that interacts with two other components:

1. *Scheduling classes* are used to decide which task runs next. The kernel supports different scheduling policies (completely fair scheduling, real-time scheduling, and scheduling of the idle task when there is nothing to do), and scheduling classes allow for implementing these policies in a modular way: Code from one class does not need to interact with code from other classes.

   When the scheduler is invoked, it queries the scheduler classes which task is supposed to run next.

2. After a task has been selected to run, a low-level *task switch* must be performed. This requires close interaction with the underlying CPU.

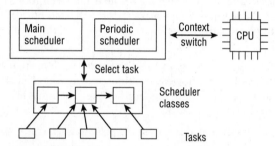

Figure 2-13: Overview of the components of the scheduling subsystem.

Every task belongs to exactly one of the scheduling classes, and each scheduling class is responsible to manage their tasks. The generic scheduler itself is not involved in managing tasks at all; this is completely delegated to the scheduler classes.

Elements in the Task Structure

There are several scheduling-relevant elements in the task structure of each process.

```
<sched.h>
struct task_struct {
...
        int prio, static_prio, normal_prio;
        unsigned int rt_priority;

        struct list_head run_list;
        const struct sched_class *sched_class;
        struct sched_entity se;

        unsigned int policy;
        cpumask_t cpus_allowed;
        unsigned int time_slice;
...
}
```

❑ Not all processes on a system are equally important: Less urgent tasks should receive less attention, while important work should be done as quickly as possible. To determine the importance of a particular task, it is equipped with a relative priority.

However, the task structure employs three elements to denote the priority of a process: `prio` and `normal_prio` indicate the dynamic priorities, `static_prio` the static priority of a process. The *static priority* is the priority assigned to the process when it was started. It can be modified with the `nice` and `sched_setscheduler` system calls, but remains otherwise constant during the process' run time.

`normal_priority` denotes a priority that is computed based on the static priority and the scheduling policy of the process. Identical static priorities will therefore result in different normal priorities depending on whether a process is a regular or a real-time process. When a process forks, the child process will inherit the normal priority.

However, the priority considered by the scheduler is kept in `prio`. A third element is required because situations can arise in which the kernel needs to temporarily boost the priority of a process. Since these changes are not permanent, the static and normal priorities are unaffected by this. How the three priorities depend on each other is slightly subtle, and I discuss this in detail below.

❑ `rt_priority` denotes the priority of a real-time process. Note that this does not replace the previously discussed values! The lowest real-time priority has value 0, whereas the highest priority is 99. Higher values correspond to higher priorities. The convention used here is different from the convention used for nice values.

❑ `sched_class` denotes the scheduler class the process is in.

❑ The scheduler is not limited to schedule processes, but can also work with larger entities. This allows for implementing *group scheduling*: This way, the available CPU time can first be distributed between general process groups (e.g., all processes can be grouped according to their owner), and the assigned time is then again distributed within the group.

This generality requires that the scheduler does not directly operate on processes but works with *schedulable entities*. An entity is represented by an instance of `sched_entity`.

In the simplest case, scheduling is performed on a per-process level, and this is the case we concentrate on initially. Since the scheduler is designed to work on schedulable entities, each process must look to it like such an entity. `se` therefore embeds an instance of `sched_entity` on which the scheduler operates in each task struct (notice that `se` is *not* a pointer because the entity is embedded in the task!).

❑ `policy` holds the scheduling policy applied to the process. Linux supports five possible values:

    ❑ `SCHED_NORMAL` is used for normal processes on which our description focuses. They are handled by the completely fair scheduler. `SCHED_BATCH` and `SCHED_IDLE` are also handled by the completely fair scheduler but can be used for less important tasks. `SCHED_BATCH` is for CPU-intensive batch processes that are not interactive. Tasks of this type are disfavored in scheduling decisions: They will never preempt another process handled by the CF scheduler and will therefore not disturb interactive tasks. The class is well suited for situations in which the static priority of a task is not desired to be decreased with `nice`, but when the task should nevertheless not influence the interactivity of a system.

    `SCHED_IDLE` tasks will also be of low importance in the scheduling decisions, but this time because their relative weight is always minimal (this will become clear when I discuss how the kernel computes task weights that reflect their priority).

Note that SCHED_IDLE is, despite its name, *not* responsible to schedule the idle task. The kernel provides a separate mechanism for this purpose.

❑   SCHED_RR and SCHED_FIFO are used to implement soft real-time processes. SCHED_RR implements a round robin method, while SCHED_FIFO uses a first in, first out mechanism. These are not handled by the completely fair scheduler class, but by the real-time scheduler class, which is discussed in Section 2.7 in greater length.

The auxiliary function rt_policy is used to decide if a given scheduling policy belongs to the real-time class (SCHED_RR and SCHED_FIFO) or not. task_has_rt_policy determines this property for a given task.

kernel/sched.c
```
static inline int rt_policy(int policy)
static inline int task_has_rt_policy(struct task_struct *p)
```

❑   cpus_allowed is a bit field used on multiprocessor systems to restrict the CPUs on which a process may run.[22]

❑   run_list and time_slice are required for the round-robin real-time scheduler, but not for the completely fair scheduler. run_list is a list head used to hold the process on a run list, while time_slice specifies the remaining time quantum during which the process may use the CPU.

The TIF_NEED_RESCHED flag discussed above is just as important for the scheduler as the specific scheduler elements held in the task structure. If this flag is set for an active process, the scheduler knows that the CPU is to be withdrawn from the process — either voluntarily or by force — and granted to a new process.

Scheduler Classes

Scheduler classes provide the connection between the generic scheduler and individual scheduling methods. They are represented by several function pointers collected in a special data structure. Each operation that can be requested by the global scheduler is represented by one pointer. This allows for creation of the generic scheduler without any knowledge about the internal working of different scheduler classes.

Without extensions required for multiprocessor systems (I will come back to these later), the structure looks as follows:

<sched.h>
```
struct sched_class {
        const struct sched_class *next;

        void (*enqueue_task) (struct rq *rq, struct task_struct *p, int wakeup);
        void (*dequeue_task) (struct rq *rq, struct task_struct *p, int sleep);
        void (*yield_task) (struct rq *rq);

        void (*check_preempt_curr) (struct rq *rq, struct task_struct *p);

        struct task_struct * (*pick_next_task) (struct rq *rq);
        void (*put_prev_task) (struct rq *rq, struct task_struct *p);
```

---

[22]The bitmap can be set using the sched_setaffinity system call.

```
        void (*set_curr_task) (struct rq *rq);
        void (*task_tick) (struct rq *rq, struct task_struct *p);
        void (*task_new) (struct rq *rq, struct task_struct *p);
};
```

An instance of `struct sched_class` must be provided for each scheduling class. Scheduling classes are related in a flat hierarchy: Real-time processes are most important, so they are handled before completely fair processes, which are, in turn, given preference to the idle tasks that are active on a CPU when there is nothing better to do. The next element connects the `sched_class` instances of the different scheduling classes in the described order. Note that this hierarchy is already set up at compile time: There is no mechanism to add new scheduler classes dynamically at run time.

The operations that can be provided by each scheduling class are as follows:

❏   `enqueue_task` adds a new process to the run queue. This happens when a process changes from a sleeping into a runnable state.

❏   `dequeue_task` provides the inverse operation: It takes a process off a run queue. Naturally, this happens when a process switches from a runnable into an un-runnable state, or when the kernel decides to take it off the run queue for other reasons — for instance, because its priority needs to be changed.

    Although the term *run queue* is used, the individual scheduling classes need not represent their processes on a simple queue. In fact, recall from above that the completely fair scheduler uses a red-black tree for this purpose.

❏   When a process wants to relinquish control of the processor voluntarily, it can use the `sched_yield` system call. This triggers `yield_task` to be called in the kernel.

❏   `check_preempt_curr` is used to preempt the current task with a newly woken task if this is necessary. The function is called, for instance, when a new task is woken up with `wake_up_new_task`.

❏   `pick_next_task` selects the next task that is supposed to run, while `put_prev_task` is called before the currently executing task is replaced with another one. Note that these operations are *not* equivalent to putting tasks on and off the run queue like `enqueue_task` and `dequeue_task`. Instead, they are responsible to give the CPU to a task, respectively, take it away. Switching between different tasks, however, still requires performing a low-level context switch.

❏   `set_curr_task` is called when the scheduling policy of a task is changed. There are also some other places that call the function, but they are not relevant for our purposes.

❏   `task_tick` is called by the periodic scheduler each time it is activated.

❏   `new_task` allows for setting up a connection between the `fork` system call and the scheduler. Each time a new task is created, the scheduler is notified about this with `new_task`.

The standard functions `activate_task` and `deactivate_task` are provided to enqueue and dequeue a task by calling the aforementioned functions. Additionally, they keep the kernel statistics up to date.

kernel/sched.c
```
static void enqueue_task(struct rq *rq, struct task_struct *p, int wakeup)
static void dequeue_task(struct rq *rq, struct task_struct *p, int sleep)
```

When a process is registered on a run queue, the `on_rq` element of the embedded `sched_entity` instance is set to 1, otherwise to 0.

Besides these, the kernel defines the convenience method `check_preempt_curr` to call the `check_preempt_curr` method of the scheduling class that is associated with a given task:

kernel/sched.c
```
static inline void check_preempt_curr(struct rq *rq, struct task_struct *p)
```

Userland applications do not directly interact with scheduling classes. They only know of the constants `SCHED_xyz` as defined above. It is the kernel's job to provide an appropriate mapping between these constants and the available scheduling classes. `SCHED_NORMAL`, `SCHED_BATCH`, and `SCHED_IDLE` are mapped to `fair_sched_class`, while `SCHED_RR` and `SCHED_FIFO` are associated with `rt_sched_class`. Both `fair_sched_class` and `rt_sched_class` are instances of `struct sched_class` that represent, respectively, the completely fair and the realtime scheduler. The contents of these instances will be shown when I discuss the respective scheduler classes in detail.

Run Queues

The central data structure of the core scheduler that is used to manage active processes is known as the *run queue*. Each CPU has its own run queue, and each active process appears on just one run queue. It is not possible to run a process on several CPUs at the same time.[23]

The run queue is the starting point for many actions of the global scheduler. Note, however, that processes are not directly managed by the general elements of the run queue! This is the responsibility of the individual scheduler classes, and a class-specific sub-run queue is therefore embedded in each run queue.[24]

Run queues are implemented using the following data structure. To simplify matters, I have omitted several statistical elements that do not directly influence the work of the run queue, and also the elements required on multiprocessor systems.

kernel/sched.c
```
struct rq {
        unsigned long nr_running;
        #define CPU_LOAD_IDX_MAX 5
        unsigned long cpu_load[CPU_LOAD_IDX_MAX];
...

        struct load_weight load;

        struct cfs_rq cfs;
        struct rt_rq rt;

        struct task_struct *curr, *idle;

        u64 clock;

...
};
```

❑ `nr_running` specifies the number of runnable processes on the queue — regardless of their priority or scheduling class.

---

[23]However, threads originating from the same process can execute on different processors as task management makes no important distinction between processes and threads.

[24]For readers familiar with earlier versions of the kernel, it might be interesting to know the scheduler class run queues replace the lists of *active* and *expired* tasks that were utilized by the previous $O(1)$ scheduler.

❑ `load` provides a measure for the current load on the run queue. The queue load is essentially proportional to the number of currently active processes on the queue, where each process is additionally weighted by its priority. The speed of the virtual per-run queue clock is based on this information. Since computing the load and other related quantities is an important component of the scheduling algorithm, I devote Section 2.5.3 below to a detailed discussion of the mechanisms involved.

❑ `cpu_load` allows for tracking the load behavior back into the past.

❑ `cfs` and `rt` are the embedded sub-run queues for the completely fair and real-time scheduler, respectively.

❑ `curr` points to the task structure of the process currently running.

❑ `idle` points to the task structure of the idle process called when no other runnable process is available — the idle thread.

❑ `clock` and `prev_raw_clock` are used to implement the per-run queue clock. The value of `clock` is updated each time the periodic scheduler is called. Additionally, the kernel provides the standard function `update_rq_clock` that is called from many places in the scheduler that manipulate the run queue, for instance, when a new task is woken up in `wakeup_new_task`.

All run queues of the system are held in the `runqueues` array, which contains an element for each CPU in the system. On single-processor systems, there is, of course, just one element because only one run queue is required.

kernel/sched.c
```
static DEFINE_PER_CPU_SHARED_ALIGNED(struct rq, runqueues);
```

The kernel also defines a number of convenient macros, which are self-explanatory.

kernel/sched.c
```
#define cpu_rq(cpu)      (&per_cpu(runqueues, (cpu)))
#define this_rq()        (&__get_cpu_var(runqueues))
#define task_rq(p)       cpu_rq(task_cpu(p))
#define cpu_curr(cpu)    (cpu_rq(cpu)->curr)
```

Scheduling Entities

Since the scheduler can operate with more general entities than tasks, an appropriate data structure is required to describe such an entity. It is defined as follows:

<sched.h>
```
struct sched_entity {
        struct load_weight load; /* for load-balancing */
        struct rb_node run_node;
        unsigned int on_rq;

        u64 exec_start;
        u64 sum_exec_runtime;
        u64 vruntime;
        u64 prev_sum_exec_runtime;
...
}
```

The structure can contain many more statistical elements if support for scheduler statistics has been compiled into the kernel, and also has some more elements if group scheduling is enabled. The part that is interesting for us right now, however, boils down to what you see above. The meaning of the individual elements is as follows:

❑ load specifies a weight for each entity that contributes to the total load of the queue. Computing the load weight is an important task of the scheduler because the speed of the virtual clock required for CFS will ultimately depend on it, so I discuss the method in detail in Section 2.5.3.

❑ run_node is a standard tree element that allows the entity to be sorted on a red-black tree.

❑ on_rq denotes whether the entity is currently scheduled on a run queue or not.

❑ When a process is running, the consumed CPU time needs to be recorded for the completely fair scheduler. sum_exec_runtime is used for this purpose. Tracking the run time is done cumulatively, in update_curr. The function is called from numerous places in the scheduler, for instance, when a new task is enqueued, or from the periodic tick. At each invocation, the difference between the current time and exec_start is computed, and exec_start is updated to the current time. The difference interval is added to sum_exec_runtime.

The amount of time that has elapsed on the virtual clock during process execution is accounted in vruntime.

❑ When a process is taken off the CPU, its current sum_exec_runtime value is preserved in prev_exec_runtime. The data will later be required in the context of process preemption. Notice, however, that preserving the value of sum_exec_runtime in prev_exec_runtime does *not* mean that sum_exec_runtime is reset! The old value is kept, and sum_exec_runtime continues to grow monotonically.

Since each task_struct has an instance of sched_entity embedded, a task is a schedulable entity. Notice, however, that the inverse statement is not true in general: A schedulable entity need not necessarily be a task. However in the following we are concerned only with task scheduling, so for now we can equate scheduling entities and tasks. Keep in mind that this is not true in general, though!

2.5.3 Dealing with Priorities

Priorities are deceptively simple from the userspace point of view: After all, they seem to be just a range of numbers. The in-kernel reality is unfortunately somewhat different, and comparatively much effort is required to work with priorities.

Kernel Representation of Priorities

The static priority of a process can be set in userspace by means of the nice command, which internally invokes the nice system call.[25] The nice value of a process is between −20 and +19 (inclusive). Lower values mean higher priorities. Why this strange range was chosen is shrouded in history.

The kernel uses a simpler scale ranging from 0 to 139 inclusive to represent priorities internally. Again, lower values mean higher priorities. The range from 0 to 99 is reserved for real-time processes. The nice values [−20, +19] are mapped to the range from 100 to 139, as shown in Figure 2-14. Real-time processes thus always have a higher priority than normal processes can ever have.

---

[25]setpriority is an alternative system call for setting process priority. It is able to modify not only the priority of an individual thread but also the priorities of all threads in a thread group or of all processes of a specific user, selected by means of the UID.

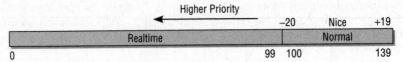

Figure 2-14: Kernel priority scale.

The following macros are used to convert between the different forms of representation (MAX_RT_PRIO specifies the maximum priority of real-time processes, and MAX_PRIO is the maximal priority value for regular processes):

```
<sched.h>
#define MAX_USER_RT_PRIO        100
#define MAX_RT_PRIO             MAX_USER_RT_PRIO
#define MAX_PRIO                (MAX_RT_PRIO + 40)
#define DEFAULT_PRIO            (MAX_RT_PRIO + 20)


kernel/sched.c
#define NICE_TO_PRIO(nice)      (MAX_RT_PRIO + (nice) + 20)
#define PRIO_TO_NICE(prio)      ((prio) - MAX_RT_PRIO - 20)
#define TASK_NICE(p)            PRIO_TO_NICE((p)->static_prio)
```

Computing Priorities

Recall that it is not sufficient to consider just the static priority of a process, but that three priorities must be taken into account: dynamic priority (task_struct->prio), normal priority (task_struct->normal_prio), and static priority (task_struct->static_prio). These priorities are related to each other in interesting ways, and in the following I discuss how.

static_prio is the starting point of the calculations. Assume that it has been already set and that the kernel now wants to compute the other priorities. This is done by a one-liner:

```
p->prio = effective_prio(p);
```

The auxiliary function effective_prio performs the following operations:

```
kernel/sched.c
static int effective_prio(struct task_struct *p)
{
        p->normal_prio = normal_prio(p);
        /*
         * If we are RT tasks or we were boosted to RT priority,
         * keep the priority unchanged. Otherwise, update priority
         * to the normal priority:
         */
        if (!rt_prio(p->prio))
                return p->normal_prio;
        return p->prio;
}
```

First of all, the normal priority is computed and stored in normal_priority. This side effect allows for setting both prio and normal_prio with a single function invocation. Another helper function, rt_prio,

94

checks if the normal priority is in the real-time range, that is, smaller than RT_RT_PRIO. Notice that the check is not related to any scheduling class, but only to the numerical value of the priority.

Assume for now that we are dealing with a regular process that is not subjected to real-time scheduling. In this case, normal_prio just returns the static priority. The effect is then simple: All three priority values have the same value, namely, that of the static priority!

Things are different for real-time tasks, however. Observe how the normal priority is computed:

kernel/sched.c
```
static inline int normal_prio(struct task_struct *p)
{
        int prio;

        if (task_has_rt_policy(p))
                prio = MAX_RT_PRIO-1 - p->rt_priority;
        else
                prio = __normal_prio(p);
        return prio;
}
```

The normal priority needs to be computed differently for regular tasks and real-time tasks. The computation performed in __normal_prio is only valid for a regular task. Real-time tasks, instead, compute the normal priority based on their rt_priority setting. Because higher values of rt_priority denote higher real-time priorities, this runs counter to the kernel-internal representation of priorities, where *lower* values mean *higher* priorities. The proper in-kernel priority value is therefore given by MAX_RT_PRIO-1 - p->rt_priority. Notice that this time, the detection of a real-time task is, in contrast to effective_prio, *not* based on any priority, but on the scheduling policy set in the task_struct.

What does __normal_priority do? The function is really simple; it just returns the static priority:

kernel/sched.c
```
static inline int __normal_prio(struct task_struct *p)
{
        return p->static_prio;
}
```

Now one can certainly wonder why an extra function is used for this purpose. There is a historical reason: Computing the normal priority in the old $\mathcal{O}(1)$ scheduler was a much trickier business. Interactive tasks had to be detected and their priority boosted, while non-interactive tasks had to be penalized to obtain good interactive behavior of the system. This required numerous heuristic calculations that either did the job well — or failed at it. The new scheduler, thankfully, does not require such magical calculations anymore.

However, one question remains: Why does the kernel base the real-time check in effective_prio on the numerical value of the priority instead of using task_has_rt_policy? This is required for non-real-time tasks that have been temporarily boosted to a real-time priority, which can happen when RT-Mutexes are in use. [26]

---

[26] Real-time mutexes allow for protection of dangerous parts of the kernel against concurrent access by multiple processors. However, a phenomenon called *priority inversion*, in which a process with lower priority executes even though a process with higher priority is waiting for the CPU, can occur. This can be solved by temporarily boosting the priority of processes. Refer to the discussion in Section 5.2.8 for more details about this problem.

Finally, Table 2-3 summarizes the result of the calculations for different types of tasks.

Table 2-3: Computing Priorities for Various Task Types.

Task type / priority	`static_prio`	`normal_prio`	`prio`
Non-real-time task	`static_prio`	`static_prio`	`static_prio`
Priority-boosted non-real-time task	`static_prio`	`static_prio`	`prio` as before
Real-time task	`static_prio`	`MAX_RT_PRIO-1-rt_priority`	`prio` as before

`p->prio` is set with the method shown above when a newly created task is woken up with `wake_up_new_task`, and when the static priority was changed using the `nice` system call.

Notice that when a process forks off a child, the current static priority will be inherited from the parent. The dynamic priority of the child, that is, `task_struct->prio`, is set to the normal priority of the parent. This ensures that priority boosts caused by RT-Mutexes are not transferred to the child process.

Computing Load Weights

The importance of a task is not only specified by its priority, but also by the load weight stored in `task_struct->se.load`. `set_load_weight` is responsible to compute the load weight depending on the process type and its static priority.

The load weight is contained in the data structure `load_weight`:

```
<sched.h>
struct load_weight {
        unsigned long weight, inv_weight;
};
```

The kernel not only keeps the load itself, but also another quantity that can be used to perform divisions by the weight.[27]

The general idea is that every process that changes the priority by one nice level down gets 10 percent more CPU power, while changing one nice level up gives 10 percent CPU power less. To enforce this policy, the kernel converts priorities to weight values. Let's first see the table:

```
kernel/sched.c
static const int prio_to_weight[40] = {
 /* -20 */     88761,     71755,     56483,     46273,     36291,
 /* -15 */     29154,     23254,     18705,     14949,     11916,
 /* -10 */      9548,      7620,      6100,      4904,      3906,
 /*  -5 */      3121,      2501,      1991,      1586,      1277,
 /*   0 */      1024,       820,       655,       526,       423,
```

---

[27]Since a normal `long` is used, the kernel cannot directly store 1/`weight`, but has to resort to a technique that allows for performing the division with a multiplication and bit shifting. The details are not of interest here, however.

```
/*    5 */          335,         272,        215,        172,        137,
/*   10 */          110,          87,         70,         56,         45,
/*   15 */           36,          29,         23,         18,         15,
};
```

The array contains one entry for each nice level in the range $[0, 39]$ as used by the kernel. The multiplier between the entries is 1.25. To see why this is required, consider the following example. Two processes A and B run at nice level 0, so each one gets the same share of the CPU, namely, 50 percent. The weight for a nice 0 task is 1,024 as can be deduced from the table. The share for each task is $\frac{1024}{1024+1024} = 0.5$, that is, 50 percent as expected.

If task B is re-niced by one priority level, it is supposed to get 10 percent less CPU share. In other words, this means that A will get 55 percent and B will get 45 percent of the total CPU time. Increasing the priority by 1 leads to a decrease of its weight, which is then $1,024/1.25 \approx 820$. The CPU share A will get now is therefore $\frac{1024}{1024+820} \approx 0.55$, whereas B will have $\frac{820}{1024+820} \approx 0.45$ — a 10 percent difference as required.

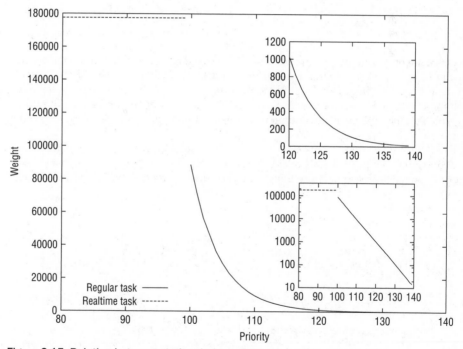

Figure 2-15: Relation between static priority and load for regular and real-time processes.

The code that performs the conversion also needs to account for real-time tasks. These will get double of the weight of a normal task. SCHED_IDLE tasks, on the other hand, will always receive a very small weight:

kernel/sched.c
```
#define WEIGHT_IDLEPRIO          2
#define WMULT_IDLEPRIO           (1 << 31)
```

```
static void set_load_weight(struct task_struct *p)
{
        if (task_has_rt_policy(p)) {
                p->se.load.weight = prio_to_weight[0] * 2;
                p->se.load.inv_weight = prio_to_wmult[0] >> 1;
                return;
        }

        /*
         * SCHED_IDLE tasks get minimal weight:
         */
        if (p->policy == SCHED_IDLE) {
                p->se.load.weight = WEIGHT_IDLEPRIO;
                p->se.load.inv_weight = WMULT_IDLEPRIO;
                return;
        }

        p->se.load.weight = prio_to_weight[p->static_prio - MAX_RT_PRIO];
        p->se.load.inv_weight = prio_to_wmult[p->static_prio - MAX_RT_PRIO];
}
```

The kernel not only computes the weight itself, but also stores the value required for division. Notice that allowing 10 percent more CPU time per priority change leads to an *exponential* behavior of the weight (and the related CPU times), which is illustrated in Figure 2-15. The upper inset in the figure shows the graph for a restricted region of regular priorities. The lower inset employs a logarithmic scale on the y axis. Note that the function is discontinuous at the transition point from regular to real-time processes.

Recall that not only processes, but also run queues are associated with a load weight. Every time a process is added to a run queue, the kernel calls inc_nr_running. This not only ensures that the run queue keeps track of how many processes are running, but also adds the process weight to the weight of the run queue:

kernel/sched.c
```
static inline void update_load_add(struct load_weight *lw, unsigned long inc)
{
        lw->weight += inc;
}

static inline void inc_load(struct rq *rq, const struct task_struct *p)
{
        update_load_add(&rq->load, p->se.load.weight);
}

static void inc_nr_running(struct task_struct *p, struct rq *rq)
{
        rq->nr_running++;
        inc_load(rq, p);
}
```

Corresponding functions (dec_nr_running, dec_load, and update_load_sub) are called when a process is removed from the run queue.

2.5.4 Core Scheduler

As mentioned above, scheduler implementation is based on two functions — the periodic scheduler and the main scheduler function. These distribute CPU time on the basis of the priorities of the available processes; this is why the overall method can also be referred to as *priority scheduling* — although this is a very general term, naturally. I discuss how priority scheduling is implemented in this section.

The Periodic Scheduler

The periodic scheduler is implemented in `scheduler_tick`. The function is automatically called by the kernel with the frequency `HZ` if system activity is going on. If no processes are waiting to be scheduled, the tick can also be turned off to save power on computers where this is a scarce resource, for instance, laptops or small embedded systems. The mechanism underlying periodic actions is discussed in Chapter 15. The function has two principal tasks.

1. To manage the kernel scheduling-specific statistics relating to the whole system and to the individual processes. The main actions performed involve incrementing counters and are of no particular interest to us.

2. To activate the periodic scheduling method of the scheduling class responsible for the current process.

kernel/sched.c
```
void scheduler_tick(void)
{
        int cpu = smp_processor_id();
        struct rq *rq = cpu_rq(cpu);
        struct task_struct *curr = rq->curr;
...
        __update_rq_clock(rq)
        update_cpu_load(rq);
```

The first part of the function deals with updating the run queue clock. This is delegated to `__update_rq_clock`, which essentially advances the `clock` time stamp of the current instance of `struct rq`. The function has to deal with some oddities of hardware clocks, but these are not relevant for our purposes. `update_cpu_load` then deals with updating the `cpu_load[]` history array of the run queue. This essentially shifts the previously stored load values one array position ahead, and inserts the present run queue load into the first position. Additionally, the function introduces some averaging to ensure that the contents of the load array do not exhibit large discontinuous jumps.

Thanks to the modular structure of the scheduler, the main work is really simple, as it can be completely delegated to the scheduler-class-specific method:

kernel/sched.c
```
        if (curr != rq->idle)
                curr->sched_class->task_tick(rq, curr);
}
```

How `task_tick` is implemented depends on the underlying scheduler class. The completely fair scheduler, for instance, will in this method check if a process has been running for too long to avoid large latencies, but I discuss this in detail below. Readers familiar with the old time-slice-based scheduling method should be aware, however, that this is *not* equivalent to an expiring time slice — they do not exist anymore in the completely fair scheduler.

If the current task is supposed to be rescheduled, the scheduler class methods set the `TIF_NEED_RESCHED` flag in the task structure to express this request, and the kernel fulfills it at the next opportune moment.

The Main Scheduler

The main scheduler function (`schedule`) is invoked directly at many points in the kernel to allocate the CPU to a process other than the currently active one. After returning from system calls, the kernel also checks whether the reschedule flag `TIF_NEED_RESCHED` of the current process is set — for example, the flag is set by `scheduler_tick` as mentioned above. If it is, the kernel invokes `schedule`. The function then assumes that the currently active task is definitely to be replaced with another task.

Before I discuss `schedule` in detail, I need to make one remark that concerns the `__sched` prefix. This is used for functions that can potentially call schedule, including the `schedule` function itself. The declaration looks as follows:

```
void __sched some_function(...) {
    ...
        schedule();
    ...
}
```

The purpose of the prefix is to put the compiled code of the function into a special section of the object file, namely, `.sched.text` (see Appendix C for more information on ELF sections). This information enables the kernel to ignore all scheduling-related calls when a stack dump or similar information needs to be shown. Since the scheduler function calls are not part of the regular code flow, they are of no interest in such cases.

Let's come back to the implementation of the main scheduler `schedule`. The function first determines the current run queue and saves a pointer to the task structure of the (still) active process in `prev`.

```
kernel/sched.c
asmlinkage void __sched schedule(void)
{
        struct task_struct *prev, *next;
        struct rq *rq;
        int cpu;

need_resched:
        cpu = smp_processor_id();
        rq = cpu_rq(cpu);
        prev = rq->curr;
    ...
```

As in the periodic scheduler, the kernel takes the opportunity to update the run queue clock and clears the reschedule flag `TIF_NEED_RESCHED` in the task structure of the currently running task.

```
kernel/sched.c
        __update_rq_clock(rq);
        clear_tsk_need_resched(prev);
    ...
```

Again thanks to the modular structure of the scheduler, most work can be delegated to the scheduling classes. If the current task was in an interruptible sleep but has received a signal now, it must be promoted to a running task again. Otherwise, the task is deactivated with the scheduler-class-specific methods (deactivate_task essentially ends up in calling sched_class->dequeue_task):

kernel/sched.c
```
        if (unlikely((prev->state & TASK_INTERRUPTIBLE) &&
        unlikely(signal_pending(prev)))) {
                prev->state = TASK_RUNNING;
        } else {
                deactivate_task(rq, prev, 1);
        }
    ...
```

put_prev_task first announces to the scheduler class that the currently running task is going to be replaced by another one. Note that this is *not* equivalent to taking the task off the run queue, but provides the opportunity to perform some accounting and bring statistics up to date. The next task that is supposed to be executed must also be selected by the scheduling class, and pick_next_task is responsible to do so:

```
        prev->sched_class->put_prev_task(rq, prev);
        next = pick_next_task(rq, prev);
    ...
```

It need not necessarily be the case that a new task has been selected. If only one task is currently able to run because all others are sleeping, it will naturally be left on the CPU. If, however, a new task has been selected, then task switching at the hardware level must be prepared and executed.

kernel/sched.c
```
        if (likely(prev != next)) {
                rq->curr = next;
                context_switch(rq, prev, next);
        }
    ...
```

context_switch is the interface to the architecture-specific methods that perform a low-level context switch.

The following code checks if the reschedule bit of the current task is set, and the scheduler jumps to the label described above and the search for a new process recommences:

kernel/sched.c
```
        if (unlikely(test_thread_flag(TIF_NEED_RESCHED)))
                goto need_resched;
    }
```

Notice that the above piece of code is executed in two different contexts: When no context switch has been performed, it is run directly at the end of the schedule function. If, however, a context switch has been performed, the current process will stop running *right before* this point — the new task has taken over the CPU. However, when the previous task is reselected to run later on, it will resume its execution directly at this point. Since prev will not point to the proper process in this case, the current thread needs to be found via current by test_thread_flag.

Interaction with fork

Whenever a new process is created using the fork system call or one of its variants, the scheduler gets a chance to hook into the process with the sched_fork function. On a single-processor system, the function performs essentially three actions: Initialize the scheduling-related fields of the new process, set up data structures (this is rather straightforward), and determine the dynamic priority of the process:

kernel/sched.c
```
/*
 * fork()/clone()-time setup:
 */
void sched_fork(struct task_struct *p, int clone_flags)
{
        /* Initialize data structures */
...

        /*
         * Make sure we do not leak PI boosting priority to the child:
         */
        p->prio = current->normal_prio;
        if (!rt_prio(p->prio))
                p->sched_class = &fair_sched_class;
...
}
```

By using the *normal* priority of the parent process as the *dynamic* priority of the child, the kernel ensures that any temporary boosts of the parent's priority are not inherited by the child. Recall that the dynamic priority of a process can be temporarily modified when RT-Mutexes are used. This effect must not be transferred to the child. If the priority is not in the real-time range, the process will always start out in the completely fair scheduling class.

When a new task is woken up using wake_up_new_task, a second opportunity for the scheduler to interact with task creation presents itself: The kernel calls the task_new function of the scheduling class. This gives an opportunity to enqueue the new process into the run queue of the respective class.

Context Switching

Once the kernel has selected a new process, the technical details associated with multitasking must be dealt with; these details are known collectively as *context switching*. The auxiliary function context_switch is the dispatcher for the required architecture-specific methods.

kernel/sched.c
```
static inline void
context_switch(struct rq *rq, struct task_struct *prev,
               struct task_struct *next)
{
        struct mm_struct *mm, *oldmm;

        prepare_task_switch(rq, prev, next);
        mm = next->mm;
        oldmm = prev->active_mm;
..
```

Immediately before a task switch, the `prepare_arch_switch` hook that must be defined by every architecture is called from `prepare_task_switch`. This enables the kernel to execute architecture-specific code to prepare for the switch. Most supported architectures (with the exception of Sparc64 and Sparc) do not use this option because it is not needed.

The context switch proper is performed by invoking two processor-specific functions:

1. `switch_mm` changes the memory context described in `task_struct->mm`. Depending on the processor, this is done by loading the page tables, flushing the translation lookaside buffers (partially or fully), and supplying the MMU with new information. Because these actions go deep into CPU details, I do not intend to discuss their implementation here.

2. `switch_to` switches the processor register contents and the kernel stack (the virtual user address space is changed in the first step, and as it includes the user mode stack, it is not necessary to change the latter explicitly). This task also varies greatly from architecture to architecture and is usually coded entirely in assembly language. Again, I ignore implementation details.

   Because the register contents of the userspace process are saved on the kernel stack when kernel mode is entered (see Chapter 14 for details), this need not be done explicitly during the context switch. And because each process first begins to execute in kernel mode (at that point during scheduling at which control is passed to the new process), the register contents are automatically restored using the values on the kernel stack when a return is made to userspace.

Remember, however, that kernel threads do not have their own userspace memory context and execute on top of the address space of a random task; their `task_struct->mm` is NULL. The address space "borrowed" from the current task is noted in `active_mm` instead:

kernel/sched.c
```
if (unlikely(!mm)) {
        next->active_mm = oldmm;
        atomic_inc(&oldmm->mm_count);
        enter_lazy_tlb(oldmm, next);
} else
        switch_mm(oldmm, mm, next);
...
```

`enter_lazy_tlb` notifies the underlying architecture that exchanging the userspace portion of the virtual address space is not required. This speeds up the context switch and is known as the *lazy TLB* technique.

If the previous task was a kernel thread (i.e., prev->mm is NULL), its `active_mm` pointer must be reset to NULL to disconnect it from the borrowed address space:

kernel/sched.c
```
        if (unlikely(!prev->mm)) {
                prev->active_mm = NULL;
                rq->prev_mm = oldmm;
        }
    ...
```

Finally, the task switch is finished with `switch_to`, which switches the register state and the stack — the new process will be running after the call:

kernel/sched.c

```
        /* Here we just switch the register state and the stack. */
        switch_to(prev, next, prev);

        barrier();
        /*
         * this_rq must be evaluated again because prev may have moved
         * CPUs since it called schedule(), thus the 'rq' on its stack
         * frame will be invalid.
         */
        finish_task_switch(this_rq(), prev);
}
```

The code following after `switch_to` will only be executed when the current process is selected to run next time. `finish_task_switch` performs some cleanups and allows for correctly releasing locks, which, however, we will not discuss in detail. It also gives individual architectures another possibility to hook into the context switching process, but this is only required on a few machines. The `barrier` statement is a directive for the compiler that ensures that the order in which the `switch_to` and `finish_task_switch` statements are executed is not changed by any unfortunate optimizations (see Chapter 5 for more details).

Intricacies of `switch_to`

The interesting thing about `finish_task_switch` is that the cleanups are performed for the task that has been active before the running task has been selected for execution. Notice that this is not the task that has initiated the context switch, but some random other task in the system! The kernel must find a way to communicate this task to the `context_switch` routine, and this is achieved with the `switch_to` macro. It must be implemented by every architecture and has a very unusual calling convention: Two variables are handed over, but in *three* parameters! This is because not only two, but three processes are involved in a context switch. The situation is illustrated in Figure 2-16.

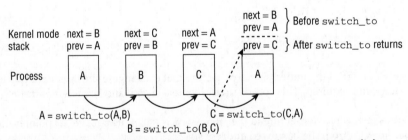

Figure 2-16: Behavior of the `prev` and `next` variables during context switches.

Suppose that three processes A, B, and C are running on the system. At some point in time, the kernel decides to switch from A to B, then from B to C, and then from C back to A again. Before each `switch_to` call, the pointers `next` and `prev` located on the stacks of the individual processes are set such that `prev` points to the *currently* running process, while `next` points to the process that will be running next. To perform the switch from `prev` to `next`, the first two arguments are completely sufficient for `switch_to`. For process A, `prev` points to A and `next` points to B.

A problem arises when A is selected to execute again. Control will return to the point after `switch_to`, and if the stack were restored to the exact state it had before the switch, `prev` and `next` would still point to the same values as before the switch — namely, `next=B` and `prev=A`. In this situation, the kernel would not know that process C has actually run before process A.

Therefore, the low-level task switch routine must feed the previously executing task to `context_switch` when a new task is selected. Since control flow comes back to the middle of the function, this cannot be done with regular function return values, and that is why a three-parameter *macro* is used. However, the conceptional effect is the same as if `switch_to` were a function of two arguments that would return a pointer to the previously executing process. What `switch_to` essentially does is

```
prev = switch_to(prev,next)
```

where the `prev` value returned is *not* the `prev` value used as the argument, but the process that executed last in time. In the above example, process A would feed `switch_to` with A and B, but would obtain `prev=C` as result. How the kernel implements this behavior depends on the underlying architecture, but it is obvious that the kernel can reconstruct the desired information by considering the kernel mode stacks of both processes — which are naturally simultaneously available to the kernel, which can access all memory at will.

Lazy FPU Mode

Because the speed of context switching plays a major role in system performance, the kernel uses a trick to reduce the CPU time needed. Floating-point registers (and other extended registers not used by the kernel; e.g., the SSE2 registers on IA-32 platforms) are not saved unless they are actually used by the application and are not restored unless they are required. This is known as the *lazy FPU* technique. Its implementation differs from platform to platform because assembly language code is used, but the basic principle is always the same. It should also be noted that, regardless of platform, the contents of the floating-point registers are *not* saved on the process stack but in its thread data structure. I illustrate this technique by means of an example.

For the sake of simplicity, let us assume this time that there are only two processes, A and B, on the system. Process A is running and uses floating-point operations. When the scheduler switches to process B, the contents of the floating-point registers of A are saved in the thread data structure of the process. However, the values in these registers are *not* immediately replaced with the values for process B.

If B does not perform any floating-point operations during its time slice, A sees its former register contents when it is next activated. The kernel is therefore spared the effort of explicitly restoring register values, and this represents a time-saving.

If, however, B does perform floating-point operations, this fact is reported to the kernel so that it can fill the registers with the appropriate values from the thread data structure. Consequently, the kernel saves and restores floating-point register contents only when needed and wastes no time on superfluous operations.

2.6   The Completely Fair Scheduling Class

All information that the core scheduler needs to know about the completely fair scheduler is contained in `fair_sched_class`:

kernel/sched_fair.c

```
static const struct sched_class fair_sched_class = {
        .next = &idle_sched_class,
        .enqueue_task = enqueue_task_fair,
        .dequeue_task = dequeue_task_fair,
        .yield_task = yield_task_fair,

        .check_preempt_curr = check_preempt_wakeup,

        .pick_next_task = pick_next_task_fair,
        .put_prev_task = put_prev_task_fair,
...
        .set_curr_task = set_curr_task_fair,
        .task_tick = task_tick_fair,
        .task_new = task_new_fair,
};
```

We have seen in the previous discussion when these functions are called by the main scheduler and will examine in the following how they are implemented for CFS.

2.6.1   Data Structures

First, I need to introduce how the CFS run queue looks. Recall that an instance is embedded into each per-CPU run queue of the main scheduler:

kernel/sched.c

```
struct cfs_rq {
        struct load_weight load;
        unsigned long nr_running;

        u64 min_vruntime;

        struct rb_root tasks_timeline;
        struct rb_node *rb_leftmost;

        struct sched_entity *curr;
}
```

The individual elements have the following meaning:

❑   `nr_running` counts the number of runnable processes on the queue, and `load` maintains the cumulative load values of them all. Recall that you have already encountered the load calculation in Section 2.5.3.

❑   `min_vruntime` tracks the minimum virtual run time of all processes on the queue. This value forms the basis to implement the virtual clock associated with a run queue. The name is slightly confusing because `min_vruntime` can actually be bigger than the `vruntime` setting of the leftmost tree element as it needs to increase monotonically, but I will come back to this when I discuss how the value is set in detail.

❑ `tasks_timeline` is the base element to manage all processes in a time-ordered red-black tree. `rb_leftmost` is always set to the leftmost element of the tree, that is, the element that deserves to be scheduled most. The element could, in principle, be obtained by walking through the red-black tree, but since usually only the leftmost element is of interest, this speeds up the average time spent searching the tree.

❑ `curr` points to the schedulable entity of the currently executing process.

2.6.2 CFS Operations

Let us now turn our attention to how the scheduling methods provided by the CF scheduler are implemented.

The Virtual Clock

I discussed in the Introduction that the completely fair scheduling algorithm depends on a virtual clock that measures the amount of time a waiting process would have been allowed to spend on the CPU on a completely fair system. However, no virtual clock can be found anywhere in the data structures! This is because all required information can be inferred from the existing real-time clocks combined with the load weight associated with every process. All calculations related to the virtual clock are performed in `update_curr`, which is called from various places in the system including the periodic scheduler. The code flow diagram in Figure 2-17 provides an overview of what the function does.

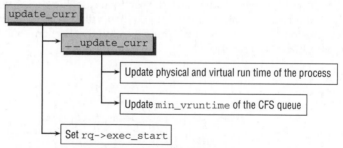

Figure 2-17: Code flow diagram for `update_curr`.

First of all, the function determines the currently executing process of the run queue and also obtains the real clock value of the main scheduler run queue, which is updated at each scheduler tick (`rq_of` is an auxiliary function to determine the instance of `struct rq` that is associated with a CFS run queue):

```
static void update_curr(struct cfs_rq *cfs_rq)
{
        struct sched_entity *curr = cfs_rq->curr;
        u64 now = rq_of(cfs_rq)->clock;
        unsigned long delta_exec;

        if (unlikely(!curr))
                return;
...
```

If no process is currently executing on the run queue, there is obviously nothing to do. Otherwise, the kernel computes the time difference between the last update of the load statistics and now, and delegates the rest of the work to __update_curr.

kernel/sched_fair.c
```
            delta_exec = (unsigned long)(now - curr->exec_start);

            __update_curr(cfs_rq, curr, delta_exec);
            curr->exec_start = now;
    }
```

Based on this information, __update_curr has to update the physical and virtual time that the current process has spent executing on the CPU. This is simple for the physical time. The time difference just needs to be added to the previously accounted time:

kernel/sched_fair.c
```
static inline void
__update_curr(struct cfs_rq *cfs_rq, struct sched_entity *curr,
              unsigned long delta_exec)
{
        unsigned long delta_exec_weighted;
        u64 vruntime;

        curr->sum_exec_runtime += delta_exec;
    ...
```

The interesting thing is how the non-existing virtual clock is emulated using the given information. Once more, the kernel is clever and saves some time in the common case: For processes that run at nice level 0, virtual and physical time are identical by definition. When a different priority is used, the time must be weighted according to the load weight of the process (recall that Section 2.5.3 discussed how process priority and load weight are connected):

kernel/sched_fair.c
```
            delta_exec_weighted = delta_exec;
            if (unlikely(curr->load.weight != NICE_0_LOAD)) {
                    delta_exec_weighted = calc_delta_fair(delta_exec_weighted,
                                                          &curr->load);
            }
            curr->vruntime += delta_exec_weighted;
    ...
```

Neglecting some rounding and overflow checking, what calc_delta_fair does is to compute the value given by the following formula:

$$\text{delta\_exec\_weighted} = \text{delta\_exec} \times \frac{\text{NICE\_0\_LOAD}}{\text{curr->load.weight}}$$

The inverse weight values mentioned above can be brought to good use in this calculation. Recall that more important tasks with higher priorities (i.e., lower nice values) will get *larger* weights, so the virtual run time accounted to them will be *smaller*. Figure 2-18 illustrates the connection between real and virtual time for various priorities. One can also see from the formula that the virtual and physical time are *identical* for nice 0 tasks with priority 120, that is, if current->load.weight is NICE_0_LOAD. Notice that the inset in Figure 2-18 uses a double logarithmic plot to show a wider range of priorities.

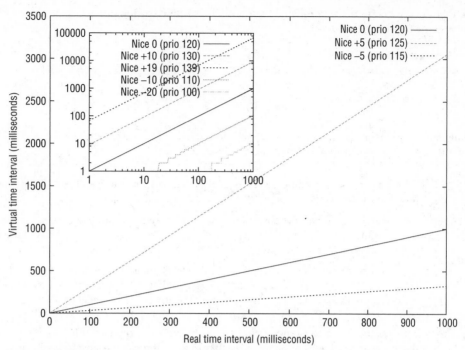

Figure 2-18: Relation between real and virtual time for processes depending on their priority/nice level.

Finally, the kernel needs to set min_vruntime. Care is taken to ensure that the value is increasing monotonically.

kernel/sched_fair.c

```
        /*
         * maintain cfs_rq->min_vruntime to be a monotonically increasing
         * value tracking the leftmost vruntime in the tree.
         */
        if (first_fair(cfs_rq)) {
                vruntime = min_vruntime(curr->vruntime,
                                __pick_next_entity(cfs_rq)->vruntime);
        } else
                vruntime = curr->vruntime;

        cfs_rq->min_vruntime =
                max_vruntime(cfs_rq->min_vruntime, vruntime);
}
```

first_fair is a helper function that checks if the tree has a leftmost element, that is, if any process is waiting on the tree to be scheduled. If so, the kernel obtains its vruntime, which is the smallest of all elements in the tree. If no leftmost element is in the tree because it is empty, the virtual run time of the current process is used instead. To ensure that the per-queue min_vruntime is monotonic increasing, the kernel sets it to the larger of both values. This means that the per-queue min_vruntime is only updated if it is exceeded by the vruntime of one of the elements on the tree. With this policy, the kernel ensures that min_vrtime can only increase, but never decrease.

One really crucial point of the completely fair scheduler is that sorting processes on the red-black tree is based on the following key:

kernel/sched_fair.c
```
static inline s64 entity_key(struct cfs_rq *cfs_rq, struct sched_entity *se)
{
        return se->vruntime - cfs_rq->min_vruntime;
}
```

Elements with a smaller key will be placed more to the left, and thus be scheduled more quickly. This way, the kernel implements two antagonistic mechanisms:

1. When a process is running, its vruntime will steadily increase, so it will finally move rightward in the red-black tree.

Because vruntime will increase *more slowly* for more important processes, they will also move rightward more slowly, so their chance to be scheduled is bigger than for a less important process — just as required.

2. If a process sleeps, its vruntime will remain unchanged. Because the per-queue min_vruntime increases in the meantime (recall that it is monotonic!), the sleeper will be placed more to the left after waking up because the key got *smaller*.[28]

In practice, both effects naturally happen simultaneously, but this does not influence the interpretation. Figure 2-19 illustrates the different movement mechanisms on the red-black tree graphically.

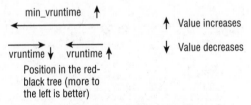

Figure 2-19: Influence of the per-entity and per-queue virtual times on the placement of processes in the red-black tree.

Latency Tracking

The kernel has a built-in notion of what it considers a good scheduling latency, that is, the interval during which every runnable task should run at least once.[29] It is given in sysctl_sched_latency, which can be controlled via /proc/sys/kernel/sched_latency_ns and defaults to, respectively, 20,000,000 ns (nanoseconds) and 20 ms (milliseconds). A second control parameter, sched_nr_latency, controls the number of active processes that are at most handled in one latency period. If the number of active processes grows larger than this bound, the latency period is extended linearly. sched_nr_latency can be indirectly controlled via sysctl_sched_min_granularity, which can be set via /proc/sys/kernel/sched_min_granularity_ns. The default value is 4,000,000 ns, that is, 4 ms, and sched_nr_latency is

---

[28]This is slightly different for short sleepers, but I consider this situation when I discuss the exact mechanism.

[29]Caution: This has nothing to do with time slices, which were used by the old scheduler!

computed as `sysctl_sched_latency/sysctl_sched_min_granularity` each time one of the values is changed.

`__sched_period` determines the length of the latency period, which is usually just `sysctl_sched_latency`, but is extended linearly if more processes are running. In this case, the period length is

$$\text{sysctl\_sched\_latency} \times \frac{\text{nr\_running}}{\text{sched\_nr\_latency}}.$$

Distribution of the time among active processes in one latency period is performed by considering the relative weights of the respective tasks. The slice length for a given process as represented by a schedulable entity is computed as follows:

kernel/sched_fair.c
```
static u64 sched_slice(struct cfs_rq *cfs_rq, struct sched_entity *se)
{
        u64 slice = __sched_period(cfs_rq->nr_running);

        slice *= se->load.weight;
        do_div(slice, cfs_rq->load.weight);

        return slice;
}
```

Recall that the run queue load weight accumulates the load weights of all active processes on the queue. The resulting time slice is given in real time, but the kernel sometimes also needs to know the equivalent in virtual time.

kernel/sched_fair.c
```
static u64 __sched_vslice(unsigned long rq_weight, unsigned long nr_running)
{
        u64 vslice = __sched_period(nr_running);

        vslice *= NICE_0_LOAD;
        do_div(vslice, rq_weight);

        return vslice;
}

static u64 sched_vslice(struct cfs_rq *cfs_rq)
{
   return __sched_vslice(cfs_rq->load.weight, cfs_rq->nr_running);
}
```

Recall that a real-time interval `time` for a process with a given `weight` has the length

$$\text{time} \times \frac{\text{NICE\_0\_LOAD}}{\text{weight}},$$

and this is also used to transfer the latency interval portion.

Now we have everything in place to discuss the various methods that must be implemented by CFS to interact with the global scheduler.

2.6.3 Queue Manipulation

Two functions are available to move elements to and from the run queue: `enqueue_task_fair` and `dequeue_task_fair`. Let us concentrate on placing new tasks on the run queue first.

Besides pointers to the generic run queue and the task structure in question, the function accepts one more parameter: `wakeup`. This allows for specifying if the task that is enqueued has only recently been woken up and changed into the running state (`wakeup` is 1 in this case), or if it was runnable before (`wakeup` is 0 then). The code flow diagram for `enqueue_task_fair` is shown in Figure 2-20.

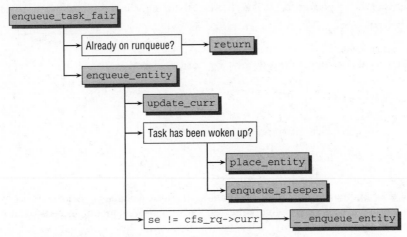

Figure 2-20: Code flow diagram for `enqueue_task_fair`.

If the task is already on the run queue as signaled by the `on_rq` element of `struct sched_entity`, nothing needs to be done. Otherwise, the work is delegated to `enqueue_entity`, where the kernel takes the opportunity to update the statistics with `updater_curr`.

If the task has recently been running, its virtual run time is still valid, and (unless it is currently executing) it can be directly included into the red-black tree with `__enqueue_entity`. This function requires some mechanics to handle the red-black tree, but it can rely on standard methods of the kernel (see Appendix C for more information) and is thus not very interesting. The essential point is that the process is placed at the proper position, but this has already been ensured before by setting the `vruntime` field of the process, and by the constant `min_vruntime` updates performed by the kernel for the queue.

If the process has been sleeping before, the virtual run time of the process is first adjusted in `place_entity`[30]:

kernel/sched_fair.c
```
static void
place_entity(struct cfs_rq *cfs_rq, struct sched_entity *se, int initial)
```

---

[30]Note that the real kernel sources will execute portions of the code depending on outcomes of `sched_feature` queries. The CF scheduler supports some "configurable" features, but they can only be turned on and off in debugging mode — otherwise, the set of features is fixed. I will therefore ignore the feature selection mechanism and consider only those that are always compiled in and active.

```
{
        u64 vruntime;

        vruntime = cfs_rq->min_vruntime;

        if (initial)
                vruntime += sched_vslice_add(cfs_rq, se);

        if (!initial) {
                vruntime -= sysctl_sched_latency;
                vruntime = max_vruntime(se->vruntime, vruntime);
        }

        se->vruntime = vruntime;
}
```

The function distinguishes between two cases depending on the value of `initial`. This parameter is only set if a new task is added to the system, but that's not the case here: `initial` is zero (I will come back to the other case when I discuss `task_new_fair` below).

Since the kernel has promised to run all active processes at least once within the current latency period, the `min_vruntime` of the queue is used as the base virtual time, and by subtracting `sysctl_sched_latency`, it is ensured that the newly awoken process will only run after the current latency period has been finished.

However, if the sleeper has accumulated a large unfairness as indicated by a large `se_vruntime` value, the kernel must honor this. If `se->vruntime` is larger than the previously computed difference, it is kept as the `vruntime` of the process, which leads to a leftward placement on the red-black tree — recall that large `vruntime` values are good to schedule early!

Let us go back to `enqueue_entity`: After `place_entity` has determined the proper virtual run time for the process, it is placed on the red-black tree with `__enqueue_entity`. I have already noted before that this is a purely mechanical function that uses standard methods of the kernel to sort the task into the red-black tree.

2.6.4 Selecting the Next Task

Selecting the next task to run is performed in `pick_next_task_fair`. The code flow diagram is shown in Figure 2-21.

If no tasks are currently runnable on the queue as indicated by an empty `nr_running` counter, there is little to do and the function can return immediately. Otherwise, the work is delegated to `pick_next_entity`.

If a leftmost task is available in the tree, it can immediately be determined using the `first_fair` helper function, and `__pick_next_entity` extracts the `sched_entity` instance from the red-black tree. This is done using the `container_of` mechanism because the red-black tree manages instances of `rb_node` that are embedded in `sched_entity`s.

Now the task has been selected, but some more work is required to mark it as the running task. This is handled by `set_next_entity`.

kernel/sched_fair.c

```
static void
set_next_entity(struct cfs_rq *cfs_rq, struct sched_entity *se)
{
        /* 'current' is not kept within the tree. */
        if (se->on_rq) {
                __dequeue_entity(cfs_rq, se);
        }
...
```

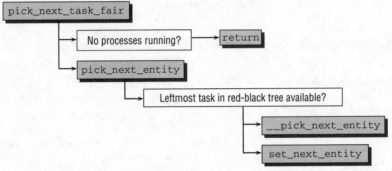

Figure 2-21: Code flow diagram for `pick_next_task_fair`.

The currently executing process is not kept on the run queue, so __dequeue_entity removes it from the red-black tree, setting the leftmost pointer to the next leftmost task if the current task has been the leftmost one. Notice that in our case, the process has been on the run queue for sure, but this need not be the case when set_next_entity is called from different places.

Although the process is not contained in the red-black tree anymore, the connection between process and run queue is not lost, because curr marks it as the running one now:

kernel/sched_fair.c

```
        cfs_rq->curr = se;
        se->prev_sum_exec_runtime = se->sum_exec_runtime;
}
```

Because the process is now the currently active one, the real time spent on the CPU will be charged to sum_exec_runtime, so the kernel preserves the previous setting in prev_sum_exec_runtime. Note that sum_exec_runtime is *not* reset in the process. The difference sum_exec_runtime - prev_sum_exec_runtime does therefore denote the real time spent executing on a CPU.

2.6.5 Handling the Periodic Tick

This aforementioned difference is important when the periodic tick is handled. The formally responsible function is task_tick_fair, but the real work is done in entity_tick. Figure 2-22 presents the code flow diagram.

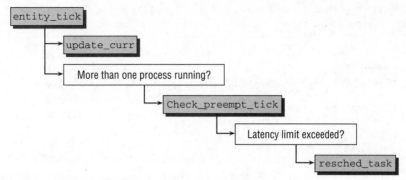

Figure 2-22: Code flow diagram for `entity_tick`.

First of all, the statistics are — as always — updated using `update_curr`. If the `nr_running` counter of the queue indicates that fewer than two processes are runnable on the queue, nothing needs to be done. If a process is supposed to be preempted, there needs to be at least another one that *could* preempt it. Otherwise, the decision is left to `check_preempt_tick`:

kernel/sched_fair.c
```
static void
check_preempt_tick(struct cfs_rq *cfs_rq, struct sched_entity *curr)
{
        unsigned long ideal_runtime, delta_exec;

        ideal_runtime = sched_slice(cfs_rq, curr);
        delta_exec = curr->sum_exec_runtime - curr->prev_sum_exec_runtime;
        if (delta_exec > ideal_runtime)
                resched_task(rq_of(cfs_rq)->curr);
}
```

The purpose of the function is to ensure that no process runs longer than specified by its share of the latency period. This length of this share in real-time is computed in `sched_slice`, and the real-time interval during which the process has been running on the CPU is given by `sum_exec_runtime - prev_sum_exec_runtime` as explained above. The preemption decision is thus easy: If the task has been running for longer than the desired time interval, a reschedule is requested with `resched_task`. This sets the `TIF_NEED_RESCHED` flag in the task structure, and the core scheduler will initiate a rescheduling at the next opportune moment.

2.6.6   Wake-up Preemption

When tasks are woken up in `try_to_wake_up` and `wake_up_new_task`, the kernel uses `check_preempt_curr` to see if the new task can preempt the currently running one. Notice that the core scheduler is not involved in this process! For completely fair handled tasks, the function `check_preempt_wakeup` performs the desired check.

The newly woken task need not necessarily be handled by the completely fair scheduler. If the new task is a real-time task, rescheduling is immediately requested because real-time tasks always preempt CFS tasks:

kernel/sched_fair.c
```
static void check_preempt_wakeup(struct rq *rq, struct task_struct *p)
{
        struct task_struct *curr = rq->curr;
        struct cfs_rq *cfs_rq = task_cfs_rq(curr);
        struct sched_entity *se = &curr->se, *pse = &p->se;
        unsigned long gran;

        if (unlikely(rt_prio(p->prio))) {
                update_rq_clock(rq);
                update_curr(cfs_rq);
                resched_task(curr);
                return;
        }
    ...
```

The most convenient cases are SCHED_BATCH tasks — they do not preempt other tasks by definition.

kernel/sched.c
```
        if (unlikely(p->policy == SCHED_BATCH))
                return;
    ...
```

When a running task is preempted by a new task, the kernel ensures that the old one has at least been running for a certain minimum amount of time. The minimum is kept in sysctl_sched_wakeup_granularity, which crossed our path before. Recall that it is per default set to 4 ms. This refers to real time, so the kernel first needs to convert it into virtual time if required:

kernel/sched_fair.c
```
        gran = sysctl_sched_wakeup_granularity;
        if (unlikely(se->load.weight != NICE_0_LOAD))
                gran = calc_delta_fair(gran, &se->load);
    ...
```

If the virtual run time of the currently executing task (represented by its scheduling entity se) is larger than the virtual run time of the new task plus the granularity safety, a rescheduling is requested:

kernel/sched_fair.c
```
        if (pse->vruntime + gran < se->vruntime)
                resched_task(curr);
}
```

The added "buffer" time ensures that tasks are not switched too frequently so that not too much time is spent in context switching instead of doing real work.

2.6.7 Handling New Tasks

The last operation of the completely fair scheduler that we need to consider is the hook function that is called when new tasks are created: task_new_fair. The behavior of the function is controllable with the parameter `sysctl_sched_child_runs_first`. As the name might suggest, it determined if a newly created child process should run before the parent. This is usually beneficial, especially if the child performs an `exec` system call afterward. The default setting is 1, but this can be changed via `/proc/sys/kernel/sched_child_runs_first`.

Initially, the function performs the usual statistics update with `update_curr` and then employs the previously discussed `place_entity`:

kernel/sched_fair.c
```
static void task_new_fair(struct rq *rq, struct task_struct *p)
{
        struct cfs_rq *cfs_rq = task_cfs_rq(p);
        struct sched_entity *se = &p->se, *curr = cfs_rq->curr;
        int this_cpu = smp_processor_id();

        update_curr(cfs_rq);
        place_entity(cfs_rq, se, 1);
   ...
```

In this case, `place_entity` is, however, called with `initial` set to 1, which amounts to computing the initial `vruntime` with `sched_vslice_add`. Recall that this determines the portion of the latency interval that belongs to the process, but converted to virtual time. This is the scheduler's initial debt to the process.

kernel/sched_fair.c
```
        if (sysctl_sched_child_runs_first && curr->vruntime < se->vruntime) {
                swap(curr->vruntime, se->vruntime);
        }

        enqueue_task_fair(rq, p, 0);
        resched_task(rq->curr);
}
```

If the virtual run time of the parent (represented by `curr`) is less than the virtual run time of the child, this would mean that the parent runs before the child — recall that small virtual run times favor left positions in the red-black tree. If the child is supposed to run before the parent, the virtual run times of both need to be swapped.

Afterward, the child is enqueued into the run queue as usual, and rescheduling is requested.

2.7 The Real-Time Scheduling Class

As mandated by the POSIX standard, Linux supports two real-time scheduling classes in addition to "normal" processes. The structure of the scheduler enables real-time processes to be integrated into the kernel without any changes in the core scheduler — this is a definitive advantage of scheduling classes.[31]

Now is a good place to recall some of the facts discussed a long time ago. Real-time processes can be identified by the fact that they have a *higher* priority than normal processes — accordingly, their `static_prio` value is always *lower* than that of normal processes, as shown in Figure 2-14. The `rt_task` macro is

---

[31]The completely fair scheduler needs to be aware of real-time processes in the wake-up preemption code, but this requires only very little effort.

provided to establish whether a given task is a real-time process or not by inspecting its priority, and `task_has_rt_policy` checks if the process is associated with a real-time scheduling policy.

2.7.1 Properties

Real-time processes differ from normal processes in one essential way: If a real-time process exists in the system and is runnable, it will always be selected by the scheduler — unless there is another real-time process with a higher priority.

The two available real-time classes differ as follows:

❑ *Round robin* processes (`SCHED_RR`) have a time slice whose value is reduced when they run if they are normal processes. Once all time quantums have expired, the value is reset to the initial value, but the process is placed at the end of the queue. This ensures that if there are several `SCHED_RR` processes with the same priority, they are always executed in turn.

❑ *First-in, first-out* processes (`SCHED_FIFO`) do not have a time slice and are permitted to run as long as they want once they have been selected.

It is evident that the system can be rendered unusable by badly programmed real-time processes — all that is needed is an endless loop whose loop body never sleeps. Extreme care should therefore be taken when writing real-time applications.[32]

2.7.2 Data Structures

The scheduling class for real-time tasks is defined as follows:

kernel/sched-rt.c
```
const struct sched_class rt_sched_class = {
        .next = &fair_sched_class,
        .enqueue_task = enqueue_task_rt,
        .dequeue_task = dequeue_task_rt,
        .yield_task = yield_task_rt,

        .check_preempt_curr = check_preempt_curr_rt,

        .pick_next_task = pick_next_task_rt,
        .put_prev_task = put_prev_task_rt,

        .set_curr_task = set_curr_task_rt,
        .task_tick = task_tick_rt,
};
```

The implementation of the real-time scheduler class is simpler than the completely fair scheduler. Only roughly 250 lines of code compared to 1,100 for CFS are required!

The core run queue also contains a sub-run queue for real-time tasks as embedded instance of struct `rt_rq`:

---

[32]Notice that this situation will be eased with the introduction of real-time group scheduling in kernel 2.6.25, which was still under development when this book was written.

kernel/sched.c
```
struct rq {
...
        t_rq rt;
...
}
```

The run queue is very straightforward — a linked list is sufficient[33]:

kernel/sched.c
```
struct rt_prio_array {
        DECLARE_BITMAP(bitmap, MAX_RT_PRIO+1); /* include 1 bit for delimiter */
        struct list_head queue[MAX_RT_PRIO];
};

struct rt_rq {
        struct rt_prio_array active;
};
```

All real-time tasks with the same priority are kept in a linked list headed by `active.queue[prio]`, and the bitmap `active.bitmap` signals in which list tasks are present by a set bit. If no tasks are on the list, the bit is not set. Figure 2-23 illustrates the situation.

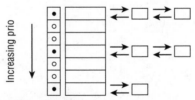

Figure 2-23: Run queue of the real-time scheduler.

The analog of `update_cur` for the real-time scheduler class is `update_curr_rt`: The function keeps track of the time the current process spent executing on the CPU in `sum_exec_runtime`. All calculations are performed with real times; virtual times are not required. This simplifies things a lot.

2.7.3 Scheduler Operations

To enqueue and dequeue tasks is simple: The task is placed or respectively removed from the appropriate list selected by `array->queue + p->prio`, and the corresponding bit in the bitmap is set if at least one task is present, or removed if no tasks are left on the queue. Notice that new tasks are always queued at the end of each list.

The two interesting operations are how the next task is selected and how preemption is handled. Consider `pick_next_task_rt`, which handles selection of the next task first. The code flow diagram is shown in Figure 2-24.

---

[33]SMP systems require some more elements for load balancing, but these do not concern us here.

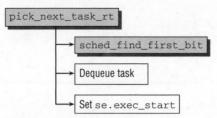

Figure 2-24: Code flow diagram for pick_next_task_rt.

`sched_find_first_bit` is a standard function that finds the first set bit in `active.bitmap` — this means that higher real-time priorities (which result in lower in-kernel priorities) are handled before lower real-time priorities. The first task on the selected list is taken out, and `se.exec_start` is set to the current real-time clock value of the run queue — that's all that is required.

The implementation of the periodic tick is likewise simple. `SCHED_FIFO` tasks are easiest to handle: They can run as long as they like and must pass control to another task explicitly by using the `yield` system call:

kernel/sched.c
```
static void task_tick_rt(struct rq *rq, struct task_struct *p)
{
        update_curr_rt(rq);

        /*
         * RR tasks need a special form of timeslice management.
         * FIFO tasks have no timeslices.
         */
        if (p->policy != SCHED_RR)
                return;
...
```

If the current process is a round robin process, its time slice is decremented. When the time quantum is not yet exceeded, nothing more needs to be done — the process can keep running. Once the counter reverts to 0, its value is renewed to `DEF_TIMESLICE`, which is set to `100 * HZ / 1000`, that is, 100 ms. If the task is not the only task in its list, it is requeued to the end. Rescheduling is requested as usual by setting the `TIF_NEED_RESCHED` flag with `set_tsk_need_resched`:

kernel/sched-rt.c
```
        if (--p->time_slice)
                return;

        p->time_slice = DEF_TIMESLICE;

        /*
         * Requeue to the end of queue if we are not the only element
         * on the queue:
         */
        if (p->run_list.prev != p->run_list.next) {
```

```
                        requeue_task_rt(rq, p);
                        set_tsk_need_resched(p);
              }
      }
```

The `sched_setscheduler` system call must be used to convert a process into a real-time process. This call is not discussed at length because it performs only the following simple tasks:

- ❏ It removes the process from its current queue using `deactivate_task`.
- ❏ It sets the real-time priority and the scheduling class in the task data structure.
- ❏ It reactivates the task.

If the process was not previously on any run queue, only the scheduling class and the new priority value need be set; deactivation and reactivation are unnecessary.

Note that changing the scheduler class or priority is only possible without constraints if the `sched_setscheduler` system call is performed by a process with root rights (or, equivalently, the capability `CAP_SYS_NICE`). Otherwise, the following conditions apply:

- ❏ The scheduling class can only be changed from `SCHED_NORMAL` to `SCHED_BATCH` or vice versa. A change to `SCHED_FIFO` is impossible.
- ❏ Only the priority of processes with the same UID or EUID as the EUID of the caller can be changed. Additionally, the priority may only be decreased, but not increased.

2.8   Scheduler Enhancements

So far, we have only considered scheduling on real-time systems — naturally, Linux can do slightly better. Besides support for multiple CPUs, the kernel also provides several other enhancements that relate to scheduling, discussed in the following sections. Notice, however, that these enhancements add much complexity to the scheduler, so I will mostly consider simplified situations that illuminate the essential principle, but do not account for all boundary cases and scheduling oddities.

2.8.1   SMP Scheduling

On multiprocessor systems, the kernel must consider a few additional issues in order to ensure good scheduling:

- ❏ The CPU load must be shared as fairly as possible over the available processors. It makes little sense if one processor is responsible for three concurrent applications while another has only the idle task to deal with.
- ❏ The *affinity* of a task to certain processors in the system must be selectable. This makes it possible, for example, to bind a compute-intensive application to the first three CPUs on a 4-CPU system while the remaining (interactive) processes run on the fourth CPU.

❑ The kernel must be able to migrate processes from one CPU to another. However, this option must be used with great care because it can severely impair performance. CPU caches are the biggest problem on smaller SMP systems. For *really* big systems, a CPU can be located literally some meters away from the memory previously used, so access to it will be very costly.

The affinity of a task to particular CPUs is defined in the cpus_allowed element of the task structure specified above. Linux provides the sched_setaffinity system call to change this assignment.

Extensions to the Data Structures

The scheduling methods that each scheduler class must provide are augmented by two additional functions on SMP systems:

```
<sched.h>
struct sched_class {
...
#ifdef CONFIG_SMP
        unsigned long (*load_balance) (struct rq *this_rq, int this_cpu,
                        struct rq *busiest, unsigned long max_load_move,
                        struct sched_domain *sd, enum cpu_idle_type idle,
                        int *all_pinned, int *this_best_prio);

        int (*move_one_task) (struct rq *this_rq, int this_cpu,
                        struct rq *busiest, struct sched_domain *sd,
                        enum cpu_idle_type idle);
#endif
...
}
```

Despite their names, the functions are, however, not directly responsible to handle load balancing. They are called by the core scheduler code whenever the kernel deems rebalancing necessary. The scheduler class-specific functions then set up an iterator that allows the generic code to walk through all processes that are potential candidates to be moved to another queue, but the internal structures of the individual scheduler classes must *not* be exposed to the generic code because of the iterator. load_balance employs the generic function load_balance, while move_one_task uses iter_move_one_task. The functions serve different purposes:

❑ iter_move_one_task picks one task off the busy run queue busiest and moves it to the run queue of the current CPU.

❑ load_balance is allowed to distribute multiple tasks from the busiest run queue to the current CPU, but must not move more load than specified by max_load_move.

How is load balancing initiated? On SMP systems, the scheduler_tick periodic scheduler function invokes the trigger_load_balance function on completion of the tasks required for all systems as described above. This raises the SCHEDULE_SOFTIRQ softIRQ (the software analog to hardware interrupts; see Chapter 14 for more details), which, in turn, guarantees that run_rebalance_domains will be run in due time. This function finally invokes load balancing for the current CPU by calling rebalance_domains. The time flow is illustrated in Figure 2-25.

To perform rebalancing, the kernel needs some more information. Run queues are therefore augmented with additional fields on SMP systems:

kernel/sched.c

```
struct rq {
...
#ifdef CONFIG_SMP
        struct sched_domain *sd;
        /* For active balancing */
        int active_balance;
        int push_cpu;
        /* cpu of this runqueue: */
        int cpu;

        struct task_struct *migration_thread;
        struct list_head migration_queue;
#endif
...
}
```

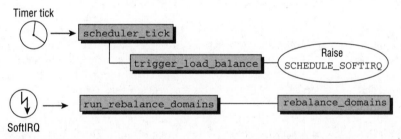

Figure 2-25: Time flow for initiation of load balancing on SMP systems.

Run queues are CPU-specific, so cpu denotes the processor to which the run queue belongs. The kernel provides one *migration thread* per run queue to which migration requests can be posted — they are kept on the list migration_queue. Such requests usually originate from the scheduler itself, but can also become necessary when a process is restricted to a certain set of CPUs and must not run on the one it is currently executing on anymore. The kernel tries to balance run queues periodically, but if this fails to be satisfactory for a run queue, then active balancing must be used. active_balance is set to a nonzero value if this is required, and cpu notes the processor from which the request for active balancing initiates.

Furthermore, all run queues are organized in *scheduling domains*. This allows for grouping CPUs that are physically adjacent to each other or share a common cache such that processes should preferably be moved between them. On "normal" SMP systems, however, all processors will be contained in one scheduling domain. I will therefore not discuss this structure in detail, but only mention that it contains numerous parameters that can be set via /proc/sys/kernel/cpuX/domainY. These include the minimal and maximal time interval after which load balancing is initiated, the minimal imbalance for a queue to be re-balanced, and so on. Besides, the structure also manages fields that are set at run time and that allow the kernel to keep track when the last balancing operation has been performed, and when the next will take place.

So what does `load_balance` do? The function checks if enough time has elapsed since the last re-balancing operation, and initiates a new re-balancing cycle if necessary by invoking `load_balance`. The code flow diagram for this function is shown in Figure 2-26. Notice that I describe a simplified version because the SMP scheduler has to deal with a very large number of corner cases that obstruct the view on the essential actions.

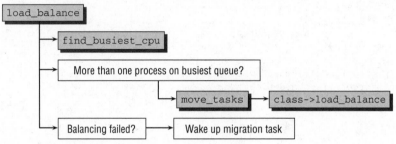

Figure 2-26: Code flow diagram for `load_balance`.

First of all, the function has to identify which queue has most work to do. This task is delegated to `find_busiest_queue`, which is called for a specific run queue. The function iterates over the queues of all processors (or, to be precise, of all processors in the current scheduling group) and compares their load weights. The busiest queue is the queue with the largest value found in the end.

Once `find_busiest_queue` has identified a very busy queue, and if at least one task is running on this queue (load balancing will otherwise not make too much sense), a suitable number of its tasks are migrated to the current queue using `move_tasks`. This function, in turn, invokes the scheduler-class-specific `load_balance` method.

When selecting potential migration candidates, the kernel must ensure that the process in question

❑   is not running at the moment or has just finished running because this fact would cancel out the benefits of the CPU caches currently filled with the process data.

❑   may execute on the processor associated with the current queue on the grounds of its CPU affinity.

If balancing failed (e.g., because all tasks on the remote queue have a higher kernel-internal priority value, i.e., a lower nice priority), the migration thread that is responsible for the busiest run queue is woken up. To ensure that active load balancing is performed that is slightly more aggressive than the method tried now, `load_balance` sets the `active_balance` flag of the busiest run queue and also notes the CPU from which the request originates in `rq->cpu`.

The Migration Thread

The migration thread serves two purposes: It must fulfill migration requests originating from the scheduler, and it is used to implement active balancing. This is handled in a kernel thread that executes `migration_thread`. The code flow diagram for the function is shown in Figure 2-27.

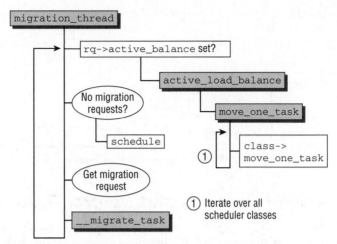

Figure 2-27: Code flow diagram for `migration_thread`.

`migration_thread` runs an infinite loop and sleeps when there is nothing to do. First of all, the function checks if active balancing is required, and if this is the case, `active_load_balance` is called to satisfy this request. The function tries to move one task from the current run queue to the run queue of the CPU that initiated the request for active balancing. It uses `move_one_task` for this purpose, which, in turn, ends up calling the scheduler-class specific `move_one_task` functions of all scheduler classes until one of them succeeds. Note that these functions try to move processes more aggressively than `load_balance`. For instance, they do not perform the previously mentioned priority comparison, so they are more likely to succeed.

Once the active load balancing is finished, the migration thread checks if any migration requests from the scheduler are pending in the `migrate_req` list. If none is available, the thread can reschedule. Otherwise, the request is fulfilled with `__migrate_task`, which performs the desired process movement directly without further interaction with the scheduler classes.

Core Scheduler Changes

Besides the additions discussed above, some changes to the existing methods are required in the core scheduler on SMP systems. While numerous small details change all over the place, the most important differences as compared to uniprocessor systems are the following:

❑ When a new process is started with the `exec` system call, a good opportunity for the scheduler to move the task across CPUs arises. Naturally, it has not been running yet, so there cannot be any negative effects on the CPU cache by moving the task to another CPU. `sched_exec` is the hook function invoked by the `exec` system call, and the code flow diagram is shown in Figure 2-28.

`sched_balance_self` picks the CPU that is currently least loaded (and on which the process is also allowed to run). If this is not the current CPU, then `sched_migrate_task` forwards an according migration request to the migration thread using `sched_migrate_task`.

❑ The scheduling granularity of the completely fair scheduler scales with the number of CPUs. The more processors present in the system, the larger the granularities that can be employed. Both `sysctl_sched_min_granularity` and `sysctl_sched_latency` for `sysctl_sched_min_` granularity are multiplied by the correction factor $1 + \log_2(\texttt{nr\_cpus})$, where nr_cpus represents the number of available CPUs. However, they must not exceed 200 ms. sysctl_sched_wakeup_granularity is also increased by the factor, but is not bounded from above.

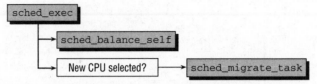

Figure 2-28: Code flow diagram for sched_exec.

2.8.2 Scheduling Domains and Control Groups

In the previous discussion of the scheduler code, we have often come across the situation that the scheduler does not deal directly with processes, but with *schedulable entities*. This allows for implementing *group scheduling*: Processes are placed into different groups, and the scheduler is first fair among these groups and then fair among all processes in the group. This allows, for instance, granting identical shares of the available CPU time to each user. Once the scheduler has decided how much time each user gets, the determined interval is then distributed between the users' processes in a fair manner. This naturally implies that the more processes a user runs, the less CPU share each process will get. The amount of time for the user in total is not influenced by the number of processes, though.

Grouping tasks between users is not the only possibility. The kernel also offers *control groups*, which allow — via the special filesystem cgroups — creating arbitrary collections of tasks, which may even be sorted into multiple hierarchies. The situation is illustrated in Figure 2-29.

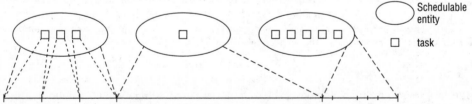

Figure 2-29: Overview of fair group scheduling: The available CPU time is first distributed fairly among the scheduling groups, and then between the processes in each group.

To reflect the hierarchical situation within the kernel, struct sched_entity is augmented with an element that allows for expressing this hierarchy:

<sched.h>
```
struct sched_entity {
...
#ifdef CONFIG_FAIR_GROUP_SCHED
        struct sched_entity *parent;
...
#endif
...
}
```

This substructure of scheduling entities must be considered by all scheduling-class-related operations. Consider, for instance, how the code to enqueue a task in the completely fair scheduler really looks:

kernel/sched_fair.c
```
static void enqueue_task_fair(struct rq *rq, struct task_struct *p, int wakeup)
{
        struct cfs_rq *cfs_rq;
        struct sched_entity *se = &p->se;

        for_each_sched_entity(se) {
                if (se->on_rq)
                        break;
                cfs_rq = cfs_rq_of(se);
                enqueue_entity(cfs_rq, se, wakeup);
                wakeup = 1;
        }
}
```

for_each_sched_entity traverses the scheduling hierarchy defined by the parent elements of sched_entity, and each entity is enqueued on the run queue.

Notice that for_each_sched_entity will resolve to a trivial loop that executes the code contained in the loop body exactly once when support for group scheduling is not selected, so the behavior described in the previous discussion is regained.

2.8.3 Kernel Preemption and Low Latency Efforts

Let us now turn our attention to kernel preemption, which allows for a smoother experience of the system, especially in multimedia environments. Closely related are low latency efforts performed by the kernel, which I will discuss afterward.

Kernel Preemption

As described above, the scheduler is invoked before returning to user mode after system calls or at certain designated points in the kernel. This ensures that the kernel, unlike user processes, cannot be interrupted unless it explicitly wants to be. This behavior can be problematic if the kernel is in the middle of a relatively long operation — this may well be the case with filesystem, or memory-management-related tasks. The kernel is executing on behalf of a specific process for a long amount of time, and other processes do not get to run in the meantime. This may result in deteriorating system latency, which users experience as "sluggish" response. Video and audio dropouts may also occur in multimedia applications if they are denied CPU time for too long.

These problems can be resolved by compiling the kernel with support for *kernel preemption*. This allows not only userspace applications but also the kernel to be interrupted if a high-priority process has some things to do. Keep in mind that kernel preemption and preemption of userland tasks by other userland tasks are two different concepts!

Kernel preemption was added during the development of kernel 2.5. Although astonishingly few changes were required to make the kernel preemptible, the mechanism is not as easy to implement as preemption of tasks running in userspace. If the kernel cannot complete certain actions in a single operation — manipulation of data structures, for instance — *race conditions* may occur and render the system inconsistent. The same problems arise on multiprocessor systems discussed in Chapter 5.

The kernel may not, therefore, be interrupted at all points. Fortunately, most of these points have already been identified by SMP implementation, and this information can be reused to implement kernel preemption. Problematic sections of the kernel that may only be accessed by one processor at a time are protected by so-called *spinlocks*: The first processor to arrive at a dangerous (also called critical) region acquires the lock, and releases the lock once the region is left again. Another processor that wants to access the region in the meantime has to wait until the first user has released the lock. Only then can it acquire the lock and enter the dangerous region.

If the kernel can be preempted, even uniprocessor systems will behave like SMP systems. Consider that the kernel is working inside a critical region when it is preempted. The next task also operates in kernel mode, and unfortunately also wants to access the same critical region. This is effectively equivalent to two processors working in the critical region at the same time and must be prevented. Every time the kernel is inside a critical region, kernel preemption must be disabled.

How does the kernel keep track of whether it can be preempted or not? Recall that each task in the system is equipped with an architecture-specific instance of struct thread_info. The structure also includes a *preemption counter*:

```
<asm-arch/thread_info.h>
struct thread_info {
    ...
            int preempt_count;    /* 0 => preemptable, <0 => BUG */
    ...
}
```

The value of this element determines whether the kernel is currently at a position where it may be interrupted. If preempt_count is zero, the kernel can be interrupted, otherwise not. The value must not be manipulated directly, but only with the auxiliary functions dec_preempt_count and inc_preempt_count, which, respectively, decrement and increment the counter. inc_preempt_count is invoked each time the kernel enters an important area where preemption is forbidden. When this area is exited, dec_preempt_count decrements the value of the preemption counter by 1. Because the kernel can enter some important areas via different routes — particularly via nested routes — a simple Boolean variable would not be sufficient for preempt_count. When multiple dangerous regions are entered one after another, it must be made sure that *all* of them have been left before the kernel can be preempted again.

The dec_preempt_count and inc_preempt_count calls are integrated in the synchronization operations for SMP systems (see Chapter 5). They are, in any case, already present at all relevant points of the kernel so that the preemption mechanism can make best use of them simply by reusing the existing infrastructure.

Some more routines are provided for preemption handling:

❑ preempt_disable disables preemption by calling inc_preempt_count. Additionally, the compiler is instructed to avoid certain memory optimizations that could lead to problems with the preemption mechanism.

❑ preempt_check_resched checks if scheduling is necessary and does so if required.

❑ preempt_enable enables kernel preemption, and additionally checks afterward if rescheduling is necessary with preempt_check_resched.

❑ preempt_disable_no_resched disables preemption, but does not reschedule.

At some points in the kernel, the protection by the normal SMP synchronization methods is not sufficient. This happens, for instance, when per-CPU variables are modified. On a real SMP system, this requires no form of protection because only one processor can by definition operate with the variable — every other CPU in the system has its own instance and does not need to fiddle with the instance of the current processor. However, kernel preemption would allow that two different code paths on the same processor would access the variable quasi-concurrently, which would have the same result as if two independent processors would manipulate the value. Preemption must therefore be explicitly disabled in these situations using manual incovations of `preempt_disable` and `preempt_disable`.

Note, however, that the `get_cpu` and `put_cpu` functions mentioned in the Introduction will automatically disable kernel preemption, so no extra precautions are necessary if per-CPU variables are accessed using this mechanism.

How does the kernel know if preemption is required? First of all, the `TIF_NEED_RESCHED` flag must be set to signalize that a process is waiting to get CPU time. This is honored by `preempt_check_resched`:

\<preempt.h\>
```
#define preempt_check_resched() \
do { \
        if (unlikely(test_thread_flag(TIF_NEED_RESCHED))) \
                preempt_schedule(); \
} while (0)
```

Recall that the function is called when preemption is re-enabled after it had been disabled, so this is a good time to check if a process wants to preempt the currently executing kernel code. If this is the case, it should be done as quickly as possible — without waiting for the next routine call of the scheduler.

The central function for the preemption mechanism is `preempt_schedule`. The simple desire that the kernel be preempted as indicated by `TIF_NEED_RESCHED` does not yet guarantee that this is *possible* — recall that the kernel could currently still be inside a critical region, and must not be disturbed. This is checked by `preempt_reschedule`:

kernel/sched.c
```
asmlinkage void __sched preempt_schedule(void)
{
        struct thread_info *ti = current_thread_info();
        /*
         * If there is a non-zero preempt_count or interrupts are disabled,
         * we do not want to preempt the current task. Just return..
         */
        if (unlikely(ti->preempt_count || irqs_disabled()))
                return;
        ...
```

If the preemption counter is greater than 0, then preemption is still disabled, and consequently the kernel may not be interrupted — the function terminates immediately. Neither is preemption possible if the kernel has disabled hardware IRQs at important points where processing must be completed in a single operation. `irqs_disabled` checks whether interrupts are disabled or not, and if they are disabled, the kernel must not be preempted.

The following steps are required if preemption is possible:

kernel/sched.c
```
do {
        add_preempt_count(PREEMPT_ACTIVE);

        schedule();

        sub_preempt_count(PREEMPT_ACTIVE);
        /*
         * Check again in case we missed a preemption opportunity
         * between schedule and now.
         */
} while (unlikely(test_thread_flag(TIF_NEED_RESCHED)));
```

Before the scheduler is invoked, the value of the preemption counter is set to `PREEMPT_ACTIVE`. This sets a flag bit in the preemption counter that has such a large value that it is never affected by the regular preemption counter increments as illustrated by Figure 2-30. It indicates to the `schedule` function that scheduling was not invoked in the normal way but as a result of a kernel preemption. After the kernel has rescheduled, code flow returns to the current task — possibly after some time has elapsed, because the preempting task will have run in between — the flag bit is removed again.

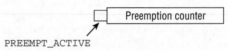

PREEMPT_ACTIVE

Figure 2-30: The per-process preemption counter.

I ignored the implications of this flag for `schedule` before, so I have to discuss it now. Recall that the scheduler deactivates a task with `deactivate_task` if it is not in a runnable state at the moment. In fact, this operation is skipped if the scheduling was initiated via the preemption mechanism as can be seen if `PREEMPT_ACTIVE` is set in the preemption counter:

kernel/sched.c
```
asmlinkage void __sched schedule(void) {
...
        if (prev->state && !(preempt_count() & PREEMPT_ACTIVE)) {
                if (unlikely((prev->state & TASK_INTERRUPTIBLE) &&
                                     unlikely(signal_pending(prev)))) {
                        prev->state = TASK_RUNNING;
                } else {
                        deactivate_task(rq, prev, 1);
                }
        }
...
}
```

This ensures that the next task is selected as quickly as possible without the hassle of deactivating the current one. If a high-priority task is waiting to be scheduled, it will be picked by the scheduler class and will be allowed to run.

This method is only one way of triggering kernel preemption. Another possibility to activate preemption is after a hardware IRQ has been serviced. If the processor returns to kernel mode after handling the IRQ (return to user mode is not affected), the architecture-specific assembler routine checks whether the value of the preemption counter is 0 — that is, if preemption is allowed — and whether the reschedule flag is set — exactly as in `preempt_schedule`. If both conditions are satisfied, the scheduler is invoked, this time via `preempt_schedule_irq` to indicate that the preemption request originated from IRQ context. The essential difference between this function and `preempt_schedule` is that `preempt_schedule_irq` is called with IRQs disabled to prevent recursive calls for simultaneous IRQs.

As a result of the methods described in this section, a kernel with enabled preemption is able to replace processes with more urgent ones faster than a normal kernel could.

Low Latency

Naturally, the kernel is interested in providing good latency times even if kernel preemption is not enabled. This can, for instance, be important in network servers. While the overhead introduced by kernel preemption is not desired in such an environment, the kernel should nevertheless respond to important events with reasonable speed. If, for example, a network request comes in that needs to be serviced by a daemon, then this should not be overly long delayed by some database doing heavy I/O operations. I have already discussed a number of measures offered by the kernel to reduce this problem: scheduling latency in CFS and kernel preemption. Real-time mutexes as discussed in Chapter 5 also aid in solving the problem, but there is one more scheduling-related action that can help.

Basically, long operations in the kernel should not occupy the system completely. Instead, they should check from time to time if another process has become ready to run, and thus call the scheduler to select the process. This mechanism is independent of kernel preemption and will reduce latency also if the kernel is built without explicit preemption support.

The function to initiate conditional rescheduling is `cond_resched`. It is implemented as follows:

kernel/sched.c
```
int __sched cond_resched(void)
{
        if (need_resched() && !(preempt_count() & PREEMPT_ACTIVE)) {
                __cond_resched();
                return 1;
        }
        return 0;
}
```

`need_resched` checks if the `TIF_NEED_RESCHED` flag is set, and the code additionally ensures that the kernel is not currently being preempted already[34] and rescheduling is thus allowed. Should both conditions be fulfilled, then `__cond_resched` takes care of the necessary details to invoke the scheduler.

How can `cond_resched` be used? As an example, consider the case in which the kernel reads in memory pages associated with a given memory mapping. This could be done in an endless loop that terminates after all required data have been read:

```
for (;;)
        /* Read in data */
        if (exit_condition)
                continue;
```

---

[34]Additionally, the function also makes sure that the system is completely up and running, which is, for instance, not the case if the system has not finished booting yet. Since this is an unimportant corner case, I have omitted the corresponding check.

If a large number of read operations is required, this can consume a sizeable amount of time. Since the process runs in kernel space, it will not be deselected by the scheduler as in the userspace case, taken that kernel preemption is not enabled. This can be improved by calling cond_resched in every loop iteration:

```
for (;;)
        cond_resched();
        /* Read in data */
        if (exit_condition)
                continue;
```

The kernel has been carefully audited to find the longest-running functions, and calls to cond_resched have been put in the appropriate places. This ensures higher responsiveness even without explicit kernel preemption.

Following a long-time tradition for Unix kernels, Linux has supported task states for both interruptible and uninterruptible sleeps. During the 2.6.25 development cycle, however, another state was added: TASK_KILLABLE.[35] Tasks in this state are sleeping and do not react to non-fatal signals, but can — in contrast to TASK_UNINTERRUPTIBLE — be killed by fatal signals. At the time of writing, almost all places in the kernel that would provide apt possibilities for killable sleeps are still waiting to be converted to the new form.

The scheduler has seen a comparatively large number of cleanups during the development of kernels 2.6.25 and 2.6.26. A new feature added during this period is real-time group scheduling. This means that real-time tasks can now also be handled by the group scheduling framework introduced in this chapter.

Additionally, the scheduler documentation was moved into the dedicated directory Documentation/ scheduler/, and obsolete files documenting the old $\mathcal{O}(1)$ scheduler have been removed. Documentation on real-time group scheduling can be found in Documentation/scheduler/sched-rt-group.txt.

2.9 Summary

Linux is a multiuser and multitasking operating system, and thus has to manage multiple processes from multiple users. In this chapter, you have learned that processes are a very important and fundamental abstraction of Linux. The data structure used to represent individual processes has connections with nearly every subsystem of the kernel.

You have seen how Linux implements the traditional fork/exec model inherited from UNIX to create new processes that are hierarchically related to their parent, and have also been introduced to Linux-specific extensions to the traditional UNIX model in the form of namespaces and the clone system call. Both allow for fine-tuning how a process perceives the system, and which resources are shared between parent and child processes. Explicit methods that enable otherwise separated processes to communicate are discussed in Chapter 5.

Additionally, you have seen how the available computational resources are distributed between processes by the scheduler. Linux supports pluggable scheduling modules, and these are used to implement completely fair and POSIX soft real-time scheduling policies. The scheduler decides when to switch between which tasks, and is augmented by architecture-specific routines to implement the context switching proper.

Finally, I have discussed how the scheduler must be augmented to service systems with multiple CPUs, and how kernel preemption and low-latency modifications make Linux handle time-constrained situations better.

---

[35] Actually, TASK_KILLABLE is not a completely new task state, but an extension to TASK_UNINTERRUPTIBLE. The effect is, however, identical.

3

Memory Management

Memory management is one of the most complex and at the same time most important parts of the kernel. It is characterized by the strong need for cooperation between the processor and the kernel because the tasks to be performed require them to collaborate very closely. Chapter 1 provided a brief overview of the various techniques and abstractions used by the kernel in the implementation of memory management. This chapter examines the technical aspects of implementation in detail.

3.1 Overview

Memory management implementation covers many areas:

- ❑   Management of physical pages in memory.

- ❑   The buddy system to allocate memory in large chunks.

- ❑   The slab, slub, and slob allocators to allocate smaller chunks of memory.

- ❑   The `vmalloc` mechanism to allocate non-contiguous blocks of memory.

- ❑   The address space of processes.

As we know, the virtual address space of the processor is in general divided into two parts by the Linux kernel. The lower and larger part is available to user processes, and the upper part is reserved for the kernel. Whereas the lower part is modified during a context switch (between two user processes), the kernel part of virtual address space always remains the same. On IA-32 systems, the address space is typically divided between user processes and the kernel in a ratio of 3 : 1; given a virtual address space of 4 GiB, 3 GiB would be available to userspace and 1 GiB for the kernel. This ratio can be changed by modifying the relevant configuration options. However, this has advantages only for very specific configurations and applications. For purposes of our further investigations, I assume a ratio of 3 : 1 for now, but will come back to different ratios later.

The available physical memory is mapped into the address space of the kernel. Accesses with virtual addresses whose offset to the start of the kernel area does not exceed the size of the available RAM are therefore *automatically* associated with physical page frames. This is practical because memory allocations in the kernel area always land in physical RAM when this scheme is adopted. However, there is one problem. The virtual address space portion of the kernel is necessarily smaller than the maximum theoretical address space of the CPU. If there is more physical RAM than can be mapped into the kernel address space, the kernel must resort to the highmem method to manage "super fluous" memory. On IA-32 systems, up to 896 MiB of RAM can be managed directly; anything above this figure (up to a maximum of 4 GiB) can only be addressed by means of highmem.

4 GiB is the maximum memory size that can be addressed on 32-bit systems ($2^{32} = 4$ GiB). If a trick is used, modern IA-32 implementations — Pentium PRO and higher — can manage up to 64 GiB of memory if PAE mode is enabled. PAE stands for page address extension *and provides additional bits for memory pointers. However, not all 64 GiB can be addressed at the same time, only sections of 4 GiB each.*

Because most memory management data structures can only be allocated in the range between 0 and 1 GiB, there is a practical limit to the maximum memory size and this is less than 64 GiB. The exact value varies according to kernel configuration. For example, it is possible to allocate third-level page table entries in highmem to reduce the load on the normal zone.

Because IA-32 systems with memory in excess of 4 GiB are a rarity and the 64-bit architecture AMD64 that has for all practical purposes replaced IA-32 offers a much cleaner solution to this problem, I won't bother discussing the second highmem mode here.

Highmem mode is not required on 64-bit machines because the available address space is gigantic, even if physical addressing is limited to a smaller number of bits, for example, 48 or 52. Given that exactly the same was thought of the 4-GiB address space on 32-bit systems just a few years ago, one could argue that it would merely seem to be a matter of time before the limits of 64-bit systems are reached, although 16 EiB *should* suffice for some time. But you never know . . . .

> **The use of highmem pages is problematic only for the kernel itself. The kernel must first invoke the `kmap` and `kunmap` functions discussed below to map the highmem pages into its virtual address space before it can use them — this is not necessary with normal memory pages. However, for userspace processes, it makes absolutely no difference if the pages are highmem or normal pages because they are always accessed via page tables and never directly.**

There are two types of machine that manage physical memory in different ways:

1. UMA machines (*uniform memory access*) organize available memory in a contiguous fashion (possibly with small gaps). Each processor (in a symmetric multiprocessor system) is able to access each memory area equally quickly.

2. NUMA machines (*non-uniform memory access*) are always multiprocessor machines. Local RAM is available to each CPU of the system to support particularly fast access. The processors are linked via a bus to support access to the local RAM of other CPUs — this is naturally slower than accessing local RAM.

   Examples of such systems are Alpha-based WildFire servers and NUMA-Q machines from IBM.

Figure 3-1 illustrates the difference between the two approaches.

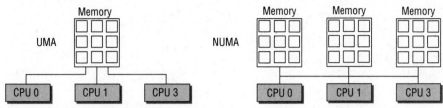

Figure 3-1: UMA and NUMA systems.

A mix of both machine types with discontiguous memory is also possible. Such a mix would then represent a UMA system whose RAM is not contiguous but has large holes. Here it is often helpful to apply the principles of NUMA organization to make memory access simpler for the kernel. In fact, the kernel distinguishes three configuration options — FLATMEM, DISCONTIGMEM, and SPARSEMEM. SPARSEMEM and DISCONTIGMEM serve practically the same purpose, but in the view of developers, differ in the quality of their code — SPARSEMEM is regarded as more experimental and less stable but does feature performance optimizations. Discontiguous memory is presumed to be more stable, but is not prepared for new features like memory hotplugging.

In the following sections, we restrict ourselves largely to FLATMEM because this memory organization type is used on most configurations and is also usually the kernel default. The fact that we do not discuss the other options is no great loss because all memory models make use of practically the same data structures.

Real NUMA systems will set the configuration option CONFIG_NUMA, and the memory management codes will differ between the two variants. Since the flat memory model will not make sense on NUMA machines, only discontiguous and sparse memory will be available. Notice that the configuration option NUMA_EMU allows AMD64 systems with a flat memory to enjoy the full complexities of NUMA systems by splitting the memory into fake NUMA zones. This can be useful for development when no real NUMA machine is available — for some reason, these tend to be rather costly.

This book focuses on the UMA case, and does not consider CONFIG_NUMA. This does not mean that the NUMA data structures can be completely neglected. Since UMA systems can choose the configuration option CONFIG_DISCONTIGMEM if their address space contains large holes, then more than one memory node can also be available on systems that do not employ NUMA techniques otherwise.

Figure 3-2 summarizes the various possible choices for the configuration options related to memory layout.

Notice that we will come across the term *allocation order* quite often in the following discussion. It denotes the binary logarithm of the number of pages that are contained in a memory region. An order 0 allocation consists of one page, an order two allocation of $2^1 = 2$ pages, an order three allocation of $2^2 = 4$ pages, and so on.

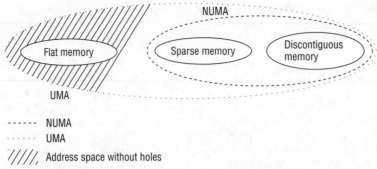

————— NUMA

· · · · · · UMA

///// Address space without holes

Figure 3-2: Overview of possible memory setups for flat, sparse, and discontiguous memory on UMA and NUMA machines.

3.2 Organization in the (N)UMA Model

The various architectures supported differ greatly in terms of how they manage memory. Owing to the intelligent design of the kernel and, in some cases, intervening compatibility layers, these differences are so well concealed that generic code can usually ignore them. As discussed in Chapter 1, a major issue is the varying number of indirection levels for page tables. A second key aspect is the division into NUMA and UMA systems.

The kernel uses identical data structures for machines with uniform and non-uniform memory access so that the individual algorithms need make little or no distinction between the various forms of memory arrangement. On UMA systems, a single NUMA node is introduced to help manage the entire system memory. The other parts of memory management are led to believe that they are working with a pseudo-NUMA system.

3.2.1 Overview

Before we look at the data structures used to organize memory in the kernel, we need to define a few concepts because the terminology is not always easy to understand. Let's first consider NUMA systems. This will enable us to show that it is very easy to reduce them to UMA systems.

Figure 3-3 is a graphic illustration of the memory partitioning described below (the situation is somewhat simplified, as you will see when we examine the data structures closely).

First, RAM memory is divided into *nodes*. A node is associated with each processor of the system and is represented in the kernel by an instance of pg_data_t (these data structures are defined shortly).

Each node is split into *zones* as further subdivisions of memory. For example, there are restrictions as to the memory area that can be used for DMA operations (with ISA devices); only the first 16 MiB are suitable. There is also a highmem area that cannot be mapped directly. Between these is the ''normal'' memory area for universal use. A node therefore comprises up to three zones. The kernel introduces the following constants to distinguish between them.

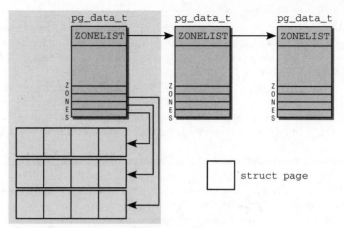

Figure 3-3: Memory partitioning in NUMA systems.

The kernel introduces the following constants to enumerate all zones in the system:

<mmzone.h>
```
enum zone_type {
#ifdef CONFIG_ZONE_DMA
        ZONE_DMA,
#endif
#ifdef CONFIG_ZONE_DMA32
        ZONE_DMA32,
#endif
        ZONE_NORMAL,
#ifdef CONFIG_HIGHMEM
        ZONE_HIGHMEM,
#endif
        ZONE_MOVABLE,
        MAX_NR_ZONES
};
```

❑   ZONE_DMA for DMA-suitable memory. The size of this region depends on the processor type. ON IA-32 machines, the limit is the classical 16 MiB boundary imposed by ancient ISA devices. But also, more modern machines can be affected by this.

❑   ZONE_DMA32 for DMA-suitable memory in a 32-bit addressable area. Obviously, there is only a difference between the two DMA alternatives on 64-bit systems. On 32-bit machines, this zone is empty; that is, its size is 0 MiB. On Alphas and AMD64 systems, for instance, this zone ranges from 0 to 4 GiB.

❑   ZONE_NORMAL for normal memory mapped directly in the kernel segment. This is the only zone guaranteed to be possible present on all architectures. It is, however, not guaranteed that the zone must be equipped with memory. If, for instance, an AMD64 system has 2 GiB of RAM, then all of it will belong to ZONE_DMA32, and ZONE_NORMAL will be empty.

❑   ZONE_HIGHMEM for physical memory that extends beyond the kernel segment.

> Depending on the compile-time configuration, some zones need not be considered.
> 64-bit systems, for instance, do not require a high memory zone, and the DMA32 zone
> is only required on 64-bit systems that also support 32-bit peripheral devices that
> can only access memory up to 4 GiB.

The kernel additionally defines a pseudo-zone ZONE_MOVABLE, which is required when efforts are made to prevent fragmentation of the physical memory. We will look closer into this mechanism in Section 3.5.2.

MAX_NR_ZONES acts as an end marker if the kernel wants to iterate over all zones present in the system.

Each zone is associated with an array in which the physical memory pages belonging to the zone — known as *page frames* in the kernel — are organized. An instance of struct page with the required management data is allocated for each page frame.

The nodes are kept on a singly linked list so that the kernel can traverse them.

For performance reasons, the kernel always attempts to perform the memory allocations of a process on the NUMA node associated with the CPU on which it is currently running. However, this is not always possible — for example, the node may already be full. For such situations, *each* node provides a fallback list (with the help of struct zonelist). The list contains other nodes (and associated zones) that can be used as alternatives for memory allocation. The further back an entry is on the list, the less suitable it is.

What's the situation on UMA systems? Here, there is just a single node — no others. This node is shown against a gray background in the figure. Everything else is unchanged.

3.2.2 Data Structures

Now that I have explained the relationship between the various data structures used in memory management, let's look at the definition of each.

Node Management

pg_data_t is the base element used to represent a node and is defined as follows:

```
<mmzone.h>
typedef struct pglist_data {
        struct zone node_zones[MAX_NR_ZONES];
        struct zonelist node_zonelists[MAX_ZONELISTS];
        int nr_zones;
        struct page *node_mem_map;
        struct bootmem_data *bdata;

        unsigned long node_start_pfn;
        unsigned long node_present_pages; /* total number of physical pages */
        unsigned long node_spanned_pages; /* total size of physical page
                                            range, including holes */
        int node_id;
        struct pglist_data *pgdat_next;
        wait_queue_head_t kswapd_wait;
        struct task_struct *kswapd;
        int kswapd_max_order;
} pg_data_t;
```

- ❏ `node_zones` is an array that holds the data structures of the zones in the node.

- ❏ `node_zonelists` specifies alternative nodes and their zones in the order in which they are used for memory allocation if no more space is available in the current zone.

- ❏ The number of different zones in the node is held in `nr_zones`.

- ❏ `node_mem_map` is a pointer to an array of `page` instances used to describe all physical pages of the node. It includes the pages of all zones in the node.

- ❏ During system boot, the kernel needs memory even before memory management has been initialized (memory must also be reserved to initialize memory management). To resolve this problem, the kernel uses the boot memory allocator described in Section 3.4.3. `bdata` points to the instance of the data structure that characterizes the boot memory allocator.

- ❏ `node_start_pfn` is the logical number of the first page frame of the NUMA node. The page frames of *all* nodes in the system are numbered consecutively, and each frame is given a number that is globally unique (not just unique to the node).

  `node_start_pfn` is always 0 in a UMA system because there is only one node whose first page frame is therefore 0. `node_present_pages` specifies the number of page frames in the zone and `node_spanned_pages` the size of the zone in page frames. This value need not necessarily be the same as `node_present_pages` because there may be holes in the zone that are not backed by a real page frame.

- ❏ `node_id` is a global node identifier. All NUMA nodes in the system are numbered starting from 0.

- ❏ `pgdat_next` links the nodes in the system on a singly linked list whose end is indicated, as usual, by a null pointer.

- ❏ `kswapd_wait` is the wait queue for the swap daemon needed when swapping frames out of the zone (Chapter 18 deals with this at length). `kswapd` points to the task structure of the swap daemon responsible for the zone. `kswapd_max_order` is used in the implementation of the swapping subsystem to define the size of the area to be freed and is currently of no interest.

The association between the node and the zones it contains and the fallback list shown in Figure 3-3 is established by means of arrays at the beginning of the data structure.

> These are not the usual pointers to arrays. The array data are held in the node structure itself.

The zones of the node are held in `node_zones[MAX_NR_ZONES]`. The array always has three entries, even if the node has fewer zones. If the latter is the case, the remaining entries are filled with null elements.

Node State Management

If more than one node can be present on the system, the kernel keeps a bitmap that provides state information for each node. The states are specified with a bitmask, and the following values are possible:

```
<nodemask.h>
enum node_states {
        N_POSSIBLE,           /* The node could become online at some point */
        N_ONLINE,             /* The node is online */
        N_NORMAL_MEMORY,      /* The node has regular memory */
#ifdef CONFIG_HIGHMEM
```

```
            N_HIGH_MEMORY,              /* The node has regular or high memory */
#else
            N_HIGH_MEMORY = N_NORMAL_MEMORY,
#endif
            N_CPU,                      /* The node has one or more cpus */
            NR_NODE_STATES
};
```

The states `N_POSSIBLE`, `N_ONLINE`, and `N_CPU` are required for CPU and memory hotplugging, but these features are not considered in this book. Essential for memory management are the flags `N_HIGH_MEMORY` and `N_NORMAL_MEMORY`. While the first one announces that the zone is equipped with memory that may be either regular or high memory, `N_NORMAL_MEMORY` is only set if non-highmem memory is present on a node.

Two auxiliary functions are provided to set or clear, respectively, a bit in the bit-field or a specific node:

\<nodemask.h\>
```
void node_set_state(int node, enum node_states state)
void node_clear_state(int node, enum node_states state)
```

Additionally, the macro `for_each_node_state(__node, __state)` allows for iterating over all nodes that are in a specific state, and `for_each_online_node(node)` iterates over all active nodes.

If the kernel is compiled to support only a single node, that is, using the flat memory model, the node bitmap is not present, and the functions to manipulate it resolve to empty operations that simply do nothing.

Memory Zones

The kernel uses the `zones` structure to describe a zone. It is defined as follows:

\<mmzone.h\>
```
struct zone {
        /* Fields commonly accessed by the page allocator */
        unsigned long           pages_min, pages_low, pages_high;

        unsigned long           lowmem_reserve[MAX_NR_ZONES];

        struct per_cpu_pageset  pageset[NR_CPUS];

        /*
         * free areas of different sizes
         */
        spinlock_t              lock;
        struct free_area        free_area[MAX_ORDER];

        ZONE_PADDING(_pad1_)

        /* Fields commonly accessed by the page reclaim scanner */
        spinlock_t              lru_lock;
        struct list_head        active_list;
        struct list_head        inactive_list;
        unsigned long           nr_scan_active;
        unsigned long           nr_scan_inactive;
        unsigned long           pages_scanned;      /* since last reclaim */
```

```
        unsigned long           flags;              /* zone flags, see below */

        /* Zone statistics */
        atomic_long_t           vm_stat[NR_VM_ZONE_STAT_ITEMS];

        int prev_priority;

        ZONE_PADDING(_pad2_)
        /* Rarely used or read-mostly fields */

        wait_queue_head_t       * wait_table;
        unsigned long           wait_table_hash_nr_entries;
        unsigned long           wait_table_bits;

        /* Discontig memory support fields. */
        struct pglist_data      *zone_pgdat;
        unsigned long           zone_start_pfn;

        unsigned long           spanned_pages;  /* total size, including holes */
        unsigned long           present_pages;  /* amount of memory (excluding holes) */

        /*
         * rarely used fields:
         */
        char                    *name;
} ____cacheline_maxaligned_in_smp;
```

The striking aspect of this structure is that it is divided into several sections separated by ZONE_PADDING. This is because zone structures are very frequently accessed. On multiprocessor systems, it commonly occurs that different CPUs try to access structure elements at the same time. Locks (examined in Chapter 5) are therefore used to prevent them interfering with each, and giving rise to errors and inconsistencies. The two spinlocks of the structure — zone->lock and zone->lru_lock — are often acquired because the kernel very frequently accesses the structure.[1]

Data are processed faster they are is held in a cache of the CPU. Caches are divided into lines, and each line is responsible for various memory areas. The kernel invokes the ZONE_PADDING macro to generate "padding" that is added to the structure to ensure that each lock is in its own cache line. The compiler keyword __cacheline_maxaligned_in_smp is also used to achieve optimal cache alignment.

The last two sections of the structure are also separated from each other by padding. As neither includes a lock, the primary aim is to keep the data in a cache line for quick access and thus to dispense with the need for loading the data from RAM memory, which is a slow process. The increase in size due to the padding structures is negligible, particularly as there are relatively few instances of zone structures in kernel memory.

What is the meaning of the structure elements? Since memory management is a complex and comprehensive part of the kernel, it is not possible to cover the exact meaning of all elements at this point — a good part of this and of following chapters will be devoted to understanding the associated data structures and mechanisms. What I can provide, however, is an overview that gives a taste of the problems I am about to discuss. A large number of forward references is nevertheless unavoidable.

---

[1]The locks are therefore known as *hotspots*. In Chapter 17, some tricks that are used by the kernel to reduce the pressure on these hotspots are discussed.

❑ `pages_min`, `pages_high`, and `pages_low` are "watermarks" used when pages are swapped out. The kernel can write pages to hard disk if insufficient RAM memory is available. These three elements influence the behavior of the swapping daemon.

   ❑ If more than `pages_high` pages are free, the state of the zone is ideal.

   ❑ If the number of free pages falls below `pages_low`, the kernel begins to swap pages out onto the hard disk.

   ❑ If the number of free pages falls below `pages_min`, the pressure to reclaim pages is increased because free pages are urgently needed in the zone. Chapter 18 will discuss various means of the kernel to find relief.

The importance of these watermarks will mainly show in Chapter 18, but they also come into play in Section 3.5.5.

❑ The `lowmem_reserve` array specifies several pages for each memory zone that are reserved for critical allocations that must not fail under any circumstances. Each zone contributes according to its importance. The algorithm to calculate the individual contributions is discussed in Section 3.2.2.

❑ `pageset` is an array to implement per-CPU hot-n-cold page lists. The kernel uses these lists to store fresh pages that can be used to satisfy implementations. However, they are distinguished by their cache status: Pages that are most likely still cache-hot and can therefore be quickly accessed are separated from cache-cold pages. The next section discusses the `struct per_cpu_pageset` data structure used to realize this behavior.

❑ `free_area` is an array of data structures of the same name used to implement the buddy system. Each array element stands for contiguous memory areas of a fixed size. Management of free memory pages contained in each area is performed starting from `free_area`.

The employed data structures merit a discussion of their own, and Section 3.5.5 covers the implementation details of the buddy system in depth.

❑ The elements of the second section are responsible for cataloging the pages used in the zone according to activity. A page is regarded as *active* by the kernel if it is accessed frequently; an inactive page is obviously the opposite. This distinction is important when pages need to be swapped out. If possible, frequently used pages should be left intact, but superfluous inactive pages can be swapped out without impunity.

The following elements are involved:

   ❑ `active_list` collects the active pages, and `inactive_list` the inactive pages (page instances).

   ❑ `nr_scan_active` and `nr_scan_inactive` specify how many active and inactive pages are to be scanned when reclaiming memory.

   ❑ `pages_scanned` specifies how many pages were unsuccessfully scanned since the last time a page was swapped out.

   ❑ `flags` describes the current status of the zone. The following flags are allowed:

     <mmzone.h>

```
typedef enum {
        ZONE_ALL_UNRECLAIMABLE,         /* all pages pinned */
        ZONE_RECLAIM_LOCKED,            /* prevents concurrent reclaim */
```

```
        ZONE_OOM_LOCKED,                    /* zone is in OOM killer zonelist */
} zone_flags_t;
```

It is also possible that none of these flags is set. This is the normal state of the zone.
`ZONE_ALL_UNRECLAIMABLE` is a state that can occur when the kernel tries to reuse some
pages of the zone (*page reclaim*, see Chapter 18), but this is not possible at all because
all pages are *pinned*. For instance, a userspace application could have used the `mlock`
system call to instruct the kernel that pages must not be removed from physical memory,
for example, by swapping them out. Such a page is said to be pinned. If all pages in a
zone suffer this fate, the zone is unreclaimable, and the flag is set. To waste no time, the
swapping daemon scans zones of this kind very briefly when it is looking for pages to
reclaim.[2]

On SMP systems, multiple CPUs could be tempted to reclaim a zone concurrently. The
flag `ZONE_RECLAIM_LOCKED` prevents this: If A CPU is reclaiming a zone, it set the flag. This
prevents other CPUs from trying.

`ZONE_OOM_LOCKED` is reserved for an unfortunate situation: If processes use up so much
memory that essential operations cannot be completed anymore, then the kernel will try
to select the worst memory eater and kill it to obtain more free pages. The flag prevents
multiple CPUs from getting into their way in this case.

The kernel provides three auxiliary functions to test and set zone flags:

<mmzone.h>
```
void zone_set_flag(struct zone *zone, zone_flags_t flag)
int zone_test_and_set_flag(struct zone *zone, zone_flags_t flag)
void zone_clear_flag(struct zone *zone, zone_flags_t flag)
```

`zone_set_flag` and `zone_clear_flag` set and clear a certain flag, respectively. `zone_test_`
`and_set_flag` first tests if a given flag is set and does so if not. The old state of the flag is
returned to the caller.

❑ `vm_stat` keeps a plethora of statistical information about the zone. Since most of the information kept in there will not make much sense at the moment, a detailed discussion is
   deferred to Section 17.7.1. For now, it suffices to know that the information is updated from
   places all over the kernel. The auxiliary function `zone_page_state` allows for reading the
   information in `vm_stat`:

   <vmstat.h>
   ```
   static inline unsigned long zone_page_state(struct zone *zone,
                                  enum zone_stat_item item)
   ```

   `item` can, for instance, be `NR_ACTIVE` or `NR_INACTIVE` to query the number of active and
   inactive pages stored on `active_list` and `inactive_list` discussed above. The number of
   free pages in the zone is obtained with `NR_FREE_PAGES`.

❑ `prev_priority` stores the priority with which the zone was scanned in the last scan operation until sufficient page frames were freed in `try_to_free_pages` (see Chapter 17). As
   you shall also see in Chapter 17, the decision as to whether mapped pages are swapped out
   depends on this value.

---

[2]However, scanning cannot be totally dispensed with because the zone may contain reclaimable pages again at some time
in the future. If so, the flag is removed and the `kswapd` daemon treats the zone again like any other zone.

❑ `wait_table`, `wait_table_bits`, and `wait_table_hash_nr_entries` implement a wait queue for processes waiting for a page to become available. While the details of this mechanism are shown in Chapter 14, the intuitive notion holds pretty well: Processes queue up in a line to wait for some condition. When this condition becomes true, they are notified by the kernel and can resume their work.

❑ The association between a zone and the parent node is established by `zone_pgdat`, which points to the corresponding instance of `pg_list_data`.

❑ `zone_start_pfn` is the index of the first page frame of the zone.

❑ The remaining three fields are rarely used, so they've been placed at the end of the data structure.

  `name` is a string that holds a conventional name for the zone. Three options are available at present: `Normal`, `DMA`, and `HighMem`.

  `spanned_pages` specifies the total number of pages in the zone. However, not all need be usable since there may be small holes in the zone as already mentioned. A further counter (`present_pages`) therefore indicates the number of pages that are actually usable. Generally, the value of this counter is the same as that for `spanned_pages`.

Calculation of Zone Watermarks

Before calculating the various watermarks, the kernel first determines the minimum memory space that must remain free for critical allocations. This value scales nonlinearly with the size of the available RAM. It is stored in the global variable `min_free_kbytes`. Figure 3-4 provides an overview of the scaling behavior, and the inset — which does not use a logarithmic scale for the main memory size in contrast to the main graph — shows a magnification of the region up to 4 GiB. Some exemplary values to provide a feeling for the situation on systems with modest memory that are common in desktop environments are collected in Table 3-1. An invariant is that not less than 128 KiB but not more than 64 MiB may be used. Note, however, that the upper bound is only necessary on machines equipped with a *really* satisfactory amount of main memory.[3] The file `/proc/sys/vm/min_free_kbytes` allows reading and adapting the value from userland.

Filling the watermarks in the data structure is handled by `init_per_zone_pages_min`, which is invoked during kernel boot and need not be started explicitly.[4]

`setup_per_zone_pages_min` sets the `pages_min`, `pages_low`, and `pages_high` elements of `struct zone`. After the total number of pages outside the highmem zone has been calculated (and stored in `lowmem_pages`), the kernel iterates over all zones in the system and performs the following calculation:

mm/page_alloc.c
```
void setup_per_zone_pages_min(void)
{
        unsigned long pages_min = min_free_kbytes >> (PAGE_SHIFT - 10);
        unsigned long lowmem_pages = 0;
        struct zone *zone;
        unsigned long flags;
```

---

[3]In practice, it will be unlikely that such an amount of memory is installed on a machine with a single NUMA node, so it will be hard to actually reach the point where the cutoff is required.

[4]The functions are not only called from here, but are also invoked each time one of the control parameters is modified via the proc filesystem.

```
...
        for_each_zone(zone) {
                u64 tmp;

                tmp = (u64)pages_min * zone->present_pages;
                do_div(tmp,lowmem_pages);
                if (is_highmem(zone)) {
                        int min_pages;

                        min_pages = zone->present_pages / 1024;
                        if (min_pages < SWAP_CLUSTER_MAX)
                                min_pages = SWAP_CLUSTER_MAX;
                        if (min_pages > 128)
                                min_pages = 128;
                        zone->pages_min = min_pages;
                } else {
                        zone->pages_min = tmp;
                }

                zone->pages_low = zone->pages_min + (tmp >> 2);
                zone->pages_high = zone->pages_min + (tmp >> 1);
        }
}
```

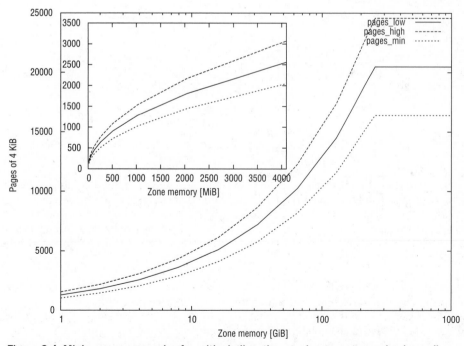

Figure 3-4: Minimum memory size for critical allocations and zone watermarks depending on the main memory size of a machine (`pages_min` is nothing other than `min_free_kbytes` in units of pages).

Table 3-1: Correlation between Main Memory Size and Minimum Memory Available for Critical Allocations.

Main memory	Reserve
16 MiB	512 KiB
32 MiB	724 KiB
64 MiB	1024 KiB
128 MiB	1448 KiB
256 MiB	2048 KiB
512 MiB	2896 KiB
1024 MiB	4096 KiB
2048 MiB	5792 KiB
4096 MiB	8192 KiB
8192 MiB	11584 KiB
16384 MiB	16384 KiB

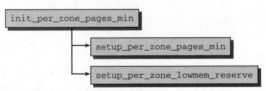

Figure 3-5: Code flow diagram for `init_per_zone_pages_min`.

The lower bound for highmem zones, `SWAP_CLUSTER_MAX`, is an important quantity for the whole page reclaim subsystem as discussed in Chapter 17. The code there often operates batchwise on page clusters, and `SWAP_CLUSTER_MAX` defines the size of such clusters. Figure 3-4 shows the outcome of the calculations for various main memory sizes. Since high memory is not very relevant anymore these days (most machines with large amounts of RAM use 64-bit CPUs), I have restricted the graph to show the outcomes for regular zones.

Computing `lowmem_reserve` is done in `setup_per_zone_lowmem_reserve`. The kernel iterates over all nodes of the system and calculates the minimum reserve for each zone of the node by dividing the total number of page frames in the zone by `sysctl_lowmem_reserve_ratio[zone]`. The default settings for the divisor are 256 for low memory and 32 for high memory.

Hot-N-Cold Pages

The `pageset` element of `struct zone` is used to implement a hot-n-cold allocator. The kernel refers to a page in memory as *hot* if it is in a CPU cache and its data can therefore be accessed quicker than if it were in RAM. Conversely, a *cold* page is not held in cache. As each CPU has one or more caches on multiprocessor systems, management must be separate for each CPU.

> **Even though a zone belongs to a specific NUMA node and is therefore associated with a specific CPU, the caches of other CPUs may include pages from this zone — ultimately, each processor can access *all* pages in the system, albeit at different speeds. The zone-specific data structure must therefore cater not only for the CPU associated with the NUMA node of the zone but also for all other CPUs in the system.**

`pageset` is an array that holds as many entries as the maximum possible number of CPUs that the system can accommodate.

<mmzone.h>
```
struct zone {
        ...
        struct per_cpu_pageset  pageset[NR_CPUS];
        ...
};
```

`NR_CPUS` is a configurable pre-processor constant defined at compilation time. Its value is always 1 on uniprocessor systems, but on a kernel compiled for SMP systems, it may be between 2 and 32 (or 64 on 64-bit systems).

> **The value does not reflect the number of CPUs actually present in a system but the maximum number of CPUs supported by the kernel.**

The array elements are of type `per_cpu_pageset`, which is defined as follows:

<mmzone.h>
```
struct per_cpu_pageset {
        struct per_cpu_pages pcp[2];    /* 0: hot.  1: cold */
} ____cacheline_aligned_in_smp;
```

The structure consists of an array with two entries, the first to manage hot and the second to manage cold pages.

The useful data are held in `per_cpu_pages`.[5]

<mmzone.h>
```
struct per_cpu_pages {
        int count;              /* number of pages in the list */
        int high;               /* high watermark, emptying needed */
        int batch;              /* chunk size for buddy add/remove */
        struct list_head list;  /* the list of pages */
};
```

---

[5]Kernel 2.6.25, which was still under development when this book was written, will replace the separate lists for hot and cold pages by a single list. Hot pages will be kept at the beginning, while cold pages will be placed at the end. The change was introduced after measurements had shown that having two separate lists would not provide substantial benefits compared to a single list.

Whereas count keeps a record of the number of pages associated with the element, high is a watermark. If the value of count exceeds high, this indicates that there are too many pages in the list. No explicit watermark for low fill states is used: When no elements are left, the list is refilled.

list is a doubly linked list that holds the per-CPU pages and is handled using standard methods of the kernel.

If possible, the per-CPU caches are not filled with individual pages but with multipage chunks. batch is a guideline to the number of pages to be added in a single pass.

Figure 3-6 illustrates graphically how the data structures of the per-CPU cache are filled on a dual-processor system.

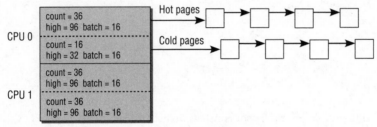

Figure 3-6: Per-CPU cache on a dual-processor system.

How watermarks are calculated and how the cache data structures are initialized are discussed in more detail in Section 3.4.2.

Page Frames

Page frames represent the smallest unit of system memory, and an instance of struct page is created for each page in RAM. Kernel programmers take care to keep this structure as small as possible because the memory of systems even with a moderate RAM configuration is broken down into a *very* large number of pages. For instance, an IA-32 system working with a standard page size of 4 KiB has around 100,000 pages given a main memory size of 384 MiB. Although this memory size is certainly not excessively large for today's standards, the number of pages is already considerable.

This is why the kernel makes great efforts to keep struct page as small as possible. The sheer number of pages in a typical system causes even small changes in the structure to lead to a large increase in the amount of physical memory required to keep all page instances.

Keeping the structure small is not exactly simplified by the ubiquity of pages: They are used in many parts of memory management, and for varying applications. While one part of the kernel absolutely depends on a specific piece of information being available in struct page, this could be useless for another part, which itself depends a different piece of information, which could again be completely useless for the other part, and so on . . . .

A C union lends itself naturally as a remedy for this problem, even if clarity of struct page is not increased at first. Consider an example: A physical page can be mapped into the virtual address space via page tables from multiple places, and the kernel wants to keep track of how many places map the page. For this end, a counter in struct page counts the number of mappings. If a page is used by the slub allocator (a means to subdivide complete pages into into smaller portions, see Section 3.6.1), then it is guaranteed to be only used by the kernel and not from somewhere else, so the map count information is superfluous. Instead, the kernel can reinterpret the field to denote how many small memory objects into which a page is subdivided are in use. The double interpretation looks as follows in the data structure definition:

<mm_types.h>
```
struct page {
...
        union {
                atomic_t _mapcount; /* Count of ptes mapped in mms,
                                     * to show when page is mapped
                                     * & limit reverse map searches.
                                     */
                unsigned int inuse; /* SLUB: Nr of objects */
        };
...
}
```

Note that `atomic_t` and `unsigned int` are two different data types — the first allows for changing values atomically, that is, safe against concurrent access, while the second is a classical integer. `atomic_t` provides 32 bits,[6] and an integer also provides this many bits on each architecture supported by Linux. Now it could be tempting to "simplify" the definition as follows:

```
struct page {
...
        atomic_t counter;
...
}
```

This would be *bad* style, though, and is completely unacceptable to the kernel developers. The slub code does not need atomicity to access its object counter, and this should also be reflected in the data type. And, most importantly, readability of the code will suffer in both subsystems. While `_mapcount` and `inuse` provide a clear and concise description of what the element is about, `counter` could mean almost everything.

Definition of page

The structure is defined as follows:

<mm.h>
```
struct page {
        unsigned long flags;            /* Atomic flags, some possibly
                                         * updated asynchronously */
        atomic_t _count;                /* Usage count, see below. */
        union {
                atomic_t _mapcount; /* Count of ptes mapped in mms,
                                     * to show when page is mapped
                                     * & limit reverse map searches.
                                     */
```

---

[6]Before kernel 2.6.3, this was not true. The Sparc architecture could only provide 24 bits for atomic manipulation, so the generic code for all architecture needed to stick to this limit. Luckily, this problem has been resolved now by improvements in the Sparc specific code.

```
                    unsigned int inuse; /* SLUB: Nr of objects */
        };
        union {
            struct {
                unsigned long private;              /* Mapping-private opaque data:
                                                     * usually used for buffer_heads
                                                     * if PagePrivate set; used for
                                                     * swp_entry_t if PageSwapCache;
                                                     * indicates order in the buddy
                                                     * system if PG_buddy is set.
                                                     */
                struct address_space *mapping;  /* If low bit clear, points to
                                                 * inode address_space, or NULL.
                                                 * If page mapped as anonymous
                                                 * memory, low bit is set, and
                                                 * it points to anon_vma object:
                                                 * see PAGE_MAPPING_ANON below.
                                                 */
            };
...
            struct kmem_cache *slab; /* SLUB: Pointer to slab */
            struct page *first_page; /* Compound tail pages */
        };
        union {
                pgoff_t index; /* Our offset within mapping. */
                void *freelist; /* SLUB: freelist req. slab lock */
        };
        struct list_head lru;              /* Pageout list, eg. active_list
                                            * protected by zone->lru_lock !
                                            */
#if defined(WANT_PAGE_VIRTUAL)
        void *virtual;                     /* Kernel virtual address (NULL if
                                              not kmapped, ie. highmem) */
#endif /* WANT_PAGE_VIRTUAL */
};
```

The elements slab, freelist, and inuse are used by the slub allocator. We do not need to be concerned with these special arrangements, and they are not used if support for the slub allocator is not compiled into the kernel, so I omit them in the following discussion to simplify matters.

Each page frame is described by this structure in an architecture-independent format that does not depend on the CPU type used. Besides the slub elements, the page structure includes several other elements that can only be explained accurately in the context of kernel subsystems discussed elsewhere. I shall nevertheless provide an overview of the contents of the structure, even though this means referencing later chapters.

❑   flags stores architecture-independent flags to describe page attributes. I discuss the different flag options below.

❑   _count is a usage count indicating the number of references to this page in the kernel. When its value reaches 0, the kernel knows that the page instance is not currently in use and can therefore be removed. If its value is greater than 0, the instance should on no account be removed from memory. If you are not familiar with reference counters, you should consult Appendix C for further information.

❑ _mapcount indicates how many entries in the page table point to the page.

❑ lru is a list head used to keep the page on various lists that allow grouping the pages into different categories, most importantly active and inactive pages. Especially the discussion in Chapter 18 will come back to these lists.

❑ The kernel allows for combining multiple adjacent pages into a larger *compound page*. The first page in the cluster is called the *head page*, while all other pages are named *tail page*. All tail pages have first_page set to point to the head page.

❑ mapping specifies the address space in which a page frame is located. index is the offset within the mapping. Address spaces are a very general concept used, for example, when reading a file into memory. An address space is used to associate the file contents (data) with the areas in memory into which the contents are read. By means of a small trick,[7] mapping is able to hold not only a pointer, but also information on whether a page belongs to an anonymous memory area that is not associated with an address space. If the bit with numeric value 1 is set in mapping, the pointer does *not* point to an instance of address_space but to another data structure (anon_vma) that is important in the implementation of reverse mapping for anonymous pages; this structure is discussed in Section 4.11.2. Double use of the pointer is possible because address_space instances are always aligned with sizeof(long); the least significant bit of a pointer to this instance is therefore 0 on all machines supported by Linux.

The pointer can be used directly if it points normally to an instance of address_space. If the trick involving setting the least significant bit to 1 is used, the kernel can restore the pointer by means of the following operation:

```
anon_vma = (struct anon_vma *) (mapping - PAGE_MAPPING_ANON)
```

❑ private is a pointer to "private" data ignored by virtual memory management. The pointer can be employed in different ways depending on page usage. It is mostly used to associate the page with data buffers as described in the following chapters.

❑ virtual is used for pages in the highmem area, in other words, for pages that cannot be directly mapped into kernel memory. virtual then accepts the *virtual* address of the page.

As the pre-processor statement #ifdef{WANT_PAGE_VIRTUAL} shows, the virtual element is only part of struct page if the corresponding pre-processor constant is defined. Currently, this is only the case for a few architectures, namely, Motorola m68k, FRV, and Extensa.

All other architectures adopt a different scheme of addressing virtual pages. At the heart of this is a hash table used to find the address of all highmem pages. Section 3.5.8 deals with the appropriate techniques in more detail. Handling the hash table requires some mathematical operations that are slow on the aforementioned machines, so they chose the direct approach.

Architecture-Independent Page Flags

The different attributes of a page are described by a series of page flags stored as bits in the flags element of struct page. The flags are independent of the architecture used and cannot therefore provide CPU- or machine-specific information (this information is held in the page table itself as is shown below).

Not only are the individual flags defined with the help of the pre-processor in page-flags.h, but also macros are generated to set, delete, and query the flags. In doing so, the kernel conforms to a universal

---

[7]The trick borders on the unscrupulous but helps save space in one of the most frequently needed kernel structures.

naming scheme; for example, the PG_locked constant defines the bit position in flags to specify whether a page is locked or not. The following macros are available to manipulate the bit:

❑ PageLocked queries whether the bit is set.

❑ SetPageLocked sets the PG_locked bit, regardless of its previous state.

❑ TestSetPageLocked sets the bit, but also returns its old value.

❑ ClearPageLocked deletes the bit regardless of its previous state.

❑ TestClearPageLocked deletes the bit and returns its old value.

There is an identical set of macros to perform the operations shown on the appropriate bit for the other page flags. The macros are implemented atomically. Although some of them are made up of several statements, special processor commands are used to ensure that they act as if they were a single statement; that is, they cannot be interrupted as this would result in race conditions. (Chapter 14 describes how race conditions arise and how they can be prevented.)

Which page flags are available? The following list includes the most important flags (again, their meanings become clear in later chapters):

❑ PG_locked specifies whether a page is locked. If the bit is set, other parts of the kernel are not allowed to access the page. This prevents race conditions in memory management, for example, when reading data from hard disk into a page frame.

❑ PG_error is set if an error occurs during an I/O operation involving the page.

❑ PG_referenced and PG_active control how actively a page is used by the system. This information is important when the swapping subsystem has to select which page to swap out. The interaction of the two flags is explained in Chapter 18.

❑ PG_uptodate indicates that the data of a page have been read without error from a block device.

❑ PG_dirty is set when the contents of the page have changed as compared to the data on hard disk. For reasons of performance, pages are not written back immediately after each change. The kernel therefore uses this flag to note which pages have been changed so that they can be flushed later.

Pages for which this flag has been set are referred to as *dirty* (generally, this means that the data in RAM and the data on a secondary storage medium such as a hard disk have not been synchronized).

❑ PG_lru helps implement page reclaim and swapping. The kernel uses two least recently used lists[8] to distinguish between active and inactive pages. The bit is set if the page is held on one of these lists. There is also a PG_active flag that is set if the page is on the list of active pages. Chapter 18 discusses this important mechanism in detail.

❑ PG_highmem indicates that a page is in high memory because it cannot be mapped permanently into kernel memory.

❑ PG_private must be set if the value of the private element in the page structure is non-NULL. Pages that are used for I/O use this field to subdivide the page into *buffers* (see Chapter 16 for more information), but other parts of the kernel find different uses to attach private data to a page.

---

[8]Frequently used entries are automatically in the foremost positions on this type of list, whereas inactive entries are always moved toward the end of the list.

❏ PG_writeback is set for pages whose contents are in the process of being written back to a block device.

❏ PG_slab is set for pages that are part of the slab allocator discussed in Section 3.6.

❏ PG_swapcache is set if the page is in the swap cache; in this case, private contains an entry of type swap_entry_t (further details are provided in Chapter 18).

❏ When the available amount of memory gets smaller, the kernel tries to periodically *reclaim* pages, that is, get rid of inactive, unused pages. Chapter 18 discusses the details. Once the kernel has decided to reclaim a specific page, this is announced by setting the PG_reclaim flag.

❏ PG_buddy is set if the page is free and contained on the lists of the buddy system, that is, the core of the page allocation mechanism.

❏ PG_compound denotes that the page is part of a larger compound page consisting of multiple adjacent regular pages.

A number of standard macros are defined to check if a page has a specific bit is set, or to manipulate a bit. Their names follow a certain pattern:

❏ PageXXX(page) checks if a page has the PG_XXX bit set. For instance, PageDirty checks for the PG_dirty bit, while PageActive checks for PG_active, and so on.

❏ To set a bit if it is not set and return the previous value, SetPageXXX is provided.

❏ ClearPageXXX unconditionally deletes a specific bit.

❏ TestClearPageXXX clears a bit if it is set, but also returns the previously active value.

Notice that these operations are implemented atomically. Chapter 5 discusses what this means in more detail.

Often it is necessary to wait until the state of a page changes, and then resume work. Two auxiliary functions provided by the kernel are of particular interest for us:

```
<pagemap.h>
void wait_on_page_locked(struct page *page);
void wait_on_page_writeback(struct page *page)
```

Assume that one part of the kernel wants to wait until a locked page has been unlocked. wait_on_page_locked allows for doing this. While how this is technically done is discussed in Chapter 14, it suffices to know here that after calling the function, the kernel will go to sleep if the page is locked. Once the page becomes unlocked, the sleeper is automatically woken up and can continue its work.

wait_on_page_writeback works similarly, but waits until any pending writeback operations in which the data contained in the page are synchronized with a block device — a hard disk, for instance — have been finished.

3.3 Page Tables

Hierarchically linked page tables are used to support the rapid and efficient management of large address spaces. The principle behind this approach and the benefits it brings as compared to linear addressing are discussed in Chapter 1. Here we take a closer look at the technical aspects of implementation.

Recall that page tables are used to establish an association between the virtual address spaces of user processes and the physical memory of the system (RAM, page frames). The structures discussed so far serve to describe the structure of RAM memory (partitioning into nodes and zones) and to specify the number and state (used or free) of the page frames contained. Page tables are used to make a uniform virtual address space available to each process; the applications see this space as a contiguous memory area. The tables also map the virtual pages used into RAM, thus supporting the implementation of shared memory (memory shared by several processes at the same time) and the swapping-out of pages to a block device to increase the effective size of usable memory without the need for additional physical RAM.

Kernel memory management assumes four-level page tables — regardless of whether this is the case for the underlying processor. The best example where this assumption is *not* true is IA-32 systems. By default, this architecture uses only a two-level paging system — assuming the PAE extensions are not used. Consequently, the third and fourth levels must be emulated by architecture- specific code.

Page table management is split into two parts, the first architecture-*dependent*, the second architecture-*independent*. Interestingly, all data structures and almost all functions to manipulate them are defined in architecture-specific files. Because there are some big differences between CPU-specific implementations (owing to the various CPU concepts used), I won't go into the low-level details for the sake of brevity. Extensive knowledge of the individual processors is also required, and the hardware documentation for each processor family is generally spread over several books. Appendix A describes the IA-32 architecture in more detail. It also discusses, at least in summary form, the architecture of the other important processors supported by Linux.

The descriptions of data structures and functions in the following sections are usually based on the interfaces provided by the architecture-dependent files. The definitions can be found in the header files `include/asm-`*arch*`/page.h` and `include/asm-`*arch*`/pgtable.h` referred to in abbreviated form as `page.h` and `pgtable.h` below. Since AMD64 and IA-32 are unified into one architecture but exhibit a good many differences when it comes to handling page tables, the definitions can be found in two different files: `include/asm-x86/page_32.h` and `include/asm-x86/page_64.h`, and similar for `pgtable_xx.h`. When aspects relating to a specific architecture are discussed, I make explicit reference to the architecture. All other information is equally valid for all architectures even if the definitions of the associated structures are architecture-specific.

3.3.1   Data Structures

In C, the `void*` data type is used to specify a pointer to any byte positions in memory. The number of bits required differs according to architecture. All common processors (including all those on which Linux runs) use either 32 or 64 bits.

The kernel sources assume that `void*` and `unsigned long` have the same number of bits so that they can be mutually converted by means of typecasts without loss of information. This assumption — expressed formally as `sizeof(void*) == sizeof(unsigned long)` — is, of course, true on all architectures supported by Linux.

Memory management prefers to use variables of type `unsigned long` instead of `void` pointers because they are easier to handle and manipulate. Technically, they are both equally valid.

Breakdown of Addresses in Memory

Addresses in virtual memory are split into five parts as required by the structure of the four-level page tables (four table entries to select the page and an index to indicate the position within the page).

Not only the length but also the way in which the address is split are different on the individual architectures. The kernel therefore defines macros to break down the address into its individual components.

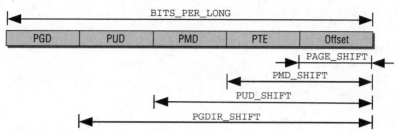

Figure 3-7: Breakdown of a virtual address.

Figure 3-7 shows how the positions of the address elements are defined by bit shifts. BITS_PER_LONG specifies the number of bits used for an unsigned long variable and therefore also for a generic pointer to virtual address space.

At the end of each pointer there are several bits to specify the position within the selected frame page. The number of bits required is held in PAGE_SHIFT.

PMD_SHIFT specifies the *total* number of bits used by a page *and* by an entry in the last level of the page tables. This number can be subtracted from PAGE_SHIFT to determine the number of bits required by an entry in the last hierarchy level of the page table. More important is the fact that the value indicates the size of the partial address space managed by an entry in the middle page table, namely, 2^{PMD_SHIFT} bytes.

PUD_SHIFT adds together the bit lengths of PAGE_OFFSET and PMD_SHIFT, whereas PGDIR_SHIFT combines the bit lengths of PAGE_OFFSET, PUD_SHIFT, and PMD_SHIFT with the bit number of an entry in the page middle directory. The value is the binary logarithm of the size of the partial address space that can be addressed via an entry in the page global directory.

The number of pointers that can be stored in the various directories of the page table is also determined by macro definitions. PTRS_PER_PGD specifies the number of entries in the page global directory, PTRS_PER_PMD the number in the page middle directory, PTRS_PER_PUD the number in the page upper directory, and PTRS_PER_PTE the number in the page table entry.

> Architectures with two-level page tables define **PTRS_PER_PMD** and **PTRS_PER_PUD** as 1. This persuades the remaining parts of the kernel that they are working with four-level page translation although only two pages are used — the page middle and page upper directories are effectively eliminated because they have only a single entry. Because only a very few systems use a four-level page table, the kernel uses the header file **include/asm-generic/pgtable-nopud.h** to hold all the declarations needed to simulate the presence of a fourth page table. The header file **include/asm-generic/pgtable-nopmd.h** is also available to simulate the presence of a third page table level on systems with two-level address translation.

The size of the address area that can be addressed with pointers of n-bit length is 2^n bytes. The kernel defines additional macro variables to hold the values calculated so that it is unnecessary to repeat the calculations time and time again. The variables are defined as follows:

```
#define PAGE_SIZE       (1UL << PAGE_SHIFT)
#define PUD_SIZE        (1UL << PUD_SHIFT)
#define PMD_SIZE        (1UL << PMD_SHIFT)
#define PGDIR_SIZE      (1UL << PGDIR_SHIFT)
```

The value 2^n is easily calculated in the binary system by shifting a bit n positions to the left starting from position 0. The kernel uses this "trick" at many places. Those of you unfamiliar with bit arithmetic will find relevant explanations in Appendix C.

include/asm-x86/pgtable_64.h
```
#define PGDIR_SHIFT 39
#define PTRS_PER_PGD 512

#define PUD_SHIFT 30
#define PTRS_PER_PUD 512

#define PMD_SHIFT 21
#define PTRS_PER_PMD 512
```

The macros PTRS_PER_XXX specify how many pointers (i.e., different values) a given directory entry can represent. Since AMD64 employs 9 bits for each directory, $2^9 = 512$ pointers fit into each.

The kernel also needs a means of extracting the individual components from a given address. The kernel uses the bitmasks defined below to do this.

```
#define PAGE_MASK       (~(PAGE_SIZE-1))
#define PUD_MASK        (~(PUD_SIZE-1))
#define PMD_MASK        (~(PMD_SIZE-1))
#define PGDIR_MASK      (~(PGDIR_SIZE-1))
```

The masks are applied on a given address by simple bitwise addition.

Format of Page Tables

The size of the entries in the page tables has been established by the above definitions but not their structure. The kernel provides four data structures (defined in page.h) to represent the entry structures.

❑   pgd_t for entries of the global directory.

❑   pud_t for entries of the page upper directory.

❑   pmd_t for entries of the page middle directory.

❑   pte_t for direct page table entries.

The standard functions to analyze page table entries are listed in Table 3-2. (Depending on architecture, some functions are implemented as macros and others as inline functions; I make no distinction between the two below.)

Table 3-2: Functions for Analyzing Page Table Entries.

Function	Description
pgd_val pud_val pmd_val pte_val pgprot_val	Convert a variable of type pte_t and so on to an unsigned long number.
__pgd __pud __pmd __pte __pgprot	Do the reverse of pdg_val and so on: They convert an unsigned long number into a variable of type pdg_t and so on.
pgd_index pud_index pmd_index pte_index	Yield the address of the next-level table starting from a memory pointer and a page table entry.
pgd_present pud_present pmd_present pte_present	Check whether the _PRESENT bit of the corresponding entry is set. This is the case when the page or page table addressed is in RAM memory.
pgd_none pud_none pmd_none pte_none	Do the logical reverse of the xxx_present functions. If they return a true value, the searched page is *not* in RAM.
pgd_clear pud_clear pmd_clear pte_clear	Delete the passed page table entry. This is usually done by setting it to zero.
pgd_bad pud_bad pmd_bad	Check whether entries of the page middle, upper, and global directories are invalid. They are used for safety purposes in functions that receive input parameters from the outside where it cannot be assumed that the parameters are valid.
pmd_page pud_page pte_page	Return the address of the page structure holding the data on the page or the entries of the page middle directories.

How do the offset functions work? Let us consider pmd_offset as an example. It requires as parameter an entry from the page global directory (src_pgd) and an address in memory. It returns an element from one of the page middle directories.

```
src_pmd = pmd_offset(src_pgd, address);
```

PAGE_ALIGN is another standard macro that must be defined by each architecture (typically in `page.h`). It expects an address as parameter and "rounds" the address so that it is exactly at the start of the next page. If the page size is 4,096, the macro always returns an integer multiple of this size; PAGE_ALIGN(6000) = 8192 = 2× 4,096, PAGE_ALIGN(0x84590860) = 0x84591000 = 542,097 × 4,096. The alignment of addresses to page boundaries is important to ensure that best use is made of the cache resources of the processor.

Although C structures are used to represent entries in page tables, most consist of just a single element — typically `unsigned long` — as an example of AMD64 architecture shows:[9]

include/asm-x86_64/page.h
```
typedef struct { unsigned long pte; } pte_t;
typedef struct { unsigned long pmd; } pmd_t;
typedef struct { unsigned long pud; } pud_t;
typedef struct { unsigned long pgd; } pgd_t
```

`structs` are used instead of elementary types to ensure that the contents of page table elements are handled only by the associated helper functions and never directly. The entries may also be constructed of several elementary variables. In this case, the kernel is obliged to use a `struct`.[10]

> The virtual address is split into several parts that are used as an index into the page table in accordance with the familiar scheme. The individual parts are therefore less than 32 or 64 bits long, depending on the word length of the architecture used. As the excerpt from the kernel sources shows, the kernel (and therefore also the processor) uses 32- or 64-bit types to represent entries in the page tables (regardless of table level). This means that not all bits of a table entry are required to store the useful data — that is, the base address of the next table. The superfluous bits are used to hold additional information. Appendix A describes the structure of the page tables on various architectures in detail.

PTE-Specific Entries

Each final entry in the page table not only yields a pointer to the memory location of the page, but also holds additional information on the page in the superfluous bits mentioned above. Although these data are CPU-specific, they usually provide at least some information on page access control. The following elements are found in most CPUs supported by the Linux kernel:

❑ _PAGE_PRESENT specifies whether the virtual page is present in RAM memory. This need not necessarily be the case because pages may be swapped out into a swap area as noted briefly in Chapter 1.

The structure of the page table entry is usually different if the page is not present in memory because there is no need to describe the position of the page in memory. Instead, information is needed to identify and find the swapped-out page.

---

[9]The definitions for IA-32 are similar. However, only pte_t and pgd_t, which are defined as `unsigned long`, make an effective contribution. I use the code example for AMD64 because it is more regular.

[10]When IA-32 processors use PAE mode, they define pte_t as, for example, **typedef struct { unsigned long pte_low, pte_high; }**. 32 bits are then no longer sufficient to address the complete memory because more than 4 GiB can be managed in this mode. In other words, the available amount of memory can be larger than the processor's address space.

Since pointers are, however, still only 32 bits wide, an appropriate subset of the enlarged memory space must be chosen for userspace applications that do still only see 4 GiB each.

❑ _PAGE_ACCESSED is set automatically by the CPU each time the page is accessed. The kernel regularly checks the field to establish how actively the page is used (infrequently used pages are good swapping candidates). The bit is set after either read or write access.

❑ _PAGE_DIRTY indicates whether the page is "dirty," that is, whether the page contents have been modified.

❑ _PAGE_FILE has the same numerical value as _PAGE_DIRTY, but is used in a different context, namely, when a page is *not* present in memory. Obviously, a page that is not present cannot be dirty, so the bit can be reinterpreted: If it is not set, then the entry points to the location of a swapped-out page (see Chapter 18). A set _PAGE_FILE is required for entries that belongs to nonlinear file mappings which are discussed in Section 4.7.3.

❑ If _PAGE_USER is set, userspace code is allowed to access the page. Otherwise, only the kernel is allowed to do this (or when the CPU is in system mode).

❑ _PAGE_READ, _PAGE_WRITE, and _PAGE_EXECUTE specify whether normal user processes are allowed to read the page, write to the page, or execute the machine code in the page.

Pages from kernel memory must be protected against writing by user processes.

There is, however, no assurance that even pages belonging to user processes can be written to, for example, if the page contains executable code that may not be modified — either intentionally or unintentionally.

Architectures that feature less finely grained access rights define the _PAGE_RW constant to allow or disallow read and write access in combination if no further criterion is available to distinguish between the two.

❑ IA-32 and AMD64 provide _PAGE_BIT_NX to label the contents of a page as *not executable* (this protection bit is only available on IA-32 systems if the page address extensions for addressing 64 GiB memory are enabled). It can prevent, for example, execution of code on stack pages that can result in security gaps in programs because of intentionally provoked buffer overflows if malicious code has been introduced. The NX bit cannot prevent buffer overflow but can suppress its effects because the process refuses to run the malicious code. Of course, the same result can also be achieved if the architectures themselves provide a good set of access authorization bits for memory pages, as is the case with some (unfortunately not very common) processors.

Each architecture must provide two things to allow memory management to modify the additional bits in pte_t entries — the data type __pgprot in which the additional bits are held, and the pte_modify function to modify the bits. The above pre-processor symbols are used to select the appropriate entry.

The kernel also defines various functions to query and set the architecture-dependent state of memory pages. Not all functions can be defined by all processors because of lack of hardware support for a given feature.

❑ pte_present checks if the page to which the page table entry points is present in memory. This function can, for instance, be used to detect if a page has been swapped out.

❑ pte_dirty checks if the page associated with the page table entry is dirty, that is, its contents have been modified since the kernel checked last time. Note that this function may only be called if pte_present has ensured that the page is available.

❑ pte_write checks if the kernel may write to the page.

❑   `pte_file` is employed for nonlinear mappings that provide a different view on file contents by manipulating the page table (this mechanism is discussed in more detail in Section 4.7.3). The function checks if a page table entry belongs to such a mapping.

> `pte_file` may only be invoked if `pte_present` returns `false`; that is, the page associated with the page table entry is *not* present in memory.

Since the generic code relies on `pte_file`, it must also be defined if an architecture does not support nonlinear mappings. In this case, the function always returns 0.

A summary of all functions provided to manipulate PTE entries can be found in Table 3-3.

Table 3-3: Functions for Processing the Architecture-Dependent State of a Memory Page

Function	Description
pte_present	Is the page present?
pte_read	May the page be read from within userspace?
pte_write	May the page be written to?
pte_exec	May the data in the page be executed as binary code?
pte_dirty	Is the page dirty; that is, have its contents been modified?
pte_file	Does the PTE belong to a nonlinear mapping?
pte_young	Is the access bit (typically _PAGE_ACCESS) set?
pte_rdprotect	Removes read permission for the page.
pte_wrprotect	Deletes write permission for the page.
pte_exprotect	Removes permission to execute binary data in the page.
pte_mkread	Sets read permission.
pte_mkwrite	Sets write permission.
pte_mkexec	Permits execution of page contents.
pte_mkdirty	Marks the page as dirty.
pte_mkclean	"Cleans" the page; that is, usually deletes the _PAGE_DIRTY bit.
pte_mkyoung	Sets the accessed bit — _PAGE_ACCESSED on most architectures.
pte_mkold	Deletes the accessed bit.

The functions often appear in groups of three to set, delete, and query a specific attribute, for instance, write permission for a page. The kernel assumes that access to page data can be regulated in three different ways — by means of write, read, and execution permission. (Execution permission indicates that page binary data may be executed as machine code in the same way as programs are executed.) However, this assumption is a little too optimistic for some CPUs. IA-32 processors support only two control modes to allow reading and writing. In this case, the architecture-dependent code tries to emulate the desired semantics as best it can.

3.3.2 Creating and Manipulating Entries

Table 3-4 lists all functions for creating new page table entries.

Table 3-4: Functions for Creating New Page Table Entries

Function	Description
mk_pte	Creates a pte entry; a page instance and the desired page access permissions must be passed as parameters.
pte_page	Yields the address of the page instance belonging to the page described by the page table entry.
pgd_alloc pud_alloc pmd_alloc pte_alloc	Reserve and initialize memory to hold a complete page table (not just a single entry).
pgd_free pud_free pmd_free pte_free	Free the memory occupied by the page table.
set_pgd set_pud set_pmd set_pte	Set the value of an entry in a page table.

The functions in the table must be implemented by all architectures to enable memory management code to create and destroy page tables.

3.4 Initialization of Memory Management

In the context of memory management, *initialization* can have multiple meanings. On many CPUs, it is necessary to explicitly set the memory model suitable for the Linux kernel, for example, by switching to *protected mode* on IA-32 systems, before it is possible to detect the available memory and register it with the kernel. In the course of initialization, it is also necessary to set up the data structures of memory management, and much more. Because the kernel needs memory before memory management is fully initialized, a simple additional form of memory management is used during the boot process and is discarded thereafter.

As the CPU-specific parts of memory management initialization employ many minor, subtle details of the underlying architecture that reveal little of interest about the structure of the kernel and are simply best practices in assembly language programming, let's concern ourselves in this section only with initialization work on a higher level. The key aspect is initialization of the pg_data_t data structure (and its subordinate structures) introduced in Section 3.2.2 because this is already machine-independent.

The primary purpose of the aforementioned processor-specific operations whose details we will ignore is to investigate how much memory is available in total and how it is shared between the individual nodes and zones of the system.

3.4.1 Data Structure Setup

Initialization of the data structures is launched from within the start_kernel global start routine that is executed after kernel loading to render the various subsystems operational. As memory management is a very important kernel component, it is initialized almost immediately after architecture-specific setup, which is responsible for the technical details of detecting memory and establishing how it is distributed in the system (Section 3.4.2 deals briefly with the implementation of system-*dependent* initialization on IA-32 systems). At this point, an instance of pgdat_t has been generated for each system memory mode to hold information on how much memory there is in the node and how it is distributed over the node zones. The architecture-specific NODE_DATA macro implemented on all platforms is used to query the pgdat_t instance associated with a NUMA node by reference to the number of the instance.

Prerequisites

Since the majority of systems have just one memory node, only systems of this type are examined below. What is the situation on such systems? To ensure that memory management code is portable (so that it can be used on UMA and NUMA systems alike), the kernel defines a single instance of pg_data_t (called contig_page_data) in mm/page_alloc.c to manage all system memory. As the file pathname suggests, this is not a CPU-specific implementation; in fact, it is adopted by most architectures. The implementation of NODE_DATA is now even simpler.

```
<mmzone.h>
#define NODE_DATA(nid)          (&contig_page_data)
```

Although the macro has a formal parameter for selecting a NUMA node, the same data are always returned — there is just one pseudo-node.

The kernel can also rely on the fact that the architecture-dependent initialization code has set the numnodes variable to the number of nodes present in the system. This number is 1 on UMA systems because only one (formal) node is present.

At compilation time, pre-processor statements select the correct definitions for the particular configuration.

System Start

Figure 3-8 shows a code flow diagram for start_kernel. It includes only the system initialization functions associated with memory management.

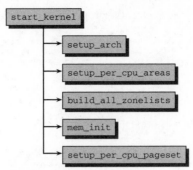

Figure 3-8: Kernel initialization in the view of memory management.

Let's take a closer look at the functions invoked in the sections below after first summarizing their tasks as follows:

❑ setup_arch is an architecture-specific set-up function responsible for, among other things, initialization of the boot allocator.

❑ On SMP systems, setup_per_cpu_areas initializes per-CPU variables defined statically in the source code (using the per_cpu macro) and of which there is a separate copy for each CPU in the system. Variables of this kind are stored in a separate section of the kernel binaries. The purpose of setup_per_cpu_areas is to create a copy of these data for each system CPU.

This function is a null operation on non-SMP systems.

❑ build_all_zonelists sets up the node and zone data structures (see below).

❑ mem_init is another architecture-specific function to disable the bootmem allocator and perform the transition to the actual memory management functions, as discussed shortly.

❑ kmem_cache_init initializes the in-kernel allocator for small memory regions.

❑ setup_per_cpu_pageset allocates memory for the first array element of the pageset arrays from struct zone mentioned above. Allocating the first array element means, in other words, for the first system processor. All memory zones of the system are taken into account.

The function is also responsible for setting the limits for the hot-n-cold allocator discussed at length in Section 3.5.3.

Notice that the pageset arrays members of other CPUs on SMP systems will be initialized when they are activated.

Node and Zone Initialization

build_all_zonelists builds the data structures required to manage nodes and their zones. Interestingly, it can be implemented by the macros and abstraction mechanisms introduced above regardless of whether it runs on a NUMA or UMA system. This works because the executed functions are available in two flavors: one for NUMA systems and one for UMA systems.

Since this little trick is often used by the kernel, I will briefly discuss it. Suppose that a certain task must be performed differently depending on the compile-time configuration. One possibility would be using two different functions and select the proper one each time it is called with some pre-processor conditionals:

```
void do_something() {
...
#ifdef CONFIG_WORK_HARD
        do_work_fast();
#else
        do_work_at_your_leisure();
#endif
...
}
```

Since this requires using the pre-processor each time the function is called, this approach is considered bad style by the kernel developers. A much more elegant solution is to define the function itself differently depending on the chosen configuration:

```
#ifdef CONFIG_WORK_HARD
void do_work() {
        /* Get going, fast! */
...
}

#else
void do_work() {
        /* Relax, take it easy */
...
}
#endif
```

Notice that the same name is employed for both implementations because they can never be active at the same time. Calling the proper function is now not more complicated than calling a regular function:

```
void do_something() {
...
        do_work();   /* Work hard or not, depending on configuration /*
...
}
```

Clearly, this variant is much more readable and is always preferred by the kernel developers (in fact, patches using the first style will have a very hard time getting into the mainline kernel, if at all).

Let us go back to setting up the zone lists. The portion of build_all_zonelists that is currently of interest to us (there is some more work to do for the page group mobility extensions to the page allocator, but I will discuss this separately below) delegates all work to __build_all_zonelists, which, in turn, invokes build_zonelists for each NUMA node in the system.

mm/page_alloc.c
```
static int __build_all_zonelists(void *dummy)
{
        int nid;
```

```
for_each_online_node(nid) {
        pg_data_t *pgdat = NODE_DATA(nid);

        build_zonelists(pgdat);
...
}
return 0;
}
```

for_each_online_node iterates over all active nodes in the system. As UMA systems have only one node, build_zonelists is invoked just once to create the zone lists for the whole of memory. NUMA systems must invoke the function as many times as there are nodes; each invocation generates the zone data for a different node.

build_zonelists expects as parameter a pointer to a pgdat_t instance containing all existing information on the node memory configuration and holding the newly created data structures.

On UMA systems, NODE_DATA *returns the address of* contig_page_data.

The task of the function is to establish a ranking order between the zones of the node currently being processed and the other nodes in the system; memory is then allocated according to this order. This is important if no memory is free in the desired node zone.

Let us look at an example in which the kernel wants to allocate high memory. It first attempts to find a free segment of suitable size in the highmem area of the current node. If it fails, it looks at the regular memory area of the node. If this also fails, it tries to perform allocation in the DMA zone of the node. If it cannot find a free area in any of the three local zones, it looks at other nodes. In this case, the alternative node should be as close as possible to the primary node to minimize performance loss caused as a result of accessing non-local memory.

The kernel defines a memory hierarchy and first tries to allocate "cheap" memory. If this fails, it gradually tries to allocate memory that is "more costly" in terms of access and capacity.

The high memory (highmem) range is cheapest because no part of the kernel depends on memory allocated from this area. There is no negative effect on the kernel if the highmem area is full — and this is why it is filled first.

The situation in regular memory is different. Many kernel data structures *must* be held in this area and cannot be kept in highmem. The kernel is therefore faced with a critical situation if regular memory is completely full — as a result, memory is not allocated from this area until there is no free memory in the less critical highmem area.

Most costly is the DMA area because it is used for data transfer between peripherals and the system. Memory allocation from this area is therefore a last resort.

The kernel also defines a ranking order among the alternative nodes as seen by the current memory nodes. This helps determine an alternative node when all zones of the current node are full.

The kernel uses an array of zonelist elements in pg_data_t to represent the described hierarchy as a data structure.

<mmzone.h>
```
typedef struct pglist_data {
  ...
        struct zonelist node_zonelists[MAX_ZONELISTS];
...
} pg_data_t;

#define MAX_ZONES_PER_ZONELIST (MAX_NUMNODES * MAX_NR_ZONES)
struct zonelist {
  ...
        struct zone *zones[MAX_ZONES_PER_ZONELIST + 1];     // NULL delimited
};
```

The node_zonelists array makes a separate entry available for every possible zone type. This entry contains a fallback list of type zonelist whose structure is discussed below.

Because the fallback list must include all zones of all nodes, it consists of MAX_NUMNODES * MAX_NZ_ZONES entries, plus a further element for a null pointer to mark the end of the list.

The task of creating a fallback hierarchy is delegated to build_zonelists, which creates the data structures for each NUMA node. It requires as parameter a pointer to the relevant pg_data_t instance. Before I discuss the code in detail, let us recall one thing mentioned above. Since we have restricted our discussion to UMA systems, why would it be necessary to consider multiple NUMA nodes? Indeed, the code shown below will be replaced with a different variant by the kernel if CONFIG_NUMA is set. However, it is possible that an architecture selects the discontiguous or sparse memory option on UMA systems. This can be beneficial if the address space contains large holes. The memory "blocks" created by such holes can best be treated using the data structures provided by NUMA. This is why we have to deal with them here.

A large external loop first iterates over all node zones. Each loop pass looks for the zone entry for the i-th zone in the zonelist array in which the fallback list is held.

mm/page_alloc.c
```
static void __init build_zonelists(pg_data_t *pgdat)
{
        int node, local_node;
        enum zone_type i,j;

        local_node = pgdat->node_id;
        for (i = 0; i < MAX_NR_ZONES; i++) {
                struct zonelist *zonelist;

                zonelist = pgdat->node_zonelists + i;

                j = build_zonelists_node(pgdat, zonelist, 0, j);
  ...
}
```

The array element of node_zonelists is addressed by means of pointer manipulation, a perfectly legal practice in C. The actual work is delegated to build_zonelist_node. When invoked, it first generates the fallback order within the local node.

mm/page_alloc.c
```
static int __init build_zonelists_node(pg_data_t *pgdat, struct zonelist *zonelist,
                                       int nr_zones, enum zone_type zone_type)
{
        struct zone *zone;

        do {
                zone = pgdat->node_zones + zone_type;
                if (populated_zone(zone)) {
                        zonelist->zones[nr_zones++] = zone;
                }
                zone_type--;

        } while (zone_type >= 0);
        return nr_zones;
}
```

The fallback list entries are ordered by means of the `zone_type` parameter that specifies the zone from which memory is best taken and is calculated using `highest_zone` as shown. Recall that it can have one of the following values: `ZONE_HIGHMEM`, `ZONE_NORMAL`, `ZONE_DMA`, or `ZONE_DMA32`. `nr_zone` denotes the position in the fallback list at which filling new entries starts. The caller has passed 0 since there is no entry in the list yet.

The kernel then iterates over all zones from costly to less costly. In each step, `populated_zone` ensures that `zone->present_pages` is greater than 0 for the selected zone; that is, whether there are pages in the zone. If so, a pointer to the `zone` instance previously determined is added at the current position within the zone list `zonelist->zones`. The current position in the zone list is held in `nr_zone`.

At the end of each step, the zone type is decremented by 1; in other words, it is set to a more costly zone type. For example, if the start zone is `ZONE_HIGHMEM`, decrementing by 1 ensures that the next zone type used is `ZONE_NORMAL`.

Consider a system with the zones `ZONE_HIGHMEM`, `ZONE_NORMAL`, and `ZONE_DMA`. In the first run of `build_zonelists_node`, the following assignments are made:

```
zonelist->zones[0] = ZONE_HIGHMEM;
zonelist->zones[1] = ZONE_NORMAL;
zonelist->zones[2] = ZONE_DMA;
```

Figure 3-9 illustrates this for the case in which a fallback list for node 2 of a system is successively filled. There are a total of four nodes in the system (`numnodes = 4`); k = `ZONE_HIGHMEM` also applies.

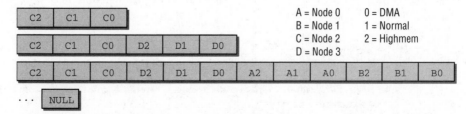

Figure 3-9: Successive filling of the fallback list.

After the first step, the allocation targets in the list are highmem, followed by normal memory and finally the DMA zone of the second node.

The kernel must then establish the order in which the zones of the other nodes in the system are used as fallback targets.

mm/page_alloc.c
```
static void __init build_zonelists(pg_data_t *pgdat)
{
    ...
                for (node = local_node + 1; node < MAX_NUMNODES; node++) {
                        j = build_zonelists_node(NODE_DATA(node), zonelist, j, i);
                }
                for (node = 0; node < local_node; node++) {
                        j = build_zonelists_node(NODE_DATA(node), zonelist, j, i);
                }

                zonelist->zones[j] = NULL;
        }
    }
}
```

The first loop successively iterates over all nodes with a *higher* number than the node being processed. In our example, there are four nodes numbered $0, 1, 2$, and 3 and therefore only node number 3 is left. New entries are added to the fallback list by `build_zonelists_node`. This is where the meaning of j comes into play. After the fallback targets in the local node had been found, the value of the variable was 3; this is used as the starting position for the new entries. If node number 3 also consists of three zones, the situation after invocation of `build_zonelists` is as shown in the second step of Figure 3-9.

The second `for` loop then generates the entries for all nodes with *lower* numbers than the current node. In our example, these nodes have the numbers 0 and 1. If three zones are also present in these nodes, the fallback list situation is as shown in the lower part of Figure 3-9.

The number of entries in the fallback list is never known exactly because the zone configurations may be different in the various nodes of the system. The last entry is therefore assigned a null pointer to explicitly mark the end of the list.

For any node m of a total number of N nodes, the kernel always selects the order $m, m + 1, m + 2, \ldots, N, 0, 1, \ldots, m - 1$ for the fallback nodes. This ensures that no node is overused (as compared, e.g., to an unchanging fallback list independent of m).

Figure 3-10 shows the fallback lists built for the third node in a system with four nodes.

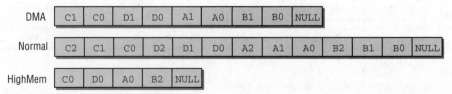

Figure 3-10: Finished fallback lists.

Section 3.5.5 discusses the implementation of the buddy system that makes use of the fallback lists generated here.

3.4.2 Architecture-Specific Setup

The initialization of memory management on IA-32 systems is in some aspects a very subtle undertaking that must overcome a few historical obstacles associated with the processor architecture. These include, for example, switching the processor from normal mode to *protected mode* to grant the CPU access to the 32-bit world — a legacy from the days when compatibility with 16-bit 8086 processors was important. Similarly, paging is not enabled by default and must be activated manually, which, for instance, involves fiddling with the `cr0` register of the processor. However, these subtleties are of no interest to us; you are referred to the appropriate reference manuals.

Notice that our focus on the IA-32 architecture does not mean that the things discussed in the following will be completely disconnected from all other architectures supported by the kernel. Quite the opposite is the case: Even if many details will be unique to the IA-32 architecture, many other architectures do things in a similar way. It's just necessary to choose one particular architecture as an example, and since IA-32 has not only been around for quite some time, but was also the architecture initially supported by Linux, this is reflected in the kernel's general design. Although there is a clear tendency of the kernel toward 64-bit platforms, many aspects can still be traced to its IA-32 roots.

Another reason why we pick the IA-32 architecture as an example is for practical purposes: Since the address space is only 4 GiB large, all addresses can be described with comparatively compact hexadecimal numbers, which are simply easier to read and work with than the long values required by 64-bit architectures.

Interestingly, the IA-32 architecture does not exist as a separate architecture starting with kernel 2.6.24 anymore! It was merged with the AMD64 architecture to form a new, unified x86 architecture. Although both are now constrained to the single architecture-specific directory `arch/x86`, a good many differences still remain. This is why many files are available in two variants: `file_32.c` for IA-32, and `file_64.c` for AMD64. The existence of two different files for each subarchitecture is something that is only temporarily tough. Future development will ensure that finally a single file will contain code for both architectures.

Since the unified architecture promotes the AMD64 architecture (even more) to one of the most important architectures supported by the kernel, I will also consider how architecture-specific details differ for AMD64 compared to IA-32. Owing to the large number of architectures supported by the kernel, it is not possible to discuss the specific details for all of them here. Considering one 32- and one 64-bit architecture in the following will, however, provide the taste of how Linux does things in both worlds, and lay the fundamentals to understand the approaches by other architectures.

Arrangement of the Kernel in Memory

Before discussing the individual memory initialization operations, we need to examine the situation in RAM after the boot loader has copied the kernel into memory and the assembler part of the initialization routines has completed. I concentrate on the default case in which the kernel is loaded to a fixed position in physical RAM that is determined at compile time.

It is also possible to configure the initial position of the kernel binary in physical RAM if the crash dump mechanism is enabled. Additionally, some embedded systems will require this ability. The configuration option PHYSICAL_START determines the position in RAM in this case, subjected to physical alignment specified by the configuration option PHYSICAL_ALIGN.

Additionally, the kernel can be built as a *relocatable* binary, and the physical start address given at compile time is completely ignored in this case. The boot loader can decide where to put the kernel. Since both options are either only required in corner cases or are still considered experimental, I will not discuss them any further.

Figure 3-11 shows the lowest megabytes of physical RAM memory in which the various parts of the kernel image reside.

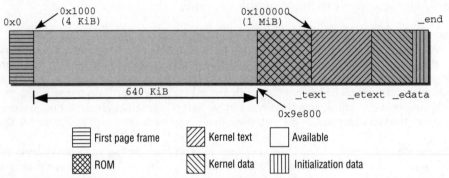

Figure 3-11: Arrangement of the Linux kernel in RAM memory.

The figure shows the first megabytes of physical memory — how much is exactly required depends on how big the kernel binary is. The first 4,096 KiB — the first page frame — are omitted because they are often reserved for the BIOS. The next 640 KiB would be usable in principle, but are again not used for kernel loading. The reason is that this area is immediately followed by an area reserved for the system into which various ROM ranges are mapped (typically the system BIOS and the graphic card ROM). It is not possible to write to these areas. However, the kernel should always be loaded into a contiguous memory range, and this would be possible only for kernels smaller than 640 KiB if the start address of RAM memory were used as the start position for the kernel image.

To resolve these problems, IA-32 kernels use 0x100000 as the start address; this corresponds to the start of the first megabyte in RAM memory. There is sufficient contiguous memory at this point to hold the entire kernel.

The memory occupied by the kernel is split into several sections whose bounds are held in variables.

❑   _text and _etext are the start and end address of the text section that contains the compiled kernel code.

❑   The data section in which most kernel variables are kept is located between _etext and _edata.

❑   Initialization data no longer needed after the kernel boot process is finished (among others, e.g., the BSS segment that contains all static global variables initialized to 0) are held in the last section, which extends from _edata to _end. Once kernel initialization has completed, most of the data can be removed from memory leaving more space for applications. The interval is split into smaller subintervals to control what can be removed and what cannot, but this is not of importance for our purposes now.

Although the variables used to define section bounds are defined in the kernel source code (arch/x86/kernel/setup_32.c), *no values are assigned to them at this point. This is simply not possible. How can the compiler know at compilation time how large the kernel will be? The exact value is only established when the object files are linked, and it is then patched into the binary file. This action is controlled by* arch/arch/vmlinux.ld.S *(for IA-32, the file is* arch/x86/vmlinux_32.ld.S*), where the kernel memory layout is also defined.*

The exact value varies according to kernel configuration as each configuration has text and data sections of different sizes — depending on which parts of the kernel are enabled and which are not used. Only the start address (_text) is always the same.

Each time the kernel is compiled, a file named System.map is generated and stored in the source base directory. Besides the addresses of all other (global) variables, procedures, and functions defined in the kernel, this file also includes the values of the constants shown in Figure 3-11,

```
wolfgang@meitner> cat System.map
...
c0100000 A _text
...
c0381ecd A _etext
...
c04704e0 A _edata
...
c04c3f44 A _end
...
```

All values have the offset 0xC0000000, which is the start address of the kernel segment if the standard 3 : 1 split between user and kernel address space is chosen. The addresses are virtual addresses because RAM memory is mapped into the virtual address space as a linear mapping starting at this address. The corresponding physical addresses are obtained by subtraction from 0xC0000000.

/proc/iomem also provides information on the sections into which RAM memory is divided.

```
wolfgang@meitner> cat /proc/iomem
00000000-0009e7ff : System RAM
0009e800-0009ffff : reserved
000a0000-000bffff : Video RAM area
000c0000-000c7fff : Video ROM
000f0000-000fffff : System ROM
00100000-17cefffff : System RAM
  00100000-00381ecc : Kernel code
  00381ecd-004704df : Kernel data
...
```

The kernel image begins above the first megabyte (0x00100000). The size of the code is approximately 2.5 MiB, and the data section accounts for about 0.9 MiB.

The same information is also available for AMD64 systems. Here the kernel starts 2 MiB after the first page frame, and physical memory is mapped into the virtual address space from `0xffffffff80000000` onward. The relevant entries in `System.map` are as follows:

```
wolfgang@meitner> cat System.map
ffffffff80200000 A _text
...
ffffffff8041fc6f A _etext
...
ffffffff8056c060 A _edata
...
ffffffff8077548c A _end
```

This information is also contained in `/proc/iomem` for the running kernel:

```
root@meitner # cat /proc/iomem
...
00100000-cff7ffff : System RAM
  00200000-0041fc6e : Kernel code
  0041fc6f-0056c05f : Kernel data
  006b6000-0077548b : Kernel bss
...
```

Initialization Steps

Which system-specific steps must the kernel perform once it has been loaded into memory and the assembler parts of initialization have been completed? Figure 3-12 shows a code flow diagram of the individual actions.

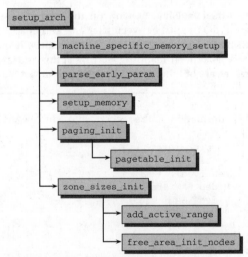

Figure 3-12: Code flow diagram for memory initialization on IA-32 systems.

The figure includes only those function calls associated with memory management. All others are unimportant in this context and are therefore omitted. Recall that `setup_arch` is invoked from within `start_kernel`, as already noted in Section 3.4.1.

`machine_specific_memory_setup` is first invoked to create a list with the memory regions occupied by the system and the free memory regions. Because the way in which this information is obtained differs slightly between the "subarchitectures" of the IA-32 family,[11] the kernel provides a machine-specific function that is defined in `include/asm-x86/mach-type/setup.c`. type can then stand for `default`, `voyager`, or `visws`; I discuss only the default situation.

A map provided by the BIOS and showing the individual memory regions is used in this case.

> These are not the same regions as in the NUMA concept but are areas occupied by system ROM, for example, or by ACPI functions.

When the system is booted, the regions found are displayed by the kernel function `print_memory_map`.

```
wolfgang@meitner> dmesg
...
BIOS-provided physical RAM map:
 BIOS-e820: 0000000000000000 - 000000000009e800 (usable)
 BIOS-e820: 000000000009e800 - 00000000000a0000 (reserved)
 BIOS-e820: 00000000000c0000 - 00000000000cc000 (reserved)
 BIOS-e820: 00000000000d8000 - 0000000000100000 (reserved)
 BIOS-e820: 0000000000100000 - 0000000017cf0000 (usable)
 BIOS-e820: 0000000017cf0000 - 0000000017cff000 (ACPI data)
 BIOS-e820: 0000000017cff000 - 0000000017d00000 (ACPI NVS)
 BIOS-e820: 0000000017d00000 - 0000000017e80000 (usable)
 BIOS-e820: 0000000017e80000 - 0000000018000000 (reserved)
 BIOS-e820: 00000000ff800000 - 00000000ffc00000 (reserved)
 BIOS-e820: 00000000fff00000 - 0000000100000000 (reserved)
...
```

If this information is not provided by the BIOS (this may be the case on some older machines), the kernel itself generates a table to mark memory in the ranges 0–640 KiB and 1 MiBend as usable.

The kernel then analyzes the command line with `parse_cmdline_early`, concentrating on arguments like `mem=XXX[KkmM]`, `highmem=XXX[kKmM]`, or `memmap=XXX[KkmM]""@XXX[KkmM]` arguments. The administrator can overwrite the size of available memory or manually define memory areas if the kernel calculates an incorrect value or is provided with a wrong value by the BIOS. This option is only of relevance on older computers. `highmem=` permits overwriting of the highmem size value detected. It can be used on machines with a very large RAM configuration to limit available RAM size — as it sometimes yields performance gains.

---

[11] There are not only "normal" IA-32 computers but also custom products of Silicon Graphics and NCR that, although they consist mainly of standard components, take a different approach to some things — including memory detection. Because these machines are either very old (Voyager from NCR) or not in widespread use (Visual Workstation from SGI), I won't bother with their oddities.

The next major step is performed in setup_memory of which there are two versions; one for systems with contiguous memory (in arch/x86/kernel/setup_32.c) and one for machines with discontiguous memory (in arch/x86/mm/discontig_32.c). They both have the same effect although their implementations differ.

❑ The number of physical pages available (per node) is determined.

❑ The bootmem allocator is initialized (Section 3.4.3 describes the implementation of the allocator in detail).

❑ Various memory areas are then reserved, for instance, for the initial RAM disk needed when running the first userspace processes.

paging_init initializes the kernel page tables and enables paging since it is not active by default on IA-32 machines.[12] *Execute Disable Protection* is also enabled if supported by the processor and if the kernel was compiled with PAE support; unfortunately, the feature is otherwise not available. By calling pagetable_init, the function also ensures that the direct mapping of physical memory into the kernel address space is initialized. All page frames in low memory are directly mapped to the virtual memory region above PAGE_OFFSET. This allows the kernel to address a good part of the available memory without having to deal with page tables anymore. More details about paging_init and the whole mechanism behind it are discussed below.

Calling zone_sizes_init initializes the pgdat_t instances of all nodes of the system. First a comparatively simple list of the available physical memory is prepared using add_active_range. The architecture-independent function free_are_init_nodes then uses this information to prepare the full-blown kernel data structures. Since this is a very important step that has numerous implications for how the kernel manages page frames at run time, it is discussed in more detail in Section 3.5.3.

Notice that the memory-related initialization sequence is quite similar on AMD64 machines, as the code flow diagram in Figure 3-13 shows.

The basic memory setup does not require any machine-type-specific handling, but can always be done with setup_memory_region. Information about the available RAM is given by the so-called E820 map supplied from the BIOS. After parsing the command-line options relevant for the early boot process, a simple list of the available memory is created by add_active called from e820_register_active_region, which, in turn, just walks over the information provided by parsing the E820 map above.

The kernel then calls init_memory_mapping to directly map the available physical memory into the virtual address space portion of the kernel starting from PAGE_OFFSET. contig_initmem_init is responsible to activate the bootmem allocator.

The last function in the list, paging_init, is actually a misnomer: It does not initialize paging, but has to deal with some set-up routines for sparse memory systems that are not interesting for our purposes. The important thing, however, is that the function also calls free_area_init_nodes, which is as in the IA-32 case responsible to initialize the data structures required to manage physical page frames by the kernel. Recall that this is an architecture-independent function and relies on the information provided by add_active_range as mentioned above. A detailed discussion of how free_area_init_nodes sets up memory follows in Section 3.5.3.

---

[12]All addresses are interpreted linearly if paging is not explicitly enabled.

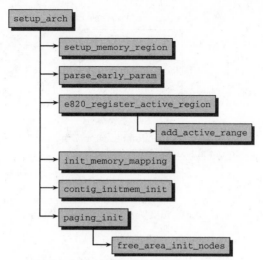

Figure 3-13: Code flow diagram for memory initialization on AMD64 systems.

Initialization of Paging

`paging_init` is responsible for setting up the page tables that can be used only by the kernel and are not accessible in userspace. This has far-reaching effects on the way in which access to memory is regulated between normal applications and the kernel itself. It is therefore important to explain the purpose of the function before looking closely at its implementation.

As noted in Chapter 1, on IA-32 systems the kernel typically divides the total available virtual address space of 4 GiB in a ratio of 3 : 1. The lower 3 GiB are available for user-mode applications, and the upper gigabyte is reserved exclusively for the kernel. Whereas the current system context is irrelevant when assigning the virtual address space of the kernel, each process has its own specific address space.

The major reasons for this division are as follows:

❑   When execution of a user application switches to kernel mode (this always happens when, e.g., a system call is used or a periodic timer interrupt is generated), the kernel must be embedded in a reliable environment. It is therefore essential to assign part of the address space exclusively to the kernel.

❑   The physical pages are mapped to the start of the kernel address space so that the kernel can access them directly without the need for complicated page table operations.

If all physical pages were mapped into the address space accessible to userspace processes, this would lead to serious security problems if several applications were running on the system. Each application would then be able to read and modify the memory areas of other processes in physical RAM. Obviously this must be prevented at all costs.

While the virtual address portion employed for userland processes changes with every task switch, the kernel portion is always the same. The situation is summarized in Figure 3-14.

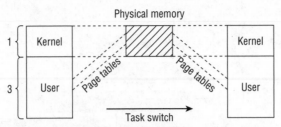

Figure 3-14: Connection between virtual and physical address space on IA-32 processors.

Division of Address Space

Division of address space in a ratio of 3 : 1 is only an approximate reflection of the situation in the kernel as the kernel address space itself is split into various sections. Figure 3-15 graphically illustrates the situation.

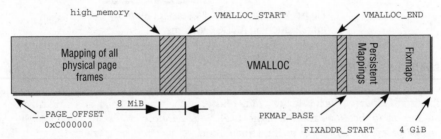

Figure 3-15: Division of the kernel address space on IA-32 systems.

> The figure shows the structure of the page table entries used to manage the fourth gigabyte of virtual address space. It indicates the *purpose* of each area of *virtual address space, and this has nothing to do with the assignment of physical RAM.*

The first section of the address space is used to map all physical pages of the system into the virtual address space of the kernel. Because this address space begins at an offset of `0xC0000000` — the frequently mentioned 3 GiB — each virtual address x corresponds to the physical address $x - 0xC0000000$, and is therefore a simple linear shift.

As the figure shows, the *direct mapping* area extends from `0xC0000000` to the `high_memory` address whose exact value I discuss shortly. As intimated in Chapter 1, there is a problem with this scheme. Because the virtual address space of the kernel comprises only 1 GiB, a maximum of 1 GiB of RAM memory can be mapped. The fact that the maximum memory configuration on IA-32 systems (without PAE) can be up to 4 GiB raises the question of what to do with the remaining memory.

Here's the bad news. The kernel cannot map the whole of physical memory at once if it is larger than 896 MiB.[13] This value is even less than the previously stated maximum limit of 1 GiB because

---

[13]It would also be possible to get rid of the split completely by introducing *two* 4 GiB address spaces, one for the kernel and one for each userspace program. However, context switches between kernel and user mode are more costly in this case.

the kernel must reserve the last 128 MiB of its address space for other purposes which I explain shortly. Adding these 128 MiB to the 896 MiB of direct RAM mapping results in a total virtual kernel address space of 1,024 MiB = 1 GiB. The kernel uses the two frequently employed abbreviations "normal" and "highmem" to distinguish between pages that can be mapped directly and those than cannot.

The kernel port must provide two macros for each architecture to translate between physical and virtual addresses in the identity-mapped part of virtual kernel memory (ultimately this is a platform-dependent task).[14]

❑   __pa(vaddr) returns the physical address associated with the virtual address vaddr.

❑   __va(paddr) yields the virtual address corresponding to the physical address paddr.

Both functions operate with void pointers and with unsigned longs because both data types are equally valid for the representation of memory addresses.

> *Caution: The functions are* not *valid to deal with arbitrary addresses from the virtual address space, but only* work for the identity-mapped part! *This is why they can usually be implemented with simple linear transformations and do not require a detour over the page tables.*

IA-32 maps the page frames into the virtual address space starting from PAGE_OFFSET, and correspondingly the following simple transformation is sufficient:

include/asm-x86/page_32.h
```
#define __pa(x) ((unsigned long)(x)-PAGE_OFFSET)
#define __va(x) ((void *)((unsigned long)(x)+PAGE_OFFSET))
```

For what purpose does the kernel use the last 128 MiB of its address space? As Figure 3-15 shows, it is put to three uses:

1. Virtually contiguous memory areas that are *not* contiguous in physical memory can be reserved in the *vmalloc* area. While this mechanism is commonly used with user processes, the kernel itself tries to avoid non-contiguous physical addresses as best it can. It usually succeeds because most of the large memory blocks are allocated for the kernel at boot time when RAM is not yet fragmented. However, on systems that have been running for longer periods, situations can arise in which the kernel requires physical memory but the space available is not contiguous. A prime example of such a situation is when modules are loaded dynamically.

2. *Persistent mappings* are used to map non-persistent pages from the highmem area into the kernel. Section 3.5.8 takes a close look at this topic.

3. *Fixmaps* are virtual address space entries associated with a fixed but freely selectable page in physical address space. In contrast to directly mapped pages that are associated with RAM memory by means of a fixed formula, the association between a virtual fixmap address and the position in RAM memory can be freely defined and is then always observed by the kernel.

---

[14]The kernel places only two conditions on the functions that must remain as invariants; $x_1 < x_2 \Rightarrow$ __**va**$(x_1) <$ __**va**(x_2) must be valid (for any physical addresses x_i), and __**va**(__**pa**$(x)) = x$ must be valid for any addresses x within the direct mapping.

Two pre-processor symbols are important in this context: __VMALLOC_RESERVE sets the size of the vmalloc area, and MAXMEM denotes the maximum possible amount of physical RAM that can be directly addressed by the kernel.

The splitting of memory into the individual areas is controlled by means of the constants shown in Figure 3-15. The constants may have different values depending on the kernel and system configuration. The bound of the direct mappings is specified by high_memory.

arch/x86/kernel/setup_32.c
```
static unsigned long __init setup_memory(void)
{
...
#ifdef CONFIG_HIGHMEM
        high_memory = (void *) __va(highstart_pfn * PAGE_SIZE - 1) + 1;
#else
        high_memory = (void *) __va(max_low_pfn * PAGE_SIZE - 1) + 1;
#endif
...
}
```

max_low_pfn specifies the number of memory pages present on systems with less than 896 MiB. The value is also limited upwards to the maximum number of pages that fit in 896 MiB (the exact calculation is given in find_max_low_pfn). If highmem support is enabled, high_memory indicates the bound between two memory areas, which is always at 896 MiB.

There is a gap with a minimum size of VMALLOC_OFFSET between the direct mapping of all RAM pages and the area for non-contiguous allocations.

include/asm-x86/pgtable_32.h
```
#define VMALLOC_OFFSET  (8*1024*1024)
```

This gap acts as a safeguard against any kernel faults. If *out of bound* addresses are accessed (these are unintentional accesses to memory areas that are no longer physically present), access fails and an exception is generated to report the error. If the vmalloc area were to immediately follow the direct mappings, access would be successful and the error would not be noticed. There should be no need for this additional safeguard in stable operation, but it is useful when developing new kernel features that are not yet mature.

VMALLOC_START and VMALLOC_END define the start and end of the vmalloc area used for physically non-contiguous kernel mappings. The values are not defined directly as constants but depend on several parameters.

include/asm-x86/pgtable_32.h
```
#define VMALLOC_START    (((unsigned long) high_memory + \
                          2*VMALLOC_OFFSET-1) & ~(VMALLOC_OFFSET-1))
#ifdef CONFIG_HIGHMEM
# define VMALLOC_END     (PKMAP_BASE-2*PAGE_SIZE)
#else
# define VMALLOC_END     (FIXADDR_START-2*PAGE_SIZE)
#endif
```

The start address of the vmalloc area depends on how much virtual address space memory is used for the direct mapping of RAM (and therefore on the `high_memory` variable defined above). The kernel also takes account of the fact that there is a gap of *at least* `VMALLOC_OFFSET` between the two areas and that the vmalloc area begins at an address divisible by `VMALLOC_OFFSET`. This results in the offset values shown in Table 3-5 for different memory configuration levels between 128 and 135 MiB; the offsets start a new cycle at 136 MiB.

Table 3-5: `VMALLOC_OFFSET` **Values for Different RAM Sizes**

Memory (MiB)	Offset (MiB)
128	8
129	15
130	14
131	13
132	12
133	11
134	10
135	9

Where the vmalloc area ends depends on whether highmem support is enabled — if it is not, no space is needed for persistent kernel mappings because the whole of RAM memory can be permanently mapped. Depending on configuration, the area therefore ends either at the start of the persistent kernel mappings or at the start of the fixmap area; two pages are always left as a safety gap to the vmalloc area.

The start and end of the persistent kernel mappings are defined as follows:

```
include/asm-x86/highmem.h
#define LAST_PKMAP 1024
#define PKMAP_BASE ( (FIXADDR_BOOT_START - PAGE_SIZE*(LAST_PKMAP + 1)) & PMD_MASK )
```

`PKMAP_BASE` defines the start address (the calculation is made relative to the fixmap area using some constants that are discussed shortly). `LAST_PKMAP` defines the *number* of pages used to hold the mappings.

The last memory section is occupied by *fixed mappings*. These are addresses that point to a *random* location in RAM memory. In contrast to linear mapping at the start of the fourth gigabyte, the correlation between virtual address and position in RAM memory is not preordained with this type of mapping but can be freely defined, even though it cannot be changed later. The fixmap area fills the virtual address space right up to its top end.

include/asm-x86/fixmap_32.h
```
#define __FIXADDR_TOP    0xfffff000
#define FIXADDR_TOP      ((unsigned long)__FIXADDR_TOP)
#define __FIXADDR_SIZE   (__end_of_permanent_fixed_addresses << PAGE_SHIFT)
#define FIXADDR_START    (FIXADDR_TOP - __FIXADDR_SIZE)
```

The advantage of fixmap addresses is that at compilation time, the address acts like a constant whose physical address is assigned when the kernel is booted. Addresses of this kind can be de-referenced faster than when normal pointers are used. The kernel also ensures that the page table entries of fixmaps are not flushed from the TLB during a context switch so that access is always made via fast cache memory.

A constant is created for each fixmap address and must appear in the enum list called fixed_addresses.

include/asm-x86/fixmap_32.h
```
enum fixed_addresses {
        FIX_HOLE,
        FIX_VDSO,
        FIX_DBGP_BASE,
        FIX_EARLYCON_MEM_BASE,
#ifdef CONFIG_X86_LOCAL_APIC
        FIX_APIC_BASE,   /* local (CPU) APIC) —  required for SMP or not */
#endif
...
#ifdef CONFIG_HIGHMEM
        FIX_KMAP_BEGIN, /* reserved pte's for temporary kernel mappings */
        FIX_KMAP_END = FIX_KMAP_BEGIN+(KM_TYPE_NR*NR_CPUS)-1,
#endif
...
        FIX_WP_TEST,
        __end_of_fixed_addresses
};
```

The kernel provides the fix_to_virt function to calculate the virtual address of a fixmap constant.

include/asm-x86/fixmap_32.h
```
 static __always_inline unsigned long fix_to_virt(const unsigned int idx)
 {
         if (idx >= __end_of_fixed_addresses)
                 __this_fixmap_does_not_exist();

         return __fix_to_virt(idx);
 }
```

The if query is totally removed by compiler optimization mechanisms — this is possible because the function is defined as an inline function, and only constants are used in the query. Such optimization is necessary because otherwise fixmap addresses would be no better than normal pointers. A formal check is made to ensure that the required fixmap address is in the valid area. __end_of_fixed_adresses is the last element of fixed_addresses and defines the maximum possible number. The pseudo-function __this_fixmap_does_not_exist (for which no definition exists) is invoked if the kernel accesses an invalid address. When the kernel is linked, this leads to an error message indicating that no image can be generated because of undefined symbols. Consequently, kernel faults of this kind are detected at compilation time and not when the kernel is running.

When a valid fixmap address is referenced, the comparison in the `if` query yields a positive value. Since both comparison objects are constants, the query need not be executed and is therefore removed.

`__fix_to_virt` is defined as a macro. Owing to the `inline` property of `fix_to_virt`, it is copied directly to the point in the code where the fixmap address query is executed. This macro is defined as follows:

include/asm-x86/fixmap_32.h
```
#define __fix_to_virt(x)          (FIXADDR_TOP - ((x) << PAGE_SHIFT))
```

Starting *at the top* (and not from the bottom as usual), the kernel goes back *n* pages to determine the virtual address of the *n*-th fixmap entry. As, once again, only constants are used in this calculation, the compiler is able to compute the result at compilation time. The address in RAM at which the corresponding virtual address is located has not yet been occupied as a result of the above division of memory.

The association between the fixmap address and physical page in memory is established by `set_fixmap(fixmap, page_nr)` and `set_fixmap_nocache` (whose implementation is not discussed). They simply associate the corresponding entry in the page tables with a page in RAM. Unlike `set_fixmap`, `set_fixmap_nocache` disables hardware caching for the page involved as this is sometimes necessary.

Notice that some other architectures also provide fixmaps, including AMD64.

Alternative Division

Dividing virtual address space in a 3 : 1 ratio is not the only option. Relatively little effort is needed to select a different division because all bounds are defined by constants in the sources. For some purposes it may be better to split the address space symmetrically, 2 GiB for user address space and 2 GiB for kernel address space. `__PAGE_OFFSET` must then be set to `0x80000000` instead of the typical default of `0xC0000000`. This division is useful when the system performs tasks that require a large amount of memory for the kernel but little for the user processes (such tasks are rare). As any change to how memory is divided requires recompilation of all userspace applications, the configuration statements include no option to split memory differently, although this would be easy to do in principle.

Basically, it is possible to split memory by manually modifying the kernel sources, but the kernel offers some default splitting ratios. `__PAGE_OFFSET` is then defined as follows:

include/asm-x86/page_32.h
```
#define __PAGE_OFFSET          # ((unsigned long)CONFIG_PAGE_OFFSET)
```

Table 3-6 collects all possibilities for splitting the virtual address space and the resulting maximal amount of RAM that can be mapped.

Splitting the kernel in ratios other than 3 : 1 can make sense in specific scenarios, for instance, for machines that mainly run code in the kernel — think about network routers. The general case, however, is best served with a 3 : 1 ratio.

Splitting the Virtual Address Space

`paging_init` is invoked on IA-32 systems during the boot process to split the virtual address space as described above. The code flow diagram is shown in Figure 3-16.

Table 3-6: Different Splitting Ratios for the IA-32 Virtual Address Space, and the Resulting Maximum Identity-Mapped Physical Memory.

Ratio	CONFIG_PAGE_OFFSET	MAXMEM(MiB)
3 : 1	0xC0000000	896
≈ 3 : 1	0xB0000000	1152
2 : 2	0x80000000	1920
≈ 2 : 2	0x78000000	2048
1 : 3	0x40000000	2944

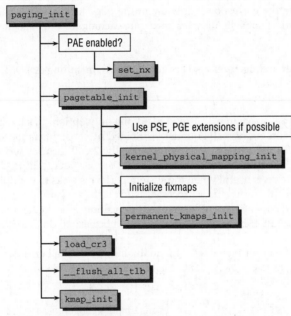

Figure 3-16: Code flow diagram for `paging_init`.

`pagetable_init` first initializes the page tables of the system using `swapper_pg_dir` as a basic (this variable was previously used to hold the provisional data). Two extensions available on all modern IA-32 variants are then enabled (only a few very old Pentium implementations do not support these).

❏ Support for large memory pages. The size of specially marked pages is 4 MiB instead of the usual 4 KiB. This option is used for kernel pages because they are never swapped out. Increasing the page size means that fewer page table entries are needed, and this has a positive impact on the translation lookaside buffers (TLBs), which are then less burdened with kernel data.

❏ If possible, kernel pages are provided with a further attribute (_PAGE_GLOBAL) that is why the __PAGE_GLOBAL bit is activated in the __PAGE_KERNEL and __PAGE_KERNEL_EXEC variables. These variables specify the flags set for the kernel itself when pages are allocated; these settings are therefore automatically transferred to the kernel pages.

The TLB entries of pages with a set _PAGE_GLOBAL bit are not flushed from the TLBs during context switches. Since the kernel is always present at the same location in the virtual address space, this enhances system performance, a welcome effect as kernel data must be made available as quickly as possible.

Mapping of the physical pages (or of the first 896 MiB, as discussed above) into virtual address space as of PAGE_OFFSET is done with the help of kernel_physical_mapping_init. The kernel successively scans all relevant entries of the various page directories and sets the pointers to the correct values.

Then the areas for fixmap entries and the persistent kernel mappings are set up. Again, this equates to filling the page tables with appropriate values.

Once page table initialization with pagetable_init has been concluded, the cr3 register is supplied with a pointer to the page global directory used (swapper_pg_dir). This is necessary to activate the new page tables. Reassigning the cr3 register has exactly this effect on IA-32 machines.

The TLB entries must also be flushed because they still contain boot memory allocation data. __flush_all_tlb does the necessary work. In contrast to TLB flushes during context switches, pages with a _PAGE_GLOBAL bit are also flushed.

kmap_init initializes the global variable kmap_pte. The kernel uses this variable to store the page table entry for the area later used to map pages from the highmem zone into kernel address space. Besides, the address of the first fixmap area for highmem kernel mappings is stored in the global variable kmem_vstart.

Initialization of the Hot-n-Cold Cache

I have already mentioned the per-CPU (or hot-n-cold) cache in Section 3.2.2.. Here we deal with the initialization of the associated data structures and the calculation of the "watermarks" used to control cache filling behavior.

zone_pcp_init is responsible for initializing the cache. The kernel calls the function from free_area_init_nodes, which is, in turn, invoked during boot on both IA-32 and AMD64.

mm/page_alloc.c
```
static __devinit void zone_pcp_init(struct zone *zone)
{
        int cpu;
        unsigned long batch = zone_batchsize(zone);

        for (cpu = 0; cpu < NR_CPUS; cpu++) {
                setup_pageset(zone_pcp(zone,cpu), batch);
        }
        if (zone->present_pages)
                printk(KERN_DEBUG " %s zone: %lu pages, LIFO batch:%lu\n",
                        zone->name, zone->present_pages, batch);
}
```

Once the batch size (which is the basis for calculating the minimum and maximum fill level) has been determined with zone_batchsize, the code iterates over all CPUs in the system and invokes setup_pageset to fill the constants of each per_cpu_pageset instance. The zone_pcp macro used when this function is invoked selects the pageset instance of the zone associated with the CPU currently being examined.

Let us take a closer look at how the watermark is calculated.

mm/page_alloc.c
```
static int __devinit zone_batchsize(struct zone *zone)
{
        int batch;

        batch = zone->present_pages / 1024;
        if (batch * PAGE_SIZE > 512 * 1024)
                batch = (512 * 1024) / PAGE_SIZE;
        batch /= 4;
        if (batch < 1)
                batch = 1;

        batch = (1 << (fls(batch + batch/2)-1)) - 1;

        return batch;
}
```

The code calculates batch so that it corresponds to roughly 25 percent of a thousandth of the pages present in the zone. The shift operation also ensures that the value calculated has the form $2^n - 1$ because it has been established empirically that this minimizes cache aliasing effects for most system loads. fls is a machine-specific operation to yield the last set bit of a value. Note that this alignment will cause the resulting values to deviate from 25 percent of one-thousandth the zones pages. The maximal deviation arises for that case batch = 22. Since $22 + 11 - 1 = 32$, fls will find bit 5 as last set bit in the number, and $1 << 5 - 1 = 31$. Because the deviation will usually be smaller, it can be neglected for all practical purposes.

The batch size does not increase when the memory in the zone exceeds 512 MiB. For systems with a page size of 4,096 KiB, for instance, this limit is reached when more than 131,072 pages are present. Figure 3-17 shows how the batch size evolves with the number of pages present in a zone.

The batch value makes sense when we consider how batch is used to calculate the cache limits in setup_pageset.

mm/page_alloc.c
```
inline void setup_pageset(struct per_cpu_pageset *p, unsigned long batch)
{
        struct per_cpu_pages *pcp;

        memset(p, 0, sizeof(*p));

        pcp = &p->pcp[0];                    /* hot */
        pcp->count = 0;
        pcp->high = 6 * batch;
        pcp->batch = max(1UL, 1 * batch);
        INIT_LIST_HEAD(&pcp->list);
```

```
        pcp = &p->pcp[1];                /* cold*/
        pcp->count = 0;
        pcp->high = 2 * batch;
        pcp->batch = max(1UL, batch/2);
        INIT_LIST_HEAD(&pcp->list);
    }
```

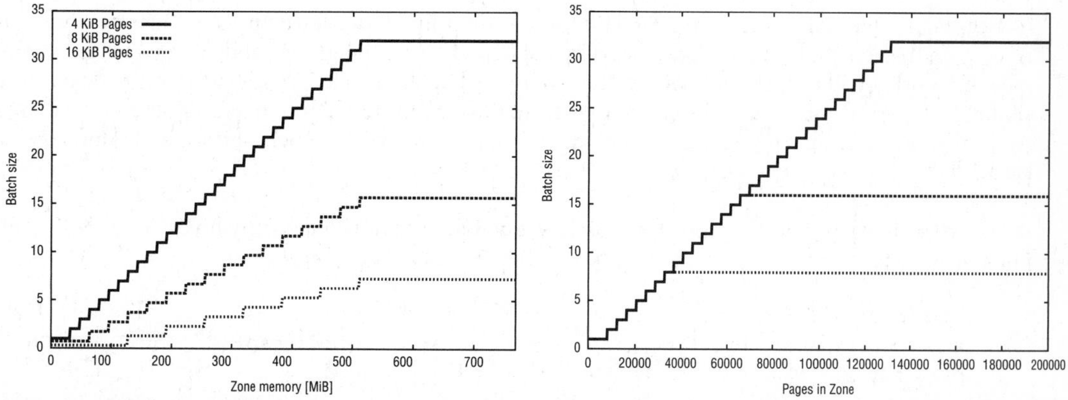

Figure 3-17: Batch sizes dependent on the amount of memory present (left-hand side) on the zone for various page sizes. The graph on the right-hand side shows the dependency against the number of pages present in a zone.

As the lower limit used for hot pages is 0 and the upper limit is 6*batch, the average number of pages in the cache will be around 4*batch because the kernel tries to not let the caches drain too much. batch*4, however, corresponds to a thousandth of the total number of zone pages (this is also the reason why zone_batchsize tried to optimize the batch size for 25 percent of one-thousandth of the total pages). The size of the L2 cache on IA-32 processors is in the range between 0.25 and 2 MiB, so it makes no sense to keep much more memory in a hot-n-cold cache than would fit into this space. As a rule of thumb, the cache size is one-thousandth of the main memory size; consider that current systems are equipped with between 1 and 2 GiB of RAM per CPU, so the rule is reasonable. The computed batch size will thus likely allow that the pages on the hot-n-cold cache fit into the CPU's L2 cache.

The watermarks of the cold list are slightly lower because cold pages not held in the cache are used only for actions that are *not* performance-critical (such actions are, of course, in the minority in the kernel,). Only double of the batch value is used as the upper limit.

The pcp->batch size determines how many pages are used at once when the list needs to be refilled. For performance reasons, a whole chunk of pages rather than single pages is added to the list.

The number of pages in each zone is output at the end of zone_pcp_init together with the calculated batch sizes as shown in the boot logs (for a system with 4 GiB of RAM in the example below).

```
root@meitner # dmesg | grep LIFO
    DMA zone: 2530 pages, LIFO batch:0
    DMA32 zone: 833464 pages, LIFO batch:31
    Normal zone: 193920 pages, LIFO batch:31
```

Registering Active Memory Regions

I noted above that initialization of the zone structures is an extensive task. Luckily this task is identical on all architectures. While kernel versions before 2.6.19 had to set up the required data structures on a per-architecture basis, the approach has become more modular in the meantime: The individual architectures only need to register a very simple map of all active memory regions, and generic code then generates the main data structures from this information.

Notice that individual architectures can still decide to set up all data structures on their own without relying on the generic framework provided by the kernel. Since both IA-32 and AMD64 let the kernel do the hard work, I will not discuss this possibility any further. Any architecture that wants to enjoy the possibilities offered by the generic framework must set the configuration option ARCH_POPULATES_NODE_MAP. After all active memory regions are registered, the rest of the work is then performed by the generic kernel code.

An active memory region is simply a memory region that does not contain any holes. add_active_range must be used to register a region in the global variable early_node_map.

mm/page_alloc.c
```
static struct node_active_region __meminitdata early_node_map[MAX_ACTIVE_REGIONS];
static int __meminitdata nr_nodemap_entries;
```

The number of currently registered regions is denoted by nr_nodemap_entries. The maximal number of distinct regions is given by MAX_ACTIVE_REGIONS. The value can be set by the architecture-specific code using CONFIG_MAX_ACTIVE_REGIONS. If not, the kernel allows for registering 256 active regions per default (or 50 regions per NUMA node if it is running on a system with more than 32 nodes). Each region is described by the following data structure:

<mmzone.h>
```
struct node_active_region {
        unsigned long start_pfn;
        unsigned long end_pfn;
        int nid;
};
```

start_pfn and end_pfn denote the first and last page frame in a continuous region, and nid is the NUMA ID of the node to which the memory belongs. UMA systems naturally set this to 0.

An active memory region is registered with add_active_range:

mm/page_alloc.c
```
void __init add_active_range(unsigned int nid, unsigned long start_pfn,
                                       unsigned long end_pfn)
```

When two adjacent regions are registered, then add_active_regions ensures that they are merged to a single one. Besides, the function does not present any surprises.

Recall from Figures 3-12 and 3-13 that the function is called from zone_sizes_init on IA-32 systems, and in e820_register_active_regions on AMD64 systems. Thus I will briefly discuss these functions.

Registering Regions on IA-32

Besides calling `add_active_range`, the function `zone_sizes_init` stores the boundaries of the different memory zones in terms of page frames.

arch/x86/kernel/setup_32.c
```
void __init zone_sizes_init(void)
{
        unsigned long max_zone_pfns[MAX_NR_ZONES];
        memset(max_zone_pfns, 0, sizeof(max_zone_pfns));
        max_zone_pfns[ZONE_DMA] =
                virt_to_phys((char *)MAX_DMA_ADDRESS) >> PAGE_SHIFT;
        max_zone_pfns[ZONE_NORMAL] = max_low_pfn;
#ifdef CONFIG_HIGHMEM
        max_zone_pfns[ZONE_HIGHMEM] = highend_pfn;
        add_active_range(0, 0, highend_pfn);
#else
        add_active_range(0, 0, max_low_pfn);
 #endif

        free_area_init_nodes(max_zone_pfns);
}
```

`MAX_DMA_ADDRESS` is the highest suitable memory address for DMA operations. The constant is declared as `PAGE_OFFSET+0x1000000`. Recall that the physical pages are mapped into the virtual starting from `PAGE_OFFSET`, and the first 16 MiB — hexadecimal `0x1000000` — are suitable for DMA operations. Conversion with `virt_to_phys` yields the address in physical memory, and shifting right by `PAGE_SHIFT` bits effectively divides this figure by the page size and produces the number of pages that can be used for DMA. Unsurprisingly, the result is 4,096 since IA-32 uses pages of 4 KiB.

`max_low_pfn` and `highend_pfn` are global constants to specify the highest page number in the low (usually ≤ 896 MiB if $3:1$ split of the address space is used) and high memory ranges that were filled before.

Notice that `free_area_init_nodes` will combine the information in `early_mem_map` and `max_zone_pfns`: The active ranges for each memory region are selected, and architecture-independent data structures are constructed.

Registering Regions on AMD64

Registering the available memory is split between two functions on AMD64. The active memory regions are registered as follows:

arch/x86/kernel/e820_64.c
```
e820_register_active_regions(int nid, unsigned long start_pfn,
                                                unsigned long end_pfn)
 {
        unsigned long ei_startpfn;
        unsigned long ei_endpfn;
        int i;
```

```
                    for (i = 0; i < e820.nr_map; i++)
                    if (e820_find_active_region(&e820.map[i],
                                                start_pfn, end_pfn,
                                                &ei_startpfn, &ei_endpfn))
                            add_active_range(nid, ei_startpfn, ei_endpfn);
        }
```

Essentially the code iterates over all regions provided by the BIOS and finds the active region for each entry. This is interesting because `add_active_range` is potentially called multiple times in contrast to the IA-32 variant.

Filling in `max_zone_pfns` is handled by `paging_init`:

arch/x86/mm/init_64.c
```
void __init paging_init(void)
{
        unsigned long max_zone_pfns[MAX_NR_ZONES];
        memset(max_zone_pfns, 0, sizeof(max_zone_pfns));
        max_zone_pfns[ZONE_DMA] = MAX_DMA_PFN;
        max_zone_pfns[ZONE_DMA32] = MAX_DMA32_PFN;
        max_zone_pfns[ZONE_NORMAL] = end_pfn;
...
        free_area_init_nodes(max_zone_pfns);
}
```

The page frame boundaries for the 16- and 32-bit DMA regions are stored in pre-processor symbols that translate the 16 MiB and 4 GiB ranges into page frames:

include/asm-x86/dms_64.h
```
/* 16MB ISA DMA zone */
#define MAX_DMA_PFN ((16*1024*1024) >> PAGE_SHIFT)

/* 4GB broken PCI/AGP hardware bus master zone */
#define MAX_DMA32_PFN ((4UL*1024*1024*1024) >> PAGE_SHIFT)
```

`end_pfn` is the largest page frame number detected. Since AMD64 does not require high memory, the corresponding entry in `max_zone_pfns` remains NULL.

Address Space Setup on AMD64

The address space setup on AMD64 systems is easier than for IA-32 in some respects, but unfortunately also harder in others. While having a 64-bit virtual address space allows for avoiding oddities like high memory, things are complicated by another factor: The address space spanned by 64 bits is so large that there are currently simply no applications that would require this. Current implementations therefore implement a smaller *physical address space* that is only 48 bits wide. This allows for simplifying and speeding up address translation without losing flexibility: 2^{48} bits still allows addressing 256 TiB, or $256 \times 1{,}024$ GiB — which is plenty even for Firefox!

While the physical address space is restricted to 48 bits, addressing the virtual address space is still performed with 64-bit pointers, and the space therefore has to span 64 bits formally. This raises a problem, though: Some parts of the virtual address space cannot be addressed because effectively only 48 bits can be handled.

Since future hardware implementations might support larger physical address spaces, it is not possible to simply to remap the subset that is not addressable to a different subset of the address space. Suppose that any program would rely on pointers into the unimplemented address space to be remapped to some part of the regular address space. Next-generation processors that implement more physical address bits would lead to a different behavior and thus break all existing code.

Clearly, accessing the unimplemented regions must be hindered by the processor. One possibility to enforce this would be to forbid use of all virtual addresses larger than the physical address space. This, however, is not the approach chosen by the hardware designers. Their solution is based on a *sign extension* approach, which is illustrated in Figure 3-18.

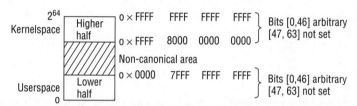

Figure 3-18: Possible virtual versus implemented physical address space on AMD64 machines.

The first 47 bits of a virtual address, that is, [0, 46], can be arbitrarily set. Bits in the range [47, 63], however, always need to have the same value: Either all are 0, or all are 1. Such addresses are called *canonical*. They divide the total address space into three parts: a lower half, a higher half, and a forbidden region in between. Together both portions form an address space that spans exactly 2^{48} bits. The address space for the lower half is [0x0, 0x0000 7FFF FFFF FFFF], while the subset for the top half is [0xFFF 800 0000 0000, 0xFFFF FFFF FFFF FFFF]. Notice that 0x0000 7FFF FFFF FFFF is a binary number with the lower 47 bits set to 1 and all other bits not set, so it is the last address before the non-addressable region. Similarly, 0xFFFF 8000 0000 0000 has the bits [48, 63] set and is thus the first valid address in the higher half.

Partitioning the virtual address space into two parts is nothing the kernel is afraid of: It actually relies on a separation of the address space into kernel and user parts on most architectures.[15] The separation enforced by the AMD64 therefore lends itself naturally to implement the separation between user and kernel address space. Figure 3-19 shows how the Linux kernel lays out the virtual address space on AMD64 machines.[16]

The complete lower half of the accessible address space is used as userspace, while the complete upper half is reserved for the kernel. Since both spaces are huge, no fiddling with splitting ratios and the like is required.

The kernel address space starts with a guard hole to prevent incidental access on the non-canonical portion of the address space that would result in a general protection exception raised by the processor. Physical pages are identity-mapped into kernel space starting from PAGE_OFFSET. 2^{46} bits (as specified by MAXMEM) are reserved for physical page frames. This amounts to 16 TiB of memory.

---

[15]There are also machines that allow a different approach. UltraSparc processors provide different virtual address spaces for user and kernel space per default, so a separation of one address space into two components is not required.

[16]The kernel sources contain some documentation about the address space layout in Documentation/x86_64/mm.txt.

include/asm-x86/pgtable_64.h
```
#define __AC(X,Y) (X##Y)
#define _AC(X,Y) __AC(X,Y)

#define __PAGE_OFFSET _AC(0xffff810000000000, UL)
#define PAGE_OFFSET __PAGE_OFFSET
#define MAXMEM _AC(0x3fffffffffff, UL)
```

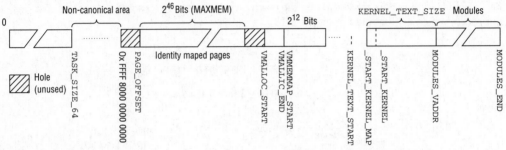

Figure 3-19: Organization of the virtual address space on AMD64 systems. The image is not drawn to scale, naturally.

Note that _AC is used to mark a given constant with a suffix. _AC(17,UL) becomes (17UL), for instance, which makes the constant an *unsigned long*. This can be handy in C code, but is not allowed in assembler code, where the _AC macro directly resolves to the given value without postfix.

Another guard hole is placed between the identity-mapped region and the area for vmalloc area, which lies between VMALLOC_START and VMALLOC_END:

include/asm-x86/pgtable_64.h
```
#define VMALLOC_START _AC(0xffffc20000000000, UL)
#define VMALLOC_END _AC(0xffffe1ffffffffff, UL)
```

The *virtual memory map* (VMM) area immediately behind the vmalloc area is 1 TiB in size. It is only useful on kernels that use the sparse memory model. Converting between virtual and physical page frame number via pfn_to_page and page_to_pfn can be costly on such machines because all holes in the physical address space must be taken into account. Starting with kernel 2.6.24, a simpler solution is offered by generic code in mm/sparse-memmap.c: The page tables for the VMM area are set up such that all struct page instances located in physical memory are mapped into the area *without* any holes. This provides a virtually contiguous area in which only the active memory regions are included. The MMU therefore automatically aids the translation between virtual and physical numbers that does not need to be concerned with holes anymore. This accelerates the operation considerably.

Besides simplifying the translation between physical and virtual page numbers, the technique also has benefits for the implementation of the auxiliary functions virt_to_page and page_address, because the required calculations are likewise simplified.

The kernel text is mapped into the region starting from __START_KERNEL_MAP, with a compile-time con-figurable offset given by CONFIG_PHYSICAL_START. Setting the offset is required for a relocatable kernel, but it is ensured that the resulting address __START_KERNEL is aligned with __KERNEL_ALIGN. The region reserved for the kernel binary is KERNEL_TEXT_SIZE, currently defined to 40 MiB.

include/asm-x86/page_64.h
```
#define __PHYSICAL_START        CONFIG_PHYSICAL_START
#define __KERNEL_ALIGN          0x200000

#define __START_KERNEL          (__START_KERNEL_map + __PHYSICAL_START)
#define __START_KERNEL_map      _AC(0xffffffff80000000, UL)
#define KERNEL_TEXT_SIZE        (40*1024*1024)
#define KERNEL_TEXT_START       _AC(0xffffffff80000000, UL)
```

Finally, some space to map modules into must be provided, and this is in the region from MODULES_VADDR to MODULES_END:

include/asm-x86/pgtable_64.h
```
#define MODULES_VADDR _AC(0xffffffff88000000, UL)
#define MODULES_END _AC(0xfffffffffff00000, UL)
#define MODULES_LEN (MODULES_END - MODULES_VADDR)
```

The available amount of memory is computed in MODULES_LEN; currently, this amounts to approximately 1,920 MiB.

3.4.3   Memory Management during the Boot Process

Although memory management is not yet initialized, the kernel needs to reserve memory during the boot process so that it can create various data structures. A *bootmem allocator* that assigns memory in the early boot phase is used to do this.

Obviously, what is required is a system that focuses on simplicity rather than on performance and universality. Kernel developers therefore decided to implement a *first-fit* allocator as the simplest conceivable way of managing memory in the boot phase.

A bitmap with (at least) as many bits as there are physical pages present in the system is used to manage pages. Bit value 1 indicates a used page and 0 a free page.

When memory needs to be reserved, the allocator scans the bitmap bit by bit until it finds a position big enough to hold a sufficient number of contiguous pages, literally the first-best or first-fit position.

This procedure is not very efficient because the bit chain must be scanned right from the start for each allocation. It cannot therefore be used for memory management once the kernel has been fully initialized. The buddy system (used in conjunction with the slab, slub, or slob allocator) is a far better alternative, as discussed in Section 3.5.5.

Data Structures

Even the first-fit allocator has to manage some data. The kernel provides an instance of the bootmem_data structure (for each node in the system) for this purpose. Of course, the memory needed for the structure *cannot* be reserved dynamically but must already be allocated to the kernel at compilation time.

Reservation is implemented in a CPU-independent way on UMA systems (NUMA systems employ architecture-specific solutions). The `bootmem_data` structure is defined as follows:

<bootmem.h>
```
typedef struct bootmem_data {
        unsigned long node_boot_start;
        unsigned long node_low_pfn;
        void *node_bootmem_map;
        unsigned long last_offset;
        unsigned long last_pos;
        unsigned long last_success;

        struct list_head list;
} bootmem_data_t;
```

When I use the term *page* below, I always mean a physical page frame.

❑　`node_boot_start` holds the number of the first page in the system; this is zero for most architectures.

❑　`node_low_pfn` is the number of the last page of the physical address space that can be managed directly; in other words, it is the end of `ZONE_NORMAL`.

❑　`node_bootmem_map` is a pointer to the memory area in which the allocation bitmap is stored. On IA-32 systems, the memory area immediately following the kernel image is used for this purpose. The corresponding address is held in the `_end` variable, which is automatically patched into the kernel image during linking.

❑　`last_pos` is the number of the page last allocated. `last_offset` is used as an offset within the page if not all of the page memory was requested. This enables the bootmem allocator to assign memory areas that are smaller than a complete page (the buddy system cannot do this).

❑　`last_success` specifies the point in the bitmap at which allocation was last successful and is used as the starting point for new reservations. Although this makes the first-fit algorithm a little faster, it is still no real substitute for more sophisticated techniques.

❑　Systems with discontinuous memory can require more than one bootmem allocator. This is typically the case on NUMA machines that register one bootmem allocator per node, but it would, for instance, also be possible to register one bootmem allocator for each continuous memory region on systems where the physical address space is interspersed with holes.

　　A new boot allocator is registered with `init_bootmem_core`, and the list of all registered allocators is headed by the global variable `bdata_list`.

On UMA systems, the single `bootmem_t` instance required is called `contig_bootmem_data`. It is associated with `contig_page_data` by means of the `bdata` element.

mm/page_alloc.c
```
static bootmem_data_t contig_bootmem_data;
struct pglist_data contig_page_data = { .bdata = &contig_bootmem_data };
```

Initialization

Initializing the bootmem allocator is an architecture specific process that additionally depends on the memory layout of the machine in question. As discussed above, IA-32 uses `setup_memory`, which calls `setup_bootmem_allocator` to initialize the bootmem allocator, whereas AMD64 uses `contig_initmem_init`.

The code flow diagram in Figure 3-20 illustrates the individual steps involved in the initialization of the bootmem allocator on IA-32 systems, and the corresponding diagram for AMD64 is shown in Figure 3-21.

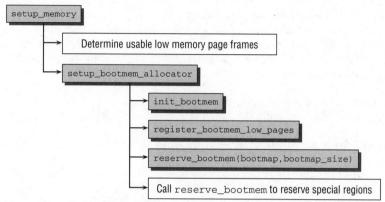

Figure 3-20: Initialization of the bootmem allocator on IA-32 machines.

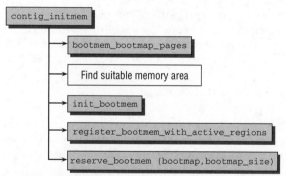

Figure 3-21: Initialization of the bootmem allocator on AMD64 machines.

Initialization for IA-32

`setup_memory` analyzes the detected memory regions to find the maximal page frame number in the low memory region; high memory is of no use for the bootmem allocator because it is too complicated to handle. The global variable `max_low_pfn` holds the number of the highest mappable page. The kernel reports the amount of memory found in its boot logs.

```
wolfgang@meitner> dmesg
...
0MB HIGHMEM available.
511MB LOWMEM available.
...
```

Based on this information, `setup_bootmem_allocator` is then responsible to initiate all necessary steps to initialize the bootmem allocator. It first invokes the generic function `init_bootmem`, which itself is a front end for `init_bootmem_core`.

The purpose of `init_bootmem_core` is to perform the first initialization step of the bootmem allocator. The previously detected range of low-memory page frames is entered in the responsible `bootmem_data_t` instance, in this case, `contig_bootmem_data`. All pages are initially marked as used in the bitmap `contig_bootmemdata->node_bootmem_map`. Because `init_bootmem_core` is an architecture-independent function, it cannot yet know which pages are available for use and which are not. Some need special handling for architectural reasons, for example, page 0 on IA-32 systems. Some are already used, for instance, by the kernel image. The pages that can actually be used must be explicitly marked by the architecture-dependent code.

This marking is done with two architecture-specific functions: `register_bootmem_low_pages` frees all potentially usable memory pages by setting the corresponding bits in the bitmap to 0 so that the pages are marked as unused. IA-32 systems are supported in this task by the BIOS, which provides the kernel with a list of all usable memory areas — the e820 map — at an earlier point during initialization.

Since the bootmem allocator requires some memory pages to manage the reservation bitmap, these must be reserved first by calling `reserve_bootmem`.

However, there are still more regions that are already in use and must be marked accordingly. For this purpose, `reserve_bootmem` registers the corresponding pages after the event. The exact number of regions that must be registered depends highly on the kernel configuration. It is, for instance, required to reserve the zeroth page because this page is a special BIOS page on many machines that is required for some machine-specific functions to work properly. Other `reserve_bootmem` calls reserve configuration-dependent memory areas, for ACPI data or SMP boot-time configurations, for instance.

Initialization for AMD64

While the technical details of bootmem initialization differ on AMD64, the general structure is rather similar to the IA-32 case. This time `contig_initmem` is the responsible dispatcher.

First of all, `bootmem_bootmap_bitmap` computes the number of pages required for the bootmem bitmap. Using the information provided by the BIOS in the e820 map, this allows — as on IA-32 — for finding a continuous memory region of suitable size that is populated with proper RAM pages.

This information is then filled into the architecture-independent bootmem data structure using `init_bootmem`. As before, the function marks all pages as reserved, and the free pages must now be selected. `free_bootmem_with_active_regions` can once more use the information in the e820 map to free all memory regions that were reported as usable by the BIOS. Finally, a single call to `reserve_bootmem` is sufficient to register the space required for the bootmem allocation bitmap. In contrast to IA-32, it is not required to reserve space for legacy information on magical places in memory.

Interface to the Kernel

Allocating Memory

The kernel provides a variety of functions for reserving memory during initialization. The following functions are available on UMA systems:

❑ `alloc_bootmem(size)` and `alloc_bootmem_pages(size)` reserve memory whose size is expressed by `size` in `ZONE_NORMAL`; data are aligned so that memory begins either at an ideal position for the L1 cache or on a page boundary.

> Even though the name **`alloc_bootmem_pages`** suggests that the required size is specified in page units, **`_pages`** refers only to the *alignment* of the data.

❑ `alloc_bootmem_low` and `alloc_bootmem_low_pages` operate in the same ways as the above functions but take the area `ZONE_DMA` that is suitable for DMA operations as their source. Consequently, the functions should only be used when DMA memory is required.

Basically the same API applies for NUMA systems, but the suffix `_node` is appended to the function name. As compared with the UMA functions, an additional parameter is required to specify which node is used for memory reservation.

These functions are all front ends for `__alloc_bootmem`, which delegates the real work to `__alloc_bootmem_nopanic`. Since more than one bootmem allocator can be registered (recall that they are all kept in a global list), `__alloc_bootmem_core` iterates over all of them until one succeeds.

On NUMA systems, `__alloc_bootmem_node` is used to implement the API functions. First, work is passed on to `__alloc_bootmem_core` to try the allocation on the specific bootmem allocator of the node. If this fails, the function falls back to `__alloc_bootmem`, which tries all nodes.

mm/bootmem.c
```
void * __init __alloc_bootmem(unsigned long size, unsigned long align,
                              unsigned long goal)
```

`__alloc_bootmem` requires three parameters to describe a request: `size` is the size of the desired memory area, `align` indicates the alignment of the data, and `goal` specifies the start address at which the search for a suitable free area is to begin. The front ends use the function as follows:

<bootmem.h>
```
#define alloc_bootmem(x) \
        __alloc_bootmem((x), SMP_CACHE_BYTES, __pa(MAX_DMA_ADDRESS))
#define alloc_bootmem_low(x) \
        __alloc_bootmem((x), SMP_CACHE_BYTES, 0)
#define alloc_bootmem_pages(x) \
        __alloc_bootmem((x), PAGE_SIZE, __pa(MAX_DMA_ADDRESS))
#define alloc_bootmem_low_pages(x) \
        __alloc_bootmem((x), PAGE_SIZE, 0)
```

The desired allocation size (x) is forwarded unchanged to __alloc_bootmem, but there are two options for alignment in memory: SMP_CACHE_BYTES aligns the data on most architectures so that they are ideally positioned in the L1 cache (despite its name the constant is, of course, also defined on uniprocessor systems). PAGE_SIZE aligns the data on the page boundaries. The latter alignment is ideal for allocating one or more complete pages, but the former produces better results when parts of pages are allocated.

The distinction between low and normal memory is made by means of the start address. Searches for DMA-suitable memory begins at the address 0, whereas requests for normal memory with RAM are processed from MAX_DMA_ADDRESS upward (__pa translates the memory address into a page number).

__alloc_bootmem_core is a relatively extensive function (efficiency is not required during booting) that I won't discuss in detail as the main thing it does is to implement the first-fit algorithm already described. However, the allocator has been enhanced to permit reservation not only of complete memory pages but also smaller parts thereof.

The function performs the following (outline) actions:

1. Starting at goal, the page bitmap is scanned for a free area to satisfy the allocation request.

2. If the page found immediately follows the last allocated page held in bootmem_data->last_pos, the kernel checks by reference to bootmem_data->last_offset whether the required memory (including the space needed to align the data) can be allocated in the last page or can at least start there.

3. The bits of the newly allocated pages in the block bitmap are set to 1. The number of the last page allocated is also stored in bootmem_data->last_pos. If the page is not fully allocated, the appropriate offset is held in bootmem_data->last_offset; otherwise, this value is set to 0.

Releasing Memory

The kernel provides the free_bootmem function to free memory. It requires two parameters — the start address and the size of the area to be freed. The name of the equivalent function on NUMA systems is not surprisingly free_bootmem_node; it expects an additional parameter to define the appropriate node.

```
<bootmem.h>
void free_bootmem(unsigned long addr, unsigned long size);
void free_bootmem_node(pg_data_t *pgdat,
                       unsigned long addr,
                       unsigned long size);
```

Both versions delegate their work to __free_bootmem_core. Only whole pages can be freed because the bootmem allocator does not keep any information about page divisions. The kernel uses __free_bootmem_core to first calculate the pages whose contents are *fully* held in the area to be freed. Pages whose contents are only held in part in this area are ignored. The corresponding entries in the page bitmap are set to 0 to conclude page freeing.

This procedure conceals the risk that a page is not freed if parts of its contents are returned in successive requests. If the first half of a page and at some time later the second half of the same page are freed, the allocator has no way of knowing that the entire page is no longer in use and can therefore be freed. The page simply remains "in use," although this is not the case. Nevertheless, this is not a big problem because free_bootmem is very rarely used. Most memory areas allocated during system initialization are intended for basic data structures that are needed throughout kernel run time and are therefore never relinquished.

Disabling the Bootmem Allocator

The bootmem allocator must be disabled once system initialization has progressed so far that the buddy system allocator can assume responsibility for memory management; after all, memory cannot be managed by two allocators at the same time. Disabling is done by `free_all_bootmem` on UMA systems and by `free_all_bootmem_node` on NUMA systems. Both need to be invoked by the architecture-specific initialization code after the buddy system has been set up.

The page bitmap of the bootmem allocator is first scanned, and every unused page is freed. The interface to the buddy system is the `__free_pages_bootmem` function that is invoked for each freed page. The function relies internally on the standard function `__free_page`. It enables the pages to be incorporated in the data structures of the buddy system, where they are managed as free pages and are available for allocation.

Once the page bitmap has been fully scanned, the memory space it occupies must also be removed. Thereafter, only the buddy system can be used for memory allocation.

Releasing Initialization Data

Many kernel code chunks and data tables are needed only during the system initialization phase. For example, it is not necessary to keep data structure initialization routines in kernel memory for permanently linked drivers. They are no longer needed once the structures have been set up. Similarly, hardware databases that drivers need to detect their devices are no longer required once the associated devices have been identified.[17]

The kernel provides two "attributes" (`__init` and `__initcall`) to label initialization functions and data. These must be placed before the function or data declarations. For instance, the probing routine of the (fictitious ...) network card HyperHopper2000 is no longer used once the system has been initialized.

```
int __init hyper_hopper_probe(struct net_device *dev)
```

The `__init` attribute is inserted between the return type and name in the function declaration.

Data sections can likewise be labeled as initialization data. For example, the fictitious network card driver requires a few strings in the system initialization phase only; thereafter the strings can be discarded.

```
static char search_msg[] __initdata = "%s: Desperately looking for HyperHopper at address %x...";
static char stilllooking_msg[] __initdata = "still searching...";
static char found_msg[] __initdata = "found.\n";
static char notfound_msg[] __initdata = "not found (reason = %d)\n";
static char couldnot_msg[] __initdata = "%s: HyperHopper not found\n";
```

`__init` and `__initdata` cannot be implemented using normal C means so that the kernel once again has to resort to special GNU C compiler statements. The general idea behind the implementation of

---

[17]At least for compiled-in data and devices that are not hotpluggable. If devices are added to the system dynamically, the data tables cannot, of course, be discarded as they may be required later.

initialization functions is to keep the data in a specific part of the kernel image that can be completely removed from memory when booting has finished. The following macros are defined with this in mind:

<init.h>
```
#define __init      __attribute__ ((__section__ (".init.text"))) __cold
#define __initdata  __attribute__ ((__section__ (".init.data")))
```

__attribute__ is a special GNU C keyword to permit the use of attributes. The __section__ attribute is used to instruct the compiler to write the subsequent data or function into the respective .init.data and .init.text sections of the binary file (those of you unfamiliar with the structure of ELF files are referred to Appendix E). The prefix __cold also instructs the compiler that paths leading to the function will be unlikely, that is, that the function won't be called very often, which is usually the case for initialization functions.

The readelf tool can be used to display the individual sections of the kernel image.

```
wolfgang@meitner> readelf - sections vmlinux
There are 53 section headers, starting at offset 0x2c304c8:

Section Headers:
  [Nr] Name              Type            Address           Offset
       Size              EntSize         Flags  Link  Info  Align
  [ 0]                   NULL            0000000000000000  00000000
       0000000000000000  0000000000000000         0     0     0
  [ 1] .text             PROGBITS        ffffffff80200000  00200000
       000000000021fc6f  0000000000000000  AX     0     0     4096
  [ 2] __ex_table        PROGBITS        ffffffff8041fc70  0041fc70
       0000000000003e50  0000000000000000  A      0     0     8
  [ 3] .notes            NOTE            ffffffff80423ac0  00423ac0
       0000000000000024  0000000000000000  AX     0     0     4
  ...
  [28] .init.text        PROGBITS        ffffffff8067b000  0087b000
       000000000002026e  0000000000000000  AX     0     0     1
  [29] .init.data        PROGBITS        ffffffff8069b270  0089b270
       000000000000c02e  0000000000000000  WA     0     0     16
  ...
```

To release initialization data from memory, it is not necessary for the kernel to know the nature of the data — which data and functions are held in memory and what purpose they serve is totally irrelevant. The only information of relevance is the addresses in memory at which the data and functions begin and end.

Because this information is not available at compilation time, it is patched in when the kernel is linked. I have already mentioned this technique at other places in this chapter. To support it, the kernel defines the variable pair __init_begin and __init_end, whose names reveal their meanings.

free_initmem is responsible for freeing the memory area defined for initialization purposes and returning the pages to the buddy system. The function is called right at the end of the boot process immediately before init starts the first process in the system. The boot logs include a message indicating how much memory was freed.

```
wolfgang@meitner> dmesg
...
Freeing unused kernel memory: 308k freed
...
```

In comparison with today's typical main memory sizes, the approximately 300 KiB freed are not gigantic but are a significant contribution. The removal of initialization data is important, particularly on hand-held or embedded systems, which, by their very nature, make do with little memory.

3.5 Management of Physical Memory

Responsibility for memory management is assumed by the buddy system once kernel initialization has been completed. The buddy system is based on a relatively simple but nevertheless surprisingly powerful algorithm that has been with us for almost 40 years. It combines two key characteristics of a good memory allocator — speed and efficiency.

3.5.1 Structure of the Buddy System

An instance of `struct page` is available for each physical page of memory (a page frame) in the system. Each memory zone is associated with an instance of `struct zone` that holds the central array for managing buddy data.

```
<mmzone.h>
struct zone {
...
        /*
         * free areas of different sizes
         */
        struct free_area        free_area[MAX_ORDER];
...
};
```

free_area is an auxiliary data structure we have not yet met. It is defined as follows:

```
<mmzone.h>
struct free_area {
        struct list_head free_list[MIGRATE_TYPES];
        unsigned long nr_free;
};
```

nr_free specifies the number of free page blocks in the current area (counting is page by page for the zeroth area, by two-page pairs for order 1, by sets of four pages for order 2, etc.). free_list is used to link page lists. As discussed in Chapter 1, the page lists contain contiguous memory areas of the same size. While the definition provides more than one page list, I ignore this fact for a moment and come back to why there are different lists below.

The *order* is a very important term in buddy systems. It describes the quantified units in which memory can be allocated. The size of a memory block is 2^{order}, where order may extend from 0 to MAX_ORDER.

<mmzone.h>
```
#ifndef CONFIG_FORCE_MAX_ZONEORDER
#define MAX_ORDER 11
#else
#define MAX_ORDER CONFIG_FORCE_MAX_ZONEORDER
#endif
#define MAX_ORDER_NR_PAGES (1 << (MAX_ORDER - 1))
```

The typical value of this constant is 11, which means that the maximum number of pages that can be requested in a single allocation is $2^{11} = 2,048$. However, this value can be changed manually if the FORCE_MAX_ZONEORDER configuration option is set by the architecture-specific code. For example, the gigantic address spaces on IA-64 systems allow for working with MAX_ORDER = 18, whereas ARM or v850 systems use smaller values such as 8 or 9. This, however, is not necessarily caused by little memory supported by the machine, but can also be because of memory alignment requirements. Or, as the Kconfig configuration file for the V850 architecture puts it:

arch/v850/Kconfig
```
# The crappy-ass zone allocator requires that the start of allocatable
# memory be aligned to the largest possible allocation.
config FORCE_MAX_ZONEORDER
        int
        default 8 if V850E2_SIM85E2C || V850E2_FPGA85E2C
```

The indices of the individual elements of the free_area[] array are also interpreted as order parameters and specify how many pages are present in the contiguous areas on a shared list. The zeroth array element lists sections with one page ($2^0 = 1$), the first lists page pairs ($2^1 = 2$), the third manages sets of 4 pages, and so on.

How are the page areas linked? The list element of the *first* page in the block is used to keep the blocks in a list. As a result, there is no need to introduce a new data structure to group pages that are physically contiguous — otherwise, they wouldn't be in a block. Figure 3-22 illustrates the situation graphically.

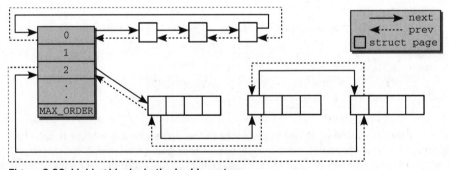

Figure 3-22: Linking blocks in the buddy system.

The buddies *need not* be linked with each other. If a block is broken down into two blocks of half the size during allocation, the kernel automatically adds the unused half to the list of next smaller blocks. If, at some point in the future, both blocks are not in use after memory has been freed, their addresses can be referenced to automatically determine whether they are buddies. This minimal administrative effort is a major advantage of the buddy system.

Memory management based on the buddy system is concentrated on a single memory zone of a node, for instance, the DMA or high-memory zone. However, the buddy systems of all zones and nodes are linked via the allocation fallback list. Figure 3-23 illustrates this relationship.

When a request for memory cannot be satisfied in the preferred zone or node, first another zone in the same node, and then another node is picked to fulfill the request.

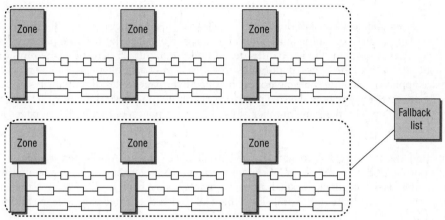

Figure 3-23: Relationship between buddy system and memory zones/nodes.

Finally, note that information about the current state of the buddy system is available in /proc/buddyinfo:

```
wolfgang@meitner> cat /proc/buddyinfo
Node 0, zone      DMA      3      5      7      4      6      3      3      3      1      1      1
Node 0, zone    DMA32    130    546    695    271    107     38      2      2      1      4    479
Node 0, zone   Normal     23      6      6      8      1      4      3      0      0      0      0
```

The number of free entries per allocation order is printed for each zone, and the order increases from left to right. The information shown above is taken from an AMD64 system with 4 GiB of RAM.

3.5.2 Avoiding Fragmentation

In the simplified explanation given in the Introduction, one doubly linked list was sufficient to satisfy all the needs of the buddy system. This has, indeed, been the situation until kernel 2.6.23. During the development of the kernel 2.6.24, the buddy system has, however, seen the integration of patches disputed among the kernel developers for an unusually long amount of time. Since the buddy system is one of the most venerable components of the kernel, changes are not accepted lightly.

Grouping Pages by Mobility

The basic principle of the buddy system has been discussed in the Introduction, and the scheme has, indeed, worked very well during the last couple of years. However, there is one issue that has been a long-standing problem with Linux memory management: After systems have been up and running for longer times, physical memory tends to become fragmented. The situation is depicted in Figure 3-24.

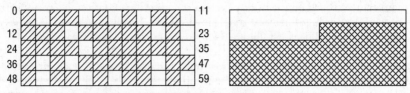

Figure 3-24: Fragmentation of physical memory.

Assume that the memory consists of 60 pages — clearly, this is not going to be the key component to the next supercomputer, but is fair enough for the sake of example. The free pages are scattered across the address space on the left-hand side. Although roughly 25 percent of the physical memory is still unallocated, the largest continuous free area is only a single page. This is no problem for userspace applications: Since their memory is mapped over page tables, it will always appear continuous to them irrespective of how the free pages are distributed in physical memory. The right-hand side shows the situation with the same number of used and free pages, but with all free pages located in a continuous area.

Fragmentation is, however, a problem for the kernel: Since (most) RAM is identity-mapped into the kernel's portion of the address space, it cannot map an area larger than a single page in this scenario. While many kernel allocations are small, there is sometimes the need to allocate more than a single page. Clearly, the situation on the right-hand side, where all reserved and free pages are in continuous regions, would be preferable.

Interestingly, problems with fragmentation can already occur when most of the memory is still unallocated. Consider the situation in Figure 3-25. Only 4 pages are reserved, but the largest contiguous area that can be allocated is 8 pages because the buddy system can only work that allocation ranges that are powers of 2.

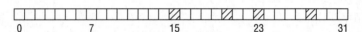

Figure 3-25: Memory fragmentation where few reserved pages prevent the allocation of larger contiguous blocks.

I have mentioned that memory fragmentation only concerns the kernel, but this is only partially true: Most modern CPUs provide the possibility to work with huge pages whose page size is much bigger than for regular pages. This has benefits for memory-intensive applications. When bigger pages are used, the translation lookaside buffer has to handle fewer entries, and the chance of a TLB cache miss is reduced. Allocating huge pages, however, requires free contiguous areas of physical RAM!

Fragmentation of physical memory has, indeed, belonged to the weaker points of Linux for an unusually long time span. Although many approaches have been suggested, none could satisfy the demanding needs of the numerous workloads that Linux has to face without having too great an impact on others. During the development of kernel 2.6.24, means to prevent fragmentation finally found their way into the kernel. Before I discuss their strategy, one point calls for clarification: Fragmentation is also known from filesystems, and in this area the problem is typically solved by defragmentation tools: They analyze the filesystem and rearrange the allocated blocks such that larger continuous areas arise. This approach would also be possible for RAM, in principle, but is complicated by the fact that many physical pages cannot be moved to an arbitrary location. Therefore, the kernel's approach is *anti-fragmentation*: Try to prevent fragmentation as well as possible from the very beginning.

How does anti-fragmentation work? To understand the approach, we must be aware that the kernel distinguishes three different types of reserved pages:

❑ *Non-movable pages* have a fixed position in memory and cannot be moved anywhere else. Most allocations of the core kernel fall into this category.

❑ *Reclaimable pages* cannot be moved directly, but they can be deleted and their contents regenerated from some source. Data mapped from files fall into this category, for instance.

Reclaimable pages are periodically freed by the kswapd daemon depending on how often they are accessed. This is a complicated process that merits a detailed discussion of its own: Chapter 18 that describes page reclaim in detail. In the meanwhile, it suffices to know that the kernel will take care of removing reclaimable pages when they start to use up too much RAM.

It is also possible to initiate page reclaim when there is an acute shortage of memory, that is, when an allocation has failed. You will see further below when the kernel deems it necessary to do so.

❑ *Movable pages* can be moved around as desired. Pages that belong to userspace applications fall into this category. They are mapped via page tables. If they are copied into a new location, the page table entries can be updated accordingly, and the application won't notice anything.

A page has a certain *mobility* depending into which of the three categories it falls. The anti-fragmentation technique used by the kernel is based on the idea of grouping pages with identical mobility together. Why does this approach help to reduce fragmentation? Recall from Figure 3-25 that a page that cannot be moved somewhere else can prevent continuous allocations in an otherwise nearly completely empty RAM area. By distributing pages onto different lists depending on their mobility, this situation is prevented. For instance, a non-movable page cannot be located in the middle of a block of movable pages and effectively prevent any larger part of the block from being used.

Imagine that most of the free pages in Figure 3-25 belong to the reclaimable category, while the reserved pages are non-movable. If the pages had been collected on two different lists, the situation might, however, look as shown in Figure 3-26. It is still hard to find a large continuous free space for non-movable pages, but much easier for reclaimable pages.

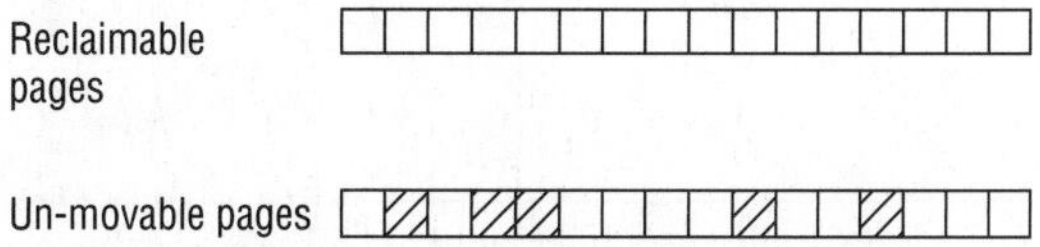

Figure 3-26: Memory fragmentation is reduced by grouping pages together depending on their mobility.

Note, however, that the memory is not partitioned into different mobility regions from the very beginning. They will be populated at run time. A second approach of the kernel *does* partition the memory into regions for movable and non-movable allocations, and I will discuss how this works below. Such a partitioning, however, is not essential for the approach described here.

Data Structure

Although the anti-fragmentation technique used by the kernel is highly effective, it has astonishingly little impact on code and data structures of the buddy allocator. The kernel defines some macros to represent the different migrate types:

```
<mmzone.h>
#define MIGRATE_UNMOVABLE 0
#define MIGRATE_RECLAIMABLE 1
#define MIGRATE_MOVABLE 2
#define MIGRATE_RESERVE 3
#define MIGRATE_ISOLATE 4 /* can't allocate from here */
#define MIGRATE_TYPES 5
```

The types `MIGRATE_UNMOVABLE`, `MIGRATE_RECLAIMABLE`, and `MIGRATE_MOVABLE` have already been introduced. `MIGRATE_RESERVE` provides an emergency memory reserve if an allocation request cannot be fulfilled from the mobility-specific lists (it is filled during initialization of the memory subsystem with `setup_zone_migrate_reserve`, but I will not go into detail about this). `MIGRATE_ISOLATE` is a special virtual zone that is required to move physical pages across NUMA nodes. On large systems, it can be beneficial to bring physical pages closer to the CPUs that use them most. `MIGRATE_TYPES`, finally, is also not a zone, but just denotes the number of migrate types.

The core adjustment to the buddy system data structures is that the free list is broken into a `MIGRATE_TYPE` number of lists:

```
<mmzone.h>
struct free_area {
        struct list_head free_list[MIGRATE_TYPES];
        unsigned long nr_free;
};
```

`nr_free` counts the number of free pages on *all* lists, but a specific free list is provided for each migrate type. The macro `for_each_migratetype_order(order, type)` can be used to iterate over the migrate types of all allocation orders.

What happens if the kernel cannot fulfill an allocation request for a given migrate type? A similar problem has already occurred before, namely, when we considered what happens when an allocation cannot be fulfilled from a specific NUMA zone. The kernel proceeds similarly as in this case by providing a fallback list regulating which migrate types should be used next if a request cannot be fulfilled from the desired list:

mm/page_alloc.c
```
/*
 * This array describes the order lists are fallen back to when
 * the free lists for the desirable migrate type are depleted
 */
static int fallbacks[MIGRATE_TYPES][MIGRATE_TYPES-1] = {
        [MIGRATE_UNMOVABLE]   = { MIGRATE_RECLAIMABLE, MIGRATE_MOVABLE, MIGRATE_RESERVE },
        [MIGRATE_RECLAIMABLE] = { MIGRATE_UNMOVABLE, MIGRATE_MOVABLE, MIGRATE_RESERVE },
        [MIGRATE_MOVABLE]     = { MIGRATE_RECLAIMABLE, MIGRATE_UNMOVABLE, MIGRATE_RESERVE },
        [MIGRATE_RESERVE]     = { MIGRATE_RESERVE, MIGRATE_RESERVE, MIGRATE_RESERVE },
                                /* Never used */
};
```

The data structure is mostly self-explanatory: When the kernel wants to allocate un-movable pages, but the corresponding list is empty, then it falls back to reclaimable pages, then to movable pages, and finally to the emergency reserve.

Global Variables and Auxiliary Functions

While page mobility grouping is always compiled into the kernel, it only makes sense if enough memory that can be distributed across multiple migrate lists is present in a system. Since on each migrate list a suitable amount of memory should be present, the kernel needs a notion of "suitable." This is provided by the two global variables `pageblock_order` and `pageblock_nr_pages`. The first denotes an allocation order that is considered to be "large," and `pageblock_nr_pages` denotes the corresponding number of pages for this allocation order. Usually the the page order is selected to be the order of huge pages if such are provided by the architecture:

```
<pageblock-flags.h>
#define pageblock_order HUGETLB_PAGE_ORDER
```

On the IA-32 architecture, huge pages are 4 MiB in size, so each huge page consists of 1,024 regular pages and `HUGETLB_PAGE_ORDER` is defined to be 10. The IA-64 architecture, in contrast, allows varying regular and huge page sizes, so the value of `HUGETLB_PAGE_ORDER` depends on the kernel configuration.

If an architecture does not support huge pages, then the second highest allocation order is taken as a large order:

```
<pageblock-flags.h>
#define pageblock_order (MAX_ORDER-1)
```

Page migration will not provide any benefits if each migrate type cannot at least be equipped with one large page block, so the feature is turned off by the kernel if too little memory is available. This is checked in the function `build_all_zonelists`, which is used to initialize the zone lists. If not enough memory is available, the global variable `page_group_by_mobility` is set to 0, otherwise to 1.[18]

How does the kernel know to which migrate type a given allocation belongs? As you will see in Section 3.5.4, details about each memory allocation are specified by an *allocation mask*. The kernel provides two flags that signal that the allocated memory will be movable (`__GFP_MOVABLE`) or reclaimable (`__GFP_RECLAIMABLE`). If none of these flags is specified, the allocation is assumed to be non-movable. The following auxiliary function converts between allocation flags and their corresponding migrate types:

```
<gfp.h>
static inline int allocflags_to_migratetype(gfp_t gfp_flags)
{
        if (unlikely(page_group_by_mobility_disabled))
                return MIGRATE_UNMOVABLE;

        /* Group based on mobility */
        return (((gfp_flags & __GFP_MOVABLE) != 0) << 1) |
                ((gfp_flags & __GFP_RECLAIMABLE) != 0);
}
```

---

[18]Note that systems not only with little memory but also with extremely large page sizes can be affected by this since the check is performed on a pages-per-list basis.

If page mobility has been disabled, all pages will be kept in the unmovable zone. Otherwise, the return value of the function can be directly used as an array index in `free_area.free_list`.

Finally, note that each memory zone provides a special field that allows for tracking properties of page blocks with `pageblock_nr_pages` pages. Since this is currently only used by the page mobility code, I have not introduced this feature before:

```
<mmzone.h>
struct zone {
...
        unsigned long *pageblock_flags;
...
}
```

During initialization, the kernel automatically ensures that for each page block group in the zone, sufficient space is available in `pageblock_flags` to store `NR_PAGEBLOCK_BITS` bits. Currently, 3 bits are required to denote the migrate type of the page range:

```
<pageblock-flags.h>
/* Macro to aid the definition of ranges of bits */
#define PB_range(name, required_bits) \
        name, name ## _end = (name + required_bits) - 1

/* Bit indices that affect a whole block of pages */
enum pageblock_bits {
        PB_range(PB_migrate, 3), /* 3 bits required for migrate types */
        NR_PAGEBLOCK_BITS
};
```

`set_pageblock_migratetype` is responsible to set the migrate type for a page block headed by `page`:

```
mm/page_alloc.c
void set_pageblock_migratetype(struct page *page, int migratetype)
```

The `migratetype` argument can be constructed by the auxiliary function `allocflags_to_migratetype` introduced above. Notice that it is essential that the migrate type of a page is always preserved and not just available when the page is located in the buddy system. When memory is released, the pages must be put back to the proper migrate list, and this is only possible because the required information can be obtained with `get_pageblock_migratetype`.

Finally, notice that the current state of page distribution across the migrate lists can be found in `/proc/pagetypeinfo`:

```
wolfgang@meitner> cat /proc/pagetypeinfo
Page block order: 9
Pages per block:  512
```

```
Free pages count per migrate type at order      0    1    2    3    4    5    6    7    8    9   10
Node    0, zone      DMA, type    Unmovable      0    0    1    1    1    1    1    1    1    1    0
Node    0, zone      DMA, type  Reclaimable      0    0    0    0    0    0    0    0    0    0    0
Node    0, zone      DMA, type      Movable      3    5    6    3    5    2    2    2    0    0    0
Node    0, zone      DMA, type      Reserve      0    0    0    0    0    0    0    0    0    0    1
Node    0, zone      DMA, type       <NULL>      0    0    0    0    0    0    0    0    0    0    0
Node    0, zone    DMA32, type    Unmovable     44   37   29    1    2    0    1    1    0    1    0
Node    0, zone    DMA32, type  Reclaimable     18   29    3    4    1    0    0    0    1    1    0
Node    0, zone    DMA32, type      Movable      0    0  191  111   68   26   21   13    7    1  500
Node    0, zone    DMA32, type      Reserve      0    0    0    0    0    0    0    0    0    1    2
Node    0, zone    DMA32, type       <NULL>      0    0    0    0    0    0    0    0    0    0    0
Node    0, zone   Normal, type    Unmovable      1    5    1    0    0    0    0    0    0    0    0
Node    0, zone   Normal, type  Reclaimable      0    0    0    0    0    0    0    0    0    0    0
Node    0, zone   Normal, type      Movable      1    4    0    0    0    0    0    0    0    0    0
Node    0, zone   Normal, type      Reserve     11   13    7    8    3    4    2    0    0    0    0
Node    0, zone   Normal, type       <NULL>      0    0    0    0    0    0    0    0    0    0    0

Number of blocks type     Unmovable   Reclaimable      Movable       Reserve         <NULL>
Node 0, zone       DMA            1             0            6             1              0
Node 0, zone     DMA32           13            18         2005             4              0
Node 0, zone    Normal           22            10          351             1              0
```

Initializing Mobility-Based Grouping

During the initialization of the memory subsystem, `memmap_init_zone` is responsible to handle the `page` instances of a memory zone. The function does some standard initializations that are not too interesting, but one thing is essential: All pages are initially marked to be movable!

mm/page_alloc.c
```c
void __meminit memmap_init_zone(unsigned long size, int nid, unsigned long zone,
unsigned long start_pfn, enum memmap_context context)
{
        struct page *page;
        unsigned long end_pfn = start_pfn + size;
        unsigned long pfn;

        for (pfn = start_pfn; pfn < end_pfn; pfn++) {
...
                if ((pfn & (pageblock_nr_pages-1)))
                        set_pageblock_migratetype(page, MIGRATE_MOVABLE);
...
        }
```

As discussed in Section 3.5.4, the kernel favors large page groups when pages must be "stolen" from different migrate zones from those the allocation is intended for. Because all pages initially belong to the movable zone, stealing pages is required when regular, unmovable kernel allocations are performed.

Naturally, not too many movable allocations will have been performed during boot, so chances are good that the allocator can pick maximally sized blocks and transfer them from the movable to the non-movable list. Because the blocks have maximal size, no fragmentation is introduced into the movable zone!

All in all, this avoids situations in which kernel allocations that are done during boot (and which often last for the whole system uptime) are spread across the physical RAM such that other allocation types are fragmented — one of the most important goals of the page mobility grouping framework.

The Virtual Movable Zone

Grouping pages by mobility order is one possible method to prevent fragmentation of physical memory, but the kernel additionally provides another means to fight this problem: the virtual zone ZONE_MOVABLE. The mechanism has even found its way into the kernel during the development of kernel 2.6.23, one release before the mobility grouping framework was merged. In contrast to mobility grouping, the ZONE_MOVABLE feature must be explicitly activated by the administrator.

The basic idea is simple: The available physical memory is partitioned into one zone used for movable allocations, and one zone used for non-movable allocations. This will automatically prevent any non-movable pages from introducing fragmentation into the movable zone.

This immediately raises the question of how the kernel is supposed to decide how the available memory will be distributed between the two competitors. Clearly, this asks too much of the poor kernel, so the system administrator has to make the decision. After all, a human can predict much better which scenarios the machine will handle and what the expected distribution of allocations into the various types will be.

Data Structures

The kernelcore parameter allows for specifying the amount of memory used for non-movable allocations, that is, for allocations that can neither be reclaimed nor migrated. The remaining memory is used for movable allocations. After parsing the parameter, the result is stored in the global variable required_kernelcore.

It is also possible to use the parameter movablecore to control the amount of memory that is used for movable memory. The size of required_kernelcore will be computed accordingly. If wise guys specify both parameters simultaneously, the kernel computes required_kernelcore as before, and takes the larger one of the computed and specified value.

Depending on the architecture and the kernel configuration, the new zone ZONE_MOVABLE is located above the high-memory or regular-memory zone:

```
<mmzone.h>
enum zone_type {
...
        ZONE_NORMAL
#ifdef CONFIG_HIGHMEM
        ZONE_HIGHMEM,
```

```
#endif
        ZONE_MOVABLE,
        MAX_NR_ZONES
};
```

In contrast to all other zones in the system, ZONE_MOVABLE is not associated with any memory range that is of significance to the hardware. Indeed, the zone is filled with memory taken from either the highmem or the regular zone, and accordingly we call ZONE_MOVABLE a virtual zone in the following.

The auxiliary function find_zone_movable_pfns_for_nodes is used to compute the amount of memory that goes into ZONE_MOVABLE. If neither the kernelcore nor movablecore parameter was specified, find_zone_movable_pfns_for_nodes leaves ZONE_MOVABLE empty, and the mechanism is not active.

Two things must be considered with respect to how many pages are taken from a physical zone and used for ZONE_MOVABLE:

❑   The memory for non-movable allocations is spread evenly across all memory nodes.

❑   Only memory from the highest zone is used. On 32-bit systems with much memory, this will usually be ZONE_HIGHMEM, but for 64-bit systems, ZONE_NORMAL or ZONE_DMA32 will be used.

The actual computation is rather lengthy, but not very interesting, so I do not consider it in detail. What matters are the results:

❑   The physical zone from which pages for the virtual zone ZONE_MOVABLE are taken is stored in the global variable movable_zone.

❑   For each node, the page frame in the movable zone from which onward the memory belongs to ZONE_MOVABLE is in zone_movable_pfn[node_id].

mm/page_alloc.c
```
unsigned long __meminitdata zone_movable_pfn[MAX_NUMNODES];
```

The kernel ensures that these pages will be used to satisfy allocations that fall into the responsibility of ZONE_MOVABLE.

Implementation

How are the data structures described so far brought to use? As with the page migration approach, allocation flags play a crucial role. They are discussed below in Section 3.5.4 in more detail. Here, it suffices to say that all movable allocations must specify both __GFP_HIGHMEM *and* __GFP_MOVABLE.

Since the kernel determines the zone from which an allocation is fulfilled by the allocation flags, it can select ZONE_MOVABLE when the said flags are set. This is the only change required to integrate ZONE_MOVABLE into the buddy system! The rest is done by generic routines that work on all zones, discussed below.

3.5.3 Initializing the Zone and Node Data Structures

Until now, we have only seen how the kernel detects the available memory in the system in the architecture-specific code. The association with higher-level structures — zones and nodes — needs to be constructed from this information. Recall that architectures are required to established the following information during boot:

❏ The page frame boundaries of the various zones in the system as stored in the max_zone_pfn array.

❏ The distribution of page frames across nodes as stored in the global variable early_node_map.

Managing Data Structure Creation

Starting with kernel 2.6.10, a generic framework was provided to transfer this information into the node and zone data structures expected by the buddy system; before this, each architecture had to set up the structures on its own. Today, it suffices to set up the aforementioned simple structures and leave the hard work to free_area_init_nodes. Figure 3-27 shows an overview of the process, and Figure 3-28 shows the code flow diagram for free_area_init_nodes.

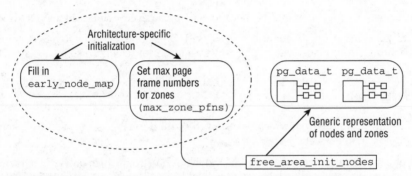

Figure 3-27: Overview of the interplay between architecture-specific and generic kernel code for setting up node and zone data memory management data structures.

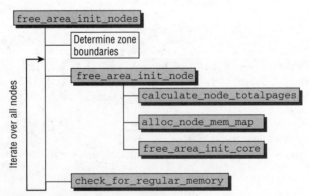

Figure 3-28: Code flow diagram for free_area_init_nodes.

`free_area_init_nodes` first has to analyze and rewrite the information provided by the architecture-specific code. Among others, the numbers of the lowest and highest page frames that can be *used* — in contrast to the principal boundaries specified in `zone_max_pfn` and `zone_min_pfn` — need to be obtained for each zone. Two global arrays are used to store the information:

mm/page_alloc.c
```
static unsigned long __meminitdata arch_zone_lowest_possible_pfn[MAX_NR_ZONES];
static unsigned long __meminitdata arch_zone_highest_possible_pfn[MAX_NR_ZONES]
```

First of all, however, `free_area_init_nodes` sorts the entries in `early_node_map` by their first page frame `start_pfn`.

mm/page_alloc.c
```
void __init free_area_init_nodes(unsigned long *max_zone_pfn)
{
        unsigned long nid;
        enum zone_type i;

        /* Sort early_node_map as initialisation assumes it is sorted */
        sort_node_map();
    ...
```

Sorting the entries makes life easier for the following tasks, but is not particularly complicated, so it is not required to inspect `sort_node_map` further. Just note that the kernel provides a generic heap sort implementation in `lib/sort.c` that is employed by the function.

The information passed to `free_area_init_nodes` in `max_zone_pfn` records the maximal page frame numbers that can be contained in each zone. `free_area_init_nodes` prepares a more convenient representation of this information by providing page frame intervals of the form [low, high] for each zone in the aforementioned global variables (I omit initialization of these variables with zero bytes):

mm/page_alloc.c
```
        arch_zone_lowest_possible_pfn[0] = find_min_pfn_with_active_regions();
        arch_zone_highest_possible_pfn[0] = max_zone_pfn[0];

        for (i = 1; i < MAX_NR_ZONES; i++) {
                if (i == ZONE_MOVABLE)
                        continue;
                arch_zone_lowest_possible_pfn[i] =
                        arch_zone_highest_possible_pfn[i-1];
                arch_zone_highest_possible_pfn[i] =
                        max(max_zone_pfn[i], arch_zone_lowest_possible_pfn[i]);
        }
```

The auxiliary function `find_min_pfn_with_active_regions` is used to find the smallest registered usable page frame for the lowest registered zone. This need not necessarily be ZONE_DMA, but can, for instance, also be ZONE_NORMAL if the machine does not require DMA memory. The maximum page frame for the smallest zone can be directly taken from the information provided by `max_zone_pfn`.

The intervals for the other zones are then constructed in a straightforward manner: The *smallest* page frame for the *n*-th zone is the *largest* page frame of the previous (*n* − 1) zone. The largest page frames for the current zone are already available in max_zone_pfn.

mm/page_alloc.c
```
        arch_zone_lowest_possible_pfn[ZONE_MOVABLE] = 0;
        arch_zone_highest_possible_pfn[ZONE_MOVABLE] = 0;

        /* Find the PFNs that ZONE_MOVABLE begins at in each node */
...
        find_zone_movable_pfns_for_nodes(zone_movable_pfn);
```

Since ZONE_MOVABLE is a virtual zone and not associated with real hardware zones, the zone boundaries are always set to zero. Recall from above that it only exists if any of the kernel command-line parameter kernelcore or movablecore was specified. The movable zone for each node starts above a certain page frame number of a specific zone for each node. The corresponding numbers are computed in find_zone_movable_pfns_for_nodes.

Some information about the determined page frame intervals is proudly presented to the user. This includes, for instance, the following (the output is taken on an AMD64 system with 4 GiB of RAM):

```
root@meitner # dmesg
...
Zone PFN ranges:
  DMA             0 ->     4096
  DMA32        4096 ->  1048576
  Normal    1048576 ->  1245184
...
```

The remaining portion of free_area_init_nodes iterates over all nodes to set up the data structures for each.

mm/page_alloc.c
```
        /* Print information about zones */
...
        /* Initialise every node */
        for_each_online_node(nid) {
                pg_data_t *pgdat = NODE_DATA(nid);
                free_area_init_node(nid, pgdat, NULL,
                                find_min_pfn_for_node(nid), NULL);

                /* Any memory on that node */
                if (pgdat->node_present_pages)
                        node_set_state(nid, N_HIGH_MEMORY);
                check_for_regular_memory(pgdat);
        }
}
```

The code iterates over all active nodes and delegates setting up the data structures for each to free_area_init_node. The function requires the first available page frame as a parameter, and find_min_pfn_for_node extracts this information from the early_node_map array.

If the node is equipped with memory as indicated by the `node_present_pages` field, this is reflected in the node bitmap by setting the `N_HIGH_MEMORY` flag. Recall from Section 3.2.2 that the flag — despite its name — only signals that *either* regular *or* high memory is present on the node, so `check_for_regular_memory` checks if pages in any zone below `ZONE_HIGHMEM` are present and sets the flag `N_NORMAL_MEMORY` in the node bitmap accordingly.

Creating Data Structures for Each Node

Once the zone boundaries have been determined, `free_area_init_nodes` creates the data structures for the individual zones iteratively by calling `free_area_init_node`. Several helper functions are required for this purpose.

`calculate_node_totalpages` first calculates the total number of pages in the node by summing up the pages in the individual zones. In the case of contiguous memory, this could be done in `zones_size_init`, but `calculate_zone_totalpages` also takes holes in the zone into account. The number of pages found for each node is output in a short message when the system is booted. The example below is taken from a UMA system with 512 MiB of RAM.

```
wolfgang@meitner> dmesg
...
On node 0 totalpages: 131056
...
```

`alloc_node_mem_map` is responsible for initializing a simple but nevertheless very important data structure. As noted above, there is an instance of `struct page` for every physical memory page in the system. Initialization of this structure is performed by `alloc_node_mem_map`.

mm/page_alloc.c
```
static void __init_refok alloc_node_mem_map(struct pglist_data *pgdat)
{
        /* Skip empty nodes */
        if (!pgdat->node_spanned_pages)
                return;

        if (!pgdat->node_mem_map) {
                unsigned long size, start, end;
                struct page *map;

                start = pgdat->node_start_pfn & ~(MAX_ORDER_NR_PAGES - 1);
                end = pgdat->node_start_pfn + pgdat->node_spanned_pages;
                end = ALIGN(end, MAX_ORDER_NR_PAGES);
                size = (end - start) * sizeof(struct page);
                map = alloc_remap(pgdat->node_id, size);
                if (!map)
                        map = alloc_bootmem_node(pgdat, size);
                pgdat->node_mem_map = map + (pgdat->node_start_pfn - start);
        }

        if (pgdat == NODE_DATA(0))
                mem_map = NODE_DATA(0)->node_mem_map;
}
```

Empty nodes with no pages can obviously be skipped. If the memory map has not already been set up by architecture-specific code (this can happen, e.g., on IA-64 systems), then the memory required for all instances of struct page associated with the node must be allocated. Individual architectures can provide a specific function for this purpose. This is, however, currently only the case for IA-32 with a discontiguous memory configuration. On all other configurations, the regular boot memory allocator is used to perform the allocation. Notice that the code aligns the memory map with the maximal allocation order of the buddy system because this is required for all calculations to work properly.

A pointer to this space is held not only in the pglist_data instance but also in the global variable mem_map — providing the node just examined is the zeroth node of the system (always the case on a system with just one memory node). mem_map is a global array that we will come across frequently in our description of memory management.

mm/memory.c
```
struct page *mem_map;
```

The heavy work involved in the initialization of zone data structures is carried out by free_area_init_core, which iterates over all zones of the node one after the other.

mm/page_alloc.c
```
static void __init free_area_init_core(struct pglist_data *pgdat,
               unsigned long *zones_size, unsigned long *zholes_size)
{
        enum zone_type j;
        int nid = pgdat->node_id;
        unsigned long zone_start_pfn = pgdat->node_start_pfn;
...

        for (j = 0; j < MAX_NR_ZONES; j++) {
               struct zone *zone = pgdat->node_zones + j;
               unsigned long size, realsize, memmap_pages;

               size = zone_spanned_pages_in_node(nid, j, zones_size);
               realsize = size - zone_absent_pages_in_node(nid, j,
                                                   zholes_size);
...
```

The true size of the zone is obtained by correcting the number of spanned pages with the number of holes. Both quantities are computed by two helper functions, which I will not bother to discuss in more detail. Their complexity naturally depends on the memory model and configuration options chosen, but ultimately all variants do not provide any unexpected surprises.

mm/page_alloc.c
```
...
               if (!is_highmem_idx(j))
                       nr_kernel_pages += realsize;
               nr_all_pages += realsize;

               zone->spanned_pages = size;
               zone->present_pages = realsize;
...
               zone->name = zone_names[j];
...
               zone->zone_pgdat = pgdat;
```

```
                          /* Initialize zone fields to default values,
                           * and call helper functions */
      ...
      }
```

The kernel uses two global variables to keep track of how many pages are present in the system: nr_kernel_pages counts all identity mapped pages, while nr_all_pages also includes high-memory pages.

The task of the remaining part of free_area_init_core is to initialize the list heads of the zone structure and to initialize the various structure members to 0. Of particular interest are two helper functions invoked:

❑ zone_pcp_init initializes the per-CPU caches for the zone as discussed extensively in the next section.

❑ init_currently_empty_zone initializes the free_area lists and sets all page instances of pages belonging to the zone to their initial defaults. memmap_init_zone as discussed above is invoked to initialize the pages of the zone. Also recall that all pages are attributed to MIGRATE_MOVABLE in the beginning.

Additionally, the free lists are initialized in zone_init_free_lists:

mm/page_alloc.c
```
static void __meminit zone_init_free_lists(struct pglist_data *pgdat,
struct zone *zone, unsigned long size)
{
        int order, t;
        for_each_migratetype_order(order, t) {
                INIT_LIST_HEAD(&zone->free_area[order].free_list[t]);
                zone->free_area[order].nr_free = 0;
        }
}
```

The number of free pages (nr_free) is still currently defined as 0, and this obviously does not reflect the true situation. The correct value is not set until the bootmem allocator is disabled and normal buddy allocation comes into effect.

3.5.4 Allocator API

As far as the interface to the buddy system is concerned, it makes no difference whether a NUMA or a UMA architecture is used as the call syntax is the same for both. Common to all functions is the fact that pages can only be allocated in integer powers of 2. For this reason, the desired memory size is *not* specified as parameter as it would be in the malloc function of the C standard library or in the bootmem allocator. Instead, the order of the allocation must be specified, and this causes the buddy system to reserve 2^{order} pages in memory. Finer-grained allocation in the kernel is only possible with the help of the slab allocator (or alternatively, the slub or slob allocators), which builds on the buddy system (Section 3.6 gives further details).

❑ alloc_pages(mask, order) allocates 2^{order} pages and returns an instance of struct page to represent the start of the reserved block. alloc_page(mask) is a shorter notation for order = 0 if only one page is requested.

❏ `get_zeroed_page(mask)` allocates a page and returns a `page` instance but fills the page with zeros (with all other functions, page contents are undefined after allocation).

❏ `__get_free_pages(mask, order)` and `__get_free_page(mask)` work in the same way as the above functions but return the virtual address of the reserved memory chunk instead of a `page` instance.

❏ `get_dma_pages(gfp_mask, order)` allows for obtaining pages suitable for DMA.

If allocation fails because insufficient memory is free to satisfy the request, all the above functions return either a null pointer (`alloc_pages` and `alloc_page`) or the value 0 (`get_zeroed_page`, `__get_free_pages`, and `__get_free_page`). The kernel must therefore check the result returned after *every* allocation attempt. This practice is not different from any well-designed userland applications, but neglecting the check in the kernel will lead to much more severe failures.

The kernel provides other memory management functions in addition to the buddy system functions. They build on layers that are used as a basis by the buddy system but do not belong to the buddy allocator itself. These functions are `vmalloc` and `vmalloc_32`, which use page tables to map discontiguous memory into kernel address space so that it appears to be contiguous. There is also a set of functions of the `kmalloc` type to reserve memory areas smaller than a complete page. Their implementation is discussed separately in later sections of this chapter.

Four slightly different functions are defined to return pages no longer needed in memory to the kernel.

❏ `free_page(struct page*)` and `free_pages(struct page*, order)` return one or 2^{order} pages to memory management. The start of the memory area is indicated by means of a pointer to the first `page` instance of the area.

❏ `__free_page(addr)` and `__free_pages(addr, order)` operate in the same way as the functions just mentioned but use a virtual memory address instead of a `page` instance to select the memory area to be returned.

Allocation Masks

What is the meaning of the `mask` parameter that is mandatory for all functions? As we know from Section 3.2.1, Linux divides memory into zones. The kernel provides what is known as *zone modifiers* (defined in the least significant 4 bits of a mask) to specify the zone from which the pages are to be taken for purposes of memory allocation.

```
<gfp.h>
/* Zone modifiers in GFP_ZONEMASK (see linux/mmzone.h - low three bits) */
#define __GFP_DMA      ((__force gfp_t)0x01u)
#define __GFP_HIGHMEM  ((__force gfp_t)0x02u)
#define __GFP_DMA32 ((__force gfp_t)0x04u)
...
#define __GFP_MOVABLE ((__force gfp_t)0x100000u) /* Page is movable */
```

These constants are familiar from Section 3.4.1 in which the creation of fallback lists is discussed. The abbreviation GFP stands for *get free pages*. `__GFP_MOVABLE` does not represent a physical memory zone, but instructs the kernel that an allocation should be fulfilled from the special virtual zone `ZONE_MOVABLE`.

Interestingly, there is no __GFP_NORMAL constant, although the main burden of allocation falls on this zone. The kernel takes account of this fact by providing a function that calculates the highest memory zone compatible with the given allocation flags. Allocations can then be made from this zone and from those below it.

mm/page_alloc.c

```
static inline enum zone_type gfp_zone(gfp_t flags)
{
#ifdef CONFIG_ZONE_DMA
        if (flags & __GFP_DMA)
                return ZONE_DMA;
#endif
#ifdef CONFIG_ZONE_DMA32
        if (flags & __GFP_DMA32)
                return ZONE_DMA32;
#endif
        if ((flags & (__GFP_HIGHMEM | __GFP_MOVABLE)) ==
                        (__GFP_HIGHMEM | __GFP_MOVABLE))
                return ZONE_MOVABLE;
#ifdef CONFIG_HIGHMEM
        if (flags & __GFP_HIGHMEM)
                return ZONE_HIGHMEM;
#endif
        return ZONE_NORMAL;
}
```

Because the way in which the zone modifiers are interpreted may not immediately appear to be intuitive, Table 3-7 shows an example of the function results when the zones for DMA and DMA32 are identical. Assume that the __GFP_MOVABLE modifier is not set in the following:

If both __GFP_DMA and __GFP_HIGHMEM are *not* set, ZONE_NORMAL is first scanned, followed by ZONE_DMA. If __GFP_HIGHMEM is set and __GFP_DMA is not set, the result is that all three zones are scanned starting with ZONE_HIGHMEM. If __GFP_DMA is set, it is irrelevant to the kernel whether __GFP_HIGHMEM is set or not. Only ZONE_DMA is used in both cases. This is reasonable because the simultaneous use of __GFP_HIGHMEM and __GFP_DMA makes no sense. Highmem is never DMA-suitable.

Table 3-7: Correlation between Zone Modifiers and Zones Scanned

Modifier	Zones scanned
Empty	ZONE_NORMAL, ZONE_DMA
__GFP_DMA	ZONE_DMA
__GFP_DMA & __GFP_HIGHMEM	ZONE_DMA
__GFP_HIGHMEM	ZONE_HIGHMEM, ZONE_NORMAL, ZONE_DMA

Setting __GFP_MOVABLE will not influence the kernel's decision unless it is specified together with __GFP_HIGHMEM. In this case, the special virtual zone ZONE_MOVABLE will be used to satisfy a memory request. This behavior is essential for the anti-fragmentation strategy of the kernel as outlined.

A few flags can be set in the mask in addition to the zone modifiers. Figure 3-29 shows the layout of the mask and the constants associated with the bit positions. __GFP_DMA32 appears several times because it may be located at different places.

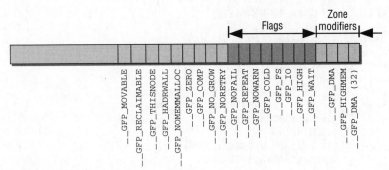

Figure 3-29: Layout of a GFP mask.

In contrast to the zone modifiers, the additional flags do *not* limit the RAM segments from which memory can be allocated, but they do alter the behavior of the allocator. For example, they modify how aggressively a search is made for free memory. The following flags are defined in the kernel sources:

<gfp.h>

```
/* Action modifiers - doesn't change the zoning */
#define __GFP_WAIT        ((__force gfp_t)0x10u)    /* Can wait and reschedule? */
#define __GFP_HIGH        ((__force gfp_t)0x20u)    /* Should access emergency pools? */
#define __GFP_IO          ((__force gfp_t)0x40u)    /* Can start physical IO? */
#define __GFP_FS          ((__force gfp_t)0x80u)    /* Can call down to low-level FS? */
#define __GFP_COLD        ((__force gfp_t)0x100u)   /* Cache-cold page required */
#define __GFP_NOWARN      ((__force gfp_t)0x200u)   /* Suppress page allocation failure warning */
#define __GFP_REPEAT      ((__force gfp_t)0x400u)   /* Retry the allocation.  Might fail */
#define __GFP_NOFAIL      ((__force gfp_t)0x800u)   /* Retry for ever.  Cannot fail */
#define __GFP_NORETRY     ((__force gfp_t)0x1000u)  /* Do not retry.  Might fail */
#define __GFP_NO_GROW     ((__force gfp_t)0x2000u)  /* Slab internal usage */
#define __GFP_COMP        ((__force gfp_t)0x4000u)  /* Add compound page metadata */
#define __GFP_ZERO        ((__force gfp_t)0x8000u)  /* Return zeroed page on success */
#define __GFP_NOMEMALLOC  ((__force gfp_t)0x10000u) /* Don't use emergency reserves */
#define __GFP_HARDWALL    ((__force gfp_t)0x20000u) /* Enforce hardwall cpuset memory allocs */
#define __GFP_THISNODE    ((__force gfp_t)0x40000u) /* No fallback, no policies */
#define __GFP_RECLAIMABLE ((__force gfp_t)0x80000u) /* Page is reclaimable */
#define __GFP_MOVABLE     ((__force gfp_t)0x100000u) /* Page is movable */
```

Some of the constants shown are used only in rare situations, so I won't discuss them. The meanings of the most important constants are as follows:

❑ __GFP_WAIT indicates that the memory request may be interrupted; that is, the scheduler is free to select another process during the request, or the request can be interrupted by a more important event. The allocator is also permitted to wait for an event on a queue (and to put the process to sleep) before memory is returned.

❑ __GFP_HIGH is set if the request is very important, that is, when the kernel urgently needs memory. This flag is always used when failure to allocate memory would have massive consequences for the kernel resulting in a threat to system stability or even a system crash.

> **Despite the similarity in name, __GFP_HIGH has nothing to do with __GFP_HIGHMEM and must not be confused with it.**

❑ __GFP_IO specifies that the kernel can perform I/O operations during an attempt to find fresh memory. In real terms, this means that if the kernel begins to swap out pages during memory allocation, the selected pages may be written to hard disk only if this flag is set.

❑ __GFP_FS allows the kernel to perform VFS operations. This must be prevented in kernel layers linked with the VFS layer because interactions of this kind could cause endless recursive calls.

❑ __GFP_COLD is set if allocation of a "cold" page that is *not* resident in the CPU cache is required.

❑ __GFP_NOWARN suppresses a kernel failure warning if allocation fails. There are very few occasions when this flag is useful.

❑ __GFP_REPEAT automatically retries a failed allocation but stops after a few attempts. __GFP_NOFAIL retries the failed allocation until it succeeds.

❑ __GFP_ZERO returns a page filled with zero bytes if allocation succeeds.

❑ __GFP_HARDWALL is meaningful on NUMA systems only. It limits memory allocation to the nodes associated with the CPUs assigned to a process. The flag is meaningless if a process is allowed to run on all CPUs (this is the default). It only has an explicit effect if the CPUs on which a process may run are limited.

❑ __GFP_THISNODE also only makes sense on NUMA systems. If the bit is set, then fallback to other nodes is not permitted, and memory is guaranteed to be allocated on either the current node or on an explicitly specified node.

❑ __GFP_RECLAIMABLE and __GFP_MOVABLE are required by the page mobility mechanism. As their names indicate, they mark that the allocated memory will be reclaimable or movable, respectively. This influences from which sublist of the freelist the page or pages will be taken.

As the flags are used in combination and hardly ever on their own, the kernel classifies them into groups containing appropriate flags for a variety of standard situations. If at all possible, one of the following groups should always be used for memory allocation outside of memory management itself. (This requirement is reinforced by the fact that the names of the predefined groups do not begin with a double underscore — the usual convention for internal data and definitions in the kernel sources.)

```
<gfp.h>
#define GFP_ATOMIC          (__GFP_HIGH)
#define GFP_NOIO            (__GFP_WAIT)
#define GFP_NOFS            (__GFP_WAIT | __GFP_IO)
#define GFP_KERNEL          (__GFP_WAIT | __GFP_IO | __GFP_FS)
#define GFP_USER            (__GFP_WAIT | __GFP_IO | __GFP_FS | __GFP_HARDWALL)
#define GFP_HIGHUSER        (__GFP_WAIT | __GFP_IO | __GFP_FS | __GFP_HARDWALL | \
                             __GFP_HIGHMEM)
#define GFP_HIGHUSER_MOVABLE   (__GFP_WAIT | __GFP_IO | __GFP_FS | \
                                __GFP_HARDWALL | __GFP_HIGHMEM | \
                                __GFP_MOVABLE)
#define GFP_DMA             __GFP_DMA
#define GFP_DMA32           __GFP_DMA32
```

❑ The meaning of the first three combinations is clear. GFP_ATOMIC is used for atomic allocations that may not be interrupted on any account and may also draw on the "emergency reserves" of memory. GFP_NOIO and GFP_NOFS explicitly exclude I/O operations and access to the VFS layer, respectively, but may be interrupted because __GFP_WAIT is set.

❑ GFP_KERNEL and GFP_USER are the default settings for kernel and user allocations, respectively. Their failure is not an immediate threat to system stability. GFP_KERNEL is far and away the most frequently used flag in the kernel sources.

❑ GFP_HIGHUSER is an extension of GFP_USER that is also used on behalf of userspace. It also permits the use of high-memory areas that can no longer be mapped directly. There is no disadvantage to using highmem pages because the address space of user processes is always organized by means of nonlinear page table assignments. GFP_HIGHUSER_MOVABLE is similar to GFP_HIGHUSER in purpose, but allocations will be satisfied from the virtual zone ZONE_MOVABLE.

❑ GFP_DMA is used for DMA allocations and is currently a simple synonym for __GFP_DMA; GFP_DMA32 is likewise a synonym for __GFP_GMA32.

Allocation Macros

Through the use of flags, zone modifiers, and the various allocation functions, the kernel offers a very flexible system of memory reservation. Nevertheless, all interface functions can be traced back to a single base function (alloc_pages_node).

alloc_page and __get_free_page that reserve a single page are defined with the help of macros, as is alloc_pages.

```
<gfp.h>
#define alloc_page(gfp_mask) alloc_pages(gfp_mask, 0)
...
#define __get_free_page(gfp_mask) \
                __get_free_pages((gfp_mask),0)

<mm.h>
#define __get_dma_pages(gfp_mask, order) \
                __get_free_pages((gfp_mask) | GFP_DMA,(order))
```

Neither is the implementation of get_zeroed_page particularly difficult. alloc_pages used with the __GFP_ZERO flag reserves a page already filled with null bytes — only the address of the memory area associated with the page need be returned.

The `clear_page` standard function that must be implemented by all architectures helps `alloc_pages` fill pages with null bytes.[19]

`__get_free_pages` accesses `alloc_pages`, while `alloc_pages`, in turn, resorts to `alloc_pages_node`:

<gfp.h>
```
#define alloc_pages(gfp_mask, order) \
                alloc_pages_node(numa_node_id(), gfp_mask, order)
```

mm/page_alloc.c
```
fastcall unsigned long __get_free_pages(gfp_t gfp_mask, unsigned int order)
{
        struct page * page;
        page = alloc_pages(gfp_mask, order);
        if (!page)
                return 0;
        return (unsigned long) page_address(page);
}
```

In this case, a proper function is used instead of a macro because the `page` instance returned by `alloc_pages` still remains to be translated into a memory address using the helper function `page_address`. At this point it is enough for us to know that the function yields the linear memory address of a page associated with the passed `page` instance. This is problematic with highmem pages, so I discuss the details of the function in Section 3.5.7.

The unification of all API functions to a common base function — `alloc_pages` — is thus complete. Figure 3-30 shows the relationships among the various functions in a graphical overview.

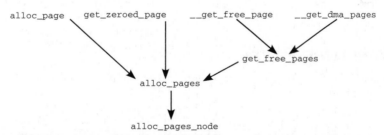

Figure 3-30: Relationships among the allocation functions of the buddy system.

`page_cache_alloc` and `page_cache_alloc_cold` are also convenience functions to yield cache-warm and cache-cold pages, respectively, by setting the `__GFP_COLD` modifier accordingly.

Similarly, the memory-freeing functions can be reduced to a central function (`__free_pages`) invoked with different parameters:

<gfp.h>
```
#define __free_page(page) __free_pages((page), 0)
#define free_page(addr) free_pages((addr),0)
```

---

[19]Of course, pages could be filled with zeros by generic processor-independent code, but most CPUs feature special commands that do this much faster.

The relationship between `free_pages` and `__free_pages` is established by means of a function instead of a macro because the virtual address must first be converted to a pointer to `struct page`.

mm/page_alloc.c
```
void free_pages(unsigned long addr, unsigned int order)
{
        if (addr != 0) {
                __free_pages(virt_to_page(addr), order);
        }
}
```

`virt_to_page` converts virtual memory addresses to pointers to `page` instances. Basically, this is the reverse of the `page_address` helper function introduced above.

Figure 3-31 summarizes the relationships among the various memory-freeing functions in a graphical overview.

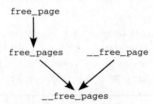

Figure 3-31: Relationships among the memory-freeing functions of the buddy system.

3.5.5 Reserving Pages

All API functions lead back to `alloc_pages_node`, which is a kind of "launch pad" for central implementation of the buddy system.

<gfp.h>
```
static inline struct page *alloc_pages_node(int nid, gfp_t gfp_mask,
                                            unsigned int order)
{
        if (unlikely(order >= MAX_ORDER))
                return NULL;

        /* Unknown node is current node */
        if (nid < 0)
                nid = numa_node_id();

        return __alloc_pages(gfp_mask, order,
                NODE_DATA(nid)->node_zonelists + gfp_zone(gfp_mask));
}
```

Just a simple check is carried out to ensure that no overly large memory chunk is allocated. If a negative node ID (which does not exist) is specified, the kernel automatically uses the ID that belongs to the currently executing CPU. Work is then delegated to `__alloc_pages` to which an appropriate set of parameters is passed. Notice that `gfp_zone` is used to select the zone from which the allocation is supposed to be fulfilled. This is an important detail that can easily be missed!

The kernel sources refer to this `__alloc_pages` as the "heart of the buddy system" because it deals with the essential aspects of allocation. Since a heart is an important thing to have, I shall introduce the function in detail below.

Selecting Pages

Let us therefore turn our attention to how page selection works.

Helper Functions

First, we need to define some flags used by the functions to control behavior when various watermarks are reached.

mm/page_alloc.c
```
#define ALLOC_NO_WATERMARKS      0x01 /* don't check watermarks at all */
#define ALLOC_WMARK_MIN          0x02 /* use pages_min watermark */
#define ALLOC_WMARK_LOW          0x04 /* use pages_low watermark */
#define ALLOC_WMARK_HIGH         0x08 /* use pages_high watermark */
#define ALLOC_HARDER             0x10 /* try to alloc harder */
#define ALLOC_HIGH               0x20 /* __GFP_HIGH set */
#define ALLOC_CPUSET             0x40 /* check for correct cpuset */
```

The first flags indicate which watermark applies when the decision is made as to whether pages can be taken or not. By default (that is, there is no *absolute* need for more memory because of pressure exerted by other factors), pages are taken only when the zone still contains at least `zone->pages_high` pages. This corresponds to the `ALLOC_WMARK_HIGH` flag. `ALLOC_WMARK_MIN` or `_LOW` must be set accordingly in order to use the low (`zone->pages_low`) or minimum (`zone->pages_min`) setting instead. `ALLOC_HARDER` instructs the buddy system to apply the allocation rules more generously when memory is urgently needed; `ALLOC_HIGH` relaxes these rules even more when highmem is allocated. Finally, `ALLOC_CPUSET` tells the kernel to note that memory must be taken only from the areas associated with the CPUs that the current process is allowed to use — of course, this option only makes sense on NUMA systems.

The flag settings are applied in the `zone_watermark_ok` function, which checks whether memory can still be taken from a given zone depending on the allocation flags set.

mm/page_alloc.c
```
int zone_watermark_ok(struct zone *z, int order, unsigned long mark,
                      int classzone_idx, int alloc_flags)
{
        /* free_pages my go negative - that's OK */
        long min = mark
        long free_pages = zone_page_state(z, NR_FREE_PAGES) - (1 << order) + 1;
        int o;

        if (alloc_flags & ALLOC_HIGH)
                min -= min / 2;
        if (alloc_flags & ALLOC_HARDER)
                min -= min / 4;
```

```
                    if (free_pages <= min + z->lowmem_reserve[classzone_idx])
                            return 0;
                    for (o = 0; o < order; o++) {
                            /* At the next order, this order's pages become unavailable */
                            free_pages -= z->free_area[o].nr_free << o;

                            /* Require fewer higher order pages to be free */
                            min >>= 1;

                            if (free_pages <= min)
                                    return 0;
                    }
                    return 1;
        }
```

Recall that `zone_per_state` allows for accessing the per-zone statistics. In this case, the number of free pages is obtained.

Once the `ALLOC_HIGH` and `ALLOC_HARDER` flags have been interpreted (they reduce the minimum mark by a half or quarter of the current value, which makes the allocation effectively try hard or even harder), the function checks whether the number of free pages is less than the desired minimum plus the emergency reserve specified in `lowmem_reserve`. If not, the code iterates over all orders less than the current order and subtracts all pages in the current zone from `free_pages` (the o-fold left shift is necessary because `nr_free` stores the free page *blocks*). At the same time, the required number of free pages is halved for each zone. The allocation is freed if the kernel establishes that not enough pages are present after iterating over all low-memory zones.

`get_page_from_freelist` is another important helper function used by the buddy system. It refers to the flags set and the allocation order to decide whether allocation can be made; if so, it initiates actual page allocation.[20]

mm/page_alloc.c
```
static struct page *
get_page_from_freelist(gfp_t gfp_mask, unsigned int order,
                struct zonelist *zonelist, int alloc_flags)
{
        struct zone **z;
        struct page *page = NULL;
        int classzone_idx = zone_idx(zonelist->zones[0]);
        struct zone *zone;
...
        /*
         * Scan zonelist, looking for a zone with enough free.
         * See also cpuset_zone_allowed() comment in kernel/cpuset.c.
         */
        z = zonelist->zones;

        do {
...
                zone = *z;
```

---

[20]Notice that NUMA systems use a zone list cache that accelerates scanning through the zones. Although the cache is not active on UMA systems, it has some influence on the code below that I have removed for the sake of simplicity.

```
              if ((alloc_flags & ALLOC_CPUSET) &&
                      !cpuset_zone_allowed_softwall(zone, gfp_mask))
                          continue;

      if (!(alloc_flags & ALLOC_NO_WATERMARKS)) {
              unsigned long mark;
              if (alloc_flags & ALLOC_WMARK_MIN)
                      mark = zone->pages_min;
              else if (alloc_flags & ALLOC_WMARK_LOW)
                      mark = zone->pages_low;
              else
                      mark = zone->pages_high;
              if (!zone_watermark_ok(zone, order, mark,
                          classzone_idx, alloc_flags))
                      continue;
      }

      ...
```

A pointer to the fallback list is passed as parameter to the function. This list determines the order in which the other zones (and nodes) of the system are scanned if no pages are free in the desired zone. The layout and meaning of this data structure are discussed extensively in Section 3.4.1.

The subsequent do loop does more or less exactly what would intuitively be expected as the simplest way of finding a suitable free memory block — it iterates over all zones of the fallback list. First of all, the ALLOC_* flags are interpreted (cpuset_zone_allowed_softwall is another helper function to check whether the given zone belongs to the allowed CPUs for the process). zone_watermark_ok then checks each zone to find out if enough pages are present and attempts to allocate a contiguous memory block. If one of these two conditions is not met — either there are not enough free pages or the request cannot be satisfied with *contiguous* pages — the next zone in the fallback list is checked in the same way.

If the zone is suitable for the current request, buffered_rmqueue tries to remove the desired number of pages from it:

mm/page_alloc.c

```
      ...
              page = buffered_rmqueue(*z, order, gfp_mask);
              if (page) {
                      zone_statistics(zonelist, *z);
                      break;
              }
      } while (*(++z) != NULL);
      return page;
}
```

We take a closer look at buffered_rmqueue in Section 3.5.4. If page removal was successful, the page(s) can be returned to the caller. Otherwise, the loop starts anew, and the next best zone is selected.

Allocation Control

As mentioned above, __alloc_pages is the main function of the buddy system. Now that we have dealt with all preparatory work and described all possible flags, we turn our attention to the relatively complex implementation of the function that is one of the lengthier parts of the kernel. Complexity arises above all when too little memory is available to satisfy a request or when available memory is slowly running out. If sufficient memory is available, the necessary work is quickly done as the start of the code shows.

mm/page_alloc.c
```
struct page * fastcall
__alloc_pages(gfp_t gfp_mask, unsigned int order,
              struct zonelist *zonelist)
{
        const gfp_t wait = gfp_mask & __GFP_WAIT;
        struct zone **z;
        struct page *page;
        struct reclaim_state reclaim_state;
        struct task_struct *p = current;
        int do_retry;
        int alloc_flags;
        int did_some_progress;

        might_sleep_if(wait);

restart:
        z = zonelist->zones;  /* the list of zones suitable for gfp_mask */

        if (unlikely(*z == NULL)) {
        /*
         * Happens if we have an empty zonelist as a result of
         * GFP_THISNODE being used on a memoryless node
         */
                return NULL;
        }

        page = get_page_from_freelist(gfp_mask|__GFP_HARDWALL, order,
                                zonelist, ALLOC_WMARK_LOW|ALLOC_CPUSET);
        if (page)
                goto got_pg;
...
```

In the simplest scenario, allocation of a fresh memory area involves a single invocation of `get_page_from_freelist` to return the required number of pages (which is handled by the code at the label `got_pg`).

The first memory allocation attempt is not particularly aggressive. A failure to find memory in any of the zones means that there isn't much memory left but requires more than a moderate increase in effort from the kernel to find more memory (the big guns are brought out later).

mm/page_alloc.c
```
...
        for (z = zonelist->zones; *z; z++)
                wakeup_kswapd(*z, order);

        alloc_flags = ALLOC_WMARK_MIN;
        if ((unlikely(rt_task(p)) && !in_interrupt()) || !wait)
                alloc_flags |= ALLOC_HARDER;
        if (gfp_mask & __GFP_HIGH)
```

```
                    alloc_flags |= ALLOC_HIGH;
          if (wait)
              alloc_flags |= ALLOC_CPUSET;

          page = get_page_from_freelist(gfp_mask, order, zonelist, alloc_flags);
          if (page)
                  goto got_pg;
   ...
   }
```

The kernel again iterates over all zones in the fallback list and invokes the `wakeup_kswapd` each time. As its name suggests, this function wakes the `kswapd` daemon responsible for swapping out pages. The task of the swapping daemons is complex and is therefore described in a separate chapter (Chapter 18). All you need note here is that fresh memory can be obtained by, for example, shrinking kernel caches and page reclaim, that is, writing back or swapping out rarely used pages. Both measures are initiated by the daemon.

Once the swapping daemon has been woken, the kernel starts a new attempt to find a suitable memory chunk in one of the zones. This time it goes about its search more aggressively by adjusting the allocation flags to more promising values for the particular situation. In doing so, it reduces the watermark to its minimum value. `ALLOC_HARDER` is set for real-time processes and for calls with `__GFP_WAIT` that may not go to sleep. A further call of `get_page_from_freelist` with a changed set of flags tries to obtain the desired pages.

If this also fails, the kernel resorts to more drastic measures:

mm/page_alloc.c
```
rebalance:
        if (((p->flags & PF_MEMALLOC) || unlikely(test_thread_flag(TIF_MEMDIE)))
                  && !in_interrupt()) {
              if (!(gfp_mask & __GFP_NOMEMALLOC)) {
nofail_alloc:
                  /* go through the zonelist yet again, ignoring mins */
                  page = get_page_from_freelist(gfp_mask, order,
                      zonelist, ALLOC_NO_WATERMARKS);
                  if (page)
                          goto got_pg;
                  if (gfp_mask & __GFP_NOFAIL) {
                          congestion_wait(WRITE, HZ/50);
                          goto nofail_alloc;
                  }
              }
              goto nopage;
          }
   ...
```

If `PF_MEMALLOC` is set or if the `TIF_MEMDIE` flag is set for the task (in both cases, the kernel must not be in the interrupt context). `get_page_from_freelist` tries once more to obtain the desired pages, but this time, watermarks are completely ignored because `ALLOC_NO_WATERMARKS` is set. Whereas the `PF_MEMALLOC` condition usually only applies when the call for more memory originates from the allocator itself, `TIF_MEMDIE` is set when a thread has just been hit by the OOM killer.

The search can come to an end here for two reasons:

1. __GFP_NOMEMALLOC is set. This flag prohibits using the emergency reserve (which can well be if the watermarks are ignored), so calling get_page_from_freelist without obeying the watermarks is forbidden. The kernel can do nothing more than fail ultimately in this case by jumping to the noopage label, where the failure is reported to the user with a kernel message, and a NULL pointer is returned to the caller.

2. get_page_from_freelist fails despite watermarks being ignored. In this case, the search is also aborted and terminates with an error message. However, if __GFP_NOFAIL is set, the kernel goes into an endless loop (implemented by branching back to the nofail_alloc label) to first wait (by means of congestion_wait) for the end of "congestion" in the block layer, which can arise when pages are reclaimed (see Chapter 18). Allocation is then attempted again until it succeeds.

If PF_MEMALLOC is not set, the kernel still has some more options to try, but these require going sleep. This is necessary to allow kswapd to make some progress.

The kernel now enters on a *slow path* where time-consuming operations begin. A prerequisite is that the __GFP_WAIT flag is set in the allocation mask because the subsequent actions can put the process to sleep.

mm/page_alloc.c

```
        /* Atomic allocations - we can't balance anything */
        if (!wait)
                goto nopage;

        cond_schedule();
...
```

Recall that wait is 1 if the bit is set, and 0 otherwise. If this flag is not set, allocation is aborted at this point. Before further attempts are made, the kernel provides the opportunity of rescheduling by means of cond_resched. This prevents too much time being spent searching for memory so that other tasks are left unfulfilled.

The paging mechanism provides an as-yet-unused option for swapping rarely used pages out to a block medium to create more space in RAM. However, this option is very time-consuming and can sleep. try_to_free_pages is the respective helper function that attempts to find pages that are currently not urgently needed and can therefore be swapped out. It is invoked after the PF_MEMALLOC flag has been set for the task to indicate to the remaining kernel code that all subsequent memory allocations are needed *in the search for memory*.

mm/page_alloc.c

```
        /* We now go into synchronous reclaim */
        p->flags |= PF_MEMALLOC;
...
        did_some_progress = try_to_free_pages(zonelist->zones, order, gfp_mask);
...
        p->flags &= ~PF_MEMALLOC;

        cond_resched();
...
```

The call is framed by code that sets the above PF_MEMALLOC flag. It may be necessary for try_to_free_pages to allocate new memory for its own work. As this additional memory is needed to obtain fresh memory (a rather paradoxical situation), the process should, of course, enjoy maximum priority in terms of memory management from this point on — this is achieved by setting the above flag.

> *Recall that only a few lines ago, a very aggressive attempt at memory allocation was tried conditioned on* PF_MEMALLOC *being set.*

Besides, setting the flag ensures that try_to_free_pages is not called recursively because __alloc_pages will already have aborted before if PF_MEMALLOC is set.

try_to_free_pages is itself a lengthy and complex function whose implementation I won't discuss here. Instead, see Chapter 18, which includes a detailed description of the underlying mechanism. At the moment, it is sufficient to know that the function selects pages not recently in very active use and writes them to the swap area to free space in RAM memory. The number of freed pages by try_to_free_pages is returned as the result.

---

try_to_free_pages acts only on the node containing the desired zone. All other nodes are ignored.

If more than one page is to be allocated, pages from the per-CPU cache are brought back into the buddy system:

mm/page_alloc.c
```
        if (order != 0)
                drain_all_local_pages();
```

How this is technically done is not of relevance here, so it is not necessary to discuss drain_all_local_pages in detail.

The next kernel action — could it be any different — is to invoke get_page_from_freelist to attempt allocation again if some pages could be freed by try_to_free_pages:

mm/page_alloc.c
```
        if (likely(did_some_progress)) {
                page = get_page_from_freelist(gfp_mask, order,
                                                zonelist, alloc_flags);
                if (page)
                        goto got_pg;
        } else if ((gfp_mask & __GFP_FS) && !(gfp_mask & __GFP_NORETRY)) {
...
```

If the kernel may perform calls that affect the VFS layer and is not hindered by GFP_NORETRY, the out-of-memory (OOM) killer is invoked:

mm/page_alloc.c
```
                /* The OOM killer will not help higher order allocs so fail */
                if (order > PAGE_ALLOC_COSTLY_ORDER) {
                        clear_zonelist_oom(zonelist);
```

```
                              goto nopage;
                }

                out_of_memory(zonelist, gfp_mask, order);
                goto restart;
        }
}
```

Without going into the details of implementation, note that `out_of_memory` picks one task that the kernel deems particularly guilty of reserving all the memory — and kills it. This, hopefully, will lead to a good number of free pages, and the allocation is retried by jumping to the label `restart`. However, it is unlikely that killing a process will immediately lead to a continuous range of more than $2^{PAGE\_COSTLY\_ORDER}$ pages (where `PAGE_COSTLY_ORDER_PAGES` is usually set to 3), so the kernel spares one innocent task's life if such a big allocation was requested, does not perform out-of-memory killing, and admits failure by jumping to `nopage`.

What happens if `__GFP_NORETRY` is set or the kernel is not allowed to use operations that might affect the VFS layer? In this case, the size of the desired allocation comes in:

mm/page_alloc.c

```
...
        do_retry = 0;
        if (!(gfp_mask & __GFP_NORETRY)) {
                if ((order <= PAGE_ALLOC_COSTLY_ORDER) ||
                                              (gfp_mask & __GFP_REPEAT))
                        do_retry = 1;
                if (gfp_mask & __GFP_NOFAIL)
                        do_retry = 1;
        }
        if (do_retry) {
                congestion_wait(WRITE, HZ/50);
                goto rebalance;
        }
        nopage:
        if (!(gfp_mask & __GFP_NOWARN) && printk_ratelimit()) {
                printk(KERN_WARNING "%s: page allocation failure."
                        " order:%d, mode:0x%x\n",
                        p->comm, order, gfp_mask);
                dump_stack();
                show_mem();
        }
got_pg:
        return page;
}
```

The kernel goes into an endless loop if the allocation size is less than $2^{PAGE\_ALLOC\_COSTLY\_ORDER} = 8$ pages, or the `__GFP_REPEAT` flag is set. `GFP_NORETRY` must naturally not be set in both cases since the caller does not like to retry the allocation in this case. The kernel branches back to the `rebalance` label that introduces the *slow path* and remains there until a suitable memory chunk is finally found — with reservations of this size, the kernel can assume that the endless loop won't last all that long. Beforehand, the kernel invokes `congestion_wait` to wait for the block layer queues to free up (see Chapter 6) so that it has a chance to swap pages out.

The kernel also goes into the above endless loop if the desired allocation order is greater than 3 but the `__GFP_NOFAIL` flag is set — the flag does not allow failing on any account.

If this is not the case, the kernel gives up and can do nothing more than return a NULL pointer to the user, and print a warning message that a memory request could not be fulfilled.

Removing the Selected Pages

Two things remain to be done once the kernel has found a suitable zone with sufficient free pages for the allocation. First, it must be checked whether the pages are *contiguous* (up to now it only knows *how many* free pages there are). And second, the pages must be removed from the free_lists in the buddy fashion, and this may make it necessary to break up and rearrange memory regions.

The kernel delegates this work to buffered_rmqueue as discussed in the previous section. Figure 3-32 shows the essential steps of the function.

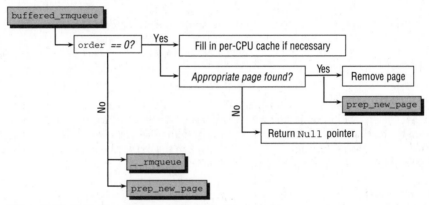

Figure 3-32: Code flow diagram for **buffered_rmqueue**.

The kernel performs optimization if only a single page is to be allocated, that is, if the allocation order is 0 because $2^0 = 1$. The page is not taken directly from the buddy system but from the per-CPU page cache (recall that this cache provides a CPU-local list of cache-hot and cache-cold pages; the required data structures are described in Section 3.2.2).

As usual, some variables need to be set up first:

mm/page_alloc.c
```
static struct page *
buffered_rmqueue(struct zone *zone, int order, gfp_t gfp_flags)
{
        unsigned long flags;
        struct page *page;
        int cold = !!(gfp_flags & __GFP_COLD);
        int migratetype = allocflags_to_migratetype(gfp_flags);
```

If GFP_COLD is set in the allocation flags, then a cache-cold page must be taken from the per-CPU allocator if any exists. The double negation ensures that cold is either 0 or 1.[21] It is also essential to determine the

---

[21]If just gfp_flags & __GFP_COLD were used, then the numerical value of cold would be the bit value of __GFP_COLD if the flag is set. This would not allow using cold as an index into a binary array.

migrate list from the allocation flags. The previously introduced function `allocflags_to_migratetype` (see Section 3.5.2) comes in handy here.

When only a single page is desired, the kernel tries to speed up the request with the help of the per-CPU cache. If the cache is empty, the kernel takes the opportunity to check the cache fill level.

mm/page_alloc.c
```
again:
        if (order == 0) {
                struct per_cpu_pages *pcp;

                page = NULL;
                pcp = &zone_pcp(zone, get_cpu())->pcp[cold];
                if (!pcp->count)
                        pcp->count = rmqueue_bulk(zone, 0,
                                        pcp->batch, &pcp->list);
                        if (unlikely(!pcp->count))
                                goto failed;
        }
    ...
```

Once the appropriate (i.e., hot or cold) per-CPU list for the current processor has been selected, `rmqueue_bulk` is invoked to refill the cache. I won't reproduce the function here as it simply removes pages from the normal buddy system and adds them to the cache. However, it is important to note that `buffered_rmqueue` stores the migrate type of the page in the `private` element of `struct page`. This will become important when pages are taken off the cache:

mm/page_alloc.c
```
                /* Find a page of the appropriate migrate type */
                list_for_each_entry(page, &pcp->list, lru)
                        if (page_private(page) == migratetype)
                                break;

                /* Allocate more to the pcp list if necessary */
                if (unlikely(&page->lru == &pcp->list)) {
                        pcp->count += rmqueue_bulk(zone, 0,
                                        pcp->batch, &pcp->list, migratetype);
                        page = list_entry(pcp->list.next, struct page, lru);
                }

                list_del(&page->lru);
                pcp->count--
        } else {
                page = __rmqueue(zone, order);
                if (!page)
                        goto failed;
        }
    ...
```

The kernel iterates over all pages on the per-CPU cache and checks if the page of the desired migrate type is available. This need not be the case if the cache has been refilled by a previous call with pages of a different migrate type. If no suitable page is found, some more pages with the currently desired migrate type are added to the cache, and one page is removed from the per-CPU list and processed further below.

If more than one page is to be allocated (as handled in the `else` branch), the kernel calls `__rmqueue` to select a suitable page block from the zone's buddy lists. If necessary, the function automatically breaks down larger blocks and puts unused parts back in the lists (how this is done is described below). Caution: It can be the case that there are enough free pages in the zone to satisfy the allocation request, but that the pages are *not contiguous*. In this case, `__rmqueue` fails, and a `NULL` pointer is returned.

Since all failures are handled by jumping to the label `failed`, it is guaranteed that `page` points to a valid sequence of pages once the kernel gets to the current point. Before the pointer can be returned, `prep_new_page` has to prepare the pages for life in the kernel (note that the function returns a positive value if something is wrong with the selected pages; in this case, the allocation is restarted from the beginning):

mm/page_alloc.c
```
        if (prep_new_page(page, order, gfp_flags))
                goto again;
        return page;
failed:
...
        return NULL;
}
```

`prep_new_page` performs several checks on the pages to ensure that they leave the allocator in a perfect state — this means, in particular, that the page must not be in use in existing mappings and no incorrect flags like `PG_locked` or `PG_buddy` may be set because this would imply that the page is in use somewhere else and should not be on the free list. Normally, however, no error should occur because this would imply a kernel error elsewhere. The function also sets the following default flags used for each new page:

mm/page_alloc.c
```
static int prep_new_page(struct page *page, int order, gfp_t gfp_flags)
{
        page->flags &= ~(1 << PG_uptodate | 1 << PG_error | 1 << PG_readahead |
                        1 << PG_referenced | 1 << PG_arch_1 |
                        1 << PG_owner_priv_1 | 1 << PG_mappedtodisk);
...
```

The meanings of the individual bits are given in Section 3.2.2. `prep_new_page` is also invoked to set the reference counters of the first `page` instance involved to the initial value of 1. Besides, some more work is required depending on the page flags:

mm/page_alloc.c
```
        if (gfp_flags & __GFP_ZERO)
                prep_zero_page(page, order, gfp_flags);

        if (order && (gfp_flags & __GFP_COMP))
                prep_compound_page(page, order);

        return 0;
}
```

❑ If `__GFP_ZERO` is set, `prep_zero_page` fills the page with zero bytes using an efficient, architecture-specific function.

❑ If `__GFP_COMP` is set and more than one page has been requested, the kernel must group the pages into *compound pages*. The first page is called the *head page*, while all other pages are called *tail pages*. The structure of compound pages is shown in Figure 3-33.

All pages are identified as compound pages by the `PG_compound` bit. The `private` elements of the `page` instance of *all* pages — even the head page itself — point to the head page. Besides, the kernel needs to store information on how to free the compound page. This requires both a function to free the page and information on how many pages compose the compound page. The LRU list element of the first tail page is abused for this purpose: A pointer to a destructor function is thus kept in `lru.next`, while the allocation order is stored in `lru.prev`. Notice that the `lru` element cannot be used for this purpose because it is required if the compound page is to be kept on a kernel list.

Why is this information required? The kernel can combine multiple adjacent physical pages to a so-called huge-TLB page. When a userland application works with large chunks of data, many processors allow using huge-TLB pages to keep the data in memory. Since the page size of a huge-TLB page is larger than the regular page size, this reduces the amount of information that must be stored in the translation lookaside buffer (TLB), that, in turn, reduces the probability of a TLB cache miss — and thus speeds things up.[22] However, huge-TLB pages need to be freed differently than compound pages composed of multiple regular pages, so an explicit destructor is required. `free_compound_pages` is used for this purpose. The function essentially determines the page order stored in `lru.prev` and frees the pages one after another when the compound page is freed.

The auxiliary function `prep_compound_page` is used to arrange the described structure.

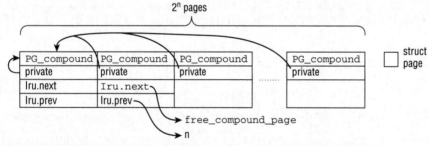

Figure 3-33: Higher-order allocations generate compound pages in which the individual pages are linked.

The `__rmqueue` Helper Function

The kernel uses the `__rmqueue` function (whose purpose is evident from the preceding description), which acts as a gatekeeper to penetrate into the innermost core of the buddy system:

mm/page_alloc.c
```
static struct page *__rmqueue(struct zone *zone, unsigned int order,
                                            int migratetype)
```

---

[22]Huge-TLB pages are created at boot time and kept in a special cache. The kernel parameter hugepages allows for specifying how many huge-TLB pages are to be created, and applications can request them via the special filesystem hugetlbfs. The library `libhugetlbfs` allows userland applications to use huge-TLB pages without direct interference with this filesystem.

```
{
        struct page *page;

        page = __rmqueue_smallest(zone, order, migratetype);

        if (unlikely(!page))
                page = __rmqueue_fallback(zone, order, migratetype);

        return page;
}
```

By reference to the desired allocation order, the zone from which the pages are to be removed, and the migrate type, __rmqueue_smalles scans the page lists until it finds a suitable contiguous chunk of memory. When it does this, buddies can be split as described in Chapter 1. Should the desired migrate list not be able to satisfy the request, then other migrate lists are tried as an emergency measure in __rmqueue_fallback.

The implementation of __rmqueue_smallest is not very long. Essentially, it consists of a loop that iterates over the list of migrate-type-specific free pages list of the zone in ascending order until an appropriate entry is found.

mm/page_alloc.c
```
static struct page *__rmqueue_smallest(struct zone *zone, unsigned int order,
int migratetype)
{
        unsigned int current_order;
        struct free_area * area;
        struct page *page;

        /* Find a page of the appropriate size in the preferred list */
        for (current_order = order; current_order < MAX_ORDER; ++current_order) {
                area = &(zone->free_area[current_order]);
                if (list_empty(&area->free_list[migratetype]))
                        continue;

                page = list_entry(area->free_list[migratetype].next,
                                                    struct page, lru);
                list_del(&page->lru);
                rmv_page_order(page);
                area->nr_free--;
                __mod_zone_page_state(zone, NR_FREE_PAGES, - (1UL << order));
                expand(zone, page, order, current_order, area, migratetype);
                return page;
        }

        return NULL;
}
```

The search begins at the entry for the desired allocation order. Smaller areas are of no use because the pages allocated must be contiguous. Recall that all pages of a given allocation order are again subdivided into migrate-type-specific lists, and the proper one is selected.

Checking for a suitable chunk of memory is very simple: If an element is present in the examined list, it can be used because it contains as many contiguous pages as needed. Otherwise, the kernel selects the next higher allocation order and continues the search there.

Once a memory chunk has been removed from the list with `list_del`, its removal must be noted by decrementing the `nr_free` element of `struct free_area` by 1. The per-zone statistics of the current zone must also be updated accordingly with `__mod_zone_page_state`. `rmv_page_order` is a helper function that deletes the `PG_buddy` bit from the page flags — the page is not contained in the buddy system anymore — and sets the `private` element of `struct page` to 0.

If the memory chunk to be allocated is smaller than the selected range of contiguous pages, that is, if the pages stem from a higher allocation order than required because no suitable smaller block was available, it must be split into smaller segments in accordance with the principles of the buddy system. This is done by the `expand` function.

mm/page_alloc.c
```
static inline struct page *
expand(struct zone *zone, struct page *page,
        int low, int high, struct free_area *area)
        int migratetype)
{
        unsigned long size = 1 << high;

        while (high > low) {
                area--;
                high--;
                size >>= 1;
                list_add(&page[size].lru, &area->free_list[migratetype]);
                area->nr_free++;
                set_page_order(&page[size], high);
        }
        return page;
}
```

This function uses a whole range of parameters. The meanings of `page`, `zone`, and `area` are obvious. `index` specifies the index position of the buddy pair in the allocation bitmap, `low` is the desired allocation order, and `high` indicates the order from which the memory found was taken. `migratetype` sticks to its name and denotes the migrate type.

It is best to look at the code step-by-step to understand how it works. Let us assume the following situation: A block with `order = 3` is to be allocated. There is no block of this size in RAM, so the kernel selects a block with `order = 5` instead. For the sake of simplicity, this is located at *index = 0*. The function is therefore invoked with the following parameters.

```
expand(page,index=0,low=3,high=5,area)
```

Figure 3-34 illustrates the steps described below that are needed to split the page (the previous contents of the `free_area` lists are not shown, only the new pages).

1. The value of `size` is initialized to $2^{high} = 2^5 = 32$. The allocated memory area has already been removed from the `free_area` list in `__rmqueue` and is therefore shown with dashed lines in Figure 3-34.

2. In the first loop pass, the kernel switches to the migrate-type-specific `free_area` list with the next smaller memory units, namely, `area=4`. Analogously, the area size reduces to `size=16`

(calculated by `size >> 1`). The front half of the initial area is inserted in the `free_area` list for `order=4`.

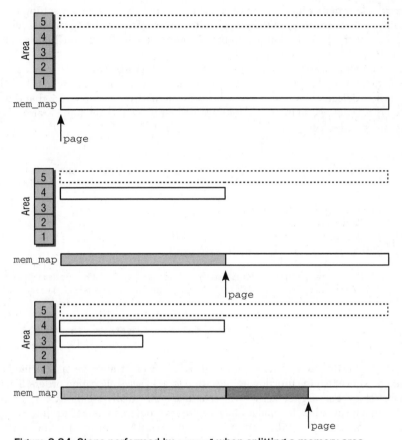

Figure 3-34: Steps performed by **expand** when splitting a memory area.

> Only the first **page** instance of a memory area is needed by the buddy system for management purposes; the size of the area is derived automatically from the list in which the page is located.

3. The index of the rear memory area with `size = 16` can be calculated by adding `size` to `index`, thus skipping the next 16 bits in the allocation bitmap. Because all `page` instances are in linear succession in memory, the pointer to `page` must also be increased by 16 to arrive at the corresponding `page` instance. The position of the `page` pointer is indicated by an arrow in Figure 3-34.

4. The next loop pass places the first half of the remaining 16 units on the `free_area` list with `size=8`. Both `index` and `page` are then increased by 8 units. The function has now arrived at the desired size unit, and the `page` pointer can be returned as the result. From the figure, it is evident that the last 8 pages of the original area of 32 pages are used; all other pages are in the appropriate `free_area` lists of the buddy system.

The kernel always uses the migrate-type-specific `free_area` list and does not change the migrate type of any page during the process.

The `set_page_order` helper function invoked in each step is responsible for setting the `private` flag of the first instance of `struct page` in each block to the order currently being processed and for assigning the `PG_buddy` bit to the page. This indicates that the block is managed by the buddy system.

If no contiguous memory area is available on the migrate-type-specific list, `__rmqueue_smallest` returns a `NULL` pointer. The kernel then tries to fulfill the request using other migrate lists based on the fallback order. The task is delegated to `__rmqueue_fallback`. Recall from Section 3.5.2 that the fallback order for migrate types is defined in the `fallbacks` array. First of all, the function iterates once again over the various allocation order lists:

mm/page_alloc.c
```
static struct page *__rmqueue_fallback(struct zone *zone, int order,
                                                   int start_migratetype)
{
        struct free_area * area;
        int current_order;
        struct page *page;
        int migratetype, i;

        /* Find the largest possible block of pages in the other list */
        for (current_order = MAX_ORDER-1; current_order >= order;
                                        --current_order) {
                for (i = 0; i < MIGRATE_TYPES - 1; i++) {
                        migratetype = fallbacks[start_migratetype][i];
...
```

However, not just the desired migrate type, but also different migrate types as specified in the fallback list are considered. Notice that the function iterates from *large* to *small* allocation orders! This is done contrary to the usual strategy, because the kernel wants to take a maximally big block out of foreign allocation lists if this cannot be avoided. If smaller blocks were favored, this would introduce fragmentation into the other zone because blocks of different migrate types would be mixed, and this is clearly undesired.

The special zone `MIGRATE_RESERVE` contains emergency reservations and requires special treatment, discussed below. If the free list for the currently considered migrate type contains free page blocks, the request can be satisfied from there:

mm/page_alloc.c
```
                        /* MIGRATE_RESERVE handled later if necessary */
                        if (migratetype == MIGRATE_RESERVE)
                                continue;

                        area = &(zone->free_area[current_order]);
                        if (list_empty(&area->free_list[migratetype]))
                                continue;

                        page = list_entry(area->free_list[migratetype].next,
                                        struct page, lru);
                        area->nr_free--;
...
```

Recall that migrate lists are the basis for the page mobility approach that is used to keep memory fragmentation as low as possible. Low memory fragmentation means that larger contiguous page blocks are available even after the system has been running for a longer time. As discussed in Section 3.5.2, the notion of *how* big a larger block is given by the global variable pageblock_order, which defines the order for a large block.

If it is required to break a block of free pages from another migration list, the kernel has to choose what to do with the remaining pages. If the rest itself qualifies as a large block, it makes sense to transfer the whole block to the migrate list of the allocation type to mitigate fragmentation.

The kernel is more aggressive about moving free pages from one migrate list to another if an allocation is performed for reclaimable memory. Allocations of this type often appear in bursts, for instance, when updatedb is running, and could therefore scatter many small reclaimable portions across all migrate lists. To avoid this situation, remaining pages for MIGRATE_RECLAIMABLE allocations are always transferred to the reclaimable migrate list.

The kernel implements the described policy as follows:

mm/page_alloc.c

```
/*
 * If breaking a large block of pages, move all free
 * pages to the preferred allocation list. If falling
 * back for a reclaimable kernel allocation, be more
 * agressive about taking ownership of free pages
 */
if (unlikely(current_order >= (pageblock_order >> 1)) ||
            start_migratetype == MIGRATE_RECLAIMABLE) {
    unsigned long pages;
    pages = move_freepages_block(zone, page,
                                start_migratetype);

    /* Claim the whole block if over half of it is free */
    if (pages >= (1 << (pageblock_order-1)))
            set_pageblock_migratetype(page,
                                    start_migratetype);

    migratetype = start_migratetype;
}
    . . .
```

move_freepages tries to move the *complete* page block with $2^{pageblock\_order}$ pages in which the current allocation is contained to the new migrate list. However, only free pages (i.e., those with the PG_buddy bit set) are moved. Additionally, move_freepages also obeys zone boundaries, so the total number of pages can be smaller than a complete large page block. If, however, more than one-half of a large page block is free, then set_pageblock_migratetype claims the complete block (recall that the function always works on groups with pageblock_nr_pages pages).

Finally, the kernel can remove the page block from the list, and use expand to place the unused parts of a larger block back on the buddy system.

mm/page_alloc.c

```
/* Remove the page from the freelists */
list_del(&page->lru);
```

```
                       rmv_page_order(page);
                       __mod_zone_page_state(zone, NR_FREE_PAGES,
                                                   -(1UL << order));
    . . .

                       expand(zone, page, order, current_order, area, migratetype);
                       return page;
               }
           }
    . . .
```

Notice that the new migrate type is used by expand if the kernel has decided to change it before. Otherwise, the remainders are put back onto their original migrate list.

Finally, one more scenario must be considered: What if the allocation cannot be satisfied despite all page orders and all migrate types have been taken into account? In this case, the kernel can try to fulfill the allocation from the MIGRATE_RESERVE list, which serves as a last resort:

mm/page_alloc.c
```
       /* Use MIGRATE_RESERVE rather than fail an allocation */
       return __rmqueue_smallest(zone, order, MIGRATE_RESERVE);
}
```

3.5.6 Freeing Pages

__free_pages is the base function used to implement all functions of the kernel API. Its code flow diagram is shown in Figure 3-35.

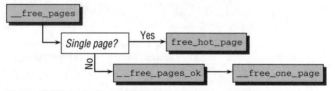

Figure 3-35: Code flow diagram for __free_pages.

__free_pages first establishes whether a single page or a larger contiguous block is to be freed. If a single page is freed, it is not returned to the buddy system but is placed in the per-CPU cache — in the warm list for all pages that are highly likely to reside in the CPU cache. For this purpose, the kernel provides the free_hot_page helper function, which is a parameter conversion function for free_hot_cold_page that is invoked in turn.

If free_hot_cold_page determines that the number of pages in the per-CPU cache exceeds the limit set by pcp->count, a whole batch of pages — whose size is specified by pcp->batch — is returned to the buddy system. This strategy is known as *lazy coalescing*. It prevents large numbers of wasteful coalescing operations that would be carried out if single pages were returned to the buddy system and then immediately split to satisfy subsequent allocation requests. The free_pages_bulk function is used to return pages to the buddy system.

If the lazy coalescing limit is not exceeded, the page is simply kept on the per-CPU cache. However, it is important that the `private` element be set to the migrate type of the page. As described, this allows allocations fulfilled from the per-CPU cache to pick only pages of the proper migrate type.

If more than one page is freed, then `__free_pages` delegates work (after a detour that is not interesting for our purposes) to `__free_pages_ok` and finally to `__free_one_page`. Despite the name, the function not only handles freeing of single pages, but also takes compound pages into account.

mm/page_alloc.c
```
static inline void __free_one_page (struct page *page,
                struct zone *zone, unsigned int order)
```

This function is the cornerstone of memory freeing. The relevant area is added to the appropriate `free_area` list of the buddy system. When buddy pairs are freed, the function coalesces them into a contiguous area that is then placed in the next higher `free_area` list. If this reunites a further buddy pair, it is also coalesced and moved to a higher list. This procedure is repeated until all possible buddy pairs have been coalesced and the changes have been propagated upward as far as possible.

However, this doesn't answer the question as to how the kernel knows that both parts of a buddy pair are located on the list of free pages. To place a page group back into the buddy system, the kernel must be able to compute two things: the address of the potential buddy and the index of the combined page group if both buddies can be recombined. Two auxiliary functions are provided for this purpose:

mm/page_alloc.c
```
static inline struct page *
__page_find_buddy(struct page *page, unsigned long page_idx, unsigned int order)
{
        unsigned long buddy_idx = page_idx ^ (1 << order);

        return page + (buddy_idx - page_idx);
}

static inline unsigned long
__find_combined_index(unsigned long page_idx, unsigned int order)
{
        return (page_idx & ~(1 << order));
}
```

It is advantageous to remember that the operator ^ performs a bitwise XOR operation. The calculations performed by the function will be clarified by an example immediately.

First, we need to introduce one more helper function, though. The page index of the buddy is not enough. The kernel must also ensure that all pages, belonging to the buddy are free and thus contained in the buddy system to be able to merge both pairs:

mm/page_alloc.c
```
static inline int page_is_buddy(struct page *page, struct page *buddy,
                          int order)
{
```

```
        ...
            if (PageBuddy(buddy) && page_order(buddy) == order) {
                return 1;
            }
            return 0;
        }
```

If the first page of the buddy group is in the buddy system, then the PG_buddy bit of the corresponding struct page instance is set. This, however, is not sufficient to reunite two buddies: When freeing a page group with 2^{order} pages, the kernel must ensure that 2^{order} pages of the second buddy are contained in the buddy system. This is easy to check because the page order of the free group is stored in the first private element of the struct page instance of a free group, and page_order reads this value. Note that page_is_buddy is slightly more complicated in reality because it needs to account for memory holes, but this is omitted to simplify matters.

Table 3-8: Calculations When a Page is Placed Back into the Buddy System.

order	page_idx	buddy_index – page_index	__find_combined_index
0	10	1	10
1	10	-2	8
2	8	4	8
3	8	-8	0

The following code determines whether a buddy pair can be coalesced:

mm/page_alloc.c
```
static inline void __free_one_page(struct page *page,
struct zone *zone, unsigned int order)
{
        int migratetype = get_pageblock_migratetype(page);
        ...
        while (order < MAX_ORDER-1) {
                unsigned long combined_idx;
                struct page *buddy;

                buddy = __page_find_buddy(page, page_idx, order);
                if (!page_is_buddy(page, buddy, order))
                        break; /* Move the buddy up one level. */

                list_del(&buddy->lru);
                zone->free_area[order].nr_free--;
                rmv_page_order(buddy);
                combined_idx = __find_combined_index(page_idx, order);
                page = page + (combined_idx - page_idx);
                page_idx = combined_idx;
                order++;
        }
        ...
```

The routine tries to free a page group of order `order`. Because it is possible not only that the current group can be merged with its direct buddy, but also that higher-order buddies can be merged, the kernel needs to find the maximal allocation order for which this is possible.

The action of the code is best understood by means of an example. Imagine that an order 0 allocation, that is, a single page, is freed, and let this page have the page index 10. The required calculations are found in Table 3-8, and Figure 3-36 visualizes the process step-by-step. We assume that page 10 is the last missing link that allows for coalescing two buddies of order 3 to form a new range of order 4.

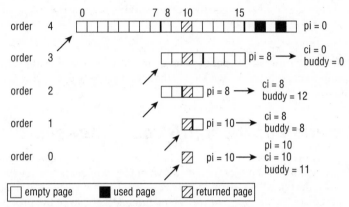

Figure 3-36: Returning a page into the buddy system can cause higher-order allocations to be coalesced. pi stands for `page_index`, while ci denotes `combined_index`.

The first loop pass finds page number 11 as the buddy for page 10. Since not the page number of the buddy, but a pointer to the corresponding `page` instance is required, the difference `buddy_idx` - `page_idx` is of relevance: It denotes the difference between the current page and its buddy, and adding it to the `page` pointer will deliver a pointer to the `page` instance of the buddy.

This pointer is required by `page_is_buddy` to check if the buddy is free. As per Figure 3-36, this is luckily the case, so the buddies can be combined. This requires that page number 11 is temporarily removed from the buddy system because it will be reintegrated as part of a larger block later. The `page` instance is taken off the free list, and `rmv_page_order` clears the `PG_buddy` flag and the private data.

Computing the index of the combined group in `__find_combined_index` delivers 10, because the 2-page buddy block starts at this page number. At the end of each loop step, the `page` pointer is set to point to the first page in the new buddy group, but in this case, nothing needs to be modified.

The next loop pass works similarly, but now for `order=1`; that is, the kernel tries to combine two 2-page buddies into a 4-page group. The buddy of the [10, 11] page group starts at page number 8, so the difference `buddy_index` - `page_index` is negative. Naturally, there's nothing preventing a buddy from being on the left-hand side of the current page group. The combined index of the merged group is 8, so the `page` pointer has to be updated accordingly after `page_is_buddy` has ensured that all pages of the new buddy (i.e., pages 8 and 9) are contained in the buddy system.

The loop continues until the order 4. This page group cannot be merged with its buddy because the buddy is not empty, as the figure shows. Consequently, `page_is_buddy` does not allow for merging the two regions, and the loop is left.

Finally, the $2^4 = 16$ page region must now be placed on the free lists of the buddy system. This is not very complicated:

mm/page_alloc.c
```
            set_page_order(page, order);
            list_add(&page->lru,
                    &zone->free_area[order].free_list[migratetype]);
            zone->free_area[order].nr_free++;
    }
```

Notice that the allocation order of the page group is preserved in the `private` element of the first `page` instance of the group. This way the kernel knows that not only page 0, but also the whole range $[0, 15]$, is free and in the buddy system.

3.5.7 Allocation of Discontiguous Pages in the Kernel

Physically contiguous mappings are best for the kernel for the reasons given above, but they cannot always be used successfully. When a larger chunk of memory is allocated, it may be that it is not available in a contiguous block despite all efforts made to avoid this situation. This is not a problem in userspace because normal processes are designed to use the paging mechanism of the processor even though this is costly in terms of speed and TLBs.

The same technique can also be applied in the kernel. As discussed in Section 3.4.2, the kernel reserves a chunk of its virtual address space so that it can set up contiguous mappings in them.

As Figure 3-37 shows, a memory zone for the management of discontiguous memory on IA-32 follows the direct mapping of the first 892 MiB of RAM after an intervening safety gap of 8 MiB. This segment has all the properties of a linear address space; the pages assigned to it can be located anywhere in RAM memory. This is achieved by modifying the kernel page tables responsible for this area.

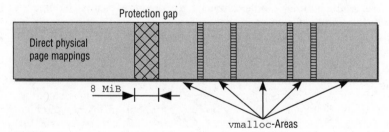

Figure 3-37: `vmalloc` area in the kernel's virtual address space on IA-32 systems.

A self-contained area separated from the other areas by a memory page is assigned to each `vmalloc` allocation. Like the boundary between direct mappings and the `vmalloc` area, the purpose of this is to safeguard against incorrect memory access operations; these occur only as a result of kernel faults and should be reported by a system error message rather than allowing the data of other kernel parts to be overwritten unnoticed. Because this separation is made in virtual address space, no valuable real memory pages are wasted.

Reserving Memory with vmalloc

vmalloc is the interface function used by the kernel code to request memory that is not necessarily contiguous in physical memory but is always linear in virtual memory.

<vmalloc.h>
```
void *vmalloc(unsigned long size);
```

Just one parameter is required to specify the size of the required memory area — in contrast to the functions discussed earlier, the size unit is not pages but bytes, as is common in userspace programming.

The best-known example of vmalloc use is in the module implementation of the kernel. Because modules can be loaded at any time, there is no guarantee — particularly if the system has been up and running for a long time — that sufficient contiguous memory will be available for the sometimes voluminous module data. This problem can be circumvented by using vmalloc if sufficient memory can be pieced together from smaller chunks.

vmalloc is also invoked at about 400 other places in the kernel, particularly in device and sound drivers.

Because the memory pages used for vmalloc must in any case be actively mapped in kernel address space, it is obviously preferable to use pages from ZONE_HIGHMEM for this purpose. This allows the kernel to conserve the more valuable lower zones without incurring any added disadvantages. For this reason, vmalloc (along with the mapping functions discussed in Section 3.5.8) is one of the few occasions when the kernel is able to use highmem pages for its own purposes (and not for userspace applications).

Data Structures

When it manages the vmalloc area in virtual memory, the kernel must keep track of which sections are in use and which are free. To this end, it defines a data structure to hold all used sections in a linked list.

> **The kernel uses an important data structure called vm_area_struct to manage the virtual address space contents of a userspace process. Despite the similarity of name and purpose, these two structures must not be confused.**

<vmalloc.h>
```
struct vm_struct {
        struct vm_struct        *next;
        void                    *addr;
        unsigned long           size;
        unsigned long           flags;
        struct page             **pages;
        unsigned int            nr_pages;
        unsigned long           phys_addr;
};
```

There is an instance of the structure in kernel memory for each area allocated with vmalloc. The meanings of the structure elements are as follows:

❏ addr defines the start address of the allocated area in virtual address space; size indicates the size of the area. A complete allocation plan of the vmalloc area can be drawn up on the basis of this information.

❏ flags stores the — almost inevitable — flag set associated with the memory section. It is used only to specify the memory area type and currently accepts one of the three values below.

  ❏ VM_ALLOC specifies that the area was created by vmalloc.

  ❏ VM_MAP is set to indicate that an existing collection of pages was mapped into the contiguous virtual address space.

  ❏ VM_IOREMAP indicates that an (almost) random physical memory area was mapped into the vmalloc area; this is an architecture-specific operation.

  Section 3.5.7 shows how the latter two values are employed.

❏ pages is a pointer to an array of page pointers. Each element represents the page instance of a physical page mapped into virtual address space.

  nr_pages specifies the number of entries in pages and therefore the number of memory pages involved.

❏ phys_addr is required only if physical memory areas described by a physical address are mapped with ioremap. This information is held in phys_addr.

❏ next enables the kernel to hold all sections in the vmalloc area on a singly linked list.

Figure 3-38 shows an example of how the structure is used. Three physical pages whose (fictitious) positions in RAM are 1,023, 725 and 7,311 are mapped one after the other. In the virtual vmalloc area, the kernel sees them as a contiguous memory area starting at the VMALLOC_START + 100.

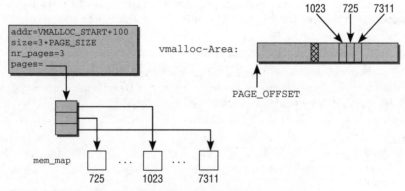

Figure 3-38: Mapping physical pages into the vmalloc area.

Creating a `vm_area`

Before a new virtual memory area can be created, it is necessary to find a suitable location for it. A linked list with instances of `vm_area` manages the sections already created in the `vmalloc` area. The global variable `vmlist` defined in `mm/vmalloc` is the list head.

mm/vmalloc.c
```
struct vm_struct *vmlist;
```

The kernel provides the `get_vm_area` helper function in `mm/vmalloc`; it acts as a parameter-preparation front end for `__get_vm_area`. In turn, the latter function is a frontend for `__get_vm_area_node` that does the actual work. On the basis of the size information for the area, the function tries to find a suitable place in the virtual `vmalloc` space.

As a safety gap of 1 page (guard page) is inserted between each `vmalloc` area, the kernel first increases the `size` specification by the appropriate amount.

mm/vmalloc.c
```
struct vm_struct *__get_vm_area_node(unsigned long size, unsigned long flags,
                           unsigned long start, unsigned long end, int node)
{
        struct vm_struct **p, *tmp, *area;
...
        size = PAGE_ALIGN(size);
....
        /*
         * We always allocate a guard page.
         */
        size += PAGE_SIZE;
...
```

The `start` and `end` parameters are set to `VMALLOC_START` and `VMALLOC_END`, respectively, by the calling functions.

A loop then iterates over all elements of the `vmlist` list to find a suitable entry.

mm/vmalloc.c
```
        for (p = &vmlist; (tmp = *p) != NULL ;p = &tmp->next) {
                if ((unsigned long)tmp->addr < addr) {
                        if((unsigned long)tmp->addr + tmp->size >= addr)
                                addr = ALIGN(tmp->size +
                                                (unsigned long)tmp->addr, align);
                        continue;
                }
                if ((size + addr) < addr)
                        goto out;
                if (size + addr <= (unsigned long)tmp->addr)
                        goto found;
                addr = ALIGN(tmp->size + (unsigned long)tmp->addr, align);
```

```
            if (addr > end - size)
                    goto out;
    }
...
```

The kernel finds a suitable position if `size+addr` is less than the start address of the area just examined (held in `tmp->addr`). The new list element is then initialized with the appropriate values and is added to the `vmlist` linked list.

mm/vmalloc.c
```
found:
            area->next = *p;
            *p = area;

            area->flags = flags;
            area->addr = (void *)addr;
            area->size = size;
            area->pages = NULL;
            area->nr_pages = 0;
            area->phys_addr = 0;

            return area;
...
    }
```

A null pointer is returned to indicate failure if no suitable memory area is found.

The `remove_vm_area` function removes an existing area from the `vmalloc` address space.

<vmalloc.h>
```
struct vm_struct *remove_vm_area(void *addr);
```

The function expects as a parameter the virtual start address of the area to be removed. To find the area, the kernel must successively scan the list elements of `vmlist` until it finds a match. The corresponding `vm_area` instance can then be removed from the list.

Allocating a Memory Area

Allocation of a non-continuous memory area is initiated by `vmalloc`. This is simply a front-end function to supply `__vmalloc` with suitable parameters and to directly invoke `__vmalloc_node`. The associated code flow diagram is shown in Figure 3-39.

Implementation is divided into three parts. First, `get_vm_area` finds a suitable area in the `vmalloc` address space. Then individual pages are allocated from physical memory, and finally, these pages are mapped contiguously into the `vmalloc` area — and VM allocation is done.

The full code need not be reproduced here because it is riddled with boring safety checks.[23] What is interesting is the allocation of the physical memory area (ignore the possibility that there may not be enough physical pages available).

---

[23]This, however, does not mean that you should avoid safety checks in your own code!

mm/vmalloc.c
```
void *__vmalloc_area_node(struct vm_struct *area, gfp_t gfp_mask,
                              pgprot_t prot, int node)
{
...
        for (i = 0; i < area->nr_pages; i++) {
                if (node < 0)
                        area->pages[i] = alloc_page(gfp_mask);
                else
                        area->pages[i] = alloc_pages_node(node, gfp_mask, 0);
        }
...
        if (map_vm_area(area, prot, &pages))
                goto fail;
        return area->addr;
...
}
```

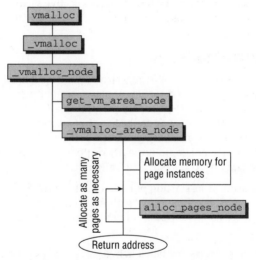

Figure 3-39: Code flow diagram for vmalloc.

If an explicit node is specified from which the pages are to be allocated, the kernel invokes alloc_pages_node. Otherwise, pages are taken from the current node using alloc_page.

The pages are removed from the buddy system of the relevant node; when this is done, vmalloc sets gfp_mask to GFP_KERNEL | __GFP_HIGHMEM — the kernel instructs memory management to take the pages from ZONE_HIGHMEM if possible. The reasons for this were given above: Pages from the lower-memory areas are more valuable and should therefore not be wasted for vmalloc allocations that could just as well be satisfied with high-memory pages.

Memory is taken from the buddy system, and gfp_mask is set to GFP_KERNEL | __GFP_HIGHMEM so that the kernel instructs memory management to take the pages from ZONE_HIGHMEM if possible. We have already seen the reasons.

> Memory is not allocated from the buddy system in a single chunk but page-by-page. This is a key aspect of **vmalloc**. If it were certain that a contiguous allocation could be made, there would be no need to use **vmalloc**. After all, the whole purpose of the function is to reserve large memory chunks even though they may not be contiguous owing to fragmentation of the available memory. Splitting the allocation into the smallest possible units — in other words, individual pages — ensures that **vmalloc** will still work even when physical memory is fragmented.

The kernel invokes map_vm_area to map the scattered physical pages contiguously into the virtual vmalloc area. This function iterates over the reserved physical pages and allocates the required number of entries in the various page directories and in the page tables.

Some architectures require flushing of the CPU caches after the page tables have been modified. The kernel therefore invokes the flush_cache_vmap whose definition is architecture-specific. Depending on CPU type, this includes the required low-level assembler statements to flush the cache, an invocation of flush_cache_all (if there is no function to flush selective virtually mapped areas), or an empty procedure if the CPU is not reliant on cache flushing, as is the case with IA-32.

Alternative Mapping Methods

Besides vmalloc, there are other ways of creating virtually contiguous mappings. All are based on the __vmalloc function discussed above or make use of a very similar mechanism (not discussed here).

❑ vmalloc_32 works in the same way as vmalloc but ensures that the physical memory used can always be addressed by means of regular 32-bit pointers. This is important if an architecture can address more memory than would normally be possible on the basis of its word length; this is the case, for example, on IA-32 systems with enabled PAE.

❑ vmap uses a page array as its starting point to create a virtually contiguous memory area. In contrast to vmalloc, the physical memory location is not allocated implicitly but must be passed ready-made to the function. Mappings of this kind can be recognized by the VM_MAP flag in their vm_map instance.

❑ Unlike all mapping methods described above, ioremap is a processor-specific function that must be implemented on all architectures. It enables a chunk taken from the physical address space used by the system buses for I/O operations to be mapped into the address space of the kernel.

This function is used predominantly in device drivers to make the address areas used for communication with the peripherals available to the rest of the kernel (and, of course, to itself).

Freeing Memory

Two functions return memory to the kernel — vfree for areas allocated by vmalloc and vmalloc_32, and vunmap for mappings created using vmap or ioremap. Both lead back to __vunmap.

mm/vmalloc.c
```
void __vunmap(void *addr, int deallocate_pages)
```

addr indicates the start address of the area to be freed, and deallocate_pages specifies whether the physical pages associated with the area are to be returned to the buddy system. vfree sets the parameter to 1, whereas vunmap sets it to 0 because in this case only the mappings are removed but the associated physical pages are not returned to the buddy system. Figure 3-40 shows the code flow diagram for __vunmap.

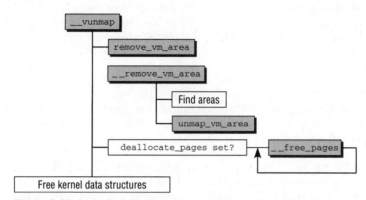

Figure 3-40: Code flow diagram for __vunmap.

It is not necessary to explicitly state the size of the area to be freed because this can be derived from the information in vmlist. The first task of __vunmap is therefore to scan this list in __remove_vm_area (invoked by remove_vm_area after completion of locking) in order to find the associated entry.

The vm_area instance found is used by unmap_vm_area to remove the entries no longer needed from the page tables. In the same way as when memory is reserved, the function works its way through the various hierarchy levels of page management, but this time removes the entries involved. It also updates the CPU caches.

If the __vunmap function parameter deallocate_pages is set to a true value (in vfree), the kernel iterates over all elements of area->pages in which there are pointers to the page instances of the physical pages involved. __free_page is invoked for each entry to return the page to the buddy system.

Finally, the kernel data structures used to manage the memory area must be returned.

3.5.8 Kernel Mappings

Although the vmalloc family of functions can be used to map pages from the highmem area into the kernel (these are then not usually directly visible in kernel space), this is not the actual purpose of these functions. It is important to underline this fact because the kernel provides other functions for the explicit mapping of ZONE_HIGHMEM pages into kernel space, and these are unrelated to the vmalloc mechanism; this is, therefore, a common source of confusion.

Persistent Kernel Mappings

The kmap function must be used if highmem pages are to be mapped into kernel address space for a longer period (as a *persistent mapping*). The page to be mapped is specified by means of a pointer to page as the function parameter. The function creates a mapping when this is necessary (i.e., if the page really is a highmem page) and returns the address of the data.

This task is simple if highmem support is not enabled. In this case, all pages can be accessed directly so it is only necessary to return the page address; there is no need to create a mapping explicitly.

The situation is more complicated if highmem pages are actually present. As with vmalloc, the kernel must first establish an association between the highmem pages and the addresses at which they are mapped. An area in virtual address space must also be reserved to map the pages, and finally, the kernel must keep track of which parts of the virtual area are already in use and which are still free.

Data Structures

As discussed in Section 3.4.2, the IA-32 kernel reserves a region that follows on from the vmalloc area and extends from PKMAP_BASE to FIXADDR_START. This area is used for persistent mappings. The schemes used by different architectures are similar.

pkmap_count (defined in mm/highmem.m) is an integer array with LAST_PKMAP positions that contain an entry for each page that can be persistently mapped. It is, in fact, a usage counter for the mapped pages with slightly unusual semantics. The number of users in the kernel is not counted, but the number of users plus 1. If the value of the counter is 2, the mapped page is used at just one point in the kernel. The counter value 5 indicates that there are four users. Expressed more generally, the counter value n stands for $n - 1$ users in the kernel.

As with classic usage counters, 0 means that the associated page is not in use. Counter value 1 has a special meaning. The page associated with the position has already been mapped but cannot be used because the TLB of the CPU has not been updated and access would either fail or be directed to an incorrect address.

The kernel makes use of the following data structure to create the association between the page instances of the physical pages and their position in the virtual memory area:

mm/highmem.c
```
struct page_address_map {
        struct page *page;
        void *virtual;
        struct list_head list;
};
```

This structure is used to create the page⟶virtual mapping (hence the name of the structure). page holds a pointer to the page instance in the global mem_map array, and virtual specifies the allocated position in the kernel virtual address space.

For ease of organization, the mappings are kept in a hash table where the list element is used to set up an overflow list to handle hash collisions.

The hash table is implemented by means of the page_address_htable array, not discussed further here. The hash function is page_slot from mm/highmen.c, which determines the page address on the basis of the page instance. page_address is the front-end function to determine the address of a given page instance using the data structures just described:

mm/highmem.c
```
void *page_address(struct page *page)
```

Figure 3-41 outlines the interplay between the above data structures.

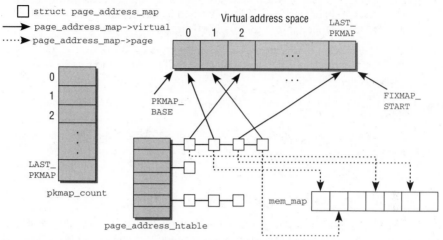

Figure 3-41: Data structures for managing persistent mappings.

Finding Page Addresses

page_address first checks whether the passed page instance is in normal memory or high memory. If the former applies, the page address can be calculated from the position of page in the mem_map array. In the latter case, the above hash table is referenced to find the virtual address.

Creating a Mapping

The kmap function must be used to create a mapping by means of a page pointer.[24] It is only a front end to establish whether the desired page really is in highmem. If not, the address yielded by page_address is returned as the result. Otherwise, the kernel delegates work to kmap_high, which is defined as follows:

mm/highmem.c
```
void fastcall *kmap_high(struct page *page)
{
        unsigned long vaddr;

        vaddr = (unsigned long)page_address(page);
        if (!vaddr)
                vaddr = map_new_virtual(page);
        pkmap_count[PKMAP_NR(vaddr)]++;
        return (void*) vaddr;
}
```

---

[24]This function resides not only in arch/x86/mm/highmem_32.c but also in include/asm-ppc/highmem.h and include/asm-sparc/highmem.h with practically the same definition.

The `page_address` function discussed above first checks whether the page is already mapped. If it does not return a valid address, the page must be mapped using `map_new_virtual`. The function performs the following main steps:

1. The `pkmap_count` array is scanned backward from the last used position (held in the global variable `last_pkmap_nr`) until a free position is found. If no position is free, the function sleeps until another part of the kernel performs an unmapping.

   When the maximum index of `pkmap_count` is reached, the search begins at position 0. In this case, the `flush_all_zero_pkmaps` function is also invoked to flush the caches (you will see this shortly).

2. The page tables of the kernel are modified so that the page is mapped at the desired position. However, the TLB is not updated.

3. The usage counter for the new position is set to 1. As stated above, this means that the page is reserved but cannot be used because the TLB entries are not current.

4. `set_page_address` adds the page to the data structures of the persistent kernel mappings.

The function returns the virtual address of the newly mapped page as its result.

On architectures that do not require high-memory pages (or if `CONFIG_HIGHMEM` is not set), a generic version of `kmap` is used to return only the page address without changing anything in virtual memory.

```
<highmem.h>
static inline void *kmap(struct page *page)
{
        might_sleep();
        return page_address(page);
}
```

Unmapping

Pages mapped with `kmap` must be unmapped using `kunmap` when they are no longer needed. As usual, this function first checks whether the relevant page (identified by means of its `page` instance) is actually in high memory. If so, work is delegated to `kunmap_high` from `mm/highmem.c`, whose main task is to decrement the counter at the corresponding position in the `pkmap_count` array (I won't discuss the details).

> **This mechanism can never reduce the counter value to less than 1; this means that the associated page is not freed. This is because of the additional usage counter increment required to ensure correct handling of the CPU cache as discussed above.**

The `flush_all_zero_pkmaps` also mentioned above is key to the final freeing of a mapping; it is always invoked when the search for a free position in `map_new_virtual` starts from the beginning. It is responsible for three actions:

1. `flush_cache_kmaps` performs a flush on the kernel mappings (on most architectures that require explicit flushing, the complete CPU cache is flushed using `flush_cache_all`) because the global page tables of the kernel are changed.[25]

---

[25]This is a very costly operation that fortunately is not required on many processor architectures. In this case, it is defined as a null operation as described in Section 3.7.

2. `pkmap_count` is scanned in full. Entries with counter value 1 are set to 0, and the associated entry is deleted from the page table, thus finally removing the mapping.

3. Finally, all TLB entries present for the `PKMAP` area are flushed using the `flush_tlb_kernel_range` function.

Temporary Kernel Mappings

The `kmap` function just described must not be used in interrupt handlers because it can sleep. If there are no free positions in the `pkmap` array, it goes to sleep until the situation improves. The kernel therefore provides an alternative mapping function that executes atomically and is logically named `kmap_atomic`. A major advantage of this function is that it is faster than a normal `kmap`. However, it must *not* be used in code that can potentially go to sleep. It is therefore ideal for short code sections that quickly require a temporary page.

The definition of `kmap_atomic` is architecture-specific for IA-32, PPC, and Sparc32, but the three implementations differ only in very minor details. Their prototype is identical.

```
void *kmap_atomic(struct page *page, enum km_type type)
```

`page` is a pointer to the management structure of the highmem page, and `type` defines the type of mapping required.[26]

```
<asm-arch/kmap_types.h>
enum km_type {
    KM_BOUNCE_READ,
    KM_SKB_SUNRPC_DATA,
...
    KM_PTE0,
    KM_PTE1,
...
    KM_SOFTIRQ1,
    KM_TYPE_NR
};
```

The fixmap mechanism discussed in Section 3.4.2 makes the memory needed to create atomic mappings available in the kernel address space. An area that can be used to map highmem pages is set up between `FIX_KMAP_BEGIN` and `FIX_KMAP_END` in the `fixed_addresses` array. The exact position is calculated on the basis of the CPU currently active and the desired mapping type.

```
idx = type + KM_TYPE_NR*smp_processor_id();
vaddr = __fix_to_virt(FIX_KMAP_BEGIN + idx);
```

In the fixmap area, there is a "window" for each processor in the system. It contains just one entry for each mapping type, as demonstrated in Figure 3-42 (`KM_TYPE_NR` is not a separate type but simply indicates how many entries there are in `km_type`). This arrangement makes it clear why functions may not block when they use `kmap_atomic`. If they did, another process could create a mapping of the same type behind their backs and overwrite the existing entries.

---

[26]The contents of the structure differ according to architecture, but the differences are so insignificant that they are not worth describing.

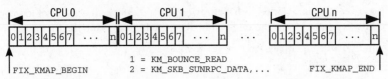

Figure 3-42: Mapping high-memory pages by means of fixed mappings.

Once the appropriate index has been calculated using the formula specified above and the associated fixmap address has been found, all the kernel need do is modify the page tables accordingly and flush the TLBs to put the changes into effect.

The kunmap_atomic function unmaps an existing atomic mapping from virtual memory by reference to its type and virtual address simply by deleting the corresponding entry in the page tables.

Mapping Functions on Machines without Highmem

Many architectures do not support high memory because they don't need it — 64-bit architectures head this list. However, to permit use of the above functions without having to constantly distinguish between highmem and non-highmem architectures, the kernel defines several macros that implement compatible functions in normal memory (these are also used when highmem support is disabled on highmem-capable machines).

```
<highmem.h>
#ifdef CONFIG_HIGHMEM
...
#else
static inline void *kmap(struct page *page)
{
        might_sleep();
        return page_address(page);
}

#define kunmap(page) do { (void) (page); } while (0)
#define kmap_atomic(page, idx)          page_address(page)
#define kunmap_atomic(addr, idx)        do { } while (0)
#endif
```

3.6 The Slab Allocator

Every C programmer is familiar with malloc and all its related functions in the standard library; they are frequently invoked by most programs to reserve a few bytes of memory.

The kernel must also frequently allocate memory but cannot resort to the standard library functions. The buddy system resources described above support the allocation of memory in pages, but this unit is much too big. If space is needed for a string with 10 characters, reserving a full page with 4 KiB or more is not only wasteful but absolutely unacceptable. The obvious solution is to split the memory in a page into smaller units that can then hold large numbers of small objects.

To this end, it is necessary to introduce new management mechanisms that place a greater overhead on the kernel. To minimize the impact of this extra burden on system performance, the implementation of the management layer should be as compact as possible so that there is little noticeable effect on the caches and TLBs of the processor. At the same time, the kernel must ensure that memory is utilized speedily and efficiently. Not only Linux but look-alikes and all other operating systems face this problem. Over the course of time, some good solutions and some bad solutions have been proposed and are described in the general operating system literature (e.g., [Tan07]).

One such proposal — slab allocation — has proved to be very efficient for many workloads. It was devised and implemented for Solaris 2.4 by Jeff Bonwick, a Sun employee. Because he publicly documented his method [Bon94], it was also possible to implement a version for Linux.

The provision of smaller memory blocks is not the only task of the slab allocator. Owing to its structure, it also serves as a *cache* for objects that are frequently allocated and then released. By setting up a slab cache, the kernel is able to keep a store of objects at the ready for subsequent use, even in an initialized state, if so desired. For instance, the kernel must frequently generate new instances of struct fs_struct to manage the filesystem data associated with a process (see Chapter 8). The memory blocks occupied by instances of this type are reclaimed just as often (when a process terminates). In other words, the kernel tends to allocate and release **sizeof{fs_struct}** memory blocks with great regularity. The slab allocator keeps the returned memory blocks on an internal list and does not immediately give them back to the buddy system. A recently returned block is then used when a new request is received for a fresh instance of the object. This has two advantages. First, handling time is shorter because the kernel need not apply the buddy system algorithms. Second, because the memory blocks are still "fresh," there is a strong probability that they are still in one of the CPU caches.

The slab allocator also has two further benefits:

❑ Calls to the buddy system are operations that have a considerable impact on the data and instruction caches of the system. The more the kernel wastes these resources, the less they are available for userspace processes. The more lightweight slab allocator dispenses with the need for calls to the buddy system wherever possible and helps prevent undesirable cache "contamination."

❑ Data stored in pages delivered directly by the buddy system is always clustered around addresses divisible by powers of 2 (many other allocation methods that divide pages into smaller blocks share this characteristic). This has a negative impact on CPU cache utilization because some cache lines are overused owing to this kind of address distribution and others are almost empty. This disadvantage can be even more drastic on multiprocessor systems if different memory addresses are transferred on different buses because some buses may be congested, while others are little used.

By means of *slab coloring*, the slab allocator is able to distribute objects uniformly to achieve uniform cache utilization, as demonstrated below.

> *That frequently used kernel objects are kept in the CPU cache is a desired effect. The earlier comment that the large cache and TLB footprints of the buddy system are negative in terms of the slab allocator related to the fact that* unimportant *data land in the CPU cache and* important *data are displaced — a situation that should naturally be prevented.*

> **The term *color* is used in the metaphorical sense. It has nothing to do with colors but represents a certain offset by which the objects in the slab are shifted to place them in a different cache line.**

Where does the name *slab* allocator come from? The objects managed in each cache are combined into larger groups covering one or more contiguous page frames. Such groups are called *slabs*; each cache consists of several such slabs.

3.6.1 Alternative Allocators

Although the slab allocator works well for many possible workloads, there are naturally situations in which it fails to provide optimal performance. Problems arise when slab allocation is used on machines that range on the borders of the current hardware scale: tiny embedded systems and large, massively parallel systems equipped with huge amounts of RAM. In the second case, the large amount of metadata required by the slab allocator can become a problem: developers have reported that many gigabytes of memory are required only for the slab data structures on large systems. For embedded systems, the total footprint and complexity of slab allocation can simply be too much.

To cope with such situations, two drop-in replacements for the slab allocator were added during the development of kernel 2.6:

❏ The *slob* allocator is especially optimized for low code size. It is centered around a simple linked lists of blocks (thus its name). To allocate memory, a likewise simple first-fit algorithm is used.

With only roughly 600 lines, the total footprint of the slob allocator is very small. Naturally, it is not the most efficient allocator in terms of speed and is definitely not designed to be used on large-scale systems.

❏ The *slub* allocator tries to minimize the required memory overhead by packing page frames into groups and to manage these groups by overloading unused fields in `struct page`. While this certainly does not simplify the definition of this structure, as you have seen before, the effort is justified by the better performance of slub in contrast to slab on large machines.

Since slab allocation is the default option used by most kernel configurations, alternative allocators are not discussed in detail. It is, however, important to emphasize that the rest of the kernel need not be concerned about which low-level allocator is chosen. The visible front end is identical for all allocators. Each must implement a certain set of functions for memory allocation and caching:

❏ `kmalloc`, `__kmalloc`, and `kmalloc_node` as general (node-specific) allocation functions.

❏ `kmem_cache_alloc`, `kmem_cache_alloc_node` as (node-specific) providers of specific kernel caches.

The behavior of these functions is included in the following discussion of the slab allocator. Using these standard functions, the kernel can provide further convenience functions that do not require specific knowledge about how memory is managed internally — for instance, `kcalloc` to allocate memory for arrays, or `kzalloc` to allocate a memory region that is filled with zero bytes. The situation is illustrated in Figure 3-43.

Regular kernel code just needs to include `slab.h` to enjoy all standard kernel functions for memory allocation. The build system will ensure that the allocator chosen at compile time is used to fulfill the desired requests.

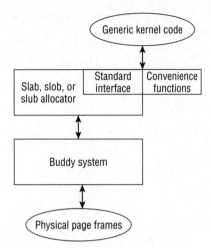

Figure 3-43: Connection between the buddy system, general-purpose allocators, and the interface to generic kernel code.

3.6.2 Memory Management in the Kernel

The general allocation and freeing functions of the kernel have similar names to their equivalents in the C standard library and are employed in exactly the same way.

❑   kmalloc(size, flags) reserves a memory area of size bytes and returns a void pointer to the start of the area. If insufficient memory is available (a very improbable situation in the kernel but one that must always be catered for), a null pointer is the result.

   The flags argument specifies the area from which memory is to be selected using the GFP_ constants discussed in Section 3.5.4, for example, GFP_DMA for a DMA-suitable memory area.

❑   **kfree{*ptr}** frees the memory area pointed at by *ptr.

In contrast to the situation in userspace programming, the kernel also includes the percpu_alloc and percpu_free functions to reserve and free the desired memory area for each system CPU (and *not* specifically for the CPU currently active).[27]

kmalloc is used at thousands of places in the kernel sources, but the pattern is always the same. The memory area reserved with kmalloc is converted to the correct type by means of a typecast and is then assigned to a pointer variable.

```
info = (struct cdrom_info *) kmalloc (sizeof (struct cdrom_info), GFP_KERNEL);
```

The task of setting up and using caches is not especially difficult from the programmer's point of view. A suitable cache must first be created with kmem_cache_create, then the objects it contains can be allocated

---

[27]Older kernel versions have used the functions alloc_percpu and free_percpu for this purpose, but since these functions do not support CPU hotplugging, they are only supported for compatibility reasons and should not be used in new code.

and freed using `kmem_cache_alloc` and `kmem_cache_free`. The slab allocator is automatically responsible for interaction with the buddy system to reserve the required pages.

A list of all active caches is held in `/proc/slabinfo` (the output below omits a few less important columns for reasons of space).[28]

```
wolfgang@meitner> cat /proc/slabinfo
slabinfo - version: 2.1
# name                 <active_objs> <num_objs> <objsize> <objperslab> <pagesperslab> : tunables
<limit> <batchcount> <sharedfactor> : slabdata <active_slabs> <num_slabs> <sharedavail>
nf_conntrack_expect        0        0    224   18  1 : tunables  0  0  0 : slabdata      0      0   0
UDPv6                     16       16    960    4  1 : tunables  0  0  0 : slabdata      4      4   0
TCPv6                     19       20   1792    4  2 : tunables  0  0  0 : slabdata      5      5   0
xfs_inode              25721    25725    576    7  1 : tunables  0  0  0 : slabdata   3675   3675   0
xfs_efi_item              44       44    352   11  1 : tunables  0  0  0 : slabdata      4      4   0
xfs_efd_item              44       44    360   11  1 : tunables  0  0  0 :
slabdata        4        4      0
...
kmalloc-128              795      992    128   32  1 : tunables  0  0  0 : slabdata     31     31   0
kmalloc-64             19469    19584     64   64  1 : tunables  0  0  0 : slabdata    306    306   0
kmalloc-32              2942     2944     32  128  1 : tunables  0  0  0 : slabdata     23     23   0
kmalloc-16              2869     3072     16  256  1 : tunables  0  0  0 : slabdata     12     12   0
kmalloc-8               4075     4096      8  512  1 : tunables  0  0  0 : slabdata      8      8   0
kmalloc-192             2940     3276    192   21  1 : tunables  0  0  0 : slabdata    156    156   0
kmalloc-96               754      798     96   42  1 : tunables  0  0  0 : slabdata     19     19   0
```

The file columns contain the following information in addition to a string that identifies each cache (and also ensures that no identical caches are created):

❑ Number of active objects in the cache.

❑ Total number of objects in the cache (used and unused).

❑ Size of the managed objects in bytes.

❑ Number of objects in a slab.

❑ Pages per slab.

❑ Number of active slabs.

❑ Object number allocated when the kernel decides to make more memory available to a cache. (A larger memory block is allocated in one chunk so that the required interaction with the buddy system is worthwhile.) This value is also used as the block size when shrinking the cache.

---

[28] Additional information on slab allocator statistics is output if the `CONFIG_DEBUG_SLAB` option is set at compilation time.

In addition to easily identified cache names such as `unix_sock` (for domain sockets, i.e., objects of type `struct unix_sock`), there are other fields called `kmalloc-size`. (Machines that provide DMA memory also include caches for DMA allocations, but these are not present in the above example.) These are the basis of the `kmalloc` function in which the kernel provides slab caches for various memory sizes that, with few exceptions, are in power-of-2 steps between $2^5 = 32$ (for machines with 4 KiB page size), respective 64 (for all other machines), and 2^{25} bytes. The upper bound can also be considerably smaller and is set by `KMALLOC_MAX_SIZE`, which, in turn, is computed based on the page size of the system and the maximally allowed allocation order:

```
<slab.h>
#define KMALLOC_SHIFT_HIGH ((MAX_ORDER + PAGE_SHIFT - 1) <= 25 ? \
(MAX_ORDER + PAGE_SHIFT - 1) : 25)

#define KMALLOC_MAX_SIZE (1UL << KMALLOC_SHIFT_HIGH)
#define KMALLOC_MAX_ORDER (KMALLOC_SHIFT_HIGH - PAGE_SHIFT)
```

Each time `kmalloc` is invoked, the kernel finds the most suitable cache and allocates one of its objects to satisfy the request for memory as best it can (if no cache fits exactly, larger objects are always allocated but never smaller objects).

The difference between the slab allocator and cache outlined above quickly disappears in the concrete implementation, so much so that both terms are used synonymously in the further course of the book. Section 3.6.5 looks at the details of `kmalloc` after discussing the implementation of the slab allocator.

3.6.3 The Principle of Slab Allocation

The slab allocator is made up of a closely interwoven network of data and memory structures that is not easy to untangle at first sight. It is therefore important to obtain an overview of the relationships between the structures before moving on to examine the implementation.

Basically, the slab cache consists of the two components shown in Figure 3-44: a cache object to hold the management data and slabs to hold the managed objects.

Each cache is responsible for just one object type, instances of `struct unix_sock`, for example, or general buffers. The number of slabs in each cache varies according to the number of pages used, the object size, and the number of objects managed. Section 3.6.4 goes into the details of how cache sizes are calculated.

All caches in the system are also kept in a doubly linked list. This gives the kernel the opportunity to traverse all caches one after the other; this is necessary, for example, when shrinking cache memory because of an impending memory shortage.

Fine Structure of the Cache

If we look more closely at the cache structure, we note further details of importance. Figure 3-45 provides an overview of the cache components.

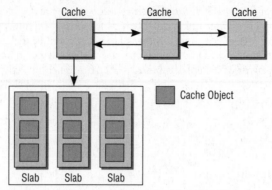

Figure 3-44: Components of the slab allocator.

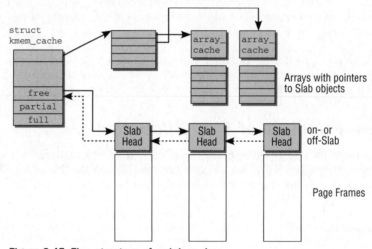

Figure 3-45: Fine structure of a slab cache.

Besides management data (such as the number of used and free objects or flag registers), the cache structure includes two elements of special significance:

❏   A pointer to an array in which the last freed objects can be kept for each specific CPU.

❏   Three list heads per memory node under which slabs can be listed. The first list contains `full` slabs, the second `partially free` slabs, and the third `free` slabs.

The cache structure points to an array that contains as many entries as there are CPUs in the system. Each element is a pointer to a further structure known as an *array cache*, which contains the management data for the particular system CPU (and not for the cache as a whole). The memory area immediately following the management data contains an array with pointers to as-yet-unused objects in the slabs.

The per-CPU pointers are important to best exploit the CPU caches. The LIFO principle (last in, first out) is applied when objects are allocated and returned. The kernel assumes that an object just returned is still in the cache and allocates it again as quickly as possible (in response to the next request). Only when the per-CPU caches are empty are free objects from the slabs used to refill them.

This results in a three-level hierarchy for object allocation within which both the allocation cost and the negative impact of the operation on caches and TLBs rise from level to level:

1. Per-CPU objects in the CPU cache.

2. Unused objects from an existing slab.

3. Unused objects from a new slab just reserved using the buddy system.

Fine Structure of Slabs

Objects are not listed continuously in slabs but are distributed according to a rather complicated scheme. Figure 3-46 illustrates the details.

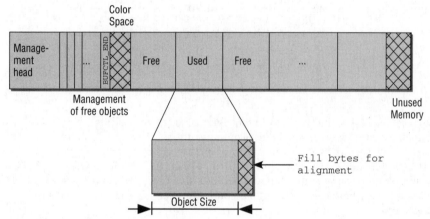

Figure 3-46: Fine structure of a slab.

The size used for each object does not reflect its exact size. Instead, the size is rounded to fulfill certain alignment criteria. Two alternatives are possible:

❑ Using the flag SLAB_HWCACHE_ALIGN at slab creation time, the slab user can request that objects are aligned to hardware cache lines. The alignment is then performed along the value returned by cache_line_size, which returns the processor-specific size of the L1 cache.

If objects are smaller than half of the cache line size, then more than one object is fit into one cache line.

❑ If alignment along hardware cache lines is not requested, then the kernel ensures that objects are aligned with BYTES_PER_WORD — the number of bytes needed to represent a void pointer.

On 32-bit processors, 4 bytes are required for a void pointer. Consequently, for an object with 6 bytes, $8 = 2 \times 4$ bytes are needed, and objects with 15 bytes require $16 = 4 \times 4$ bytes. The superfluous bytes are referred to as *fill bytes*.

Fill bytes speed access to the objects in a slab. Memory access is faster on almost all architectures if aligned addresses are used. This compensates for the disadvantage of higher memory requirements entailed by the use of fill bytes.

The management structure holding all the management data (and the list element to link with the cache lists) is located at the start of each slab. It is immediately followed by an array that includes an (integer) entry for each object in the slab. The entries are only of significance if the associated object is *not* allocated. In this case, it specifies the index of the next free object. Because the number of the free object with the lowest number is also stored in the management structure at the start of the slab, the kernel is easily able to find all objects currently available without having to use linked lists or other complicated associations.[29] The last array entry is always an end marker with the value BUFCTL_END.

Figure 3-47 illustrates the situation graphically.

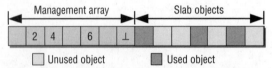

Figure 3-47: Management of the free objects in a slab.

In most cases, the size of the slab area (minus the management head) is not divisible by the (possibly padded) object size without a remainder. Consequently, a little superfluous memory is available to the kernel and is used to give the slab a "color" in the form of an offset as described above. The slab members of a cache are given different offsets to position the data in different cache lines with the result that the free memory at the start and end of a slab varies. When the offset is calculated, the kernel must take other alignment factors into account, for instance, alignment of the data on the L1 cache (discussed below).

The management data can be positioned either on the slab itself or in an external memory area allocated using kmalloc.[30] Which alternative the kernel selects depends on the size of the slab and of the objects used. The corresponding selection criteria are discussed shortly. The association between the management data and slab memory is easy to establish because the slab header contains a pointer to the start of the slab data area (regardless of whether it is *on-slab* or *off-slab*).

Figure 3-48 shows the situation when the data are not on the slab itself (as it is in Figure 3-46) but in external memory.

And finally, the kernel needs a way of identifying the slab (and therefore the cache in which an object resides) by reference to the object itself. On the basis of an object's physical memory address, it is not difficult to find the associated page and therefore the matching page instance in the global mem_map array. As we already know, the page structure includes a list element used to manage the page in

---

[29] The original implementation of the slab allocator in the SunOS operating system kernel uses a linked list to keep track of the free objects.

[30] This requires special precautions when the kmalloc caches are initialized because obviously kmalloc cannot be invoked there yet. This and other *chicken-and-egg* problems of slab initialization are discussed below.

various lists. As this is not necessary for pages on the slab cache, the pointers can be used for other purposes:

❑   `page->list.next` points to the management structure of the cache in which the page resides.

❑   `page->list.prev` points to the management structure of the slab on which the page is held.

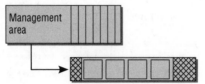

Management area

Figure 3-48: Slab with external (*off-slab*) slab header.

Setting or reading this information is concealed behind the `set_page_slab` and `get_page_slab`, respectively, `_cache` functions to lower the *hack value* of this convention.

mm/slab.c
```
void page_set_cache(struct page *page, struct kmem_cache *cache)
struct kmem_cache *page_get_cache(struct page *page)

void page_set_slab(struct page *page, struct slab *slab)
struct slab *page_get_slab(struct page *page)
```

Additionally, the kernel sets the page flag `PG_SLAB` for each physical page, that is allocated for the slab allocator.

3.6.4   Implementation

Various data structures are used to implement the slab allocator as described above. Although this does not appear to be difficult, the code is not always easy to read or understand. This is because many memory areas need to be manipulated using pointer arithmetic and type-casting — not necessarily one of the areas of C famed for its clarity. The code is also pervaded with pre-processor statements because the slab system features numerous debugging options. [31] Some of these are listed below:

❑   **Red Zoning** — An additional memory area filled with a known byte pattern is placed at the start and end of each object. If this pattern is overwritten, programmers will note when analyzing kernel memory that their code accesses memory areas that don't belong to them.

❑   **Object Poisoning** — Objects are filled with a predefined pattern when a slab is created and freed. If it is noted at object allocation that this pattern is changed, programmers know that unauthorized access has already taken place.

For the sake of simplicity and to focus attention on the big picture rather than minor details, let's restrict our description below to a "pure" slab allocator that doesn't make use of the above options.

---

[31] The `CONFIG_DEBUG_SLAB` configuration option must be set at compilation time to enable debugging. However, this significantly slows allocator performance.

Data Structures

Each cache is represented by an instance of the kmem_cache structure defined in mm/slab.c. The structure is not normally visible at other points of the kernel because it is defined in a C header and not in a header file. This is because users of the cache need not know in detail how the cache is implemented. It is sufficient to regard slab caches as mechanisms for the efficient creation and release of objects of a specific type by means of a set of standard functions.

The contents of the structure are as follows:

mm/slab.c
```
struct kmem_cache {
/* 1) per-cpu data, touched during every alloc/free */
        struct array_cache *array[NR_CPUS];
/* 2) Cache tunables. Protected by cache_chain_mutex */
        unsigned int batchcount;
        unsigned int limit;
        unsigned int shared;

        unsigned int buffer_size;
        u32 reciprocal_buffer_size;
/* 3) touched by every alloc & free from the backend */

        unsigned int flags; /* constant flags */
        unsigned int num; /* # of objs per slab */


/* 4) cache_grow/shrink */
        /* order of pgs per slab (2^n) */
        unsigned int gfporder;

        /* force GFP flags, e.g. GFP_DMA */
        gfp_t gfpflags;

        size_t colour; /* cache colouring range */
        unsigned int colour_off; /* colour offset */
        struct kmem_cache *slabp_cache;
        unsigned int slab_size;
        unsigned int dflags; /* dynamic flags */

        /* constructor func */
        void (*ctor)(struct kmem_cache *, void *);

/* 5) cache creation/removal */
        const char *name;
        struct list_head next;

/* 6) statistics */
...

        struct kmem_list3 *nodelists[MAX_NUMNODES];
};
```

This lengthy structure is divided into multiple parts as indicated by the comments in the kernel sources.[32]

The initial elements are concerned with CPU-specific data accessed by the kernel during each allocation, touched upon in Section 3-46.

❑   `array` is a pointer to an array with an entry for each CPU in the system. Each entry contains a further pointer to an instance of the `array_cache` structure discussed below.

❑   `batchcount` specifies the number of objects to be taken from the slabs of a cache and added to the per-CPU list if it is empty. It also indicates the number of objects to be allocated when a cache is grown.

❑   `limit` specifies the maximum number of objects that may be held in a per-CPU list. If this value is exceeded, the kernel returns the number of objects defined in `batchcount` to the slabs (if the kernel then shrinks the caches, memory is returned from the slabs to the buddy system).

❑   `buffer_size` specifies the size of the objects managed in the cache.[33]

❑   Suppose that the kernel has a pointer to an element in a slab and wants to determine the corresponding object index. The easiest way to do this is to divide the offset of the pointer compared to the start of the slab area by the object size. Consider, for example, that a slab area starts at memory location 100, each object requires 5 bytes, and the object in question is located at memory position 115. The offset between the slab start and the object is $115 - 100 = 15$, so the object index is $15/5 = 3$. Unfortunately, divisions are slow on some older machines.

Since multiplications are much faster on these machines, the kernel uses the so-called *Newton-Raphson* technique, which requires only multiplications and bit shifts. While the mathematical details are not interesting for our purposes (they can be found in any standard textbook), we need to know that instead of computing `C = A/B`, the kernel can also employ `C = reciprocal_divide(A, reciprocal_value(B))` — both functions are provided as library routines. Since the object size in a slab is constant, the kernel can store the recpirocal value of `buffer_size` in `recpirocal_buffer_size`, which can be used later when the division must be computed.

The kernel provides an instance of `array_cache` for each system processor. This structure is defined as follows:

mm/slab.c
```
struct array_cache {
        unsigned int avail;
        unsigned int limit;
        unsigned int batchcount;
        unsigned int touched;
        spinlock_t lock;
        void *entry[];
};
```

---

[32]If slab debugging is enabled, another part with statistical information gathered by the kernel concludes the structure.
[33]If slab debugging is enabled, the buffer size can differ from the object size because extra padding (in addition to the padding used to align the objects properly) is introduced per element. In this case, a second variable denotes the real size of the object.

The meanings of `batchcount` and `limit` are as given above. The values of `kmem_cache_s` are applied (normally unchanged) as defaults for the per-CPU values used for cache refill or emptying.

`avail` holds the number of elements currently available. `touched` is set to 1 when an element is removed from the cache, whereas cache shrinking causes `touched` to be set to 0. This enables the kernel to establish whether a cache has been accessed since it was last shrunk and is an indicator of the importance of the cache. The last element is a dummy array without an entry to facilitate access to the cache elements following each `array_cache` instance in memory.

The third and fourth parts of `kmem_cache` contain all the variables needed to manage the slabs and are required when the per-CPU caches are filled or emptied.

❑ `nodelists` is an array that contains an entry for each possible node in the system. Each entry holds an instance of `struct kmem_list3` that groups the three slab lists (full, free, partially free) together in a separate structure discussed below.

The element must be placed at the end of the structure. While it formally always has `MAX_NUMNODES` entries, it is possible that fewer nodes are usable on NUMA machines. The array thus requires fewer entries, and the kernel can achieve this at run time by simply allocating less memory than the array formally requires. This would not be possible if `nodelists` were placed in the middle of the structure.

On UMA machines, this is not much of a concern because only a single node will ever be available.

❑ `flags` is a flag register to define the global properties of the cache. Currently, there is only one flag bit. `CFLGS_OFF_SLAB` is set when the management structure is stored outside the slab.

❑ `objsize` is the size of the objects in the cache, including all fill bytes added for alignment purposes.

❑ `num` holds the maximum number of objects that fit into a slab.

❑ `free_limit` specifies the upper limit of free objects in a cache after it has been shrunk (if there is no reason to shrink the cache during normal operation, the number of free objects may exceed this value).

The list heads to manage the slab lists are kept in a separate data structure defined as follows:

mm/slab.c
```
struct kmem_list3 {
        struct list_head slabs_partial; /* partial list first, better asm code */
        struct list_head slabs_full;
        struct list_head slabs_free;
        unsigned long free_objects;
        unsigned int free_limit;
        unsigned int colour_next; /* Per-node cache coloring */
        spinlock_t list_lock;
        struct array_cache *shared; /* shared per node */
        struct array_cache **alien; /* on other nodes */
        unsigned long next_reap; /* updated without locking */
        int free_touched; /* updated without locking */
};
```

The meanings of the first three list heads are clear from the explanations in the above sections. `free_objects` indicates the total number of free objects in all slabs of `slabs_partial` and `slabs_free`.

`free_touched` indicates whether the cache is active or not. When an object is taken from the cache, the kernel sets the value of this variable to 1; when the cache is shrunk, the value is reset to 0. However, the kernel only shrinks a cache if `free_touched` has been set to 0 *beforehand*, because the value 1 indicates that another part of the kernel has just taken objects from the cache and thus it is not advisable to shrink it.

> This variable applies for the whole cache unlike the per-CPU `touched` element.

`next_reap` defines a time interval that the kernel must allow to elapse between two attempts to shrink the cache. The idea is to prevent degradation of system performance due to frequent cache shrinking and growing operations as can happen in certain load situations. This technique is only used on NUMA systems and will thus not concern us any further.

`free_limit` specifies the maximum number of unused objects permitted on all slabs.

The structure is concluded by pointers to `array_cache` instances that are either shared per node or originate from other nodes. This is of relevance on NUMA machines but, for the sake of simplicity, this won't be discussed in detail.

The third part of `kmem_cache` contains all variables needed to grow (and shrink) the cache.

❑ `gfporder` specifies the slab size as a binary logarithm of the number of pages, or, expressed differently, the slab comprises 2^{gfporder} pages.

❑ The three `colour` elements hold all relevant data for slab coloring.

`colour` specifies the maximum number of colors and `colour_next` the color to use for the next slab created by the kernel. Note, however, that this value is specified as an element of `kmem_list3`. `colour_off` is the basic offset multiplied by a color value to obtain the absolute offset. This is again required for NUMA machines — UMA systems could keep `colour_next` in `struct kmem_cache`. Placing the next color in a node-specific structure, however, allows coloring slabs added on the same node sequentially, which is beneficial for the local caches.

Example: If there are five possible colors $(0, 1, 2, 3, 4)$ and the offset unit is 8 bytes, the kernel can use the following offset values: $0 \times 8 = 0, 1 \times 8 = 8, 2 \times 8 = 16, 3 \times 8 = 24$ and $4 \times 8 = 32$ bytes.

Section 3.6.4 examines how the kernel determines the possible settings for slab colors. Besides, note that the kernel sources, in contrast to this book, spell *colour* properly, at least from the British point of view.

❑ If the slab head is stored outside the slab, `slabp_cache` points to the general cache from which the required memory is taken. If the slab head is on-slab, `slabp_cache` contains a null pointer.

❑ `dflags` is a further set of flags that describe the "dynamic properties" of the slab, but currently no flags are defined.

❑ `ctor` is a pointer to a constructor function that is invoked when objects are created. This method is well known in object-oriented languages such as C++ and Java. Former kernel versions did offer the ability to specify an additional destructor function, but since this opportunity was not used, it has been dropped during the development of kernel 2.6.22.

The fifth and last part (statistics fields that are of no further interest for our purposes) of `struct kmem_cache` consists of two further elements:

❏ `name` is a string containing a human-readable name for the cache. It is used, for example, to list the available caches in `/proc/slabinfo`.

❏ `next` is a standard list element to keep all instances of `kmem_cache` on the global list `cache_chain`.

Initialization

At first sight, initialization of the slab system does not appear to be especially complicated because the buddy system is already fully enabled and no other particular restrictions are imposed on the kernel. Nevertheless, there is a *chicken-and-egg* problem[34] because of the structure of the slab allocator.

To initialize the slab data structures, the kernel needs memory blocks that are much smaller than a complete page and are therefore best allocated by `kmalloc`. And here's the crux: `kmalloc` only functions if the slab system is already enabled.

To be more accurate, the problem lies with the initialization of the per-CPU caches for `kmalloc`. Before these caches can be initialized, `kmalloc` must be available to reserve the required memory space, and `kmalloc` itself is just in the process of being initialized. In other words, `kmalloc` can only be initialized once `kmalloc` has been initialized — an impossible scenario. The kernel must therefore resort to a few tricks.

The `kmem_cache_init` function is used to initialize the slab allocator. It is invoked during the kernel initialization phase (`start_kernel`) once the buddy system is enabled. However, on multiprocessor systems, the boot CPU is running and the other CPUs are not yet initialized. `kmem_cache_init` employs a multistep process to activate the slab allocator step-by-step:

1. `kmem_cache_init` creates the first slab cache in the system to generate memory for instances of `kmem_cache`. To this end, the kernel uses mainly static data created at compilation time; in fact, a static data structure (`initarray_cache`) is used as a per-CPU array. The name of this cache is `cache_cache`.

2. `kmem_cache_init` then initializes the general caches that serve as a source for `kmalloc`. For this purpose, `kmem_cache_create` is invoked for each cache size required. The function first needs only the `cache_cache` cache already created; however, when the per-CPU caches are to be initialized, the function must resort to `kmalloc`, and this is not yet possible.

To resolve this problem, the kernel uses the `g_cpucache_up` variable, which can accept one of four values (`NONE`, `PARTIAL_AC`, `PARTIAL_L3`, or `FULL`) to reflect the state of `kmalloc` initialization.

Initially the state of the kernel is `NONE`. When the smallest `kmalloc` cache (which provides memory blocks of 32 bytes on machines with 4 KiB memory pages; if other page sizes are used, the smallest allocation size is 64 bytes; the exact definition of existing sizes is given in Section 3.6.5) is initialized, a static variable is again used for the per-CPU cache data.

---

[34]*Chicken-and-egg problems* are encountered where something cannot happen until a second thing does, and the second thing cannot happen until the first does. For example, B must be present in order to initialize A, but A must be present to initialize B. It's the age-old question of which came first, the chicken or the egg?

If you are a scientist, you can also use the term *causality dilemma*, which expresses exactly the same, but sounds much more educated . . . .

The state in g_cpucache_up is then set to PARTIAL_AC, meaning that array_cache instances can be allocated immediately. If the initialized size is also sufficient to allocate kmem_list3 instances, the state immediately changes to PARTIAL_L3. Otherwise, this only happens when the next larger cache has been initialized.

The per-CPU data of the remaining kmalloc caches can now be created with kmalloc as an instance of arraycache_init, as only the smallest kmalloc area is needed for this purpose.

mm/slab.c
```
struct arraycache_init {
        struct array_cache cache;
        void * entries[BOOT_CPUCACHE_ENTRIES];
};
```

3. In the last step of kmem_cache_init, all statically instantiated elements of the data structures used up to present are replaced with dynamically allocated version created using kmalloc. The state of g_cpucache_up is now FULL, indicating that the slab allocator is ready for use.

Creating Caches

kmem_cache_create must be invoked to create a new slab cache. This function requires a large set of parameters.

mm/slab.c
```
struct kmem_cache *
kmem_cache_create (const char *name, size_t size, size_t align,
        unsigned long flags,
        void (*ctor)(struct kmem_cache *, void *))
```

Besides a human-readable name that subsequently appears in /proc/slabinfo, the function requires the size of the managed objects in bytes, an offset used when aligning data (align, in almost all cases 0), a set of flags in flags, and constructor/destructor functions in ctor and dtor.

Creation of a new cache is a lengthy procedure, as the code flow diagram for kmem_cache_create in Figure 3-49 shows.

Several parameter checks are carried out to ensure that no invalid specifications are used (e.g., an object size with fewer bytes than a processor word, a slab without name, etc.) before the first important step is carried out — calculation of the required alignment. First, the object size is rounded up to a multiple of the word length of the processor used:

mm/slab.c
```
kmem_cache_t *
kmem_cache_create (...) {
...
        if (size & (BYTES_PER_WORD-1)) {
                size += (BYTES_PER_WORD-1);
                size &= ~(BYTES_PER_WORD-1);
        }
```

Object alignment (in align) is typically also based on the processor word length. However, if the SLAB_HWCACHE_ALIGN flag is set, the kernel aligns the data as recommended by the architecture-specific function cache_line_size. It also attempts to pack as many objects as possible in a cache line by halving the alignment factor as long as this is possible for the given object size. As a result, 2, 4, ... objects fit into a cache line instead of a single object.

mm/slab.c
```
          /* 1) arch recommendation: */
          if (flags & SLAB_HWCACHE_ALIGN) {
                  /* Default alignment: as specified by the arch code.
                   * Except if an object is really small, then squeeze multiple
                   * objects into one cacheline.
                   */
                  ralign = cache_line_size();
                  while (size <= ralign/2)
                          ralign /= 2;
          } else {
                  ralign = BYTES_PER_WORD;
          }
    ...
```

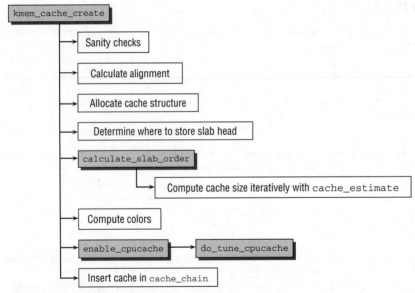

Figure 3-49: Code flow diagram for `kmem_cache_create`.

The kernel also takes account of the fact that some architectures require a minimum boundary for the alignment of data as defined by ARCH_SLAB_MINALIGN; the alignment required by users is also accepted.

mm/slab.c
```
          /* 2) arch mandated alignment */
          if (ralign < ARCH_SLAB_MINALIGN) {
                  ralign = ARCH_SLAB_MINALIGN;
          }
          /* 3) caller mandated alignment */
          if (ralign < align) {
```

```
                ralign = align;
        }
        /* 4) Store it. */
        align = ralign;
...
```

A new instance of `struct kmem_cache` is allocated once the data alignment has been calculated (a separate slab cache named `cache_cache` is provided to perform allocation).

The decision as to whether to store the slab head on-slab or off-slab (see Section 3.6.3) is relatively simple. If the object size is more than one-eighth of a page frame, the head is stored off-slab, otherwise on the slab itself.

mm/slab.c

```
        if (size >= (PAGE_SIZE>>3))
                /*
                 * Size is large, assume best to place the slab management obj
                 * off-slab (should allow better packing of objs).
                 */
                flags |= CFLGS_OFF_SLAB;

        size = ALIGN(size, align);
...
```

The slab header can also be stored off-slab for smaller objects by explicitly setting `CFLGS_OFF_SLAB` in the `kmem_cache_create` call.

Finally, the object `size` is increased until it corresponds to the alignment calculated above.

Up to now we have only defined the size of the objects but not of the slab. In the next step, an attempt is therefore made to find a suitable number of pages that is neither too small nor too big. Too few objects on a slab increase administrative overhead and render the method less efficient, while overlarge slab areas are detrimental to the buddy system.

The kernel tries to find the ideal slab size in an iterative process implemented in `calculate_slab_order`. Based on the given object size, `cache_estimate` calculates the number of objects, the wasted space, and the space needed for coloring for a specific number of pages. The function is invoked in a loop until the kernel is satisfied with the results.

By systematic trial and error, `cache_estimate` finds a slab arrangement that can be described by the following elements: `size` is the object size, `gfp_order` the order for page allocation, `num` the number of objects on the slab, and `wastage` the space that is "wasted" with this order and is therefore no longer available for useful data (of course, `wastage` < `size` always applies; otherwise, another object could be fitted on the slab). `head` specifies how much space is required for the slab head. This layout corresponds to the following formula:

```
PAGE_SIZE<<gfp_order = head + num*size + left_over
```

If the slab head is stored off-slab, the value of `head` is 0 because no space need be reserved for head. If it is stored on-slab, the value is calculated as follows:

```
head = sizeof(struct slab) + num*sizeof(kmem_bufctl_t)
```

273

As discussed in Section 3.6.3, each slab head is followed by an array with as many entries as there are objects on the slab. The kernel refers to this array to find the position of the next free object. The data type used to do this is kmem_bufctl_t, which is nothing more than an ordinary unsigned int variable appropriately abstracted by typedef.

The number of objects num is used to calculate the head size; this is needed to determine the number of objects in a slab — and is another example of the chicken-and-egg problem. The kernel solves this problem by systematically incrementing the number of objects to check whether a given configuration still fits in the available space.

cache_estimate is repeatedly invoked in a while loop, and each time the available gfp_order is incremented by 1 — thus doubling the slab size each time starting with a single page frame. The kernel terminates the loop and is satisfied with the result if *one* of the following conditions applies:

❑   8*left_over is less than the size of the slab; that is, less than one-eighth of the space is wasted.

❑   gfp_order is greater than or equal to the value stored in slab_break_gfp_order. slab_break_gfp_order has the value BREAK_GFP_ORDER_LO = 1 if the machine has less than 32 MiB of main memory; otherwise, its value is BREAK_GFP_ORDER_HI = 2.

❑   The management head is stored off-slab, and the number of objects is greater than the value stored in offslab_limit. offslab_limit specifies the maximum number of kmem_bufctl_t instances that can be held together with an instance of struct slab in a memory block reserved with kmalloc. If the number of objects in a slab exceeds this value, it is no longer possible to reserve the required space, with the result that gfp_order is decremented by 1, the data are recalculated, and the loop is exited.

Of course, the kernel always makes sure that there is space for at least one object on the slab, as a cache with no objects makes little sense.

The size of the slab head is rounded to ensure that the entry immediately following the head is properly aligned.

mm/slab.c
```
. . .
        slab_size = ALIGN(cachep->num*sizeof(kmem_bufctl_t)
                           + sizeof(struct slab), align);
. . .
```

ALIGN(x,y) is a standard macro provided by the kernel that computes the required space that is sufficient to store the object x, but is additionally an integer-valued multiple of align. Table 3-9 provides some exemplary alignment calculations.

If sufficient free space is available to store the slab head on-slab although it should actually be stored off-slab, the kernel gladly makes use of the opportunity. The CFLGS_OFF_SLAB is deleted, and the head is stored on the slab despite the earlier decision to do the opposite or despite the default setting.

The following steps are performed to color the slab:

mm/slab.c
```
        cachep->colour_off = cache_line_size();
        /* Offset must be a multiple of the alignment. */
```

```
        if (cachep->colour_off < align)
                cachep->colour_off = align;
        cachep->colour = left_over/cachep->colour_off;
    ...
```

The kernel uses the size of an L1 cache that can be determined using the architecture-specific `cache_line_size` function as an offset. It must also be ensured that the offset is a multiple of the alignment used — otherwise, the alignment effect would be lost.

Table 3-9: Examplary Calculations of the Alignment on 4- and 8-Byte Boundaries

Object size x	Alignment y	ALIGN(x,y)
1	4	8
4	4	8
5	8	8
8	8	8
9	12	16
12	12	16
13	16	16
16	16	16
17	20	24
19	20	24

The color of the slab (i.e., the number of potential offset values) is calculated by dividing the free space on the slab (known as the `left_over`) by the color offset (`colour_off`) without a remainder.

For example, on an older IA-32 machine, the kernel produces the following results for a cache that manages 256-byte objects aligned on the hardware cache with SLAB_HWCACHE_ALIGN:

- 15 objects are managed on a slab (num = 15).
- One page is used (gfp_order = 0).
- There are five possible colors (colour = 5), and an offset of 32 bytes is used for each color (colour_off = 32).
- The slab head is stored on-slab.

Now that we have dealt with the slab arrangement, there are still two more things to do when creating a new slab cache in kmem_cache_create:

❑ The per-CPU caches must be generated. This task is delegated to enable_cpucache (the layout and structure of these caches are described in Section 3.6.4). First, the kernel defines the number of object pointers in the cache depending on the object size:

$$0 < \text{size} \leq 256 : 120 \text{ objects}$$

$$256 < \text{size} \leq 1024 : 54 \text{ objects}$$

$$1024 < \text{size} \leq \text{PAGE\_SIZE} : 24 \text{ objects}$$

$$\text{PAGE\_SIZE} < \text{size} : 8 \text{ objects}$$

$$\text{size} > 131072 : 1 \text{ object}$$

Allocation of the required memory for each processor — an instance of array_cache and an array of pointers to objects with the calculated number of elements — as well as initialization of the data structures is delegated to do_tune_cpucache. A particularly interesting aspect is that the batchcount field is always set to half the calculated number of objects in the cache.

This regulates the number of objects processed in one go when a cache is filled.

❑ To conclude initialization, the initialized kmem_cache instance is added to a globally linked list whose list head (cache_chain) is defined in mm/slab.c.

Allocating Objects

kmem_cache_alloc is invoked to obtain objects from a specific cache. Like all malloc functions, it yields either a pointer to the reserved memory area or a null pointer if allocation fails. The function requires two parameters — the cache from which the object is to be obtained and a flag variable to accurately describe the allocation characteristics.

<slab.h>
```
void *kmem_cache_alloc (kmem_cache_t *cachep, gfp_t flags)
```

Any of the GFP_ values mentioned in Section 3.5.4 can be specified for the flags.[35]

As the code flow diagram in Figure 3-50 shows, kmem_cache_alloc is based on the internal function __cache_alloc that requires the same parameters and can be invoked without further ado (this structure was adopted to merge the implementation of kmalloc and kmem_cache_alloc as quickly as possible, as demonstrated in Section 3.6.5). However, __cache_allloc is also only a front-end function to perform all necessary locking operations. The actual work is delegated to ____cache_alloc (with four underscores), as shown in Figure 3-50 (actually, the function do_cache_alloc stands between __cache_alloc and ____cache_alloc, but is only required on NUMA systems).

The figure clearly shows that work can follow one of two paths; the first, which is the more frequent and more convenient of the two, is taken if there are free objects in the per-CPU cache. However, if all objects are in use, the cache must be refilled, and in the worst-case scenario, this means that a new slab must be created.

---

[35]Notice that the kernel used to provide a differently named set of constants (SLAB_ATOMIC, SLAB_DMA, etc.) with the same numerical values. These have been dropped during the development of kernel 2.6.20 and cannot be used anymore.

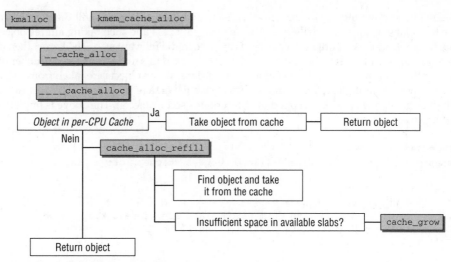

Figure 3-50: Code flow diagram for `kmem_cache_alloc`.

Selecting a Cached Object

____cache_alloc can check relatively easily if an object is in the per-CPU cache, as the following code excerpt shows:

mm/slab.c
```
static inline void *____cache_alloc(kmem_cache_t *cachep, gfp_t flags)
{
        ac = ac_data(cachep);
        if (likely(ac->avail)) {
                ac->touched = 1;
                objp = ac->entry[--ac->avail];
        }
        else {
                objp = cache_alloc_refill(cachep, flags);
        }

return objp;
```

cachep is a pointer to the kmem_cache_t instance of the cache used. The ac_data macro yields the associated array_cache instance for the currently active CPU by returning cachep->array[smp_processor_id()].

As the objects in memory immediately follow the array_cache instance, the kernel can access them easily with the help of the dummy array at the end of the structure without the explicit need for pointer arithmetic. The object is removed from the cache by decrementing ac->avail.

Refilling the Per-CPU Cache

The workload is heavier when there are no more objects in the per-CPU cache. The refill operations needed in this situation are located in cache_alloc_refill, which is invoked when the allocation cannot be satisfied directly from the per-CPU cache.

The kernel must now find `array_cache->batchcount` unused objects to refill the per-CPU cache by first scanning the list of all partially free slabs (`slabs_partial`) and then taking all free objects one after another by `slab_get_obj` until no more objects are free in the relevant slab. The kernel then performs the same procedure on all other slabs in the `slabs_partial` list. If this finds the desired number of objects, the kernel iterates over the `slabs_free` list of all unused slabs. When objects are taken from a slab, the kernel must also ensure that it places them on the correct slab list (`slabs_full` or `slabs_partial`, depending on whether the slab was totally emptied or still contains some objects). The above is implemented by the following code:

mm/slab.c
```
static void *cache_alloc_refill(kmem_cache_t *cachep, gfp_t flags)
{
...
        while (batchcount > 0) {
            /* Select list from which slabs are to be taken
               (first slabs_partial, then slabs_free) */
            ...

            slabp = list_entry(entry, struct slab, list);
            while (slabp->inuse < cachep->num && batchcount--) {
                /* get obj pointer */
                ac->entry[ac->avail++] = slab_get_obj(cachep, slabp,
                                                      node);
            }
            check_slabp(cachep, slabp);

            /* move slabp to correct slabp list: */
            list_del(&slabp->list);
            if (slabp->free == BUFCTL_END)
                    list_add(&slabp->list, &l3->slabs_full);
            else
                    list_add(&slabp->list, &l3->slabs_partial);
        }
...
}
```

The key to removing one slab element after another is in `slab_get_obj`:

mm/slab.c
```
static void *slab_get_obj(struct kmem_cache *cachep, struct slab *slabp,
                          int nodeid)
{
        void *objp = index_to_obj(cachep, slabp, slabp->free);
        kmem_bufctl_t next;

        slabp->inuse++;
        next = slab_bufctl(slabp)[slabp->free];
        slabp->free = next;

        return objp;
}
```

Recall from Figure 3-47 that the kernel uses an interesting system to keep track of free entries: The index of the free object that is currently under consideration is stored in `slabp->free`, and the index of the next free object, is kept in the management array.

Obtaining the object that belongs to a given index is a matter of some simple pointer manipulation performed in `index_to_obj`. `slab_bufctl` is a macro that yields a pointer to the `kmem_bufctl` array after `slabp`.

Let us return to `cache_alloc_grow`. If no free object is found although all slabs have been scanned, the cache must be enlarged using `cache_grow`. This is a costly operation examined in the next section.

Growing the Cache

Figure 3-51 shows the code flow diagram for `cache_grow`.

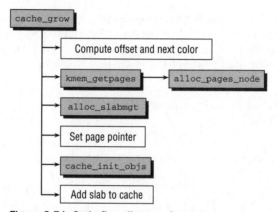

Figure 3-51: Code flow diagram for `cache_grow`.

The arguments of `kmem_cache_alloc` are passed to `cache_grow`. It is also possible to specify an explicit node from which the fresh memory pages are to be supplied.

The color and offset are first calculated:

mm/slab.c
```
static int cache_grow(struct kmem_cache *cachep,
            gfp_t flags, int nodeid, void *objp)
{
...
        l3 = cachep->nodelists[nodeid];
...
        offset = l3->colour_next;
        l3->colour_next++;
        if (l3->colour_next >= cachep->colour)
                l3->colour_next = 0;
        offset *= cachep->colour_off;
...
}
```

The kernel restarts counting at 0 when the maximum number of colors is reached; this automatically results in a zero offset.

The required memory space is allocated page-by-page by the buddy system using the kmem_getpages helper function. The sole purpose of this function is to invoke the alloc_pages_node function discussed in Section 3.5.4 with the appropriate parameters. The PG_slab bit is also set on each page to indicate that the page belongs to the buddy system. When a slab is used to satisfy short-lived or reclaimable allocations, the flag __GFP_RECLAIMABLE is passed down to the buddy system. Recall from Section 3.5.2 that this is important to allocate the pages from the appropriate migrate list.

The allocation of the management head for the slab is not very exciting. The relevant alloc_slabmgmt function reserves the required space if the head is stored off-slab; if not, the space is already reserved on the slab. In both situations, the colouroff, s_mem, and inuse elements of the slab data structure must be initialized with the appropriate values.

The kernel then establishes the associations between the pages of the slab and the slab or cache structure by invoking slab_map_pages. This function iterates over all page instances of the pages newly allocated for the slab and invokes page_set_cache and page_set_slab for each page. These two functions manipulate (or misuse) the lru element of a page instance as follows:

mm/slab.c

```
static inline void page_set_cache(struct page *page, struct kmem_cache *cache)
{
        page->lru.next = (struct list_head *)cache;
}
static inline void page_set_slab(struct page *page, struct slab *slab)
{
        page->lru.prev = (struct list_head *)slab;
}
```

cache_init_objs initializes the objects of the new slab by invoking the constructor for each object assuming it is present. (As only a very few parts of the kernel make use of this option, there is normally little to do in this respect.) The kmem_bufctl list of the slab is also initialized by storing the value $i + 1$ at array position i: because the slab is as yet totally unused, the next free element is always the next consecutive element. As per convention, the last array element holds the constant BUFCTL_END.

The slab is now fully initialized and can be added to the slabs_free list of the cache. The number of new objects generated is also added to the number of free objects in the cache (cachep->free_objects).

Freeing Objects

When an allocated object is no longer required, it must be returned to the slab allocator using kmem_cache_free. Figure 3-52 shows the code flow diagram of this function.

kmem_cache_free immediately invokes __cache_free and forwards its arguments unchanged. (Again the reason is to prevent code duplication in the implementation of kfree, as discussed in Section 3.6.5.)

As with allocation, there are two alternative courses of action depending on the state of the per-CPU cache. If the number of objects held is below the permitted limit, a pointer to the object in the cache is stored.

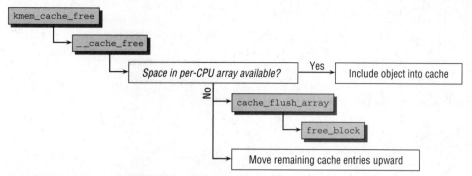

Figure 3-52: Code flow diagram for `kmem_cache_free`.

mm/slab.c
```
static inline void __cache_free(kmem_cache_t *cachep, void *objp)
{
...
        if (likely(ac->avail < ac->limit)) {
                ac->entry[ac->avail++] = objp;
                return;
        } else {
                cache_flusharray(cachep, ac);
                ac->entry[ac->avail++] = objp;
        }
}
```

If not, some objects (the exact number is given by `array_cache->batchcount`) must be moved from the cache back into the slabs starting with the array elements with the lowest numbers — because the cache implementation applies the LIFO principle, these are objects that have been in the array longest and whose data are therefore least likely still to be held in the CPU cache.

Implementation is delegated to `cache_flusharray`. In turn, this function invokes `free_block` to move the objects from the cache to their original slabs and shifts the remaining objects in the cache to the start of the array. For example, if there is space for 30 objects in the cache and the `batchcount` is 15, the objects at positions 0 to 14 are moved back into the slabs. The remaining objects numbered 15 to 29 are shifted upward in the cache so that they now occupy positions 0 to 14.

Moving objects from the cache back onto the slabs is instructive, so it's well worth taking a closer look at `free_block`. The arguments required by this function are the `kmem_cache_t` instance of the cache, a pointer to an array consisting of pointers to the objects in the cache, an integer to indicate the number of objects in the array, and the node whose memory is just being processed.

The function iterates over all objects in `objpp` after the number of unused objects in the cache data structure has been updated.

mm/slab.c
```
static void free_block(kmem_cache_t *cachep, void **objpp, int nr_objects,
                    int node)
{
        int i;
```

```
                struct kmem_list3 *13;

        for (i = 0; i < nr_objects; i++) {
                void *objp = objpp[i];
                struct slab *slabp;
    ...
```

The following operations must be performed for each object:

mm/slab.c
```
                slabp = virt_to_slab(objp)
                13 = cachep->nodelists[node];
                list_del(&slabp->list);
                slab_put_obj(cachep, slabp, objp, node);
                slabp->inuse--;
                13->free_objects++;
```

Before it can be established to which slab an object belongs, it is first necessary to invoke `virt_to_page` to find the page in which the object is located. The association with the slab is determined using `page_get_slab` as discussed above.

The slab is (temporarily) removed from the lists of the cache. `slab_put_obj` is used to reflect this action in the freelist: The first object to be used for allocation purposes is the one just removed, and the next object in the list is the one that was previously first.

Thereafter, the slab is reinserted in the linked lists of the cache:

mm/slab.c
```
    ...
                /* fixup slab chains */
                if (slabp->inuse == 0) {
                        if (13->free_objects > 13->free_limit) {
                                13->free_objects -= cachep->num;
                                slab_destroy(cachep, slabp);
                        } else {
                                list_add(&slabp->list, &13->slabs_free);
                        }
                } else {
                        list_add(&slabp->list, &13->slabs_partial);
                }
        }
}
```

The slab is normally placed on the `slabs_free` list if, after deletion, all objects in the slab are unused (`slab->inuse == 0`).

> *Exception: The number of free objects in the cache is above the predefined limit* `cachep->free_limit`.
> *In this case, the complete slab is returned to the buddy system using* `slab_destroy`.

The slab is inserted into the `slabs_partial` list of the cache if it contains both used and unused objects.

Destroying Caches

The `kmem_cache_destroy` function must be invoked to destroy a complete cache in which there are only unused objects. This function is needed primarily when removing modules that want to return all memory space allocated to them.[36]

Since the implementation itself reveals nothing new, we will confine ourselves to outlining the main steps needed to remove a cache:

❑ The slabs on the `slabs_free` list are scanned successively. The destructor is first invoked for each object on each slab, and then the slab memory space is returned to the buddy system.

❑ The memory space for the per-CPU caches is freed.

❑ The data are removed from the `cache_cache` list.

3.6.5   General Caches

The `kmalloc` and `kfree` functions must be used to allocate and free memory in the classic sense rather than objects. These are the kernel equivalents to the `malloc` and `free` functions from the C standard library in userspace.[37]

I have already noted several times that `kmalloc` and `kfree` are implemented as slab allocator front-ends and mimic the semantics of `malloc`/`free` as best they can. We can therefore deal with their implementation succinctly.

Implementation of `kmalloc`

The base of `kmalloc` is an array that groups slab caches for memory areas of graded sizes. The array entries are instances of the `cache_sizes` data structure that is defined as follows:

```
<slab_def.h>
struct cache_sizes {
        size_t            cs_size;
        kmem_cache_t      *cs_cachep;
        kmem_cache_t      *cs_dmacachep;
#ifdef CONFIG_ZONE_DMA
        struct kmem_cache *cs_dmacachep;
#endif
}
```

`size` specifies the size of the memory area for which the entry is responsible. There are two slab caches for each size, one of which supplies DMA-suitable memory.

The statically defined `malloc_sizes` array groups the available sizes essentially using powers of 2 between $2^5 = 32$ and $2^{25} = 131,072$, depending on the setting of `KMALLOC_MAX_SIZE` as discussed above.

---

[36]This is not mandatory. If a module wants to obtain persistent memory that is preserved between unloading a module and reloading the next time (assuming, of course, that the system is not rebooted in the meantime), it can retain a cache so that the data it contains are available for reuse.

[37]Use of `printk`, `kmalloc` and `kfree` in userspace programs is an unmistakable sign of too much contact with kernel programming.

mm/slab.c
```
static struct cache_sizes malloc_sizes[] = {
#define CACHE(x) { .cs_size = (x) },
#if (PAGE_SIZE == 4096)
        CACHE(32)
#endif
        CACHE(64)
#if L1_CACHE_BYTES < 64
        CACHE(96)
#endif
        CACHE(128)
#if L1_CACHE_BYTES < 128
        CACHE(192)
#endif
        CACHE(256)
        CACHE(512)
        CACHE(1024)
        CACHE(2048)
        CACHE(4096)
        CACHE(8192)
        CACHE(16384)
        CACHE(32768)
        CACHE(65536)
        CACHE(131072)
#if KMALLOC_MAX_SIZE >= 262144
        CACHE(262144)
#endif
#if KMALLOC_MAX_SIZE >= 524288
        CACHE(524288)
#endif
...
#if KMALLOC_MAX_SIZE >= 33554432
        CACHE(33554432)
        CACHE(ULONG_MAX)
```

There is always a cache for allocations up to the maximum size that can be represented in an `unsigned long` variable. However, this cache (in contrast to all others) is not filled with elements in advance; this allows the kernel to ensure that each giant allocation is satisfied with freshly allocated memory pages. As allocations of this size can request the entire memory of the system, a corresponding cache would not be particularly useful. However, this kernel approach makes sure that very large allocation requests can be satisfied if sufficient memory is available.

The pointers to the corresponding caches are not initially filled. They are assigned their correct value when initialization is performed with `kmem_cache_init`.

`kmalloc` from `<slab_def.h>` first checks whether a constant is specified as the memory size; in this case, the required cache can be determined statically at compilation time, and this delivers speed gains. If not, `__kmalloc` is invoked to find the cache of matching size. The function is a parameter-conversion front end for `__do_kmalloc`:

mm/slab.c
```
void *__do_kmalloc(size_t size, gfp_t flags)
{
        kmem_cache_t *cachep;
```

```
        cachep = __find_general_cachep(size, flags);
        if (unlikely(ZERO_OR_NULL_PTR(cachep)))
                return NULL;
        return __cache_alloc(cachep, flags);
}
```

Once `__find_general_cachep` has found a suitable cache (it iterates over all possible `kmalloc` sizes to find a matching cache), the heavy work is delegated to the `__cache_alloc` function discussed above.

Implementation of `kfree`

`kfree` is likewise easy to implement:

mm/slab.c
```
void kfree(const void *objp)
{
        kmem_cache_t *c;
        unsigned long flags;

        if (unlikely(ZERO_OR_NULL_PTR(objp)))
                return;
        c = virt_to_cache(objp));
        __cache_free(c, (void*)objp);
}
```

`kfree` hands over the actual work to the `__cache_free` function also discussed above once the cache associated with the memory pointer has been found.

3.7   Processor Cache and TLB Control

Caches are crucial in terms of overall system performance, which is why the kernel tries to exploit them as effectively as possible. It does this primarily by skillfully aligning kernel data in memory. A judicious mix of normal functions, inline definitions, and macros also helps extract greater performance from the processor. The compiler optimizations discussed in Appendix C also make their contribution.

However, the above aspects affect the cache only indirectly. Use of the correct alignment for a data structure *does indeed* have an effect on the cache but only implicitly — active control of the processor cache is not necessary.

Nevertheless, the kernel features some commands that act directly on the cache and the TLB of the processor. However, they are not intended to boost system efficiency but to maintain the cache *contents* in a consistent state and to ensure that no entries are incorrect and out-of-date. For example, when a mapping is removed from the address space of a process, the kernel is responsible for removing the corresponding entries from the TLBs. If it failed to do so and new data were added at the position previously occupied by the mapping, a read or write operation to the virtual address would be redirected to the incorrect location in physical memory.

The hardware implementation of caches and TLBs differs significantly from architecture to architecture. The kernel must therefore create a view on TLBs and caches that takes adequate account of the different approaches without neglecting the specific properties of each architecture.

❑ The meaning of the *translation lookaside buffer* is abstracted to refer to a mechanism that translates a virtual address into a physical address.[38]

❑ The kernel regards a *cache* as a mechanism that provides rapid access to data by reference to a *virtual* address without the need for a request to RAM memory. There is not always an explicit difference between data and instruction caches. The architecture-specific code is responsible for any differentiation if its caches are split in this manner.

It is not necessary for each processor type to implement every control function defined by the kernel. If a function is not required, its invocation can be replaced with an empty operation (**do {} while (0)**) that is optimized away by the compiler. This is very frequently the case with cache-related operations because, as above, the kernel assumes that addressing is based on virtual addresses. The resultant problems do not occur in physically organized caches so that it is not usually necessary to implement the cache control functions.

The following functions must be made available (even if only as an empty operation) by each CPU-specific part of the kernel in order to control the TLBs and caches[39]:

❑ `flush_tlb_all` and `flush_cache_all` flush the *entire* TLB/cache. This is only required when the page tables of the kernel (and not of a userspace process) are manipulated because a modification of this kind affects not only all processes but also all processors in the system.

❑ `flush_tlb_mm(struct mm_struct *mm)` and `flush_cache_mm` flush all TLB/cache entries belonging to the address space `mm`.

❑ `flush_tlb_range(struct vm_area_struct *vma, unsigned long start, unsigned long end)` and `flush_cache_range(vma, start, end)` flush all entries from the TLB/cache between the `start` and `end` virtual addresses in the address range `vma->vm_mm`.

❑ `flush_tlb_page(struct vm_area_struct *vma, unsigned long page)` and `flush_cache_page(vma, page)` flush all entries from the TLB/cache whose virtual addresses are in an interval that begins at `page` and consists of `PAGE_SIZE` bytes.

❑ `update_mmu_cache(struct vm_area_struct *vma, unsigned long address, pte_t pte)` is invoked after a page fault has been handled. It inserts information in the memory management unit of the processor so that the entry at the virtual address `address` is described by the page table entry `pte`.

This function is needed only if there is an external MMU. Typically, the MMU is integrated into the processor, but MIPS processors, for example, have external MMUs.

The kernel makes no distinction between data and instruction caches. If a distinction is required, the processor-specific code can reference the `VM_EXEC` flag in `vm_area_struct->flags` to ascertain whether the cache contains data or instructions.

The `flush_cache_` and `flush_tlb_` functions very often occur in pairs; for instance, when the address space of a process is duplicated using `fork`.

kernel/fork.c
```
flush_cache_mm(oldmm);
...
```

---

[38]Whether TLBs are the only hardware resource for doing this or whether other alternatives (e.g., page tables) are provided is irrelevant.

[39]The following description is based on the documentation by David Miller [Mil] in the kernel sources.

```
/* Manipulate page tables */
...
flush_tlb_mm(oldmm);
```

The sequence of operations — cache flushing, memory manipulation, and TLB flushing — is important for two reasons:

❏ If the sequence were reversed, another CPU in a multiprocessor system could take the wrong information from the process table after the TLBs have been flushed but before the correct information is supplied.

❏ Some architectures require the presence of "virtual-to-physical" transformation rules in the TLB when the cache is flushed (caches with this property are referred to as *strict*). flush_tlb_mm must execute *after* flush_cache_mm to guarantee that this is the case.

Some control functions apply specifically to data caches (flush_dcache_ ...) or instruction caches (flush_icache_ ...).

❏ flush_dcache_page(struct page *page) helps prevent alias problems that arise if a cache may contain several entries (with different virtual addresses) that point to the same page in memory. It is always invoked when the kernel writes to a page in the page cache or when it wants to read data from a page that is also mapped in userspace. This routine gives each architecture in which alias problems can occur an opportunity to prevent such problems.

❏ flush_icache_range(unsigned long start, unsigned long end) is invoked when the kernel writes data to kernel memory (between start and end) for subsequent execution. A standard example of this scenario is when a module is loaded into the kernel. The binary data are first copied to RAM and are then executed. flush_icache_range ensures that data and instruction caches do not interfere with each other if implemented separately.

❏ flush_icache_user_range(*vma, *page, addr, len) is a special function for the ptrace mechanism. It is needed to propagate changes to the address space of a traced process.

It is beyond the scope of this book to discuss the implementation details of the cache and TLB control functions. Too much background knowledge on the structure of the underlying processor (and the subtle problems involved) would be required for a full understanding of the implementation details.

3.8 Summary

This chapter has discussed many aspects of memory management. Our focus lies on physical memory management, but the connection between virtual and physical memory via page tables has also been covered. Although the architecture-specific details in this area differ greatly among the various architectures supported by Linux, an architecture-independent set of data structures and functions allows generic code to manipulate the page tables. However, some architecture-specific code is required before the generic view is enabled, and this code runs during the boot process.

Once the kernel is up and running, memory management is handled by two layers: The buddy system is responsible for the management of physical page frames, while the slab allocator must handle small allocations and provides an in-kernel equivalent to the malloc function family known from userland programming.

The buddy system is centered around the idea of splitting and recombining larger continuous blocks of pages. When a continuous area becomes free, the kernel notices this automatically, and can use it once the need for a corresponding allocation arises. Since this is unfortunately not sufficient to prevent fragmentation of physical memory after longer uptimes in a satisfactory manner, recent kernels have acquired anti-fragmentation techniques that allow grouping pages by their mobility, on the one hand, and augment the kernel with a new virtual memory zone, on the other hand. Both help to avoid fragmentation by essentially decreasing the chance that coalescing of larger regions is prohibited by allocated blocks in their middle.

The slab allocator is implemented on top of the buddy system. It does not only allow to allocate small chunks of memory for arbitrary use, but additionally offers the possibility to create specific caches for often used data structures.

Initializing memory management is challenging because the data structures employed by the subsystem itself also require memory, which must be allocated from somewhere. We have seen how the kernel solves the situation by introducing a very simple boot memory allocator that is shut down after the proper allocation routines function fully.

While we have mostly focused on physical memory here, the next chapter will discuss how the virtual address space is managed by the kernel.

Virtual Process Memory

The virtual address space of userland processes is an important abstraction of Linux: It allows the same view of the system to each running process, and this makes it possible for multiple processes to run simultaneously without interfering with the memory contents of the others. Additionally, it allows various advanced programming techniques like memory mappings. In this chapter, I will discuss how these concepts are realized in the kernel. This also requires an examination of the connection between page frames of the available physical RAM and pages in all virtual process address spaces: The *reverse mapping* technique helps to track which virtual pages are backed by which physical page, and *page fault handling* allows filling the virtual address space with data from block devices on demand.

4.1 Introduction

All the memory management methods discussed in the preceding chapter were concerned either with the organization of physical memory or management of the virtual kernel address space. This section examines the methods required by the kernel to manage the virtual *user* address space. For a variety of reasons, some of which are given below, this is more complex than managing kernel address space:

- ❏ Each application has its own address space that is segregated from all other applications.

- ❏ Usually only a few sections of the large linear address space available to each userspace process are actually used, and they may also be some distance from each other. The kernel needs data structures to efficiently manage these (randomly) spread sections.

- ❏ Only the smallest part of the address space is directly associated with physical pages. Infrequently used parts are linked with pages only when necessary.

- ❏ The kernel has trust in itself, but not in user processes. For this reason, each operation to manipulate user address space is accompanied by various checks to ensure that programs cannot acquire more rights than are due to them and thus endanger system stability and security.

❑ The `fork-exec` model used under UNIX to generate new processes (described in Chapter 2) is not very powerful if implemented carelessly. The kernel must therefore concentrate on managing user address spaces as efficiently as possible by resorting to a few tricks.

Most of the ideas discussed below are based on the assumption that the system has a *memory management unit* (or MMU) that supports the use of virtual memory. This is, in fact, the situation on all "normal" processors. However, during the development of Linux 2.5, three architectures that do not provide an MMU were added to the kernel sources — V850E, H8300, and m68knommu. Another one (blackfin) was added during the development of kernel 2.6.22. Some of the functions examined below are not available on these CPUs, and the interface to the outside returns error messages because the underlying mechanisms are not implemented in the kernel and cannot be implemented owing to the lack of processor support. The information below covers only machines with MMU. I do not deal with the oddities and modifications needed for MMU-less architectures.

4.2 Virtual Process Address Space

The virtual address space of each process starts at address 0 and extends to `TASK_SIZE - 1`; the kernel address space begins above this. On IA-32 systems with $2^{32} = 4$ GiB, the total address space is usually split in a 3:1 ratio on which we focus in the information below. The kernel is assigned 1 GiB, while 3 GiB is available to *each* userspace process. Other ratios are possible but yield benefits only on very specific configurations and with certain work loads, as discussed above.

A very important aspect relating to system integrity is that user programs may access only the lower part of the overall address space but *not* the kernel part. Neither is it possible for a user process to manipulate parts of the address space of another process without previous "agreement," simply because these parts are invisible to it.

The contents of the virtual address space portion of the kernel are always the same regardless of which user process is currently active. Depending on hardware, this is achieved either by manipulating the page tables of user processes so that the upper part of the virtual address space always appears to be identical or by instructing the processor itself to provide a separate address space for the kernel, which is mapped above each user address space. Recall that this is visualized in Figure 1-3 in the Introduction.

The virtual address space is made up of many sections of varying sizes that serve different purposes and must be handled differently. For example, in most cases, it is not permitted to modify the text segment, but it must be possible to execute its contents. On the other hand, it must be possible to modify the contents of a text file mapped into the address space but not to execute such contents as this doesn't make sense — it's just data and not machine code.

4.2.1 Layout of the Process Address Space

The virtual address space is populated by a number of regions. How they are distributed is architecture-specific, but all approaches have the following elements in common:

❑ The binary code of the code currently running. This code is normally referred to as *text* and the area of virtual memory in which it is located as a *text segment*.[1]

❑ The code of dynamic libraries used by the program.

---

[1]This is *not* the same as a hardware segment, which is featured in some architectures and acts as a separate address space. It is simply the linear address space area used to hold the data.

- ❑ The heap where global variables and dynamically generated data are stored.
- ❑ The stack used to hold local variables and to implement function and procedure calls.
- ❑ Sections with environment variables and command-line arguments.
- ❑ Memory mappings that map the contents of files into the virtual address space.

Recall from Chapter 2 that each process in the system is equipped with an instance of struct mm_struct that can be accessed via the task structure. This instance holds memory management information for the process:

<mm_types.h>
```
struct mm_struct {
...
        unsigned long (*get_unmapped_area) (struct file *filp,
                                unsigned long addr, unsigned long len,
                                unsigned long pgoff, unsigned long flags);
...
        unsigned long mmap_base; /* base of mmap area */
        unsigned long task_size; /* size of task vm space */
...
        unsigned long start_code, end_code, start_data, end_data;
        unsigned long start_brk, brk, start_stack;
        unsigned long arg_start, arg_end, env_start, env_end;
...
}
```

The start and end of the virtual address space area consumed by the executable code are marked by start_code and end_code. Similarly, start_data and end_data mark the region that contains initialized data. Notice that the size of these areas does not change once an ELF binary has been mapped into the address space.

The start address of the heap is kept in start_brk, while brk denotes the current end of the heap area. While the start is constant during the lifetime of a process, heap size and thus the value of brk will vary.

The position of the argument list and the environment is described by arg_start and arg_end, respectively, env_start and env_end. Both regions reside in the topmost area of the stack.

mmap_base denotes the starting point for memory mappings in the virtual address space, and get_unmapped_area is invoked to find a suitable place for a new mapping in the mmap area.

task_size — variable names don't lie — stores the task size of the corresponding process. For native applications, this will usually be TASK_SIZE. However, 64-bit architectures are often binary-compatible with their predecessors. If a 32-bit binary is executed on a 64-bit machine, then task_size describes the effective task size visible to the binary.

The individual architectures can influence the layout of the virtual address space by several configuration options:

- ❑ If an architecture wants to choose between different possibilities for how the mmap area is arranged, it needs to set HAVE_ARCH_PICK_MMAP_LAYOUT and provide the function arch_pick_mmap_layout.

❑ When a new memory mapping is created, the kernel needs to find a suitable place for it unless a specific address has been specified by the user. If the architecture wants to choose the proper location itself, it must set the pre-processor symbol HAVE_ARCH_UNMAPPED_AREA and define the function arch_get_unmapped_area accordingly.

❑ New locations for memory mappings are usually found by starting the search from lower memory locations and progressing toward higher addresses. The kernel provides the default function arch_get_unmapped_area_topdown to perform this search, but if an architecture wants to provide a specialized implementation, it needs to set the pre-processor symbol HAVE_ARCH_GET_UNMAPPED_AREA.

❑ Usually, the stack grows from bottom to top. Architectures that handle this differently need to set the configuration option CONFIG_STACK_GROWSUP.[2] In the following, only stacks that grow from top to bottom are considered.

Finally, we need to consider the task flag PF_RANDOMIZE. If it is set, the kernel does not choose fixed locations for stack and the starting point for memory mappings, but varies them randomly each time a new process is started. This complicates, for instance, exploiting security holes that are caused by buffer overflows. If an attacker cannot rely on a fixed address where the stack can be found, it will be much harder to construct malicious code that deliberately manipulates stack entries after access to the memory region has been gained by a buffer overflow.

Figure 4-1 illustrates how the aforementioned components are distributed across the virtual address space on most architectures.

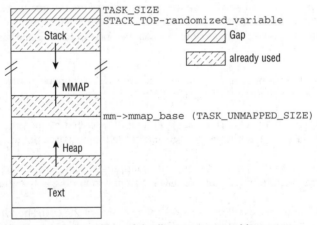

Figure 4-1: Composition of the linear process address space.

---

[2]Currently only PA-Risc processors require this option. The constants in the kernel thus have a slight tendency toward a situation where the stack grows from downward, albeit the PA-Risc code is not quite satisfied with that, as we can read in include/asm-parisc/a.out.h:

```
/* XXX: STACK_TOP actually should be STACK_BOTTOM for parisc. * prumpf *\
```

The funny thing is that "prumpf" is not a grumpy sign of discontent, but an abbreviation for a developer, Philipp Rumpf :-)

How the text segment is mapped into the virtual address space is determined by the ELF standard (see Chapter E for more information about this binary format). A specific starting address is specified for each architecture: IA-32 systems start at `0x08048000`, leaving a gap of roughly 128 MiB between the lowest possible address and the start of the text mapping that is used to catch `NULL` pointers. Other architectures keep a similar hole: UltraSparc machines use `0x100000000` as the starting point of the text segment, while AMD64 uses `0x0000000000400000`. The heap starts directly above the text segment and grows upward.

The stack starts at `STACK_TOP`, but the value is decremented by a small random amount if `PF_RANDOMIZE` is set. `STACK_TOP` must be defined by each architecture, and most set it to `TASK_SIZE` — the stack starts at the highest possible address of the user address space. The argument list and environment of a process are stored as initial stack elements.

The region for memory mappings starts at `mm_struct->mmap_base`, which is usually set to `TASK_UNMAPPED_BASE`, needing to be defined by every architecture. In nearly all cases, `TASK_SIZE/3` is chosen. Note that the start of the mmap region is not randomized if the default kernel approach is used.

Using the described address space layout works very well on machines that provide a large virtual address space. However, problems can arise on 32-bit machines. Consider the situation on IA-32: The virtual address space ranges from 0 to `0xC0000000`, so 3 GiB are available for each user process. `TASK_UNMAPPED_BASE` starts at `0x4000000`, that is, at 1 GiB. Unfortunately, this implies that the heap can only consume roughly 1 GiB before it crashes right into the mmap area, which is clearly not a desirable situation.

The problem is caused by the memory mapping region that is located in the middle of the virtual address space. This is why a new virtual address space layout for IA-32 machines (in addition to the classical one, which can still be used) was introduced during the development of kernel 2.6.7. It is illustrated in Figure 4-2.

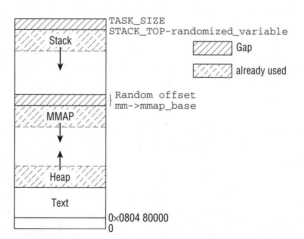

Figure 4-2: Layout of the virtual address space on IA-32 machines when the mmap region is expanded from top to bottom.

The idea is to limit the maximal stack size to a fixed value. Since the stack is bounded, the region into which memory mappings are installed can then be started immediately below the end of the stack. In contrast to the classical approach, it now expands *from top to bottom*. Since the heap is still located in the lower region of the virtual address space and grows upward, both mmap region and heap can expand until there is really no portion of the virtual address space left. To ensure that the stack does not collide with the mmap region, a safety gap is installed between both.

4.2.2 Creating the Layout

The address space of a task is laid out when an ELF binary is loaded with `load_elf_binary` — recall that the function is used by the `exec` system call. Loading an ELF file is cluttered with numerous technical details that are not interesting for our purposes, so the code flow diagram in Figure 4-3 concentrates on the steps required to set up the virtual memory region.

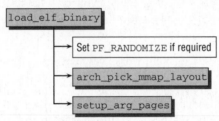

Figure 4-3: Code flow diagram for
`load_elf_binary`.

Address space randomization is enabled if the global variable `randomize_va_space` is set to 1. This is usually the case, but is disabled for Transmeta CPUs because it has a negative speed impact on such machines. Besides, the user can use `/proc/sys/kernel/randomize_va_space` to disable the feature.

The address space layout is selected in `arch_pick_mmap_layout`. If the architecture does not provide a specific function, the kernel's default routine sets up the address space as shown in Figure 4-1. It is, however, more interesting to observe how IA-32 chooses between the classical and the new alternative:

```
arch/x86/mm/mmap_32.c
void arch_pick_mmap_layout(struct mm_struct *mm)
{
        /*
         * Fall back to the standard layout if the personality
         * bit is set, or if the expected stack growth is unlimited:
         */
        if (sysctl_legacy_va_layout ||
                        (current->personality & ADDR_COMPAT_LAYOUT) ||
                        current->signal->rlim[RLIMIT_STACK].rlim_cur == RLIM_INFINITY)
        {

                mm->mmap_base = TASK_UNMAPPED_BASE;
                mm->get_unmapped_area = arch_get_unmapped_area;
                mm->unmap_area = arch_unmap_area;
        } else {
                mm->mmap_base = mmap_base(mm);
```

```
                    mm->get_unmapped_area = arch_get_unmapped_area_topdown;
                    mm->unmap_area = arch_unmap_area_topdown;
            }
    }
```

The old layout is chosen if the user has explicitly instructed to do so via /proc/sys/kernel/legacy_va_layout, if a binary that was compiled for a different UNIX flavor that requires the old layout is executed, or — most importantly — the stack may grow infinitely. This makes it difficult to find a bound for the stack below which the mmap region can start.

In the classical case, the start of the mmap area is at TASK_UNMAPPED_BASE, which resolves to 0x4000000, and the standard function arch_get_unmapped_area (despite its name, the function is not necessarily architecture-specific, but there's also a standard implementation available in the kernel) is used to grow new mappings from bottom to top.

When the new layout is used, memory mappings grow from top to bottom. The standard function arch_get_unmapped_area_topdown (which I will not consider in detail) is responsible for this. More interesting is how the base address for memory mappings is chosen:

arch/x86/mm/mmap_32.c
```
#define MIN_GAP (128*1024*1024)
#define MAX_GAP (TASK_SIZE/6*5)

static inline unsigned long mmap_base(struct mm_struct *mm)
{
        unsigned long gap = current->signal->rlim[RLIMIT_STACK].rlim_cur;
        unsigned long random_factor = 0;

        if (current->flags & PF_RANDOMIZE)
                random_factor = get_random_int() % (1024*1024);

        if (gap < MIN_GAP)
                gap = MIN_GAP;
        else if (gap > MAX_GAP)
                gap = MAX_GAP;

        return PAGE_ALIGN(TASK_SIZE - gap - random_factor);
}
```

The lowest possible stack location that can be computed from the maximal stack size can be used as the start of the mmap area. However, the kernel ensures that the stack spans at least 128 MiB. Additionally, it is ensured that at least a small portion of the address space is not taken up by the stack if a gigantic stack limit is specified.

If address space randomization is requested, the position is modified by a random offset of maximally 1 MiB. Additionally, the kernel ensures that the region is aligned along the page frame size because this is required by the architecture.

At a first glance, one could assume that life is easier for 64-bit architectures because they should not have to choose between different address layouts — the virtual address space is so large that collisions of heap and mmap region are nearly impossible.

However, the definition of `arch_pick_mmap_layout` for the AMD64 architecture shows that another complication arises:

arch/x86_64/mmap.c
```
void arch_pick_mmap_layout(struct mm_struct *mm)
{
#ifdef CONFIG_IA32_EMULATION
        if (current_thread_info()->flags & _TIF_IA32)
                return ia32_pick_mmap_layout(mm);
#endif
        mm->mmap_base = TASK_UNMAPPED_BASE;
        if (current->flags & PF_RANDOMIZE) {
                /* Add 28bit randomness which is about 40bits of address space
                   because mmap base has to be page aligned.
                   or ~1/128 of the total user VM
                   (total user address space is 47bits) */
                unsigned rnd = get_random_int() & 0xfffffff;
                mm->mmap_base += ((unsigned long)rnd) << PAGE_SHIFT;
        }
        mm->get_unmapped_area = arch_get_unmapped_area;
        mm->unmap_area = arch_unmap_area;
}
```

If binary emulation for 32-bit applications is enabled, any process that runs in compatibility mode should see the same address space as it would encounter on a native machine. Therefore, `ia32_pick_mmap_layout` is used to lay out the address space for 32-bit applications. The function is an identical copy of `arch_pick_mmap_layout` for IA-32 systems, as discussed above.

The classic layout for virtual address space is always used on AMD64 systems so that there is no need to distinguish between the various options. Address space randomization is performed by shifting the otherwise fixed `mmap_base` if the `PF_RANDOMIZE` flag is set.

Let us go back to `load_elf_binary`. Finally, the function needs to create the stack at the appropriate location:

<fs/binfmt_elf.c>
```
static int load_elf_binary(struct linux_binprm *bprm, struct pt_regs *regs)
{
...
        retval = setup_arg_pages(bprm, randomize_stack_top(STACK_TOP),
                executable_stack);
...
}
```

The standard function `setup_arg_pages` is used for this purpose. I will not discuss it in detail because it is only technical. The function requires the top of the stack as a parameter. This is given by the architecture-specific constant `STACK_TOP`, but `randomize_stack_top` ensures that the address is changed by a random amount if address space randomization is required.

4.3 Principle of Memory Mappings

Because the total virtual address space of all user processes is *substantially* larger than the available RAM memory, only the most frequently used elements can be associated with a physical page frame. This is not a problem because most programs occupy only a small part of the memory actually available to them. Let's look at the situation in which a file is manipulated by a text editor. Typically, the user is only bothered with the end of the file so although the complete file is mapped into memory, only a few pages are actually used to store the data at the end of the file. As for the beginning of the file, the kernel need only keep the information in address space about where on the disk to find the data and how to read them when they are required.

The situation is similar with the text segment — only part of it is always needed. If we stay with the example of the text editor, only the code for the central editing function is required. Other parts — the Help system or the obligatory Web and e-mail client common to all programs — are only loaded when explicitly required by the user.[3]

The kernel must provide data structures to establish an association between the regions of the virtual address space and the places where the related data are located. In the case of a mapped text file, for example, the virtual memory area must be associated with the area on the hard disk in which the filesystem has stored the contents of the file. This is illustrated in Figure 4-4.

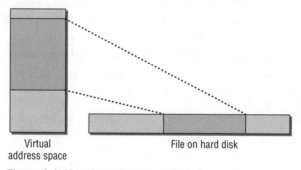

Virtual
address space   File on hard disk

Figure 4-4: Mapping a file into virtual memory.

Of course, I have shown the situation in simplified form because file data are not generally stored contiguously on hard disk but are distributed over several smaller areas (this is discussed in Chapter 9). The kernel makes use of the `address_space` data structure[4] to provide a set of methods to read data from a *backing store* — from a filesystem, for example. `address_spaces` therefore form an auxiliary layer to represent the mapped data as a contiguous linear area to memory management.

Allocating and filling pages on demand is known as *demand paging*. It is based on interaction between the processor and the kernel using a variety of data structures as shown in Figure 4-5.

---

[3]I assume that all program parts reside in a single, large binary file. Of course, program parts can also be loaded at the explicit request of the program itself, but I do not discuss this here.

[4]Unfortunately, the names for the virtual address space and the address space indicating how the data are mapped are identical.

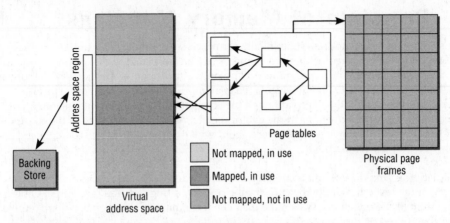

Figure 4-5: Interaction of data structures during demand paging.

❑ A process tries to access a memory address that is in user address space but cannot be resolved using the page tables (there is no associated page in RAM memory).

❑ The processor then triggers a page fault that is forwarded to the kernel.

❑ The kernel runs through the process address space data structures responsible for the area in which the fault occurred to find the appropriate backing store or to establish that access was, indeed, incorrect.

❑ A physical page is allocated and filled with the requisite data from the backing store.

❑ The physical page is incorporated into the address space of the user process with the help of the page tables, and the application resumes.

These actions are transparent to user processes; in other words, the processes don't notice whether a page is actually available or must first be requested by means of demand paging.

4.4 Data Structures

Recall that `struct mm_struct` is important — it provides all necessary information to lay out a task in memory as discussed before. Additionally, it includes the following elements for management of all memory regions in the virtual address space of a user process.

```
<mm_types.h>
struct mm_struct {
        struct vm_area_struct * mmap;          /* list of VMAs */
        struct rb_root mm_rb;
        struct vm_area_struct * mmap_cache;    /* last find_vma result */
...
}
```

The following sections discuss the meanings of the entries.

4.4.1 Trees and Lists

Each region is described by an instance of `vm_area_struct`, and the regions of a process are sorted in two ways:

1. On a singly linked list (starting with `mm_struct->mmap`).

2. In a red-black tree whose root element is located in `mm_rb`.

`mmap_cache` is a cache for the region last handled; its meaning will become clear in Section 4.5.1.

Red-black trees are binary search trees whose nodes also have a color (red or black). They exhibit all the properties of normal search trees (and can therefore be scanned very efficiently for a specific element). The red-black property also simplifies re-balancing.[5] Readers unfamiliar with this concept are referred to Appendix C, which deals extensively with the structure, properties, and implementation of red-black trees.

The start and end addresses describe each region in virtual user address space. The existing regions are included in the linked list in ascending order of start address. Scanning the list to find the region associated with a particular address is a very inefficient operation if there are a very large number of regions (as is the case with data-intensive applications). The individual instances of `vm_area_struct` are therefore also managed in a red-black tree, which speeds up scanning considerably.

To add a new region, the kernel first searches the red-black tree for the region immediately preceding the new region. With its help, it can add the new region to the tree and also to the linear list without having to explicitly scan the list (the algorithm used by the kernel to add new regions is discussed at length in Section 4.5.3). Finally, the situation in memory is illustrated in Figure 4-6. Notice that the representation of the tree is only symbolic and does not reflect the real layout, which is more complicated.

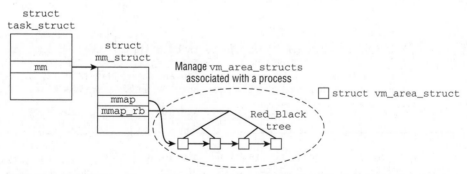

Figure 4-6: Association of `vm_area_struct` instances with the virtual process space of a process.

---

[5]All important tree operations (add, delete, find) can be performed in $\mathcal{O}(\log n)$, where n is the number of elements in the tree.

4.4.2 Representation of Regions

Each region is represented by an instance of vm_area_struct, which is defined (in simplified form) as
follows:

<mm_types.h>

```
struct vm_area_struct {
        struct mm_struct * vm_mm;        /* The address space we belong to. */
        unsigned long vm_start;          /* Our start address within vm_mm. */
        unsigned long vm_end;            /* The first byte after our end address
                                            within vm_mm. */

        /* linked list of VM areas per task, sorted by address */
        struct vm_area_struct *vm_next;

        pgprot_t vm_page_prot;           /* Access permissions of this VMA. */
        unsigned long vm_flags;          /* Flags, listed below. */

        struct rb_node vm_rb;

        /*
         * For areas with an address space and backing store,
         * linkage into the address_space->i_mmap prio tree, or
         * linkage to the list of like vmas hanging off its node, or
         * linkage of vma in the address_space->i_mmap_nonlinear list.
         */
        union {
                struct {
                        struct list_head list;
                        void *parent;    /* aligns with prio_tree_node parent */
                        struct vm_area_struct *head;
                } vm_set;

                struct raw_prio_tree_node prio_tree_node;
        } shared;

        /*
         * A file's MAP_PRIVATE vma can be in both i_mmap tree and anon_vma
         * list, after a COW of one of the file pages.  A MAP_SHARED vma
         * can only be in the i_mmap tree.  An anonymous MAP_PRIVATE, stack
         * or brk vma (with NULL file) can only be in an anon_vma list.
         */
        struct list_head anon_vma_node; /* Serialized by anon_vma->lock */
        struct anon_vma *anon_vma;       /* Serialized by page_table_lock */

        /* Function pointers to deal with this struct. */
        struct vm_operations_struct * vm_ops;

        /* Information about our backing store: */
        unsigned long vm_pgoff;          /* Offset (within vm_file) in PAGE_SIZE
                                            units, *not* PAGE_CACHE_SIZE */
        struct file * vm_file;           /* File we map to (can be NULL). */
        void * vm_private_data;          /* was vm_pte (shared mem) */
};
```

The individual elements have the following meanings:

❑ vm_mm is a back-pointer to the mm_struct instance to which the region belongs.

❑ vm_start and vm_end specify the virtual start and end addresses of the region in userspace.

❑ The linear linking of all vm_area_struct instances of a process is achieved using vm_next, whereas incorporation in the red-black tree is the responsibility of vm_rb.

❑ vm_page_prot stores the access permissions for the region in the constants discussed in Section 3.3.1, which are also used for pages in memory.

❑ vm_flags is a set of flags describing the region. I discuss the flags that can be set below.

❑ A mapping of a file into the virtual address space of a process is uniquely determined by the interval in the file and the corresponding interval in memory. To keep track of all intervals associated with a process, the kernel uses a linked list and a red-black tree as described above.

However, it is also necessary to go the other way round: Given an interval in a file, the kernel sometimes needs to know all processes into which the interval is mapped. Such mappings are called *shared mappings*, and the C standard library, which is used by nearly every process in the system, is a prime example of why such mappings are necessary.

To provide the required information, all vm_area_struct instances are additionally managed in a *priority* tree, and the elements required for this are contained in shared. As you can easily imagine from the rather complicated definition of this structure member, this is a tricky business, which is discussed in detail in Section 4.4.3 below.

❑ anon_vma_node and anon_vma are used to manage shared pages originating from anonymous mappings. Mappings that point to the same pages are held on a doubly linked list, where anon_vma_node acts as the list element.

There are several of these lists, depending on how many sets of mappings there are that share different physical pages. The anon_vma element serves as a pointer to the management structure that is associated with each list and comprises a list head and an associated lock.

❑ vm_ops is a pointer to a collection of methods used to perform various standard operations on the region.

<mm.h>
```
struct vm_operations_struct {
        void (*open)(struct vm_area_struct * area);
        void (*close)(struct vm_area_struct * area);
        int (*fault)(struct vm_area_struct *vma, struct vm_fault *vmf);
        struct page * (*nopage)(struct vm_area_struct * area, unsigned long
                                address, int *type);
...
};
```

❑ open and close are invoked when a region is created and deleted, respectively. They are not normally used and have null pointers.

❑ However, fault is very important. If a virtual page is not present in an address space, the automatically triggered page fault handler invokes this function to read the corresponding data into a physical page that is mapped into the user address space.

❑ nopage is the kernel's old method to respond to page faults that is less flexible than fault. The element is still provided for compatibility reasons, but should not be used in new code.

❏ vm_pgoffset specifies an offset for a file mapping when not all file contents are to be mapped (the offset is 0 if the whole file is mapped).

> The offset is not expressed in bytes but in multiples of **PAGE_SIZE**. On a system with pages of 4 KiB, an offset value of 10 equates to an actual byte offset of 40,960. This is reasonable because the kernel only supports mappings in whole-page units, and smaller values would make no sense.

❏ vm_file points to the file instance that describes a mapped file (it holds a null pointer if the object mapped is not a file). Chapter 8 discusses the contents of the file structure at length.

❏ Depending on mapping type, vm_private_data can be used to store private data that are not manipulated by the generic memory management routines. (The kernel ensures only that the element is initialized with a null pointer when a new region is created.) Currently, only a few sound and video drivers make use of this option.

vm_flags stores flags to define the properties of a region. They are all declared as pre-processor constants in <mm.h>.

❏ VM_READ, VM_WRITE, VM_EXEC, and VM_SHARED specify whether page contents can be read, written, executed, or shared by several processes.

❏ VM_MAYREAD, VM_MAYWRITE, VM_MAYEXEC, and VM_MAYSHARE determine whether the VM_* flags may be set. This is required for the mprotect system call.

❏ VM_GROWSDOWN and VM_GROWSUP indicate whether a region can be extended downward or upward (to lower/higher virtual addresses). Because the heap grows from bottom to top, VM_GROWSUP is set in its region; VM_GROWSDOWN is set for the stack, which grows from top to bottom.

❏ VM_SEQ_READ is set if it is likely that the region will be read sequentially from start to end; VM_RAND_READ specifies that read access may be random. Both flags are intended as "prompts" for memory management and the block device layer to improve their optimizations (e.g., page readahead if access is primarily sequential. Chapter 8 takes a closer look at this technique).

❏ If VM_DONTCOPY is set, the relevant region is not copied when the fork system call is executed.

❏ VM_DONTEXPAND prohibits expansion of a region by the mremap system call.

❏ VM_HUGETLB is set if the region is based on huge pages as featured in some architectures.

❏ VM_ACCOUNT specifies whether the region is to be included in the calculations for the *overcommit* features. These features restrict memory allocations in various ways (refer to Section 4.5.3 for more details).

4.4.3 The Priority Search Tree

Priority search trees are required to establish a connection between a region in a file and all virtual address spaces into which the region is mapped. To understand how this connection is established, we need to introduce some data structures of the kernel, which will be discussed in more detail and within a more general context in the following chapters.

Additional Data Structures

Every open file (and every block device, because these can also be memory-mapped via device special files) is represented by an instance of `struct file`. This structure, in turn, contains a pointer to an *address space* object as represented by `struct address_space`. This object is the basis of the priority search tree (*prio tree*) by which the connection between mapped intervals and the address spaces into which these are mapped is established. The definition of both structures is as follows (I only show the elements required for our purposes here):

<fs.h>
```
struct address_space {
        struct inode *host; /* owner: inode, block_device */
...

        struct prio_tree_root i_mmap; /* tree of private and shared mappings */
        struct list_head i_mmap_nonlinear;/*list VM_NONLINEAR mappings */
...
}
```

<fs.h>
```
struct file {
...

        struct address_space *f_mapping;
...
}
```

Additionally, each file and each block device are represented by an instance of `struct inode`. In contrast to `struct file`, which is the abstraction for a file opened by the `open` system call, the inode represents the object in the filesystem itself.

<fs.h>
```
struct inode {
...

        struct address_space *i_mapping;
...
}
```

Notice that only mapped file intervals are discussed below although, it is also possible to map different things, for instance, direct intervals in raw block devices, without a detour over filesystems. When a file is opened, the kernel sets `file->f_mapping` to `inode->i_mapping`. This allows multiple processes to access the same file without directly interfering with the other processes: `inode` is a file-specific data structure, while `file` is local to a given process.

These data structures are connected with each other, and Figure 4-7 provides an overview about the situation in memory. Notice that the representation of the tree is only symbolic and does not reflect the actual, complicated tree layout.

Given an instance of `struct address_space`, the kernel can infer the associated inode, which, in turn, allows for access to the backing store on which the file data are stored. Usually, the backing store will be a block device; the details are discussed in Chapter 9. Section 4.6 and Chapter 16 are devoted to discussing more about address spaces. Here it suffices to know that the address space is the base element of a priority tree that contains all vm_area_struct instances describing the mapping of an interval of the file associated with the inode into some virtual address space. Since each instance of struct vm_area contains a pointer to the mm_struct of the process to which it belongs, the desired connection is set up! Note that vm_area_structs can also be associated with an address space via a doubly linked list headed by i_mmap_nonlinear. This is required for *nonlinear mappings*, which I neglect for now. I will come back to them in Section 4.7.3, though.

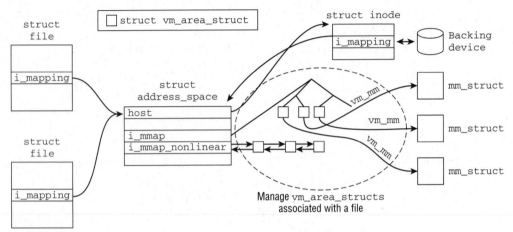

Figure 4-7: Tracking the virtual address spaces into which a given interval of a file is mapped with the help of a priority tree.

Recall that Figure 4-6 shows how vm_area_struct instances are organized in a linked list and a red-black tree. It is important to realize that these are the *same* vm_area_struct instances that are managed in the prio tree. While keeping vm_area_structs in two or more data structures at the same time is no problem for the kernel at all, it is nearly impossible to visualize. Therefore, keep in mind that a given instance of struct vm_area can be contained in two data structures: One establishes a connection between a region in the virtual address space of a process to the data in the underlying file, and one allows for finding all address spaces that map a given file interval.

Representing Priority Trees

Priority trees allow for management of the vm_area_struct instances that represent a particular interval of the given file. This requires that the data structure cannot only deal with *overlapping*, but also with *identical* file intervals. The situation is illustrated in Figure 4-8: Two processes map the region [7, 12] of a file into their virtual address space, while a third process maps the interval [10, 30].

Managing overlapping intervals is not much of a problem: The boundaries of the interval provide a unique index that allows for storing each interval in a unique tree node. I will not discuss in detail how this is implemented by the kernel because it rather similar to radix trees (see Appendix C for more details). It suffices to know that if intervals B, C, and D are completely contained in another interval A, then A will be the parent element of B, C, and D.

However, what happens if multiple *identical* intervals must be included in the prio tree? Each prio tree node is represented by the raw_prio_tree_node instance, which is *directly included* in each `vm_ area_struct` instance. Recall, however, that it is in a union with a `vm_set`. This allows for associating a list of `vm_sets` (and thus `vm_area_structs`) with a prio tree node. Figure 4-9 illustrates the situation in memory.

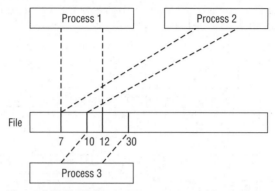

Figure 4-8: Multiple processes can map identical or overlapping regions of a file into their virtual address space.

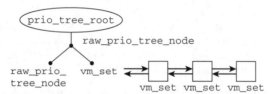

Figure 4-9: Interrelation of data structures in the management of shared identical mappings.

When an interval is inserted into the prio tree, the kernel proceeds as follows:

❑ When the `vm_area_struct` instance is linked into the prio tree as a node, `prio_tree_node` is used to establish the necessary associations. To check whether there is a `vm_area_struct` in the tree, the kernel exploits the fact that the `parent` element of `vm_set` coincides with the last structure element of `prio_tree_node` — the data structures are coordinated accordingly. Since `parent` is not used within `vm_set`, the kernel can use `parent != NULL` to check whether the current `vm_area_struct` member is in a tree.

The definition of `prio_tree_node` also ensures that the `head` element of `vmset` does *not* overlap with `prio_tree_node` so that both can be used together, although they are actually combined in a `union`.

The kernel therefore uses `vm_set.head` to point to the first element on the list of `vm_area_struct` instances that belong to a shared mapping.

❑ If the above list of shared mappings contains a `vm_area_struct`, `vm_set.list` is used as the list head to list all regions affected.

Section 4.5.3 discusses the technical details of how the kernel goes about inserting new regions.

4.5 Operations on Regions

The kernel provides various functions to manipulate the regions of a process. Creating and deleting regions (and finding a suitable memory location for a new region) are standard operations needed when setting up or removing a mapping. The kernel is also responsible for performing optimizations when managing the data structures, as shown in Figure 4-10.

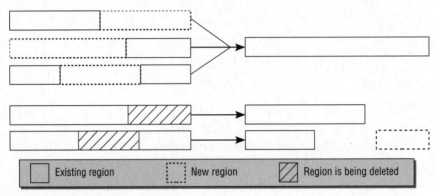

Figure 4-10: Operations on regions.

❑ When a new region is added immediately before or after an existing region (and therefore also between two existing regions), the kernel merges the data structures involved into a single structure — but, of course, *only* if the access permissions for all the regions involved are identical and contiguous data are mapped from the same backing store.

❑ If a deletion is made at the start or end of a region, the existing data structure must be truncated accordingly.

❑ If a region *between* two other regions is deleted, the existing data structure is reduced in size, and a new data structure is created for the resultant new region.

A further important standard operation is the search for a region associated with a specific virtual address in userspace. Before explaining the optimizations mentioned above, let's discuss the helper function used to do this.

4.5.1 Associating Virtual Addresses with a Region

By reference to a virtual address, `find_vma` finds the first region in user address space whose end is *after* the given address and therefore satisfies the `addr < vm_area_struct->vm_end` condition. As parameters, the function requires not only the virtual address (`addr`) but also a pointer to the `mm_struct` instance of the relevant process whose address space is to be scanned.

<mm/mmap.c>
```
struct vm_area_struct * find_vma(struct mm_struct * mm, unsigned long addr)
{
        struct vm_area_struct *vma = NULL;

        if (mm) {
                /* Check the cache first. */
```

```
        /* (Cache hit rate is typically around 35%.) */
        vma = mm->mmap_cache;
        if (!(vma && vma->vm_end > addr && vma->vm_start <= addr)) {
                struct rb_node * rb_node;

                rb_node = mm->mm_rb.rb_node;
                vma = NULL;

                while (rb_node) {
                        struct vm_area_struct * vma_tmp;

                        vma_tmp = rb_entry(rb_node,
                                        struct vm_area_struct, vm_rb);

                        if (vma_tmp->vm_end > addr) {
                                vma = vma_tmp;
                                if (vma_tmp->vm_start <= addr)
                                        break;
                                rb_node = rb_node->rb_left;
                        } else
                                rb_node = rb_node->rb_right;
                }
                if (vma)
                        mm->mmap_cache = vma;
        }
        return vma;
}
```

The kernel first checks whether the region last processed and now held in mm->mmap_cache contains the required address — that is, whether its end is after the required address and its start is before. If so, the kernel does not execute the if block and immediately returns the pointer to the region.

If not, the red-black tree must be searched step by step. rb_node is the data structure used to represent each node in the tree. rb_entry enables the "useful data" (in this case, an instance of vm_area_struct) to be removed from the node.

The root element of the tree is located in mm->mm_rb.rb_node. If the end address of the associated region is less than the required address and the start address is greater than the required address, the kernel has found the appropriate element and can exit the while loop to return a pointer to the vm_area_struct instance. Otherwise, the search is resumed at the

❑   *left child* if the end address of the current region is *after* the required address,

or at the

❑   *right child* if the end address of the region is *before* the required address.

As the root elements of the tree have null pointers as child elements, it is easy for the kernel to decide when to terminate the search and return a null pointer as an error message.

If a suitable region is found, a pointer to it is stored in mmap_cache because there is a strong likelihood that the next find_vma call will search for a neighboring address in the same region.

find_vma_intersection is another helper function to establish whether an interval bounded by start_addr and end_addr is fully within an existing region. It builds on find_vma and is easily implemented as follows:

<mm.h>
```
static inline
struct vm_area_struct * find_vma_intersection(struct mm_struct * mm,
                                              unsigned long start_addr,
                                              unsigned long end_addr)
{
        struct vm_area_struct * vma = find_vma(mm, start_addr);

        if (vma && end_addr <= vma->vm_start)
                vma = NULL;
        return vma;
}
```

4.5.2 Merging Regions

When a new region is added to the address space of a process, the kernel checks whether it can be merged with one or more existing regions as shown in Figure 4-10.

vm_merge merges a new region with the surrounding regions if this is possible. It requires numerous parameters.

mm/mmap.c
```
struct vm_area_struct *vma_merge(struct mm_struct *mm,
                    struct vm_area_struct *prev, unsigned long addr,
                    unsigned long end, unsigned long vm_flags,
                    struct anon_vma *anon_vma, struct file *file,
                    pgoff_t pgoff, struct mempolicy *policy)
{
        pgoff_t pglen = (end - addr) >> PAGE_SHIFT;
        struct vm_area_struct *area, *next;
...
```

mm is the address space instance of the relevant process and prev the region immediately *before* the new region. rb_parent is the parent element of the region in the red-black search tree.

addr, end, and vm_flags describe the start, end, and flags of the new region as their names suggest. If the region belongs to a file mapping, file contains a pointer to the file instance that identifies the file. pgoff specifies the offset of the mapping within the file data. Since policy is required on NUMA systems only, I won't discuss it further.

The technical details of implementation are very straightforward. A check is first made to ascertain whether the end address of the predecessor region corresponds to the start address of the new region. If so, the kernel must then check that the flags and the mapped file are identical for both regions, that the offsets of file mappings are such that a contiguous region results, that both regions do not contain anonymous mappings, and that both regions are mutually compatible.[6] This is done using the

---

[6]The regions cannot be merged if two file mappings follow each other without a hole but map non-contiguous sections of the file.

can_vma_merge_after helper function. The work of merging a region with its predecessor region looks like this:

mm/mmap.c
```
        if (prev && prev->vm_end == addr &&
                        can_vma_merge_after(prev, vm_flags,
                                              anon_vma, file, pgoff)) {
    ...
```

If it can, the kernel then checks whether the successor region can and must be merged.

mm/mmap.c
```
            /*
             * OK, it can.  Can we now merge in the successor as well?
             */
            if (next && end == next->vm_start &&
                            can_vma_merge_before(next, vm_flags,
                                    anon_vma, file, pgoff+pglen) &&
                            is_mergeable_anon_vma(prev->anon_vma,
                                              next->anon_vma)) {
                    vma_adjust(prev, prev->vm_start,
                                next->vm_end, prev->vm_pgoff, NULL);
            } else
                    vma_adjust(prev, prev->vm_start,
                                  end, prev->vm_pgoff, NULL);
            return prev;
        }
```

The first difference as compared to the previous case is that can_vma_merge_before is used instead of can_vma_merge_after to check whether the two regions can be merged. If both the predecessor and the successor region can be merged with the current region, it must also be ensured that the anonymous mappings of the predecessor can be merged with those of the successor before a single region consisting of all three regions can be created.

In both cases, the helper function vma_adjust is invoked to perform final merging; it appropriately modifies all data structures involved — the priority tree and the vm_area_struct instances — as well as deallocating the instances of these structures that are no longer needed.

4.5.3   Inserting Regions

insert_vm_struct is the standard function used by the kernel to insert new regions. The actual work is delegated to two helper functions, as the code flow diagram in Figure 4-11 shows.

find_vma_prepare is first invoked to obtain the information listed below by reference to the start address of the new region and of the address space involved (mm_struct).

❑   The vm_area_struct instance of the preceding address space.

❑   The parent node (in the red-black tree) in which the node for the new region is held.

❑   The leaf node (of the red-black tree) that contains the region itself.

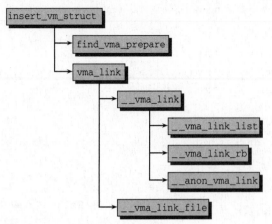

**Figure 4-11: Code flow diagram for
`insert_vm_struct`.**

It's common knowledge that C permits functions to return just one variable — consequently, the above function returns only a pointer to the successor region as its direct result; the remaining information is supplied by means of pointer arguments.

The information found is sufficient to incorporate the new region into the existing data structures of the process using `vma_link`. After some preparatory work, the function delegates the real work to `insert_vm_struct`, which performs three insert operations as the code flow diagram shows.

❏ `__vma_link_list` puts the new region on the linear list of regions of the process; only the predecessor and successor region found using `find_vma_prepare` are needed to do this.[7]

❏ `__vma_link_rb` links the new region into the data structures of the red-black tree, as the name suggests.

❏ `__anon_vma_link` adds the `vm_area_struct` instance to the linked list of anonymous mappings discussed above.

Finally, `__vma_link_file` links the relevant `address_space` and the mapping in the case of file mappings and also adds the region to the prio tree using `vma_prio_tree_insert`, which handles multiple identical regions as described above.

4.5.4 Creating Regions

Before a new memory region can be inserted into the data structures, the kernel must establish where there is enough free space in virtual address space for a region of a given size. This job is assigned to the `get_unmapped_area` helper function.

---

[7]If there is no predecessor region because the new region is the new start region or because no regions are defined for the address space, the information in the red-black tree is used to set the pointers correctly.

mm/mmap.c
```
unsigned long
get_unmapped_area(struct file *file, unsigned long addr, unsigned long len,
                  unsigned long pgoff, unsigned long flags)
```

The arguments are self-explanatory. The implementation of the function is of no further interest as the actual work is delegated to the architecture-specific helper function stored in the mm_struct instance of the current process.[8]

Recall from Section 4.2 that different mapping functions are used depending on the layout of the virtual process address space. Here I consider the standard function arch_get_unmapped_area that is employed on most systems.

arch_get_unmapped_area first has to check whether the MAP_FIXED flag is set, indicating that the mapping is to be created at a fixed address. If so, the kernel ensures only that the address satisfies alignment requirements (page-by-page) and that the interval is fully within the available address space.

If no desired area was specified, the kernel tries to find a suitable section in the virtual memory area of the process by invoking arch_get_unmapped_area. If a particular preferred (as opposed to a fixed) address is specified, the kernel checks whether the region overlaps with an existing region. If not, the address can be returned as the target.

mm/mmap.c
```
unsigned long
arch_get_unmapped_area(struct file *filp, unsigned long addr,
                  unsigned long len, unsigned long pgoff, unsigned long flags)
{
        struct mm_struct *mm = current->mm;
...

        if (addr) {
                addr = PAGE_ALIGN(addr);
                vma = find_vma(mm, addr);
                if (TASK_SIZE - len >= addr &&
                    (!vma || addr + len <= vma->vm_start))
                        return addr;
        }
...
```

Otherwise, the kernel must try to find a free area of the right size by iterating over the available regions of the process. In doing so, it checks whether a cached area from previous scans could be used.

mm/mmap.c
```
        if (len > mm->cached_hole_size) {
                start_addr = addr = mm->free_area_cache;
        } else {
                start_addr = addr = TASK_UNMAPPED_BASE;
                mm->cached_hole_size = 0;
        }
...
```

---

[8]Files can also be equipped with a special-purpose mapping function. This is, for instance, used by the frame-buffer code to allow direct manipulation of the video memory when a frame-buffer device file is mapped into memory. However, because the kernel generally uses the standard implementation, I won't bother to discuss other more specific routines.

The actual iteration begins either at the address of the last "hole" in the virtual address space or at the global start address TASK_UNMAPPED_BASE.

mm/mmap.c

```
full_search:
        for (vma = find_vma(mm, addr); ; vma = vma->vm_next) {
                /* At this point:  (!vma || addr < vma->vm_end). */
                if (TASK_SIZE - len < addr) {
                        /*
                         * Start a new search - just in case we missed
                         * some holes.
                         */
                        if (start_addr != TASK_UNMAPPED_BASE) {
                                addr = TASK_UNMAPPED_BASE;
                                start_addr = addr;
                                mm->cached_hole_size = 0;
                                goto full_search;
                        }
                        return -ENOMEM;
                }
                if (!vma || addr + len <= vma->vm_start) {
                        /*
                         * Remember the place where we stopped the search:
                         */
                        mm->free_area_cache = addr + len;
                        return addr;
                }
                if (addr + mm->cached_hole_size < vma->vm_start)
                        mm->cached_hole_size = vma->vm_start - addr;
                addr = vma->vm_end;
        }
}
```

If the search continues to the end of the user address space (TASK_SIZE) and no suitable area is found, the kernel returns an -ENOMEM error that must be forwarded to userspace for processing by the relevant application, as it indicates that insufficient virtual address space memory is available to satisfy the request. If memory is found, its virtual start address is returned.

The version for top-down allocation, arch_get_unmapped_area_topdown, progresses similarly, but the search direction is, of course, reversed. We need not bother with the details of implementation here.

4.6 Address Spaces

Memory mappings of files can be regarded as mappings between two different address spaces to simplify the work of (system) programmers. One address space is the virtual memory address space of the user process, the other is the address space spanned by the filesystem.

When the kernel creates a mapping, it must create a link between the address spaces to support communication between the two — in the form of read and write requests. The vm_operations_struct structure with which we are familiar from Section 4.4.2 is first used to do this. It provides an operation to read pages not yet in physical memory although their contents have already been mapped there.

However, the operation has no information on the mapping type or on its properties. As there are numerous kinds of file mappings (regular files on different filesystem types, device files, etc.), more information is required. In fact, the kernel needs a more detailed description of the address space of the data source.

The `address_space` structure mentioned briefly above is defined for this purpose and contains additional information on a mapping. Recall that the connection between files, address spaces, and inodes has been shown in Figure 4-7. Some of the data structures involved are explained in future chapters, and thus their relationships are not dealt with here; let us simply state that each file mapping has an associated instance of `address_space`.

Neither is the exact definition of `struct address_space` relevant at this point; it is discussed in more detail in Chapter 16. Here it is sufficient to know that each address space has a set of address space operations held as function pointers in the structure shown below (only the most important entries are reproduced).

```
<fs.h>
struct address_space_operations {
        int (*writepage)(struct page *page, struct writeback_control *wbc);
        int (*readpage)(struct file *, struct page *);
...
        /* Write back some dirty pages from this mapping. */
        int (*writepages)(struct address_space *, struct writeback_control *);

        /* Set a page dirty. Return true if this dirtied it */
        int (*set_page_dirty)(struct page *page);

        int (*readpages)(struct file *filp, struct address_space *mapping,
        struct list_head *pages, unsigned nr_pages);
...
};
```

A detailed description of the structure can also be found in Chapter 16.

❏ `readpage` reads a single page from the underlying block medium into RAM memory; `readpages` performs the same task for several pages at once.

❏ `writepage` writes the contents of a page from RAM memory back to the corresponding location on a block device to permanently save changes.

❏ `set_page_dirty` indicates that the contents of a page have been changed and no longer match the original contents on the block device.

How is the link between `vm_operations_struct` and `address_space` established? There is no static link to assign an instance of each structure to the other structure. Nevertheless, both are linked by the standard implementations that the kernel provides for `vm_operations_struct` and that are used by almost all filesystems.

```
mm/filemap.c
struct vm_operations_struct generic_file_vm_ops = {
        .fault = filemap_fault,
};
```

The implementation of `filemap_fault` uses the `readpage` method of the underlying mapping and therefore adopts the above `address_space` concept, as you will see in the concept description in Chapter 8.

4.7 Memory Mappings

Now that we are familiar with the data structures and address space operations related to memory mappings, we move on in this section to examine the interaction between the kernel and the applications when mappings are created. As we know, the C standard library features the `mmap` function to install mappings. Two system calls — `mmap` and `mmap2` — are provided on the kernel side. Some architectures implement both versions [e.g., IA-64, and Sparc(64)], others only the first (AMD64) or only the second (IA-32). Both have the same set of parameters.

```
asmlinkage unsigned long sys_mmap{2}(unsigned long addr, unsigned long len,
        unsigned long prot, unsigned long flags, unsigned long fd,
        unsigned long off)
```

Both calls create a mapping of length `len` at position `pos` in the virtual user address space whose access permissions are defined in `prot`. `flags` is a flag set used to set a number of parameters. The relevant file is identified by means of its file descriptor in `fd`.

The difference between `mmap` and `mmap2` lies in the meaning of the offset (`off`). In both calls, it indicates the point in the file at which mapping is to begin. For `mmap`, the position is specified in bytes, whereas the unit used by `mmap2` is pages (`PAGE_SIZE`) — this enables file sections to be mapped even if the file is larger than the address space available.

Typically, the C standard library provides only a single function for the creation of memory mappings by applications. This function call is then translated internally to the system call appropriate to the architecture.

The `munmap` system call is invoked to remove a mapping. There is no need for a `munmap2` system call because no file offset is required — just the virtual address of the mapping.

4.7.1 Creating Mappings

The call syntax for `mmap` and `mmap2` has already been introduced above, so I only need briefly list the most important flags that can be set:

❑   `MAP_FIXED` specifies that no other address than the one given may be used for the mapping. If this flag is not set, the kernel is free to change the desired address if, for example, a mapping already resides there (the existing mapping would otherwise be overwritten).

❑   `MAP_SHARED` must be used when an object (usually a file) is to be shared between several processes.

❑   `MAP_PRIVATE` creates a private mapping that is separated from the contents of the source — write operations on the mapped region have no effect on the data in the file.

❑   `MAP_ANONYMOUS` creates an *anonymous* mapping that is not associated with any data source — the `fd` and `off` parameters are ignored. This type of mapping can be used to allocate `malloc`-like memory for applications.

A combination of PROT_EXEC, PROT_READ, PROT_WRITE, and PROT_NONE values can be used to define access permission in prot. Not all combinations are implemented for all processors, with the result that the region may be granted more rights than those specified. Although the kernel does its best to set the desired mode, it can only guarantee that the access permissions set are not more restrictive than those specified.

For the sake of simplicity, the description below deals only with sys_mmap2 (sys_mmap behaves in a very similar way on most other architectures: all arrive in the do_mmap_pgoff function discussed below). In line with the convention discussed in Chapter 13, the function serves as the entry point for the mmap2 system call and immediately delegates work to do_mmap2. There the kernel references the file descriptor to find the file instance with all the characteristic data of the file being processed (Chapter 8 examines this data structure more closely). The remaining work is delegated to do_mmap_pgoff.

do_mmap_pgoff is an architecture-*independent* function defined in mm/mmap.c. Figure 4-12 shows the associated code flow diagram.

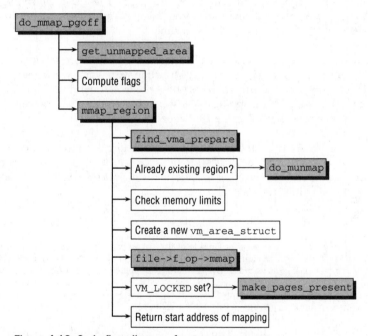

Figure 4-12: Code flow diagram for do_mmap_pgoff.

do_mmap_pgoff used to be one of the longest functions in the kernel. It is now effectively split into two parts, which are, however, still rather voluminous. One part has to thoroughly check the parameters of the user application, and the second part has to take a very large number of special situations and subtleties into consideration. As the latter make no valuable contribution to a general understanding of the mechanism involved, we look only at a representative standard situation — mapping of a regular file with MAP_SHARED — to avoid bloating our description, and the code flow diagram also applies just for this case.

The `get_unmapped_area` function described in Section 4.5.4 is first invoked to find a suitable area for the mapping in the virtual address space. Recall that the application may specify a fixed address for the mapping, suggest an address, or leave the choice of address to the kernel.

`calc_vm_prot_bits` and `calc_vm_flag_bits` combine the flags and access permission constants specified in the system call in a joint flag set that is easier to handle in the subsequent operations (the `MAP_` and `PROT_` flags are "translated" into flags with the prefix `VM_`).

mm/mmap.c
```
vm_flags = calc_vm_prot_bits(prot) | calc_vm_flag_bits(flags) |
               mm->def_flags | VM_MAYREAD | VM_MAYWRITE | VM_MAYEXEC;
```

What is most interesting is that the kernel includes the value of `def_flags` in the flag set after removing it from the `mm_struct` instance of the currently running process. `def_flags` has the value 0 or `VM_LOCK`. The former brings about no change to the resulting flag set, whereas `VM_LOCK` means that pages subsequently mapped in cannot be swapped out (the implementation of swapping is discussed in Chapter 18). To set the value of `def_flags`, the process must issue the `mlockall` system call, which uses the mechanism described above to prevent all future mappings from being swapped out, even if this was not requested explicitly by means of the `VM_LOCK` flag at creation time.

After the arguments have been checked and all required flags have been set up, the remaining work is delegated to `mmap_region`. The `find_vma_prepare` function with which we are familiar from Section 4.5.3 is invoked to find the `vm_area_struct` instances of the predecessor and successor areas and the data for the entry in the red-black tree. If a mapping already exists at the specified mapping point, it is removed by means of `do_munmap` (as described in the section below).

`vm_enough_memory` is invoked[9] if either the `MAP_NORESERVE` flag is not set or the value of the kernel parameter `sysctl_overcommit_memory`[10] is set to `OVERCOMMIT_NEVER`, that is, when overcommiting is not allowed. The function chooses whether to allocate the memory needed for the operation. If it selects against, the system call terminates with `-ENOMEM`.

---

[9]Using `security_vm_enough_memory`, which calls `__vm_enough_memory` over varying paths depending on the security framework in use.

[10]`sysctl_overcommit_memory` can be set with the help of the `/proc/sys/vm/overcommit_memory`. Currently there are three overcommit options. 1 allows an application to allocate as much memory as it wants, even more than is permitted by the address space of the system. 0 means that heuristic overcommitting is applied with the result that the number of usable pages is determined by adding together the pages in the page cache, the pages in the swap area, and the unused page frames; requests for allocation of a smaller number of pages are permitted. 2 stands for the strictest mode, known as *strict overcommitting*, in which the permitted number of pages that can be allocated is calculated as follows:

```
allowed = (totalram_pages - hugetlb) * sysctl_overcommit_ratio / 100;
allowed += total_swap_pages;
```

Here `sysctl_overcommit_ratio` is a configurable kernel parameter that is usually set to 50. If the total number of pages used exceeds this value, the kernel refuses to perform further allocations.

Why does it make sense to allow an application to allocate more pages than can ever be handled in principle? This is sometimes required for scientific applications. Some tend to allocate *huge* amounts of memory without actually requiring it — but, in the opinion of the application authors, it seems good to have it *just in case*. If the memory will, indeed, never be used, no physical page frames will ever be allocated, and no problem arises.

Such a programming style is clearly bad practice, but unfortunately this is often no criterion for the value of software. Writing clean code is usually not rewarding in the scientific community outside computer science. There is only immediate interest that a program works for a given configuration, while efforts to make programs future-proof or portable do not seem to provide immediate benefits and are therefore often not valued at all.

Once the kernel has granted the desired memory, the following steps are taken:

1. Allocation and initialization of a new `vm_area_struct` instance that is inserted in the list/tree data structures of the process.

2. Creation of the mapping with the file-specific function `file->f_op->mmap`. Most filesystems use `generic_file_mmap` for this purpose; all it does is set the `vm_ops` element of the mapping to `generic_file_vm_ops`.

   ```
   vma->vm_ops = &generic_file_vm_ops;
   ```

   The definition of `generic_file_vm_ops` is given in Section 4.5.3. Its key element is `filemap_fault`, which is invoked when an application accesses the mapped area but the corresponding data are not yet in RAM memory. `filemap_fault` enlists the help of low-level routines of the underlying filesystem to fetch the desired data and — transparently to the application — read them into RAM memory. In other words, the mapped data are not read in immediately when the mapping is created but only when they are actually needed.

   Chapter 8 takes a closer look at the implementation of `filemap_fault`.

If `VM_LOCKED` is set — either explicitly with system call flags or implicitly by means of the `mlockall` mechanism — the kernel invokes `make_pages_present` to successively scan the pages of the mapping and to trigger a page fault for each so that their data are read in. Of course, this means that the performance gain of deferred reading is lost, but the kernel makes sure that the pages are *always* in memory after a mapping has been created — after all, the `VM_LOCKED` flag prevents them from being swapped out, so they must be first in.

The start address of the new mapping is then returned to conclude the system call.

`do_mmap_pgoff` performs several checks (not described in detail here) at various points in addition to the actions described above. If one of the checks fails, the operation is terminated, and the system call returns to userspace with an error code.

❑ **Accounting** — The kernel keeps statistics on the number of pages a process uses for mappings. As it is possible to limit process resources, the kernel must always ensure that the permitted value is not exceeded. There is also a maximum number of mappings per process.

❑ **Extensive security and plausibility checks** must be carried out to prevent the applications from setting invalid parameters or parameters that could threaten system stability. For example, no mappings may be created that are larger than the virtual address space or extend beyond the boundaries of virtual address space.

4.7.2 Removing Mappings

The `munmap` system call, which requires two parameters — the start address and length of the area to be unmapped, must be used to remove an existing mapping from virtual address space. `sys_munmap` is the entry point for the system call; it delegates its work in the usual way to the `do_munmap` function defined in `mm_mmap.c`. (Further implementation information is shown in the associated code flow diagram in Figure 4-13.)

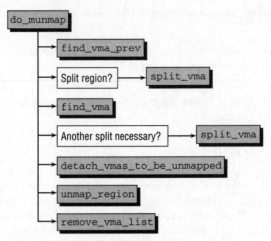

Figure 4-13: Code flow diagram for do_munmap.

The kernel must first invoke `find_vma_prev` to try to find the `vm_area_struct` instance for the region to be unmapped. This function operates in exactly the same way as `find_vma` discussed in Section 4.5.1, but it not only finds the `vm_area_struct` matching the address, but also returns a pointer to the predecessor region.

If the start address of the area to be unmapped is not precisely at the start of the region found by `find_vma_prev`, only part but not the whole of the mapping is unmapped. Before the kernel does this, it must first divide the existing mapping into several parts. The front part of the mapping that is not to be unmapped is first split off by `split_vma`. This is a helper function I won't bother discussing because all it does is perform standard operations on familiar data structures. It simply allocates a new instance of `vm_area_struct`, fills it with the data of the old region, and adjusts the boundaries. The new region is inserted into the data structures of the process.

The same procedure is repeated for the rear part of the mapping if the old region is not to be unmapped right up to its end.

The kernel then invokes `detach_vmas_to_be_unmapped` to draw up a list of all regions to be unmapped. Because an unmapping operation can involve any area of address space, it may well be that several successive regions are affected. The kernel has ensured that only complete regions are affected by splitting the areas at the start and the end.

`detach_vmas_to_be_unmapped` iterates over the linear list of `vm_area_struct` instances until the whole area is covered. The `vm_next` element of the structures is briefly "misused" to link the regions to be unmapped with each other. The function also sets the mmap cache to `NULL`, thus invalidating it.

Two final steps follow. First, `unmap_region` is invoked to remove all entries from the page tables associated with the mapping. When this is done, the kernel must also make sure that the relevant entries are removed from the translation lookaside buffer or are rendered invalid. Second, the space occupied by the `vm_area_struct` instances is freed with `remove_vma_list` to finally remove the mapping from the kernel.

4.7.3 Nonlinear Mappings

As just demonstrated, normal mappings map a continuous section from a file into a likewise continuous section of virtual memory. If various parts of a file are mapped in a different sequence into an otherwise contiguous area of virtual memory, it is generally necessary to use several mappings, which is more costly in terms of resources (particularly in `vm_area_structs`). A simpler way of achieving the same result[11] is to use nonlinear mappings as introduced during the development of 2.5. The kernel features a separate system call specifically for this purpose.

mm/fremap.c
```
long sys_remap_file_pages(unsigned long start, unsigned long size,
           unsigned long __prot, unsigned long pgoff, unsigned long flags)
```

The system call allows for rearranging pages in a mapping such that the order in memory is not identical with the order in the file. This is achieved *without* moving the memory contents around, but is instead performed by manipulating the page tables of the process.

`sys_remap_file_pages` enables an existing mapping at position `pgoff` and with a size of `size` to be moved to a new position in virtual memory. `start` identifies the mapping whose pages are to be moved, and thus must fall into the address of an already existing mapping. It also specifies the new position into which the pages identified by `pgoff` and `size` are supposed to be moved.

If a nonlinear mapping is swapped out, the kernel must ensure that the offsets are still present when the mapping is swapped back in again. The information needed to do this is stored in the page table entries of the pages swapped out and must be referenced when they are swapped back in, as we shall see below. But how is the information encoded? Two components are used:

1. The `vm_area_struct` instances of all installed nonlinear mappings are stored in a list headed by the `i_mmap_nonlinear` element of `struct address_space`. The individual `vm_area_structs` on the list can employ `shared.vm_set.list` as list element because a nonlinear VMA will not be present on the standard prio tree.

2. The page table entries for the region in question are populated with special entries. These are constructed such that they look like PTEs of pages that are not present, but contain additional information identifying them as PTEs for nonlinear mappings. When the page described by the PTE is accessed, a page fault is generated, and the correct page can be read in.

Naturally, page table entries cannot be modified at will, but must adhere to conventions imposed by the underlying architecture. To create nonlinear PTEs, help by the architecture-specific code is required, and three functions must be defined:

1. `pgoff_to_pte` takes a file offset encoded as a page number and encodes it into a format that can be stored in a page table.

2. `pte_to_pgoff` can decode a file offset encoded in a page table.

---

[11] Even though there appears to be very little need for this, there are various large databases that use operations of this kind to represent data transactions.

3. `pte_file(pte)` checks if a given page table entry is used to represent a nonlinear mapping. This especially allows for distinguishing a page table entry of a nonlinear mapping from a page table entry for a regular swapped-out page when a page fault occurs.

The pre-processor constant `PTE_FILE_MAX_BITS` denotes how many bits of a page table entry can be used to store a file offset. Since this constant will usually be smaller than the word size of the processor because some status bits in the PTE are required by the architecture and to distinguish it from swap-PTEs, the range of a file that can be remapped is, in general, smaller than the maximally possible file size.

Since the layout of non-present page table entries is not plagued by any historical oddities on IA-64, the way nonlinear PTEs are implemented is particularly clean, so I present it as an example, which is illustrated in Figure 4-14.

include/asm-ia64/pgtable.h
```
#define PTE_FILE_MAX_BITS 61
#define pte_to_pgoff(pte) ((pte_val(pte) << 1) >> 3)
#define pgoff_to_pte(off) ((pte_t) { ((off) << 2) | _PAGE_FILE })
```

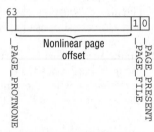

Figure 4-14: Representing nonlinear mappings in page table entries on IA-64 systems.

Swap identifiers are 64 bits long. Bit 0 must be zero because the page is not present, and bit 1 represents `_PAGE_FILE` to indicate that the entry belongs to a nonlinear mapping in contrast to a swap specifier. The last bit, that is, 63, is reserved for the `_PAGE_PROTNONE` bit.[12] Consequently, this leaves 61 bits raw capacity to represent the nonlinear page offset.

`pte_to_pgoff` first extracts the value stored in the page table entry with `pte_val` as provided by the architecture-specific code. Performing one left-shift and two right-shifts is a simple method to extract the bits at position [2, 62]. When a PTE representing a nonlinear mapping is constructed, the kernel needs to shift the offset into the bit range starting at bit 2, and must additionally ensure that `_PTE_FILE` is set to identify it as a nonlinear mapping in contrast to a regular swapped-out identifier.

The essential steps of `sys_remap_file_pages` are summarized in the code flow diagram in Figure 4-15.

---

[12] A page with this bit set was marked as completely inaccessible by the mmap system call. While such pages do not need to be backed by a physical page frame (they are not accessible, so what should be read from or written to the page?), the kernel nevertheless has to mark somehow that they must not be accessed, and the aforementioned bit provides this capability.

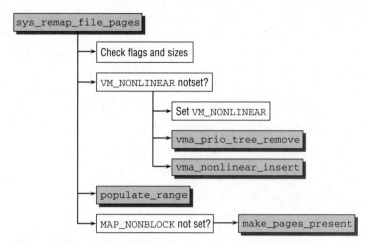

Figure 4-15: Code flow diagram for `sys_remap_file_pages`.

After all flags have been checked and the kernel has ensured that the range to be remapped is valid, the vm_area_struct instance of the target region is selected by find_vma. If the destination has not been nonlinearly remapped before, the flag VM_NONLINEAR is not set in vm_area_struct->vm_flags. In this case, the linear mapping has to be removed from the prio tree with vma_prio_tree_remove, and it is inserted into the list of nonlinear mappings using vma_nonlinear_insert.

The crucial step is to install the modified page table entries. The auxiliary routine populate_range is responsible for this:

mm/fremap.c
```
static int populate_range(struct mm_struct *mm, struct vm_area_struct *vma,
unsigned long addr, unsigned long size, pgoff_t pgoff)
{
        int err;
...
```

The mapping is described by vma. The region starting currently at page offset pgoff with length length is to be remapped to address addr. Since this can involve multiple pages, the kernel needs to iterate over all of them and install new page table entries with install_file_pte:

mm/fremap.c
```
        do {
                err = install_file_pte(mm, vma, addr, pgoff, vma->vm_page_prot);
                if (err)
                        return err;

                size -= PAGE_SIZE;
                addr += PAGE_SIZE;
                pgoff++;
        } while (size);

        return 0;
}
```

`install_file_pte` first removes any existing page table entry with `zap_file_pte` and then constructs a new entry using the helper function `pgoff_to_pte`, which encodes a given file offset into a format suitable for a PTE:

mm/fremap.c
```
static int install_file_pte(struct mm_struct *mm, struct vm_area_struct *vma,
                unsigned long addr, unsigned long pgoff, pgprot_t prot)
{
        pte_t *pte;
...
        if (!pte_none(*pte))
                zap_pte(mm, vma, addr, pte);

        set_pte_at(mm, addr, pte, pgoff_to_pte(pgoff));
...
}
```

The final step in `sys_remap_file_pages` is to read in the pages of the mapping if this is desired (it can be prevented by setting the flag `MAP_NONBLOCK`). This is done using `make_present_pages`, which acts as if a page fault would have occurred for each single page in the mapping, and triggers reading the data from the underlying block device.

4.8 Reverse Mapping

The data structures already discussed enable the kernel to establish a link between a virtual and a physical address (via the page tables) and between a memory region of a process and its virtual page addresses. What is still missing is a link between a physical page and the processes to which the page belongs (or, to be more accurate, to the page table entries of all processes that use the page). This is the very link that is needed when swapping pages out (see Chapter 18) in order to update all processes that use the page because the fact that the page has been swapped out must be noted in their page tables.

In this context, it is necessary to distinguish between two similar terms:

1. When a page is mapped, it is associated with a process but need not necessarily be in active use.

2. The number of *references* to a page indicates how actively the page is used. In order to determine this number, the kernel must first establish a link between a page and all its users and must then resort to a few tricks to find out how actively the page is used.

The first task is therefore to create a link between a page and all points at which it is mapped. To do this, the kernel uses a few additional data structures and functions and adopts a *reverse mapping* approach.[13]

All mapping actions described above are concerned only with virtual pages, and there was therefore no need (and no way) to create reverse mappings. The discussion of how the kernel handles page faults and

---

[13]Reverse mappings were first introduced during the development of kernel 2.5. They were available as separate patches for 2.4 but had never been included in the standard sources. Swapping-out of shared pages is much more complicated and inefficient without this mechanism because the shared page had to be kept in a special cache until the kernel had chosen separately (and independently) to swap the page out for all processes involved. The implementation of the reverse mapping algorithm was also heavily revised during the development of kernel 2.6.

assigns physical pages to hold mapping data in Section 4.10 notes that there is then a need for reverse mapping.

4.8.1 Data Structures

The kernel uses lean data structures to minimize management overhead for reverse mappings. The `page` structure (discussed in Section 3.2.2) contains a single element to implement reverse mapping.

```
mm.h
struct page {
....
        atomic_t _mapcount;              /* Count of ptes mapped in mms,
                                          * to show when page is mapped
                                          * & limit reverse map searches.
                                          */

...
};
```

`_mapcount` *indicates at how many points the page is shared. The original value of the counter is −1. It is assigned the value 0 when the page is inserted in the reverse mapping data structures and is incremented by 1 for each additional user. This enables the kernel to check quickly how many users are using the page in addition to the owner.*

Obviously, this isn't much help because the purpose of reverse mapping is to find all points at which the physical page is used by reference to a given `page` instance. Consequently, two other data structures have a role to play:

1. The priority search tree in which each region belonging to a non-anonymous mapping is embedded

2. The linked lists of anonymous areas that lead back to the same pages in memory

The elements needed to generate both data structures are integrated in `vm_area_struct` — these are the `shared` union as well as `anon_vma_node` and `anon_vma`. To refresh the reader's memory, I reproduce the corresponding section from `vm_area_struct` below.

```
mm.h
struct vm_area_struct {
...
        /*
         * For areas with an address space and backing store,
         * linkage into the address_space->i_mmap prio tree, or
         * linkage to the list of like vmas hanging off its node, or
         * linkage of vma in the address_space->i_mmap_nonlinear list.
         */
        union {
                struct {
                        struct list_head list;
                        void *parent;   /* aligns with prio_tree_node parent */
                        struct vm_area_struct *head;
                } vm_set;

                struct raw_prio_tree_node prio_tree_node;
```

```
            } shared;

            /*
             * A file's MAP_PRIVATE vma can be in both i_mmap tree and anon_vma
             * list, after a COW of one of the file pages.  A MAP_SHARED vma
             * can only be in the i_mmap tree.  An anonymous MAP_PRIVATE, stack
             * or brk vma (with NULL file) can only be in an anon_vma list.
             */
            struct list_head anon_vma_node; /* Serialized by anon_vma->lock */
            struct anon_vma *anon_vma;       /* Serialized by page_table_lock */
    ...
    }
```

The trick employed by the kernel when implementing reverse mapping is not to store a direct link between a page and the associated users but only the association between a page and the *region* in which the page is located. All other regions in which the page is included (and therefore all users) can be found by means of the data structures just mentioned. This method is also known as *object-based reverse mapping* because no direct link between page and user is stored; instead, a further object (the regions in which the page is located) is interposed between the two.

4.8.2 Creating a Reverse Mapping

When a reverse mapping is created, it is necessary to distinguish between two alternatives — anonymous pages and pages with file-based mappings. This is understandable because the data structures used to manage both alternatives also differ.

> The information below only covers working with **page** instances to be inserted into the reverse mapping scheme. Other parts of the kernel are responsible for adding the relevant **vm_area_structs** to the data structures discussed above (priority tree and anon list); for example, by invoking **vma_prio_tree_insert** that is used (directly or indirectly) at several places in the kernel.

Anonymous Pages

There are two ways of inserting an anonymous page into the reverse mapping data structures. page_add_new_anon_rmap must be invoked for new anonymous pages. page_add_anon_rmap is the right option for pages that are already reference-counted. The only difference between these alternatives is that the former sets the mapping counter page->_mapcount to 0 (reminder: the initial value of _mapcount is 0 for newly initialized pages), and the latter increments the counter by 1. Both functions then merge into __page_set_anon_rmap.

```
mm/rmap.c
void __page_set_anon_rmap(struct page *page,
        struct vm_area_struct *vma, unsigned long address)
{
        struct anon_vma *anon_vma = vma->anon_vma;

        anon_vma = (void *) anon_vma + PAGE_MAPPING_ANON;
        page->mapping = (struct address_space *) anon_vma;

        page->index = linear_page_index(vma, address);
}
```

The address of the `anon_vma` list head is stored in the `mapping` element of the `page` instance after `PAGE_MAPPING_ANON` has been added to the pointer. This enables the kernel to distinguish between anonymous pages and pages with a regular mapping by checking whether the least significant bit is 0 (if `PAGE_MAPPING_ANON` is not set) or 1 (if `PAGE_MAPPING_ANON` is set) as discussed above. Recall that this trick is valid because the lowest-order bit of a page pointer is guaranteed to be zero because of alignment requirements.

Pages with a File-Based Mapping

Work is even simpler for pages of this type, as the following code excerpt shows:

mm/rmap.c
```
void page_add_file_rmap(struct page *page)
{
        if (atomic_inc_and_test(&page->_mapcount))
                __inc_zone_page_state(page, NR_FILE_MAPPED);
}
```

Basically, all that needs to be done is to increment the `_mapcount` variable atomically and update the per-zone statistics.

4.8.3 Using Reverse Mapping

The real benefits of reverse mapping do not become clear until Chapter 18, which examines the implementation of swapping. There we will see that the kernel defines the `try_to_unmap` function, which is invoked to delete a specific physical page from the page tables of *all* processes by which the page is used. It is apparent that this is only possible with the data structures just described. Nevertheless, the implementation is influenced by many details of the swap layer, and this is why I won't go into how `try_to_unmap` works at this point.

`page_referenced` is an important function that puts the data structures of the reverse mapping scheme to good use. It counts the number of processes that have *actively* used a shared page recently by accessing it — this is different from the number of regions into which the page is mapped. Whereas the second quantity is mostly static, the first changes rapidly if the page is in active use.

The function is a multiplexer that invokes `page_referenced_anon` for anonymous pages or `page_referenced_file` for pages from a file-based mapping. Both try to establish at how many places a page is used, but each adopts a different approach owing to the different underlying data structures.

Let's first look at the version for anonymous pages. We first need the `page_lock_anon_vma` helper function to find the associated list of regions by reference to a specific `page` instance (by reading the information discussed in the previous section from the data structure).

<mm/rmap.c>
```
static struct anon_vma *page_lock_anon_vma(struct page *page)
{
        struct anon_vma *anon_vma = NULL;
        unsigned long anon_mapping;

        anon_mapping = (unsigned long) page->mapping;
        if (!(anon_mapping & PAGE_MAPPING_ANON))
                goto out;
```

```
        if (!page_mapped(page))
              goto out;

    anon_vma = (struct anon_vma *) (anon_mapping - PAGE_MAPPING_ANON);

    return anon_vma;
}
```

Once the code has ensured that the `page->mapping` pointer actually points to an `anon_vma` instance using the by-now-familiar trick (the least significant bit of the pointer must be set), `page_mapped` checks whether the page has been mapped at all (`page->_mapcount` must then be greater than or equal to 0). If so, the function returns a pointer to the `anon_vma` instance associated with the page.

`page_referenced_anon` makes use of this knowledge as follows:

mm/rmap.c
```
static int page_referenced_anon(struct page *page)
{
        unsigned int mapcount;
        struct anon_vma *anon_vma;
        struct vm_area_struct *vma;
        int referenced = 0;

        anon_vma = page_lock_anon_vma(page);
        if (!anon_vma)
                return referenced;

        mapcount = page_mapcount(page);
        list_for_each_entry(vma, &anon_vma->head, anon_vma_node) {
                referenced += page_referenced_one(page, vma, &mapcount);
                if (!mapcount)
                        break;
        }

        return referenced;
}
```

Once the matching `anon_vma` instance has been found, the kernel iterates over all regions in the list and invokes `page_referenced_one` for each one to return the number of places at which the page is used (some corrections are required when the system is swapping pages in and out, but these are not of interest here and are discussed in Section 18.7). The results are added together for all pages before the total is returned.[14]

`page_referenced_one` performs its task in two steps:

1. It finds the page table entry that points to the page. This is possible because not only the `page` instance but also the associated `vm_area_struct` is passed to `page_referenced_one`. The position in virtual address space at which the page is mapped can be determined from the latter variable.

---

[14]The kernel terminates its work when the number of references reaches the number of mappings held in `mapcount` as it makes no sense to continue searching. `page_referenced_one` automatically decrements the `mapcount` counter passed for each referenced page.

2. It checks whether the _PAGE_ACCESSED bit is set in the page table entry and then deletes the bit. This flag is set on each access to the page by the hardware (with the additional support of the kernel if required by the particular architecture). The reference counter is incremented by 1 if the bit is set; otherwise, it is left unchanged. As a result, frequently used pages have a high number of references, and the opposite is true for rarely used pages. The kernel is therefore able to decide immediately whether a page is important based on the number of references.

The approach adopted for checking the number of references for pages with file-based mapping is similar.

mm/rmap.c
```
static int page_referenced_file(struct page *page)
{
...
        mapcount = page_mapcount(page);

        vma_prio_tree_foreach(vma, &iter, &mapping->i_mmap, pgoff, pgoff) {
                if ((vma->vm_flags & (VM_LOCKED|VM_MAYSHARE))
                                == (VM_LOCKED|VM_MAYSHARE)) {
                        referenced++;
                        break;
                }
                referenced += page_referenced_one(page, vma, &mapcount);
                if (!mapcount)
                        break;
        }

...

        return referenced;
}
```

The kernel invokes vm_prio_tree_foreach to iterate over all elements of the priority tree that store a region where the relevant page is included. As above, page_referenced_one is invoked for each page in order to collect all references. If a page is locked into memory (with VM_LOCKED) and may be shared by processes (VM_MAYSHARE), the reference value is increased further because pages of this kind should not be swapped out and are therefore given a bonus.

4.9 Managing the Heap

Managing the *heap* — the memory area of a process used to dynamically allocate variables and data — is not directly visible to application programmers because it relies on various helper functions of the standard library (the most important of which is malloc) to reserve memory areas of any size. The classic interface between malloc and the kernel is the brk system call that expands/shrinks the heap. Recent malloc implementations (such as those of the GNU standard library) now use a combined approach that operates with brk and anonymous mappings. This approach delivers better performance and certain advantages when returning larger allocations.

The heap is a contiguous memory area that grows from bottom to top when expanded. The `mm_struct` structure already mentioned includes the start and the current end address (`start_brk` and `brk`) of the heap in virtual address space.

```
<mm_types.h>
struct mm_struct {
...
        unsigned long start_brk, brk, start_stack;
...
};
```

The `brk` system call expects just a single parameter to specify the new end address of the heap in virtual address space (it can, of course, be smaller than the previous value if the heap is to be shrunk).

As usual, the entry point for the implementation of the `brk` system call is the `sys_brk` function, whose code flow diagram is shown in Figure 4-16.

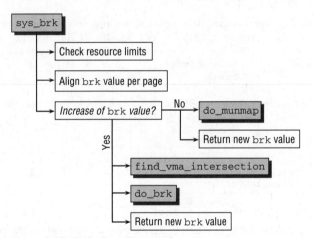

Figure 4-16: Code flow diagram for **sys_brk**.

The `brk` mechanism is not another independent kernel concept but is implemented on the basis of anonymous mappings to reduce internal overhead. Many of the functions to manage memory mappings discussed in the preceding sections can therefore be reused to implement `sys_brk`.

After it has been checked that the new desired address for `brk` is actually within the heap limits, the first important action of `sys_brk` is to align the request to page size.

```
mm/mmap.c
asmlinkage unsigned long sys_brk(unsigned long brk)
{
        unsigned long rlim, retval;
        unsigned long newbrk, oldbrk;
        struct mm_struct *mm = current->mm;
```

```
       ...
              newbrk = PAGE_ALIGN(brk);
              oldbrk = PAGE_ALIGN(mm->brk);
       ...
```

This code ensures that the new (and, as a precaution, the old) value of brk is a multiple of the system page size. In other words, a page is the smallest memory area that can be reserved with brk.[15]

do_munmap, with which we are familiar from Section 4.7.2, is invoked when it is necessary to shrink the heap.

<mm/mmap.c>
```
              /* Always allow shrinking brk. */
              if (brk <= mm->brk) {
                     if (!do_munmap(mm, newbrk, oldbrk-newbrk))
                            goto set_brk;
                     goto out;
              }
       ...
```

If the heap is to be enlarged, the kernel must first check whether the new size is outside the limit set as the maximum heap size for the process. find_vma_intersection then checks whether the enlarged heap would overlap with an existing mapping of the process; if so, it returns without doing anything.

<mm/mmap.c>
```
              /* Check against existing mmap mappings. */
              if (find_vma_intersection(mm, oldbrk, newbrk+PAGE_SIZE))
                     goto out;
       ...
```

Otherwise, the actual work of enlarging the heap is delegated to do_brk. The new value of mm->brk is always returned regardless of whether it is larger, smaller, or unchanged as compared to the old value.

<mm/mmap.c>
```
              /* Ok, looks good - let it rip. */
              if (do_brk(oldbrk, newbrk-oldbrk) != oldbrk)
                     goto out;
set_brk:
              mm->brk = brk;
out:
              retval = mm->brk;
              return retval;
       }
```

We need not discuss do_brk separately as essentially it is a simplified version of do_mmap_pgoff and reveals no new aspects. Like the latter, it creates an anonymous mapping in user address space but omits some safety checks and the handling of special situations to improve code performance.

---

[15]It is therefore essential to interpose a further allocator function in userspace to split the page into smaller areas; this is the task of the C standard library.

4.10 Handling of Page Faults

The association between virtual and physical memory is not established until the data of an area are actually needed. If a process accesses a part of virtual address space not yet associated with a page in memory, the processor automatically raises a *page fault* that must be handled by the kernel. This is one of the most important and complex aspects of memory management simply because a myriad of details must be taken into account. For example, the kernel must ascertain the following:

❑   Was the page fault caused by access to a valid address from the user address space, or did the application try to access the protected area of the kernel?

❑   Does a mapping exist for the desired address?

❑   Which mechanism must be used to obtain the data for the area?

Figure 4-17 shows an initial overview of the potential paths the kernel may follow when handling page faults.

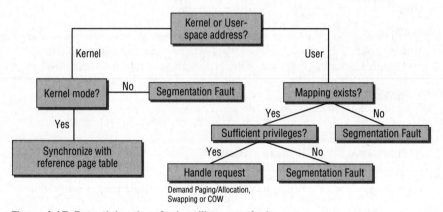

Figure 4-17: Potential options for handling page faults.

As demonstrated below, the individual actions are much more complicated because the kernel must not only guard against malicious access from userspace but must also take note of many minor details; on top of this, it must not allow the page handling operations to degrade system performance unnecessarily.

The implementation of page fault handling varies from processor to processor. Because the CPUs employ different memory management concepts, the details of page fault generation also differ. Consequently, the handler routines in the kernel are located in the architecture-specific source code segments.

We confine ourselves below to a detailed description of the approach adopted on the IA-32 architecture. Implementation on most other CPUs is at least similar.

An assembler routine in `arch/x86/kernel/entry_32.S` serves as the entry point for page faults but immediately invokes the C routine `do_page_fault` from `arch/x86/mm/fault_32.c`. (A routine of the same name is present in the architecture-specific sources of most CPUs.[16,17]) Figure 4-18 shows the code flow diagram of this extensive routine.

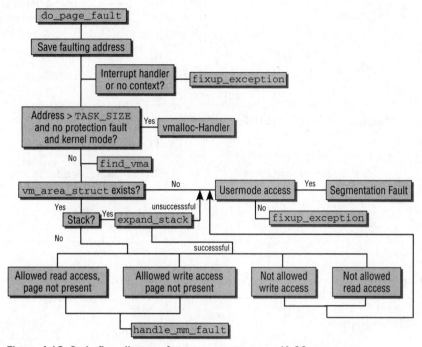

Figure 4-18: Code flow diagram for `do_page_fault` on IA-32 processors.

This situation is complex, so it is necessary to examine the implementation of do_page_fault very closely.

Two parameters are passed to the routine — the register set active at the time of the fault, and an error code (long error_code) that supplies information on the cause of the fault. Currently, only the first three bits (0, 1, and 2) of error_code are used; their meanings are given in Table 4-1.

arch/x86/mm/fault_32.c
```
fastcall void __kprobes do_page_fault(struct pt_regs *regs,
                                      unsigned long error_code)
{
        struct task_struct *tsk;
        struct mm_struct *mm;
```

---

[16]As usual, Sparc processors are the odd man out. There the name of the function is do_sparc_fault (Sparc32), do_sun4c_fault (Sparc32 sun4c), or do_sparc64_fault (UltraSparc). ia64_do_page_fault is used on IA-64 systems.
[17]Note that the code for IA-32 and AMD64 will be unified in kernel 2.6.25, which was still under development when this book was written. The remarks given here also apply for the AMD64 architecture.

```
        struct vm_area_struct * vma;
        unsigned long address;
        unsigned long page;
        int write, si_code;
        int fault;
...

        /* get the address */
        address = read_cr2();
...
```

Table 4-1: Meaning of Page Fault Error Codes on IA-32

Bit	Set (1)	Not set (0)
0	No page present in RAM	Protection fault (insufficient access permission)
1	Read access	Write access
2	Privileged kernel mode	User mode

Once a large number of variables have been declared for subsequent use, the kernel stores the address of the location that triggered the fault in address.[18]

arch/i386/mm/fault.c
```
        tsk = current;

        si_code = SEGV_MAPERR;

        /*
         * We fault-in kernel-space virtual memory on-demand. The
         * 'reference' page table is init_mm.pgd.
         *
         * NOTE! WE MUST NOT take any locks for this case. We may
         * be in an interrupt or a critical region, and should
         * only copy the information from the master page table,
         * nothing more.
         *
         * This verifies that the fault happens in kernel space
         * (error_code & 4) == 0, and that the fault was not a
         * protection error (error_code & 9) == 0.
         */
        if (unlikely(address >= TASK_SIZE)) {
                if (!(error_code & 0x0000000d) && vmalloc_fault(address) >= 0)
                        return;
                /*
                 * Don't take the mm semaphore here. If we fixup a prefetch
                 * fault we could otherwise deadlock.
```

---

[18]On IA-32 processors, the address is held in register CR2, whose contents are copied to address by read_cr2. The processor-specific details are of no interest.

```
        */
      goto bad_area_nosemaphore;
   }
...
```

A `vmalloc` fault is indicated if the address is outside user address space. The page tables of the process must therefore be synchronized with the information in the kernel's master page table. Naturally, this is only permitted if access took place in kernel mode and the fault was not triggered by a protection error; in other words, neither bit 2 nor bits 3 and 0 of the error code may be set.[19]

The kernel uses the auxiliary function `vmalloc_fault` to synchronize the page tables. I won't show the code in detail because all it does is copy the relevant entry from the page table of `init` — this is the kernel master table on IA-32 systems — into the current page table. If no matching entry is found there, the kernel invokes `fixup_exception` in a final attempt to recover the fault; I discuss this shortly.

The kernel jumps to the `bad_area_nosemaphore` label if the fault was triggered during an interrupt (see Chapter 14) or in a kernel thread (see Chapter 14) that does not have its own context and therefore no separate instance of `mm_struct`.

arch/i386/mm/fault.c
```
      mm = tsk->mm;

      /*
       * If we're in an interrupt, have no user context or are running in an
       * atomic region then we must not take the fault..
       */
      if (in_atomic() || !mm)
            goto bad_area_nosemaphore;
...
bad_area_nosemaphore:
      /* User mode accesses just cause a SIGSEGV */
      if (error_code & 4) {
...
            force_sig_info_fault(SIGSEGV, si_code, address, tsk);
            return;
      }


no_context:
      /* Are we prepared to handle this kernel fault? */
      if (fixup_exception(regs))
            return;
```

A segmentation fault is output if the fault originates from userspace (indicated by the fact that bit 4 is set in `error_code`). If, however, the fault originates from kernel space, `fixup_exception` is invoked. I describe this function below.

If the fault does not occur in an interrupt or without a context, the kernel checks whether the address space of the process contains a region in which the fault address lies. It invokes the `find_vma` function, which we know from Section 4.5.1 to do this.

---

[19]This is checked by `!(error_code & 0x0000000d)`. Because $2^0 + 2^2 + 2^3 = 13 = 0\mathrm{xd}$, neither bit 2 *nor* bits 3 and 0 may be set.

arch/i386/mm/fault.c

```
        vma = find_vma(mm, address);
        if (!vma)
                goto bad_area;
        if (vma->vm_start <= address)
                goto good_area;
        if (!(vma->vm_flags & VM_GROWSDOWN))
                goto bad_area;
...
        if (expand_stack(vma, address))
                goto bad_area;
```

good_area and bad_area are labels to which the kernel jumps once it has discovered whether the address is valid or invalid.

The search can yield various results:

❑   No region is found whose end address is after address, in which case access is invalid.

❑   The fault address is within the region found, in which case access is valid and the page fault is corrected by the kernel.

❑   A region is found whose end address is after the fault address but the fault address is *not* within the region. There may be two reasons for this:

   1. The VM_GROWSDOWN flag of the region is set; this means that the region is a stack that grows from top to bottom. expand_stack is then invoked to enlarge the stack accordingly. If it succeeds, 0 is returned as the result, and the kernel resumes execution at good_area. Otherwise, access is interpreted as invalid.

   2. The region found is not a stack, so access is invalid.

good_area follows on immediately after the above code.

arch/i386/mm/fault.c

```
...
good_area:
        si_code = SEGV_ACCERR;
        write = 0;
        switch (error_code & 3) {
                default:        /* 3: write, present */
                    /* fall through */
                case 2:         /* write, not present */
                    if (!(vma->vm_flags & VM_WRITE))
                            goto bad_area;
                    write++;
                    break;
                case 1:         /* read, present */
                    goto bad_area;
                case 0:         /* read, not present */
                    if (!(vma->vm_flags & (VM_READ | VM_EXEC)))
                            goto bad_area;
        }
...
```

The presence of a mapping for the fault address does not necessarily mean that access is actually permitted. The kernel must check the access permissions by examining bits 0 and 1 (because $2^0 + 2^1 = 3$). The following situations may apply:

❑ VM_WRITE must be set in the event of a write access (bit 1 set, cases 3 and 2). Otherwise, access is invalid, and execution resumes at bad_area.

❑ In the event of a read access to an existing page (Case 1), the fault must be a permission fault detected by the hardware. Execution then resumes at bad_area.

❑ If a read access is made to a page that doesn't exist, the kernel must check whether VM_READ or VM_EXEC is set, in which case access is valid. Otherwise, read access is denied, and the kernel jumps to bad_area.

If the kernel does not explicitly jump to bad_area, it works its way down through the case statement and arrives at the handle_mm_fault call that immediately follows; this function is responsible for correcting the page fault (i.e., reading the required data).

arch/i386/mm/fault.c

```
...
  survive:
        /*
         * If for any reason at all we couldn't handle the fault,
         * make sure we exit gracefully rather than endlessly redo
         * the fault.
         */
        fault = handle_mm_fault(mm, vma, address, write);
        if (unlikely(fault & VM_FAULT_ERROR)) {
                if (fault & VM_FAULT_OOM)
                        goto out_of_memory;
                else if (fault & VM_FAULT_SIGBUS)
                        goto do_sigbus;
                BUG();
        }
        if (fault & VM_FAULT_MAJOR)
                tsk->maj_flt++;
        else
                tsk->min_flt++;

        return;
  ...
  }
```

handle_mm_fault is an architecture-*independent* routine for selecting the appropriate fault correction method (demand paging, swap-in, etc.) and for applying the method selected (we take a close look at the implementation and the various options of handle_mm_fault in Section 4.11).

If the page is created successfully, the routine returns either VM_FAULT_MINOR (the data were already in memory) or VM_FAULT_MAJOR (the data had to be read from a block device). The kernel then updates the process statistics.

However, faults may also occur when a page is created. If there is insufficient physical memory to load the page, the kernel forces termination of the process to at least keep the system running. If a permitted access to data fails for whatever reason — for instance, if a mapping is accessed but has been shrunk by another process in the meantime and is no longer present at the given address — the SIGBUS signal is sent to the process.

4.11 Correction of Userspace Page Faults

Once the architecture-specific analysis of the page fault has been concluded and it has been established that the fault was triggered at a permitted address, the kernel must decide on the appropriate method to read the required data into RAM memory. This task is delegated to handle_mm_fault, which is no longer dependent on the underlying architecture but is implemented system-independently within the memory management framework. The function ensures that page table entries for all directory levels that lead to the faulty PTE are present. The function handle_pte_fault analyzes the reason for the page fault. entry is a pointer to the relevant page table element (pte_t).

mm/memory.c
```
static inline int handle_pte_fault(struct mm_struct *mm,
                struct vm_area_struct *vma, unsigned long address,
                pte_t *pte, pmd_t *pmd, int write_access)
{
        pte_t entry;
        spinlock_t *ptl;

        if (!pte_present(entry)) {
                if (pte_none(entry)) {
                        if (vma->vm_ops) {
                                return do_linear_fault(mm, vma, address,
                                        pte, pmd, write_access, entry);
                        }
                        return do_anonymous_page(mm, vma, address,
                                                pte, pmd, write_access);
                }
                if (pte_file(entry))
                        return do_nonlinear_fault(mm, vma, address,
                                        pte, pmd, write_access, entry);
                return do_swap_page(mm, vma, address,
                                        pte, pmd, write_access, entry);
        }
...
}
```

Three cases must be distinguished if the page is not present in physical memory [!pte_present(entry)].

1. If no page table entry is present (page_none), the kernel must load the page from scratch — this is known as *demand allocation* for anonymous mappings and *demand paging* for file-based mappings. This does not apply if there is no vm_operations_struct registered in vm_ops — in this case, the kernel must return an anonymous page using do_anonymous_page.

2. If the page is marked as not present but information on the page is held in the page table, this means that the page has been swapped out and must therefore be swapped back in from one of the system swap areas (*swap-in* or *demand paging*).

3. Parts of nonlinear mappings that have been swapped out cannot be swapped in like regular pages because the nonlinear association must be restored correctly. The function `pte_file` allows for checking if the PTE belongs to a nonlinear mapping, and `do_nonlinear_fault` handles the fault.

A further potential case arises if the region grants write permission for the page but the access mechanisms of the hardware *do not* (thus triggering the fault). Notice that since the page is present in this case, the above `if` case is executed and the kernel drops right through to the following code:

mm/memory.c
```
        if (write_access) {
                if (!pte_write(entry))
                        return do_wp_page(mm, vma, address,
                                          pte, pmd, ptl, entry);
                entry = pte_mkdirty(entry);
        }
    ...
```

`do_wp_page` is responsible for creating a copy of the page and inserting it in the page tables of the process — with write access permission for the hardware. This mechanism is referred to as *copy on write* (COW, for short) and is discussed briefly in Chapter 1. When a process forks, the pages are not copied immediately but are mapped into the address space of the process as "read-only" copies so as not to spend too much time in the (wasteful) copying of information. A separate copy of the page is not created for the process until write access actually takes place.

The sections below take a closer look at the implementation of the fault handler routines invoked during page fault correction. They do not cover how pages are swapped in from a swap area by means of `do_swap_page`, as this topic is discussed separately in Chapter 18 and requires additional knowledge of the structure and organization of the swap layer.

4.11.1 Demand Allocation/Paging

Allocation of pages on demand is delegated to `do_linear_fault`, which is defined in `mm/memory.c`. After some parameter conversion, the work is delegated to `__do_fault`, and the code flow diagram of this function is shown in Figure 4-19.

First of all, the kernel has to make sure that the required data are read into the faulting page. How this is handled depends on the file that is mapped into the faulting address space, and therefore a file-specific method is invoked to obtain the data. Usually, it is stored in `vm->vm_ops->fault`. Since earlier kernel versions used a method with a different calling convention, the kernel must account for the situation in which some code has not yet been updated to stick to the new convention. Therefore, the old variant `vm->vm_ops->nopage` is invoked if no `fault` method is registered.

Most files use `filemap_fault` to read in the required data. The function not only reads in the required data, but also implements readahead functionality, which reads in pages ahead of time that will most likely be required in the future. The mechanisms needed to do this are introduced in Chapter 16, which discusses the function in greater length. At the moment, all we need to know is that the kernel reads the data from the backing store into a physical memory page using the information in the `address_space` object.

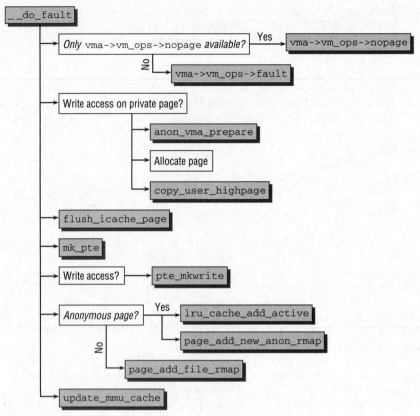

Figure 4-19: Code flow diagram for __do_fault.

Given the `vm_area_struct` region involved, how can the kernel choose which method to use to read the page?

1. The mapped `file` object is found using `vm_area_struct->vm_file`.

2. A pointer to the mapping itself can be found in `file->f_mapping`.

3. Each address space has special address space operations from which the `readpage` method can be selected. The data are transferred from the file into RAM memory using `mapping->a_ops->readpage(file, page)`.

If write access is required, the kernel has to distinguish between shared and private mappings. For private mappings, a copy of the page has to be prepared.

mm/memory.c
```
static int __do_fault(struct mm_struct *mm, struct vm_area_struct *vma,
            unsigned long address, pmd_t *pmd,
            pgoff_t pgoff, unsigned int flags, pte_t orig_pte)
{
...
```

```
            /*
             * Should we do an early C-O-W break?
             */
            if (flags & FAULT_FLAG_WRITE) {
                    if (!(vma->vm_flags & VM_SHARED)) {
                            anon = 1;
                            if (unlikely(anon_vma_prepare(vma))) {
                                    ret = VM_FAULT_OOM;
                                    goto out;
                            }
                            page = alloc_page_vma(GFP_HIGHUSER_MOVABLE,
                                                  vma, address);
    ...
                    }
                    copy_user_highpage(page, vmf.page, address, vma);
            }

    ...
```

A new page must be allocated once a new `anon_vma` instance has been created for the region with `anon_vma_prepare` (the pointer to the old region is redirected to the new region in `anon_vma_prepare`). The high memory area is preferably used for this purpose as it presents no problems for userspace pages. `copy_user_highpage` then creates a copy of the data (routines for copying data between kernel and userspace are discussed in Section 4.13).

Now that the position of the page is known, it must be added to the page table of the process and incorporated in the reverse mapping data structures. Before this is done, a check is made to ensure that the page contents are visible in userspace by updating the caches with `flush_icache_page`. (Most processors don't need to do this and define an empty operation.)

A page table entry that normally points to a read-only page is generated using the `mk_pte` function discussed in Section 3.3.2. If a page with write access is created, the kernel must explicitly set write permission with `pte_mkwrite`.

How pages are integrated into the reverse mapping depends on their type. If the page generated when handling the write access is anonymous, it is added to the active area of the LRU cache using `lru_cache_add_active` (Chapter 16 examines the caching mechanisms used in more detail) and then integrated into the reverse mapping with `page_add_new_anon_rmap`. `page_add_file_rmap` is invoked for all other pages associated with a file-based mapping. Both functions are discussed in Section 4.8. Finally, the MMU cache of the processor has to be updated if required because the page tables have been modified.

4.11.2 Anonymous Pages

`do_anonymous_page` is invoked to map pages not associated with a file as a backing store. Except that no data must be read into a page, the procedure hardly differs from the way in which file-based data are mapped. A new page is created in the highmem area, and all its contents are deleted. The page is then added to the page tables of the process, and the caches/MMU are updated.

Notice that earlier kernels distinguished between read-only and write access to anonymous mappings: In the first case, a single, global page filled with zero bytes was used to satisfy read requests to anonymous regions. During the development of kernel 2.6.24, this behavior has, however, been dropped because measurements have shown that the performance gain is negligible, while larger systems can experience several problems with shared zero mappings, which I do not want to discuss in detail here.

4.11.3 Copy on Write

Copy on write is handled in do_wp_page, whose code flow diagram is shown in Figure 4-20.

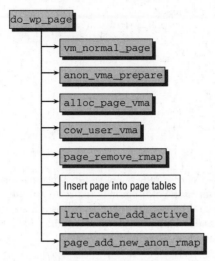

Figure 4-20: Code flow diagram for do_wp_page.

Let's examine a slightly simplified version in which I have omitted potential interference with the swap cache as well as some corner cases, since this would complicate the situation without revealing anything insightful about the mechanism itself.

The kernel first invokes vm_normal_page to find the struct page instance of the page by reference to the page table entry — essentially, this function builds on pte_pfn and pfn_to_page, which must be defined on all architectures. The former finds the page number for an associated page table entry, and the latter determines the page instance associated with the page number. This is possible because the COW mechanism is invoked only for pages that actually reside in memory (otherwise, they are first automatically loaded by one of the other page fault mechanisms).

After obtaining a reference on the page with page_cache_get, anon_vma_prepare then prepares the data structures of the reverse mapping mechanism to accept a new anonymous area. Since the fault originates from a page filled with useful data that must be copied to a new page, the kernel invokes alloc_page_vma to allocate a fresh page. cow_user_page then copies the data of the faulted page into the new page to which the process may subsequently write.

The reverse mapping to the original read-only page is then removed using page_remove_rmap. The new page is added to the page tables, at which point the CPU caches must also be updated.

The final actions involve placing the newly allocated pages on the active list of the LRU cache using lru_cache_add_active and inserting them in the reverse mapping data structures by means of page_add_anon_rmap. Thereafter, the userspace process can write to the page to its heart's content.

4.11.4   Getting Nonlinear Mappings

Page fault handling for nonlinear mappings is much shorter than when the methods described above are used:

mm/memory.c
```
static int do_nonlinear_fault(struct mm_struct *mm, struct vm_area_struct *vma,
                unsigned long address, pte_t *page_table, pmd_t *pmd,
                int write_access, pte_t orig_pte)
{
...
        pgoff = pte_to_pgoff(orig_pte);
        return __do_fault(mm, vma, address, pmd, pgoff, flags, orig_pte);
}
```

Since the faulting address is not linearly associated with the contents of the mapped file, the desired position must be obtained from the information in the PTE that was previously encoded with pgoff_to_pte. Now comes the time to put this information to use: pte_to_pgoff analyzes the page table entry and obtains the desired page-sized offset into the file.

Once the address within the file is known, reading in the required data can be pursued as for regular page faults. The kernel thus hands off the work to the previously discussed function __do_page_fault and is done.

4.12   Kernel Page Faults

When kernel address space is accessed, page faults can be triggered by various conditions as described below.

❏   A programming error in the kernel has caused an incorrect address to be accessed — this is a genuine bug. Of course, this should never happen in stable versions[20] but does occur occasionally in developer versions.

❏   The kernel accesses an invalid address passed as a system call parameter from userspace.

❏   The page fault was triggered by access to an area allocated using vmalloc.

The first two conditions are genuine errors against which the kernel must guard by performing additional checks. The vmalloc situation is a legitimate reason for a page fault that must be corrected. Modifications in the vmalloc address space are not transmitted to the page tables of a process until a corresponding page fault has occurred; the appropriate access information must be copied from the master page table. Although this is not a difficult operation, it is strongly architecture-dependent, so I won't discuss it here.

The *exception fixup* mechanism is a last resort when handling page faults not due to accessing vmalloc area. At some points, the kernel makes preparations for intercepting incorrect accesses that are made for a legitimate reason — for example, when copying address data from userspace addresses passed as system call parameters.

---

[20]In fact, errors of this kind very rarely occur because — as you might have already noted — Linux is an extremely stable system . . .

Copying is performed by various central functions, such as `copy_from_user`, which is discussed in the next section. At present, it is sufficient to know that access to the incorrect address may occur at only a few places in the kernel.

When data are copied to or from userspace, page faults may occur if access is made to an address in virtual address space that is not associated with a physical page. We are already familiar with this situation in user mode. When an application accesses a virtual address, the kernel automatically and transparently returns a physical page using the demand paging mechanism discussed above. If access takes place in kernel mode, the fault must likewise be corrected, albeit using slightly different means.

Each time a page fault occurs, the cause of the fault and the address in the code currently executing are output. This enables the kernel to compile a list of all risky chunks of code that may carry out unauthorized memory access operations. This "exception table" is created when the kernel image is linked and is located between `__start_exception_table` and `__end_exception_table` in the binary file. Each entry corresponds to an instance of `struct exception_table`, which, although architecture-dependent, is almost always structured as follows:

```
<include/asm-x86/uaccess_32.h>
struct exception_table_entry
{
        unsigned long insn, fixup;
};
```

`insn` specifies the position in virtual address space at which the kernel expects the fault; `fixup` is the code address at which execution resumes when the fault occurs.

`fixup_exception` is used to search the exception tables and is defined as follows on IA-32 systems:

```
arch/x86/mm/extable_32.c
int fixup_exception(struct pt_regs *regs)
{
        const struct exception_table_entry *fixup;

        fixup = search_exception_tables(regs->eip);
        if (fixup) {
                regs->eip = fixup->fixup;
                return 1;
        }

        return 0;
}
```

`regs->eip` points to the `EIP` register that, on IA-32 processors, contains the address of the code segment where the fault was triggered. `search_exception_tables` scans the exception table for a suitable entry.[21]

---

[21]To be more accurate, several tables are scanned — the main kernel table and the tables registered by modules loaded dynamically at kernel run time. As the mechanisms used are practically the same, it's not worth describing their minor differences.

When a fixup routine is found, the instruction pointer is set to the corresponding memory location. The kernel executes the routine found after `fixup_exception` returns with `return`.

What happens if there is no fixup routine? This indicates a genuine kernel fault that is handled by the code in `do_page_fault`, which follows the (unsuccessful) call of `search_exception_table` and results in a kernel oops. It looks like this on IA-32 processors:

arch/x86/mm/fault_32.c
```
fastcall void __kprobes do_page_fault(struct pt_regs *regs,
                                      unsigned long error_code)
{
...
no_context:
        /* Are we prepared to handle this kernel fault?  */
        if (fixup_exception(regs))
                return;
...
        /*
         * Oops. The kernel tried to access some bad page. We'll have to
         * terminate things with extreme prejudice.
         */
...
        if (address < PAGE_SIZE)
                printk(KERN_ALERT "BUG: unable to handle kernel NULL "
                                "pointer dereference");
        else
                printk(KERN_ALERT "BUG: unable to handle kernel paging"
                                " request");
        printk(" at virtual address %08lx\n",address);
        printk(KERN_ALERT "printing eip: %08lx ", regs->eip);

        page = read_cr3();
        page = ((__typeof__(page) *) __va(page))[address >> PGDIR_SHIFT];
        printk("*pde = %08lx ", page);
...
        tsk->thread.cr2 = address;
        tsk->thread.trap_no = 14;
        tsk->thread.error_code = error_code;
        die("Oops", regs, error_code);
        do_exit(SIGKILL);
...
```

If a virtual address between 0 and `PAGE_SIZE - 1` is accessed, the kernel reports an invalid `NULL` pointer de-reference. Otherwise, the user is informed that a paging request could not be satisfied in kernel memory — this is a kernel bug in both cases. Additional information is also output to help debug the fault and to supply hardware-specific data; `die` prints the contents of the current registers (among other things).

Thereafter, the current process is forced to terminate with `SIGKILL` to save whatever can be saved (in many cases, the system is rendered unusable by a fault of this kind).

4.13   Copying Data between Kernel and Userspace

The kernel often needs to copy data from userspace to kernel space; for example, when lengthy data structures are passed indirectly in system calls by means of pointers. There is a similar need to write data in the reverse direction from kernel space to userspace.

This cannot be done simply by passing and de-referencing pointers for two reasons. First, userspace programs must not access kernel addresses; and second, there is no guarantee that a virtual page belonging to a pointer from userspace is really associated with a physical page. The kernel therefore provides several standard functions to cater for these special situations when data are exchanged between kernel space and userspace. They are shown in summary form in Table 4-2.

Table 4-2: Standard Functions for Exchanging Data between Userspace and Kernel Space

Function	Meaning
`copy_from_user(to, from, n)` `__copy_from_user`	Copies a string of n bytes from `from` (userspace) to `to` (kernel space).
`get_user(type *to, type* ptr) __get_user`	Reads a simple variable (`char`, `long`, ...) from `ptr` to `to`; depending on pointer type, the kernel decides automatically to transfer 1, 2, 4, or 8 bytes.
`strncopy_from_user(to, from, n)` `__strncopy_from_user`	Copies a null-terminated string with a maximum of n characters from `from` (userspace) to `to` (kernel space).
`put_user(type *from, type *to)` `__put_user`	Copies a simple value from `from` (kernel space) to `to` (userspace); the relevant value is determined automatically from the pointer type passed.
`copy_to_user(to, from, n)` `__copy_to_user`	Copies n bytes from `from` (kernel space) to `to` (userspace).

Table 4-3 lists additional helper functions for working with strings from userspace. These functions are subject to the same restrictions as the functions for copying data.

> **get_user** and **put_user** function correctly only when applied to pointers to "simple" data types such as **char, int,** and so on. They do not function with compound data types or arrays because of the pointer arithmetic required (and owing to the necessary implementation optimizations). Before **structs** can be exchanged between userspace and kernel space, it is necessary to copy the data and then convert it to the correct type by means of typecasts.

Table 4-3: Standard Functions for Working with Strings in Userspace Data

Function	Meaning
clear_user(to, n) __clear_user	Fills the next n bytes after to with zeros.
strlen_user(s) __strlen_user	Gets the size of a null-terminated string in userspace (including the terminating character).
strnlen_user(s, n) __strnlen_user	Gets the size of a null-terminated string but restricts the search to a maximum of n characters.

As the tables show, there are two versions of most of the functions. In the versions *without* preceding underscores, access_user is also invoked to perform checks on the userspace address; the checks carried out differ from architecture to architecture. For example, one check ensures that a pointer really points to a position in the user segment; another invokes handle_mm_fault if pages are not found in memory to make sure that data are read in for processing. All functions also apply the fixup mechanism described above to detect and correct page faults.

The functions are implemented mainly in assembler language. They are extremely performance-critical because they are invoked so frequently. The exception code must also be integrated using complicated GNU C constructions to embed assembler and linker directives in the code. It is not my intention to discuss the implementation of the individual functions in detail.

A checker tool was added to the compilation process during the development of kernel 2.5. It analyzes the sources to check whether userspace pointers can be de-referenced directly without the need for the above functions. The pointers originating from userspace must be labeled with the keyword __user so that the tool knows which pointers to check. One particular example is the chroot system call, which expects a filename as argument. Many, many more places in the kernel contain similarly marked arguments from userspace.

```
<fs/open.c>
asmlinkage long sys_chroot(const char __user * filename) {
...
}
```

Address space randomization has been augmented further during the development of kernel 2.6.25. It is now possible to randomize the address of the heap, traditionally called *brk address*. The randomization is, however, only performed if the new configuration option COMPAT_BRK is not set because some ancient propgrams are not compatible with a randomized heap address. On the technical level, brk randomization works as all other randomization techniques introduced in this chapter.

4.14 Summary

You have seen that handling the virtual address space of userland processes is a very important part of the Linux kernel. I have introduced you to the general structure of address spaces and how they are managed by the kernel, and you have learned how they are partitioned into regions. These allow for describing the contents of the virtual memory space of userland processes and form the backbone for linear and nonlinear memory mappings. Besides, they are connected with paging, which helps to manage the connection between physical and virtual memory.

Since the virtual address space of each userland process is different but the virtual address space portion of the kernel always remains the same, some effort is required to exchange data between both, and I have introduced you to the mechanisms required for this purpose.

5

Locking and Interprocess Communication

As a multitasking system, Linux is able to run several processes at the same time. Normally, the individual processes must be kept as separate as possible so that they do not interfere with each other. This is essential to protect data and to ensure system stability. However, there are situations in which applications must communicate with each other; for example,

❑ when data generated by one process are transferred to another.

❑ when data are shared.

❑ when processes are forced to wait for each other.

❑ when resource usage needs to be coordinated.

These situations are handled using several classic techniques that were introduced in System V and have since proven their worth, so much so that they are now part and parcel of Linux. Because not only userspace applications but also the kernel itself are faced with such situations — particularly on multiprocessor systems — various kernel-internal mechanisms are in place to handle them.

If several processes share a resource, they can easily interfere with each other — and this must be prevented. The kernel therefore provides mechanisms not only for sharing data but also for coordinating access to data. Again, the kernel employs mechanisms adopted from System V.

Resources need to be protected not only in userspace applications but especially in the kernel itself. On SMP systems, the individual CPUs may be in kernel mode at the same time and, theoretically, may want to manipulate all existing data structures. To prevent the CPUs from getting into each other's way, it is necessary to protect some kernel areas by means of *locks*; these ensure that access is restricted to one CPU at a time.

5.1 Control Mechanisms

Before describing the various interprocess communication (*IPC*) and data synchronization options of the kernel, let's briefly discuss the ways in which communicating processes can interfere with each other — and how this can be prevented. Our discussion is restricted to basic and central aspects. For detailed explanations and numerous examples of classic problems, see the general textbooks on operating systems that are available on the market.

5.1.1 Race Conditions

Let us consider a system that reads data from an external device via two interfaces. Independent data packets arrive via both interfaces at irregular intervals and are saved in separate files. To log the order of arrival of the data packets, a number is added at the end of each filename to indicate the "serial number" of the packet. A typical sequence of filenames would be `act1.fil`, `act2.fil`, `act3.fil`, and so on. A separate variable is used to simplify the work of both processes. This variable is held in a memory page shared by both processes and specifies the next unused serial number (for the sake of simplicity, I refer to this variable as `counter` below).

When a packet arrives, the process must perform a few actions to save the data correctly:

1. It reads the data from the interface.
2. It opens a file with the serial number `count`.
3. It increments the serial number by 1.
4. It writes the data to the file and closes it.

Why should errors occur with this system? If each process strictly observes the above procedure and increments the status variable at the appropriate places, the procedure should obviously function correctly not just with two but with any number of processes.

As a matter of fact, it *will* function correctly in most cases — and this is where the real difficulty lies with distributed programming — but it won't in certain circumstances. Let us set a trap by calling the processes that read data from the interfaces *process 1* and *process 2*:

Our scenario begins with a number of files to which a serial number has been added, say, 12 files in all. The value of `counter` is therefore 13. Obviously a bad omen . . .

Process 1 receives data from the interface as a new block has just arrived. Dutifully it opens a file with the serial number 13 just at the moment when the scheduler is activated and decides that the process has had enough CPU time and must be replaced with another process — in this case, process 2. Note that at this time, process 1 has read but not yet incremented the value of `counter`.

Once process 2 has started to run, it too receives data from its interface and begins to perform the necessary actions to save these data. It reads the value of `counter`, increments it to 14, opens a file with serial number 13, writes the data to the file, and terminates.

Soon it's the turn of process 1 again. It resumes where it left off and increments the value of `counter` by 1, from 14 to 15. Then it writes its data to the previously opened file with serial number 13 — and, in doing so, overwrites the existing data of process 2.

This is a double mishap — a data record is lost, and serial number 14 is not used.

The program sequence could be modified to prevent this error by changing the individual steps after data have been received. For example, processes could increment the value of `counter` immediately after reading its value and before opening a file. However, closer examination of suggestions of this kind quickly lead to the conclusion that it is always possible to devise situations that result in a fatal error. If we look at our suggestion, it soon becomes clear that an inconsistency is generated if the scheduler is invoked between reading `counter` and incrementing its value.

Situations in which several processes interfere with each other when accessing resources are generally referred to as *race conditions*. Such conditions are a central problem in the programming of distributed applications because they cannot usually be detected by systematic trial and error. Instead, a thorough study of source code (coupled with intimate knowledge of the various paths that code can take) and a generous supply of intuition are needed to find and eliminate them.

Situations leading to race conditions are few and far between, thus begging the question as to whether it's worth making the — sometimes very considerable — effort to protect code against their occurrence.

In some environments (electronic aircraft control, monitoring of vital machinery, or dangerous equipment), race conditions may prove to be fatal in the literal sense of the word. But even in routine software projects, protection against potential race conditions is an important contribution to program quality and user satisfaction. As part of improved multiprocessor support in the Linux kernel, much effort has been invested in pinpointing areas where dangers lurk and in providing suitable protection. Unexpected system crashes and mysterious errors owing to lack of protection are simply unacceptable.

5.1.2 Critical Sections

The essence of the problem is as follows: Processes are interrupted at points where they shouldn't be if they are to do their work correctly. Obviously, a potential solution is to mark the relevant code section so that it can no longer be interrupted by the scheduler. Although this approach would work in principle, there are several inherent problems. Under certain circumstances, a faulty program would be unable to find its way out of the marked code section and would fail to relinquish the CPU, thus making the computer unusable. We must therefore reject this solution out of hand.[1]

The solution to the problem does not necessarily require that the critical section not be interrupted. Processes may well be interrupted in a critical section *as long as no other process enters the section*. This strict prohibition ensures that values cannot be changed by several processes at the same time and is referred to as *mutual exclusion*. Only one process may enter a critical area of code at a given time.

There are many ways of designing a mutual exclusion method of this kind (regardless of the technical implementation). However, all must ensure that the exclusion principle functions under all circumstances. It must depend neither on the *number* nor on the *speed* of the processors involved. If this were the case (and the solution were therefore only available on a given computer system with a specific hardware configuration), the solution would be impracticable because it would not provide general protection — and this is exactly what is needed. Processes should not be allowed to block each other and come to a permanent stop. Although this is a desirable goal, it cannot always be achieved by technical means as you will see below. It is often up to the programmer to think ahead so that the problem does not occur.

Which principles are applied to support a mutual exclusion method? A multitude of different solutions have been proposed in the history of multitasking and multiuser systems, all with their specific

---

[1] The kernel itself can (and must) reserve the right to disable interrupts at certain points to seal itself off completely from external or periodic events. This is not, however, possible for user processes.

advantages and disadvantages. Some solutions are of an academic nature, and some have found their way into practice in various operating systems — one solution has been adopted in most systems and is therefore worth discussing in detail.

Semaphores

Semaphores were designed by E. W. Dijkstra in 1965. At first glance, they provide a surprisingly simple solution to all kinds of interprocess communication problems — but their use calls for experience, intuition, and caution.

Basically, *semaphores* are simply specially protected variables that can represent both positive and negative integers; their initial value is 1.

Two standard operations are defined to manipulate semaphores — up and down. They are used to control entry to and exit from critical code areas, where it is assumed that competing processes have equal access to the semaphores.

When a process wants to enter critical code, it invokes the down function. This decrements the value of the semaphore by 1; that is, it sets it to 0 and executes the dangerous section of code. Once it has performed the programmed actions, the up function is invoked to increment the value of the semaphore by 1 — thus resetting it to its original value. Semaphores are characterized by two special features:

1.   When a second process tries to enter the critical code section, it too must first perform a down operation on the semaphore. Because a first process has already entered the code section, the value of the semaphore is 0. This causes the second process to "sleep" on the semaphore. In other words, it waits until the first process has exited the relevant code.

     It is of particular importance in the implementation of the down operation that it is handled as *an elementary step* from the perspective of the application. It cannot then be interrupted by a scheduler call, and this means that race conditions cannot occur. In the view of the kernel, querying the variable and modifying its value are two different actions but are seen by the user as an atomic unit.

     When a process sleeps on a semaphore, the kernel puts it in the blocked state and also places it on a wait list with all other processes waiting on the semaphore.

2.   When a process exits the critical code section, it performs the up operation. This not only increments the value of the semaphore (to 1), but also selects a process sleeping on it. This process is now able to safely begin execution of the critical code after resuming and completing its down operation to decrement the semaphore value to 0.

This procedure would not be possible without the special support of the kernel because a userspace library cannot guarantee that the down operation will not be interrupted. Before describing the implementation of the corresponding functions, it is first necessary to discuss the mechanisms that the kernel itself uses to protect critical code sections. These mechanisms are the basis for the protection facilities exported to user programs.

Semaphores work well in userland, and could in principle also be used to solve all kinds of in-kernel locking problems. But they are not: Performance is one of the foremost goals of the kernel, and despite the fact that semaphores might seem simple to implement at a first glance, their overhead is usually too large for the kernel. This is why a plethora of different locking and synchronization mechanisms are available for use in the kernel, which I discuss in the following.

5.2 Kernel Locking Mechanisms

The kernel requires no explicit mechanisms to facilitate the distributed use of memory areas because it has unrestricted access to the full address space. On multiprocessor systems (or similarly, on uniprocessor systems with enabled kernel preemption; see Chapter 2), this gives rise to a few problems. If several processors are in kernel mode at the same time, they can access the same data structure simultaneously — and this is exactly what causes the problem described in the previous sections.

In the first SMP-capable version of the kernel, the solution to this problem was very simple. Only one processor at a time was ever allowed to be in kernel mode. Consequently, uncoordinated parallel access to data was automatically ruled out. Unfortunately, this method was obviously not very efficient and was quickly dropped.

Nowadays, the kernel uses a fine-grained network of locks for the explicit protection of individual data structures. If processor A is manipulating data structure X, processor B may perform any other kernel actions — but it may not manipulate X.

The kernel provides various locking options for this purpose, each optimized for different kernel data usage patterns.

❏ **Atomic Operations** — These are the simplest locking operations. They guarantee that simple operations, such as incrementing a counter, are performed atomically without interruption even if the operation is made up of several assembly language statements.

❏ **Spinlocks** — These are the most frequently used locking option. They are designed for the short-term protection of sections against access by other processors. While the kernel is waiting for a spinlock to be released, it repeatedly checks whether it can acquire the lock without going to sleep in the meantime (*busy waiting*). Of course, this is not very efficient if waits are long.

❏ **Semaphores** — These are implemented in the classical way. While waiting for a semaphore to be released, the kernel goes to sleep until it is woken. Only then does it attempt to acquire the semaphore. *Mutexes* are a special case of semaphores — only one user at a time can be in the critical region protected by them.

❏ **Reader/Writer Locks** — These are locks that distinguish between two types of access to data structures. Any number of processors may perform concurrent *read* access to a data structure, but write access is restricted to a single CPU. Naturally, the data structure cannot be read while it is being written.

The sections below discuss the implementation and usage of these options in detail. Their deployment is omnipresent over all the kernel sources, and locking has become a very important aspect of kernel development, both for fundamental core kernel code as well as for device drivers. Nevertheless, when I discuss specific kernel code in this book, I will mostly omit locking operations except if locks are employed in an unusual way, or if special locking requirements must be fulfilled. But why do we omit this aspect of the kernel in other chapters if it is important? Most of you will certainly agree that this book does not belong to the thinner specimen on your bookshelves, and adding a detailed discussion of locking in all subsystems would certainly not be the ultimate diet for the book. More important, however, is that in most cases a discussion of locking would obstruct and complicate the view on the essential working of a particular mechanism. My main concern, however, is to provide exactly this to you.

Fully understanding the use of locks requires line-by-line familiarity with all kernel code affected by the locks, and this is something a book cannot provide — in fact, something that it *should not even try*:

The source code of Linux is readily available, and there's no need to fill page after page with material that you cannot only easily inspect yourself on your computer, but that is additionally subject to permanent change in many details. So it is much better to equip you with a solid understanding of the *concepts* that are naturally much less likely to change rapidly. Nevertheless, this chapter will provide you with everything necessary to understand how protection against concurrency is implemented in specific subsystems, and together with the explanations about the design and working of these, you will be well equipped to dive into the source code, read, and modify it.

5.2.1 Atomic Operations on Integers

The kernel defines the `atomic_t` data type (in `<asm-`*arch*`/atomic.h>`) as the basis for atomic operations with integer counters. In the view of the kernel, these are operations that are performed as if they consisted of a single assembly language instruction. A short example, in which a counter is incremented by 1, is sufficient to demonstrate the need for operations of this kind. On the assembly language level, incrementation is usually performed in three steps:

1. The counter value is copied from memory into a processor register.
2. The value is incremented.
3. The register data are written back to memory.

Problems may occur if this operation is performed on a second processor at the same time. Both processors read the value in memory simultaneously (e.g., 4), increment it to 5, and write the new value back to memory. However, the correct value in memory should be 6 because the counter was incremented twice.

All processors supported by the kernel provide means of performing operations of this kind atomically. In general, special lock instructions are used to prevent the other processors in the system from working until the current processor has completed the next action. Equivalent mechanisms that produce the same effect may also be used.[2]

To enable platform-independent kernel parts to use atomic operations, the architecture-specific code must provide the operations listed in Table 5-1 that manipulate variables of type `atomic_t`. Because, on some systems, these operations are much slower than normal C operations, they should not be used unless really necessary.

As an understanding of operation implementation presupposes a deep knowledge of the assembler facilities of the individual CPUs, I do not deal with this topic here (each processor architecture provides special functions to implement operations).

> **It is not possible to mix classic and atomic operations. The operations listed in Table 5-1 do *not* function with normal data types such as int or long, and conversely standard operators such as ++ do not work with `atomic_t` variables.**

It should also be noted that atomic variables may be initialized only with the help of the `ATOMIC_INIT` macro. Because the atomic data types are ultimately implemented with normal C types, the kernel encapsulates standard variables in a structure that can no longer be processed with normal operators such as ++.

---

[2]The required instruction is actually called `lock` on IA-32 systems.

\<asm-arch/atomic.h\>
```
typedef struct { volatile int counter; } atomic_t;
```

Table 5-1: Atomic Operations

Operation	Effect
`atomic_read(atomic_t *v)`	Reads the value of the atomic variable.
`atomic_set(atomic_t *v, int i)`	Sets v to i.
`atomic_add(int i, atomic_t *v)`	Adds i to v.
`atomic_add_return(int i, atomic_t *v)`	Adds i to v and returns the result.
`atomic_sub(int i, atomic_t *v)`	Subtracts i from v.
`atomic_sub_return(int i, atomic_t *v)`	Subtracts i from v and returns the result.
`atomic_sub_and_test(int i, atomic_t *v)`	Subtracts i from v. Returns a true value if the result is 0, otherwise `false`.
`atomic_inc(atomic_t *v)`	Subtracts 1 from v.
`atomic_inc_and_test(atomic_t *v)`	Adds 1 to v. Returns `true` if the result is 0, otherwise `false`.
`atomic_dec(atomic_t *v)`	Subtracts 1 from v.
`atomic_dec_and_test(atomic_t *v)`	Subtracts 1 from v. Returns `true` if the result is 0, otherwise `false`.
`atomic_add_negative(int i, atomic_t *v)`	Adds i to v. Returns `true` if the result is less than 0, otherwise `false`.
`atomic_add_negative(int i, atomic_t *v)`	Adds i to v and returns `true` if the result is negative, otherwise `false`.

If the kernel was compiled without SMP support, the operations described are implemented in the same way as for normal variables (only `atomic_t` encapsulation is observed) because there is no interference from other processors.

The kernel provides the `local_t` data type for SMP systems. This permits atomic operations *on a single CPU*. To modify variables of this kind, the kernel basically makes the same functions available as for the `atomic_t` data type, but it is then necessary to replace `atomic` with `local`.

Notice that atomic variables are well suited for integer operations, but not so for bit operations. Each architecture therefore has to define a set of bit manipulation operations, and these also work atomically to provide coherence across processors on SMP systems. The available operations are summarized in Section A.8.

5.2.2   Spinlocks

Spinlocks are used to protect short code sections that comprise just a few C statements and are therefore quickly executed and exited. Most kernel data structures have their own spinlock that must be acquired when critical elements in the structure are processed. Although spinlocks are omnipresent in the kernel sources, I omit them in most pieces of code shown in this book. They do not provide any valuable insight into how the kernel functions but make the code more difficult to read, as explained above. Nevertheless, it is important that code *is* equipped with appropriate locks!

Data Structures and Usage

Spinlocks are implemented by means of the `spinlock_t` data structure, which is manipulated essentially using `spin_lock` and `spin_unlock`. There are a few other spinlock operations: `spin_lock_irqsave` not only acquires the spinlock but also disables the interrupts on the local CPU, and `spin_lock_bh` also disables softIRQs (see Chapter 14). Spinlocks acquired with these operations must be released by means of their counterpart; `spin_unlock_bh` and `spin_unlock_irqsave`, respectively. Once again, implementation is almost fully in (strongly architecture-dependent) assembly language and is therefore not discussed here.

Spinlocks are used as follows:

```
spinlock_t lock = SPIN_LOCK_UNLOCKED;
...
spin_lock(&lock);
/* Critical section */
spin_unlock(&lock);
```

`SPIN_LOCK_UNLOCKED` must be used in its unlocked state to initialize the spinlock. `spin_lock` takes account of two situations:

1. If `lock` is not yet acquired from another place in the kernel, it is reserved for the current processor. Other processors may no longer enter the following area.

2. If `lock` is already acquired by another processor, `spin_lock` goes into an endless loop to repeatedly check whether `lock` has been released by `spin_unlock` (thus the name *spin*lock). Once this is the case, `lock` is acquired, and the critical section of code is entered.

`spin_lock` is defined as an atomic operation to prevent race conditions arising when spinlocks are acquired.

Additionally, the kernel provides the two methods `spin_trylock` and `spin_trylock_bh`. They try to obtain a lock, but will not block if it cannot be immediately acquired. When the locking operation has succeeded, they return a nonzero value (and the code is protected by the spinlock), but otherwise they return 0. In this case, the code is *not* protected by the lock.

Two points must be noted when using spinlocks:

1. If a lock is acquired but no longer released, the system is rendered unusable. All processors — including the one that acquired the lock — sooner or later arrive at a point where they must enter the critical region. They go into the endless loop to wait for lock release, but this never happens. This produces a *deadlock*, and the grim name suggests that it's something that should be avoided.

2. On no account should spinlocks be acquired for a longer period because all processors waiting for lock release are no longer available for other productive tasks (the situation with semaphores is different, as you will see shortly).

> **Code that is protected by spinlocks *must not* go to sleep.** This rule is not so simple to obey as it seems: It is not complicated to avoid going to sleep actively, but it must also be ensured that none of the functions that are called inside a spinlocked region can go to sleep! One particular example is the `kmalloc` function: Usually the requested memory will be returned straight away, but when the kernel is short on memory, the function *can* go to sleep, as discussed in Chapter 3. Code that makes the mistake of allocating memory inside a spinlocked region will thus work perfectly fine most of the time, but sometimes cause a failure. Naturally, such problems are *very* hard to reproduce and debug. Therefore, you should pay great attention to which functions you call inside a spinlocked region, and make sure that they cannot go to sleep in any circumstance.

On uniprocessor systems, spinlocks are defined as empty operations because critical sections cannot be entered by several CPUs at the same time. However, this does *not* apply if kernel preemption is enabled. If the kernel is interrupted in a critical region and this region is then entered by another process, this has exactly the same effect as if the region were actually being executed by two processors on SMP systems. This is prevented by a simple trick — kernel preemption is disabled when the kernel is in a critical region protected by a spinlock. When a uniprocessor kernel is compiled with enabled kernel preemption, `spin_lock` is (basically) equivalent to `preempt_disable` and `spin_unlock` to `preempt_enable`.

> **Spinlocks cannot be acquired more than once from the current holder!** This is especially important when functions that call other functions that each operate with the same lock. If a lock has already been acquired and a function is called that tries to again acquire it although the current code path is already holding the lock, a deadlock will occur — the processor will wait for itself to release the lock, and this might take a while ...

Finally, notice that the kernel itself also provides some notes on how to use spinlocks in `Documentation/spinlocks.txt`.

5.2.3 Semaphores

Semaphores that are used in the kernel are defined by the structure below. Userspace semaphores are implemented differently, as described in Section 5.3.2.

```
<asm-arch/semaphore.h>
struct semaphore {
        atomic_t count;
        int sleepers;
        wait_queue_head_t wait;
};
```

355

Although the structure is defined in an architecture-dependent header file, most architectures use the structure shown.

- ❑ count specifies how many processes may be in the critical region protected by the semaphore at the same time. count == 1 is used in most cases (semaphores of this kind are also known as *mutex* semaphores because they are used to implement *mutual exclusion*).

- ❑ sleepers specifies the number of processes waiting to be allowed to enter the critical region. Unlike spinlocks, waiting processes go to sleep and are not woken until the semaphore is free; this means that the relevant CPU can perform other tasks in the meantime.

- ❑ wait is used to implement a queue to hold the task structures of all processes sleeping on the semaphore (Chapter 14 describes the underlying mechanisms).

In contrast to spinlocks, semaphores are suitable for protecting longer critical sections against parallel access. However, they should not be used to protect shorter sections because it is very costly to put processes to sleep and wake them up again — as happens when the semaphore is contended.

In most cases, the full potential of semaphores is not required, but they are used in the form of mutexes, which are nothing other than binary semaphores. To simplify this case, the kernel provides the macros DECLARE_MUTEX, which declare a binary semaphore that starts out unlocked with count = 1.[3]

```
DECLARE_MUTEX(mutex)
...
down(&mutex);
/* Critical section */
up(&mutex);
```

The usage counter is decremented with down when the critical section is entered. When the counter has reached 0, no other process may enter the section.

When an attempt is made to acquire a *reserved* semaphore with down, the current process is put to sleep and placed on the wait queue associated with the semaphore. At the same time, the process is placed in the TASK_UNINTERRUPTIBLE state and cannot receive signals while waiting to enter the critical region. If the semaphore is *not reserved*, the process may immediately continue without being put to sleep and enters the critical region, but not without reserving the semaphore first.

up must be called when the critical region is exited. The routine is responsible for waking one of the processes sleeping on the semaphore — this process is then allowed to enter the critical section, and all other processes continue to sleep.

In addition to down, two other operations are used to reserve a semaphore (unlike spinlocks, only one up function is available and is used to exit the section protected by a semaphore):

- ❑ down_interruptible works in the same way as down but places the task in the TASK_INTERRUPTIBLE state if the semaphore could not be acquired. As a result, the process can be woken by signals while it is sleeping.[4]

---

[3]Note that earlier kernel versions also provided the macro DECLARE_MUTEX_LOCKED to initialize a locked semaphore, but this variant has been removed during the development of kernel 2.6.24 because it was only required for operations that can be better implemented by *completions*, as discussed in Section 14.4.

[4]If the semaphore is acquired, the function returns 0. If the process is interrupted by a signal without acquiring the semaphore, -EINTR is returned.

❏ down_trylock attempts to acquire a semaphore. If it fails, the process does not go to sleep to wait for the semaphore but continues execution normally. If the semaphore is acquired, the function returns a false value, otherwise a true value.

In addition to mutex variables that can be used in the kernel only, Linux also features so-called *futexes* (*fast userspace mutex*) that consist of a combination of kernel and user mode. These provide mutex functionality for userspace processes. However, it must be ensured that they are used and manipulated as quickly and efficiently as possible. For reasons of space, I dispense with a description of their implementation, particularly as they are not especially important for the kernel itself. See the manual page futex(2) for more information.

5.2.4 The Read-Copy-Update Mechanism

Read-copy-update (RCU) is a rather new synchronization mechanism that was added during the development of kernel 2.5, but has been very favorably accepted by the kernel community. It is by now used in numerous places all over the kernel. RCU performs very well in terms of performance impact, if at a slight cost in memory requirements, which is, however, mostly negligible. This is a good thing, but good things are always accompanied by a number of not-so-good things. This time, it's the constraints that RCU places on potential users:

❏ Accesses to the shared resource should be Read Only most of the time, and writes should be correspondingly rare.

❏ The kernel cannot go to sleep within a region protected by RCU.

❏ The protected resource must be accessed via a pointer.

The principle of RCU is simple: The mechanism keeps track of all users of the pointer to the shared data structure. When the structure is supposed to change, a copy (or a new instance that is filled in appropriately, this does not make any difference) is first created and the change is performed there. After all previous readers have finished their reading work on the old copy, the pointer can be replaced by a pointer to the new, modified copy. Notice that this allows read access to happen concurrently with write updates!

Core API

Suppose that a pointer ptr points to a data structure that is protected by RCU. It is forbidden to simply de-reference the pointer, but rcu_dereference(ptr) must be invoked before and the *result* be de-referenced. Additionally, the code that de-references the pointer and uses the result needs to be embraced by calls to rcu_read_lock and rcu_read_unlock:

```
rcu_read_lock();

p = rcu_dereference(ptr);
if (p != NULL) {
        awesome_function(p);
}

rcu_read_unlock();
```

> The de-referenced pointer may not be used outside the region protected by
> rcu_read_lock() ... rcu_read_unlock(), nor may it be used for write access!

If the object pointed at by `ptr` has to be modified, this must be done with `rcu_assign_pointer`:

```
struct super_duper *new_ptr = kmalloc(...);

new_ptr->meaning = xyz;
new_ptr->of = 42;
new_ptr->life = 23;

rcu_assign_pointer(ptr, new_ptr);
```

In RCU terminology, this *publishes* the pointer, and subsequent read operations will see the new structure instead of the old one.

> **If updates can come from many places in the kernel, protection against concurrent write operations must be provided using regular synchronization primitives, for instance, spinlocks. While RCU protects readers from writers, it does not protect writers against writers!**

What happens to the old structure once the new value has been published? After all readers are gone, the kernel can get rid of the memory — but it needs to know when this is safe to do. RCU provides two more functions for this purpose:

❑ `synchronize_rcu()` waits until all existing readers have finished their work. After the function returns, it is safe to free the memory associated with the old pointer.

❑ `call_rcu` can be used to register a function that is called after all existing readers to a shared resource are gone. This requires that an instance of `rcu_head` is embedded — and not just accessible via a pointer — into the data stucture protected by RCU:

```
struct super_duper {
        struct rcu_head head;
        int meaning, of, life;
};
```

The callback gets the `rcu_head` of the object passed as parameter and can use the `container_of` mechanism to access the object.

kernel/rcupdate.c
```
void fastcall call_rcu(struct rcu_head *head,
                       void (*func)(struct rcu_head *rcu))
```

List Operations

Generic pointers are not the only objects that can be protected by RCU. The kernel also provides standard functions that allow for protecting doubly linked lists by the RCU mechanism, and this is the most prominent application within the kernel. Additionally, hash lists that consist of `struct hlist_head` and `struct hlist_node` pairs can also be protected by RCU.

The nice thing about list protection by RCU is that the standard list elements can still be used — it is only necessary to invoke the RCU variants of standard functions to iterate over lists and change and delete list elements. The names of the functions are easy to remember: Just append `_rcu` to the standard functions.

\<list.h\>
```
static inline void list_add_rcu(struct list_head *new, struct list_head *head)
static inline void list_add_tail_rcu(struct list_head *new,
                                     struct list_head *head)
static inline void list_del_rcu(struct list_head *entry)
static inline void list_replace_rcu(struct list_head *old,
                                    struct list_head *new)
```

❑   `list_add_rcu` adds a new element `new` to the beginning of a list headed by `head`, while `list_add_tail_rcu` adds it to the end.

❑   `list_replace_rcu` replaces the list element `old` with `new`.

❑   `list_del_rcu` removes the element `entry` from its list.

Most importantly, `list_for_each_rcu` allows for iterating over all elements of a list. The variant `list_for_each_rcu_safe` is even safe against element removal.

> *Both operations must be enclosed in a* `rcu_read_lock() ... rcu_read_unlock()` *pair.*

Notice that the kernel provides a large amount of documentation about RCU by the creator of the mechanism. It is located in `Documentation/RCU` and makes for a very interesting read — especially because it is not outdated like many other texts included in the kernel. The documents not only provide information about how RCU is implemented, but additionally introduce some further standard functions not covered here because their use in the kernel is not so common.

5.2.5 Memory and Optimization Barriers

Modern compilers and processors will try to squeeze every bit of performance out of code, and readers will certainly agree that this is a good thing. However, as with every good thing, there is also a drawback to consider (maybe you've heard this before in this chapter). One particular technique to achieve better performance is to *reorder* instructions. This can be perfectly fine, as long as the result is identical. However, it can be hard to decide for a compiler or processor *if* the result of a reordering will really match the intended purpose, especially if side effects need to be considered — a thing at which machines are naturally suboptimal compared to humans. Side effects are, however, a common and necessary effect when data are written to I/O registers.

While locks are sufficient to ensure *atomicity*, they cannot always guarantee *time ordering* of code that is subjected to optimizations by compilers and processors. And, in contrast to race conditions, this problem not only affects SMP systems, but also uniprocessor machines.

The kernel provides several functions to prevent both the processor and the compiler from reordering code:

❑   `mb()`, `rmb()`, and `wmb()` insert hardware memory barriers into the code flow. `rmb()` is a *read memory barrier*. It guarantees that all read operations issued *before* the barrier are completed before any read operations *after* the barrier are carried out. `wmb` does the same thing, but this time for write accesses. And, as you have guessed, `mb()` combines both effects.

❑   `barrier` inserts an *optimization* barrier. This instructs the compiler to assume that all memory locations in RAM stored in CPU registers that were valid before the barrier are invalid after the barrier. Essentially, this means that the *compiler* does not process any read or write requests following the barrier before read or write requests issued before the barrier have been completed.

The CPU can still reorder the time flow!

❑ `smb_mb()`, `smp_rmb()`, and `smp_wmb()` act as the hardware memory barriers described above, but only when they are used on SMP systems. They generate a software barrier on uniprocessor systems instead.

❑ `read_barrier_depends()` is a special form of a read barrier that takes dependencies among read operations into account. If a read request *after* the barrier depends on data for which a read request is performed *before* the barrier, then both compiler and hardware must not reorder these requests.

Notice that all commands presented above will have an impact on run-time performance. This is only natural because if optimizations are disabled, things tend to run slower than with optimizations, which is the whole purpose of optimizing code. Most of you will agree, though, the code that runs a little slower but does the right thing is preferable to code that is fast — and wrong.

One particular application for optimization barriers is the kernel preemption mechanism. Note that the `preempt_disable` increments the preemption counter and thus disables preemption, while `preempt_enable` reenables preemption again by decreasing the preemption counter. Code inside a region embraced by these commands is protected against preemption. Consider the following code:

```
preempt_disable();
function_which_must_not_be_preempted();
preempt_enable();
```

It would be quite inconvenient if the compiler would decide to rearrange the code as follows:

```
function_which_must_not_be_preempted();
preempt_disable();
preempt_enable();
```

Another possible reordering would be likewise suboptimal:

```
preempt_disable();
preempt_enable();
function_which_must_not_be_preempted();
```

In both cases, the non-preemptible part *could* be preempted. Therefore, `preempt_disable` inserts a memory barrier after the preemption counter has been incremented:

```
<preempt.h>
#define preempt_disable() \
do { \
        inc_preempt_count(); \
        barrier(); \
} while (0)
```

This prevents the compiler from swapping `inc_preempt_count()` with any of the following statements. Likewise, `preempt_enable` has to insert an optimization barrier before preemption is enabled again:

```
<preempt.h>
#define preempt_enable() \
do { \
```

```
        ...
                barrier(); \
                preempt_check_resched(); \
        } while (0)
```

This measure protects against the second erroneous reordering shown above.

All barrier commands discussed so far are made available by including `<system.h>`. You might have gotten the impression that memory barriers are notoriously complicated to use, and your perception serves you well, indeed — getting memory and optimization barriers right can be a very tricky business. It should therefore be noted that memory barriers are not particularly favored by some kernel maintainers, and code using them will have a hard time finding its way into mainline. So it's always worth a try to see if things cannot be done differently without barriers. This is possible because locking instructions will on many architectures also act as memory barriers. However, this needs to be checked for the specific cases that require memory barriers, and general advice is hard to give.

5.2.6   Reader/Writer Locks

The mechanisms described above have one disadvantage. They do not differentiate between situations in which data structures are simply read and those in which they are actively manipulated. Usually, any number of processes are granted concurrent read access to data structures, whereas write access must be restricted exclusively to a single task.

The kernel therefore provides additional semaphore and spinlock versions to cater for the above — these are known accordingly as *Reader/Writer* semaphores and Reader/Writer spinlocks.

The `rwlock_t` data type is defined for Reader/Writer spinlocks. Locks must be acquired in different ways in order to differentiate between read and write access.

❑   `read_lock` and `read_unlock` must be executed before and after a critical region to which a process requires read access. The kernel grants any number of read processes concurrent access to the critical region.

❑   `write_lock` and `write_unlock` are used for write access. The kernel ensures that only one writer (and no readers) is in the region.

An `_irq` `_irqsave` variant is also available and functions in the same way as normal spinlocks. Variants ending in `_bh` are also available. They disable software interrupts, but leave hardware interrupts still enabled.

Read/write semaphores are used in a similar way. The equivalent data structure is `struct rw_semaphore`, and `down_read` and `up_read` are used to obtain read access to the critical region. Write access is performed with the help of `down_write` and `up_write`. The `_trylock` variants are also available for all commands — they also function as described above.

5.2.7   The Big Kernel Lock

A relic of earlier days is the option of locking the entire kernel to ensure that no processors run in parallel in kernel mode. This lock is known as the *big kernel lock* but is most frequently referred to by its abbreviation, *BKL*.

The complete kernel is locked using `lock_kernel`; its unlocking counterpart is `unlock_kernel`.

A special feature of the BKL is that its lock depth is also counted. This means that `lock_kernel` can be invoked even when the kernel has already been locked. The matching unlocking operation (`unlock_kernel`) must then be invoked the same number of times to unlock the kernel so that other processors can enter it.

Although the BKL is still present at more than 1,000 points in the kernel, it is an obsolete concept whose use is deprecated by kernel developers because it is a catastrophe in terms of performance and scalability. New code should *on no account* use the lock but should instead adopt the finer-grained options described above. Nevertheless, it will be a few more years before the BKL finally disappears — if ever at all.[5] The kernel sources summarize the situation well:

lib/kernel_lock.c
```
/*
 * lib/kernel_lock.c
 *
 * This is the traditional BKL - big kernel lock. Largely
 * relegated to obsolescence, but used by various less
 * important (or lazy) subsystems.
 */
```

Notice that SMP systems and UP systems with kernel preemption allow for preempting the big kernel lock if the configuration option `PREEMPT_BKL` is set, although I will not discuss this mechanism further. While this helps to decrease kernel latency, it is not a cure for the problems created by the BKL and should only be seen as an emergency measure that serves as good as possible as an interim solution.

5.2.8 Mutexes

Although semaphores can be used to implement the functionality of mutexes, the overhead imposed by the generality of semaphores is often not necessary. Because of this, the kernel contains a separate implementation of special-purpose mutexes that are not based on semaphores. Or, to be precise, the kernel contains two implementations of mutexes: A classical variant, and real-time mutexes that allow for solving priority inversion problems. I discuss both approaches in the following.

Classical Mutexes

The basic data structure for classical mutexes is defined as follows:

<mutex.h>
```
struct mutex {
        /* 1: unlocked, 0: locked, negative: locked, possible waiters */
        atomic_t                count;
        spinlock_t              wait_lock;
        struct list_head        wait_list;
};
```

The concept is rather simple: `count` is 1 if the mutex is unlocked. The locked case distinguishes between two situations. If only a single process is using the mutex, then `count` is set to 0. If the mutex is locked and any processes are waiting on the mutex to be unlocked (and need be awoken when this happens), `count` is negative. This special casing helps to speed up the code because in the usual case, no one will be waiting on the mutex.

---

[5]During the development of kernel 2.6.26, a special kernel tree whose purpose is to speed up BKL removal was created, and hopefully progress will be accelerated by this measure.

There are two ways to define new mutexes:

1. Static mutexes can be generated at compile time by using DEFINE_MUTEX (be sure not to confuse this with DECLARE_MUTEX from the semaphore-based mutexes!).

2. mutex_init dynamically initializes a new mutex at run time.

mutex_lock and mutex_unlock are used to lock and unlock a mutex, respectively. In addition, the kernel also provides the function mutex_trylock, which tries to obtain the mutex, but will return immediately if this fails because the mutex is already locked. Finally, mutex_trylock can be used to check if a given mutex is locked or not.

Real-Time Mutexes

Real-time mutexes (RT-mutexes) are another form of mutex supported by the kernel. They need to be explicitly enabled at compile time by selecting the configuration option CONFIG_RT_MUTEX. In contrast to regular mutexes, they implement *priority inheritance*, which, in turn, allows for solving (or, at least, attenuating) the effects of *priority inversion*. Both are well-known effects, respectively, methods and are discussed in most operating systems textbooks.

Consider a situation in which two processes run on a system: A has high priority, and C has low priority. Assume the C has acquired a mutex and is happily operating in the protected region, with no intention of leaving it sometime in the near future. However, shortly after C has entered the protected region, A also tries to obtain the mutex that protects it — and has to wait, because C has already acquired the mutex. This causes the *higher*-priority process A to wait for the *lower*-priority process C.

Things can get worse when a third process B with a priority between A and C enters the field. Suppose that C still holds the lock, and A is waiting for it. Now B gets ready to run. Because it has a higher priority than C, it can preempt C. But it has also effectively preempted A, although this process has a higher priority than B. If B continues to stay runnable, it can prevent A from running for a long time, because C will finish its operation only slowly. B therefore acts as if it had a higher priority than A. This unfortunate situation is referred to as *unbounded priority inversion*.

This problem can be solved by priority inheritance: When a high-priority process blocks on a mutex that is currently held by a low-priority process, the priority of C (in our example) is temporarily *boosted* to the priority of A. If B starts to run now, it will only get as much CPU time as if it were competing with A, thus setting priorities straight again.

The definition of a RT-mutex is tantalizingly close to the definition of a regular mutex:

```
<rtmutex.h>
struct rt_mutex {
        spinlock_t wait_lock;
        struct plist_head wait_list;
        struct task_struct *owner;
};
```

The mutex owner is denoted by owner, and wait_lock provides the actual protection. All waiting processes are enqueued on wait_list. The decisive change in contrast to regular mutexes is that the tasks on the waiter lists are sorted by priority. Whenever the waiter list changes, the kernel can consequently adjust the priority of the owner up or down. This requires an interface to the scheduler that is provided by the function rt_mutex_setprio. The function updates the dynamic priority task_struct->prio, but leaves the normal priority `task_struct->normal_priority` untouched. If you are confused by these terms, it might be a good idea to refresh yourself with the discussion of the scheduler in Chapter 2.

Besides, the kernel provides several standard functions (`rt_mutex_init`, `rt_mutex_lock`, `rt_mutex_unlock`, `rt_mutex_trylock`) that work exactly as for regular mutexes and thus need not be discussed any further.

5.2.9 Approximate Per-CPU Counters

Counters can become a bottleneck if a system is equipped with a large number of CPUs: Only one CPU at a time may modify the value; all other CPUs need to wait for the operation to finish until they can access the counter again. If a counter is frequently visited, this has a severe impact on system performance.

For some counters, it is not necessary to know the exact value at all times. An approximation of the value serves quite as well as the proper value would do. This insight can be used to accelerate counter manipulation on SMP systems by introducing per-CPU counters. The basic idea is depicted in Figure 5-1: The proper counter value is stored at a certain place in memory, and an array with one entry for every CPU in the system is kept below the memory location of the proper value.

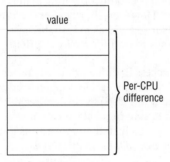

Figure 5-1: Data stucture for approximate per-CPU counters.

If a processor wants to modify the value of the counter by adding or subtracting a number n, it does not perform this modification by directly changing the counter value because this would require locking out other CPUs from accessing the counter, a potentially time-consuming operation. Instead, the desired modification is stored in the CPU-specific entry of the array associated with the counter. If, for instance, the value 3 was supposed to be added to the counter, the entry +3 would be stored in the array. If the same CPU wants to substract a number (say, 5) from the counter at some other time, it also does not perform the operation directly on the counter, but on the value in the CPU-specific array: 5 is subtracted from 2, and the new value is thus −2. If any processor reads the counter value, it is not entirely accurate. If the original value was 15, then it would be 13 after the previously mentioned modifications, but is still 15. If one wants to know the value only approximately, 13 is still a good approximation to 15.

If the changes in one of the CPU-specific array elements sum up to a value above or below a threshold that is considered to be large, the proper counter value is changed. In this case, the kernel needs to make sure that the access is protected by appropriate locking. But since this change now occurs only seldom, the cost of the locking operation is not so important anymore.

As long as the counter changes only moderately, the mean value received from read operations in this scheme is quite close to the proper value of the counter.

The kernel implements per-CPU counters with the help of the following data structure:

<percpu_counter.h>
```
struct percpu_counter {
        spinlock_t lock;
        long count;
        long *counters;
};
```

`count` is the proper value of the counter, and `lock` is a spinlock to protect the counter when the exact value is required. The CPU-specific array buffering counter manipulations is given by `counters`.

The threshold value that triggers the modification of the proper counter depends on the number of CPUs found in the system:

<percpu_counter.h>
```
#if NR_CPUS >= 16
#define FBC_BATCH        (NR_CPUS*2)
#else
#define FBC_BATCH        (NR_CPUS*4)
#endif
```

The following functions are available to modify approximate per-CPU counters:

<percpu_counter.h>
```
static inline void percpu_counter_add(struct percpu_counter *fbc, s64 amount)
static inline void percpu_counter_dec(struct percpu_counter *fbc)
static inline s64 percpu_counter_sum(struct percpu_counter *fbc)
static inline void percpu_counter_set(struct percpu_counter *fbc, s64 amount)
static inline void percpu_counter_inc(struct percpu_counter *fbc)
static inline void percpu_counter_dev(struct percpu_counter *fbc)
```

❏ `percpu_counter_add` and `percpu_counter_dec` modify the counter by a given increment or decrement. The change is propagated to the proper counter if the accumulated changes surpass the threshold as given by `FBC_BATCH`.

❏ `percpu_counter_read` reads the current value of the counter without considering changes made by the individual CPUs.

❏ `percpu_counter_inc` and `percpu_counter_inc` are shortcuts to, respectively, increment and decrement an approximate counter by 1.

❏ `percpu_counter_set` sets the counter to a specific value.

❏ `percpu_counter_sum` computes the exact value.

5.2.10 Lock Contention and Fine-Grained Locking

After having discussed the numerous locking primitives provided by the kernel, let us briefly address some of the problems related to locking and kernel scalability. While multiprocessor systems were nearly completely unknown to the average user only a decade ago, they are present on nearly every desktop today. Scalability of Linux on systems with more than a single CPU has therefore become a very important goal. This needs especially to be taken into account when locking rules are designed for a piece of kernel code. Locking needs to fulfill two purposes that are often hard to achieve simultaneously:

1. Code must be protected against concurrent access, which would lead to failures.

2. The impact on performance must be as little as possible.

Having both things at the same time is especially complicated when data are heavily used by the kernel. Consider a really important data structure that is accessed very often — the memory management subsystem contains such structures, for instance, but also the networking code and many other components of the kernel. If the whole data structure (or, even worse, multiple data structures, or a whole driver, or a whole subsystem[6]) is protected by only a single lock, than chances are high that the lock is acquired by some other part of the system when one part want to get hold of it. *Lock contention* is said to be high in this case, and the lock becomes a *hotspot* of the kernel. To remedy this situation, it is customary to identify independent parts of a data structure and use *multiple* locks to protect the elements. This solution is known as *fine-grained locking*. While the approach is beneficial for scalability on really big machines, it raises two other problems:

1. Taking many locks increases the overhead of an operation, especially on smaller SMP machines.

2. When a data structure is protected by multiple locks, then cases naturally arise that an operation needs to access two protected regions simultaneously, and multiple locks must be held at the same time. This makes it necessary to obey a certain *lock ordering*, which mandates in which order locks are to be acquired and released. If not, then again deadlocks will be the result! Since the code paths through the kernel can be complicated and interwoven, it is especially hard to ensure that all cases are right.

Achieving fine-grained locking for good scalability while making sure to avoid deadlocks is therefore currently among the kernel's foremost challenges.

5.3 System V Interprocess Communication

Linux uses mechanisms introduced in System V (SysV) to support interprocess communication and synchronization for user processes. System calls provide various routines to enable user libraries (typically the C standard library) to implement the required operations.

In addition to semaphores, the SysV scheme of interprocess communication includes an option for exchanging messages and sharing memory areas between processes in accordance with a controlled pattern as described below.[7]

5.3.1 System V Mechanisms

The three IPC mechanisms of System V UNIX (semaphores, message queues, and shared memory) reflect three very different concepts but have one thing in common. They all make use of system-wide resources

---

[6]This is not so ridiculous as it may first sound, but the initial SMP-capable kernels even went one step further: After all, the big kernel lock protects *all* of the kernel!

[7]The POSIX standard has now introduced similar structures in a more modern form. I do not discuss these because most applications still use SysV mechanisms.

that can be shared by several processes at the same time. This would seem to be logical for IPC mechanisms but nevertheless should not be taken for granted. For example, the mechanisms could have been designed in such a way as to ensure that only the threads of a program or a structure generated by a `fork` are able to access shared SysV objects.

Before individual SysV elements can be accessed by various independent processes, they must be uniquely identifiable in the system. To this end, each IPC structure is assigned a number when it is created. Each program with knowledge of this magic number is able to access the corresponding structure. If independent applications are to communicate with each other, this number is usually permanently compiled into the individual programs. An alternative is to dynamically generate a magic number that is guaranteed to be unique (statically assigned numbers cannot be guaranteed to be unique). The standard library provides several functions to do this (see the relevant system programming manuals for detailed information).

A privilege system based on the system adopted for file access permissions is used to access IPC objects. Each object has a user ID and a group ID that depend on the UID/GID under which the program that generated the IPC object is running. Read and write permissions are assigned at initialization. As with normal files, these govern access for three different user classes — owner, group, and others. Detailed information on how this is done is provided in the corresponding system programming manuals.

The flag 0666 must be specified to create a semaphore that grants all possible access permissions (owner, group, and all other users have read and write permissions).

5.3.2 Semaphores

System V semaphores are implemented using `sem/sem.c` in conjunction with the header file `<sem.h>`. These semaphores are not related in any way to the kernel semaphores described above.

Using System V Semaphores

The System V interface for using semaphores is anything but intuitive because the concept of a semaphore has been expanded well beyond its actual definition. Semaphores are no longer treated as simple variables to support atomic execution of predefined operations. Instead, a System V semaphore now refers to a whole set of semaphores, which allows not just one but several operations to be performed at the same time (although they appear to be atomic to users). It is, of course, possible to request a semaphore set with just a single semaphore and to define functions that simulate the behavior of simple operations. The following sample program shows how semaphores are used:

```
#include<stdio.h>
#include<sys/types.h>
#include<sys/ipc.h>
#include<sys/sem.h>

#define SEMKEY 1234L      /* Identifier */
#define PERMS  0666       /* Access permission: rwrwrw */

struct sembuf op_down[1] = { 0, -1 , 0 };
struct sembuf op_up[1] = { 0, 1 , 0 };

int semid = -1;    /* Semaphore identifier */
int res;           /* Result of semaphore operations */
```

```
void init_sem() {
  /* Test whether semaphore already exists */
  semid = semget(SEMKEY, 0, IPC_CREAT | PERMS);
  if (semid < 0) {
    printf("Create the semaphore\n");

    semid = semget(SEMKEY, 1, IPC_CREAT | PERMS);
    if (semid < 0) {
      printf("Couldn't create semaphore!\n");
      exit(-1);
    }

    /* Initialize with 1 */
    res = semctl(semid, 0, SETVAL, 1);
  }
}

void down() {
  /* Perform down operation */
  res = semop(semid, &op_down[0], 1);
}

void up() {
  /* Perform up operation */
  res = semop(semid, &op_up[0], 1);
}


int main(){
  init_sem();
  /* Normal program code. */

  printf("Before critical code\n");
  down();
  /* Critical code */
  printf("In critical code\n");
  sleep(10);
  up();

  /* Remaing program code */
  return 0;
}
```

A new semaphore with a permanently defined magic number (1234) is first created in main for purposes of identification within the system. Because several copies of the program are to run in parallel, it is necessary to test whether a corresponding semaphore already exists. If not, one is created. This is done using the semget system call to reserve a semaphore set. It requires the following parameters: the magic number (SEMKEY), the number of semaphores in the set (1), and the desired access permissions. The above sample program creates a semaphore set with just a single semaphore. The access permissions indicate that all users have both read and write access to the semaphore.[8] Then the value of the single semaphore in the semaphore set is initialized to 1 using the semctl system call. The semid variable identifies the semaphore in the kernel (it can be obtained with the help of the magic number of any other program).

---

[8] IPC_CREAT is a system constant that must be "ORed" with the access number to specify that a new semaphore is to be created.

0 specifies that we want to manipulate the semaphore with identifier 0 in our semaphore set (this is the only semaphore in our set). The meaning of SETVAL, 1 is obvious — the semaphore value is to be set to 1.[9]

The familiar up and down operations are implemented by procedures of the same name. How the semaphore value is modified in the SysV scheme is interesting. Operations are performed using the semop system call, and, as usual, the semid variable is used to identify the desired semaphore. Of particular note are the last two arguments. One is a pointer to an array with sembuf elements, each of which represents a semaphore operation. The number of operations in the array is defined by an integer argument because the kernel cannot otherwise identify the operations.

Entries in the sembuf array consist of three elements with the following meanings:

1. The first entry serves to select the semaphore in the semaphore set.

2. The second entry specifies the desired operation. 0 waits until the value of the semaphore reaches 0; a positive number is added to the value of the semaphore (and corresponds to releasing a resource; the process cannot go to sleep with this action); a negative number is used to request resources. If the absolute value is less than the value of the semaphore, its (absolute) value is subtracted from the current semaphore value without sleeping on the semaphore; otherwise, the process blocks until the semaphore value reaches a value that allows the operation to be performed.

3. The third entry is a flag used for fine control of the operation.

The behavior of a semaphore can be simulated by using 1 and -1 as numeric arguments. down tries to subtract 1 from the semaphore counter (and goes to sleep when the semaphore value reaches 0), while up adds 1 to the semaphore value and therefore corresponds to releasing a resource.

The code yields the following result:

```
wolfgang@meitner> ./sema
Create the semaphore
Before the critical code
In the critical code
```

The program creates the semaphore, enters the critical code, and waits there for 10 seconds. Before the code is entered, a down operation is performed to decrement the semaphore value to 0. A second process started during the wait period is not allowed to enter critical code.

```
wolfgang@meitner> ./sema
Before the critical code
```

Any attempt to enter critical code triggers a down operation, which tries to subtract 1 from the semaphore value. This fails because the current value is 0. The process goes to sleep on the semaphore. It is not woken until the first process has released the resource by means of an up operation (and the semaphore value has reverted to 1). It can then decrement the semaphore value and enter the critical code.

Data Structures

The kernel uses several data structures to describe the current status of all registered semaphores and to build a kind of network. They are responsible not only for managing the semaphores and their

---

[9]For the sake of simplicity, we do not query for errors in our sample program.

characteristics (value, read, and write permissions, etc.), but also for associating semaphores with waiting processes by means of a waiting list.

Starting with kernel 2.6.19, the IPC mechanism is aware of namespaces (see Chapter 2 for more information about this concept). Managing IPC namespaces is, however, simple because they are not hierarchically related. A given task belongs to the namespace pointed at by `task_struct->nsproxy->ipc_ns`, and the initial default namespace is implemented by the static `ipc_namespace` instance `init_ipc_ns`. Each namespace carries essentially the following information:

<ipc.h>
```
struct ipc_namespace {
 ...
        struct ipc_ids *ids[3];

        /* Resource limits */
 ...
}
```

I have omitted a large number of elements devoted to observing resource consumption and setting resource limits. The kernel, for instance, restricts the maximum number of shared memory pages, the maximum size for a shared memory segment, the maximum number of message queues, and so on. All restrictions apply on a per-namespace basis and are documented in the manual pages `msgget(2)`, `shmget(2)`, and `semget(2)`, so I will not discuss them further here. All are implemented by simple counters.

More interesting is the array `ids`. One array position per IPC mechanism — shared memory, semaphores, and messages — exists, and each points to an instance of `struct ipc_ids` that is the basis to keep track of the existing IPC objects per category. To prevent getting lost in search of the proper array index per category, the kernel provides the auxiliary functions `msg_ids`, `shm_ids`, and `sem_ids`. But just in case you were wondering, semaphores live in position 0, followed by message queues and then by shared memory.

`struct ipc_ids` is defined as follows:

ipc/util.h
```
struct ipc_ids {
        int in_use;
        unsigned short seq;
        unsigned short seq_max;
        struct rw_semaphore rw_mutex;
        struct idr ipcs_idr;
};
```

The first elements hold general information on the status of the IPC objects:

❑   `in_use` holds the number of IPC objects currently in use.

❑   `seq` and `seq_id` allow generating userspace IPC identifiers sequentially. Note that the identifiers are not identical with the sequence numbers, though. The kernel identifies an IPC object internally with an identifier managed per resource type, that is, one identifier for message queues, one for semaphores, and one for shared memory objects. Each time a new IPC object is created, the sequence number is incremented by 1 (wrapping is handled automatically).

The identifier visible to userland is given by `s*SEQ_MULTIPLIER+i`, where `s` is the current sequence number and `i` is the kernel-internal identifier. The sequence multiplier is set to the upper limit for IPC objects. If an internal ID is reused, a different userspace identifier is generated this way because the sequence number is reused. This minimizes the risk of using a wrong resource when a stale ID is passed from userland.

❏ `rw_mutex` is a kernel semaphore. It is used to implement semaphore operations and safeguards against race conditions in userspace. The mutex appropriately protects the data structures that contain, for instance, the semaphore value.

Each IPC object is represented by an instance of `kern_ipc_perm` to which we come in a moment. Each object has a kernel-internal ID, and `ipcs_idr` is used to associate an ID with a pointer to the corresponding `kern_ipc_perm` instance. Since the number of used IPC objects can grow and shrink dynamically, a static array would not serve well to manage the information, but the kernel provides a radix-tree-like (see Appendix C) standard data structure in `lib/idr.c` for this purpose. How the entries are managed in detail is not relevant for our purposes; it suffices to know that each internal ID can be associated with the respective `kern_ipc_perm` instance without problems.

The elements of `kern_ipc_perm` hold information on semaphore "owners" and on access permissions.

<ipc.h>
```
struct kern_ipc_perm
{
        int             id;
        key_t           key;
        uid_t           uid;
        gid_t           gid;
        uid_t           cuid;
        gid_t           cgid;
        mode_t          mode;
        unsigned long   seq;
};
```

The structure can be used not only for semaphores but also for other IPC mechanisms. You will come across it frequently in this chapter.

❏ `key` holds the magic number used by user programs to identify the semaphore, and `id` is the kernel-internal identifier.

❏ `uid` and `gid` specify the user and group ID of the owner. `cuid` and `cgid` hold the same data for the process that generated the semaphore.

❏ `seq` is a sequence number that was used when the object was reserved.

❏ `mode` holds the bitmask, which specifies access permissions in accordance with the owner, group, others scheme.

The above data structures are not sufficient to keep all information required for semaphores. A special per-task element is required:

<sched.h>
```
struct task_struct {
...
#ifdef CONFIG_SYSVIPC
```

```
/* ipc stuff */
        struct sysv_sem sysvsem;
#endif
...
};
```

Note that the SysV code is only compiled into the kernel if the configuration option CONFIG_SYSVIPC is set. The sysv_sem data structure is used to encapsulate a further element.

sem.h
```
struct sysv_sem {
        struct sem_undo_list *undo_list;
};
```

The only member, undo_list, is used to permit semaphore manipulations that can be undone. If a process crashes after modifying a semaphore, the information held in the list is used to return the semaphore to its state prior to modification. The mechanism is useful when the crashed process has made changes after which processes waiting on the semaphore can no longer be woken. By undoing these actions (using the information in the undo list), the semaphore can be returned to a consistent state, thus preventing deadlocks. I won't bother with the details here, however.

sem_queue is another data structure that is used to associate a semaphore with a sleeping process that wants to perform a semaphore operation but is not allowed to do so at the moment. In other words, each instance of the data structure is an entry in the list of pending operations.

<sem.h>
```
struct sem_queue {
        struct sem_queue *      next;    /* next entry in the queue */
        struct sem_queue **     prev;    /* previous entry in the queue, *(q->prev) == q */
        struct task_struct*     sleeper; /* this process */
        struct sem_undo *       undo;    /* undo structure */
        int                     pid;     /* process id of requesting process */
        int                     status;  /* completion status of operation */
        struct sem_array *      sma;     /* semaphore array for operations */
        int                     id;      /* internal sem id */
        struct sembuf *         sops;    /* array of pending operations */
        int                     nsops;   /* number of operations */
        int                     alter;   /* does the operation alter the array? */
};
```

For each semaphore, there is exactly one queue that manages all sleeping processes associated with the semaphore. The queue is not implemented using standard kernel facilities but manually by means of next and prev pointers.

❑   sleeper is a pointer to the task structure of the process waiting for permission to perform a semaphore operation.

❑   pid specifies the PID of the waiting process.

❑   id holds the kernel-internal semaphore identifier.

❏ `sops` is a pointer to an array that holds the pending semaphore operations (a further data structure discussed below is used to describe the operations themselves). The number of operations (i.e., the size of the array) is defined in `sops`.

❏ `alter` indicates whether the operations alter the value of the semaphore (e.g., a status query leaves the value unchanged).

`sma` holds a pointer to an instance of the data structure used to manage the semaphore status.

\<sem.h\>
```
struct sem_array {
        struct kern_ipc_perm    sem_perm;       /* permissions .. see ipc.h */
        time_t                  sem_otime;      /* last semop time */
        time_t                  sem_ctime;      /* last change time */
        struct sem              *sem_base;      /* ptr to first semaphore in array */
        struct sem_queue        *sem_pending;   /* pending operations to be processed */
        struct sem_queue        **sem_pending_last; /* last pending operation */
        struct sem_undo         *undo;          /* undo requests on this array */
        unsigned long           sem_nsems;      /* no. of semaphores in array */
};
```

There is exactly one instance of this data structure in the system for each semaphore set. The instance is used to manage all the semaphores that make up the set.

❏ Semaphore access permissions are held in `sem_perm` of the familiar `kern_ipc_perm` type. This must be located at the beginning of the structure so that a trick can be used involving the `ipc_ids->entries` arrays employed to manage all semaphore sets. Because the individual elements point to areas in which sufficient memory is reserved not only for `kern_ipc_perm` but also for `sem_array`, the kernel can switch between both representations by means of typecasts.

This trick is also used for other SysV-IPC objects, as you will see further below.

❏ `sem_nsems` specifies the number of semaphores in a user semaphore.

❏ `sem_base` is an array, each of whose entries describes a semaphore in the set. It holds the current semaphore value and the PID of the process that last accessed it.

\<sem.h\>
```
struct sem {
        int     semval;         /* current value */
        int     sempid;         /* pid of last operation */
};
```

❏ `sem_otime` specifies the time of the last access to the semaphore in jiffies (including, e.g., information queries). `sem_ctime` specifies the time the semaphore value was last changed.

❏ `sem_pending` points to a linked list of pending semaphore operations. The list consists of `sem_queue` instances. `sem_pending_last` is used to quickly access the last element in the list, whereas `sem_pending` points to the start of the list.

Figure 5-2 shows the interplay between the data structures involved.

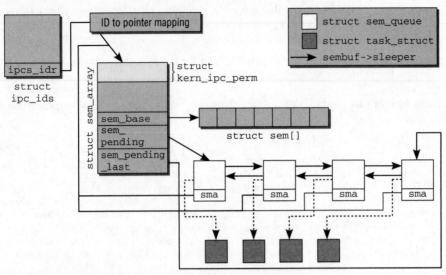

Figure 5-2: Interplay between the semaphore data structures.

Starting from the `sem_ids` instance obtained from the current namespace, the kernel travels via `ipcs_idr` to the ID-to-pointer database and looks up the required instance of `kern_ipc_perm`. The `kern_ipc_perm` entry can be type-cast into an instance of type `sem_array`. The current status of the semaphore is indicated by linking with two further structures.

❑   The pending operations are managed in a linked list of `sem_queue` instances. Processes that are sleeping while waiting for operation execution can also be determined from this list.

❑   An array of `struct sem` instances is used to hold the values of the individual semaphores of the set.

Not shown is the information for managing undo operations because it is not particularly interesting and would complicate matters unnecessarily.

`kern_ipc_perm` is the first element of the data structure for managing IPC objects not only for semaphores but also for message queues and shared memory objects. It enables the kernel to use the same code to check access permissions in all three cases.

Each `sem_queue` element contains a pointer to an array of `sem_ops` instances that describe in detail the operations to be performed on the semaphore. (An array of `sem_ops` instances is used because several operations can be performed on the semaphores in a semaphore set using a single `semctl` call.)

<sem.h>
```
struct sembuf {
        unsigned short  sem_num;        /* semaphore index in array */
        short           sem_op;         /* semaphore operation */
        short           sem_flg;        /* operation flags */
};
```

This definition brings to mind the sample code shown in Section 5.3.2. It is exactly the same data structure used by the program to describe an operation on a semaphore. It holds not only the number of the semaphore in the semaphore set (`sem_num`) but also the desired operation (`sem_op`) and a number of operation flags (`sem_flg`).

Implementing System Calls

All operations on semaphores are performed using a single system call named `ipc`. This call is used not only for semaphores but also to manipulate message queues and shared memory. Its first parameter delegates the actual multiplex work to other functions. These functions are as follows for semaphores:

- ❑ `SEMCTL` performs a semaphore operation and is implemented in `sys_semctl`.

- ❑ `SEMGET` reads the semaphore identifier; `sys_semget` is the associated implementation.

- ❑ `SEMOP` and `SEMTIMEDOP` are responsible for incrementing and decrementing the semaphore value; the latter enables a time-out to be specified.

The use of a single system call to delegate work to multiple other functions is a relic of early days.[10] Some architectures to which the kernel was later ported (e.g., IA-64 and AMD64) dispense with the implementation of the `ipc` multiplexer and use the above "subfunctions" directly as system calls. Older architectures like IA-32 still provide the multiplexer, but individual system calls for the variants have been added during the development of kernel 2.5. Since the implementation is generic, all architectures benefit from this. `sys_semtimedop` offers the functionality of `sys_ipc` for `SEMOP` and `SEMTIMEDOP`, and `sys_semctl` and `sys_semget` are direct implementations of `SEMCTL` and `SEMGET`, respectively.

Notice that the operations that get an IPC object are, however, quickly reunited, as Figure 5-3 illustrates. This is possible because the data structures to manage IPC objects are generic and not dependent on a particular IPC type as described above.

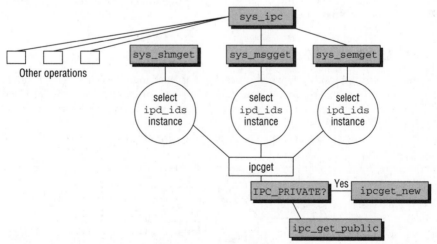

Figure 5-3: The system calls to obtain IPC objects can be unified by a common helper function.

---

[10]The kernel comment "This is really horribly ugly" for `sys_ipc` *does* have a cause.

Permission Checks

IPC objects are protected by the same mechanisms that apply to regular file-based objects. Access rights can be separately specified for the owner of an object, the group, and all other users. Furthermore, the possible rights are reading, writing, and executing. `ipcperms` is responsible for checking if permissions are given for a certain operation on any of the possible IPC objects. It is defined as follows:

ipc/util.c
```
int ipcperms (struct kern_ipc_perm *ipcp, short flag)
{        /* flag will most probably be 0 or S_...UGO from <linux/stat.h> */
         int requested_mode, granted_mode, err;
...
         requested_mode = (flag >> 6) | (flag >> 3) | flag;
         granted_mode = ipcp->mode;
         if (current->euid == ipcp->cuid || current->euid == ipcp->uid)
                 granted_mode >>= 6;
         else if (in_group_p(ipcp->cgid) || in_group_p(ipcp->gid))
                 granted_mode >>= 3;
         /* is there some bit set in requested_mode but not in granted_mode? */
         if ((requested_mode & ~granted_mode & 0007) &&
             !capable(CAP_IPC_OWNER))
                 return -1;
         return security_ipc_permission(ipcp, flag);
}
```

The requested mode (`request_mode`) contains the requested flags bit-triples as a threefold copy. `granted_mode` initially holds the mode bits of the IPC object. Depending on whether the user himself, a member of the group, or someone else wants to perform a specific operation, the contents of `granted_mode` are shifted to the right such that the appropriate bit-triple resides in the low three bits. If the last three bits of `requested_mode` and `granted_mode` disagree, permission is denied accordingly. `securit_ipc_permission` hooks into other security frameworks like SELinux, which are potentially active but need not concern us here.

5.3.3   *Message Queues*

Another way of communicating between processes is to exchange messages. This is done using the message queue mechanism, whose implementation is based on the System V model. There are some commonalities between message queues and semaphores as far as data structures are concerned.

The functional principle of messages queues is relatively simple, as Figure 5-4 shows.

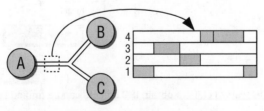

Figure 5-4: Functional principle of System V
message queues.

A process usually referred to as the *sender* generates messages and writes them to a queue, while one or more other processes (logically known as *receivers*) retrieve them from the queue. The individual message elements contain the message text and a (positive) number to implement several types within a message queue. Receivers can retrieve messages on the basis of the number (e.g., they can specify that they will accept only messages with the number 1 or messages up to the number 5). Once a message has been read, the kernel deletes it from the queue. Even if several processes are listening in on a channel, each message can be read by one process only.

Messages with the same number are processed in FIFO order (*first in, first out*). Messages placed on the queue first are retrieved first. However, if messages are read selectively, the FIFO order no longer applies.

> Sender and receiver need not be running at the same time in order to communicate via message queues. For example, a sender process can open a queue, write messages on it, and terminate its work. A receiver process started after the sender has terminated can still access the queue and (by reference to the message number) retrieve the messages intended for it. The messages are held by the kernel in the intervening period.

Message queues are also implemented using a network of data structures similar to those already discussed. The starting point is the appropriate `ipc_ids` instance of the current namespace.

Again, the internal ID numbers are formally associated with `kern_ipc_perm` instances, but as in the semaphore case, a different data type (`struct msg_queue`) is obtained as a result of type conversion. The structure is defined as follows:

```
<msg.h>
struct msg_queue {
        struct kern_ipc_perm q_perm;
        time_t q_stime;                 /* last msgsnd time */
        time_t q_rtime;                 /* last msgrcv time */
        time_t q_ctime;                 /* last change time */
        unsigned long q_cbytes;         /* current number of bytes on queue */
        unsigned long q_qnum;           /* number of messages in queue */
        unsigned long q_qbytes;         /* max number of bytes on queue */
        pid_t q_lspid;                  /* pid of last msgsnd */
        pid_t q_lrpid;                  /* last receive pid */

        struct list_head q_messages;
        struct list_head q_receivers;
        struct list_head q_senders;
};
```

The structure includes status information as well as queue access permissions.

❑ `q_stime`, `q_rtime` and `q_ctime` specify the last send, receive, and change time (if queue properties are changed).

❑ `q_cbytes` specifies the number of bytes currently used by the messages in the queue.

❑ q_qbytes specifies the maximum number of bytes that may be used by the messages in the queue.

❑ q_num specifies the number of messages in the queue.

❑ q_lspid is the PID of the last sender process; q_lrpid is the PID of the last receiver process.

Three standard lists of the kernel are used to manage sleeping senders (q_senders), sleeping receivers (q_receivers), and the messages themselves (q_messages). Each uses its own separate data structures as list elements.

Each message in q_messages is encapsulated in an instance of msg_msg.

ipc/msg.c
```
struct msg_msg {
        struct list_head m_list;
        long  m_type;
        int m_ts;              /* message text size */
        struct msg_msgseg* next;
        /* the actual message follows immediately */
};
```

m_list is used as a list element to link the individual messages; the other elements are used to manage the message itself.

❑ m_type specifies the message type and is used as described to support several types per queue.

❑ m_ts specifies the message text size in bytes.

❑ next is needed to hold long messages requiring more than one memory page.

There is no explicit field in which the message itself is stored. Because (at least) one page is always reserved for each message and the msg_msg instance is held at the beginning of this page, the remaining space can be used to store the message text, as shown in Figure 5-5.

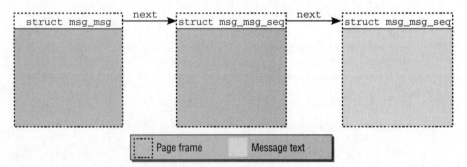

Figure 5-5: Managing an IPC message in memory.

The maximum number of bytes available for the message text in a msg_msg page is calculated by subtracting the size of the structure from the size of a memory page.

ipc/msgutils.c
```
#define DATALEN_MSG     (PAGE_SIZE-sizeof(struct msg_msg))
```

Longer messages must be spread over several pages with the help of the next pointer. This points to an instance of msg_msgseq that is also situated at the beginning of a page, as shown in Figure 5-5. It is defined as follows:

ipc/msgutils.c
```
struct msg_msgseg {
        struct msg_msgseg* next;
        /* the next part of the message follows immediately */
};
```

Again, the message text immediately follows the data structure instance. next is used to enable the message to be spread over any number of pages.

Both sender and receiver processes can go to sleep when communicating via message queues — senders while they are attempting to write a message on a queue whose maximum capacity has already been reached; receivers when they want to retrieve a message from a queue although none has arrived.

Sleeping senders are placed on the q_senders list of msg_queue using the following data structure:

ipc/msg.c
```
struct msg_sender {
        struct list_head list;
        struct task_struct* tsk;
};
```

list is a list element, and tsk is a pointer to the corresponding task structure. No additional information is required because the sender process goes to sleep during the sys_msgsnd system call — which can also be activated via sys_ipc — used to send the message and automatically repeats the send operation when it is woken.

The data structure to hold the receiver process in the q_receivers list is a little longer.

ipc/msg.c
```
struct msg_receiver {
        struct list_head        r_list;
        struct task_struct      *r_tsk;

        int                     r_mode;
        long                    r_msgtype;
        long                    r_maxsize;

        struct msg_msg *volatile r_msg;
};
```

It holds not only a pointer to the corresponding task structure but also the descriptors of the expected message (above all, the message type r_msgtype) and a pointer to a msg_msg instance into which the data are copied if available.

Figure 5-6 illustrates the interplay of the message queue data structures (for the sake of clarity, the list of sleeping senders is not shown).

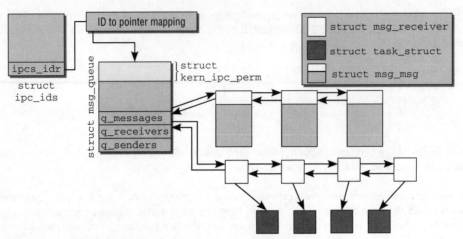

Figure 5-6: Data structures for System V message queues.

5.3.4 Shared Memory

From the user and kernel perspective, *shared memory* — the third and final SysV concept for interprocess communication — uses similar structures for its implementation to the first two mechanisms described above. Its essential aspects do not differ from those of semaphores and message queues.

❑ Applications request an IPC object that can be accessed via a common magic number and a kernel-internal identifier via the current namespace.

❑ Access to memory can be restricted by means of a system of privileges.

❑ System calls are used to allocate memory that is associated with the IPC object and that can be accessed by all processes with the appropriate authorization.

Kernel-side implementation also adopts very similar concepts to those described above. I will therefore make do with a brief description of the data structures shown in Figure 5-7.

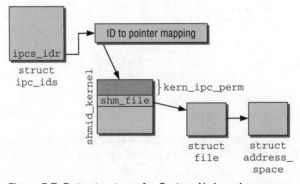

Figure 5-7: Data structures for System V shared memory.

Once again, a combination of kern_ipc_perm and shmid_kernel held in the entries array of the smd_ids global variable is used to facilitate management of the access permissions to the IPC object. A dummy file linked with the corresponding instance of shmid_kernel via shm_file is created for each shared memory object. The kernel uses the pointer smh_file->f_mapping to access the address space object (struct address_space) used to create anonymous mappings as described in Chapter 4. The page tables of the processes involved are set up so that each process is able to access the areas linked with the region.

5.4 Other IPC Mechanisms

There are other traditional ways of exchanging messages and data between processes in addition to the IPC mechanisms adopted from System V UNIX. Whereas the SysV options are primarily of interest to application programmers, practically all users who have ever worked with the shell will know signals and pipes.

5.4.1 Signals

Signals are an older form of communication than the SysV mechanisms. Although they provide fewer options, they are generally very suited to their purpose. The underlying concept is very simple — the kill command sends a signal to a process identified by its PID. The number of the signal is specified using -s sig and is a positive integer whose maximum size varies depending on processor type. The two most frequently used variants of the command are kill without a signal number, which politely requests the process to terminate (the process is free to ignore the signal), and kill -9, which is the equivalent of a signature on an execution warrant (and results in certain death).

In the past, 32-bit systems supported a maximum of 32 signals, but this restriction has now been lifted, and all signals listed on the kill manual page are now supported. Nevertheless, all the "classic" signals occupy the first 32 positions on the list. They are followed by new signals introduced for real-time processes.

Processes must install handler routines to process signals. These are invoked when signals are sent to the processes (but there are several signals such as SIGKILL whose behavior cannot be overridden). If no explicit handler routine is installed, the kernel uses a default handler implementation.

Signals introduce several special features that must always be kept in mind. A process can decide to *block* specific signals (sometimes referred to as the *masking* of signals). If this happens, the signal is ignored until the process decides to remove the block. There is therefore no guarantee that a process will be aware that a signal has been sent to it. When a signal is blocked, the kernel places it on a *pending* list. If the same signal is blocked more than once, only a single occurrence of the signal is placed on the pending list. No matter how many identical signals are sent, the process receives just one occurrence of the signal when it removes the block.

The SIGKILL signal cannot be blocked and cannot be handled by a process-specific handler function. It cannot be overridden because it is the last resort to remove an out-of-control process from the system. This contrasts with the SIGTERM signal, which can be dealt with by a user-defined signal handler — after all, the signal is just a polite request to the process to stop work as soon as possible. If a handler is installed for this signal, the program is, for example, given the opportunity to save data or to ask users whether they really want to exit the program. SIGKILL does not provide such opportunities because the kernel brings the process to an immediate and abrupt end.

The init process is granted a special status. The kernel ignores any SIGKILL signals sent to it. Because this process is of particular importance to the entire system, it may not be forced to terminate — not even unintentionally.

Implementing Signal Handlers

The `sigaction` system call is used to install a new handler function.

```
#include<signal.h>
#include<stdio.h>

/* Handler function */
void handler(int sig) {
  printf("Receive signal: %u\n", sig);
};

int main(void) {
  struct sigaction sa;
  int count;

  /* Initialize the signal handler structure */
  sa.sa_handler = handler;
  sigemptyset(&sa.sa_mask);
  sa.sa_flags = 0;

  /* Assign a new handler function to the SIGTERM signal */
  sigaction(SIGTERM, &sa, NULL);

  sigprocmask(&sa.sa_mask); /* Accept all signals */
  /* Block and wait until a signal arrives */
  while (1) {
    sigsuspend(&sa.sa_mask);
    printf("loop\n");
  }

  return 0;
};
```

If no user-specific handler function is assigned to a signal, the kernel automatically installs predefined functions to provide reasonable standard operations and to deal with the specific situation.

The definition of the field of type `sigaction` used to describe the new handler is platform-specific but has practically the same contents on all architectures.

<asm-*arch*/signal.h>
```
struct sigaction {
        __sighandler_t sa_handler;
        unsigned long sa_flags;
...
        sigset_t sa_mask;                /* mask last for extensibility */
};
```

❑　　　`sa_handler` is a pointer to the handler function invoked by the kernel when a signal arrives.

❑　　　`sa_mask` contains a bitmask with exactly one bit for each signal available in the system. It is used to block other signals during execution of the handler routine. On completion of the routine, the kernel resets the list of blocked signals to its value prior to signal handling.

❑　　　`sa_flags` contains additional flags to specify how the signal must be handled; these are documented in various system programming manuals.

The prototype of functions that act as signal handlers is as follows:

```
<asm-generic/signal.h>
typedef void __signalfn_t(int);
typedef __signalfn_t __user *__sighandler_t;
```

The parameter accepts the number of the signal received so that the same handler function can be installed for different signals.[11]

The signal handler is installed using the `sigaction` system call, which (in our example) replaces the default handler for SIGTERM with the user-defined `handler` function.

Processes can set a global mask to specify which signals are to be blocked while the handler is running. A bit chain is used to indicate that a signal is either blocked (bit value 1) or not blocked (bit value 0). The sample program sets all bit positions to 0 so that all signals sent to the process from the outside can be received while the handler is running.

The last step in the program is to wait for a signal using the `sigsuspend` system call. The process is placed in the blocked state (see Chapter 2) and sleeps until woken by the arrival of a signal; it is then immediately put to sleep again (by the `while` loop). The main code need not concern itself with signal handling because this is done automatically by the kernel in conjunction with the handler function. The approach shown is a good example of how to avoid the deprecated practice of *busy waiting*.[12]

If the SIGTERM signal is sent to the process using `kill`, the process is not terminated as it normally would be; instead, it outputs the number of the received signal (15) and continues to run because, as desired, the signal was forwarded to the user-defined handler routine and not to the default implementation of the kernel.

Implementing Signal Handling

All signal-related data are managed with the help of a linked data structure consisting of several C structures. Its entry point is the `task_struct` task structure, which includes various signal-relevant fields.

```
<sched.h>
struct task_struct {
...
/* signal handlers */
        struct signal_struct *signal;
        struct sighand_struct *sighand;

        sigset_t blocked;
        struct sigpending pending;

        unsigned long sas_ss_sp;
        size_t sas_ss_size;
...
};
```

---

[11] Another version that passes more information exists for handler functions used with POSIX real-time signals.

[12] Instead of repeatedly running through an empty loop to wait for a signal (a senseless waste of CPU time because the process is always running in this approach), the program can happily devote itself to doing nothing without burdening the CPU — the kernel automatically wakes the process when the signal arrives and can use CPU time more profitably in the meantime.

Although signal handling takes place in the kernel, the installed signal handlers run in user mode — otherwise, it would be very easy to introduce malicious or faulty code into the kernel and undermine the system security mechanisms. Generally, signal handlers use the user mode stack of the process in question. However, POSIX mandates the option of running signal handlers on a stack set up specifically for this purpose (using the sigaltstack system call). The address and size of this additional stack (which must be explicitly allocated by the user application) are held in sas_ss_sp and sas_ss_size, respectively.[13]

The sighand element with the following structure is used to manage information on the signal handlers installed. The underlying structure is essentially defined as follows:

<sched.h>
```
struct sighand_struct {
        atomic_t                count;
        struct k_sigaction      action[_NSIG];
};
```

count holds the number of processes that share the instance. As described in Chapter 2, it is possible to specify in the clone operation that parent and child process share the same signal handler so that there is no need to copy the data structure.

The installed signal handlers are held in the action array that has _NSIG elements. _NSIG specifies the number of different signals that can be handled. This figure is 64 on most platforms, but there are exceptions — Mips, for instance, which supports 128 signals.

Each element contains an instance of the k_sigaction structure to specify the properties of a signal as seen by the kernel. On some platforms, the kernel has more information on signal handlers than is available for userspace applications. Normally, k_sigaction has a single element that includes the familiar sigaction structure.

<asm-*arch*/signal.h>
```
struct k_sigaction {
        struct sigaction sa;
};
```

If no user-defined handler routine is installed for a signal (this means that the default routine is used instead), the sa.sa_handler flag is set to SIG_DFL. In this case, the kernel performs one of four standard actions depending on the signal type:

❑ **Ignore** — Nothing happens.

❑ **Terminate** — Terminates the process or process group.

❑ **Stop** — Places the process in the TASK_STOPPED state.

❑ **Core Dump** — Creates a core dump of the address space and writes it to a core file for processing, for example, by a debugger.

---

[13]Signal handlers that use this stack must be installed using the SA_ONSTACK flag. Since this mechanism is rarely used, I will not bother discussing it here.

Table 5-2 shows which signals are assigned to which default handler. The corresponding information can be obtained from the macros SIG_KERNEL_ONLY_MASK, SIG_KERNEL_COREDUMP_MASK, SIG_KERNEL_IGNORE_MASK, and SIG_KERNEL_STOP_MASK in <signal.h>.

Table 5-2: Default Actions for Standard Signals

Action	Signals
Ignore	SIGCONT, SIGCHLD, SIGWINCH, SIGURG
Terminate	SIGHUP, SIGINT, SIGKILL, SIGUSR1, SIGUSR2, SIGALRM, SIGTERM, SIGVTALRM, SIGPROF, SIGPOLL, SIGIO, SIGPWR and all real-time signals.
Stop	SIGSTOP, SIGTSTP, SIGTTIN, SIGTTOU
Core dump	SIGQUIT, SIGILL, SIGTRAP, SIGABRT, SIGBUS, SIGFPE, SIGSEGV, SIGXCPU, SIGXFSZ, SIGSYS, SIGXCPU, SIGEMT

All blocked signals are defined by the blocked element of the task structure. The sigset_t data type used is a bitmask that must contain (at least) as many positions as the number of signals supported. For this purpose, the kernel uses an array of unsigned longs whose size is calculated on the basis of _NSIG and _NSIG_BPW (bits per word).

<asm-*arch*/signal.h>
```
#define _NSIG           64
#define _NSIG_BPW       32
#define _NSIG_WORDS     (_NSIG / _NSIG_BPW)

typedef struct {
        unsigned long sig[_NSIG_WORDS];
} sigset_t;
```

pending is the final task structure element of relevance for signal handling. It creates a linked list of all signals raised and still to be handled by the kernel. The following data structure is used:

<signal.h>
```
struct sigpending {
        struct list_head list;
        sigset_t signal;
};
```

list manages all pending signals in a doubly linked list, while signal, with the bitmask described above, specifies the numbers of all signals still to be handled. The list elements are instances of type sigqueue, which is essentially defined as follows:

<signal.h>
```
struct sigqueue {
        struct list_head list;
        siginfo_t info;
};
```

The individual entries are linked by means of list. The siginfo_t data structure contains more detailed information on the pending signals.

\<asm-generic/siginfo.h>
```
typedef struct siginfo {
        int si_signo;
        int si_errno;
        int si_code;

        union {
          /* Signal-specific information */
          struct { ... } _kill;
          struct { ... } _timer;    /* POSIX.1b timers */
          struct { ... } _rt;       /* POSIX.1b signals */
          struct { ... } _sigchld;
          struct { ... } _sigfault; /* SIGILL, SIGFPE, SIGSEGV, SIGBUS */
          struct { ... } _sigpoll;
        } _sifields;
} siginfo_t;
```

❑   `si_signo` holds the signal number.

❑   `si_errno` has a non-zero value if the signal was raised as a result of an error; otherwise, its value is 0.

❑   `si_code` returns detailed information on the origin of the signal; we are interested only in the distinction between user signal (`SI_USER`) and kernel-generated signal (`SI_KERNEL`).

❑   Additional information needed by the kernel to handle some signals is held in the `_sifield` union. For example, `_sigfault` contains the userspace address of the instruction that raised the signal.

Because a very large number of data structures are used, Figure 5-8 gives an overview of how they are interlinked.

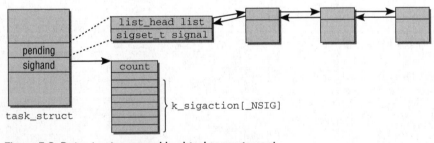

Figure 5-8: Data structures used in signal management.

Implementing Signal Handling

Table 5-3 shows an overview of the most important system calls used by the kernel to implement signal handling. In practice, there are a few more, some for historical reasons, some to ensure compatibility with various standards — above all, POSIX.

Although the signal mechanism appears to be very simple, its implementation is made more complicated by the many subtleties and details that must be taken into account. Because these reveal no significant information on the implementation structure, I will not discuss specific cases but restrict myself to a description of the key mechanisms.

Table 5-3: Some System Calls Relating to Signals

System call	Function
kill	Sends a signal to all processes of a process group.
tkill	Sends a signal to a single process.
sigpending	Checks whether there are pending signals.
sigprocmask	Manipulates a bitmask of blocked signals.
sigsuspend	Sleeps until a specific signal is received.

Sending Signals

Despite their names, kill and tkill send any signal to a process group or to a single process, respectively. As both functions are basically identical,[14] I discuss only sys_tkill, whose code flow diagram is shown in Figure 5-9.

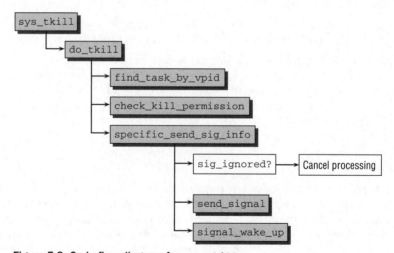

Figure 5-9: Code flow diagram for **sys_tkill**.

---

[14]sys_kill sends the signal to several processes that are interpreted according to the form of the PID passed.

❏   pid > 0 sends the signal to the process with the specified PID.

❏   pid = 0 sends the signal to all members of the process group of the task that sent the signal.

❏   pid = −1 sends the signal to all processes with pid > 1.

❏   pid = −pgrp < −1 sends the signal to all members of the pgrp process group.

Once `find_task_by_vpid` has found the task structure of the target process, the kernel delegates the job of checking whether the process has the permissions needed to send the signal to `check_kill_permission`, which uses the following query:

kernel/signal.c
```
static int check_kill_permission(int sig, struct siginfo *info,
                                  struct task_struct *t)
{
...
        if ((info == SEND_SIG_NOINFO || (!is_si_special(info) && SI_FROMUSER(info)))
                && ((sig != SIGCONT) ||
                    (task_session_nr(current) != task_session_nr(t)))
                && (current->euid ^ t->suid) && (current->euid ^ t->uid)
                && (current->uid ^ t->suid) && (current->uid ^ t->uid)
                && !capable(CAP_KILL))
                    return -EPERM;
...
}
```

It could be helpful to remember that the ^ operator implements an XOR operation, but otherwise the checks are rather straightforward.

The remaining signal handling work is passed on to `specific_send_sig_info`.

❏   If the signal is blocked (this can be checked with `sig_ignored`), handling is aborted immediately to prevent further waste of time.

❏   `send_signal` generates a new `sigqueue` instance (using the cache `sigqueue_cachep`), which is filled with the signal data and added to the sigpending list of the target process.

❏   If the signal is delivered successfully and is not blocked, the process is woken with `signal_wake_up` so that it is available for selection by the scheduler. The `TIF_SIGPENDING` flag is also set to indicate to the kernel that it must deliver signals to the process.

Although the signal is sent after these actions, it does not trigger the signal handler. How this is done is described below.

Processing the Signal Queue

Signal queue processing is not triggered by a system call but is initiated by the kernel each time a switch is made from kernel mode to user mode, as mentioned in Chapter 14. Implementation is naturally very architecture-specific because processing is initiated in the assembly language code of `entry.s`. Regardless of the particular architecture, the ultimate effect of the actions performed is to invoke the `do_signal` function, which, although also platform-specific, behaves in much the same way on all systems.

❏   `get_signal_to_deliver` gathers all information on the next signal to be delivered. It also removes the signal from the process-specific pending list.

❏   `handle_signal` manipulates the user mode stack of the process so that the signal handler is run and not the normal program code after switching from kernel to user mode. This complicated approach is necessary because the handler function may not be executed in kernel mode.

The stack is also modified so that the `sigreturn` system call is invoked when the handler function terminates. How this is done depends on the particular architecture, but the kernel either writes the required machine code instructions to execute the system call directly onto the stack, or uses some glue that is available in userspace.[15] This routine is responsible for restoring the process context so that the application can continue to run when the next switch is made to user mode.

Figure 5-10 illustrates the chronological flow and the various switches between user and kernel mode during signal handler execution.

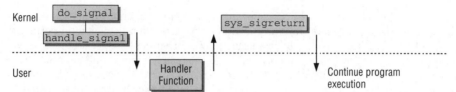

Figure 5-10: Signal handler execution.

5.4.2 Pipes and Sockets

Pipes and sockets are popular interprocess communication mechanisms. I provide only an overview of how both concepts work because both make intense use of other kernel subsystems. Pipes use objects of the virtual filesystem, while sockets use various network functions and also the virtual filesystem.

Shell users are familiar with pipes in command lines such as

```
wolfgang@meitner> prog | ghostscript | lpr -
```

which use the output of one process as input for another process, the pipe being responsible for data transport. As the name suggests, a *pipe* is a connection used to exchange data. One process feeds data into one end of the pipe, and another takes the data out at the other end for further processing. Several processes can be joined together by a series of individual pipes.

When pipes are generated via the shell, there is always one read and one write process. Applications must invoke the pipe system call to generate pipes. The call returns two file descriptors — one for the read end and one for the write end of the pipe. Because both descriptors exist in the same process, the process can initially only send messages to itself, and this is not very practical.

Pipes exist as a data object in process address space — and are retained when a process is duplicated with fork or clone. It is this very characteristic that programs exploit. Once the exec system call has replaced the child process with another program, there is a communication link between two different applications (the pipe descriptors must be directed to standard input and output or the dup system call must be invoked to ensure that the file descriptors are not closed when exec is called).

Sockets are also objects that return a file descriptor when initialized in the kernel and can then be handled as normal files. However, unlike pipes, they can be used bidirectionally and to communicate with remote

---

[15]On IA-32 machines, this glue code can, for instance, be found in the vsyscall page, which is mapped into every user address space. It assists the C standard library in finding the fastest way to perform system calls on a given machine by providing the required machine code instructions. The kernel decides at boot time which method is used best, and maps the page into the address space of each userland process. The page also includes the required code to execute the aforementioned sigreturn system call.

systems connected via a network (this does not mean that they cannot be used to support communication between two processes located on the same system).

Socket implementation is one of the rather more complex parts of the kernel because extensive abstraction mechanisms are needed to hide the details of communication. From a user point of view, there is no great difference whether communication is between two local processes on the same system or between applications running on computers located in different continents. The implementation of this amazing mechanism is discussed in depth in Chapter 12.

During the development of kernel 2.6.26, the architecture-specific implementation of semaphores has been replaced with a generic variant. Naturally, the generic implementation performs slightly less efficient than optimized code, but since semaphores are not in very widespread use across the kernel (mutexes are much more common), this does not really matter. The definition of `struct semaphore` has been moved to `include/linux/semaphore.h`, and all operations are implemented in `kernel/semaphore.c`. Most importantly, the semaphore API has not changed, so existing code will run without modifications.

Another change introduced during the development of kernel 2.6.26 concerns the implementation of spinlocks. Because these locks are by definition supposed to be uncontended in the average case, the kernel did not make any efforts to achieve fairness among multiple waiters, i.e., the order in which tasks waiting for a spinlock to become unlocked are allowed to run after the lock is released by the current holder was undefined. Measurements have, however, shown that this can lead to unfairness problems on machines with a larger number of processors, e.g., 8-CPU systems. Since machines of this kind are not uncommon anymore nowadays, the implementation of spinlocks has been changed such that the order in which multiple waiters are allowed to obtain the lock is the same order in which they arrived. The API was also left unchanged in this case, so existing code will again run without modifications.

5.5   Summary

While systems with more than one CPU were oddities only a few years ago, recent achievements of semiconductor engineering have changed this drastically. Thanks to multi-core CPUs, SMP computers are not only found in specialized niches like number crunching and supercomputing, but on the average desktop. This creates some unique challenges for the kernel: More than one instance of the kernel can run simultaneously, and this requires coordinated manipulation of shared data structures. The kernel provides a whole set of possibilities for this purpose, which I have discussed in this chapter. They range from simple and fast spinlocks to the powerful read-copy-update mechanism, and allow for ensuring correctness of parallel operations while preserving performance. Choosing the proper solution is important, and I have also discussed the need to select an appropriate design that ensures performance by fine-grained locking, but does not lead to too much overhead on smaller machines.

Similar problems as in the kernel arise when userland tasks communicate with each other. Besides providing means that allow otherwise separated processes to communicate, the kernel must also make means of synchronization available to them. I have discussed how the mechanisms originally invented in System V UNIX are implemented in the Linux kernel.

6

Device Drivers

Device drivers are a key area of the kernel as many users judge operating system performance primarily by the number of peripherals for which drivers are available and how effectively they are supported. Consequently, large parts of the kernel sources are devoted to the implementation of device drivers.

Device drivers build on many different mechanisms provided by the central kernel (this is why drivers are sometimes referred to as kernel "applications"). The immense number of drivers in the Linux kernel means that it is impossible to discuss all (or even a few) in detail. Fortunately, this is not necessary. The structures of the drivers are generally very similar — regardless of device — so that in this chapter we need only discuss a few key aspects common to all drivers. Since the objective of this book is to cover all important parts of the kernel, this chapter omits some of the more specific points of driver writing which would require a book of its own. However, two books that focus solely on driver writing are currently available. The classic text in this area is *Linux Device Drivers* by Corbet et al. [CRKH05]. We can recommend it wholeheartedly to anyone interested in or charged with writing a device driver. A recent addition to kernel hackers' bookshelves is *Essential Linux Device Drivers* by Venkateswaran [Ven08]. Developers who are able to read German will certainly also enjoy *Linux Gerätetreiber* by Quade and Kunst [QK06]. The quoted references are complementary to this book. Here, we document *how* the kernel sets up and manages data structures and generic infrastructure for device drivers. Also, we discuss routines that are provided to support device drivers. Device driver books, on the other hand, focus on how to *use* these routines to actually create new drivers, but are not so much interested in how the underlying foundations are implemented.

6.1 I/O Architecture

Communication with peripherals is usually referred to as *input* and *output*, abbreviated I/O in the literature. The kernel must deal with three problem areas when implementing I/O for peripherals. Firstly, the hardware must be addressed using a variety of methods depending on the specific device type and model. Secondly, the kernel must provide user applications and system tools with ways of accessing the various devices. Wherever possible, a uniform scheme should be adopted to keep programming effort within limits and to ensure that applications are able to interoperate regardless of the particular hardware approach. Thirdly, userspace needs to know which devices are available in the kernel.

Communication with peripherals is layered as illustrated in Figure 6-1.

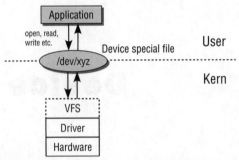

Figure 6-1: Layer model for addressing peripherals.

Access to each individual device is performed via abstraction layers arranged hierarchically. At the bottom of the hierarchy is the device itself, which is attached to other devices and the system CPU by means of a bus system. Communication with the kernel follows this path.

Before we examine the relevant algorithms and structures in the Linux kernel, it is worthwhile taking a brief look at how expansion hardware generally works. For detailed descriptions, readers are referred to hardware-specific publications such as [MD03].

6.1.1 Expansion Hardware

Hardware devices may be attached to the system in various ways; internal slots on the motherboard or external connectors are the most common methods. Of course, expansions can also be accommodated directly on the system board; this method has gained in popularity over the last few years. Whereas in the 80386 era it was quite usual to house the hard disk controller as an expansion board in a special slot on the motherboard, server boards are now commonplace; they are able to accommodate networks, USB, SCSI, graphic cards, and the like without the need for bulky plug-in cards. This trend toward miniaturization is being pushed even further in handhelds and mini-laptops. As far as the kernel is concerned, it generally makes no difference *how* a peripheral is attached to the rest of the system because these details are abstracted from the hardware.

Bus Systems

Even though the spectrum of peripherals — ranging from CD writers, modems, and ISDN boards to cameras and sound cards — may appear to be unlimited, they all share one thing in common. They are not attached directly to the CPU; instead, they are connected via a *bus* that is responsible for communication between the device and the CPU and also between the individual devices. There are numerous ways of implementing buses,[1] most of which are supported by Linux. We list a representative selection below.

❏ **Peripheral Component Interconnect** (PCI) — The main system bus used on many architectures. As such, we will take a closer look at its special features and its implementation in the kernel in the further course of this chapter. PCI devices are placed in slots on the motherboard of the system. Modern versions of the bus also support hotplugging so that devices can be connected and disconnected while the system is running (although this option is rarely used, it is supported in the kernel sources). PCI achieves maximum transfer speeds of a few hundred megabytes per second and thus covers a wide range of application.

❏ **Industrial Standard Architecture** (ISA) — An older bus that (unfortunately) is still in widespread use. Because it is very simple in terms of its electronics, it is easy for electronics enthusiasts or small companies to design and manufacture additional hardware. This was indeed the intention when IBM introduced this bus in the early days of PCs. However, over time it gave rise to more and more problems and has now finally been replaced in more advanced systems. ISA is tied very closely to the particular features of the IA-32 architecture (and to those of its predecessors) but may also be used with other processors.

❏ **SBus** — This is a very advanced bus but already has quite a few years under its belt. It was designed by SUN as a non-proprietary or open bus but was unable to establish a position for itself on other architectures. Even though more recent UltraSparc-based models by SUN are moving more in the direction of PCI, the SBus still plays an important role on older SparcStations and is supported by Linux for this reason.

❏ **IEEE1394** — This is obviously not an easy name to market. This bus is therefore referred to as *FireWire* by some manufacturers and as *I.link* by others. It has several very interesting technical features including planned hotplug capability and the potential for very high transfer rates. IEEE1394 is an external bus used predominantly in laptops of the higher price range to provide a high-speed expansion option.

❏ **Universal Serial Bus** (USB) — This is also an external bus in widespread use and with very high market acceptance. The main features of this bus are its hotplug capability and its ability to detect new hardware automatically. Its maximum speed is only moderate but sufficient for devices such as CD writer, keyboard, and mouse. A new version of the bus (2.0) delivers much faster maximum speeds but is practically unchanged in terms of software (the differences on the hardware level are much more dramatic, but fortunately we needn't bother with them here).

The topology of USB systems is unusual because the devices are not arranged in a single chain but in a tree structure; this fact is noticeable in the way the devices are addressed in the kernel. *USB hubs* are used as nodes to which further devices (and further hubs) can be connected. Another unusual feature of USB is the option of reserving a fixed bandwidth for individual devices; this is an important factor when it is necessary to implement a uniform data stream.

❏ **Small Computer System Interface** (SCSI) — This bus used to be called the *bus for professionals* because of the high cost of the associated peripherals. Because SCSI supports high data throughput, it is used mainly to address hard disks in server systems based on the most varied of

---

[1]To be strictly accurate, buses are used not only to communicate with peripherals but also to exchange data with basic system components such as RAM memory. However, because buses have more to do with hardware and electronics and present no problems to the software and the kernel, I don't discuss them in detail here.

processor architectures. It is rarely used in workstation systems because its electrical installation is very complicated as compared to other buses (each SCSI chain must be terminated in order to function correctly).

❑ **Parallel and Serial Interfaces** — These are present in most architectures regardless of the design of the overall system. These are extremely simple and very slow connections to the outside world and have been with us for an eternity. They are used to address slow devices such as printers, modems, and keyboards that place no great performance demands on the system.

Regardless of the processor architecture employed, systems usually have not just one but a combination of buses. Current PC designs generally include two PCI buses interconnected by a *bridge*. For compatibility reasons, they sometimes also feature an ISA bus (mostly with just one slot). Some buses such as USB or FireWire cannot be operated as main buses but always require a further system bus via which data are passed to the processor. Figure 6-2 shows how different buses are linked in a system.

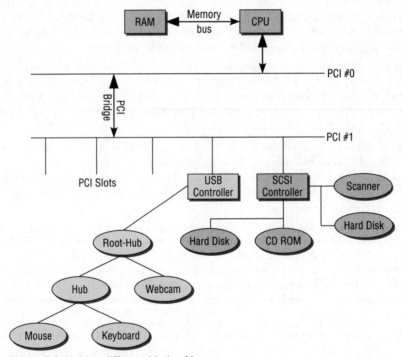

Figure 6-2: Linking different kinds of buses.

Interaction with the Peripherals

Let us turn our attention to the methods that are available to communicate with peripherals. There are several ways of communicating with the hardware attached to the system.

I/O Ports

One option is to use the I/O ports found on IA-32 and many other architectures. In this case, the kernel sends data to an I/O controller. The device for which the data are intended then is identified by means of a unique port number, and the data are forwarded to the attached device for processing. A separate virtual address space managed by the processor is used for the management of all I/O addresses. However, it must also be supported by the remaining system hardware.

> The I/O address space is *not* usually linked with normal system memory. This often gives rise to confusion because ports can also be mapped into memory.

There are different types of ports. Some are Read Only and some are Write Only, but typically they operate bidirectionally so that data can be exchanged in both directions between the processor (and therefore the application and the kernel) and the peripheral.

On IA-32 architectures, the port address space consists of 2^{16} (i.e., approximately 64,000) different 8-bit addresses that are uniquely identified by means of numbers ranging from 0x0 to 0xFFFFH. Each resulting port has a device assigned to it or is unused. It is not possible for several peripherals to share a port.

In view of today's complex technology, 8 bits is not much when it comes to exchanging data with external units. For this reason, it is possible to combine two successive 8-bit ports into a 16-bit port. Furthermore, two successive 16-bit ports (in reality, four successive 8-bit ports) can be regarded as a 32-bit port. The processor features suitable assembler statements to perform input and output operations.

Each processor type implements access to its ports differently. Consequently, the kernel must provide an appropriate abstraction layer. Commands such as outb (to write a byte), outw (to write a word), and inb (to read a byte) are implemented in asm-*arch*/io.h. These are very processor-specific definitions so there is no need to discuss them here.[2]

I/O Memory Mapping

Programmers must address many devices in a similar way to RAM memory. For this reason, modern processors provide the option of *memory mapping* of I/O ports in which the port addresses of a specific peripheral are mapped into normal memory, where they can be manipulated with the same statements used to handle regular memory. Graphic cards typically use this type of operation because it is easier to process extensive image data with normal processor commands than with specific port commands. System buses such as PCI are also often addressed by means of mapped I/O addresses.

To work with memory mappings, I/O ports must first be mapped into regular system memory (using processor-specific routines). Because the methods used to do this differ greatly between the various underlying architectures, the kernel once again provides a small abstraction layer consisting primarily of the ioremap and iounmap commands to map and unmap I/O areas. I don't deal specifically with their implementation.

Polling and Interrupts

Besides the technical details of access to peripheral devices, another question is also interesting. How does the system know whether and when data are ready to be read from a device? There are two ways of finding out — by means of polling or by using interrupts.

Polling is the less elegant alternative, but the strategy behind polling is very simple. The device is repeatedly asked if data are available — when this is the case, the processor then fetches the data. It's more than

---

[2]Nevertheless, the implementation of the I/O functions for IA-32 processors is interesting from a certain point of view because include/asm-i386/io.h delves quite deeply into the pre-processor's box of tricks.

evident that this is not very sparing on resources. Much system run time is needed to check the status of peripherals, to the detriment of more important tasks.

Interrupts are the better alternative. Each CPU provides *interrupt lines* that are shared between the individual system devices (several devices may also share an interrupt but I discuss this below). Each interrupt is identified by a unique number, and the kernel makes a *service routine* available for each interrupt used.

Interrupts suspend normal system work, thus drawing attention to themselves. A peripheral raises an interrupt when data are ready to be processed by the kernel or (indirectly) by an application program. With this method the system need no longer constantly check whether new data are available because it is notified automatically by the peripheral when this is the case.

Interrupt handling and implementation are complex topics whose details are discussed separately in Chapter 14.

Device Control via Buses

Not all devices are addressed directly by I/O statements but via a bus system. How this is done varies according to the bus and devices used. Rather than going into specific details, I describe the basic differences between the various approaches here.

Not all device classes can be attached to all bus systems. For example, it is possible to connect hard disks and CD writers but not graphic cards to an SCSI interface. However, the latter can be housed in PCI slots. In contrast, hard disks must be attached to a PCI bus via another interface (typically IDE).

The different bus types are called *system* and *expansion* buses (I won't bother with their technical details). The differences in hardware implementation are not important for the kernel (and are therefore of no relevance when programming device drivers). Only the way in which the buses and attached peripherals are addressed is relevant.

In the case of the system bus — a PCI bus on many processor types and system architectures — I/O statements and memory mappings are used to communicate with the bus itself and with the devices attached to it. The kernel also provides several commands for device drivers to invoke special bus functions — querying a list of available devices, reading or setting configuration information in a uniform format, and so on — that are platform-independent and that simplify driver development because their code can be used unchanged on various platforms.

Expansion buses such as USB, IEEE1394, and SCSI exchange data and commands with attached devices by means of a clearly defined bus protocol. The kernel communicates with the bus itself via I/O statements or memory mappings[3] and makes platform-independent routines available to enable the bus to communicate with the attached devices.

Communication with bus-attached devices need not be performed in kernel space in the form of a device driver but in some cases may also be implemented from userspace. Prime examples are SCSI writers that are typically addressed by the `cdrecord` tool. This tool generates the required SCSI commands, sends them to the corresponding device via the SCSI bus with the help of the kernel, and processes the information and responses generated and returned by the device.

---

[3]The buses are often plug-in cards in a PCI slot and must be addressed accordingly.

6.2 Access to Devices

Device special files (often referred to as *device files*) are used to access expansion devices. These files are not associated with a data segment on hard disk or on any other storage medium but establish a link with a device driver in order to support communication with the expansion device. As far as the application is concerned, there is little difference between processing regular files and device files. Both are handled by exactly the same library functions. However, for more convenient handling, several additional commands are provided to perform actions on device files that are not possible on regular files.

6.2.1 Device Files

Let us examine the approach adopted by reference to a modem attached to a serial interface. The name of the corresponding device file is /dev/ttyS0. The device is identified not by means of its filename but by means of the major and minor number of the file; these numbers are managed as special attributes in the filesystem.

The same tools used to read and write regular files are employed to write data to or read results from a device file. For instance,

```
wolfgang@meitner> echo "ATZ" > /dev/ttyS0
```

sends an initialization string to a modem connected to the first serial interface.

6.2.2 Character, Block, and Other Devices

The ways in which data are exchanged between peripherals and the system can be classified into several categories. Some devices are better suited to character-oriented exchange because the volumes of data transferred are low. Others are better able to handle data blocks with a fixed number of bytes. The kernel makes a distinction between character and block devices. The former category includes serial interfaces and text consoles, while the latter covers hard disks, CD-ROM devices, and the like.

Identifying Device Files

Both the above types can be distinguished by reference to the properties of their device files. Let us look at some members of the /dev directory.

```
wolfgang@meitner> ls -l /dev/sd{a,b} /dev/ttyS{0,1}
brw-r----- 1 root disk 8,  0 2008-02-21 21:06 /dev/sda
brw-r----- 1 root disk 8, 16 2008-02-21 21:06 /dev/sdb
crw-rw---- 1 root uucp 4, 64 2007-09-21 21:12 ttyS0
crw-rw---- 1 root uucp 4, 65 2007-09-21 21:12 ttyS1
```

In many aspects, the above output is not different from that for regular files, particularly as concerns the access permissions. However, there are two important differences.

❏ The letter preceding the access permissions is either b or c to denote *block* and *character* devices, respectively.

❏ Instead of the file size, two figures are given; these are the *major number* and *minor number*. Together they form a unique number that allows the kernel to find the corresponding device driver.

Names are assigned to device files because users (humans) find it easier to remember symbolic names rather than numbers. However, the actual functionality of a device file is *not* denoted by its name but exclusively by its major and minor number. Neither is the directory in which a device file is located of any relevance. (Nevertheless, a standard way of naming files has been adopted.) mknod is used to create device files. How this is done is described in the standard literature on system administration.

The kernel employs the major and minor numbers to identify the matching driver. The reason why two numbers are used is because of the general structure of a device driver. Firstly, the system may include several devices of the same type that are managed by a single device driver (it wouldn't make sense to load the same code into the kernel more than once). Secondly, devices of the same category can be combined so that they can be inserted logically into the kernel's data structures.

The major number is used to address the device driver itself. For instance, as we can see in the above example, the major number of the first SATA controller on which disks sda and sdb are located is 8. The individual devices of the drive (that is, the primary and secondary disk) are designated by the different minor numbers; 0 for sda and 16 for sdb. Why is there such a big gap between both numbers? Let's look at the remaining files that refer to the sda disk in the /dev directory.

```
wolfgang@meitner> ls -l /dev/sda*
brw-r----- 1 root disk 8,  0 2008-02-21 21:06 /dev/sda
brw-r----- 1 root disk 8,  1 2008-02-21 21:06 /dev/sda1
brw-r----- 1 root disk 8,  2 2008-02-21 21:06 /dev/sda2
brw-r----- 1 root disk 8,  5 2008-02-21 21:06 /dev/sda5
brw-r----- 1 root disk 8,  6 2008-02-21 21:06 /dev/sda6
brw-r----- 1 root disk 8,  7 2008-02-21 21:06 /dev/sda7
```

As you know, individual *partitions* of a disk can be addressed by means of device files /dev/sda1, /dev/sda2, and so on, whereas /dev/sda refers to the *entire* disk. Consecutive minor numbers are used to identify partitions so that the driver is able to distinguish between the different versions. A single driver can reserve more than one major number. If two SATA buses are present in the system, the second SATA channel gets a different major number from the first one.

The division just described also applies for character devices, which are likewise represented by a major and a minor number. For example, the major number of the driver for the serial interface is 4, and the individual interfaces have a minor number from 64 onward.

Each major number is allocated to *both* a block device and a character device. Consequently, the information needed to select the correct driver is not unique unless both the number and the type of the device (block or char) are specified.

In the early days of Linux, major numbers were allocated in a very lax way (at the time, there were only a small number of drivers), but the allocation of major and minor numbers for new drivers is now regulated by a more or less official organization. Drivers that did not use the major numbers registered in this list to identify their devices cannot and are not included in the standard distribution of kernel sources.

The current list can be obtained at http://www.lanana.org. This rather strange-sounding URL stands for *Linux assigned name and numbers authority*. The standard distribution of kernel sources also includes the file `Documentation/devices.txt` with current data at the time of kernel release. Pre-processor constants, which are easier to read than the raw number, are defined in `<major.h>`. The numbers here are synchronized with the assignments in the LANANA list, but not all LANANA-assigned numbers also have a pre-processor symbol. SCSI disks (as required by SATA devices) and TTY devices with major numbers 8 and 4, respectively, are represented by the following pre-processor symbols:

```
<major.h>
...
#define TTY_MAJOR          4
...
#define SCSI_DISK0_MAJOR   8
...
```

Dynamic Creation of Device Files

Traditionally the device nodes in `/dev` were created statically on a disk-based filesystem. With more and more supported devices, more and more entries had to be installed and managed — around 20,000 entries for typical distributions. Most of these entries are not necessary on an average system, which contains only a handful of devices — especially compared to the 20,000 available device nodes. Nearly all distributions have thus switched to managing the contents of `/dev` with udevd, a daemon that allows dynamic device file creation from userland.

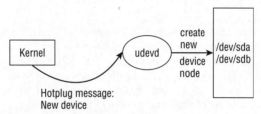

Figure 6-3: Managing device nodes from userspace with udevd.

The basic idea of udevd is depicted in Figure 6-3. Even if the device files are managed from userland, support from the kernel is an absolute necessity: It is impossible to determine which devices are available in the system otherwise.

Whenever the kernel detects a device, a kernel object (`kobject`; see Chapter 1) is created. The object is exported to userland with the help of the sysfs filesystem (see Section 10.3 for more details). Additionally, the kernel sends a hotplug message to userspace, as is discussed in Section 7.4.

When a new device is found during startup or attached at run time (like USB sticks), the hotplug messages generated by the kernel include which major and minor numbers the driver assigns for the device. All the udevd daemon needs to do is listen to these messages. When a new device is registered, the entries in `/dev` are created, and the device can be accessed from userland.

Since the introduction of the udev mechanism, `/dev` is not contained on a disk-based filesystem anymore, but uses tmpfs — a slight variation on the RAM-disk filesystem ramfs. This implies that device nodes are not persistent across system boots. When a device is removed during the downtime, the corresponding device node will not be contained in `/dev` anymore. Since it will also not be created anew — there is no message from the kernel that the device was registered since it is not present in the system anymore — this ensures that no old and obsolete devices files are aggregated in `/dev`. Although nothing would prevent udevd from working on a disk-based filesystem, this would not really make sense.

In addition to the task outlined above, the udev daemon also assumes some more responsibilities like ensuring that device nodes for specific devices always have the same name irrespective of the device topology. For instance, users usually desire to have the same device node for USB sticks independent of when and where they are plugged in. Refer to the manual page udevd(5) for more information on how the udev daemon handles such cases — this is a pure userspace problem and nothing the kernel needs to be concerned about.

6.2.3 Device Addressing Using Ioctls

Even though character and block devices generally fit snugly in the structures of the filesystem and therefore conform to the UNIX philosophy that "everything is a file," some tasks are very difficult to perform using only input and output commands. These involve checking device-specific functions and properties that are not within the general file framework. A prime example is setting the configuration of a device.

If is, of course, possible to carry out such tasks by defining "magic" strings with special meanings and using generic read and write functions. For example, an approach of this kind can be used with a floppy disk drive to support software ejection. The device driver could monitor the data stream to the device and eject the disk from the drive when it encounters the string floppy: eject. Special codes can likewise be defined for other tasks.

This method has one obvious disadvantage. What happens if a text file containing the above string is written to floppy disk (the text may be part of an operating guide for the disk drive)? The driver would eject the disk — to the annoyance of the user because this is not what is wanted. Naturally, it is possible to prevent this situation by having a userspace application check that the string does not appear in the text or by masking it if it does (an appropriate method would also have to be defined to do this too). This whole process is not only a waste of time and resources but lacks elegance and sophistication.[4]

The kernel must therefore provide a way of supporting special device properties without having recourse to normal Read and Write commands. One way of doing this is to introduce special system calls. However, this a deprecated practice among kernel developers and is therefore used only for a few very popular devices. A more appropriate solution goes by the name of *IOCTL*, which stands for *input output control interface* and is a general interface for configuring and modifying specific device characteristics. There's also a third alternative available: Sysfs, a file system that hierarchically represents all devices of the system, and also provides means to set parameters for these devices. More information about this mechanism is contained in Section 10.3. For now, I will stick to the slightly more old-fashioned, but still valid IOCTL method.

Ioctls are implemented by means of a special method that can be used to process files. This method produces the desired results when applied to device files but has no effect when used with regular files. Chapter 8 discusses how the implementation fits into the virtual filesystem schema. All we need to know at this point is that each device driver is free to define an ioctl routine that enables control data to be transferred separately from the actual input/output channel.

How are ioctls employed from a user and programming point of view? The standard libraries provide the ioctl function to direct an ioctl command to an opened file by means of a specific code. The

---

[4]For historical reasons, some drivers do employ this method. It is used widely with terminals to transfer control characters to modify device properties such as text color, cursor position, and so on.

implementation of this function is based on the `ioctl` system call that is handled by `sys_ioctl` in the kernel (see Chapter 13 for information on the implementation of system calls).

fs/ioctl.c
```
asmlinkage long sys_ioctl(unsigned int fd, unsigned int cmd, unsigned long arg)
{
...
}
```

The ioctl code (`cmd`) is passed to an opened file identified by its file descriptor (`fd`) in the form of a more or less easily readable pre-processor constant. A third parameter (`arg`) transfers further information (detailed tables of all ioctls and parameters supported by the kernel are provided in numerous manuals on system programming). Section 6.5.9 discusses the kernel-side implementation of ioctls in more detail.

Network Cards and Other Devices

Character and block devices are not the only device categories managed by the kernel. Network cards occupy a special position in the kernel because they do not fit into this category scheme (Chapter 12 deals extensively with why this is so). This is revealed by the fact that there are no device files for network cards. Instead, user programs must use sockets to communicate with network cards, the sockets being an abstraction layer to provide an abstract view of all network cards. Access takes place by means of the `socketcall` system call invoked by the network-related functions of the standard library to support communication and interaction with the kernel.

There are also other system devices that do not have device files; these are accessed either by specially defined system calls or are simply not accessed from userspace. An example of the latter is all expansion buses such as USB and SCSI. Although these are addressed by a device driver, the corresponding functions are made available within the kernel only (accordingly, USB expansion cards do not have device files via which they can be addressed). It is left to lower-level device drivers to provide functions that are exported into userspace.

6.2.4 Representation of Major and Minor Numbers

For historical reasons, there are two ways of managing the major and minor numbers of a device in a compound data type. During the development of 2.6, a 16-bit integer (typically `unsigned short`) was used to represent major and minor numbers. The integer was split in a 1:1 ratio, that is, 8 bits for the major number and 8 bits for the minor number. This meant that exactly 256 major numbers and 256 minor numbers were possible. This is not sufficient on today's much bigger systems — one need only consider the example of SCSI storage arrays comprising a very large number of hard disks.

The 16-bit integer definition was therefore replaced with a 32-bit integer (`dev_t` is the associated abstract type), but this had certain consequences. It was realized that 16 bits are more than enough for the major numbers. As a result, 12 bits were reserved for the major and 20 for the minor numbers. This gave rise to the following problems.

❑ Many drivers make the incorrect assumption that only 16 bits are available to represent the numbers.

❑ Device file numbers stored on old filesystems use only 16 bits but must still function correctly. The problem of the now non-symmetrical division of bits between major and minor numbers must therefore be resolved.

The first problem can be eliminated by revising the driver, but the second is of a more fundamental nature. To come to terms with the new situation, the kernel uses the division of the userspace-visible device number data type u32 shown in Figure 6-4.

❑ In the kernel itself the bit range 0 — 19, that is, 20 bits are used for the minor number. This leaves 12 bits in the range 20 — 31 for the major number.

❑ When it is necessary to represent a dev_t externally, the 8 bits from the range 0 — 7 are used for the first part of the minor number, the next 12 bits (range 8 — 19) for the major number, and the last 12 bits (range 20 — 31) for the missing part of the minor number.

The old layout consists of 16 bits evenly split between major and minor numbers. If both major and minor are less than 255, the new representation is compatible with the old version.

Code that sticks to these functions to convert between dev_t and external representations will require no changes should the internal data type be changed once more in the future.

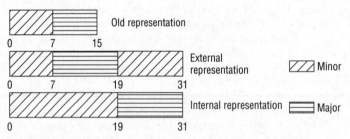

Figure 6-4: Division of a device number into major and minor parts.

The advantage of this split is that the first 16 bits of the data structure can be interpreted as an old device specification; this is important for reasons of compatibility.

The kernel provides the functions/macros listed below (and defined in <kdev_t.h>) to extract information from the u32 representation and convert between u32 and dev_t.

❑ MAJOR and MINOR extract the major and minor number, respectively, from a dev_t.

❑ MKDEV(major, minor) generates a dev_t type from the major and minor numbers.

❑ new_encode_dev converts dev_t to u32 in the external representation mentioned above.

❑ new_decode_dev converts the external representation to dev_t.

❑ old_encode_dev and old_decode_dev switches between a number of type u16, that is, the old representation, and the modern dev_t representation.

The prototypes are as follows.

```
<kdev_t.h>
u16 old_encode_dev(dev_t dev);
dev_t old_decode_dev(u16 val);
u32 new_encode_dev(dev_t dev);
dev_t new_decode_dev(u32 dev);
```

6.2.5   Registration

The kernel has a natural interest in knowing which character and block devices are available in the system, thus a database needs to be maintained. Additionally, an interface for driver writers to submit new entries into the database must be provided.

Data Structures

Let us turn our attention to the data structures used to manage devices.

The Device Database

Although block and character devices can and do behave very differently from each other, the databases employed to keep track of all available devices are identical. This is natural since both block and character devices are identified by a unique device number. Nevertheless, the database keeps track of different objects dependent on whether block or character devices are managed.

❑   Each character device is represented by an instance of struct cdev.

❑   struct genhd is used to manage partitions of block devices and plays a role similar to that of cdev for character devices. This is reasonable since a block device without partitions can also be seen as a block device with a single, large partition!

For now, it is sufficient to know that each block and character device is represented by an instance of the respective data structure. Their contents do not matter here as we will have a closer look at them below. Instead, it is important to see how the kernel keeps track of all available cdev and genhd instances. Figure 6-5 summarizes the situation graphically.

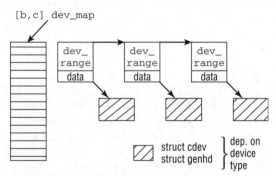

Figure 6-5: Device database to keep track of all block and character devices.

A global array — bdev_map for block and cdev_map for character devices — is used to implement a hash table, which employs the device major number as hash key. Both cdev_map and bdev_map are instances of the same data structure, struct kobj_map. The hashing method is quite simple: major % 255. This works well since currently only a very limited number of devices has major numbers larger than 255, so hash collisions are rare. The definition of struct kobj_map also includes the definition of the hash list elements struct probe.

drivers/base/map.c
```
struct kobj_map {
        struct probe {
                struct probe *next;
                dev_t dev;
                unsigned long range;
                struct module *owner;
                kobj_probe_t *get;
...
                void *data;
        } *probes[255];
        struct mutex *lock;
};
```

The mutex `lock` serializes access to the hash table. The elements of `struct probe` are as follows:

- `next` connects all hash elements in a singly linked list.

- `dev` denotes the device number. Recall that both major and minor numbers are contained in this datum.

- The consecutive range of minor numbers is stored in `range`. The minor numbers associated to the device are thus given by `MINORS(DEV)` + range - 1.

- `owner` points to the module (if any) providing the device driver.

- `get` points to a function that returns the `kobject` instance associated with the device. Usually, this task is rather straightforward, but it may become more involved if device mappers are in use.

- The distinction between block and character devices is made by `data`. For character devices, it points to an instance of `struct cdev`, while `struct genhd` is the pointer destination for block devices.

Character Device Range Database

A second database is for character devices only. It is used to manage device number range allocation to drivers. A driver can either request a dynamic device number, or it can specify a range that is supposed to be acquired. In the first case, the kernel needs to find a free range, while in the second case, it must be ensured that the desired range does not overlap with any existing region.

Again a hash table is employed to keep track of previously allocated device number ranges, and again the major number is used as hash key. The data structure in question looks as follows:

fs/char_dev.c
```
static struct char_device_struct {
        struct char_device_struct *next;
        unsigned int major;
        unsigned int baseminor;
        int minorct;
        char name[64];
        struct file_operations *fops;
        struct cdev *cdev;                      /* will die */
} *chrdevs[CHRDEV_MAJOR_HASH_SIZE];
```

The way entries are organized is quite similar to the techniques employed for struct kobj_map above. next links all elements on the same hash line (major_to_index computes the hash position given a major number). You will have guessed that major specifies the major number, while baseminor is the smallest minor number in a consecutive range of minorct minor numbers. name provides an identifier for the device. Usually, this name is chosen similar to the name of the device special file used for the device, but this is no strict requirement. fops points to the file_operations associated with the device, and cdev provides a link with struct cdev, which is discussed in Section 6.4.1.

Registration Procedures

Now consider how block and character devices are registered.

Character Devices

Registering a block device in the kernel requires two steps:

❑ Register or allocate a range of device numbers. If the driver wants to use a specified range of device numbers, register_chrdev_region must be employed, while alloc_chrdev_region lets the kernel choose an apt range. The prototypes are as follows:

<fs.h>
```
int register_chrdev_region(dev_t from, unsigned count, const char *name)
int alloc_chrdev_region(dev_t *dev, unsigned baseminor, unsigned count,
                        const char *name);
```

When a new range is allocated with alloc_chrdev_region, the smallest minor number and the size of the desired range have to be specified in baseminor and count. The selected major number is returned in dev. Note that struct cdev is *not* required to register or allocate device numbers.

❑ After a device number range has been obtained, the device needs to be activated by adding it to the character device database. This requires initializing an instance of struct cdev with cdev_init, followed by a call to cdev_add. The prototypes of the functions are defined as follows:

<cdev.h>
```
void cdev_init(struct cdev *cdev, const struct file_operations *fops);
int cdev_add(struct cdev *p, dev_t dev, unsigned count);
```

fops in cdev_init contains pointers to the operations that handle the actual communication with the device. count in cdev_add denotes how many minors the device provides.

Observe, for instance, how the FireWire video driver activates a character device (the driver has already registered the major number IEEE1394_VIDEO1394_DEV with 16 minor numbers before).

drivers/ieee1394/video1394.c
```
static struct cdev video1394_cdev;

cdev_init(&video1394_cdev, &video1394_fops);
...
ret = cdev_add(&video1394_cdev, IEEE1394_VIDEO1394_DEV, 16);
```

After cdev_add returns successfully, the device is alive and active.

Since all registration functions discussed above manipulate the database data structures in a straightforward way, I do not bother to discuss their code explicitly.

In ancient times long long ago, the standard registration function for character devices used to be `register_chrdev`. It is still supported for backward compatibility, and quite a number of drivers have not been updated to the new interface as described above. New code, however, should not employ it![5] The function does also not work for device numbers larger than 255.

Block Devices

Registering block devices requires only a single call to `add_disk`. To describe the device properties, an instance of `struct genhd` is required as a parameter; this structure is discussed in Section 6.5.1.

Earlier kernel versions required block devices to be registered using `register_blkdev`, which has the following prototype:

<fs.h>
```
int register_blkdev(unsigned int major, const char *name);
```

`name` is usually identical to the device filename, but can be any arbitrary valid string. Although it is not necessary to call the function anymore today, it is still possible. The benefit is that the block device will show up in `/proc/devices`.

6.3 Association with the Filesystem

With few exceptions, device files are handled by standard functions in the same way as regular files. They are managed in the virtual filesystem discussed in Chapter 8. Both regular files and device files are accessed via an absolutely identical interface.

6.3.1 Device File Elements in Inodes

Each file in the virtual file system is associated with just one inode that manages the file properties. Since the inode data structure is very lengthy, I don't reproduce it in full here but only include the elements relevant to device drivers.

<fs.h>
```
struct inode {
        ...
        dev_t                   i_rdev;
        ...
        umode_t                 i_mode;
        ...
        struct file_operations  *i_fop;
        ...
        union {
...
```

---

[5]When `register_chrdev` is used, no handling of `struct cdev` is necessary since this is automatically managed. The reason is simple: The `cdev` abstraction was not available in the kernel at the time `register_chrdev` was designed, so old drivers cannot know anything about it.

```
                struct block_device *i_bdev;
                struct cdev *i_cdev;
        };
        ...
    };
```

❑ To uniquely identify that device associated with a device file, the kernel stores the file type (block- or character-oriented) in i_mode and the major and minor numbers in i_rdev. These two items of information are combined in the kernel into a single variable of type dev_t.

> The definition of this data type is by no means set in stone but may be modified if kernel developers deem it necessary. For this reason, only the two helper functions imajor and iminor — which expect a pointer to an inode instance as parameter — should be used to extract the major and minor number from i_rdev.

❑ i_fop is a collection of file operations such as open, read, and write used by the virtual filesystem to work with the block device (the exact definition of the structure is given in Chapter 8).

❑ Depending on whether the inode represents a block or a character device, i_bdev or i_cdev point to more specific information, which is discussed further below.

6.3.2 Standard File Operations

When a device file is opened, the various filesystem implementations invoke the init_special_inode function to create the inode for a block or character device file.[6]

fs/inode.c
```
void init_special_inode(struct inode *inode, umode_t mode, dev_t rdev)
{
        inode->i_mode = mode;
        if (S_ISCHR(mode)) {
                inode->i_fop = &def_chr_fops;
                inode->i_rdev = rdev;
        } else if (S_ISBLK(mode)) {
                inode->i_fop = &def_blk_fops;
                inode->i_rdev = rdev;
        }
        else
                printk(KERN_DEBUG "init_special_inode: bogus i_mode (%o)\n",
                        mode);
}
```

The underlying filesystem must return the major and minor numbers of a device in addition to the device type (block or character) passed in mode. The inode is supplied with different file operations depending on device type.

6.3.3 Standard Operations for Character Devices

The situation with character devices is initially very unclear because only a single file operation is made available.

---

[6]For the sake of simplicity, I omit the creation of inodes for sockets and fifos as these are not relevant in this context.

fs/devices.c
```
struct file_operations def_chr_fops = {
        .open = chrdev_open,
};
```

Character devices differ considerably. The kernel cannot therefore initially provide more than one operation because each device file requires a separate, custom set of operations. The main task of the `chrdev_open` function is therefore to fill the structure with the missing function pointers appropriate to the opened device so that meaningful operations can be performed on the device file and ultimately on the device itself.

6.3.4   Standard Operations for Block Devices

Block devices conform to a much more uniform scheme. This allows the kernel to provide a much larger selection of operations right from the start. These are grouped together in a general structure called `blk_fops`.

fs/block_dev.c
```
const struct file_operations def_blk_fops = {
        .open           = blkdev_open,
        .release        = blkdev_close,
        .llseek         = block_llseek,
        .read           = do_sync_read,
        .write          = do_sync_write,
        .aio_read       = generic_file_aio_read,
        .aio_write      = generic_file_aio_write_nolock,
        .mmap           = generic_file_mmap,
        .fsync          = block_fsync,
        .unlocked_ioctl = block_ioctl,
        .splice_read    = generic_file_splice_read,
        .splice_write   = generic_file_splice_write,
};
```

Read and write operations are performed by generic kernel routines. The caches generally present in the kernel are used automatically for block devices.

> `file_operations` must not be used with `block_device_operations` although both are similarly structured. Although `file_operations` is used by the VFS layer to communicate with userspace, the routines it contains invoke the functions in `block_device_operations` to implement communication with the block device. The `block_device_operations` must be implemented specifically for each block device to abstract the device properties, but the same `file_operations` that build on these can be used for all block devices.

In contrast to character devices, block devices are not fully described by the above data structures, because access to block devices is not performed in response to each individual request but is efficiently managed by a refined and complex system of caches and request lists. The caches are operated predominantly by general kernel code, but the request lists are managed by the block device layer. When I discuss possible block device driver operations at greater length, you will see further structures used to manage the request queue, which collects and arranges statements addressed to the relevant device.

6.4   Character Device Operations

The hardware of character devices is usually very simple, and, not surprisingly, the associated drivers are not very difficult to implement.

6.4.1   Representing Character Devices

Recall that character devices are represented by struct cdev. We have seen how the kernel keeps a database of all active cdev instances, but have not yet looked into the content of the structure. It is defined as follows:

```
<cdev.h>
struct cdev {
        struct kobject kobj;
        struct module *owner;
        const struct file_operations *ops;
        struct list_head list;
        dev_t dev;
        unsigned int count;
};
```

kobj is a kernel object embedded in the structure. As usual, it is used for general management of the data structure. owner points to the module (if any) that provides the driver, and ops is a list of file operations that implement specific operations to communicate with the hardware. dev specifies the device number, and count denotes how many minors are associated with the device. list allows for implementing a list of all inodes that represent device special files for the device.

Initially, the file operations for character devices are limited to just a single method for opening the associated device file (always the first action when using a driver). Logically, let's examine this method first.

6.4.2   Opening Device Files

chrdev_open from fs/devices.c is the generic function for opening character devices. Figure 6-6 shows the associated code flow diagram.

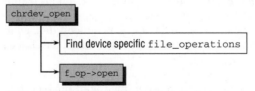

Figure 6-6: Code flow diagram for chrdev_open.

Assume that the inode that represents the device file has not been opened before. Given the device number, kobject_lookup queries the character device database introduced in Section 6.2.5 and returns the kobject instance associated with the driver. This, in turn, allows for obtaining the cdev instance.

With the `cdev` instance for the device in hand, the kernel also has access to the device-specific `file_operations` via cdev->ops. Various connections between data structures are then set up like Figure 6-7.

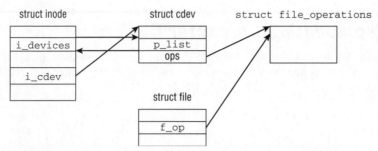

Figure 6-7: Relations between data structures for the representation of character devices.

❑   inode->i_cdev points to the selected `cdev` instance. When the inode is opened next time, the character device database need not be queried *anymore* because the cached value can be used.

❑   The inode is added to cdev->list (i_devices is used as the list element in the inode).

❑   file->f_ops, that is, the file_operations for struct file, are set to point to the file_operations instance given by struct cdev.

The (now device-specific) open method of the new `file_operations` from `struct file` is then invoked to carry out the required initialization tasks on the device (some peripherals need to negotiate operating details by means of handshaking before they are used for the first time). The function can also be used to make the data structure changes needed for a specific minor number.

Let us consider the example of a character device with major number 1. According to the LANANA standard, this device has 10 different minor numbers; each provides a different function each provides a different function, each of which relates to memory access operations. Table 6-1 lists a few minor numbers together with the associated filenames and functions.

Some devices will be familiar, particularly the /dev/null device. Without going into the details of the individual minor numbers, it is clear from the device descriptions that there are considerable differences between the functions implemented, even though they are all concerned with memory access. It is therefore not surprising that, again, only a single function pointer is defined in the `file_operations` structure of the `chrdevs` entry; open points to memory_open after one of the above files has been opened.

The procedure is defined in drivers/char/mem.c and implements a dispatcher that distinguishes between the individual devices by reference to the minor number and selects the appropriate `file_operations`. Figure 6-8 illustrates how the file operations change when a memory device is opened.

The functions gradually reflect the special features of the device. Initially, only the general procedure for opening character devices is known. This is then replaced by a special procedure to open the memory-related device files. The function pointers are then refined even further depending on the minor number selected. The end products do not necessarily use identical functions, as the examples of `null_fops` (for `/dev/null`) and `random_fops` (for `/dev/random`) demonstrate.

Table 6-1: Minor Numbers for Major 1 (Memory Access).

Minor	File	Description
1	/dev/mem	Physical memory
2	/dev/kmem	Virtual kernel address space
3	/dev/null	Bit bucket
4	/dev/port	Access to I/O ports
5	/dev/zero	Source for null characters
8	/dev/random	Non-deterministic random generator

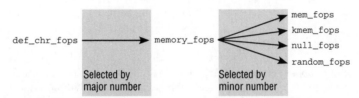

Figure 6-8: File operations when memory devices are opened.

drivers/char/mem.c
```
static struct file_operations null_fops = {
        .llseek         = null_lseek,
        .read           = read_null,
        .write          = write_null,
        .splice_write   = splice_write_null,
};
```

drivers/char/random.c
```
struct file_operations random_fops = {
        .read           = random_read,
        .write          = random_write,
        .poll           = random_poll,
        .ioctl          = random_ioctl,
};
```

The same approach is adopted for other device types. A specific set of file operations is first installed on the basis of the major number. These operations can then be replaced by other operations selected according to the minor number.

6.4.3   *Reading and Writing*

The actual work of reading from and writing to character device files is not an especially interesting task because of the links already established between the virtual file and the device driver code. Calling the read and write operations of the standard library issues the system calls discussed in Chapter 8 to ultimately invoke the relevant operations (primarily read and write) in the file_operations structure. The specific implementation of these methods varies according to device and cannot be generalized.

The above memory devices have it easy because they need not bother with interaction with concrete peripherals but simply invoke other kernel functions to do their work for them.

For example, the /dev/null device uses the read_null and write_null procedures to implement read and write operations on the bit bucket. A quick look at the kernel sources will confirm that the implementation of these functions is really *very* simple.

drivers/char/mem.c
```
static ssize_t read_null(struct file * file, char __user * buf,
                         size_t count, loff_t *ppos)
{
        return 0;
}

static ssize_t write_null(struct file * file, const char __user * buf,
                          size_t count, loff_t *ppos)
{
        return count;
}
```

Reading from the null device returns nothing, and this is easy to implement; the result returned is a data stream with a length of 0 bytes. Data written to the device are simply ignored, but a successful write operation is reported for data of any length.

More complicated character devices supply functions that read and write meaningful results. The generic mechanism, however, is unchanged.

6.5   Block Device Operations

Block devices account for the second large group of peripherals supported via the VFS interface of the kernel. Unfortunately, the situation faced by block device drivers is more complicated than that for character devices. This is caused by a range of circumstances, above all by the need for continuous speed adjustment occasioned by the design of the block device layer, by the way in which block devices work, and by the historical development of the block device layer.

Block devices differ fundamentally from character devices in three principle areas.

❑   Access can be performed at any point within the data. This can but need not be the case with character devices.

❑   Data are always transferred in fixed-size blocks. Even if a single byte is requested, the device driver must always fetch a complete block from the device. In contrast, character devices are able to return individual bytes.

❑   Accesses to block devices are massively cached; that is, read data are kept in memory and are accessed from there if they are needed again. Write operations are also delayed by using caches.

This makes no sense on character devices (such as keyboards); each read request must be satisfied by genuine interaction with the device.

We use two terms repeatedly below — block and sector. A *block* is a byte sequence of a specific size used to hold data transferred between the kernel and a device; the size of the block can be modified by software means. A *sector* is a fixed hardware unit and specifies the smallest amount of data that can be transferred by a device. A block is nothing more than a sequence of successive sectors; consequently, the block size must always be an integer multiple of the sector size. As a sector is a hardware-specific constant, it is also used to specify the position of a data block on a device. The kernel regards each block device as a linear list of integer-numbered sectors or blocks.

Today, almost all common block devices have a sector size of 512 bytes, which equates to a block size of 512, 1,024, 2,048 or 4,096. It should, however, be noted that the maximum block size is limited by the memory page size of the particular architecture. IA-32 systems support a maximum block size of 4,096 bytes because the memory page size is 4,096 bytes. On the other hand, IA-64 and Alpha systems are able to handle blocks with 8,192 bytes.

The relative freedom of choice with regard to block size has advantages for many block device applications as you will see when examining, for example, how filesystems are implemented. Filesystems may divide the hard disk into blocks of different sizes in order to optimize performance when many small files or few large files are involved. Implementation is made much easier because the filesystem is able to match the transfer block size to its own block size.

The block device layer is not only responsible for addressing the block devices but also for carrying out other tasks to enhance the performance of all block devices in the system. Such tasks include the implementation of *readahead* algorithms that read data from a block device speculatively in advance when the kernel assumes that the data will be required shortly by an application program.

The block device layer must provide buffers and caches to hold the readahead data if they are not required immediately. Such buffers and caches are not reserved solely for readahead data but are also used to temporarily store frequently needed block device data.

The list of tricks and optimizations performed by the kernel when addressing block devices is long and beyond the scope of this chapter. What is more important is to sketch the various components of the block device layer and demonstrate how they interact.

6.5.1   Representation of Block Devices

Block devices have a set of characteristic properties managed by the kernel. The kernel uses what is known as *request queue management* to support communication with devices of this kind as effectively as possible. This facility enables requests to read and write data blocks to be buffered and rearranged. The results of requests are likewise kept in caches so that the data can be read and reread in a very efficient way. This is useful when a process repeatedly accesses the same part of a file or when different processes access the same data in parallel.

A comprehensive network of data structures as described below is needed to perform these tasks. Figure 6-9 shows an overview of the various elements of the block layer.

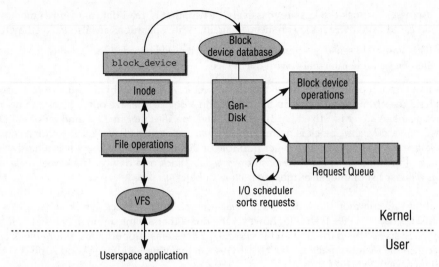

Figure 6-9: Overview of the block device layer.

Raw block devices are represented by struct block_device, which I discuss further below. Since this structure is managed in an interesting way by the kernel, we need to take a close look at this first.

By convention, the kernel stores the block_device instance associated with a block device immediately in front of the block device's inode. This behavior is implemented by the following data structure:

fs/block_dev.c
```
struct bdev_inode {
        struct block_device bdev;
        struct inode vfs_inode;
};
```

All inodes that represent block devices are kept on the bdev pseudo-filesystem (see Section 8.4.1), which is not visible to userland. This allows for using standard VFS functions to work with the collection of block device inodes.

In particular, this is exploited by the auxiliary function bdget. Given a device number represented by a dev_t, the function searches through the pseudo-filesystem to see if a corresponding inode already exists and returns a pointer to it. Thanks to struct bdev_inode, this immediately allows for finding the block_device instance for the device. If the inode does not yet exist because the device has not been opened before, bdget and the pseudo-filesystem automatically ensure that a new bdev_inode is allocated and set up properly.

In contrast to the character device layer, the block device layer provides comprehensive queueing functions as demonstrated by the *request queue* associated with each device. Queues of this kind are the reason for most of the complexity of the block device layer. As Figure 6-9 shows, the individual array entries (in simplified form) contain pointers to various structures and procedures whose most important elements are as follows:

❑ A wait queue to hold both read and write requests to the device.

❑ Function pointers to the I/O scheduler implementation used to rearrange requests.

❏ Characteristic data such as sector and block size or device capacity.

❏ The *generic hard disk* abstraction genhd that is available for each device and that stores both partitioning data and pointers to low-level operations.

Each block device must provide a probe function that is registered with the kernel either directly by means of register_blkdev_range or indirectly via the gendisk object discussed below using add_disk. The function is invoked by the filesystem code to find the matching gendisk object.

Read and write requests to block devices do not immediately cause the corresponding operations to be executed. Instead, they are collected and transferred to the device later in a kind of concerted action. For this reason, no specific functions to perform the read and write operations are held in the file_operations structure for the corresponding device files. Instead, they contain generic versions such as generic_read_file and generic_write_file, which are discussed in Chapter 8.

What is remarkable is that *exclusively* generic functions are used — a distinctive feature of block devices. In character devices these functions are represented by driver-specific versions. All hardware-specific details are handled when requests are executed; all other functions work with an abstracted queue and receive their results from buffers and caches that do not interact with the underlying device until it is absolutely necessary. The path from the read or write system call to actual communication with a peripheral device is therefore long and complex.

6.5.2 Data Structures

Until now, I have only gently touched the data structures required to represent block devices within the kernel. Now I am going to dissect them in detail.

Block Devices

The core properties of a block device are represented by — the name says it all — struct block_device. Let us discuss this structure first and afterward examine how it fits into a network with various other structures.

```
<fs.h>
struct block_device {
        dev_t bd_dev; /* not a kdev_t - it's a search key */
        struct inode * bd_inode; /* will die */
        int bd_openers;
    ...
        struct list_head bd_inodes;
        void * bd_holder;
    ...
        struct block_device * bd_contains;
        unsigned bd_block_size;
        struct hd_struct * bd_part;

        unsigned bd_part_count;
        int bd_invalidated;
        struct gendisk * bd_disk;
        struct list_head bd_list;
    ...
        unsigned long bd_private;
};
```

❑ The device number for the block device is stored in bd_dev.[7]

❑ A link back to the inode that represents the block device in the bdev pseudo-filesystem is given by bd_inode (basically, this could also be obtained using bdget, so the information is redundant, and the field will be removed in a future kernel version).

❑ bd_inodes heads a list of all inodes that represent device special files for the block device.

> **These inodes represent regular files and must not be confused with the bdev inode, which represents the block device itself!**

❑ bd_openers counts how often the block device has been opened with do_open.

❑ bd_part points to a specialized data structure (struct hd_struct) that represents the partition contained on the block device. I will come back to this representation in a moment.

❑ bd_part_count does *not* count the number of partitions as could be assumed. Instead, it is a usage count that states from how many places in the kernel partitions within the device have been referenced.

This is necessary when partitions are rescanned with rescan_partitions: If bd_part_count is greater than zero, rescanning is refused because the old partitions are still in use.

❑ bd_invalidated is set to 1 if the partition information in the kernel is invalid because it has changed on disk. Next time the device is opened, the partition tables will be rescanned.

❑ bd_disk provides another abstraction layer that also allows for partitioning hard disks. This mechanism is examined in the following section.

❑ bd_list is a list element that allows for keeping track of all block_device instances available in the system. The list is headed by the global variable all_bdevs. This allows for iterating over all block devices without querying the block device database.

❑ bd_private can be used to store holder-specific data with each block_device instance.

> As the term holder-specific implies, only the current holder of the block_device instance may use bd_private. To become a holder, bd_claim needs to be successfully called on the block device. bd_claim is successful if bd_holder is a NULL pointer, that is, if no holder is yet registered. In this case, bd_holder points to the current holder, which can be an arbitrary address in kernel space. Calling bd_claim signalizes to other parts of the kernel that they essentially do not have any business with the block device anymore.

There are no fixed rules on which part of the kernel can hold a block device. The Ext3 filesystem, for instance, claims the block device which represents an external journal of a mounted filesystem, and the superblock is registered as a holder. If a partition is used as a swap space, then the swapping code holds the partition after it is activated with the swapon system call.

---

[7]The comment on data type kdev_t is included for historical reasons. When development work started on 2.6 the kernel used two different data types (dev_t and kdev_t) to represent device numbers inside and outside the kernel.

When a block device is opened for using `blkdev_open` and exclusive use is requested as discussed in Section 6.5.4, the `file` instance associated with the device file claims the block device.

It is interesting to observe that there are currently no users of `bd_private` field in the kernel sources. The `bd_claim` mechanism, however, is still useful even if no holder needs to associate private data with a block device currently.

A block device is released with `bd_release`.

Generic Hard Disks and Partitions

While `struct block_device` represents a block device toward the device driver level, another abstraction emphasizes the connection with generic kernel data structures. From this point of view, the block devices by themselves are not interesting. Instead, the notion of a hard disk, possibly with subpartitions, is more useful. The partition information on a device is independent of the `block_device` instances that represent the partitions. Indeed, when a disk is added to the system, the kernel reads and analyzes the partition information on the underlying block device but does not create the `block_device` instances for the individual partitions. For these reasons, the kernel uses the following data structure to provide a representation for generic partitioned hard disks (some fields related to statistics bookkeeping have been omitted):

<genhd.h>
```
struct gendisk {
        int major;                         /* major number of driver */
        int first_minor;
        int minors;                        /* maximum number of minors, =1 for
                                            * disks that can't be partitioned. */
        char disk_name[32];                /* name of major driver */
        struct hd_struct **part;           /* [indexed by minor] */
        int part_uevent_suppress;
        struct block_device_operations *fops;
        struct request_queue *queue;
        void *private_data;
        sector_t capacity;
        int flags;
        struct device *driverfs_dev;
        struct kobject kobj;
...
};
```

❑   `major` specifies the major number of the driver; `first_minor` and `minors` indicate the range within which minor numbers may be located (we already know that each partition is allocated its own minor number).

❑   `disk_name` gives a name to the disk. It is used to represent the disk in sysfs and in `/proc/partitions`.

❑   `part` is an array consisting of pointers to `hd_struct`, whose definition is given below. There is one entry for each disk partition.

❑   If `part_uevent_suppress` is set to a positive value, no hotplug events are sent to userspace if changes in the partition information of the device are detected. This is only used for the initial partition scan that occurs before the disk is fully integrated into the system.

❑ `fops` is a pointer to device-specific functions that perform various low-level tasks. I discuss these below.

❑ `queue` is needed to manage request queues, which I discuss below.

❑ `private_data` is a pointer to private driver data not modified by the generic functions of the block layer.

❑ `capacity` specifies the disk capacity in sectors.

❑ `driverfs_dev` identifies the hardware device to which the disk belongs. The destination is an object of the driver model, which is discussed in Section 6.7.1.

❑ `kobj` is an integrated `kobject` instance for the generic kernel object model as discussed in Chapter 1.

For each partition, there is an instance of `hd_struct` to describe the key data of the partition within the device. Again, I present a slightly simplified version of the data structure to focus on the essential features.

\<genhd.h\>
```
struct hd_struct {
        sector_t start_sect;
        sector_t nr_sects;
        struct kobject kobj;
...
};
```

`start_sect` and `nr_sects` define the start sector and the size of the partition on the block device, thus describing the partition uniquely (for the sake of brevity, other elements used for statistical purposes are omitted). `kobj` associates the object with the generic object model, as usual.

The `parts` array is filled by various routines that examine the partition structure of the hard disk when it is registered. The kernel supports a large number of partitioning methods to support coexistence with most other systems on many architectures. I won't bother describing how they are implemented because they differ only in the details of how information is read from disk and analyzed.

> **Although `gendisks` represent partitioned disks, they can as well represent devices without any partitions.**

It is also important to note that instances of `struct gendisk` may not be individually allocated by drivers. Instead, the auxiliary function `alloc_disk` must be used:

\<genhd.h\>
```
struct gendisk *alloc_disk(int minors);
```

Given the number of minors for the device, calling this function automatically allocates the `genhd` instance equipped with sufficient space for pointers to `hd_structs` of the individual partitions.

Only memory for the pointers is added; the partition instances are only allocated when an actual partition is detected on the device and added with `add_partition`.

Additionally, `alloc_disk` integrates the new disk into the device model data structures.

Consequently, `gendisks` must not be destroyed by simply `freeing` them. Use `del_gendisk` instead.

Connecting the Pieces

The previously introduced data structures — struct block_device, struct gendisk, and struct hd_struct — are directly connected with each other. Figure 6-10 shows how.

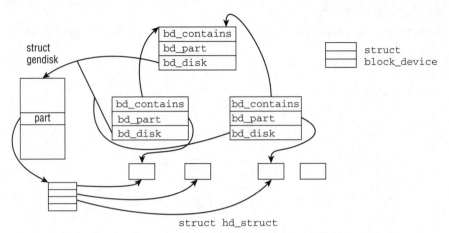

Figure 6-10: Connection between block devices, generic hard disks, and partitions.

For each partition of a block device that has already been opened, there is an instance of struct block_device. The objects for partitions are connected with the object for the complete device via bd_contains. All block_device instances contain a link to their generic disk data structure gen_disk via bd_disk. Note that while there are multiple block_device instances for a partitioned disk, one gendisk instance is sufficient.

The gendisk instance points to an array with pointers to hd_structs. Each represents one partition. If a block_device represents a partition, then it contains a pointer to the hd_struct in question — the hd_struct instances are shared between struct gendisk and struct block_device.

Additionally, generic hard disks are integrated into the kobject framework as shown in Figure 6-11. The block subsystem is represented by the kset instance block_subsystem. The kset contains a linked list on which the embedded kobjects of each gendisk instance are collected.

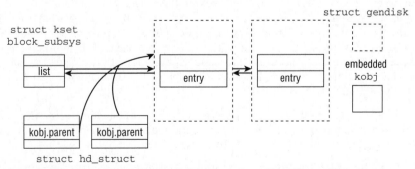

Figure 6-11: Integration of generic hard disks with the generic kernel object framework.

Partitions represented by `struct hd_struct` also contain an embedded `kobject`. Conceptually, partitions are subelements of a hard disk, and this is also captured in the data structures: The `parent` pointer of the `kobject` embedded in every `hd_struct` points to the `kobject` of the generic hard disk.

Block Device Operations

Operations specific to a class of block devices are collected in the following (slightly simplified) data structure:

```
<fs.h>
struct block_device_operations {
        int (*open) (struct inode *, struct file *);
        int (*release) (struct inode *, struct file *);
        int (*ioctl) (struct inode *, struct file *, unsigned, unsigned long);
...
        int (*media_changed) (struct gendisk *);
        int (*revalidate_disk) (struct gendisk *);
...
        struct module *owner;
};
```

`open`, `release` and `ioctl` have the same meaning as the equivalent functions in `file_operations` and are used to open and close files, and to send special commands to a block device.

> **The functions are not invoked directly by the VFS code but indirectly by the operations contained in the standard file operations for block devices, `def_blk_fops`.**

The remaining elements of `block_device_operations` list the options available only to block devices.

❏ `media_changed` checks whether the storage medium has been changed as can happen with devices such as floppy disks and ZIP drives (hard disks do not usually support this function because they cannot normally be exchanged …). The routine is provided for internal use in the kernel to prevent inconsistencies owing to careless user interaction. Data loss is inevitable if a floppy disk is removed from the drive without first having been unmounted and if the data in the cache have not been synchronized with the contents on the disk in the meantime. The situation is even worse if a user removes a floppy disk whose changes have not yet been written back and inserts a new floppy with different contents. When writeback finally takes place, the contents of the new floppy are destroyed or at least severely compromised — this should be prevented at all costs because it compounds the fact that the data on the first floppy have already been lost. The kernel can, indeed, prevent such loss by invoking `check_media_change` at the appropriate points in the code.

❏ As its name suggests, `revalidate_disk` is called to revalidate the device. Currently, this is only necessary when an old medium is removed and replaced with a new medium without first performing a correct unmount followed by a new mount.

The `owner` field holds a pointer to a module structure in memory if the driver is implemented as a module. Otherwise, it contains a `NULL` pointer.

Request Queues

Read and write requests to block devices are placed on a queue known as a *request queue*. The `gendisk` structure includes a pointer to the device-specific queue, which is represented by the following data type.

```
<blkdev.h>
struct request_queue
{
        /*
         * Together with queue_head for cacheline sharing
         */
        struct list_head        queue_head;
        struct list_head        *last_merge;
        elevator_t              elevator;
        struct request_list     rq;             /* Queue request freelists */

        request_fn_proc         *request_fn;
        make_request_fn         *make_request_fn;
        prep_rq_fn *prep_rq_fn;
        unplug_fn *unplug_fn;
        merge_bvec_fn *merge_bvec_fn;
        prepare_flush_fn *prepare_flush_fn;
        softirq_done_fn *softirq_done_fn;
  ...


        /*
         * Auto-unplugging state
         */
        struct timer_list       unplug_timer;
        int                     unplug_thresh;  /* After this many requests */
        unsigned long           unplug_delay;   /* After this many jiffies */
        struct work_struct      unplug_work;

        struct backing_dev_info backing_dev_info;
  ...
        /* queue needs bounce pages for pages above this limit */
        unsigned long           bounce_pfn;
        int                     bounce_gfp;

        unsigned long           queue_flags;

        /* queue settings */
        unsigned long           nr_requests;    /* Max # of requests */
        unsigned int            nr_congestion_on;
        unsigned int            nr_congestion_off;
        unsigned int            nr_batching;

        unsigned short          max_sectors;
        unsigned short          max_hw_sectors;
        unsigned short          max_phys_segments;
        unsigned short          max_hw_segments;
        unsigned short          hardsect_size;
        unsigned int            max_segment_size;
};
```

queue_head is the central list head used to construct a doubly linked list of requests — each element is of the data type request discussed below and stands for a request to the block device to read or fetch data. The kernel rearranges the list to achieve better I/O performance (several algorithms are provided to perform I/O scheduler tasks as described below). As there are various ways of resorting requests, the elevator element[8] groups the required functions together in the form of function pointers. I shall come back to this structure further below.

rq serves as a cache for request instances. struct request_list is used as a data type; in addition to the cache itself, it provides two counters to record the number of available free input and output requests.

The next block in the structure contains a whole series of function pointers and represents the central request handling area. The parameter settings and return type of the function are defined by typedef macros (struct bio manages the transferred data and is discussed below).

```
<blkdev.h>
typedef void (request_fn_proc) (struct request_queue *q);
typedef int (make_request_fn) (struct request_queue *q, struct bio *bio);
typedef int (prep_rq_fn) (struct request_queue *, struct request *);
typedef void (unplug_fn) (struct request_queue *);

typedef int (merge_bvec_fn) (struct request_queue *, struct bio *, struct bio_vec *);
typedef void (prepare_flush_fn) (struct request_queue *, struct request *);
typedef void (softirq_done_fn)(struct request *);
```

The kernel provides standard implementations of these functions that can be used by most device drivers. However, each driver must implement its own request_fn function because this represents the main link between the request queue management and the low-level functionality of each device — it is invoked when the kernel processes the current queue in order to perform pending read and write operations.

The first four functions are responsible to manage the request queue:

❑ request_fn is the standard interface for adding new requests to the queue. The function is automatically called by the kernel when the driver is supposed to perform some work like reading data from or writing data to the underlying device. In kernel nomenclature, this function is also referred to as *strategy routine*.

❑ make_request_fn creates new requests. The standard kernel implementation of this function adds the request to the request list as you will see below. When there are enough requests in the list, the driver-specific request_fn function is invoked to process them together.

The kernel allows device drivers to define their own make_request_fn functions because some devices (RAM disks, for example) do not make use of queues as data can be accessed in any sequence without impairing performance, or they might know better than the kernel how to deal with requests and would not benefit from the standard methods (volume managers, for example). However, this practice is rare.

❑ prep_rq_fn is a request preparation function. It is not used by most drivers and is therefore set to NULL. If it is implemented, it generates the hardware commands needed to prepare a request before the actual request is sent. The auxiliary function blk_queue_prep_rq sets prep_rq_fn in a given queue.

---

[8]This term is slightly confusing because none of the algorithms used by the kernel implements the classic elevator method. Nevertheless, the basic objective is similar to that of elevators.

❑ `unplug_fn` is used to unplug a block device. A plugged device does not execute requests but collects them and sends them when it is unplugged. Used skillfully, this method enhances block layer performance. The remaining three functions are slightly more specialized.

❑ `merge_bvec_fn` determines if it is allowed to augment an existing request with more data. Since request queues usually have fixed size limits for their requests, the kernel can use these to answer the question. However, more specialized drivers — especially compound devices — may have varying limits so that they need to provide this function. The kernel provides the auxiliary routine `blk_queue_merge_bvec` to set `merge_bvec_fn` for a queue.

❑ `prepare_flush_fn` is called to prepare flushing the queue, that is, before all pending requests are executed in one go. Devices can perform necessary cleanups in this method.

The auxiliary function `blk_queue_ordered` is available to equip a request queue with a specific method.

❑ Completing requests, that is, ending all I/O, can be a time-consuming process for large requests. During the development of 2.6.16, the possibility to complete requests asynchronously using SoftIRQs (see Chapter 14 for more details on this mechanism) was added. Asynchronous completion of a request can be demanded by calling `blk_complete_request`, and `softirq_done_fn` is in this case used as a callback to notify the driver that the completion is finished.

The kernel provides the standard function `blk_init_queue_node` to generate a standard request queue. The only management function that must be provided by the driver itself in this case is `request_fn`. Any other management issues are handled by standard functions. Drivers that implement request management this way are required to call `blk_init_queue_node` and attach the resulting `request_queue` instance to their `gendisk` *before* `add_disk` is called to activate the disk.

Request queues can be plugged when the system is overloaded. New requests then remain unprocessed until the queue is unplugged (this is called *queue plugging*). The `unplug_` elements are used to implement a timer mechanism that automatically unplugs a queue after a certain period of time. `unplug_fn` is responsible for actual unplugging.

`queue_flags` is used to control the internal state of the queue with the help of flags.

The last part of the `request_list` structure contains information that describes the managed block device in more detail and reflects the hardware-specific device settings. This information is always in the form of numeric values; the meaning of the individual elements is given in Table 6-2.

`nr_requests` indicates the maximum number of requests that may be associated with a queue; we come back to this topic in Chapter 17.

6.5.3 Adding Disks and Partitions to the System

After having introduced numerous data structures that build up the block layer, everything is set to examine in more detail how generic hard disks are added to the system. As mentioned above, `add_disk` is provided for this purpose. A discussion of the implementation follows an examination of how partitions are added to the kernel's data structures using `add_partition`.

Table 6-2: Hardware Characteristics of a Request Queue.

Element	Meaning
max_sectors	Specifies the maximum number of sectors that the device can process in a single request; the sector size of the specific device (hardsect_size) is used as the size unit.
max_segment_size	Maximum segment size (in bytes) for a single request.
max_phys_segments	Specifies the maximum number of non-continuous segments for scatter-gather requests used to transport non-contiguous data.
max_hw_segments	Same as max_phys_segments but takes into account any remappings that may be made by a (possible) I/O MMU. The constant specifies the maximum number of address/length pairs that the driver can pass to the device.
hardsect_size	Specifies the physical sector size with which the device operates. This value is almost always 512; only a few very new devices use different settings.

Adding Partitions

add_partition is responsible for adding a new partitions into the generic hard disk data structures. I shall discuss a slightly simplified version here. First of all, a new instance of struct hd_struct is allocated and filled with some basic information about the partition:

fs/partitions/check.c
```
void add_partition(struct gendisk *disk, int part, sector_t start, sector_t len, int flags)
{
        struct hd_struct *p;

        p = kzalloc(sizeof(*p), GFP_KERNEL);
...
        p->start_sect = start;
        p->nr_sects = len;
        p->partno = part;
...
```

After assigning a name that shows up, for instance, in sysfs, the partition's kernel object parent is set to be the generic hard disk object. In contrast to complete disks, the ktype is not ktype_block, but ktype_part. This allows for distinguishing uevents (see Section 7.4) that originate from disks from uevents that originate from partitions:

fs/partitions/check.c
```
        kobject_set_name(&p->kobj, "%s%d",
        kobject_name(&disk->kobj),part);

        p->kobj.parent = &disk->kobj;
        p->kobj.ktype = &ktype_part;
...
```

Adding the new object with `kobject_add` makes it a member of the block subsystem, and consequently, the sysfs entries that provide information about the partition appear in `/sys/block`. Finally, the generic hard disk object must be modified to point to the new partition:

fs/partitions/check.c
```
        kobject_init(&p->kobj);
        kobject_add(&p->kobj);

        disk->part[part-1] = p;
}
```

Adding Disks

Figure 6-12 shows the code flow diagram for `add_disk`. A three-stage strategy is employed.

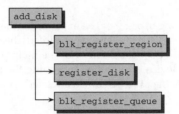

Figure 6-12: Code flow diagram for `add_disk`.

First of all, calling `blk_register_region` ensures that the desired device number range is not yet allocated. More interesting work is performed in `register_disk`. After the kernel object is supplied with a name, a new `block_device` instance for the device is obtained with `bdget_disk` (the function is a parameter conversion front end for `bdget`).

Until now, nothing is known about the partitions of the device. To remedy this situation, the kernel calls several procedures that end up in `rescan_partitions` (see the discussion of the exact call chain in the next section). The function tries to identify the partitions on the block device by trial and error. The global array `check_part` contains pointers to functions that are able to identify one particular partition type. On standard computers, usually PC Bios or EFI partitions will be used, but support is also available for more esoteric types like SGI Ultrix or Acorn Cumana partitions. Each of these functions is allowed to have a look at the block device,[9] and if a known partition scheme is detected, the `check_part` function returns this information to `rescan_partitions`. Here, `add_partition` as discussed above is called for each detected partition.

6.5.4   Opening Block Device Files

When a user application opens the device file of a block device, the virtual filesystem invokes the `open` function of the `file_operations` structure and arrives at `blkdev_open`. Figure 6-13 shows the associated code flow diagram.

---

[9]Note that this implies that reading data from the block device is already required to work when the device is registered with `disk_add`!

425

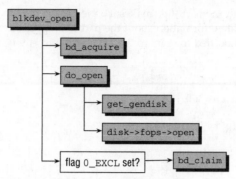

Figure 6-13: Code flow diagram for blkdev_open.

bd_acquire first finds the matching block_device instance for the device. The pointer to the instance can be read directly from inode->i_bdev if the device has already been used. Otherwise, it is created using the dev_t information. Afterward do_open carries out the main portion of the task, described below. If exclusive access to the block device is requested by setting the flag O_EXCL, then the block device is claimed with bd_claim. This sets the file instance associated with the device file as current holder of the block device.

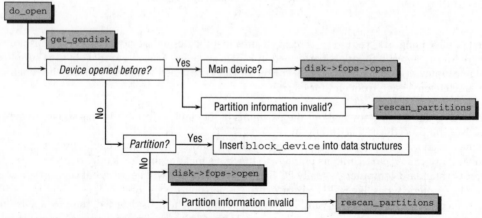

Figure 6-14: Code flow diagram for do_open.

The first step of do_open is to call get_gendisk. This delivers the gendisk instance that belongs to the block device. Recall that the gendisk structure describes the partitions of the block device as discussed in Section 6.2.5. However, if the block device is opened for the first time, the information is not yet complete. Nevertheless, the device-specific block_device_operations that are required to work with the device can already be found in the generic hard disk structure.

The kernel then needs to proceed differently depending on the type and state of the block device, as is shown in Figure 6-14. Things are simpler if the block device has been opened before, as can be inferred from the openers count block_device->bd_openers.

❑ `disk->fops->open` invokes the appropriate `open` function for the file to perform hardware-specific initialization tasks.

❑ If the partition information has become invalid as indicated by `block_device->bd_invalidated`, `rescan_partitions` is called to re-read the partition information. Partition information can become invalid if a removable medium is exchanged.

If the device has not been opened before, some more work is required. First suppose that not a partition, but the main block device is opened — which may nevertheless contain partitions. In this case, the required actions are modulo some bookkeeping details identical to the case shown above: `disk->fops->open` handles the low-level work of opening the device, and `rescan_partitions` reads the partition table if the existing information is invalid.

This is, however, usually the first time that partition information is read in. When a new disk is registered using `add_disk`, the kernel sets `gendisk->bd_invalidated` to 1, which signals an invalid partition table on the block device (in fact, since there is no partition table at all, it cannot really be called *valid*!). Then a fake file is constructed as a parameter passed to `do_open`, and this, in turn, triggers reading the partition table.

If the opened block device represents a partition that has not been opened before, the kernel needs to associate the `block_device` instance for the partition with the `block_device` that contains the partition. Essentially this works as follows:

fs/block_dev.c
```
struct hd_struct *p;
struct block_device *whole;
whole = bdget_disk(disk, 0);
...
bdev->bd_contains = whole;
p = disk->part[part - 1];
...
bdev->bd_part = p;
```

After finding the `block_device` instance that represents the whole disk that includes the partition, a link between partition and container is set up using `block_device->bd_contains`. Note that the kernel can find the whole block device starting from the partition's block device, but not vice versa! Additionally, the partition information in `hd_struct` is now shared between the generic hard disk and the `block_device` instance for the partition, as indicated in Figure 6-10.

6.5.5 Request Structure

The kernel provides its own data structure to describe a request to a block device.

<blkdev.h>
```
struct request {
        struct list_head queuelist;
        struct list_head donelist;

        struct request_queue *q;

        unsigned int cmd_flags;
```

```
                enum rq_cmd_type_bits cmd_type;
    ...
                sector_t sector;               /* next sector to submit */
                sector_t hard_sector;         /* next sector to complete */
                unsigned long nr_sectors;     /* no. of sectors left to submit */
                unsigned long hard_nr_sectors; /* no. of sectors left to complete */
                /* no. of sectors left to submit in the current segment */
                unsigned int current_nr_sectors;

                /* no. of sectors left to complete in the current segment */
                unsigned int hard_cur_sectors;

                struct bio *bio;
                struct bio *biotail;
    ...
                void *elevator_private;
                void *elevator_private2;

                struct gendisk *rq_disk;
                unsigned long start_time;

                unsigned short nr_phys_segments;
                unsigned short nr_hw_segments;
    ...
                unsigned int cmd_len;
    ...
    };
```

The very nature of a request is to be kept on a request queue. Such queues are implemented using doubly linked lists, and `queuelist` provides the required list element.[10] `q` points back to the request queue to which the request belongs, if any.

Once a request is completed, that is, when all required I/O operations have been performed, it can be queued on a completed list, and `donelist` provides the necessary list element.

The structure includes three elements to indicate the exact position of the data to be transferred.

❑ `sector` specifies the start sector at which data transfer begins.

❑ `current_nr_sectors` indicates the number of sectors to transfer for the current request.

❑ `nr_sectors` specifies the number of sector requests still pending.

`hard_sector`, `hard_cur_sectors`, and `hard_nr_sectors` have the same meaning but relate to the actual hardware and not to a virtual device. Usually, both variable collections have the same values, but differences may occur when RAID or the Logical Volume Manager is used because these combine several physical devices into a single virtual device.

When scatter-gather operations are used, `nr_phys_segments` and `nr_hw_segments` specify, respectively, the number of segments in a request and the number of segments used after possible re-sorting by an I/O MMU.

---

[10]This is only necessary for asynchronous request completion. Normally the list is not required.

Like most kernel data types, requests are equipped with pointers to private data. In this case, not only one, but two elements (`elevator_private` and `elevator_private2`) are available! They can be set by the I/O scheduler — traditionally called *elevator* — which currently processes the request.

BIOs are used to transfer data between the system and a device. Their definition is examined below.

❑   `bio` identifies the current BIO instance whose transfer has not yet been completed.

❑   `biotail` points to the last request, since a list of BIOs may be used in a request.

A request can be used to transmit control commands to a device (more formally, it can be used as *packet command carrier*). The desired commands are listed in the `cmd` array. We have omitted several entries related to bookkeeping required in this case.

The flags associated with a request are split into two parts. `cmd_flags` contains a set of generic flags for the request, and `cmd_type` denotes the type of request. The following request types are possible:

<blkdev.h>
```
enum rq_cmd_type_bits {
        REQ_TYPE_FS             = 1,      /* fs request */
        REQ_TYPE_BLOCK_PC,               /* scsi command */
        REQ_TYPE_SENSE,                  /* sense request */
        REQ_TYPE_PM_SUSPEND,             /* suspend request */
        REQ_TYPE_PM_RESUME,              /* resume request */
        REQ_TYPE_PM_SHUTDOWN,            /* shutdown request */
        REQ_TYPE_FLUSH,                  /* flush request */
        REQ_TYPE_SPECIAL,                /* driver defined type */
        REQ_TYPE_LINUX_BLOCK,            /* generic block layer message */
    ...
};
```

The most common request type is `REQ_TYPE_FS`: It is used for requests that actually transfer data to and from a block device. The remaining types allow for sending various types of commands as documented in the source comments to a device.

Besides the type, several additional flags characterize the request type:

<blkdev.h>
```
enum rq_flag_bits {
        __REQ_RW,               /* not set, read. set, write */
        __REQ_FAILFAST,         /* no low level driver retries */
        __REQ_SORTED,           /* elevator knows about this request */
        __REQ_SOFTBARRIER,      /* may not be passed by ioscheduler */
        __REQ_HARDBARRIER,      /* may not be passed by drive either */
        __REQ_FUA,              /* forced unit access */
        __REQ_NOMERGE,          /* don't touch this for merging */
        __REQ_STARTED,          /* drive already may have started this one */
        __REQ_DONTPREP,         /* don't call prep for this one */
        __REQ_QUEUED,           /* uses queueing */
        __REQ_ELVPRIV,          /* elevator private data attached */
        __REQ_FAILED,           /* set if the request failed */
        __REQ_QUIET,            /* don't worry about errors */
        __REQ_PREEMPT,          /* set for "ide_preempt" requests */
```

```
      __REQ_ORDERED_COLOR,    /* is before or after barrier */
      __REQ_RW_SYNC,          /* request is sync (O_DIRECT) */
      __REQ_ALLOCED,          /* request came from our alloc pool */
      __REQ_RW_META,          /* metadata io request */
      __REQ_NR_BITS,          /* stops here */
};
```

__REQ_RW is especially important because it indicates the direction of data transfer. If the bit is set, data are written; if not, data are read. The remaining bits are used to send special device-specific commands, to set up barriers,[11] or to transfer control codes. Their meaning is concisely described by the kernel commentary, so I need not add anything further.

6.5.6 BIOs

Before giving an exact definition of BIOs, it is advisable to discuss their underlying principles as illustrated in Figure 6-15.

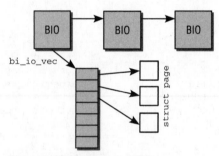

Figure 6-15: Structure of BIOs.

The central management structure (`bio`) is associated with a vector whose individual entries each point to a memory page (caution: *Not* the address in memory but the `page` instance belonging to the page). These pages are used to receive data from and send data to the device.

> It is explicitly possible to use highmem pages that are not directly mapped in the
> kernel and cannot therefore be addressed via virtual kernel addresses. This is
> useful when data are copied directly to userspace applications that are able to access
> the highmem pages using their page tables.

The memory pages can but need not be organized contiguously; this facilitates the implementation of scatter-gather operations.

BIOs have the following (simplified) structure in the kernel sources:

<bio.h>
```
struct bio {
        sector_t                bi_sector;
        struct bio              *bi_next;        /* request queue link */
```

---

[11]If a device comes across a barrier in a request list, all still pending requests must be fully processed before any other actions can be performed.

```
        struct block_device     *bi_bdev;
...
        unsigned short           bi_vcnt;        /* how many bio_vec's */
        unsigned short           bi_idx;         /* current index into bvl_vec */

        unsigned short           bi_phys_segments;
        unsigned short           bi_hw_segments;

        unsigned int             bi_size;        /* residual I/O count */
...
        struct bio_vec          *bi_io_vec;      /* the actual vec list */

        bio_end_io_t            *bi_end_io;

        void                    *bi_private;
...
};
```

❑   `bi_sector` specifies the sector at which transfer starts.

❑   `bi_next` combines several BIOs in a singly linked list associated with a request.

❑   `bi_bdev` is a pointer to the block device data structure of the device to which the request belongs.

❑   `bi_phys_segments` and `bi_hw_segments` specify the number of segments in a transfer before and after remapping by the I/O MMU.

❑   `bi_size` indicates the total size of the request in bytes.

❑   `bi_io_vec` is a pointer to the I/O vectors, and `bi_vcnt` specifies the number of entries in the array. `bi_idx` denotes which array entry is currently being processed.

The structure of the individual array elements is as follows:

<bio.h>
```
struct bio_vec {
        struct page      *bv_page;
        unsigned int     bv_len;
        unsigned int     bv_offset;
};
```

`bv_page` points to the `page` instance of the page used for data transfer. `bv_offset` indicates the offset within the page; typically this value is 0 because page boundaries are normally used as boundaries for I/O operations.

`len` specifies the number of bytes used for the data if the whole page is not filled.

❑   `bi_private` is not modified by the generic BIO code and can be used for driver-specific information.

❑   `bi_destructor` points to a destructor function invoked before a `bio` instance is removed from memory.

❑   `bi_end_io` must be invoked by the device driver when hardware transfer is completed. This gives the block layer the opportunity to do clean-up work or wake sleeping processes that are waiting for the request to end.

6.5.7 Submitting Requests

In this section, I discuss the mechanism that the kernel provides to submit data requests to peripheral devices. This also involves buffering and reordering requests to reduce disk head seek movements, for example, or to boost performance by bundling operations. Also covered are the operation of the device driver, which interacts with the specific hardware in order to process requests, and the general code of the virtual filesystem that is associated with device files and therefore with user applications and other parts of the kernel. As you will see in Chapters 16 and 8, the kernel employs caches to retain data already read from block devices for future reuse if the same request is submitted repeatedly. We are not interested in this particular aspect here. Instead, we will examine how the kernel goes about submitting a physical request to a device to read or write data.

The kernel submits a request in two steps.

❑ It creates a `bio` instance to describe the request and then embeds the instance in a request that is placed on a request queue.

❑ It processes the request queue and carries out the actions described by the `bio`.

Creating a new `bio` instance is not particularly interesting as all it involves is filling the desired locations on a block device and providing page frames to hold and transfer the relevant data. I won't bother with the details.

Once a BIO has been created, `make_request_fn` is invoked to generate a new request for insertion on the request queue.[12] The requests are submitted by `request_fn`.

The implementation of these actions reside in `block/ll_rw_blk.c` up to kernel 2.6.24. The strange-sounding filename is an abbreviation of *low level read write handling for block devices*. Later kernels split the implementation into a number of smaller files named by the scheme `block/blk-*.c`.

Creating Requests

`submit_bio` is the key function that creates a new request based on a passed `bio` instance and finally places it on the request queue of the driver using `make_request_fn`. Figure 6-16 shows the associated code flow diagram. Let's consider a simplified version first, but come back later to address some problems that can arise in certain cases, and how the kernel solves them with a little trick.

The function is invoked at various places in the kernel to initiate physical data transfers. `submit_bio` simply updates the kernel statistics, the actual work being delegated to `__generic_make_request` after a detour over `generic_make_request`, which is explained below. The work is done in three steps after a few sanity checks have been performed (one such check establishes, for example, whether the request exceeds the physical capabilities of the device).

❑ The request queue of the block device to which the request refers is found using `bdev_get_queue`.

❑ If the device is partitioned, the request is remapped with `blk_partition_remap` to ensure that the correct area is read or written. This enables the remaining kernel to treat individual partitions in the same way as independent, non-partitioned devices. If a partition starts at sector *n* and

---

[12]Or to store the request elsewhere if the driver has explicitly replaced the default implementation with its own function.

access is to be made to sector *m* within the partition, a request must be created to access sector *m* + *n* of the block device. The correct offset for the partition is held in the `parts` array of the `gendisk` instance associated with the queue.

❑ `q->make_request_fn` generates a `request` by reference to the `bio` and forwards it to the device driver. The kernel standard function (`__make_request`) is invoked for most devices.

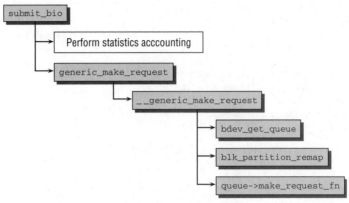

Figure 6-16: Code flow diagram for `submit_bio`.

I have announced above that this approach can cause problems, and they manifest themselves exactly at this point. Some block drivers in the kernel — MD and the device mapper — cannot use the standard function supplied by the kernel and implement their own functions. These, however, call `generic_make_request` recursively!

While recursive function calls are no problem in userspace, they can become problematic in the kernel since only very limited stack space is available. Therefore a way to limit the maximal recursion depth to a sane value needs to be devised. To understand how this is done, observe first that the `task_struct`, which represents central data for each process (refer to Chapter 2), also contains two elements related to BIO handling:

<sched.h>
```
struct task_struct {
...
/* stacked block device info */
        struct bio *bio_list, **bio_tail;
...
}
```

The pointers are used to limit the maximal recursion depth to one — without losing any of the submitted BIOs, naturally. If `__generic_make_request` or some subfunction calls `generic_make_request`, the code flow will return before the next recursive call to `__generic_make_request`. To understand how, we need to take a look at the implementation of `generic_make_request` (recall that `current` points to the `task_struct` instance of the currently running process).

block/ll_rw_blk.c
```
void generic_make_request(struct bio *bio)
{
        if (current->bio_tail) {
                /* make_request is active */
```

433

```
                    *(current->bio_tail) = bio;
                    bio->bi_next = NULL;
                    current->bio_tail = &bio->bi_next;
                    return;
          }

     do {
                    current->bio_list = bio->bi_next;
                    if (bio->bi_next == NULL)
                           current->bio_tail = &current->bio_list;
                    else
                           bio->bi_next = NULL;
                    __generic_make_request(bio);
                    bio = current->bio_list;
          } while (bio);
          current->bio_tail = NULL; /* deactivate */
   }
```

The method is simple, yet creative. Figure 6-17 shows how the data structures evolve over time.

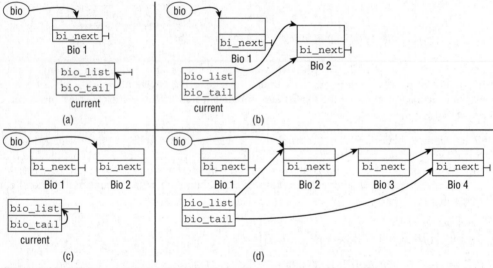

Figure 6-17: BIO lists evolving under recursive calls to `generic_make_request`.

current->bio_tail is initialized to NULL, so we can skip the first conditional block. One bio instance is submitted, and the data structures look as in Figure 6-17(a). bio points to the submitted BIO, while current->bio_list is NULL and current_bio_tail point to the address of current_bio_tail. Note that the following pictures in the figure will always consider the local bio variable of the first function call to generic_make_request — not any variables in later stack frames.

Now suppose that __generic_make_request does recursively call generic_make_request to submit a BIO instance, which we call BIO 2. How do the data structures look when __generic_make_request returns? Consider the action of the recursive call: Since current->bio_tail is not a NULL pointer anymore, the initial if-block in generic_make_request is processed. current->bio_list then points to the second BIO, and current->bio_tail points at the address of the bi_next of BIO 2. Thus the data structure looks as in Figure 6-17(b) when __generic_make_request returns.

The do loop is now executed a second time. Before the second — iterative! — call to __generic_make_request, the data structure looks as in Figure 6-17(c), and the second bio instance is processed. If no more BIOs are submitted recursively, the job is done afterward.

The method also works if __generic_make_request calls generic_make_request more than once. Imagine that three additional BIOs are submitted. The resulting data structure is depicted in Figure 6-17(d). If no more BIOs are submitted afterward, the loop processes the existing BIO instances one after another and then returns.

After having resolved the difficulties with recursive generic_make_request calls, we can go on to examine the default make_request_fn implementation __make_request. Figure 6-18 shows the code flow diagram.[13]

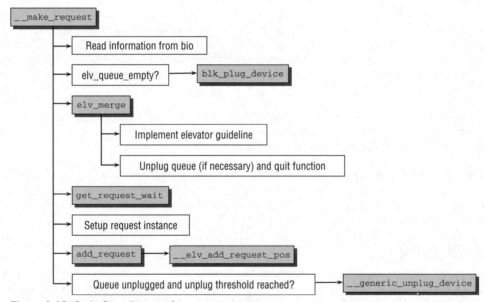

Figure 6-18: Code flow diagram for __make_request.

Once the information needed to create the request has been read from the passed bio instance, the kernel invokes elv_queue_empty to check whether the elevator queue is currently empty. If so, work is made easier as there is no need to merge the request with existing requests (because none is present).

If there are pending requests in the queue, elv_merge is called to invoke the elevator_merge_fn function of the elevator element associated with the request queue (Section 6.5.8 deals with the implementation of I/O schedulers). At this point, we are interested only in the result of the function. It returns a pointer to the request list position at which the new request is to be inserted. The I/O scheduler also specifies whether and how the request is to be coalesced with existing requests.

---

[13] As a slight simplification, I omit bounce buffer handling. Older hardware might only be able to transfer data into some specific region in memory. In this case, the kernel initiates the transfer to go into this region and copies the result to some more apt place after the transfer is finished.

❑   ELEVATOR_BACK_MERGE and ELEVATOR_FRONT_MERGE cause the new request to be coalesced with the request at the found position in the request list. ELEVATOR_BACK_MERGE merges the new data after the data of the existing request, ELEVATOR_FRONT_MERGE before the data.

The existing element is modified to produce a merged request covering the desired areas.

❑   ELEVATOR_NO_MERGE finds out that the request cannot be coalesced with existing elements on the request queue and must therefore be added on its own.

These are the only actions that an elevator can take; it cannot influence the request queue in any other way. This clearly demonstrates the difference between I/O and CPU schedulers. Although both are faced with a very similar problem, the solutions they provide diverge greatly.

Once the elevator requirements have been satisfied (as far as this is possible), the kernel must generate a new request.

get_request_wait allocates a new request instance that is then filled with data from the bio using init_request_from_bio. If the queue is still empty (this is checked by elv_queue_empty), it is plugged with blk_plug_device. This is how the kernel prevents the queue from being processed after each new request; instead, it collects requests for read and/or write operations and executes them in a single action. I discuss the mechanism used shortly.

After a few kernel statistics have been updated with __elv_add_request_pos, add_request adds the request to the request list (this leads to the I/O scheduler-specific elevator_add_req_fn function) at the position selected by the above I/O scheduler call.

If a request is to be processed synchronously (BIO_RW_SYNC must then be set in the bio instance of the request), the kernel must unplug the queue using __generic_unplug_device to ensure that the request can, in fact, be handled synchronously. Requests of this kind are seldom used because they negate the effect of I/O scheduling.

Queue Plugging

In terms of performance, it is, of course, desirable to re-sort individual requests and merge them into larger units to optimize data transfer. Obviously, this only works if the queue contains several requests that can be merged. The kernel must therefore first collect a few requests in the queue before it can process them in a single operation; this automatically generates opportunities for merging.

The kernel uses *queue plugging* to intentionally prevent requests from being processed. A request queue may be in one of two states — either free or plugged. If it is free, the requests waiting in the queue are processed. Otherwise, new requests are added to the list but not processed. The QUEUE_FLAG_PLUGGED flag in the queue_flags element of request_queue is set when a queue is plugged; the kernel provides the blk_queue_plugged helper function to check this flag.

In the description of __make_request, I already noted that the kernel plugs a queue with blk_plug_device but does not explicitly unplug the queue if no synchronous request is sent. How is it possible to ensure that queues will be processed again at some time in the future? The solution is to be found in blk_plug_device.

drivers/block/ll_rw_blk.c
```
 void blk_plug_device(request_queue_t *q)
{
...
        if (!test_and_set_bit(QUEUE_FLAG_PLUGGED, &q->queue_flags)) {
                mod_timer(&q->unplug_timer, jiffies + q->unplug_delay);
...
        }
}
```

This section of code ensures that the unplug timer of the queue is enabled after `q->unplug_delay` jiffies [typically `(3 * HZ) / 1000`, or 3 milliseconds]; in turn, this invokes `blk_unplug_timeout` to unplug the queue.

A second mechanism is also available to unplug the queue. If the number of current read and write requests (stored in the two entries of the `count` array of the request list) corresponds to the threshold specified by `unplug_thresh`, `__generic_unplug_device` is invoked in `elv_insert`[14] to trigger unplugging so that waiting requests are processed.

`__generic_unplug_device` is not very complicated.

block/ll_rw_blk.c
```
void __generic_unplug_device(request_queue_t *q)
{
...
        if (!blk_remove_plug(q))
                return;

        q->request_fn(q);
}
```

`request_fn` is invoked to process the waiting requests after `blk_remove_plug` has removed the plug of the queue and the timer used for automatic unplugging (`unplug_timer`) is set. That's all that need be done!

The kernel is also able to perform unplugging manually when important I/O operations are pending. This ensures that important read operations, for example, are carried out immediately if data are urgently required. This situation arises when synchronous requests (mentioned briefly above) need to be satisfied.

Executing Requests

The device-specific `request_fn` function is invoked when the requests in the request queue are ready to be processed. This is a very hardware-specific task so the kernel does not provide a default implementation. Instead, it always uses the method passed when the queue was registered with `blk_dev_init`.

Nevertheless, the structure of the `request` function described below is similar in most device drivers. I assume a situation in which there are several requests in the request queue.

---

[14]`elv_insert` is an internal function of the elevator implementation and is called at various points in the kernel.

`sample_request` is a hardware-independent sample routine for `request_fn` that illustrates the basic steps performed by all drivers.

```
void sample_request (request_queue_t *q)
        int status;
        struct request *req;

        while ((req = elv_next_request(q)) != NULL)
        if (!blk_fs_request(req))
            end_request(req, 0);
            continue;

        status = perform_sample_transfer(req);
                end_request(req, status);
```

The basic layout of the strategy function is simple; `elv_next_request` — embedded in a `while` loop — is used to read the requests sequentially from the queue. Transfer itself is carried out by `perform_sample_transfer`. `end_request` is a standard kernel function to delete the request from the request queue, to update the kernel statistics, and to execute any completions (see Chapter 5) waiting in `request->completion`. Also invoked is the BIO-specific `bi_end_io` function to which the kernel can assign a cleanup that depends on the purpose of the BIO.

As BIOs can be used to transfer not only data but also diagnostics information, the driver must invoke `blk_fs_request` to check whether, in fact, data are to be transferred — for the sake of simplicity, I ignore all other types of transfer.

The hardware-specific actions in genuine drivers are typically segregated into separate functions to keep code concise. I have adopted the same approach in our sample strategy function. The hardware-specific functions that would be found in a genuine driver are replaced with comments in `perform_sample_transfer`.

```
int perform_transfer(request *req)
    switch(req->cmd)
    case READ:
      /* Perform hardware-specific reading of data */
      break;
    case WRITE:
      /* Perform hardware-specific writing of data */
      break;
    default:
      return -EFAULT;
```

The `cmd` field is referenced to establish whether the request is for a read or write operation. The appropriate actions are then taken to transfer the data between the system and the hardware.

6.5.8   I/O Scheduling

The various algorithms employed in the kernel for scheduling and reordering I/O operations are known as *I/O schedulers* (in contrast to normal process schedulers or packet schedulers for traffic shaping in networks). Traditionally, I/O schedulers are also called *elevators*. They are represented by a collection of functions grouped together in the following data structure[15]:

---

[15]The kernel also defines `typedef struct elevator_s elevator_t`.

<elevator.h>
```
struct elevator_ops
{
        elevator_merge_fn *elevator_merge_fn;
        elevator_merged_fn *elevator_merged_fn;
        elevator_merge_req_fn *elevator_merge_req_fn;

        elevator_dispatch_fn *elevator_dispatch_fn;
        elevator_add_req_fn *elevator_add_req_fn;
        elevator_activate_req_fn *elevator_activate_req_fn;
        elevator_deactivate_req_fn *elevator_deactivate_req_fn;

        elevator_queue_empty_fn *elevator_queue_empty_fn;
        elevator_completed_req_fn *elevator_completed_req_fn;

        elevator_request_list_fn *elevator_former_req_fn;
        elevator_request_list_fn *elevator_latter_req_fn;

        elevator_set_req_fn *elevator_set_req_fn;
        elevator_put_req_fn *elevator_put_req_fn;

        elevator_may_queue_fn *elevator_may_queue_fn;

        elevator_init_fn *elevator_init_fn;
        elevator_exit_fn *elevator_exit_fn;
};
```

The I/O scheduler is not only responsible for request reordering but also for the complete management of the request queue.

❑   `elevator_merge_fn` checks whether a new request can be coalesced with an existing request as described above. It also specifies the position at which a request is inserted in the request queue.

❑   `elevator_merge_req_fn` coalesces two requests into a single request; `elevator_merged_fn` is invoked *after* two requests have been merged (it performs clean-up work and returns management data of the I/O scheduler that are no longer needed because of the merge to the system).

❑   `elevator_dispatch_fn` selects which request from a given request queue should be dispatched next.

❑   `elevator_add_req_fn` and `elevator_remove_req_fn` add and remove a request to/from the request queue.

❑   `elevator_queue_empty_fn` checks whether the queue contains requests ready for processing.

❑   `elevator_former_req_fn` and `elevator_latter_req_fn` find the predecessor and successor request of a given request; this is useful when performing merging.

❑   `elevator_set_req_fn` and `elevator_put_req_fn` are invoked when a new request is instantiated and returned to memory management (at this point in time the requests are not yet or no longer associated with any queue or have been satisfied). The functions give the I/O scheduler the opportunity to allocate, initialize, and return management data structures.

❑   `elevator_init_fn` and `elevator_exit_fn` are invoked when a queue is initialized and returned; their effect is the same as that of a constructor or destructor.

Each elevator is encapsulated in the following data structure that holds further management information for the kernel:

```
<elevator.h>
struct elevator_type
{
        struct list_head list;
        struct elevator_ops ops;
        struct elv_fs_entry *elevator_attrs;
        char elevator_name[ELV_NAME_MAX];
        struct module *elevator_owner;
};
```

The kernel keeps all elevators in a doubly linked standard list implemented by means of the `list` element (the list head is represented by the global variable `elv_list`). Each elevator is also given a human-readable name that can be used to select the elevator from userspace. Attributes that will appear in sysfs are kept in `elevator_attrs`. They can be used to tune the elevator behavior on a per-disk basis.

The kernel implements a whole series of I/O schedulers. However, device drivers may overwrite specific functions of the schedulers for their own purposes or even implement their own schedulers. The elevators have the following properties.

❏ `elevator_noop` is a very simple I/O scheduler that adds incoming requests to the queue one after the other for processing on a "first come, first served" basis. Requests are merged but not reordered. The noop I/O scheduler (*no operation*) is only a good choice for intelligent hardware that can reorder requests by itself. It is also reported to be a good scheduler for devices where there are no moving parts and thus no seek times — flash disks, for instance.

❏ `iosched_deadline` serves two purposes: it tries to minimize the number of disk seeks (i.e., movement of the read/write heads) and also does its best to ensure that requests are processed within a certain time. In the latter case, the kernel's timer mechanism is used to implement an "expiry time" for the individual requests. In the former case, lengthy data structures (red-black trees and linked lists) are used to analyze requests so that they can be reordered with the minimum of delay, thus reducing the number of disk seeks.

❏ `iosched_as` implements the *anticipatory scheduler*, which — as its name suggests — anticipates process behavior as far as possible. Naturally, this is not an easy goal, but the scheduler tries to achieve it by assuming that read requests are not totally independent of each other. When an application submits a read request to the kernel, the assumption is then made that a second related request will be submitted within a certain period. This is important if the read request is submitted in a period during which the disk is busy with write operations. To ensure satisfactory interaction, the write operations are deferred, and preference is given to the read operations. If writing is resumed immediately, a disk seek operation is required but is negated by a new read request arriving shortly afterward. In this case, it is better to leave the disk head in its position after the first read request and to wait briefly for the next read request — if a second read request does not arrive, the kernel is free to resume write operations.

❏ `iosched_cfq` provides *complete fairness queuing*. It is centered around several queues into which all requests are sorted. Requests from a given process always end up on the same queue. Time slices are allocated for each of the queues, and a round robin algorithm is used to process the queue. This ensures that the I/O bandwidth is shared in a fair manner between the different queues. If the number of queues is bigger than or equal to the number of processes doing simultaneous I/O, this implies that the bandwidth is also fairly distributed between the processes. Some practical problems (like multiple processes being mapped to identical queues, varying request sizes, different I/O priorities, etc.) make the distribution not completely fair, but basically, the method achieves its goal to a good extent.

The deadline scheduler was the default scheduler almost up to the end of development of 2.5 but was replaced with the anticipatory scheduler until 2.6.17. From 2.6.18 onward, the Completely Fair Queuing scheduler is the default choice.

For reasons of space, I shall not deal with the implementation details of each scheduler. It should be noted, however, that the deadline scheduler is much less complicated than the anticipatory scheduler but delivers practically identical performance in most situations.

6.5.9 Implementation of Ioctls

Ioctls permit the use of special device-specific functions that cannot be accessed by normal read and write operations. This form of support is implemented by means of the `ioctl` system call that can be used with regular files (detailed descriptions of how it is used are provided in the many system programming manuals).

As expected, the system call is implemented in `sys_ioctl`, but the main work is done in `vfs_ioctl`. Figure 6-19 shows the associated code flow diagram.

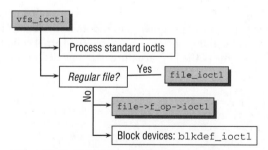

Figure 6-19: Code flow diagram for `sys_ioctl`.

The desired ioctl is specified by means of a passed constant; typically, symbolic pre-processor constants are used for this purpose.

Two situations must be distinguished once the kernel has checked whether one of the standard ioctls has been applied (these are available for all files in the system regardless of type); for example, whether the file descriptor is to be closed when `exec` is executed (see Chapter 2).

❑ If the file is a regular file, `file_ioctl` is invoked. The function first checks a number of standard ioctls that are always implemented for this file type (`FIGETBSZ`, for example, to query the block size used by the file). `do_ioctl` is then used to invoke the file-specific `ioctl` function in the `file_operations` (if it exists) to process the ioctl (regular files do not usually provide a `ioctl` function so that the system call returns an error code).

❑ If the file is not a regular file, `do_ioctl` and therefore the file-specific `ioctl` methods are invoked immediately; the method for block device files is `blkdev_ioctl`.

`blkdev_ioctl` also implements some ioctls that must be available for all block devices; for instance, a request to read the partitioning data or a method of determining the total size of the device. Thereafter the device-specific ioctls are processed by invoking the `ioctl` method in the `file_operations` of the `gendisk` instance. This is where driver-specific commands, such as the eject medium command for CD-ROMs, are implemented.

6.6 Resource Reservation

I/O ports and *I/O memory* are two conceptual ways of supporting communication between device drivers and devices. So that the various drivers do not interfere with each other, it is essential to *reserve* ports and I/O memory ranges prior to use by a driver. This ensures that several device drivers do not attempt to access the same resources.

6.6.1 Resource Management

Let us first examine the data structures and functions for managing resources.

Tree Data Structures

Linux provides a generalized framework to help build data structures in memory. These structures describe the resources available in the system and enable the kernel code to manage and allocate the resources. Significantly, the name of the key structure is `resource`; it is defined as follows:

```
<ioport.h>
struct resource {
        resource_size_t start;
        resource_size_t end;
        const char *name;
        unsigned long flags;
        struct resource *parent, *sibling, *child;
};
```

`name` stores a string so that the resource can be given a meaningful name. It has no relevance for the kernel but is useful when a resource list (in the `proc` filesystem) is output in readable form.

The resource itself is characterized by the three parameters below. `start` and `end` specify a general area marked by unsigned `long` numbers; even though theoretically the contents of the two numbers can be interpreted freely, they usually represent an area in an address space. `flags` enables the resource and its current state to be described more precisely.

Of particular interest are the three pointers to other `resource` structures. These enable a tree-like hierarchy to be established in which the pointers are often arranged as you will see below.

Figure 6-20 illustrates how the *parent*, *child*, and *sibling* pointers are arranged in a tree structure that is reminiscent of the process network discussed in Chapter 2.

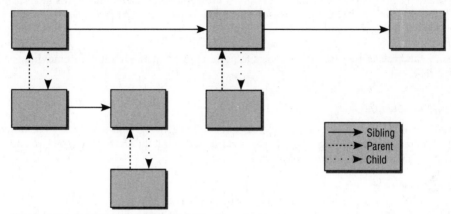

Figure 6-20: Resource management in a tree structure.

The rules for linking the *parent*, *child*, and *sibling* elements are simple.

❑   Each child has *just one* parent.

❑   A parent can have any number of children.

❑   All children with the same parent are linked on the list of siblings.

The following must be noted when the data structure is represented in memory.

❑   Even though there may be a pointer from each child to the parent, there is always only a single pointer from the parent to the first child. All other children can be reconstructed from the sibling list.

❑   The pointer to the parent may also be NULL, in which case there is no higher-level element.

How can this hierarchical structure be used for device drivers? Let us look at the example of a system bus to which a network card is attached. The card supports *two* outputs, each of which is assigned a specific memory area for data input and output. The bus itself also has a I/O memory area, sections of which are used by the network card.

This scheme fits perfectly into the tree hierarchy. The bus memory area that theoretically occupies the (fictitious) range between 0 and 1,000 acts as the root element (the uppermost parent element). The network card lays claim to the memory area between 100 and 199 and is a child of the root element (the bus itself). The child elements of the network card represent the individual network outputs to which the I/O ranges from 100 to 149 and from 150 to 199 are assigned. The originally large resource area is repeatedly subdivided into smaller sections, each of which represents a layer of an abstraction model. Consequently, child elements can be used to partition the area into ever smaller and ever more specific sections.

Requesting and Releasing Resources

To ensure that resources — regardless of kind — are deployed reliably, the kernel must feature a mechanism to allocate and subsequently release them. Once a resource has been allocated, it may not be used by any other driver.

Requesting and releasing a resource equates to nothing more than adding and removing entries from a resource tree.[16]

Requesting Resources

The kernel provides the __request_resource function to request a resource area.[17] The function expects a series of parameters including a pointer to the parent element, the start and end address of the resource area, and a string to hold the name of the area.

kernel/resource.c
```
static struct resource * request_resource(struct resource *root,
                                          struct resource *new);
```

The purpose of the function is to allocate a request instance and fill it with the data passed. Checks are also performed to detect obvious errors (start address bigger than the end address, for example) that would render the request useless and would abort the action. request_resource is responsible only for the requisite locking. The heavy work is delegated to __request_resource. It scans the existing resources consecutively to add the new resource at the correct position or to reveal conflicts with areas already allocated. It does this by running through the list of siblings. The new resource instance is inserted if the required resource area is free, thus reserving the resource. Reservation fails if the area is not free.

> *The children of a specific parent are scanned on one sibling level only. The kernel does not scan the list of children downward.*

If a resource cannot be reserved, the driver automatically knows that it is already in use and is therefore not available at the moment.

Releasing Resources

The release_resource function is invoked to release a resource that is in use.

kernel/resource.c
```
void release_resource(struct resource *old)
```

---

[16]It is important to note that many system resources *could* be addressed without the need to reserve them. With few exceptions, processors have no way of enforcing resource reservation. The functions described below should therefore be employed in the interests of a clean programming style, although it would be possible to dispense with reservations in most cases.

[17]The kernel sources include other functions for allocating resources for reasons of compatibility, but they should no longer be used in new code. There are also functions that *search* for resources of a certain size so that areas still free are filled automatically. I won't discuss these extended options as they are used only at a few places in the kernel.

6.6.2 I/O Memory

One of the most important aspects of the resource concept deals with how I/O memory is distributed because this is the main way on all platforms (with the exception of IA-32, where great importance is attached to I/O ports) of communicating with peripherals.

I/O memory includes not only the memory regions used directly to communicate with expansion devices but also the regular RAM and ROM memory available to the system and included in the resource list (which can be displayed using the `iomem` file in the `proc` filesystem).

```
wolfgang@meitner> cat /proc/iomem
00000000-0009e7ff : System RAM
0009e800-0009ffff : reserved
000a0000-000bffff : Video RAM area
000c0000-000c7fff : Video ROM
000f0000-000fffff : System ROM
00100000-07cefffff : System RAM
  00100000-002a1eb9 : Kernel code
  002a1eba-0030cabf : Kernel data
07cf0000-07cfefff : ACPI Tables
07cf0000-07cfefff : ACPI Tables
07cff000-07cfffff : ACPI Non-volatile Storage
...
f4000000-f407ffff : Intel Corp. 82815 CGC [Chipset Graphics Controller]
f4100000-f41fffff : PCI Bus #01
  f4100000-f4100fff : Intel Corp. 82820 (ICH2) Chipset Ethernet Controller
    f4100000-f4100fff : eepro100
  f4101000-f41017ff : PCI device 104c:8021 (Texas Instruments)
...
```

All allocated I/O memory addresses are managed in a resource tree that uses the global kernel variable `iomem_resource` as its root. Each text indentation represents a child level. All entries with the same indentation level are siblings and are linked as such. Figure 6-21 shows the parts of the data structures in memory from which the information in the `proc` filesystem is obtained.

However, reservation of a memory region is not the only action needed when using I/O memory. Depending on bus system and processor type, it may be necessary to map the address space of an expansion device into kernel address space before it can be accessed (this is known as *software I/O mapping*). This is achieved by setting up the system page tables appropriately using the `ioremap` kernel function, which is available at various points in the kernel sources and whose definition is architecture-specific. The likewise architecture-specific `iounmap` function is provided to unmap mappings.

Implementation requires, in part, long and complex manipulation of the process tables. I won't therefore discuss it in detail, particularly as it varies greatly from system to system and is not important for an understanding of device drivers. What's more important is that — in general terms — a physical address is mapped into the virtual address space of the processor so that it can be used by the kernel. As applied to device drivers, this means that the address space of an expansion bus is mapped into the address space of the CPU, where it can then be manipulated using normal memory access functions.

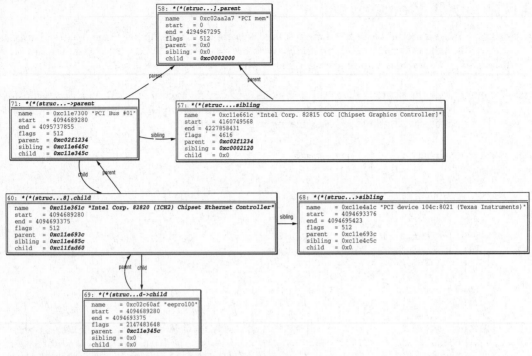

Figure 6-21: Allocated resources of a PCI network card.

> Even after I/O areas have been mapped, it is necessary on some platforms to use special methods rather than direct pointer de-referencing to access the individual memory areas. Table 6-3 shows the functions declared to do this on all platforms (generally in `<asm-arch/io.h>`). They should always be used by portable drivers even if they boil down to simple pointer de-referencing on some architectures because no other steps are needed to communicate with the I/O areas (as on IA-32 systems, for example).

6.6.3 I/O Ports

I/O ports are a popular way of communicating with devices and buses, above all in the IA-32 world. As with I/O memory, the required region must first be registered before it can be accessed by a driver in good faith — unfortunately, the processor is again unable to check whether this has been done.

`ioport_resource` from `kernel/resource.c` acts as the root element of a resource tree. The `ioports` file in the `proc` filesystem reveals the reserved port addresses.

```
wolfgang@meitner> cat /proc/ioports
0000-001f : dma1
0020-003f : pic1
0040-005f : timer
0060-006f : keyboard
...
```

```
0170-0177 : ide1
...
0378-037a : parport0
03c0-03df : vga+
...
0cf8-0cff : PCI conf1
1800-180f : Intel Corp. 82820 820 (Camino 2) Chipset IDE U100 (-M)
  1800-1807 : ide0
  1808-180f : ide1
1810-181f : Intel Corp. 82820 820 (Camino 2) Chipset SMBus
1820-183f : Intel Corp. 82820 820 (Camino 2) Chipset USB (Hub A)
...
3000-3fff : PCI Bus #01
  3000-303f : Intel Corp. 82820 (ICH2) Chipset Ethernet Controller
    3000-303f : eepro100
```

Table 6-3: Functions for Accessing I/O Memory Areas.

Function	Meaning
readb(addr)	
readw(addr)	
readl(addr)	Reads a byte, word, or long from the specified I/O address addr.
writeb(val, addr)	
writew(val, addr)	
writel(val, addr)	Writes a byte, word, or long value specified by val to the I/O address addr.
memcpy_fromio(dest, src, num)	Moves num bytes from the I/O addresss src to dest in normal address space.
memcpy_toio(dst, src, nun)	Copies num bytes from dst in normal address space to src in the I/O area.
memset_io(addr, value, count)	Fills count bytes with value starting at position addr.

Again the kernel makes use of indentation to reflect the parent/child and sibling relationships. The list was generated on the same system as the I/O memory areas shown above. It is interesting that the list includes not only standard system components such as keyboard and timer but also a few familiar devices from the I/O mapping such as the Ethernet controller — after all, there's no reason why a device cannot be addressed via ports and I/O memory.

Usually ports must be accessed by means of special processor commands on the assembler level. The kernel therefore provides corresponding macros to make a system-independent interface available to driver programmers. They are listed in Table 6-4.

447

Table 6-4: Functions for Accessing I/O Ports.

Function	Meaning
insb(port, addr, num)	
insl(port, addr, num)	
insw(port, addr, num)	Reads num bytes, words, or longs from port port to the address addr of the regular address space.
outsb(port, addr, num)	
outsb(port, addr, num)	
outsb(port, addr, num)	Writes num bytes, words, or longs from the virtual address addr to the port port.

> The functions are declared and implemented (usually by means of access to "normal" I/O memory) even on architectures that make no use of ports in order to simplify driver development for various architectures.

6.7 Bus Systems

Whereas expansion devices are addressed by device drivers that communicate with the remaining code only via a fixed set of interfaces and therefore have no effect on the core kernel sources, the kernel is also responsible for a more basic issue — *how* devices are attached to the rest of the system by means of buses.

Bus drivers are much more closely linked with the central kernel code than drivers for specific devices can ever be. Also, there is no standardized interface via which a bus driver makes its functions and options available to associated drivers. This is because the hardware techniques used differ greatly between the various bus systems. However, this does not mean that the code responsible for managing the different buses has no commonalities. Similar buses adopt similar concepts, and the generic *driver model* has been introduced to manage all system buses in a collection of central data structures, reducing them as far as possible to the smallest common denominator.

The kernel supports a large number of buses, sometimes on several hardware platforms, sometimes on just a single platform. It is therefore impossible to discuss all versions in detail. I shall therefore limit us to a close examination of the PCI bus since its design is relatively modern, it features all the common and key elements of a powerful system bus, and it is used on most architectures supported by Linux. I shall also discuss the widely used and system-independent USB for external peripherals.[18]

---

[18]Whether this is a classical bus is a matter of controversy because USB does not offer the functionality of a *system* bus but is reliant on an additional distribution mechanism "within the computer." I take a pragmatic approach and am little concerned with this controversial issue.

6.7.1 The Generic Driver Model

Modern bus systems may differ in the details of their layout and structure, but they have much in common, a fact that is reflected in the data structures in the kernel. Many elements are used in all buses (and in the associated device data structures). During the development of 2.6, a generic driver model (*device model*) was incorporated into the kernel to prevent unnecessary duplication. Properties common to all buses are packed into special data structures that are associated with the bus-specific elements and can be processed by generic methods.

The generic driver model is heavily based on the generic object model as discussed in Chapter 1, and has thus also strong connections with the sysfs filesystem as examined in Section 10.3.

Representation of Devices

The driver model features a special data structure to represent the generic device properties of practically all bus types.[19] This structure is embedded directly in the bus-specific data structures and not by means of a reference — as is the case with the kobjects introduced above. Its (simplified) definition is as follows:

```
<device.h>
struct device {
        struct klist            klist_children;
        struct klist_node       knode_parent;          /* node in sibling list */
        struct klist_node       knode_driver;
        struct klist_node       knode_bus;
        struct device   * parent;

        struct kobject kobj;
        char    bus_id[BUS_ID_SIZE];    /* position on parent bus */
...

        struct bus_type * bus;          /* type of bus device is on */
        struct device_driver *driver;   /* which driver has allocated this
                                           device */
        void            *driver_data;   /* data private to the driver */
        void            *platform_data; /* Platform specific data, device
                                           core doesn't touch it */
...
        void    (*release)(struct device * dev);
};
```

The klist and klist_node data structures used are enhanced versions of the familiar list_head data structures to which locking and reference management elements have been added. klist is a list head and klist_node a list element. Various list manipulation operations implemented by means of this mechanism are located in <klist.h>. The associated code is rather technical, but does not offer any deep insight into the kernel, so I won't discuss it here, particularly as lists of this kind are used only for the generic device model but not by the remainder of the kernel.

---

[19]Devices of all relatively modern buses include such properties, and this will not change in new bus designs. Older buses that do not comply with the model are regarded as exceptions.

More interesting are the elements of `struct device`, which have the following meanings:

❑ The embedded `kobject` controls generic object properties as discussed above.

❑ Various elements are used to build hierarchical relationships between devices. `klist_children` is the head of a linked list with all lower-level devices of the specified device. `knode_parent` is used as a list element if the device itself is included on such a list. `parent` points to the `device` instance of the parent element.

❑ Since a device driver is able to serve more than one device (when, for example, two identical cards are installed in the system), `knode_driver` is used as a list element to list the `device` instances of all managed devices. `driver` points to the data structure of the device driver that controls the device (more on this below).

❑ `bus_id` uniquely specifies the position of the device on the hosting bus (the format used varies between bus types). For example, the position of devices on a PCI bus is uniquely defined by a string with the following format: `<bus number>:<slot number>.<function number>`.

❑ `bus` is a pointer to the data structure instance of the bus (more below) on which the device is located.

❑ `driver_data` is a private element of the driver that is not modified by generic code. It can be used to point to specific data that do not fit into the general scheme but are needed to work with the device. `platform_data` and `firmware_data` are also private elements that can be used to associate architecture-specific data and firmware information with a device; they are also left untouched by the generic driver model.

❑ `release` is a destructor function to free the allocated resources to the kernel when the device (or `device` instance) is no longer in use.

The kernel provides the `device_register` standard function to add a new device to the kernel data structures. This function is examined below. The `device_get` and `device_put` function pair counts the references.

The generic driver model also makes a separate data structure available for device drivers.

```
<driver.h>
struct device_driver {
        const char              * name;
        struct bus_type         * bus;

        struct kobject          kobj;
        struct klist            klist_devices;
        struct klist_node       knode_bus;
...
        int     (*probe)        (struct device * dev);
        int     (*remove)       (struct device * dev);
        void    (*shutdown)     (struct device * dev);
        int     (*suspend)      (struct device * dev, pm_message_t state);
        int     (*resume)       (struct device * dev);
};
```

The meanings of the elements are as follows:

- ❑ name points to a text string to uniquely identify the driver.

- ❑ bus points to an object that represents the bus and provides bus-specific operations (see closer look at this below).

- ❑ klist_devices is the head of a standard list that includes the device instances of all devices controlled by the driver. The individual devices are interlinked by means of devices->knode_devices.

- ❑ knode_bus is used to link all devices on a common bus.

- ❑ probe is a function to check whether a device that can be handled by the device driver is present in the system.

- ❑ remove is invoked to remove a device from the system.

- ❑ shutdown, suspend, and resume are used for power management.

Drivers are registered with the system using the driver_register standard function of the kernel discussed below.

Representation of Buses

The generic driver model represents not only devices but also buses using a further data structure that is defined as follows:

```
<device.h>
struct bus_type {
        const char              * name;
...
        struct kset             subsys;
        struct kset             drivers;
        struct kset             devices;
        struct klist            klist_devices;
        struct klist            klist_drivers;
...
        int             (*match)(struct device * dev, struct device_driver * drv);
        int             (*uevent)(struct device *dev, struct kobj_uevent_env *env);
        int             (*probe)(struct device * dev);
        int             (*remove)(struct device * dev);
        void            (*shutdown)(struct device * dev);
        int             (*suspend)(struct device * dev, pm_message_t state);
...
        int             (*resume)(struct device * dev);
...
};
```

- ❑ name is a text name for the bus. It is especially used to identify the bus in the sysfs filesystem.

- ❑ All devices and drivers associated with the bus are managed as sets using the drivers and devices entries. The kernel also generates two lists (klist_devices and klist_drivers) to hold the same data. The lists enable all resources (devices and drivers) to be scanned quickly, and the ksets ensure automatic integration into the sysfs filesystem. subsys provides a connection with the bus subsystem. Accordingly buses appear in /sys/bus/busname.

❑ match points to a function that attempts to find a matching driver for a given device.

❑ add is used to inform a bus that a new device has been added to the system.

❑ probe is invoked when it is necessary to link a driver with a device. This function checks whether the device is actually present in the system.

❑ remove removes the link between a driver and a device. This happens, for example, when a hot-pluggable device is removed from the system.

❑ shutdown, suspend, and resume are power management functions.

Registration Procedures

To clarify how the data structures for buses, devices, and device drivers are connected with each other, it is useful to examine the registration procedures for each type. Some technical details like error handling are omitted in the following to highlight the essential points. Naturally, the functions make extensive use of methods provided by the generic device model.

Registering Buses

Before devices and their drivers can be registered, a bus is required. Thus we start with bus_register, which adds a new bus to the system. First of all, the new bus is added to the bus subsystem via the embedded subsys kset:

drivers/base/bus.c
```
int bus_register(struct bus_type * bus)
{
        int retval;

        retval = kobject_set_name(&bus->subsys.kobj, "%s", bus->name);
        bus->subsys.kobj.kset = &bus_subsys;
        retval = subsystem_register(&bus->subsys);
...
```

The bus wants to know all about both its devices and their drivers, so the bus registers kernel sets for them. Both have bus as parent and drivers ksets:

drivers/base/bus.c
```
        kobject_set_name(&bus->devices.kobj, "devices");
        bus->devices.kobj.parent = &bus->subsys.kobj;
        retval = kset_register(&bus->devices);

        kobject_set_name(&bus->drivers.kobj, "drivers");
        bus->drivers.kobj.parent = &bus->subsys.kobj;
        bus->drivers.ktype = &driver_ktype;
        retval = kset_register(&bus->drivers);
...
}
```

Registering Devices

Registering devices consists of two separate steps as Figure 6-22 shows: Initializing the data structures of the device, and including it into the data structure network.

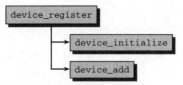

Figure 6-22: Code flow diagram for `device_register`.

`device_initialize` mainly adds the new device to the device subsystem by `kobj_set_kset_s(dev, devices_subsys)`.

`device_add` requires a little more effort. First of all, the parent/child relationship specified via `device->parent` is brought over to the generic kernel object hierarchy:

drivers/base/core.c
```
int device_add(struct device *dev)
{
        struct device *parent = NULL;
...
        parent = get_device(dev->parent);
        kobj_parent = get_device_parent(dev, parent);
        dev->kobj.parent = kobj_parent;
...
```

Registering the device in the devices subsystem requires a simple call to `kobject_add` since subsystem membership was already set in `device_initialize`.

drivers/base/core.c
```
        kobject_set_name(&dev->kobj, "%s", dev->bus_id);
        error = kobject_add(&dev->kobj);
...
```

Afterward `bus_add_device` adds links within sysfs — one in the bus directory that points to the device, and one in the device directory which points to the bus subsystem. `bus_attach_device` tries to autoprobe the device. If a suitable driver can be found, the device is added to `bus->klist_devices`. The device is also added to the child list of the parent (before that, the device knew its parent, but the parent did not know the child).

drivers/base/core.c
```
        error = bus_add_device(dev);
        bus_attach_device(dev);
        if (parent)
                klist_add_tail(&dev->knode_parent, &parent->klist_children);
...
}
```

Registering Device Drivers

After performing some sanity checks and initialization work, `driver_register` employs `bus_add_driver` to add a new driver to a bus. Once more, the driver is first equipped with a name and then registered in the generic data structure framework:

drivers/base/bus.c
```
int bus_add_driver(struct device_driver *drv)
{
        struct bus_type * bus = bus_get(drv->bus);
        int error = 0;
...

        error = kobject_set_name(&drv->kobj, "%s", drv->name);
        drv->kobj.kset = &bus->drivers;
        error = kobject_register(&drv->kobj);
...
```

If the bus supports autoprobing, `driver_attach` is called. The function iterates over all devices on the bus and checks if the driver feels responsible for any of them using the driver's `match` function. Finally, the driver is added to the list of all drivers registered with the bus.

drivers/base/bus.
```
        if (drv->bus->drivers_autoprobe)
                error = driver_attach(drv);
...
        klist_add_tail(&drv->knode_bus, &bus->klist_drivers);
...
}
```

6.7.2 The PCI Bus

PCI is short for *peripheral component interconnect*, a standard bus developed by Intel that has quickly established itself as a very popular bus among component manufacturers and architecture vendors, not because of a skillful marketing strategy but on the basis of its technical merits. It was designed to combat one of the worst plagues ever to affect the (programming) world — the ISA bus.[20] The following goals were formulated to compensate for the deficiencies inherent in the ISA bus design once and for all:

❑ Support for high transfer bandwidths to cater to multimedia applications with large data streams.

❑ Simple and easily automated configuration of attached peripherals.

❑ Platform independence; that is, not tied to a specific processor type or system platform.

Several versions of the PCI specification exist, as enhancements have been added to cover more recent technical developments — for example, one of the last major "updates" relates to support for hotplugging (the addition and removal of devices while the system is up and running).

---

[20]ISA stands for *industrial standard architecture*. This bus was developed by a large association of hardware vendors in response to IBM's attempts to suppress the manufacture of expansion devices through the introduction of the patented and proprietary microchannel. The ISA bus system is of very simple design to facilitate the use of expansion cards; in fact, it is so simple that even amateur electronics enthusiasts are able to develop suitable expansion hardware — something that is practically inconceivable with today's modern designs. It does, however, exhibit serious deficiencies in terms of bus programming and device driver addressing that are due in part to the totally different computer technology situation of the time and in part to the bus design, which can by no means be regarded as forward-looking.

As a result of the processor-independent nature of the PCI specification, the bus is used not only on IA-32 systems (and their more or less direct successors IA-64 and AMD64) but also on other complementary architectures such as PowerPC, Alpha, or SPARC — justified by the need to enjoy the benefits of the numerous inexpensive expansion cards produced for the bus.

Layout of a PCI System

Before discussing how PCI is implemented in the kernel, let us examine the major principles on which the bus is based. Readers who require more detailed descriptions are referred to the many textbooks on hardware technology (e.g., [BH01]).

Identification of Devices

Each device on one of the PCI buses of the system is identified by a set of three numbers.

❑   The *bus number* is the number of the bus to which the device is assigned; numbering starts at 0 as usual. The PCI specification permits a maximum of 255 buses per system.

❑   The *device number* is a unique identifying number within a bus. A maximum of 32 devices can be attached to a bus. Devices on different buses may have the same device number.

❑   The *function number* is used to implement devices with more than one expansion device (in the classical sense) on a single plug-in card. For example, two network cards can be housed on a plug-in card for reasons of space, in which case the individual interfaces are designated by different function numbers. Much used in laptops are multifunction chipsets, which are attached to the PCI and integrate a whole range of expansions (IDE controller, USB controller, modem, network, etc.) in a minimum of space; these expansions must also be kept apart by means of the function number. The PCI standard defines the maximum number of function units on a device as eight.

Each device is uniquely identified by a 16-bit number, where 8 bits are reserved for the bus number, 5 for the device number, and 3 for the function number. Drivers need not bother with this extremely compact notation because the kernel builds a network of data structures that contains the same information but is much easier to handle from a C point of view.

Address Spaces

Three address spaces support communication with PCI devices.

❑   The I/O space is described by 32 bits and therefore provides a maximum of 4 GB for the port addresses used to communicate with the device.

❑   Depending on processor type, either 32 or 64 bytes are available for data space; of course, the latter is supported only on CPUs with a corresponding word length. The devices present in the system are split over the two memory areas and therefore have unique addresses.

❑   The configuration space contains detailed information on the type and characteristics of the individual devices in order to dispense with the need for dangerous autoprobing.[21]

The address spaces are mapped to different locations in the system's virtual memory according to processor type so that the kernel and the device drivers are able to access the corresponding resources.

---

[21]Autoprobing is the "automatic detection" of devices by sending data to various addresses and waiting for the system to respond in order to recognize the cards present in the system. This was one of the many evils of the ISA bus.

Configuration Information

In contrast to many of its predecessors, the PCI bus is a jumper-free system. In other words, expansion devices can be fully configured by software means and without user intervention.[22] To support such configuration, each PCI device has a 256-byte-long configuration space with information on the special characteristics and requirements of the device. Even though 256 bytes may at first appear to be a paltry figure given current memory configuration levels, a large amount of information can be stored, as shown in Figure 6-23, which illustrates the layout of the configuration space as required by the PCI specification.

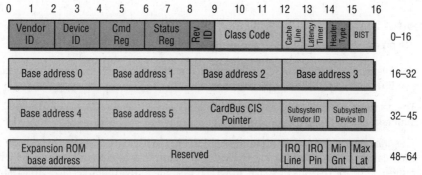

Figure 6-23: Layout of the PCI configuration space.

> Although the structure must be 256 bytes in length, only the first 64 bytes are standardized. The remainder are freely available and are typically used to exchange additional information between the device and the driver. The structure of this information is (or should be) defined in the hardware documentation. It should also be noted that not all information in the first 64 bytes is mandatory; some items are optional and may be filled with zeros if they are not required by a device. The mandatory items are highlighted in darker gray in the figure.

The *vendor ID* and *device ID* uniquely identify the vendor and device type. Whereas the former is assigned by the PCI Special Interest Group (an industry consortium) to identify individual companies,[23] the latter can be freely selected by the vendors — they alone are responsible for ensuring that there are no overlaps in their address space. Taken together the two IDs are often referred to as the *signature* of a device. Two additional fields with similar names — *subsystem vendor ID* and *subsystem device ID* — may also be used to more accurately describe generic interfaces. The *revision ID* enables a distinction to be made between various device revision levels. This helps users select device driver versions where known hardware faults have been eliminated or where new features have been added.

The *class code* field is used to assign devices to various function groups and is split into two parts. The first 8 bits indicate the base class and the remaining 16 bits a subclass of the base class. Examples of base classes and their subclasses are given below (I use the names of the corresponding constants in `<pci_ids.h>`).

---

[22]Some readers may well remember the ISA "game" where the cards, mostly miserably documented, were configured by manually adjusting resources by means of jumpers.

[23]The ID for Intel is `0x8086` ...

❑   Mass storage (`PCI_BASE_CLASS_STORAGE`)

   ❑   SCSI controller (`PCI_CLASS_STORAGE_SCSI`)

   ❑   IDE controller (`PCI_CLASS_STORAGE_IDE`)

   ❑   RAID controller (to combine multiple disk drives) (`PCI_CLASS_STORAGE_RAID`)

❑   Network (`PCI_BASE_CLASS_NETWORK`)

   ❑   Ethernet (`PCI_BASE_NETWORK_ETHERNET`)

   ❑   FDDI (`PCI_BASE_NETWORK_FDDI`)

❑   System components (`PCI_BASE_CLASS_SYSTEM`)

   ❑   DMA controller (`PCI_CLASS_SYSTEM_DMA`)

   ❑   Real-time clock (`PCI_CLASS_SYSTEM_RTC`)

The six base address fields each comprise 32 bits and are used to define the addresses for communication between the PCI device and the rest of the system. When 64-bit devices are involved (as can happen on Alpha and Sparc64 systems), two base address fields are always merged to describe the position in memory; this halves the number of possible base addresses to three. As far as the kernel is concerned, the only remaining field of any relevance is the IRQ number, which can accept any value between 0 and 255 to specify the interrupt used by the device. A value of 0 indicates that the device does not use interrupts.

> **Even though the PCI standard supports up to 255 interrupts, the number that can actually be used is generally limited by the specific architecture. Methods such as interrupt sharing (discussed in Chapter 5) must then be employed on such systems to support the use of more devices than there are IRQ lines.**

The remaining fields are used by the hardware and not by the software so I won't bother explaining their meanings.

Implementation in the Kernel

The kernel provides an extensive framework for PCI drivers that can be roughly divided into two categories.

❑   Initialization of the PCI system (and, depending on system, the assignment of resources) together with the provision of corresponding data structures to reflect the contents and capabilities of the individual buses and devices so that they can be manipulated easily

❑   Standardized function interfaces to support access to all PCI options

PCI system initialization sometimes differs greatly between the individual system types. For example, IA-32 systems allocate all relevant PCI resources themselves with the help of the BIOS at boot time so that there's little left for the kernel to do. As Alpha systems have no BIOS nor any suitable equivalent, this must be done manually by the kernel. Consequently, when describing the relevant data structures in kernel memory, I shall make the assumption that all PCI devices and buses have already been fully initialized.

Data Structures

The kernel provides several data structures to manage the system's PCI structures. They are declared in <pci.h> and are interlinked by a network of pointers. I give an overview of the structure elements below before moving on to take a closer look at their definitions.

❑ The individual buses in the system are represented by instances of pci_bus.

❑ The pci_dev structure is provided for individual devices, cards, and function units.

❑ Each driver is described by an instance of pci_driver.

The kernel makes two global list_heads available to head the network of PCI data structures (both are defined in <pci.h>).

❑ pci_root_buses lists all the PCI buses in the system. It is the starting point when the data structures are scanned "downward" to find all devices attached to the individual buses.

❑ pci_devices links all PCI devices in the system without taking the bus structure into account. This is useful when a driver wants to search for all devices it supports because the topology is of no interest in this situation (it is, of course, possible to find the bus associated with a device using the many links between the PCI data structures, as you will see below).

Representation of Buses

Each PCI bus is represented in memory by an instance of the pci_bus data structure, which is defined as follows:

<pci.h>
```
#define PCI_BUS_NUM_RESOURCES 8

struct pci_bus {
        struct list_head node;          /* node in list of buses */
        struct pci_bus  *parent;        /* parent bus this bridge is on */
        struct list_head children;      /* list of child buses */
        struct list_head devices;       /* list of devices on this bus */
        struct pci_dev  *self;          /* bridge device as seen by parent */
        struct resource *resource[PCI_BUS_NUM_RESOURCES];
                                        /* address space routed to this bus */

        struct pci_ops  *ops;           /* configuration access functions */
        void            *sysdata;       /* hook for sys-specific extension */
        struct proc_dir_entry *procdir; /* directory entry in /proc/bus/pci */

        unsigned char   number;         /* bus number */
        unsigned char   primary;        /* number of primary bridge */
        unsigned char   secondary;      /* number of secondary bridge */
        unsigned char   subordinate;    /* max number of subordinate buses */

        char            name[48];
...
};
```

The structure is divided into function sections as indicated by the source code formatting.

The first section includes all elements that create links with other PCI data structures. node is a list element used to keep all buses on the global list mentioned above. parent is a pointer to the data structure of the higher-level bus. There may be just one parent bus. The subordinate or child buses must be managed on a linked list with children as the list head.

All attached devices are likewise managed in a linked list headed by devices.

With the exception of bus 0, all system buses can be addressed only via a PCI bridge that functions like a normal PCI device. The self element provides each bus with a pointer to a pci_dev instance that describes the bridge.

The sole purpose of the resource array is to hold the address areas occupied by the bus in virtual memory; each array element contains an instance of the above resource structure. Since the array contains four entries, a bus can reserve just as many different address spaces to communicate with the rest of the system (the array dimension does, of course, conform to the PCI standard). The first element contains the address area for I/O ports. The second always holds the I/O memory area.

The second block first lists a large number of function pointers concentrated in the ops element. These are a collection of functions invoked to access the configuration space, examined more closely below. The sysdata element enables the bus structure to be associated with hardware-specific and therefore driver-specific functions, although the kernel rarely makes use of this option. Finally, procdir provides an interface to the proc filesystem so that /proc/bus/pci can be used to export information on the individual buses to userspace.

The next block contains numeric information. number is a consecutive number that uniquely identifies the bus in the system. subordinate is the maximum number of subordinate buses that the particular bus may have. The name field holds a text name for the bus (e.g., PCI Bus #01) but may also be left blank.

A list of all system buses is compiled when the PCI subsystem is initialized. The buses are linked together in two different ways. The first involves a linear list starting with the above-mentioned root_buses global variable and including all the buses in the system. The node element acts as the list head.

The two-dimensional topology structure of the PCI buses in the form of a tree is facilitated by the parent and children structure members.

Device Management

The struct pci_dev data structure described in this section is the key structure used to represent the individual PCI devices in the system.

> In this context, the kernel interprets the term *device* to mean not only expansion cards but also the PCI bridges used to connect buses to each other. There are not only bridges to interlink PCI buses but also (on older systems) bridges to link PCI buses with ISA buses.

<pci.h>
```
struct pci_dev {
        struct list_head global_list;   /* node in list of all PCI devices */
        struct list_head bus_list;      /* node in per-bus list */
```

```
        struct pci_bus  *bus;          /* bus this device is on */
        struct pci_bus  *subordinate;  /* bus this device bridges to */

        void            *sysdata;      /* hook for sys-specific extension */
        struct proc_dir_entry *procent; /* device entry in /proc/bus/pci */

        unsigned int    devfn;         /* encoded device & function index */
        unsigned short  vendor;
        unsigned short  device;
        unsigned short  subsystem_vendor;
        unsigned short  subsystem_device;
        unsigned int    class;         /* 3 bytes: (base,sub,prog-if) */
        u8              revision;      /* PCI revision, low byte of class word */
        u8              hdr_type;      /* PCI header type ('multi' flag masked out) */
        u8              pcie_type;     /* PCI-E device/port type */
        u8              rom_base_reg;  /* which config register controls the ROM */
        u8              pin;           /* which interrupt pin this device uses */

        struct pci_driver *driver;     /* which driver has allocated this
        device */
...
        struct  device  dev;          /* Generic device interface */

        /* device is compatible with these IDs */
        unsigned short vendor_compatible[DEVICE_COUNT_COMPATIBLE];
        unsigned short device_compatible[DEVICE_COUNT_COMPATIBLE];

        int             cfg_size;      /* Size of configuration space */

        /*
         * Instead of touching interrupt line and base address registers
         * directly, use the values stored here. They might be different!
         */
        unsigned int    irq;
        struct resource resource[DEVICE_COUNT_RESOURCE]; /* I/O and memory
        regions + expansion ROMs */
...
};
```

The first elements of the structure are dedicated to implementing links by means of lists or trees. global_list and bus_list are two list heads to place the device on the global device list (headed by pci_devices) or on the bus-specific device list (headed by pci_bus->devices).

The bus element is used for backward linking between device and bus. It contains a pointer to the pci_bus instance to which the device is assigned. A second link to a bus is held in subordinate, which only has a valid value if the device represented is a PCI-to-PCI bridge that interconnects two PCI buses (otherwise it contains a null pointer). If this is the case, subordinate is used to point to the data structure of the "subordinate" PCI bus.

The next two elements are less interesting — sysdata is used to store driver-specific data, and procentry to manage the proc entry for the device. Neither does the next block hold any surprises. All elements between devfn and rom_base_reg simply store PCI configuration space data already mentioned above. They are filled with data read from the hardware when the system is initialized. It is then no longer necessary to fetch these data from the configuration space for subsequent operations since they can be obtained quickly and easily from the data structure.

`driver` points to the driver used to control the device; I discuss the `struct pci_driver` data structure used to do this shortly. Each PCI driver is uniquely identified by an instance of this structure. A link to the generic *device model* is also a must for PCI devices and is established by means of the `dev` element.

`irq` specifies the number of the interrupt used by the device, and `resource` is an array that holds the instances of the `resources` reserved by the driver for I/O memory.

Driver Functions

The third and final basic data structure that forms the PCI layer is called `pci_driver`. It is used to implement PCI drivers and represents the interface between generic kernel code and the low-level hardware driver for a device. Each PCI driver must pack its functions into this interface so that the kernel is able to control the available drivers consistently.

The structure is defined as follows (for the sake of simplicitiy I have omitted the entries required to implement power management):

\<pci.h\>
```
struct pci_driver {
...
        char *name;
        const struct pci_device_id *id_table;   /* must be non-NULL for probe to be called */
         int  (*probe)  (struct pci_dev *dev, const struct pci_device_id *id);   /* New device
inserted */
        void (*remove) (struct pci_dev *dev);   /* Device removed (NULL if not a hot-plug capable
driver) */
...
        struct device_driver    driver;
...
};
```

The meaning of the first two elements is self-evident. `name` is a text identifier for the device (typically, the name of the module in which the driver is implemented), and `driver` establishes the link to the generic device model.

The most important aspect of the PCI driver structure is support for detection, installation, and removal of devices. Two function pointers are available for this purpose: `probe`, which checks whether a PCI device is supported by the driver (this procedure is known as *probing* and explains the name of the pointer); and `remove`, which helps remove a device. Removal of PCI devices only makes sense if the system supports hotplugging (which is not usually the case).

A driver must know for which devices it is responsible. The (sub)device and (sub)vendor IDs discussed above are used to uniquely identify the devices supported in a list to which the kernel refers to ascertain which devices are supported by the driver. A further data structure named `pci_device_id` is used to implement the list. This structure is of great importance in the PCI subsystem and is discussed below. Since a driver can support various (more or less compatible) devices, the kernel supports a whole search list of device IDs.

Registering Drivers

PCI drivers can be registered by means of `pci_register_driver`. The function is quite primitive. Its prime task is to fill a few remaining fields of a `pci_device` instance to which relevant functions have already been assigned. This instance is passed to the generic device layer using `driver_register`, whose mode of operation was discussed above.

More interesting than the registration process is the filling of the `pci_device` structure in the individual drivers as this involves not only defining the above functions that define the interfaces between the driver and the generic kernel code but also creating a list of all devices whose (sub)device and (sub)vendor IDs indicate that they are suitable for the driver.

As already noted above, the `pci_device_id` data structure whose definition is given below has a decisive role to play in this context.

```
<mod_devicetable.h>
struct pci_device_id {
        __u32 vendor, device;          /* Vendor and device ID or PCI_ANY_ID*/
        __u32 subvendor, subdevice;    /* Subsystem ID's or PCI_ANY_ID */
        __u32 class, class_mask;       /* (class,subclass,prog-if) triplet */
        unsigned long driver_data;     /* Data private to the driver */
};
```

You are familiar with the elements of this structure from the description of the PCI configuration space. By defining specific constants, a driver is able to refer to a particular chipset/device; `class_mask` also allows classes to be filtered by reference to a bitmask.

In many cases, it is neither necessary nor desirable to describe *just one* device. If a large number of compatible devices is supported, this would quickly result in endless declaration lists in the driver sources; these would be difficult to read and would have the tangible disadvantage that a compatible device may not be found simply because it is not included in the list of supported devices. The kernel therefore provides the wildcard constant `PCI_ANY_ID` that matches any identifier of a PCI device. Let us look at how this is used in the following example for the eepro100 driver (a widely used network card chipset from Intel):

```
drivers/net/e100/e100_main.c
#define INTEL_8255X_ETHERNET_DEVICE(device_id, ich) {\
        PCI_VENDOR_ID_INTEL, device_id, PCI_ANY_ID, PCI_ANY_ID, \
        PCI_CLASS_NETWORK_ETHERNET << 8, 0xFFFF00, ich }
static struct pci_device_id e100_id_table[] = {
        INTEL_8255X_ETHERNET_DEVICE(0x1029, 0),
        INTEL_8255X_ETHERNET_DEVICE(0x1030, 0),
        INTEL_8255X_ETHERNET_DEVICE(0x1031, 3),
        INTEL_8255X_ETHERNET_DEVICE(0x1032, 3),
        INTEL_8255X_ETHERNET_DEVICE(0x1033, 3),
...
        INTEL_8255X_ETHERNET_DEVICE(0x245D, 2),
        INTEL_8255X_ETHERNET_DEVICE(0x27DC, 7),
        { 0, }
};
```

Each macro expansion of `INTEL_8255X_ETHERNET_DEVICE` generates an entry in the table. The individual elements of the entry are given in the sequence in which they are declared in `pci_device_id`.

`0x8086` is the vendor ID for Intel, the manufacturer of the chipset (the driver could also have used the pre-processor constant `PCI_VENDOR_ID_INTEL` defined with the same value). Each entry holds a specific device ID that identifies all versions currently on the market. Subvendor and subdevice ID are of no relevance and are therefore represented by `PCI_ANY_ID`; this means that any subvendor or any subdevice is recognized as valid.

The kernel provides the `pci_match_id` function to compare the PCI device data with the data in an ID table. It refers to the given ID table of a `pci_dev` instance to ascertain whether the device is included in the table.

drivers/pci/pci-driver.c
```
const struct pci_device_id *pci_match_id(const struct pci_device_id *ids,
                                         struct pci_dev *dev);
```

A match is found when all elements in an ID table entry and all elements in the device configuration are identical. If a field in the ID table contains the special entry `PCI_ANY_ID`, *every* value in the corresponding field of the `pci_device` instance is interpreted as a match.

6.7.3 USB

USB (*Universal Serial Bus*) was developed at the end of the '90s of what is now the last century as an external bus to satisfy ever-more-demanding PC requirements and to produce solutions for new computer types such as handhelds, PDAs, and the like. As a universal external bus, USB delivers its benefits when used in conjunction with devices requiring low to medium data transfer rates such as mice, Webcams, and keyboards. However, more broadband-intensive devices such as external hard disks, CD-ROMs, and CD writers can also be operated on USB buses. The maximum transfer rate for USB 1.1 is limited to 12 MBit/second but Version 2.0 of the standard supports higher rates of up to 480 MBit/second.

When the bus was designed, special attention was focused on ease of use for inexperienced computer users. As a consequence, hotplugging and the associated transparent installation of drivers are core aspects of the USB design. In contrast to earlier PCI hotplug cards (which were difficult to obtain) and PCMCIA/PC cards (which were little used because of their high price), USB is the first bus that has made the hotplugging capabilities of the kernel available to a wide audience.

Features and Mode of Operation

There are three versions of the USB standard. The most important are the first version (1.0) and its successor (1.1), as most hardware has adopted this standard. The more recent version (2.0) is designed to eliminate the speed disadvantages of USB as compared with other external buses (primarily FireWire), and is nowadays in widespread use. Kernel support is available for both protocols. The in-kernel data structures employed to manage devices are identical for all versions, and since I will concentrate on these in the following, I will not be much concerned with the technical differences between the different versions of the standard.

What are the special features of USB as compared to other buses? In addition to ease of use for end-users, mention must be made of the topological structure used to sort attached devices, which is reminiscent of network structures. Starting from a single root controller, devices are connected via hubs in a tree-like structure, as illustrated in Figure 6-24. Up to 127 terminal devices can be attached to a system in this manner.

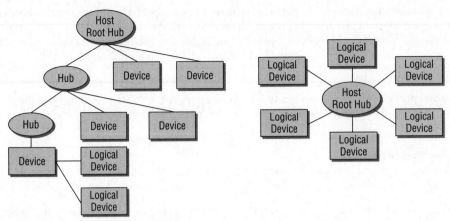

Figure 6-24: Topology of a USB system.

A device is never connected directly to the host controller but always via a hub. To ensure that drivers have a uniform view of the situation, the kernel replaces the root controller with a small emulation layer so that the rest of the system sees the controller as a virtual hub; this simplifies the development of drivers.

> The fact that the devices in a USB system are physically arranged in a tree structure is only of relevance to specific parts of the USB subsystem. The drivers for terminal devices need not concern themselves with whether a device is connected directly to the root hub or via five intervening hubs. Each device on the bus is assigned a unique number for communication purposes, and, as a result, the USB driver sees all devices as being connected *directly* to the root hub. The right-hand part of Figure 6-24 shows the logical view of the structure as seen by a device driver.

USB is not explicitly tied to a specific processor or system architecture but can, in principle, be used on all platforms — even if, as usual, the PC platform is primarily responsible for the popularity of the bus. Because USB interfaces are also available as PCI plug-in cards (which, as standard, use a motherboard chip connected to the PCI system bus via a bridge), all architectures that support PCI cards (in the main, Sparc64, Alpha, etc.) are automatically able to support USB.

Due care should be exercised when using the term *device* in the context of USB because it splits into three levels.

❑ A *device* is anything that the user can connect to the USB bus — for example, a videocamera with integrated microphone or the like. As this example shows, a device may consist of several function units that can be controlled by different drivers.

❑ Each device is made up of one or more *configurations* that govern the global characteristics of the device. For instance, a device may feature two interfaces, one of which is used if power is supplied from the bus, the other if an external power supply is used.

❑ In turn, each configuration consists of one or more *interfaces*, each of which provides different setting options. Three interfaces are conceivable for a videocamera — microphone only enabled, camera only enabled, or both enabled. The bandwidth requirements of the device may differ according to the interface selected.

❑ And finally, each interface may have one or more *end points* that are controlled by a driver. There are situations in which a driver controls all end points of a device but each end point may require a different driver. In our example above, the end points are the imaging video unit and the microphone. Another common example of a device with two different end points is a USB keyboard that integrates a USB hub to permit the connection of other devices (a hub is ultimately a special kind of USB device).

All USB devices are classified in categories; this is reflected in the fact that the source code for the individual drivers is kept separate in the kernel sources. `drivers/usb/` contains a number of subdirectories with the following contents:

❑ `image` for graphics and video devices such as digital cameras, scanners, and the like.

❑ `input` for input and output devices for communication with computer users. Classic representatives of this category include not only keyboards and mice but also touch screens, data gloves, and the like.

❑ `media` for the numerous multimedia devices that have come to the fore in the last few years.

❑ `net` for network cards that are attached to the computer by means of USB and are therefore often referred to as *adapters* that bridge the gap between Ethernet and USB.

❑ `storage` for all mass storage devices such as hard disks and the like.

❑ `class` includes all drivers support devices of one of the standard classes defined for USB.

❑ `core` contains drivers for host adapters to which a USB chain is attached.

Roughly speaking, the driver sources originate from the following three areas: *standard devices* such as keyboards, mice, and the like that can always be supported by the same driver, regardless of device vendor; *proprietary* hardware such as MP3 players and other gadgets that require special drivers; and drivers for *host adapters* that are attached to the rest of the system via a different bus system (typically PCI) and that establish the connection (also physical) to the USB device chain.

The USB standard defines four different transfer modes, each of which must be explicitly catered for by the kernel.

❑ *Control transfer* involves the transfer of control information needed (primarily) for the initial configuration of a device. This type of communication must be safe and reliable but requires only a narrow bandwidth. The various control commands are transferred by means of pre-defined tokens whose symbolic names such as `GET_STATUS`, `SET_INTERFACE`, and so on have been defined and documented in the USB standard. In the kernel sources they can all be found in <usb.h>, where they are prefixed with `USQ_REQ_` — to prevent namespace problems — and declared as pre-processor constants. The standard mandates a minimum set of commands that all devices must understand. However, vendors are free to add further device-specific commands that must be used and understood by their own drivers.

❑ *Bulk transfers* send individual data packets that can take up the full bus bandwidth. In this mode, data transfer takes place with the security guaranteed by the bus; in other words, data sent always reach their destination unchanged.[24] Devices such as scanners or mass storage expansions use this mode.

❑ *Interrupt transfers* are similar to bulk transfers but are repeated at periodic intervals. The interval length can be freely defined (within certain limits) by the driver. This transfer mode is used by preference by network cards and similar devices.

❑ A special role is played by *isochronous transfer* as this is the only way of setting up a transfer that although unreliable makes use of a fixed, pre-defined bandwidth (in certain respects, this mode can be compared with the datagram technique for network cards as discussed in Chapter 12). This transfer mode is best used in situations where it is important to guarantee a continuous data stream and where the occasional loss of data is acceptable. A prime example of where this mode is used are Webcams that send video data via the USB bus.

Management of Drivers

The USB bus system is implemented in two layers in the kernel.

❑ A driver must be available for the host adapter. The adapter must provide a connection option for the USB chain and assume responsibility for electrical communication with the terminated devices; the adapter itself must be connected to another system bus (currently, three different host adapter types called OHCI, EHCI, and UHCI are available; they cover all controller types offered on the market).

❑ Device drivers communicate with individual USB devices and export their functionality to other parts of the kernel respectively into userspace. These drivers interact with the host controllers via a standardized interface so that the controller type is irrelevant to the USB driver. Any other approach is obviously impractical because it would then be necessary to develop a host controller-dependent driver for each USB device.

Below I shall examine the structure and mode of operation of USB drivers. In doing so, I shall regard the host controller simply as a transparent interface without discussing the details of its implementation.

Although the structure and layout of the USB subsystem are closely based on the USB standard in terms of the contents of data structures and the names of constants, account must be taken of several subtle details during the practical development of USB drivers. To keep the following information as concise as possible, I shall limit our discussion to the core aspects of the USB subsystem. Consequently, I have "relieved" the data elements I examine of their less relevant members. Once the structure of the subsystem has become clear, it is a simple matter to look up the corresponding details in the kernel sources.

The USB subsystem performs four principal tasks.

❑ Registering and managing the device drivers present.

❑ Finding a suitable driver for a USB device plus initialization and configuration.

❑ Representing the device tree in kernel memory.

❑ Communicating with the device (exchanging data).

---

[24]Assuming, of course, that there are no hardware faults or other effects of *force majeure*.

The following data structures are associated with the items in this list.

The usb_driver structure is the starting point of the collaboration between the USB device driver and the rest of the kernel (above all the USB layer).

```
<usb.h>
struct usb_driver {
        const char *name;

        int (*probe) (struct usb_interface *intf,
                     const struct usb_device_id *id);
        void (*disconnect) (struct usb_interface *intf);
        int (*ioctl) (struct usb_interface *intf, unsigned int code,
                     void *buf);
    ...
        const struct usb_device_id *id_table;
    ...
        struct usbdrv_wrap drvwrap;
    ...
};
```

The name and owner fields fulfill the usual management purposes. The former holds the name of the driver, which must be unique within the kernel (the filename of the module is normally used). The latter creates an association between usb_driver and the module structure if the driver has been added to the kernel as a module. The usual embedded driver object is hidden in another structure this time.

```
<usb.h>
struct usbdrv_wrap {
        struct device_driver driver;
        int for_devices;
};
```

The extra data structure allows distinguishing between interface drivers (for_devices is zero in this case) and proper device drivers.

Of special interest are the function pointers probe and disconnect. Together with id_table, they form the backbone of the hotplugging capabilities of the USB subsystem. When the host adapter detects that a new device has been inserted, a *probing* process is started to find a suitable device driver.

The kernel then traverses all elements of the device tree to ascertain whether any driver is interested. This presupposes, of course, that a driver has not already been assigned to the device. If a driver has been allocated, the device is skipped.

The kernel first scans the list of all devices that are supported by the driver and are included in its id_table list. This approach is familiar because USB devices (like PCI devices) can be uniquely identified by a number. Once a match has been found between device and table, the driver-specific probe function is invoked to perform further checks and initialization work.

If no match is found between the device ID and the list of drivers, the kernel skips to the next driver and need not invoke the function stored in probe.

The ID table is made up of several instances of the following structure, which describes a USB device by means of several identifiers:

```
<mod_devicetable.h>
struct usb_device_id {
        /* which fields to match against? */
        __u16           match_flags;

        /* Used for product specific matches; range is inclusive */
        __u16           idVendor;
        __u16           idProduct;
        __u16           bcdDevice_lo;
        __u16           bcdDevice_hi;

        /* Used for device class matches */
        __u8            bDeviceClass;
        __u8            bDeviceSubClass;
        __u8            bDeviceProtocol;

        /* Used for interface class matches */
        __u8            bInterfaceClass;
        __u8            bInterfaceSubClass;
        __u8            bInterfaceProtocol;
    ...
};
```

`match_flags` is used to specify which fields of the structure are to be compared with the device data; various pre-processor constants are defined for this purpose. For example, `USB_DEVICE_ID_MATCH_VENDOR` indicates that the `idVendor` field is to be checked, and `USB_DEVICE_ID_MATCH_DEV_PROTOCOL` instructs the kernel to check the protocol field. The meaning of the other fields of `usb_device_id` is self-explanatory.

The association between driver and device is established not only when a new device is added to the system but also when a new driver is loaded. The same approach is adopted as described above. The starting point is the `usb_register` routine, which must be invoked to register a new USB driver.

The `probe` and `remove` functions work with interfaces that are described by a separate data structure (`usb_interface`). Besides interface characteristics, these include pointers to the associated device, the driver, and the USB class to which the interface belongs. It is not therefore necessary to go into the details of the data structure definition.

Representation of the Device Tree

A further data structure is needed to represent the USB device tree and the various device characteristics in the kernel.

```
<usb.h>
struct usb_device {
        int                   devnum;        /* Address on USB bus */
        char                  devpath [16];  /* Use in messages: /port/port/... */
        enum usb_device_state state;         /* configured, not attached, etc */
        enum usb_device_speed speed;         /* high/full/low (or error) */
    ...
```

```
            unsigned int toggle[2];          /* one bit for each endpoint
                                              * ([0] = IN, [1] = OUT) */

            struct usb_device *parent;        /* our hub, unless we're the root */
            struct usb_bus *bus;              /* Bus we're part of */

            struct device dev;                /* Generic device interface */

            struct usb_device_descriptor descriptor;/* Descriptor */
            struct usb_host_config *config;   /* All of the configs */

            struct usb_host_config *actconfig;/* the active configuration */
...
            u8 portnum;                       /* Parent port number (origin 1) */

...

            /* static strings from the device */
            char *product;                    /* iProduct string, if present */
            char *manufacturer;               /* iManufacturer string, if present */
            char *serial;                     /* iSerialNumber string, if present */
...
            int maxchild;                     /* Number of ports if hub */
            struct usb_device *children[USB_MAXCHILDREN];
...
    };
```

❑   devnum holds the unique number of the device (globally unique in the entire USB tree). state
    and speed indicate the state (attached, configured, etc.) and the speed of the device. The USB
    standard defines three possible values for the speed: USB_SPEED_LOW and USB_SPEED_FULL for
    USB 1.1 and USB_SPEED_HIGH for USB 2.0.

❑   devpath specifies the position of the device in the topology of the USB tree. The port numbers
    of all hubs that must be traversed to move from the root element to the device are stored in the
    individual array entries.

❑   parent points to the data structure of the hub on which the device is attached, and bus points
    to the corresponding data structure of the bus. Both fields therefore supply information on the
    topology of the USB chain.

❑   dev establishes the link to the generic device model.

❑   descriptor groups together the characteristic data that describe a USB device in a further data
    structure (which includes things like vendor ID, product ID, device class, etc.).

❑   actconfig points to the current configuration of the device, and config lists all possible alterna-
    tives.

❑   usbfs_entry is used to link with the USB filesystem that is normally mounted at /proc/bus/usb
    and provides access to the devices from userspace.

❑   product, manufacturer, and serial point to ASCII strings with the product name, the manufac-
    turer, and a serial number for the device, all of which are supplied by the hardware itself.

❑   Two more elements are relevant if the current device is a hub: maxchild specifies how many
    ports the hub has (i.e., how many devices can be attached), and children contains a collection of
    pointers to their usb_device instances. These elements define the topology of the USB tree.

> Even though up to now I have always spoken of just *one* USB device tree, there may
> be several such trees in kernel memory (that do not share the same root element).
> This happens when a computer has several USB host controllers. The root elements
> of all buses are kept in a separate list named `usb_bus_list` that is defined in
> `drivers/usb/core/hcd.c`.

The elements in the bus list are represented by the following data structure:

```
<usb.h>
struct usb_bus {
        struct device *controller;
        int busnum;                     /* Bus number (in order of reg) */
        char *bus_name;                 /* stable id (PCI slot_name etc) */

...

        struct usb_devmap devmap;       /* device address allocation map */
        struct usb_device *root_hub;    /* Root hub */
        struct list_head bus_list;      /* list of busses */

...

        struct dentry *usbfs_dentry;         /* usbfs dentry entry for the bus */

...
};
```

The data structure has two elements that uniquely identify the bus: `busnum` is an integer number assigned sequentially when buses are registered, and `bus_name` is a pointer to a short string holding a unique name. `controller` stores a pointer to the `device` instance of the hardware device that implements the bus.

Not only devices but also the buses themselves appear in the USB filesystem mentioned above. `usb_bus` must therefore also include a pointer to the `dentry` instance to create the requisite link to the virtual filesystem.

The middle elements of the data structure contain the most interesting data which link the available buses with each other and also the attached devices. They also provide a standardized connection to the underlying host controllers, thus abstracting the controllers as seen by the remaining USB layer.

❑　`bus_list` is a list element used to manage all `usb_bus` instances on a linked list.

❑　`root_hub` is a pointer to the data structure of the (virtual) root hub that represents the root element of the bus's device tree.

❑　`devmap` is a bitmap list with a (minimum) length of 128 bits. It is used to keep track of which USB numbers have already been allocated and which are still free.

> *Reminder: Each USB device on a number is assigned a unique integer number when it is inserted. The standard specifies a maximum of 128 devices on a bus.*

The `usb_devnum` structure type used is simply an array of `unsigned long` elements that serves no other purpose than to ensure that at least 128 consecutive bits are available.

To communicate with underlying controller hardware, a *USB request block* is used. Such blocks are used to exchange data with USB devices in all possible forms of transfer (isochronous transfer, etc.).

```
drivers/usb/core/hcd.h
int usb_hcd_submit_urb (struct urb *urb, gfp_t mem_flags) ;
```

URBs have not always been used to communicate and exchange data with USB devices. In earlier versions of the USB system, there were various interfaces for each type of transfer — not something that made the programming of device drivers any easier. In this old approach, the implementation of isochronous transfers was riddled with errors. A group of kernel developers therefore decided not only to totally rewrite the driver for the host adapter used at the time but also to fully redesign the entire USB layer.[25] URBs are something of an oddity in the Linux kernel in the sense that their design was lifted from the USB implementation of MS Windows, otherwise so unloved in Linux circles. There are differences in detail, but the basic concept is the same in both operating systems. Of course, it goes without saying that the Linux version has far fewer bugs ...

The exact layout of URBs is not particularly interesting for our purposes, so I will dispense with a close examination of the associated `struct urb` structure. The many references to the details of and difference between the individual transfer types means that the structure is difficult to understand without a comprehensive knowledge of USB data transfer, and a detailed description of the structure is beyond the scope of this book.

As it is, USB device drivers rarely come into contact with `urb` instances but instead make use of a whole set of macros and helper functions to facilitate filling in URBs for requests and the reading of returned data. This requires in-depth knowledge of the operation of USB devices and is therefore not discussed here.

6.8 Summary

Device drivers comprise the largest part of the Linux kernel sources. Nevertheless, I did not consider the implementation of individual drivers in this chapter, but focused on the *framework* provided by the kernel for this purpose instead. This is reasonable because device drivers can be seen as "kernel applications" that are built on top of this framework.

You have learned that device drivers can essentially be grouped into two categories: Character devices that transfer a stream of bytes to and from the kernel, and block devices that require a more complicated request management. Both, however, do interact with userland applications by means of device special files that allow them to access the services of drivers with regular file I/O operations.

Finally, I have also discussed how I/O memory and port resources are handled by the kernel, and have discussed how bus systems connect devices with the computer and with other devices. This also included a presentation of the generic device and driver model, which allows both kernel and userspace applications to enjoy a unified picture of the available resources.

---

[25]In allusion to the date of the patch, the authors of the new layer refer to this rewrite as the "USB October revolution" ...

7

Modules

Modules are an efficient way of adding device drivers, filesystems and other components dynamically into the Linux kernel without having to build a new kernel or reboot the system. They remove many of the restrictions constantly raised as arguments against monolithic architectures by, above all, micro-kernel proponents. These arguments concern primarily the lack of dynamic extensibility. In this chapter, we examine how the kernel interacts with the modules; in other words, how they are loaded and unloaded and how the kernel detects the interdependencies between various modules. It is therefore necessary to deal in some detail with the structure of module binary files (and their ELF structure).

7.1 Overview

Modules have many advantages,[1] of which the following are worthy of particular mention:

❏ By using modules, distributors are able to pre-compile a comprehensive collection of drivers without bloating the size of the kernel image beyond bounds. After automatic hardware detection or user prompting, the installation routine selects the appropriate modules and adds them into the kernel.

   This enables even inexperienced users to install drivers for system devices without having to build a new kernel. This represents a major step toward (and perhaps even a prerequisite for) wider acceptance of Linux systems.

❏ Kernel developers can pack experimental code into modules that can be unloaded and reloaded after each modification. This allows new features to be tested quickly without having to reboot the system each time.[2]

License issues can also be resolved with the help of modules. As is generally known, the source code of the Linux kernel is available under the GNU General Public License (Version 2), one of the

---

[1]And also some disadvantages. However, these are so minor that they are of little consequence.

[2]Unless, of course, the system has crashed in the meantime, and this is said to happen when developing drivers.

first and most widely used Open Source licenses.[3] A major problem is the fact that for a variety of reasons — which may or may not be sensible and justified — many hardware manufacturers keep the documentation needed to control their add-on devices under wraps or require developers to sign "nondisclosure agreements" in which they, in turn, promise to keep secret the source code they write using information in the documentation and not to reveal it to the public. This means that the driver cannot be included in official kernel sources whose source code is always open.

This problem can be solved — at least from a technical point of view — by using binary modules that are passed on in compiled form only but not in source code. Control of proprietary hardware is possible using this approach, but most kernel developers are not happy with this situation because using open code has many advantages. The sweeping success of the Linux kernel is certainly a prime example.

Modules can be inserted almost seamlessly into the kernel, as illustrated in Figure 7-1. The module code exports functions that can be used by other kernel modules (and also by code permanently compiled into the kernel). The link between the module and the remaining parts of the kernel can, of course, be broken when the code needs to be unloaded; I discuss the technical details in the sections below.

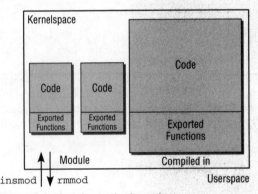

Figure 7-1: Modules in the kernel.

7.2 Using Modules

To add and remove modules, there are several system calls that are normally addressed using the tools of the modutils package that is installed on practically every system.[4]

7.2.1 Adding and Removing

From the user point of view, modules can be added into a running kernel by two different system programs: modprobe and insmod. The former takes into account the dependencies that arise between individual modules when a module depends on the functions of one or more partner modules. In contrast, insmod loads only a single module into the kernel, and this module may depend only on the code already

---

[3]To counter the criticisms levied by license purists: GPL does not, of course, stand for Open Source but for free software. However, because the details are of a legal rather than a technical nature, I do not consider them here.
[4]Notice that during the development of kernel 2.5, the module implementation was revised from top to bottom. The userspace interface differs completely from the old version, which also necessitated a full rewrite of the modutils.

in the kernel, regardless of whether the code was generated dynamically by modules or is permanently compiled into the kernel.

`modprobe` also accesses `insmod` internally once it has identified the additional modules needed for the desired module. Before discussing how this is implemented, I will first describe the mode of operation of `insmod` on which work with modules in userspace is based.

The actions needed when loading a module show strong similarities with the linking of application programs by means of `ld` and with the use of dynamic libraries with `ld.so`. Externally, modules are just normal relocatable object files, as a `file` call will quickly confirm:

```
wolfgang@meitner> file vfat.ko
vfat.ko: ELF 64-bit LSB relocatable, x86-64, version 1 (SYSV), not stripped
```

They are, of course, neither executable files nor program libraries as normally found in system programming; however, the basic structure of the binary module file is based on the same scheme also used for the above purposes.

The output of the `file` command indicates that the module file is *relocatable*, a familiar term in userspace programming. *Relocatable* files have no function references to absolute addresses but point only to *relative* addresses within the code and can therefore be loaded at any offsets in memory provided the addresses are modified accordingly by the dynamic linker `ld.so`. The same applies for kernel modules. Addresses are again given in relative and not absolute units. However, it is the kernel itself and not the dynamic loader that performs relocation.

Whereas in earlier kernel versions (up to 2.4) modules had to be loaded in a multistep process (reservation of memory in the kernel, followed by relocation of data in userspace and copying of the binary code into the kernel), only one system call — `init_module` — is now needed to perform all actions in the kernel itself.

When the system call is processed, the module code is first copied from the kernel into kernel memory; this is followed by relocation and the resolution of as yet undefined references in the module. These occur because the module uses functions that are permanently compiled into the kernel and whose addresses are not known at compilation time.

Handling Unresolved References

In order to work with the remaining parts of the kernel, modules must use functions provided by the kernel. These may be general auxiliary functions such as `printk` or `kmalloc` used by almost every kernel part. More specific functions associated with the module functionality must also be used. The `ramfs` module enables a filesystem to be made available in memory (usually known as RAM disk) and must therefore — like any other code used to implement file systems — call the `register_filesystem` function to add itself to the list of available filesystems in the kernel. The module also makes use of (among others) the `generic_file_read` and `generic_file_write` standard functions that are present in the kernel code and that are used by most kernel filesystems.

A similar situation arises when libraries are used in userspace. Programs use functions defined in an external library by storing pointers to the functions — but not the implementation of the function itself — in their own binary code (of course, other symbol types such as global variables can appear instead of functions). References are resolved for static libraries when the program is linked (using `ld`) and for dynamic libraries when the binary file is loaded (using `ld.so`).

The nm tool can be used to generate a list of all external functions in a module (or in any object file). The following example shows a number of functions that are used in the romfs module but are labeled as external references:

```
wolfgang@meitner> nm romfs.ko
        U generic_read_dir
        U generic_ro_fops
        ...
        U printk
        ...
        U register_filesystem
        ...
```

The U in the output stands for an *unresolved* reference. Note that if your kernel was not built with KALLSYMS_ALL enabled, generic_ro_fops will not be visible. Only symbols of functions but no other symbols like constant structures as generic_ro_fops are included in this case.

It is clear that these functions are defined in kernel base code and are therefore already held in memory. But how can the matching addresses needed to resolve the reference be found? For this purpose, the kernel provides a list of all exported functions; this list shows the memory addresses together with the corresponding function names and can be accessed via the proc filesystem, this being the purpose of the file /proc/kallsyms[5]:

```
wolfgang@meitner> cat /proc/kallsyms | grep printk
ffffffff80232a7f T printk
```

The function references shown in the above example can be fully resolved using the following information, all of which is held in the symbol table of the kernel:

```
fffffc0000324aa0 T printk
fffffc00003407e0 T generic_file_write
ffffffff8043c710 R generic_ro_fops
fffffc0000376d20 T register_filesystem
```

A T denotes that the symbol is located in the text segment, while D determines it to be in the data segment. Refer to Appendix E for more information on the layout of object files.

Logically, the information in the symbol table differs not only according to kernel configuration but also from processor to processor. In our example, we used an AMD64 system. Searching through the symbol table on an IA-32 CPU, for example, would produce the following picture:

```
c0119290 T printk
c012b7b0 T generic_read_dir
c0129fc0 D generic_ro_fops
c0139340 T register_filesystem
```

The addresses are not only shorter (after all, IA-32 use a word length of 32 bits) but, logically, point to different locations.

---

[5]Notice that because the reference is resolved in the kernel itself and not in userspace, this file is available for information purposes but is not used by the module utilities.

7.2.2 Dependencies

A module can also depend on one or more other modules. Let us take a look at the vfat module that depends on the fat module because the latter includes several functions that do not make a distinction between the two variants of the filesystem.[6] In the view of the object file vfat.o, all this means is that there are code references to functions defined in fat.o. The advantages of this approach are obvious. Because the code for handling a VFAT filesystem differs only in a few routines from that for handling a FAT filesystem, a large part of the code can be used by both modules. This not only reduces space requirements in system memory but also makes the source code shorter, more readable, and easier to maintain.

The nm tool illustrates the situation clearly:

```
wolfgang@meitner> nm vfat.ko
...
        U fat_alloc_new_dir
        U fat_attach
...

wolfgang@meitner> nm fat.ko
...

0000000000001bad T fat_alloc_new_dir
0000000000004a67 T fat_attach
...
```

I have selected two examples: fat_alloc_new_dir and fat_attach (fat also provides many other functions used by vfat). As the output of nm shows, the two functions are listed in the vfat module as unresolved references, whereas in fat.o, they appear together with their (still unrelocated) addresses in the object file.

Naturally, it makes no sense to patch these addresses into the object code of vfat.ko because the functions would be somewhere totally different in memory after relocation of fat.ko. Of greater interest are the addresses of the functions *after* the fat module is added. This information is exported to userspace by /proc/kallsyms but is still held directly in the kernel. For both the permanently compiled part of the kernel and for all subsequently added modules, there is an array whose entries assign symbols to their addresses in virtual address space.

The following items are relevant when adding modules into the kernel:

❑ The symbol list of the functions provided by the kernel can be dynamically extended when modules are loaded. As you will see below, modules can specify exactly which functions in their code are to be released for general use and which may be used internally only.

❑ The order in which modules are added into the kernel is important if there are interdependencies between the modules. If, for example, an attempt is made to load the vfat module before fat is in the kernel, the attempt will fail because the addresses of a number of functions cannot be resolved (and the code would not run).

---

[6]FAT (*file allocation table*) is the very simple filesystem used by MS-DOS and still used for diskettes; vfat is a (minimal) enhancement with an identical basic structure that supports filenames up to 255 characters long and no longer restricts them to the old $8 + 3$ schema.

Dependencies between modules can make the situation extremely complex during dynamic extension of the kernel if users are not aware of the specific structure of the inter-module dependencies. Whereas in our example this does not present a problem, or at least not for interested and technically versed users, it can be very laborious to find the correct module loading sequence if there are complex dependencies. A means of automatically analyzing the dependencies between modules is therefore required.

The `depmod` tool in the `modutils` standard tool collection is used to calculate the dependencies between the modules of a system. The program usually runs each time the system is booted or after new modules have been installed. The dependencies found are stored in a list. By default, they are written to the file `/lib/modules/`*version*`/modules.dep`. The format is not complicated; the name of the binary file of the module is noted, and this is followed by the filenames of all modules that contain code needed for correct execution of the module first named. The entry for the `vfat` module therefore looks like this:

```
wolfgang@meitner> cat modules.dep | grep vfat
/lib/modules/2.6.24/kernel/fs/vfat/vfat.ko: /lib/modules/2.6.24/kernel/fs/fat/fat.ko
```

This information is processed by `modprobe`, which is used to insert modules into the kernel if existing dependencies are to be resolved automatically. The strategy is simple: `modprobe` reads in the contents of the dependency file, searches for the line in which the desired module is described, and compiles a list of prerequisite modules. Because these modules may, in turn, depend on other modules, a search is made for their entries in the dependency file, and then the entries are checked; this procedure is continued until the names of all prerequisite modules are known. The actual task of inserting all modules involved into the kernel is delegated to the `insmod` tool.[7]

The most interesting question still remains unanswered. How can dependencies between modules be identified? To solve this problem, `depmod` employs no special features of kernel modules but simply uses the information shown above. This information can be read not only from modules but also from normal executable files or libraries using `nm`.

`depmod` analyzes the binary code of all available modules, generates a list for each that includes all defined symbols and all unresolved references, and finally compares these lists with each other. If module A contains a symbol that is found in module B as an unresolved reference, this means that B depends on A — and this fact will be duly acknowledged by means of an entry in the form `B: A` in the dependency file. Most symbols to which the modules refer are not defined in other modules but in the kernel itself. For this reason, the file `/lib/modules/`*version*`/System.map` is generated (likewise using `depmod`) when modules are installed. This file lists all symbols exported by the kernel. If it contains an unresolved symbol of a module, this is not a problem because it will be resolved automatically when the module is loaded. If the symbol cannot be found in the file or in another module, the module may not be added into the kernel because it refers to external functions not implemented anywhere.

7.2.3 Querying Module Information

Additional sources of information are text descriptions that specify the purpose and usage of modules and are stored directly in the binary files. They can be queried using the `modinfo` tool in the `modutils` distribution. Various items of data are stored:

❑   Author of the driver, usually with an e-mail address. This information is useful, particularly for bug reports (besides granting the developer some personal satisfaction).

❑   A brief description of the driver function.

---

[7]It is, of course, also necessary to check whether a module is already resident in the kernel — logically, it need not then be added.

❑   Configuration parameters that can be passed to the module; possibly with a description of the exact meaning of the parameters.

❑   The designation of the device supported (e.g., fd for floppy disk).

❑   The license under which the module is distributed.

A separate list is also provided in the module information to accept a list of different device types supported by the driver.

Querying module information using the modinfo tool is not difficult, as the following example shows:

```
wolfgang@meitner> /sbin/modinfo 8139too
filename:       /lib/modules/2.6.24/kernel/drivers/net/8139too.ko
version:        0.9.28
license:        GPL
description:    RealTek RTL-8139 Fast Ethernet driver
author:         Jeff Garzik <jgarzik@pobox.com>
srcversion:     1D03CC1F1622811EB8ACD9E
alias:          pci:v*d00008139sv000013D1sd0000AB06bc*sc*i*
...
alias:          pci:v000010ECd00008139sv*sd*bc*sc*i*
depends:
vermagic:       2.6.24 SMP mod_unload
parm:           debug:8139too bitmapped message enable number (int)
parm:              multicast_filter_limit:8139too maximum number of filtered multicast addresses
(int)
parm:           media:8139too: Bits 4+9: force full duplex, bit 5: 100Mbps (array of int)
parm:           full_duplex:8139too: Force full duplex for board(s) (1) (array of int)
```

The kernel does not demand that developers supply this information in every module, although this is good programming practice and should be done for new drivers. Many older modules do not provide all the above fields, and developers are generally quite happy to omit detailed descriptions of possible parameters. However, in most cases, there is at least a brief description, the name of the (main) author, and a note on the software license under which the driver is distributed.

How can this additional information be incorporated in the binary module file? In all binary files that use the ELF format (see Appendix E), there are various units that organize the binary data into different categories — technically these are known as *sections*. To allow information on the module to be added, the kernel introduces a further section named .modinfo. As you will see below, this process is relatively transparent to the module programmer because a set of simple macros is provided to insert the data into the binary file. Naturally, the presence of this additional information does not change the behavior of the code because the .modinfo sections are ignored by all programs that handle modules but are not interested in the information.

Why is information on the module license used stored in the binary file? The reason is not (unfortunately) a technical one but is of a legal nature. Because the kernel source code is covered by the GNU GPL license, there are several legal problems surrounding the use of modules distributed in binary code only. In this respect, the GPL license is somewhat difficult to interpret.[8] For this reason, I do not intend to deal with the legal implications here — this is best left to the legal departments of large software manufacturers. It is enough to know that such modules may use only the kernel functions explicitly provided (in contrast, there are also functions that are explicitly provided for GPL-compatible modules only). The standard set

---

[8]Some programmers suggest that there are more interpretations of GPL than there are programs distributed under the license.

is perfectly adequate to program standard drivers — if, however, the module wants to delve deeply into the depths of the kernel, it must use other functions, and with some licenses this is prohibited for legal reasons. The modprobe tool must take this situation into consideration when new modules are used. This is why it checks the licenses and rejects illegal link actions.

Most developers (and also users) are not particularly happy about the fact that some manufacturers distribute their drivers in binary modules. This not only makes it difficult to debug kernel errors, but also has an adverse effect on ongoing driver development because it is necessary to rely on manufacturers to eliminate bugs or implement new functions. At this point, it is not my intention to waste your time with the many and varied aspects of manufacturer behavior. I simply refer you to the countless discussions that have taken place, are still taking place, and will doubtless take place in the future on the various Internet channels (not least on the kernel mailing list, see Appendix F).

7.2.4 *Automatic Loading*

Generally, module loading is initiated from userspace, either by the user or by means of automated scripts. To achieve greater flexibility in the handling of modules and to improve transparency, the kernel itself is also able to request modules.

Where is the catch? It is not difficult for the kernel to insert the binary code once it has access to it. However, it cannot do this without further help from userspace. The binary file must be localized in the filesystem, and dependencies must be resolved. Because this is far easier to do in userspace than in kernel space, the kernel has an auxiliary task known as kmod to which these tasks are delegated. Note that kmod is not a permanent daemon, but is only initiated by the kernel on demand.

Let us examine a scenario that demonstrates the advantages of kernel-initiated module loading. It is assumed that the VFAT filesystem is available as a module only and is not permanently integrated into the kernel. If a user issues the following command for mounting a diskette:

```
wolfgang@meitner> mount -t vfat /dev/fd0 /mnt/floppy
```

before the vfat module is loaded into the kernel, an error message would normally be returned indicating that the corresponding filesystem is not supported because it is not registered with the kernel. However, in practice this is not the case. The diskette is mounted without any problem, even if the module is not loaded. When the mount call terminates, the required modules are located in the kernel.

How is this possible? When the kernel processes the mount system call, it discovers that no information on the desired filesystem — vfat — is present in its data structures. It therefore attempts to load the corresponding module using the request_module function whose exact structure is discussed in Section 7.4.1. This function uses the kmod mechanism to start the modprobe tool, which then inserts the vfat module in the usual way. In other words, the kernel relies on an application in userspace that, in turn, uses kernel functions to add the module as illustrated in Figure 7-2.

Once this has been done, the kernel again tries to obtain information on the desired filesystem; as a result of the modprobe call, this information is now held in its data structures if, of course, the module actually exists — if not, the system call terminates with a corresponding error code.

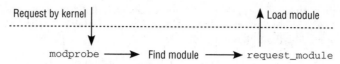

Figure 7-2: Automatic module loading.

`request_module` calls are located at various points throughout the kernel sources; with their help, the kernel attempts to make functions delegated to modules accessible as transparently as possible by adding the code automatically as needed and without user interaction.

Situations can arise in which it is not possible to uniquely define which module is required to provide the desired functionality. Consider the case that a USB stick is added to the system. The host controller driver recognizes the new device. The module that needs to be loaded is `usb-storage`, but how can the kernel know this? The solution to the problem is a small "database" that is attached to every module. The contents describe which devices are supported by the module. In case of USB devices, this is a list of supported interface types, manufacturer IDs, or any similar piece of information that identifies the device. Modules that provide a driver for PCI devices, as another example, also use the unique IDs associated with the device. The module provides a list of all supported devices.

The database information is provided via *module aliases*. These are generic identifiers for modules that encode the described pieces of information. The macro MODULE_ALIAS is used to generate module aliases.

<modules.h>
```
/* Generic info of form tag = "info" */
#define MODULE_INFO(tag, info) __MODULE_INFO(tag, tag, info)

/* For userspace: you can also call me... */
#define MODULE_ALIAS(_alias) MODULE_INFO(alias, _alias)
```

<moduleparam.h>
```
#define __MODULE_INFO(tag, name, info)                              \
static const char __module_cat(name,__LINE__)[]                     \
  __attribute_used__                                                \
  __attribute__((section(".modinfo"),unused)) = __stringify(tag) "=" info
```

The alias provided to MODULE_ALIAS is stored in the `.modinfo` section of the module binary. If a module provides several different services, appropriate aliases are inserted directly. The code for RAID 4, 5, and 6 is contained in the same module, for instance.

drivers/md/raid5.c
```
MODULE_ALIAS("md-personality-4"); /* RAID5 */
MODULE_ALIAS("md-raid5");
MODULE_ALIAS("md-raid4");
MODULE_ALIAS("md-level-5");
MODULE_ALIAS("md-level-4");
MODULE_ALIAS("md-personality-8"); /* RAID6 */
MODULE_ALIAS("md-raid6");
MODULE_ALIAS("md-level-6");
```

More important than direct aliases is the inclusion of device databases. The kernel provides the macro MODULE_DEVICE_TABLE to implement such databases. The device table for the 8139too module that was shown above is created by the following code:

drivers/net/8139too.c
```
static struct pci_device_id rtl8139_pci_tbl[] = {
        {0x10ec, 0x8139, PCI_ANY_ID, PCI_ANY_ID, 0, 0, RTL8139 },
        {0x10ec, 0x8138, PCI_ANY_ID, PCI_ANY_ID, 0, 0, RTL8139 },
        {0x1113, 0x1211, PCI_ANY_ID, PCI_ANY_ID, 0, 0, RTL8139 },
...

        {PCI_ANY_ID, 0x8139, 0x13d1, 0xab06, 0, 0, RTL8139 },

        {0,}
};

MODULE_DEVICE_TABLE (pci, rtl8139_pci_tbl);
```

The macro provides a standardized name in the module binary by which the table can be accessed:

<module.h>
```
#define MODULE_GENERIC_TABLE(gtype,name)                     \
extern const struct gtype##_id __mod_##gtype##_table         \
  __attribute__ ((unused, alias(__stringify(name))))
```

<module.h>
```
#define MODULE_DEVICE_TABLE(type,name)            \
  MODULE_GENERIC_TABLE(type##_device,name)
```

In the case of PCI, this generates the ELF symbol __mod_pci_device_table, which is an alias for rtl8139_pci_tbl.

When modules are built, a conversion script (scripts/mod/file2alias.c) parses the device tables for the different bus systems (PCI, USB, IEEE1394, ...) — which have all different formats — and generates MODULE_ALIAS entries for the database entries. This allows treating device databases entries in the same way as module aliases without having to duplicate the database information. Since the conversion process basically consists of parsing an ELF file and doing some string rewriting, I will not discuss it in greater detail here. The output looks as follows for the 8139too module:

drivers/net/8139too.mod.c
```
MODULE_ALIAS("pci:v000010ECd00008139sv*sd*bc*sc*i*");
MODULE_ALIAS("pci:v000010ECd00008138sv*sd*bc*sc*i*");
MODULE_ALIAS("pci:v00001113d00001211sv*sd*bc*sc*i*");
...
MODULE_ALIAS("pci:v00001743d00008139sv*sd*bc*sc*i*");
MODULE_ALIAS("pci:v0000021Bd00008139sv*sd*bc*sc*i*");
MODULE_ALIAS("pci:v*d00008139sv000010ECsd00008139bc*sc*i*");
MODULE_ALIAS("pci:v*d00008139sv00001186sd00001300bc*sc*i*");
MODULE_ALIAS("pci:v*d00008139sv000013D1sd0000AB06bc*sc*i*");
```

Providing module aliases forms the basis to solve the automatic module loading problem, but is not yet completely sufficient. The kernel needs some support from userspace. After the kernel has noticed that it needs a module for a device with specific properties, it needs to pass an appropriate request to a userspace daemon. This daemon then seeks the apt module and inserts it into the kernel. Section 7.4 describes how this is implemented.

7.3 Inserting and Deleting Modules

Two system calls form the interface between the userspace tools and the module implementation of the kernel:

- ❑ init_module — Inserts a new module into the kernel. All the userspace tool needs do is provide the binary data. All further steps (particularly relocation and symbol resolution) are performed in the kernel itself.

- ❑ delete_module — Removes a module from the kernel. A prerequisite is, of course, that the code is no longer in use and that no other modules are employing functions exported from the module.

There is also a function named request_module (*not* a system call) that is used to load modules from the kernel side. It is required not only to load modules but also to implement hotplug capabilities.

7.3.1 Module Representation

Before looking more closely at the implementation of the module-related functions, it is necessary to explain how modules (and their properties) are represented in the kernel. As usual, a set of data structures is defined to do this.

Not surprisingly, the name of the most important structure is module; an instance of this structure is allocated for each module resident in the kernel. It is defined as follows:

```
<module.h>
struct module
{
        enum module_state state;

        /* Member of list of modules */
        struct list_head list;

        /* Unique handle for this module */
        char name[MODULE_NAME_LEN];
...
        /* Exported symbols */
        const struct kernel_symbol *syms;
        unsigned int num_syms;
        const unsigned long *crcs;

        /* GPL-only exported symbols. */
        const struct kernel_symbol *gpl_syms;
        unsigned int num_gpl_syms;
        const unsigned long *gpl_crcs;
...
```

```
               /* symbols that will be GPL-only in the near future. */
               const struct kernel_symbol *gpl_future_syms;
               unsigned int num_gpl_future_syms;
               const unsigned long *gpl_future_crcs;

               /* Exception table */
               unsigned int num_exentries;
               const struct exception_table_entry *extable;

               /* Startup function. */
               int (*init)(void);

               /* If this is non-NULL, vfree after init() returns */
               void *module_init;

               /* Here is the actual code + data, vfree'd on unload. */
               void *module_core;

               /* Here are the sizes of the init and core sections */
               unsigned long init_size, core_size;

               /* The size of the executable code in each section.  */
               unsigned long init_text_size, core_text_size;
   ...
               /* Arch-specific module values */
               struct mod_arch_specific arch;

               unsigned int taints; /* same bits as kernel:tainted */
   ...
               #ifdef CONFIG_MODULE_UNLOAD
               /* Reference counts */
               struct module_ref ref[NR_CPUS];

               /* What modules depend on me? */
               struct list_head modules_which_use_me;

               /* Who is waiting for us to be unloaded */
               struct task_struct *waiter;

               /* Destruction function. */
               void (*exit)(void);
               #endif

               #ifdef CONFIG_KALLSYMS
               /* We keep the symbol and string tables for kallsyms. */
               Elf_Sym *symtab;
               unsigned long num_symtab;
               char *strtab;

               /* Section attributes */
               struct module_sect_attrs *sect_attrs;

               /* Notes attributes */
               struct module_notes_attrs *notes_attrs;
```

```
        #endif

        /* Per-cpu data. */
        void *percpu;

        /* The command line arguments (may be mangled). People like
        keeping pointers to this stuff */
        char *args;
};
```

As this source code extract shows, the structure definition depends on the kernel configuration settings:

❑   KALLSYMS is a configuration option (but only for embedded systems — it is always enabled on regular machines) that holds in memory a list of *all* symbols defined in the kernel itself and in the loaded modules (otherwise only the exported functions are stored). This is useful if oops messages (which are used if the kernel detects a deviation from the normal behavior, for example, if a NULL pointer is de-referenced) are to output not only hexadecimal numbers but also the names of the functions involved.

❑   In contrast to kernel versions prior to 2.5, the ability to unload modules must now be configured explicitly. The required additional information is not included in the module data structure unless the configuration option MODULE_UNLOAD is selected.

Other configuration options that occur in conjunction with modules but do not change the definition of struct module are as follows:

❑   MODVERSIONS enables version control; this prevents an obsolete module whose interface definitions no longer match those of the current version from loading into the kernel. Section 7.5 deals with this in more detail.

❑   MODULE_FORCE_UNLOAD enables modules to be removed from the kernel by force, even if there are still references to the module or the code is being used by other modules. This brute force method is never needed in normal operation but can be useful during development.

❑   KMOD enables the kernel to automatically load modules once they are needed. This requires some interaction with the userspace, which is described below in the chapter.

The elements of struct module have the following meaning:

❑   state indicates the current state of the module and can assume one of the values of module_state:

<module.h>
```
enum module_state
{
        MODULE_STATE_LIVE,
        MODULE_STATE_COMING,
        MODULE_STATE_GOING,
};
```

During loading, the state is MODULE_STATE_COMING. In normal operation (after completion of all initialization tasks), it is MODULE_STATE_LIVE; and while a module is being removed, it is MODULE_STATE_GOING.

❑   `list` is a standard list element used by the kernel to keep all loaded modules in a doubly linked list. The `modules` global variable defined in `kernel/module.c` is used as list header.

❑   `name` specifies the name of the module. This name must be unique because it is referenced, for example, to select the module to be unloaded. In this element, the name of the binary file is usually given without the suffix `.ko` − `vfat`, for example, for the VFAT filesystem.

❑   `syms`, `num_syms`, and `crc` are used to manage the symbols exported by the module. `syms` is an array of `num_syms` entries of the `kernel_symbol` type and is responsible for assigning identifiers (`name`) to memory addresses (`value`):

<module.h>
```
struct kernel_symbol
{
        unsigned long value;
        const char *name;
};
```

`crcs` is also an array with `num_syms` entries that store checksums for the exported symbols needed to implement version control (see Section 7.5).

❑   When symbols are exported, the kernel considers not only symbols that may be used by all modules regardless of their license, but also symbols that may be used only by modules with GPL and GPL-compatible licenses. The third category consists of modules that may at present still be used by modules with any license, but will be made GPL-only in the near future. The `gpl_syms`, `num_gpl_syms` and `gpl_crcs` elements are provided for GPL-only symbols, while `gpl_future_syms`, `num_gpl_future_syms` and `gpl_future_crcs` serve for future GPL-only symbols. They have the same meaning as the entries discussed above but are responsible for managing symbols that may be used only by GPL-compatible modules now or in the future.

Two more sets of symbols (which are for brevity's sake omitted from the structure definition above) are described by the structure members `unused_gpl_syms` and `unused_syms`, together with the corresponding counter and checksum members. The sets are used to store (GPL-only) symbols that are exported, but unused by in-tree kernel modules. The kernel prints a warning message when an out-of-tree module nevertheless uses a symbol of this type.

❑   If a module defines new exceptions (see Chapter 4), their description is held in the `extable` array. `num_exentries` specifies the number of entries in the array.

❑   `init` is a pointer to a function called when the module is initialized.

❑   The binary data of a module are divided into two parts: the initialization part and the core part. The former contains everything that can be discarded after loading has terminated (e.g., the initialization functions). The latter contains all data needed during the current operation. The start address of the initialization part is held in `module_init` and comprises `init_size` bytes, whereas the core area is described by `module_core` and `core_size`.

❑   `arch` is a processor-specific hook that, depending on the particular system, can be filled with various additional data needed to run modules. Most architectures do not require any additional information and therefore define `struct mod_arch_specific` as an empty structure that is removed by the compiler during optimization.

❑   `taints` is set if a module taints the kernel. *Tainting* means that the kernel suspects the module of doing something harmful that could prevent correct kernel operation. Should a kernel panic[9]

---

[9]A kernel panic is triggered when a fatal internal error occurs that does not allow resumption of regular operations.

occur, then the error diagnosis will also contain information about why the kernel is tainted. This helps developers to distinguish bug reports coming from properly running systems and those where something was already suspicious.

The function `add_taint_module` is provided to taint a given instance of `struct module`. A module can taint the kernel for two reasons:

❑ `TAINT_PROPRIETARY_MODULE` is used if a module with a proprietary license, or a license that is not compatible with the GPL, is loaded into the kernel. Since the source code for proprietary modules is most likely not available, kernel developers will not be willing to fix kernel bugs that appear in possibly even completely unrelated kernel areas. The module might have done arbitrary things to the kernel that cannot be tracked, so the bugs might well have been introduced by the module.

Note that the kernel provides the function `license_is_gpl_compatible` to decide whether a given license is compatible with the GPL.

> **All licenses are, in contrast to the usual habit, not specified by constants, but by C strings.**

❑ `TAINT_FORCED_MODULE` denotes that the module was forcibly loaded. Forced loading can be requested if no version information (also called *version magic*) is present in the module, or if the module and kernel disagree about the version of some symbol.

❑ `license_gplok` is a Boolean variable that specifies whether the module license is GPL-compatible; in other words, whether GPL-exported functions may be used or not. The flag is set when the module is inserted into the kernel. How the kernel judges a license to be compatible with the GPL or not is discussed below.

❑ `module_ref` is used for reference counting. There is an entry in the array for each CPU of the system; this entry specifies at how many other points in the system the module is used. The data type `module_ref` used for the individual array elements contains only one entry, which should, however, be aligned on the L1 cache:

<mm.h>
```
struct module_ref
{
        local_t count;
} ____cacheline_aligned;
```

The kernel provides the `try_module_get` and `module_put` functions to increment or decrement the reference counter. It is also possible to use `__module_get` to increment the reference count if the caller is sure that the module is not being unloaded right now. `try_module_get`, in contrast, ensures that this is really the case.

❑ `modules_which_use_me` is used as a list element in the data structures that describe the inter-module dependencies in the kernel. Section 7.3.2 goes into greater detail.

❑ `waiter` is a pointer to the task structure of the process that caused the module to be unloaded and is now waiting for the action to terminate.

❑ `exit` is the counterpart to `init`. It is a pointer to a function called to perform module-specific clean-up work (e.g., releasing reserved memory areas) when a module is removed.

❑ `symtab`, `num_symtab` and `strtab` are used to record information on *all* symbols of the module (not only on the explicitly exported symbols).

❏ `percpu` points to per-CPU data that belong to the module. It is initialized when the module is loaded.

❏ `args` is a pointer to the command-line arguments passed to the module during loading.

7.3.2 Dependencies and References

A *relationship* exists between two modules A and B if B uses functions provided by A. This relationship can be viewed in two different ways.

1. B depends on A. B cannot be loaded unless A is already resident in kernel memory.

2. A references B. In other words, B cannot be removed from the kernel unless A has been removed — or unless all other modules that reference B have disappeared. In the kernel, this kind of relationship is described as *A uses B*.

To correctly manage these dependencies, the kernel needs to introduce a further data structure:

kernel/modules.c
```
struct module_use
{
        struct list_head list;
        struct module *module_which_uses;
};
```

The dependency network is set up together with the `modules_which_use_me` element of the `module` data structure. A new instance of `module_use` is created for each module A that uses functions in module B. This instance is added to the `modules_which_use_me` list of B. `module_which_uses` points to the `module` instance of A. On the basis of this information, the kernel can easily find out which other kernel modules are used by a particular module.

As the relationship described is not immediately clear, Figure 7-3 provides a graphic example to illustrate the situation.

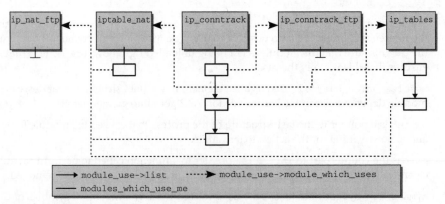

Figure 7-3: Data structures for managing dependencies between modules.

I have selected a number of modules from the Netfilter package for this example. The dependency file modules.dep includes the following dependencies found when the modules were compiled[10]:

```
ip_tables.ko:
iptable_nat.ko:        ip_conntrack.ko    ip_tables.ko
ip_nat_ftp.ko:         iptable_nat.ko     ip_tables.ko      ip_conntrack.ko
ip_conntrack.ko:
ip_conntrack_ftp.ko:   ip_conntrack.ko
```

Although ip_nat_ftp and ip_conntrack_ftp depend on several other modules, they do not have any modules that depend *on them*, which is why the modules_which_use_me element of their module instance is a null pointer.

ip_tables does not have any dependencies on other modules and can therefore be loaded into the kernel on its own. However, there are two modules that depend on ip_tables: iptable_nat and ip_nat_ftp. An instance of module_use is created for each; these are placed in the list of the modules_which_use_me element of ip_tables. Their module_which_use pointers point to ip_nat_ftp and iptable_nat, as shown in Figure 7-3.

Three modules depend on ip_conntrack, which is why its modules_which_use_me list contains three instances of module_use with pointers to iptable_nat, ip_nat_ftp, and ip_conntrack_ftp.

> The kernel data structures indicate only which other modules depend on a particular module — they are not suitable (at least not without looking through the list of all modules and reanalyzing the information in the list) for finding out which modules already need to be resident in the kernel before a specific new module can be loaded. However, this is not necessary because it is sufficient that the information is present in userspace; and, thanks to modules.dep, this is the case.

If an attempt is made to load a module for which it was not possible to resolve all symbols because dependent modules are not present, the kernel returns an error code and aborts loading. However, no effort is made to load the prerequisite modules from the kernel side. This is the sole responsibility of the modprobe userspace tool.

Only two calls of modprobe are needed to insert the displayed modules into the kernel:

```
wolfgang@meitner> /sbin/modprobe ip_nat_ftp
wolfgang@meitner> /sbin/modprobe ip_conntrack_ftp
```

When ip_nat_ftp is inserted, ip_conntrack, ip_tables and iptable_nat are automatically added because they are listed as prerequisites in modules.dep. ip_conntrack_ftp can then be added without explicit resolution of dependencies because the requisite ip_conntrack module was automatically inserted into the kernel when ip_nat_ftp was loaded.

Manipulating Data Structures

The kernel provides the already_uses function to test whether module A requires another module B:

kernel/module.c
```
/* Does a already use b? */
static int already_uses(struct module *a, struct module *b)
```

---

[10]To improve readability, I have not specified the files with their full pathnames as they would appear in modules.dep. Additionally, the example is slightly simplified.

```
        {
                struct module_use *use;

                list_for_each_entry(use, &b->modules_which_use_me, list) {
                        if (use->module_which_uses == a) {
                                return 1;
                        }
                }
                return 0;
        }
```

If A depends on B, the `modules_which_use_me` list of B must contain a pointer to the `module` instance of A. This is why the kernel looks through the list step by step and checks the pointers in `module_which_uses`. If a matching entry is found — in other words, if the dependency really exists — 1 is returned; otherwise, the function terminates and returns 0.

`use_module` is used to establish the relation between A and B — module A needs module B to function correctly. It is implemented as follows:

kernel/module.c
```
/* Module a uses b */
static int use_module(struct module *a, struct module *b)
{
        struct module_use *use;
...
        if (b == NULL || already_uses(a, b)) return 1;

        if (!strong_try_module_get(b))
                return 0;

        use = kmalloc(sizeof(*use), GFP_ATOMIC);
        if (!use) {
                printk("%s: out of memory loading\n", a->name);
                module_put(b);
                return 0;
        }

        use->module_which_uses = a;
        list_add(&use->list, &b->modules_which_use_me);
...
        return 1;
}
```

`already_uses` first checks whether the relation has already been established. If so, the function can return immediately (a `NULL` pointer as a dependent module is also interpreted as meaning that the relation already exists). If not, the reference counter of B is incremented so that it can no longer be removed — after all, A insists on its presence. The `strong_try_module_get` used for this purpose is a wrapper around the aforementioned `try_module_get` function; it deals with the situation in which the module is in the process of being loaded:

kernel/module.c
```
static inline int strong_try_module_get(struct module *mod)
{
        if (mod && mod->state == MODULE_STATE_COMING)
```

```
                    return 0;
            return try_module_get(mod);
    }
```

It is not complicated to establish the relation. A new instance of `module_use`, whose `module_which_uses` pointer is set to the module instance of A, is created. The new `module_use` instance is added to the `list` list of B.

7.3.3 Binary Structure of Modules

Modules use the ELF binary format, which features several additional sections not present in normal programs or libraries. In addition to a few compiler-generated sections that are not relevant for our purposes (mainly relocation sections), modules consist of the following ELF sections[11]:

❑   The `__ksymtab`, `__ksymtab_gpl`, and `__ksymtab_gpl_future` sections contain a symbol table with all symbols exported by the module. Whereas the symbols in the first-named section can be used by all kernel parts regardless of the license, symbols in `__kysmtab_gpl` may be used only by GPL-compatible parts, and those in `__ksymtab_gpl_future` only by GPL-compatible parts in the future.

❑   `__kcrctab`, `__kcrctab_gpl`, and `__kcrctab_gpl_future` contain checksums for all (GPL, or future-GPL) exported functions of the module. `__versions` includes the checksums for *all* references used by the module from external sources.

> The above sections are not created unless the version control feature was enabled when the kernel was configured.

Section 7.5 deals in more detail with how version information is generated and used.

❑   `__param` stores information on the parameters accepted by a module.

❑   `__ex_table` is used to define new entries for the exception table of the kernel in case the module code needs this mechanism.

❑   `.modinfo` stores the names of all other modules that must reside in the kernel before a module can be loaded — in other words, the names of all modules that the particular module depends on.

In addition, each module can hold specific information that can be queried using the `modinfo` userspace tool, particularly the name of the author, a description of the module, license information, and a list of parameters.

❑   `.exit.text` contains code (and possibly data) required when the module is removed from the kernel. This information is not kept in the normal text segment so that the kernel need not load it into memory if the option for removing modules was not enabled in the kernel configuration.

❑   The initialization functions (and data) are stored in `.init.text`. They are held in a separate section because they are no longer needed after completion of initialization and can therefore be removed from memory.

❑   `.gnu.linkonce.this_module` provides an instance of `struct module`, which stores the name of the module (`name`) and pointers to the initialization and clean-up functions (`init` and `cleanup`) in the binary file. By referring to this section, the kernel recognizes whether a specific binary file is a module or not. If it is missing, file loading is rejected.

---

[11] `readelf -S module.ko` lists all the sections in a module object.

Some of the above sections cannot be generated until the module itself and possibly all other kernel modules have been compiled, for example, the section that lists all module dependencies. Because no explicit dependency information is given in the source code, the kernel must get this information by analyzing non-resolved references of the module involved as well as the exported symbols of all other modules.

A multistep strategy is therefore adopted for generating modules:

1. First, all C files in the source code of a module are compiled into normal .o object files.

2. Once the object files have been generated for all modules, the kernel can analyze them. The additional information found (e.g., on module dependencies) is stored in a separate file that is also compiled into a binary file.

3. The two binary files are linked and thus produce the final module.

Appendix B describes the kernel build process in detail and deals with problems encountered when compiling modules.

Initialization and Cleanup Functions

The module initialization and clean-up functions are stored in the `module` instance in the `.gnu.linkonce.module` section. The instance is located in the abovementioned autogenerated extra file for each module. It is defined as follows[12]:

```
module
module.mod.c
struct module __this_module
__attribute__((section(".gnu.linkonce.this_module"))) = {
 .name = KBUILD_MODNAME,
 .init = init_module,
#ifdef CONFIG_MODULE_UNLOAD
 .exit = cleanup_module,
#endif
 .arch = MODULE_ARCH_INIT,
};
```

KBUILD_MODNAME contains the name of the module and is only defined if the code is compiled as a module. If the code is to be permanently bound into the kernel, no __this_module object is generated because no post-processing of the module object is performed. MODULE_ARCH_INIT is a pre-processor symbol that can point to architecture-specific initialization methods for modules. This is currently only required for m68k CPUs.

The `module_init` and `module_exit` macros in `init.h>` are used to define the init and exit functions.[13] Each module includes code of the following kind that defines the init/exit functions[14]:

---

[12]The attribute directive of the GNU C compiler is used to place the data in the desired section. Other uses of this directive are described in Appendix C.

[13]The macros define init_module and exit_module functions that are created as aliases — a GCC enhancement — for the actual initialization and clean-up functions. This trick enables the kernel to always use the same names to refer to the functions; however, programmers can choose whichever names they want.

[14]If the code is not compiled as a module, module_init and module_exit convert the functions into regular init/exit calls.

```
#ifdef MODULE
static int __init xyz_init(void) {
  /* Initialization code */
}

static void __exit xyz_cleanup (void) {
    /* Cleanup code */
}

module_init(xyz_init);
module_exit(xyz_exit);
#endif
```

The __init and __exit prefixes help place the two functions in the right sections of the binary code:

<init.h>
```
#define __init          __attribute__ ((__section__ (".init.text"))) __cold
#define __initdata      __attribute__ ((__section__ (".init.data")))
#define __exitdata      __attribute__ ((__section__(".exit.data")))
#define __exit_call     __attribute_used__ __attribute__ ((__section__ (".exitcall.exit")))
```

The data variants are used to place data (in contrast to functions) in the .init and .exit section.

Exporting Symbols

The kernel provides two macros for exporting symbols — EXPORT_SYMBOL and EXPORT_SYMBOL_GPL. As their names suggest, a distinction is made between exporting general symbols and exporting symbols that may be used only by GPL-compatible code. Again, their purpose is to place the symbols in the appropriate section of the module binary image:

<module.h>
```
/* For every exported symbol, place a struct in the __ksymtab section */
#define __EXPORT_SYMBOL(sym, sec) \
        extern typeof(sym) sym; \
        __CRC_SYMBOL(sym, sec) \
        static const char __kstrtab_##sym[] \
        __attribute__((section("__ksymtab_strings"))) \
        = MODULE_SYMBOL_PREFIX #sym; \
        static const struct kernel_symbol __ksymtab_##sym \
        __attribute_used__ \
        __attribute__((section("__ksymtab" sec), unused)) \

#define EXPORT_SYMBOL(sym)                                       \
        __EXPORT_SYMBOL(sym, "")

#define EXPORT_SYMBOL_GPL(sym)                                   \
        __EXPORT_SYMBOL(sym, "_gpl")

#define EXPORT_SYMBOL_GPL_FUTURE(sym)                            \
        __EXPORT_SYMBOL(sym, "_gpl_future")
```

At first glance, the definition is anything but clear. Its effect is therefore illustrated by reference to the following example:

```
EXPORT_SYMBOL(get_rms)
/****************************************************************/
EXPORT_SYMBOL_GPL(no_free_beer)
```

The above code is processed by the pre-processor and then looks something like this:

```
static const char __kstrtab_get_rms[]
    __attribute__((section("__ksymtab_strings"))) = "get_rms";

static const struct kernel_symbol __ksymtab_get_rms
    __attribute_used__ __attribute__((section("__ksymtab" ""), unused)) =
        (unsigned long)&get_rms, __kstrtab_get_rms


/****************************************************************/

static const char __kstrtab_no_free_beer[]
    __attribute__((section("__ksymtab_strings"))) = "no_free_beer";

static const struct kernel_symbol __ksymtab_no_free_beer
    __attribute_used__ __attribute__((section("__ksymtab" "_gpl"), unused)) =
        (unsigned long)&no_free_beer, __kstrtab_no_free_beer
```

Two code sections are generated for each exported symbol. They serve the following purpose:

❏   __kstrtab_*function* is stored in the __ksymtab_strings section as a statically defined variable. Its value is a string that corresponds to the name of the (*function*) function.

❏   A kernel_symbol instance is stored in the __ksymtab (or __kstrtab_gpl) section. It consists of a pointer to the exported function and a pointer to the entry just created in the string table.

This allows the kernel to find the matching code address by reference to the function name in the string; this is needed when resolving references, as is discussed in Section 7.3.4.

MODULE_SYMBOL_PREFIX can be used to assign a prefix to all exported symbols of a module; this is necessary on some architectures (but most define an empty string as the prefix).

__CRC_SYMBOL is used when kernel version control is enabled for exported functions (refer to Section 7.5 for further details); otherwise, it is defined as an empty string as I have assumed here for simplicity's sake.

General Module Information

The .modinfo section of a module includes general information set using MODULE_INFO:

<module.h>
```
#define MODULE_INFO(tag, info) __MODULE_INFO(tag, tag, info)
```

<moduleparam.h>
```
#define __MODULE_INFO(tag, name, info)                              \
    static const char __module_cat(name,__LINE__)[]                 \
```

```
__attribute_used__                                                        \
__attribute__((section(".modinfo"),unused)) = __stringify(tag) "=" info
```

In addition to this general macro that generates `tag = info` entries, there are a range of macros that create entries with pre-defined meanings. These are discussed below.

Module License

The module license is set using `MODULE_LICENSE`:

<module.h>
```
#define MODULE_LICENSE(_license) MODULE_INFO(license, _license)
```

The technical implementation is not particularly stunning. More interesting is the question as to which license types are classified as GPL-compatible by the kernel.

- ❑ GPL and GPLv2 stand for the second version of the GNU Public License; in the first definition, any later version of the license (that may not yet exist) may also be used.

- ❑ GPL and additional rights must be used if further clauses, which must be compatible with the free software definition software, have been added to the GPL.

- ❑ Dual BSD/GPL, Dual MIT/GPL, or Dual MPL/GPL are used for modules whose sources are available under a dual license (GPL combined with the Berkeley, MIT, or Mozilla license).

- ❑ Proprietary modules (or modules whose license is not compatible with GPL) must use Proprietary.

- ❑ unspecified is used if no explicit license is specified.

Author and Description

Each module should contain brief information about the author (with e-mail address, if possible) and a description of the purpose of the module:

<module.h>
```
#define MODULE_AUTHOR(_author) MODULE_INFO(author, _author)
#define MODULE_DESCRIPTION(_description) MODULE_INFO(description, _description)
```

Alternative Name

MODULE_ALIAS(alias) is used to give a module alternative names (alias) by which it can be addressed in userspace. This mechanism enables a distinction to be made between, for example, alternative drivers, when only one of the drivers can be used although externally they all implement the same functionality. It is also essential for constructing systematic names. This enables, for instance, assigning one or more alias names to a module. These aliases specify the identification numbers of all PCI devices that are supported by the module. When such a device is found in the system, the kernel can (with the help of the userspace) automatically insert the corresponding module.

Elementary Version Control

Some indispensable version control information is always stored in the .modinfo section, regardless of whether the version control feature is enabled or disabled. This allows a distinction to be made between various kernel configurations that have a drastic impact on the entire code and therefore need a separate set of modules. The following code is linked into each module during the second phase of module compilation:

module.mod.c
```
MODULE_INFO(vermagic, VERMAGIC_STRING);
```

`VERMAGIC_STRING` is a string that indicates the key features of the kernel configuration:

<vermagic.h>
```
#define VERMAGIC_STRING \
        UTS_RELEASE " " \
        MODULE_VERMAGIC_SMP MODULE_VERMAGIC_PREEMPT \
        MODULE_VERMAGIC_MODULE_UNLOAD MODULE_ARCH_VERMAGIC
```

A copy of `VERMAGIC_STRING` is stored in the kernel itself and in each module; a module may only be loaded if both variants match. This means that the following must be identical in the module and in the kernel:

❑   The SMP configuration (enabled or not)

❑   The preemption configuration (enabled or not)

❑   The compiler version used

❑   An architecture-specific constant

On IA-32 systems, the processor type is used as the architecture-specific constant because some very different features are available. For example, a module compiled with special optimization for Pentium 4 processors cannot be inserted into an Athlon kernel.

The kernel version is stored but is ignored when the comparison is made. Modules with different kernel versions whose remaining version string matches can be loaded with no problem; for example, modules of 2.6.0 can be loaded into a kernel with version 2.6.10.

7.3.4   Inserting Modules

The `init_module` system call is the interface between userspace and kernel and is used to load new modules.

kernel/module.c
```
asmlinkage long
sys_init_module(void __user *umod, unsigned long len, const char __user *uargs)
```

The call requires three parameters — a pointer to the area in user address space in which the binary code of the module is located (`umod`), its length (`len`), and a pointer to a string that specifies the module parameters. From the userspace viewpoint, inserting a module is very simple because all that need be done is to read in the module binary code and to issue a system call.

System Call Implementation

Figure 7-4 shows the code flow diagram for `sys_init_module`.

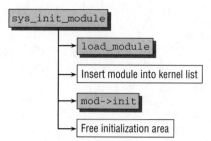

Figure 7-4: Code flow diagram for
`sys_init_module`.

The binary data are transferred into the kernel address space using `load_module`. All required relocations are performed, and all references are resolved. The arguments are converted into a form that is easy to analyze (a table of `kernel_param` instances), and an instance of the `module` data structure is created with all the necessary information on the module.

Once the `module` instance created in the `load_module` function has been added to the global `modules` list, all the kernel need do is to call the module initialization function and free the memory occupied by the initialization data.

Loading Modules

The real difficulties are encountered when implementing `load_module` — the kernel comment "do all the hard work" for the function is quite right. This is a very comprehensive function (with more than 350 lines) that assumes the following tasks:

- ❑ Copying module data (and arguments) from userspace into a *temporary* memory location in kernel address space; the relative addresses of the ELF sections are replaced with absolute addresses of the temporary image.

- ❑ Finding the positions of the (optional) sections

- ❑ Ensuring that the version control string and the definition of `struct module` match in the kernel and module

- ❑ Distributing the existing sections to their final positions in memory

- ❑ Relocating symbols and resolving references. Any version control information linked with the module symbols is noted.

- ❑ Processing the arguments of the module

`load_module` is the cornerstone of the module loader, which is why I deal in greater detail with the most important code sections.

> The information below makes frequent reference to special features of the ELF format. The data structures made available for this format by the kernel are also often used. Appendix E discusses both in detail.

kernel/module.c
```
static struct module *load_module(void __user *umod,
                                   unsigned long len,
                                   const char __user *uargs)
```

```
{
        Elf_Ehdr *hdr;
        Elf_Shdr *sechdrs;
        char *secstrings, *args, *modmagic, *strtab = NULL;
        unsigned int i;
        unsigned int symindex = 0;
        unsigned int strindex = 0;
        unsigned int setupindex;
        unsigned int exindex;
        unsigned int exportindex;
        unsigned int modindex;
        unsigned int obsparmindex;
        unsigned int infoindex;
        unsigned int gplindex;
        unsigned int crcindex;
        unsigned int gplcrcindex;
...

        struct module *mod;
        long err = 0;
...

        if (copy_from_user(hdr, umod, len) != 0) {
                err = -EFAULT;
                goto free_hdr;
        }
...

        /* Convenience variables */
        sechdrs = (void *)hdr + hdr->e_shoff;
        secstrings = (void *)hdr + sechdrs[hdr->e_shstrndx].sh_offset;
```

Once a large number of variables has been defined, the kernel loads the module binary data into kernel memory using copy_from_user (I have dispensed with some index variables for ELF sections and information on error handling — and will do so in the following sections — so as not to add unnecessarily to the volume of this description).

hdr then points to the start address of the binary data, in other words, to the ELF header of the module.

sechdrs and secstring are set so that they point to the positions in memory where information on the existing ELF sections and the string table with the section names is located. The *relative* value in the ELF header is added to the *absolute* address of the module in the kernel address space to determine the correct position (we will come across this procedure frequently).

Rewriting Section Addresses

The addresses of all sections in the binary code are then rewritten into absolute values in the temporary image[15]:

kernel/module.c
```
for (i = 1; i < hdr->e_shnum; i++) {
...
        /* Mark all sections sh_addr with their address in the
```

---

[15] e_shnum indicates the number of sections, sh_addr is the address of a section, and sh_offset is the identifier of the section in the section table as described in detail in Appendix E.

```
                temporary image. */
        sechdrs[i].sh_addr = (size_t)hdr + sechdrs[i].sh_offset;

        /* Internal symbols and strings. */
        if (sechdrs[i].sh_type == SHT_SYMTAB) {
                symindex = i;
                strindex = sechdrs[i].sh_link;
                strtab = (char *)hdr + sechdrs[strindex].sh_offset;
        }
    }
```

Iteration through all sections is used to find the position of the symbol table (the only section whose type is SHT_SYMTAB) and of the associated symbol string table whose section is linked with the symbol table using the ELF link feature.

Finding Section Addresses

In section .gnu.linkonce.this_module, there is an instance of struct module (find_sec is an auxiliary function that finds the index of an ELF section by reference to its name):

module/kernel.c
```
modindex = find_sec(hdr, sechdrs, secstrings,
                        ".gnu.linkonce.this_module");
...
mod = (void *)sechdrs[modindex].sh_addr;
```

mod now points to an instance of struct module in which the name and the pointers to the initialization and clean-up functions are supplied but whose remaining elements are still initialized with NULL or 0.

find_sec is also used to find the index positions of the remaining module sections (they are held in the *section* index variable defined above):

kernel/module.c
```
/* Optional sections */
exportindex = find_sec(hdr, sechdrs, secstrings, "__ksymtab");
gplindex = find_sec(hdr, sechdrs, secstrings, "__ksymtab_gpl");
gplfutureindex = find_sec(hdr, sechdrs, secstrings, "__ksymtab_gpl_future");
...
versindex = find_sec(hdr, sechdrs, secstrings, "__versions");
infoindex = find_sec(hdr, sechdrs, secstrings, ".modinfo");
pcpuindex = find_pcpusec(hdr, sechdrs, secstrings);
```

The module loader then calls the architecture-specific function mod_frob_arch_sections used by some architectures to manipulate the contents of the individual sections. Because this is not usually needed (the function is defined accordingly as a *no-operation*), it is not discussed here.

Organizing Data in Memory

layout_sections is used to decide which sections of the module are to be loaded at which positions in memory or which modules must be copied from their temporary address. The sections are split into two parts: *core* and *init*. While the first contains all code sections required during the entire run time of the module, the kernel places all initialization data and functions in a separate part that is removed when loading is completed.

Module sections are not transferred to their final memory position unless the SHF_ALLOC flag is set in their header.[16] For example, this flag is not set for sections with debugging information (produced when the gcc option -g is used) because these data need not be present in memory and can be read from the binary file if needed.

layout_sections checks whether the name of a section contains the .init string. This enables a distinction to be made between initialization code and regular code; accordingly, the start position of the section refers to the core or to the init section.

The result of layout_sections is communicated using the following elements:

❑   sh_entsize in the ELF section data structure, of which there is one instance for each section, indicates the relative position of the section in the core or initialization area. If a section is not to be loaded, the value is set to ~0UL.

To then differentiate between initialization and core sections, the INIT_OFFSET_MASK bit (defined by (1UL << (BITS_PER_LONG-1))) is set in sh_entsize. This stores the relative position of all init modules.

❑   core_size is used to transfer the total code size that is to reside in the kernel permanently, at least until the module is unloaded. init_size totals the volumes of all sections that are required for module initialization.

Transferring Data

Now that section distribution in memory is clear, the required memory space is reserved and initialized with null bytes:

kernel/module.c
```
/* Do the allocs. */
ptr = module_alloc(mod->core_size);
...
memset(ptr, 0, mod->core_size);
mod->module_core = ptr;

ptr = module_alloc(mod->init_size);
...
memset(ptr, 0, mod->init_size);
mod->module_init = ptr;
```

module_alloc is an architecture-specific function for allocating module memory. In most cases, it is implemented by directly calling vmalloc or one of its variants as described in Chapter 3. In other words, the module resides in the memory area of the kernel that is mapped via page tables and not directly.

The data of all sections of the SHF_ALLOC type are then copied to their final memory area using the information obtained by layout_sections; the sh_addr elements of each section are also set to the final position of the section (previously they pointed to the section position in the temporary module area).

Querying the Module License

Technically insignificant but important from a legal point of view — the module license can now be read from the .modinfo section and placed in the module data structure:

---

[16]This is not quite correct because the kernel also defines a specific order for the various sections on the basis of their flags. However, I need not discuss this here.

kernel/module.c
```
set_license(mod, get_modinfo(sechdrs, infoindex, "license"));
```

`set_license` checks whether the license used is GPL-compatible (by comparing its name with the string in section 7.3.3):

kernel/module.c
```
static void set_license(struct module *mod, const char *license)
{
        if (!license)
                license = "unspecified";

        if (!license_is_gpl_compatible(license)) {
                if (!(tainted & TAINT_PROPRIETARY_MODULE))
                        printk(KERN_WARNING "%s: module license '%s' taints "
                        "kernel.\n", mod->name, license);
                add_taint_module(mod, TAINT_PROPRIETARY_MODULE);
        }
}
```

If the license found is not GPL-compatible, the `TAINT_PROPRIETARY_MODULE` flag is set in the `tainted` global variable via `add_taint_module`, which also taints the module via the `taints` field in `struct module`. `license_is_gpl_compatible` determines which licenses are considered to be GPL-compatible at the moment:

kernel/module.c
```
static inline int license_is_gpl_compatible(const char *license)
{
        return (strcmp(license, "GPL") == 0
                || strcmp(license, "GPL v2") == 0
                || strcmp(license, "GPL and additional rights") == 0
                || strcmp(license, "Dual BSD/GPL") == 0
                || strcmp(license, "Dual MIT/GPL") == 0
                || strcmp(license, "Dual MPL/GPL") == 0);
}
```

In an additional step, the kernel is also tainted if the module `ndiswrapper` or `driverwrapper` is loaded into the kernel. Although these modules would comply with the kernel by their own license, their purpose is to load binary data into the kernel (Windows drivers for wireless networking cards in the case of `ndiswrapper`). This is incompatible with the kernel's license and must thus require tainting.

Resolving References and Relocation

The next step is to continue with processing of the module symbols. This task is delegated to the `simplify_symbols` auxiliary function that iterates through all symbols in the symbol table[17]:

kernel/module.c
```
static int simplify_symbols(Elf_Shdr *sechdrs,
                            unsigned int symindex,
                            const char *strtab,
                            unsigned int versindex,
```

---

[17]The number of symbols is determined by dividing the size of the symbol table by the size of an entry.

```
                       unsigned int pcpuindex,
                       struct module *mod)
{
        Elf_Sym *sym = (void *)sechdrs[symindex].sh_addr;
        unsigned long secbase;
        unsigned int i, n = sechdrs[symindex].sh_size / sizeof(Elf_Sym);
        int ret = 0;

        for (i = 1; i < n; i++) {
                switch (sym[i].st_shndx) {
```

Different symbol types must be handled differently. This is easiest for absolutely defined symbols because nothing need be done:

kernel/module.c

```
                case SHN_ABS:
                        /* Don't need to do anything */
                        DEBUGP("Absolute symbol: 0x%08lx\n",
                                (long)sym[i].st_value);
                        break;
```

Undefined symbols must be resolved (I deal below with the corresponding `resolve_symbol` function that returns the matching address for a given symbol):

kernel/module.c

```
                case SHN_UNDEF:
                        sym[i].st_value
                          = resolve_symbol(sechdrs, versindex,
                                          strtab + sym[i].st_name, mod);

                        /* Ok if resolved.  */
                        if (sym[i].st_value != 0)
                                break;
                        /* Ok if weak.  */
                        if (ELF_ST_BIND(sym[i].st_info) == STB_WEAK)
                                break;

                        printk(KERN_WARNING "%s: Unknown symbol %s\n",
                                mod->name, strtab + sym[i].st_name);
                        ret = -ENOENT;
                        break;   strtab + sym[i].st_name, mod);
```

If the symbol cannot be resolved because no matching definition is available, `resolve_symbol` returns 0. This is OK if the symbol is defined as *weak* (see Appendix E); otherwise, the module cannot be inserted because it references symbols that do not exist.

All other symbols are resolved by looking up their value in the symbol table of the module:

kernel/module.c

```
                default:
                        secbase = sechdrs[sym[i].st_shndx].sh_addr;
                        sym[i].st_value += secbase;
```

```
                     break;
             }
     }

     return ret;
}
```

The next step in module loading is to place the table of (GPL-) exported symbols in the kernel by setting the num_syms, syms and crcindex elements (or their GPL equivalents) to the corresponding memory locations of the binary data:

kernel/module.c
```
/* Set up EXPORTed & EXPORT_GPLed symbols (section 0 is 0 length) */
mod->num_syms = sechdrs[exportindex].sh_size / sizeof(*mod->syms);
mod->syms = (void *)sechdrs[exportindex].sh_addr;
if (crcindex)
        mod->crcs = (void *)sechdrs[crcindex].sh_addr;
mod->num_gpl_syms = sechdrs[gplindex].sh_size / sizeof(*mod->gpl_syms);
mod->gpl_syms = (void *)sechdrs[gplindex].sh_addr;
if (gplcrcindex)
        mod->gpl_crcs = (void *)sechdrs[gplcrcindex].sh_addr;
mod->num_gpl_future_syms = sechdrs[gplfutureindex].sh_size /
                                 sizeof(*mod->gpl_future_syms);
mod->gpl_future_syms = (void *)sechdrs[gplfutureindex].sh_addr;
if (gplfuturecrcindex)
        mod->gpl_future_crcs = (void *)sechdrs[gplfuturecrcindex].sh_addr;
```

Symbols marked as unused are handled identically so that we omit the corresponding code. Relocation is then performed, and again, the kernel iterates through all module sections. Depending on section type (SHT_REL or SHT_RELA), either apply_relocate or apply_relocate_add is called to perform relocation. Depending on processor type, there is usually only one type of relocation (general relocation or add relocation; see Appendix E). However, let's not go into the details of relocation because this would involve discussing a large number of architecture-specific subtleties.

module_finalize then offers a further architecture-specific hook that allows the individual implementations to perform system-specific finalization tasks. On IA-32 systems, for example, some slower assembly language instructions of older processor types are replaced with newer, faster instructions, if this is possible.

Parameter processing is performed by parse_args, which converts the passed string of the foo=bar,bar2 baz=fuz wiz type into an array of kernel_param instances. A pointer to this array, which can be processed by the module initialization function, is stored in the args element of the module data structure.

As a final step, load_module installs module-related files into sysfs and frees temporary memory occupied by the initial copy of the binary code.

Resolving References

resolve_symbol is used to resolve undefined symbol references. It is primarily a wrapper function, as the code flow diagram in Figure 7-5 indicates.

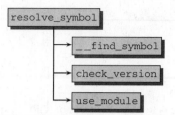

Figure 7-5: Code flow diagram for `resolve_symbol`.

Actual resolution of the symbol is performed in __find_symbol. The kernel first looks through all symbols permanently compiled into the kernel:

kernel/module.c
```
static unsigned long __find_symbol(const char *name,
                                   struct module **owner,
                                   const unsigned long **crc,
                                   int gplok)
{
        struct module *mod;
        const struct kernel_symbol *ks;

        /* Core kernel first. */
        *owner = NULL;
        ks = lookup_symbol(name, __start___ksymtab, __stop___ksymtab);
        if (ks) {
                *crc = symversion(__start___kcrctab, (ks - __start___ksymtab));
                return ks->value;
        }
...
```

The helper function lookup_symbol(name, start, end) searches through the symbol table found between start and end and checks if an entry with a given name can be found. symversion is an auxiliary macro. If the MODVERSIONS option is enabled, it extracts the corresponding entry from the CRC table; otherwise, it returns 0.

The code to search in further sections is basically identical to the code shown above, so we don't list it explicitly here. If gplok is set to 1 because the module uses a GPL-compatible license, the GPL symbols of the kernel located between __start___ksymtab_gpl and __stop___kysmtab_gpl are scanned if no matching information is found in the generally accessible symbols. If this fails, the future GPL-exported symbols are searched. If this still fails, the unused symbols as well as the unused GPL symbols are searched. Should the symbol be present in these section, the kernel uses it to resolve the dependency but prints out a warning because the symbol is bound to disappear sooner or later, so any modules using the symbol will stop working at this point.

If the search is still unsuccessful, the exported symbols of the modules already loaded are scanned:

kernel/module.c
```
        /* Now try modules. */
        list_for_each_entry(mod, &modules, list) {
```

```
        *owner = mod;
        ks = lookup_symbol(name, mod->syms, mod->syms + mod->num_syms);
        if (ks) {
                *crc = symversion(mod->crcs, (ks - mod->syms));
                return ks->value;
        }

        if (gplok) {
                ks = lookup_symbol(name, mod->gpl_syms,
                                        mod->gpl_syms + mod->num_gpl_syms);
                if (ks) {
                        *crc = symversion(mod->gpl_crcs,
                                                (ks - mod->gpl_syms));
                        return ks->value;
                }
        }

        ...
        /* Try unused symbols etc. */
        ...

    }
    return 0;
}
```

Each module stores its exported symbols in the mod->syms array, which has the same structure as the symbol array of the kernel.

If the module is GPL-compatible, all GPL-exported symbols of the modules are scanned; this is done in exactly the same way as the above search, but mod->gpl_syms is used as the database. If this remains unsuccessful, the kernel tries the remaining symbol sections.

> **The kernel sets the owner parameter of __find_symbol to the module data structure of the second module that is presently being processed. This serves to create a dependency between modules when a symbol is resolved with the help of another module.**

0 is returned if the kernel cannot resolve the symbol.

Let's return to resolve_symbol. If __find_symbol is successful, the kernel first uses check_version to determine whether the checksums match (this function is discussed in Section 7.5). If the symbol used originates from another module, a dependency between the two modules is established by means of the familiar use_module function; this prevents the referenced module from being removed as long as the symbol just loaded is still in memory.

7.3.5 Removing Modules

Removing modules from the kernel is much simpler than inserting them, as shown by the code flow diagram of sys_delete_module in Figure 7-6.

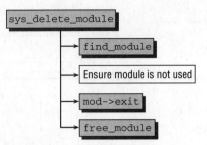

Figure 7-6: Code flow diagram for
`sys_delete_module`.

The system call identifies a module by its name, which must be passed as a parameter[18]:

kernel/module.c
```
asmlinkage long
sys_delete_module(const char __user *name_user, unsigned int flags)
```

First, the kernel must find the matching `module` instance by using `find_module` to look through the list of all registered modules.

It must then be ensured that the module is not required by any other modules:

kernel/module.c
```
        if (!list_empty(&mod->modules_which_use_me)) {
                /* Other modules depend on us: get rid of them first. */
                ret = -EWOULDBLOCK;
                goto out;
        }
```

It is sufficient to check whether the list is empty because a link is automatically established via the `modules_which_use_me` element described above each time a symbol is referenced by another module.

Once it has been established that the reference counter has returned to 0, the module-specific clean-up function is called, and memory space occupied by the module data is freed by means of `free_module`.

7.4 Automation and Hotplugging

Modules can be loaded not only on the initiative of the user or by means of an automated script, but can also be requested by the kernel itself. There are two situations where this kind of loading is useful:

1. The kernel establishes that a required function is not available. For example, a filesystem needs to be mounted but is not supported by the kernel.

The kernel can attempt to load the required module and then retry file mounting.

2. A new device is connected to a hotpluggable bus (USB, FireWire, PCI, etc.). The kernel detects the new device and automatically loads the module with the appropriate driver.

---

[18]Two flags can be passed in addition to the name: O_TRUNC, which indicates that the module may also be removed from the kernel "by force" (despite, e.g., the fact that the reference counter is positive); O_NONBLOCK, which specifies that the operation must be performed without blocking. To keep things simple, the flags are not discussed here.

The implementation of this feature is interesting because, in both cases, the kernel relies on utilities in userspace. On the basis of the information provided by the kernel, the utilities find the appropriate module and insert it into the kernel in the usual way.

7.4.1 Automatic Loading with *kmod*

request_module in kernel/kmod.c is the main function for automatic kernel-initiated module loading. The name of a module (or a generic placeholder[19]) is passed to this function.

Module requests must be built into the kernel explicitly — logically at points where attempts are made to reserve a particular resource but fail because no driver is available. At the moment, there are about 100 such points in the kernel. The IDE driver, for example, attempts to load required drivers when probing for existing devices. The module name of the desired driver must be specified directly to do this:

drivers/ide/ide-probe.c
```
if (drive->media == ide_disk)
        request_module("ide-disk");
...
if (drive->media == ide_floppy)
        request_module("ide-floppy");
```

If a particular protocol family is not available, the kernel must make do with a general request:

net/socket.c
```
if (net_families[family]==NULL)
{
        request_module("net-pf-%d",family);
}
```

Whereas automatic module loading in earlier kernel versions (up to 2.0) was the responsibility of a separate daemon that had to be started explicitly in userspace, loading is now implemented by kernel means — but the kernel still requires a utility in userspace to insert modules. /sbin/modprobe is used by default. The tool was mentioned above when discussing how the manual insertion of modules is used by default. It is not my intention to consider with the numerous tool control options available when automatically inserting modules. Instead, see the comprehensive system administration literature on on this subject.

Figure 7-7 shows the code flow diagram for request_module.

The function requires a minimal environment in which the modprobe process executes (with full root permissions):

kernel/kmod.c
```
char *argv[] = { modprobe_path, "-q", "--", module_name, NULL };
static char *envp[] = { "HOME=/",
                        "TERM=linux",
                        "PATH=/sbin:/usr/sbin:/bin:/usr/bin",
                        NULL };
```

---

[19]This is a service name that is not associated with a particular hardware. For example, the kernel determines that a network module for a certain protocol family is needed, but not linked into the kernel. Because it only knows the number of the protocol family, but not the name of the module that provides support for this family number, the kernel uses net-pf-X as the module name — X denotes the family number. The modules.alias file assigns the appropriate module name for the particular family. net-pf-24, for instance, resolves to pppoe.

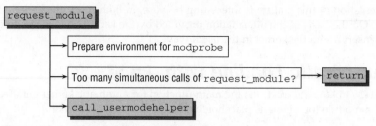

Figure 7-7: Code flow diagram for `request_module`.

The default value for `modprobe_path` is `/sbin/modprobe`. However, this value can be changed via the `proc` filesystem (`/proc/sys/kernel/modprobe`) or the corresponding Sysctl. The name of the required module is passed as a command-line argument.

If `modprobe` itself builds on a service implemented in a module,[20] the kernel goes into a recursive endless loop because `modprobe` instances are started repeatedly. To prevent this, the kernel uses the global variable `kmod_concurrent`, which is incremented by 1 each time `modprobe` is called. The operation is terminated when the lesser of the two values `MAX_KMOD_CONCURRENT` — the default is 50 — or `max_threads/2` is exceeded.

`call_usermodehelper` is then called to start the utility in userspace. Via some detours over functions that are not described in further detail here, the function declares a new work queue entry (see Chapter 14) and adds it to the work queue of the `khelper` kernel thread. When the queue entry is processed, `____call_usermodehelper` is called. This function is, in turn, responsible to run the `modprobe` application, which inserts the desired module into the kernel using the method described above.

7.4.2 Hotplugging

When a new device is connected (or removed) at a hotpluggable bus, the kernel, again with the help of a userspace application, ensures that the correct driver is loaded. In contrast to normal module insertion, it is necessary to perform several additional tasks (e.g., the right driver must be found by reference to a device identification string, or configuration work must be carried out). For this reason, another tool (usually `/sbin/udevd`[21]) is used in place of `modprobe`.

Note that the kernel provides messages to userspace not only when devices are inserted and removed, but also for a much more generic set of events. When, for instance, a new hard disk is connected to the system, the kernel does not just provide information about this event, but also sends notifications about partitions that have been found on the device. Every component of the device model can send registration and unregistration events to the userland. Since this results in a rather large and comprehensive set of messages that can be potentially passed on from the kernel, I do not want to describe them all in detail.

---

[20]In other words, `modprobe` is dependent on a service in a module; accordingly, the kernel issues an instruction to `modprobe` to load the module — and this, in turn, causes `modprobe` to instruct the kernel to start `modprobe` to load the module.

[21]For former versions of the kernel, `/sbin/hotplug` was used as the only hotplug agent. With the introduction of the device model and its maturation during the development of 2.6, `udevd` is now the method of choice for most distributions. Nevertheless, the kernel does provide generic messages and is not tied to a particular mechanism in userspace. In some places, the kernel still calls the program registered in `uevent_helper`, which can be set to `/sbin/hotplug` — the setting is accessible via `/proc/sys/kernel/hotplug`. Setting the value to an empty string disables the mechanism. Since it is only needed during early boot or for some very specific configurations (mostly systems where networking is completely disabled), I will not consider it any further.

Instead, we focus on a specific example illustrating the basic mechanism. Consider that a USB memory stick is attached to the system, but the module that provides USB mass storage support has not yet been loaded into the kernel. Additionally, the distribution wants to automatically mount the device so that the user can immediately access it without further ado. The following steps are necessary to achieve this:

❑ The USB host controller detects a new device on the bus and reports this to the device driver. The host controller allocates a new device and calls usb_new_device to register it.

❑ usb_new_device triggers kobject_uevent to be called.[22] This function calls the subsystem-specific event notification procedure registered in the kobject instance for the object in question.

❑ For USB device objects, usb_uevent is used as the notification function. The function prepares a message that contains all necessary information for udevd to react properly to the insertion of the new USB mass storage device.

The udevd daemon allows inspection of all messages received from the kernel. Observe the following log of the communication that takes place when a new USB stick is plugged into the system.

```
root@meitner # udevmonitor --environment
...
UEVENT[1201129806.368892] add        /devices/pci0000:00/0000:00:1a.7/usb7/7-4/7-4:1.0
(usb)
ACTION=add
DEVPATH=/devices/pci0000:00/0000:00:1a.7/usb7/7-4/7-4:1.0
SUBSYSTEM=usb
DEVTYPE=usb_interface
DEVICE=/proc/bus/usb/007/005
PRODUCT=951/1600/100
TYPE=0/0/0
INTERFACE=8/6/80
MODALIAS=usb:v0951p1600d0100dc00dsc00dp00ic08isc06ip50
SEQNUM=1830
```

The first message is generated by the abovementioned function usb_uevent. Every message consists of identifier/value pairs that determine what is going on inside the kernel. Since a new device is added to the system, the value for ACTION is add. DEVICE denotes where the information about the device can be found in the USB filesystem, and PRODUCT offers some information about vendor and device. The most important field in this case is INTERFACE because this determines the interface class to which the new device belongs. The USB standard reserves 8 for mass storage devices:

<usb_ch9.h>
```
#define USB_CLASS_MASS_STORAGE          8
```

The field MODALIAS contains all generic pieces of information that are available about the device. It is encoded in a string that is obviously not designed for the human eye, but can easily be parsed by a computer. It is generated as follows (add_uevent_var is a helper function that adds a new identifier/value pair to a hotplug message).

drivers/usb/core/usb.c
```
add_uevent_var(env,
        "MODALIAS=usb:v%04Xp%04Xd%04Xdc%02Xdsc%02Xdp%02Xic%02Xisc%02Xip%02X",
```

---

[22]The precise call path is usb_new_device → device_add → kobject_uevent.

```
                    le16_to_cpu(usb_dev->descriptor.idVendor),
                    le16_to_cpu(usb_dev->descriptor.idProduct),
                    le16_to_cpu(usb_dev->descriptor.bcdDevice),
                    usb_dev->descriptor.bDeviceClass,
                    usb_dev->descriptor.bDeviceSubClass,
                    usb_dev->descriptor.bDeviceProtocol,
                    alt->desc.bInterfaceClass,
                    alt->desc.bInterfaceSubClass,
                    alt->desc.bInterfaceProtocol));
```

By comparing the value of MODALIAS against the aliases provided by the modules, udevd can find the proper module that needs to be inserted. In this case, usb-storage is the right choice because the following alias matches the requirements:

```
wolfgang@meitner> /sbin/modinfo usb-storage
...
alias:            usb:v*p*d*dc*dsc*dp*ic08isc06ip50*
...
```

The asterisks are placeholders for arbitrary values as in normal regular expressions, and the last part of the alias (ic08isc06ip50*) is identical with the MODALIAS value. Thus the alias matches, and udevd can insert the usb-storage module into the kernel. How does udevd know which aliases a given module has? It relies on the program depmod, which scans all available modules, extracts the alias information, and stores them in the text file /lib/modules/2.6.x/modules.alias.

The story, however, has not come to an end here. After the USB mass storage module has been inserted into the kernel, the block layer recognizes the device and the partitions contained on it. This leads to another notification.

```
root@meitner # udevmonitor
...
UDEV  [1201129811.890376] add       /block/sdc/sdc1 (block)
UDEV_LOG=3
ACTION=add
DEVPATH=/block/sdc/sdc1
SUBSYSTEM=block
MINOR=33
MAJOR=8
PHYSDEVPATH=/devices/pci0000:00/0000:00:1a.7/usb7/7-4/7-4:1.0/host7/target7:0:0/7:0:0:0
PHYSDEVBUS=scsi
SEQNUM=1837
UDEVD_EVENT=1
DEVTYPE=partition
ID_VENDOR=Kingston
ID_MODEL=DataTraveler_II
ID_REVISION=PMAP
ID_SERIAL=Kingston_DataTraveler_II_5B67040095EB-0:0
ID_SERIAL_SHORT=5B67040095EB
ID_TYPE=disk
ID_INSTANCE=0:0
ID_BUS=usb
ID_PATH=pci-0000:00:1a.7-usb-0:4:1.0-scsi-0:0:0:0
ID_FS_USAGE=filesystem
ID_FS_TYPE=vfat
```

```
ID_FS_VERSION=FAT16
ID_FS_UUID=0920-E14D
ID_FS_UUID_ENC=0920-E14D
ID_FS_LABEL=KINGSTON
ID_FS_LABEL_ENC=KINGSTON
ID_FS_LABEL_SAFE=KINGSTON
DEVNAME=/dev/sdc1
DEVLINKS=/dev/disk/by-id/usb-Kingston_DataTraveler_II_5B67040095EB-0:0-part1
/dev/disk/by-path/pci-0000:00:1a.7-usb-0:4:1.0-scsi-0:0:0:0-part1
/dev/disk/by-uuid/0920-E14D /dev/disk/by-label/KINGSTON
```

The message provides information about the name of the newly detected partition (/dev/sdc1) and the filesystem that is found on the partition (vfat). This is enough for udevd to automatically mount the filesystem and make the USB stick accessible.

7.5 Version Control

Constantly changing kernel sources naturally has implications for driver and module programming — particularly in the context of proprietary binary-only drivers; and it is these implications that are discussed in this section.

When new features are implemented or overall design is revised, it is often necessary to modify the interfaces between the individual parts of the kernel to cope with the new situation or to support a range of performance and design improvements. Of course, developers do their best, whenever possible, to restrict changes to internal functions not directly used by drivers. However, this does not rule out occasional modifications to the "public" interfaces. Naturally, the module interface is also affected by such changes.

When drivers are made available in the source code, this does not present a problem so long as an industrious kernel hacker can be found to adapt the code to the new structures — with most drivers, this can be done in a matter of days (if not hours). Since there is no explicit "development kernel" anymore, it is unavoidable that interface changes are introduced between two stable revisions of the kernel, but since the in-tree code can be easily updated, this does not pose a particular problem.

The situation is different with drivers distributed by manufacturers in binary only. Users are forced to rely on the goodwill of the manufacturers and must wait until a new driver has been developed and released. This approach gives rise to a whole range of problems, two of which are technical [23] and therefore of particular interest to us:

❑   If the module uses an obsolete interface, not only is correct module functioning impaired, but also there is a great likelihood that the system will crash.

❑   Because the interfaces differ for SMP and single-processor systems, two binary versions are needed, and again this can cause the system to crash if the wrong one is loaded.

Of course, these arguments also apply if Open Source modules in binary only are used. Sometimes, this is the only option available to technically less experienced users until manufacturers offer an appropriate update.

---

[23]There is a wealth of detailed information on moral, ethical, and ideological issues on the Internet.

The need for module version control is therefore apparent. But which is the best approach? The simplest solution would be to introduce a constant stored in both the kernel and module. The value of the constant would be incremented each time an interface changes. The kernel would not accept a module unless the interface number in the module and in the kernel were identical; this would solve the version problem. This approach works in principle but is not very intelligent. If an interface *not* used by a module is changed, it can no longer be loaded although it would function perfectly.

For this reason, a finely grained method is used to take account of changes in the individual kernel procedures. The actual module and kernel implementation is not relevant. What is relevant is that the call interface may not change if a module is to function with different kernel versions.[24] The method used is striking in its simplicity, but its mechanism is perfectly capable of solving version control problems.

7.5.1   Checksum Methods

The basic idea is to use a CRC checksum generated using the parameters of a function or procedure. The checksum is an 8-byte figure that requires four letters in hexadecimal notation. If the function interface is modified, so is the checksum. This enables the kernel to deduce that the new version is no longer compatible with the old version.

The checksum is not a mathematically unique sum — (different procedures could be mapped to the same checksum because there are more combinations (in fact, an infinite number) derived from procedure parameters than there are checksums available (namely, 2^{32}). In practice, this is not a problem because the likelihood that a function interface has the same checksum after several of its parameters have been changed is low.

Generating a Checksum

The genksym tool that comes with the kernel sources and is automatically created at compilation time is used to generate a function checksum. To demonstrate how it works, let's use the following header file, which contains an exported function definition:

```
#include<linux/sched.h>
#include<linux/module.h>
#include<linux/types.h>

int accelerate_task(long speedup, struct task_struct *task);

EXPORT_SYMBOL(accelerate_task);
```

The function definition contains a compound structure as a parameter, and this makes the work of genksyms more difficult. When the definition of the structure changes, the checksum of the function also changes. In order to analyze the contents of the structure, it is a given that the contents must be known. Consequently, input for genksyms is made up exclusively of files that have been processed by the pre-processor and therefore contain the required include files in which the appropriate definitions are located.

---

[24]This presupposes, of course, that the name of the function changes when the semantics of its code change but that the interface definition remains unchanged.

The following call is needed to generate the checksum of the exported function[25]:

```
wolfgang@meitner> gcc -E test.h -D__GENKSYMS__ -D__KERNEL__ | genksyms > test.ver
```

The contents of `test.ver` are then as follows:

```
wolfgang@meitner> cat test.ver
__crc_accelerate_task = 0x3341f339 ;
```

If the definition of `accelerate_task` changes because, for example, an integer is used as the first parameter, the checksum also changes: in this case, `genksym` calculates `0xbb29f607`.

If several symbols are defined in a file, `genksyms` generates several checksums. The resulting file has the following sample contents for the `vfat` module:

```
wolfgang@meitner> cat .tmp_vfat.ver
__crc_vfat_create = 0x50fed954 ;
__crc_vfat_unlink = 0xe8acaa66 ;
__crc_vfat_mkdir = 0x66923cde ;
__crc_vfat_rmdir = 0xd3bf328b ;
__crc_vfat_rename = 0xc2cd0db3 ;
__crc_vfat_lookup = 0x61b29e32 ;
```

This is a script for the linker `ld` whose significance in the compilation process is explained below.

Linking Into Modules and the Kernel

The kernel must incorporate the information supplied by `genksym` in the binary code of a module in order to use it later; how this is done is discussed in the following.

Exported Functions

Recall that `__EXPORT_SYMBOL` calls the `__CRC_SYMBOL` macro internally, as discussed in Section 7.3.3. This is defined as follows when version control is enabled:

```
<module.h>
#define __CRC_SYMBOL(sym, sec)                                  \
        extern void *__crc_##sym __attribute__((weak));         \
        static const unsigned long __kcrctab_##sym              \
        __attribute_used__                                      \
        __attribute__((section("__kcrctab" sec), unused))       \
        = (unsigned long) &__crc_##sym;
```

When `EXPORT_SYMBOL(get_shorty)` is called, `__CRC_SYMBOL` expands as follows:

```
extern void *__crc_get_richard __attribute__((weak));
static const unsigned long __kcrctab_get_shorty
    __attribute_used__
    __attribute__((section("__kcrctab" ""), unused)) =
    (unsigned long) &__crc_get_shorty;
```

---

[25]For simplicity's sake, the parameters for matching the include paths to the kernel sources are not shown; also, in a genuine module compilation, `-DMODULE`, for example, would also be specified. Refer to the output of `make modules` for details.

As a result, the kernel creates two objects in the binary file:

❑ The undefined void pointer __crc_*function* is located in the normal symbol table of the module. [26]

❑ A pointer to the variable just defined is stored under krcrtab_*function* in the __kcrctab section of the file.

When the module is linked (in the first phase of module compilation), the linker uses the .ver file generated by genksyms as a script. This supplies the __crc_*function* symbols with the values in the script. The kernel reads them in later. If another module refers to one of these symbols, the kernel uses the information shown here to ensure that both refer to the same version.

Unresolved References

Naturally it is not sufficient to store only the checksums of the exported functions of a module. It is more important to note the checksums of all symbols *used* because these must be compared with the versions made available by the kernel when modules are inserted.

In the second part of module compilation,[27] the following steps are performed to insert version information for all referenced symbols of a module into the module binary files:

1. modpost is called as follows:

```
wolfgang@meitner> scripts/modpost vmlinux module1 module2 module3 ...
modulen
```

Not only the name of the kernel image but also the names of all previously generated .o module binaries are specified. modpost is a utility that comes with the kernel sources. It produces two lists, a global list containing all symbols made available (regardless of whether by the kernel or by a module), and a specific list for each module with all unresolved module references.

2. modprobe then iterates through all modules and tries to find the unresolved references in the list of all symbols. This succeeds if the symbol is defined either by the kernel itself or in another module.

A new *module*.mod.c file is created for each module. Its contents look like this (for the vfat module, e.g.):

```
wolfgang@meitner> cat vfat.mod.c
#include <linux/module.h>
#include <linux/vermagic.h>
#include <linux/compiler.h>

MODULE_INFO(vermagic, VERMAGIC_STRING);

struct module __this_module
__attribute__((section(".gnu.linkonce.this_module"))) =
.name = KBUILD_MODNAME,
```

---

[26]The weak attribute creates a (*weakly*) linked variable. If it is not supplied with a value, no error is reported — as it would be for a normal variable. It is ignored instead. This is necessary because genksyms does not generate a checksum for some symbols.

[27]In the first part of compilation, all module source files were compiled into .o object files that contain version information on the exported symbols but not the referenced symbols.

```
 .init = init_module,
#ifdef CONFIG_MODULE_UNLOAD
 .exit = cleanup_module,
#endif
 .arch = MODULE_ARCH_INIT,
};

static const struct modversion_info ____versions[]
__attribute_used__
__attribute__((section("__versions"))) =
        0x8533a6dd, "struct_module" ,
        0x21ab58c2, "fat_detach" ,
        0xd8ec2862, "__mark_inode_dirty" ,
...
        0x3c15a491, "fat_dir_empty" ,
        0x9a290a43, "d_instantiate" ,
};

static const char __module_depends[]
__attribute_used__
__attribute__((section(".modinfo"))) =
"depends=fat";
```

In the file, two variables located in different sections of the binary file are defined:

a. All symbols referenced by the module — together with the checksum that they need and that was copied from the symbol definition in the kernel or in another module — are stored in the `modversions_info` array in the `__modversions` section. When a module is inserted, this information is used to check whether the running kernel has the correct versions of the required symbols.

b. A list of all modules on which the processed module depends is located in the `module_depends` array in the `.modinfo` section. In our example, the VFAT module depends on the FAT module.
It is a simple matter for `modprobe` to create the depends list. If module A references a symbol that is not defined in the kernel itself but in another module B, the name of B is noted in the depends list of A.

3. In the last step, the kernel compiles the resulting `.mod.o` file into an object file and links it with the existing `.o` object file of the module using `ld`; the resulting file is named *module*.`ko` and is the finished kernel module that can be loaded with `insmod`.

7.5.2   *Version Control Functions*

Above I noted that the kernel uses the auxiliary function `check_version` to determine whether the symbol versions required by a module match the versions made available by the kernel.

This function requires several parameters: a pointer to the section header of the (`sechdrs`) module, the index of the `__version` section, the name of the processed symbol (`symname`), a pointer to the module data structure (`mod`), and a pointer to the checksum (`crc`) that the kernel provides for the symbol and that is supplied by `__find_symbol` when the symbol is resolved.

kernel/module.c
```
static int check_version(Elf_Shdr *sechdrs,
                         unsigned int versindex,
                         const char *symname,
                         struct module *mod,
                         const unsigned long *crc)
{
        unsigned int i, num_versions;
        struct modversion_info *versions;

        /* Exporting module didn't supply crcs?  OK, we're already tainted. */
        if (!crc)
                return 1;
...
```

If the module (from which the symbol to be resolved originates) does not provide any CRC information, the function returns 1 directly. This means that the version check was successful — if no information is available, the check cannot fail.

Otherwise the kernel iterates through all symbols referenced by the module, searches for the corresponding entry and compares the checksum returned in `versions[i].crc` by the module with the (`crc`) returned by the kernel. If the two match, the kernel returns 1; if not, a warning message is issued and the function terminates with 0:

kernel/module.c
```
        versions = (void *) sechdrs[versindex].sh_addr;
        num_versions = sechdrs[versindex].sh_size
                / sizeof(struct modversion_info);

        for (i = 0; i < num_versions; i++) {
                if (strcmp(versions[i].name, symname) != 0)
                        continue;

                if (versions[i].crc == *crc)
                        return 1;
                printk("%s: disagrees about version of symbol %s\n",
                        mod->name, symname);
                return 0;
        }
```

If the symbol is not found in the version table of the module, no version requirements are applied. As a result, the function again returns 1 for success. However, the aforementioned `tainted` global variable and the instance of `struct module` for the module in question are supplied with `TAINT_FORCED_MODULE` to note for later that a symbol without version information was used.

kernel/module.c
```
        /* Not in module's version table.  OK, but that taints the kernel. */
        if (!(tainted & TAINT_FORCED_MODULE)) {
                printk("%s: no version for \"%s\" found: kernel tainted.\n",
                        mod->name, symname);
                add_taint_module(mod, TAINT_FORCED_MODULE);
        }
        return 1;
}
```

7.6 Summary

Modules allow us to extend the functionalities provided by the kernel at run time. Considering the extensive number of drivers available in the kernel, this is an important mechanism because only the really required code needs to be active. However, not only device drivers, but all except the most fundamental parts of the kernel can be configured as modules.

I have discussed how dependencies between modules are detected and can be resolved, how modules are represented in binary files, and how they are loaded into and unloaded from the kernel. Additionally, I have described how the kernel can automatically request modules when a particular feature is accessed from userland, but the corresponding code is not present in the kernel. This requires some interaction with userland to resolve which module is required.

Finally, I have shown how the kernel can protect itself against modules that are compiled against a different kernel version and that might employ an incompatible set of functions with the help of module version control.

8

The Virtual Filesystem

Typically, a full Linux system consists of somewhere between several thousand and a few million files that store programs, data, and all kinds of information. Hierarchical directory structures are used to catalog and group files together. Various approaches are adopted to permanently store the required structures and data.

Every operating system has at least one "standard filesystem" that features functions, some good, some less so, to carry out required tasks reliably and efficiently. The Second/Third Extended Filesystem that comes with Linux is a kind of standard filesystem that has proved itself to be very robust and suitable for everyday use over the past few years. Nevertheless, there are other filesystems written for or ported to Linux, all of which are acceptable alternatives to the Ext2 standard. Of course, this does not mean that programmers must apply different file access methods for each filesystem they use — this would run totally counter to the concept of an operating system as an abstraction mechanism.

To support various native filesystems and, at the same time, to allow access to files of other operating systems, the Linux kernel includes a layer between user processes (or the standard library) and the filesystem implementation. This layer is known as the *Virtual File System*, or *VFS* for short.[1] Figure 8-1 shows the significance of the layer.

The task of VFS is not a simple one. On the one hand, it is intended to provide uniform ways of manipulating files, directories, and other objects. On the other, it must be able to come to terms with the concrete implementations of the various approaches, which differ in part not only in specific details but also in their overall design. However, the rewards are high because VFS adds substantial flexibility to the Linux kernel.

The kernel supports more than 40 filesystems of various origins — ranging from the FAT filesystem from the MS-DOS era through UFS (Berkeley UNIX) and iso9660 for CD-ROMs to network filesystems such as coda and NFS and virtual versions such as procfs.

---

[1]The term *virtual filesystem switch* is also used occasionally.

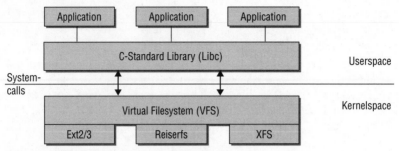

Figure 8-1: VFS layer for filesystem abstraction.

8.1 Filesystem Types

Filesystems may be grouped into three general classes:

1. **Disk-based filesystems** are the classic way of storing files on nonvolatile media to retain their contents between sessions. In fact, most filesystems have evolved from this category. Some well-known examples are Ext2/3, Reiserfs, FAT, and iso9660. All make use of block-oriented media and must therefore answer the question, how to store file contents and structure information on the directory hierarchies. Of no interest to us here is the way in which communication takes place with the underlying block device — the corresponding device drivers in the kernel provide a uniform interface for this purpose. From the filesystem point of view, the underlying devices are nothing more than a list of storage blocks for which an appropriate organization scheme must be adopted.

2. **Virtual filesystems** are generated in the kernel itself and are a simple way of enabling userspace programs to communicate with users. The proc filesystem is the best example of this class. It requires no storage space on any kind of hardware device; instead, the kernel creates a hierarchical file structure whose entries contain information on a particular part of the system. The file /proc/version, for example, has a nominal length of 0 bytes when viewed with the ls command.

   ```
   wolfgang@meitner> ls -l /proc/version
   -r--r--r--    1 root     root              0 May 27 00:36 /proc/version
   ```

   However, if the file contents are output with cat, the kernel generates a list of information on the system processor; this list is extracted from the data structures in kernel memory.

   ```
   wolfgang@meitner> cat /proc/version
   Linux version 2.6.24 (wolfgang@schroedinger) (gcc version 4.2.1 (SUSE Linux))
   #1 Tue Jan 29 03:58:03 GMT 2008
   ```

3. **Network filesystems** are a Halfway House between disk-based and virtual filesystems. They permit access to data on a computer attached to the local computer via a network. In this case, the data are, in fact, stored on a hardware device on a different system. This means that the kernel need not be concerned with the details of file access, data organization, and hardware communication — this is taken care of by the kernel of the remote computer. All operations on files in this filesystem are carried out over a network connection. When a process writes data to a file, the data are sent to the remote computer using a specific protocol

(determined by the network filesystem). The remote computer is then responsible for storing the transmitted data and for informing the sender that the data have arrived.

Nevertheless, the kernel needs information on the size of files, their position within the directory hierarchy, and other important characteristics, even when it is working with network filesystems. It must also provide functions to enable user processes to perform typical file-related operations such as open, read, or delete. As a result of the VFS layer, userspace processes see no difference between a local filesystem and a filesystem available only via a network.

8.2 The Common File Model

The VFS not only provides methods and abstractions for filesystems, but also supports a uniform view of the objects (or *files*) in the filesystem. Even though the meaning of the term *file* may appear to be clear, there are many small, often subtle differences in detail owing to the underlying implementations of the individual filesystems. Not all support the same functions, and some operations (which are indispensable for "normal" files) make no sense when applied to certain objects — *named pipes*, for instance — which are also integrated into VFS.

Not every filesystem supports all abstraction types in VFS. Device files cannot be stored in filesystems originating from other systems (i.e., FAT) because the latter do not cater to objects of this kind.

Defining a minimum common model that supports only those functions implemented by *all* filesystems in the kernel is not practical because many essential features would be lost or would only be accessible via filesystem-specific paths. This would negate the benefits of a virtual abstraction layer. The VFS answer is quite the opposite — a structure model consisting of all components that mirror a powerful filesystem. However, this model exists only virtually and must be adapted to each filesystem using a variety of objects with function pointers. All implementations must provide routines that can be adapted to the structures defined by the VFS and can therefore act as a go-between between the two views.

Naturally, the structure of the virtual filesystem is not a product of fantasy but is based on structures used to describe classical filesystems. The VFS layer was also organized to clearly resemble the Ext2 filesystem. This makes life more difficult for filesystems based on totally different concepts (e.g., the Reiser filesystem or XFS) but delivers speed gains when working with Ext2fs because practically no time is lost converting between Ext2 and VFS structures.

When working with files, the central objects differ in kernel space and userspace. For user programs, a file is identified by a *file descriptor*. This is an integer number used as a parameter to identify the file in all file-related operations. The file descriptor is assigned by the kernel when a file is opened and is valid only within a process. Two different processes may therefore use the same file descriptor, but it does not point to the same file in both cases. Shared use of files on the basis of the same descriptor number is not possible.

The *inode* is key to the kernel's work with files. Each file (and each directory) has just one inode, which contains metadata such as access rights, date of last change, and so on, and also pointers to the file data. However, and this may appear to be slightly strange, the inode does *not* contain one important item of information — the filename. Usually, it is assumed that the name of a file is one of its major characteristics and should therefore be included in the object (inode) used to manage it. I explain why this is not so in the following section.

8.2.1   Inodes

How can directory hierarchies be represented by data structures? As already noted, inodes are central to file implementation, but are also used to implement directories. In other words, directories are just a special kind of file and must be interpreted correctly.

The elements of an inode can be grouped into two classes:

1.   Metadata to describe the file status; for example, access permissions or date of last change
2.   A data segment (or a pointer to data) in which the actual file contents are held; text in the case of a text file

To demonstrate how inodes are used to structure the directory hierarchy of the filesystem, let's look at how the kernel goes about finding the inode of /usr/bin/emacs.

Lookup starts at the root inode, which represents the root directory / and must always be known to the system. The directory is represented by an inode whose data segment does not contain normal data but only the root directory entries. These entries may stand for files or other directories. Each entry consists of two elements.

1.   The number of the inode in which the data of the next entry are located
2.   The name of the file or directory

All inodes of the system have a specific number by which they are uniquely identified. The association between filename and inode is established by this number.

The first step in the lookup operation is to find the inode of the subdirectory usr. The data field of the root inode are scanned until an entry named usr is found (if lookup fails, a "File not found" error is returned). The associated inode can be localized by reference to the inode number.

The above step is repeated, but this time a search is made for a data entry with the name bin so that the inode can be identified by its inode number. The name sought in its data entry is emacs. Again, this returns the number of an inode — which, in this case, represents a file and not a directory. Figure 8-2 shows the situation at the end of the lookup process (the path taken is indicated by pointers between the objects).

The file contents of the last inode differ from those of the three previous inodes. Each of the first three represents a directory and therefore contains a list of its subdirectories and files. The inode associated with the emacs file stores the contents of the file in the data segment.

Although the basic idea of a step-by-step file lookup process is the same in the actual implementation of the VFS, there are a few differences in detail. For example, caches are used to speed the lookup operations because frequent opening of files is a slow process. In addition, the VFS layer must communicate with the underlying filesystems that supply the actual information.

8.2.2   Links

Links are used to establish connections between filesystem objects that do not fit into the classic tree model. There are two types of link — *symbolic* and *hard*.

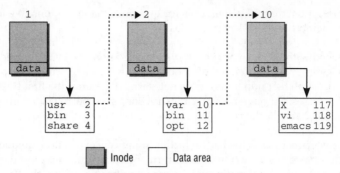

Figure 8-2: Lookup operation for `/usr/bin/emacs`.

Symbolic links can be regarded as "direction pointers" (at least by user programs) to indicate the presence of a file at a particular location, although — as we all know — the actual file resides somewhere else.

Sometimes the name *soft link* is used for links of this kind. This is because the link and link target are not tightly coupled with each other. A link can be imagined as a directory entry that does not contain any data but just a pointer to a filename. The link is retained when the target file is deleted. A separate inode is used for each symbolic link. The data segment of the inode contains a character string that gives the name of the link target.

With symbolic links, it is possible to distinguish between the original file and the link. This is not the case with hard links. Once a hard link has been created, it is no longer possible to establish which filename is the original and which is the hard link. When a hard link is created, a directory entry is generated whose associated inode uses an existing inode number.

Deleting a symbolic link is not difficult, but the situation with hard links is a little trickier. Let us assume that a hard link (B) shares the same inode with the original file (A). A user now wants to delete A; this normally destroys the associated inode together with its data segment so that it can be released and subsequently overwritten. Access to B is then no longer possible because the associated inode and file information no longer exists. Of course, this is not desirable behavior.

It can be prevented by a counter incorporated in the inode. The counter is incremented each time a hard link to the file is created. If one of the hard links or, indeed, the original file (because it is impossible to differentiate between the two) is deleted, the counter is decremented by 1. Only when the counter has reverted to 0 is it certain that the inode is no longer in use and can therefore be removed from the system.

8.2.3 Programming Interface

The interface between user processes and the kernel implementation of the VFS is formed, as usual, by system calls, most of which involve the manipulation of files, directories, and filesystems in general. At this point, we will not concern ourselves with the specific details of system programming as these are the subject of many other publications such as [SR05] and [Her03].

The kernel provides more than 50 system calls for the above manipulations. We look only at the most important calls to demonstrate the key principles.[2]

Files must be opened with the open or openat system call before they can be used. The kernel returns a non-negative integer number to userland after opening the file successfully. The assigned file descriptor numbers start at 3. Recall that numbering does not start at 0 because the first three file descriptors are reserved for all processes, although no explicit instructions need be given. 0 represents standard input, 1 standard output, and 2 standard error.

Once a file has been opened, its name has no further significance. It is now uniquely identified by its file descriptor, which is passed as a parameter to all further library functions (and therefore to system calls). While file descriptors were traditionally sufficient to identify a file within the kernel, this is not the case anymore. Since the introduction of multiple namespaces and containers, multiple file descriptors with the same numerical value can coexist in the kernel. A unique representation is provided by a special data structure (struct file), discussed below.

We see this in the close part of the sample program that closes the "connection" to a file (and returns the file descriptor so that it can be used for files to open other files in the future). read also expects the file descriptor as its first parameter so that it can identify the source from which to read data.

The current position within an open file is held in the *file pointer*, which is an integer that specifies the offset from the start of the file. The pointer can be set to any value for *random access files* as long as the value remains within the file limits. This supports random access to the file data. Other file types — *named pipes* or *device files* for character devices, for instance — prohibit this. They may only be read sequentially from beginning to end.

Various flags (such as O_RDONLY) are specified to define the *access mode* when a file is opened. More detailed explanations are given in all works on system programming.

8.2.4 Files as a Universal Interface

UNIX is based on just a few judiciously selected paradigms. A very important "metaphor" threads its way through the kernel (and particularly through the VFS), particularly with regard to the implementation of input and output mechanisms.

Everything is a file.

OK, let's admit it: There are, of course, a few exceptions to this rule (e.g., network devices), but most functions exported by the kernel and employed by user programs can be reached via the file interface defined by the VFS. The following is a selection of kernel subsystems that use files as their central means of communication:

❏   Character and block devices

❏   Pipes between processes

---

[2]Communication with files is carried out not only by means of file descriptors but also with the help of *streams*. The latter provide a convenient interface. They are, however, implemented in the C standard library and not in the kernel. Internally they make use of normal file descriptors.

❑   Sockets for all network protocols

❑   Terminals for interactive input and output

Note that some of the objects are not necessarily linked with an entry in a filesystem. Pipes, for instance, are generated by special system calls and then managed by the kernel in the data structures of the VFS without having a "real" filesystem entry that can be accessed with typical commands such as rm, ls, and so on.[3]

Of particular interest (above all, in the context of Chapter 6) are device files to access block and character devices. These are real files that typically reside in the /dev directory. Their contents are generated dynamically by the associated device driver when a read or write operation is performed.

8.3   Structure of the VFS

Now that we are familiar with the basic structure of the VFS and the interface to users, we turn our attention to the implementation details. A large number of sometimes very lengthy data structures are involved in the implementation of the VFS interface. It is therefore best to sketch out a rough overview of the components and how they are interlinked.

8.3.1   Structural Overview

The VFS consists of two components — files and filesystems — that need to be managed and abstracted.

File Representation

As noted above, inodes are the means of choice for representing file contents and associated metadata. In theory, only one (albeit very long) data structure with all the requisite data would be needed to implement this concept. In practice, the data load is spread over a series of smaller, clearly laid out structures whose interplay is illustrated in Figure 8-3.

No fixed functions are used to abstract access to the underlying filesystems. Instead, function pointers are required. These are held in two structures that group together related functions.

1.   **Inode Operations** — Create links, rename files, generate new file entries in a directory, and delete files.

2.   **File Operations** — Act on the data contents of a file. They include obvious operations such as read and write, but also operations such as setting file pointers and creating memory mappings.

Other structures in addition to the ones above are needed to hold the information associated with an inode. Of particular significance is the data field that is linked with each inode and stores either the contents of the file or a table of directory entries. Each inode also includes a pointer to the superblock object of the underlying filesystem used to perform operations such as the manipulation of the inodes themselves (these operations are also implemented by arrays of function pointers, as we will see shortly). Information on filesystem features and limits can also be provided.

---

[3]Named pipes do have an entry in the filesystem so that they can be accessed.

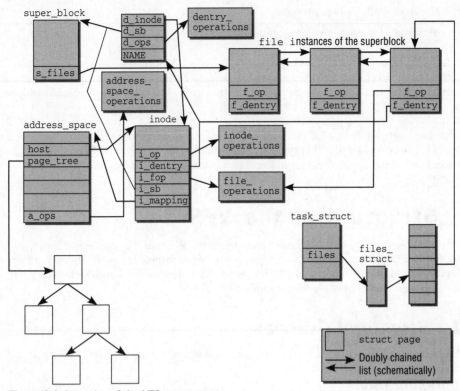

Figure 8-3: Interplay of the VFS components.

Because opened files are always assigned to a specific system process, the kernel must store the connection between the file and the process in its data structures. As discussed briefly in Chapter 2, the task structure includes an element in which all opened files are held (via a roundabout route). This element is an array that is accessed using the file descriptor as an index. The objects it contains are not only linked with the inode of the corresponding file, but also have a pointer to an element of the *dentry cache* used to speed lookup operations.

The individual filesystem implementations are also able to store their own data (that is not manipulated by the VFS layer) in the VFS inode.

Filesystem and Superblock Information

The supported filesystem types are linked by means of a special kernel object that features a method of reading the *superblock*. As well as key information on the filesystem (block size, maximum file size, etc.), the superblock contains function pointers to read, write, and manipulate inodes.

The kernel also creates a list of the superblock instances of all active filesystems. I use the term *active* instead of *mounted* because, in certain circumstances, it is possible to use a single superblock for several mount points.[4]

---

[4]When a filesystem of a block device is mounted at several points in the directory hierarchy.

Whereas each filesystem appears just once in `file_system_type`, there may be several instances of a superblock for the same filesystem type in the list of superblock instances because several filesystems of the same type can be stored on various block devices or partitions. Most systems have, for example, both a root and a home partition, which may be on different partitions of the hard disk but normally use the same filesystem type. Only one occurrence of the filesystem type need appear in `file_system_type`, but the superblocks for both mounts are different, although the same filesystem is used in both cases.

An important element of the superblock structure is a list with all modified inodes of the relevant filesystem (the kernel refers to these rather disrespectfully as *dirty* inodes). Files and directories that have been modified are easily identified by reference to this list so that they can be written back to the storage medium. Writeback must be coordinated and kept to a necessary minimum because it is a very time-consuming operation (hard disks, floppy disk drives, and other media are very slow as compared to other system components). On the other hand, it is fatal to write back modified data too infrequently because a system crash (or, more likely in the case of Linux, a power outage) results in irrecoverable data loss. The kernel scans the list of dirty blocks at periodic intervals and transfers changes to the underlying hardware.[5]

8.3.2 Inodes

The inode structure of the VFS is as follows:

```
<fs.h>
struct inode {
        struct hlist_node       i_hash;
        struct list_head        i_list;
        struct list_head        i_sb_list;
        struct list_head        i_dentry;
        unsigned long           i_ino;
        atomic_t                i_count;
        unsigned int            i_nlink;
        uid_t                   i_uid;
        gid_t                   i_gid;
        dev_t                   i_rdev;
        unsigned long           i_version;
        loff_t                  i_size;
        struct timespec         i_atime;
        struct timespec         i_mtime;
        struct timespec         i_ctime;
        unsigned int            i_blkbits;
        blkcnt_t                i_blocks;
        umode_t                 i_mode;

        struct inode_operations *i_op;
        const struct file_operations    *i_fop; /* former ->i_op->default_file_ops */
        struct super_block      *i_sb;
        struct address_space    *i_mapping;
        struct address_space    i_data;
```

---

[5]There are additional caches between the raw hardware and the kernel, as described in Chapter 6.

```
        struct dquot            *i_dquot[MAXQUOTAS];

        struct list_head        i_devices;
        union {
                struct pipe_inode_info *i_pipe;
                struct block_device *i_bdev;
                struct cdev *i_cdev;
        };

        int                     i_cindex;

        __u32                   i_generation;

        unsigned long           i_state;
        unsigned long           dirtied_when;   /* jiffies of first dirtying */

        unsigned int            i_flags;

        atomic_t                i_writecount;
        void                    *i_security;
};
```

The structure opens with several list heads that are used to manage each inode instance according to category. We look at the significance of the individual lists below in this section.

Before explaining the meanings of the individual structural members, it is worth remembering that the inode structure examined here was designed for processing *in memory* and therefore includes a few elements that are *not* present in the stored inodes. They are created dynamically or generated by the kernel itself when the information on the low-level filesystem is read in.

There are also filesystems such as FAT and Reiserfs that do not use inodes in the classic sense and must therefore generate the information shown here by extracting it from the data they themselves contain.

The majority of the elements are dedicated to managing simple status information; for example, i_atime, i_mtime, and t_ctime store the time of the last *access*, the time of the last *modification*, and the time of the last inode *change*. *Modification* is taken to mean a change to the data contents associated with the inode. A change must be made to the inode structure itself (or to an attribute of the file) to bring about a change to i_ctime.

The file length in bytes is stored in i_size. i_blocks specifies the value in blocks. The latter value is a characteristic of the filesystem rather than of the file itself. When many filesystems are created, a block size can be selected as the minimum unit for storage space allocation on the hardware medium (the default for the Ext2 filesystem is 4,096 bytes per block, but smaller or larger values may be chosen — Chapter 9 discusses this in more detail). The file size in blocks could therefore also be calculated using the information on the filesystem block size and the file size in bytes. This is not done, but for convenience, the file size is included in the inode structure.

Each VFS inode (for a given filesystem) is identified by a unique number held in i_ino. i_count is a usage counter to specify how many processes are accessing the same inode structure. (Inodes are used simultaneously when, for example, a process duplicates itself with fork, as demonstrated in Chapter 2.) i_nlink is the counter used to record the total number of *hard* links that are using the inode.

File access and ownership rights are held in i_mode (file type and access permissions) and in i_uid and i_gid (the UID and GID associated with the file).

i_rdev is needed when the inode represents a device file. It indicates the device with which communication is to take place. Note that i_rdev is only a number, not a data structure! The information contained in this number is, however, sufficient to find everything interesting about the device. For block devices, this would be an instance of struct block_device, as is discussed in Chapter 6.[6]

If the inode represents a device special file, then the elements contained in the anonymous union that follows i_rdev contain pointers to specialized data structures about the devices.

i_bdev is used for block devices, i_pipe contains relevant information for inodes used to implement pipes, and i_cdev is utilized for character devices. Since an inode cannot represent more than one type of device at a time, it is safe to keep i_pipe, i_bdev, and i_cdev in a union. i_devices is also connected to device file handling: It allows a block or character device to keep a list of inodes that represent a device file over which it can be accessed. While in many cases a single device file per device will suffice, there are also numerous possibilities — chroot'ed environments, for instance — where a given block or character device will be accessible via more than one device file and thus more than one inode.

Most of the remaining elements point to compound data types whose meanings are discussed below in this chapter.

Inode Operations

The kernel provides a large number of functions for performing operations on inodes. A set of function pointers is defined to abstract the operations because data are manipulated by the specific filesystem implementation. The call interface always remains the same, although the actual work is carried out by implementation-specific functions.

The inode structure has two pointers (i_op and i_fop) to arrays that implement the above abstraction. One relates to the inode-specific operations, and the other provides file operations. A reference to the file operations structure is included not only in the inode structure but also in the file structure. We take a closer look at this after we have examined how files are represented in the kernel. Here, suffice it to say that file operations deal with manipulating the data contained in a file, while inode operations are responsible for managing the structural operations (e.g., deleting a file) and metadata associated with files (e.g., attributes).

All inode operations are grouped together in the following structure:

<fs.h>
```
struct inode_operations {
        int (*create) (struct inode *,struct dentry *,int, struct nameidata *);
        struct dentry * (*lookup) (struct inode *,struct dentry *, struct nameidata *);
        int (*link) (struct dentry *,struct inode *,struct dentry *);
        int (*unlink) (struct inode *,struct dentry *);
        int (*symlink) (struct inode *,struct dentry *,const char *);
        int (*mkdir) (struct inode *,struct dentry *,int);
        int (*rmdir) (struct inode *,struct dentry *);
```

---

[6]The auxiliary function bdget can be used to construct an instance of block_device given the device identifier in i_rdev.

```
    int (*mknod) (struct inode *,struct dentry *,int,dev_t);
    int (*rename) (struct inode *, struct dentry *,
    struct inode *, struct dentry *);
    int (*readlink) (struct dentry *, char __user *,int);
    void * (*follow_link) (struct dentry *, struct nameidata *);
    void (*put_link) (struct dentry *, struct nameidata *, void *);
    void (*truncate) (struct inode *);
    int (*permission) (struct inode *, int, struct nameidata *);
    int (*setattr) (struct dentry *, struct iattr *);
    int (*getattr) (struct vfsmount *mnt, struct dentry *, struct kstat *);
    int (*setxattr) (struct dentry *, const char *,const void *,size_t,int);
    ssize_t (*getxattr) (struct dentry *, const char *, void *, size_t);
    ssize_t (*listxattr) (struct dentry *, char *, size_t);
    int (*removexattr) (struct dentry *, const char *);
    void (*truncate_range)(struct inode *, loff_t, loff_t);
    long (*fallocate)(struct inode *inode, int mode, loff_t offset,
                      loff_t len);
}
```

In most cases, the meaning of the element is clear from the name of the function pointer. The strong similarity with the names of the corresponding system calls and userspace tools is intentional. For example, rmdir deletes directories, rename renames filesystem objects, and so on.

Nevertheless, not all names can be traced back to familiar standard commands:

❑   lookup finds the inode instance of a filesystem object by reference to its name (expressed as a string).

❑   link is invoked to delete a file. However, as described above, the delete operation is not carried out if the hard link reference counter indicates that the inode is in use by more than one file.

❑   The xattr functions create, read, and delete extended attributes not supported in the classicUNIX model. They are used, for example, in the implementation of access control lists (ACLs).

❑   truncate changes the size of the specified inode. The function accepts just one parameter — the data structure of the inode to be processed. The new file size must be set manually in the i_size element of the inode structure before the function is invoked.

❑   truncate_range allows for truncating a range of blocks (i.e., for punching holes into files), but this operation is currently only supported by the shared memory filesystem.

❑   follow_link follows a symbolic link by finding the inode of the target file. Because symbolic links may go beyond filesystem boundaries, the implementation of the routine is usually very short, and work is quickly delegated to generic VFS routines that complete the task.

❑   fallocate is used to pre-allocate space for a file, which can in some circumstances lead to performance benefits. However, only very recent filesystems (like Reiserfs or Ext4) support this operation.

struct dentrys are used as parameters throughout the function prototypes. A struct dentry is a standardized data structure that may represent a filename or a directory. It also establishes the important link between a filename and its inode. We examine the structure extensively below when we discuss the dentry cache, which is of great relevance to VFS implementation. At the moment, we can simply regard a `dentry` as a structure with information on a filename and its inode.

Inode Lists

Each inode has a `i_list` list head element to store the inode on a list. Depending on the state of the inode, three main cases are possible:

1. The inode exists in memory but is not linked to any file and is not in active use.

2. The inode structure is in memory and is being used for one or more tasks, usually to represent a file. The value of both counters (`i_count` and `i_nlink`) must be greater than 0. The file contents and the inode metadata are identical to the information on the underlying block device; that is, the inode has not been changed since the last synchronization with the storage medium.

3. The inode is in active use. Its data contents have been changed and therefore differ from the contents on the storage medium. Inodes in this state are described as *dirty*.

In `fs/inode.c`, the kernel defines two global variables for use as list heads — `inode_unused` for valid but no longer active inodes (the first category in the above list), and `inode_in_use` for all used but unchanged inodes (the second category). The dirty inodes (third category) are held in a superblock-specific list.

A fourth, less frequent possibility arises when all inodes associated with a superblock are invalidated. This happens when a media change has been detected for a removable device such that previously used inodes become meaningless, or when a filesystem was remounted. In all cases, the code ends up in the function `invalidate_inodes`, and the invalidated inodes are kept on a local list that does not have any further relevance for the VFS code.

Each inode appears not only in the state-specific list but also in a hash table to support quick access by reference to the inode number and superblock — this combination is unique throughout the system. The hash table is an array that can be accessed with the help of the global variable `inode_hashtable` (also from `fs/inode.c`). The table is initialized during booting in the `inode_init` function from `fs/inode.c`. The messages output indicate the size of the array calculated on the basis of the available RAM.

```
wolfgang@meitner> dmesg
...
Inode-cache hash table entries: 262144 (order: 9, 2097152 bytes)
...
```

The `hash` function from `fs/inode.c` is used to compute the hash sum (I won't describe the implementation of the hash method). It combines the inode number and the address of the superblock object into a unique number that is guaranteed to reside within the reserved index range of the hash table.[7] Collisions are resolved as usual by means of an overflow list. The inode element `i_hash` is used to manage the overflow elements.

In addition to the hash table, inodes are also kept on a per-superblock list headed by `super_block->s_inodes`. `i_sb_list` is used as the list element.

---

[7]There are, however, filesystems in which there is no guarantee that inodes can be identified by reference to their number and associated superblock. In this situation, additional elements must be scanned (using filesystem-specific methods); `ilookup5` is provided as a front end for this purpose. Currently, the function is not in widespread use except for sysfs and some rarely used filesystems like OCFS2, but external code for more esoteric filesystems is able to access it.

However, the superblock manages more inode lists that are managed independently of i_sb_list (Section 8.4.1 takes a closer look at the definition of struct super_block). If an inode is dirty, that is, its content has been modified, it is listed on a dirty list headed by super_block->s_dirty with the list element i_list. This has the advantage that it is not necessary to scan *all* inodes of the system when writing back data (data writeback is also often referred to as *synchronization*) — it suffices to consider all inodes on the dirty list. Two more lists (headed by super_block->s_io and super_block->s_more_io) use the same list element i_list. They contain inodes that have been selected to be written back to disk and are waiting for this to happen.

8.3.3 Process-Specific Information

File descriptors (which are nothing more than integer numbers) are used to uniquely identify opened files within a process. This assumes that the kernel is capable of establishing a link between the descriptors in the user process and the structures used internally. The elements needed to do this are included in the task structure of each process.

```
<sched.h>
struct task_struct {
...
/* file system info */
        int link_count, total_link_count;
        ...
/* filesystem information */
        struct fs_struct *fs;
/* open file information */
        struct files_struct *files;
/* namespaces */
        struct nsproxy *nsproxy;
...
}
```

The integer elements link_count and total_link_count are used to prevent endless loops when looking up circularly chained links as I will demonstrate in Section 8.4.2.

The filesystem-related data of a process are stored in fs. These data include, for example, the current working directory and information on chroot restrictions, which I discuss in Section 8.3.4.

Since the kernel allows for simultaneously running multiple containers that mimic independent systems, every resource that seems "global" to the container is wrapped up by the kernel and separately managed for every container. The virtual filesystem is also affected because each container can face a different mount hierarchy. The corresponding information is contained in ns_proxy->mnt_namespace (see Section 8.3.4).

files contains the process file descriptors examined in the section below.

Associated Files

The file element of the task structure is of type files_struct. The definition is as follows:

```
<sched.h>
struct files_struct {
        atomic_t count;
        struct fdtable *fdt;
```

```
        struct fdtable fdtab;

        int next_fd;
        struct embedded_fd_set close_on_exec_init;
        struct embedded_fd_set open_fds_init;
        struct file * fd_array[NR_OPEN_DEFAULT];
};
```

next_fd denotes the number of the file descriptor that will be used when a new file is opened. close_on_exec_init and open_fds_init are bitmaps. close_on_exec contains a set bit for all file descriptors that will be closed on exec. open_fds_init is the initial set of file descriptors. struct embedded_fd_set is just a simple unsigned long encapsulated in a special structure.

<file.h>
```
struct embedded_fd_set {
        unsigned long fds_bits[1];
};
```

fd_array contains a pointer to an instance of struct file for every open file; I will discuss this structure in a moment.

By default, the kernel allows each process to open NR_OPEN_DEFAULT files. This value is defined in include/linux/sched.h with the default setting of BITS_PER_LONG. On 32-bit systems, the initial number of files is therefore 32; 64-bit systems can handle 64 files simultaneously. If a process attempts to open more files at the same time, the kernel must increase the memory space for various elements of files_struct that are used to manage information on all files associated with the process.

The most important information is contained in fdtab. The kernel defines another data structure for this purpose.

<file.h>
```
struct fdtable {
        unsigned int max_fds;
        struct file ** fd;      /* current fd array */
        fd_set *close_on_exec;
        fd_set *open_fds;
        struct rcu_head rcu;
        struct files_struct *free_files;
        struct fdtable *next;
};
```

Both an instance of this structure itself and a pointer to an instance are included in struct files_struct because the RCU mechanism is used to enable lock-free reading of these data structures, which speeds up things. Before I come back to how this is done, I need to introduce the meaning of the elements:

max_fds specifies the current maximum number of file objects and file descriptors that the process can handle. There are no fundamental upper limits because both values can be increased if necessary (providing they do not exceed the value specified by Rlimit — but this has nothing to do with the file structure). Although the same number of file objects and file descriptors is always used, the kernel must define different maximum numbers. This is due to the way in which the associated data structures are managed. I explain this below, but first have to clarify what the remaining members of the structure mean:

❑   `fd` is an array of pointers to `file` structures that manage all information on an opened file. The file descriptor of the userspace process acts as an array index. The current size of the array is defined by `max_fds`.

❑   `open_fds` is a pointer to a bit field that manages the descriptors of all currently opened files. There is just one bit for each possible file descriptor; if it is set to 1, the descriptor is in use; otherwise, it is unused. The current maximum number of bit positions is specified by `max_fdset`.

❑   `close_on_exec` is also a pointer to a bit field that holds the descriptors of all files to be closed on the `exec` system call (see Chapter 2).

At a first glance, some information seems to be duplicated between `struct fdtable` and `struct files_struct`: the close-on-exec and open file descriptor bitmap as well as the `file` array. This is not the case because the elements in `file_struct` are real instances of some data structure, while the elements of `fdtable` are pointers. Indeed, `fd`, `open_fds`, and `close_on_exec` are initialized so that they point to these three elements in the structure. As a result, the `fd` array contains `NR_OPEN_DEFAULT` entries; `close_on_exec` and `open_fds` are represented by bitmaps with `BITS_PER_LONG` entries initially as I mentioned above. Since `NR_OPEN_DEFAULT` is set to `BITS_PER_LONG`, all share the same size. Should the need for more open files arise, the kernel allocates an instance of `fd_set` to replace the initial `embedded_fd_set`. `fd_set` is defined as follows:

```
<posix_types.h>
#define __NFDBITS       (8 * sizeof(unsigned long))
#define __FD_SETSIZE    1024
#define __FDSET_LONGS   (__FD_SETSIZE/__NFDBITS)

typedef struct {
        unsigned long fds_bits [__FDSET_LONGS];
} __kernel_fd_set;

typedef __kernel_fd_set         fd_set;
```

Note that `struct embedded_fd_set` can be typecast into `struct fd_set`. In this sense, `embedded_fd_set` is a shrunken version of `fd_set` that can be used in the same way but requires less space.

If one of the initial limits for the bitmaps or the `fd` array is too low, the kernel can expand the relevant elements by making the pointers point to correspondingly larger structures. The arrays are expanded in different steps — this explains why there are different maximum values for the descriptor numbers and file elements in the structure.

One component used for the definition of `files_struct` still needs to be discussed: `struct file`. The structure holds characteristic information on a file as seen by the kernel. Slightly simplified, it is defined as follows:

```
<fs.h>
struct file {
        struct list_head        fu_list;
        struct path f_path;
#define f_dentry f_path.dentry
```

```
#define f_vfsmnt f_path.mnt
        const struct file_operations    *f_op;
        atomic_t                f_count;
        unsigned int            f_flags;
        mode_t                  f_mode;
        loff_t                  f_pos;
        struct fown_struct      f_owner;
        unsigned int            f_uid, f_gid;
        struct file_ra_state    f_ra;

        unsigned long           f_version;
...
        struct address_space    *f_mapping;
...
};
```

The elements have the following meanings:

❏ f_uid and f_gid specify the UID and the GID of the user.

❏ f_owner contains information on the process working with the file (and therefore determines the PID to which SIGIO signals are sent to implement asynchronous input and output).

❏ The readahead characteristics are held in f_ra. These values specify if and how file data are to be read in anticipation before they are actually requested (readahead improves system performance).

❏ The mode passed when a file is opened (generally read, write, or read *and* write access) is held in the f_mode field.

❏ f_flags specifies additional flags that can be passed on the open system call.

❏ The current position of the file pointer (which is important for sequential read operations or when reading a specific file section) is held in the f_pos variable as a byte offset from the beginning of the file.

❏ f_path encapsulates two pieces of information:

   ❏ An association between filename and inode

   ❏ Information about the mounted filesystem in which the file resides

The path data structure is defined as follows:

<namei.h>
```
struct path {
        struct vfsmount *mnt;
        struct dentry *dentry;
};
```

struct dentry provides a connection between filename and inode. I discuss it in Section 8.3.5. Information about the mounted filesystem is contained in struct vfs_mount, discussed in Section 8.4.1.

Since former kernel versions did not use struct path but had explicit dentry and vfsmount members in struct file, corresponding helper macros are required ensuring that code that is not yet updated continues to work.

❑ f_op specifies the functions invoked for file operations (see Section 8.3.4).

❑ f_version is used by filesystems to check whether a file instance is still compatible with the contents of the associated inode. This is important to ensure the consistency of cached objects.

❑ mapping points to the address space mapping that belongs to the inode instance with which the file is associated. Usually, it is a shorthand for inode->i_mapping, but filesystems or other subsystems of the kernel may modify it for their purposes, which I will not discuss any further.

Every superblock provides an s_list list head element to hold file objects — linked by means of file->f_list. The list includes all opened files of the filesystem represented by the superblock. It is scanned when, for example, a filesystem in Read/Write mode is to be remounted in Read Only mode. Of course, this cannot be done if files are still open in Write mode — and the kernel checks this list to find out.[8]

file instances can be reserved with get_empty_filp, which employs its own cache and pre-initializes the instances with essential data.

Increasing the Initial Limits

Whenever the kernel opens a file or does some other action that could need more entries in file_struct than initially provided, it calls expand_files. The function checks if an enlargement is necessary and calls expand_fdtable if this is the case. The function is — slightly simplified — implemented as follows.

fs/file.c
```
static int expand_fdtable(struct files_struct *files, int nr)
{
        struct fdtable *new_fdt, *cur_fdt;

        spin_unlock(&files->file_lock);
        new_fdt = alloc_fdtable(nr);
        spin_lock(&files->file_lock);

        copy_fdtable(new_fdt, cur_fdt);
        rcu_assign_pointer(files->fdt, new_fdt);
        if (cur_fdt->max_fds > NR_OPEN_DEFAULT)
                free_fdtable(cur_fdt);

        return 1;
}
```

alloc_fdtable allocates a file descriptor table with the maximal number of possible entries and also reserves memory for the enlarged bitmaps — it only makes sense to increase all components at the same time. After this, the function copies the previous contents of the file descriptor table into the new, enlarged instance. Switching the pointer files_fdt to the new instance is handled by the RCU function rcu_assign_pointer as described in Chapter 5. After this, the old file descriptor table can be freed.

---

[8]Actually, this is slightly more complicated in reality because the RCU mechanism is used to make the freeing of file instances more efficient. Since this only complicates things, but does not add new insights. I am not going to discuss it any further.

8.3.4   File Operations

Files must not only be able to store information, but must also allow this information to be manipulated. From the user viewpoint, manipulation is performed by functions of the standard library. These instruct the kernel to execute system calls, which then perform the required operations. Of course, the interface may not differ for each filesystem implementation. The VFS layer therefore provides abstracted operations that link general file objects with the low-level mechanisms of the underlying filesystem.

The structure used to abstract the file operations must be kept as general as possible or as necessary to cater for a wide range of target files. At the same time, it must not feature too many specialized operations that are useful for one particular file type but not for the rest. Nevertheless, the special requirements of the various files (normal files, device files, etc.) must be satisfied in order to exploit their capabilities to the full.

Each `file` instance includes a pointer to an instance of the `struct file_operations` structure that holds function pointers to all possible file operations. This structure is defined as follows:

<fs.h>
```
struct file_operations {
        struct module *owner;
        loff_t (*llseek) (struct file *, loff_t, int);
        ssize_t (*read) (struct file *, char __user *, size_t, loff_t *);
        ssize_t (*write) (struct file *, const char __user *, size_t, loff_t *);
        ssize_t (*aio_read) (struct kiocb *, const struct iovec *, unsigned long, loff_t);
        ssize_t (*aio_write) (struct kiocb *, const struct iovec *, unsigned long, loff_t);
        int (*readdir) (struct file *, void *, filldir_t);
        unsigned int (*poll) (struct file *, struct poll_table_struct *);
        int (*ioctl) (struct inode *, struct file *, unsigned int, unsigned long);
        long (*unlocked_ioctl) (struct file *, unsigned int, unsigned long);
        long (*compat_ioctl) (struct file *, unsigned int, unsigned long);
        int (*mmap) (struct file *, struct vm_area_struct *);
        int (*open) (struct inode *, struct file *);
        int (*flush) (struct file *, fl_owner_t id);
        int (*release) (struct inode *, struct file *);
        int (*fsync) (struct file *, struct dentry *, int datasync);
        int (*aio_fsync) (struct kiocb *, int datasync);
        int (*fasync) (int, struct file *, int);
        int (*lock) (struct file *, int, struct file_lock *);
        ssize_t (*sendpage) (struct file *, struct page *, int, size_t, loff_t *, int);
        unsigned long (*get_unmapped_area)(struct file *, unsigned long, unsigned long,
                                           unsigned long, unsigned long);
        int (*check_flags)(int);
        int (*dir_notify)(struct file *filp, unsigned long arg);
        int (*flock) (struct file *, int, struct file_lock *);
        ssize_t (*splice_write)(struct pipe_inode_info *, struct file *, loff_t *, size_t,
                                unsigned int);
        ssize_t (*splice_read)(struct file *, loff_t *, struct pipe_inode_info *, size_t,
                               unsigned int);
};
```

The `owner` entry is used only if a filesystem has been loaded as a module and is not compiled into the kernel. This entry then points to the data structure representing the module in memory.

Most pointer names reveal the task that they perform (there are also many identically named system calls that invoke the corresponding function in a more direct way).

- ❑ `read` and `write` read and write data — How could it be otherwise? They make use of the file descriptor, a buffer (in which the Read/Write data reside) and an offset to specify the position within the file. A further pointer indicates the number of bytes to be read or written.

- ❑ `aio_read` is used for asynchronous read operations.

- ❑ `open` opens a file; this corresponds to associating a `file` object with an inode.

- ❑ `release` is invoked when the usage counter of a `file` object reaches 0; in other words, when no one is using the file. This allows low-level implementations to release memory and cache contents no longer needed.

- ❑ Files can be accessed very easily if their contents are mapped into the virtual address space of a process. This is done by `mmap`, whose mode of operation is discussed in Chapter 3.

- ❑ `readdir` reads the contents of directories and is therefore only available for objects of this type.

- ❑ `ioctl` is used to communicate with hardware devices and can therefore only be applied to device files (not to other objects because these contain a null pointer). This method is used when it is necessary to send control commands to a device (the `write` function is used to send data). Even though the function has the same name and the same call syntax for all peripherals, the actual commands differ depending on the hardware-specific situation.

- ❑ `poll` is used with the `poll` and `select` system calls needed to implement synchronous I/O multiplexing. What does this mean? The `read` function is used when a process is waiting for input data from a file object. If no data are available (this may be the case when the process is reading from an external interface), the call blocks until data become available. This could result in unacceptable situations if there are no more data to be read and the `read` function blocks forever.

  The `select` system call, which is also based on the `poll` method, comes to the rescue. It sets a time-out to abort a read operation after a certain period during which no new data arrive. This ensures that program flow is resumed if no further data are available.

- ❑ `flush` is invoked when a file descriptor is closed, which goes hand in hand with decrementing a usage counter — this time the counter need not be 0 (as with `release`). This function is required by network filesystems to conclude transmissions.

- ❑ `fsync` is used by the `fsync` and `fdatasync` system calls to initiate synchronization of file data in memory with that on a storage medium.

- ❑ `fasync` is needed to enable and disable signal-controlled input and output (processes are notified of changes in the file object by means of signals).

- ❑ `readv` and `writev` are used in the implementation of the system calls of the same name for reading and writing vectors. *Vectors* are basically structures that provide a non-contiguous memory area to hold results or initial data. This technique is known as *fast scatter-gather*. It is used to dispense with the need for multiple `read` and `write` calls that would impair performance.

- ❑ The `lock` function enables files to be locked. It synchronizes concurrent file access by several processes.

- ❑ `revalidate` is used by network filesystems to ensure consistency of remote data after a media change.

❑ check_media_change is only available for device files and checks whether there has been a media change since the last access. Prime examples are the block-device files for CD-ROMs and floppies that can be exchanged by users (hard disks are not usually exchanged).

❑ sendfile exchanges data between two file descriptors by means of the sendfile system call. As sockets (see Chapter 12) are also represented by file descriptors, this function is also used for the simple, efficient exchange of data over networks.

❑ splice_read and splice_write are used to transfer data from a pipe into a file and vice versa. Since the methods are currently only used by the system call splice2, I will not discuss them any further.

An object that uses the structure shown here as an interface need not implement all operations. To take a concrete example, pipes between processes provide only a few operations because the remaining operations make no sense at all — pipes cannot read directory contents, so readdir is not available, for instance.

There are two ways of specifying that a certain method is not available — either by assigning a null pointer to the function pointer or by invoking a dummy that simply returns an error value.

For example, the following file_operations instance is provided for block devices (see Chapter 6):

fs/block_dev.c
```
const struct file_operations def_blk_fops = {
        .open = blkdev_open,
        .release = blkdev_close,
        .llseek = block_llseek,
        .read = do_sync_read,
        .write = do_sync_write,
        .aio_read = generic_file_aio_read,
        .aio_write = generic_file_aio_write_nolock,
        .mmap = generic_file_mmap,
        .fsync = block_fsync,
        .unlocked_ioctl = block_ioctl,
        .splice_read = generic_file_splice_read,
        .splice_write = generic_file_splice_write,
};
```

The Ext3 filesystem uses a different set of functions.

fs/ext3/file.c
```
const struct file_operations ext3_file_operations = {
        .llseek = generic_file_llseek,
        .read = do_sync_read,
        .write = do_sync_write,
        .aio_read = generic_file_aio_read,
        .aio_write = ext3_file_write,
        .ioctl = ext3_ioctl,
        .mmap = generic_file_mmap,
        .open = generic_file_open,
        .release = ext3_release_file,
        .fsync = ext3_sync_file,
        .splice_read = generic_file_splice_read,
        .splice_write = generic_file_splice_write,
};
```

Although different pointers are assigned to the two objects, they share some common features — functions whose name begins with `generic_`. These are general helper functions of the VFS layer, a few of which are discussed in Section 8.5.

Directory Information

Other process-specific data must be managed in addition to the list of open file descriptors. Every `task_struct` instance therefore includes a pointer to a further structure of type `fs_struct`.

```
<fs_struct.h>
struct fs_struct {
        atomic_t count;
        int umask;
        struct dentry * root, * pwd, * altroot;
        struct vfsmount * rootmnt, * pwdmnt, * altrootmnt;
};
```

`umask` represents the standard mask used to set permissions for a new file. Its value can be read or set using the `umask` command. The system call of the same name does this internally.

The `dentry` elements of the structure point to the name of a directory, and `vfsmount` represents a mounted filesystem (the exact definition of the data structures is given below).

There are three dentry and three VFS mount elements with similar names. In fact, the entries are linked in pairs.

❑ `root` and `rootmnt` specify the root directory and the filesystem of the relevant process. Normally these are the `/` directory and the root filesystem of the system. This situation is, of course, different for processes locked into a certain subdirectory by `chroot` (and implicitly by the system call of the same name). A subdirectory is then used instead of the global root directory, and the process sees this subdirectory as its own new root directory.

❑ `pwd` and `pwdmnt` specify the *present working directory* and the VFS mount structure of the filesystem. Both change dynamically when the process changes its present directory; this happens frequently (`cd` command) when working with a shell. Whereas the value of `pwd` changes with each `chdir` system call,[9] `pwdmnt` is only modified when the territory of a new mount point is entered. Let us look at an example where a floppy disk drive is mounted at `/mnt/floppy`. A user starts working with the shell in the root directory (`/`) and switches to the appropriate directory by successively entering the `cd /mnt` and `cd floppy` commands. Both commands change the data in `fs_struct`.

  ❑ `cd /mnt` changes the `pwd` entry but leaves the `pwdmnt` entry unchanged — we are still in root directory territory.

  ❑ `cd floppy` changes the value of `pwd` and of `pwdmnt` because a switch has been made to a new directory and the territory of a new filesystem has been entered.

❑ The `altroot` and `altrootmnt` elements are used when implementing *personalities*; they permit the creation of an emulation environment for binary programs so that they have the impression they are working with an operating system other than Linux. For example, this method is

---

[9]The only exception is a switch to the `.` directory.

used on Sparc systems to emulate SunOS; special files and libraries needed for emulation are installed in a directory (usually `/usr/gnemul/`). Information on this path is stored in the `alt` elements.

The above directory is always scanned first when searching for a file so that libraries or system files of the emulation are found before the Linux originals (these are searched afterward). This supports the parallel use of different libraries for different binary formats. Since this technique is rarely used, I won't discuss it further.

VFS Namespaces

Recall from Chapter 2 that the kernel provides the possibility to implement containers. A single system can provide many containers, but processes trapped in a container cannot see the world outside and do not have any information about their fellow containers. The containers are completely independent of each other, and from the VFS point of view, this implies that mounted filesystems need to be tracked separately for each container. A single global view is not sufficient.

A *VFS namespace* is the collection of all mounted filesystems that make up the directory tree of a container.[10]

Normally, forked or cloned processes inherit the namespace of their parent process. However, the `CLONE_NEWNS` flag can be set to create a new VFS namespace (in the following, I drop the distinction between *VFS namespace* and *namespace*, although the kernel also provides non-VFS namespaces). If the new namespace is modified, changes are not propagated to processes belonging to a different namespace. Neither do changes to other namespaces affect the new namespace.

Recall that `struct task_struct` contains a member element, `nsproxy`, which is responsible for namespace handling.

The kernel uses the following (slightly simplified) structure to manage namespaces. One of the namespaces is the VFS namespace.

```
<nsproxy.h>
struct nsproxy {
...
        struct mnt_namespace *mnt_ns;
...
};
```

The amount of information required to implement a VFS namespace is comparatively little:

```
<mnt_namespace.h>
struct mnt_namespace {
        atomic_t              count;
        struct vfsmount *     root;
        struct list_head      list;
...
};
```

---

[10]Note that `chroot` environments do not require a separate namespace. Although they cannot access the complete directory tree, they are affected by changes to their superordinate namespace — unmounting a directory, for example — if the changes are in their territory.

count is a usage counter to specify the number of processes using the namespace. root points to the vfsmount instance of the root directory, and list is the start of a doubly linked list that holds all vfsmount instances linked by their mnt_list elements.

Namespace manipulation operations such as mount and umount do not act on a global data structure of the kernel (as was previously the case). Instead, they manipulate the namespace instance of the current process that can be accessed via the task structure element of the same name. The change affects all members because all processes of a namespace share the same namespace instance.

8.3.5 Directory Entry Cache

Owing to slow block media, it can take quite some time to find the inode associated with a filename. Even if the device data are already in the page cache (see Chapter 16), it is nonsensical to repeat the full lookup operation each time.

Linux uses the *directory entry cache* (*dentry cache*, for short) to provide quick access to the results of a previous full lookup operation (we take a closer look at this in Section 8.4.2). The cache is built around struct dentry, which has already been mentioned a few times.

Once the VFS — together with the filesystem implementations — has read the data of a directory or file entry, a dentry instance is created to cache the data found.

Dentry Structure

The structure is defined as follows:

```
<dcache.h>
struct dentry {
        atomic_t d_count;
        unsigned int d_flags;           /* protected by d_lock */
        spinlock_t d_lock;              /* per dentry lock */
        struct inode *d_inode;          /* Where the name belongs to - NULL is
                                         * negative */
        /*
         * The next three fields are touched by __d_lookup.  Place them here
         * so they all fit in a cache line.
         */
        struct hlist_node d_hash;       /* lookup hash list */
        struct dentry *d_parent;        /* parent directory */
        struct qstr d_name;

        struct list_head d_lru;         /* LRU list */
        union {
                struct list_head d_child;       /* child of parent list */
                struct rcu_head d_rcu;
        } d_u;
        struct list_head d_subdirs;     /* our children */
        struct list_head d_alias;       /* inode alias list */
        unsigned long d_time;           /* used by d_revalidate */
        struct dentry_operations *d_op;
        struct super_block *d_sb;       /* The root of the dentry tree */
        void *d_fsdata;                 /* fs-specific data */
```

```
                int d_mounted;
                unsigned char d_iname[DNAME_INLINE_LEN_MIN];     /* small names */
        };
```

The dentry instances form a network to map the structure of the filesystem. All files and subdirectories associated with a dentry instance for a given directory are included in the d_subdirs list (also as dentry instances); d_child in the child elements links the instances.[11]

However, the topology of the filesystem is not mapped in full because the dentry cache only ever contains a small extract of it. The most frequently used files and directories are held in memory. In principle, it would be possible to generate dentry entries for *all* filesystem objects, but RAM space and performance reasons militate against this.

As frequently noted, the main purpose of the dentry structure is to establish a link between a filename and its associated inode. Three elements are used to do this:

1. d_inode is a pointer to the relevant inode instance.

> A null pointer is used for **d_inode** if a **dentry** object is created for a nonexistent filename. This helps speed lookup for nonexistent filenames which takes just as long as lookup for files that actually exist.

2. d_name specifies the name of the file. qstr is a kernel string wrapper. It stores the actual char* string as well as its length and hash sum; this makes it easier to handle.

> No absolute filenames are stored, only the last component — for example, only emacs for /usr/bin/emacs — the reason being that the directory hierarchy is already mapped by the above list structure.

3. If a filename consists of only a few characters, it is held in d_iname instead of in dname to speed up access.

The *minimum* length up to which a filename is still regarded as "short" is specified by DNAME_INLINE_NAME_LEN and is (at least) 16 characters. However, the kernel can sometimes accommodate longer filenames because the element is at the end of the structure and the cache line with the data may still have space available (this depends on the architecture and the processor type).

The remaining elements have the following meanings:

❑ d_flags can contain several flags defined in include/linux/dcache.h. However, only two of them are relevant for our purposes: DCACHE_DISCONNECTED specifies that a dentry is currently not connected to the dentry tree of the superblock. DCACHE_UNHASHED states that the dentry instance is not contained in the hash table of any inode. Note that both flags are completely independent of each other.

---

[11]The RCU element that shares a union with the list head comes into play when list elements are deleted, but is not interesting for our purposes.

❑ d_parent is a pointer to the parent directory in whose d_subdirs list the dentry instance is located. In the root directory (which has no parent directory), d_parent points to its own dentry instance.

❑ d_mounted is set to 1 if the dentry object represents a mount point; otherwise, its value is 0.

❑ d_alias links the dentry objects of identical files. This situation arises when links are used to make the file available under two different names. This list is linked from the corresponding inode by using its i_dentry element as a list head. The individual dentry objects are linked by d_alias.

❑ d_op points to a structure with function pointers to provide various operations for dentry objects. The operations must be implemented by the underlying filesystems. I discuss the structure contents below.

❑ s_sb is a pointer to the filesystem superblock instance to which the dentry object belongs. The pointer enables the individual dentry instances to be distributed over the available (and mounted) filesystems. The dentry tree can be split into several subtrees because each superblock structure contains a pointer to the dentry element of the directory on which the filesystem is mounted.

All active instances of dentry in memory are held in a hash table implemented using the global variable dentry_hashtable from fs/dcache.c. An overflow chain implemented with d_hash is used to resolve hash collisions. I refer to this hash table as the *global dentry hash table* in the following.

The kernel also has a second dentry list headed by the global variable dentry_unused (also initialized in fs/dcache.c). Which entries does this list contain? All dentry instances whose usage counter (d_count) has reached 0 (and are therefore no longer used by any process) are automatically placed on this list. You will see how the list is managed in the next section, which deals with the structure of the dentry cache.

> **Dentry objects are very convenient when the kernel needs to obtain information on files, but they are not the principal object for representing files and their contents — this role is assigned to inodes. For example, there is no way of ascertaining whether a file was modified or not by reference to a dentry object. It is essential to look at the corresponding inode instance to find out — and this instance is easy to find using the dentry object.**

Cache Organization

The dentry structures not only make working with filesystem structures easier, but are also crucial to system performance. They accelerate work with the VFS by keeping communication with the underlying filesystem implementations to a minimum.

Each request forwarded to the underlying implementations by the VFS leads to the creation of a new dentry object to hold the request results. These objects are held in a cache so that they can be accessed faster the next time they are needed and operations can be performed more quickly. How is the cache organized? It comprises the following two components to organize dentry objects in memory:

1. A hash table (dentry_hashtable) containing all dentry objects.

2. An LRU (*least recently used*) list in which objects no longer used are granted a last period of grace before they are removed from memory.

Recall that the hash table is implemented in keeping with the classical pattern. The function d_hash from fs/dcache.c is used to determine the hash position of a dentry object.

Handling of the LRU list is a bit trickier. The list is headed by the global variable dentry_unused, and the objects it contains are linked by the d_lru element of struct dentry.

dentry objects are placed on the LRU list when their usage counter (d_count) has reached 0 — this indicates that no application is actively using the object. New entries are always placed at the beginning of the list. In other words, the further back an entry is in the list, the older it is — the classic LRU principle. The prune_dcache function is invoked from time to time, for instance, when a filesystem is unmounted or when the kernel needs more memory. Old objects are removed and memory is freed. Note that it can temporarily happen that dentry objects are on the unused list although they are in active use and their usage count is bigger than zero. This is because the kernel does some optimizations: When a dentry that was on the unused list comes back into use, it is not immediately taken off the unused list since this saves some locking and thus increases performance. Operations like prune_dcache, which are costly anyway, make up for this: When they encounter an object with positive usage count, they just remove it from the list, but do not free it.

Because LRU list objects are still simultaneously present in the hash table, they can be found by lookup operations searching for the entry they represent. Once an entry is found, the object is removed from the LRU list because it is now in active use. The usage counter is also incremented.

Dentry Operations

The dentry_operations structure holds function pointers to various filesystem-specific operations that can be performed on dentry objects. The structure is defined as follows:

```
<dcache.h>
struct dentry_operations {
        int (*d_revalidate)(struct dentry *, struct nameidata *);
        int (*d_hash) (struct dentry *, struct qstr *);
        int (*d_compare) (struct dentry *, struct qstr *, struct qstr *);
        int (*d_delete)(struct dentry *);
        void (*d_release)(struct dentry *);
        void (*d_iput)(struct dentry *, struct inode *);
        char *(*d_dname)(struct dentry *, char *, int);
};
```

❑ d_iput releases an inode from a dentry object no longer in use (in the default implementation, the usage counter is decremented, and the inode is removed from the various lists once the counter reaches 0).

❑ d_delete is invoked after the last reference has been removed (when d_count reaches 0).

❑ d_release is invoked before a dentry object is finally deleted. The two default implementations for d_release and d_delete do nothing.

❑ d_hash calculates hash values that can be used to place objects in the dentry hash table.

❑ d_compare compares the filenames of two dentrys. Whereas VFS performs a simple string comparison, filesystems can override this behavior to suit their own requirements. For example, the filenames in the FAT implementation are not case-sensitive. As no distinction is made between uppercase and lowercase, a simple string match would return an incorrect result. A FAT-specific function must be provided in this case.

❏   d_revalidate is of particular relevance for network filesystems. It checks whether the structure set up by the individual dentry objects in memory still reflects the current situation. Because the underlying filesystem is not directly linked with the kernel/VFS and all information must be gathered via a network connection, some dentrys may no longer be valid as a result of changes to the filesystem made at the other end. This function ensures consistency.

As inconsistencies of this kind do not usually occur in local filesystems, the default implementation in VFS does nothing when d_revalidate is invoked.

As the functions in the preceding list are not implemented by most filesystems, the convention is that the operations are always replaced with the VFS default implementation if a null pointer is found for a function.

Standard Functions

Several auxiliary functions that ease handling dentry objects are provided by the kernel. Their implementation is mostly an exercise in list management and data structure handling, so I won't bother to discuss their code. It is, however, important to show their prototypes and describe their effect since we will come across them frequently in discussing implementation of VFS operations. The following auxiliary functions require a pointer to struct dentry as parameter. Each performs one simple operation.

❏   dget needs to be called whenever a dentry instance is put to use by some part of the kernel. Calling dget increments the reference count of the object; that is, it acquires a reference to it.

❏   dput is the counterpart to dget: It must be called when a dentry instance is not required any more by a user in the kernel.

The function decrements the usage count of a dentry object. If the count drops to zero, the dentry_operations->d_delete method is called if it is available. Additionally, the instance is unhashed from the global dentry hash using d_drop, and also taken away from the LRU list and put on the unused list.

If the object is not contained in the hash when dput is called, it is deleted from memory via kfree.

❏   d_drop unhashes a dentry instance from the global dentry hash tables. It is automatically called from dput if the usage count drops to zero, but can also be called manually if a dentry cache object needs to be invalidated. __d_drop is a variant of d_drop that does not automatically handle locking.

❏   d_delete unhashes a dentry object using __d_drop if it is still contained on the global dentry hash tables. If only one user for the object remains, dentry_iput is also called to decrement the usage count of the inode associated with the dentry object.

d_delete is usually called immediately before dput. This ensures that the dentry object will be erased by dput since it is not on the global dentry hash anymore.

Some helper functions are more complicated, so it's best to inspect their prototypes.[12]

```
<dcache.h>
extern void d_instantiate(struct dentry *, struct inode *);

struct dentry * d_alloc(struct dentry *, const struct qstr *);
struct dentry * d_alloc_anon(struct inode *);

struct dentry * d_splice_alias(struct inode *, struct dentry *);

static inline void d_add(struct dentry *entry, struct inode *inode);
struct dentry * d_lookup(struct dentry *, struct qstr *);
```

❏ d_instantiate associates a dentry instance with an inode. This means setting the d_inode field and adding the dentry to the list headed by inode->i_dentry.

❏ d_add instantiates a dentry object by using d_instantiate. Additionally, the object is added to the global inode hash table dentry_hashtable.

❏ d_alloc allocates memory for a new instance of struct dentry as the name does suggest. The fields are initialized, and if a parent dentry is given, the superblock pointer for the new dentry is taken from the parent. Additionally, the new dentry is added to the subdirectory list of the parent headed by parent->d_subdirs.

❏ d_alloc_anon allocates memory for an instance of struct dentry but does not set up any connections with a parent dentry — this is why no such parameter is required in contrast to d_alloc. The new dentry is added to two lists: the superblock-specific list of anonymous dentry objects headed by super_block->s_anon and the list of all dentry instances associated with the inode, which is headed by inode->i_dentry.

Note that if the inode already contains a disconnected dentry as allocated by a previous call to d_alloc_anon, this copy is used instead of creating a new instance.

❏ d_splice_alias splices a disconnected dentry into the dentry tree. The inode parameter required by the function denotes the inode to which the dentry is supposed to be associated.

For inodes that represent any filesystem object other than directories, it suffices to call d_add. For directories, the function ensures that only a single dentry alias is present, which requires some more administrative work that I won't bother to discuss in detail.

❏ d_lookup takes the dentry instance of a directory and searches for a dentry object that represents a file with name.

8.4 Working with VFS Objects

The data structures described above act as a basis for working with the VFS layer. We examine this layer in the following sections. Let us first focus on mounting and unmounting filesystems (and filesystem

---

[12]More auxiliary functions are defined in <dentry.h> and implemented in fs/dcache.c. Since they are not so frequently used, I will not discuss them here, but refer to the documentation associated with them for more information.

registration, which is a prerequisite for these actions). I then introduce the most important and most interesting functions involving files and all other objects represented via the same interfaces.

We start with the system calls used by the standard library to communicate with the kernel.

8.4.1 Filesystem Operations

Whereas file operations are part of the standard repertoire of all applications, actions on filesystems are restricted to just a few system programs, namely, the mount and umount programs[13] for mounting and unmounting filesystems.

A further important aspect must also be taken into consideration. Filesystems are implemented in modular form in the kernel; this means that they can be compiled into the kernel as modules (see Chapter 7) or can be totally ignored by compiling the kernel without support for a particular filesystem version — given the fact that there are about 50 filesystems, it would make little sense to keep the code for all of them in the kernel.

Consequently, each filesystem must register with the kernel before it is used so that Linux has an overview of the available filesystems and can invoke the required mount functions.

Registering Filesystems

When a filesystem is registered with the kernel, it makes no difference whether the code is compiled as a module or is permanently compiled into the kernel. The technical approach is the same in both cases, regardless of the time of registration (permanently compiled filesystems are registered at boot time, modular filesystems when the relevant module is loaded into the kernel).

register_filesystem from fs/super.c is used to register a filesystem with the kernel. The structure of the function is very simple. All filesystems are stored in a (singly) linked list, and the name of each filesystem is stored as a string in a list object. When a new filesystem is registered with the kernel, this list is scanned element-by-element until either the end of the list is reached or the required filesystem is found. In the latter case, an appropriate error message is returned (a filesystem cannot be registered twice); otherwise, the object describing the new filesystem is placed at the end of the list and is therefore registered with the kernel.

The structure used to describe a filesystem is defined as follows:

```
<fs.h>
struct file_system_type {
        const char *name;
        int fs_flags;
        struct super_block *(*get_sb) (struct file_system_type *, int,
                                const char *, void *, struct vfsmount *);
        void (*kill_sb) (struct super_block *);
        struct module *owner;
        struct file_system_type * next;
        struct list_head fs_supers;
};
```

---

[13]In earlier UNIX versions, this command was logically called unmount, but the first n has been lost in the long history of this operating system.

name holds the filesystem name as a string (and therefore contains values such as `reiserfs`, `ext3`, and the like). `fs_flags` are flags used, for example, to indicate Read Only mounting, to disallow setuid/setgid execution, or to make other fine adjustments. `owner` is a pointer to a module structure that only contains a value if the filesystem was loaded as a module (a null pointer indicates a filesystem permanently compiled into the kernel).

The available filesystems are linked by means of the `next` element, which *cannot* use standard list functions because the list is linked in one direction only.

The most interesting entries are `fs_supers` and the function pointer `get_sb`. A superblock structure is created in memory for each mounted filesystem. This structure holds relevant information on the filesystem itself and on the mount point. Because several filesystems *of the same type* can be mounted (the best example is of a filesystem of the same type on the home and root partition), several superblock structures exist for a single filesystem type and are grouped together in a linked list. `fs_supers` is the corresponding list head. Further details are provided in the information below on filesystem mounting.

Also of great importance for the mount process is the function (stored in the `get_sb`) for reading the superblock of the underlying storage medium. Logically, this function depends on the specific filesystem and cannot be implemented as an abstraction. Neither can the function be held in the above `super_operations` structure because the superblock object and the pointer to this structure are not created until `get_sb` is invoked.

`kill_super` performs clean-up work when a filesystem type is no longer needed.

Mounting and Unmounting

Mounting and unmounting directory trees is much more complex than simply registering filesystems because the actions required on kernel-internal data structures are considerably more complicated than adding objects to a linked list. Filesystem mounting is initiated by the `mount` system call. Before discussing the individual steps in detail, we need to clarify which tasks must be performed to mount a new filesystem in an existing directory tree. We also need to look at the data structure used to describe mount points.

VFS Mount Structures

UNIX employs a single filesystem hierarchy into which new filesystems can be integrated, as shown in Figure 8-4.

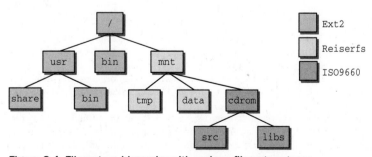

Figure 8-4: Filesystem hierarchy with various filesystem types.

The illustration shows three different filesystems. The global root directory / uses the Ext2 filesystem (see Chapter 9), /mnt has a Reiserfs, and /mnt/cdrom uses the ISO9660 format commonly used on CD-ROMs. This scenario can be queried using mount.

```
wolfgang@meitner> mount
/dev/hda7 on / type ext2 (rw)
/dev/hda3 on /mnt type reiserfs (rw)
/dev/hdc on /mnt/cdrom type iso9660 (ro,noexec,nosuid,nodev,user=wolfgang)
```

The /mnt and /mnt/cdrom directories are known as *mount points* because this is where filesystems are attached (mounted). Each mounted filesystem has a local root directory that contains the system directories (the source and libs directories in the case of a CD-ROM). When a directory is mounted, the contents of the mount point are replaced with the relative root directory of the mounted filesystem. The previous directory data disappear until the new directory is unmounted (naturally, the data in the old filesystem remain unchanged but can no longer be accessed).

Mounts can be nested as in our example. The CD-ROM is mounted in the directory /mnt/cdrom. This means that the relative root directory of the ISO9660 filesystem is mounted within a Reiser filesystem and is therefore totally divorced from the Second Extended Filesystem used for the global root directory.

The child–parent relationship common to other parts of the kernel is also used to better describe the relationship between two filesystems. Ext2 is the parent filesystem of the Reiserfs in /mnt. /mnt/cdrom contains the child filesystem of /mnt, which is unrelated to the Ext2 root filesystem (at least from this point of view).

The platform for each mounted filesystem is an instance of the vfsmount structure, which is defined as follows:

<mount.h>
```
struct vfsmount {
        struct list_head mnt_hash;
        struct vfsmount *mnt_parent; /* fs we are mounted on */
        struct dentry *mnt_mountpoint; /* dentry of mountpoint */
        struct dentry *mnt_root; /* root of the mounted tree */
        struct super_block *mnt_sb; /* pointer to superblock */
        struct list_head mnt_mounts; /* list of children, anchored here */
        struct list_head mnt_child; /* and going through their mnt_child */
        int mnt_flags;
        /* 4 bytes hole on 64bits arches */
        char *mnt_devname; /* Name of device e.g. /dev/dsk/hda1 */
        struct list_head mnt_list;
        struct list_head mnt_expire; /* link in fs-specific expiry list */
        struct list_head mnt_share; /* circular list of shared mounts */
        struct list_head mnt_slave_list;/* list of slave mounts */
        struct list_head mnt_slave; /* slave list entry */
        struct vfsmount *mnt_master; /* slave is on master->mnt_slave_list */
        struct mnt_namespace *mnt_ns; /* containing namespace */
        /*
         * We put mnt_count & mnt_expiry_mark at the end of struct vfsmount
         * to let these frequently modified fields in a separate cache line
         * (so that reads of mnt_flags wont ping-pong on SMP machines)
         */
```

```
        atomic_t mnt_count;
        int mnt_expiry_mark; /* true if marked for expiry */
    };
```

mnt_mntpoint is the dentry structure of the mount point *in the parent directory* in which the filesystem was mounted; the relative root directory of the filesystem itself is stored in mnt_root. Two dentry instances represent the same directory (namely, the mount point). This means that it is not necessary to delete the previous mount point information from memory and make it available again once the filesystem has been unmounted. When I discuss the mount system call, the need for two dentry entries will become crystal clear.

The mnt_sb pointer creates a link to the associated superblock (of which there is exactly one instance for each *mounted* filesystem); mnt_parent points to the vfsmount structure of the parent filesystem.

The parent–child relationships are represented by a linked list implemented by two elements of the structure. The mnt_mounts list head is the starting point for the list of child filesystems. The individual list elements are linked by the mnt_child field.

Each vfsmount instance of the system can be identified in two further ways. All mounted filesystems of a namespace are held in a linked list headed by namespace->list. The individual objects are linked by the mnt_list element. I ignore the topology here because all mounts are performed one after the other.

Various filesystem-independent flags can be set in nmt_flags. The following constants list all possible flags:

<mount.h>
```
#define MNT_NOSUID 0x01
#define MNT_NODEV 0x02
#define MNT_NOEXEC 0x04
#define MNT_NOATIME 0x08
#define MNT_NODIRATIME 0x10
#define MNT_RELATIME 0x20

#define MNT_SHRINKABLE 0x100

#define MNT_SHARED 0x1000 /* if the vfsmount is a shared mount */
#define MNT_UNBINDABLE 0x2000 /* if the vfsmount is a unbindable mount */
#define MNT_PNODE_MASK 0x3000 /* propagation flag mask *
```

The first block is concerned with classic properties like disallowing setuid execution or the existence of device files on the mount, or how access time handling is managed. MNT_NODEV is set if the mounted filesystem is virtual, that is, does not have a physical backing device. MNT_SHRINKABLE is a specialty of NFS and AFS that is used to mark submounts. Mounts with this mark are allowed to be automatically removed.

The last block contains flags that indicate shared and unbindable mounts. Refer to Section 8.4.1 for more details on what these types are good for.

A hash table called mount_hashtable and defined in fs/namespace.c is also used. The overflow list is implemented as a linked list with mnt_hash. The address of the vfsmount instance and the address of the associated dentry object are used to calculate the hash sum. mnt_namespace is the namespace to which the mount belongs.

A usage counter is implemented with `mnt_count`. Whenever a `vfsmount` instance is not required anymore, the counter must be decreased with `mntput`. `mntget` is the counterpart that needs to be called when the instance is taken in use.

The remaining fields are used to implement several novel mount types that were mostly introduced during the development of kernel 2.6. `mnt_slave`, `mnt_slave_list`, and `mnt_master` serve to realize slave mounts. The master mount keeps all slave mounts on a linked list for which `mnt_slave_list` is used as the list head, while `mnt_slave_list` serves as the list element. All slave mounts point back to their master via `mnt_master`.

Shared mounts are easier to represent. All the kernel needs to do is to keep all shared peer mounts on a circular list. `mnt_share` serves as the list element for this.

Mount expiration is handled with `mnt_expiry_mark`. The element is used to indicate if the mount is unused. `mnt_expire` allows for placing all mounts that are subjected to auto-expiration on a linked list. Section 8.4.1 discusses the implementation of expiring mounts.

Finally, `mnt_ns` points at the namespace to which the mount belongs.

Superblock Management

The mount structures themselves are not the only objects generated in memory when new filesystems are mounted. The mount operation starts by reading a structure called a *superblock*. I mentioned this structure several times above without bothering to define it properly. I do this now.

The `read_super` function pointer stored in the `file_system_type` objects returns an object of type `super_block` that represents a superblock in memory. It is generated with the help of the low-level implementation.

The structure definition is very long. I therefore reproduce a simplified version below (which itself is anything but lean).

```
<fs.h>
struct super_block {
        struct list_head        s_list;         /* Keep this first */
        dev_t                   s_dev;          /* search index; _not_ kdev_t */
        unsigned long           s_blocksize;
        unsigned char           s_blocksize_bits;
        unsigned char           s_dirt;
        unsigned long long      s_maxbytes;     /* Max file size */
        struct file_system_type *s_type;
        struct super_operations *s_op;
        unsigned long           s_flags;
        unsigned long           s_magic;
        struct dentry           *s_root;
        struct xattr_handler    **s_xattr;

        struct list_head        s_inodes;       /* all inodes */
        struct list_head        s_dirty;        /* dirty inodes */
        struct list_head        s_io;           /* parked for writeback */
        struct list_head        s_more_io;      /* parked for more writeback */
        struct list_head        s_files;
```

```
        struct block_device    *s_bdev;
        struct list_head        s_instances;

        char s_id[32];                          /* Informational name */
        void                    *s_fs_info;     /* Filesystem private info */

        /* Granularity of c/m/atime in ns.
           Cannot be worse than a second */
        u32                     s_time_gran;
};
```

❏   `s_blocksize` and `s_blocksize_bits` specify the block size of the filesystem (this is of particular interest for data organization on hard disk, etc., as discussed in Chapter 9). Basically, the two variables represent the same information expressed in different ways. The unit for `s_blocksize` is kilobytes, whereas `_bits` stores the corresponding log2 value.[14]

❏   `s_maxbytes` holds the maximum file size that the filesystem can handle and therefore varies from implementation to implementation.

❏   `s_type` points to the `file_system_type` instance (discussed in Section 8.4.1), which holds general type information on the filesystem.

❏   `s_root` associates the superblock with the dentry entry of the global root directory as seen by the filesystem.

> Only the superblocks of normally visible filesystems point to the dentry instance of the / (root) directory. Versions for filesystems that have special functions and do not appear in the regular directory hierarchy (e.g., pipe or socket filesystems) point to special entries that *cannot* be accessed by normal file commands.

Code that deals with filesystem objects often needs to check if a filesystem is mounted or not, and `s_root` provides a possibility to do this. If it is NULL, then the filesystem is a pseudo-filesystem that is only visible within the kernel. Otherwise, the filesystem is visible in userspace.

❏   `xattr_handler` is a pointer to the structure that determines the functions to use for handling extended attributes.

❏   `s_dev` and `s_bdev` specify the block device on which the data of the underlying filesystem reside. The former uses the internal kernel number, whereas the latter is a pointer to the `block_device` structure in memory that is used to define device operations and capabilities in more detail (Chapter 6 takes a closer look at both types).

   The `s_dev` entry is always supplied with a number (even for virtual filesystems that do not require block devices). In contrast, the `s_bdev` pointer may also contain a null pointer.

❏   `s_fs_info` is a pointer to private data of the filesystem implementation and is not manipulated by the VFS.

❏   `s_time_gran` specifies the maximal granularity that is possible for the various time stamps supported by the filesystem. The value is identical for all time stamps and is given in nanoseconds, that is, the 10^{-9}-th part of a second.

---

[14]Standard Ext2 filesystems use 1,024 KiB so that `s_blocksize` holds the value `1024` and `s_blocksize_bits` the value `10` (because $2^{10} = 1,024$).

Two list heads group together inodes and files associated with the superblock.

❏   s_dirty is a list head for the list of "dirty" inodes (discussed in Section 8.3.2) used to achieve major speed gains when synchronizing memory contents with the data on the underlying storage medium. Not *all* inodes need be scanned to write back changes — only those that have been modified and therefore appear in this list. This field must not be confused with s_dirt, which is not a list head, but a simple integer variable. It is set to 1 if the superblock was altered in any way and needs to be written back to disk. Otherwise, it is 0.

❏   s_files is a series of file structures listing all opened files of the filesystem represented by the superblock. The kernel references this list when unmounting filesystems. If it still contains files opened for writing, the filesystem is still in use, and the unmount operation fails with an appropriate error message.

The first element of the structure is also a list element called s_list that is used to group together all superblock elements in the system. The list is headed by the global variable super_blocks defined in fs/super.c.

Finally, the individual superblocks are linked in a further list that combines all instances representing filesystems *of the same type*, regardless of the underlying block devices but with the condition that the filesystem type is the same for all elements. The list head is the fs_supers element of the file_system_type structure discussed in Section 8.4.1. s_instances links the individual elements.

s_op points to a structure with function pointers that, in the familiar VFS manner, provide a generic interface with operations for working with superblocks. The implementation of the operations must be provided by the underlying low-level code of the filesystems.

The structure is defined as follows:

\<fs.h\>
```
struct super_operations {
        struct inode *(*alloc_inode)(struct super_block *sb);
        void (*destroy_inode)(struct inode *);

        void (*read_inode) (struct inode *);

        void (*dirty_inode) (struct inode *);
        int (*write_inode) (struct inode *, int);
        void (*put_inode) (struct inode *);
        void (*drop_inode) (struct inode *);
        void (*delete_inode) (struct inode *);
        void (*put_super) (struct super_block *);
        void (*write_super) (struct super_block *);
        int (*sync_fs)(struct super_block *sb, int wait);
        void (*write_super_lockfs) (struct super_block *);
        void (*unlockfs) (struct super_block *);
        int (*statfs) (struct super_block *, struct kstatfs *);
        int (*remount_fs) (struct super_block *, int *, char *);
        void (*clear_inode) (struct inode *);
        void (*umount_begin) (struct super_block *);

        int (*show_options)(struct seq_file *, struct vfsmount *);
        int (*show_stats)(struct seq_file *, struct vfsmount *);
};
```

The operations in the structure do not change the contents of inodes but control the way in which inode data are obtained and returned to the underlying implementations. The structure also includes methods for carrying out relatively extensive tasks such as remounting filesystems. As the names of the function pointers clearly indicate the actions performed by the functions, I describe them in a very cursory fashion below.

❑ read_inode reads inode data; strangely, it requires a pointer to an inode structure but no other parameters. How does the function then know which inode to read? The answer is relatively simple. The i_ino field of the passed inode holds an inode number that uniquely identifies the desired inode in the filesystem. The routines of the low-level implementation read this value, fetch the relevant data from the storage medium, and fill the remaining fields of the inode object.

❑ dirty_inode marks the passed inode structure as "dirty" because its data have been modified.

❑ delete_inode deletes the inode from memory and from the underlying storage medium.

> As you will see when examining the filesystem implementations, deleting an inode from a storage medium causes the pointer to the associated data blocks to be removed but leaves the file data untouched (they are overwritten at an unspecified time in the future). Knowledge of the filesystem structure coupled with physical access to the computer are therefore sufficient to restore deleted files — and this could be a problem where sensitive data are concerned.

❑ put_inode decrements the inode usage counter in memory when a process finishes using the data.

> The object cannot be removed from memory until all users have invoked this function and the counter has reached 0.

❑ clear_inode is invoked internally by the VFS when there is no further use for an inode. It frees all associated memory pages still containing data. clear_inode is not implemented by all filesystems as these are able to release memory in other ways.

❑ write_super and write_super_lockfs write the superblock to the storage medium. The difference between the two functions is the way in which they use kernel locking. The kernel must select the function appropriate to the situation. I won't bother discussing the detailed differences in code because both alternatives do basically the same work.

❑ unlockfs is used by the Ext3 and Reiserfs journaling filesystem to ensure correct interaction with the Device Mapper Code.

❑ remount_fs remounts a mounted filesystem with modified options (this happens at boot time, e.g., to allow Write access to the root filesystem previously mounted with Read Only access).

❑ put_super removes private information of the superblock from memory when a filesystem is unmounted and the data are no longer needed.

❑ statfs delivers statistics information on the filesystem — for instance, the number of used and unused data blocks or the maximum length of filenames. It works hand-in-hand with the system call of the same name.

❑ umount_begin is used only by networking filesystems (NFS, CIFS, and 9fs) and userspace filesystems (FUSE). It permits communication with the remote partner *before* the unmounting operation is started. It is invoked only when a filesystem is forced to unmount; in other words, it is only used when MNT_FORCE forces the kernel to perform the umount operation, although there are still references to the filesystem.

❑ sync_fs synchronizes the filesystem data with the data on the underlying block device.

❑ show_options is used by the proc filesystem to display the filesystem mount options. show_stats provides filesystem statistics for the same purpose.

The Mount System Call

The point of entry for the mount system call is the sys_mount function defined in fs/namespace.c. Figure 8-5 shows the associated code flow diagram.

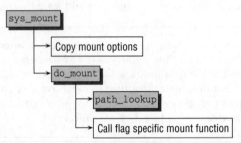

Figure 8-5: Code flow diagram for sys_mount.

The approach described here is used only to mount a new filesystem in an existing root filesystem. A modified version of the above algorithm mounts the root filesystem itself, but is not sufficiently interesting to merit a separate description (its code can be found in mount_root in init/do_mounts.c).

After the mount options (type, device, and options) have been copied from userspace by sys_mount, the kernel transfers control to do_mount, where the information passed is analyzed, and the relevant flags are set. This is also where the dentry entry of the mount point is found using the path_lookup function discussed below.

do_mount acts as a multiplexer to delegate work that still needs to be done to various mount type-dependent functions.

❑ do_remount modifies the options of a filesystem already mounted (MS_REMOUNT).

❑ do_loopback is invoked to mount a filesystem via the loopback interface (the MS_BIND flag is required to do this).[15]

❑ do_move_mount (MS_MOVE) is used to move a mounted filesystem.

❑ do_change_type is responsible for handling shared, slave, and unbindable mounts by changing the mount flags or building up the required data structure connections between the vfsmount instances involved.

❑ do_new_mount handles normal mount operations. This is the default situation, so no special flags are required.

---

[15]A loopback mount involves mounting a filesystem whose data reside in a file and not on a normal block device. This is useful to quickly test new filesystems or to check CD-ROM filesystems before writing them to CD.

It's worth taking a closer look at do_new_mount because it is used so frequently. Its code flow diagram is shown in Figure 8-6.

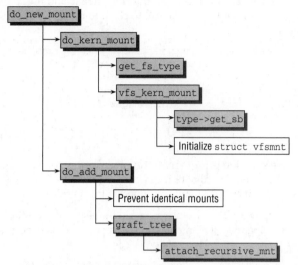

Figure 8-6: Code flow diagram for **do_new_mount**.

do_new_mount splits into two parts — do_kern_mount and do_add_mount:

❑ The initial task of do_kern_mount is to find the matching file_system_type instance using get_fs_type. The helper function scans the linked list of registered filesystems mentioned above and returns the correct entry. If no matching filesystem is found, the routine automatically tries to load the corresponding module (see Chapter 7).

After this, vfs_kern_mount invokes the filesystem-specific get_sb function to read the associated superblock that is returned as an instance of struct super_block.

❑ do_add_mount handles some necessary locking and ensures that a filesystem is not mounted to the same place multiple times (notwithstanding that, it is certainly possible to mount the same filesystem at multiple *different* places). The main work is delegated to graft_tree. The newly mounted filesystem is added to the namespace of the parent mount by calling attach_recursive_mount. The function is essentially defined as follows:

fs/namespace.c
```
static int attach_recursive_mnt(struct vfsmount *source_mnt,
                    struct nameidata *nd, struct nameidata *parent_nd)
{
        struct vfsmount *dest_mnt = nd->mnt;
        struct dentry *dest_dentry = nd->dentry;
...
        mnt_set_mountpoint(dest_mnt, dest_dentry, source_mnt);
        commit_tree(source_mnt);
...
}
```

nameidata is a structure used to group together a vfsmnt instance and a dentry instance. In this case, the structure holds the dentry instance of the mount point and the vfsmnt instance of the filesystem in which the directory was *previously* located, that is, before the new mount was performed.

`mnt_set_mountpoint` ensures that both the `mnt_parent` and the `mnt_mountpoint` element of the *new* `vfsmnt` instance `child_mount` are set to point to the old elements:

fs/namespace.c
```
void mnt_set_mountpoint(struct vfsmount *mnt, struct dentry *dentry,
                        struct vfsmount *child_mnt)
{
        child_mnt->mnt_parent = mntget(mnt);
        child_mnt->mnt_mountpoint = dget(dentry);
        dentry->d_mounted++;
}
```

This enables the situation prior to mounting to be reconstructed when the kernel unmounts a filesystem. The `d_mounted` value of the *old* `dentry` instance is incremented so that the kernel is able to recognize that a filesystem is mounted at this point.

In addition, the new `vfsmnt` instance is added to the global hash table and to the child list of the previous entry using the list elements discussed above. This is performed by `commit_tree`:

fs/namespace.c
```
static void commit_tree(struct vfsmount *mnt)
{
        struct vfsmount *parent = mnt->mnt_parent;
...
        list_add_tail(&mnt->mnt_hash, mount_hashtable +
                                hash(parent, mnt->mnt_mountpoint));
        list_add_tail(&mnt->mnt_child, &parent->mnt_mounts);
...
}
```

Shared Subtrees

The mechanisms I have discussed so far covered the standard mount cases that are available on any UNIX system. However, Linux supports some more advanced possibilities that allow for gaining more power from namespaces. Since they were only introduced during the development of 2.6 (2.6.16, to be precise), their use is still somewhat limited, so I will briefly review their basic principle before I discuss the implementation. For specific details on potential applications and a precise description of the shared subtree semantics of the mount tool, see the manual page `mount(8)`. Another detailed investigation of the features provided by shared subtrees can be found on `http://lwn.net/Articles/159077/`.

The extended mount options (which I collectively call *shared subtrees*) implement several new attributes for mounts:

❑ **Shared Mounts** — A set of mounted filesystems between which mount events are propagated. If a new filesystem is mounted into one member of the set, the mount is replicated into all other members of the set.

❑ **Slave Mounts** — Similar to shared mounts, except that the symmetry between all members of the set is removed. One mount in the set is especially distinguished as the master mount. All mount operations in the master mount propagate into the slave mounts, but mount operations in the slaves do not propagate back into the master.

❏   **Unbindable Mounts** — Cannot be cloned through a bind operation.

❏   **Private Mounts** — essentially a new name for the classical mount type known from UNIX: They can be mounted on multiple places across the filesystem, but mounts propagate neither to nor from them.

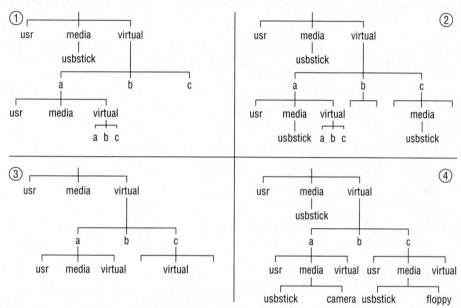

Figure 8-7: Illustration of some features provided by shared subtrees.

Consider a filesystem that is mounted on multiple places across the filesystem. This is a standard feature of UNIX and Linux and can be achieved with the old framework discussed so far. Imagine the situation depicted in the top-left part of Figure 8-7: The directory /virtual contains three identical bind mounts of the root filesystem in /virtual/a, /virtual/b, and /virtual/c. However, it could be desirable that any medium mounted in /media will also be visible in /virtual/user/media, even if the medium was added after the mount structure has been established. The solution is to replace the bind mounts by shared mounts: In this case, any filesystem mounted in /media in any of the peers (/, /file/virtual/a/, /file/virtual/b/, and /file/virtual/c/) will be visible in all of them. The top-right part of Figure 8-7 shows the directory tree in this situation.

If the filesystem structure presented above is used as a basis for containers, each user of a container can see all other containers by looking at the contents of /virtual/name/virtual! Usually, this is not desired.[16] A remedy to the problem is provided by turning /virtual into an unbindable subtree: Its contents can then not be seen anymore in bind mounts, and the users trapped in the containers will not see anything that lives outside their world. The bottom-left part of Figure 8-7 illustrates the situation.

---

[16]Note that many of the problems presented here can also be solved to some extent by using more refined variants of binding mounts or proper access control, but usually, some drawbacks or limitations will come along with these solutions. The possibilities offered by shared subtrees are usually more powerful.

Another issue arises when all container users are supposed to see devices mounted on /media, for instance, a USB stick in /media/usbstick. This clearly works if /media is shared between the containers, but has one drawback: Any container user will see the media mounted by any other container. Turning /media into a slave mount keeps the desired features (mount events propagating from /), but isolates the containers from each other. As the bottom-right part of Figure 8-7 shows, the camera mounted by user A cannot be seen in any other container, while the USB stick mount point propagates downward into all subdirectories of /virtual.

Recall that the data structures that are the basis for shared subtrees were described in Section 8.4.1. Let us thus now turn our attention to the required extensions of the mount implementation. If one of the flags MS_SHARED, MS_PRIVATE, MS_SLAVE, or MS_UNBINDABLE is passed to the mount system call, then do_mount calls do_change_type to change the type of a given mount. The function is essentially implemented as follows:

fs/namespace.c
```
static int do_change_type(struct nameidata *nd, int flag)
{
        struct vfsmount *m, *mnt = nd->mnt;
        int recurse = flag & MS_REC;
        int type = flag & ~MS_REC;
...
for (m = mnt; m; m = (recurse ? next_mnt(m, mnt) : NULL))
        change_mnt_propagation(m, type);
return 0;
}
```

The mount type for the path given in nd is changed using change_mnt_propagation; if the MS_REC flag is set, the mount types of all submounts are changed recursively. next_mnt provides an iterator that allows for traversing all submounts of a given mount.

change_mnt_propagation is responsible to set the appropriate propagation flag for an instance of struct vfsmount.

fs/pnode.c
```
void change_mnt_propagation(struct vfsmount *mnt, int type)
{
        if (type == MS_SHARED) {
                set_mnt_shared(mnt);
                return;
        }
        do_make_slave(mnt);
        if (type != MS_SLAVE) {
                list_del_init(&mnt->mnt_slave);
                mnt->mnt_master = NULL;
                if (type == MS_UNBINDABLE)
                        mnt->mnt_flags |= MNT_UNBINDABLE;
        }
}
```

This is simple for shared mounts: It suffices to set the flag MNT_SHARED with the auxiliary function set_mnt_shared.

If a slave — or a private or unbindable mount — has to be established, the kernel has to rearrange the mount data structure such that the `vfsmount` instance under consideration is turned into a slave mount. This is done by `do_make_slave`. The function proceeds in several steps:

1. A master for the mount itself and any possible slave mounts needs to be found. First, the kernel searches among the shared-mount peers; the first one with the same root dentry is taken as the new master. If no such peer exists, the first element in the peer list is used.

2. If a new master has been found, both the mount under consideration and all its slave mounts are made slaves of the new master.

3. If the kernel could not find a new master, all slave mounts of the mount under consideration are freed — they do not have a master anymore.

In any case, the `MNT_SHARED` flag is also removed.

After `do_make_slave` has performed these rearrangements, `change_mnt_propagation` needs some more steps for unbindable and private mounts.[17] In both cases, the mount is deleted from a slave list if it should be on one, and the master is set to NULL — neither mount type has a master. For unbindable mounts, the `MNT_UNBINDABLE` flag is set to identify it as such.

Shared subtrees obviously also influence the kernel behavior when new mounts are added to the system. The crucial steps are taken in `attach_recursive_mnt`. Recall that the function has already been touched on before, but the presentation was simplified. This time, I also include the effects of shared subtrees.[18] First of all, the function needs to check into which mounts the mount event is supposed to propagate.

fs/namespace.c
```
static int attach_recursive_mnt(struct vfsmount *source_mnt,
struct nameidata *nd, struct nameidata *parent_nd)
{
        LIST_HEAD(tree_list);
        struct vfsmount *dest_mnt = nd->mnt;
        struct dentry *dest_dentry = nd->detnry;
        struct vfsmount *child, *p;

        if (propagate_mnt(dest_mnt, dest_dentry, source_mnt, &tree_list))
                return -EINVAL;
...
```

`propagate_mnt` iterates over all slave and shared mounts of the mount destination and mounts the new filesystem into them using `mnt_set_montpoint`. All mount points that are affected by this are returned in `tree_list`.

---

[17]Since the function has already returned to the caller in the case of shared mounts, only these mount types remain and can be different from MS_SLAVE in the `if` conditional.

[18]Note that we also perform a slight simplification this time since we only consider add mounts, but no move mounts where an existing mount is shifted from one place in the filesystem hierarchy to another.

If the destination mount point is a shared mount, then the new mount and all its submounts need to become shared as well:

fs/namespace.c
```
        if (IS_MNT_SHARED(dest_mnt)) {
                for (p = source_mnt; p; p = next_mnt(p, source_mnt))
                        set_mnt_shared(p);
        }
    . . .
```

Finally, the kernel needs to finish the mount process by calling `mnt_set_mountpoint` and `commit_tree` to introduce the changes into the data structures as discussed for regular mounts. Note, however, that `commit_tree` needs to be called for every mount that has been propagated to shared peers or slave mounts (`mnt_set_mountpoint` for these mounts has already been called in `propagate_mnt`):

fs/namespace.c
```
        mnt_set_mountpoint(dest_mnt, dest_dentry, source_mnt);
        commit_tree(source_mnt);

        list_for_each_entry_safe(child, p, &tree_list, mnt_hash) {
          list_del_init(&child->mnt_hash);
          commit_tree(child);
        }

        return 0;
    }
```

The umount System Call

Filesystems are unmounted by the `umount` system call, whose entry point is `sys_umount` from `fs/namespace.c`. Figure 8-8 shows the associated code flow diagram.

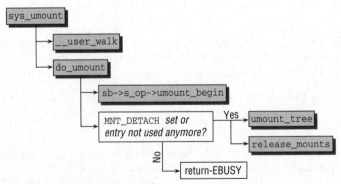

Figure 8-8: Code flow diagram for `sys_umount`.

First, `__user_walk` finds the `vfsmnt` instance and the `dentry` instance of the mount point, which are packed in a `nameidata` structure.[19]

---

[19] `__user_walk` invokes the `path_walk` function after the pathname has been copied into kernel space.

The actual work is delegated to `do_umount`.

❏ If a superblock-specific `umount_begin` function is defined, it is invoked. This allows, for instance, network filesystems to terminate communication with the remote partner before an unmount is forced.

❏ `umount_tree` is invoked if the mounted filesystem is no longer needed (this is indicated by the usage counter) *or* if `MNT_DETACH` was specified to force a filesystem unmount. The real work is delegated to `umount_tree` and `release_mounts`. Essentially, the first one is responsible for decrementing the counter `d_mounted`, while the latter one uses the data stored in `mnt_mountpoint` and `mnt_parent` to restore the original state before the new filesystem was mounted. The structures of the previously mounted filesystem are also removed from the kernel lists.

Automatic Expiration

The kernel also provides some infrastructure to allow automatic expiration of mounts. When a mount is not used by any process or the kernel itself, it will be automatically removed from the VFS mount tree if automatic expiration is used. Currently the NFS and AFS network filesystems use this offer. All `vfsmount` instances of submounts that are supposed to expire automatically must be collected on a linked list that uses `vfsmount->mnt_expire` to chain the elements together.

It then suffices to periodically apply `mark_mounts_for_expiry` on the list. The function scans through all entries. A mount is unused if its usage count is 1, that is, if it is only referenced by the parent mount. When such an unused mount is found, `mnt_expiry_mark` is set. When `mark_mounts_for_expiry` finds an unused entry with `mnt_expiry_mark` set on the next list traversal, the mount is removed from the namespace.

Note that the `mntput` is responsible to clear `mnt_expiry_mark`. This ensures that a mount that has already been on the expiration list but became used again is not immediately expired when it becomes once more unused. The code flow is as follows:

1. An unused mount is marked for expiry by `mark_mounts_for_expiry`.

2. After this, the mount comes into use again, so its `mnt_count` is increased. This prevents `mark_mounts_for_expiry` from removing the mount from the namespace despite the expiration mark still being set.

3. When the usage count is decreased with `mntput`, the function will also ensure that the expiration mark is removed. The `mark_mounts_for_expiry` circle can thus commence as usual.

Pseudo-Filesystems

Filesystems do not necessarily require an underlying block medium. They can either use memory as backing store, as is the case for ramfs and tmpfs, or can require no backing store at all, as procfs and sysfs do — their contents are generated synthetically from information contained in the kernel's data structures. While filesystems of this type are already quite distinct from the traditional concepts, it is still possible to take a further step forward. How? All filesystems, be they virtual or not, have one common property: They are visible to userspace in the form of files and directories. However, this property is not sacrosanct. *Pseudo*-filesystems are filesystems that cannot be mounted and are thus never directly visible in userland.

This does not seem overly useful at a first glance. What is a filesystem good for if it does not export anything to userland? While files and directories are, indeed, one possible and without doubt useful representation of the contents of a filesystem, they are not the only one. It is also perfectly valid to think of a filesystem solely in terms of inodes! Files and directories are only a front end in this picture, and they can be omitted without any loss of information.

Except visibility to userland. But this does not really concern the kernel. On some occasions, the need can arise to internally group inodes together, and userland need not know anything about this. The kernel, however, can benefit from organizing such collections in the form of filesystems because all standard auxiliary functions that work for regular filesystems will automatically work for such collections as well.

Particular examples of pseudo-filesystems are bdev to manage inodes that represent block devices, pipefs to handle pipes, and sockfs to deal with sockets. All appear in /proc/filesystems, but cannot be mounted:

```
root@meitner # cat /proc/filesystems
...
nodev   bdev
...
nodev   sockfs
nodev   pipefs
...
root@meitner # mount -t bdev bdev /mnt/bdev
mount: wrong fs type, bad option, bad superblock on bdev,
       missing codepage or helper program, or other error
       In some cases useful info is found in syslog - try
       dmesg | tail  or so
```

The kernel provides the mount flag MS_NOUSER to prevent a filesystem from being mounted. Apart from this, all filesystem mechanisms work as discussed in this chapter. The kernel can mount a pseudo-filesystem with kern_mount or kern_mount_data. This ends up in vfs_kern_mount, which integrates the filesystem data into the VFS data structures.

When a filesystem is mounted from userland, do_kern_mount is not sufficient. Integration of the files and directories into the user-visible representation is afterward handled by graft_tree. The method, however, refuses to perform its job if the flag MS_NOUSER is set:

fs/namespace.c
```
static int graft_tree(struct vfsmount *mnt, struct nameidata *nd)
{
...
        if (mnt->mnt_sb->s_flags & MS_NOUSER)
                return -EINVAL;
...
}
```

Nevertheless, structure and contents of the pseudo-filesystem are available to the kernel. The filesystem library provides some means to write pseudo-filesystems with little effort, and I will come back to this in Section 10.2.4.

8.4.2 File Operations

Operations with complete filesystems are an important aspect of the VFS layer but occur comparatively rarely — because, with the exception of removable devices, filesystems are mounted during the boot process and are unmounted at shutdown. More usual are frequently repeated operations on files by all system processes.

To permit universal access to files regardless of the filesystem used, the VFS provides interface functions for file processing in the form of various system calls as already noted above. This section concentrates on the most common operations performed by processes when working with files.

Finding Inodes

A major operation is the finding of an inode by reference to a given filename. This provides us with an opportunity to examine the *lookup* mechanism used to find this information.

The `nameidata` structure is used to pass parameters to the lookup function and to hold the lookup result. We encountered this structure above without actually defining it, so let's do this now.

```
<fs.h>
struct nameidata {
        struct dentry    *dentry;
        struct vfsmount  *mnt;
        struct qstr      last;
        unsigned int     flags;
...
}
```

❑   `dentry` and `mnt` contain the data of the required filesystem entry after completion of lookup.

❑   `flags` holds flags to fine-tune the lookup operation. I will come back to these when I describe the lookup algorithm.

❑   `last` contains the name to be looked up. It is a *quick string* that, as described above, includes not only the string itself but also the length of the string and a hash value.

The kernel uses the `path_lookup` function to find any path or filename.

```
fs/namei.c
int fastcall path_lookup(const char *name, unsigned int flags,
                    struct nameidata *nd)
```

In addition to the required `name` and the lookup `flags`, the function expects a pointer to a `nameidata` instance that is used as "working memory" for interim results.

First, the kernel uses the `nameidata` instance to define the starting point for lookup. If the name begins with /, the `dentry` and `vfsmnt` instances of the current root directory are used (note must be taken of any active `chroot` cage); otherwise, the current working directory data obtained from the task structure are used.

link_path_walk is a front end for the __link_path_walk function, which works its way through the directory levels. With approximately 200 lines, this function is one of the longest parts of the kernel. Figure 8-9 shows its code flow diagram — much simplified because I have ignored minor aspects.

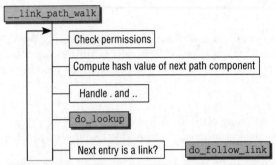

Figure 8-9: Code flow diagram for __link_path_walk.

The function is made up of a large loop to process a filename or pathname component-by-component. The name is broken down into its individual components (each separated by one or more slashes) inside the loop. Each component represents a directory name with the exception of the last, which is always a filename.

Why is the code for __link_path_walk so long? Unfortunately, finding the inode associated with a given filename is more complicated than it would at first appear and is made more difficult because the following must be taken into account:

❑ One file can reference another by means of a symbolic link, and the lookup code must cater for this possibility by being able to recognize and break cyclic link loops.

❑ Mount points must be detected, and the lookup operation must be redirected accordingly.

❑ The access rights of all directories on the path to the target filename must be checked. The process must have the appropriate rights, or the operation is aborted with an error message.

❑ Strangely formulated but correct names such as /./usr/bin/../local/././bin//emacs[20] must be resolved correctly.

Let us take a look at the actions performed in each loop pass until the specified file or directory name has been fully processed and the matching inode has been found. The mnt and dentry values of the nameidata instance are filled with the values of either the root directory or the working directory and are the starting point for further actions in which the following steps are carried out:

❑ Checking if the current process is granted permission to enter the directory depends on whether the inode under inspection defines the permission method in its inode_operations. If this is not the case, exec_lite is used to make the decision. Depending on the credentials of the process, the function selects the proper parts of the file's mode mask and checks if the MAY_EXEC bit is set (certain capabilities are also taken into account, but I omit this here for simplicity).

---

[20]This could have been written as /usr/local/bin/emacs.

If the inode defines a specific `permission` method, then `exec_permission_light` tells this to the callee by returning `_EAGAIN`. In this case, `vfs_permission` is used to decide whether the process has the rights needed to switch to the specified directory. `vfs_permission` just calls the `permission` function, and this, in turn, invokes the `permission` method stored in the `inode_operations` structure. Section 8.5.3 discusses permission-checking in further detail.

❑ The name is scanned character-by-character until the kernel arrives at one (or more) slashes (`/`). These are skipped because only the name itself is of interest. If, for example, the name of the file is `/home/wolfgang/test.txt`, only the `home`, `wolfgang`, and `test.txt` components are relevant — the slashes simply separate the components from each other. One name component is processed in each loop pass.

Each character of a component is used by the `partial_name_hash` function to calculate an incremental hash sum. This sum is translated into the final hash value when all characters of a path component are known and is then stored in a `qstr` instance.

❑ A dot (`.`) as a path component indicates the current directory and is very easy to process. The kernel simply skips to the next cycle of the lookup loop because the position in the directory hierarchy has not changed.

❑ Dot dot (`..`) is a little more difficult to handle, so this task is delegated to the `follow_dotdot` function. When the lookup operation is in the root directory of the process, it has no effect because there is no parent directory to which it could switch.

Otherwise, two options are available. If the current directory is *not* the root directory of a mount point, the `d_parent` entry of the current `dentry` object can be used as a new directory because it always represents the parent directory. If, however, the current directory is the root directory of a mounted filesystem, the information held in `mnt_mountpoint` and `mnt_parent` is used to define the new `dentry` and `vfsmount` object. `follow_mount` and `lookup_mnt` are used to retrieve the required information.

❑ If the directory component is a normal file, the kernel can find the corresponding `dentry` instance (and therefore the corresponding inode) in one of two ways. Either the desired information is in the dentry cache and can be accessed with minimum delay, or it must be found by the low-level implementation of the filesystem, and the appropriate data structures must be constructed. `do_lookup` is responsible for distinguishing between these two situations (discussed shortly) and returns the desired `dentry` instance. Note that mount points are also detected in this step.

❑ The last step in the processing of a path component is the kernel check to determine whether the component is a symbolic link.

How does the kernel establish whether a `dentry` structure is a symbolic link? Only inodes used to represent symbolic links[21] include the `lookup` function in the inode operations. Otherwise, the field is assigned a null pointer.

`do_follow_link` is used as a VFS layer front-end to follow the link, as discussed below.

The loop is repeated until the end of the filename is reached — the kernel recognizes this by the fact that the pathname contains no further `/`. Using the means described above, the last component is also resolved into a `dentry` entry that is returned as the result of the `link_path_walk` operation.

---

[21]Hard links require no special treatment in lookup code because they are indistinguishable from normal files.

Implementation of `do_lookup`

`do_lookup` starts from a path component and the `nameidata` instance with the data of the initial directory and returns the associated inode.

The kernel first attempts to find the inode in the dentry cache using the `__d_lookup` function described in Section 8.3.5. Even if a matching element is found, this does not necessarily mean that it is current — the `d_revalidate` function in the `dentry_operations` of the underlying filesystem must be invoked to check whether it is still valid. If so, it is returned as the result of the cache search. If not, a lookup operation must be initiated in the low-level filesystem. The same operation is used when no entry is found in the cache.

`real_lookup` performs the filesystem-specific lookup action. Its work involves allocating data structures in memory (to hold the lookup result) and, above all, invoking the filesystem-specific `lookup` function made available by the inode operation structure `inode_operations`.

If the required directory exists, the result received by the kernel is a filled `dentry` instance; otherwise, a null pointer is returned. Note that Chapter 9 describes in greater detail how filesystems perform low-level lookups.

`do_lookup` also needs to take care of following mount points. If a valid `dentry` is found in the cache, `__follow_mount` takes care of this. As discussed in Section 8.4.1, the kernel records the fact that a filesystem is mounted by incrementing the `d_mounted` structure element of the associated `dentrys`. To ensure that mounting has the desired effect, the kernel must take this fact into account when traversing the directory structure. This is done by invoking `__follow_mount`, whose implementation is surprisingly simple (the `path` structure used as argument collects the required pointers to the `vfsmount` and `dentry` instances of the mount point).[22]

fs/namei.c
```
static int __follow_mount(struct path *path)
{
        int res = 0;
        while (d_mountpoint(path->dentry)) {
                struct vfsmount *mounted = lookup_mnt(path->mnt, path->dentry);
                if (!mounted)
                        break;
                path->mnt = mounted;
                path->dentry = mounted->mnt_root;
                res = 1;
        }
        return res;
}
```

How does this loop work? A check is first made to ascertain whether the current `dentry` instance is a mount point. In this context, the `d_mountpoint` macro need only check whether the value of `d_mounted` is greater than 0. The `lookup_mount` function extracts the `vfsmount` instance of the mounted filesystem from the `mount_hashtable` discussed in Section 8.4.1. The `mnt_root` field of the mounted filesystem is used as the new value for the `dentry` structure; all this means is that the root directory of the mounted filesystem is used as the mount point — and this is exactly what we want to achieve.

---

[22]I have omitted the required locking and reference counting operations, which would make the code less readable.

A `while` loop caters to the fact that several filesystems can be mounted one after the other where the last system mounted conceals all the others.

Implementation of `do_follow_link`

When the kernel follows symbolic links, it must note that users may construct cyclic structures (intentionally or not), as the following example shows:

```
wolfgang@meitner> ls -l a b c
lrwxrwxrwx    1 wolfgang users         1 Mar   8 22:18 a -> b
lrwxrwxrwx    1 wolfgang users         1 Mar   8 22:18 b -> c
lrwxrwxrwx    1 wolfgang users         1 Mar   8 22:18 c -> a
```

a, b, and c form an endless loop. This could be exploited to render the system unusable if the kernel did not take appropriate precautions.

In fact, the kernel recognizes the situation and aborts processing.

```
wolfgang@meitner> cat a
cat: a: Too many levels of symbolic links
```

A further problem with symbolic links is the fact that the link target may be located on a different filesystem from the link source. This results in a linkage between filesystem-specific code and VFS functions that doesn't normally occur. Low-level code for following links then references VFS functions, whereas normally only the reverse occurs (the VFS invokes low-level functions of the individual implementations).

Figure 8-10 shows the code flow diagram for `do_follow_link`.

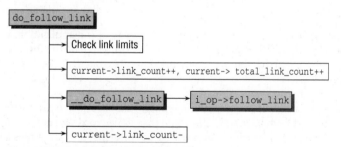

Figure 8-10: Code flow diagram for `do_follow_link`.

The `task_struct` structure includes two count variables used to follow links.

```
<sched.h>
struct task_struct {
...
/* file system info */
        int link_count, total_link_count;
...
};
```

link_count prevents recursive loops, and total_link_count limits the maximum number of links in a pathname. By default, the kernel permits MAX_NESTED_LINKS (usually set to 8) recursive and 40 consecutive links — the latter constant is hardcoded and not definable via a pre-processor symbol.

At the beginning of the do_follow_link routine, the kernel first checks whether the maximum value of either of the counters has been exceeded. If so, do_follow_link is aborted with the error code -ELOOP.

If not, both counters are incremented by 1, and the filesystem-specific follow_link routine is invoked to follow the current link. If the link does not point to a further link (and the function therefore simply returns the new dentry entry), the value of link_count is decremented by 1 as shown in the following code segment:

fs/namei.c
```
static inline int do_follow_link(struct dentry *dentry, struct nameidata *nd)
{
       . . .
       current->link_count++;
       current->total_link_count++;
       err = __do_follow_link(path, nd);
       current->link_count--;
       . . .
}
```

When is the value of total_link_count reset? Not at all — at least not during lookup for a single path component. Because this counter is a mechanism to limit the *total number* of links used (which need not be recursive to reach a high figure), the counter is reset to 0 when lookup is initiated for a *full* path or filename in path_walk (this function is called by do_path_lookup). *Every* symbolic link in the lookup operation (not just recursive links) adds to its value.

Opening Files

Files must be opened before reading or writing. In the view of the application, this is done by the open function of the standard library, which returns a file descriptor.[23] The function uses the identically named open system call, which invokes the sys_open function in fs/open.c. The associated code flow diagram is shown in Figure 8-11.

As a first step, force_o_largefile checks if the flag O_LARGEFILE should always be set irregardless of which flags were passed from userland. This is the case if the word size of the underlying processor is not 32 bits, that is, a 64-bit system. Such systems use 64-bit indexing, and large files are thus the only sensible default on them. The proper work of opening the file is then delegated to do_sys_open.

In the kernel, each opened file is represented by a file descriptor that acts as a position index for a process-specific array (task_struct->files->fd_array). This array contains an instance of the abovementioned file structure with all necessary file information for each opened file. For this reason, get_unused_fd_flags is first invoked to find a used file descriptor.

Because a string with the name of the file is used as a system call parameter, the main problem is to find the matching inode. The procedure described above does this.

---

[23]It would also be possible to use openat, which opens a file relative to a directory. The mechanisms are, however, more or less identical.

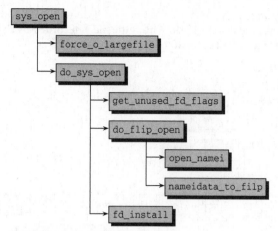

Figure 8-11: Code flow diagram for **sys_open**.

do_filp_open finds the file inode with the support of two helper functions.

1. open_namei invokes the path_lookup function to find the inode and performs several additional checks (e.g., to ascertain whether the application is trying to open a directory as if it were a regular file). If a new filesystem entry needs to be created, the function also applies the current default settings for the permission bits as stored in the process's umask (current->fs->umask).

2. nameidata_to_filp initializes the readahead structure, places the newly generated file instance on the s_files list of the superblock (see Section 8.4.1), and invokes the open function in the file_operations structure of the underlying filesystem.

fd_install must then install the file instance in files->fd from the task structure of the process before control is transferred back to the user process to which the file descriptor is returned.

Reading and Writing

Once a file has been successfully opened, a process either reads or modifies the data it contains using the read and write system calls provided by the kernel. As usual, the entry routines are called sys_read and sys_write, and both are implemented in fs/read_write.c.

Read

The read function requires three parameters — the file descriptor, a buffer to hold data, and a length argument to specify the number of characters to be read. The parameters are passed directly to the kernel.

For the VFS layer, reading from a file is not particularly difficult, as Figure 8-12 illustrates.

By reference to the file descriptor number, the kernel (using the fget_light function from fs/file_table.c) is able to find the file instance associated with the task structure of the process.

After finding the current position in the file with file_pos_read (the routine just needs to return the value of file->f_pos), the read operation itself is delegated to vfs_read. This routine invokes either the file-specific read routine `file->f_op->read` or — if it doesn't exist — the generic helper function `do_sync_read`. After this, the new position within the file is recorded by `file_pos_write` — again, the routine just needs to bring `file->f_pos` to the current position.

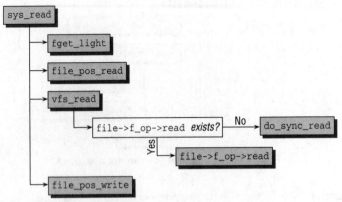

Figure 8-12: Code flow diagram for `sys_read`.

Reading data involves a sophisticated system of buffers and caches to increase system performance. I therefore deal extensively with this topic in Chapter 16. Chapter 9 examines how filesystems implement the read routine.

Write

The structure of the `write` system call is just as simple as that of the `read` routine. Both code flow diagrams are identical except that the `f_op->write` and `do_sync_write` functions are used instead of their read equivalents.

From a formal point of view, `sys_write` requires the same parameters as `sys_read` — a file descriptor, a pointer variable, and a length specification (expressed as an integer number). Obviously, their meanings are slightly different. The pointer does not point to a buffer area in which the data to be read are stored but to the data to be written to the file. The length argument specifies the length of these data in bytes.

Write operations are likewise directed through the cache system of the kernel (we discuss this topic extensively in Chapter 16).

8.5 Standard Functions

Useful resources of the VFS layer are the standard functions provided to read and write data. These operations are more or less identical for all filesystems. If the blocks in which the data reside are known, the page cache is first consulted. If the data are not held there, a read request is submitted to the relevant block device. Implementing these operations for every single filesystem would result in a massive duplication of code that must be prevented at all costs.

Most filesystems include the do_sync_read[24] and do_sync_write standard routines in the read and write pointers of their file_operations instance.

The routines are strongly associated with other kernel subsystems (block layer and page cache in particular) and must also handle many potential flags and special situations. As a result, their implementation is not always the source of true clarity and sublimeness (comment in the kernel: this is really ugly ...). For this reason, I examine slightly simplified versions below; these focus on the main path usually traversed so that important aspects are not obscured by a wealth of details. Nevertheless, I have still found it necessary to make many references to routines in other chapters (and in other subsystems).

8.5.1 Generic Read Routine

generic_file_read is the library routine used by almost all filesystems to read data. It reads data *synchronously*; in other words, it guarantees that the desired data are in memory when the function returns to the caller. This is achieved by delegating the actual read operation to an asynchronous routine and waiting until it ends. Slightly simplified, the function is implemented as follows:

mm/filemap.c
```
ssize_t do_sync_read(struct file *filp, char __user *buf, size_t len, loff_t *ppos)
{
        struct iovec iov = { .iov_base = buf, .iov_len = len };
        struct kiocb kiocb;
        ssize_t ret;

        init_sync_kiocb(&kiocb, filp);
        kiocb.ki_pos = *ppos;
        kiocb.ki_left = len;

        ret = filp->f_op->aio_read(&kiocb, &iov, 1, kiocb.ki_pos);

        if (-EIOCBQUEUED == ret)
                ret = wait_on_sync_kiocb(&kiocb);
        *ppos = kiocb.ki_pos;
        return ret;
}
```

init_sync_kiocb initializes a kiocb instance that controls the asynchronous I/O operation; its detailed contents are of little interest here.[25] The real work is delegated to the filesystem-specific asynchronous read operation that is stored in aio_read of struct file_operations. Usually generic_file_aio_read, which I discuss shortly, is used. However, the routine performs work asynchronously, so there is no guarantee that the data have already been read when the routine returns to the caller.

---

[24]In former kernel versions, the standard read and write operations used to be generic_file_read and generic_file_write, but they have been replaced by the variants I am about to discuss.

[25]Asynchronous I/O operations are used to submit a read or write request to the kernel. These requests are not satisfied immediately but are queued in a list. The code flow then returns immediately to the calling function (in contrast to the regular I/O operations implemented here). In this case, the calling function has the impression that the result is returned immediately because it does not notice the delay involved in performing the operation. The data can be queried later after the request has been dealt with asynchronously.

Asynchronous operations are not performed with file handles but with I/O control blocks. Consequently, an instance of the corresponding data type must first be generated with init_sync_kiocb. Currently, asynchronous I/O is used only by very few applications (e.g., large databases), so it's not worth going into the details.

The -EIOCBQUEUED return value indicates that the read request was queued and not yet processed. In this case, wait_on_sync_kiocb waits until the data are in memory. The function can check this by referring to the initialized control block. The process is put to sleep while it is waiting so that the CPU is available for other tasks. For the sake of simplicity, I do not differentiate between synchronous or asynchronous termination of the read operation in the following description.

Asynchronous Reading

generic_file_aio_read from mm/filemap.c reads data asynchronously. The associated code flow diagram is shown in Figure 8-13.

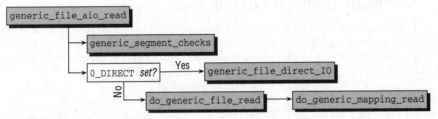

Figure 8-13: Code flow diagram for **generic_file_aio_read**.

After generic_segment_checks has ensured that the read request contains valid parameters, two possible Read modes are distinguished.

1. If the flag O_DIRECT is set, data are read without using the page cache. generic_file_direct_IO must then be used.

2. Otherwise, do_generic_file_read — a front end for do_generic_mapping_read — is used. This converts the read request for a file into a read operation with a mapping.

Reading from Mappings

Figure 8-14 shows the code flow diagram for do_generic_mapping_read.

The function uses the mapping mechanism described in Chapter 3 to map the desired section of the file onto pages in memory. It consists of a large endless loop that continues to read pages until all file data have been transferred into memory if the data are not already in any cache.

Each loop pass performs the following actions:

❑ First of all, find_get_page checks if the page is already contained in the page cache. If this fails, a synchronous readahead request is issued by calling page_cache_sync_readahead.

❑ Since the readahead mechanism has most likely ensured that the data are by now in the cache, find_get_page is used to find the page once again. There's still a small chance that this fails again and that the page has to be read in manually, which is handled by jumping to the label no_cached_page. I will deal with this below. Usually, however, the page will have been read in at this point.

❑ If the page flag PG_readahead is set — the kernel can check this with ReadaheadPage — an asynchronous readahead operation must be started with page_cache_async_readahead. Note that this is different from the synchronous readahead operation started before: Now the kernel does not wait for the readahead operation to complete, but performs the reading whenever it finds time. The readahead mechanism is considered in more detail in Chapter 16.4.5.

❑   Although the page is in the page cache, the data may not be current; this can be checked using Page_Uptodate.

If the page is not up-to-date, it must be re-read using mapping->a_ops->readpage. The function pointer normally points to mpage_readpage. After this call, the kernel knows for sure that the page is filled with the most recent data.

The access to the page must be marked with mark_page_accessed; this is important to determine page activity when it is necessary to swap data out of RAM. (Swapping is discussed in Chapter 18.) The actor routine (usually file_read_actor) maps the appropriate page into userspace address space. I won't bother going into the details of how this is done.[26]

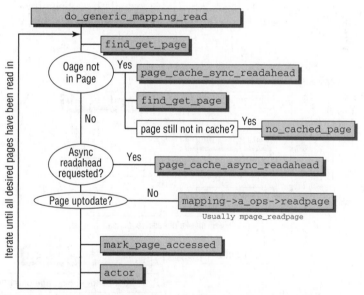

Figure 8-14: Code flow diagram for `do_generic_mapping_read`.

If the readahead mechanism has not already read the desired page in anticipation, the function is forced to do it itself. The no_cached_page section of do_generic_mapping_read is used for this purpose. Its code flow diagram is shown in Figure 8-15.[27]

Once page_cache_alloc_cold has reserved a cache-cold page, it is inserted in the LRU list of the page cache via add_to_page_cache_lru as described in Chapter 16. The mapping->a_ops->readpage method provided by the mapping is used to read the data. Usually, the function pointer points to mpage_readpage, which I deal with in Chapter 16. Finally, mark_page_accessed tells the accounting system that the page has been accessed.

---

[27]Except to say that the copy_to_user routine discussed in Chapter 3 is used.

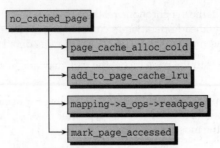

Figure 8-15: Code flow diagram for no_cached_page.

8.5.2 The fault Mechanism

Memory mappings normally invoke the filemap_fault standard routine provided by the VFS layer to read pages not held in cache. Figure 8-16 shows the code flow diagram of this function.

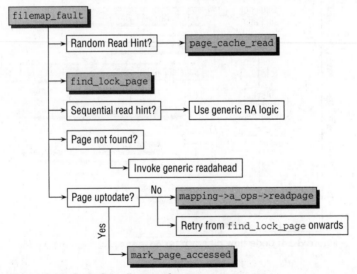

Figure 8-16: Code flow diagram for filemap_fault.

As the diagram illustrates, the implementation exhibits several parallels with the generic_file_read mechanism just discussed.

First, the function checks if the virtual memory area to which the page belongs contains a hint that accesses are mostly random and not in any predictable order. This hint is given if the VM_RAND_READ is set; this can be checked with the helper macro VM_RandomReadHint. Note that the madvise system call (not discussed here) can be invoked to advise memory management which access pattern will be most likely. If a random read pattern is expected, the kernel directly calls page_cache_read to allocate a new page in the page cache and issue a read request.

Independent of the expected read pattern, the `find_get_page` function checks whether the page is already in the page cache. Afterward, the kernel handles a sequential read hint that could be associated with the VM area to which the page belongs.[28] The generic readahead logic that is used in this case consists of the following code sequence:

mm/filemap.c
```
if (VM_SequentialReadHint(vma)) {
        if (!page) {
                page_cache_sync_readahead(mapping, ra, file,
                                                vmf->pgoff, 1);
                page = find_lock_page(mapping, vmf->pgoff);
                if (!page)
                        goto no_cached_page;
        }
        if (PageReadahead(page)) {
                page_cache_async_readahead(mapping, ra, file, page,
                                                vmf->pgoff, 1);
        }
}
```

The mechanism is identical with the mechanism used in `do_generic_mapping_read`. When the page cannot be found with synchronous readahead, the jump to `no_cached_page` employs `page_cache_read` to allocate a new page in the page cache and issue a read request. Afterward, the code retries the operation from the first call to `find_lock_page` onward. Obviously, this requires using C's `goto` feature.

Let's go back to the code snippet shown above. If the page was present in the system, it has originated from a previous readahead operation. As discussed in Chapter 16.4.5., the readahead mechanism marks a page near the end of a readahead window, that is, a range of files that is read in before a process actually requests them. Once this page is reached, then asynchronous readahead should be started to read in pages speculatively. The required mark is the `PG_readahead` bit (which can be checked with `PageReadahead`), and the function responsible to perform asynchronous readahead is `page_cache_async_readahead`. Again, notice that more details about this mechanism are discussed in Chapter 16.4.5.

If no sequential readahead hint was given and the page could not be found in the page cache, the generic readahead mechanism needs to be invoked. Slightly simplified, it is implemented as follows:

mm/filemap.c
```
if (!page) {
        unsigned long ra_pages;
...
        ra_pages = max_sane_readahead(file->f_ra.ra_pages);
        if (ra_pages) {
                pgoff_t start = 0;

                if (vmf->pgoff > ra_pages / 2)
                        start = vmf->pgoff - ra_pages / 2;
                do_page_cache_readahead(mapping, file, start, ra_pages);
        }
```

---

[28]It sounds odd that the kernel checks for a sequential read hint even if a random read hint was found only a couple of steps before, and the check could in this case be, in fact, avoided. However, the structure of `filemap_fault`, which contains a quite liberal use of `goto`, can lead to this situation.

```
        page = find_lock_page(mapping, vmf->pgoff);
        if (!page)
                goto no_cached_page;
}
```

`max_sane_readahead` computes a sensible upper bound on the number of pages that are supposed to be read in in advance. If this number is greater than zero, `do_page_cache_readahead` is invoked to allocate pages in the page cache and read in the data. Since afterward there is sufficient hope the desired page is in the page cache, `find_lock_page` once again tries to locate it there. Should this again fail, the kernel jumps to `no_cached_page` as described before.

If the page is by now contained in the page cache, it is necessary to ensure that the page is up-to-date. If it is not, it is re-read using the `readpage` method of the mapping, and retries the page access again starting from the call to `find_lock_page` further above. Otherwise, it suffices to call `mark_page_accessed` to mark the page as active.

8.5.3   Permission-Checking

`vfs_permission` is the VFS layer's standard function to check if access to a given inode is allowed for a certain right. This right can be `MAY_READ`, `MAY_WRITE`, or `MAY_EXEC`. `vfs_permission` is just a wrapper function for parameter conversion; the real work is delegated to `permission`. First of all, the function ensures that Write access to Read Only filesystems and immutable files is forbidden:

fs/namei.c
```
int permission(struct inode *inode, int mask, struct nameidata *nd)
{
        int retval, submask;

        if (mask & MAY_WRITE) {
                umode_t mode = inode->i_mode;

                /* Nobody gets write access to a read-only fs. */
                if (IS_RDONLY(inode) &&
                    (S_ISREG(mode) || S_ISDIR(mode) || S_ISLNK(mode)))
                        return -EROFS;

                /* Nobody gets write access to an immutable file. */
                if (IS_IMMUTABLE(inode))
                        return -EACCES;
        }
        ...
```

After this, the real work is either delegated to a filesystem-specific permission-checking routine if one exists, or to `generic_permission`:

fs/namei.c
```
        ...
        /* Ordinary permission routines do not understand MAY_APPEND. */
        submask = mask & ~MAY_APPEND;
        if (inode->i_op && inode->i_op->permission)
                retval = inode->i_op->permission(inode, submask, nd);
        else
```

```
            retval = generic_permission(inode, submask, NULL);

    if (retval)
            return retval;

    return security_inode_permission(inode, mask, nd);
}
```

If any of these denies the permission to access the object in the desired way, the error code is immediately returned. If they grant permission, that is, if their result is zero, it is still necessary to call the appropriate security hook via security_inode_permission, which delivers the final verdict.

Note that most filesystems rely on generic_permission, but can pass a special handler function to perform ACL-based permission checks. Thus, generic_permission not only requires the inode in question and the permission request as parameters, but also a callback function check_acl for ACL checks. First of all, the kernel needs to find out if it should use the inode rights for user, group, or other.

❑   If the filesystem UID of the current process is the same as the UID of the inode, then the permission set of the owner needs to be used.

❑   If the GID of the inode is contained in the list of groups to which the current process belongs, then the group permissions need to be used.

❑   If both conditions fail, the permissions for "other" need to be used.

This is implemented as follows:

fs/namei.c
```
int generic_permission(struct inode *inode, int mask,
            int (*check_acl)(struct inode *inode, int mask))
{
    umode_t                     mode = inode->i_mode;

    if (current->fsuid == inode->i_uid)
            mode >>= 6;
    else {
            if (IS_POSIXACL(inode) && (mode & S_IRWXG) && check_acl) {
                    int error = check_acl(inode, mask);
                    if (error == -EACCES)
                            goto check_capabilities;
                    else if (error != -EAGAIN)
                            return error;
            }

            if (in_group_p(inode->i_gid))
                    mode >>= 3;
    }
    ...
```

Checking for the fsuid is simple. If the fsuid agrees with the UID of the file, then the mode value needs to be shifted by six positions such that the bits for "owner" are now the least significant ones.

Checking the fsgid is slightly more involved because all groups to which the process belongs need to be considered, so this is delegated to the (not discussed) helper function in_group_p. Should this be successful, the mode value needs to be shifted by three places such that the mode bits for "group" are now the least significant ones. Note that the kernel may also need to perform an ACL check, which is described below.

If both UID and GID checks fail, then no shifting of the mode bits is performed, and the bits for "other" remain the least significant ones.

The discretionary access control (DAC) check is then performed on the chosen permission bits as follows:

fs/namei.c
```
    . . .
            if (((mode & mask & (MAY_READ|MAY_WRITE|MAY_EXEC)) == mask))
                    return 0;
    . . .
```

If the required permissions mask is allowed by the mode permission bits, then a zero is returned. This signals that the operation is allowed.

Failure of the DAC check does not yet mean that the desired operation is forbidden since capabilities might still allow it. The kernel tests this as follows:

fs/namei.c
```
    . . .
    check_capabilities:
            /*
             * Read/write DACs are always overridable.
             * Executable DACs are overridable if at least one exec bit is set.
             */
            if (!(mask & MAY_EXEC) ||
                (inode->i_mode & S_IXUGO) || S_ISDIR(inode->i_mode))
                    if (capable(CAP_DAC_OVERRIDE))
                            return 0;

            /*
             * Searching includes executable on directories, else just read.
             */
            if (mask == MAY_READ || (S_ISDIR(inode->i_mode) && !(mask & MAY_WRITE)))
                    if (capable(CAP_DAC_READ_SEARCH))
                            return 0;

            return -EACCES;
    }
```

If the process possesses the capability DAC_CAP_OVERRIDE, the desired permission is granted if any of the following conditions holds:

❑   Read or Write access, but *not* Execution access was requested.

❑   Any of the three possible execution bits is set.

❑   The inode represents a directory.

The other capability that comes into play is CAP_DAC_READ_SEARCH, which grants the process the right to override DAC decisions when reading files and searching directories. If the capability is present, then access is granted if any of the following conditions holds:

❏   A Read operation was requested.

❏   The inode in question is a directory, and no Write access was requested.

Finally, the question remains how ACLs are taken into account. If the inode in question has an ACL associated with it (checked by IS_POSIXACL) and a permission check callback for ACLs was passed to generic_permission, the callback is utilized right after the fsuid of the current task is compared with the UID of the file in question. If the desired access is denied, then process capabilities might still allow it. (Note that the DAC check can be skipped if an ACL callback is given because the standard DAC check is included in the ACL check.) Otherwise, the result of the ACL check is directly returned.

8.6   Summary

One of the core concepts of UNIX is that nearly every resource can be represented by a file, and Linux has inherited this point of view. Files are therefore very prominent members of the kernel world, and a considerable effort goes into their representation. This chapter has introduced the virtual filesystem, a glue layer that sits between deeper kernel layers and userland. It provides various abstract data structures to represent files and inodes, and implementations of real filesystems must fill in these structures such that applications can always use the same interface to access and manipulate files irregardless of the underlying filesystem.

I have discussed how filesystems are mounted into the filesystem tree visible for userland applications, and have additionally shown how shared subtrees can be used to create different views of the "global" filesystem depending on the namespace. You have also learned that the kernel employs a number of pseudo-filesystems that are not visible to userland, but nevertheless contain some information that is interesting for internal purposes.

Opening files requires a traversal of the file tree, and you have seen how this problem is solved by the VFS layer. Once a file has been opened, it can be written to and read from, and you have also seen how the VFS is involved in these operations.

Finally, you have learned that the kernel provides some generic standard functions that make things easier for real filesystems like Ext3, as discussed in the next chapter, and how the kernel ensures that only appropriately privileged users may access objects located in the filesystem.

9

The Extended Filesystem Family

The structure and layout of the interfaces and data structures of the Virtual Filesystem discussed in Chapter 8 define a framework within which filesystem implementations must operate. However, this does not dictate that the same ideas, approaches, and concepts must be adopted by every filesystem when files are organized on block devices to store their contents permanently. Quite the opposite: Linux supports a wide variety of concepts including those that are easy to implement and understand but are not particularly powerful (e.g., the Minix filesystem); the proven Ext2 filesystem, which is used by millions; specific versions designed to support RAM- and ROM-based approaches; highly available cluster filesystems; and modern, tree-based filesystems with rapid restoration of consistency by means of transaction journals. No other operating system offers this versatility.

The techniques used differ considerably even though they can all be addressed — from both the user and kernel sides — via an identical interface, thanks to the virtual filesystem. Because of the large number of filesystems supported, every single implementation cannot be discussed here — not even briefly. Instead, this chapter focuses on the extended filesystem family, that is, the Ext2 and Ext3 filesystems. They illustrate the key concepts underlying the development of filesystems.

9.1 Introduction

Ext3 and Ext3 can be briefly characterized as follows:

❑ The **Second Extended Filesystem** — This has been with Linux from the early days and has proved itself as the backbone of many server and desktop systems, where it has done a very good job. The design of the Ext2 filesystem makes use of structures very similar to those used in the virtual filesystem, simply because it was developed with optimized interoperation with Linux in mind. It can be — and is — used with other operating systems, though.

❑ The **Third Extended Filesystem** — This is an evolutionary development of Ext2. It is still mostly compatible with Ext2, but provides an extension — journaling — that is especially helpful to recover from system crashes. This chapter also takes a brief look at the journal mechanism of Ext3. As compared with Ext2, this features several interesting options, but the basic filesystem principles are unchanged.

While most installations nowadays prefer Ext3 to Ext2, it nevertheless makes sense to discuss Ext2 first: Since the code need not implement any journaling functionalities, it is often simpler as compared to the Ext3 implementation, and thus makes the essential principles easier to understand. Besides journaling, both variants are otherwise nearly completely identical, and many general improvements that originate from Ext3 have been back-ported to Ext2.

One specific problem — fragmentation — is encountered in the management of storage space for disk-based filesystems. Available space becomes more and more fragmented as files are removed and new ones are added — particularly if the files are very small. Because this has a negative impact on access speed, filesystems must try to keep fragmentation to a minimum.

A second important requirement is to put storage space to efficient use, and here the filesystem must make a compromise. Full use of space can only be achieved at the cost of large amounts of management data that must also be stored on disk. This cancels out any benefit gained from more compact data storage and may even make the situation worse. Wasteful use of disk capacity should also be avoided — the advantages of less management data are lost because space is not used efficiently. The various filesystem implementations address this problem differently. Often, administrator-configured parameters are introduced to optimize the filesystem for anticipated usage patterns (e.g., a predominantly large number of big files or small files).

Maintaining the consistency of file contents is also a key issue that requires careful thought during the planning and implementation of filesystems. Even the most stable of kernels can give up the ghost unexpectedly, not only because of software errors, but also owing to power outages, hardware faults, and the like. Even if mishaps of this kind cause irrecoverable errors (e.g., changes are lost if they are still cached in RAM and have not been written back to disk), the implementation must make every effort to rectify damage as quickly and as comprehensively as possible. At minimum, it must be able to restore the filesystem to a usable state.

Finally, speed is also a vital ingredient when assessing the quality of filesystems. Even if hard disks are extremely slow as compared to the CPU or RAM, a badly implemented filesystem can certainly apply the brakes to system speed.

9.2 Second Extended Filesystem

Even though Linux is neither a clone nor a further development of the educational Minix, many parts of the early Linux kernel (and "early" by now means roughly a decade ago!) clearly reflected its Minix heritage. The first filesystem the Linux kernel had to deal with was a direct adaptation of the Minix system. This had primarily practical reasons because Linux was originally developed on a Minix system before it was capable of hosting itself. We have come a long way since then.

The code of the Minix filesystem may have been valuable in educational terms, but it left a lot to be desired in terms of performance.[1] Many standard features of commercial UNIX systems were simply

---

[1]Note that the situation has changed somewhat with with the introduction of Minix 3, which has explicitly been designed to be usable on embedded devices and similar systems with little computing power. Most people, however, still seem to prefer embedded Linux distributions for these purposes.

not supported by the Minix filesystem — for example, the length of filenames was still restricted to 14 characters — rather short, but still better than the 8.3 scheme supported by another operating system that was quite ubiquitous at that time!

This fact promoted the development of the *Extended Filesystem*, which, although a great improvement on the Minix filesystem, still had clear deficits in terms of performance and functionality as compared to commercial filesystems.[2] Only with the development of the second version of this file system, known unsurprisingly as the *Second Extended Filesystem* or Ext2 for short, was an extremely powerful filesystem available that neither then nor now needed to fear comparison with commercial products. Its design was influenced primarily by the *Fast File System* (FFS) from the BSD world (described in detail in [MBKQ96]).

The Ext2 filesystem focused on high performance and on the goals summarized below and defined by the filesystem authors in [CTT]:

❑ Support for variable block sizes to enable the filesystem to cope with anticipated usage (many big files or many small files).

❑ Fast symbolic links, whose link target is stored in the inode itself (and not in the data area) if the name of the target is short enough.

❑ Integration of extensions into the design without having to reformat and reload the hard disk to migrate from the old to the new version.

❑ Minimization of the effect of system crashes by means of a sophisticated strategy of data manipulation on the storage medium. The filesystem can normally be restored to a state in which auxiliary tools (`fsck`) are at least able to repair it so that it can be used again. (This does not exclude the possibility that data are lost.)

❑ Use of special attributes (not found in classic UNIX filesystems) to label files as unchangeable. These allow important configuration files, for example, to be protected from unintentional changes — even by the superuser.

Today, these features are standard requirements for any filesystem that is used on production machines. Many new filesystems that were devised after Ext2 provide much additional functionality. Nevertheless, the extended filesystem family is still quite apt for a large range of applications. One particular advantage should not be underestimated: The code for Ext2 is very compact compared with that for more modern filesystems. Less than 10,000 lines suffice for the implementation, compared with more than 30,000 for JFS and roughly 90,000 for XFS.

9.2.1 Physical Structure

Various structures, defined as C data types in the kernel, must be created to hold filesystem data — file contents, representation of the directory hierarchy, and associated administration data such as access permissions or user and group affiliations, as well as metadata to manage filesystem-internal information. This is necessary so that data can be read from block devices for analysis. Obviously persistent copies of these structures need to reside on the hard disk so that data are not lost between working sessions and are still available the next time the kernel is activated. Because hard disk and RAM requirements differ, there

---

[2]Another filesystem of the time that has now fallen into oblivion (and for which kernel support has long been withdrawn) is the Xia filesystem, an enhancement of the Minix filesystem. The author nevertheless still has fond memories of using this filesystem for one of his first Linux installations, a choice that did not prove to be very visionary ...

are usually two versions of a data structure — one for persistent storage on disk, the other for working with memory.

In the sections below, the frequently used word *block* has two different meanings:

❑ On the one hand, some filesystems reside on block-oriented devices that — as explained in Chapter 6 — do not transfer individual characters but entire data blocks.

❑ On the other, the Second Extended Filesystem is a *block-based* filesystem that divides the hard disk into several blocks, all of the same size, to manage metadata and the actual file contents. This means that the structure of the underlying storage medium is imposed on the structure of the filesystem and this naturally influences the design of the algorithms and data structures used. This chapter takes a closer look at this influence.

One aspect is of particular importance when dividing the hard disk into fixed-sized blocks — files may occupy only integer multiples of the block size. Let us look at the impact of this situation by reference to Figure 9-1, in which, for simplicity's sake, we assume a block size of 5 units. We want to store three files whose sizes are 2, 4, and 11 units.

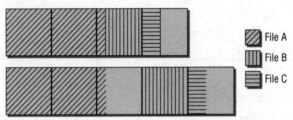

File A

File B

File C

Figure 9-1: File distribution in block-based filesystems.

The clearly more effective method of dividing existing storage space is applied in the upper part, where the contents of the individual files are spread as compactly as possible across the available blocks. However, this method is not used in practice because it has a major disadvantage.[3] The information needed to manage the file boundaries within the individual blocks would be so voluminous that it would immediately cancel out any advantage gained as compared to the wasteful assignment of blocks in the right part of the figure. As a result, each file occupies not only the space needed for its data but also the space left over when the block size is rounded up to the next integer multiple.

Structure Overview

Let's first take a bird's eye view of the C structures used to manage data to get a clear picture of the functions of the individual components and the interplay among them. Figure 9-2 shows the contents of a block group, a central element of the Ext2 filesystem.

A block group is the basic element that accommodates the further structures of the filesystem. Each filesystem consists of a very large number of block groups arranged one after the other on the hard disk as shown in Figure 9-3.

---

[3]"Not used" is not strictly accurate because a diluted form of this scheme that, to a certain extent, allows the use of a single block to hold several small files is under development and may be included as standard in future versions of the Ext2/3 filesystem. Although the basic infrastructure for such *fragments* is included in the code, it is not yet implemented.

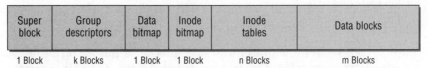

Figure 9-2: Block group of the Second Extended Filesystem.

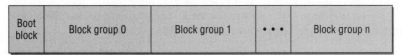

Figure 9-3: Boot sector and block groups on a hard disk.

The boot sector is a hard disk area whose contents are automatically loaded by the BIOS and executed when the system is powered up. It includes a boot loader[4] that permits selection of one of the systems installed on the computer and is also responsible for continuing the boot process. Obviously, this area must not be filled with filesystem data. Boot loaders are not needed on all systems. On systems where they are, they are usually located at the beginning of the hard disk so that later partitions are not affected.

The remaining space on the disk is occupied by successive block groups that store filesystem metadata and the useful data of the individual files. As Figure 9-2 clearly illustrates, each block group contains a great deal of redundant information. Why does the Ext2 filesystem accept this waste of space? There are two reasons why the additional space is justified:

❑ If the superblock is destroyed by a system crash, all information on filesystem structure and contents is lost. This information can be recovered only with great difficulty (perhaps not at all by most users) if redundant copies are available.

❑ By keeping file and management data closer together, the number of movements and associated travel of the read/write head are reduced, and this improves filesystem performance.

In practice, data are not duplicated in each block group, and the kernel works only with the first copy of the superblock; generally, this is sufficient. When a filesystem check is performed, the data of the first superblock are spread over the remaining superblocks, where it can be read in an emergency. Because this method also consumes a large amount of storage space, later versions of Ext2 adopt the *sparse superblock* technique. Superblocks are no longer kept in each block group of the filesystem but are written only to groups 0 and 1 as well as to all other groups whose ID can be represented as a power of 3, 5, and 7.

The superblock data are cached in memory so that the kernel is not forced to repeatedly read this information from hard disk — this is, of course, much faster. The second point made above is also no longer relevant because seeks between the individual superblock entries are no longer necessary.

Although it was assumed when designing the Ext2 filesystem that the two issues above would have a strong impact on filesystem performance and security, it was later discovered that this is not the case. The modifications described above were made for this reason.

---

[4]LILO on IA-32, MILO on Alpha, SILO on Sparc, and so on.

What is the purpose of the individual structures in the block groups? Before answering this question, it is best to briefly summarize their meaning:

❑ The *superblock* is the central structure for storing meta-information on the filesystem itself. It includes information on the number of free and used blocks, block size, current filesystem status (needed when booting the system in order to detect a previous crash), and various time stamps (e.g., time of last filesystem mount, time of last write operation). It also includes a magic number so that the mount routine can establish whether the filesystem is of the correct type.

The kernel uses only the superblock of the first block group to read filesystem meta-information, even if there are superblock objects in several block groups.

❑ The *group descriptors* contain information that reflects the status of the individual block groups of the filesystem, for instance, information on the number of free blocks and inodes of the group. *Each* block group includes group descriptors for *all* block groups of the filesystem.

❑ *Data block and inode bitmaps* are used to hold long bit strings. These structures contain exactly 1 bit for each data block and each inode to indicate whether the block or inode is free or in use.

❑ The *inode table* contains all block group inodes that hold all metadata associated with the individual files and directories of the filesystem.

❑ As the name suggests, the *data block section* contains the useful data of the files in the filesystem.

Whereas inodes and block bitmaps always occupy an entire block, the remaining elements consist of several blocks. The exact number depends not only on the options selected when creating the filesystem but also on the size of the storage medium.

The similarity of these structures with the elements of the virtual filesystem (and the general concept of UNIX filesystems as discussed in Chapter 8) is unmistakable. Even though many problems, such as directory representation, are solved by adopting this structure, the Ext2 filesystem still needs to address several tricky issues.

A key problem in filesystem implementation is the fact that the individual files may differ drastically — in terms of their size and purpose. While files with multimedia contents (e.g., videos) or large databases can easily consume hundreds of megabytes or even gigabytes, small configuration files often take up just a handful of bytes. There are also different types of meta-information. For example, the information stored for device files differs from that for directories, regular files, or named pipes.

If filesystem contents are manipulated in memory only, these problems are not as serious as when data are stored on slow external media. High-speed RAM is able to set up, scan, and modify the required structures in no time at all, whereas the same operations are much slower and much more costly on hard disk.

The structures used to store data must be designed to optimally satisfy all filesystem requirements — not always an easy task on hard disks, particularly with regard to capacity utilization and access speed. The Second Extended Filesystem therefore resorts to the tricks and dodges described below.

Indirection

Even though the Ext2 filesystem adopts the classic UNIX scheme of implementing files by means of linked inodes, further problems of little consequence in an abstract concept need to be addressed. Hard disks are divided into blocks that are occupied by files. How many blocks a particular file occupies depends on the size of the file contents (and, of course, on the size of the block itself).

Like system memory, which, in the view of the kernel, is divided into pages of equal size and is addressed by unique numbers or pointers, all hard disk blocks are uniquely identified by a number. This enables the file metadata stored in the inode structure to be associated with the file contents located in the data block sections on hard disk. The link between the two is established by storing the addresses of the data blocks in the inode.

> **Files do not necessarily occupy successive data blocks (although this would be desirable for performance reasons) but are spread over the entire hard disk.**

A closer examination of this concept quickly reveals a problem. Maximum file size is limited by the number of block numbers that can be held in the inode structure. If this number is too small, less space is needed to manage the inode structures, but, at the same time, only small-sized files can be represented.

Increasing the number of blocks in the inode structure does not solve the problem, as the following quick calculation proves. The size of a data block is 4 KiB. To hold a file comprising 700 MiB, the filesystem would need approximately 175,000 data blocks. If a data block can be uniquely identified by a 4-byte number, the inode would need 175,000 × 4 bytes to store the information on all data blocks — this is impracticable because a large portion of disk space would be given over to storing inode information. What's more, most of this space would not be needed by most files, whose average size would be less than 700 MiB.

This is, of course, an age-old problem and is not Linux-specific. Fortunately, all UNIX filesystems including Ext2 feature a proven solution known as *indirection*.[5]

With indirection, only a few bytes of the inode hold pointers to blocks — just enough to ensure that an average small-size file can be represented. With larger files, pointers to the individual data blocks are stored indirectly, as illustrated graphically in Figure 9-4.

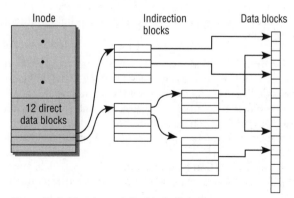

Figure 9-4: Simple and double indirection.

---

[5]Even the relatively primitive Minix filesystem supports indirection.

This approach permits the flexible storage of large and small files because the size of the area in which data block pointers is stored can be varied dynamically as a function of the actual size of the file. The inode itself is always of a fixed size, and additional data blocks needed for purposes of indirection are allocated dynamically.

Let's first take a look at the situation with a small file. The pointers stored directly in the inode are sufficient to identify all data blocks, and the inode structure occupies little hard disk space because it contains just a few pointers.

Indirection is used if the file is bigger and there aren't enough primary pointers for all blocks. The filesystem reserves a data block on the hard disk — not for file data but for additional block pointers. This block is referred to as a *single indirect block* and can accept hundreds of additional block pointers (the actual number varies according to the size of the block; Table 9-1 lists possible values for Ext2). The inode must include a pointer to the first indirection block so that it can be accessed. Figure 9-4 shows that in our example this pointer immediately follows the direct block pointers. The size of the inode always remains constant; the space needed for the additional pointer block is of some consequence with larger files but represents no additional overhead for small files.

Table 9-1: Block and File Sizes in the Second Extended Filesystem

Block size	Maximum file size
1,024	16 GiB
2,048	256 GiB
4,096	2 TiB

The further progress of indirection is evident from the illustration. Adding to available space by means of indirection must also come up against its limits when files get larger and larger. The next logical step is therefore to use double indirection. Again, a hard disk block is reserved to store pointers to data blocks. However, the latter do not store useful data but are arrays that hold pointers to other data blocks that, in turn, store the useful file data.

Using double indirection dramatically increases manageable space per file. If a data block holds pointers to 1,000 other data blocks, double indirection enables 1,000 × 1,000 data blocks to be addressed. Of course, the method has a downside because access to large files is more costly. The filesystem must first find the address of the indirection block, read a further indirection entry, look for the relevant block, and find the pointer to the data block address. There is therefore a trade-off between the ability to handle files of varying sizes and the associated reduction in speed (the larger the file, the slower the speed).

As Figure 9-4 shows, double indirection is not the end of the road. The kernel offers triple indirection to represent really *gigantic* files. This is an extension of the principle of simple and double indirection and is not discussed here.

Triple indirection takes maximum file size to such heights that other kernel-side problems crop up, particularly on 32-bit architectures. Because the standard library uses `long` variables with a length of

32 bits to address positions within a file, this restricts maximum file size to 2^{32} bits, which corresponds to 2 GiB and is less than can be managed with triple indirection in the Ext2 filesystem. To cope with this drawback, a special scheme was introduced to access large files; this not only has an impact on the routines of the standard library, but must also be taken into account in the kernel sources.

Fragmentation

The similarity between memory management and disk storage in terms of their block structure means that they share the familiar problem of fragmentation discussed in Chapter 3. Over time, many files of a filesystem are deleted at random positions on the disk, and new ones are added. This inevitably leads to fragmentation of free disk space into chunks of different sizes, as illustrated in Figure 9-5.

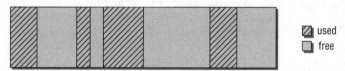

Figure 9-5: Fragmentation in filesystems.

Although the situation illustrated may well be exaggerated, it clearly indicates the nature of the problem. There are still 12 blocks free on the hard disk, but the longest contiguous unit is 5 blocks. What happens when a program wants to save data occupying a total of 7 blocks to disk? Or what about when it is necessary to add data to an existing file and the data blocks beyond the end of the file are already occupied by other data?

The answer is obvious. The data are spread over different areas of the disk and become fragmented. It is important that this be done transparently to the user process. Processes accessing a file *always* see the file as a continuous linear structure, regardless of the degree of data fragmentation on the hard disk. This is reminiscent of the way in which a processor presents working memory to processes, the difference being that there is no automatic hardware instance to ensure linearization on behalf of the filesystem. The code of the filesystem itself is responsible for this task.

Of course, this does not present any basic difficulty when direct pointers or simple, double, and triple indirection are used to point to the file data blocks. The data block numbers are always uniquely identified by the information in the pointers. From this point of view, it is irrelevant whether the data blocks are sequential or are spread randomly across the entire hard disk.

However, there is a noticeable difference in access speed. If all file blocks are contiguous on the hard disk (this is desirable), movement of the read/write head when reading data is reduced to a minimum, thus boosting the speed of data transfer. If the opposite is true — and the file blocks are distributed across the disk — the read/write head is forced to constantly traverse the disk in order to read the data, and this slows access.

Consequently, the Second Extended Filesystem does its best to prevent fragmentation. When fragmentation cannot be avoided, it attempts to keep the individual file blocks in the same block group.[6] It is very helpful if the filesystem is not filled to capacity and is operated with appropriate reserves; more file storage options are then available, and this automatically reduces susceptibility to fragmentation.

---

[6]The `defrag.ext2` system tool analyzes Ext2 partitions and reorganizes fragmented data in a contiguous structure.

9.2.2 Data Structures

Now that we have considered the structural principles underlying the Ext2 filesystem, let's take a closer look at the data structures used to implement and store data on the hard disk. As noted above, the structures on the hard disk have counterparts in memory. These are used in addition to the virtual filesystem structures, first to support communication with the filesystem and to simplify the management of important data, and second to buffer metadata to speed up work with the filesystem.

Superblock

The *superblock* is the central structure in which all characteristic data of the filesystem are kept. Its contents are the first thing the kernel sees when mounting a filesystem. Data are read using the ext2_read_super routine (located in fs/ext2/super.c) invoked by means of the read_super function pointer in the file_system_type structure discussed in Chapter 8. The actions performed by this routine are analyzed in Section 9.2.4. The structure and layout of the superblock on the hard disk concern us here.

The relatively extensive ext2_super_block structure is used to define the superblock as follows:

```
<ext2_fs.h>
struct ext2_super_block {
        __le32  s_inodes_count;         /* Inodes count */
        __le32  s_blocks_count;         /* Blocks count */
        __le32  s_r_blocks_count;       /* Reserved blocks count */
        __le32  s_free_blocks_count;    /* Free blocks count */
        __le32  s_free_inodes_count;    /* Free inodes count */
        __le32  s_first_data_block;     /* First Data Block */
        __le32  s_log_block_size;       /* Block size */
        __le32  s_log_frag_size;        /* Fragment size */
        __le32  s_blocks_per_group;     /* # Blocks per group */
        __le32  s_frags_per_group;      /* # Fragments per group */
        __le32  s_inodes_per_group;     /* # Inodes per group */
        __le32  s_mtime;                /* Mount time */
        __le32  s_wtime;                /* Write time */
        __le16  s_mnt_count;            /* Mount count */
        __le16  s_max_mnt_count;        /* Maximal mount count */
        __le16  s_magic;                /* Magic signature */
        __le16  s_state;                /* File system state */
        __le16  s_errors;               /* Behaviour when detecting errors */
        __le16  s_minor_rev_level;      /* minor revision level */
        __le32  s_lastcheck;            /* time of last check */
        __le32  s_checkinterval;        /* max. time between checks */
        __le32  s_creator_os;           /* OS */
        __le32  s_rev_level;            /* Revision level */
        __le16  s_def_resuid;           /* Default uid for reserved blocks */
        __le16  s_def_resgid;           /* Default gid for reserved blocks */
        /*
         * These fields are for EXT2_DYNAMIC_REV superblocks only.
         *
         * Note: the difference between the compatible feature set and
         * the incompatible feature set is that if there is a bit set
         * in the incompatible feature set that the kernel doesn't
         * know about, it should refuse to mount the filesystem.
         *
         * e2fsck's requirements are more strict; if it doesn't know
```

```
   * about a feature in either the compatible or incompatible
   * feature set, it must abort and not try to meddle with
   * things it doesn't understand...
   */
  __le32  s_first_ino;          /* First non-reserved inode */
  __le16   s_inode_size;        /* size of inode structure */
  __le16  s_block_group_nr;     /* block group # of this superblock */
  __le32  s_feature_compat;     /* compatible feature set */
  __le32  s_feature_incompat;   /* incompatible feature set */
  __le32  s_feature_ro_compat;  /* readonly-compatible feature set */
  __u8    s_uuid[16];           /* 128-bit uuid for volume */
  char    s_volume_name[16];    /* volume name */
  char    s_last_mounted[64];   /* directory where last mounted */
  __le32  s_algorithm_usage_bitmap; /* For compression */
  /*
   * Performance hints.  Directory preallocation should only
   * happen if the EXT2_COMPAT_PREALLOC flag is on.
   */
  __u8    s_prealloc_blocks;    /* Nr of blocks to try to preallocate*/
  __u8    s_prealloc_dir_blocks; /* Nr to pre-allocate for dirs */
  __u16   s_padding1;
  /*
   * Journaling support valid if EXT3_FEATURE_COMPAT_HAS_JOURNAL set.
   */
  ...
  __u32   s_reserved[190];      /* Padding to the end of the block */
};
```

The elements at the end of the structure are not shown because they are not used by Ext2 and are relevant only in Ext3. Why this is so is explained in Section 9.3.

It is necessary to clarify various matters relating to the data types of these elements before going on to define the meanings of the individual fields. As can be seen, the data types of most of the fields are named __le32, __le16, and so on. These are, without exception, integers of an *absolutely defined* bit length that are represented in little endian byte order.[7]

Why are no elementary C types used? Recall that different processors represent elementary types by means of different bit lengths. Using elementary types would thus result in different superblock formats depending on processor type — which is clearly no good. When removable media are swapped between different computer systems, the metadata must always be stored in the same format, regardless of processor type.

Other parts of the kernel also need data types of a guaranteed bit length that does *not* differ from processor to processor. For this reason, the architecture-specific files contain include/asm-*arch*/types.h definitions for a series of types from __s8 to __u64 to control mapping onto the correct elementary data types of the CPU type used. The endian-specific types are directly based on these definitions.

However, use of the correct *length* of a data type is, in itself, not enough. As established in Chapter 1, the arrangement of the most significant and least significant parts of a multibyte data type also differs depending on CPU type — again, we are faced with the problem of big and little endianness.

---

[7]The distinction between little and big endian numbers does not influence the number of bits. The information can be used by automated source code analysis tools to ensure that no mistakes are made when the quantities are, for example, inspected bitwise.

To ensure filesystem portability between systems, the designers of the Ext2 filesystem decided to store all numerical values of the superblock structure in little endian arrangement on the hard disk. When data are read into memory, the kernel is therefore responsible for converting this format into the native format of the CPU. The two files `byteorder/big_endian.h` and `byteorder/little_endian.h` provide routines for converting between the individual CPU types. Because the data of Ext2 filesystems are stored in little endian format by default, no conversion is necessary on CPU types such as IA-32 and AMD64. This delivers a slight speed advantage over systems such as Sparc that are forced to swap the order of the bytes for types with more than 8 bits.[8]

The superblock structure itself consists of an extensive collection of numbers to characterize the general properties of the filesystem. Its size is always 1,024 bytes. This is achieved by padding the end of the structure with a filler element (`s_reserved`).

Because the meaning of most entries is clear from the element name or associated comment, only those that are of interest and not self-explanatory are discussed.

❑ `s_log_block_size` is the binary logarithm of the block size used divided by 1,024. Currently, the three values 0, 1, and 2 are used, giving block sizes of $2^0 \times 1,024 = 1,024$, $2^1 \times 1,024 = 2,048$, and $2^2 \times 1,024 = 4,096$ bytes. Minimum and maximum block sizes are currently limited to `1024` and `4096`, respectively, by means of the kernel constants `EXT2_MIN_BLOCK_SIZE` and `EXT2_MAX_BLOCK_SIZE`.[9]

The desired block size must be specified during filesystem creation with `mke2fs`. It cannot be changed during current operation as it represents a fundamental filesystem constant. The system administrator must decide on a reasonable block size commensurate with the anticipated use of the filesystem. A balance must be struck between wasted storage space and costly administration effort — no simple undertaking. Nevertheless, nearly all distributions relieve the administrator from this burden and provide reasonable default settings based on heuristic experience.

❑ `s_blocks_per_group` and `s_inodes_per_group` define the number of blocks and inodes in each block group. These values must also be fixed when the filesystem is created because they cannot be modified thereafter. In most cases, it is advisable to use the default settings selected by `mke2fs`.

❑ A magic number is stored in the `s_magic` field. This number ensures that a filesystem to be mounted really is of type Ext2. It is stored with the value `0xEF53` in `EXT2_SUPER_MAGIC` (in `ext2_fs.h`). The `s_rev_level` and `s_minor_rev_level` fields accept a revision number to differentiate between filesystem versions.

> **Even though a Second Extended Filesystem may be uniquely identifiable by this number, there is still no guarantee that the kernel can really mount it in Read/Write mode (or even in Read mode). Because Ext2 supports a series of optional and/or incompatible extensions (as you will see shortly), it is necessary to check several other fields in addition to the magic number field before a filesystem can be mounted.**

---

[8]The endianness of a CPU has no effect on file contents if files are interpreted byte-by-byte as is the case, for example, with text files (in files of this kind, numbers are stored as a text string, thus avoiding the problem of endianness). Sound files, on the other hand, must often be converted between different representations using appropriate tools — `sox`, for example — because the arrangement of bits is of relevance for binary interpretation of the data.

[9]Note that the upper limit is currently not checked by the kernel.

❑ The `s_def_resuid` and `s_def_resgid` fields specify the user and group IDs of a system user for whom a certain number of blocks has been exclusively reserved. The corresponding number is stored in `s_r_blocks_count`.

No other user may use these blocks. What purpose does this serve? By default, both `s_def_resuid` and `s_ref_gid` are set to 0; this corresponds to the system superuser (or root user). This user is able to write to filesystems that normal users see as already being full. This additional free space is usually referred to as the *root reserve*.

If this protection were not provided, it could happen, for instance, that certain daemons or servers running under the root ID could no longer be started, thus rendering the system unusable. Take, for example, the ssh server, which has to create a status file when a login is performed. If the hard disk were totally full, no user — not even a system administrator — would be able to log in. This would be a major catastrophe, particularly on remote systems such as Internet servers.

The root reserve (usually ≈ 5% of available space is set aside when a filesystem is created) helps prevent such mishaps and provides the superuser (or any other user if the UID/GID is changed accordingly in the above variables) with a safety margin to ensure that at least actions can be taken to counter overfilling of the hard disk.

❑ Filesystem consistency checks are performed with the help of three variables: `s_state`, `s_lastcheck`, and `s_checkinterval`. The first is used to specify the current state of the filesystem. When a partition is properly unmounted, its state is set to `EXT2_VALID_FS` (in `ext2_fs.h`) to indicate to the `mount` program that the partition is OK. If the filesystem was not correctly unmounted (because, e.g., the computer was shut down by switching off the power), the variable still indicates the state to which it was set directly after the filesystem was mounted, namely, `EXT2_ERROR_FS`. In this case, an `e2fsck` consistency check is triggered automatically.

Incorrect unmounting is not the only reason for initiating a consistency check. The date of the last check is recorded in `s_lastcheck`. If `s_checkinterval` has elapsed since this date, a check is enforced even if the filesystem is in a clean state.

A third (and the most frequently used) way of enforcing a consistency check is implemented with the help of counters called `s_max_mnt_count` and `s_mnt_count`. The latter counts the number of mount operations since the last check and the first the maximum number of mounts that may be performed between two checks. When this value is exceeded, a consistency check with `e2fsck` is initiated.

❑ The Ext2 filesystem was certainly not perfect when it was introduced and (like any other software product) never will be. Ongoing technological development brings constant changes and modifications to systems — understandably, these should be as easy as possible to integrate into existing schemes. After all, nobody wants to have to completely rebuild a system every 2 weeks to enjoy the benefits of a new function. Care was therefore taken during design of the Ext2 filesystem to ensure ease of integration of new features into the old design. For this reason, three elements of the superblock structure are dedicated to describing additional features: `s_feature_compat`, `s_feature_incompat`, and `s_feature_ro_compat`. As the names of the variables indicate, there are three different classes into which new functions are grouped.

  ❑ **Compatible Features** (`s_feature_compat`) — Can be used by new versions of the filesystem code and have no negative impact (or functional impairment) on older versions. Examples of this kind of enhancement are the journal introduced in Ext3 (discussed extensively in Section 9.3) and the provision of ACLs (*access control lists*) to support finer-grained assignments of permissions than is possible with the classic UNIX Read/Write/Execute system for user/group/others. The full list of all enhancements known to each kernel version is located in `ext2_fs.h` in the form of pre-processor definitions named **EXT2_FEATURE_COMPAT_*FEATURE***.

Kernel 2.6.24 includes the following compatible features:

<ext2_fs.h>

```
#define EXT2_FEATURE_COMPAT_DIR_PREALLOC   0x0001
#define EXT2_FEATURE_COMPAT_IMAGIC_INODES  0x0002
#define EXT3_FEATURE_COMPAT_HAS_JOURNAL    0x0004
#define EXT2_FEATURE_COMPAT_EXT_ATTR       0x0008
#define EXT2_FEATURE_COMPAT_RESIZE_INO     0x0010
#define EXT2_FEATURE_COMPAT_DIR_INDEX      0x0020
#define EXT2_FEATURE_COMPAT_ANY            0xffffffff
```

The `EXT2_FEATURE_COMPAT_ANY` constant can be used to test whether *any* feature of this category is present.

❑ **Read-Only Features** — Are enhancements that do not impair read access to a filesystem when an obsolete version of the filesystem code is used. Write access, however, does result in errors and inconsistencies in the filesystem. If a Read Only feature is set using `s_feature_ro_compat`, the partition can be mounted in Read Only mode, and write access is prohibited.

One example of a Read Only-compatible enhancement is the *sparse superblock* feature, which saves space by not storing a superblock in every block group of a partition. Because, in general, the kernel uses only the (still present) superblock copy in the first block group, there is no difference in terms of read access as modifications would be made to the remaining — now no longer existent — superblock copies when the filesystem is unmounted and could therefore overwrite important data.

As for the compatible features, a list of all known variants for the current kernel version is provided in `ext2_fs.h`. Again, pre-processor variables with the name **EXT2_FEATURE_RO_COMPAT_*FEATURE*** are defined to assign a unique numeric value to each enhancement or extension.

<ext2_fs.h>

```
#define EXT2_FEATURE_RO_COMPAT_SPARSE_SUPER   0x0001
#define EXT2_FEATURE_RO_COMPAT_LARGE_FILE     0x0002
#define EXT2_FEATURE_RO_COMPAT_BTREE_DIR      0x0004
#define EXT2_FEATURE_RO_COMPAT_ANY            0xffffffff
```

❑ **Incompatible features** (`s_incompat_features`) — With regard to old versions render a filesystem unusable if old code is used. A filesystem cannot be mounted if an enhancement of this kind, which the kernel does not understand, is present. **EXT2_FEATURE_INCOMPAT_*FEATURE*** macros assign numeric values to the incompatible enhancements. An example of this kind of enhancement is "on the fly" compression that stores all files in packed form — compressed file contents are meaningless, in both Read and Write mode, to filesystem code that cannot unpack them.

Other incompatible features are:

ext2_fs.h

```
#define EXT2_FEATURE_INCOMPAT_COMPRESSION    0x0001
#define EXT2_FEATURE_INCOMPAT_FILETYPE       0x0002
#define EXT3_FEATURE_INCOMPAT_RECOVER        0x0004
#define EXT3_FEATURE_INCOMPAT_JOURNAL_DEV    0x0008
#define EXT2_FEATURE_INCOMPAT_META_BG        0x0010
#define EXT2_FEATURE_INCOMPAT_ANY            0xffffffff
```

All three field elements are bitmaps whose individual bits represent a specific kernel enhancement. This enables the kernel to determine (by means of comparisons with pre-defined constants) which of the features it knows can be used on a filesystem. It is also able to scan the entries for features it doesn't know (these are marked by bits set at positions it doesn't know) and to decide, according to category, how to handle the filesystem.

> Some elements of the structure are not used by the Ext2 code as they are provided for future enhancements envisaged when the structure was designed. This is intended to dispense with the need to reformat filesystems when new features are added. Reformatting is often impracticable on heavily loaded server systems.

In the further course of the present description, reference is made to some of these fields when discussing potential enhancements to existing functionality.

Group Descriptor

As Figure 9-2 shows, each block group has a collection of group descriptors arranged directly after the superblock. The information they hold reflects the contents of each block group of the filesystem and therefore relates not only to the data blocks associated with the local block group but also to the data and inode blocks of other block groups.

The data structure used to define a single group descriptor is much shorter than the superblock structure, as the following section of kernel source code demonstrates:

<ext2_fs.h>
```
struct ext2_group_desc
{
        __le32  bg_block_bitmap;            /* Blocks bitmap block */
        __le32  bg_inode_bitmap;            /* Inodes bitmap block */
        __le32  bg_inode_table;       /* Inodes table block */
        __le16  bg_free_blocks_count;  /* Free blocks count */
        __le16  bg_free_inodes_count;  /* Free inodes count */
        __le16  bg_used_dirs_count;    /* Directories count */
        __le16  bg_pad;
        __le32  bg_reserved[3];
};
```

The kernel uses a copy of this structure for each block group described in the group descriptor collection.

The contents of each group descriptor include not only status entries indicating the number of free blocks (bg_free_blocks_count), and inodes (bg_free_inodes_count) as well as the number of directories (bg_used_dirs_count), but also, and more importantly, two pointers to blocks containing the bitmaps needed to organize used and free blocks and inodes. These are called bg_block_bitmap and bg_inode_bitmap and are implemented by means of a 32-bit number that uniquely describes a block on the hard disk.

The block to which bg_block_bitmap refers is not used to store data. Each of its bits stands for a data block of the current block group. If a bit is set, the block is being used by the filesystem; otherwise, the block is available. Because the position at which the first data block is located is known and all data blocks are in linear sequence, it is easy for the kernel to convert between bit positions in the block bitmap and the associated block positions.

The same method is applied for the inode pointer bg_inode_bitmap. It, too, points to a block whose individual bits are used to describe all inodes of a block group. Because it is also known in which blocks the inode structures are located and how big the inode structure is, the kernel can convert between the bitmap entries and the associated positions on the hard disk (see also Figure 9-2).

Each block group contains not just one but a large number of group descriptor structures — a copy for each block group in the filesystem. From each block group, it is therefore possible to determine the following information for *every single* block group in the system:

❑   The position of the block and inode bitmaps.

❑   The position of the inode table.

❑   The number of free blocks and inodes.

The blocks used as block and inode bitmaps are not, however, duplicated in each block group for all other block groups: in fact, there is only one occurrence of them in the system. Each block group has a *local* block for the block bitmap and an extra block for the inode bitmap. Nevertheless, all data and inode bitmaps of the remaining groups can be accessed from *every* block group because their position can be determined with the help of the entries in the group descriptor.

Because the filesystem block size is variable, the number of blocks that can be represented by a block bitmap also changes accordingly. If the block size is set to 2,048 bytes, each block has exactly $2{,}048 \times 8 = 16{,}384$ *bits* that can be used to describe the state of data blocks. Similarly, block sizes of 1,024 and 4,096 bytes mean that exactly 8,192 and 32,768 blocks can be managed. This data are summarized in Table 9-2.

In our example, we use only 2 bytes to store the block bitmap so that exactly 16 blocks can be addressed. The data blocks that hold the actual contents of the filesystem files (and the data used for indirection) are at the end of the block group.

Table 9-2: Maximum Sizes in a Block Group

Block size	Number of blocks
1,024	8,192
2,048	16,384
4,096	32,768

The division of a partition into block groups makes sense for systematic reasons and also brings tangible benefits in terms of speed. The filesystem always attempts to store the contents of a file in a single block group to minimize the travel of the read/write head between inode, block bitmap, and data blocks. Normally, this can be achieved, but there are, of course, situations in which files are spread over several block groups because there is not enough space in a single block group. Because, depending on block size, a block group can accept only a certain number of data blocks, there are maximum limits for file sizes (see Table 9-2). If these are exceeded, files must be spread over several block groups at the price of longer read/write head travel and reduced performance.

Inodes

Each block group also contains an inode bitmap and a local inode table that may extend over several blocks. The bitmap contents relate to the local block group and are not copied to any other point in the filesystem.

The inode bitmap is used to provide an overview of the used and free inodes of a group. As usual, each inode is represented as "used" or "free" by means of a single bit. The inode data are stored in the inode table with the help of a large number of sequential inode structures. How these data are held on the storage medium is defined by the following lengthier structure:

<ext2_fs.h>
```
struct ext2_inode {
        __le16  i_mode;         /* File mode */
        __le16  i_uid;          /* Low 16 bits of Owner Uid */
        __le32  i_size;         /* Size in bytes */
        __le32  i_atime;        /* Access time */
        __le32  i_ctime;        /* Creation time */
        __le32  i_mtime;        /* Modification time */
        __le32  i_dtime;        /* Deletion Time */
        __le16  i_gid;          /* Low 16 bits of Group Id */
        __le16  i_links_count;  /* Links count */
        __le32  i_blocks;       /* Blocks count */
        __le32  i_flags;        /* File flags */
        union {
                struct {
                        __le32  l_i_reserved1;
                } linux1;
                struct {
                ...
                } hurd1;
                struct {
                ...
                } masix1;
        } osd1;                         /* OS dependent 1 */
        __le32  i_block[EXT2_N_BLOCKS];/* Pointers to blocks */
        __le32  i_generation;   /* File version (for NFS) */
        __le32  i_file_acl;     /* File ACL */
        __le32  i_dir_acl;      /* Directory ACL */
        __le32  i_faddr;        /* Fragment address */
        union {
                struct {
                        __u8    l_i_frag;       /* Fragment number */
                        __u8    l_i_fsize;      /* Fragment size */
```

```
                        __u16    i_pad1;
                        __le16   l_i_uid_high;    /* these 2 fields    */
                        __le16   l_i_gid_high;    /* were reserved2[0] */
                        __u32    l_i_reserved2;
                } linux2;
                struct {
                ...
                } hurd2;
                struct {
                ...
                } masix2;
        } osd2;                                   /* OS dependent 2 */
};
```

The structure includes three operating-system-specific unions that accept different data, depending on use. The Ext2 filesystem is used not only in Linux but also in the HURD kernel[10] of the GNU project and in the Masix experimental operating system (one of the principal authors of Ext2 was involved in the development of Masix). The structure in the preceding code shows only the Linux-specific elements; the data of other operating systems are beyond the scope of this book.

At the beginning of the structure there is a whole host of data on the properties of the file characterized by the inode. Many of these data will be familiar from Chapter 8, where the structure of a generalized virtual filesystem inode is discussed.

❏ i_mode saves the access rights (in accordance with the usual UNIX scheme of user, group, others) and the file type (directory, device file, etc.).

❏ Time stamps with the following meanings are held in ctime, atime, mtime, and dtime:

  ❏ atime gives the time of the last file access.

  ❏ mtime gives the time of the last file change.

  ❏ ctime gives the time of the last inode change.

  ❏ dtime gives the time of file deletion.

  All time stamps are stored in the conventional UNIX format to indicate the number of seconds elapsed since midnight on 1 January 1970.

❏ The user and group ID consist of 32 bits and are, for historical reasons, split into two fields. The lower-order part is in i_uid and i_gid, and the higher-order parts are in l_i_uid_high and l_i_gid_high.

  Why is this rather strange approach adopted instead of two simple 32-bit numbers? When the Ext2 filesystem was conceived, 16-bit numbers were adequate for user and group IDs because this permitted a maximum of $2^{16} = 65,536$ users. At the time, this figure seemed to be large enough, but this assumption was proved to be wrong, particularly on *very* large systems such as commercial mail servers. To support enhancement to 32 bits without the need for a new filesystem format, a 32-bit entry from the Linux-specific osd1 field was split into two 16-bit parts that had been reserved for enhancements. Used in conjunction with the existing data, these permit

---

[10]Hurd = Hird of UNIX replacing daemons, Hird = Hurd of interfaces representing depth — a recursive acronym. The Hurd is well known for announcements of its developers that it will be finished in half a year — or so. Unfortunately, this tradition had already been established nearly a decade ago, and a final (or at least usable) version is still far on the horizon.

the representation of a 32-bit wide user and group identifier so that $2^{32} = 4,294,967,296$ users can be supported.

❑ i_size and i_blocks specify the file size in bytes and blocks, where 512 bytes is always assumed as the block size (this unit has nothing to do with the low-level block size of the filesystem and is always constant). At first glance, it would be easy to suppose that i_blocks can always be derived from i_size. However, owing to optimization of the Ext2 filesystem, this is not the case. The *file holes* method is used to ensure that files with longer empty sections do not waste space. It keeps the space used by holes to a minimum and requires two fields to store the byte and block length of a file.

❑ The pointers to the data blocks of a file are held in the i_block array that comprises EXT2_N_BLOCKS. By default, this value is set to 12 + 3. The first 12 elements are used for direct block addressing and the last three for implementing simple, double, and triple indirection. Although theoretically this value can be changed at compilation time, this is not advisable because it produces incompatibility with all other standard formats of Ext2.

❑ i_links_count is a counter to specify the number of hard links that point to an inode.

❑ i_file_acl and i_dir_acl support implementation of *access control lists* that permit finer-grained control of access rights than is possible with the classic UNIX approach.

❑ Some elements of the inode are already defined but not yet in use. They are available for future enhancements. For example, i_faddr, l_i_fsize and l_i_fsize are provided to store fragmentation data so that the contents of several small files can be allocated to a single block.

How many inodes are there in each block group? The answer depends on the settings at filesystem creation time. The number of inodes per block group can be set to any (reasonable) value when the filesystem is created. This number is held in the s_inodes_per_group field. Because the inode structure has a constant size of 120 bytes, this information and the block size can be used to determine the number of blocks with inode structures. Regardless of the block size, the default setting is 128 inodes per block group, an acceptable value for most scenarios.

Directories and Files

Now that the principal aspects of infrastructure have been explained, let's discuss the representation of directories that define the topology of filesystems. As noted in Chapter 8, directories — as in classic UNIX filesystems — are nothing more than special files with pointers to inodes and their filenames to represent files and subdirectories in the current directory. This is also true in the Second Extended Filesystem. Each directory is represented by an inode to which data blocks are assigned. The blocks contain structures to describe the directory entries. The data structure needed to do this is defined as follows in the kernel sources:

```
<ext2_fs.h>
struct ext2_dir_entry_2 {
        __le32  inode;                   /* Inode number */
        __le16  rec_len;                 /* Directory entry length */
        __u8    name_len;                /* Name length */
        __u8    file_type;
        char    name[EXT2_NAME_LEN];     /* File name */
};

typedef struct ext2_dir_entry_2 ext2_dirent;
```

The `typedef` statement allows the shorter `ext2_dirent` to be used in place of `struct ext2_dir_entry_2` in the kernel sources.

The names of the individual fields are more or less self-explanatory because they are directly based on the scheme introduced in Chapter 8. `inode` is a pointer to the inode of the directory entry; `name_len` is the length of the directory entry string. The name itself is held in the `names[]` array and may be up to `EXT2_NAME_LEN` characters long (the default value is 255).

> **Because the length of a directory entry must always be a multiple of 4, names may be padded with up to three zero bytes (i.e., bytes with ASCII value 0). No zero bytes need be added if the length of the name is divisible by 4 without a remainder.**

`file_type` specifies the directory entry type. This variable accepts one of the values defined in the following `enum` structure:

```
<ext2_fs.h>
535
enum {
        EXT2_FT_UNKNOWN,
        EXT2_FT_REG_FILE,
        EXT2_FT_DIR,
        EXT2_FT_CHRDEV,
        EXT2_FT_BLKDEV,
        EXT2_FT_FIFO,
        EXT2_FT_SOCK,
        EXT2_FT_SYMLINK,
        EXT2_FT_MAX
};
```

`EXT2_FT_REG_FILE` is used most frequently because it indicates a regular file (whose contents are of no relevance). `EXT2_FT_DIR` also occurs often and represents directories. The other constants denote character-special and block-special files (`BLKDEV` and `CHRDEV`), FIFOs (named pipes; `FIFO`), sockets (`SOCK`), and symbolic links (`SYMLINK`).

`rec_len` is the only field in the directory structure whose meaning is not so obvious. It is an offset pointer indicating the number of bytes between the end of the `rec_len` field and the end of the *next* `rec_len` field. This enables the kernel to scan directories efficiently by jumping from one name to the next. By reference to an example, Figure 9-6 shows how different directory entries are represented on hard disk.

`ls` lists the contents of directories as follows:

```
wolfgang@meitner> ls -la
total 20
drwxr-xr-x    3 wolfgang users      4096 Feb 14 12:12 .
drwxrwxrwt   13 wolfgang users      8192 Feb 14 12:12 ..
brw-r--r--    1 wolfgang users   3,    0 Feb 14 12:12 harddisk
lrwxrwxrwx    1 wolfgang users        14 Feb 14 12:12 linux -> /usr/src/linux
-rw-r--r--    1 wolfgang users        13 Feb 14 12:12 sample
drwxr-xr-x    2 wolfgang users      4096 Feb 14 12:12 sources
```

inode	rec_len	name_len	file_type	name									
	12	1	2	.	\0	\0	\0						
	12	2	2	.	.h	\0	\0						
	16	8	4	h	a	r	d	d	i	s	k		
	32	5	7	l	i	n	u	x	\0	\0	\0		
	16	6	2	d	e	l	d	i	r	\0	\0		
	16	6	1	s	a	m	p	l	e	\0	\0		
	16	7	2	s	o	u	r	c	e	\0	\0		

Figure 9-6: Representation of files and directories in the Second Extended Filesystem.

The first two entries are always . and .. to point to the current and parent directory. The meaning of the rec_len field in Figure 9-6 is also clear. It indicates the number of bytes to be skipped after the end of the rec_len field to get to the start of the next entry, beginning with name_len.

The filesystem code makes use of this information when deleting entries from a directory. To make it unnecessary to shift the contents of the entire inode, rec_len of the entry *before* the entry to be deleted is set to a value that points to the entry *after* the entry to be deleted. The preceding list of directory contents does not include an entry for the deldir directory shown in Figure 9-6 because this directory was deleted. The value of the rec_len field in the entry before deldir is 32, and this directs the filesystem code to the next but one entry (sample) when it scans the directory contents. The detailed mechanisms used to delete files/inodes are described in Section 9.2.4.

Naturally, files are also represented by inodes. It is clear how regular data files are represented, but there are a number of file types where the filesystem must exercise special care. These include symbolic links, device files, named pipes, and sockets.

The type of a file is not defined in the inode itself but in the file_type field of the parent directory entry. Nevertheless, the contents of an inode differ according to the file type it represents. It should be noted that only directories and regular files[11] occupy data blocks on the hard disk. All other types are fully described by the information in the inode.

❑   *Symbolic links* are saved in their entirety in the inode if the name of the link target is less than 60 characters long. Because the inode itself does not provide a field for the target name of symbolic links (this would, in fact, be a massive waste of space), a trick is used. The i_block structure normally used to hold the addresses of file blocks consists of 15 32-bit entries (a total of $15 \times 4 = 60$ bytes), is assigned a new role and stores the target name of symbolic links.

If the target name comprises more than 60 characters, the filesystem allocates a data block to store the string.

---

[11] And also links with targets comprising more than 60 characters.

❑ *Device files*, *named pipes*, and *persistent sockets* are also fully described by the information in the inode. In memory, data also required are held in the inode structure of the VFS (`i_cdev` for character devices and `i_rdev` for block devices; all information can be reconstructed from these). On the hard disk the first element of the data pointer array `i_data[0]` is used to store the additional information; this does not cause any problems because device files require no data blocks; the same trick is used as with symbolic links.

Data Structures in Memory

To dispense with the need to constantly read administration structures from slow hard disks, Linux saves the most important information that these structures contain in special data structures that reside permanently in RAM. Access is considerably faster, and less interaction with the hard disk is required. Then why aren't all filesystem management data held in RAM (with writeback of changes to disk at regular intervals)? Although theoretically this would be possible, it does not work in practice because so much memory would be required to hold all block and inode bitmaps of a large hard disk with several gigabytes — as found on many computers today.

The virtual filesystem provides an element named u in the `struct super_block` and `struct inode` structures. This element is used by the various filesystem implementations to store information not already included in the filesystem-independent contents of the structure. The Second Extended Filesystem uses the `ext2_sb_info` and `ext2_inode_info` structures for the same purpose. The latter is of no particular interest as compared to its counterpart on the hard disk.

`ext2_sb_info` is defined as follows:

```
<ext2_fs_sb.h>
struct ext2_sb_info {
        unsigned long s_frag_size;      /* Size of a fragment in bytes */
        unsigned long s_frags_per_block;/* Number of fragments per block */
        unsigned long s_inodes_per_block;/* Number of inodes per block */
        unsigned long s_frags_per_group;/* Number of fragments in a group */
        unsigned long s_blocks_per_group;/* Number of blocks in a group */
        unsigned long s_inodes_per_group;/* Number of inodes in a group */
        unsigned long s_itb_per_group;  /* Number of inode table blocks per group */
        unsigned long s_gdb_count;      /* Number of group descriptor blocks */
        unsigned long s_desc_per_block; /* Number of group descriptors per block */
        unsigned long s_groups_count;   /* Number of groups in the fs */
        unsigned long s_overhead_last; /* Last calculated overhead */
        unsigned long s_blocks_last; /* Last seen block count */
        struct buffer_head * s_sbh;     /* Buffer containing the super block */
         struct ext2_super_block * s_es; /* Pointer to the super block in the buffer
*/
        struct buffer_head ** s_group_desc;
        unsigned long  s_mount_opt;
        unsigned long  s_sb_block;
        uid_t s_resuid;
        gid_t s_resgid;
        unsigned short s_mount_state;
        unsigned short s_pad;
        int s_addr_per_block_bits;
        int s_desc_per_block_bits;
        int s_inode_size;
        int s_first_ino;
```

```
       spinlock_t s_next_gen_lock;
       u32 s_next_generation;
       unsigned long s_dir_count;
       u8 *s_debts;
       struct percpu_counter s_freeblocks_counter;
       struct percpu_counter s_freeinodes_counter;
       struct percpu_counter s_dirs_counter;
       struct blockgroup_lock s_blockgroup_lock;
   };
```

What is interesting in the structure definition is the fact that machine-specific data types can be used in place of the bit-oriented variants (u32, etc.). This is because it is not necessary to be able to swap different forms of data representation in memory between machines. Although most elements of the structure are already familiar from the on-disk superblock, some elements are found only in the RAM variant.

❑   s_mount_opt holds the mount options, and the current mount state is saved in s_mount_state. The following flags are available for s_mount_opt:

<ext2_fs.h>
```
#define EXT2_MOUNT_CHECK          0x0001  /* Do mount-time checks */
#define EXT2_MOUNT_OLDALLOC       0x0002  /* Don't use the new Orlov
                                             allocator */
#define EXT2_MOUNT_GRPID          0x0004  /* Create files with directory's
                                             group */
#define EXT2_MOUNT_DEBUG          0x0008  /* Some debugging messages */
#define EXT2_MOUNT_ERRORS_CONT    0x0010  /* Continue on errors */
#define EXT2_MOUNT_ERRORS_RO      0x0020  /* Remount fs ro on errors */
#define EXT2_MOUNT_ERRORS_PANIC   0x0040  /* Panic on errors */
#define EXT2_MOUNT_MINIX_DF       0x0080  /* Mimics the Minix statfs */
#define EXT2_MOUNT_NOBH           0x0100  /* No buffer_heads */
#define EXT2_MOUNT_NO_UID32       0x0200  /* Disable 32-bit UIDs */
#define EXT2_MOUNT_XATTR_ER      0x4000   /* Extended user attributes */
#define EXT2_MOUNT_POSIX_ACL     0x8000   /* POSIX Access Control Lists */
#define EXT2_MOUNT_XIP 0x010000 /* Execute in place */
#define EXT2_MOUNT_USRQUOTA 0x020000 /* user quota */
#define EXT2_MOUNT_GRPQUOTA 0x040000 /* group quota */
#define EXT2_MOUNT_RESERVATION 0x080000 /* Preallocation */
```

To check a given ext2_sb_info instance sb for a mount option opt, the macro test_opt(sb,opt) is provided. The calling syntax is somewhat unusual: The mount option is not specified by the pre-processor constant, but only by the part without EXT2_MOUNT_. To check, for instance, if pre-allocation is required or not requires the following code: test_opt(sb,RESERVATION). Keep this especially in mind when greping through the kernel sources, or analyzing them with LXR: Searching for EXT2_MOUNT_RESERVATION will only reveal the definition of the pre-processor symbol, but none of its uses. Searching for RESERVATION instead delivers the desired hits.

❑   If the superblock is not read from the default block 1, but from some other block (in case the first one should be damaged), the corresponding (relative) block is stored in s_sb_block.

❑   The statfs system call (and most users as well) is interested in the number of blocks a filesystem provides. That means the number of blocks that can be used to store data. Unavoidably, some space needs to be sacrificed for filesystem management data like superblocks or block group descriptors. Computing the net block number is easy: the kernel just needs to subtract the number of management blocks from the number of blocks available for the filesystem. Albeit simple, the operation is costly (the kernel needs to iterate over all block groups), so `s_overhead_last` and `s_blocks_last` are used to cache the last computed value for the number of management blocks and the totally available blocks.

Note that the values usually remain constant. Once they have been computed, they can nevertheless change if the filesystem is resized while being mounted. But resizing is seldomly used and requires an external kernel patch, so it will not be discussed any further.

❑ `s_dir_count` indicates the total number of directories; this is needed for implementation of the Orlov allocator discussed in Section 9.2.4. Because this value is not saved in the on-disk structure, it must be determined each time a filesystem is mounted. The kernel provides the `ext2_count_dirs` function for this purpose.

❑ `s_debts` is a pointer to an array of 8-bit numbers (generally, `short`s) with a separate entry for each block group. The Orlov allocator uses this array to keep a balance between file and directory inodes in a block group (this is discussed in greater depth in Section 9.2.4).

❑ The `percpu_counter` instances at the end of the structure provide approximate, but fast and scalable counters for the free blocks and inodes and the number of directories. The implementation of such counters is discussed in Section 5.2.9.

In kernel versions up to 2.4, `ext2_sb_info` included additional elements to cache the block and inode bitmaps. Because of their size, it was not possible (or at least not reasonable) to keep them all in memory at the same time. As a result, an LRU method was used to keep only the most frequently used elements in RAM. In the meantime, this specific cache implementation has been rendered superfluous because accesses to block devices are now cached automatically by the kernel, even if only a single block (and not an entire page) is read. Chapter 16 discusses the implementation of the new caching scheme in detail when describing `__bread`.

Pre-allocation

To increase the performance of block allocation, the second extended filesystem employs a mechanism known as *pre-allocation*. Whenever a number of new blocks is requested for a file, not just the absolutely necessary blocks are allocated. Blocks for consecutive allocations are additionally spied out and marked for later use *without* being finally allocated. The kernel ensures that reserved areas don't overlap. This saves time when new allocations are made and prevents fragmentation, especially when multiple files grow concurrently. It should be emphasized that pre-allocation does not lead to poorer use of the available disk space. A region pre-allocated by one inode can at any time be overwritten by another inode if the need arises. However, the kernel tries to be polite and avoid this. One can think of pre-allocation as an additional layer before the final block allocation that determines how the available space *could* be put to good use. Pre-allocation is a suggestion, while allocation is final.

Several data structures are required to implement this mechanism. The reservation window itself is not very complicated: It uses a start and end block to specify a reserved region. The following data structure reflects this:

```
<ext2_fs_sb.h>
struct ext2_reserve_window {
        ext2_fsblk_t _rsv_start; /* First byte reserved */
        ext2_fsblk_t _rsv_end; /* Last byte reserved or 0 */
};
```

The window needs to be integrated with the other Ext2 data structures. Recall that both `struct ext2_inode` and `struct ext2_sb_info` contain fields that point to information about pre-allocation.

fs/ext2/ext2.h
```
struct ext2_inode_info {
...
        struct ext2_block_alloc_info *i_block_alloc_info;
...
}
```

<ext2_fs_sb.h>
```
struct ext2_sb_info {
...
        spinlock_t s_rsv_window_lock;
        struct rb_root s_rsv_window_root;
        struct ext2_reserve_window_node s_rsv_window_head;
...
}
```

The pre-allocation information for each individual inode is contained in `struct ext2_block_alloc_info` and `struct ext2_reserve_window_node`, which are defined as follows:

<ext2_fs_sb.h>
```
struct ext2_reserve_window_node {
        struct rb_node rsv_node;
        __u32 rsv_goal_size;
        __u32 rsv_alloc_hit;
        struct ext2_reserve_window rsv_window;
};

struct ext2_block_alloc_info {
        /* information about reservation window */
        struct ext2_reserve_window_node rsv_window_node;

        __u32 last_alloc_logical_block;
        ext2_fsblk_t last_alloc_physical_block;
};
```

The data structures are heavily interconnected and embedded within each other, but Figure 9-7 helps to keep track.

All instances of `ext2_reserve_window_node` are collected in a red-black tree headed by `ext2_sb_info->s_rsv_window_root` (refer to Appendix C for more information about such trees). The tree nodes are embedded into `ext2_reserve_window` via `rsv_node`.

The red-black tree allows for sorting the elements by their reservation window borders. This allows the kernel to quickly find reservations into which a given goal block falls. Additionally, `ext2_reserve_window_node` contains the following information:

❏ The desired size of the allocation window is given by `rsv_goal_size`. Note that the ioctl `EXT2_IOC_SETRSVSZ` can be used to set the value from userland, while `EXT2_IOC_GETRESVZ` retrieves the current setting. The maximum allowed reservation window size is `EXT2_MAX_RESERVE_BLOCKS`, usually defined to 1,027.

❑ rsv_alloc_hits keeps track of the pre-allocation hits, that is, how many allocations were performed from within the reservation window.

❑ Most importantly, the reserve window itself is given by rsv_window.

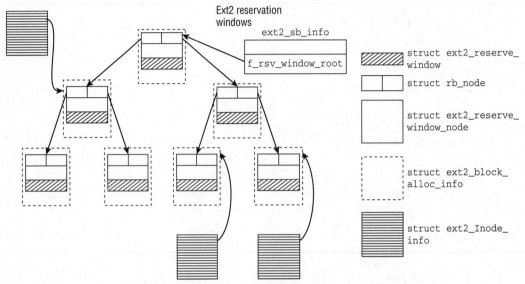

Figure 9-7: Data structures used by the pre-allocation mechanism.

If an inode is equipped with pre-allocation information, then ext2_inode_info->i_block_alloc_info points to an instance of struct ext2_block_alloc_info. In addition to an embedded instance of ext2_reserve_window_node that brings the connection with the red-black tree, the data structure contains information about the last allocated block: last_alloc_logical_block denotes the file-relative number of the last allocated block, while last_alloc_physical_block stores the corresponding physical number on the block device.

9.2.3 Creating a Filesystem

Filesystems are not created by the kernel itself but by the mke2fs userspace tool. Although I am more concerned with the work of the kernel, I discuss this important aspect of filesystem work briefly below. mk2efs not only shares the space on a partition between management information and useful data, but also creates a simple directory structure on the storage medium so that the filesystem can be mounted.

Which management information is meant? When a newly formatted[12] Ext2 partition is mounted, it already contains a standard subdirectory named lost+found to hold defective blocks of the data

---

[12]It is, of course, possible to argue about the subtle difference between low-level formatting and filesystem creation and to insist on a distinction between the two terms. I take a pragmatic approach and use both terms synonymously, as most UNIX users do, because there is no danger of confusing the two.

medium (thanks to the quality of today's hard disks, it is almost always empty). This involves the following steps:

1. An inode and a data block are reserved and initialized for the root directory. The data block contains a file list with three entries: ., .., and lost+found. As this is the root directory, both . and .. point back to the root inode that represents the root directory.

2. An inode and a data block are also reserved for the lost+found directory, which has only two entries: .. points back to the root inode and ., as usual, points to the inode of the directory itself.

Although mke2fs is designed for use with block special files, it is possible to use a regular file on a data medium to create a filesystem. This is because of the "everything is just a file philosophy" of UNIX according to which the same routines can be used to handle regular files and block special devices, at least from the userspace perspective. Using regular files instead of block special files is a very good way of experimenting with filesystem structures without having to access existing filesystems with possibly important data or without having to bother with slow floppy disk drives. For this reason, I briefly discuss the steps involved below.

First, a file of arbitrary size is created using the dd standard utility.

```
wolfgang@meitner> dd if=/dev/zero of=img.1440 bs=1k count=1440
1550+0 records in
1440+0 records out
```

This creates a file with a size of 1.4 MiB, the same capacity as a 3.5-inch floppy disk. The file contains only zero bytes (with ASCII value 0) generated by /dev/zero.

mke2fs now creates a filesystem on the file:

```
wolfgang@meitner> /sbin/mke2fs img.1440
mke2fs 1.40.2 (12-Jul-2007)
img.1440 is not a block special device.
Proceed anyway? (y,n) y
File System label=
OS type: Linux
Block size=1024 (log=0)
Fragment size=1024 (log=0)
184 inodes, 1440 blocks
72 blocks (5.00%) reserved for the super user
First data block=1
Maximum file system blocks=1572864
1 block group
8192 blocks per group, 8192 fragments per group
184 inodes per group
...
```

The data in img.1440 can be viewed using a hex editor to draw conclusions on the filesystem structure. od and hexedit are classic examples of such editors, but all distributions include numerous alternatives ranging from Spartan text-mode tools to sophisticated, user-friendly graphic applications.

An empty filesystem is not very interesting, so we need a way of filling the sample filesystem with data. This is done by mounting the filesystem using the loopback interface, as shown in the following example:

```
wolfgang@meitner> mount -t ext2 -o loop=/dev/loop0 img.1440 /mnt
```

The filesystem can then be manipulated in such a way as to give the impression that it is located on a regular partition of a block device. All changes are transferred to img.1440 and can be examined there.

9.2.4 Filesystem Actions

As demonstrated in Chapter 8, the association between the virtual filesystem and specific implementations is established in the main by three structures that include a series of function pointers; this association must be implemented by all filesystems.

❑ Operations for manipulating the contents of a file are stored in file_operations.

❑ Operations for processing the file objects themselves are held in inode_operations

❑ Operations with generalized address spaces are stored in address_space_operations.

The Ext2 filesystem features various instances of file_operations for different file types. Naturally, the most frequently used variant is for regular files and is defined as follows:

fs/ext2/file.c
```
struct file_operations ext2_file_operations = {
        .llseek         = generic_file_llseek,
        .read           = do_sync_read,
        .write          = do_sync_write,
        .aio_read       = generic_file_aio_read,
        .aio_write      = generic_file_aio_write,
        .ioctl          = ext2_ioctl,
        .mmap           = generic_file_mmap,
        .open           = generic_file_open,
        .release        = ext2_release_file,
        .fsync          = ext2_sync_file,
        .readv          = generic_file_readv,
        .splice_read    = generic_file_splice_read,
        .splice_write   = generic_file_splice_write,
};
```

Most entries hold pointers to the standard functions of VFS discussed in Chapter 8.

Directories also have their own file_operations instance — which is much shorter because many file operations make no sense if applied to directories.

fs/ext2/dir.c
```
struct file_operations ext2_dir_operations = {
        .llseek         = generic_file_llseek,
        .read           = generic_read_dir,
        .readdir        = ext2_readdir,
        .ioctl          = ext2_ioctl,
        .fsync          = ext2_sync_file,
};
```

Fields not shown are automatically initialized with NULL pointers by the compiler.

The inode operations are initialized as follows for regular files:

fs/ext2/file.c
```
struct inode_operations ext2_file_inode_operations = {
        .truncate       = ext2_truncate,
        .setxattr       = generic_setxattr,
        .getxattr       = generic_getxattr,
        .listxattr      = ext2_listxattr,
        .removexattr    = generic_removexattr,
        .setattr        = ext2_setattr,
        .permission     = ext2_permission,
};
```

More inode operations are available for directories.

fs/ext2/namei.c
```
struct inode_operations ext2_dir_inode_operations = {
        .create         = ext2_create,
        .lookup         = ext2_lookup,
        .link           = ext2_link,
        .unlink         = ext2_unlink,
        .symlink        = ext2_symlink,
        .mkdir          = ext2_mkdir,
        .rmdir          = ext2_rmdir,
        .mknod          = ext2_mknod,
        .rename         = ext2_rename,
        .setxattr       = generic_setxattr,
        .getxattr       = generic_getxattr,
        .listxattr      = ext2_listxattr,
        .removexattr    = generic_removexattr,
        .setattr        = ext2_setattr,
        .permission     = ext2_permission,
};
```

Filesystem and block layers are linked by the address_space_operations discussed in Chapter 4. In the Ext2 filesystem, these operations are filled with the following entries[13]:

fs/ext2/inode.c
```
struct address_space_operations ext2_aops = {
        .readpage       = ext2_readpage,
        .readpages      = ext2_readpages,
        .writepage      = ext2_writepage,
        .sync_page      = block_sync_page,
        .write_begin    = ext2_write_begin,
        .write_end      = generic_write_end,
        .bmap           = ext2_bmap,
        .direct_IO      = ext2_direct_IO,
        .writepages     = ext2_writepages,
};
```

---

[13]There is a second version of address space operations named ext2_nobh_aops; it contains only functions in which the page cache manages without buffer_heads. These functions are used (predominantly on machines with gigantic RAM configurations) when the mount option nobh is specified. This is a seldom used option not discussed here.

A fourth structure (super_operations) is used for interaction with the superblock (reading, writing, and allocating inodes). Its values are as follows for the Ext2 filesystem:

fs/ext2/super.c
```
static struct super_operations ext2_sops = {
        .alloc_inode    = ext2_alloc_inode,
        .destroy_inode  = ext2_destroy_inode,
        .read_inode     = ext2_read_inode,
        .write_inode    = ext2_write_inode,
        .delete_inode   = ext2_delete_inode,
        .put_super      = ext2_put_super,
        .write_super    = ext2_write_super,
        .statfs         = ext2_statfs,
        .remount_fs     = ext2_remount,
        .clear_inode    = ext2_clear_inode,
        .show_options   = ext2_show_options,
};
```

It is neither possible nor does it make sense to discuss the details of all functions listed in the above structures. Instead, the sections below are restricted to an examination of the most important functions that illustrate the key mechanisms and principles of the Ext2 implementation. You are encouraged to look up the remaining functions in the kernel sources: they are not hard to understand with the background which is provided in the following sections.

Mounting and Unmounting

Recall from Chapter 8 that the kernel requires a further structure to hold mount and unmount information when working with filesystems — the information is not provided in any of the structures discussed above. The file_system_type structure is used for this purpose and is defined as follows for the Second Extended File System:

fs/ext2/super.c
```
static struct file_system_type ext2_fs_type = {
        .owner          = THIS_MODULE,
        .name           = "ext2",
        .get_sb         = ext2_get_sb,
        .kill_sb        = kill_block_super,
        .fs_flags       = FS_REQUIRES_DEV,
};
```

Chapter 8 explained that the mount system call invokes the function in get_sb to read the superblock of a filesystem. The Second Extended Filesystem relies on a standard function of the virtual filesystem (get_sb_bdev) to do this:

fs/ext2/super.c
```
static int ext2_get_sb(struct file_system_type *fs_type,
        int flags, const char *dev_name, void *data, struct vfsmount *mnt)
{
        return get_sb_bdev(fs_type, flags, dev_name, data, ext2_fill_super, mnt);
}
```

A function pointer to `ext2_fill_super` is passed as a parameter for `get_sb_bdev`. This function fills a superblock object with data that must be read from the hard disk if there is no suitable superblock object in memory.[14] In this section, we need therefore only examine the `ext2_fill_super` function in `fs/ext2/super.c`. Its code flow diagram is shown in Figure 9-8.

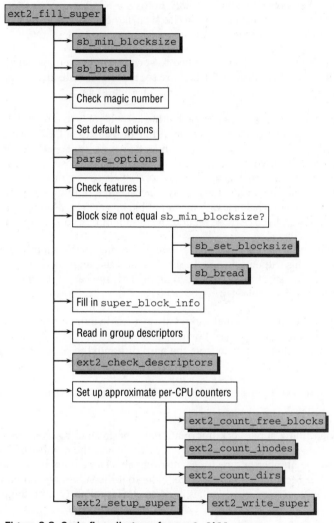

Figure 9-8: Code flow diagram for `ext2_fill_super`.

`ext2_fill_super` starts by setting an initial block size for reading the superblock. Because the block size used *in the file system* is not yet known, the kernel first attempts to find the minimum possible value with the help of `sb_min_blocksize`. This function normally sets 1,024 bytes as the block size. If, however, the block device has a larger minimum block size, this is used instead.

---

[14]This is naturally only the case when the desired filesystem is already mounted on the system but needs to be mounted somewhere else, a comparatively rare occurrence.

The data block in which the superblock is located is then read by sb_bread. This is a wrapper for the __bread function described in Chapter 16. A simple typecast converts the raw data returned by the function into an instance of type ext2_super_block.[15]

A check is now made to establish whether the partition used actually contains a Second Extended Filesystem. The magic number stored in the superblock holds the required information. Its value must match that of the EXT2_SUPER_MAGIC constant. If the check fails, the mount operation is aborted, and an error message indicates that an attempt was made to mount a non-Ext2 filesystem.

parse_options analyzes the parameters passed to specify mount options (such as the use of access control lists or enhanced attributes). All values are set to their defaults before this is done to ensure that not specifying an option is equivalent to specifying the default value.

A check of the filesystem features reveals whether the kernel is able to mount the filesystem at all, in Read and Write mode, or in Read mode only (the enhancement features of Ext2 are discussed in Section 9.2.2). The bit strings stored in s_feature_ro_compat and s_feature_incompat are compared with the corresponding kernel constants. Two constants are defined for this purpose: EXT2_FEATURE_INCOMPAT_SUPP contains all incompatible features together, while EXT2_FEATURE_RO_COMPAT contains all bits for compatible features that can only be handled Read Only. Filesystem mounting is rejected if bits are set whose meaning is not clear to the kernel or if any incompatible bits are set. Mounting is also rejected if any of the bits in EXT2_FEATURE_RO_COMPAT are set and the mount options do not specify the Read Only flag.

If the filesystem block size stored in s_blocksize does not match the initially specified minimum value, the hard disk is set to this value using set_blocksize, and the superblock is read again. The work of the kernel is simplified if the same block size is used in the filesystem and for data transfer because filesystem blocks can then be read in a single step.

Meta-information on the filesystem that should always reside in memory is held in the ext2_sb_info data structure (described in Section 9.2.2), which is now filled. Generally, this information comprises simple value allocations that copy data from the hard disk into the corresponding elements of the data structure.

The group descriptors are then read in block-by-block and checked for consistency by ext2_check_descriptors.

The last steps when filling superblock information are performed by ext2_count_free_blocks, ext2_count_free_inodes, and ext2_count_dirs, which count the number of free blocks, the number of free inodes, and the number of directories, respectively. These numbers are needed by the Orlov allocator discussed in Section 9.2.4, for instance. Note that the values are stored in an approximative counter that starts with correct initial values, but can deviate slightly from the proper count during operation.

Control is now transferred to ext2_setup_super, which runs several final checks and outputs appropriate warnings (if, e.g., a filesystem is mounted in an inconsistent state, or if the maximum number of mounts without a consistency check has been exceeded). As a final step, ext2_write_super writes the contents of the superblock back to the underlying storage medium. This is necessary because some superblock values are modified during the mount operation — the mount count and date of last mount, for example.

---

[15]An offset must be added if the superblock doesn't start at a hardware sector boundary.

Reading and Generating Data and Indirection Blocks

Once the filesystem has been mounted, user processes can invoke the functions in Chapter 8 to access file contents. The required system calls are first forwarded to the VFS layer, which, depending on file type, invokes the appropriate routine of the underlying filesystem.

As mentioned at the beginning of this section, a large number of low-level functions are available for this purpose. Not all variants are discussed in detail here but only the central basic actions that make up the major part of the code in user applications — generating, opening, reading, closing, and deleting files and directory objects. Both file-specific and inode-specific operations are used to this end. Often the virtual filesystem provides default actions (such as `generic_file_read` and `generic_file_mmap`); these use only a few elementary functions of the low-level filesystem to perform higher abstracted tasks. This discussion is restricted to the required interfaces of the Ext2 file system "upward" to the virtual filesystem; these include primarily the reading and writing of data blocks associated with a specific position in a file. From the VFS perspective, the purpose of a filesystem is to establish the link between file contents and the corresponding blocks on the associated storage medium.

Finding Data Blocks

`ext2_get_block` is the key function for associating the Ext2 implementation with the default functions of the virtual filesystem. It should be remembered that all filesystems wishing to use the VFS standard functions must define a function of type `get_block_t` with the following signature:

```
<fs.h>
typedef int (get_block_t)(struct inode *inode, sector_t iblock,
                          struct buffer_head *bh_result, int create);
```

This function not only reads blocks (as its name suggests), but also *writes* blocks from memory to a block medium. When it does the latter, it may under certain circumstances also be necessary to generate new blocks, and this behavior is controlled by the `create` parameter.

The function used by ext2 is `ext2_get_block`. It is a front end to the more universal `ext2_get_blocks` that performs the important task of finding blocks. Its code flow diagram is shown in Figure 9-9, where the actions needed to create blocks (`create==true`) are initially ignored.

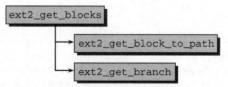

**Figure 9-9: Code flow diagram for
`ext2_get_block` (reading a block).**

The operation is split into three small steps. The first auxiliary function invoked is `ext2_block_to_path`, which concerns itself with finding the "path" to a data block by reference to its position in the file. As explained in Section 9.2.1, the Ext2 filesystem uses up to three levels of indirection to manage file data blocks.

In this context, the term *path* means the path through the descriptor tables to arrive at the desired data block.

This information can be obtained without I/O interaction with the data block. All that is needed is the position of the block in the file and the filesystem block size that is stored in the superblock data structure and need not be read in explicitly.

ext2_block_to_path performs a step-by-step comparison. If the data block number is smaller than the number of direct blocks (EXT2_NDIR_BLOCKS), it is returned without modification because the block can be addressed directly.[16]

If not, a calculation is made — with the help of the block size — to determine how many pointers to blocks fit in a single block. The number of direct blocks is added to the result of the calculation to obtain the maximum possible number of blocks in a file whose contents can be addressed by means of simple indirection. If the number of the desired block is smaller than this value, an array with *two* block numbers is returned. The first entry contains the number of the simple indirection block, and the second specifies the address of the pointer in the indirection block.

The same scheme is adopted to cater for double and triple indirection. An additional entry is added to the returned array for each further level of indirection.

The number of array entries used to describe the position of a block in the indirection network is referred to as the *path length*. Logically, the path length increases as the number of indirection levels grows.

Up to now, use has been made only of the filesystem block size, and the filesystem has not had to perform actual I/O operations on the hard disk. To find the absolute address of a data block, the path defined in the path array must be followed, and this entails reading data from the hard disk.

ext2_get_branch in fs/ext2/inode.c follows a known path to finally arrive at a data block. This task is relatively straightforward. sb_bread reads the indirection blocks one after the other. The data in each block and the offset value known from the path are used to find the pointer to the next indirection block. This procedure is repeated until the code reaches a pointer to a data block that is returned as the result of the function. This absolute address is used by higher-level functions such as block_read_full_page to read the block contents.

Requesting New Blocks

The situation becomes more complicated when it is necessary to process a block that has not yet been allocated. Before this situation can arise, a process must write to a file, thereby enlarging it; whether classic system calls or memory mapping are used to do this is irrelevant. In all cases, ext2_get_blocks is invoked to request new blocks for the file. Conceptually, adding new blocks to a file is composed of four tasks:

❑   After detecting that new blocks are necessary, the kernel needs to decide if and how many levels of indirection are required to associate the new blocks with the file.

❑   Free blocks must be found on the storage medium and reserved.

❑   The freshly allocated blocks must be added to the block list of the file.

---

[16]Reminder: File blocks are numbered linearly starting at 0.

❑ To achieve better performance, the kernel also performs block reservation. This means that for regular files, a number of blocks is pre-allocated. If the need for further blocks arises, they are preferably allocated from the pre-allocated area.

The code flow diagram for `ext2_get_blocks` in Figure 9-10 shows how the first and third tasks are done: detecting that new blocks are required, deciding which level of indirection is required, and adding the newly allocated blocks with the file. I leave the remaining two tasks for below.

The following diagram is a little bit more complicated than the simpler version in Figure 9-9, where the fact that a data block could be located *outside* the available range is ignored. Figure 9-10 shows the situation that arises when `ext2_get_blocks` needs to request new blocks.

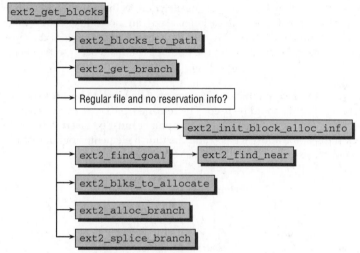

Figure 9-10: Code flow diagram for **ext2_get_blocks** (creation of a block).

The path array passed as a function argument is structured in accordance with the familiar method because it doesn't make any difference whether a block is available in a file or not. Only the position within the file and the block size of the filesystem must be known in order to set up the path.

The difference as compared with the `ext2_get_blocks` version above does not become apparent until the `ext2_get_branch` function is invoked. Whereas previously a NULL pointer was returned to indicate a successful search, the address of the last indirection block is now returned as the starting point for extending the file if the desired data block is outside the previously valid range.

To understand the situation where a new block is created, it is necessary to take a closer look at how `ext2_get_branch` works because a new data structure is introduced:

fs/ext2/inode.c
```
typedef struct {
        __le32   *p;
        __le32   key;
        struct buffer_head *bh;
} Indirect;
```

While key indicates the block number, p is a pointer to the address in memory where the key resides. A buffer head (bh) is used to keep the block data in memory.

In the case of a fully filled Indirect instance, the information on the block number is stored redundantly in key and in *p. This again becomes clear when we examine the auxiliary function to fill Indirect:

fs/ext2/inode.c
```
static inline void add_chain(Indirect *p, struct buffer_head *bh, u32 *v)
{
        p->key = *(p->p = v);
        p->bh = bh;
}
```

If, when traversing the block path, ext2_get_branch detects that there is no pointer to the next indirection level (or to a data block if direct allocation is used), an incomplete Indirect instance is returned. Although the p element points to the position where the number of the next indirection or data block should be located in the indirection block, the number itself is 0 because the block has not yet been allocated.

Figure 9-11 illustrates this fact graphically. The fourth data block to be addressed by the simple indirection block is not present but should be used. The returned Indirect instance contains a pointer to the position in the indirection block where the block number must be inserted (namely, 1,003 because the indirection block starts at the address 1,000 and the fourth element is of interest). However, the value of the key is 0 because the associated data block has not yet been allocated.

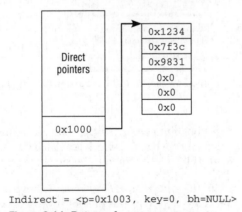

Indirect = <p=0x1003, key=0, bh=NULL>

Figure 9-11: Return of ext2_get_branch.

Now that the position in the indirection chain in which no further blocks are allocated is clear, the Second Extended Filesystem must find out where there is space in the partition to add one or more new blocks to the file. This is not a trivial task because ideally the blocks of a file should be contiguous or, if this is not feasible, at least as close together as possible. This ensures that fragmentation is minimized and results not only in better utilization of hard disk capacity but in faster read/write operations because read/write head travel is reduced.

Several steps are involved in searching for a new block. A search is first made for a *goal* block; from the perspective of the filesystem, this block is the ideal candidate for allocation. The search for a global block is based on general principles only and does not take account of the actual situation in the filesystem. The ext2_find_goal function is invoked to search for the best new block. When searching is performed, it is necessary to distinguish between two situations:

❑ When the block to be allocated logically immediately follows the block last allocated in the file (in other words, data are to be written contiguously), the filesystem tries to write to the next physical block on the hard disk. This is obvious — if data are stored sequentially in a file, they should if at all possible be stored contiguously on the hard disk.

❑ If the position of the new logical block is not immediately after the last allocated block, the ext2_find_near function is invoked to find the most suitable new block. Depending on the specific situation, it finds a block close to the indirection block or at least in the same cylinder group. I won't bother with the details here.

Once it has these two pieces of information (the position in the indirection chain in which there are no further data blocks, and the desired address of the new block), the kernel sets about reserving a block on the hard disk. Of course, there is no guarantee that the desired address is really free, so the kernel may have to be satisfied with poorer alternatives, which unavoidably entails data fragmentation.

Not only might new data blocks be required — it can also be the case that some blocks are required to hold indirection information. ext2_blks_to_allocate computes the *total* number of new blocks, that is, the sum of data and (single, double, and triple) indirection blocks. The allocation proper is then done by ext2_alloc_branch. The parameters passed to this function include the desired address of the new block, information on the last incomplete part of the indirection chain, and the number of indirection levels still missing up to the new data block. Expressed differently, the function returns a linked list of indirection and data blocks that can be added to the existing indirection list of the filesystem. Last but not least, ext2_slice_branch adds the resulting hierarchy (or, in the simplest case, the new data block) to the existing network and performs several relatively unimportant updates on Ext2 data structures.

Block Allocation

ext2_alloc_branch is responsible to allocate the required blocks for a given new path and set up the chain that connects them. At a first glance, this seems an easy task, as the code flow diagram in Figure 9-12 might suggest.

The function calls ext2_alloc_blocks, which, in turn relies on ext2_new_blocks to reserve the required new blocks. Since the function always allocates consecutive blocks, one single call might not be sufficient to obtain the total number of required blocks. If the filesystem becomes fragmented, it can be that no such consecutive region is available. However, this is no problem: ext2_new_block is called multiple times until at least the number of blocks that is required for the indirection mechanism has been allocated. The surplus blocks can be used as data blocks.

Finally, ext2_alloc_branch need only set up the Indirect instances for the indirection blocks, and it is done.

Obviously, the hard work is hidden in ext2_new_blocks. The code flow diagram in Figure 9-13 proves that this is really the case!

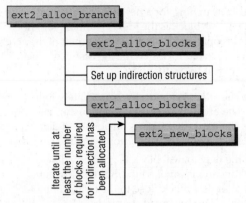

Figure 9-12: Code flow diagram for
`ext2_alloc_branch`.

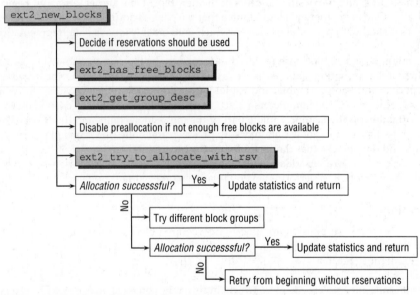

Figure 9-13: Code flow diagram for `ext2_new_blocks`.

Recall that Ext2 supports pre-allocation, and this needs to be partly handled in `ext2_new_blocks`. Since the mechanism is already complicated enough without the details of pre-allocation, let's first consider it without this extra complexity. We will come back to how pre-allocation works exactly afterward.

Consider the prototype of `ext2_new_blocks` (note that `ext2_fsblk_t` is `typedef`'d to `unsigned long` and represents a block number).

fs/ext2/balloc.c
```
ext2_fsblk_t ext2_new_blocks(struct inode *inode, ext2_fsblk_t goal,
                    unsigned long *count, int *errp)
{
...
```

inode represents the inode for which the allocation is performed, while count designates the desired number of blocks. Since the function returns the number of the first block in the allocated block sequence, possible error codes cannot be passed as a function result, thus the pointer errp is used. Finally, the goal parameter allows for specifying a *goal block*. This provides a hint to the allocation code about which block would be preferred. This is only a suggestion: Should this block not be available, then any other block can be selected.

First of all, the function decides if the pre-allocation mechanism should be used and a reserved, but not yet allocated area be created. The choice is simple: If the inode is equipped with information for pre-allocation, then use it; otherwise, not.

Allocations only make sense if the filesystem contains at least one free block, and ext2_has_free_blocks checks this. If the condition is not fulfilled, the allocation can immediately be canceled.

In a world where all wishes come true, the goal block will be free, but in reality, this need not be the case. In fact, the goal block need not even be a valid block at all, and the kernel needs to check this (es is the ext2_super_block instance for the filesystem under consideration).

fs/ext2/balloc.c
```
        if (goal < le32_to_cpu(es->s_first_data_block) ||
            goal >= le32_to_cpu(es->s_blocks_count))
                goal = le32_to_cpu(es->s_first_data_block);

        group_no = (goal - le32_to_cpu(es->s_first_data_block)) /
                    EXT2_BLOCKS_PER_GROUP(sb);
        goal_group = group_no;
retry_alloc:
        gdp = ext2_get_group_desc(sb, group_no, &gdp_bh);
```

If the goal block is not within a valid range, the first data block of the filesystem is picked as the new goal. In any case, the block group of the goal block is computed. ext2_get_group_desc provides the corresponding group descriptor.

Afterward, a little bookkeeping for the pre-allocation mechanism is again necessary. If reservations are enabled but the free space is not sufficient to fulfill it, then the mechanism is turned off. By calling ext2_try_to_allocate_with_rsv, the kernel then tries to actually reserve the desired data blocks — possibly using the reservation mechanism. As promised, this function is discussed below.

For now, let us just observe the two possible outcomes:

1. The allocation was successful. In this case, ext2_new_blocks needs to update the statistical information, but is otherwise done and can return to the caller.
2. If the request could not be satisfied in the current block group, then all other block groups are tried. If this still fails, the whole allocation is restarted *without* the pre-allocation mechanism in case it was still turned on at this point — recall that it might have been turned off by default or in the previous course of action.

Pre-allocation Handling

In the hierarchy of ext2 allocation functions, we've come as deep down as ext2_try_to_allocate_with_rsv. However, there's good news: The kernel source code cheers us up by remarking that this is "the main function used to allocate a new block and its reservation window." We're almost done! Note that now might also be a good opportunity to remember the pre-allocation data structures introduced in Section 9.2.2 since they form the core of the reservation window mechanism.

The code flow diagram for `ext2_try_to_allocate_rsv` is shown in Figure 9-14. Basically, the function handles some reservation window issues and passes the proper allocation down to `ext2_try_to_allocate`, the last link in the chain. `ext2_try_to_allocate_with_rsv` has no direct connection with the inode for which the allocation is performed, but the reservation window is passed as a parameter. If a `NULL` pointer is given instead, this means that the reservation mechanism is not supposed to be used.

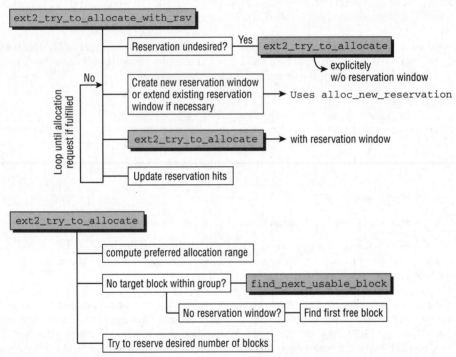

Figure 9-14: Code flow diagram for `ext2_try_to_allocate_with_rsv`.

Thus the first check is to determine whether using pre-allocation is desired or possible at all. Should this not be the case, then `ext2_try_to_allocate` can be called immediately. Likewise, the function also has a parameter for the reservation information, and if a `NULL` pointer is passed instead, no pre-allocation will be used. If a reservation window exists, the kernel checks if the pre-allocation information needs to be updated, and does so if necessary. In this case, `ext2_try_to_allocate` is called with the order to use the reservation window.

After calling `ext2_try_to_allocate`, the reservation hit statistics need to be updated by `ext2_try_to_allocate_with_rcv` in case an allocation could be performed in the allocation window. If the required number of blocks could be allocated, we are finished. Otherwise, the reservation window settings are readapted, and `ext2_try_to_allocate` is called again.

By what criteria does the kernel update the reservation window? Observe the allocation loop:

fs/etc2/balloc.c
```
static ext2_grpblk_t
ext2_try_to_allocate_with_rsv(struct super_block *sb, unsigned int group,
struct buffer_head *bitmap_bh, ext2_grpblk_t grp_goal,
struct ext2_reserve_window_node * my_rsv,
unsigned long *count)
{
...
group_first_block = ext2_group_first_block_no(sb, group);
group_last_block = group_first_block + (EXT2_BLOCKS_PER_GROUP(sb) - 1);
...
        while (1) {
                if (rsv_is_empty(&my_rsv->rsv_window) || (ret < 0) ||
                        !goal_in_my_reservation(&my_rsv->rsv_window,
                                                grp_goal, group, sb)) {
                        if (my_rsv->rsv_goal_size < *count)
                                my_rsv->rsv_goal_size = *count;
                        ret = alloc_new_reservation(my_rsv, grp_goal, sb,
                                                group, bitmap_bh);

                        if (!goal_in_my_reservation(&my_rsv->rsv_window,
                                                grp_goal, group, sb))
                                grp_goal = -1;
                } else if (grp_goal >= 0) {
                        int curr = my_rsv->rsv_end -
                                        (grp_goal + group_first_block) + 1;

                        if (curr < *count)
                                try_to_extend_reservation(my_rsv, sb,
                                                *count - curr);
                }

...

                ret = ext2_try_to_allocate(sb, group, bitmap_bh, grp_goal,
                                        &num, &my_rsv->rsv_window);
                if (ret >= 0) {
                        my_rsv->rsv_alloc_hit += num;
                        *count = num;
                        break; /* succeed */
                }
                num = *count;
        }
        return ret;
}
```

If either there is no reservation associated with the file (checked by rsv_is_empty) or the desired goal block is not within the current reservation window (checked by goal_in_my_reservation), the kernel needs to create a new reservation window. This task is delegated to alloc_new_reservation, which contains the goal block. A more detailed discussion of the function follows below. Although alloc_new_reservation will try to find a region that contains the goal block, this might not be possible. In this case, grp_goal is set to −1, which signifies that no desired goal should be used.

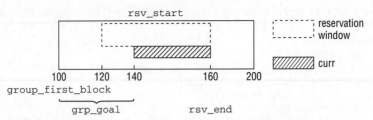

Figure 9-15: Check if a desired allocation can be fulfilled with a given reservation window.

If the file is equipped with a reservation window and a goal block is specified (as checked by the condition grp_goal > 0), the kernel has to check if the desired allocation will fit into the existing reservation. Starting from the desired allocation goal that specifies a block number *relative* to the beginning of the group, the code computes the number of blocks until the end of the block group. The calculation is illustrated in Figure 9-15. If the desired allocation as given by count is larger than the possible region, the reservation window is increased with try_to_extend_reservation. The function simply queries the pre-allocation data structures to see if no other reservation window prevents the current window to grow, and does so if possible.

Finally, the kernel can pass the allocation request together with the (possibly modified) reservation window to ext2_try_to_allocate. While the function guarantees that a consecutive number of blocks is allocated if some free space can be found, it cannot guarantee that the desired number of blocks is available. This has some implications on the returned values. While the first allocated block is returned as the direct function result, the number of allocated blocks must be passed upward via the pointer num.

If some space could be allocated, ret is larger than or equal to zero. The kernel then needs to update the allocation hit counter rsv_alloc_hit and return the number of allocated blocks via the count pointer. If the allocation has failed, the loop needs to start again. Since ret is negative in this case, the kernel allocates a new reservation window in the next run as guaranteed by the condition ret < 0 in the initial if conditional. Otherwise, everything runs again as described.

Finally, ext2_try_to_allocate is responsible for the low-level allocation that directly interacts with the block bitmaps. Recall that the function can work with a reservation window or not. The kernel now needs to search through the block bitmap, and thus an interval for the search needs to be determined. Note that the boundaries are specified *relative to the current block group*. This means that numbering starts from zero. A number of scenarios is distinguished, and Figure 9-16 illustrates various cases.

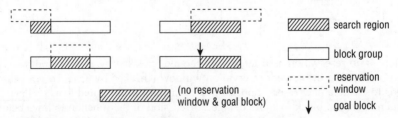

Figure 9-16: Search interval selection for block allocation in ext2_try_to_allocate.

❏ If a reservation window is available and the reservation starts within the block group, the absolute block number needs to be converted into a relative start position. For instance, if the block group starts at block 100 and the reservation window at block 120, the relative start block within the group is block 20.

If the reservation window starts *before* the block group, block number 0 is used as the starting point.

If the reservation window goes beyond the current block group, the search interval is restricted to the last block of the block group.

❏ If no reservation window is present, but a goal block is given, the goal can be directly used as the start block.

If no reservation window is available and no goal block is specified, the search starts from block 0. In both cases, the end of the block group is used as the end block of the search.

`ext2_try_to_allocate` then proceeds as follows:

fs/ext2/balloc.c
```
# static int
# ext2_try_to_allocate(struct super_block *sb, int group,
# struct buffer_head *bitmap_bh, ext2_grpblk_t grp_goal,
# unsigned long *count,
# struct ext2_reserve_window *my_rsv)
# {
...
        ext2_grpblk_t start, end;
...
        /* Determine start and end */
...
repeat:
        if (grp_goal < 0) {
                grp_goal = find_next_usable_block(start, bitmap_bh, end);
...
                if (!my_rsv) {
                        int i;

                        for (i = 0; i < 7 && grp_goal > start &&
                                        !ext2_test_bit(grp_goal - 1,
                                                        bitmap_bh->b_data);
                                i++, grp_goal--)
                                ;

                }
        }
start = grp_goal;
...
```

If no goal block was given (`grp_goal < 0`), the kernel uses `find_next_usable_block` to find the first free bit in the previously selected interval in the block allocation bitmap.

`find_next_usable_block` first performs a bitwise search up to the next 64-bit boundary.[17] This tries to find a free block near the allocation goal. If one is available, the function returns the bit position.

---

[17]If the starting block is zero, then `find_next_usable_block` assumes that no goal block was given and does not perform the near-goal search. Instead, it starts immediately with the next search step.

If no free bit is found near the desired goal, the search is not performed bitwise, but bytewise to increase performance. A free byte corresponds to eight successive zeros or eight free file blocks. If a free byte is found, the address of the first bit is returned. As a last resort, a bitwise scan over the whole range is performed. This equates to searching for a single, isolated free block and is, of course, the worst-case scenario, which, unfortunately, cannot always be avoided.

Let us go back to `ext2_try_to_allocate`. Since the bit might originate from a bytewise search, the last seven preceding bits are scanned for a free area. (A larger number of preceding bits is not possible because the kernel would then have found a free byte in the previous step.) The newly allocated block is always shifted as far to the left as possible to ensure that the free area to its right is as large as possible.

What now remains to be done is a simple bitwise traversal of the block bitmap. In each step, a block is added to the allocation if the bit is not set. Recall that allocating a block is equivalent to setting the corresponding bit in the block bitmap to one. The traversal stops when either an occupied block is encountered or a sufficient number of blocks has been allocated.

fs/ext2/balloc.c

```
        if (ext2_set_bit_atomic(sb_bgl_lock(EXT2_SB(sb), group), grp_goal,
                                                bitmap_bh->b_data)) {
            /*
             * The block was allocated by another thread, or it was
             * allocated and then freed by another thread
             */
            start++;
            grp_goal++;
            if (start >= end)
                    goto fail_access;
            goto repeat;
        }
        num++;
        grp_goal++;
        while (num < *count && grp_goal < end
                && !ext2_set_bit_atomic(sb_bgl_lock(EXT2_SB(sb), group),
                                    grp_goal, bitmap_bh->b_data)) {
            num++;
            grp_goal++;
        }
        *count = num;
        return grp_goal - num;
fail_access:
        *count = num;
        return -1;
    }
```

The only complication stems from the fact that the initial bit might have been allocated by another process between the time it was chosen and when the kernel tries to allocate it. In this case, both the starting position and group goal are increased by 1, and the search started again.

Creating New Reservations

Above, it was mentioned that `alloc_new_reservation` is employed to create new reservation windows. This is an important task now discussed in detail. An overview of the function is presented in Figure 9-17.

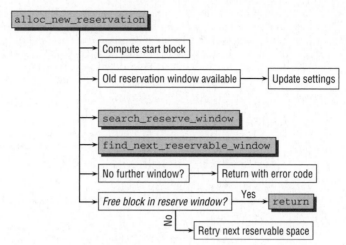

Figure 9-17: Code flow diagram for `alloc_new_reservation`.

First, `alloc_new_reservation` determines the block from which the search for a reservation window starts.

fs/ext2/balloc.c

```
static int alloc_new_reservation(struct ext2_reserve_window_node *my_rsv,
            ext2_grpblk_t grp_goal, struct super_block *sb,
            unsigned int group, struct buffer_head *bitmap_bh)
{
        struct ext2_reserve_window_node *search_head;
        ext2_fsblk_t group_first_block, group_end_block, start_block;
        ext2_grpblk_t first_free_block;
        struct rb_root *fs_rsv_root = &EXT2_SB(sb)->s_rsv_window_root;
        unsigned long size;
        int ret;

        group_first_block = ext2_group_first_block_no(sb, group);
        group_end_block = group_first_block + (EXT2_BLOCKS_PER_GROUP(sb) - 1);

        if (grp_goal < 0)
                start_block = group_first_block;
        else
                start_block = grp_goal + group_first_block;

        size = my_rsv->rsv_goal_size;
    ...
```

If the inode is already equipped with a reservation window, the allocation hit counter is evaluated and the window resized accordingly:

fs/ext2/balloc.c

```
        if (!rsv_is_empty(&my_rsv->rsv_window)) {
                /*
                 * if the old reservation is cross group boundary
                 * and if the goal is inside the old reservation window,
```

627

```
       * we will come here when we just failed to allocate from
       * the first part of the window. We still have another part
       * that belongs to the next group. In this case, there is no
       * point to discard our window and try to allocate a new one
       * in this group(which will fail). we should
       * keep the reservation window, just simply move on.
       */

     if ((my_rsv->rsv_start <= group_end_block) &&
                   (my_rsv->rsv_end > group_end_block) &&
                   (start_block >= my_rsv->rsv_start))
              return -1;

     if ((my_rsv->rsv_alloc_hit >
          (my_rsv->rsv_end - my_rsv->rsv_start + 1) / 2)) {
            /*
             * if the previously allocation hit ratio is
             * greater than 1/2, then we double the size of
             * the reservation window the next time,
             * otherwise we keep the same size window
             */
            size = size * 2;
            if (size > EXT2_MAX_RESERVE_BLOCKS)
                   size = EXT2_MAX_RESERVE_BLOCKS;
            my_rsv->rsv_goal_size= size;
     }
  }
...
```

The kernel code precisely states what is going on (and especially why this is going on), and for a change, there's nothing further to add.

If new boundaries for the window have been computed (or if there has not been a reservation window before), search_reserve_window checks if a reserve window that contains the allocation goal is already present. If this is not the case, the window before the allocation goal is returned. The selected window is used as a starting point for find_next_reservable_window, which tries to find a suitable new reservation window. Finally, the kernel checks if the window contains at least a single free bit. If not, it does not make any sense to pre-allocate space, so the window is discarded. Otherwise, the function returns successfully.

Creating and Deleting Inodes

Inodes must also be created and deleted by low-level functions of the Ext2 filesystem. This is necessary when a file or directory is created (or deleted) — the core code of the two variants hardly differs.

Let's begin with the creation of a file or directory. As explained in Chapter 8, the open and mkdir system calls are available for this purpose. They work through the various functions of the virtual filesystem to arrive at the create and mkdir functions, each of which is pointed to by a function pointer in the file-specific instance of inode_operations. The ext2_create and ext2_mkdir functions are inserted as described in Section 9.2.4. Both functions are located in fs/ext2/namei.c. The flow of both actions is shown in the code flow diagrams in Figures 9-18 and 9-19.

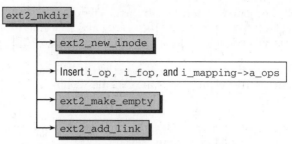

Figure 9-18: Code flow diagram for `ext2_mkdir`.

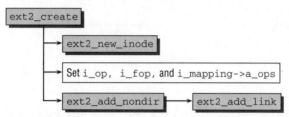

Figure 9-19: Code flow diagram for `ext2_create`.

Let us first examine how new directories are created using `mkdir`. The kernel passes via the VFS function `vfs_mkdir` to the `ext2_mkdir` low-level function with the following signature.

fs/ext2/namei.c
```
static int ext2_mkdir(struct inode * dir, struct dentry * dentry, int mode)
```

`dir` is the directory in which the new subdirectory is to be created, and `dentry` specifies the pathname of the new directory. `mode` specifies the access mode of the new directory.

Once `ext2_new_inode` has reserved a new inode at a suitable place on the hard disk (the section below describes how the kernel finds the most suitable location with the help of the Orlov allocator), it is provided with the appropriate file, inode, and address space operations.

fs/ext2/namei.c
```
static int ext2_mkdir(struct inode * dir, struct dentry * dentry, int mode)
{
...
        inode->i_op = &ext2_dir_inode_operations;
        inode->i_fop = &ext2_dir_operations;
        if (test_opt(inode->i_sb, NOBH))
                inode->i_mapping->a_ops = &ext2_nobh_aops;
        else
                inode->i_mapping->a_ops = &ext2_aops;

...
}
```

ext2_make_empty fills the inode with the default . and .. entries by generating the corresponding file structures and writing them to the data block. Then ext2_add_link adds the new directory to the existing directory data of the initial inode in the format described in Section 9.2.2.

New files are created in a similar way. The sys_open system call arrives at vfs_create, which again invokes the ext2_create low-level function of the Ext2 filesystem.

Once it has allocated a new inode on the hard disk by means of ext2_new_inode, the appropriate file, inode, and address space structures are added, this time using the variants for regular files, that is, ext2_file_inode_operations and ext2_file_operations.

> **There is no difference between the address space operations for directory inodes and file inodes.**

Responsibility for adding the new file to the directory hierarchy is assumed by ext2_add_nondir, which immediately invokes the familiar ext2_add_link function.

Registering Inodes

When directories and files are created, the ext2_new_inode function is used to find a free inode for the new filesystem entry. However, the search strategy varies according to situation — this can be distinguished by the mode argument (S_IFDIR is set for directories but not for regular files).

The search itself is not performance-critical, but it is very important for filesystem performance that the inode be optimally positioned to permit rapid access to data. For this reason, this section is devoted to an examination of the inode distribution strategy adopted by the kernel.

The kernel applies three different strategies:

1. Orlov allocation for directory inodes.
2. Classic allocation for directory inodes. This is only used if the oldalloc option is passed to the kernel, which disables Orlov allocation. Normally, Orlov allocation is the default strategy.
3. Inode allocation for regular files.

The three options are investigated below.

Orlov Allocation

A standard scheme proposed and implemented for the OpenBSD kernel by Grigoriv Orlov is used to find a directory inode. The Linux version was developed later. The goal of the allocator is to ensure that directory inodes of child directories are in the same block group as the parent directory so that they are physically closer to each other and costly hard disk seek operations are minimized. Of course, not *all* directory inodes should end up in the same block group because they would then be too far away from their associated data.

The scheme distinguishes whether a new directory is to be created directly in the (global) root directory or at another point in the filesystem, as the code flow diagram for find_group_orlov in Figure 9-20 shows.

While entries for subdirectories should be as close to the parent directory as possible, subdirectories of the filesystem root should be diverted as well as possible. Otherwise, directories would again accumulate in a distinguished block group.

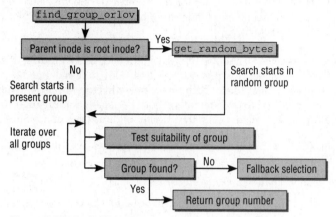

Figure 9-20: Code flow diagram for `find_group_orlov`.

Let's first take a look at the standard situation in which a new subdirectory is to be created at some point in the directory tree (and not in the root directory). This corresponds to the right-hand branch in Figure 9-20. The kernel computes several variables used as criteria to establish the suitability of a block group to accommodate the desired directory node (I took the liberty of rearranging the code a little to make it easier to understand):

fs/ext2/ialloc.c
```
int ngroups = sbi->s_groups_count;
int inodes_per_group = EXT2_INODES_PER_GROUP(sb);

freei = percpu_counter_read_positive(&sbi->s_freeinodes_counter);
avefreei = freei / ngroups;
free_blocks = percpu_counter_read_positive(&sbi->s_freeblocks_counter);
avefreeb = free_blocks / ngroups;
ndirs = percpu_counter_read_positive(&sbi->s_dirs_counter);

blocks_per_dir = (le32_to_cpu(es->s_blocks_count)-free_blocks) / ndirs;

max_dirs = ndirs / ngroups + inodes_per_group / 16;
min_inodes = avefreei - inodes_per_group / 4;
min_blocks = avefreeb - EXT2_BLOCKS_PER_GROUP(sb) / 4;

max_debt = EXT2_BLOCKS_PER_GROUP(sb) / max(blocks_per_dir, BLOCK_COST);
if (max_debt * INODE_COST > inodes_per_group)
        max_debt = inodes_per_group / INODE_COST;
if (max_debt > 255)
        max_debt = 255;
if (max_debt == 0)
        max_debt = 1;
```

avefreei and `avefreeb` denote the number of free inodes and blocks (which can be read from the approximative per-CPU counters associated with the superblock) divided by the number of groups. The values thus specify the average number of free inodes and blocks per group. This explains the prefix `ave`.

`max_dirs` specifies the absolute upper limit for the number of directory inodes in a block group. `min_inodes` and `min_blocks` define the minimum number of free inodes or blocks in a group before a new directory may be created.

`debt` is a numeric value between 0 and 255. It is saved for each block group in the `ext2_sb_info` filesystem instance that makes the `s_debts` array available (`ext2_sb_info` is defined in Section 9.2.2). The value is incremented by 1 (in `ext2_new_inode`) each time a new directory inode is created, and is decremented by 1 when the inode is required for a different purpose — usually for a regular file. The value of `debt` is therefore an indication of the ratio between the number of directories and inodes in a block group.

Starting at the block group of the parent entry, the kernel iterates over all block groups until the following criteria are met:

❑ There are no more than `max_ndir` directories.

❑ No less than `min_inodes` inodes and `min_blocks` data blocks are free.

❑ The `debt` value does not exceed `max_debt`; that is, the number of directories does not get out of hand.

If just one of these criteria is *not* satisfied, the kernel skips the current block group and checks the next:

fs/ext2/ialloc.c
```
for (i = 0; i < ngroups; i++) {
        group = (parent_group + i) % ngroups;
        desc = ext2_get_group_desc (sb, group, NULL);
        if (!desc || !desc->bg_free_inodes_count)
                continue;
        if (sbi->s_debts[group] >= max_debt)
                continue;
        if (le16_to_cpu(desc->bg_used_dirs_count) >= max_dirs)
                continue;
        if (le16_to_cpu(desc->bg_free_inodes_count) < min_inodes)
                continue;
        if (le16_to_cpu(desc->bg_free_blocks_count) < min_blocks)
                continue;
        goto found;
}
```

Division without a remainder (%) at the beginning of the loop ensures that the search is resumed at the first block group once the last block group of the partition is reached.

Once a suitable group is found (which is automatically as close as possible to the parent group unless the inode there has been removed), the kernel need only update the corresponding statistics counters and return the group number. If no group matches the requirements, the search is repeated with the help of a less demanding "fallback" algorithm:

fs/ext2/ialloc.c
```
fallback:
for (i = 0; i < ngroups; i++) {
```

```
        group = (parent_group + i) % ngroups;
        desc = ext2_get_group_desc (sb, group, &bh);
        if (!desc || !desc->bg_free_inodes_count)
                continue;
        if (le16_to_cpu(desc->bg_free_inodes_count) >= avefreei)
                goto found;
}

...

return -1;
```

Again, the kernel starts at the parent group. The directories are scanned one after the other. However, this time the kernel accepts the first group that contains more than the average number of inodes (specified by avefreei).

This method is modified slightly when a new subdirectory is created in the root directory of the system, as illustrated by the left-hand branch of the code flow diagram in Figure 9-20 above.

To spread the directory inodes across the filesystem as uniformly as possible, the immediate subdirectories of the root directory are distributed statistically over the block groups. The kernel uses get_random_bytes to select a random number that is trimmed to the maximum number of existing block groups by dividing (without remainder) by ngroups. The kernel then iterates as follows over the randomly selected groups and subsequent groups:

fs/ext2/ialloc.c
```
get_random_bytes(&group, sizeof(group));
parent_group = (unsigned)group % ngroups;
for (i = 0; i < ngroups; i++) {
        group = (parent_group + i) % ngroups;
        desc = ext2_get_group_desc (sb, group, &bh);
        if (!desc || !desc->bg_free_inodes_count)
            continue;
        if (le16_to_cpu(desc->bg_used_dirs_count) >= best_ndir)
                continue;
        if (le16_to_cpu(desc->bg_free_inodes_count) < avefreei)
                continue;
        if (le16_to_cpu(desc->bg_free_blocks_count) < avefreeb)
                continue;
        best_group = group;
        best_ndir = le16_to_cpu(desc->bg_used_dirs_count);
        best_desc = desc;
        best_bh = bh;
}
```

While, again, the minimum number of free inodes or blocks must not be below the limit set by avefreei and avefreeb, the kernel also ensures that the number of free directories is not greater than or equal to best_ndir. The value is initially set to the value of inodes_per_group but is always updated to the lowest value encountered by the kernel during its search. The winner is the block group that has the fewest entries and that also satisfies the other two conditions.

If a suitable group is found, the kernel updates the statistics and returns the group number selected. Otherwise, the fallback mechanism comes into effect to find a less qualified block group.

Classic Directory Allocation

Kernel versions up to and including 2.4 did not use Orlov allocation, but the technique described below, called *classic* allocation. Ext2 filesystems can be mounted using the `oldalloc` option, which sets the `EXT2_MOUNT_OLDALLOC` bit in the `s_mount_opt` field of the superblock. The kernel then no longer uses the Orlov allocator but resorts to the classic scheme of allocation.[18]

How does the classic scheme work? The block groups of the system are scanned in a forward search, and particular attention is paid to two conditions:

1. Free space should still be available in the block group.

2. The number of directory inodes should be as small as possible compared to other inodes in the block group.

In this scheme, directory inodes are typically spread as uniformly as possible across the entire filesystem.

If none of the block groups satisfies requirements, the kernel restricts selection to groups with above average amounts of free space and from these chooses those with the fewest directory inodes.

Inode Allocation for Other Files

A simpler scheme known as *quadratic hashing* is applied when searching for an inode for regular files, links, and all file types other than directories. It is based on a forward search starting at the block group of the directory inode of the directory in which the new file is to be created. The first block group found with a free inode is reserved.

The block group in which the directory inode is located is searched first. Let's assume its group ID is start. If it does not have a free inode, the kernel scans the block group with the number $start + 2^0$, then $start + 2^0 + 2^1$, $start + 2^0 + 2^1 + 2^2$, and so on. A higher power of 2 is added to the group number in each step, which results in the sequence $1, 1 + 2, 1 + 2 + 4, 1 + 2 + 4 + 8, \cdots = 1, 3, 7, 15, \ldots$.

Usually, this method quickly finds a free inode. However, if no free inode is returned on an (almost hopelessly) overfilled filesystem, the kernel scans *all* block groups in succession to ensure that every effort is made to find a free inode. Again, the first block group with a free inode is selected. If absolutely no inodes are free, the action is aborted with a corresponding error code.[19]

Deleting Inodes

Both directory inodes and file inodes can be deleted, and, from the perspective of the filesystem, both actions are much simpler than allocating inodes.

Let us first look at how directories are deleted. After the appropriate system call (`rmdir`) has been invoked, the code meanders through the kernel and finally arrives at the `rmdir` function pointer of the `inode_operations` structure, which, for the Ext2 filesystem, contains `ext2_rmdir` from `fs/ext2/namei.c`.

---

[18]In terms of compatibility with old kernel versions, it makes no difference whether directory inodes are reserved with the Orlov allocator or not because the format of the filesystem remains unchanged.

[19]In practice, this situation hardly ever occurs because the hard disk would have to contain a gigantic number of small files, and this is very rarely the case on standard systems. A more realistic situation (often encountered in practice) is that all data blocks are full, but a large number of inodes are still free.

Two main actions are needed to delete a directory:

1. First, the entry in the directory inode of the parent directory is deleted.

2. Then the data blocks assigned on the hard disk (an inode and the associated data blocks with the directory entries) are released.

As the code flow diagram in Figure 9-21 shows, this is done in a few steps.

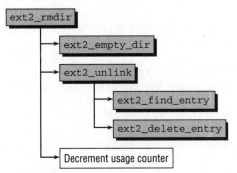

**Figure 9-21: Code flow diagram for
`ext2_rmdir`.**

To ensure that the directory to be deleted no longer contains any files, the contents of its data block are checked using the `ext2_empty_dir` function. If the kernel finds only the entries for `.` and `..`, the directory is released for deletion. Otherwise, the action is aborted, and an error code (`-ENOTEMPTY`) is returned.

Removal of the directory entry from the parent directory is delegated to the `ext2_unlink` function. This entry is found in the directory table using the `ext2_find_entry` function, which scans the individual directory entries one after the other (the scheme adopted for storing entries is described in Section 9.2.2). If a matching entry is found, the function returns an instance of `ext2_dir_entry_2` to identify it uniquely.

`ext2_delete_entry` removes the entry from the directory table. As described in Section 9.2.2, the data are not physically deleted from the table. Instead, the `rec_len` field of the `ext2_dir_entry_2` structure is set in such a way that the entry is skipped when the table is traversed. As already noted, this approach yields substantial benefits in terms of speed, as actual deletion would necessitate rewriting a large amount of data.

This has both advantages and disadvantages. By inspecting the filesystem structures on the hard disk (assuming the corresponding permissions to read and write raw data on the partition) it is possible to recover a deleted file by reactivating the directory entry by resetting the `rec_len` field of its predecessor — if, of course, the allocated blocks have not been overwritten with other data in the meantime. If sensitive data are deleted, this can prove to be a final lifeline and, of course, a source of danger because a little technical know-how is all that is needed to access the data if the data blocks have not yet been overwritten.[20]

The kernel has now removed the directory entry from the filesystem, but the data blocks for the inode and directory contents are still marked as occupied. When are they released?

---

[20]Explicitly overwriting the file with null bytes before deletion is a remedy.

In this context, care should be exercised because of the structure of UNIX filesystems, as explained in Chapter 8. If hard links are used, users have access to inodes (and therefore to the associated data blocks) under several names in the system. However, the nlink counter in the inode structure keeps a record of how many hard links point to an inode.

The filesystem code decrements this counter by 1 each time a link to the inode is deleted. When the counter value reaches 0, there are no remaining hard links to the inode, and it can therefore be finally released. Once again it should be noted that only the corresponding bit in the inode bitmap is set to 0; the associated data are still present in the block and can potentially be used to reconstruct the file contents.

> The data blocks associated with the inode have not yet been released. This is not done until all references to the inode data structure have been returned with iput.

What is the difference between deleting a regular file and deleting a directory? Most of the above actions (with the exception of ext2_empty_dir) do not specifically relate to directories and can be used for general inode types. In fact, the procedure used to delete non-directories is very similar to the one described above. Starting with the unlink system call, the VFS vfs_unlink function is invoked to initiate the file-specific inode_operations->unlink operation. For the Second Extended Filesystem, this operation is ext2_unlink, which is described above. Everything said there also applies for deleting regular files, links, and so on.

Removing Data Blocks

In the delete operations described above, the data blocks remain untouched, partly because of the hard link problem. Removal of data blocks is closely associated with the reference counting of inode objects because two conditions must be satisfied before the data blocks can actually be deleted:

1. The link counter nlink must be zero to ensure that there are no references to the data in the filesystem.

2. The usage counter (i_count) of the inode structure must be flushed from memory.

The kernel uses the iput function to decrement the reference counter for the memory object. It therefore makes sense to introduce a check at this point to establish whether the inode is still needed and to remove it if not. This is a standard function of the virtual filesystem not discussed in detail here because the only aspect of interest is that the kernel invokes the ext2_delete_inode function to release the data associated with the inode on the hard disk (iput also returns memory data structures and memory pages reserved for data). This function builds primarily on two other functions — ext2_truncate, which releases the data blocks associated with the inode (regardless of whether the inode represents a directory or a regular file); and ext2_free_inode, which releases the memory space occupied by the inode itself.

> **Neither function deletes the space occupied on the hard disk or overwrites it with null bytes. They simply release the corresponding positions in the block or inode bitmap.**

Since both functions reverse the technique used to create files, their implementation need not be discussed here.

Address Space Operations

In Section 9.2.4, the address space operations associated with the Ext2 filesystem are discussed. For the most part, functions whose names are prefixed with `ext2_` are assigned to the individual function pointers. At first glance, it could therefore be assumed that they are all special implementations for the Second Extended Filesystem.

However, this is not the case. Most of the functions make use of standard implementations of the virtual filesystem, which uses the function discussed in Section 9.2.4 as an interface to the low-level code. For example, the implementation of `ext2_readpage` is as follows:

fs/ext2/inode.c
```
static int ext2_readpage(struct file *file, struct page *page)
{
        return mpage_readpage(page, ext2_get_block);
}
```

This is simply a transparent front end for the `mpage_readpage` standard function (introduced in Chapter 16) whose parameters are a pointer to `ext2_get_block` and the memory page to be processed.

`ext2_writepage` is used to write memory pages and is similar in terms of its implementation:

fs/ext2/inode.c
```
static int ext2_writepage(struct page *page, struct writeback_control *wbc)
{
        return block_write_full_page(page, ext2_get_block, wbc);
}
```

Again, a standard function described in Chapter 16 is used. This function is associated with the low-level implementation of the Ext2 filesystem using `ext2_get_block`.

Most other address space functions provided by the Ext2 filesystem are implemented via similar front ends that use `ext2_get_block` as a go-between. It is therefore not necessary to discuss additional Ext2-specific implementations because the functions described in Chapter 8 together with the information on `ext2_get_block` in Section 9.2.4 are all we need to know about address space operations.

9.3 Third Extended Filesystem

The third extension to the Ext filesystem, logically known as *Ext3*, features a *journal* in which actions performed on the filesystem data are saved. This helps to considerably shorten the run time of `fsck` following a system crash.[21] Since the underlying filesystem concepts not related to the new journal mechanism have remained unchanged in the third version of the filesystem, I will discuss only the new Ext3 capabilities. However, for reasons of space, I will not delve too deeply into their technical implementation.

The transaction concept originates from the database sector, where it helps guarantee data consistency if operations are not completed. The same consistency problem (which is not specific to Ext) arises in

---

[21]On filesystems with several hundred gigabytes, consistency checks may take a few hours depending on system speed. This downtime is not acceptable on servers. But even PC users appreciate the fact that consistency checks take just a few seconds rather than several minutes.

filesystems. How can the correctness and consistency of metadata be ensured if filesystem operations are interrupted unintentionally — for example, in the event of a power outage or if a user switches a computer off without shutting it down first?

9.3.1 Concepts

The basic idea of Ext3 is to regard each operation on the filesystem metadata as a *transaction* that is saved in a *journal* before it is performed. Once the transaction has terminated (i.e., when the desired modifications to the metadata have been made), the associated information is removed from the journal. If a system error occurs after transaction data have been written to the journal — but before (or during) performance of the actual operations — the pending operations are carried out in their entirety the next time the filesystem is mounted. The filesystem is then automatically in a consistent state. If the interruption occurs *before* the transaction is written to the journal, the operation itself is not performed because the information on it is lost when the system is restarted, but at least filesystem consistency is retained.

However, Ext3 cannot perform miracles. It is still possible to lose data because of a system crash. Nevertheless, the filesystem can always be restored to a consistent state very quickly afterward.

The additional overhead needed to log transactions is, of course, reflected in the performance of Ext3, which does not quite match that of Ext2. The kernel is able to access the Ext3 filesystem in three different ways in order to strike a suitable balance between performance and data integrity in all situations:

1. In *writeback* mode, only changes to the metadata are logged to the journal. Operations on useful data bypass the journal. This mode guarantees highest performance but lowest data protection.

2. In *ordered* mode only changes to the metadata are logged to the journal. However, changes to useful data are grouped and are always made *before* operations are performed on the metadata. This mode is therefore slightly slower than Writeback mode.

3. In *journal* mode, changes not only to metadata but also to useful data are written to the journal. This guarantees the highest level of data protection but is by far the slowest mode (except in a few pathological situations). The chance of losing data is minimized.

The desired mode is specified in the `data` parameter when the filesystem is mounted. The default is `ordered`.

As already stated, the Ext3 filesystem is designed to be fully compatible with Ext2 — not only downward but also (as far as possible) upward. The journal therefore resides in a special file with (as usual) its own inode. This enables Ext3 filesystems to be mounted on systems that support only Ext2. Even existing Ext2 partitions can be converted to Ext3 quickly and, above all, without the need for complicated data copying operations — a major consideration on server systems.

The journal can be held not only in a special file but also on a separate partition, but the details are not discussed here.

The kernel includes a layer called a *journaling block device* (JBD) layer to handle journals and associated operations. Although this layer can be used on different filesystems, currently it is used only by Ext3. All other journaling filesystems such as ReiserFS, XFS, and JFS have their own mechanisms. In the sections below, therefore, JBD and Ext3 are regarded as a single unit.

Log Records, Handles, and Transactions

Transactions are not a monolithic structure used to implement the transaction concept. Owing to the structure of filesystems (and also for performance reasons), it is necessary to break a transaction down into smaller units, as shown in Figure 9-22.

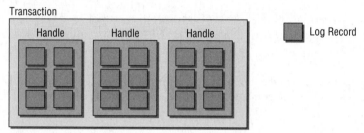

Figure 9-22: Interaction of transactions, log records, and handles.

❑ *Log records* are the smallest units that can be logged. Each represents an individual update to a block.

❑ *(Atomic) handles* group together several log records on the system level. For example, if a write request is issued using the `write` system call, all log records involved in this operation are grouped into a handle.

❑ *Transactions* are groupings of several handles that ensure better performance.

9.3.2 Data Structures

Whereas transactions include data with system-wide validity, each handle is always associated with a specific process. For this reason, the familiar task structure discussed in Chapter 2 includes an element that points to the current process handle:

```
<sched.h>
struct task_struct {
...
/* journaling file system info */
        void *journal_info;
...
}
```

The JBD layer automatically assumes responsibility for converting the `void` pointer to a pointer to `handle_t`. The `journal_current_handle` auxiliary function is used to read the active handle of the current process.

`handle_t` is a `typedef` to the `struct handle_s` data type used to define a handle (a simplified version is shown):

<jbd.h>
```
typedef struct handle_s          handle_t;        /* Atomic operation type */
```

<jbd.h>
```
struct handle_s
{
        /* Which compound transaction is this update a part of? */
        transaction_t         *h_transaction;

        /* Number of remaining buffers we are allowed to dirty: */
        int                   h_buffer_credits;
...
};
```

`h_transaction` is a pointer to the transaction data structure with which the handle is associated, and `h_buffer_credits` specifies how many free buffers are still available for journal operations (discussed shortly).

The kernel provides the `journal_start` and `journal_stop` functions that are used in pairs to label a code section whose operation is to be regarded as atomic by the journal layer:

```
handle_t *handle = journal_start(journal, nblocks);
/* Perform operations to be regarded as atomic */
journal_stop(handle);
```

The functions can be nested, but it must be ensured that `journal_stop` is invoked the same number of times as `journal_start`. The kernel provides the wrapper function `ext3_journal_start`, which takes a pointer to the inode in question as a parameter to infer the associated journal. With this information, `journal_start` is called. While `journal_start` is usually not used directly, `ext3_journal_start` is used all over the Ext3 code.

Each handle consists of various log operations, each of which has its own buffer head (see Chapter 16) to save the change — even if only a single bit is modified in the underlying filesystem. What appears at first glance to be a massive waste of memory is compensated by higher performance because buffers are processed very efficiently.

The data structure is defined (in greatly simplified form) as follows:

<journal_head.h>
```
struct journal_head {
        struct buffer_head *b_bh;

        transaction_t *b_transaction;
        struct journal_head *b_tnext, *b_tprev;
```

❑   `b_bh` points to the buffer head that contains the operation data.

❑   `b_transaction` references the transaction to which the log entry is assigned.

❑   `b_tnext` and `b_tprev` help implement a doubly linked list of all logs associated with an atomic operation.

The JBD layer provides `journal_dirty_metadata` to write modified metadata to the journal:

fs/jbd/transaction.c
```
int journal_dirty_metadata(handle_t *handle, struct buffer_head *bh)
```

The matching `journal_dirty_data` function writes useful data to the journal and is used in `data` mode.

Transactions are represented by a dedicated data structure; again a much simplified version is shown:

<jbd.h>
```
typedef transaction_s transaction_t;

struct transaction_s
{
        journal_t               *t_journal;
        tid_t                   t_tid;

        enum {
                T_RUNNING,
...
                T_FLUSH,
                T_COMMIT,
                T_FINISHED
        }                       t_state;

        struct journal_head     *t_buffers;
        unsigned long           t_expires;
        int t_handle_count;
};
```

❑   `t_journal` is a pointer to the journal to which the transaction data are written (for the sake of simplicity, the data structure used is not discussed because it is overburdened with technical details).

❑   Each transaction can have different states that are held in `t_state`:

    ❑   `T_RUNNING` indicates that new atomic handles can be added to the journal.

    ❑   `T_FLUSH` indicates that log entries are being written at the moment.

    ❑   `T_COMMIT` indicates when all data have been written to disk, but the metadata still need to be processed.

    ❑   `T_FINISHED` indicates that all log entries have been written safely to disk.

❑   `t_buffers` points to the buffers associated with the transaction.

❑   `t_expires` specifies the time by which the transaction data must have been physically written to the journal. The kernel uses a timer that expires by default 5 seconds after the transaction has been generated.

❑   `t_handle_count` indicates the number of handles associated with the transaction.

The Ext3 code uses ''checkpoints'' at which a check is made to ascertain whether the changes in the journal have been written to the filesystem. If they have, the data in the journal are no longer needed and can be removed. During normal operation, the contents of the journal play no active role. Only if a system crash occurs are the journal data used to reconstruct changes to the filesystem and return it to a consistent state.

As compared to the original definition in Ext2, several elements have been added to the superblock data structure of Ext3 to support the journal functions:

```
<ext3_fs_sb.h>

struct ext3_sb_info {
...
        /* Journaling */
        struct inode * s_journal_inode;
        struct journal_s * s_journal;
        unsigned long s_commit_interval;
        struct block_device *journal_bdev;
};
```

As noted, the journal can be held both in a file and on its own partition. Depending on the option chosen, either `s_journal_inode` or `journal_bdev` is used to reference its location. `s_commit_interval` specifies the frequency with which data are transferred from memory into the journal, and `s_journal` points to the journal data structure.

9.4 Summary

Filesystems are used to organize file data on physical block devices like hard disks to store information persistently across reboots. The second and third extended filesystems have been the standard working horses of Linux for many years, and you have seen their implementation and how they represent data on disks in detail.

After describing the basic challenges that filesystems have to face, you have seen the on-disk and in-kernel structures of the second extended file system. You have learned how filesystem objects are managed by inodes, and how data blocks that provide storage space for files are handled. Various important filesystem operations like creating new directories were also discussed in detail.

Finally, you have been introduced to the journaling mechanisms of Ext3, the evolutionary successor of Ext2.

10

Filesystems without Persistent Storage

Traditionally, filesystems are used to store data persistently on block devices. However, it is also possible to use filesystems to organize, present, and exchange information that is not stored on block devices, but dynamically generated by the kernel. This chapter examines some of them:

❑ The *proc filesystem* enables the kernel to generate information on the state and configuration of the system. This information can be read from normal files by users and system programs without the need for special tools for communication with the kernel; in some cases, a simple `cat` is sufficient. Data can not only be read from the kernel, but also sent to it by writing character strings to a file of the `proc` filesystem. `echo "value" > /proc/file` — there's no easier way of transferring information from userspace to the kernel.

This approach makes use of a *virtual* filesystem that generates file information "on the fly," in other words, only when requested to do by read operations. A dedicated hard disk partition or some other block storage device is not needed with filesystems of this type.

In addition to the `proc` filesystem, the kernel provides many other virtual filesystems for various purposes, for example, for the management of all devices and system resources cataloged in the form of files in hierarchically structured directories. Even device drivers can make status information available in virtual filesystems, the USB subsystem being one such example.

❑ *Sysfs* is one particularly important example of another virtual filesystem that serves a similar purpose to procfs on the one hand, but is rather different on the other hand. Sysfs is, per convention, always mounted at /sys, but there is nothing that would prevent including it in other places. It was designed to export information from the kernel into userland at a highly structured level. In contrast to procfs, it was not designed for direct human use because the information is deeply and hierarchically nested. Additionally, the files do not always contain information in ASCII text form, but may well use unreadable binary strings. The filesystem is, however, very useful for tools that want to gather detailed information about the hardware present in a system and the topological connection between the devices.

It is also possible to create sysfs entries for kernel objects that use `kobjects` (see Chapter 1 for more information) with little effort. This gives userland easy access to important core kernel data structures.

❑ Small filesystems that serve a specific purpose can be constructed from standard functions supplied by the kernel. The in-kernel library that provides the required functions is called *libfs*. Additionally, the kernel provides means to implement sequential files with ease. Both techniques are put together in the debugging filesystem debugfs, which allows kernel developers to quickly export values to and import values from userland without the hassle of having to create custom interfaces or special-purpose filesystems.

10.1 The `proc` Filesystem

As mentioned at the beginning of this chapter, the `proc` filesystem is a *virtual* filesystem whose information cannot be read by a block device. Information is generated dynamically only when the contents of a file are read.

Using the `proc` filesystem, information can be obtained on the kernel subsystems (e.g., memory utilization, peripherals attached, etc.) and kernel behavior can be modified without the need to recompile the sources, load modules, or reboot the system. Closely related to this filesystem is the system control mechanism — *sysctl* for short — which has been frequently referenced in previous chapters. The `proc` filesystem provides an interface to all options exported using this mechanism, thus allowing parameters to be modified with little effort. No special communication programs need be developed — all that is required is a shell and the standard `cat` and `echo` programs.

Usually, the process data filesystem (its full name) is mounted in /proc, from which it obviously derives its more frequently used abbreviated name (procFS). Nevertheless, it is worth noting that the filesystem — like any other filesystem — can be mounted at any other point in the file tree, although this would be unusual.

The section below describes the layout and contents of the `proc` filesystem to illustrate its functions and options before we move on to examine its implementation details.

10.1.1 Contents of /proc

Although the size of the `proc` filesystem varies from system to system (different data are exported depending on hardware configuration, and different architectures affect its contents) it nevertheless contains a large number of deeply nested directories, files, and links. However, this wealth of information can be grouped into a few larger categories:

❑ Memory management

❑ Characteristic data of system processes

❑ Filesystems

❑ Device drivers

❑   System buses

❑   Power management

❑   Terminals

❑   System control parameters

Some of these categories are very different in nature (and the above list is by no means comprehensive) and share few common features. In the past, this information overload was a latent but ever-present source of criticism (which occasionally erupted violently) of the proc filesystem concept. It may well be useful to provide data by means of a virtual filesystem, but a *more* structured approach would have been appreciated . . . .

The trend in kernel development is away from the provision of information by the proc filesystem and toward the exporting of data by a problem-specific but likewise virtual filesystem. A good example of this is the USB filesystem which is used to export many types of status information on the USB subsystem into userspace without "overburdening" /proc with new entries. Additionally, the Sysfs filesystem allows for presenting a hierarchical view not only of the device tree (by *device*, I mean system buses, PCI devices, CPUs, etc.), but also of important kernel objects. Sysfs is discussed in Section 10.3.

On the kernel mailing list, the addition of new entries to /proc is viewed with deep suspicion and is the subject of controversial discussion. New code has a far better chance of finding its way into the sources if it does *not* use /proc. Of course, this does not mean that the proc filesystem will gradually become superfluous. In fact, the opposite is true. Today, /proc is as important as ever not only when installing new distributions, but also to support (automated) system administration.

The following sections give a *brief* overview of the various files in /proc and the information they contain. Again, I lay no claim to completeness and discuss only the most important elements found on all supported architectures.

Process-Specific Data

Each system process, regardless of its current state, has a subdirectory (with the same name as the PID) that contains information on the process. As the name suggests, the original intention of the "process data system" (proc for short) was to deliver process data.

What information is held in the process-specific directories? A simple ls -l command paints an initial picture:

```
wolfgang@meitner> cd /proc/7748
wolfgang@meitner> ls -l
total 0
dr-xr-xr-x 2 wolfgang users 0 2008-02-15 04:22 attr
-r-------- 1 wolfgang users 0 2008-02-15 04:22 auxv
--w------- 1 wolfgang users 0 2008-02-15 04:22 clear_refs
-r--r--r-- 1 wolfgang users 0 2008-02-15 00:37 cmdline
-r--r--r-- 1 wolfgang users 0 2008-02-15 04:22 cpuset
lrwxrwxrwx 1 wolfgang users 0 2008-02-15 04:22 cwd -> /home/wolfgang/wiley_kbook
-r-------- 1 wolfgang users 0 2008-02-15 04:22 environ
lrwxrwxrwx 1 wolfgang users 0 2008-02-15 01:30 exe -> /usr/bin/emacs
dr-x------ 2 wolfgang users 0 2008-02-15 00:56 fd
dr-x------ 2 wolfgang users 0 2008-02-15 04:22 fdinfo
```

```
-rw-r--r-- 1 wolfgang users 0 2008-02-15 04:22 loginuid
-r--r--r-- 1 wolfgang users 0 2008-02-15 04:22 maps
-rw------- 1 wolfgang users 0 2008-02-15 04:22 mem
-r--r--r-- 1 wolfgang users 0 2008-02-15 04:22 mounts
-r-------- 1 wolfgang users 0 2008-02-15 04:22 mountstats
-r--r--r-- 1 wolfgang users 0 2008-02-15 04:22 numa_maps
-rw-r--r-- 1 wolfgang users 0 2008-02-15 04:22 oom_adj
-r--r--r-- 1 wolfgang users 0 2008-02-15 04:22 oom_score
lrwxrwxrwx 1 wolfgang users 0 2008-02-15 04:22 root -> /
-rw------- 1 wolfgang users 0 2008-02-15 04:22 seccomp
-r--r--r-- 1 wolfgang users 0 2008-02-15 04:22 smaps
-r--r--r-- 1 wolfgang users 0 2008-02-15 00:56 stat
-r--r--r-- 1 wolfgang users 0 2008-02-15 01:30 statm
-r--r--r-- 1 wolfgang users 0 2008-02-15 00:56 status
dr-xr-xr-x 3 wolfgang users 0 2008-02-15 04:22 task
-r--r--r-- 1 wolfgang users 0 2008-02-15 04:22 wchan
```

Our example shows the data for an `emacs` process with the PID 7,748 as used to edit the LaTeX sources of this book.

The meanings of most entries are evident from the filename. For instance, `cmdline` is the command line used to start the process — that is, the name of the program including all parameters as a string:

> **The kernel does not use normal blanks to separate elements but NUL bytes as used in C to indicate the end of a string.**

```
wolfgang@meitner> cat cmdline
emacsfs.tex
```

The `od` tool can be used to convert the data to a readable format:

```
wolfgang@meitner> od -t a /proc/7748/cmdline
0000000   e   m   a   c   s nul   f   s   .   t   e   x nul
0000015
```

The above output makes it clear that the process was called by `emacs fs.tex`.

The other files contain the following data:

❏   `environ` indicates all environment variables set for the program; again, NUL characters are used as separators instead of blanks.

❏   All memory mappings to libraries (and to the binary file itself) used by the process are listed in text form in `maps`. In the case of `emacs`, an excerpt from this file would look like this (I use a regular text format without NUL characters):

```
wolfgang@meitner> cat maps
00400000-005a4000 r-xp 00000000 08:05 283752
/usr/bin/emacs
007a3000-00e8c000 rw-p 001a3000 08:05 283752
/usr/bin/emacs
00e8c000-018a1000 rw-p 00e8c000 00:00 0                              [heap]
2af4b085d000-2af4b0879000 r-xp 00000000 08:05 1743619
```

```
/lib64/ld-2.6.1.so
...
4003a000-40086000 r-xp 00000000 03:02 131108    /usr/lib/libcanna.so.1.2
40086000-4008b000 rwxp 0004b000 03:02 131108    /usr/lib/libcanna.so.1.2
4008b000-40090000 rwxp 4008b000 00:00 0
40090000-400a0000 r-xp 00000000 03:02 131102    /usr/lib/libRKC.so.1.2
400a0000-400a1000 rwxp 00010000 03:02 131102    /usr/lib/libRKC.so.1.2
400a1000-400a3000 rwxp 400a1000 00:00 0
400a3000-400e6000 r-xp 00000000 03:02 133514    /usr/X11R6/lib/libXaw3d.so.8.0
400e6000-400ec000 rwxp 00043000 03:02 133514    /usr/X11R6/lib/libXaw3d.so.8.0
400ec000-400fe000 rwxp 400ec000 00:00 0
400fe000-4014f000 r-xp 00000000 03:02 13104     /usr/lib/libtiff.so.3.7.3
4014f000-40151000 rwxp 00051000 03:02 13104     /usr/lib/libtiff.so.3.7.3
40151000-4018f000 r-xp 00000000 03:02 13010     /usr/lib/libpng.so.3.1.2.8
4018f000-40190000 rwxp 0003d000 03:02 13010     /usr/lib/libpng.so.3.1.2.8
40190000-401af000 r-xp 00000000 03:02 9011      /usr/lib/libjpeg.so.62.0.0
401af000-401b0000 rwxp 0001e000 03:02 9011      /usr/lib/libjpeg.so.62.0.0
401b0000-401c2000 r-xp 00000000 03:02 12590     /lib/libz.so.1.2.3
401c2000-401c3000 rwxp 00011000 03:02 12590     /lib/libz.so.1.2.3
...
2af4b7dc1000-2af4b7dc3000 rw-p 00001000 08:05 490436
/usr/lib64/pango/1.6.0/modules/pango-basic-fc.so
2af4b7dc3000-2af4b7e07000 r--p 00000000 08:05 1222118
/usr/share/fonts/truetype/arial.ttf
2af4b7e4d000-2af4b7e53000 r--p 00000000 08:05 211780
/usr/share/locale-bundle/en_GB/LC_MESSAGES/glib20.mo
2af4b7e53000-2af4b7e9c000 rw-p 2af4b7e07000 00:00 0
7ffffa218000-7ffffa24d000 rw-p 7ffffa218000 00:00 0                    [stack]
ffffffffff600000-ffffffffff601000 r-xp 00000000 00:00 0               [vdso]
```

❑   status returns general information on process status in text form.

```
wolfgang@meitner> cat status
Name:    emacs
State:   S (sleeping)
SleepAVG:        98%
Tgid:    7748
Pid:     7748
PPid:    4891
TracerPid:       0
Uid:     1000    1000    1000    1000
Gid:     100     100     100     100
FDSize: 256
Groups: 16 33 100
VmPeak:    140352 kB
VmSize:    139888 kB
VmLck:          0 kB
VmHWM:      28144 kB
VmRSS:      27860 kB
VmData:     10772 kB
VmStk:        212 kB
VmExe:       1680 kB
VmLib:      13256 kB
VmPTE:        284 kB
Threads:        1
SigQ:    0/38912
```

```
SigPnd: 0000000000000000
ShdPnd: 0000000000000000
SigBlk: 0000000000000000
SigIgn: 0000000000000000
SigCgt: 00000001d1817efd
CapInh: 0000000000000000
CapPrm: 0000000000000000
CapEff: 0000000000000000
Cpus_allowed:    00000000,00000000,00000000,0000000f
Mems_allowed:    00000000,00000001
```

Information is provided not only on UID/GID and other process numbers but also on memory allocation, process capabilities, and the state of the individual signal masks (pending, blocked, etc.).

❏   stat and statm contain — as a consecutive sequence of numbers — more status information on the process and its memory consumption.

The fd subdirectory contains files with numbers as names; these represent the individual file descriptors of the process. A symbolic link points to the position in the filesystem that is associated with the file descriptor, assuming it is a file in the proper sense. Other elements such as pipes that are also addressed via file descriptors are given a link target in the form pipe:[1434].

Similarly, symbolic links point to files and directories associated with the process:

❏   cwd points to the current working directory of the process. If users have the appropriate rights, they can switch to this directory using

cd cwd

without needing to know which directory it is.

❏   exe points to the binary file with the application code. In our example, it would point to /usr/bin/emacs

❏   root points to the root directory of the process. This need not necessarily be the global root directory (see the chroot mechanism discussed in Chapter 8).

General System Information

Not only the subdirectories of /proc contain information but also the directory itself. General information relating to no specific kernel subsystem (or shared by several subsystems) resides in files in /proc.

Some of these files were mentioned in earlier chapters. For example, iomem and ioports provide information on memory addresses and ports used to communicate with devices, as discussed in Chapter 6. Both files contain lists in text form:

```
wolfgang@meitner> cat /proc/iomem
00000000-0009dbff : System RAM
  00000000-00000000 : Crash kernel
0009dc00-0009ffff : reserved
000c0000-000cffff : pnp 00:0d
000e4000-000fffff : reserved
00100000-cff7ffff : System RAM
  00200000-004017a4 : Kernel code
  004017a5-004ffdef : Kernel data
```

```
cff80000-cff8dfff : ACPI Tables
cff8e000-cffdffff : ACPI Non-volatile Storage
cffe0000-cfffffff : reserved
d0000000-dfffffff : PCI Bus #01
  d0000000-dfffffff : 0000:01:00.0
    d0000000-d0ffffff : vesafb
...
fee00000-fee00fff : Local APIC
ffa00000-ffafffff : pnp 00:07
fff00000-ffffffff : reserved
100000000-12fffffff : System RAM


wolfgang@meitner> cat /proc/ioports
0000-001f : dma1
0020-0021 : pic1
0040-0043 : timer0
0050-0053 : timer1
0060-006f : keyboard
0070-0077 : rtc
0080-008f : dma page reg
00a0-00a1 : pic2
...
e000-efff : PCI Bus #03
  e400-e40f : 0000:03:00.0
    e400-e40f : libata
  e480-e483 : 0000:03:00.0
    e480-e483 : libata
  e800-e807 : 0000:03:00.0
    e800-e807 : libata
  e880-e883 : 0000:03:00.0
    e880-e883 : libata
  ec00-ec07 : 0000:03:00.0
    ec00-ec07 : libata
```

Similarly, some files provide a rough overview of the current memory management situation. `buddyinfo` and `slabinfo` supply data on current utilization of the buddy system and slab allocator, and `meminfo` gives an overview of general memory usage — broken down into high and low memory, free, allocated and shared areas, swap and writeback memory, and so on. `vmstat` yields further memory management characteristics including the number of pages currently in each memory management subsystem.

The `kallsyms` and `kcore` entries support kernel code debugging. The former holds a table with the addresses of all global kernel variables and procedures including their addresses in memory:

```
wolfgang@meitner> cat /proc/kallsyms
...
ffffffff80395ce8 T skb_abort_seq_read
ffffffff80395cff t skb_ts_finish
ffffffff80395d08 T skb_find_text
ffffffff80395d76 T skb_to_sgvec
ffffffff80395f6d T skb_truesize_bug
ffffffff80395f89 T skb_under_panic
ffffffff80395fe4 T skb_over_panic
ffffffff8039603f t copy_skb_header
ffffffff80396273 T skb_pull_rcsum
```

649

```
ffffffff803962da T skb_seq_read
ffffffff80396468 t skb_ts_get_next_block
...
```

kcore is a dynamic core file that "contains" all data of the running kernel — that is, the entire contents of main memory. It is no different from the normal core files that are saved for debugging purposes when a fatal error in user applications generates a core dump. The current state of a running system can be inspected using a debugger together with the binary file. Many of the figures in this book illustrating the interplay among the kernel data structures were prepared using this method. Appendix 2 takes a closer look at how available capabilities can be used with the help of the GNU gdb debugger and the ddd graphical user interface.

interrupts saves the number of interrupts raised during the current operation (the underlying mechanism is described in Chapter 14). On an IA-32 quad-core server, the file could look like this:

```
wolfgang@meitner> cat /proc/interrupts
           CPU0       CPU1       CPU2       CPU3
  0:    1383211    1407764    1292884    1364817   IO-APIC-edge      timer
  1:          0          1          1          0   IO-APIC-edge      i8042
  8:          0          1          0          0   IO-APIC-edge      rtc
  9:          0          0          0          0   IO-APIC-fasteoi   acpi
 12:          1          3          0          0   IO-APIC-edge      i8042
 16:       8327       4251     290975     114077   IO-APIC-fasteoi   libata, uhci_hcd:usb1
 18:          0          1          0          0   IO-APIC-fasteoi   ehci_hcd:usb2, uhci_hcd:usb4,
                                                                     uhci_hcd:usb7
 19:          0          0          0          0   IO-APIC-fasteoi   uhci_hcd:usb6
 21:          0          0          0          0   IO-APIC-fasteoi   uhci_hcd:usb3
 22:     267439      93114      10575       5018   IO-APIC-fasteoi   libata, libata, HDA Intel
 23:          0          0          0          0   IO-APIC-fasteoi   uhci_hcd:usb5, ehci_hcd:usb8
4347:         12         17          7      77445   PCI-MSI-edge      eth0
NMI:          0          0          0          0
LOC:    5443482    5443174    5446374    5446306
ERR:          0
```

Not only the number of interrupts but also the name of the device or driver responsible for the interrupt are given for each interrupt number.

Last but not least, I must mention loadavg and uptime, which display, respectively, the average system loading (i.e., the length of the run queue) during the last 60 seconds, 5 minutes, and 15 minutes; and the system uptime — the time elapsed since system boot.

Network Information

The /proc/net subdirectory supplies data on the various network options of the kernel. The information held there is a colorful mix of protocol and device data and includes several interesting entries as follows:

❑ Statistics on UDP and TCP sockets are available for IPv4 in udp and tcp; the equivalent data for IPv6 are held in udp6 and tcp6. UNIX sockets are logged in unix.

❑ The ARP table for backward resolution of addresses can be viewed in the arp file.

❑ dev holds statistics on the volume of data transferred via the network interfaces of the system (including the loopback software interface). This information can be used to check the transmission quality of the network because it also includes incorrectly transmitted and rejected packages as well as collision data.

Some network card drivers (e.g., for the popular Intel PRO/100 chipset) create additional subdirectories in /proc/net with more detailed hardware-specific information.

System Control Parameters

The system control parameters used to check and modify the behavior of the kernel dynamically make up the lion's share of entries in the proc filesystem. However, this interface is not the only way of manipulating data — this can also be done using the sysctl system call. This requires more effort because it is first necessary to write a program to support communication with the kernel via the system call interface. As a result, the numeric sysctl mechanism was tagged as being obsolete during development of 2.5 (the kernel outputs a warning message to this effect each time sysctl is invoked) and was planned to be dropped at some point. Removing the system call has, however, created a controversial discussion, and up to 2.6.25, the call is still in the kernel — although a message warns the user that it is deprecated.

The sysctl system call is not really needed because the /proc interface is a kernel data manipulation option of unrivaled simplicity. The sysctl parameters are managed in a separate subdirectory named /proc/sys, which is split into further subdirectories in line with the various kernel subsystems:

```
wolfgang@meitner> ls -l /proc/sys
total 0
dr-xr-xr-x 0 root root 0 2008-02-15 04:29 abi
dr-xr-xr-x 0 root root 0 2008-02-15 04:29 debug
dr-xr-xr-x 0 root root 0 2008-02-14 22:26 dev
dr-xr-xr-x 0 root root 0 2008-02-14 22:22 fs
dr-xr-xr-x 0 root root 0 2008-02-14 22:22 kernel
dr-xr-xr-x 0 root root 0 2008-02-14 22:22 net
dr-xr-xr-x 0 root root 0 2008-02-14 22:26 vm
```

The subdirectories contain a series of files that reflect the characteristic data of the associated kernel subsystems. For example, /proc/sys/vm includes the following entries:

```
wolfgang@meitner> ls -l /proc/sys/vm
total 0
-rw-r--r-- 1 root root 0 2008-02-17 01:32 block_dump
-rw-r--r-- 1 root root 0 2008-02-16 20:55 dirty_background_ratio
-rw-r--r-- 1 root root 0 2008-02-16 20:55 dirty_expire_centisecs
-rw-r--r-- 1 root root 0 2008-02-16 20:55 dirty_ratio
-rw-r--r-- 1 root root 0 2008-02-16 20:55 dirty_writeback_centisecs
...
-rw-r--r-- 1 root root 0 2008-02-17 01:32 swappiness
-rw-r--r-- 1 root root 0 2008-02-17 01:32 vfs_cache_pressure
-rw-r--r-- 1 root root 0 2008-02-17 01:32 zone_reclaim_mode
```

Unlike the files discussed earlier, the contents of the files in these directories can not only be read, but also supplied with new values by means of normal file operations. For instance, the vm subdirectory includes a swappiness file to indicate how "aggressively" the swapping algorithm goes about its job of swapping out pages. The default value is 60, as shown when the file contents are output using cat:

```
wolfgang@meitner> cat /proc/sys/vm/swappiness
60
```

651

However, this value can be modified by issuing the following command (as root user):

```
wolfgang@meitner> echo "80" > /proc/sys/vm/swappiness
wolfgang@meitner> cat /proc/sys/vm/swappiness
80
```

As discussed in Chapter 18, the higher the swappiness value the more aggressively will the kernel swap out pages; this can lead to better performance at certain system load levels.

Section 10.1.8 describes in detail the implementation used by the kernel to manipulate parameters in the proc filesystem.

10.1.2   Data Structures

Once again there are a number of central data structures around which the code used to implement the process data filesystem is built. These include the structures of the virtual filesystem discussed in Chapter 8. proc makes generous use of these, simply because, as a filesystem itself, it must be integrated into the VFS layer of the kernel.

There are also proc-specific data structures to organize the data provided in the kernel. An interface to the subsystems of the kernel must also be made available to enable the kernel to extract required information from its structures before it is supplied to userspace by means of /proc.

Representation of proc Entries

Each entry in the proc filesystem is described by an instance of proc_dir_entry whose (abbreviated) definition is as follows:

```
<proc_fs.h>
struct proc_dir_entry {
        unsigned int low_ino;
        unsigned short namelen;
        const char *name;
        mode_t mode;
        nlink_t nlink;
        uid_t uid;
        gid_t gid;
        loff_t size;
        struct inode_operations * proc_iops;
        const struct file_operations * proc_fops;
        get_info_t *get_info;
        struct module *owner;
        struct proc_dir_entry *next, *parent, *subdir;
        void *data;
        read_proc_t *read_proc;
        write_proc_t *write_proc;
  ...
};
```

Because each entry is given a filename, the kernel uses two elements of the structure to store the corresponding information: name is a pointer to the string in which the name is held, and namelen specifies the length of the name. Also adopted from the classic filesystem concept is the numbering of all inodes using `low_ino`. The meaning of `mode` is the same as in normal filesystems because the element reflects the type of the entry (file, directory, etc.), and the assignment of access rights in accordance with the classic "owner, group, others" scheme by means of the appropriate constants in `<stat.h>`. `uid` and `gid` specify the user ID and group ID to which the file belongs. Both are usually set to 0, which means that the root user is the owner of almost all `proc` files.

The usage counter common to most data structures is implemented by `count`, which indicates the number of points at which the instance of a data structure is used in the kernel to ensure that the structure is not freed inadvertently.

`proc_iops` and `proc_fops` are pointers to instances of types `inode_operations` and `file_operations` discussed in Chapter 8. They hold operations that can be performed on an inode or file and act as an interface to the virtual filesystem that relies on their presence. The operations used depend on the particular file type and are discussed in more detail below.

The file size in bytes is saved in the `size` element. Because `proc` entries are generated dynamically, the length of a file is not usually known in advance; in this case, the value 0 is used.

If a `proc` entry is generated by a dynamically loaded module, `module` contains a reference to the associated module data structure in memory (if the entry was generated by compiled-in code, `module` holds a null pointer).

The following three elements are available to control the exchange of information between the virtual filesystem (and ultimately userspace) and the various `proc` entries or individual kernel subsystems.

❑ `get_info` is a function pointer to the relevant subsystem routine that returns the desired data. As with normal file access, the offset and length of the desired range can be specified so that it is not necessary to read the full data set. This is useful, for example, for the automated analysis of `proc` entries.

❑ `read_proc` and `write_proc` point to functions to support the reading of data from and the writing of data to the kernel. The parameters and return values of the two functions are specified by the following type definition:

<proc_fs.h>
```
typedef int (read_proc_t)(char *page, char **start, off_t off,
                          int count, int *eof, void *data);
typedef int (write_proc_t)(struct file *file, const char __user *buffer,
                           unsigned long count, void *data);
```

Whereas data are read on the basis of memory pages (of course, an offset and the length of the data to be read can also be specified), the writing of data is based on a `file` instance. Both routines have an additional `data` argument that is defined when a new `proc` entry is registered and is passed as a parameter each time the routine is invoked (the `data` element of `proc_dir_entry` holds the data argument). This means that a single function can be registered as the read/write routine for *several* `proc` entries; the code can then distinguish the various cases by reference to the `data` argument (this is not possible with `get_info` because no data argument is passed). This tactic has already been adopted in preceding chapters to prevent the unnecessary duplication of code.

Recall that there is a separate instance of `proc_dir_entry` for each entry in the `proc` filesystem. They are used by the kernel to represent the hierarchical structure of the filesystem by means of the following elements:

- ❑ `nlink` specifies the number of subdirectories and symbolic links in a directory. (The number of files of other types is irrelevant.)

- ❑ `parent` is a pointer to the directory containing a file (or subdirectory) represented by the current `proc_dir_entry` instance.

- ❑ `subdir` and `next` support the hierarchical arrangement of files and directories. `subdir` points to the first entry of a directory (which, in spite of the name of the element, can be *either* a file *or* a directory), and `next` groups all common entries of a directory in a singly linked list.

proc inodes

The kernel provides a data structure called `proc_inode` to support an inode-oriented view of the `proc` filesystem entries. This structure is defined as follows:

```
<proc_fs.h>
union proc_op {
        int (*proc_get_link)(struct inode *, struct dentry **, struct vfsmount **);
        int (*proc_read)(struct task_struct *task, char *page);
};

struct proc_inode {
        struct pid *pid;
        int fd;
        union proc_op op;
        struct proc_dir_entry *pde;
        struct inode vfs_inode;
};
```

The purpose of the structure is to link the `proc`-specific data with the inode data of the VFS layer. `pde` contains a pointer to the `proc_dir_entry` instance associated with each entry; the meaning of the instance was discussed in the previous section. At the end of the structure there is an instance of `inode`.

> **This is the actual data, *not* a pointer to an instance of the structure.**

This is exactly the same data used by the VFS layer for inode management. In other words, directly before each instance of an `inode` structure linked with the `proc` filesystem, there are additional data in memory that can be extracted from a given instance of `proc_inode` using the container mechanism. Because the kernel frequently needs to access this information, it defines the following auxiliary procedure:

```
<proc_fs.h>
static inline struct proc_inode *PROC_I(const struct inode *inode)
{
        return container_of(inode, struct proc_inode, vfs_inode);
}
```

This returns the inode-specific data associated with a VFS inode. Figure 10-1 illustrates the situation in memory.

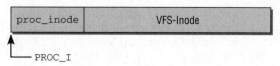

Figure 10-1: Connection between struct proc_inode and struct inode.

The remaining elements of the structure are only used if the inode represents a process-specific entry (which is therefore located in the proc/*pid* directory). Their meanings are as follows:

❑ pid is a pointer to the pid instance of a process. Because it is possible to access a large amount of process-specific information this way, it is clear why a process-specific inode should be directly associated with this data.

❑ proc_get_link and proc_read (which are collected in a union because only one at a time makes sense) are used to get process-specific information or to generate links to process-specific data in the Virtual Filesystem.

❑ fd holds the filedescriptor for which a file in /proc/<pid>/fd/ presents information. With the help of fd, all files in this directory can use the same file_operations.

The meanings and use of these elements are discussed in detail in Section 10.1.7.

10.1.3 Initialization

Before the proc filesystem can be used, it must be mounted with mount, and the kernel must set up and initialize several data structures to describe the filesystem structure in kernel memory. Unfortunately, the appearance and contents of /proc differ substantially from platform to platform and from architecture to architecture, and the code is crammed with #ifdef pre-processor statements that select code sections according to the particular situation. Although this practice is frowned upon, it simply cannot be avoided.

Because initialization differences relate primarily to creation of the subdirectories that subsequently appear in /proc, they are not evident in Figure 10-2, which shows a code flow diagram of proc_root_init in fs/proc/root.c.

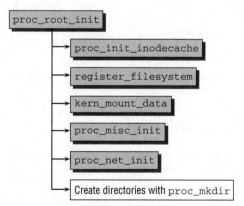

Figure 10-2: Code flow diagram for proc_root_init.

`proc_root_init` first creates a slab cache for `proc_inode` objects using `proc_init_inodecache`; these objects are the backbone of the `proc` filesystem and often need to be generated and destroyed as quickly as possible. Then the filesystem is officially registered with the kernel using the `register_filesystem` routine described in Chapter 8. And finally, `mount` is invoked to mount the filesystem.

`kern_mount_data` is a wrapper function for `do_kern_mount`, also discussed in Chapter 8. It returns a pointer to a `vfsmount` instance. The pointer is saved in the global variable `proc_mnt` for later use by the kernel.

`proc_misc_init` generates various file entries in the `proc` main directory; these are linked using special procedures to read information from the kernel data structures. Examples of these procedures are:

- ❑ loadavg (`loadavg_read_proc`)
- ❑ meminfo (`meminfo_read_proc`)
- ❑ filesystems (`filesystems_read_proc`)
- ❑ version (`version_read_proc`)

`create_proc_read_entry` is invoked for each name on this list (and for a few more, as the kernel sources show). The function creates a new instance of the familiar `proc_dir_entry` data structure whose `read_proc` entry is set to the procedure associated with each name. The implementation of most of these procedures is extremely simple, as exemplified by the `version_read_proc` procedure used to get the kernel version:

init/version.c
```
const char linux_proc_banner[] =
        "%s version %s"
        " (" LINUX_COMPILE_BY "@" LINUX_COMPILE_HOST ")"
        " (" LINUX_COMPILER ") %s\n";
```

fs/proc/proc_misc.c
```
static int version_read_proc(char *page, char **start, off_t off,
                             int count, int *eof, void *data)
{
        int len;

        len = snprintf(page, PAGE_SIZE, linux_proc_banner,
                utsname()->sysname,
                utsname()->release,
                utsname()->version);
        return proc_calc_metrics(page, start, off, count, eof, len);
}
```

The kernel string `linux_proc_banner` is written into a userspace page using `sprintf`. When this is done, the `proc_calc_metrics` auxiliary function determines the length of the data returned.

Once `proc_misc_init` has completed, the kernel uses `proc_net_init` to install a large number of networking related files in /proc/net. Since the mechanism is similar to the previous case, it is not discussed here.

Finally, the kernel invokes `proc_mkdir` to create a number of /proc subdirectories; these are required later but do not contain files at the moment. As for `proc_mkdir`, all we need to know is that the function registers a new subdirectory and returns the associated `proc_dir_entry` instance; its implementation is of no further interest. The kernel saves these instances in global variables because these data are needed later when filling the directories with files (i.e., when supplying the real information).

fs/proc_root.c
```
struct proc_dir_entry *proc_net, *proc_bus, *proc_root_fs, *proc_root_driver;

void __init proc_root_init(void)
{
...
        proc_net = proc_mkdir("sysvipc", NULL);
...

        proc_root_fs = proc_mkdir("fs", NULL);
        proc_root_driver = proc_mkdir("driver", NULL);
...

        proc_bus = proc_mkdir("bus", NULL);
}
```

Further directory initialization is no longer carried out by the `proc` layer itself but is performed by other parts of the kernel where the required information is made available. This makes it clear why the kernel uses global variables to save the `proc_dir_entry` instances of these subdirectories. The files in `proc/net` are filled, for example, by the network layer, which inserts files at many different points in the code of card drivers and protocols. Because new files are created when new cards or protocols are initialized, this can be done during the boot operation (in the case of compiled-in drivers) or while the system is running (when modules are loaded) — in any case, after initialization of the `proc` filesystem by `proc_root_init` has completed. If the kernel did not use global variables, it would have to provide functions to register subsystem-specific entries, and this is neither as clean nor as elegant as using global variables.

The system control mechanism fills `proc_sys_root` with files that are always generated when a new sysctl is defined in the kernel. Repeated reference was made to this facility in earlier chapters. A detailed description of the associated mechanism is provided in Section 10.1.8.

10.1.4 Mounting the Filesystem

Once all kernel-internal data that describe the structure and contents of the `proc` filesystem have been initialized, the next step is to mount the filesystem in the directory tree.

In the view of the system administrator in userspace, mounting `/proc` is almost the same as mounting a non-virtual filesystem. The only difference is that an arbitrary keyword (usually `proc` or `none`) is specified as the source instead of a device file:

```
root@meitner # mount -t proc proc /proc
```

The VFS-internal processes involved in mounting a new filesystem are described in detail in Chapter 8, but as a reminder are summarized below. When it adds a new filesystem, the kernel uses a linked list that is scanned to find an instance of `file_system_type` associated with the filesystem. This instance provides information on how to read in the filesystem superblock. For `proc`, the structure is initialized as follows:

fs/proc/root.c
```
static struct file_system_type proc_fs_type = {
        .name           = "proc",
```

```
        .get_sb         = proc_get_sb,
        .kill_sb        = kill_anon_super,
};
```

The filesystem-specific superblock data are used to fill a `vfsmount` structure so that the new filesystem can be incorporated in the VFS tree.

As the source code extract above shows, the superblock of the `proc` filesystem is supplied by `proc_get_sb`. The function builds on a further kernel auxiliary routine (`get_sb_single`) that enlists the help of `proc_fill_super` to fill a new instance of `super_block`.

`proc_fill_super` is not very complex and is mainly responsible for filling the `super_block` elements with defined values that never change:

fs/proc/inode.c
```
int proc_fill_super(struct super_block *s, void *data, int silent)
{
        struct inode * root_inode;
...

        s->s_blocksize = 1024;
        s->s_blocksize_bits = 10;
        s->s_magic = PROC_SUPER_MAGIC;
        s->s_op = &proc_sops;
...

        root_inode = proc_get_inode(s, PROC_ROOT_INO, &proc_root);
        s->s_root = d_alloc_root(root_inode);
...

        return 0;
}
```

The block size cannot be set and is always 1,024; as a result, `s_blocksize_bits` must always be 10 because 2^{10} equals 1,024.

With the help of the pre-processor, the magic number used to recognize the filesystem is defined as `0x9fa0`. (This number is not actually needed in the case of `proc` because data do not reside on a storage medium but are generated dynamically.)

More interesting is the assignment of the `proc_sops` superblock operations that group together the functions needed by the kernel to manage the filesystem:

fs/proc/inode.c
```
static struct super_operations proc_sops = {
        .alloc_inode    = proc_alloc_inode,
        .destroy_inode  = proc_destroy_inode,
        .read_inode     = proc_read_inode,
        .drop_inode     = generic_delete_inode,
        .delete_inode   = proc_delete_inode,
        .statfs         = simple_statfs,
        .remount_fs     = proc_remount,
};
```

The next two lines of `proc_fill_super` create an inode for the root directory and use `d_alloc_root` to convert it into a `dentry` that is assigned to the superblock instance; here it is used as the starting point for lookup operations in the mounted filesystem, as described in Chapter 8.

In the main, the `proc_get_inode` function used to create the root inode fills several inode structure values to define, for example, the owner and the access mode. Of greater interest is the static `proc_dir_entry` instance called `proc_root`; when it is initialized, it gives rise to data structures with relevant function pointers:

fs/proc/root.c
```
struct proc_dir_entry proc_root = {
        .low_ino       = PROC_ROOT_INO,
        .namelen       = 5,
        .name          = "/proc",
        .mode          = S_IFDIR | S_IRUGO | S_IXUGO,
        .nlink         = 2,
        .count         = ATOMIC_INIT(1),
        .proc_iops     = &proc_root_inode_operations,
        .proc_fops     = &proc_root_operations,
        .parent        = &proc_root,
}
```

The root inode differs from all other inodes of the `proc` file system in that it not only contains "normal" files and directories (even though they are generated dynamically), but also manages the process-specific PID directories that contain detailed information on the individual system processes, as mentioned above. The root inode therefore has its own inode and file operations, which are defined as follows:

fs/proc/root.c
```
/*
 * The root /proc directory is special, as it has the
 * <pid> directories. Thus we don't use the generic
 * directory handling functions for that..
 */
static struct file_operations proc_root_operations = {
        .read           = generic_read_dir,
        .readdir        = proc_root_readdir,
};

/*
 * proc root can do almost nothing..
 */
static struct inode_operations proc_root_inode_operations = {
        .lookup         = proc_root_lookup,
        .getattr        = proc_root_getattr,

}
```

`generic_read_dir` is a standard virtual filesystem function that returns `-EISDIR` as an error code; this is because directories cannot be handled like normal files in order to get data from them. Section 10.1.5 describes how `proc_root_lookup` functions.

10.1.5 Managing /proc Entries

Before the proc filesystem can be put to meaningful use, it must be filled with entries containing data. Several auxiliary routines are provided to add files, create directories, and so on, in order to make this job as easy as possible for the remaining kernel sections. These routines are discussed below.

> The fact that new proc entries can be easily generated should not disguise the fact that it is not accepted practice to use code to do this. Nevertheless, the simple, lean interface can be very useful for opening up a communication channel for test purposes between kernel and userspace with minimum effort.

I also discuss methods used by the kernel to scan the tree of all registered proc entries to find required information.

Creating and Registering Entries

New entries are added to the proc filesystem in two steps. First, a new instance of proc_dir_entry is created together with all information needed to describe the entry. This instance is then registered in the data structures of proc so that it is visible to the outside. Because the two steps are never carried out independently of each other, the kernel makes auxiliary functions available to combine both actions so that new entries can be generated quickly and easily.

The most frequently used function is called create_proc_entry and requires three arguments:

```
<proc_fs.h>
extern struct proc_dir_entry *create_proc_entry(const char *name, mode_t mode,
                                         struct proc_dir_entry *parent);
```

❏   name specifies the filename.

❏   mode specifies the access mode in the conventional UNIX scheme (user/group/others).

❏   parent is a pointer to the proc_dir_entry instance of the directory where the file is to be inserted.

Caution: The function fills only the essential elements of the proc_dir_entry structure. It is therefore necessary to make a few brief "manual" corrections to the structure generated.

This is illustrated by the following sample code, which generates the proc/net/hyperCard entry to supply information on a (unbelievably good) network card:

```
struct proc_dir_entry *entry = NULL;

entry = create_proc_entry("hyperCard", S_IFREG|S_IRUGO|S_IWUSR,
                          &proc_net);

if (!entry) {
        printk(KERN_ERR "unable to create /proc/net/hyperCard\n");
        return -EIO;
} else {
        entry->read_proc = hypercard_proc_read;
```

```
                entry->write_proc = hypercard_proc_write;
        }
```

Once the entry has been created, it is registered with the `proc` filesystem using `proc_register` in `fs/proc/generic.c`. The task is divided into three steps:

1. A unique `proc`-internal number is generated to give the entry its own identity. `get_inode_number` is used to return an unused number for dynamically generated entries.

2. The `next` and `parent` elements of the `proc_dir_entry` instance must be set appropriately to incorporate the new entry into the hierarchy.

3. Depending on the file type, the pointers must be set appropriately to file and inode operations if the corresponding elements of `proc_dir_entry`, `proc_iops` and `proc_fops` previously contained a null pointer. Otherwise, the value held there is retained.

Which file and inode operations are used for `proc` files? The corresponding pointers are set as follows:

fs/proc/generic.c
```
static int proc_register(struct proc_dir_entry * dir, struct proc_dir_entry * dp)
{
        if (S_ISDIR(dp->mode)) {
                if (dp->proc_iops == NULL) {
                        dp->proc_fops = &proc_dir_operations;
                        dp->proc_iops = &proc_dir_inode_operations;
                }
                dir->nlink++;
        } else if (S_ISLNK(dp->mode)) {
                if (dp->proc_iops == NULL)
                        dp->proc_iops = &proc_link_inode_operations;
        } else if (S_ISREG(dp->mode)) {
                if (dp->proc_fops == NULL)
                        dp->proc_fops = &proc_file_operations;
                if (dp->proc_iops == NULL)
                        dp->proc_iops = &proc_file_inode_operations;
        }
        ...
}
```

For regular files, the kernel uses `proc_file_operations` and `proc_file_inode_operations` to define the file and inode operation methods:

fs/proc/generic.c
```
static struct inode_operations proc_file_inode_operations = {
        .setattr        = proc_notify_change,
};
```

fs/proc/generic.c
```
static struct file_operations proc_file_operations = {
        .llseek         = proc_file_lseek,
        .read           = proc_file_read,
        .write          = proc_file_write,
};
```

Directories use the following structures:

fs/proc/generic.c
```
static struct file_operations proc_dir_operations = {
        .read                 = generic_read_dir,
        .readdir              = proc_readdir,
};
```

fs/proc/generic.c
```
/* proc directories can do almost nothing... */
static struct inode_operations proc_dir_inode_operations = {
        .lookup       = proc_lookup,
        .getattr      = proc_getattr,
        .setattr      = proc_notify_change,
};
```

Symbolic links require inode operations but not file operations:

fs/proc/generic.c
```
static struct inode_operations proc_link_inode_operations = {
        .readlink     = generic_readlink,
        .follow_link  = proc_follow_link,
};
```

Later in this section, I take a closer look at the implementation of some of the routines in the above data structures.

In addition to `create_proc_entry`, the kernel provides two further auxiliary functions for creating new proc entries. All three are short wrapper routines for `create_proc_entry` and are defined with the following parameter list:

<proc_fs.h>
```
static inline struct proc_dir_entry *create_proc_read_entry(const char *name,
        mode_t mode, struct proc_dir_entry *base,
        read_proc_t *read_proc, void * data) { ... }

static inline struct proc_dir_entry *create_proc_info_entry(const char *name,
        mode_t mode, struct proc_dir_entry *base, get_info_t *get_info) { ... }
```

`create_proc_read_entry` and `create_proc_info_entry` are used to create a new read entry. Because this can be done in two different ways (as discussed in Section 10.1.2), there must also be two routines. Whereas `create_proc_info_entry` requires a procedure pointer of type `get_info_t` that is added to the `get_info` element of `proc_dir_entry`, `create_proc_info_entry` expects not only a procedure pointer of type `read_proc_t`, but also a data pointer that enables the same function to be used as a read routine for various proc entries distinguished by reference to their data argument.

Although we are not interested in their implementation, I include below a list of other auxiliary functions used to manage proc entries:

❑   `proc_mkdir` creates a new directory.

❑   `proc_mkdir_mode` creates a new directory whose access mode can be explicitly specified.

❑   proc_symlink generates a symbolic link.

❑   remove_proc_entry deletes a dynamically generated entry from the proc directory.

The kernel sources include a sample file in Documentation/DocBook/procfs_example.c. This demonstrates the options described here and can be used as a template for writing proc routines. Section 10.1.6 includes some sample kernel source routines that are responsible for interaction between the read/write routines of the proc filesystem and the kernel subsystems.

Finding Entries

Userspace applications access proc files as if they were normal files in regular filesystems; in other words, they follow the same path as the VFS routines described in Chapter 8 when searching for entries. As discussed there, the lookup process (e.g., of the open system call) duly arrives at real_lookup, which invokes the function saved in the lookup function pointer of inode_operations to resolve the filename by reference to its individual path components. In this section, we take a look at the steps performed by the kernel to find files in the proc filesystem.

The search for entries starts at the mount point of the proc filesystem, usually /proc. In Section 10.1.2 you saw that the lookup pointer of the file_operations instance for the root directory of the process filesystem points to the proc_root_lookup function. Figure 10-3 shows the associated code flow diagram.

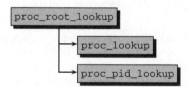

Figure 10-3: Code flow diagram for
proc_root_lookup.

The kernel uses this routine simply to distinguish between two different types of proc entries before delegating the real work to specialized routines. Entries may be files in a process-specific directory, as with /proc/1/maps. Alternatively, entries may be files registered dynamically by a driver or subsystem (e.g., /proc/cpuinfo or /proc/net/dev). It is up to the kernel to distinguish between the two.

The kernel first invokes proc_lookup to find regular entries. If the function finds the file it is looking for (by sequentially scanning the components of the specified path), everything is OK, and the lookup operation is terminated.

If proc_lookup fails to find an entry, the kernel invokes proc_pid_lookup to look in the list of process-specific entries.

These functions are not examined in detail here. All we need to know is that an appropriate inode type is returned (proc_pid_lookup is discussed again in Section 10.1.7, where the creation and structure of process-specific inodes are discussed).

10.1.6   *Reading and Writing Information*

As noted in Section 10.1.5, the kernel uses the operations stored in `proc_file_operations` to read and write the contents of regular `proc` entries. The contents of the function pointers in this structure are as follows:

fs/proc/generic.c
```
static struct file_operations proc_file_operations = {
        .llseek        = proc_file_lseek,
        .read          = proc_file_read,
        .write         = proc_file_write,
};
```

The sections below examine the read and write operations implemented by means of `proc_file_read` and `proc_file_write`.

Implementation of `proc_file_read`

Data are read from a `proc` file in three steps:

1.   A kernel memory page is allocated into which data are generated.

2.   A file-specific function is invoked to fill the kernel memory page with data.

3.   The data are copied from kernel space to userspace.

Obviously, the second step is the most important because the subsystem data and kernel data structures must be specially prepared. The other two steps are simple routine tasks. Section 10.1.2 noted that the kernel provides two function pointers to `get_info` and `read_proc` in the `proc_dir_entry` structure; these functions are used to read data, and the kernel must select the one that matches.

fs/proc/generic.c
```
proc_file_read(struct file *file, char __user *buf, size_t nbytes,
              loff_t *ppos)
{
...
                if (dp->get_info) {
                        /* Handle old net routines */
                        n = dp->get_info(page, &start, *ppos, count);
                        if (n < count)
                                eof = 1;
                } else if (dp->read_proc) {
                        n = dp->read_proc(page, &start, *ppos,
                                          count, &eof, dp->data);
                } else
                        break;
...
}
```

`page` is a pointer to the memory page allocated to hold the data in the first step.

Since a sample implementation of `read_proc` is included in Section 10.1.5, it need not be repeated here.

Implementation of proc_file_write

Writing to proc files is also a simple matter — at least from the perspective of the filesystem. The code of proc_file_write is very compact and thus is reproduced in full below.

fs/proc/generic.c
```
static ssize_t
proc_file_write(struct file * file, const char __user *buffer,
                size_t count, loff_t *ppos)
{
        struct inode *inode = file->f_dentry->d_inode;
        struct proc_dir_entry * dp;

        dp = PDE(inode);

        if (!dp->write_proc)
                return -EIO;

        return dp->write_proc(file, buffer, count, dp->data);
}
```

The PDE function needed to obtain the required proc_dir_entry instance from the VFS inode using the container mechanism is very simple. All it does is execute PROC_I(inode)->pde. As discussed in Section 10.1.2, PROC_I finds the proc_inode instance associated with an inode (in the case of proc inodes, the inode data always immediately precede the VFS inode).

Once the proc_dir_entry instance has been found, the routine registered for write purposes must be invoked with suitable parameters — assuming, of course, that the routine exists and is not assigned a null pointer.

How does the kernel implement a write routine for proc entries? This question is answered using proc_write_foobar, which is included as an example for a write handler in the kernel sources:

kernel/Documentation/DocBook/procfs_example.c
```
static int proc_write_foobar(struct file *file,
                             const char *buffer,
                             unsigned long count,
                             void *data)
{
        int len;
        struct fb_data_t *fb_data = (struct fb_data_t *)data;

        if(count > FOOBAR_LEN)
                len = FOOBAR_LEN;
        else
                len = count;

        if(copy_from_user(fb_data->value, buffer, len))
                return -EFAULT;

        fb_data->value[len] = '\0';
```

```
          /* Parse the data and perform actions in the subsystem */
          return len;
}
```

Usually, a `proc_write` implementation performs the following actions:

1. First, the length of the user input (it can be determined using the `count` parameter) must be checked to ensure that it is not longer than the reserved area.

2. The data are copied from userspace into the reserved kernel space area.

3. Information is extracted from the string. This operation is known as *parsing*, a term borrowed from compiler design. In the above example, this task is delegated to the `cpufreq_parse_policy` function.

4. Manipulations are then performed on the (sub)system in accordance with the user information received.

10.1.7 Task-Related Information

Outputting detailed information on system processes was one of the prime tasks for which the `proc` filesystem was originally designed, and this still holds true today. As demonstrated in Section 10.1.7, `proc_pid_lookup` is responsible for opening PID-specific files in `/proc/<pid>`. The associated code flow diagram is shown in Figure 10-4.

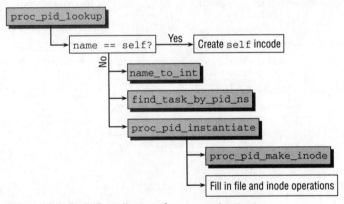

Figure 10-4: Code flow diagram for `proc_pid_lookup`.

The goal of the routine is to create an inode that acts as the first object for further PID-specific operations; this is because the inode represents the `/proc/pid` directory containing all files with process-specific information. Two cases, analyzed below, must be distinguished.

The `self` directory

Processes can be selected by explicit reference to their PIDs, but the data of the currently running process can be accessed without knowing PID by selecting the `/proc/self` directory — the kernel then automatically determines which process is currently running. For example, outputting the contents of /proc/self/map with cat produces the following result:

```
wolfgang@meitner> cat /proc/self/cmdline
cat/proc/self/cmdline
```

If a Perl script is used to read the file, the following information is obtained.

```
wolfgang@meitner> perl -e 'open(DAT, "< /proc/self/cmdline"); print(<DAT>); close(DAT);'
perl-eopen(DAT, "< /proc/self/cmdline"); print(<DAT>); close(DAT);
```

Because the script was passed to the Perl interpreter as a command-line parameter, it reproduces itself — in fact, it is almost a self-printing Perl script.[1]

The self case is handled first in proc_pid_lookup, as the code flow diagram in Figure 10-4 shows.

When a new inode instance is generated, only a few uninteresting standard fields need to be filled. Of prime importance is the fact that the statically defined proc_self_inode_operations instance is used for the inode operations:

fs/proc/base.c
```
static struct inode_operations proc_self_inode_operations = {
        .readlink      = proc_self_readlink,
        .follow_link   = proc_self_follow_link,
};
```

The self directory is implemented as a link to a PID-specific directory. As a result, the associated inode always has the same structure and does not contain any information as to *which* process it refers. This information is obtained dynamically when the link target is read (this is necessary when following or reading a link, e.g., when listing the entries of /proc). This is precisely the purpose of the two functions in proc_self_inode_operations whose implementations require just a few lines:

fs/proc/base.c
```
static int proc_self_readlink(struct dentry *dentry, char *buffer, int buflen)
{
        char tmp[30];
        sprintf(tmp, "%d", current->tgid);
        return vfs_readlink(dentry,buffer,buflen,tmp);
}

static void *proc_self_follow_link(struct dentry *dentry, struct nameidata *nd)
{
        char tmp[PROC_NUMBUF];
        sprintf(tmp, "%d", task_tgid_vnr(current));
        return ERR_PTR(vfs_follow_link(nd,tmp));
}
```

Both functions generate a string into tmp. For proc_self_readlink, it holds the thread group ID of the currently running process, which is read using current->tgid. For proc_self_follow_link, the PID that the current namespace associates with the task is used. Recall from Chapter 2 that PIDs are not unique across the system because of namespaces. Also remember that the thread group ID is identical

---

[1]Writing programs that print themselves is an old hacker's delight. A collection of such programs in a wide variety of high-level languages is available at www.nyx.net/~gthompso/quine.htm.

with the classic PID for single-threaded processes. The `sprintf` function, with which we are familiar from the C programming of userspace applications, converts the integer number into a string.

The remaining work is then delegated to standard virtual filesystem functions that are responsible for directing the lookup operation to the right places.

Selection According to PID

Let us turn our attention to how the process-specific information is selected by PID.

Creating the Directory Inode

If a PID is passed to `proc_pid_lookup` instead of `"self"`, the course of the lookup operation is as shown in the code flow diagram in Figure 10-4.

Because filenames are always processed in the form of strings but PIDs are integer numbers, the former must be converted accordingly. The kernel provides the `name_to_int` auxiliary function to convert strings consisting of digits into an integer.

The information obtained is used to find the `task_struct` instance of the desired process by means of the `find_task_by_pid_ns` function described in Chapter 2. However, the kernel cannot make the assumption that the desired process actually exists. After all, it is not unknown for programs to try to process a nonexistent PID, in which case, a corresponding error (`-ENOENT`) is reported.

Once the desired `task_struct` is found, the kernel delegates the rest of the work mostly to `proc_pid_instantiate` implemented in `fs/proc/base.c`, which itself relies on `proc_pid_make_inode`. First, a new inode is created by the `new_inode` standard function of VFS; this basically boils down to the same `proc`-specific `proc_alloc_inode` routine mentioned above that makes use of its own slab cache.

> The routine not only generates a new **struct inode** instance, but also reserves memory needed by **struct proc_inode**; the reserved memory holds a normal VFS inode as a "subobject," as noted in Section 10.1.2. The elements of the object generated are then filled with standard values.

After calling `proc_pid_make_inode`, all the remaining code in `proc_pid_instantiate` has to do is perform a couple of administrative tasks. Most important, the `inode->i_op` inode operations are set to the `proc_tgid_base_inode_operations` static structure whose contents are examined below.

Processing Files

When a file (or directory) in the PID-specific /proc/*pid* directory is processed, this is done using the inode operations of the directory, as noted in Chapter 8 when discussing the virtual filesystem mechanisms. The kernel uses the statically defined `proc_base_inode_operations` structure as the inode operations of PID inodes. This structure is defined as follows:

fs/proc/base.c
```
static const struct inode_operations proc_tgid_base_inode_operations = {
        .lookup = proc_tgid_base_lookup,
        .getattr = pid_getattr,
        .setattr = proc_setattr,
};
```

In addition to attribute handling, the directory supports just one more operation — subentry lookup.[2]

The task of `proc_tgid_base_lookup` is to return an inode instance with suitable inode operations by reference to a given name (`cmdline`, `maps`, etc.). The extended inode operations (`proc_inode`) must also include a function to output the desired data. Figure 10-5 shows the code flow diagram.

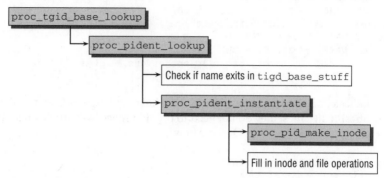

Figure 10-5: Code flow diagram for `proc_tgid_base_lookup`.

The work is delegated to `proc_pident_lookup`, which works not only for TGID files, but is a generic method for other ID types. The first step is to find out whether the desired entry exists at all. Because the contents of the PID-specific directory are always the same, a static list of all files together with a few other bits of information is defined in the kernel sources. The list is called `tgid_base_stuff` and is used to find out easily whether a desired directory entry exists or not. The array contains elements of type `pid_entry`, which is defined as follows:

fs/proc/base.c
```
struct pid_entry {
        char *name;
        int len;
        mode_t mode;
        const struct inode_operations *iop;
        const struct file_operations *fop;
        union proc_op op;
};
```

`name` and `len` specify the filename and the string length of the name, while `mode` denotes the mode bits. Additionally, there are fields for the inode and file operations associated with the entry, and a copy of `proc_op`. Recall that this contains a pointer to the `proc_get_link` or `proc_read_link` operation, depending on the file type.

Some macros are provided to ease the construction of static `pid_entry` instances:

fs/proc/base.c
```
#define DIR(NAME, MODE, OTYPE) \
        NOD(NAME, (S_IFDIR|(MODE)), \
```

---

[2]A special `readdir` method is also implemented for `proc_tgid_base_operations` (an instance of `struct file_operations`) to read a list of all files in the directory. It's not discussed here simply because every PID-specific directory always contains the same files, and therefore the same data would always be returned.

```
                        &proc_##OTYPE##_inode_operations, &proc_##OTYPE##_operations, \
                        {} )
#define LNK(NAME, OTYPE) \
        NOD(NAME, (S_IFLNK|S_IRWXUGO), \
                &proc_pid_link_inode_operations, NULL, \
                { .proc_get_link = &proc_##OTYPE##_link } )
#define REG(NAME, MODE, OTYPE) \
        NOD(NAME, (S_IFREG|(MODE)), NULL, \
                &proc_##OTYPE##_operations, {})
#define INF(NAME, MODE, OTYPE) \
        NOD(NAME, (S_IFREG|(MODE)), \
                NULL, &proc_info_file_operations, \
                { .proc_read = &proc_##OTYPE } )
```

As the names indicate, the macros generate directories, links, and regular files. INF also generates regular
files, but in contrast to REG files, they do not need to provide specialized inode operations, but need only
fill in proc_read from pid_entry->op. Observe how

```
REG("environ", S_IRUSR, environ)
/*******************************/
INF("auxv", S_IRUSR, pid_auxv)
```

is expanded to see how both types differ:

```
{ .name = ("environ"),
  .len = sizeof("environ") - 1,
  .mode = (S_IFREG|(S_IRUSR)),
  .iop = NULL,
  .fop = &proc_environ_operations,
  .op = {},
}
/*******************************/
{ .name = ("auxv"),
  .len = sizeof("auxv") - 1,
  .mode = (S_IFREG|(S_IRUSR)),
  .iop = NULL,
  .fop = &proc_info_file_operations,
  .op = { .proc_read = &proc_pid_auxv },
}
```

The macros are used to construct the TGID-specific directory entries in tgid_base_stuff:

fs/proc/base.c
```
static const struct pid_entry tgid_base_stuff[] = {
        DIR("task", S_IRUGO|S_IXUGO, task),
        DIR("fd", S_IRUSR|S_IXUSR, fd),
        DIR("fdinfo", S_IRUSR|S_IXUSR, fdinfo),
        REG("environ", S_IRUSR, environ),
        INF("auxv", S_IRUSR, pid_auxv),
        INF("status", S_IRUGO, pid_status),
        INF("limits", S_IRUSR, pid_limits),
...
        INF("oom_score", S_IRUGO, oom_score),
        REG("oom_adj", S_IRUGO|S_IWUSR, oom_adjust),
```

```
#ifdef CONFIG_AUDITSYSCALL
        REG("loginuid", S_IWUSR|S_IRUGO, loginuid),
#endif
#ifdef CONFIG_FAULT_INJECTION
        REG("make-it-fail", S_IRUGO|S_IWUSR, fault_inject),
#endif
#if defined(USE_ELF_CORE_DUMP) && defined(CONFIG_ELF_CORE)
        REG("coredump_filter", S_IRUGO|S_IWUSR, coredump_filter),
#endif
#ifdef CONFIG_TASK_IO_ACCOUNTING
        INF("io", S_IRUGO, pid_io_accounting),
#endif
};
```

The structure describes each entry by type, name, and access rights. The latter are defined using the usual VFS constants with which we are familiar from Chapter 8.

To summarize, various types of entry can be distinguished:

❑   INF-style files use a separate read_proc function to obtain the desired data. The proc_info_file_operations standard instance is used as the file_operations structure. The methods it defines represent the VFS interface that passes the data returned upward using read_proc.

❑   SYM generates symbolic links that point to another VFS file. A type-specific function in proc_get_link specifies the link target, and proc_pid_link_inode_operations forwards the data to the virtual filesystem in suitable form.

❑   REG creates regular files that use specialized inode operations responsible for gathering data and forwarding them to the VFS layer. This is necessary if the data source does not fit into the framework provided by proc_info_inode_operations.

Let us return to proc_pident_lookup. To check whether the desired name is present, all the kernel does is iterate over the array elements and compare the names stored there with the required name until it strikes lucky — or perhaps not. After it has ensured that the name exists in tgid_base_stuff, the function generates a new inode using proc_pident_instantiate, which, in turn, uses the already known proc_pid_make_inode function.

10.1.8 System Control Mechanism

Kernel behavior can be modified at run time by means of *system controls*. Parameters can be transferred from userspace into the kernel without having to reboot. The classic method of manipulating the kernel is the sysctl system call. However, for a variety of reasons, this is not always the most elegant option — one reason being that it is necessary to write a program to read arguments and pass them to the kernel using sysctl. Unfortunately, this method does not allow users to obtain a quick overview of which kernel control options are available; unlike with system calls, there is no POSIX or, indeed, any other standard that defines a standard set of sysctls to be implemented by all compatible systems. Consequently, the sysctl implementation is now regarded as outmoded and will, in the short or the long term, sink into oblivion.

To resolve this situation, Linux resorts to the proc filesystem. It exports to /proc/sys a directory structure that arranges all sysctls hierarchically and also allows parameters to be read and manipulated using simple userspace tools; cat and echo are sufficient to modify kernel run-time behavior.

This section not only examines the `proc` interface of the sysctl mechanism, but also discusses how sysctls are registered and managed in the kernel, particularly as these two aspects are closely related.

Using Sysctls

To paint a general picture of system control options and usage, I have chosen a short example to illustrate how userspace programs call on sysctl resources with the help of the `sysctl` system call. The example also shows how difficult things would be without the `proc` filesystem.

The many sysctls in every UNIX look-alike are organized into a clear hierarchical structure that mirrors the familiar tree structure used in filesystems: and it's thanks to this feature that sysctls can be exported with such ease by a virtual filesystem.

However, in contrast to filesystems, sysctls do not use strings to represent path components. Instead, they use integer numbers packed in symbolic constants. These are easier for the kernel to parse than pathnames in strings.

The kernel provides several "base categories" including `CTL_DEV` (information on peripherals), `CTL_KERN` (information on the kernel itself), and `CTL_VM` (memory management information and parameters).

`CTL_DEV` includes a subcategory named `DEV_CDROM` that supplies information on the CD-ROM drive(s) of the system (CD-ROM drives are obviously peripherals).

In `CTL_DEV/DEV_CDROM` there are several "end points" representing the actual sysctls. For example, there is a sysctl called `DEV_CDROM_INFO` which supplies general information on the capabilities of the drive. Applications wishing to access this sysctl must specify the pathname `CTL_DEV/DEV_CDROM/DEV_CDROM_INFO` to identify it uniquely. The numeric values of the required constants are defined in `<sysctl.h>`, which the standard library also used (via `/usr/include/sys/sysctl.h`).

Figure 10-6 shows a graphic excerpt from the sysctl hierarchy that also includes the path described above.

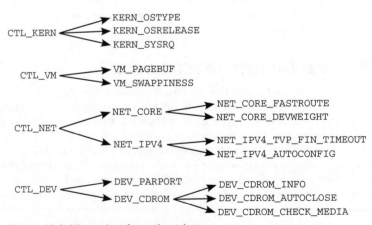

Figure 10-6: Hierarchy of sysctl entries.

The core of the code is the `sysctl` function defined by the C standard library in `/usr/include/sys/sysctl.h`:

```
int sysctl (int *names, int nlen, void *oldval,
            size_t *oldlenp, void *newval, size_t newlen)
```

The path to the sysctl is given as an integer array in which each array element represents a path component. In our example, the path is defined statically in `names`.

The kernel does not know how many path components there are and must therefore be informed explicitly by means of `nlen`; there are three components in our example.

`oldval` is a pointer to a memory area of undefined type, and `oldlenp` specifies the size of the reserved area in bytes. The kernel uses the `oldval` pointer to return the old value represented by sysctl. If this information can be read but not manipulated, its value is the same both before and after the sysctl call. In this case, `oldval` is used to read its value. Once the system call has been executed, the length of the output data is given in `oldval`; for this reason, the variable must be passed by reference and not by value.

`newval` and `newlen` also form a pair consisting of a pointer and a length specification. They are used when a sysctl allows a kernel parameter to be modified. The `newval` pointer points to the memory area where the new information is held in userspace, and `newlenp` specifies its length. A null pointer is passed for `newval` and a zero for `newlenp` in the case of read access, as in our example.

How does the sample code work? Once all parameters have been generated for the `sysctl` call (pathname and memory location to return the desired information), `sysctl` is invoked and returns an integer number as its result. 0 means that the call was successful (I skip error handling for the sake of simplicity). The data obtained are held in `oldval` and can be printed out like any normal C string using `printf`.

Data Structures

The kernel defines several data structures for managing sysctls. As usual, let's take a closer look at them before examining their implementation. Because sysctls are arranged hierarchically (each larger kernel subsystem defines its own sysctl list with its various subsections), the data structure must not only hold information on the individual sysctls and their read and write operations, it must also provide ways of mapping the hierarchy between the individual entries.

Each sysctl entry has its own `ctl_table` instance:

```
<sysctl.h>
struct ctl_table
{
        int ctl_name;                   /* Binary ID */
        const char *procname;           /* Text ID for /proc/sys, or zero */
        void *data;
        int maxlen;
        mode_t mode;
        struct ctl_table *child;
        struct ctl_table *parent;       /* Automatically set */
        proc_handler *proc_handler;     /* Callback for text formatting */
        ctl_handler *strategy;          /* Callback function for all r/w */
```

```
            struct proc_dir_entry *de;        /* /proc control block */
            void *extra1;
            void *extra2;
};
```

> The name of the structure is misleading. A *sysctl table* is an array of `sysctl` structures, whereas a single instance of the structure is called a *sysctl entry* — despite the word `table` in its name.

The meanings of the structure elements are as follows:

❏ `ctl_name` is an ID, that must be unique only on the given hierarchy level of the entry but not in the entire table.

<sysctl.h> contains countless `enums` that define sysctl identifiers for various purposes. The identifiers for the base categories are defined by the following enumeration:

<sysctl.h>
```
enum
{
        CTL_KERN=1,               /* General kernel info and control */
        CTL_VM=2,                 /* VM management */
        CTL_NET=3,                /* Networking */
        CTL_PROC=4,               /* Process info */
        CTL_FS=5,                 /* File Systems */
        CTL_DEBUG=6,              /* Debugging */
        CTL_DEV=7,                /* Devices */
        CTL_BUS=8,                /* Busses */
        CTL_ABI=9,                /* Binary emulation */
        CTL_CPU=10                /* CPU stuff (speed scaling, etc) */
...
};
```

Below `CTL_DEV`, there are entries for various device types:

<sysctl.h>
```
/* CTL_DEV names: */
enum {
        DEV_CDROM=1,
        DEV_HWMON=2,
        DEV_PARPORT=3,
        DEV_RAID=4,
        DEV_MAC_HID=5,
        DEV_SCSI=6,
        DEV_IPMI=7,
};
```

The constant 1 (and others) occurs more than once in the enumerations shown — in both `CTL_KERN` and `DEV_CDROM`. This is not a problem because the two entries are on different hierarchy levels, as shown in Figure 10-6.

❏ `procname` is a string containing a human-readable description of the entry in /proc/sys. The names of all root entries appear as directory names in /proc/sys.

```
wolfgang@meitner> ls -l /proc/sys
total 0
dr-xr-xr-x  2 root root 0 2006-08-11 00:09 debug
dr-xr-xr-x  8 root root 0 2006-08-11 00:09 dev
dr-xr-xr-x  7 root root 0 2006-08-11 00:09 fs
dr-xr-xr-x  4 root root 0 2006-08-11 00:09 kernel
dr-xr-xr-x  8 root root 0 2006-08-11 00:09 net
dr-xr-xr-x  2 root root 0 2006-08-11 00:09 proc
dr-xr-xr-x  2 root root 0 2006-08-11 00:09 sunrpc
dr-xr-xr-x  2 root root 0 2006-08-11 00:09 vm
```

If the entry is not to be exported to the proc filesystem (and is therefore only accessible using the sysctl system call), procname can also be assigned a null pointer, although this is extremely unusual.

❑ data may be assigned any value — usually a function pointer or a string — that is processed by sysctl-specific functions. The generic code leaves this element untouched.

❑ maxlen specifies the maximum length (in bytes) of data accepted or output by a sysctl.

❑ mode controls the access rights to the data and determines whether and by whom data may be read or written. Rights are assigned using the virtual filesystem constants with which you are familiar from Chapter 8.

❑ child is a pointer to an array of additional ctl_table elements regarded as children of the current element. For example, in the CTL_KERN sysctl entry, child points to a table containing entries such as KERN_OSTYPE (operating system type), KERN_OSRELEASE (kernel version number), and KERN_HOSTNAME (name of the host on which the kernel is running) because these are hierarchically subordinate to the CTL_KERN sysctl.

Because the length of the ctl_table arrays is not stored explicitly anywhere, the last entry must always be an instance of ctl_table whose entries consist of null pointers.

❑ proc_readsys is invoked when data are output via the proc interface. The kernel can output the data stored in the kernel directly, but also has the option of translating it into a more readable form (e.g., converting numeric constants into more meaningful strings).

❑ strategy is used by the kernel to read or write the value of a sysctl via the system call interface discussed above (note that proc uses different functions of its own for this purpose). ctl_handler is a typedef for a function pointer defined as follows:

<sysctl.h>
```
typedef int ctl_handler (ctl_table *table, int __user *name, int nlen,
                         void __user *oldval, size_t __user *oldlenp,
                         void __user *newval, size_t newlen);
```

In addition to the complete set of arguments used when the sysctl system call is invoked, the function also expects a pointer to the ctl_table instance where the current sysctl is located. It also needs a context-dependent void* pointer that is currently unused and to which a null pointer is therefore always assigned.

❑ The interface to the proc data is set up by de.

❑ extra1 and extra2 can be filled with proc-specific data that are not manipulated by the generic sysctl code. They are often used to define upper and lower limits for numeric arguments.

The kernel provides the `ctl_table_header` data structure to enable several sysctl tables to be maintained in a linked list that can be traversed and manipulated using the familiar standard functions. The structure is prefixed to a sysctl table in order to insert the elements needed for list management:

<sysctl.h>
```
struct ctl_table_header
{
        ctl_table *ctl_table;
        struct list_head ctl_entry;
...
};
```

`ctl_table` is a pointer to a sysctl array (consisting of `ctl_table` elements). `ctl_entry` holds the elements required to manage the list. Figure 10-7 clearly illustrates the relationship between `ctl_table_header` and `ctl_table`.[3]

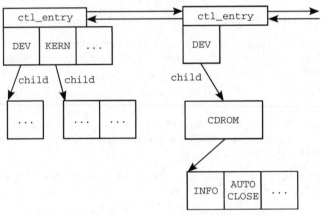

Figure 10-7: Relationship between `ctl_table_header` and `ctl_table`.

The hierarchical relationship between the various sysctl tables of the system is established by the `child` element of `ctl_table` and by the linked list implemented using `ctl_table_header`. The linkage via `child` enables a direct connection to be made between the various tables that map the sysctl hierarchy.

In the kernel it is possible to define various hierarchies in which sysctl tables are interlinked by means of `child` pointers. However, because there may be just one overall hierarchy, the individual hierarchies must be "overlaid" to form a single hierarchy. This situation is illustrated in Figure 10-7, in which there are two independent hierarchies. One is the standard kernel hierarchy containing sysctls to query, for example, the name of the host or the network status. This hierarchy also includes a container to supply information on system peripherals.

The CD-ROM driver wants to export sysctls to output information on the CD-ROM drive of the system. What is needed is a sysctl (in `/proc/sys/dev/cdrom/info` in the `proc` filesystem) that is a child of `CTL_DEV` and provides, for example, general data to describe the drive. How does the driver go about this?

---

[3]The list elements are actually below the data elements, but, for reasons of presentability, I have turned this situation "on its head" in the figure.

❑ First, a four-level hierarchy is created with the help of sysctl tables. CTL_DEV is the base level and has a child called DEV_CDROM. This also has several child elements, one of which is called DEV_CDROM_INFO.

❑ The new hierarchy is associated with the existing standard hierarchy in a linked list. This has the effect of "overlaying" the two hierarchies. Seen from userspace, it is impossible to distinguish between the hierarchies because they appear as a single overall hierarchy.

The sample program above used the sysctl described without having to know how the hierarchy is represented in the kernel. All it needs to know to access the required information is the path CTL_DEV->DEV_CDROM->DEVCDROM_INFO.

Of course, the contents of the /proc/sys directory in the proc filesystem are also constructed in such a way that the internal composition of the hierarchy is not visible.

Static Sysctl Tables

Static sysctl tables are defined for all sysctls, regardless of the system configuration.[4] The base element is the table named root_table, which acts as the root of the statically defined data:

kernel/sysctl.c

```
static ctl_table root_table[];
static struct ctl_table_header root_table_header =
        { root_table, LIST_HEAD_INIT(root_table_header.ctl_entry) };
```

The table is given a header element so that additional hierarchies can be maintained in a linked list as described above; these can be overlaid with the hierarchy defined by root_table. The root_table table defines the framework into which the various sysctls are sorted:

kernel/sysctl.c

```
static ctl_table root_table[] = {
        {
                .ctl_name       = CTL_KERN,
                .procname       = "kernel",
                .mode           = 0555,
                .child          = kern_table,
        },
        {
                .ctl_name       = CTL_VM,
                .procname       = "vm",
                .mode           = 0555,
                .child          = vm_table,
        },
#ifdef CONFIG_NET
        {
                .ctl_name       = CTL_NET,
                .procname       = "net",
                .mode           = 0555,
                .child          = net_table,
        },
#endif#
        ...
```

---

[4]Even though sysctls of this kind are implemented on all architectures, their effect may differ from architecture to architecture.

```
        {
                .ctl_name       = CTL_DEV,
                .procname       = "dev",
                .mode           = 0555,
                .child          = dev_table,
        },

        { .ctl_name = 0 }
};
```

Of course, further top-level categories can be added using the overlay mechanism described above. The kernel also selects this option, for example, for all sysctls that are assigned to the ABI (*application binary interface*) and belong to the CTL_ABI category.

The tables referenced in the definition of root_table — kern_table, net_table, and so on — are likewise defined as static arrays. Because they hold a wealth of sysctls, we ignore their lengthy definitions here, particularly as they offer little of interest besides further static ctl_table instances. Their contents can be viewed in the kernel sources, and their definitions are included in kernel/sysctl.c.

Registering Sysctls

In addition to statically initiated sysctls, the kernel features an interface for dynamically registering and unregistering new system control functions. register_sysctl_table is used to register controls and its counterpart, unregister_sysctl_table, to remove sysctl tables, typically when modules are unloaded.

The register_sysctl_table function requires one parameter — a pointer to an array of ctl_table entries in which the new sysctl hierarchy is defined. The function also comprises just a few steps. First, a new ctl_table_header is instantiated and associated with the sysctl table. The resulting construct is then added to the existing list of sysctl hierarchies.

The auxiliary function sysct_check_table is used to check that the new entry contains proper information. Basically, it ensures that no nonsense combinations are specified (i.e., directories that contain data directories that are writable) and that regular files have a valid strategy routine.

Registering a sysctl entry does not automatically create inode instances that connect the sysctl entries with proc entries. Since most sysctls are never used via proc, this wastes memory. Instead, the connection with proc files is created dynamically. Only the directory /proc/sys is created when procfs is initialized:

fs/proc/proc_sysctl.c
```
int proc_sys_init(void)
{
        proc_sys_root = proc_mkdir("sys", NULL);
        proc_sys_root->proc_iops = &proc_sys_inode_operations;
        proc_sys_root->proc_fops = &proc_sys_file_operations;
        proc_sys_root->nlink = 0;
        return 0;
}
```

The inode operations specified in proc_sys_inode_operations ensure that files and directories below /proc/sys are dynamically generated when they are needed. The contents of the structure are as follows:

fs/proc/proc_sysctl.c

```
static struct inode_operations proc_sys_inode_operations = {
        .lookup        = proc_sys_lookup,
        .permission    = proc_sys_permission,
        .setattr       = proc_sys_setattr,
};
```

Lookup operations are handled by `proc_sys_lookup`. The following approach is used to dynamically construct inodes for `proc` entries:

❑ `do_proc_sys_lookup` takes the parent `dentry` and the name of the file or directory to find the desired sysctl table entry. This involves mainly iterating over the data structures presented before.

❑ Given the `inode` of the parent directory and the sysctl table, `proc_sys_make_inode` is employed to construct the required `inode` instance. Since the new inode's inode operations are also implemented by `proc_sys_inode_operations`, it is ensured that the described method also works for new subdirectories.

The file operations for `/proc/sys` entries are given as follows:

kernel/sysctl.c

```
static const struct file_operations proc_sys_file_operations = {
        .read         = proc_sys_read,
        .write        = proc_sys_write,
        .readdir      = proc_sys_readdir,
};
```

Read and write file operations for all entries are implemented by means of standard operations.

/proc/sys File Operations

The implementations for `proc_sys_read` and `proc_sys_write` are very similar. Both require three easy steps:

1. `do_proc_sys_lookup` finds the sysctl table entry that is associated with the file in `/proc/sys`.

2. It is not guaranteed that all rights on sysctl entries are granted even to the root user. Some entries can, for instance, be only read, but are not allowed to be changed, that is, written to. Thus an extra permission check with `sysctl_perm` is required. While `proc_sys_read` needs read permission, write permission is necessary for `proc_sys_write`.

3. Calling the `proc` handler stored in the sysctl table completes the action.

`proc_handler` is assigned a function pointer when the sysctl tables are defined. Because the various sysctls are spread over several standard categories (in terms of their parameter and return values), the kernel provides standard implementations that are normally used in place of the specific function implementations. Most frequently, the following functions are used:

❑ `proc_dointvec` reads or writes integer values from or to the kernel [the exact number of values is specified by `table->maxlen/sizeof(unsigned int)`]. Only a single integer may be involved (and not a vector) if `maxlen` indicates the byte number of a single `unsigned int`.

❑ `proc_dointvec_minmax` works in the same way as `proc_dointvec`, but ensures that each number is within a minimum and maximum value range specified by `table->extra1` (minimum value) and `table->extra2` (maximum value). All values outside the range are ignored.

`proc_doulongvec_minmax` serves the same purpose, but uses values with type `unsigned long` instead of `int`.

❑ `proc_dointvec_jiffies` reads an integer table. The values are converted to jiffies. A nearly identical variant is `proc_dointvec_ms`, where the values are interpreted as milliseconds.

❑ `proc_dostring` transfers strings between kernel and userspace and vice versa. Strings that are longer than the internal buffer of an entry are automatically truncated. When data are copied into userspace, a *carriage return* (\n) is appended automatically so that a line break is added after information is output (e.g., using `cat`).

10.2 Simple Filesystems

Full-featured filesystems are hard to write and require a considerable amount of effort until they reach a usable, efficient, and correct state. This is reasonable if the filesystem is really supposed to store data on disk. However, filesystems — especially virtual ones — serve many purposes that differ from storing proper files on a block device. Such filesystems still run in the kernel, and their code is thus subjected to the rigorous quality requirements imposed by the kernel developers. However, various standard methods makes this aspect of life much easier. A small filesystem library — libfs — contains nearly all ingredients required to implement a filesystem. Developers only need to provide an interface to their data, and they are done.

Additionally, some more standard routines — in the form of the `seq_file` mechanism — are available to handle sequential files with little effort. Finally, developers might want to just export a value or two into userspace without messing with the existing filesystems like procfs. The kernel also provides a cure for this need: The debugfs filesystem allows for implementing a bidirectional debugging interface with only a few function calls.

10.2.1 Sequential Files

Before discussing any filesystem library, we need to have a look at the sequential file interface. Files in small filesystems will usually be read sequentially from start to end from userland, and their contents are created by iterating over several items. These could, for instance, be array elements. The kernel traverses the the whole array from start to end and creates a textual representation for each element. Put into kernel nomenclature, one could also call this making synthetic files from sequences of records.

The routines in `fs/seq_file.c` allow implementing such files with minimal effort. Despite their name, seeking is possible for sequential files, but the implementation is not very efficient. Sequential access — where one item is read after another — is clearly the preferred mode of access; simplicity in one aspect often comes with a price in other regards.

The kprobe mechanism contains an interface to the aforementioned debug filesystem. A sequential file presents all registered probes to userland. I consider the implementation to illustrate the idea of sequential files.

Writing Sequential File Handlers

Basically, an instance of `struct file_operations` that provides pointers to some `seq_` routines must be implemented to benefit from the sequential file standard implementation. The kprobes subsystem does this as follows:

kernel/kprobes.c
```
static struct file_operations debugfs_kprobes_operations = {
        .open           = kprobes_open,
        .read           = seq_read,
        .llseek         = seq_lseek,
        .release        = seq_release,
};
```

This instance of `file_operations` can be associated with a file by the methods discussed in Chapter 8. In the case of kprobes, the file will be created in the debugging filesystem; see Section 10.2.3.

The only method that needs to be implemented is `open`. Not much effort is required for the function, though: A simple one-liner connects the file with the sequential file interface:

kernel/kprobes.c
```
static struct seq_operations kprobes_seq_ops = {
        .start = kprobe_seq_start,
        .next  = kprobe_seq_next,
        .stop  = kprobe_seq_stop,
        .show  = show_kprobe_addr
};

static int __kprobes kprobes_open(struct inode *inode, struct file *filp)
{
        return seq_open(filp, &kprobes_seq_ops);
}
```

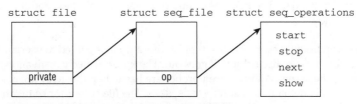

Figure 10-8: Data structures for sequential files.

`seq_open` sets up the data structures required by the sequential file mechanism. The result is shown in Figure 10-8. Recall from Chapter 8 that the `private_data` element of `struct file` can point to arbitrary data that are private to the file and not touched by the generic VFS functions. In this case, `seq_open` uses the pointer to establish a connection with an instance of `struct seq_file` that contains status information about the sequential file:

<seq_file.h>
```
struct seq_file {
        char *buf;
```

```
        size_t size;
        size_t from;
        size_t count;
        loff_t index;
...
        const struct seq_operations *op;
...
};
```

buf points to a memory buffer that allows for constructing data that go out to userland. count specifies the number of bytes remaining to be written to userland. The start position of the copy operation is denoted by from, and size gives the total number of bytes in the buffer. index is another index into the buffer. It marks the start position for the next new record that is written into the buffer by the kernel. Note that index and from can evolve differently since writing data into the buffer is different from copying these data to userspace.

The most important element from a filesystem implementor's point of view is the pointer op to an instance of seq_operations. This connects the generic sequential file implementation with routines providing file-specific contents. Four methods are required by the kernel and need to be implemented by the file provider:

<seq_file.h>
```
struct seq_operations {
        void * (*start) (struct seq_file *m, loff_t *pos);
        void (*stop) (struct seq_file *m, void *v);
        void * (*next) (struct seq_file *m, void *v, loff_t *pos);
        int (*show) (struct seq_file *m, void *v);
};
```

The first argument to the functions is always the seq_file instance in question. The start method is called whenever an operation on a sequential file is started. The position argument pos is a cursor in the file. The interpretation is left to the implementation. It could be taken as a byte offset, but can also be interpreted as an array index. The kprobes example implements all these routines as shown above, so they are discussed now.

Let us first, however, briefly describe which type of information is passed to userland — we need to know what goes out before we can discuss how it goes out. The kprobes mechanism allows for attaching probes to certain points in the kernel. All registered probes are hashed on the array kprobe_table, and the size of the array is statically defined to KPROBE_TABLE_SIZE. The file cursor for sequential files is interpreted as an index into the array, and the debug file is supposed to show information about all registered probes that must be constructed from the contents of the hash table.

The start method is simple: It just needs to check if the current cursor is beyond the array bounds.

kernel/kprobes.c
```
static void __kprobes *kprobe_seq_start(struct seq_file *f, loff_t *pos)
{
        return (*pos < KPROBE_TABLE_SIZE) ? pos : NULL;
}
```

This is simple, but closing a sequential file is even simpler: In almost all cases, nothing needs to be done!

kernel/kprobes.c
```
static void __kprobes kprobe_seq_stop(struct seq_file *f, void *v)
{
        /* Nothing to do */
}
```

The next function is called when the cursor must be updated to the next position. Besides incrementing the array index, the function must check that it does not go out of bounds:

kernel/kprobes.c
```
static void __kprobes *kprobe_seq_next(struct seq_file *f, void *v, loff_t *pos)
{
        (*pos)++;
        if (*pos >= KPROBE_TABLE_SIZE)
                return NULL;
        return pos;
}
```

A NULL pointer indicates that the end of the file is reached.

The most interesting function is show since the actual contents of the sequential file are generated here. For the sake of illustration, I present a slightly simplified version that abstracts some of the difficulties associated with kprobes that would detract from the seq_file issues:

kernel/kprobes.c
```
static int show_kprobe_addr(struct seq_file *pi, void *v)
{
        struct hlist_head *head;
        struct hlist_node *node;
        struct kprobe *p;
        const char *sym = NULL;
        unsigned int i = *(loff_t *) v;
        unsigned long offset = 0;
        char *modname, namebuf[128];

        head = &kprobe_table[i];

        hlist_for_each_entry_rcu(p, node, head, hlist) {
                sym = kallsyms_lookup((unsigned long)p->addr, NULL,
                                &offset, &modname, namebuf);
                if (sym)
                        seq_printf(pi, "%p %s+0x%x %s\n", p->addr,
                                sym, offset, (modname ? modname : " "));
                else
                        seq_printf(pi, "%p\n", p->addr);
        }
        return 0;
}
```

The current value of the file cursor is in the argument v, and the function converts it into the array index i. Data generation is done by iterating over all elements hashed on this array index. An output line is constructed for each element. Information about the probe point and the symbol that is possibly associated with the point is generated, but this is not really relevant for the example. What does matter is that instead of `printk`, `seq_printf` is used to format the information. In fact, the kernel provides some auxiliary functions that must be used for this purpose. All take a pointer to the `seq_file` instance in question as first parameter:

❑ `seq_printf` works like `printk` and can be used to format arbitrary C strings.

❑ `seq_putc` and `seq_puts`, respectively, write out a single character and a string without any formatting.

❑ `seq_esc` takes two strings. All characters in the second string that are found in the first string are replaced by their value in octal.

The special function `sec_path` allows for constructing the filename associated with a given instance of `struct dentry`. It is used by filesystem- or namespace-specific code.

Connection with the Virtual Filesystem

Up to now, I have presented everything that is required from a sequential file user. The rest, that is, connecting the operations with the virtual filesystem, is left to the kernel. To establish the connection, it is necessary to use the `seq_read` as `read` method for `file_operations` as shown above in the case of `debugfs_kprobes_operations`. The method bridges VFS and sequential files.

First of all, the function needs to obtain the `seq_file` instance from the VFS layer's `struct file`. Recall that `seq_opened` has established a connection via `private_data`.

If some data are waiting to be written out — as indicated by a positive `count` element of `struct seq_file` — , they are copied to userland with `copy_to_user`. Additionally, updating the various status elements of `seq_file` is required.

In the next step, new data are generated. After calling `start`, the kernel calls `show` and `next` one after another until the available buffer is filled. Finally, `stop` is employed, and the generated data are copied to userspace using `copy_to_user`.

10.2.2 Writing Filesystems with Libfs

Libfs is a library that provides several very generic standard routines that can be used to create small filesystems that serve one specific purpose. The routines are well suited for in-memory files without a backing store. Obviously the code cannot provide means to interact with specific on-disk formats; this needs to be handled properly by full filesystem implementations. The library code is contained in a single file, `fs/libfs.c`.

> The prototypes are defined in **<fs.h>**; there is *no* **<libfs.h>**! Routines provided by libfs are generally prefixed by **simple_**. Recall from Chapter 8 that the kernel also provides several generic filesystem routines that are prefixed by **generic_**. In contrast to libfs routines, these can also be used for full-blown filesystems.

The file and directory hierarchy of virtual filesystems that use libfs is generated and traversed using the dentry tree. This implies that during the lifetime of the filesystem, all dentries must be pinned into memory. They must not go away unless they are explicitly removed via `unlink` or `rmdir`. However, this is simple to achieve: The code only needs to ensure that all dentries always have a positive use count.

To understand the idea of libfs better, let's discuss the way directory handling is implemented. Boilerplate instances of inode and file operations for directories are provided that can immediately be reused for any virtual filesystem implemented along the lines of libfs:

fs/libfs.c

```
const struct file_operations simple_dir_operations = {
        .open           = dcache_dir_open,
        .release        = dcache_dir_close,
        .llseek         = dcache_dir_lseek,
        .read           = generic_read_dir,
        .readdir        = dcache_readdir,
        .fsync          = simple_sync_file,
};

const struct inode_operations simple_dir_inode_operations = {
        .lookup = simple_lookup,
};
```

In contrast to the convention introduced above, the names of the routines that make up `simple_dir_operations` do not start with `simple_`. Nevertheless, they are defined in `fs/libfs.c`. The nomenclature reflects that the operations solely operate on objects from the dentry cache.

If a virtual filesystem sets up a proper dentry tree, it suffices to install `simple_dir_operations` and `simple_dir_inode_operations` as file or inode operations, respectively, for directories. The libfs functions then ensure that the information contained on the tree is exported to userland via the standard system calls like `getdents`. Since constructing one representation from another is basically a mechanical task, the source code is not discussed in detail.

Instead, it is more interesting to observe how new files are added to a virtual filesystem. Debugfs (discussed below) is one filesystem that employs libfs. New files (and thus new inodes) are created with the following routine:

fs/debugfs/inode.c

```
static struct inode *debugfs_get_inode(struct super_block *sb, int mode, dev_t dev)
{
        struct inode *inode = new_inode(sb);

        if (inode) {
                inode->i_mode = mode;
                inode->i_uid = 0;
                inode->i_gid = 0;
                inode->i_blocks = 0;
                inode->i_atime = inode->i_mtime = inode->i_ctime = CURRENT_TIME;
                switch (mode & S_IFMT) {
                default:
                        init_special_inode(inode, mode, dev);
                        break;
                case S_IFREG:
                        inode->i_fop = &debugfs_file_operations;
                        break;
...
                case S_IFDIR:
```

```
                              inode->i_op = &simple_dir_inode_operations;
                              inode->i_fop = &simple_dir_operations;

                              /* directory inodes start off with i_nlink == 2
                               * (for "." entry) */
                              inc_nlink(inode);
                              break;
                      }
              }
              return inode;
      }
```

Besides allocating a new instance of struct inode, the kernel needs to decide which file and inode operations are to be associated with the file depending on the information in the access mode. For device special files, the standard routine init_special_file (not connected with libfs) is used. The more interesting cases, however, are regular files and directories. Directories require the standard file and inode operations as discussed above; this ensures with no further effort that the new directory is correctly handled.

Regular files cannot be provided with boilerplate file operations. It is at least necessary to manually specify the read, write, and open methods. read is supposed to prepare data from kernel memory and copy them into userspace, while write can be used to read input from the user and apply it somehow. This is all that is required to implement custom files!

A filesystem also requires a superblock. Thankfully for lazy programmers, libfs provides the method simple_fill_super, that can be used to fill in a given superblock:

<fs.h>
```
int simple_fill_super(struct super_block *s, int magic, struct tree_descr *files);
```

s is the superblock in question, and magic specifies a unique magic number which can be used to identify the filesystem. The files parameter provides a very convenient method to populate the virtual filesystem with what it is supposed to contain: files! Unfortunately, only files in a single directory can be specified with this method, but this is not a real limitation for virtual filesystems. More content can still be added later dynamically.

An array with struct tree_descr elements is used to describe the initial set of files. The structure is defined as follows:

<fs.h>
```
struct tree_descr {
        char *name;
        const struct file_operations *ops;
        int mode;
};
```

name denotes the filename, ops points to the associated file operations, and mode specifies the access bits.

The last entry in the list must be of the form { "", NULL, 0 }.

10.2.3 The Debug Filesystem

One particular filesystem using functions from libfs is the debug filesystem debugfs. It presents kernel developers with a possibility of providing information to userland. The information is not supposed to be compiled into production kernels. Quite in contrast, it is only an aid for developing new features. Support for debugfs is only activated if the kernel is compiled with the DEBUG_FS configuration option. Code that registers files in debugfs thus needs to be embraced by C pre-processor conditionals checking for CONFIG_DEBUG_FS.

Example

Recall the kprobes example discussed earlier in the chapter as an example for the sequential file mechanism. The resulting file is exported via debugfs in only a couple of lines — as simple as can be!

kernel/kprobes.c
```
#ifdef CONFIG_DEBUG_FS
...
static int __kprobes debugfs_kprobe_init(void)
{
        struct dentry *dir, *file;
        unsigned int value = 1;

        dir = debugfs_create_dir("kprobes", NULL);
...
        file = debugfs_create_file("list", 0444, dir, NULL,
                                &debugfs_kprobes_operations);
...
        return 0;
}
...
#endif /* CONFIG_DEBUG_FS */
```

debugfs_create_dir is used to create a new directory, and debugfs_create_file establishes a new file in this directory. debugfs_kprobes_operations was discussed above as an example for the sequential file mechanism.

Programming Interface

Since the debugfs code is very clean, simple, and well documented, it is not necessary to add remarks about the implementation. It suffices to discuss the programming interface. However, have a look at the source code, which is a very nice application of the libfs routines.

Three functions are available to create new filesystem objects:

<debugfs.h>
```
struct dentry *debugfs_create_file(const char *name, mode_t mode,
                                struct dentry *parent, void *data,
                                const struct file_operations *fops);

struct dentry *debugfs_create_dir(const char *name, struct dentry *parent);
```

```
struct dentry *debugfs_create_symlink(const char *name, struct dentry *parent,
                              const char *dest);
```

Unsurprisingly, a filesystem object can either be a regular file, a directory, or a symbolic link. Two additional operations allow for renaming and removing files:

<debugfs.h>
```
void debugfs_remove(struct dentry *dentry);

struct dentry *debugfs_rename(struct dentry *old_dir, struct dentry *old_dentry,
                struct dentry *new_dir, const char *new_name);
```

When kernel code is being debugged, the need to export and manipulate a single elementary value like an int or a long often arises. Debugfs also provides several functions that create a new file that allows for reading the value from userspace and passing a new value into the kernel. They all share a common prototype:

<debugfs.h>
```
struct dentry *debugfs_create_XX(const char *name, mode_t mode,
                struct dentry *parent, XX *value);
```

name and mode denote the filename and access mode, while parent points to the dentry instance of the parent directory. value is most important: It points to the value that is exported and can be modified by writing into the file. The function is available for several data types.

If XX is replaced by any of the standard kernel data types u8, u16, u32, or u64, a file that allows for reading but forbids changing the value is created. If x8, x16, or x32 is used, the value can also be changed from userspace.

A file that presents a Boolean value can be created by debugfs_create_bool:

<debugfs.h>
```
struct dentry *debugfs_create_bool(const char *name, mode_t mode,
                struct dentry *parent, u32 *value)
```

Finally, it is also possible to exchange short portions of binary data (conventionally called *binary blobs*) with userspace. The following function is provided for this purpose:

<debugfs.h>
```
struct dentry *debugfs_create_blob(const char *name, mode_t mode,
                                struct dentry *parent,
                                struct debugfs_blob_wrapper *blob);
```

The binary data are represented by a special data structure containing a pointer to the memory location that holds the data and the data length:

<debugfs.h>
```
struct debugfs_blob_wrapper {
        void *data;
        unsigned long size;
};
```

10.2.4 Pseudo Filesystems

Recall from Section 8.4.1 that the kernel supports pseudo-filesystems that collect related inodes, but cannot be mounted and are thus not visible in userland. Libfs also provides an auxiliary function to implement this specialized type of filesystem.

The kernel employs a pseudo-filesystem to keep track of all inodes that represent block devices:

fs/block_dev.c
```
static int bd_get_sb(struct file_system_type *fs_type,
        int flags, const char *dev_name, void *data, struct vfsmount *mnt)
{
        return get_sb_pseudo(fs_type, "bdev:", &bdev_sops, 0x62646576, mnt);
}

static struct file_system_type bd_type = {
        .name           = "bdev",
        .get_sb         = bd_get_sb,
        .kill_sb        = kill_anon_super,
};
```

The code looks as for any regular filesystem, but libfs provides the method get_sb_pseudo which ensures that the filesystem cannot be mounted from userspace. This is simple: It just needs to set the flag MS_NOUSER as discussed in Chapter 8. Besides, an instance of struct super_block is filled in, and the root inode for the pseudo-filesystem is allocated.

To use a pseudo-filesystem, the kernel needs to mount it using kern_mount or kern_mount_data. It can be used to collect inodes without the hassle of writing a specialized data structure to do so. For bdev, all inodes that represent block devices are grouped together. The collection, however, will only be visible to the kernel and not to userspace.

10.3 Sysfs

Sysfs is a filesystem for exporting kernel objects to userspace, providing the ability to not only observe properties of kernel-internal data structures, but also to modify them. Especially important is the highly hierarchical organization of the filesystem layout: The entries of sysfs originate from kernel objects (kobjects) as introduced in Chapter 1, and the hierarchical order of these is directly reflected in the directory layout of sysfs.[5] Since all devices and buses of the system are organized via kobjects, sysfs provides a representation of the system's hardware topology.

In many cases, short, human readable text strings are used to export object properties, but passing binary data to and from the kernel via sysfs is also frequently employed. Sysfs has become an alternative to the more old-fashioned IOCTL mechanism. Instead of sending cryptic ioctls into the kernel, which usually requires a C program, it is much simpler to read from or write a value to a sysfs file. A simple shell command is sufficient. Another advantage is that a simple directory listing provides a quick overview on what options can be set.

As for many virtual filesystems, sysfs was initially based on ramfs; thus, the implementation uses many techniques known from other places in the kernel. Note that sysfs is always compiled into the kernel

---

[5]The large number of extensively interconnected data structures known from the kobject mechanism is thus also directly transferred to sysfs, at least when a kobject is exported to the filesystem.

if it is configured to be active; generating it as a module is not possible. The canonical mount point for sysfs is /sys.

The kernel sources contain some documentation on sysfs, its relation to the driver model with respect to the kobject framework, and so on. It can be found in Documentation/filesystems/sysfs.txt and Documentation/filesystems/sysfs-pci.txt. An overview article by the author of sysfs himself is available in the proceedings of the Ottawa Linux Symposium 2005 on www.linuxsymposium.org/2005/linuxsymposium_procv1.pdf.

Finally, note that the connection between kobjects and sysfs is not automatically set up. Standalone kobject instances are by default not integrated into sysfs. You need to call kobject_add to make an object visible in the filesystem. If the kobject is a member of a kernel subsystem, the registration is performed automatically, though.

10.3.1 Overview

struct kobject, the related data structures, and their usage are described in Chapter 1; thus, here our discussion is restricted to a recap of the most essential points. In particular, it is important to remember that

❑ kobjects are included in a hierarchic organization; most important, they can have a *parent* and can be included in a kset. This determines where the kobject appears in the sysfs hierarchy: If a parent exists, a new entry in the directory of the parent is created. Otherwise, it is placed in the directory of the kobject that belongs to the kset the object is contained in (if both of these possibilities fail, the entry for the kobject is located directly in the top level of the system hierarchy, but this is obviously a rare case).

❑ Every kobject is represented as a directory within sysfs. The files that appear in this directory are the *attributes* of the object. The operations used to export and set attribute values are provided by the subsystem (class, driver, etc.) to which the kobject belongs.

❑ Buses, devices, drivers, and classes are the main kernel objects using the kobject mechanism; they thus account for nearly all entries of sysfs.

10.3.2 Data Structures

As usual, let's first discuss the data structures used by the sysfs implementation.

Directory Entries

Directory entries are represented by struct sysfs_dirent as defined in <sysfs.h>. It is the main data structure of sysfs; the whole implementation is centered around it. Each sysfs node is represented by a single instance of sysfs_dirent. The definition is as follows:

```
<sysfs.h>
struct sysfs_dirent {
        atomic_t s_count;
        atomic_t s_active;
        struct sysfs_dirent *s_parent;
        struct sysfs_dirent *s_sibling;
        const char *s_name;
```

```
        union {
                struct sysfs_elem_dir s_dir;
                struct sysfs_elem_symlink s_symlink;
                struct sysfs_elem_attr s_attr;
                struct sysfs_elem_bin_attr s_bin_attr;
        };

        unsigned int s_flags;
        ino_t s_ino;
        umode_t s_mode;
        struct iattr *s_iattr;
};
```

❑ `s_sibling` and `s_children` are used to capture the parent/child relationship between sysfs entries in a data structure: `s_sibling` is used to connect all children of a parent among each other, and `s_children` is used by the parent element to serve as a list head.

❑ The kernel uses `s_flags` with a twofold purpose: First, it is used to set the type of the sysfs entry. Second, it can set a number of flags. The lower 8 bits are used for the type; they can be accessed with the auxiliary function `sysfs_type`. The type can be any of SYSFS_DIR, SYSFS_KOBJ_ATTR, SYSFS_KOBJ_BIN_ATTR or SYSFS_KOBJ_LINK, depending on whether the instance is a directory, a regular respectively binary attribute, or a symbolic link.

   The remaining bits are reserved for flags. Currently, only SYSFS_FLAG_REMOVED is defined, which is set when a sysfs entry is in the process of being removed.

❑ Information about the access mode of the file associated with the `sysfs_dirent` instance is stored in `s_mode`. Attributes are described by an `iattr` instance pointed at by `s_iattr`; if this is a NULL pointer, a default set of attributes is used.

❑ `s_name` points to the filename for the file, directory, or link represented by the object.

❑ Depending on the type of the sysfs entry, different types of data are associated with it. Since an entry can only represent a single type at a time, the data structures that encapsulate the entry's payload are collected in an anonymous union. The members are defined as follows:

fs/sysfs/sysfs.h

```
struct sysfs_elem_dir {
        struct kobject *kobj;
        /* children list starts here and goes through sd->s_sibling */
        struct sysfs_dirent *children;
};

struct sysfs_elem_symlink {
        struct sysfs_dirent *target_sd;
};

struct sysfs_elem_attr {
        struct attribute *attr;
        struct sysfs_open_dirent *open;
};

struct sysfs_elem_bin_attr {
        struct bin_attribute *bin_attr;
};
```

sysfs_elem_attr and sysfs_bin_attr contain pointers to data structures that represent attributes, and are discussed in the following section. sysfs_elem_symlink implements a symbolic link. All it needs to do is provide a pointer to the target sysfs_dirent instance.

Directories are implemented with the aid of sysfs_elem_dir. children is the head of a singly linked list connecting all children via s_sibling. Note that the elements on the sibling list are sorted by s_ino in decreasing order. The relationship is illustrated in Figure 10-9.

Like any other filesystem, sysfs entries are also represented by instances of struct dentry. The connection between both layers is given by dentry->d_fsdata, which points to the sysfs_dirent instance associated with the dentry element.

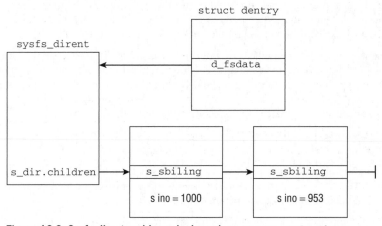

Figure 10-9: Sysfs directory hierarchy based on **struct sysfs_dirent**.

Reference counting for struct sysfs_dirent is unconventional because two reference counters are provided: s_count and s_active. The first one is a standard reference counter that needs to be incremented when the sysfs_dirent instance under consideration is required by some part of the kernel and decremented when it is not required anymore. A problem arises, though, because whenever a sysfs node is opened, the associated kobject is also referenced. Userland applications could thus prevent the kernel from deleting kobject instances by simply keeping a sysfs file open. To circumvent this, the kernel requires that an *active* reference on a sysfs_direntry is held whenever the associated internal objects (available via sysfs_elem_*) are accessed. Unsurprisingly, the active reference counter is implemented with s_active.

When a sysfs file is supposed to be deleted, access to the internal objects associated with it can be deactivated by setting the active reference counter to a negative value — the auxiliary function sysfs_dectivate is provided for this. Once the value is negative, operations on the associated kobject cannot be performed anymore. When all users of the kobject have disappeared, it can safely be deleted by the kernel. The sysfs file and thus the sysfs_dirent instance, however, can still exist — even if they do not make much sense anymore!

Active references can be obtained by sysfs_get_active or sysfs_get_active_two (for a given sysfs_direntry instance as well as its parent). They must immediately be released with `sysfs_put_active` (respectively, `sysfs_put_active_two`) as soon as the operation with the associated internal data is finished.

Attributes

Let us turn our attention to the data structures that represent attributes and the mechanisms used to declare new attributes:

Data Structures

Attributes are defined by the following data structure:

include/linu/<sysfs.h>
```
struct attribute {
        const char              * name;
        struct module           * owner;
        mode_t                  mode;
};
```

`name` provides a name for the attribute that is used as a filename in sysfs (thus attributes that belong to the same object need to have unique names), while `mode` specifies the access mode. `owner` points to the `module` instance to which the owner of the attribute belongs.

It is also possible to define a group of attributes with the aid of the following data structure:

<sysfs.h>
```
struct attribute_group {
        const char              * name;
        struct attribute        ** attrs;
};
```

`name` is a name for the group, and `attrs` points to an array of `attribute` instances terminated by a `NULL` entry.

Note that these data structures only provide a means to represent attributes, but do not specify how to read or modify them. This is covered in Section 10.3.4. The separation of representation and access method was chosen because all attributes belonging to a certain entity (e.g., a driver, a device class, etc.) are modified in a similar way, so it makes sense to transfer this group property to the export/import mechanism. Note, though, that it is customary that the `show` and `store` operations of the subsystem rely on attribute-specific show and store methods that are internally connected with the attribute and that differ on a per-attribute basis. The implementation details are left to the respective subsystem; sysfs is unconcerned about this.

For a read/write attribute, two methods denoted as `show` and `store` need to be available; the kernel provides the following data structure to keep them together:

<sysfs.h>
```
struct sysfs_ops {
        ssize_t (*show)(struct kobject *, struct attribute *,char *);
        ssize_t (*store)(struct kobject *,struct attribute *,const char *, size_t);
};
```

It is the responsibility of the code that declares a new attribute type to provide a suitable set of `show` and `store` operations.

The situation is different for binary attributes: Here, the methods used to read and modify the data are usually different for each attribute. This is reflected in the data structure, where methods for reading, writing, and memory mapping are specified explicitly:

```
<sysfs.h>
struct bin_attribute {
        struct attribute attr;
        size_t size;
        void *private;
        ssize_t (*read)(struct kobject *, struct bin_attribute *,
                        char *, loff_t, size_t);
        ssize_t (*write)(struct kobject *, struct bin_attribute *,
                        char *, loff_t, size_t);
        int (*mmap)(struct kobject *, struct bin_attribute *attr,
                    struct vm_area_struct *vma);
};
```

`size` denotes the size of the binary data associated with the attribute, and `private` is (usually) used to point to the place where the data are actually stored.

Declaring New Attributes

Many possibilities for declaring subsystem-specific attributes are spread around the kernel, but since they all share a basic structure with regard to their implementation, it is sufficient to consider one implementation as an example for the underlying mechanism. Consider, for instance, how the generic hard disk code defines a structure that unites an attribute and the associated methods to read and modify the attribute:

```
<genhd.h>
struct disk_attribute {
        struct attribute attr;
        ssize_t (*show)(struct gendisk *, char *);
        ssize_t (*store)(struct gendisk *, const char *, size_t);
};
```

The `attr` member is nothing other than an attribute as introduced before; this can be fed to sysfs whenever an instance of `attribute` is required. But note that the `show` and `store` function pointers have a different prototype from that required for sysfs!

How do the subsystem-specific attribute functions get called by the sysfs layer? The connection is made by the following struct:

```
block/genhd.c
static struct sysfs_ops disk_sysfs_ops = {
        .show   = &disk_attr_show,
        .store  = &disk_attr_store,
};
```

The `show` and `store` methods of `sysfs_ops` are called when a process wants to read from (or write to) a sysfs file as will be shown below in more detail.

When a sysfs file related to generic hard disk attributes is accessed, the kernel uses the methods disk_attr_show and disk_attr_store to read and modify the attribute values. The disk_attr_show function is called whenever the value of an attribute of this type needs to be read from the kernel; the code acts as the glue between sysfs and the genhd implementation:

block/genhd.c
```
static ssize_t disk_attr_show(struct kobject *kobj, struct attribute *attr,
                              char *page)
{
        struct gendisk *disk = to_disk(kobj);
        struct disk_attribute *disk_attr =
                container_of(attr,struct disk_attribute,attr);
        ssize_t ret = -EIO;

        if (disk_attr->show)
             •  ret = disk_attr->show(disk,page);
        return ret;
}
```

The attribute connected to the sysfs file can be used to infer the containing disk_attribute instance by using the container_of-mechanism; after the kernel has made sure that the attribute possesses a show method, it is called to transfer data from the kernel to userspace and thus from the internal data structures to the sysfs file.

Similar methods are implemented by many other subsystems, but since their code is basically identical to the example shown above, it is unnecessary to consider them in greater detail here. Instead, I will cover the steps leading to a call of the sysfs-specific show and store methods; the connection between subsystem and sysfs is left to the subsystem-specific code.

10.3.3   Mounting the Filesystem

As usual, let's start the discussion of the implementation by considering how the filesystem is mounted. The system call ends up in delegating the work to fill a superblock to sysfs_fill_super; the associated code flow diagram can be found in Figure 10-10.

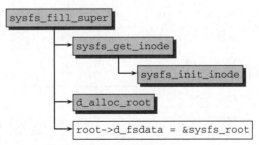

Figure 10-10: Code flow diagram for
sysfs_fill_super.

There is not too much to do for sysfs_fill_super: Some uninteresting initialization work needs to be performed first. sysfs_get_inode is then used to create a new instance of struct inode as the starting point for the whole sysfs tree. The routine can not only be used to obtain the root inode, but is a generic function that works for any sysfs entry. This routine first checks if the inode is already present in the inode hash. Because the filesystem has not been mounted before, this check will fail in our case, so `sysfs_init_inode` is used to construct a new inode instance from scratch. I will come back to this function in a moment.

The final steps are again performed in `sysfs_fill_super`. After allocating a root dentry with `d_alloc_root`, the connection between the sysfs data and the filesystem entry is established:

sysfs/mount.c
```
static int sysfs_fill_super(struct super_block *sb, void *data, int silent)
{
        struct inode *inode;
        struct dentry *root;
...
        root->d_fsdata = &sysfs_root;
        sb->s_root = root;
...
}
```

Recall that `dentry->d_fsdata` is a function pointer reserved for filesystem internal use, so sysfs is allowed to create a connection between `sysfs_dirents` and `dentry` instances this way. `sysfs_root` is a static instance of `stuct sysfs_dirent` that represents the root entry of sysfs. It is defined as follows:

sysfs/mount.c
```
struct sysfs_dirent sysfs_root = {
        .s_name = "",
        .s_count = ATOMIC_INIT(1),
        .s_flags = SYSFS_DIR,
        .s_mode = S_IFDIR | S_IRWXU | S_IRUGO | S_IXUGO,
        .s_ino = 1,
};
```

Note that `d_fsdata` always points to the associated instance of `struct sysfs_dirent`; the scheme is not only used for the root entry, but also for all other entries of sysfs. This connection allows the kernel to derive the sysfs-specific data from the generic VFS data structures.

I will now consider inode initialization in `sysfs_init_inode` in more detail as promised above. The code flow diagram for the function is depicted in Figure 10-11.

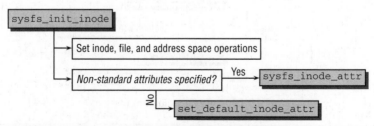

Figure 10-11: Code flow diagram for **sysfs_new_inode**.

`sysfs_init_inode` sets the inode operations such that only `setattr` is implemented by a filesystem-specific function, namely, `sysfs_setattr`. Following this, the kernel takes care of assigning the inode attributes. These can either be specified explicitly via `sysfs_dirent->iattr` or can be left to the default values if the field contains a `NULL` pointer. In this case, the following auxiliary function is used to set the default attributes:

fs/sysfs/inode.c
```
static inline void set_default_inode_attr(struct inode * inode, mode_t mode)
{
        inode->i_mode = mode;
        inode->i_uid = 0;
        inode->i_gid = 0;
        inode->i_atime = inode->i_mtime = inode->i_ctime = CURRENT_TIME;
}
```

While the access mode of the file can be arbitrarily chosen by the caller, the ownership of the file belongs to `root.root` in the default case.

Finally, the inode needs to be initialized according to the type of the sysfs entry:

fs/sysfs/inode.c
```
static void sysfs_init_inode(struct sysfs_dirent *sd, struct inode *inode)
{
...
        /* initialize inode according to type */
        switch (sysfs_type(sd)) {
        case SYSFS_DIR:
                inode->i_op = &sysfs_dir_inode_operations;
                inode->i_fop = &sysfs_dir_operations;
                inode->i_nlink = sysfs_count_nlink(sd);
                break;
        case SYSFS_KOBJ_ATTR:
                inode->i_size = PAGE_SIZE;
                inode->i_fop = &sysfs_file_operations;
                break;
        case SYSFS_KOBJ_BIN_ATTR:
                bin_attr = sd->s_bin_attr.bin_attr;
                inode->i_size = bin_attr->size;
                inode->i_fop = &bin_fops;
                break;
        case SYSFS_KOBJ_LINK:
                inode->i_op = &sysfs_symlink_inode_operations;
                break;
        default:
                BUG();
        }
...
```

Different types are distinguished by different inode and file operations.

10.3.4 File and Directory Operations

Since sysfs exposes its data structures in a filesystem, most interesting operations can be triggered with standard filesystem operations. The functions that implement the filesystem operations thus serve as a glue layer between sysfs and the internal data structures. As for every filesystem, the methods used for operations on files are collected in an instance of `struct file_operations`. For sysfs, the following selection is available:

fs/sysfs/file.c
```
const struct file_operations sysfs_file_operations = {
        .read = sysfs_read_file,
        .write = sysfs_write_file,
        .llseek = generic_file_llseek,
        .open = sysfs_open_file,
        .release = sysfs_release,
        .poll = sysfs_poll,
};
```

In the following, not only are the functions responsible for reading and writing data (`sysfs_{read,write}_file`) described, but also the method for opening files (`sysfs_open_file`) since the connection between sysfs internals and the virtual filesystem is set up there.

A rather small number of directory inode operations need to be specifically provided by sysfs:

fs/sysfs/dir.c
```
struct inode_operations sysfs_dir_inode_operations = {
        .lookup         = sysfs_lookup,
        .setattr        = sysfs_setattr,
};
```

Most operations can be handled by standard VFS operations; only directory lookup and attribute manipulation need to be taken care of explicitly. These methods are discussed in the following sections.

The picture is even simpler for inode operations for regular files; only attribute manipulation needs to be specifically taken care of:

fs/sysfs/inode.c
```
static struct inode_operations sysfs_inode_operations ={
        .setattr        = sysfs_setattr,
};
```

Opening Files

Opening a file is a rather boring operation for a regular filesystem. In the case of sysfs, it becomes more interesting because the sysfs internal data needs to be connected with the user-visible representation in the filesystem.

Data Structures

In order to facilitate the exchange of data between userland and the sysfs implementation, some buffer space needs to be available. It is provided by the following slightly simplified data structure:

fs/sysfs/file.c
```
struct sysfs_buffer {
        size_t count;
        loff_t pos;
        char * page;
```

```
        struct sysfs_ops * ops;
        int needs_read_fill;
        struct list_head list;
};
```

The contents of the structure are as follows: `count` specifies the length of the data in the buffer, `pos` denotes the present position within the data for partial reads and seeking, and `page` points to a single page used to store the data.[6] The `sysfs_ops` instance belonging to the sysfs entry is connected with an open file via the `ops` pointer of the buffer. `needs_read_fill` specifies if the contents of the buffer need to be filled or not (filling the data is performed on the first read and need not be repeated for any successive reads if no write operation was performed in the meantime).

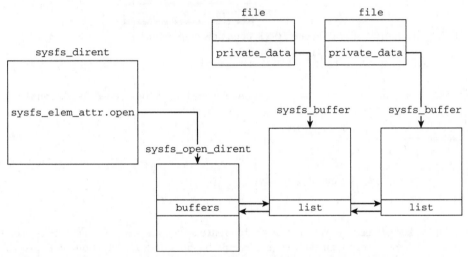

Figure 10-12: Connection between struct `sysfs_dirent`, struct `file`, and struct `sysfs_buffer`.

To understand the meaning of `list`, observe Figure 10-12, which shows how `sysfs_buffers` are connected with `struct file` and `struct sysfs_dirent`. Each open file as represented by an instance of `struct file` is connected with one instance of `sysfs_buffer` via `file->private_data`. A sysfs entry can be referenced via multiple open files, so more than one `sysf_buffer` can be associated with one instance of `struct sysfs_dirent`. All these buffers are collected in a list that uses `sysfs_buffer->list` as list element. The list is headed by an instance of `sysfs_open_dirent`. For the sake of simplicity, this structure is not discussed in great detail. Suffice it to say that it is connected with `sysfs_dirent` and heads the list of `sysfs_buffers`.

Implementation

Recall that `sysfs_file_operations` provides `sys_open_file` to be called when a file is opened. The associated code flow diagram is shown in Figure 10-13.

---

[6]The restriction to a single page is intentional because sysfs is supposed to export only *one simple* attribute per file; this will not require more space than a single page.

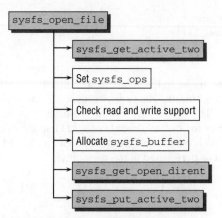

Figure 10-13: Code flow diagram for sysfs_open_file.

The first task is to find the `sysfs_ops` operations that belong to the opened file. Recall that `struct kobj_type` provides a pointer to an instance of `sysf_ops`:

<kobject.h>
```
struct kobj_type {
...
        struct sysfs_ops * sysfs_ops;
...
};
```

However, the kernel needs to obtain an active reference on the `kobject` instance that is associated with the sysfs file before the proper instance of `sysfs_ops` can be found. The function `sysfs_get_active_two` grabs the active reference as discussed above. If the `kobject` is a member of a set, then the pointer is read from the `kset` instance. Otherwise, the `kobject` itself is used as source. If neither provides a pointer to an instance of `sysfs_ops`, a generic set of operations given by `sysfs_sysfs_ops` is used. However, this is only necessary for direct kernel attributes found in `/sys/kernel`:

fs/sysfs/file.c
```
static int sysfs_open_file(struct inode *inode, struct file *file)
{
        struct sysfs_dirent *attr_sd = file->f_path.dentry->d_fsdata;
        struct kobject *kobj = attr_sd->s_parent->s_dir.kobj;
        struct sysfs_buffer * buffer;
        struct sysfs_ops * ops = NULL;
...

        /* need attr_sd for attr and ops, its parent for kobj */
        if (!sysfs_get_active_two(attr_sd))
                return -ENODEV;

        /* if the kobject has no ktype, then we assume that it is a subsystem
         * itself, and use ops for it.
         */
        if (kobj->kset && kobj->kset->ktype)
```

```
                ops = kobj->kset->ktype->sysfs_ops;
        else if (kobj->ktype)
                ops = kobj->ktype->sysfs_ops;
        else
                ops = &subsys_sysfs_ops;
    ...
```

Since all members of kernel subsystems are collected in a kset, this allows for connecting attributes at a subsystem-specific level because the same access functions are used for all elements. If the kobject under consideration is not contained in a kset, then it is still possible that it has a ktype from which the sysfs_ops can be taken. It is up to the subsystem how to implement the sysfs_ops, but the methods used are quite similar, as shown in Section 10.3.5.

If something is supposed to be written into the file, it is not sufficient to just check if the access mode bits allow this. Additionally, the entry is required to provide a store operation in the sysfs_ops. It does not make sense to grant read access if there is no function that can actually present data to userspace. A similar condition holds for read access:

fs/sysfs/file.c
```
        /* File needs write support.
         * The inode's perms must say it's ok,
         * and we must have a store method.
         */
        if (file->f_mode & FMODE_WRITE) {
                if (!(inode->i_mode & S_IWUGO) || !ops->store)
                goto err_out;
        }

        /* File needs read support.
         * The inode's perms must say it's ok, and we there
         * must be a show method for it.
         */
        if (file->f_mode & FMODE_READ) {
                if (!(inode->i_mode & S_IRUGO) || !ops->show)
                goto err_out;
        }
    ...
```

After the kernel has chosen to allow the access, an instance of sysfs_buffer is allocated, filled in with the appropriate elements, and connected to the file via file->private_data as shown below:

fs/sysfs/file.c
```
        buffer = kzalloc(sizeof(struct sysfs_buffer), GFP_KERNEL);
    ...
        mutex_init(&buffer->mutex);
        buffer->needs_read_fill = 1;
        buffer->ops = ops;
        file->private_data = buffer;

        /* make sure we have open dirent struct */
        error = sysfs_get_open_dirent(attr_sd, buffer);
    ...
        /* open succeeded, put active references */
```

```
                    sysfs_put_active_two(attr_sd);
                    return 0;
    }
```

Finally, `sysfs_get_open_dirent` connects the freshly allocated buffer with the sysfs data structures via `sysfs_open_dirent` as shown in Figure 10-12. Note that since no further access to the `kobjects` associated with the sysfs entry is required anymore, the active references can (and need!) be dropped using `sysfs_put_active_two`.

Reading and Writing File Contents

Recall that `sysfs_file_operations` specifies the methods used by the VFS to access the content of files in sysfs. After having introduced all necessary data structures for reading and writing data, it is now time to discuss these operations.

Reading

Reading data is delegated to `sysfs_read_file`; the associated code flow diagram can be found in Figure 10-14.

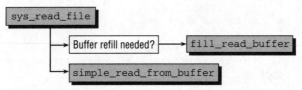

Figure 10-14: Code flow diagram for **sysfs_read_file**.

The implementation is comparatively simple: If the data buffer is not yet filled in because it is accessed for the first time or has been modified by a write operation (both indicated by `buffer->needs_read_fill`), `fill_read_buffer` needs to be called to fill the buffer first. This function is responsible for two things:

1. Allocate a (zero-filled) page frame to hold the data.

2. Call the `show` method of the `struct sysfs_ops` instance to provide the buffer contents, that is, fill in data to the page frame allocated above.

Once the buffer is filled with data, the remaining work is delegated to `simple_read_from_buffer`. As you might have guessed from the name, the task is simple and requires only some bounds checking and a memory copy operation from kernel to userspace.

Writing

To allow the reverse process, namely, writing data from user to kernel space, `sysfs_write_file` is provided. Like for the read companion, the implementation is quite simple as the code flow diagram in Figure 10-15 shows.

First, `fill_write_buffer` allocates a page frame into which the data given from userspace are copied. This sets `buffer->needs_refill` because the content of the buffer needs to be refreshed if a read request takes place after the write. The remaining work is delegated to `flush_write_buffer`; its main job is to call the `store` method provided by the `sysfs_ops` instance specific to the file.

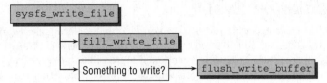

Figure 10-15: Code flow diagram for `sysfs_write_file`.

Directory Traversal

The `lookup` method of `sysfs_dir_inode_operations` is the basic building block for directory traversal. We therefore need to have a closer look at `sysfs_lookup`. Figure 10-16 provides the code flow diagram.

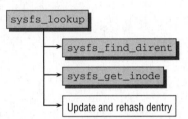

Figure 10-16: Code flow diagram for `sysfs_lookup`.

Attributes constitute the entries of a directory, and the function tries to find an attribute with a specific name that belongs to an instance of `struct sysfs_dirent`. By iterating over them and comparing names, the desired entry can be found. Recall that all attributes associated with a `kobject` are stored in a linked list whose head is `sysfs_dirent.s_dir.children`. This data structure is now brought to good use:

fs/sysfs/dir.c
```
struct sysfs_dirent *sysfs_find_dirent(struct sysfs_dirent *parent_sd,
const unsigned char *name)
{
        struct sysfs_dirent *sd;

        for (sd = parent_sd->s_dir.children; sd; sd = sd->s_sibling)
                if (!strcmp(sd->s_name, name))
                        return sd;
        return NULL;
}
```

`sysfs_find_dirent` is used by `sysfs_lookup` to find the desired `sysfs_dirent` instance for a given filename. With this in hand, the kernel then needs to establish the connection between sysfs, kernel subsystem, and the filesystem representation by attaching the `sysfs_dirent` instance of the attribute with the `dentry` instance of the attribute file.

Dentry and inode are then connected with `sysfs_get_inode`. The method resorts to `sysfs_init_inode`; this function is discussed in Section 10.3.3.

The final steps are not sysfs-specific: The inode information is filled into the `dentry`. This also requires rehashing the `dentry` on the global dentry hash.

10.3.5 Populating Sysfs

Since sysfs is an interface to export data from the kernel, only the kernel itself can populate sysfs with file and directory entries. This can be triggered from places all over the kernel, and, indeed, such operations are ubiquitous within the whole tree, which renders it impossible to cover all appearances in detail. Thus only the general methods used to connect sysfs with the internal data structures of the diverse subsystems are demonstrated; the methods used for this purpose are quite similar everywhere.

Registering Subsystems

Once more I use the generic hard disk code as an example for a subsystem that uses kobjects that are represented in sysfs. Observe that the directory /sys/block is used to represent this subsystem. For every block device available in the system, a subdirectory contains several attribute files:

```
root@meitner # ls -l /sys/block
total 0
drwxr-xr-x  4 root root 0 2008-02-09 23:26 loop0
drwxr-xr-x  4 root root 0 2008-02-09 23:26 loop1
drwxr-xr-x  4 root root 0 2008-02-09 23:26 loop2
drwxr-xr-x  4 root root 0 2008-02-09 23:26 loop3
drwxr-xr-x  4 root root 0 2008-02-09 23:26 loop4
drwxr-xr-x  4 root root 0 2008-02-09 23:26 loop5
drwxr-xr-x  4 root root 0 2008-02-09 23:26 loop6
drwxr-xr-x  4 root root 0 2008-02-09 23:26 loop7
drwxr-xr-x 10 root root 0 2008-02-09 23:26 sda
drwxr-xr-x  5 root root 0 2008-02-09 23:26 sdb
drwxr-xr-x  5 root root 0 2008-02-09 23:26 sr0
root@meitner # ls -l /sys/block/hda
total 0
-r--r--r-- 1 root root 4096 2008-02-09 23:26 capability
-r--r--r-- 1 root root 4096 2008-02-09 23:26 dev
lrwxrwxrwx 1 root root    0 2008-02-09 23:26 device -> ../../devices/pci0000:00/
0000:00:1f.2/host0/target0:0:0/0:0:0:0
drwxr-xr-x 2 root root    0 2008-02-09 23:26 holders
drwxr-xr-x 3 root root    0 2008-02-09 23:26 queue
-r--r--r-- 1 root root 4096 2008-02-09 23:26 range
-r--r--r-- 1 root root 4096 2008-02-09 23:26 removable
drwxr-xr-x 3 root root    0 2008-02-09 23:26 sda1
drwxr-xr-x 3 root root    0 2008-02-09 23:26 sda2
drwxr-xr-x 3 root root    0 2008-02-09 23:26 sda5
drwxr-xr-x 3 root root    0 2008-02-09 23:26 sda6
drwxr-xr-x 3 root root    0 2008-02-09 23:26 sda7
-r--r--r-- 1 root root 4096 2008-02-09 23:26 size
drwxr-xr-x 2 root root    0 2008-02-09 23:26 slaves
-r--r--r-- 1 root root 4096 2008-02-09 23:26 stat
lrwxrwxrwx 1 root root    0 2008-02-09 23:26 subsystem -> ../../block
--w------- 1 root root 4096 2008-02-09 23:26 uevent
```

One of the central elements behind this output is the following data structure, which connects a sysfs-specific attribute structure with genhd-specific store and show methods. Note that these methods do *not* have the signature required for the show/store methods required by sysfs; these will be provided later:

```
<genhd.h>
struct disk_attribute {
        struct attribute attr;
```

```
        ssize_t (*show)(struct gendisk *, char *);
        ssize_t (*store)(struct gendisk *, const char *, size_t);
};
```

Some attributes are attached to all objects represented by the genhd subsystem, so the kernel creates a collection of instances of disk_attribute as follows:

block/genhd.c
```
static struct disk_attribute disk_attr_uevent = {
        .attr = {.name = "uevent", .mode = S_IWUSR },
        .store  = disk_uevent_store
};
static struct disk_attribute disk_attr_dev = {
        .attr = {.name = "dev", .mode = S_IRUGO },
        .show   = disk_dev_read
};
...
static struct disk_attribute disk_attr_stat = {
        .attr = {.name = "stat", .mode = S_IRUGO },
        .show   = disk_stats_read
};

static struct attribute * default_attrs[] = {
        &disk_attr_uevent.attr,
        &disk_attr_dev.attr,
        &disk_attr_range.attr,
...
        &disk_attr_stat.attr,
...
        NULL,
};
```

The connection between the attribute-specific show/store methods and the show/store methods in sysfs_ops is made by the following structure:

block/genhd.c
```
static struct sysfs_ops disk_sysfs_ops = {
        .show   = &disk_attr_show,
        .store  = &disk_attr_store,
};
```

Without getting into any details about their implementation, note that both methods are provided with an attribute instance when called by sysfs, transform this instance into a disk_attribute, and call the show/store method associated with the specific attributes that does the low-level, subsystem-specific work.

Finally, the only thing that needs to be considered is how the set of default attributes is connected with all kobjects belonging to the genhd subsystem. For this, a kobj_type is used:

block/genhd.c
```
static struct kobj_type ktype_block = {
        .release        = disk_release,
        .sysfs_ops      = &disk_sysfs_ops,
        .default_attrs  = default_attrs,
};
```

Two further steps are necessary to connect this data structure with sysfs:

1. Create a `kset` that corresponds to the `kobj_type` by using `decl_subsys`.

2. Register the `kset` with `register_subsystem`; this function ends up in calling `kset_add` which, in turn, calls `kobject_add` to create an appropriate directory with `create_dir`. Once more, this function calls `populate_dir`, which iterates over all default attributes and creates a sysfs file for each of them.

Because subelements of generic hard disks (i.e., partitions) are connected with the kset introduced above, they automatically inherit all default attributes by virtue of the `kobject` model.

10.4 Summary

Filesystems do not necessarily need to be backed by a physical block device, but their contents can also be generated dynamically. This allows for passing information from the kernel to userland (and vice versa), which can be easily obtained by regular file I/O operations. The `/proc` filesystem was one of the first virtual filesystems used by Linux, and a more recent addition is sysfs, which presents a hierarchically structured representation of (nearly) all objects known to the kernel.

This chapter also discussed some generic routines to implement virtual filesystems and additionally considered how pseudo-filesystems that are not visible to userland carry information important for the kernel itself.

11

Extended Attributes and Access Control Lists

Many filesystems provide features that extend the standard functionality offered by the VFS layer. It is impossible for the virtual filesystem to provide specific data structures for every feature that can be imagined — fortunately, there's lots of room in our imagination, and developers are not exactly short of new ideas. Additional features that go beyond the standard UNIX file model often require an extended set of attributes associated with every filesystem object. What the kernel can provide, however, is a framework that allows filesystem-specific extensions. *Extended attributes* (xattrs) are (more or less) arbitrary attributes that can be associated with a file. Since usually every file will possess only a subset of all possible extended attributes, the attributes are stored outside the regular inode data structure to avoid increasing its size in memory and wasting disk space. This allows a really generic set of attributes without any significant impact on filesystem performance or disk space requirements.

One use of extended attributes is the implementation of *access control lists* that extend the UNIX-style permission model: They allow implementation of finer-grained access rights by not only using the concept of the classes *user*, *group*, and *others*, but also by associating an explicit list of users and their allowed operations on the file. Such lists fit naturally into the extended attribute model. Another use of extended attributes is to provide *labeling information* for SE-Linux.

11.1 Extended Attributes

From the filesystem user's point of view, an extended attribute is a name/value pair associated with objects in the filesystem. While the name is given by a regular string, the kernel imposes no restrictions on the contents of the value. It can be a text string, but may contain arbitrary binary data as well. An attribute may be defined or not (this is the case if no attribute was associated with a file). If it is defined, it may or may not have a value. No one can blame the kernel for not being liberal in this respect.

Attribute names are subdivided into namespaces. This implies that addressing attributes are required to list the namespace as well. As per notational convention, a dot is used to separate the namespace and attribute (e.g., user.mime_type). Only the basic details are covered here — it is assumed that you are familiar with the manual page attr(5), where further information about the fine points is given. The kernel uses macros to define the list of valid top-level namespaces. They are of the form XATTR_*_PREFIX. A set of accompanying macros XATTR_*_PREFIX_LEN is useful when a name string passed from the userspace needs to be compared with the namespace prefixes:

```
<xattr.h>
/* Namespaces */
#define XATTR_OS2_PREFIX "os2."
#define XATTR_OS2_PREFIX_LEN (sizeof (XATTR_OS2_PREFIX) - 1)

#define XATTR_SECURITY_PREFIX    "security."
#define XATTR_SECURITY_PREFIX_LEN (sizeof (XATTR_SECURITY_PREFIX) - 1)

#define XATTR_SYSTEM_PREFIX "system."
#define XATTR_SYSTEM_PREFIX_LEN (sizeof (XATTR_SYSTEM_PREFIX) - 1)

#define XATTR_TRUSTED_PREFIX "trusted."
#define XATTR_TRUSTED_PREFIX_LEN (sizeof (XATTR_TRUSTED_PREFIX) - 1)

#define XATTR_USER_PREFIX "user."
#define XATTR_USER_PREFIX_LEN (sizeof (XATTR_USER_PREFIX) - 1)
```

The kernel provides several system calls to read and manipulate extended attributes:

❑　setxattr is used to set or replace the value of an extended attribute or to create a new one.

❑　getxattr retrieves the value of an extended attribute.

❑　removexattr removes an extended attribute.

❑　listxattr provides a list of all extended attributes associated with a given filesystem object.

Note that all calls are also available with the prefix l; this variant does not follow symbolic links by resolving them but operates on the extended attributes of the link itself. Prefixing the calls with f does not work on a filename given by a string, but uses a file descriptor as the argument.

As usual, the manual pages provide more information about how these system calls must be used and provide the exact calling convention.

11.1.1　Interface to the Virtual Filesystem

The virtual filesystem provides an abstraction layer to the userspace such that all applications can use extended attributes regardless of how the underlying filesystem implementations store the information on disk. The following sections discuss the required data structures and system calls. Note that although the VFS provides an abstraction layer for extended attributes, this does not mean that they have to be implemented by every filesystem. In fact, quite the contrary is the case. Most filesystems in the kernel do not support extended attributes. However, it should also be noted that all filesystems that are used as Linux workhorses (ext3, reiserfs, xfs, etc.) support extended attributes.

Data Structures

Since the structure of an extended attribute is very simple, the kernel does not provide a specific data structure to encapsulate the name/value pairs; instead, a simple string is used to represent the name, while a `void`-pointer denotes the area in memory where the value resides.

Nevertheless, there need to be methods that set, retrieve, remove, and list the extended attributes. Since these operations are inode-specific, they are integrated into `struct inode_operations`:

\<fs.h\>
```
struct inode_operations {
...
        int (*setxattr) (struct dentry *, const char *,const void *,size_t,int);
        ssize_t (*getxattr) (struct dentry *, const char *, void *, size_t);
        ssize_t (*listxattr) (struct dentry *, char *, size_t);
        int (*removexattr) (struct dentry *, const char*);
...
}
```

Naturally, a filesystem can provide custom implementations for these operations, but the kernel also offers a set of generic handler functions. They are, for instance, used by the third extended filesystem, as discussed below in the chapter. Before the implementation is presented, I need to introduce the fundamental data structures. For every class of extended attributes, functions that transfer the information to and from the block device are required. They are encapsulated in the following structure:

\<xattr.h\>
```
struct xattr_handler {
        char *prefix;
        size_t (*list)(struct inode *inode, char *list, size_t list_size,
                        const char *name, size_t name_len);
        int (*get)(struct inode *inode, const char *name, void *buffer,
                size_t size);
        int (*set)(struct inode *inode, const char *name, const void *buffer,
                size_t size, int flags);
};
```

`prefix` denotes the namespace to whose attributes the operations apply: it can be any of the values introduced by `XATTR_*_PREFIX` as discussed above in the chapter. The `get` and `set` methods read and write extended attributes to the underlying block device, while `list` provides a list of all extended attributes associated with a file.

The superblock provides a link to an array of all supported handlers for the respective filesystem:

\<fs.h\>
```
struct super_block {
...
        struct xattr_handler    **s_xattr;
...
}
```

There is no fixed order in which the handlers need to appear in the array. The kernel can find the proper one by comparing the handler's `prefix` element with the namespace prefix of the extended attribute name in question. Figure 11-1 presents a graphical summary.

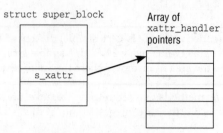

Figure 11-1: Data structures used for the generic xattr implementation.

System Calls

Recall that there are three system calls for each extended attribute operation (get, set, and list), which differ in how the destination is specified. To avoid code duplication, the system calls are structured into two parts:

1. Find the instance of `dentry` associated with the target object.

2. Delegate further processing to a function common to all three calls.

Looking up the `dentry` instance is performed by `user_path_walk`, by `user_path_walk_link`, or by reading the `dentry` pointer contained in the `file` instance, depending on which system call was used. After this, a common basis for all three system call variants has been established.

In the case of `setxattr`, the common function used for further processing is `setxattr`; the associated code flow diagram is shown in Figure 11-2.

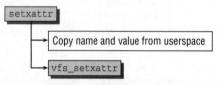

Figure 11-2: Code flow diagram for `setxattr`.

First, the routine copies both the name and the attribute value from userspace to kernel space. Since the value of the extended attribute can have arbitrary contents, the size is not predetermined. The system call has an explicit size parameter to indicate how many bytes are supposed to be read in. To avoid abuse of kernel memory, it is ensured that the size of name and value does not exceed the limits imposed by the following quantities:

```
limits.h
#define XATTR_NAME_MAX    255     /* # chars in an extended attribute name */
#define XATTR_SIZE_MAX 65536      /* size of an extended attribute value (64k) */
```

After this preparation step, further processing is delegated to `vfs_setxattr`. The associated code flow diagram is shown in Figure 11-3.

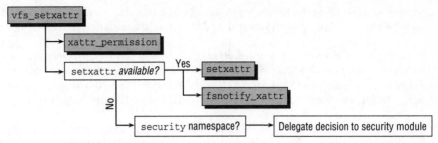

Figure 11-3: Code flow diagram for `vfs_setxattr`.

At first, the kernel needs to make sure that the user is privileged to perform the desired operation; the choice is made by `xattr_permission`. For Read-Only or immutable inodes, the operation fails immediately; otherwise, the following checks are performed:

fs/xattr.c
```
static int
xattr_permission(struct inode *inode, const char *name, int mask)
{
...
        /*
         * No restriction for security.* and system.* from the VFS.  Decision
         * on these is left to the underlying file system / security module.
         */
        if (!strncmp(name, XATTR_SECURITY_PREFIX, XATTR_SECURITY_PREFIX_LEN) ||
            !strncmp(name, XATTR_SYSTEM_PREFIX, XATTR_SYSTEM_PREFIX_LEN))
                return 0;

        /*
         * The trusted.* namespace can only accessed by a privileged user.
         */
        if (!strncmp(name, XATTR_TRUSTED_PREFIX, XATTR_TRUSTED_PREFIX_LEN))
                return (capable(CAP_SYS_ADMIN) ? 0 : -EPERM);

        /* In user.* namespace, only regular files and directories can have
         * extended attributes. For sticky directories, only the owner and
         * privileged user can write attributes.
         */
        if (!strncmp(name, XATTR_USER_PREFIX, XATTR_USER_PREFIX_LEN)) {
                if (!S_ISREG(inode->i_mode) && !S_ISDIR(inode->i_mode))
                        return -EPERM;
                if (S_ISDIR(inode->i_mode) && (inode->i_mode & S_ISVTX) &&
                    (mask & MAY_WRITE) && !is_owner_or_cap(inode))
                return -EPERM;
        }

        return permission(inode, mask, NULL);
}
```

The VFS layer does not care about attributes that live in the `security` or `system` namespace. Note that the request is *granted* if 0 is returned as result of `xattr_permission`! The kernel ignores these namespaces and delegates the choice to security modules that are included via numerous security-related calls, `security_*`, found everywhere in the kernel, or the underlying filesystem.

However, the VFS layer is concerned about the `trusted` namespace. Only a sufficiently privileged user (i.e., root or a user with appropriate capabilities) is allowed to perform operations on such attributes. For a change, the comments in the source code state precisely how the kernel thinks that attributes from the `user` namespace should be taken care of, so I need not add anything further.

Any decision for attributes from a different namespace from those processed until now is deferred to the generic `permission` function as discussed in Section 8.5.3. Note that this includes ACL checks that are implemented with the aid of extended attributes; how these checks are implemented is discussed in Section 11.2.2.

If the inode passed the permission check, `vfs_setxattr` continues as follows:

1. If a filesystem-specific `setxattr` method is available in the inode operations, it is called to perform the low-level interaction with the filesystem. After this, `fsnotify_xattr` uses the inotify mechanism to inform the userland about the extended attribute change.

2. If no `setxattr` method is available (i.e., if the underlying filesystem does not support extended attributes), but the extended attribute in question belongs to the `security` namespace, then the kernel tries to use a function that can be provided by security frameworks like SELinux. If no such framework is registered, the operation is denied.

    This allows security labels on files that reside on filesystems without extended attribute support. It is the task of the security subsystem to store the information in a reasonable way.

Note that some more hook functions of the security framework are called during the extended attribute system calls. They are omitted here since if no extra security framework like SELinux is present, they will have no effect.

Since the implementation for the system calls `getxattr` and `removexattr` nearly completely follows the scheme presented for `setxattr`, it is not necessary to discuss them in greater depth. The differences are as follows:

❑ `getxattr` does not need to use fnotify because nothing is modified.

❑ `removeattr` need not copy an attribute value, but only the name from the userspace. No special casing for the security handler is required.

The code for listing all extended attributes associated with a file differs more from this scheme, particularly because no function `vfs_listxattr` is used. All work is performed in `listxattr`. The implementation proceeds in three easy steps:

1. Adapt the maximum size of the list as given by by the userspace program such that it is not higher than the maximal size of an extended attribute list as allowed by the kernel with `XATTR_LIST_MAX`, and allocate the required memory.

2. Call `listxattr` from `inode_operations` to fill the allocated space with name/value pairs.

3. Copy the result back to the userspace.

Generic Handler Functions

Security is an important business. If wrong decisions are made, then the best security mechanisms are worth nothing. Since duplicating code increases the possibility of getting details wrong, the kernel provides generic implementations of the `inode_operation` methods for extended attribute handling on which filesystem writers can rely. As an additional benefit, this allows the filesystem people to be lazy — and concentrate their talents on things that matter much more to them than getting each and every security corner case right. The following examples look at these default implementations. As before, the code for different types of access is very similar, so the implementation of `generic_setxattr` is discussed first and the differences of the other methods afterward.

Let's get right down into the code:

fs/xattr.c
```
int
generic_setxattr(struct dentry *dentry, const char *name, const void *value, size_t size, int
flags)
{
        struct xattr_handler *handler;
        struct inode *inode = dentry->d_inode;

        if (size == 0)
                value = "";   /* empty EA, do not remove */
        handler = xattr_resolve_name(inode->i_sb->s_xattr, &name);
        if (!handler)
                return -EOPNOTSUPP;
        return handler->set(inode, name, value, size, flags);
}
```

First, `xattr_resolve_name` finds the instance of `xattr_handler` that is apt for the namespace of the extended attribute in question. If a handler exists, the `set` method is called to perform the desired set operation. Obviously, there cannot be any further generic step; `handler->set` *must* be a filesystem-specific method (the implementation of these methods for Ext3 is discussed in Section 11.1.2).

It is also not difficult to find the proper handler:

fs/xattr.c
```
static struct xattr_handler *
xattr_resolve_name(struct xattr_handler **handlers, const char **name)
{
...
        for_each_xattr_handler(handlers, handler) {
                const char *n = strcmp_prefix(*name, handler->prefix);
                if (n) {
                        *name = n;
                        break;
                }
        }
        return handler;
}
```

for_each_xattr_handler is a macro that iterates over all entries in handlers until it encounters a NULL entry. For every array element, the kernel compares the handler prefix with the namespace part of the attribute name. If there is a match, the appropriate handler has been found.

The generic implementations for the other extended attribute operations differ only slightly from the code for generic_setxattr:

❑   generic_getxattr calls handler->get instead of the handler->set.

❑   generic_removexattr calls handler->set but specifies NULL for the value and a size of 0. This triggers, per convention, removing the attribute.[1]

generic_listxattr can operate in two modes: If a NULL pointer instead of a buffer was passed to the function to hold the result, the code iterates over all handlers registered in the superblock and calls the list method for the inode in question; since list returns the number of bytes required to hold the result, they can be summed up to provide predictions about how much memory is required in total. If a buffer for the results was specified, generic_listxattr again iterates over all handlers, but this time uses the buffer to actually store the results.

11.1.2   Implementation in Ext3

Among the citizens in filesystem land, Ext3 is one of the most prominent members because it makes it understood that support for extended attributes is available and well developed. Examine the following source code to learn more about the filesystem side of extended attribute implementations. This also raises a question that has not been touched on: namely, how extended attributes are permanently stored on disk.

Data Structures

As an exemplary citizen, Ext3 starts with some good advice on coding efficiency and employs the generic implementation presented above. A number of handler functions are provided, and the following map makes it possible to access handler functions by their identification number and not by their string identifier; this simplifies many operations and allows a more efficient use of disk space because rather than the prefix string, only a simple number needs to be stored:

fs/ext3/xattr.c
```
static struct xattr_handler *ext3_xattr_handler_map[] = {
        [EXT3_XATTR_INDEX_USER]            = &ext3_xattr_user_handler,
#ifdef CONFIG_EXT3_FS_POSIX_ACL
        [EXT3_XATTR_INDEX_POSIX_ACL_ACCESS]  = &ext3_xattr_acl_access_handler,
        [EXT3_XATTR_INDEX_POSIX_ACL_DEFAULT] = &ext3_xattr_acl_default_handler,
#endif
        [EXT3_XATTR_INDEX_TRUSTED]         = &ext3_xattr_trusted_handler,
#ifdef CONFIG_EXT3_FS_SECURITY
        [EXT3_XATTR_INDEX_SECURITY]        = &ext3_xattr_security_handler,
#endif
};
```

---

[1]Note that both a NULL value *and* a size of 0 must be specified for it is possible to have empty attributes with size 0 and an empty value string (which differs from a NULL value).

Figure 11-4 presents an overview of the on-disk layout of Ext3 extended attributes.

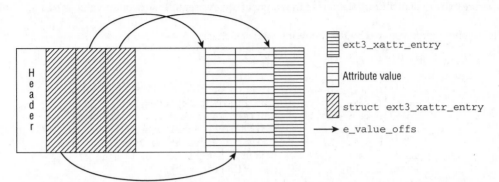

Figure 11-4: Overview of the on-disk format for extended attributes in the Ext3 filesystem.

The space consumed by the extended attributes starts with a short identification header followed by a list of entry elements. Each holds the attribute name and a pointer to the region where the associated value is stored. The list grows downward when new extended attributes are added to the file.

The values are stored at the end of the extended attribute data space; the value table grows in the opposite direction of the attribute name table. The values will, in general, not be sorted in the same order as the names, but can be in any arbitrary order.

A structure of this kind can be found in two places:

❑   The unused space at the end of the inode.

❑   A separate data block somewhere on the disk.

The first alternative is only possible if the new filesystem format with dynamic inode sizes is used (i.e., EXT3_DYNAMIC_REV); the amount of free space is stored in ext3_inode_info->i_extra_isize. Both alternatives can be used together, but the total size of all extended attribute headers and values is still limited to the sum of the space of a single block and the free space in the inode. It is not possible to use more than one additional block to store extended attributes. In practice, the space required will usually be much less than a complete disk block.

Note that it is possible for two files with identical sets of extended attributes to share the on-disk representation; this helps to save some disk space.

How do the data structures that implement this layout look? The header is defined as follows:

fs/ext3/xattr.h
```
struct ext3_xattr_header {
        __le32  h_magic;        /* magic number for identification */
        __le32  h_refcount;     /* reference count */
        __le32  h_blocks;       /* number of disk blocks used */
        __le32  h_hash;         /* hash value of all attributes */
        __u32   h_reserved[4];  /* zero right now */
};
```

The comments in the code precisely describe the meaning of the elements, and nothing more needs to be added. The only exception is h_blocks: Although this element suggests that multiple blocks can be used to store extended attribute data, it is at the moment always set to 1. Any other value is treated as an error.

Every entry is represented by the following data structure:

fs/ext3/xattr.h

```
struct ext3_xattr_entry {
        __u8    e_name_len;      /* length of name */
        __u8    e_name_index;    /* attribute name index */
        __le16  e_value_offs;    /* offset in disk block of value */
        __le32  e_value_block;   /* disk block attribute is stored on (n/i) */
        __le32  e_value_size;    /* size of attribute value */
        __le32  e_hash;          /* hash value of name and value */
        char    e_name[0];       /* attribute name */
};
```

Note that the entries are not of a uniform size because the length of the attribute names is variable; this is why the name is stored at the end of the structure; e_name_len is available to determine the name length and thus compute the size of each entry. e_value_block, together with e_value_offset, dertermines the location of the attribute value associated with the extended attribute name (if the extended attribute is stored within the inode, ext3_value_offs is used as an offset that starts at the first entry). e_name_index is used as an index into the table ext3_xattr_handler_map defined above.

Implementation

Since the handler implementation is quite similar for different attribute namespaces, the following discussion is restricted to the implementation for the user namespace; the handler functions for the other namespaces differ only little or not at all. ext3_xattr_user_handler is defined as follows:

fs/ext3/xattr_user.c

```
struct xattr_handler ext3_xattr_user_handler = {
        .prefix = XATTR_USER_PREFIX,
        .list   = ext3_xattr_user_list,
        .get    = ext3_xattr_user_get,
        .set    = ext3_xattr_user_set,
};
```

Retrieving Extended Attributes

Consider ext3_xattr_user_get first. The code is just a wrapper for a standard routine that works independently of the attribute type. Only the identification number of the type is necessary to choose the correct attributes from the set of all attributes:

fs/ext3/xattr_user.c

```
static int
ext3_xattr_user_get(struct inode *inode, const char *name,
                    void *buffer, size_t size)
{
...
        if (!test_opt(inode->i_sb, XATTR_USER))
                return -EOPNOTSUPP;
        return ext3_xattr_get(inode, EXT3_XATTR_INDEX_USER, name, buffer, size);
}
```

The test for XATTR_USER ensures that the filesystem supports extended attributes in the user namespace. It is possible to enable or disable this support at mount time.

Note that all get-type functions can be used for two purposes. If a buffer is allocated, the result is copied into it, but if a NULL pointer is given instead of a proper buffer, only the required size for the attribute value is computed and returned. This allows the calling code to first identify the size of the required allocation for the buffer. After the buffer has been allocated, a second call fills in the data.

Figure 11-5 shows the code flow diagram for ext3_xattr_get. The function is a dispatcher that first tries to find the required attribute directly in the free space of the inode with ext3_xattr_ibody_get; if this fails, ext3_xattr_block_get is used to read the value from an external attribute data block.

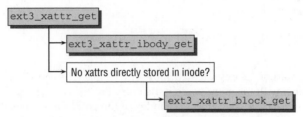

Figure 11-5: Code flow diagram for **ext3_xattr_get**.

Consider the direct search in the free inode space first. The associated code flow diagram is depicted in Figure 11-6.

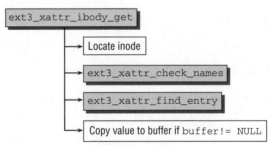

Figure 11-6: Code flow diagram for
ext3_xattr_ibody_get.

After the location of the inode is determined and access to the raw data is ascertained, ext3_xattr_check_names performs several sanity checks that ensure that the entry table is located within the free space of the inode. The real work is delegated to ext3_xattr_find_entry. Since the routine will be used on several more occasions further below, we need to discuss it in more detail.

fs/ext3/xattr.c
```
static int
ext3_xattr_find_entry(struct ext3_xattr_entry **pentry, int name_index,
                      const char *name, size_t size, int sorted)
{
        struct ext3_xattr_entry *entry;
        size_t name_len;
        int cmp = 1;
```

```
        if (name == NULL)
                return -EINVAL;
        name_len = strlen(name);
        entry = *pentry;
        for (; !IS_LAST_ENTRY(entry); entry = EXT3_XATTR_NEXT(entry)) {
                cmp = name_index - entry->e_name_index;
                if (!cmp)
                        cmp = name_len - entry->e_name_len;
                if (!cmp)
                        cmp = memcmp(name, entry->e_name, name_len);
                if (cmp <= 0 && (sorted || cmp == 0))
                        break;
        }
        *pentry = entry;
...
        return cmp ? -ENODATA : 0;
}
```

`pentry` points to the start of the extended attribute entry table. The code loops over all entries and compares the desired name with the entry name if the entry has the correct type (as indicated by `cmp == 0`, which results from subtracting the namespace index of the entry under consideration from the index of the queried entry — a slightly unconventional but nevertheless valid way to check this). Since the entries do not have a uniform size, the kernel uses `EXT3_XATTR_NEXT` to compute the address of the next entry in the table by adding the length of the actual attribute name (plus some padding that is handled by `EXT3_XATTR_LEN`) to the size of the entry data structure:

fs/ext3/xattr.h
```
#define EXT3_XATTR_NEXT(entry) \
        ( (struct ext3_xattr_entry *)( \
          (char *)(entry) + EXT3_XATTR_LEN((entry)->e_name_len)) )
```

The end of the list is marked by a zero that `IS_LAST_ENTRY` checks for.

After `ext3_xattr_find_entry` returns with the data of the desired entry, `ext3_xattr_ibody_get` needs to copy the value to the buffer given in the function arguments if it is not a `NULL` pointer; otherwise, only the size of the entry is returned.

If the desired extended attribute cannot be found within the inode, the kernel uses `ext3_xattr_block_get` to search for the entry. The associated code flow diagram is presented in Figure 11-7.

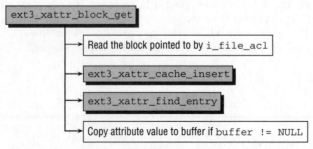

Figure 11-7: Code flow diagram for `ext3_xattr_block_get`.

The course of action is basically identical with the previously considered case where the data were located in the inode, but two modifications need to be made:

❑ The kernel needs to read the extended attribute block; the address is stored in the `i_file_acl` element of `struct ext3_inode_info`.

❑ Metadata blocks are cached by calling `ext3_xattr_cache_insert`. The kernel uses the so-called filesystem metadata block cache implemented in `fs/mbcache.c` for this.[2] Since nothing really unexpected happens there, it is not necessary to discuss the code in more detail.

Setting Extended Attributes

Setting extended attributes for the `user` namespace is handled by — you guessed it — `ext3_xattr_user_set`. As for the get operation, the function is just a wrapper for the generic helper `ext3_xattr_set`. The code flow diagram in Figure 11-8 shows that this is yet another wrapper function that is responsible for handling the interaction with the journal. The real work is delegated to `ext3_xattr_set_handle`; the associated code flow diagram can be seen in Figure 11-9.

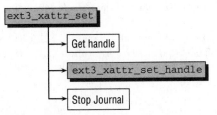

Figure 11-8: Code flow diagram for
`ext3_xattr_set`.

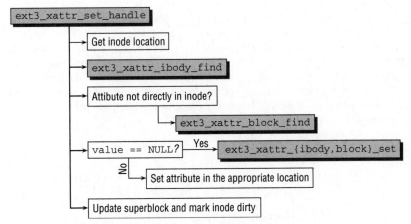

Figure 11-9: Code flow diagram for `ext3_xattr_set`.

---

[2]Although the structure of this cache is generic, it is currently only used by the extended filesystem family.

The following calling convention is used:

❏ If the data buffer passed to the function is NULL, then remove an existing extended attribute.

❏ If the data buffer contains a value, replace an existing extended attribute or create a new one. The flags XATTR_REPLACE and XATTR_CREATE can be used to indicate that the attribute must or must not exist before the call as per the documentation in the man page setxattr(2).

ext3_xattr_set_handle implements these requirements by utilizing the previously introduced framework as follows:

1. Find the location of the inode.

2. Use ext3_xattr_ibody_find to find the data of the extended attribute. If this fails, search in the external data block with ext3_xattr_block_find.

3. If no value is given, delete the attribute with ext3_xattr_ibody_set or ext3_xattr_block_set depending on whether the entry is contained in the inode or in a separate data block.

4. If a value was given, use ext3_xattr_*_set to modify the value or create a new value either within the inode or on the external data block depending on where enough space is left.

The functions ext3_xattr_ibody_set and ext3_xattr_block_set handle the low-level work of removing an entry from the data structure described in Section 11.1.2. If no value is given to update, the functions respectively create a new entry. This is primarily a matter of data structure manipulation and will not be discussed in detail here.

Listing Extended Attributes

Although the kernel includes a generic function (generic_listxattr) for listing all extended attributes associated with a file, it is not among the filesystem favorites: Only the shared memory implementation makes use of it. So let's step back a little farther to discuss the operation for Ext3.

The inode_operations instance for Ext3 lists ext3_listxattr as the handler function for listxattr. The method is just a one-line wrapper for ext3_xattr_list. This routine calls, in turn, ext3_xattr_ibody_list and ext3_xattr_block_list, depending on where extended attributes are stored. Both functions compute the location of the extended attributes and read the data, but then delegate the work to ext3_xattr_list_entries, which finally does the real work — after all, someone has to do it! It uses the previously introduced macros to iterate over all extended attributes defined for the inode, calls handler->list to retrieve the name of the attribute for each entry, and collects the results in a buffer:

fs/ext3/xattr.c
```
static int
ext3_xattr_list_entries(struct inode *inode, struct ext3_xattr_entry *entry,
                        char *buffer, size_t buffer_size)
{
        size_t rest = buffer_size;

        for (; !IS_LAST_ENTRY(entry); entry = EXT3_XATTR_NEXT(entry)) {
                struct xattr_handler *handler =
                        ext3_xattr_handler(entry->e_name_index);

                if (handler) {
```

```
                        size_t size = handler->list(inode, buffer, rest,
                                                entry->e_name,
                                                entry->e_name_len);

                if (buffer) {
                        if (size > rest)
                                return -ERANGE;
                        buffer += size;
                }
                rest -= size;
            }
    }
    return buffer_size - rest;
}
```

Since the list handler implementation is quite similar for the various attribute types, it suffices to consider the variant for the user namespace. Observe the following code:

fs/ext3/xattr_user.c
```
static size_t
ext3_xattr_user_list(struct inode *inode, char *list, size_t list_size,
                    const char *name, size_t name_len)
{
        const size_t prefix_len = sizeof(XATTR_USER_PREFIX)-1;
        const size_t total_len = prefix_len + name_len + 1;

        if (!test_opt(inode->i_sb, XATTR_USER))
                return 0;

        if (list && total_len <= list_size) {
                memcpy(list, XATTR_USER_PREFIX, prefix_len);
                memcpy(list+prefix_len, name, name_len);
                list[prefix_len + name_len] = '\0';
        }
        return total_len;
}
```

The routine copies the prefix "user." followed by the attribute name and a null byte into the buffer list and returns the number of copied bytes as result.

11.1.3 Implementation in Ext2

The implementation of extended attributes in Ext2 is quite similar to the implementation in Ext3 presented above. This is not surprising since Ext3 is a direct descendent of Ext2, but nevertheless, some features present in Ext3 that are not available in Ext2 are the source of some differences in the xattr implementation:

❑ Since Ext2 does not support dynamic inode sizes, there is not sufficient space left in the on-disk inode to store the data of extended attributes. Thus, xattrs are always stored on a separate data block. This simplifies some functions because no distinction between different locations of the extended attribute data is necessary.

❑ Ext2 does not use journaling, so all journaling-related function calls are not necessary. This also eliminates the need for some wrapper functions that are just dealing with handle operations.

Otherwise, both implementations are nearly identical; for most functions described above, a variant with the prefix `ext3_` replaced with `ext2_` is available.

11.2 Access Control Lists

POSIX access control lists (ACLs) are an extension specified in a POSIX standard to make the DAC model of Linux finer grained. As usual, I assume that you have some familiarity with the concept, but a very good overview is provided in the manual page `acl(5)`.[3] ACLs are implemented on top of extended attributes and modified with the same methods as other extended attributes are. In comparison to other xattrs whose contents are of no interest to the kernel, ACL xattrs are integrated into the inode permission checks. Although filesystems are free to choose a physical format to represent extended attributes, the kernel nevertheless defines a conversation structure to represent an access control list. The following namespaces must be used for extended attributes that carry access control lists:

```
<posix_acl_xattr.h>
#define POSIX_ACL_XATTR_ACCESS  "system.posix_acl_access"
#define POSIX_ACL_XATTR_DEFAULT "system.posix_acl_default"
```

The userland programs `getfacl`, `setfacl`, and `chacl` are used to get, set, and change the contents of an ACL. They use the standard system calls to manipulate extended attributes and do not require any non-standard interaction with the kernel. Many other utilities, for instance, `ls`, also have built-in support for dealing with access control lists.

11.2.1 Generic Implementation

The generic code for the implementation of ACLs is contained in two files: `fs/posix_acl.c` contains code to allocate new ACLs, clone ACLs, perform extended permission checks, and so on; while `fs/xattr_acl.c` holds functions to convert between extended attributes and the generic representation of ACLs, and vice versa. All generic data structures are defined in `include/linux/posix_acl.h` and `include/linux/posix_acl_xattr.h`.

Data Structures

The central data structure for in-memory representation that holds all data associated with an ACL is defined as follows:

```
<posix_acl.h>
struct posix_acl_entry {
        short                   e_tag;
        unsigned short          e_perm;
        unsigned int            e_id;
};

struct posix_acl {
        atomic_t                a_refcount;
```

---

[3]Note that another good overview about ACLs in general and the status of the implementation in various filesystems supported by Linux is given in the Usenix paper of Andreas Grünbacher [Grü03], one of the principal authors of ACL support for the Ext2 and Ext3 filesystems.

```
        unsigned int           a_count;
        struct posix_acl_entry a_entries[0];
};
```

Each entry contains a tag, a permission, and a (user or group) ID to which the ACL refers. All ACLs belonging to a given inode are collected by `struct posix_acl`. The number of ACL entries is given by `a_count`; since the array that contains all entries is located at the bottom of the structure, there is no limit on the number of entries except for the maximal size of an extended attribute. `a_refcount` is a standard reference counter.

Symbolic constants for the ACL type, the tag, and the permissions are given by the following preprocessor definitions:

<posix_acl.h>
```
/* a_type field in acl_user_posix_entry_t */
#define ACL_TYPE_ACCESS        (0x8000)
#define ACL_TYPE_DEFAULT       (0x4000)

/* e_tag entry in struct posix_acl_entry */
#define ACL_USER_OBJ           (0x01)
#define ACL_USER               (0x02)
#define ACL_GROUP_OBJ          (0x04)
#define ACL_GROUP              (0x08)
#define ACL_MASK               (0x10)
#define ACL_OTHER              (0x20)

/* permissions in the e_perm field */
#define ACL_READ               (0x04)
#define ACL_WRITE              (0x02)
#define ACL_EXECUTE            (0x01)
```

The kernel defines another set of data structures similar to the ones presented above for xattr representation of ACLs. However, this time they are supposed to be used for external interaction with userland:

<posix_acl_xattr.h>
```
typedef struct {
        __le16                 e_tag;
        __le16                 e_perm;
        __le32                 e_id;
} posix_acl_xattr_entry;

typedef struct {
        __le32                 a_version;
        posix_acl_xattr_entry  a_entries[0];
} posix_acl_xattr_header;
```

The structures used for internal and external representation are quite similar except that types with defined endianness (see Appendix A.8) and explicit bit length are used for the latter purpose; additionally, no reference counting is necessary for the on-disk representation.

Two functions to convert back and forth between the references are available: `posix_acl_from_xattr` and `posix_acl_from_xattr`. Since the translation is purely mechanical, it is not necessary to discuss it in more detail. It is, however, important to observe that they work independently of the underlying filesystem.

Permission Checks

For permission checks that involve access control lists, the kernel usually needs support from the underlying filesystems: Either they implement *all* permission checks by themselves (via the permission function of struct inode_operations), or they provide a callback method for generic_permission. The latter method is preferred by most filesystems in the kernel.

The callback is used in generic_permission as follows (note that check_acl denotes the callback function):

fs/namei.c
```
int generic_permission(struct inode *inode, int mask,
                int (*check_acl)(struct inode *inode, int mask))
{
...

                if (IS_POSIXACL(inode) && (mode & S_IRWXG) && check_acl) {
                        int error = check_acl(inode, mask);
                        if (error == -EACCES)
                                goto check_capabilities;
                        else if (error != -EAGAIN)
                                return error;
                }
...
}
```

IS_POSIXACL checks if the (mount-time) flag MS_POSIXACL is set signaling that ACLs need to be used.

Even if a filesystem provides a specialized function to perform the ACL permission check, the individual routines usually boil down to some technical work like obtaining the ACL data. The real permission checks are again delegated to the standard function posix_acl_permission provided by the kernel.

Accordingly, posix_acl_permission needs to be discussed in more detail. Given a pointer to an inode, a pointer to (the in-memory representation of) an access control list, and the right to check for (MAY_READ, MAY_WRITE or MAY_EXEC in mode), the function returns 0 if access is granted or an appropriate error code otherwise. The implementation is as follows:

fs/posix_acl.c
```
int
posix_acl_permission(struct inode *inode, const struct posix_acl *acl, int want)
{
        const struct posix_acl_entry *pa, *pe, *mask_obj;
        int found = 0;

        FOREACH_ACL_ENTRY(pa, acl, pe) {
                switch(pa->e_tag) {
                        case ACL_USER_OBJ:
                                /* (May have been checked already) */
                                if (inode->i_uid == current->fsuid)
                                        goto check_perm;
```

```
                                      break;
                          case ACL_USER:
                                  if (pa->e_id == current->fsuid)
                                          goto mask;
                                  break;
                          case ACL_GROUP_OBJ:
                                  if (in_group_p(inode->i_gid)) {
                                          found = 1;
                                          if ((pa->e_perm & want) == want)
                                                  goto mask;
                                  }
                                  break;
                          case ACL_GROUP:
                                  if (in_group_p(pa->e_id)) {
                                          found = 1;
                                          if ((pa->e_perm & want) == want)
                                                  goto mask;
                                  }
                                  break;
                          case ACL_MASK:
                                  break;
                          case ACL_OTHER:
                                  if (found)
                                          return -EACCES;
                                  else
                                          goto check_perm;
                          default:
                                  return -EIO;
                  }
          }
          return -EIO;
  ...
  }
```

The code uses the macro FOREACH_ACL_ENTRY to iterate over all ACL entries. For each entry, a suitable comparison between the file system UID (FSUID) and the appropriate part of the current process credentials (the UID/GID of the inode for _OBJ type entries and the ID specified in the ACL entry for other types). Obviously, the logic needs to be exactly as defined in the manual page acl(5).

The code involves two jump labels that are located behind the loop. The code flow ends up at mask once access has basically been granted. It still needs to be ensured, however, that no declaration of ACL_MASK follows the granting entry and denies the access right:

fs/posix_acl.c
```
  ...
  mask:
          for (mask_obj = pa+1; mask_obj != pe; mask_obj++) {
                  if (mask_obj->e_tag == ACL_MASK) {
                          if ((pa->e_perm & mask_obj->e_perm & want) == want)
                                  return 0;
                          return -EACCES;
                  }
          }
  ...
```

Victory can seem to be beguilingly close when a granting entry has been found, but the hopes are quickly annihilated when an `ACL_MASK` entry denies the access.

The following code snippet ensures that not only the rights are valid because of a proper UID or GID, but also that the desired access (read, write, or execute) is allowed by the granting entry:

fs/posix_acl.c
```
...
check_perm:
        if ((pa->e_perm & want) == want)
                return 0;
        return -EACCES;
}
```

11.2.2   Implementation in Ext3

Since ACLs are implemented on top of extended attributes and with the aid of many generic helper routines as discussed above, the implementation in Ext3 is quite concise.

Data Structures

The on-disk representation format for an ACL is similar to the in-memory representation required by the generic POSIX helper functions:

fs/ext3/acl.h
```
typedef struct {
        __le16          e_tag;
        __le16          e_perm;
        __le32          e_id;
} ext3_acl_entry;
```

The meaning of the struct members is identical to the meaning discussed above for the in-memory variant. To save disk space, a version without the `e_id` field is also defined. It is used for the first four entries of an ACL list because no specific UID/GID is required for them:

fs/ext3/acl.h
```
typedef struct {
        __le16          e_tag;
        __le16          e_perm;
} ext3_acl_entry_short;
```

A list of ACL entries is always led by a header element, which is defined as follows:

fs/ext3/acl.h
```
typedef struct {
        __le32          a_version;
} ext3_acl_header;
```

The `a_version` field would allow for distinguishing between different versions of the ACL implementation. Fortunately, the current implementation has not yet shown any weaknesses that would require introducing a new version, so revision EXT3_ACL_VERSION) — 0x0001 — is still perfectly fine. Although the field is not relevant right now, it will become important should an incompatible future version be developed.

The in-memory representation of every Ext3 inode is augmented with two fields that are relevant for the ACL implementation:

```
<ext3_fs_i.h>
struct ext3_inode_info {
...
#ifdef CONFIG_EXT3_FS_POSIX_ACL
        struct posix_acl        *i_acl;
        struct posix_acl        *i_default_acl;
#endif
...
}
```

While i_acl points to the posix_acl instance for a regular ACL list associated with an inode, i_default_acl points to the default ACL that may be associated with a directory and is inherited by subdirectories. Since all information is stored in extended attributes on disk, no extension of the disk-based struct ext3_inode is necessary.

Note that the kernel does not automatically construct the ACL information for every inode; if the information is not present in memory, the fields are set to EXT3_ACL_NOT_CACHED [defined as (void*)-1].

Conversion between On-Disk and In-Memory Representation

Two conversion functions are available to switch between the on-disk and the in-memory representation: ext3_acl_to_disk and ext3_acl_from_disk. Both are implemented in fs/ext3/acl.c.

The latter one takes the raw data as read from the information contained in the extended inode, strips off the header, and converts the data from little endian format into a format suitable for the system's CPU for every entry in the list of ACLs.

The counterpart ext3_acl_to_disk works similarly: It iterates over all entries of a given instance of posix_acl and converts the contained data from the CPU-specific format to little endian numbers with appropriate lengths.

Inode Initialization

When a new inode is created with ext3_new_inode, the initialization of the ACLs is delegated to ext3_init_acl. In addition to the transaction handle and the instance of struct inode for the new inode, the function also expects a pointer to the inode of the directory in which the new entry is created:

```
fs/ext3/acl.c
int
ext3_init_acl(handle_t *handle, struct inode *inode, struct inode *dir)
{
        struct posix_acl *acl = NULL;
        int error = 0;

        if (!S_ISLNK(inode->i_mode)) {
```

```
            if (test_opt(dir->i_sb, POSIX_ACL)) {
                    acl = ext3_get_acl(dir, ACL_TYPE_DEFAULT);
                    if (IS_ERR(acl))
                            return PTR_ERR(acl);
            }
            if (!acl)
                    inode->i_mode &= ~current->fs->umask;
    }
    ...
    }
```

The inode parameter points to the new inode, and dir shows the inode of the directory containing the file. The directory information is required because if the directory has a default ACL, the contents need also to be applied to the new file. If the superblock of the directory does not support ACLs or no default ACL is associated with it, the kernel simply applies the current umask setting of the process.

A more interesting case is when the inode's filesystem supports ACLs and a default ACL is associated with the parent directory. If the new entry is a directory, the default ACL is inherited to it:

fs/ext3/acl.c

```
    ...
            if (test_opt(inode->i_sb, POSIX_ACL) && acl) {
                    struct posix_acl *clone;
                    mode_t mode;

                    if (S_ISDIR(inode->i_mode)) {
                            error = ext3_set_acl(handle, inode,
                                            ACL_TYPE_DEFAULT, acl);
                            if (error)
                                    goto cleanup;
                    }
    ...
    }
```

ext3_set_acl is used to set the ACL contents of a specific inode; this function is discussed below in this chapter.

For all file types and not just directories, the following code remains to be executed:

fs/ext3/acl.c

```
    ...
                    clone = posix_acl_clone(acl, GFP_KERNEL);
                    error = -ENOMEM;
                    if (!clone)
                            goto cleanup;

                    mode = inode->i_mode;
                    error = posix_acl_create_masq(clone, &mode);
                    if (error >= 0) {
                            inode->i_mode = mode;
                            if (error > 0) {
                                    /* This is an extended ACL */
```

```
                                        error = ext3_set_acl(handle, inode,
                                                    ACL_TYPE_ACCESS, clone);
                        }
                    }
                    posix_acl_release(clone);
            }
    cleanup:
            posix_acl_release(acl);
            return error;
    }
```

First, a working copy of the in-memory representation of the ACL is created with posix_acl_clone. Afterward, posix_acl_create_masq is called to remove all permissions given by the mode specification of the inode creation process that are *not* granted by the default ACL. This can result in two scenarios:

1. The access mode can remain unchanged or some elements of it must be removed in order to comply with the ACL's requirements. In this case, the i_mode field of the new inode is set to the mode as computed by posix_acl_create_masq.

2. In addition to the necessity of trimming the mode, the default ACL can contain elements that cannot be represented in the regular user/group/other scheme. In this case, an ACL with extended information that provides the extra information is created for the new inode.

Retrieving ACLs

Given an instance of struct inode, ext3_get_acl can be used to retrieve an in-memory representation of the ACL. Note that another parameter (type) specifies if the default or the access inode is supposed to be retrieved. The cases are distinguished with ACL_TYPE_ACCESS and ACL_TYPE_DEFAULT. The code flow diagram for the function is shown in Figure 11-10.

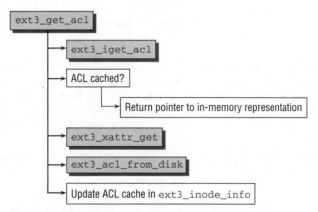

Figure 11-10: Code flow diagram for ext3_get_acl.

At first, the kernel uses the helper function ext3_iget_acl to check if the in-memory representation of the ACL is already cached in ext3_inode_info->i_acl (or, respectively, i_default_acl if the default ACL is requested). Should this be the case, the function creates a copy of the representation that can be returned as the result of ext3_get_acl.

If the ACL is not yet cached, then first `ext3_xattr_get` is called to retrieve the raw data from the extended attribute subsystem[4]; the conversion from the on-disk to the in-memory representation is performed with the aid of `ext3_acl_from_disk`. Before a pointer to this representation can be returned, the cache field in question of `ext3_inode_info` is updated so that subsequent requests can directly get the in-memory representation.

Modifying ACLs

The function `ext3_acl_chmod` is responsible for keeping ACLs up to date and consistent when the (generic) attributes of a file are changed via `ext3_setattr` that is, in turn, called by the VFS layer and thus triggered by the respective system calls from userspace. Since `ext3_acl_chmod` is called at the very end of `ext3_setattr`, the new desired mode has already been set for the classical access control part of the inode. A pointer to the instance of `struct inode` in question is thus sufficient as input data. The operational logic of `ext3_acl_chmod` is depicted in the code flow diagram in Figure 11-11.

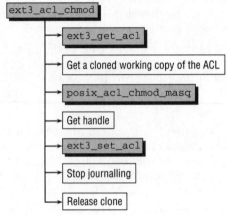

Figure 11-11: Code flow diagram for `ext3_acl_chmod`.

After retrieving a pointer to the in-memory representation of the ACL data, a clone as working copy is created using the helper function `posix_acl_clone`. The main work is delegated to `posix_acl_chmod_masq` covered below. The remaining work for the Ext3 code deals with technical issues: After a handle for the transaction has been obtained, `ext3_set_acl` is used to write back the modified ACL data. Finally, the end of the operation is announced to the journal, and the clone is released.

The generic work of updating the ACL data is performed in `posix_acl_chmod_masq` by iterating over all ACL entries. The relevant entries for the owning user and group as well as the generic entry for "other" and mask entries are updated to reflect the new situation:

```
fs/posix_acl.c
int
posix_acl_chmod_masq(struct posix_acl *acl, mode_t mode)
{
        struct posix_acl_entry *group_obj = NULL, *mask_obj = NULL;
```

---

[4]Note that there are actually two calls to `ext3_xattr_get`: The first computes how much memory is needed to hold the data, then the appropriate amount is allocated with `vmalloc`, and the second call of `ext3_xattr_get` actually transfers the desired data.

```
        struct posix_acl_entry *pa, *pe;

        /* assert(atomic_read(acl->a_refcount) == 1); */

        FOREACH_ACL_ENTRY(pa, acl, pe) {
                switch(pa->e_tag) {
                        case ACL_USER_OBJ:
                                pa->e_perm = (mode & S_IRWXU) >> 6;
                                break;

                        case ACL_USER:
                        case ACL_GROUP:
                                break;

                        case ACL_GROUP_OBJ:
                                group_obj = pa;
                                break;

                        case ACL_MASK:
                                mask_obj = pa;
                                break;

                        case ACL_OTHER:
                                pa->e_perm = (mode & S_IRWXO);
                                break;

                        default:
                                return -EIO;
                }
        }

        if (mask_obj) {
                mask_obj->e_perm = (mode & S_IRWXG) >> 3;
        } else {
                if (!group_obj)
                        return -EIO;
                group_obj->e_perm = (mode & S_IRWXG) >> 3;
        }

        return 0;
}
```

Permission Checks

Recall that the kernel provides the generic permission checking function `generic_permission`, which allows for integration of a filesystem-specific handler for ACL checks. Indeed, Ext3 makes use of this option: The function `ext3_permission` (which is, in turn, called by the VFS layer when a permission check is requested) instructs `generic_permission` to use `ext3_check_acl` for the ACL-related work:

fs/ext3/acl.c
```
int
ext3_permission(struct inode *inode, int mask, struct nameidata *nd)
{
        return generic_permission(inode, mask, ext3_check_acl);
}
```

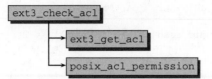

Figure 11-12: Code flow diagram for
`ext3_check_acl.`

The code flow diagram in Figure 11-12 shows that there is little to do for `ext3_check_acl`. After the ACL data have been read in by `ext3_get_acl`, all policy work is delegated to `posix_acl_permission`, which was introduced in Section 11.2.1.

11.2.3 *Implementation in Ext2*

The implementation of ACLs for Ext2 is nearly completely identical with the implementation for Ext3. The differences are even less than for extended attributes because for ACLs, the handle-related parts are not split into separate functions. Thus, by replacing `ext3_` with `ext2_` in all functions and data structures, the comments about ACLs in this chapter apply equally well for Ext2 as for Ext3.

11.3   Summary

Traditionally, the discretionary access control model is used by UNIX and Linux to decide which user may access a given resource as represented by a file in a filesystem. Although these methods work quite well for average installations, it is a very coarse-grained approach to security, and can be inappropriate in certain circumstances.

In this chapter, you have seen how ACLs provide more fine-grained means to access control for filesystem objects by attaching an explicit list of access control rules to each object.

You have also seen that ACLs are implemented on top of extended attributes, which allow augmenting filesystem objects with additional and more complex attributes than in the traditional UNIX model inherited by Linux.

12

Networks

That Linux is a child of the Internet is beyond contention. Thanks, above all, to Internet communication, the development of Linux has demonstrated the absurdity of the widely held opinion that project management by globally dispersed groups of programmers is not possible. Since the first kernel sources were made available on an ftp server more than a decade ago, networks have always been the central backbone for data exchange, for the development of concepts and code, and for the elimination of kernel errors. The kernel mailing list is a living example that nothing has changed. Everybody is able to read the latest contributions and add their own opinions to promote Linux development — assuming, of course, that the opinions expressed are reasonable.

Linux has a very cozy relationship with networks of all kinds — understandably as it came of age with the Internet. Computers running Linux account for a large proportion of the servers that build the Internet. Unsurprisingly, network implementation is a key kernel component to which more and more attention is being paid. In fact, there are very few network options that are not supported by Linux.

Implementation of network functionality is one of the most complex and extensive parts of the kernel. In addition to classic Internet protocols such as TCP, UDP, and the associated IP transport mechanism, Linux also supports many other interconnection options so that all conceivable types of computers and operating systems are able to interoperate. The work of the kernel is not made any simpler by the fact that Linux also supports a gigantic hardware spectrum dedicated to data transfer — ranging from Ethernet cards and token ring adapters to ISDN cards and modems.

Nevertheless, Linux developers have been able to come up with a surprisingly well-structured model to unify very different approaches. Even though this chapter is one of the longest in the book, it makes no claim to cover every detail of network implementation. Even an outline description of all drivers and protocols is beyond the scope of a single book — many would be needed owing to the volume of information. Not counting device drivers for network cards, the C implementation of the network layer occupies 15 MiB in the kernel sources, and this equates to more than 6,000 printed pages of code. The shear number of header files that relate to networking has motivated the kernel developers to store them not in the standard location `include/linux`, but devote the special directory `include/net` to them. Embedded in this code are many *concepts* that form the logical backbone of the network subsystem, and it is these that interest us in this chapter. Our discussion is restricted mainly to the TCP/IP implementation because it is by far the most widely used network protocol.

Of course, development of the network layer did not start with a clean sheet. Standards and conventions for exchanging data between computers had already existed for decades and were well known and well established. Linux also implements these standards to link to other computers.

12.1 Linked Computers

Communication between computers is a complex topic that raises many questions such as:

❑   How is the physical connection established? Which cables are used? Which restrictions and special requirements apply in terms of the media?

❑   How are transmission errors handled?

❑   How are individual computers identified in a network?

❑   How are data exchanged between computers connected to each other via intervening computers? And how is the best route found?

❑   How are data packaged so that they are not reliant on special features of individual computers?

❑   If there are several network services on a computer, how are they identified?

This catalog of questions could be extended at will. Unfortunately, the number of answers as well as the number of questions is almost unlimited, so that over time many suggestions have been put forward as to how to deal with specific problems. The most "reasonable" systems are those that classify problems into categories and create various layers to resolve clearly defined issues and communicate with the other layers by means of set mechanisms. This approach dramatically simplifies implementation, maintenance, and, above all, troubleshooting.

12.2 ISO/OSI and TCP/IP Reference Model

The *International Organization for Standardization* — better known as ISO — has devised a reference model that defines the various layers that make up a network. This model comprises the seven layers shown in Figure 12-1 and is called the *Open Systems Interconnection* (OSI) model.

However, the division into seven layers is too detailed for some issues. Therefore, in practice, use is often made of a second reference model in which some layers of the ISO/OSI model are combined into new layers. This model has only four layers so that its structure is simpler. It is known as the *TCP/IP reference model*, where IP stands for *Internet Protocol* and TCP for *Transmission Control Protocol*. Most of today's communication across the Internet is based on this model. Figure 12-1 compares the layers of the two models.

Each layer may speak only to the layer immediately above or below. For instance, the transport layer in the TCP/IP model may communicate only with the Internet and application layer but is totally independent of the host-to-network layer (ideally, it does not even know that such a layer exists).

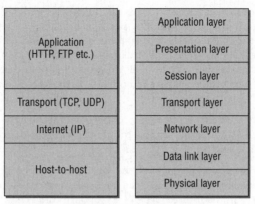

Figure 12-1: TCP/IP and ISO/OSI reference models.

The various layers perform the following tasks:

❏ The host-to-network layer is responsible for transferring information from one computer to a distant computer. It deals with the physical properties of the transmission medium[1] and with dividing the data stream into *frames* of a certain size to permit retransmission of data chunks if transmission errors occur. If several computers are sharing a transmission line, the network adapters must have a unique ID number known as a *MAC address* that is usually burned into the hardware. An agreement between manufacturers ensures that this number is globally unique. An example of a MAC address is `08:00:46:2B:FE:E8`.

In the view of the kernel, this layer is implemented by device drivers for network cards.

❏ The network layer of the OSI model is called the *Internet layer* in the TCP/IP model, but both refer basically to the same task of exchanging data between any computers in a network, not necessarily computers that are directly connected, as shown in Figure 12-2.

A direct transmission link between computers A and B is not possible because they are not physically connected to each other. The task of the network layer is therefore to find a route via which the computers can talk to each other; for example, A–E–B or A–E–C–B.

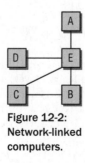

Figure 12-2: Network-linked computers.

---

[1]Predominantly coaxial cable, twisted-pair cable, and fiber optic links are used, but there is an increasing trend toward wireless transmission.

The network layer is also responsible for additional connection details such as splitting the data to be transported into packets of a specific size. This is necessary because the computers along the route may have different maximum limits to the size of the data packets they can accept. When data are sent, the data stream is split into packets that are reassembled upon receipt. This is done so that higher-level protocols can operate transparently with data units of a guaranteed size without having to bother with the specific properties of the Internet or network layer.

The network layer also assigns unique addresses within the network so that computers can talk to each other (these are not the same as the abovementioned hardware addresses because networks are usually made up of physical subnets).

In the Internet, the network layer is implemented by means of the Internet Protocol (IP), which comes in two versions (v4 and v6). At the moment, most connections are handled by IPv4, but IPv6 will replace it in the future.[2] When I speak of IP connections below, I always mean IPv4 connections.

IP uses addresses formatted like this — `192.168.1.8` or `62.26.212.10` — to address computers. These addresses are assigned by official registration authorities or providers (sometimes dynamically) or can be freely selected (within defined private ranges).

IP allows networks to be divided flexibly into *subnets* on the address level by supporting various address categories, which, depending on requirements, hold tens of millions of computers and more. However, it is not my intention to deal with this topic in detail. See the wealth of literature on network and system administration, for example, [Ste00] and [Fri02].

❑ In both models, the fourth layer is the *transport layer*. Its task is to regulate data transport between applications running on two linked computers. It is not sufficient to establish communication between the computers themselves; it is also necessary to set up a connection between the client and the server application, and this presupposes, of course, that there is an existing link between the computers. In the Internet, TCP (*Transmission Control Protocol*) or UDP (*User Datagram Protocol*) is used for this purpose. Each application interested in data in the IP layer uses a unique *port number* that uniquely identifies it on the target system. Typically, port 80 is used for web servers. Browser clients must send requests to this address to obtain the desired data. (Naturally, the client must also have a unique port number so that the web server can respond to the request, but this port number is generated dynamically.) To fully define a port address, the port number is usually appended to the IP address after a colon; for example, a web server on the computer with the address `192.168.1.8` is uniquely identifiable by the address `192.168.1.8:80`.

An additional task of this layer can (but need not) be the provision of a reliable connection over which data are transmitted in a given sequence. The above feature and the TCP protocol are discussed in Section 12.9.2.

❑ The application layer in the TCP/IP reference model is represented by layers 5 to 7 (session layer, presentation layer, and application layer) of the OSI model. As the name suggests, this layer represents the application view of a network connection. Once a communication connection has been established between two applications, this layer is responsible for the actual contents to be transferred. After all, web servers communicate with their clients differently than mail servers.

---

[2]The move to IPv6 should have already have taken place, but this is very slow in happening, particularly in the academic and commercial sectors. Perhaps the impending exhaustion of IPv4 address space will act as a spur.

A very large number of standard protocols are defined for the Internet. Usually, they are defined in *Request for Comments* (RFC) documents and must be implemented by applications wishing to use or offer a particular service. Most protocols can be tested with the `telnet` tool because they operate with simple text commands. A typical example of the communication flow between a browser and web server is shown below.

```
 wolfgang@meitner> telnet 192.168.1.20 80
Trying 192.168.1.20...
Connected to 192.168.1.20.
Escape character is '^]'.


GET /index.html HTTP/1.1
Host: www.sample.org
Connection: close



HTTP/1.1 200 OK
Date: Wed, 09 Jan 2002 15:24:15 GMT
Server: Apache/1.3.22 (Unix)
Content-Location: index.html.en
Vary: negotiate,accept-language,accept-charset
TCN: choice
Last-Modified: Fri, 04 May 2001 00:00:38 GMT
ETag: "83617-5b0-3af1f126;3bf57446"
Accept-Ranges: bytes
Content-Length: 1456
Connection: close
Content-Type: text/html
Content-Language: en

<!DOCTYPE html PUBLIC "-//W3C//DTD XHTML 1.0 Transitional//EN"
    "http://www.w3.org/TR/xhtml1/DTD/xhtml1-transitional.dtd">
<html xmlns="http://www.w3.org/1999/xhtml">
<head>
...
</html>
```

`telnet` is used to set up a TCP connection on port 80 of computer `192.168.1.20`. All user input is forwarded via the network connection to the process associated with this address (which is uniquely identified by the IP address and the port number). A response is sent once the request has been received. The contents of the desired HTML page are output together with a header with information on the document and other stuff. Web browsers use exactly the same procedure to access data transparently to users.

As a result of the systematic division of network functionality into layers, applications wishing to communicate with other computers need concern themselves with only a very few details. The actual link between the computers is implemented by lower layers, and all the application has to do is read and generate text strings — regardless of whether the two computers are sitting side by side in the same room or are located on different continents.

The layer structure of the network is reflected in the kernel by the fact that the individual levels are implemented in separate sections of code that communicate with each other via clearly defined interfaces to exchange data or forward commands.

12.3 Communication via Sockets

From the programmer's view, external devices are simply regular files under Linux (and UNIX) that are accessed by normal read and write operations, as described in Chapter 8. This simplifies access to resources because only a single, universal interface is needed.

The situation is a bit more complicated with network cards because the above scheme either cannot be adopted at all or only with great difficulty. Network cards function in a totally different way from normal block and character devices so that the typical UNIX motto that "everything is a file" no longer fully applies.[3] One reason is that many different communication protocols are used (in all layers) where many options need to be specified in order to establish a connection — and this cannot be done when device files are opened. Consequently, there are no entries for network cards in the /dev directory.[4]

Of course, the kernel must provide an interface that is as universal as possible to allow access to its network functions. This problem is not Linux-specific and gave BSD UNIX programmers headaches in the 1980s. The solution they adopted — special structures called *sockets* that are used as an interface for network implementation — has now established itself as an industry standard. Sockets are defined in the POSIX standard and are therefore also implemented by Linux.

Sockets are now used to define and set up network connections so that they can be accessed (particularly by read and write operations) using the normal means of an inode. In the view of programmers, the ultimate result of socket creation is a file descriptor that provides not only the whole range of standard functions but also several enhanced functions. The interface used for the actual exchange of data is the same for all protocols and address families.

When a socket is created, a distinction is made not only between address and protocol families but also between stream-based and datagram-based communication. What is also important (with stream-oriented sockets) is whether a socket is generated for a client or for a server program.

To illustrate the function of a socket from a user point of view, I include a short sample program to demonstrate just a few of the network programming options. Detailed descriptions are provided in numerous specialized publications, [Ste00], for example.

12.3.1 Creating a Socket

Sockets can be used not only for IP connections with different transport protocols, but also for all other address and protocol types supported by the kernel (e.g., IPX, Appletalk, local UNIX sockets, DECNet, and many other listed in <socket.h>). For this reason, it is essential to specify the desired combination when generating a socket. Although, as a relic of the past, it is possible to select any combination of partners from the address and protocol families, now only one protocol family is usually supported for each address family, and it is only possible to differentiate between stream- and datagram-oriented

---

[3]There are, however, several UNIX variants that implement network connections directly by means of device files, /dev/tcp, for example (see [Vah96]). From the application programmer's point of view and from that of the kernel itself, this is far less elegant than the socket method. Because the differences between network devices and normal devices are particularly evident when a connection is opened, network operations in Linux are only implemented by means of file descriptors (that can be processed with normal file methods) once a connection has been set up using the socket mechanism.

[4]One exception is the TUN/TAP driver, which simulates a virtual network card in userspace and is therefore very useful for debugging, for simulating network cards, or for setting up virtual tunnel connections. Because it does not communicate with any real device in order to send or receive data, this job is done by a program that communicates with the kernel via /dev/tunX or dev/tapX.

communication. For example, only TCP (for streams) or UDP (for datagram services) can be used as the transport protocol for a socket to which an Internet address such as 192.168.1.20 has been assigned.

Sockets are generated using the socket library function, which communicates with the kernel via a system call discussed in Section 12.10.3. A third argument could be used in addition to address family and communication type (stream or datagram) in order to select a protocol; however, as already stated, this is not necessary because the protocol is uniquely defined by the first two parameters. Specifying 0 for the third argument instructs the function to use the appropriate default.

Once the socket *function has been invoked, it is clear what the format of the socket address must be (or in which address family it resides), but no local address has yet been assigned to it.*

The bind function to which a sockaddr_*type* structure must be passed as an argument is used for this purpose. The structure then defines the address. Because address types differ from address family to address family, there is a different version of the structure for each family so that various requirements can be satisfied. *type* specifies the desired address type.

Internet addresses are uniquely identified by IP number and port number, which is why sockaddr_in is defined as follows:

<in.h>
```
struct sockaddr_in {
    sa_family_t          sin_family;   /* Address family     */
    __be16               sin_port;     /* Port number        */
    struct in_addr       sin_addr;     /* Internet address   */
    ...
}
```

An IP address and a port number are also needed in addition to the address family (here, AF_INET).

> **The IP address is not expected in the usual dotted decimal notation (four numbers separated by dots, i.e., 192.168.1.10), but must be specified as a number. The inet_aton library function converts an ASCII string into the format required by the kernel (and by the C library). For example, the numeric representation of the address 192.168.1.20 is 335653056. It is generated by writing the 1-byte-long sections of the IP address successively into a 4-byte data type that is then interpreted as a number. This permits the unique conversion of both representations.**

As stated in Chapter 1, CPUs apply two popular conventions for storing numeric values — little and big endian. An explicit *network byte order* corresponding to the big endian format has been defined to ensure that machines with different byte arrangements are able to communicate with each other easily. Numeric values appearing in protocol headers must therefore always be specified in this format. The fact that both the IP address and the port number consist only of numbers must be taken into account when defining the values in the sockaddr_in structure. The C library features numerous functions for converting numbers from the native format of the CPU to the network byte order (if the CPU and the network have the same byte order, the functions leave it unchanged). Good network applications always use these functions even if they are developed on big endian machines to ensure that they can be ported to different machine types.

To represent little and big endian types explicitly, the kernel provides several data types. __be16, __be32, and __be64 represent big endian numbers with 16, 32, and 64 bits, while the variants with prefix __le are analogs for little endian values. They are all defined in <types.h>. Note that both little and big endian types resolve to the same data types finally (namely, u32 and so on, as introduced in Chapter 1), but an explicit specification of the byte order allows for checking correctness of code with automated type checking tools.

12.3.2 Using Sockets

It is assumed that you are familiar with the userland side of network programming. However, to briefly illustrate how sockets represent an interface to the network layer of the kernel, I discuss two very brief sample programs, one that acts as a client for echo requests, the other as a server. A text string is sent from the client to the server and is returned unchanged. The TCP/IP protocol is used.

Echo Client

The source code for the echo client is as follows[5]:

```
#include<stdio.h>
#include<netinet/in.h>
#include<sys/types.h>
#include<string.h>

int main() {
  /* Host and port number of the echo server */
  char* echo_host = "192.168.1.20";
  int echo_port = 7;
  int sockfd;
  struct sockaddr_in *server=
      (struct sockaddr_in*)malloc(sizeof(struct sockaddr_in));

  /* Set address of server to be connected */
  server->sin_family = AF_INET;
  server->sin_port = htons(echo_port);        // Note network byte order!
  server->sin_addr.s_addr = inet_addr(echo_host);

  /* Create a socket (Internet address family, stream socket and
     default protocol) */
  sockfd = socket(AF_INET, SOCK_STREAM, 0);

  /* Connect to server */
  printf("Connecting to %s \n", echo_host);
  printf("Numeric: %u\n", server->sin_addr);
  connect(sockfd, (struct sockaddr*)server, sizeof(*server));

  /* Send message */
  char* msg = "Hello World";
  printf("\nSend: '%s'\n", msg);
  write(sockfd, msg, strlen(msg));

  /* ... and receive result */
  char* buf = (char*)malloc(1000); // Receive buffer for max. 1000 chars
  int bytes = read(sockfd, (void*)buf, 1000);
```

---

[5]To simplify matters, all error checks that would be performed in a genuine, robust implementation are omitted.

```
        printf("\nBytes received: %u\n", bytes);
        printf("Text: '%s'\n", buf);

        /* End communication (i.e. close socket) */
        close(sockfd);
}
```

The Internet superdaemon (inetd, xinetd, or similar) normally uses a built-in echo server. Consequently, the source code can be tested immediately after compilation.

```
wolfgang@meitner> ./echo_client
Connect to 192.168.1.20
Numeric: 335653056

Send: 'Hello World'

Bytes received: 11
Text: 'Hello World'
```

The following steps are performed by the client:

1. An instance of the sockaddr_in structure is generated to define the address of the server to be contacted. AF_INET indicates that it is an Internet address and the target server is precisely defined by its IP address (192.168.1.20) and port number (7).

    Also, the data from the host are converted to the network byte order. htons is used for the port number, and the inet_addr auxiliary function performs the conversion implicitly by translating the text string with a dotted decimal address into a number.

2. A socket is created in the kernel by means of the socket function, which (as shown below) is based on the socketcall system call of the kernel. The result returned is an integer number that is interpreted as a file descriptor — and can therefore be processed by all functions available for regular files, as described in Chapter 8. In addition to these operations, there are other network-specific ways of handling the file descriptor; these permit exact setting of various transmission parameters not discussed here.

3. A connection is set up by invoking the connect function in conjunction with the file descriptor and the server variable that stores the server connection data (this function is also based on the socketcall system call).

4. Actual communication is initiated by sending a text string ("Hello World" — how could it be anything else?) to the server by means of write. Writing data to a socket file descriptor is the equivalent of sending data. This step is totally independent of the server location and the protocol used to set up the connection. The network implementation ensures that the character string reaches its destination — no matter how this is done.

5. The server response is read by read, but a buffer must first be allocated to hold the data received. As a precaution, 1,000 bytes are reserved in memory, although we only expect the original string to be returned. read blocks until the server supplies a response, and it then returns the number of bytes received as an integer number.

    Because strings in C are always null-terminated, 11 bytes are received, although the message itself appears to be only 10 bytes long.

Echo Server

How sockets are used for server processes differs slightly from how they are used in clients. The following sample program demonstrates how a simple echo server can be implemented:

```c
#include<stdio.h>
#include<netinet/in.h>
#include<sys/types.h>
#include<string.h>

int main() {
  char* echo_host = "192.168.1.20";
  int echo_port = 7777;
  int sockfd;
  struct sockaddr_in *server=
      (struct sockaddr_in*)malloc(sizeof(struct sockaddr_in));

  /* Set own address */
  server->sin_family = AF_INET;
  server->sin_port = htons(echo_port);      // Note network byte order!
  server->sin_addr.s_addr = inet_addr(echo_host);

  /* Create a socket */
  sockfd = socket(AF_INET, SOCK_STREAM, 0);

  /* Bind to an address */
  if (bind(sockfd, (struct sockaddr*)server, sizeof(*server))) {
    printf("bind failed\n");
  }

  /* Enable server mode of socket */
  listen(sockfd, SOMAXCONN);

  /* ...and wait for incoming data */
  int clientfd;
  struct sockaddr_in* client =
    (struct sockaddr_in*)malloc(sizeof(struct sockaddr_in));
  int client_size = sizeof(*client);
  char* buf = (char*)malloc(1000);
  int bytes;

  printf("Wait for connection to port %u\n", echo_port);

  /* Accept a connection request */
  clientfd = accept(sockfd, (struct sockaddr*)client, &client_size);
  printf("Connected to %s:%u\n\n", inet_ntoa(client->sin_addr),
                                   ntohs(client->sin_port));
  printf("Numeric: %u\n", ntohl(client->sin_addr.s_addr));

  while(1) {    /* Endless loop */
    /* Receive transmitted data */
    bytes = read(clientfd, (void*)buf, 1000);
    if (bytes <= 0) {
      close(clientfd);
      printf("Connection closed.\n");
      exit(0);
    }
```

```
    printf("Bytes received: %u\n", bytes);
    printf("Text: '%s'\n", buf);

    /* Send response */
    write(clientfd, buf, bytes);
  }
}
```

The first section is almost the same as the client code. An instance of the sockaddr_in structure is created to hold the Internet address of the server, but this is done for a different reason. The address of the server to which the client wishes to connect is specified in the client code. In this case, the address specified is that used by the server to wait for connections. The socket is generated in exactly the same way as for the client.

In contrast to the client, the server does not actively attempt to set up a connection to another program but simply waits passively until it receives a connection request. Three library functions (again based on the universal socketcall system call) are required to set up a passive connection:

❑   bind binds the socket to an address (192.186.1.20:7777 in our example).[6]

❑   listen instructs the socket to wait passively for an incoming connection request from a client. The function creates a wait queue on which all processes wishing to establish a connection are placed. The length of the queue is defined by the second parameter. (SOMAXCONN specifies that the maximum system-internal number must be used so as not to arbitrarily restrict the maximum number of waiting processes.)

❑   The accept function accepts the connection request of the first client on the wait queue. When the queue is empty, the function blocks until a client wishing to connect is available.

Again, actual communication is performed by read and write, which use the file descriptor returned by accept.

The client connection data (supplied by accept and consisting of the IP address and port number) are output for information purposes. While the client IP address for a specific computer is fixed, the port number is selected dynamically by the computer's kernel when the connection is established.

The function of the echo server is easily imitated by reading all client input with read and writing it back with write in an endless loop. When the client closes the connection, read returns a data stream that is 0 bytes long so that the server then also terminates.

Client	Server
wolfgang@meitner> ./stream_client	wolfgang@meitner> ./stream_server
Connect to 192.168.1.20	Wait for connection on port 7777
Numeric: 335653056	
	Client: 192.168.1.10:3505
Send: 'Hello World'	Numeric: 3232235786
	Bytes received: 11
	Text: 'Hello World'
Bytes received: 11	
Text: 'Hello World'	
	Connection closed.

---

[6]Under Linux (and all other UNIX flavors), all ports between 1 and 1,024 are referred to as *reserved ports* and may be used only by processes with root rights. For this reason, we use the free port number 7,777.

A 4-tuple notation (192.168.1.20:7777, 192.168.1.10:3506) is used to uniquely identify a connection. The first element specifies the address and port of the local system, the second the address and port of the client.

An asterisk (*) is substituted if one of the elements is still undefined. A server process listening on a passive socket but not yet connected to a client is therefore denoted by 192.168.1.20:7777, *.*.

Two socket pairs are registered in the kernel once a server has duplicated itself with `fork` to handle a connection.

Listen	Established
192.168.1.20:7777, *.*	192.168.1.20:7777, 192.168.1.10:3506

Although the sockets of both server processes have the same IP address/port number combination, they are differentiated by the 4-tuple.

Consequently, the kernel must note all four connection parameters when distributing incoming and outgoing TCP/IP packets to ensure that assignments are made correctly. This task is known as *multiplexing*.

The `netstat` tool displays and checks the state of all TCP/IP connections on the system. The following sample output is produced if two clients are connected to the server:

```
wolfgang@meitner> netstat -na
Active Internet connections (servers and established)
Proto Recv-Q Send-Q Local Address        Foreign Address       State
tcp        0      0 192.168.1.20:7777    0.0.0.0:*             LISTEN
tcp        0      0 192.168.1.20:7777    192.168.1.10:3506     ESTABLISHED
tcp        0      0 192.168.1.20:7777    192.168.1.10:3505     ESTABLISHED
```

12.3.3 Datagram Sockets

UDP is a second, widely used transport protocol that builds on IP connections. UDP stands for *User Datagram Protocol* and differs from TCP in several basic areas:

❑ UDP is packet-oriented. No explicit connection setup is required before data are sent.

❑ Packets can be lost during transmission. There is no guarantee that data will actually reach their destination.

❑ Packets are not necessarily received in the same order in which they were sent.

UDP is commonly used for video conferencing, audio streaming, and similar services. Here it doesn't matter if a few packets go missing — all that would be noticed would be brief dropouts in multimedia sequences. However, like IP, UDP guarantees that the *contents* of packets are unchanged when they arrive at their destinations.

An IP address and port number can be used by a TCP and a UDP process *at the same time*. In multiplexing, the kernel ensures that only packets of the correct transport protocol are forwarded to the appropriate process.

Comparing TCP and UDP is like comparing the postal service with the telephone network. TCP corresponds to a telephone call. The calling party must set up a connection (which must be accepted by the person called) before information can be passed. During the call, all information sent is received in the same order in which it was sent.

UDP can be likened to the postal service. Packets (or letters in this analogy) can be sent to recipients without contacting them in advance for permission to do so. There is no guarantee that letters will be delivered (although both the postal service and the network will do their best). Similarly, there is no guarantee that letters will be sent or received in a particular sequence.

Those interested in further examples of the use of UDP sockets are referred to the many textbooks on network and system programming.

12.4 The Layer Model of Network Implementation

The kernel implements the network layer very similarly to the TCP/IP reference model introduced at the beginning of this chapter.

The C code is split into levels with clearly defined tasks, and each level is able to communicate only with the level immediately above and below via clearly defined interfaces. This has the advantage that various devices, transmission mechanisms, and protocols can be combined. For example, normal Ethernet cards can be used not only to set up Internet (IP) connections but also to transmit other protocols such as Appletalk or IPX without the need for any kind of modification to the device driver of the card.

Figure 12-3 illustrates the implementation of the layer model in the kernel.

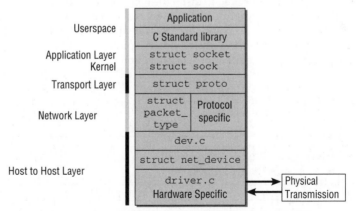

Figure 12-3: Implementation of the layer model in the kernel.

The network subsystem is one of the most comprehensive and demanding parts of the kernel. Why is this so? The answer is that it deals with a very large number of protocol-specific details and subtleties, and the code path through the layer is riddled with excessive function pointers in place of direct function

745

calls. This is unavoidable because of the numerous ways in which the layers can be combined — but this does not make the code path any clearer or easier to follow. In addition, the data structures involved are generally very closely linked with each other. To reduce complexity, the information below relates primarily to the Internet protocols.

The layer model is mirrored not only in the design of the network layer, but also in the way data are transmitted (or, to be more precise, the way in which the data generated and transmitted by the individual layers are packaged). In general, the data of each layer are made up of a header section and a data section, as shown in Figure 12-4.

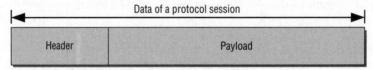

Figure 12-4: Division into header and data sections.

Whereas the header contains metadata (destination address, length, transport protocol type, etc.) on the data section, the data section itself consists of the useful data (or payload).

The base unit of transmission is the (Ethernet) frame used by the network card to transmit data. The main entry in the frame header is the hardware address of the destination system to which the data are to be transmitted and which is needed for transmission via cable.

The data of the higher-level protocol are packaged in the Ethernet frame by including the header and data tuple generated by the protocol in the data section of the frame. This is the IP layer data in Internet networks.

Because not only IP packets but also, for example, Appletalk or IPX packets can be transmitted via Ethernet, the receiving system must be able to distinguish between protocol types in order to forward the data to the correct routines for further processing. Analyzing data to find out which transport protocol is used is very time-consuming. As a result, the Ethernet header (and the headers of all other modern protocols) includes an identifier to uniquely identify the protocol type in the data section. The identifiers (for Ethernet) are assigned by an international organization (IEEE).

This division is continued for all protocols in the protocol stack. For this reason, each frame transmitted starts with a series of headers followed by the data of the application layer, as shown in Figure 12-5.[7]

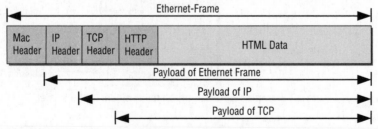

Figure 12-5: Transporting HTTP data via TCP/IP in an Ethernet frame.

---

[7]The boundary between the HTTP header and the data section is indicated by a change of shading because this distinction is made in userspace and not in the kernel.

The figure clearly illustrates that part of the bandwidth is inevitably sacrificed to accommodate control information.

12.5 Networking Namespaces

Recall from Chapter 1 that many parts of the kernel are contained in namespaces. These allow for building multiple virtual viewpoints of the system that are separated and segregated from each other. Every instance looks like a single machine running Linux, but, in fact, many such instances can operate simultaneously on a single physical machine. During the development of 2.6.24, the kernel started to adopt namespaces also for the networking subsystem. This adds some extra complexity to the networking layer because all properties of the subsystem that used to be "global" in former versions — for instance, the available network cards — need to be managed on a per-namespace basis now. If a particular networking device is visible in one namespace, it need not be available in another one.

As usual, a central structure is used to keep track of all available namespaces. The definition is as follows:

```
include/net/net_namespace.h
struct net {
        atomic_t count; /* To decided when the network
                         * namespace should be freed.
                         */
...
        struct list_head list; /* list of network namespaces */
...
        struct proc_dir_entry *proc_net;
        struct proc_dir_entry *proc_net_stat;
        struct proc_dir_entry *proc_net_root;

        struct net_device *loopback_dev; /* The loopback */

        struct list_head dev_base_head;
        struct hlist_head *dev_name_head;
        struct hlist_head *dev_index_head;
};
```

Work has only begun to make the networking subsystem fully aware of namespaces. What you see now — the situation in kernel 2.6.24 — still represents a comparatively early stage of development. Therefore, struct net will grow in size in the future as more and more networking components are transferred from a global management to a namespace-aware implementation. For now, the basic infrastructure is in place. Network devices are kept track of under consideration of namespaces, and support for the most important protocols is available. Since I have not yet discussed any specific points of the networking implementation, the structures referenced in struct net are naturally still unknown (however, I promise that this will certainly change in the course of this chapter). For now, it suffices to present a broad overview about what is handled in a namespace-aware fashion:

❑   count is a standard usage counter, and the auxiliary functions get_net and put_net are provided to obtain and release permission to use a specific net instance. When count drops to zero, the namespace is deallocated and removed from the system.

❑   All available namespaces are kept on a doubly linked list that is headed by net_namespace_list. list is used as the list element. The function copy_net_ns adds a new namespace to the list. It is automatically called when a set of new namespaces is created with create_new_namespace.

❏ Since each namespace can contain different network devices, this must also be reflected in the contents of Procfs (see Chapter 10.1). Three entries require a per-namespace handling: `/proc/net` is represented by `proc_net`, while `/proc/net/stats` is represented by `proc_net_stats`. `proc_net_root` points to the root element of the Procfs instance for the current namespace, that is, `/proc`.

❏ Each namespace may have a different loopback device, and `loopback_dev` points to the (virtual) network device that fulfills this role.

❏ Network devices are represented by `struct net_device`. All devices associated with a specific namespace are kept on a doubly linked list headed by `dev_base_head`. The devices are kept on two additional hash tables: One uses the device name as hash key (`dev_name_head`), and one uses the interface index (`dev_index_head`).

Note that there is a slight difference in terminology between devices and interfaces. While *devices* represent hardware devices that provide physical transmission capabilities, *interfaces* can be purely virtual entities, possibly implemented on top of real devices. For example, a network card could provide two interfaces.

Since the distinction between these terms is not relevant for our purposes, I use both terms interchangeably in the following.

Many components still require substantial rework to make them handle namespaces correctly, and there is still a considerable way to go until a fully namespace-aware networking subsystem will be available. For instance, kernel 2.6.25 (which was still under development when this chapter was written) will introduce initial preparations to make specific protocols aware of namespaces:

include/net/net_namespace.h
```
struct net {
...
        struct netns_packet packet;
        struct netns_unix unx;
        struct netns_ipv4 ipv4;
#if defined(CONFIG_IPV6) || defined(CONFIG_IPV6_MODULE)
        struct netns_ipv6 ipv6;
#endif
};
```

The new members like `ipv4` will store (formerly global) protocol parameters, and protocol-specific structures are introduced for this purpose. The approach proceeds step-by-step: First, the basic framework is set in place. Subsequent steps will then move global properties into the per-namespace representation; the structures are initially empty. More work along these lines is expected to be accepted into future kernel versions.

Each network namespace consists of several components, for example, the representation in Procfs. Whenever a new networking namespace is created, these components must be initialized. Likewise, some cleanups are necessary when a namespace is deleted. The kernel employs the following structure to keep track of all required initialization/cleanup tuples:

include/net/net_namespace.h
```
struct pernet_operations {
        struct list_head list;
```

```
        int (*init)(struct net *net);
        void (*exit)(struct net *net);
    };
```

The structure does not present any surprises: `init` stores an initialization function, while clean-up work is handled by `exit`. All available `pernet_operation` instances are kept on a list headed by `pernet_list`; `list` is used as the list element. The auxiliary functions `register_pernet_subsys` and `unregister_pernet_subsys` add and remove elements to and from the list, respectively. Whenever a new networking namespace is created, the kernel iterates over the list of `pernet_operation`s and calls the initialization function with the `net` instance that represents the new namespace as parameter. Cleaning up when a networking namespace is deleted is handled similarly.

Most computers will typically require only a single networking namespace. The global variable `init_net` (and in this case, the variable is *really* global and not contained in another namespace!) contains the `net` instance for this namespace. In the following, I mostly neglect namespaces to simplify matters. It suffices to keep in mind that all global functions of the network layer require a network namespace as parameter, and that any global properties of the networking subsystem may only be referenced by a detour through the namespace under consideration.

12.6 Socket Buffers

When network packets are analyzed in the kernel, the data of lower-level protocols are passed to higher-level layers. The reverse sequence applies when data are sent. The data (header and payload) generated by the various protocols are successively passed to lower layers until they are finally transmitted. As the speed of these operations is crucial to network layer performance, the kernel makes use of a special structure known as a *socket buffer*, which is defined as follows:

<skbuff.h>
```
struct sk_buff {
        /* These two members must be first. */
        struct sk_buff      *next;
        struct sk_buff      *prev;

        struct sock         *sk;
        ktime_t             tstamp;
        struct net_device   *dev;

        struct  dst_entry   *dst;

        char                cb[48];

        unsigned int        len,
                            data_len;
        __u16               mac_len,
                            hdr_len;
        union {
                __wsum csum;
                struct {
                        __u16 csum_start;
```

```
                           __u16 csum_offset;
                  };
         };
         __u32                priority;
         __u8                 local_df:1,
                              cloned:1,
                              ip_summed:2,
                              nohdr:1,
                              nfctinfo:3;
         __u8                 pkt_type:3,
                              fclone:2,
                              ipvs_property:1,
                              nf_trace:1;
         __be16               protocol;
...
         void                 (*destructor)(struct sk_buff *skb);
...
         int                  iif;
...
         sk_buff_data_t       transport_header;
         sk_buff_data_t       network_header;
         sk_buff_data_t       mac_header;

         /* These elements must be at the end, see alloc_skb() for details. */
         sk_buff_data_t       tail;
         sk_buff_data_t       end;
         unsigned char        *head,
                              *data;
         unsigned int         truesize;
         atomic_t             users;
};
```

Socket buffers are used to exchange data between the network implementation levels without having to copy packet data to and fro — this delivers considerable speed gains. The socket structure is one of the cornerstones of the network layer because it is processed on all levels both when packets are analyzed and generated.

12.6.1 *Data Management Using Socket Buffers*

Socket buffers are linked by means of the various pointers they contain with an area in memory where the data of a network packet reside, as shown in Figure 12-6. The figure assumes that we are working on a 32-bit system (the organization of a socket buffer is slightly different on a 64-bit machine, as you will see in a moment).

The basic idea of a socket buffer is to add and remove protocol headers by manipulating pointers.

❑   head and end point to the start and end of the area in memory where the data reside.

> **This area may be larger than actually needed because it is not clear how big packets will be when they are synthesized.**

❑   data and tail point to the start and end of the protocol data area.

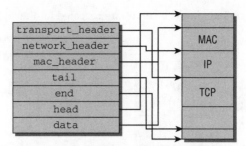

Figure 12-6: Link between socket buffer and network packet data.

❑ `mac_header` points to the start of the MAC header, while `network_header` and `transport_header` point to the header data of the network and transport layer, respectively. On systems with 32-bit word length, the data type `sk_buff_data_t` that is used for the various data components is a simple pointer:

<skbuff.h>
```
typedef unsigned char *sk_buff_data_t;
```

This enables the kernel to use socket buffers for all protocol types. Simple type conversions are necessary to interpret the data correctly, and several auxiliary functions are provided for this purpose. A socket buffer can, for example, contain a TCP or UDP packet. The corresponding information from the transport header can be extracted with `tcp_hdr`, respectively, `udp_hdr`. Both functions convert the raw pointer into an appropriate data type. Other transport layer protocols also provide helper functions of the type `XXX_hdr` that require a pointer to `struct sk_buff` and return the reinterpreted transport header data. Observe, for example, how a TCP header can be obtained from a socket buffer:

<tcp.h>
```
static inline struct tcphdr *tcp_hdr(const struct sk_buff *skb)
{
        return (struct tcphdr *)skb_transport_header(skb);
}
```

`struct tcphdr` is a structure that collects all fields contained in a TCP header; the exact layout is discussed in Section 12.9.2.

Similar conversion functions are also available for the network layer. For our purposes, `ip_hdr` is most important: It is used to interpret the contents of an IP packet.

`data` and `tail` enable data to be passed between protocol levels without requiring explicit copy operations, as shown in Figure 12-7, which demonstrates how packets are synthesized.

When a new packet is generated, the TCP layer first allocates memory in userspace to hold the packet data (header and payroll). The space reserved is larger than needed for the data so that lower-level layers can add further headers.

A socket buffer is allocated so that `head` and `end` point to the start and end of the space reserved in memory, while the TCP data are located between `data` and `tail`.

A new layer must be added when the socket buffer is passed to the IP layer. This can simply be written into the reserved space, and all pointers remain unchanged with the exception of `data`, which now points

751

to the start of the IP header. The same operations are repeated for the layers below until a finished packet is ready to be sent across the network.

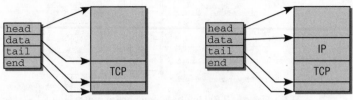

Figure 12-7: Manipulation of the socket buffer in the transition between protocol levels.

The procedure adopted to analyze packets is similar. The packet data are copied into a reserved memory area in the kernel and remain there for the duration of the analysis phase. The socket buffer associated with the packet is passed on from layer to layer, and the various pointers are successively supplied with the correct values.

The kernel provides the standard functions listed in Table 12-1 for manipulating socket buffers.

Table 12-1: Operations on Socket Buffers

Function	Meaning
alloc_skb	Allocates a new sk_buff instance.
skb_copy	Creates a copy of the socket buffer *and* associated data.
skb_clone	Duplicates a socket buffer but uses the same packet data for the original and the copy.
skb_tailroom	Returns the size of the free space at the end of the data.
skb_headroom	Returns the size of the free space at the start of the data.
skb_realloc_headroom	Creates more free space at the start of the data. The existing data are retained.

Socket buffers require numerous pointers to represent the different components of the buffer's contents. Since low memory footprint and high processing speed are essential for the network layer and thus for struct sk_buff, it is desirable to make the structure as small as possible. On 64-bit CPUs, a little trick can be used to save some space. The definition of sk_buff_data_t is changed to an integer variable:

<skbuff.h>
```
typedef unsigned int sk_buff_data_t;
```

Since integer variables require only half the memory of pointers (4 instead of 8 bytes) on such architectures, the structure shrinks by 20 bytes.[8] The information contained in a socket buffer is still the same,

---

[8]Since integers and pointers use an identical number of bits on 32-bit systems, the trick does not work for them.

though. `data` and `head` remain regular pointers, and all `sk_buff_data_t` elements are now interpreted as *offsets* relative to these pointers. A pointer to the start of the transport header is now computed as follows:

<skbuff.h>
```
static inline unsigned char *skb_transport_header(const struct sk_buff *skb)
{
        return skb->head + skb->transport_header;
}
```

It is valid to use this approach since 4 bytes are sufficient to describe memory regions of up to 4 GiB, and a socket buffer that exceeds this size will never be encountered.

Since the internal representation of socket buffers is not supposed to be visible to the generic networking code, several auxiliary functions as shown above are provided to access the elements of `struct sk_buff`. They are all defined in `<skbuff.h>`, and the proper variant is automatically chosen at compile time.

❑ `skb_transport_header(const struct sk_buff *skb)` obtains the address of the transport header for a given socket buffer.

❑ `skb_reset_transport_header(struct sk_buff *skb)` resets the start of the transport header to the start of the data section.

❑ `skb_set_transport_header(struct sk_buff *skb, const int offset)` sets the start of the transport header given the offset to the data pointer.

The same set of functions is available for the MAC and network headers by replacing `transport` with `mac` or `network`, respectively.

12.6.2 Management Data of Socket Buffers

The socket buffer structure contains not only the above pointers, but also other elements that are used to handle the associated data and to manage the socket buffer itself.

The less common elements are dicsussed in this chapter when they are needed. The most important elements are listed below.

❑ `tstamp` stores the time the packet arrived.

❑ `dev` specifies the network device on which the packet is processed. `dev` may change in the course of processing the packet — for instance, when it will leave the computer on another device at some point.

❑ The interface index number of the input device is always preserved in `iif`. Section 12.7.1 explains how to use this number.

❑ `sk` is a link to the `socket` instance (see Section 12.10.1) of the socket used to process the packet.

❑ `dst` indicates the further route of the packet through the network implementation. A special format is used (this is discussed in Section 12.8.5).

❑ `next` and `prev` hold socket buffers in a doubly linked list. The standard list implementation of the kernel is *not* used here but is replaced by a manual version.

A list head is used to implement wait queues with socket buffers. Its structure is defined as follows:

<skbuff.h>
```
struct sk_buff_head {
        /* These two members must be first. */
        struct sk_buff  *next;
        struct sk_buff  *prev;

        __u32           qlen;
        spinlock_t      lock;
};
```

qlen specifies the length of the wait queue; that is, the number of elements in the queue. next and prev of sk_buff_head and sk_buff are used to create a cyclic doubly linked list, and the list element of the socket buffer points back to the list head, as illustrated in Figure 12-8.

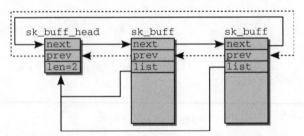

Figure 12-8: Managing socket buffers in a doubly linked list.

Packets are often placed on wait queues, for example, when they are awaiting processing or when packets that have been fragmented are reassembled.

12.7 Network Access Layer

Now that we have examined the structure of the network subsystem in the Linux kernel, we turn our attention to the first layer of the network implementation — the network access layer. This layer is primarily responsible for transferring information between computers and collaborates directly with the device drivers of network cards.

It is not my intention to discuss the implementation of the card drivers and the associated problems[9] because the techniques employed are only slightly different from those described in Chapter 6. I am much more interested in the *interface* made available by each card driver and used by the network code to provide an abstract view of the hardware.

By reference to Ethernet frames, I explain how data are represented "on the cable" and describe the steps taken between receiving a packet and passing it on to a higher layer. I also describe the steps in the reverse direction when generated packets leave the computer via a network interface.

---

[9]Even though this may be quite interesting — unfortunately not for technical reasons but for product policy reasons.

12.7.1 Representation of Network Devices

In the kernel, each network device is represented by an instance of the net_device structure. Once a structure instance has been allocated and filled, it must be registered with the kernel using register_netdev from net/core/dev.c. This function performs some initialization tasks and registers the device within the generic device mechanism. This creates a sysfs entry (see Chapter 10.3) /sys/class/net/<device>, which links to the device's directory. A system with one PCI network card and the loopback device has two entries in /sys/class/net:

```
root@meitner # ls -l /sys/class/net
total 0
lrwxrwxrwx 1 root root 0 2008-03-09 09:43 eth0 -> ../../devices/pci0000:00/0000:00:1c.5/
0000:02:00.0/net/eth0
lrwxrwxrwx 1 root root 0 2008-03-09 09:42 lo -> ../../devices/virtual/net/lo
```

Data Structure

Before discussing the contents of struct net_device in detail, let us address the question of how the kernel keeps track of the available network devices, and how a particular network device can be found. As usual, the devices are not arranged globally, but on a per-namespace basis. Recall that three mechanisms are available for each namespace net:

❑ All network devices are stored in a singly linked list with the list head dev_base.

❑ Hashing by device name. The auxiliary function dev_get_by_name(struct net *net, const char *name) finds a network device on this hash.

❑ Hashing by interface index. The auxiliary function dev_get_by_index(struct net *net, int ifindex) finds the net_device instance given the interface index.

The net_device structure holds all conceivable information on the device. It spans more than 200 lines and is one of the most voluminous structures in the kernel. As the structure is overburdened with details, a much simplified — but still quite long — version is reproduced below.[10] Here's the code:

<netdevice.h>
```
struct net_device
{
        char                    name[IFNAMSIZ];
        /* device name hash chain */
        struct hlist_node name_hlist;

        /* I/O specific fields   */
        unsigned long           mem_end;        /* shared mem end      */
        unsigned long           mem_start;      /* shared mem start    */
        unsigned long           base_addr;      /* device I/O address  */
        unsigned int            irq;            /* device IRQ number   */

        unsigned long           state;
        struct list_head        dev_list;
        int                     (*init)(struct net_device *dev);

        /* Interface index. Unique device identifier   */
```

---

[10]The kernel developers are not quite satisfied with the current state of the structure either. The source code states that "Actually, this whole structure is a big mistake".

```
int                     ifindex;

struct net_device_stats* (*get_stats)(struct net_device *dev);

/* Hardware header description */
const struct header_ops *header_ops;

unsigned short          flags;  /* interface flags (a la BSD)   */
unsigned                mtu;    /* interface MTU value          */
unsigned short          type;   /* interface hardware type      */
unsigned short          hard_header_len;        /* hardware hdr length */

/* Interface address info. */
unsigned char           perm_addr[MAX_ADDR_LEN]; /* permanent hw address */
unsigned char           addr_len;       /* hardware address length      */
int                     promiscuity;

/* Protocol specific pointers */
void                    *atalk_ptr;     /* AppleTalk link       */
void                    *ip_ptr;        /* IPv4 specific data   */
void                    *dn_ptr;        /* DECnet specific data */
void                    *ip6_ptr;       /* IPv6 specific data */
void                    *ec_ptr;        /* Econet specific data */


unsigned long           last_rx;        /* Time of last Rx      */
unsigned long           trans_start;    /* Time (in jiffies) of last Tx */

/* Interface address info used in eth_type_trans() */
unsigned char           dev_addr[MAX_ADDR_LEN]; /* hw address, (before bcast
                                        because most packets are unicast) */

unsigned char           broadcast[MAX_ADDR_LEN];        /* hw bcast add */

int (*hard_start_xmit) (struct sk_buff *skb,
                        struct net_device *dev);

/* Called after device is detached from network. */
void                    (*uninit)(struct net_device *dev);
/* Called after last user reference disappears. */
void                    (*destructor)(struct net_device *dev);

/* Pointers to interface service routines.      */
int                     (*open)(struct net_device *dev);
int                     (*stop)(struct net_device *dev);

void                    (*set_multicast_list)(struct net_device *dev);
int                     (*set_mac_address)(struct net_device *dev,
                                        void *addr);
int                     (*do_ioctl)(struct net_device *dev,
                                struct ifreq *ifr, int cmd);
int                     (*set_config)(struct net_device *dev,
                                struct ifmap *map);
int                     (*change_mtu)(struct net_device *dev, int new_mtu);
```

```
void                    (*tx_timeout) (struct net_device *dev);
int                     (*neigh_setup)(struct net_device *dev, struct neigh_parms *);

/* Network namespace this network device is inside */
struct net *nd_net;

/* class/net/name entry */
struct device dev;
```

...

The abbreviations *Rx* and *Tx* that appear in the structure are often also used in function names, variable names, and comments. They stand for *Receive* and *Transmit*, respectively, and crop up a few times in the following sections.

The name of the network device is stored in name. It consists of a string followed by a number to differentiate between multiple adapters of the same type (if, e.g., the system has two Ethernet cards). Table 12-2 lists the most common device classes.

Table 12-2: Designations for Network Devices

Name	Device class
ethX	Ethernet adapter, regardless of cable type and transmission speed
pppX	PPP connection via modem
isdnX	ISDN cards
atmX	*Asynchronous transfer mode*, interface to high-speed network cards
lo	*Loopback* device for communication with the local computer

Symbolic names for network cards are used, for example, when parameters are set using the ifconfig tool.

In the kernel, network cards have a unique index number that is assigned dynamically when they are registered and is held in the ifindex element. Recall that the kernel provides the dev_get_by_name and dev_get_by_index functions to find the net_device instance of a network card by reference to its name or index number.

Some structure elements define device properties that are relevant for the network layer and the network access layer:

❑ mtu (*maximum transfer unit*) specifies the maximum length of a transfer frame. Protocols of the network layer must observe this value and may need to split packets into smaller units.

❑ type holds the hardware type of the device and uses constants from <if_arp.h>. For example, ARPHRD_ETHER and ARPHDR_IEEE802 stand for 10 Mbit and 802.2 Ethernet, ARPHRD_APPLETLK for AppleTalk, and ARPHRD_LOOPBACK for the loopback device.

❏ `dev_addr` stores the hardware address of the device (e.g., the MAC address for Ethernet cards), and `addr_len` specifies the address length. `broadcast` is the broadcast address used to send messages to attached stations.

❏ `ip_ptr`, `ip6_ptr`, `atalk_ptr`, and so on are pointers to protocol-specific data not manipulated by the generic code.

> **Several of these pointers may have a non-null value because a network device can be used with several network protocols at the same time.**

Most elements of the `net_device` structure are function pointers to perform network card-typical tasks. Although the implementation differs from adapter to adapter, the call syntax (and the task performed) is always the same. These elements therefore represent the abstraction interface to the next protocol level. They enable the kernel to address all network cards by means of a uniform set of functions, while the low-level drivers are responsible for implementing the details.

❏ `open` and `stop` initialize and terminate network cards. These actions are usually triggered from outside the kernel by calling the `ifconfig` command. `open` is responsible for initializing the hardware registers and registering system resources such as interrupts, DMA, IO ports, and so on. `close` releases these resources and stops transmission.

❏ `hard_start_xmit` is called to remove finished packets from the wait queue and send them.

❏ `header_ops` contains a pointer to a structure that provides more function pointers to operations on the hardware header.

Most important are `header_ops->create`, which creates a new, and `header_ops->parse`, to analyze a given hardware header.

❏ `get_stats` queries statistical data that are returned in a structure of type `net_device_stats`. This structure consists of more than 20 members, all of which are numeric values to indicate, for example, the number of packets sent, received, with errors, discarded, and so on. (Lovers of statistics can query these data using `ifconfig` and `netstat -i`.)

Because the `net_device` structure provides no specific field to store the `net_device_stats` object, the individual device drivers must keep it in their private data area.

❏ `tx_timeout` is called to resolve the problem of packet transmission failure.

❏ `do_ioctl` forwards device-specific commands to the network card.

❏ `nd_det` is a pointer to the networking namespace (represented by an instance of `struct net`) to which the device belongs.

Some functions are not normally implemented by driver-specific code but are identical for all Ethernet cards. The kernel therefore makes default implementations available (in `net/ethernet/net.c`).

❏ `change_mtu` is implemented by `eth_change_mtu` and modifies the *maximum transfer unit*. The default for Ethernet is 1.5 KiB, other transmission techniques have different defaults. In some situations, it can be useful to increase or decrease this value. However, many cards do not allow this and support only the default hardware setting.

❑ The default implementation of `header_ops->create` is in `eth_header`. This function is used to generate the network access layer header for the existing packet data.

❑ `header_ops->parse` (usually implemented by `eth_header_parse`) obtains the source hardware address of a given packet.

An ioctl (see Chapter 8) is applied to the file descriptor of a socket to modify the configuration of a network device from userspace. One of the symbolic constants defined in `<sockios.h>` must be specified to indicate *which* part of the configuration is to be changed. For example, `SIOCGIFHWADDR` is responsible for setting the hardware address of a network card, but the kernel ultimately delegates this task to the `set_mac_address` function of the `net_device` instance. Device-specific constants are passed to the `do_ioctl` function. The implementation is very lengthy because of the many adjustment options but is not interesting enough for us to discuss it here.

Network devices work in two directions — they send and they receive (these directions are often referred to as *downstream* and *upstream*). The kernel sources include two driver skeletons (`isa-skeleton.c` and `pci-skeleton.c` in `drivers/net`) for use as network driver templates. Below, occasional reference is made to these drivers when we are primarily interested in their interaction with the hardware but do not want to restrict ourselves to a specific proprietary card type. More interesting than the programming of the hardware is the interfaces used by the kernel for communication purposes, which is why I focus on them below. First, we only need to introduce how network devices are registered within the kernel.

Registering Network Devices

Each network device is registered in a two-step process:

1. `alloc_netdev` allocates a new instance of `struct net_device`, and a protocol-specific function fills the structure with typical values. For Ethernet devices, this function is `ether_setup`. Other protocols (not considerd in detail) use `XXX_setup`, where possible values for `XXX` include `fddi` (fiber distributed data), `tr` (token ring), `ltalk` (localtalk), `hippi` (high-performance parallel interface), or `fc` (fiber channel).

Some in-kernel pseudo-devices implementing specific "interfaces" without being bound to particular hardware also use the `net_device` framework. `ppp_setup` initializes devices for the PPP protocol, for example. Several more `XXX_setup` functions can be found across the kernel sources.

2. Once `struct net_device` is completely filled in, it needs to be registered with `register_netdev` or `register_netdevice`. The difference between both functions is that `register_netdev` allows for working with (limited) format strings for interface names. The name given in `net_device->dev` can contain the format specifier `%d`. When the device is registered, the kernel selects a unique number that is substituted for `%d`. Ethernet devices specify `eth%d`, for instance, and the kernel subsequently creates the devices `eth0`, `eth1` ...

The convenience function `alloc_etherdev(sizeof_priv)` allocates an instance of `struct net_device` together with `sizeof_priv` bytes for private use — recall that `net_device->priv` is a pointer to driver-specific data associated with the device. Additionally, `ether_setup` mentioned above is called to set Ethernet-specific standard values.

The steps taken by `register_netdevice` are summarized in the code flow diagram in Figure 12-9.

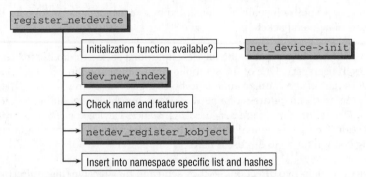

Figure 12-9: Code flow diagram for **register_netdevice.**

Should a device-specific initialization function be provided by `net_device->init`, the kernel calls it before proceeding any further. A unique *interface index* that identifies the device unambiguously within its namespace is generated by `dev_new_index`. The index is stored in `net_device->ifindex`. After ensuring that the chosen name is not already in use and no device features (see `NETIF_F_*` in `<netdevice.h>` for a list of supported features) that would contradict themselves have been specified, the new device is added to the generic kernel object model with `netdev_register_kobject`. This also creates the sysfs entries mentioned above. Finally, the device is integrated into the namespace-specific list and the device name and interface index hash tables.

12.7.2 Receiving Packets

Packets arrive at the kernel at unpredictable times. All modern device drivers use interrupts (discussed in Chapter 14) to inform the kernel (or the system) of the arrival of a packet. The network driver installs a handler routine for the device-specific interrupt so that each time an interrupt is raised — whenever a packet arrives — the kernel invokes the handler function to transfer the data from the network card into RAM, or to notify the kernel to do this some time later.

> *Nearly all cards support DMA mode and are able to transfer data to RAM autonomously. However, these data still needs to be interpreted and processed, and this is only performed later.*

Traditional Method

Currently the kernel provides two frameworks for packet reception. One of them has been in the kernel for a long time, and thus is referred to as the *traditional method*. This API suffers from problems with very-high-speed network adapters, though, and thus a new API (which is commonly referred to as NAPI[11]) has been devised by the network developers. Let us first start with the traditional methods since they are easier to understand. Besides, more adapters use the old instead of the new variant. This is fine since their physical transmission speed is not so high as to require the new methods. NAPI is discussed afterward.

---

[11]While the name describes precisely that the API is *new* in contrast to the old API, the naming scheme does not really scale well. Since NNAPI seems rather out of question, it remains interesting to see how the next new revision will be named. However, it might take a while until this problem becomes pressing since the current state of the art does not expose any severe problems that would justify the creation of another API.

Figure 12-10 shows an overview of the path followed by a packet through the kernel to the network layer functions after it arrives at the network adapter.

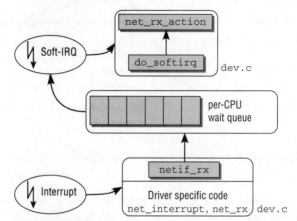

Figure 12-10: Path of an incoming packet through the kernel.

Because packets are received in the interrupt context, the handler routine may perform only essential tasks so that the system (or the current CPU) is not delayed in performing its other activities for too long.

In the interrupt context, data are processed by three short functions[12] that carry out the following tasks:

1. `net_interrupt` is the interrupt handler installed by the device driver. It determines whether the interrupt was really raised by an incoming packet (other possibilities are, e.g., signaling of an error or confirmation of a transmission as performed by some adapters). If it was, control is passed to `net_rx`.

2. The `net_rx` function, which is also card-specific, first creates a new socket buffer. The packet contents are then transferred from the network card into the buffer and therefore into RAM, where the header data are analyzed using library functions available in the kernel sources for each transmission type. This analysis determines the network layer protocol used by the packet data — IP, for instance.

3. Unlike the methods mentioned above, `netif_rx` is not a network driver-specific function but resides in `net/core/dev.c`. Its call marks the transition between the card-specific part and the universal interface of the network layer.

    The purpose of this function is to place the received packet on a CPU-specific wait queue and to exit the interrupt context so that the CPU can perform other activities.

The kernel manages the wait queues of incoming and outgoing packets in the globally defined `softnet_data` array, which contains entries of type `softnet_data`. To boost performance on multi-processor systems, wait queues are created per CPU to support parallel processing of packets. Explicit locking to protect the wait queues against concurrent access is not necessary because each CPU modifies

---

[12]`net_interrupt` and `net_rx` are names taken from the driver skeleton `isa-skeleton.c`. They have different names in other drivers.

only its own queue and cannot therefore interfere with the work of the other CPUs. Below, I ignore the multiprocessor aspect and refer only to a single "softnet_data wait queue" so as not to overcomplicate matters.

Only one element of the data structure is of interest for our purposes right now:

```
<netdevice.h>
struct softnet_data
{
...
        struct sk_buff_head     input_pkt_queue;
...
};
```

input_pkt_queue uses the sk_buff_head list head mentioned above to build a linked list of all incoming packets.

netif_rx marks the soft interrupt NET_RX_SOFTIRQ for execution (refer to Chapter 14 for more information) before it finishes its work and exits the interrupt context.

net_rx_action is used as the handler function of the softIRQ. Its code flow diagram is shown in Figure 12-11. Keep in mind that a simplified version is described here. The full story — which includes the new methods introduced for high-speed network adapters — follows below.

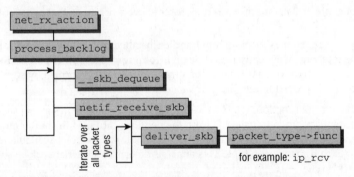

Figure 12-11: Code flow diagram for **net_rx_action**.

After a few preparatory tasks, work is passed to process_backlog, which performs the following steps in a loop. To simplify matters, assume that the loop iterates until all pending packets have been processed and is not interrupted by any other condition.

1. __skb_dequeue removes a socket buffer that is managing a received packet from the wait queue.

2. The packet type is analyzed by the netif_receive_skb function so that it can be delivered to the receive function of the network layer (i.e., to a higher layer of the network system). For this, it iterates over all network layer functions that feel responsible for the current type and calls deliver_skb for each of them.

In turn, the function uses a type-specific handler `func` that assumes further processing of the packet in the higher layers like IP.

`netif_receive_skb` also handles specialties like bridging, but it is not necessary to discuss these corner cases — at least they are corner cases on average systems — any further.

All network layer functions used to receive data from the underlying network access layer are registered in a hash table implemented by the global array `ptype_base`.[13]

New protocols are added by means of `dev_add_pack`. The entries are structures of type `packet_type` whose definition is as follows:

```
<netdevice.h>
struct packet_type {
        __be16                        type;   /* This is really htons(ether_type). */
        struct net_device             *dev;   /* NULL is wildcarded here            */
        int                           (*func) (struct sk_buff *,
                                               struct net_device *,
                                               struct packet_type *,
                                               struct net_device *);
...
        void                          *af_packet_priv;
        struct list_head              list;
};
```

`type` specifies the identifier of the protocol for the handler. `dev` binds a protocol handler to a specific network card (a null pointer means that the handler is valid for all network devices of the system).

`func` is the central element of the structure. It is a pointer to the network layer function to which the packet is passed if it has the appropriate type. `ip_rcv`, discussed below, is used for IPv4-based protocols.

`netif_receive_skb` finds the appropriate handler element for a given socket buffer, invokes its `func` function, and delegates responsibility for the packet to the network layer — the next higher level of the network implementation.

Support for High-Speed Interfaces

The previously discussed old approach to transferring packets from the network device into higher layers of the kernel works well if the devices do not support too high transmission rates. Each time a frame arrives, an IRQ is used to signalize this to the kernel. This implies a notion of "fast" and "slow." For slow devices, servicing the IRQ is usually finished before the next packet arrives. Since the next packet is also signaled by an IRQ, failing to fulfill this condition — as is often the case for "fast" devices — leads to problems. Modern Ethernet network cards operate at speeds of 10,000 MBit/s, and this would cause true interrupt storms if the old methods were used to drive them. However if a new IRQ is received while packets are still waiting to be processed, no new information is conveyed to the kernel: It was known before that packets are waiting to be processed, and it is known afterward that packets are supposed to be processed — which is not really any news. To solve this problem, NAPI uses a combination of IRQs and polling.

---

[13] Actually, another list with packet handlers is available. `ptype_all` contains packet handlers that are called for all packet types.

Assume that no packets have arrived on a network adapter yet, but start to come in at high frequency now. This is what happens with NAPI devices:

1. The first packet causes the network adapter to issue an IRQ. To prevent further packets from causing more IRQs, the driver turns off Rx IRQs for the adapter. Additionally, the adapter is placed on a *poll list*.

2. The kernel then polls the device on the poll list as long as no further packets wait to be processed on the adapter.

3. Rx interrupts are re-enabled again.

If new packets arrive while old packets are still waiting to be processed, the work is not slowed down by additional interrupts. While polling is usually a very bad technique for a device driver (and for kernel code in general), it does not have any drawbacks here: Polling is stopped when no packets need to be processed anymore, and the device returns to the normal IRQ mode of operation. No unnecessary time is wasted with polling empty receive queues as would be the case if polling without support by interrupts were used all the time.

Another advantage of NAPI is that packets can be dropped efficiently. If the kernel is sure that processing any new packets is beyond all question because too much other work needs to be performed, then packets can be directly dropped in the network adapter without being copied into the kernel at all.

The NAPI method can only be implemented if the device fulfills two conditions:

1. The device must be able to preserve multiple received packets, for instance, in a DMA ring buffer. I refer to this buffer as an *Rx* buffer in the following discussion.

2. It must be possible to disable IRQs for packet reception. However, sending packets and other management functions that possibly also operate via IRQs must remain enabled.

What happens if more than one device is present on the system? This is accounted for by a round robin method employed to poll the devices. Figure 12-12 provides an overview of the situation.

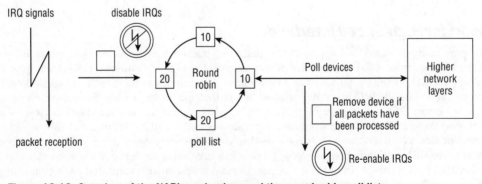

Figure 12-12: Overview of the NAPI mechanism and the round robin poll list.

Recall that it was mentioned above that a device is placed on a poll list when the initial packet arrives into an empty Rx buffer. As is the very nature of a list, the poll list can also contain more than one device.

The kernel handles all devices on the list in a round robin fashion: One device is polled after another, and when a certain amount of time has elapsed in processing one device, the next device is selected and processed. Additionally, each device carries a relative weight that denotes the importance in contrast to other devices on the poll list. Large weights are used for faster devices, while slower devices get lower weights. Since the weight specifies how many packets are processed in one polling round, this ensures that faster devices receive more attention than slower ones.

Now that the basic principle of NAPI is clear, let's discuss the details of implementation. The key change in contrast to the old API is that a network device that supports NAPI must provide a `poll` function. The device-specific method is specified when the network card is registered with `netif_napi_add`. Calling this function also indicates that the devices can and must be handled with the new methods.

<netdevice.h>
```
static inline void netif_napi_add(struct net_device *dev,
                                  struct napi_struct *napi,
                                  int (*poll)(struct napi_struct *, int),
                                  int weight);
```

`dev` points to the `net_device` instance for the device in question, `poll` specifies which function is used to poll the device with IRQs disabled, and `weight` does what you expect it to do: It specifies a relative weight for the interface. In principle, an arbitrary integer value can be specified. Usually 10- and 100-MBit drivers specify 16, while 1,000- and 10,000-MBit drivers use 64. In any case, the weight must not exceed the number of packets that can be stored by the device in the Rx buffer.

`netif_napi_add` requires one more parameter, a pointer to an instance of `struct napi_struct`. The structure is used to manage the device on the poll list. It is defined as follows:

<netdevice.h>
```
struct napi_struct {
        struct list_head poll_list;

        unsigned long state;
        int weight;
        int (*poll)(struct napi_struct *, int);
};
```

The poll list is implemented by means of a standard doubly linked kernel list, and `poll_list` is used as the list element. `weight` and `poll` have the same meaning as described above. `state` can either be `NAPI_STATE_SCHED` when the device has to be polled next time the kernel comes around to doing so, or `NAPI_STATE_DISABLE` once polling is finished and no more packets are waiting to be processed, but the device has not yet been taken off the poll list.

Note that `struct napi_struct` is often embedded inside a bigger structure containing driver-specific information about the network card. This allows for using the `container_of` mechanism to obtain the information when the kernel polls the card with the `poll` function.

Implementing Poll Functions

The poll function requires two arguments: a pointer to the `napi_struct` instance and an integer that specifies the budget, that is, how many packets the kernel allows to be processed by the driver. Since we do not want to deal with the peculiarities of any real networking card, let us discuss a pseudo-function for a very, very fast adapter that needs NAPI:

```
static int hyper_card_poll(struct napi_struct *napi, int budget)
{
        struct nic *nic = container_of(napi, struct nic, napi);
        struct net_device *netdev = nic->netdev;
        int work_done;

        work_done = hyper_do_poll(nic, budget);

        if (work_done < budget) {
                netif_rx_complete(netdev, napi);
                hcard_reenable_irq(nic);
        }

        return work_done;
}
```

After obtaining device-specific information from the container of `napi_struct`, a hardware-specific poll method — in this case, `hyper_do_poll` — is called to perform the required low-level actions to obtain the packets from the network adapter and pass them to the higher networking layers using `netif_receive_skb` as before.

`hyper_do_poll` allows processing up to `budget` packets. The function returns as result how many packets have actually been processed. Two cases must be distinguished:

❑ If the number of processed packets is less than the granted budget, then no more packets are available and the Rx buffer is empty — otherwise, the remaining packets would have been processed. As a consequence, `netif_rx_complete` signals this condition to the kernel, and the kernel will remove the device from the poll list in consequence. In turn, the driver has to re-enable IRQs by means of a suitable hardware-specific method.

❑ Although the budget has been completely used up, more packets are still waiting to be processed. The device is left on the poll list, and interrupts are *not* enabled again.

Implementing IRQ Handlers

NAPI also requires some changes in the IRQ handlers of network devices. Again, I will not resort to any specific piece of hardware, but present code for an imaginary device:

```
static irqreturn_t e100_intr(int irq, void *dev_id)
{
        struct net_device *netdev = dev_id;
        struct nic *nic = netdev_priv(netdev);

        if(likely(netif_rx_schedule_prep(netdev, &nic->napi))) {
                hcard_disable_irq(nic);
                __netif_rx_schedule(netdev, &nic->napi);
        }

        return IRQ_HANDLED;
}
```

Assume that interface-specific data are contained in `net_device->private`; this is the method used by most network card drivers. The auxiliary function `netdev_priv` is provided to access it.

Now the kernel needs to be informed that a new packet is available. A two-stage approach is required:

1. `netif_rx_schedule_prep` prepares the device to be put on the poll list. Essentially, this sets the `NAPI_STATE_SCHED` flag in `napi_struct->flags`.

2. If setting this flag succeeds (it just fails if NAPI is already active), the driver must disable IRQs with a suitable device-specific method. Invoking `__netif_rx_schedule` adds the device's `napi_struct` to the poll list and raises the softIRQ `NET_RX_SOFTIRQ`. This notifies the kernel to start polling in `net_rx_action`.

Handling the Rx SoftIRQ

After having discussed what individual device drivers are required to do for NAPI, the kernel's responsibilities remain to be investigated. `net_rx_action` is as before the handler for the softIRQ `NET_RX_SOFTIRQ`. Recall that a simplified version was shown in the preceding section. With more details about NAPI in place, we are now prepared to discuss all the details. Figure 12-13 shows the code flow diagram.

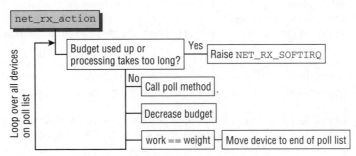

Figure 12-13: Code flow diagram for `net_rx_action`.

Essentially, the kernel processes all devices that are currently on the poll list by calling the device-specific `poll` methods for one after another. The device's weight is used as the local budget, that is, the number of packets that may be processed in a single poll step.

It must be made sure that not too much time is spent in the softIRQ handler. Processing is aborted on two conditions:

1. More than one jiffie has been spent in the handler.

2. The total number of processed packets is larger than a total budget specified by `netdev_budget`. Usually, this is set to 300, but the value can be changed via `/proc/sys/net/core/netdev_budget`.

   This budget must not be confused with the local budget for each network device! After each poll step, the number of processed packets is subtracted from the global budget, and if the value drops below zero, the softIRQ handler is aborted.

After an individual device has been polled, the kernel checks if the number of processed packets is identical with the allowed local budget. If this is the case, then the device could not obtain all waiting packets as represented by `work == weight` in the code flow diagram. The kernel moves it to the end of the poll list and will continue to poll the device after all other devices on the list have been processed. Clearly, this implements round robin scheduling between the network devices.

Implementation of the Old API on Top of NAPI

Finally, note how the old API is implemented on top of NAPI. The normal behavior of the kernel is controlled by a dummy network device linked with the softnet queue; the `process_backlog` standard function in `net/core/dev.c` is used as the poll method. If no network adapters add themselves to the poll list of the queue, it contains only the dummy adapter, and the behavior of `net_rx_action` therefore corresponds to a single call of `process_backlog` in which the packets in the queue are processed regardless of the device from which they originate.

12.7.3 Sending Packets

A finished packet is sent when a protocol-specific function of the network layer instructs the network access layer to process a packet defined by a socket buffer.

What must be noted when messages are sent from the computer? In addition to complete headers and the checksums required by the particular protocol and already generated by the higher instances, the route to be taken by the packet is of prime importance. (Even if the computer has only one network card, the kernel still has to distinguish between packets for external destinations and for the loopback link.)

Because this question can only be clarified by higher protocol instances (particularly if there is a choice of routes to the desired destination), the device driver assumes that the decision has already been made.

Before a packet can be sent to the next correct computer (normally not the same as the target computer because IP packets are usually sent via gateways unless there is a direct hardware connection), it is necessary to establish the hardware address of the receiving network card. This is a complicated process looked at more closely in Section 12.8.5. At this point, simply assume that the receiving MAC address is known. A further header for the network access layer is normally generated by protocol-specific functions.

`dev_queue_xmit` from `net/core/dev.c` is used to place the packet on the queue for outgoing packets. I ignore the implementation of the device-specific queue mechanism because it reveals little of interest on how the network layer functions. It is sufficient to know that the packet is sent a certain length of time after it has been placed on the wait queue. This is done by the adapter-specific `hard_start_xmit` function that is present as a function pointer in each `net_device` structure and is implemented by the hardware device drivers.

12.8 Network Layer

The network access layer is still quite strongly influenced by the properties of the transmission medium and the device drivers of the associated adapters. The network layer (and therefore specifically the IP Internet protocol) is almost totally divorced from the hardware properties of the network adapters. Why only almost? As you will see shortly, the layer is responsible not only for sending and receiving data, but also for forwarding and routing packets between systems not directly connected with each other. Finding the best route and selecting a suitable network device to send the packet also involves handling lower-level address families (such as hardware-specific MAC addresses), which accounts for why the layer is at least loosely associated with network cards. The assignment between the addresses of the network layer and the network access layer is made in this layer — another reason why the IP layer is not fully divorced from the hardware.

Fragmentation of larger data packets into smaller units cannot be performed without taking the underlying hardware into account (in fact, the properties of the hardware are what make this necessary in the first place). Because each transmission technique supports a maximum packet size, the IP protocol must offer ways of splitting larger packets into smaller units that can be reassembled by the receiver — unnoticed by the higher layers. The size of the fragmented packets depends on the capabilities of the particular transmission protocol.

IP was formally defined in 1981 (in RFC 791) and is therefore of ripe old age.[14] Even though the situation on the ground is not as represented in the usual company press releases that praise, for example, each new version of a spreadsheet as the greatest invention since the beginning of mankind, the last two decades have left their mark on today's technology. Deficiencies and unforeseen problems occasioned by the strong growth of the Internet are now more and more evident. This is why the IPv6 standard has been developed as the successor to the present IPv4. Unfortunately, this future standard is only slowly being adopted owing to the lack of a central control authority. In this chapter, our interest focuses on the implementation of the algorithms for Version 4, but we also take a cursory look at future practicable techniques and their implementation in the Linux kernel.

To understand how the IP protocol is implemented in the kernel, it is necessary to briefly examine how it works. Naturally, we can only touch on the relevant topics in this huge area. For detailed descriptions, see the many specialized publications, particularly [Ste00] and [Ste94].

12.8.1 IPv4

IP packets use a protocol header as shown in Figure 12-14.

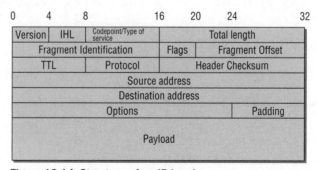

Figure 12-14: Structure of an IP header.

The meanings of the individual components of the structure are explained below.

---

[14]Even though the marketing departments of some companies suggest the opposite, the Internet is older than most of its users.

- ❑ version specifies the IP protocol version used. Currently, this field accepts the value 4 or 6. On hosts that support both versions, the version used is indicated by the transmission protocol identifier discussed in the previous chapter; this identifier also holds different values for the two versions of the protocol.

- ❑ IHL defines the header length, which is not always the same owing to the variable number of options.

- ❑ Codepoint or Type of Service is required for more complex protocol options that need not concern us here.

- ❑ Length specifies the *total length* of the packet, in other words, the length of the header plus data.

- ❑ The fragment ID identifies the individual parts of a fragmented IP packet. The fragmenting system assigns the *same* fragment ID to all parts of an original packet so that they can be identified as members of the same group. The relative arrangement of the parts is defined in the fragment offset field. The offset is specified in units of 64 bits.

- ❑ Three status bits (flags) enable and disable specific characteristics; only two of them are used.

    - ❑ DF stands for *don't fragment* and specifies that the packet must not be split into smaller units.

    - ❑ MF indicates that the present packet is a fragment of a larger packet and is followed by other fragments (the bit is set for all fragments but the last).

    The third field is "reserved for future use," which is very unlikely in view of the presence of IPv6.

- ❑ TTL stands for *Time to Live* and specifies the number of intermediate stations (or hops) along the route to the receiver.[15]

- ❑ Protocol identifies the higher-layer protocol (transport layer) carried in the IP datagram. For example, there are unique values for TCP and UDP.

- ❑ Checksum contains a checksum calculated on the basis of the contents of the header and the data. If the specified checksum does not match the figure calculated upon receipt, the packet is discarded because a transmission error has occurred.

- ❑ src and dest specify the 32-bit IP address of the source and destination.

- ❑ options is used for extended IP options, not discussed here.

- ❑ data holds the packet data (payload).

All numeric values in the IP header must be in network byte order (big endian).

In the kernel sources the header is implemented in the iphdr data structure:

```
<ip.h>
struct iphdr {
#if defined(__LITTLE_ENDIAN_BITFIELD)
        __u8    ihl:4,
                version:4;
#elif defined (__BIG_ENDIAN_BITFIELD)
        __u8    version:4,
```

---

[15]In the past, this value was interpreted as the maximum lifetime in seconds.

```
                    ihl:4;
#endif
        __u8    tos;
        __u16   tot_len;
        __u16   id;
        __u16   frag_off;
        __u8    ttl;
        __u8    protocol;
        __u16   check;
        __u32   saddr;
        __u32   daddr;
        /*The options start here. */
};
```

The ip_rcv function is the point of entry into the network layer. The onward route of a packet through the kernel is illustrated in Figure 12-15.

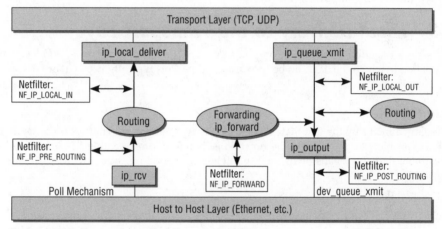

Figure 12-15: Route of a packet through the IP layer.

The program flow for send and receive operations is not always separate and may be interleaved if packets are only forwarded via the computer. The packets are not passed to higher protocol layers (or to an application) but immediately leave the computer bound for a new destination.

12.8.2 Receiving Packets

Once a packet (respectively, the corresponding socket buffer with appropriately set pointers) has been forwarded to ip_rcv, the information received must be checked to ensure that it is correct. The main check is that the checksum calculated matches that stored in the header. Other checks include, for example, whether the packet has at least the size of an IP header and whether the packet is actually IP Version 4 (IPv6 employs its own receive routine).

After these checks have been made, the kernel does not immediately continue with packet processing but allows a netfilter hook to be invoked so that the packet data can be manipulated in userspace. A netfilter hook is a kind of "hook" inserted at defined points in the kernel code to enable packets to be manipulated dynamically. Hooks are present at various points in the network subsystem, and each one has a special (*label*) — for example, NF_IP_POST_ROUTING.[16]

When the kernel arrives at a hook, the routines registered for the label are invoked in userspace. Kernel-side processing (possibly with a modified packet) is then continued in a further kernel function. Section 12.8.6 below discusses the implementation of the netfilter mechanism.

In the next step, the received IP packets arrive at a crossroads where a decision is made as to whether they are intended for the local system or for a remote computer. Depending on the answer, they must either be forwarded to one of the higher layers or transferred to the output path of the IP level (I don't bother with the third option — delivery of packets to a group of computers by means of multicast).

ip_route_input is responsible for choosing the *route*. This relatively complex decision is discussed in detail in Section 12.8.5. The result of the routing decision is that a function for further packet processing is chosen. Available functions are ip_local_deliver and ip_forward. Which is selected depends on whether the packet is to be delivered to local routines of the next higher protocol layer or is to be forwarded to another computer in the network.

12.8.3 Local Delivery to the Transport Layer

If the packet is intended for the local computer, ip_local_deliver must try to find a suitable transport layer function to which the data can be forwarded. IP packets typically use TCP or UDP as the transport layer.

Defragmentation

This is made difficult by the fact that IP packets may be fragmented. There is no certainty that a full packet is available. The first task of the function is therefore to reassemble a fragmented packet from its constituent parts by means of ip_defrag.[17] The corresponding code flow diagram is shown in Figure 12-16.

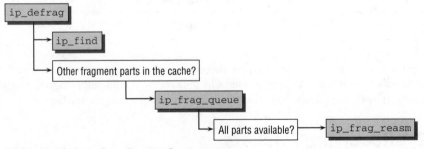

Figure 12-16: Code flow diagram for ip_defrag.

---

[16]Note that kernel 2.6.25 (which was still under development when this book was written) will change the names from NF_IP_* to NF_INET_*. This change unifies the names for IPv4 and IPv6.

[17]The kernel recognizes that a packet is fragmented either by the set fragment bit or by a non-zero value in the offset field. A zero value in the offset field indicates that this fragment is the last in the packet.

The kernel manages the fragments of an originally composite packet in a separate cache known as a *fragment cache*. In the cache, fragments that belong together are held in a separate wait queue until all fragments are present.

The `ip_find` function is then invoked. It uses a hashing procedure involving the fragment ID, source and destination address, and packet protocol identifier to check whether a wait queue has already been created for the packet. If not, a new queue is created and the packet is placed on it. Otherwise, the address of the existing queue is returned so that `ip_frag_queue` can place the packet on it.[18]

When all fragments of the packet are in the cache (i.e., the first and last fragment are present and the data in all the fragments equal the expected total length of the packet), the individual fragments are reassembled by `ip_frag_reasm`. The socket buffer is then released for further processing.

If not all fragments of a packet have arrived, `ip_defrag` returns a null pointer that terminates packet processing in the IP layer. Processing is resumed when all fragments are present.

Delivery to the Transport Layer

Let us go back to `ip_local_deliver`. After packet defragmentation, the netfilter hook `NF_IP_LOCAL_IN` is called to resume processing in `ip_local_deliver_finish`.

There the packet is passed to a transport layer function that must first be determined by reference to the protocol identifier. All protocols based on the IP layer have an instance of the structure `net_protocol` that is defined as follows:

```
include/net/protocol.h
struct net_protocol {
        int                     (*handler)(struct sk_buff *skb);
        void                    (*err_handler)(struct sk_buff *skb, u32 info);
  ...
};
```

❑   `handler` is the protocol routine to which the packets are passed (in the form of socket buffers) for further processing.

❑   `err_handler` is invoked when an ICMP error message is received and needs to be passed to higher levels.

The `inet_add_protocol` standard function is used to store each instance in the `inet_protos` array that maps the protocols onto the individual list positions using a hashing method.

Once the IP header has been "removed" by means of the usual pointer manipulations in the socket buffer, all that remains to be done is to invoke the corresponding receive routine of the network access layer stored in the `handler` field of `inet_protocol`, for example, the `tcp_v4_rcv` routine to receive TCP packets and `udp_rcv` to receive UDP packets. Section 12.9 examines the implementation of these functions.

---

[18]The fragment cache uses a timer mechanism to remove fragments from the cache. When it expires, fragments in the cache are deleted if not all fragments have arrived by then.

12.8.4 Packet Forwarding

IP packets may be delivered locally as described above, or they may leave the IP layer for forwarding to another computer without having come into local contact with the higher protocol instances. There are two categories of packet destinations:

1. Target computers in one of the local networks to which the sending computer is attached.

2. Geographically remote computers not attached to the local network and accessible only via gateways.

The second scenario is rather more complicated. The first station to which the packet is forwarded along the remaining route must be found in order to move one step closer to the final destination. Information is therefore required not only on the structure of the network in which the computer resides but also on the structure of the "adjacent" networks and associated outgoing paths.

This information is provided by *routing tables* managed by the kernel in a variety of data structures discussed in Section 12.8.5. The `ip_route_input` function invoked when a packet is received acts as the interface to the routing implementation, not only because it is able to recognize whether a packet is to be delivered locally or forwarded, but also because it also finds the route to the destination. The destination is stored in the `dst` field of the socket buffer.

This makes the work of `ip_forward` very easy, as the code flow diagram in Figure 12-17 shows.

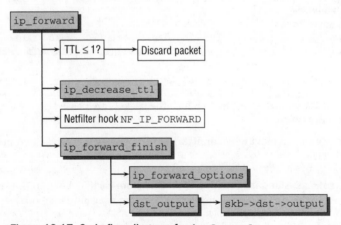

Figure 12-17: Code flow diagram for `ip_forward`.

First, the function refers to the TTL field to check whether the packet is allowed to pass through another hop. If the TTL value is less than or equal to 1, the packet is discarded; otherwise, the counter is decremented by 1. `ip_decrease_ttl` does this because changing the TTL field also means that the packet checksum must be altered.

Once the netfilter hook `NF_IP_FORWARD` has been called, the kernel resumes processing in `ip_forward_finish`. This function delegates its work to two other functions:

❑   If the packet includes additional options (not normally the case), they are processed in `ip_forward_options`.

❑   `dst_output` passes the packet to the send function selected during routing and held in `skb->dst->output`. Normally, `ip_output`, which passes the packet to the network adapter that matches the destination, is used for this purpose.[19] `ip_output` is part of the send operation for IP packets described in the next section.

12.8.5   Sending Packets

The kernel provides several functions that are used by higher protocol layers to send data via IP. `ip_queue_xmit`, whose code flow diagram, shown in Figure 12-18, is the one most frequently used.

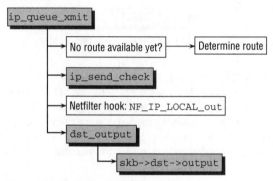

Figure 12-18: Code flow diagram for ip_queue_xmit.

The first task is to find a route for the packet. The kernel exploits the fact that all packets originating from a socket have the same destination address so that the route doesn't have to be determined afresh each time. A pointer to the corresponding data structure discussed below is linked with the socket data structure. When the first packet of a socket is sent, the kernel is required to find a new route (discussed below).

Once `ip_send_check` has generated the checksum for the packet,[20] the kernel calls the netfilter hook `NF_IP_LOCAL_OUT`. The `dst_output` function is then invoked; it is based on the destination-specific `skb->dst->output` function of the socket buffer found during routing. Normally, this is `ip_output`, which is the point where locally generated and forwarded packets are brought together.

Transition to the Network Access Layer

Figure 12-19 shows the code flow diagram of the `ip_output` function that splits the route into two parts, depending on whether a packet needs to be fragmented or not.

---

[19] A different output routine is used when, for example, IP packets are tunneled inside IP packets. This is a very special application that is rarely needed.

[20] Generation of IP checksums is time-critical and can be highly optimized by modern processors. For this reason, the various architectures provide fast assembly language implementations of their own in `ip_fast_csum`.

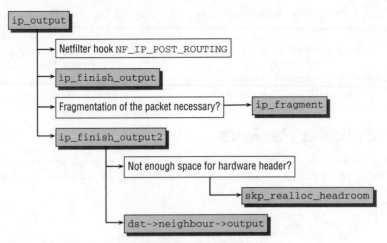

Figure 12-19: Code flow diagram for `ip_output`.

First of all, the netfilter hook `NF_IP_POST_ROUTING` is called, followed by `ip_finish_output`. I first examine the situation in which the packet fits into the MTU of the transmission medium and need not be fragmented. In this case, `ip_finish_output2` is directly invoked. The function checks whether the socket buffer still has enough space for the hardware header to be generated. If necessary, `skb_realloc_headroom` adds extra space. To complete transition to the network access layer, the `dst->neighbour->output` function set by the routing layer is invoked, normally using `dev_queue_xmit`.[21]

Packet Fragmenting

IP packets are fragmented into smaller units by `ip_fragment`, as shown in Figure 12-20.

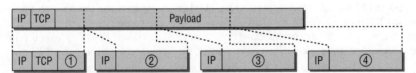

Figure 12-20: Fragmenting of an IP packet.

IP fragmenting is very straightforward if we ignore the subtleties documented in RFC 791. A data fragment, whose size is compatible with the corresponding MTU, is extracted from the packet in each cycle of a loop. A new socket buffer, whose old IP header can be reused with a few modifications, is created to hold the extracted data fragment. A common fragment ID is assigned to all fragments to support reassembly in the destination system. The sequence of the fragments is established on the basis of the fragment offset, which is also set appropriately. The *more fragments* bit must also be set. Only in the last packet of the series must this bit be set to 0. Each fragment is sent using `ip_output` after `ip_send_check` has generated a checksum.[22]

---

[21] The kernel also uses a *hard header* cache. This holds frequently needed hardware headers that are copied to the start of a packet. If the cache contains a required entry, it is output using a cache function that is slightly faster than `dst->neighbour->output`.

[22] `ip_output` is invoked via a function pointer passed to `ip_fragment` as a parameter. This means, of course, that other send functions can be selected. The bridging subsystem is the only user of this possibility, and is not discussed in more detail.

Routing

Routing is an important part of any IP implementation and is required not only to forward external packets, but also to deliver data generated locally in the computer. The problem of finding the correct path for data "out" of the computer is encountered not only with non-local addresses, but also if there are several network interfaces. This is the case even if there is only one physical network adapter — because there are also virtual interfaces such as the loopback device.

Each packet received belongs to one of the following three categories:

1. It is intended for the local host.
2. It is intended for a computer connected directly to the current host.
3. It is intended for a remote computer that can only be reached by way of intermediate systems.

The previous section discussed packets of the first category; these are passed to the higher protocol layers for further processing (this type is discussed below because all arriving packets are passed to the routing subsystem). If the destination system of a packet is connected directly to the local host, routing is usually restricted to finding the corresponding network card. Otherwise, reference must be made to the routing information to find a gateway system (and the network card associated with the gateway) via which the packet can be sent.

The routing implementation has gradually become more and more comprehensive from kernel version to kernel version and now accounts for a large part of the networking source code. Caches and lengthy hash tables are used to speed up work because many routing tasks are time-critical. This is reflected in the profusion of data structures. For reasons of space, we won't worry what the mechanisms for finding the correct routes in the kernel data structures look like. We look only at the data structures used by the kernel to communicate the results.

The starting point of routing is the `ip_route_input` function, which first tries to find the route in the routing cache (this topic is not discussed here, nor what happens in the case of multicast routing).

`ip_route_input_slow` is invoked to build a new route from the data structures of the kernel. Basically, the routine relies on `fib_lookup`, whose implicit return value (via a pointer used as a function argument) is an instance of the `fib_result` structure containing the information we want. `fib` stands for *forwarding information base* and is a table used to manage the routing information held by the kernel.

The routing results are linked with a socket buffer by means of its `dst` element that points to an instance of the `dest_entry` structure that is filled during lookup. The (very simplified) definition of the data structure is as follows:

include/net/dst.h
```
struct dst_entry
{
        struct net_device       *dev;
        int                     (*input)(struct sk_buff*);
        int                     (*output)(struct sk_buff*);
        struct neighbour        *neighbour;
};
```

❑ input and output are invoked to process incoming and outgoing packets as described above.

❑ dev specifies the network device used to process the packets.

input and output are assigned different functions depending on packet type.

❑ input is set to ip_local_deliver for local delivery and output to ip_rt_bug (the latter function simply outputs an error message to the kernel logs because invoking output for a local packet in the kernel code is an error condition that should not occur).

❑ input is set to ip_forward for packets to be forwarded, and a pointer to the ip_output function is used for output.

The neighbour element stores the IP and hardware addresses of the computer in the local network, which can be reached directly via the network access layer. For our purposes, it is sufficient to look at just a few elements of the structure:

include/net/neighbour.h
```
struct neighbour
{
        struct net_device       *dev;
        unsigned char           ha[ALIGN(MAX_ADDR_LEN, sizeof(unsigned long))];
        int                     (*output)(struct sk_buff *skb);
};
```

While dev holds the network device data structure and ha the hardware address of the device, output is a pointer to the appropriate kernel function that must be invoked to transmit a packet via the network adapter. neighbour instances are created by the ARP layer of the kernel that implements the *address resolution protocol* — a protocol that translates IP addresses into hardware addresses. Because the dst_entry structure has a pointer to neighbour instances, the code of the network access layer can invoke the output function when a packet leaves the system via the network adapter.

12.8.6 Netfilter

Netfilter is a Linux kernel framework that enables packets to be filtered and manipulated in accordance with dynamically defined criteria. This dramatically increases the number of conceivable network options — from a simple firewall through detailed analyses of network traffic to complex state-dependent filters. Because of the sophisticated netfilter design, only a few sections of network code are needed to achieve the above goals.

Extending Network Functionality

In brief, the netfilter framework adds the following capabilities to the kernel:

❑ *Packet filtering* for different flow directions (incoming, outgoing, forwarded) depending on state and other criteria.

❑ *Network address translation* (NAT) to convert source and destination addresses in accordance with certain rules. NAT can be used, for example, to implement shared Internet connections where several computers that are not attached directly to the Internet share an Internet access (this is often referred to as *masquerading* or *transparent proxy*).

❑ *Packet mangling* and *manipulation*, the splitting and modification of packets according to specific rules.

Netfilter functionality can be enhanced by modules loaded into the kernel at run time. A defined rule set informs the kernel when to use the code from the individual modules. The interface between the kernel and netfilter is kept very small to separate the two areas from each other as well as possible (and as little as necessary) in order to prevent mutual interference and improve the network code stability.

As frequently mentioned in the preceding sections, *netfilter hooks* are located at various points in the kernel to support the execution of netfilter code. These are provided not only for IPv4 but also for IPv6 and the DECNET protocol. Only IPv4 is discussed here, but the concepts apply equally to the other two protocols.

Netfilter implementation is divided into two areas:

- ❏ *Hooks* in the kernel code are used to call netfilter code and are at the heart of the network implementation.

- ❏ Netfilter modules whose code is called from within the hooks but that are otherwise independent of the remaining network code. A set of standard modules provides frequently needed functions, but user-specific functions can be defined in extension modules.

  Iptables used by administrators to configure firewall, packet filter, and similar functions are simply modules that build on the netfilter framework and provide a comprehensive, well-defined set of library functions to facilitate packet handling. I won't bother describing how the rules are activated and managed from within userspace; see the abundance of literature on network administration.

Calling Hook Functions

Functions of the network layer are interrupted by hooks at which netfilter code is executed. An important feature of hooks is that they split a function into two parts — the first part runs before the netfilter code is called, the second after. Why are two separate functions used instead of calling a specific netfilter function that executes all relevant netfilter modules and then returns to the calling function? This approach, which at first may appear to be somewhat complicated, can be explained as follows. It enables users (or administrators) to decide not to compile the netfilter functionality into the kernel, in which case, the network functions can be executed without any loss of speed. It also dispenses with the need to riddle the network implementation with pre-processor statements that, depending on the particular configuration option (netfilter enabled or disabled), select the appropriate code sections at compilation time.

Netfilter hooks are called by the NF_HOOK macro from `<netfilter.h>`. The macro is defined as follows if netfilter support is enabled in the kernel:

<netfilter.h>
```
static inline int nf_hook_thresh(int pf, unsigned int hook,
                                 struct sk_buff **pskb,
                                 struct net_device *indev,
                                 struct net_device *outdev,
                                 int (*okfn)(struct sk_buff *), int thresh,
                                 int cond)
{
        if (!cond)
                return 1;
        return nf_hook_slow(pf, hook, pskb, indev, outdev, okfn, thresh);
}
```

\<netfilter.h\>
```
#define NF_HOOK_THRESH(pf, hook, skb, indev, outdev, okfn, thresh)          \
({int __ret;                                                                \
if ((__ret=nf_hook_thresh(pf, hook, &(skb), indev, outdev, okfn, thresh, 1)) == 1)\
        __ret = (okfn)(skb);                                               \
__ret;})

#define NF_HOOK(pf, hook, skb, indev, outdev, okfn) \
        NF_HOOK_THRESH(pf, hook, skb, indev, outdev, okfn, INT_MIN)
```

The macro arguments have the following meanings:

❑   pf refers to the protocol family from which the called netfilter hook should originate. All calls in the IPv4 layer use PF_INET.

❑   hook is the hook number; possible values are defined in \<netfilter_ipv4.h\>. The values have names such as NF_IP_FORWARD and NF_IP_LOCAL_OUT in IPv4, as mentioned above.

❑   skb is the socket buffer being processed.

❑   indev and outdev are pointers to net_device instances of the network devices via which the packet enters and leaves the kernel.

   Null pointers can be assigned to these values because this information is not known for all hooks (e.g., before routing is performed, the kernel does not know via which device a packet will leave the kernel).

❑   okfn is a pointer to a function with prototype int (*okfn)(struct sk_buff *). It is executed when the netfilter hook terminates.

The macro expansion makes a detour over NF_HOOK_THRESH and nf_hook_thresh before nf_hook_slow will take care of processing the netfilter hook and calling the continuation function. This seemingly complicated way is necessary because the kernel also provides the possibility to consider only netfilter hooks whose priority is above a certain threshold and skip all others. In the case of NF_HOOK, the threshold is set to the smallest possible integer value so every hook function is considered. Nevertheless, it is possible to use NF_HOOK_THRESH directly to set a specific threshold. Since only the bridging implementation and connection tracking for IPv6 make use of this currently, I will not discuss it any further.

Consider the implementation of NF_HOOK_THRESH. First, nf_hook_thresh is called. The function checks if the condition given in cond is true. If that is not so, then 1 is directly passed to the caller. Otherwise, nf_hook_slow is called. The function iterates over all registered netfilter hooks and calls them. If the packet is accepted, 1 is returned, and otherwise some other value.

If nf_hook_thresh returned 1, that is, if the netfilter verdict was to accept the packet, then control is passed to the continuation function specified in okfn.

The IP forwarding code includes a typical NF_HOOK macro call, which we will consider as an example:

net/ipv4/in_forward.c
```
int ip_forward(struct sk_buff *skb)
{
...
        return NF_HOOK(PF_INET, NF_IP_FORWARD, skb, skb->dev, rt->u.dst.dev,
                        ip_forward_finish);
}
```

The `okfn` specified is `ip_forward_finish`. Control is passed directly to this function if the above test establishes that no netfilter hooks are registered for the combination of `PF_INET` and `NF_IP_FORWARD`. Otherwise, the relevant netfilter code is executed and control is then transferred to `ip_forward_finish` (assuming the packet is not discarded or removed from kernel control). If no hooks are installed, code flow is the same as if `ip_forward` and `ip_forward_finish` were implemented as a single, uninterrupted procedure.

The kernel makes use of the optimization options of the C compiler to prevent speed loss if netfilter is disabled. Kernel versions before 2.6.24 required that the `okfn` was defined as an *inline* function:

net/ipv4/ip_forward.c
```
static inline int ip_forward_finish(struct sk_buff *skb) {
...
}
```

This means that it is shown as a normal function, but the compiler does not invoke it by means of a classic function call (pass parameters, set instruction pointers to function code, read arguments, etc.). Instead, the entire C code is copied to the point at which the function is invoked. Although this results in a longer executable (particularly for larger functions), it is compensated by speed gains. The GNU C compiler guarantees that `inline` functions are as fast as macros if this approach is adopted.

However, starting with kernel 2.6.24, the inline definition could be removed in nearly all cases!

net/ipv4/ip_forward.c
```
static int ip_forward_finish(struct sk_buff *skb) {
...
}
```

This is possible because the GNU C compiler has become able to perform an additional optimization technique: procedure tail calls. They originate from functional languages and are, for instance, mandatory for implementations of the Scheme language. When a function is called as the last statement of another function, it is not necessary that the callee returns to the caller after it has finished its work — there is nothing left to do in the caller. This allows for performing some simplifications of the call mechanism that lead to an execution that is as fast as with the old inline mechanism, without the need to duplicate code by inlining, and thus without increasing the size of the kernel. However, this optimization is not performed by gcc for all hook functions, and a small number of them still remain inlined.

If the netfilter configuration is enabled, scanning of the `nf_hooks` array makes no sense, and the `NF_HOOK` macro is then defined differently:

include/net/netfilter.h
```
#define NF_HOOK(pf, hook, skb, indev, outdev, okfn) (okfn)(skb)
```

Invocation of the hook function is simply replaced with a call to the function defined in `okfn` (the `inline` keyword instructs the compiler to do this by copying the code). The original two functions have now merged into one, and there is no need for an intervening function call.

Scanning the Hook Table

`nf_hook_slow` is called if at least one hook function is registered and needs to be invoked. All hooks are stored in the `nf_hooks` two-dimensional array:

net/netfilter/core.c
```
struct list_head nf_hooks[NPROTO][NF_MAX_HOOKS] __read_mostly;
```

NPROTO specifies the maximum number of protocol families supported by the system (currently 34). Symbolic constants for the individual families are PF_INET and PF_DECnet; these are stored in include/linux/socket.h. It is possible to define NF_MAX_HOOKS lists with hooks for each protocol; the default is 8.

The list_head elements of the table are used as list heads for a doubly linked list that accepts nf_hook_ops instances:

<netfilter.h>
```
struct nf_hook_ops
{
        struct list_head list;

        /* User fills in from here down. */
        nf_hookfn *hook;
        struct module *owner;
        int pf;
        int hooknum;
        /* Hooks are ordered in ascending priority. */
        int priority;
};
```

In addition to the standard elements (list for linking the structure in a doubly linked list, and owner as a pointer to the module data structure of the owner module if the hook is implemented modularly), there are other elements with the following meanings:

❑   hook is a pointer to the hook function that requires the same arguments as the NF_HOOK macro:

<netfilter.h>
```
typedef unsigned int nf_hookfn(unsigned int hooknum,
                    struct sk_buff **skb,
                    const struct net_device *in,
                    const struct net_device *out,
                    int (*okfn)(struct sk_buff *));
```

❑   pf and hooknum specify the protocol family and the number associated with the hook. This information could also be derived from the position of the hook list in nf_hooks.

❑   The hooks in a list are sorted in ascending priority (indicated by priority). The full signed int range can be used to indicate the priority, but a number of preferred defaults are defined:

<netfilter_ipv4.h>
```
enum nf_ip_hook_priorities {
        NF_IP_PRI_FIRST = INT_MIN,
        NF_IP_PRI_CONNTRACK_DEFRAG = -400,
        NF_IP_PRI_RAW = -300,
        NF_IP_PRI_SELINUX_FIRST = -225,
        NF_IP_PRI_CONNTRACK = -200,
        NF_IP_PRI_MANGLE = -150,
        NF_IP_PRI_NAT_DST = -100,
        NF_IP_PRI_FILTER = 0,
        NF_IP_PRI_NAT_SRC = 100,
        NF_IP_PRI_SELINUX_LAST = 225,
        NF_IP_PRI_CONNTRACK_HELPER = INT_MAX - 2,
```

```
                    NF_IP_PRI_NAT_SEQ_ADJUST = INT_MAX - 1,
                    NF_IP_PRI_CONNTRACK_CONFIRM = INT_MAX,
                    NF_IP_PRI_LAST = INT_MAX,
            };
```

This ensures, for example, that *mangling* of packet data is always performed *before* any filter operations.

The appropriate list can be selected from the nf_hook array by reference to the protocol family and hook number. Work is then delegated to nf_iterate, which traverses the list elements and invokes the hook functions.

Activating the Hook Functions

Each hook function returns one of the following values:

❑   NF_ACCEPT accepts a packet. This means that the routine in question has made no changes to the data. The kernel continues to use the unmodified packet and lets it run through the remaining layers of the network implementation (or through subsequent hooks).

❑   NF_STOLEN specifies that the hook function has "stolen" a packet and will deal with it. As of this point, the packet no longer concerns the kernel, and it is not necessary to call any further hooks. Further processing by other protocol layers must also be suppressed.

❑   NF_DROP instructs the kernel to discard the packet. As with NF_STOLEN, no further processing by other hooks or in the network layer takes place. Memory space occupied by the socket buffer (and therefore by the packet) is released because the data it contains can be discarded — for example, packets regarded as corrupted by a hook.

❑   NF_QUEUE places the packet on a wait queue so that its data can be processed by userspace code. No other hook functions are executed.

❑   NF_REPEAT calls the hook again.

> **Ultimately, packets are not further processed in the network layer unless all hook functions return NF_ACCEPT (NF_REPEAT is never the final result). All other packets are either discarded or processed by the netfilter subsystem itself.**

The kernel provides a collection of hook functions so that separate hook functions need not be defined for every occasion. These are known as *iptables* and are used for the high-level processing of packets. They are configured using the iptables userspace tool, which is not discussed here.

12.8.7 IPv6

Even though widespread use of the Internet is a a recent phenomenon, its technical foundations have been in place for some time. Today's Internet protocol was introduced in 1981. Although the underlying standard is well thought out and forward-looking, it is showing signs of age. The explosive growth of the Internet over the past few years has thrown up a problem relating to the available address space of IPv4 — 32-bit addresses allow a maximum of 2^{32} hosts to be addressed (if subnetting and the like are ignored). Although earlier thought to be inexhaustible, this address space will no longer be sufficient in the foreseeable future because more and more devices — ranging from PDAs and laser printers to coffee machines and refrigerators — require IP addresses.

Overview and Innovations

In 1998 a new standard named IPv6 was defined[23] and is now supported by the Linux kernel in production quality. A full implementation of the protocol is located in the net/ipv6 directory. The modular and open structure of the network layer means that IPv6 can make use of the existing, mature infrastructure. As many aspects of IPv6 are similar to IPv4, a brief overview will suffice at this point.

A key change in IPv6 is a completely new packet format that uses 128-byte IP addresses, and is therefore easier and faster to process. The structure of an IPv6 packet is shown in Figure 12-21.

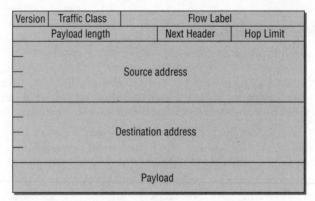

Figure 12-21: Structure of an IPv6 packet.

The structure is much simpler than that in IPv4. There are only eight header fields instead of 14. Of particular note is the absence of the fragmentation field. Although IPv6 also supports the splitting of packet data into smaller units, the corresponding information is held in an extension header pointed to by the *next header* field. Support for a variable number of extension headers makes it easier to introduce new features.

The changes between IPv4 and IPv6 have also necessitated modification of the interface via which connections are programmed. Although sockets are still used, many old and familiar functions appear under a new name to support the new options. However, this is a problem faced by userspace and C libraries and will be ignored here.

The notation of IP addresses has also changed because of the increase in address length from 32 to 128 bits. Retaining the former notation (tuples of bytes) would have resulted in extremely long addresses. Preference was therefore given to hexadecimal notation for IPv6 addresses, for example, FEDC:BA98:7654:3210:FEDC:BA98:7654:3210 and 1080:0:0:0:8:800:200C:417A. A mixture of IPv4 and IPv6 formats resulting in addresses such as 0:0:0:0:0:FFFF:129.144.52.38 is also permitted.

Implementation

What route does an IPv6 packet take when it traverses the network layer? On the lower layers, there is no change as compared with IPv4 because the mechanisms used are independent of the higher-level

---

[23]It couldn't be called IPv5 because the name had already been used to designate the STP protocol, which was defined in an RFC but never filtered through to a wide public.

protocols. Changes are apparent, however, when data are passed to the IP layer. Figure 12-22 shows a (coarse-grained) code flow diagram for IPv6 implementation.

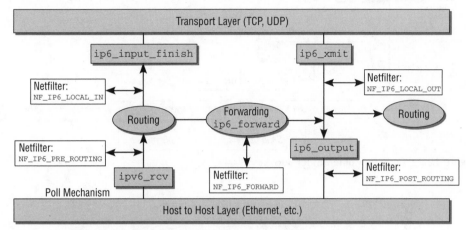

Figure 12-22: Code flow diagram for IPv6 implementation.

As the diagram shows, the structural changes between version 4 and version 6 are minor. Although the function names are different, the code follows more or less the same path through the kernel. For reasons of space, the implementation details are not discussed.[24]

12.9   Transport Layer

Two main IP-based transport protocols are used — UDP to send datagrams, and TCP to set up secure, connection-oriented services. Whereas UPD is a simple, easily implemented protocol, TCP has several well-concealed (but nevertheless well-known) booby traps and stumbling blocks that make implementation all the more complex.

12.9.1   UDP

As explained in the previous section, `ip_local_deliver` distributes the transport data contents of IP packets. `udp_rcv` from `net/ipv4/udp.c` is used to further process UDP datagram packets. The associated code flow diagram is shown in Figure 12-23.

`udp_rcv` is just a wrapper function for `__udp4_lib_rcv` since the code is shared with the implementation of the UDP-lite protocol as defined in RFC 3828.

As usual, the input parameter passed to the function is a socket buffer. Once it has been established that the packet data are intact, it is necessary to find a listening socket using `__udp4_lib_lookup`. The connection parameters can be derived from the UDP header, whose structure is shown in Figure 12-24.

---

[24]Note that the names of the netfilter hooks will be changed in the same manner as noted for IPv4 in kernel 2.6.25, which was still under development when this book was written. The constants will not be prefixed `NF_IP6_` anymore, but instead by `NF_INET_`. The same set of constants is thus used for IPv4 and IPv6.

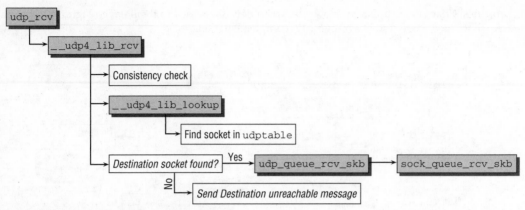

Figure 12-23: Code flow diagram for `udp_rcv`.

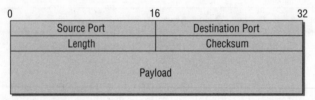

Figure 12-24: Structure of a UDP packet.

In figure 12-24, "Source" and "Destination Port" specify the port number of the source and destination system and accept values from 0 to 65,535 because each uses 16 bytes.[25] "Length" is the total length of the packet (header *and* data) in bytes, and "Checksum" holds an optional checksum.

The header of a UDP packet is represented in the kernel by the following data structure:

```
<udp.h>
struct udphdr {
        __be16    source;
        __be16    dest;
        __be16    len;
        __be16    check;
};
```

`__udp4_lib_lookup` from `net/ipv4/udp.c` is used to find a kernel-internal socket to which the packet is sent. They employ a hashing method to find and return an instance of the `sock` structure in the `udphash` global array when a listening process is interested in the packet. If they cannot find a socket, they send a *destination unreachable* message to the original system, and the contents of the packet are discarded.

Although I have not yet discussed the `sock` structure, it inevitably brings the term *socket* to mind, exactly as is intended. As we are on the borderline of the application layer, the data must be passed to userspace at some time or other using sockets as described in the sample programs at the beginning of the chapter.

---

[25]The IP address need not be specified because it is already in the IP header.

786

Note, however, that two data structures are used to represent sockets in the kernel. sock is the interface to the network access layer, and socket is the link to userspace. These rather lengthy structures are discussed in detail in the next section, which examines the part of the application layer anchored in the kernel. At the moment, we are interested only in the methods of the sock structure needed to forward data to the next higher layer. These must allow data received to be placed on a socket-specific wait queue and must also inform the receiving process that new data have arrived. Currently, the sock structure can be reduced to the following abbreviated version:

```
include/net/sock.h
/* Short version */
struct sock {
        wait_queue_head_t        *sk_sleep;
        struct sk_buff_head      sk_receive_queue;

        /* Callback */
        void                     (*sk_data_ready)(struct sock *sk, int bytes);
}
```

Control is transferred to udp_queue_rcv_skb once udp_rcv has found the appropriate sock instance and immediately afterward to sock_queue_rcv_skb, where 2 important actions are performed to complete data delivery to the application layer.

❑ Processes waiting for data delivery via the socket sleep on the sleep wait queue.

❑ Invoking skb_queue_tail inserts the socket buffer with the packet data at the end of the receive_queue list whose head is held in the socket-specific sock structure.

❑ The function pointed to by data_ready (typically, sock_def_readable if the sock instance is initialized with the standard function sock_init_data) is invoked to inform the socket that new data has arrived. It wakes all processes sleeping on sleep while waiting for data to arrive.

12.9.2 TCP

TCP provides many more functions than UDP. Consequently, its implementation in the kernel is much more difficult and comprehensive, and a whole book could easily be dedicated to the specific problems involved. The connection-oriented communication model used by TCP to support the secure transmission of data streams not only requires greater administrative overhead in the kernel, but also calls for further operations such as explicit connection setup following from negotiations between computers. The handling (and prevention) of specific scenarios as well as optimization to boost transmission performance account for a large part of TCP implementation in the kernel; all their subtleties and oddities are not discussed here.

Let's look at the three major components of the TCP protocol (connection establishment, connection termination, and the orderly transmission of data streams) by first describing the procedure required by the standard before going on to examine the implementation.

A TCP connection is always in a clearly defined state. These include the *listen* and *established* states mentioned above. There are also other states and clearly defined rules for the possible transitions between them, as shown in Figure 12-25.

At first glance, the diagram is a little confusing, not to say off-putting. However, the information it contains almost fully describes the behavior of a TCP implementation. Basically, the kernel could distinguish

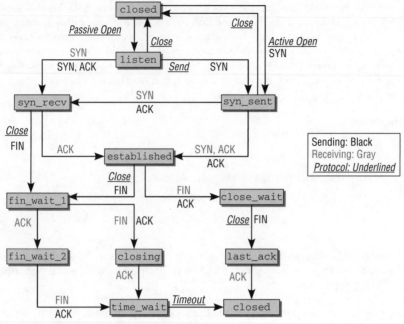

Figure 12-25: TCP state-transition diagram.

between the individual states and implement the transitions between them (using a tool known as a *finite state machine*). This is neither particularly efficient nor fast, so the kernel adopts a different approach. Nevertheless, when describing the individual TCP actions, I make repeated reference to this diagram and use it as a basis for our examination.

TCP Headers

TCP packets have a header that contains state data and other connection information. The header structure is shown in Figure 12-26.

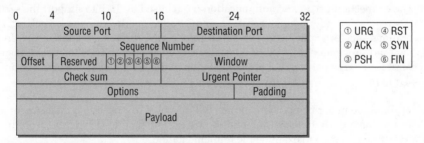

Figure 12-26: Structure of a TCP packet.

- ❏ `source` and `dest` specify the *port numbers* used. As with UDP, they consist of 2 bytes.

- ❏ `seq` is a sequence number. It specifies the position of a TCP packet within the data stream and is important when lost data need to be retransmitted.

- ❑ ack_seq holds a sequence number used when acknowledging receipt of TCP packets.

- ❑ doff stands for *data offset* and specifies the length of the TCP header structure, which is not always the same owing to the variable nature of some of the options.

- ❑ reserved is not available (and should therefore always be set to 0).

- ❑ urg (*urgent*), ack (*acknowledgment*), psh (*push*), rst (*reset*), syn (*synchronize*), and fin are *control flags* used to check, establish, and terminate connections.

- ❑ window tells the connection partner how many bytes it can send before the receiver buffer will be full. This prevents backlog when fast senders communicate with slow receivers.

- ❑ checksum is the packet checksum.

- ❑ options is a variable-length list of additional connection options.

- ❑ The actual data (or payload) follows the header. The options field may be padded because the data entry must always start at a 32-bit position (to simplify handling).

The header is implemented in the tcphdr data structure. The system endianness must be noted because a split byte field is used.

```
<tcp.h>
struct tcphdr {
        __be16 source;
        __be16 dest;
        __be32 seq;
        __be32 ack_seq;
#if defined(__LITTLE_ENDIAN_BITFIELD)
        __u16 res1:4,
        doff:4,
        fin:1,
        syn:1,
        rst:1,
        psh:1,
        ack:1,
        urg:1,
        ece:1,
        cwr:1;
#elif defined(__BIG_ENDIAN_BITFIELD)
        __u16 doff:4,
        res1:4,
        cwr:1,
        ece:1,
        urg:1,
        ack:1,
        psh:1,
        rst:1,
        syn:1,
        fin:1;
#else
#error "Adjust your <asm/byteorder.h> defines"
#endif
        __be16 window;
        __sum16 check;
        __be16 urg_ptr;
};
```

Receiving TCP Data

All TCP actions (connection setup and shutdown, data transmission) are performed by sending data packets with specific properties and various flags. Before discussing state transitions, I must first establish how the TCP data are passed to the transport layer and at what point the information in the header is analyzed.

`tcp_v4_rcv` is the entry point into the TCP layer once a packet has been processed by the IP layer. The code flow diagram for `tcp_v4_rcv` is shown in Figure 12-27.

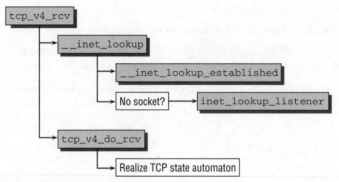

Figure 12-27: Code flow diagram for `tcp_v4_rcv`.

Each TCP socket of the system is included in one of three hash tables that accept sockets in the following states:

- ❑ Sockets that are fully connected.

- ❑ Sockets that are waiting for a connection (in the *listen* state).

- ❑ Sockets that are in the process of establishing a connection (using the three-way handshake discussed below).

After performing various checks on the packet data and copying information from the header into the control block of the socket buffer, the kernel delegates the work of finding a socket that is waiting for the packet to the `__inet_lookup` function. The only task of this function is to invoke two further functions to scan various hash tables. `__inet_lookup_established` attempts to return a connected socket. If no appropriate structure is found, the `inet_lookup_listener` function is invoked to check all listening sockets.

In both cases, the functions combine different elements of the respective connection (IP addresses of the client and server, port addresses and the kernel-internal index of the network interface) by means of hash functions to find an instance of the abovementioned `sock` type. When searching for a listening socket, a score method is applied to find the best candidate among several sockets working with wildcards. This topic is not discussed because the results simply reflect what would intuitively be regarded as the best candidate.

In contrast to UDP, work does not end but begins when the appropriate `sock` structure for the connection is found. Depending on connection state, it is necessary to perform a state transition as shown in

Figure 12-25. `tcp_v4_do_rcv` is a multiplexer that splits the code flow into different branches on the basis of the socket state.

The sections below deal with the individual options and associated actions but do not cover *all* of the sometimes tricky and seldom used oddities of the TCP protocol. For this, see specialized publications such as [WPR+01], [Ben05], and [Ste94].

Three-Way Handshake

A connection must be established explicitly between a client and a host before a TCP link can be used. As already noted, a distinction is made between *active* and *passive* connection setup.

The kernel (i.e., the kernel of both machines involved in the connection) sees the following situation immediately prior to connection establishment — the state of the client process socket is CLOSED, that of the server socket is LISTEN.

A TCP connection is set up by means of a procedure that involves the exchange of three TCP packets and is therefore known as a *three-way handshake*. As the state diagram in Figure 12-25 shows, the following actions take place:

❑   The client sends SYN to the server[26] to signal a connection request. The socket state of the client changes from CLOSED to SYN_SENT.

❑   The server receives the connection request on a listening socket and returns SYN and ACK.[27] The state of the server socket changes from LISTEN to SYN_REC.

❑   The client socket receives the SYN/ACK packet and switches to the ESTABLISHED state, indicating that a connection has been set up. An ACK packet is sent to the server.

❑   The server receives the ACK packet and also switches to the ESTABLISHED state. This concludes connection setup on both sides, and data exchange can begin.

In principle, a connection could be established using only one or two packets. However, there is then a risk of faulty connections as a result of leftover packets of old connections between the same addresses (IP addresses and port numbers). The purpose of the three-way handshake is to prevent this.

A special characteristic of TCP links immediately becomes apparent when connections are established. Each packet sent is given a sequence number, and receipt of each packet must be acknowledged by the TCP instance at the receiving end. Let us take a look at the log of a connection request to a web server[28]:

```
1 192.168.0.143 192.168.1.10  TCP  1025 > http [SYN] Seq=2895263889 Ack=0
2 192.168.1.10  192.168.0.143 TCP  http > 1025 [SYN, ACK] Seq=2882478813 Ack=2895263890
3 192.168.0.143 192.168.1.10  TCP  1025 > http [ACK] Seq=2895263890 Ack=2882478814
```

The client generates random sequence number 2895263889 for the first packet; it is stored in the SEQ field of the TCP header. The server responds to the arrival of this packet with a combined SYN/ACK packet with a new sequence number (in our example, 2882478813). What we are interested in here is the contents of the SEQ/ACK field (the numeric field, not the flag bit). The server fills this field by adding the number of bytes received +1 to the sequence number received (the underlying principle is discussed below).

---

[26]This is the name given to an empty packet with a set SYN flag.
[27]This step could be split into two parts by sending one packet with ACK and a second with SYN, but this is not done in practice.
[28]Network connection data can be captured with tools such as `tcpdump` and `wireshark`.

Together with the set ACK flag of the packet, this indicates to the client that the first packet has been received. No extra packet need be generated to acknowledge receipt of a data packet. Acknowledgment can be given in any packet in which the ACK flag is set and the `ack` field is filled.

Packets sent to establish the connection do not contain data; only the TCP header is relevant. The length stored in the `len` field of the header is therefore 0.

The mechanisms described are not specific to the Linux kernel but must be implemented by all operating systems wishing to communicate via TCP. The sections below deal more extensively with the kernel-specific implementation of the operations described.

Passive Connection Establishment

Active connection setup does not originate from the kernel itself but is triggered by receipt of a SYN packet with a connection request. The starting point is therefore the `tcp_v4_rcv` function, which, as described above, finds a listening socket and transfers control to `tcp_v4_do_rcv`, whose code flow diagram (for this specific scenario) is shown in Figure 12-28.

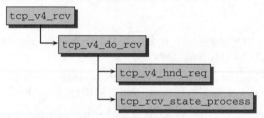

Figure 12-28: Code flow diagram for
`tcp_v4_rcv_passive`.

`tcp_v4_hnd_req` is invoked to perform the various initialization tasks required in the network layer to establish a new connection. The actual state transition takes place in `tcp_rcv_state_process`, which consists of a long `case` statement to differentiate between the possible socket states and to invoke the appropriate transition function.

Possible socket states are defined in an `enum` list:

include/net/tcp_states.h
```
enum {
  TCP_ESTABLISHED = 1,
  TCP_SYN_SENT,
  TCP_SYN_RECV,
  TCP_FIN_WAIT1,
  TCP_FIN_WAIT2,
  TCP_TIME_WAIT,
  TCP_CLOSE,
  TCP_CLOSE_WAIT,
  TCP_LAST_ACK,
  TCP_LISTEN,
  TCP_CLOSING,    /* Now a valid state */

  TCP_MAX_STATES /* Leave at the end! */
};
```

`tcp_v4_conn_request` is invoked if the socket state is `TCP_LISTEN`.[29] The function concerns itself with many details and subtleties of TCP that are not described here. What is important is the acknowledgment packet sent at the end of the function. It contains not only the set ACK flag and the sequence number of the received packet but also a newly generated sequence number and a SYN flag as required by the three-way handshake procedure. This concludes the first phase of connection setup.

The next step at the client is reception of the ACK packet that arrives at the `tcp_rcv_state_process` function via the usual path. The socket state is now `TCP_SYN_RECV`, which is handled by a separate branch of `case` differentiation. The main task of the kernel is to change the socket state to `TCP_ESTABLISHED` to indicate that a connection has now been set up.

Active Connection Establishment

Active connection setup is initiated by invoking the `open` library function by means of a userspace application that issues the `socketcall` system call to arrive at the kernel function `tcp_v4_connect`, whose code flow diagram is shown on the upper part of Figure 12-29.

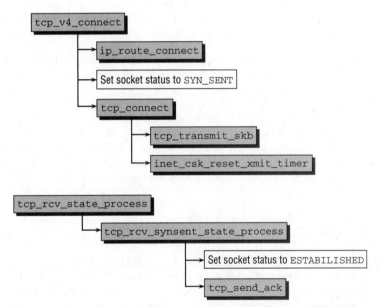

Figure 12-29: Code flow diagram for active connection establishment.

The function starts by looking for an IP route to the destination host using the framework described above. After the TCP header has been generated and the relevant values have been set in a socket buffer, the socket state changes from `CLOSED` to `SYN_SENT`. `tcp_connect`, then sends a SYN packet to the IP layer and therefore to the client. In addition, a timer is created in the kernel to ensure that packet sending is repeated if no acknowledgment is received within a certain period.

---

[29] A function pointer to an address family-specific data structure is used because the dispatcher supports both IPv4 and IPv6. As the implementation of the finite-state machine is the same for IPv4 and IPv6, a large amount of code can be saved.

Now the client must wait for server acknowledgment of the SYN packet and for a SYN packet acknowledging the connection request, which is received by means of the normal TCP mechanisms (lower part of Figure 12-29). This leads to the `tcp_rcv_state_process` dispatcher, which, in this case, directs the flow of control to `tcp_rcv_synsent_state_process`. The socket state is set to ESTABLISHED, and `tcp_send_ack` returns another ACK packet to the server to conclude connection setup.

Transmission of Data Packets

Data are transferred between computers once a connection has been set up as described above. This process is sometimes quite tricky because TCP has several features that call for comprehensive control and security procedures between the communicating hosts:

❑   Byte streams are transmitted in a guaranteed order.

❑   Lost packets are retransmitted by automated mechanisms.

❑   Data flow is controlled separately in each direction and is matched to the speeds of the hosts.

Even though initially these requirements may not appear to be very complex, a relatively large number of procedures and tricks are needed to satisfy them. Because most connections are TCP-based, the speed and efficiency of the implementation are crucial. The Linux kernel therefore resorts to tricks and optimizations, and unfortunately these don't necessarily make the implementation any easier to understand.

Before turning our attention to how data transmission is implemented over an established connection, it is necessary to discuss some of the underlying principles. We are particularly interested in the mechanisms that come into play when packets are lost.

The concept of packet acknowledgment based on sequence numbers is also adopted for normal data packets. However, sequence numbers reveal more about data transmission than mentioned above. According to which scheme are sequence numbers assigned? When a connection is set up, a random number is generated (by the kernel using `secure_tcp_sequence_number` from `drivers/char/random.c`). Thereafter a system supporting the strict acknowledgment of all incoming data packets is used.

A unique sequence number that builds on the number initially sent is assigned to each byte of a TCP transmission. Let us assume, for example, that the initial random number of the TCP system is 100. The first 16 bytes sent therefore have the sequence numbers $100, 101, \ldots, 115$.

TCP uses a *cumulative acknowledgment* scheme. This means that an acknowledgment covers a contiguous range of bytes. The number sent in the `ack` field acknowledges all bytes between the last and the current ACK number of a data stream. (The initial sequence number is used as the starting point if an acknowledgment has not yet been sent and there is therefore no last number.) The ACK number confirms receipt of all data up to and including the byte that is 1 less than the number and therefore indicates which byte is expected next. For instance, ACK number 166 acknowledges all bytes up to and including 165 and expects bytes from 166 upward in the next packet.

This mechanism is used to trace lost packets. Note that TCP does not feature an explicit re-request mechanism; in other words, the receiver cannot request the sender to retransmit lost packets. The onus is on the sender to retransmit the missing segment automatically if it does not receive an acknowledgment within a certain time-out period.

How are these procedures implemented in the kernel? We assume that the connection was established as described above so that the two sockets (on the different systems) both have the ESTABLISHED state.

Receiving Packets

The code flow diagram in Figure 12-30 shows the path taken — starting from the familiar `tcp_v4_rcv` function — when packets are received.

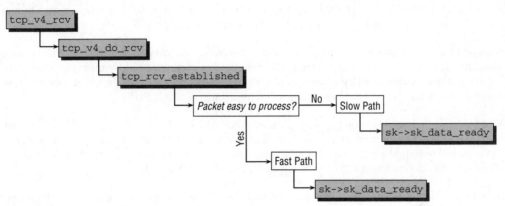

Figure 12-30: Receiving packets in TCP connections.

After control has been passed to `tcp_v4_do_rcv`, a fast path is selected (if a connection already exists) rather than entering the central dispatcher function — this is in contrast to other socket states but is logical because the transmission of data packets accounts for the lion's share of work in any TCP connection and should therefore be performed as quickly as possible. Once it has been established that the state of the destination socket is `TCP_ESTABLISHED`, the `tcp_rcv_established` function is invoked to split the control flow again. Packets that are easy to analyze are handled in the *fast path* and those with unusual options in the *slow path*.

Packets must fulfill one of the following criteria to be classified as easy to analyze:

❑   The packet must contain only an acknowledgment for the data last sent.

❑   The packet must contain the data expected next.

In addition, *none* of the following flags must be set: SYN, URG, RST, or FIN.

This description of the "best case scenario" for packets is not Linux-specific but is also found in many other UNIX variants.[30] Almost all packets fall within these categories,[31] which is why it makes sense to differentiate between a fast and a slow path.

Which operations are performed in the fast path? A few packet checks are carried out to find more complex packets and return them to the slow path. Thereafter the packet length is analyzed to ascertain whether the packet is an acknowledgment or a data packet. This is not difficult because ACK packets do not contain data and must therefore be of exactly the same length as a TCP packet header.

---

[30]This approach was developed by Van Jacobsen, a well-known network researcher, and is often referred to as the *VJ mechanism*.

[31]Today's transmission techniques are so sophisticated that very few errors occur. This was not the case in the early days of TCP. Although more faults arise on global Internet connections than in local networks, most packets can still be handled in the fast path owing to the low error rates.

The fast path code doesn't bother with processing ACK segments but delegates this task to `tcp_ack`. Here, obsolete packets and packets sent too early owing to faulty TCP implementations at the receiving end or to unfortunate combinations of transmission errors and time-outs are filtered out. The most important tasks of this function are not only to analyze new information on the connection (e.g., on the receiving window) and on other subtleties of the TCP protocol, but also to delete acknowledged data from the retransmission queue (discussed below). This queue holds all sent packets and retransmits them if they are not acknowledged by means of an ACK within a certain time period.

Because it has been established during selection of the packet for fast path handling that the data received immediately follow the previous segment, the data can be acknowledged by means of an ACK to the sender without the need for any further checks. Finally, the `sk_data_ready` function pointer stored in the socket is invoked to inform the user process that new data are available.

What is the difference between the slow path and the fast path? Owing to the many TCP options, the code in the slow path is more extensive. For this reason, I won't go into the many special situations that can arise because they are less of a kernel problem and more of a general problem of TCP connections (detailed descriptions are available in, e.g., [Ste94] and [WPR$^+$01]).

In the slow path, data cannot be forwarded directly to the socket because complicated packet option checks are necessary, and these may be followed by potential TCP subsystem responses. Data arriving out of sequence are placed on a special wait queue, where they remain until a contiguous data segment is complete. Only then can the complete data be forwarded to the socket.

Sending Packets

As seen from the TCP layer, the sending of TCP packets begins with the invocation of the `tcp_sendmsg` function by higher network instances. Figure 12-31 shows the associated code flow diagram.

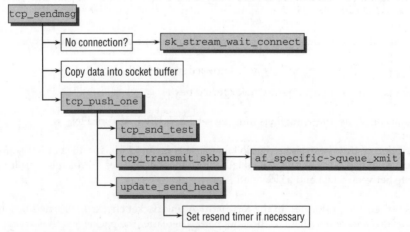

Figure 12-31: Code flow diagram for `tcp_sendmsg`.

Naturally, the state of the socket used must be TCP_ESTABLISHED before data transmission can begin. If this is not the case, the kernel waits (with the help of `wait_for_tcp_connect`) until a connection has been established. The data are then copied to the address space of the userspace process in the kernel and are used to build a TCP packet. I do not intend to discuss this complicated operation because it involves a large number of procedures, all of which are targeted at satisfying the complex requirements of the TCP protocol. Unfortunately, sending a TCP packet is not limited simply to construction of a packet header and transfer to the IP layer. It is also necessary to comply with the following (by no means exhaustive) list of demands:

❑ Sufficient space for the data must be available in the wait queue of the receiver.

❑ The ECN mechanism must be implemented to prevent connection congestion.

❑ Possible stalemate situations must be detected as otherwise communication comes to a halt.

❑ The TCP *slow-start* mechanism requires a gradual increase in packet size at the start of communication.

❑ Packets sent but not acknowledged must be retransmitted repeatedly after a certain timeout period until they are finally acknowledged by the receiver.

As the retransmission queue is a key element of reliable data transmission via a TCP connection, let's take a look here at how it actually works. After a packet has been assembled, the kernel arrives at `tcp_push_one`, which performs the following three tasks:

❑ `tcp_snd_test` checks whether the data can be sent at the present time. This may not be possible because of backlogs caused by an overloaded receiver.

❑ `tcp_transmit_skb` forwards the data to the IP layer using the address family-specific `af_specific->queue_xmit` function (`ip_queue_xmit` is used for IPv4).

❑ `update_send_head` takes care of updating some statistics. More important, it initializes the retransmit timer of the TCP segment sent. This is not necessary for every sent packet, but only for the first packet that follows after an acknowledged data region.

`inet_csk_reset_xmit_timer` is responsible for resetting the retransmit timer. The timer is the basis for resending data packets that have not been acknowledged and acts as a kind of TCP transmission guarantee certificate. If the receiver does not acknowledge data receipt within a certain period (time-out), the data are retransmitted. The kernel timer used is described in Chapter 15. The `sock` instance associated with the particular socket holds a list of retransmit timers for each packet sent. The time-out function used by the kernel is `tcp_write_timer`, which invokes the function `tcp_retransmit_timer` if an ACK is not received. The following must be noted when retransmitting segments:

❑ The connection may have been closed in the meantime. In this case, the stored packet and the timer entry are removed from kernel memory.

❑ Retransmission is aborted when more retransmit attempts have been made than specified in the `sysctl_tcp_retries2` variable.[32]

As mentioned above, the retransmit timer is deleted once an ACK has been received for a packet.

---

[32]The default for this variable is 15, but it can be modified using `/proc/sys/net/ipv4/tcp_retries2`.

Connection Termination

Like connection setup, shutdown of TCP connections is also brought about by a multistage exchange of packets, as shown in Figure 12-25. A connection can be closed in one of two ways:

1. A *graceful close* terminates the connection at the explicit request of one of the participating systems (in rare cases, both systems issue a request at the same time).

2. Termination or *abort* can be brought about by a higher protocol (because, e.g., programs have crashed).

Fortunately, since the first situation is by far the more usual, we discuss it and ignore the second.

TCP partners must exchange *four* packets to close a connection gracefully. The sequence of steps is described below.

1. The standard library function `close` is invoked in computer A to send a TCP packet whose FIN flag is set in the header. The socket of A switches to the FIN_WAIT_1 state.

2. B receives the FIN packet and returns an ACK packet. Its socket state changes from ESTAB-LISHED to CLOSE_WAIT. The socket is informed of receipt of the FIN by means of an "end of file."

3. After receipt of the ACK packet, the socket state of computer A changes from FIN_WAIT_1 to FIN_WAIT_2.

4. The application associated with the socket on computer B also executes `close` to send a FIN segment from B to A. The state of the socket of computer B then changes to `LAST_ACK`.

5. Computer A confirms receipt of the FIN with an ACK packet and first goes into the TIME_WAIT state before automatically switching to the CLOSED state after a certain period.

6. Computer B receives the ACK packet, which causes its socket also to switch to the CLOSED state.

The status transitions are performed in the central dispatcher function (`tcp_rcv_state_process`), in the path for existing connections (`tcp_rcv_established`), and in the `tcp_close` function not yet discussed.

The latter is invoked when the user process decides to call the `close` library function to close a connection. If the state of the socket is LISTEN (i.e., there is no connection to another computer), the approach is simpler because no external parties need be informed of the end of the connection. This situation is checked at the beginning of the procedure, and, if it applies, the response is a change of socket state to CLOSED.

If not, `tcp_send_fin` sends a FIN packet to the other party once the socket state has been set to FIN_WAIT_1 by the `tcp_close_state` and `tcp_set_state` call chain.[33]

---

[33]The approach is not fully compatible with the TCP standard because the socket is not actually allowed to change its state until *after* the FIN packet has been sent. However, the Linux alternative is simpler to implement and does not give rise to any problems in practice. This is why kernel developers have gone down this path as noted in a comment to this effect in `tcp_close`.

The transition from FIN_WAIT_1 to FIN_WAIT_2 is performed by the central dispatcher function `tcp_rcv_state_process` because there is no longer any need to take the fast path for existing connections. In the familiar case differentiation, a packet received with a set ACK flag triggers the transition to FIN_WAIT_2 by `tcp_set_state`. All that is now required to place the TCP connection in the TIME_WAIT state followed automatically by the CLOSED state is a FIN packet from the other party.

The status transitions of the other party that performs a passive close upon receipt of the first FIN packet follow a similar pattern. Because the first FIN packet is received when the state is ESTABLISHED, handling takes place in the slow path of `tcp_rcv_established` and involves sending an ACK to the other party and changing the socket state to TCP_CLOSING.

The next state transition (to LAST_ACK) is performed by calling the `close` library function to invoke the `tcp_close_state` function of the kernel. Only a further ACK packet from the other party is then needed to terminate the connection. This packet is also handled by the `tcp_rcv_state_process` function, which changes the socket state to CLOSED (by means of `tcp_done`), releases the memory space occupied by the socket, and thus finally terminates the connection.

> **Only the possible transition from the FIN_WAIT_1 state is described above. As the TCP finite-state machine illustrated in Figure 12-25 shows, two other alternatives are implemented by the kernel but are far less frequently used than the path I describe, reason enough not to bother with them here.**

12.10   Application Layer

Sockets are used to apply the UNIX metaphor that "everything is a file" to network connections. The interfaces between kernel and userspace sockets are implemented in the C standard library using the `socketcall` system call.

`socketcall` acts as a multiplexer for various tasks performed by various procedure, for instance, opening a socket or binding or sending data.

Linux adopts the concept of kernel sockets to make communication with sockets in userspace as simple as possible. There is an instance of the `socket` structure and the `sock` structure for every socket used by a program. These serve as an interface downward (to the kernel) and upward (to userspace). Both structures were referenced in the previous sections without defining them in detail, which is done now.

12.10.1   Socket Data Structures

The `socket` structure, slightly simplified, is defined as follows:

```
<net.h>
struct socket {
        socket_state            state;
        unsigned long           flags;
        const struct proto_ops  *ops;
        struct file             *file;
        struct sock             *sk;
        short                   type;
};
```

❑ `type` specifies the numeric identifier of the protocol type.

❑ `state` indicates the connection state of the socket by means of the following values (`SS` stands for *socket state*):

<net.h>
```
typedef enum {
    SS_FREE = 0,                /* not allocated            */
    SS_UNCONNECTED,             /* unconnected to any socket */
    SS_CONNECTING,              /* in process of connecting  */
    SS_CONNECTED,               /* connected to socket       */
    SS_DISCONNECTING            /* in process of disconnecting */
} socket_state;
```

The values listed here have *nothing* in common with the state values used by the protocols of the transport layer when connections are set up and closed. They denote general states relevant to the outside world (i.e., to user programs).

❑ `file` is a pointer to the `file` instance of a pseudo-file for communication with the socket (as discussed earlier, user applications use normal file descriptors to perform network operations).

The definition of `socket` is not tied to a specific protocol. This explains why `proto_ops` is used as a pointer to a data structure that, in turn, holds pointers to protocol-specific functions to handle the socket:

<net.h>
```
struct proto_ops {
        int             family;
        struct module   *owner;
        int             (*release)   (struct socket *sock);
        int             (*bind)      (struct socket *sock,
                                      struct sockaddr *myaddr,
                                      int sockaddr_len);
        int             (*connect)   (struct socket *sock,
                                      struct sockaddr *vaddr,
                                      int sockaddr_len, int flags);
        int             (*socketpair)(struct socket *sock1,
                                      struct socket *sock2);
        int             (*accept)    (struct socket *sock,
                                      struct socket *newsock, int flags);
        int             (*getname)   (struct socket *sock,
                                      struct sockaddr *addr,
                                      int *sockaddr_len, int peer);
        unsigned int    (*poll)      (struct file *file, struct socket *sock,
                                      struct poll_table_struct *wait);
        int             (*ioctl)     (struct socket *sock, unsigned int cmd,
                                      unsigned long arg);
        int             (*compat_ioctl) (struct socket *sock, unsigned int cmd,
                                      unsigned long arg);
        int             (*listen)    (struct socket *sock, int len);
        int             (*shutdown)  (struct socket *sock, int flags);
        int             (*setsockopt)(struct socket *sock, int level,
                                      int optname, char __user *optval, int optlen);
        int             (*getsockopt)(struct socket *sock, int level,
```

```
                                     int optname, char __user *optval, int __user *optlen);
        int             (*compat_setsockopt)(struct socket *sock, int level,
                                     int optname, char __user *optval, int optlen);
        int             (*compat_getsockopt)(struct socket *sock, int level,
                                     int optname, char __user *optval, int __user *optlen);
        int             (*sendmsg)    (struct kiocb *iocb, struct socket *sock,
                                     struct msghdr *m, size_t total_len);
        int             (*recvmsg)    (struct kiocb *iocb, struct socket *sock,
                                     struct msghdr *m, size_t total_len,
                                     int flags);
        int             (*mmap)       (struct file *file, struct socket *sock,
                                     struct vm_area_struct * vma);
        ssize_t         (*sendpage)   (struct socket *sock, struct page *page,
                                     int offset, size_t size, int flags);
};
```

Many function pointers have the same name as the corresponding functions in the C standard library. This is not a coincidence because the functions are directed to the functions stored in the pointers by means of the `socketcall` system call.

The `sock` pointer also included in the structure points to a much lengthier structure that holds additional socket management data of significance to the kernel. The structure consists of a horrendous number of elements used for sometimes very subtle or seldom required features (the original definition is almost 100 lines long). Here I make do with a much shorter and simplified version. Note that the kernel itself places the most important elements in the structure `sock_common` that is embedded into `struct sock` right at the beginning. The following code excerpt shows both structures:

include/net/sock.h
```
struct sock_common {
        unsigned short          skc_family;
        volatile unsigned char  skc_state;
        struct hlist_node       skc_node;
        unsigned int            skc_hash;
        atomic_t                skc_refcnt;
        struct proto            *skc_prot;
};

struct sock {
        struct sock_common      __sk_common;

        struct sk_buff_head     sk_receive_queue;
        struct sk_buff_head     sk_write_queue;

        struct timer_list       sk_timer;
        void                    (*sk_data_ready)(struct sock *sk, int bytes);
...
};
```

The `sock` structures of the system are organized in a protocol-specific hash table. `skc_node` is the hash linkage element, while `skc_hash` denotes the hash value.

Data are sent and received by placing them on wait queues (sk_receive_queue and sk_write_queue) that contain socket buffers.

In addition, a list of callback functions is associated with each sock structure used by the kernel to draw attention to special events or bring about state changes. Our simplified version shows only one function pointer called sk_data_ready because it is the most significant and its name has already been mentioned several times in the last few chapters. The function it contains is invoked when data arrive for handling by the user process. Typically, the value of the pointer is sock_def_readable.

There is a great danger of confusion between the ops element of type struct proto_ops in the socket structure and the prot entry of type struct proto in sock. The latter is defined as follows:

```
include/net/sock.h
struct proto {
        void                    (*close)(struct sock *sk,
                                        long timeout);
        int                     (*connect)(struct sock *sk,
                                        struct sockaddr *uaddr,
                                        int addr_len);
        int                     (*disconnect)(struct sock *sk, int flags);

        struct sock *           (*accept) (struct sock *sk, int flags, int *err);

        int                     (*ioctl)(struct sock *sk, int cmd,
                                        unsigned long arg);
        int                     (*init)(struct sock *sk);
        int                     (*destroy)(struct sock *sk);
        void                    (*shutdown)(struct sock *sk, int how);
        int                     (*setsockopt)(struct sock *sk, int level,
                                        int optname, char __user *optval,
                                        int optlen);
        int                     (*getsockopt)(struct sock *sk, int level,
                                        int optname, char __user *optval,
                                        int __user *option);
...
        int                     (*sendmsg)(struct kiocb *iocb, struct sock *sk,
                                        struct msghdr *msg, size_t len);
        int                     (*recvmsg)(struct kiocb *iocb, struct sock *sk,
                                        struct msghdr *msg,
                                        size_t len, int noblock, int flags,
                                        int *addr_len);
        int                     (*sendpage)(struct sock *sk, struct page *page,
                                        int offset, size_t size, int flags);
        int                     (*bind)(struct sock *sk,
                                        struct sockaddr *uaddr, int addr_len);
                                        struct sockaddr *uaddr, int addr_len);
...
};
```

Both structures have member elements with similar (and often identical) names although they represent different functions. Whereas the operations shown here are used for communication between the (kernel-side) socket layer and transport layer, the functions held in the function pointer block of the socket structure are designed to communicate with system calls. In other words, they form the link between user-side and kernel-side sockets.

12.10.2 Sockets and Files

Userspace processes access sockets using normal file operations once a connection has been established. How is this implemented in the kernel? Owing to the open structure of the VFS layer (as discussed in Chapter 8), very few actions are needed.

VFS inodes of the virtual filesystem are discussed in Chapter 8. Each socket is assigned an inode of this type, which is, in turn, linked with the other structures associated with normal files. The functions for manipulating files are stored in a separate pointer table:

```
<fs.h>
struct inode {
    ...
        struct file_operations  *i_fop; /* former ->i_op->default_file_ops */
    ...
}
```

As a result, file access to the file descriptor of a socket can be redirected transparently to the code of the network layer. Sockets use the following file operations:

```
net/socket.c
struct file_operations socket_file_ops = {
        .owner =          THIS_MODULE,
        .llseek =         no_llseek,
        .aio_read =       sock_aio_read,
        .aio_write =      sock_aio_write,
        .poll =           sock_poll,
        .unlocked_ioctl = sock_ioctl,
        .compat_ioctl = compat_sock_ioctl,
        .mmap =           sock_mmap,
        .open =           sock_no_open,    /* special open code to disallow open via /proc */
        .release =        sock_close,
        .fasync =         sock_fasync,
        .sendpage =       sock_sendpage,
        .splice_write = generic_splice_sendpage,
};
```

The `sock_` functions are simple wrapper routines that invoke a `sock_operations` routine as shown in the following example of `sock_mmap`:

```
net/socket.c
static int sock_mmap(struct file * file, struct vm_area_struct * vma)
{
        struct socket *sock = file->private_data;

        return sock->ops->mmap(file, sock, vma);
}
```

Inode and socket are linked by allocating one directly after the other in memory by means of the following auxiliary structure:

include/net/sock.h
```
struct socket_alloc {
        struct socket socket;
        struct inode vfs_inode;
};
```

The kernel provides two macros that perform the necessary pointer arithmetic to move from an inode to the associated socket instance (SOCKET_I) and vice versa (SOCK_INODE). To simplify the situation, whenever a socket is attached to a file, sock_attach_fd sets the private_data element of struct file so that it points to the socket instance. The sock_mmap example shown above makes use of this.

12.10.3 The `socketcall` System Call

In addition to the read and write operations of the file functions that enter the kernel by means of the system calls of the virtual filesystem where they are redirected to function pointers of the socket_file_ops structure, it is also necessary to carry out other tasks with sockets that cannot be forced into the file scheme. These include, for example, creating a socket and bind and listen calls.

For this purpose, Linux provides the socketcall system call, which is implemented in sys_socketcall and to which I have made frequent reference.

It is remarkable that there is just one system call for all 17 socket operations. This results in very different lists of arguments depending on the task in hand. The first parameter of the system call is therefore a numeric constant to select the desired call. Possible values are, for example, SYS_SOCKET, SYS_BIND, SYS_ACCEPT, and SYS_RECV. The routines of the standard library use the same names but are all redirected internally to socketcall with the corresponding constant. The fact that there is only a single system call is primarily for historical reasons.

The task of sys_socketcall is not especially difficult — it simply acts as a dispatcher to forward the system call to other functions, each of which implements a "small" system call to which the parameters are passed:

net/socket.c
```
asmlinkage long sys_socketcall(int call, unsigned long __user *args)
{
        unsigned long a[6];
        unsigned long a0,a1;
        int err;

        if(call<1||call>SYS_RECVMSG)
                return -EINVAL;

        /* copy_from_user should be SMP safe. */
        if (copy_from_user(a, args, nargs[call]))
                return -EFAULT;
...
        a0=a[0];
        a1=a[1];
```

```
switch(call)
{
        case SYS_SOCKET:
                err = sys_socket(a0,a1,a[2]);
                break;
        case SYS_BIND:
                err = sys_bind(a0,(struct sockaddr __user *)a1, a[2]);
                break;
        ...
        case SYS_SENDMSG:
                err = sys_sendmsg(a0, (struct msghdr __user *) a1, a[2]);
                break;
        case SYS_RECVMSG:
                err = sys_recvmsg(a0, (struct msghdr __user *) a1, a[2]);
                break;
        default:
                err = -EINVAL;
                break;
}
        return err;
}
```

> **Even though the target functions comply with the same naming conventions as system calls, they can be invoked only via the `socketcall` call and not by any other system call.**

Table 12-3 shows which "subcalls" of `socketcall` are available.

12.10.4 Creating Sockets

`sys_socket` is the starting point for creating a new socket. The associated code flow diagram is shown in Figure 12-32.

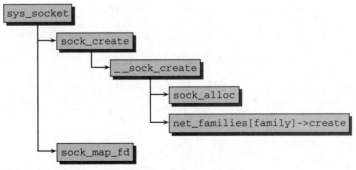

Figure 12-32: Code flow diagram for `sys_socket`.

First, a new socket data structure is created using `sock_create`, which directly calls `__sock_create`. The task of reserving the required memory is delegated to `sock_alloc`, which not only reserves space for an instance of `struct socket`, but also allocates memory for an inode instance directly below. This enables the two objects to be combined as discussed above.

All transport protocols of the kernel are grouped into the array `static struct net_proto_family *net_families[NPROTO]` defined in `net/socket.c`. (ccodesock_register is used to add new entries to the database.) The individual members provide a protocol-specific initialization function.

```
<net.h>
struct net_proto_family {
        int             family;
        int             (*create)(struct socket *sock, int protocol);
        struct module   *owner;
};
```

Table 12-3: Network-Related System Calls for Which `sys_socketcall` Acts as a Multi-plexer

Function	Meaning
sys_socket	Creates a new socket.
sys_bind	Binds an address to a socket.
sys_connect	Connects a socket with a server.
sys_listen	Opens a passive connection to listen on the socket.
sys_accept	Accepts an incoming connection request.
sys_getsockname	Returns the address of the socket.
sys_getpeername	Returns the address of the communication partner.
sys_socketpair	Creates a socket pair that can be used immediately for bidirectional communication (both sockets are on the same system).
sys_send	Sends data via an existing connection.
sys_sendto	Sends data to an explicitly specified destination address (for UDP connections).
sys_recv	Receives data.
sys_recvfrom	Receives data from a datagram socket and returns the source address at the same time.
sys_shutdown	Closes the connection.
sys_setsockopt	Returns information on the socket settings.
sys_getsockopt	Sets socket options.
sys_sendmsg	Sends messages in BSD style.
sys_recvmsg	Receives messages in BSD style.

It is exactly this function (`create`) that is invoked after memory has been reserved for the socket. `inet_create` is used for Internet connections (both TCP and UDP). It creates a new instance of a kernel-internal `sock` socket, initializes it as far as possible, and inserts it in the kernel data structures.

`map_sock_fd` generates a pseudo-file for the socket (the file operations are specified by `socket_ops`). A file descriptor is also allocated so that it can be returned as the result of the system call.

12.10.5 Receiving Data

Data are received using the `recvfrom` and `recv` system calls and the file-related `readv` and `read` functions. Because the code of each of these functions is very similar and merges at an early point, only `sys_recvfrom`, whose code flow diagram is shown in Figure 12-33, is discussed.

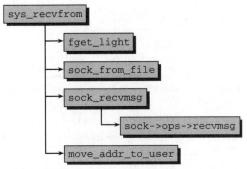

Figure 12-33: Code flow diagram for `sys_recvfrom`.

A file descriptor to identify the desired socket is passed to the system call. Consequently, the first task is to find the relevant `socket`. First, `fget_light` references the descriptor table of the task structure to find the corresponding `file` instance. `sock_from_file` determines the associated inode and ultimately the associated socket by using `SOCKET_I`.

After a few preparations (not discussed here) `sock_recvmsg` invokes the protocol-specific receive routine `sock->ops->recv_msg0`. For example, TCP uses `tcp_recvmsg` to do this. The UDP equivalent is `udp_recvmsg`. The implementation for UDP is not particularly complicated:

❑   If there is at least one packet on the receive queue (implemented by the `receive_queue` element of the `sock` structure), it is removed and returned.

❑   If the receive queue is empty, it is obvious that no data can be passed to the user process. In this case, the process uses `wait_for_packet` to put itself to sleep until data arrive.

   As the `data_ready` function of the `sock` structure is always invoked when new data arrive, the process can be woken at this point.

`move_addr_to_user` copies the data from kernel space to userspace using the `copy_to_user` functions described in Chapter 2.

The implementation for TCP follows a similar pattern but is made a little more complicated by the many details and protocol oddities.

12.10.6 Sending Data

Userspace programs also have several alternative ways of sending data. They can use two network-related system calls (`sendto` and `send`) or the `write` and `writev` functions of the file layer. Because, once again, the code in the kernel merges at a certain point, it is sufficient to examine the implementation of the first of the above calls (in the `sys_sendto` procedure in the kernel sources). The associated code flow diagram is shown in Figure 12-34.[34]

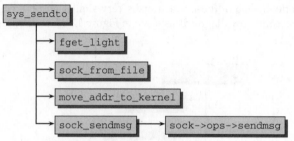

Figure 12-34: Code flow diagram for `sys_sendto`.

`fget_light` and `sock_from_file` find the relevant socket by reference to the file descriptor. The data to be sent are copied from userspace to kernel space using `move_addr_to_kernel` before `sock_sendmsg` invokes the protocol-specific send routine `sock->ops->sendmsg`. This routine generates a packet in the required format and forwards it to the lower layers.

12.11 Networking from within the Kernel

Not only userland applications have the desire and need to communicate with other hosts. The kernel could likewise be required to communicate with other computers — without explicit requests from userland to do so. This is not only useful for oddities like the in-kernel web server that used to be included with a number of releases. Network filesystems like CIFS or NCPFS depend on network communication support from within the kernel.

This, however, does not yet fulfill all communication needs of the kernel. One more piece is missing: communication between kernel components and communication between userland and kernel. The netlink mechanism provides the required framework.

12.11.1 Communication Functions

First, let us turn our attention to the in-kernel networking API. The definitions are nearly identical to the userland case:

---

[34]The sources contain some code that has to deal with the case that __sock_sendmsg can use an asynchronous request. I omit this on purpose in the code flow diagram. If the request is not directly completed in __sock_sendmsg, then wait_on_sync_kiocb is called immediately after __sock_sendmsg, and the synchronous behavior is restored.

<net.h>
```
int kernel_sendmsg(struct socket *sock, struct msghdr *msg,
                   struct kvec *vec, size_t num, size_t len);
int kernel_recvmsg(struct socket *sock, struct msghdr *msg,
                   struct kvec *vec, size_t num,
                   size_t len, int flags);

int kernel_bind(struct socket *sock, struct sockaddr *addr,
                int addrlen);
int kernel_listen(struct socket *sock, int backlog);
int kernel_accept(struct socket *sock, struct socket **newsock,
                  int flags);
int kernel_connect(struct socket *sock, struct sockaddr *addr,
                   int addrlen, int flags);
int kernel_getsockname(struct socket *sock, struct sockaddr *addr,
                       int *addrlen);
int kernel_getpeername(struct socket *sock, struct sockaddr *addr,
                       int *addrlen);
int kernel_getsockopt(struct socket *sock, int level, int optname,
                      char *optval, int *optlen);
int kernel_setsockopt(struct socket *sock, int level, int optname,
                      char *optval, int optlen);
int kernel_sendpage(struct socket *sock, struct page *page, int offset,
                    size_t size, int flags);
int kernel_sock_ioctl(struct socket *sock, int cmd, unsigned long arg);
int kernel_sock_shutdown(struct socket *sock,
                         enum sock_shutdown_cmd how);
```

With the exception of `kernel_sendmsg` and `kernel_recvmsg`, the parameters are more or less identical with the userland API, except that sockets are not specified by socket file descriptors, but directly by a pointer to an instance of `struct socket`. The implementation is simple since the functions work as simple wrapper routines around the pointers stored in the protocol operations `proto_ops` of `struct socket`:

net/socket.c
```
int kernel_connect(struct socket *sock, struct sockaddr *addr, int addrlen,
int flags)
{
        return sock->ops->connect(sock, addr, addrlen, flags);
}
```

A little care is required when the buffer space that takes received data or holds data that must be sent is specified. `kernel_sendmsg` and `kernel_recvmsg` do not access the data region directly via `struct msghdr` as in userland, but employ `struct kvec`. However, the kernel automatically provides a conversion between both representations as `kernel_sendmsg` shows.

net/socket.c
```
int kernel_sendmsg(struct socket *sock, struct msghdr *msg,
struct kvec *vec, size_t num, size_t size)
{
...
        int result;
...
        msg->msg_iov = (struct iovec *)vec;
        msg->msg_iovlen = num;
```

```
        result = sock_sendmsg(sock, msg, size);
...
        return result;
}
```

12.11.2   The Netlink Mechanism

Netlink is a networking-based mechanism that allows for communication within the kernel as well as between kernel and userland. The formal definition can be found in RFC 3549. The idea to use the networking framework to communicate between kernel and userland stems from BSD's networking sockets. Netlink sockets, however, extend the possible uses much further. The mechanism is not only used for networking purposes. By now, one of the most important users is the generic object model, which uses netlink sockets to pass all kinds of status information about what is going on inside the kernel to userland. This includes registration and removal of new devices, special events that have happened on the hardware side, and much more. While netlink used to be compilable as a module in former kernel versions, it is nowadays automatically integrated if the kernel has support for networking. This emphasizes the importance of the mechanism.

There are some alternative methods in the kernel that implement similar functionality — just think of files in procfs or sysfs. However, the netlink mechanism provides some distinct advantages compared to these approaches:

❑   No polling is required on any side. If status information were passed via a file, then the userland side would constantly need to check if any new messages have arrived.

❑   System calls and ioctls that also allow passing information from userland to the kernel are harder to implement than a simple netlink connection. Besides, there is no problem with modules using netlink services, while modules and system calls clearly do not fit together very well.

❑   The kernel can initiate sending information to userland without being requested to do so from there. This is also possible with files, but impossible with system calls or ioctls.

❑   Userspace applications do not need to use anything else than standard sockets to interact with the kernel.

Netlink supports only datagram messages, but provides bidirectional communication. Additionally, not only unicast but also multicast messages are possible. Like any other socket-based mechanism, netlink works asynchronously.

Two manual pages document the netlink mechanism: netlink(3) contains information about in-kernel macros that can be used to manipulate, access, and create netlink datagrams. The manual page netlink(7) contains generic information about netlink sockets and documents the data structures used in this context. Also note that /proc/net/netlink contains some information about the currently active netlink connections.

On the userspace side, two libraries simplify the creation of applications employing netlink sockets:

❑   libnetlink is bundled with the iproute2 packages. The library has specifically been written with routing sockets in mind. Additionally, is does not come as standalone code, but must be extracted from the package if it is to be used separately.

❑ libnl is a standalone library that has not been optimized for a particular use case. Instead, it provides support for all types of netlink connections, including routing sockets.

Data Structures

Specifying Addresses

As for every networking protocol, an address needs to be assigned to a netlink socket. The following variant of struct sockaddr represents netlink addresses:

<netlink.h>
```
struct sockaddr_nl
{
        sa_family_t nl_family; /* AF_NETLINK */
        unsigned short nl_pad; /* zero */
        __u32 nl_pid; /* port ID */
        __u32 nl_groups; /* multicast groups mask */
};
```

To distinguish between different netlink channels used by different parts of the kernel, nl_family is employed. Several different families are specified in <netlink.h>, and the list has especially grown during the development of 2.6. Currently 20 families are defined, and some examples are:

❑ NETLINK_ROUTE represents the initial purpose of netlink sockets, namely, changing routing information.

❑ NETLINK_INET_DIAG allows for monitoring IP sockets; see net/ipv4/inet_diag.c for more details.

❑ NETLINK_XFRM is used to send and receive messages related to IPSec (or, more generally, to any XFRM transformations).

❑ NETLINK_KOBJECT_UEVENT specifies the protocol for kernel to userland messages that originate from the generic object model (the reverse direction, userland to kernel, is not possible for this type of message). The channel provides the basis of the hotplugging mechanism as discussed in Section 7.4.2.

A unique identifier for the socket is provided in nl_pid. While this is always zero for the kernel itself, userspace applications conventionally use their thread group ID. Note that nl_pid explicitly does *not* represent a process ID, but can be any unique value — the thread group ID is just one particularly convenient choice.[35] nl_pid is a unicast address. Each address family can also specify different multicast groups, and nl_groups is a bitmap that denotes to which multicast addresses the socket belongs. If multicast is not supposed to be used, the field is 0. To simplify matters, I consider only unicast transmissions in the following.

Netlink Protocol Family

Recall from Section 12.10.4 that each protocol family needs to register an instance of net_proto_family within the kernel. The structure contains a function pointer that is called when a new socket is created for

---

[35]See the manual page netlink(7) on how to proceed if a userspace process wants to hold more than one netlink socket and thus requires more than one unique identifier.

the protocol family. Netlink uses `netlink_create` for this purpose.[36] The function allocates an instance of `struct sock` that is connected with the socket via `socket->sk`. However, space is not only reserved for `struct sock` but for a larger structure that is (simplified) defined as follows:

net/netlink/af_netlink.c
```
struct netlink_sock {
/* struct sock has to be the first member of netlink_sock */
        struct sock sk;
        u32 pid;
        u32 dst_pid;
...

        void (*netlink_rcv)(struct sk_buff *skb);
...
};
```

In reality, there are many more netlink-specific elements, and the above code is a selection of the most essential ones.

The `sock` instance is directly embedded into `netlink_sock`. Given an instance of `struct sock` for netlink sockets, the associated netlink-specific structure `netlink_socket` can be obtained using the auxiliary function `nlk_sk`. The port IDs of both ends of the connection are kept in `pid` and `dst_pid`. `netlink_rcv` points to a function that is called to receive data.

Message Format

Netlink messages need to obey a certain format as depicted in Figure 12-35.

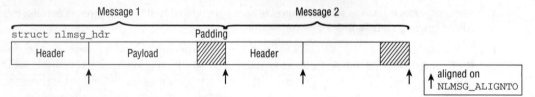

Figure 12-35: Format of a netlink message.

Each message consists of two components: the header and the payload. While the header is required to be represented by `struct nlmsghdr`, the payload can be arbitrary.[37] The required contents of the header are given by the following data structure:

<netlink.h>
```
struct nlmsghdr
{
        __u32 nlmsg_len; /* Length of message including header */
        __u16 nlmsg_type; /* Message content */
        __u16 nlmsg_flags; /* Additional flags */
```

---

[36]The protocol family operations `netlink_family_ops` point to this function. Recall from Section 12.10.4 that the creation function is automatically called when a new socket is created.

[37]The kernel offers the standard data structure `struct nlattr` if netlink is used to transport attributes. This possibility is not discussed in detail, but note that all attribute definitions and a useful set of auxiliary helper functions can be found in `include/net/netlink.h`.

```
            __u32 nlmsg_seq;  /* Sequence number */
            __u32 nlmsg_pid;  /* Sending process port ID */
    };
```

❑ The length of the total message — including header and any required padding — is stored in `nlmsg_len`.

❑ The message type is denoted by `nlmsg_type`. The value is private to the family and not inspected or modified by generic netlink code.

❑ Various flags can be stored in `nlmsg_flags`. All possible values are defined in `<netlink.h>`. For our purposes, mainly two flags are of relevance: `NLM_F_REQUEST` is set if a message contains a request to perform some specific action (as opposed to transferring just some status information), and `NLM_F_ACK` requests that an acknowledgment is sent on receiving the message and successfully processing the request.

❑ `nlmsg_seq` holds a sequence number that induces a temporal relationship amongst a series of messages.

❑ The unique port ID that identifies the sender is stored in `nlmsg_pid`.

Note that the constituents of netlink messages are always aligned to `NLMSG_ALIGNTO` (usually set to 4) byte boundaries as indicated in the figure. Since the size of `struct nlmsghdr` is currently a multiple of `NLMSG_ALIGNTO`, the alignment criterion is automatically fulfilled for the header. Padding might, however, be required behind the payload. To ensure that the padding requirements are fulfilled, the kernel introduces several macros in `<netlink.h>` that can be used to properly compute the boundaries. Since they are well documented in the manual page `netlink(3)`, the information is not repeated here.

The length of a message should fit into a single page because this places only little pressure on memory allocation. However, if pages larger the 8 KiB are used, then the message size should not exceed 8 KiB because userland should not be forced to allocate excessively big buffers to receive netlink messages. The kernel defines the constant `NLMSG_GOODSIZE`, which contains the preferred amount of total space for a message. `NLMSG_DEFAULT_SIZE` specifies how much space is available for the payload without header. When a socket buffer into which a netlink message is constructed is allocated, `NLMSG_GOODSIZE` is a good choice for its size.

Keeping Track of Netlink Connections

The kernel keeps track of all netlink connections as represented by `sock` instances using several hash tables. They are implemented around the global array `nl_table`, which contains pointers to instances of `struct netlink_table`. The actual definition of this structure does not bother us in detail because the hashing method follows a rather straightforward path:

1. Each array element of `nl_table` provides a separate hash for each protocol family member. Recall that each family member is identified by one of the constants defined by `NETLINK_XXX`, where XXX includes `ROUTE` or `KOBJECT_UEVENT`, for instance.

2. The hash chain number is determined using `nl_pid_hashfn` based on the port ID and a (unique) random number associated with the hash chain.[38]

---

[38]Actually, the situation is more complicated because the kernel rehashes the elements on the hash table when there are too many entries, but this extra complexity is ignored here.

`netlink_insert` is used to insert new entries into the hash table, while `netlink_lookup` allows for finding `sock` instances:

net/netlink/af_netlink.c
```
static int netlink_insert(struct sock *sk, struct net *net, u32 pid);
static __inline__ struct sock *netlink_lookup(struct net *net, int protocol,
                                              u32 pid);
```

Note that the hashing data structures are not designed to operate on a per-namespace basis since there is only one global structure for the whole system. Nevertheless, the code is networking-namespace-aware: When a `sock` is looked up, the code ensures that the result lives in the proper namespace. Connections with identical port IDs that originate from different namespaces can exist on the same hash chain simultaneously without problems.

Protocol-Specific Operations

Since userland applications use the standard socket interface to deal with netlink connections, the kernel must provide a set of protocol operations. They are defined as follows:

net/netlink/af_netlink.c
```
static const struct proto_ops netlink_ops = {
        .family = PF_NETLINK,
        .owner = THIS_MODULE,
        .release = netlink_release,
        .bind = netlink_bind,
        .connect = netlink_connect,
        .socketpair = sock_no_socketpair,
        .accept = sock_no_accept,
        .getname = netlink_getname,
        .poll = datagram_poll,
        .ioctl = sock_no_ioctl,
        .listen = sock_no_listen,
        .shutdown = sock_no_shutdown,
        .setsockopt = netlink_setsockopt,
        .getsockopt = netlink_getsockopt,
        .sendmsg = netlink_sendmsg,
        .recvmsg = netlink_recvmsg,
        .mmap = sock_no_mmap,
        .sendpage = sock_no_sendpage,
};
```

Programming Interface

The generic socket implementation provides most of the basic functionality required for netlink. Netlink sockets can be opened both from the kernel and from userland. In the first case, `netlink_kernel_create` is employed, while in the second case, the bind method of `netlink_ops` is triggered via the standard networking paths. For reasons of space, I do not want to discuss the implementation of the userland protocol handlers in detail, but focus on how connections are initialized from the kernel. The function requires various parameters:

net/netlink/af_netlink.c
```
struct sock *
netlink_kernel_create(struct net *net, int unit, unsigned int groups,
```

```
void (*input)(struct sk_buff *skb),
struct mutex *cb_mutex, struct module *module);
```

net denotes the networking namespace, unit specifies the protocol family member, and input is a callback function that is activated when data arrives for the socket.[39] If a NULL pointer is passed for input, the socket will only be able to transport data from kernel to userland, but not vice versa. The tasks performed in netlink_kernel_create are summarized by the code flow diagram in Figure 12-36.

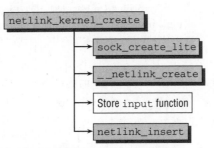

Figure 12-36: Code flow diagram for netlink_kernel_create (multicast handling is omitted).

1. All required data structures need to be allocated, especially an instance of struct socket and struct netlink_sock. sock_create_lite handles the first requirement, and allocating netlink_sock is delegated to the auxiliary function __netlink_create.

2. If an input function is specified, it is stored in netlink_sock->netlink_rcv.

3. The new sock instance is inserted into the netlink hash via netlink_insert.

Consider, for instance, how the generic object model creates a netlink socket for the uevent mechanism (refer to Section 7.4.2 on how to use this connection):

lib/kobject_uevent.c
```
static int __init kobject_uevent_init(void)
{
        uevent_sock = netlink_kernel_create(&init_net, NETLINK_KOBJECT_UEVENT,
                      1, NULL, NULL, THIS_MODULE);

...

        return 0;
}
```

Since uevent messages do not require any input from userland, it is not necessary to specify an input function.

After the socket is created, the kernel can construct sk_buff instances and send them off with either netlink_unicast or netlink_broadcast.

---

[39]There are some more parameters that are not necessary to consider in detail. groups gives the number of multicast groups, but I will not discuss the associated possibilities any further. It is also possible to specify a locking mutex (cb_mutex) that protects a netlink callback, but since I have also omitted to discuss this mechanism, you can likewise ignore this parameter. Usually, a NULL pointer is specified as mutex argument, and the kernel falls back to a default locking solution.

Naturally, things get more involved when bidirectional communication is allowed. Take, for example, the audit subsystem, which can not only send messages to userspace, but also receive some in the inverse direction. First of all, an input function is required when `netlink_kernel_create` is called:

kernel/audit.c
```
audit_sock = netlink_kernel_create(&init_net, NETLINK_AUDIT, 0,
                                   audit_receive, NULL, THIS_MODULE);
```

`audit_receive` is responsible to handle received messages stored in socket buffers. `audit_receive` is just a wrapper that ensures correct locking and dispatches the real work to `audit_receive_skb`. Since all receive functions follow a similar pattern, it is instructive to observe the code of this function:

kernel/audit.c
```
static void audit_receive_skb(struct sk_buff *skb)
{
        int err;
        struct nlmsghdr *nlh;
        u32 rlen;

        while (skb->len >= NLMSG_SPACE(0)) {
                nlh = nlmsg_hdr(skb);
...
                rlen = NLMSG_ALIGN(nlh->nlmsg_len);
...
                if ((err = audit_receive_msg(skb, nlh))) {
                        netlink_ack(skb, nlh, err);
                } else if (nlh->nlmsg_flags & NLM_F_ACK)
                        netlink_ack(skb, nlh, 0);
                skb_pull(skb, rlen);
        }
}
```

Multiple netlink messages can be contained in a single socket buffer, so the kernel needs to iterate over all of them until no more payload is left. This is the purpose of the while loop. The general structure is to process one message, remove the processed data with `skb_pull`,[40] and process the next message. Since `NLMSG_SPACE(0)` specifies the space required for the netlink header, without any payload, the kernel can easily check if more messages wait to be processed by comparing the remaining length of the socket buffer with this quantity.

For each message, the header is extracted with `nlmsg_hdr`, and the total length including padding is computed with `NLMSG_ALIGN`. `audit_receive_msg` is then responsible to analyze the audit-specific contents of the message, which does not concern us any further here. Once the data have been parsed, two alternatives are possible:

1. An error has occurred during parsing. `netlink_ack` is used to send an acknowledgment response that contains the erroneous message and the error code.

2. If the message requested to be acknowledged by setting the `NLM_F_ACK` flag, the kernel sends the desired acknowledgment again by `netlink_ack`. This time the input message is not contained in the reply because the error argument of `netlink_ack` is set to 0.

---

[40]To be precise, the function does not remove the data, but just sets the `data` pointer of the socket buffer accordingly. The effect is, however, identical.

12.12   Summary

Linux is often used to operate network servers, and consequently, its networking implementation is powerful, comprehensive, and complex. This chapter discussed the general layered structure of the networking subsystem that allows for accommodating a large number of different protocols, and provides a rich set of services.

After introducing the idea of sockets that establish the link between networking layer and userland, we have discussed socket buffers, the fundamental in-kernel data structure for representation, and processing of packets obtained and sent via networks. We then discussed how network devices are operated and also explained how NAPI helps to ensure that they reach their full possible speed.

You have then seen how an IP packet travels through the network layer and how the transport layer processes TCP and UDP packets. Ultimately, the packets end up or originate from the application layer, and we have also explored the mechanisms behind this.

The chapter closed with a discussion of how networking can be initiated from within the kernel and how the netlink mechanism allows for installing a high-speed communication link between kernel and userland.

13

System Calls

In the view of user programs, the kernel is a transparent system layer — it is always present but never really noticed. Processes don't know whether the kernel is running or not. Neither do they know which virtual memory contents are currently in RAM or which contents have been swapped out or perhaps not even read in. Nevertheless, processes are engaged in permanent interaction with the kernel to request system resources, access peripherals, communicate with other processes, read in files, and much more. For these purposes, they use standard library routines that, in turn, invoke kernel functions — ultimately, the kernel is responsible for sharing resources and services fairly and, above all, smoothly between requesting processes.

Applications therefore see the kernel as a large collection of routines that perform a wide variety of system functions. The standard library is an intermediate layer to standardize and simplify the management of kernel routines across different architectures and systems.

In the view of the kernel, the situation is, of course, a bit more complicated especially as there are several major differences between user and kernel mode, some of which were discussed in earlier chapters. Of particular note are the different virtual address spaces of the two modes and the different ways of exploiting various processor features. Also of interest is how control is transferred backward and forward between applications and the kernel, and how parameters and return values are passed. This chapter discusses such questions.

As described in previous chapters, *system calls* are used to invoke kernel routines from within user applications in order to exploit the special capabilities of the kernel. We have already examined the implementation of a number of system calls from a wide range of kernel subsystems.

First, let's take a brief look at system programming to distinguish clearly between library routines of the standard library and the corresponding system calls. We then closely examine the kernel sources in order to describe the mechanism for switching from userspace to kernel space. The infrastructure used to implement system calls is described, and special implementation features are discussed.

13.1 Basics of System Programming

Principally, system programming involves work with the standard library that provides a wide range of essential functions for developing applications. No matter what kind of applications they write, programmers have to know the basics of system programming. A simple program such as the classic `hello.c` routine, which displays "Hello, world!" or a similar text on screen, makes indirect use of system routines to output the necessary characters.

Of course, system programming need not always be done in C. There are other programming languages — such as C++, Pascal, Java, or even the dreadful FORTRAN — which also support the more or less direct use of routines from external libraries and are therefore also able to invoke standard library functions. Nevertheless, it is usual to write system programs in C simply because this fits best into the UNIX concept — all UNIX kernels are written in C, and Linux is no exception.

The standard library is not only a collection of interfaces to implement the kernel system calls; it also features many other functions that are implemented fully in userspace. This simplifies the work of programmers, who are spared the effort of constantly reinventing the wheel. And the approximately 100 MiB of code in the GNU C library must be good for something.

Because the general programming language trend is toward higher and higher levels of abstraction, the real meaning of system programming is slowly being eroded. Why bother with system details when successful programs can be built effortlessly with a few mouse clicks? A middle course is required. A short Perl script that scans a text file for a certain string will hardly want to bother with the mechanisms that open and read the text file. In this situation, a pragmatic view that somehow the data will be coaxed out of the file is sufficient. On the other hand, databases with gigabytes or terabytes of data will certainly want to know which underlying operating system mechanisms are used to access their files and raw data so that the database code can be tuned to deliver maximum performance. Supplying a giant matrix in memory with specific values is a classic example of how program performance can be significantly boosted by observing the internal structures of the operating system. The order in which values are supplied is crucial if the matrix data are spread over several memory pages. Unnecessary paging can be avoided and system caches and buffers can be put to best use depending on how the memory management subsystem manages memory.

This chapter discusses techniques that are not (or at least only to a minor extent) abstracted from the functions of the kernel — all the more so as we want to examine the internal structure of the kernel and the architectural principles used, including the interfaces to the outside world.

13.1.1 Tracing System Calls

The following example illustrates how system calls are made using the wrapper routines of the standard library:

```
#include<stdio.h>
#include<fcntl.h>
#include<unistd.h>
#include<malloc.h>

int main() {
  int handle, bytes;
  void* ptr;
```

```
    handle = open("/tmp/test.txt", O_RDONLY);

    ptr = (void*)malloc(150);

    bytes = read(handle, ptr, 150);
    printf("%s", ptr);

    close(handle);
    return 0;
}
```

The sample program opens /tmp/test.txt, reads the first 150 bytes, and writes them to standard output — a very simple version of the standard Unix head command.

How many system calls does the program use? The only ones that are immediately visible are open, read, and close (their implementation is discussed in Chapter 8). However, the print function is also implemented by system calls in the standard library. It would, of course, be possible to find out which system calls are used by reading the source code of the standard library, but this would be tedious. A simpler option is to use the strace tool, which logs all system calls issued by an application and makes this information available to programmers — this tool is indispensable when debugging programs. Naturally, the kernel must provide special support for logging system calls as discussed in Section 13.3.3 (not surprisingly, support is also provided in the form of a system call (ptrace); our only interest is in its output).

The following strace writes a list of all issued system calls to the file test.syscalls[1]:

```
wolfgang@meitner> strace -o log.txt ./shead
```

The contents of log.txt are more voluminous than you might have expected:

```
execve("./shead", ["./shead"], [/* 27 vars */]) = 0
uname(sys="Linux", node="jupiter", ...) = 0
brk(0)                                    = 0x8049750
old_mmap(NULL, 4096, PROT_READ|PROT_WRITE, ..., -1, 0) = 0x40017000
open("/etc/ld.so.preload", O_RDONLY)      = -1 ENOENT (No such file or directory)
open("/etc/ld.so.cache", O_RDONLY)        = 3
fstat64(3, st_mode=S_IFREG|0644, st_size=85268, ...) = 0
old_mmap(NULL, 85268, PROT_READ, MAP_PRIVATE, 3, 0) = 0x40018000
close(3)                                  = 0
open("/lib/i686/libc.so.6", O_RDONLY)     = 3
read(3, "\177ELF\1\1\1\0\0\0\0\0\0\0\0\0\3\0\3\0\1\0\0\0\200\302"..., 1024) = 1024
fstat64(3, st_mode=S_IFREG|0755, st_size=5634864, ...) = 0
old_mmap(NULL, 1242920, PROT_READ|PROT_EXEC, MAP_PRIVATE, 3, 0) = 0x4002d000
mprotect(0x40153000, 38696, PROT_NONE)    = 0
old_mmap(0x40153000, 24576, PROT_READ|PROT_WRITE, ..., 3, 0x125000) = 0x40153000
old_mmap(0x40159000, 14120, PROT_READ|PROT_WRITE, ..., -1, 0) = 0x40159000
close(3)                                  = 0
munmap(0x40018000, 85268)                 = 0
getpid()                                  = 10604
open("/tmp/test.txt", O_RDONLY)           = 3
brk(0)                                    = 0x8049750
```

---

[1] strace has other options to specify exactly which data are saved; they are documented in the strace(1) manual page.

```
brk(0x8049800)                          = 0x8049800
brk(0x804a000)                          = 0x804a000
read(3, "A black cat crossing your path s"..., 150) = 109
fstat64(1, st_mode=S_IFCHR|0620, st_rdev=makedev(136, 1), ...) = 0
mmap2(NULL, 4096, PROT_READ|PROT_WRITE, MAP_PRIVATE|MAP_ANONYMOUS, -1, 0) = 0x40018000
ioctl(1, TCGETS, B38400 opost isig icanon echo ...) = 0
write(1, "A black cat crossing your path s"..., 77) = 77
write(1, "                -- Groucho Marx\n", 32) = 32
munmap(0x40018000, 4096)                = 0
_exit(0)                                = ?
```

The trace log shows that the application makes a large number of system calls not explicitly listed in the source code. Consequently, the output of `strace` is not easy to read. For this reason, all lines with a direct equivalent in the C sources of the example are in italics. All other entries are generated by code added automatically at program compilation time.

The additional system calls are generated by code that is needed as a framework for launching and running the application — for example, the C standard library is dynamically mapped into the process memory area. Other calls — `old_mmap` and `unmap` — are responsible for managing the dynamic memory used by the application.

The three system calls used directly — `open`, `read`, and `close` — are translated into calls of the corresponding kernel functions.[2] Two further routines of the standard library make internal use of system calls with different names to achieve the desired effect:

❏ `malloc` is the standard function for reserving memory in the process heap area. As mentioned in Chapter 3, the `malloc` variant of the GNU library features an additional memory management facility to make effective use of the memory space allocated by the kernel.

Internally, `malloc` executes the `brk` system call whose implementation is described in Chapter 3. The system call log shows that `malloc` executes the call three times as a result of its internal algorithms — but each time with different arguments.

❏ `printf` first processes the passed arguments — in this case, a dynamic string — and displays the results with the `write` system call.

Using the `strace` tool has a further advantage — the source code of the application being traced need not be present to learn about its internal structure and how it functions.

Our small sample program shows clearly that there are strong dependencies between the application and the kernel, as indicated by the repeated use of system calls. Even scientific programs that spend most of their time number-crunching and rarely invoke kernel functions cannot manage without system calls. On the other hand, interactive applications such as `emacs` and `mozilla` make frequent use of system calls. The size of the log file for `emacs` is approximately 170 KiB for program launch alone (i.e., up to the end of program initialization).

---

[2]The GNU standard library also includes a general routine that allows system calls to be executed by reference to their numbers if no wrapper implementation is available.

13.1.2 Supported Standards

System calls are of special significance in all UNIX look-alikes. Their scope and speed and their efficient implementation play a major role in system performance. System calls are implemented extremely efficiently in Linux, as demonstrated in Section 13.3. Of equal importance are the versatility and choice of available routines to make the lives of programmers (of applications and of standard library functions) easier and to facilitate program portability between the various UNIX derivatives on source text level. In the more than 25-year history of UNIX, this has contributed to the emergence of standards and de facto standards governing the uniformity of interfaces between the various systems.

The POSIX standard (whose acronym — *Portable Operating System Interface for* UNIX — reveals its purpose) has emerged as the dominant standard. Linux and the C standard library also make every effort to comply with POSIX, which is why it is worthy of brief discussion here. Since publication of the first documents at the end of the 1980s, the standard has expanded drastically in scope (the current version fills four volumes[3]) and is now — in the opinion of many programmers — overlong and too complex.

The Linux kernel is largely compatible with the POSIX-1003.1 standard. Naturally, new developments in the standard take some time before they filter through into kernel code.

In addition to POSIX, there are other standards that are not based on the work of committees but are rooted in the development of UNIX and its look-alikes. In the history of UNIX, two major lines of development have produced two independent and autonomous systems — System V (which derives directly from the original sources of AT&T) and BSD (Berkeley Software Distribution, developed at the University of California and now strongly represented in the marketplace under the names of NetBSD, FreeBSD, and OpenBSD and the commercial offshoots, BSDI and MacOS X).

Linux features system calls from all three of the above sources — in a separate implementation, of course. The code of competing systems is not used for legal and licensing reasons alone. For example, the three well-known system calls listed below originate from the three different camps:

❏ `flock` locks a file to prevent parallel access by several processes and to ensure file consistency. This call is prescribed by the POSIX standard.

❏ BSD UNIX provides the `truncate` call to shorten a file by a specified number of bytes; Linux also implements this function under the same name.

❏ `sysfs` gathers information on the filesystems known to the kernel and was introduced in System V Release 4. Linux has also adopted this system call. However, the Linux developers might not entirely agree with the System V designers about the true value of the call — at least, the source code comment says `Whee.. Weird sysv syscall`.

Nowadays, the information is obtained much more easily by reading `/proc/filesystems`.

Some system calls are required by all three standards. For example, `time`, `gettimeofday` and `settimeofday` exist in identical form in System V, POSIX, and 4.3BSD — and consequently in the Linux kernel.

---

[3]The standard is available in electronic form at `www.opengroup.org/onlinepubs/007904975/`.

Similarly, some system calls were developed specifically for Linux and either don't exist at all in other look-alikes or have a different name. One example is the `vm86` system call, which is of fundamental importance in implementing the DOS emulator on IA-32 processors. More general calls, such as `nanosleep` to suspend process execution for very short periods of time, are also part of the Linux-specific repertoire.

In some cases, two system calls are implemented to resolve the same problem in different ways. Prime examples are the `poll` and `select` system calls; the first was introduced in System V, the latter in 4.3BSD. Ultimately, both perform the same function.

In conclusion, it's worth noting that — in spite of the name — simply implementing the POSIX standard does not produce a full UNIX system. POSIX is nothing more than a collection of *interfaces* whose concrete implementations are not mandated and need not necessarily be included in the kernel. Some operating systems therefore fully implement the POSIX standard in a normal library to facilitate UNIX application porting despite their non-UNIX design.[4]

13.1.3 Restarting System Calls

An interesting problem arises when system calls clash with signals. How are priorities assigned when it is imperative to send a signal to a process while a system call is being executed? Should the signal wait until the system call terminates, or should the call be interrupted so that the signal can be delivered as quickly as possible? The first option obviously causes fewer problems and is the simpler solution. Unfortunately, it only functions properly if *all* system calls terminate quickly and don't make the process wait for too long (as mentioned in Chapter 5, signals are always delivered when the process returns to user mode after a system call). This is not always the case. System calls not only need a certain period of time to execute, but, in the worst case, they also go to sleep (when, e.g., no data are available to `read`). This seriously delays delivery of any signals that may have occurred in the meantime. Consequently, such situations must be prevented at all costs.

If an executing system call is interrupted, which value does the kernel return to the application? In normal circumstances, there are only two situations: Either the call is successful or it fails — in which case an error code is returned so that the user process can determine the cause of the error and react appropriately. In the event of an interruption, a third situation arises: The application must be informed that the system call *would* have terminated successfully, *had* it not been interrupted by a signal during execution. In such situations, the `-EINTR` constant is used under Linux (and under other System V derivatives).

The downside of this procedure is immediately apparent. Although it is simple to implement, it forces programmers of userspace applications to explicitly check the return value of all interruptible system calls for `-EINTR` and, where this value is true, to restart the call repeatedly until it is no longer interrupted by a signal. System calls restarted in this way are called *restartable system calls*, and the technique itself is known as *restarting*.

This behavior was introduced for the first time in System V UNIX. However, it is not the only way of combining the rapid delivery of new signals and the interruption of system calls, as the approach adopted in the BSD world confirms. Let us examine what happens in the BSD kernel when a system call is interrupted by a signal.

The BSD kernel interrupts execution of the system call and switches to signal execution in user mode. When this happens, the call does *not* issue a return value but is restarted automatically by

---

[4]More recent Windows versions include a library of this kind.

the kernel once the signal handler has terminated. Because this behavior is transparent to the user application and also dispenses with repeated implementation of checks for the -EINTR return value and call restarting, this alternative is much more popular with programmers than the System V approach.

Linux supports the BSD variant by means of the SA_RESTART flag, which can be specified on a per-signal basis when handler routines are installed (see Chapter 5). The mechanism proposed by System V is used by default because the BSD mechanism also occasionally gives rise to difficulties, as the following example taken from [ME02], page 229, shows.

```c
#include <signal.h>
#include <stdio.h>
#include <unistd.h>

volatile int signaled = 0;

void handler (int signum) {
  printf("signaled called\n");
  signaled = 1;
}

int main() {
  char ch;
  struct sigaction sigact;
  sigact.sa_handler = handler;
  sigact.sa_flags = SA_RESTART;
  sigaction(SIGINT, &sigact, NULL);

  while (read(STDIN_FILENO, &ch, 1) != 1 && !signaled);
}
```

This short C program waits in a while loop until the user enters a character via standard input or until the program is interrupted by the SIGINT signal (which can be sent using kill -INT or by pressing CTRL-C). Let us examine the code flow. If the user hits a normal key that does not cause SIGINT to be sent, read yields a positive return code, namely, the number of characters read.

The argument of the while loop must return a logically false value to terminate execution. This happens if one of the two logical queries linked by && (and) is false — which is the case when

❑   A single key was pressed; read then returns 1 and the test to check that the return value is not equal to 1 returns a logically false value.

❑   The signaled variable is set to 1 because the negation of the variable (!signaled) also returns a logically false value.

These conditions simply mean that the program waits either for keyboard input or the arrival of the SIGINT signal in order to terminate.

To apply System V behavior for the code as implemented by default under Linux, it is necessary to suppress setting of the SA_RESTART flag; in other words, the line sigact.sa_flags = SA_RESTART must be deleted or commented out. Once this has been done, the program runs as described and can be terminated either by pressing a key or sending SIGINT.

The situation is more interesting if read is interrupted by the SIGINT signal and BSD behavior is activated by means of SA_RESTART, as in the sample program. In this case, the signal handler is invoked, signaled is set to 1, and a message is output to indicate that SIGINT was received — but the program is not terminated. Why? After running the handler, the BSD mechanism restarts the read call and again waits for entry of a character. The !signaled condition of the while loop does not apply and is not evaluated. The program can therefore no longer be terminated by sending the SIGNIT signal, although the code suggests that this is so.

13.2 Available System Calls

Before going into the technical details of system call implementation by the kernel (and by the userspace library), it is useful to take a brief look at the actual functions made available by the kernel in the form of system calls.

Each system call is identified by means of a symbolic constant whose platform-*dependent* definition is specified in <asm-*arch*/unistd.h>. Since not all system calls are supported on all architectures (some combinations are meaningless), the number of available calls varies from platform to platform — roughly speaking, there are always upward of 200 calls. As a result of changes to the kernel implementation of system calls over time, some calls are now superfluous, and their numbers are no longer used — the SPARC port (on 32-bit processors) boasts a large number of extinct calls that give rise to "gaps" in the list of calls.

It is simpler for programmers to group system calls into functional categories as they are not interested in their individual numbers — they are concerned only with the symbolic names and the meaning of the calls. The following *short* list — which makes no claim to be complete — gives an overview of the various categories and their most important system calls.

Process Management Processes are at the center of the system, so it's not surprising that a large number of system calls are devoted to process management. The functions provided by the calls range from querying simple information to starting new processes:

❑　fork and vfork split an existing process into two new processes as described in Chapter 2. clone is an enhanced version of fork that supports, among other things, the generation of threads.

❑　exit ends a process and frees its resources.

❑　A whole host of system calls exist to query (and set) process properties such as PID, UID, and so on.; most of these calls simply read or modify a field in the task structure. The following can be read: PID, GID, PPID, SID, UID, EUID, PGID, EGID, and PGRP. The following can be set: UID, GID, REUID, REGID, SID, SUID, and FSGID.

System calls are named in accordance with a logical scheme that uses designations such as setgid, setuid, and geteuid.

❑　personality defines the execution environment of an application and is used, for instance, in the implementation of binary emulations.

❑　ptrace enables system call tracing and is the platform on which the above strace tool builds.

❑ nice sets the priority of normal processes by assigning a number between −20 and 19 in descending order of importance. Only root processes (or processes with the CAP_SYS_NICE permission) are allowed to specify negative values.

❑ setrlimit is used to set certain resource limits, for example, CPU time or the maximum permitted number of child processes. getrlimit queries the current limits (i.e., maximum permitted values), and getrusage queries current resource usage to check whether the process is still within the defined resource limits.

Time Operations Time operations are critical, not only to query and set the current system time, but also to give processes the opportunity to perform time-based operations, as described in Chapter 15:

❑ adjtimex reads and sets time-based kernel variables to control kernel time behavior.

❑ alarm and setitimer set up alarms and interval timers to defer actions to a later time. getitimer reads settings.

❑ gettimeofday and settimeofday get and set the current system time, respectively. Unlike times, they also take account of the current time zone and daylight saving time.

❑ sleep and nanosleep suspend process execution for a defined interval; nanosleep defines high-precision intervals.

❑ time returns the number of seconds since midnight on January 1, 1970 (this date is the classic time base for UNIX systems). stime sets this value and therefore changes the current system date.

Signal Handling Signals are the simplest (and oldest) way of exchanging limited information between processes and of facilitating interprocess communication. Linux supports not only classic signals common to all UNIX look-alikes but also real-time signals in line with the POSIX standard. Chapter 5 deals with the implementation of the signal mechanism.

❑ signal installs signal handler functions. sigaction is a modern, enhanced version that supports additional options and provides greater flexibility.

❑ sigpending checks whether signals are pending for the process but are currently blocked.

❑ sigsuspend places the process on the wait queue until a specific signal (from a set of signals) arrives.

❑ setmask enables signal blocking, while getmask returns a list of all currently blocked signals.

❑ kill is used to send any signals to a process.

❑ The same system calls are available to handle real-time signals. However, their function names are prefixed with rt_. For example, rt_sigaction installs a real-time signal handler, and rt_sigsuspend puts the process in a wait state until a specific signal (from a set of signals) arrives.

In contrast to classic signals, 64 different real-time signals can be handled on all architectures — even on 32-bit CPUs. Additional information can be associated with real-time signals, and this makes the work of (application) programmers a little easier.

Scheduling Scheduling-related system calls could be grouped into the process management category because all such calls logically relate to system tasks. However, they merit a category of their own due simply to the sheer number of manipulation options provided by Linux to parameterize process behavior.

❑ setpriority and getpriority set and get the priority of a process and are therefore key system calls for scheduling purposes.

❑ Linux is noted not only for supporting different process priorities, but also for providing a wide variety of scheduling classes to suit the specific time behavior and time requirements of applications. sched_setscheduler and sched_getscheduler set and query scheduling classes. sched_setparam and sched_getparam set and query additional scheduling parameters of processes (currently, only the parameter for real-time priority is used).

❑ sched_yield voluntarily relinquishes control even when CPU time is still available to the process.

Modules System calls are also used to add and remove modules to and from the kernel, as described in Chapter 7.

❑ init_module adds a new module.

❑ delete_module removes a module from the kernel.

Filesystem All system calls relating to the filesystem apply to the routines of the VFS layer discussed in Chapter 8. From there, the individual calls are forwarded to the filesystem implementations that usually access the block layer. System calls of this kind are very costly in terms of resources and execution time.

❑ Some system calls are used as a direct basis for userspace utilities of the same name that create and modify the directory structure: chdir, mkdir, rmdir, rename, symlink, getcwd, chroot, umask, and mknod.

❑ File and directory attributes can be modified using chown and chmod.

❑ The following utilities for processing file contents are implemented in the standard library and have the same names as the system calls: open, close, read and readv, write and writev, truncate and llseek.

❑ readdir and getdents read directory structures.

❑ link, symlink, and unlink create and delete links (or files if they are the last element in a hard link); readlink reads the contents of a link.

❑ mount and umount are used to attach and detach filesystems.

❑ poll and select are used to wait for some event.

❑ execve loads a new process in place of an old process. It starts new programs when used in conjunction with fork.

Memory Management Under normal circumstances, user applications rarely or never come into contact with memory management system calls because this area is completely shielded from the standard library — by the malloc, balloc, and calloc functions in the case of C. Implementation is usually programming language-specific because each language has different dynamic memory management needs and often provides features like garbage collection that require sophisticated allocation of the memory available to the kernel.

❑ In terms of dynamic memory management, the most important call is brk, which modifies the size of the process data segment. Programs that invoke malloc or similar functions (almost all nontrivial code) make frequent use of this system call.

❑ `mmap`, `mmap2`, `munmap`, and `mremap` perform mapping, unmapping, and remapping operations, while `mprotect` and `madvise` control access to and give advice about specific regions of virtual memory.

mmap and `mmap2` differ slightly by their parameters; refer to the manual pages for more details. The GNU C library uses `mmap2` by default; `mmap` is just a userland wrapper function by now.

Depending on the `malloc` implementation, it can also be that `mmap` or `mmap2` is used internally. This works because *anonymous mappings* allow installing mappings that are not backed by a file. This approach allows for achieving more flexibility than by using `brk`.

❑ `swapon` and `swapoff` enable and disable (additional) swap space on external storage devices.

Interprocess Communication and Network Functions Because "IPC and networks" are complex issues, it would be easy to assume that a rich selection of system calls is available. As Chapters 12 and 5 show, however, the opposite is true. Only two system calls are provided to handle all possible tasks. However, a very large number of parameters is involved. The C standard library spreads them over many different functions with just a few parameters so that they are easier for programmers to handle. Ultimately, the functions are always based on the two system calls:

❑ `socketcall` deals with network questions and is used to implement socket abstraction. It manages connections and protocols of all kinds and implements a total of 17 different functions differentiated by means of constants such as `SYS_ACCEPT`, `SYS_SENDTO`, and so on. The arguments themselves must be passed as a pointer that, depending on function type, points to a userspace structure holding the required data.

❑ `ipc` is the counterpart to `socketcall` and is used for process connections local to the computer and not for connections established via networks. Because this system call need implement "only" 11 different functions, it uses a fixed number of arguments — five in all — to transfer data from userspace to kernel space.

System Information and Settings It is often necessary to query information on the running kernel and its configuration and on the system configuration. Similarly, kernel parameters need to be set and information must be saved to system log files. The kernel provides three further system calls to perform such tasks:

❑ `syslog` writes messages to the system logs and permits the assignment of different priorities (depending on message priority, userspace tools send the messages either to a permanent log file or directly to the console to inform users of critical situations).

❑ `sysinfo` returns information on the state of the system, particularly statistics on memory usage (RAM, buffer, swap space).

❑ `sysctl` is used to "fine-tune" kernel parameters. The kernel now supports an immense number of dynamically configurable options that can be read and modified using the `proc` filesystem, as described in Chapter 10.

System Security and Capabilities The traditional UNIX security model — based on users, groups, and an "omnipotent" root user — is not flexible enough for modern needs. This has led to the introduction of the capabilities system, which enables non-root processes to be furnished with additional privileges and capabilities according to a fine-grained scheme.

In addition, the *Linux security modules* subsystem (LSM) provides a general interface to support modules whose functions are invoked at various hooks in the kernel to perform security checks:

❑ `capset` and `capget` are responsible for setting and querying process capabilities.

❑ `security` is a system call multiplexer for implementing LSM.

13.3 Implementation of System Calls

In the implementation of system calls, not only the kernel source code that provides the required functions is relevant but also the *way* in which the functions are invoked. Functions are not called in the same way as normal C functions because the boundary between user and kernel mode is crossed. This raises various problems that are handled by platform-specific assembly language code. This code establishes a processor-independent state as quickly as possible to enable system calls to be implemented independently of the underlying architecture. How parameters are passed between userspace and kernel space must also be considered.

13.3.1 Structure of System Calls

Kernel code for implementing system calls is divided into two very different parts. The actual task to be performed by the system call is implemented as a C routine that is virtually no different from the remaining kernel code. The mechanism for calling the routine is packed with platform-specific features and must take numerous details into consideration — so that ultimately implementation in assembly language code is a must.

Implementation of Handler Functions

Let us first take a close look at what's behind C implementation of the actual handler functions. These functions are spread across the kernel because they are embedded in code sections to which they are most closely related in terms of their purpose. For example, all file-related system calls reside in the `fs/` kernel subdirectory because they interact directly with the virtual filesystem. Likewise, all memory management calls reside in the files of the `mm/` subdirectory.

The handler functions for implementing system calls share several formal features:

❑ The name of each function is prefixed with `sys_` to uniquely identify the function as a system call — or to be more accurate, as a handler function for a system call. Generally, it is not necessary to distinguish between handler function and system call. In the sections below, I do so only where necessary.

❑ All handler functions accept a maximum of five parameters; these are specified in a parameter list as in normal C functions (how parameters are supplied with values differs slightly from the classic approach, as you will see shortly).

❑ All system calls are executed in kernel mode. Consequently, the restrictions discussed in Chapter 2 apply, primarily that direct access to user mode memory is not permitted. Recall that `copy_from_user`, `copy_to_user`, or other functions from this family must ensure that the desired memory region is available to the kernel before doing the actual read/write operation.

Once the kernel has transferred control to the handler routine, it returns to completely neutral code that is not dependent on a particular CPU or architecture. However, there are exceptions — for various reasons, a small number of handler functions are implemented separately for each platform. When results are returned, the handler function need take no special action; a simple `return` followed by a return value is sufficient. Switching between kernel and user mode is performed by platform-specific kernel code with which the handler does not come into contact. Figure 13-1 illustrates the chronological sequence.

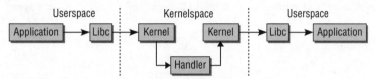

Figure 13-1: Chronological sequence of a system call.

The above approach greatly simplifies the work of programmers because handler functions are implemented in practically the same way as normal kernel code. Some system calls are so simple that they can be implemented by a single line of C code. For example, the `getuid` system call to return the UID of the current process is implemented as follows:

kernel/timer.c
```
asmlinkage long sys_getuid(void)
{
        /* Only we change this so SMP safe */
        return current->uid;
}
```

`current` is a pointer to the current instance of `task_struct` and is set automatically by the kernel. The above code returns the `uid` element (current user ID) of `task_struct`. It couldn't be simpler!

Of course, there are much more complicated system calls, some of which were discussed in preceding chapters. Implementation of the handler function itself is always short and compact. It is usual to transfer control to a more general kernel auxiliary function as soon as possible, as, for example, in the case of `read`.

fs/read_write.c
```
asmlinkage ssize_t sys_read(unsigned int fd, char __user * buf, size_t count)
{
        struct file *file;
        ssize_t ret = -EBADF;
        int fput_needed;

        file = fget_light(fd, &fput_needed);
        if (file) {
                loff_t pos = file_pos_read(file);
                ret = vfs_read(file, buf, count, &pos);
                file_pos_write(file, pos);
                fput_light(file, fput_needed);
        }

        return ret;
}
```

Here, the bulk of the work is done by `vfs_read`, as described in Chapter 8.

A third "type" of system call acts as a multiplexer. Multiplexers use constants to delegate system calls to functions that perform very different tasks. A prime example is socketcall (discussed in Chapter 12), which groups together all network-related calls.

net/socket.c
```
asmlinkage long sys_socketcall(int call, unsigned long __user *args)
{
        unsigned long a[6];
        unsigned long a0,a1;
        int err;
...
        switch(call)
        {
                case SYS_SOCKET:
                        err = sys_socket(a0,a1,a[2]);
                        break;
                case SYS_BIND:
                        err = sys_bind(a0,(struct sockaddr __user *)a1, a[2]);
                        break;
                case SYS_CONNECT:
                        err = sys_connect(a0, (struct sockaddr __user *)a1, a[2]);
                        break;
                case SYS_LISTEN:
                        err = sys_listen(a0,a1);
                        break;
...

                case SYS_RECVMSG:
                        err = sys_recvmsg(a0, (struct msghdr __user *) a1, a[2]);
                        break;
                default:
                        err = -EINVAL;
                        break;
        }
        return err;
}
```

Formally, only one void pointer is passed because the number of system call arguments varies according to the multiplexing constant. The first task is therefore to determine the required number of arguments and to fill the individual elements of the a[] array (this involves manipulating pointers and arrays and is not discussed here). The call parameter is then referenced to decide which kernel function will be responsible for further processing.

Regardless of their complexity, all handler functions have one thing in common. Each function declaration includes the additional (asmlinkage) qualifier, which is not a standard element of C syntax. asmlinkage is an assembler macro defined in <linkage.h>. What is its purpose? For most platforms, the answer is very simple — it does nothing at all!

However, the macro is used in conjunction with the GCC enhancement (__attribute__) discussed in Appendix C on IA-32 and IA-64 systems only in order to inform the compiler of the special calling conventions for the function (examined in the next section).

Dispatching and Parameter Passing

System calls are uniquely identified by a number assigned by the kernel. This is done for practical reasons that become clear when system calls are activated. All calls are handled by a *single* central piece of code that uses the number to dispatch a specific function by reference to a static table. The parameters passed are also handled by the central code so that parameter passing is implemented independently of the actual system call.

Switching from user to kernel mode — and therefore to dispatching and parameter passing — is implemented in assembly language code to cater for many platform-specific features. Owing to the very large number of architectures supported, every detail cannot be covered, and our description is therefore restricted to the widespread IA-32 architectures. The implementation approach is much the same on other processors, even though assembler details may differ.

To permit switching between user and kernel mode, the user process must first draw attention to itself by means of a special machine instruction; this requires the assistance of the C standard library. The kernel must also provide a routine that satisfies the switch request and looks after the technical details. This routine cannot be implemented in userspace because commands are needed that normal applications are not permitted to execute.

Parameter Passing

Different platforms use different assembler methods to execute system calls.[5] System call parameters are passed directly in registers on all platforms — which handler function parameter is held in which register is precisely defined. A further register is needed to define the system call number used during subsequent dispatching to find the matching handler function.

The following overview shows the methods used by a few popular architectures to make system calls:

❑   On IA-32 systems, the assembly language instruction **int $0x80** raises software interrupt 128. This is a *call gate* to which a specific function is assigned to continue system call processing. The system call number is passed in register eax, while parameters are passed in registers ebx, ecx, edx, esi, and edi.[6]

On more modern processors of the IA-32 series (Pentium II and higher), two assembly language instructions (sysenter and sysexit) are used to enter and exit kernel mode quickly. The way in which parameters are passed and returned is the same, but switching between privilege levels is faster.

To enable sysenter calls to be made faster without losing downward compatibility with older processors, the kernel maps a memory page into the top end of address space (at 0x0xffffe000). Depending on processor type, the system call code on this page includes either int 0x80 or sysenter.

---

[5]The details are easy to find in the sources of the GNU standard library by referring to the filenamed sysdeps/unix/sysv/linux/*arch*/syscall.S. The assembly language code required for the particular platform can be found under the syscall label; this code provides a general interface for invoking system calls for the rest of the library.

[6]In addition to the 0x80 call gate, kernel implementation on IA-32 processors features two other ways of entering kernel mode and executing system calls — the lcall7 and lcall27 call gates. These are used to perform binary emulation for BSD and Solaris because these systems make system calls in native mode. They differ only slightly from the standard Linux method and offer little in the way of new insight — which is why I do not bother to discuss them here.

Calling the code stored there (with `call 0xffffe000`) allows the standard library to automatically select the method that matches the processor used.

❑ Alpha processors provide a privileged system mode (PAL, *privileged architecture level*) in which various system kernel routines can be stored. The kernel employs this mechanism by including in the PAL code a function that must be activated in order to execute system calls. `call_pal PAL_callsys` transfers control flow to the desired routine. `v0` is used to pass the system call number, and the five possible arguments are held in `a0` to `a4` (note that register naming is more systematic in recent architectures than in earlier architectures such as IA-32 ...).

❑ PowerPC processors feature an elegant assembly language instruction called `sc` (system call). This is used specifically to implement system calls. Register `r3` holds the system call number, while parameters are held in registers `r4` to `r8` inclusive.

❑ The AMD64 architecture also has its own assembly language instruction with the revealing name of `syscall` to implement system calls. The system call number is held in the `raw` register, parameters in `rdi`, `rsi`, `rdx`, `r10`, `r8`, and `r9`.

Once the application program has switched to kernel mode with the help of the standard library, the kernel is faced with the task of finding the matching handler function for the system call and supplying it with the passed parameters. A table named `sys_call_table`, which holds a set of function pointers to handler routines, is available for this purpose on all (!) platforms. Because the table is generated with assembly language instructions in the data segment of the kernel, its contents differ from platform to platform. The principle, however, is always the same: by reference to the system call number, the kernel finds the appropriate position in the table at which a pointer points to the desired handler function.

System Call Table

Let us take a look at the `sys_call_table` of an Sparc64 system as defined in `arch/sparc/kernel/systlbs.S` (System call tables for other systems can be found in a file often called `entry.S` in the corresponding directory for the processor type.)

arch/sparc64/kernel/systbls.S
```
sys_call_table64:
sys_call_table:
/*0*/ .word sys_restart_syscall, sparc_exit, sys_fork, sys_read, sys_write
/*5*/ .word sys_open, sys_close, sys_wait4, sys_creat, sys_link
/*10*/ .word sys_unlink, sys_nis_syscall, sys_chdir, sys_chown, sys_mknod
/*15*/ .word sys_chmod, sys_lchown, sparc_brk, sys_perfctr, sys_lseek
/*20*/ .word sys_getpid, sys_capget, sys_capset, sys_setuid, sys_getuid
/*25*/ .word sys_vmsplice, sys_ptrace, sys_alarm, sys_sigaltstack, sys_nis_syscall
/*30*/ .word sys_utime, sys_nis_syscall, sys_nis_syscall, sys_access, sys_nice
       .word sys_nis_syscall, sys_sync, sys_kill, sys_newstat, sys_sendfile64
/*40*/ .word sys_newlstat, sys_dup, sys_pipe, sys_times, sys_nis_syscall
       .word sys_umount, sys_setgid, sys_getgid, sys_signal, sys_geteuid
/*50*/ .word sys_getegid, sys_acct, sys_memory_ordering, sys_nis_syscall, sys_ioctl
       .word sys_reboot, sys_nis_syscall, sys_symlink, sys_readlink, sys_execve
/*60*/ .word sys_umask, sys_chroot, sys_newfstat, sys_fstat64, sys_getpagesize

...
/*280*/ .word sys_tee, sys_add_key, sys_request_key, sys_keyctl, sys_openat
        .word sys_mkdirat, sys_mknodat, sys_fchownat, sys_futimesat, sys_fstatat64
/*290*/ .word sys_unlinkat, sys_renameat, sys_linkat, sys_symlinkat, sys_readlinkat
        .word sys_fchmodat, sys_faccessat, sys_pselect6, sys_ppoll, sys_unshare
```

```
/*300*/ .word sys_set_robust_list, sys_get_robust_list, sys_migrate_pages, sys_mbind,
            sys_get_mempolicy
        .word sys_set_mempolicy, sys_kexec_load, sys_move_pages, sys_getcpu, sys_epoll_pwait
/*310*/ .word sys_utimensat, sys_signalfd, sys_timerfd, sys_eventfd, sys_fallocate
```

The table definition is similar on IA-32 processors.

arch/x86/kernel/syscall_table_32.S

```
ENTRY(sys_call_table)
        .long sys_restart_syscall     /* 0 - old "setup()" system call, used for restarting */
        .long sys_exit
        .long sys_fork
        .long sys_read
        .long sys_write
        .long sys_open          /* 5 */
        .long sys_close
...
        .long sys_utimensat /* 320 */
        .long sys_signalfd
        .long sys_timerfd
        .long sys_eventfd
        .long sys_fallocate
```

The purpose of the `.long` statements is to align the table entries in memory.

The tables defined in this way have the properties of a C array and can therefore be processed using pointer arithmetic. `sys_call_table` is the base pointer and points to the start of the array, that is, to the zero entry in C terms. If a userspace program invokes the `open` system call, the number passed is 5. The dispatcher routine adds this number to the `sys_call_table` base and arrives at the fifth entry that holds the address of `sys_open` — this is the processor-independent handler function. Once the parameter values still held in registers have been copied onto the stack, the kernel calls the handler routine and switches to the processor-independent part of system call handling.

> Because the kernel mode and user mode use two different stacks, as described in Chapter 3, system call parameters cannot be passed on the stack as would normally be the case. Switching between the stacks is performed either in architecture-specific assembly language code that is called when kernel mode is entered, or is carried out automatically by the processor when the protection level is switched from user to kernel mode.

Return to User Mode

Each system call must inform the user application whether its routine was executed and with which result. It does this by means of its return code. From the perspective of the application, a normal variable is read using C programming means. However, the kernel, in conjunction with `libc`, must expend a little more effort to make things just as simple for the user process.

Meaning of Return Values

Generally, the following applies for system call return values. Negative values indicate an error, and positive values (and 0) denote successful termination.

Of course, neither programs nor the kernel itself operates with raw numbers but with symbolic constants defined with the help of the pre-processor in `include/asm-generic/errno-base.h` and `include/asm-generic/errno.h`.[7] The file named `<errno.h>` contains several additional error codes, but these are kernel-specific and are never visible to the user application. Error codes up to and including 511 are reserved for general errors; kernel-specific constants use the values above 512.

Because (not surprisingly) there are a very large number of potential errors, only a few constants are listed below:

<asm-generic/errno-base.h>
```
#define EPERM          1       /* Operation not permitted */
#define ENOENT         2       /* No such file or directory */
#define ESRCH          3       /* No such process */
#define EINTR          4       /* Interrupted system call */
#define EIO            5       /* I/O error */
#define ENXIO          6       /* No such device or address */
#define E2BIG          7       /* Argument list too long */
#define ENOEXEC        8       /* Exec format error */
#define EBADF          9       /* Bad file number */
#define ECHILD         10      /* No child processes */
...
#define EMLINK         31      /* Too many links */
#define EPIPE          32      /* Broken pipe */
#define EDOM           33      /* Math argument out of domain of func */
#define ERANGE         34      /* Math result not representable */
```

The "classic" errors that occur when working with UNIX system calls are listed in `errno-base.h`. On the other hand, `errno.h` contains more unusual error codes whose meanings are not immediately obvious even to seasoned programmers. Examples such as `EOPNOTSUPP` — which stands for "Operation not supported on transport endpoint" — and `ELNRNG` — which means "Link number out of range" — are not what might be classified as common knowledge. Some more examples:

<asm-generic/errno.h>
```
#define EDEADLK        35      /* Resource deadlock would occur */
#define ENAMETOOLONG   36      /* File name too long */
#define ENOLCK         37      /* No record locks available */
#define ENOSYS         38      /* Function not implemented */
...
#define ENOKEY         126     /* Required key not available */
#define EKEYEXPIRED    127     /* Key has expired */
#define EKEYREVOKED    128     /* Key has been revoked */
#define EKEYREJECTED   129     /* Key was rejected by service */

/* for robust mutexes */
#define EOWNERDEAD     130     /* Owner died */
#define ENOTRECOVERABLE 131    /* State not recoverable */
```

Although I just mentioned that error codes are always returned with a negative number, all codes shown here are positive. It is a kernel convention that the numbers are defined as positive but are returned as

---

[7]SPARC, Alpha, PA-RISC, and MIPS architectures define their own versions of these files because they use different numeric error codes from the remaining Linux ports. This is because of the fact that binary specifications for different platforms do not always use the same magic constants.

a negative value by adding a sign. For example, if an operation were not permitted, a handler routine would execute return -ENOPERM to yield the error code −1.

Let us examine the open system call with a particular focus on its return values (sys_open implementation is discussed in Chapter 8). What can go wrong when a file is opened? Not much, you would think. But the kernel finds nine ways of causing problems. For the individual sources of error, see the standard library documentation (and, of course, the kernel sources). The most frequent system call error codes are as follows:

❏ EACCES indicates that a file cannot be processed in the desired access mode — for example, a file cannot be opened for write access if the write bit is not set in its mode string.

❏ EEXIST is returned if an attempt is made to create a file that already exists.

❏ ENOENT means that the desired file does not exist, and the flag to allow files that do not exist to be created is not specified.

A positive number greater than zero is returned if the system call terminates successfully. As discussed in Chapter 8, this is a file handle that is used to represent the file in all subsequent operations as well as in the internal data structures of the kernel.

Linux uses the long data type to transfer results from kernel space to userspace; this is either 32 or 64 bits wide depending on processor type. One bit is used as the sign bit.[8] This causes no problems for most system calls, such as open. The positive values returned are usually so small that they fit into the range provided by long.

Unfortunately, the situation is more complicated when returning large numbers that occupy the full unsigned long space. This is the case with malloc and long if memory addresses are allocated at the top of virtual memory space. The kernel then interprets the returned pointer as a *negative* number because it overruns the positive range of signed long; this would be reported as an error even though the system call terminated successfully. How can the kernel prevent such mishaps?

As noted above, the symbolic constants for error codes that reach userspace extend only up to 511 — in other words, error codes returned in the range from −1 to −511. Consequently, all *lower* error codes are excluded and are interpreted correctly — as very high return values of successful system calls.

All that now needs to be done to successfully terminate the system call is to switch back from kernel mode to user mode. The result value is returned using a mechanism that functions similarly in the opposite direction. The C function, in which the system call handler is implemented, uses return to place the return code on the kernel stack. This value is copied into a specific processor register (eax on IA-32 systems, a3 on Alpha systems, etc.), where it is processed by the standard library and transferred to user applications.

13.3.2 Access to Userspace

Even though the kernel does its best to keep kernel space and userspace separate, there are situations in which kernel code has to access the virtual memory of user applications. Of course, this only makes sense when the kernel is performing a synchronous action initiated by a user application — write and read access by arbitrary processes not only serves no purpose, but may also produce risky results in the code currently executing.

---

[8]Of course, 2's complement notation is used to prevent errors where there are two zeros with different signs. See http://en .wikipedia.org/wiki/Two%27s_complement for more information about this format.

The processing of system calls is, of course, a classic situation in which the kernel is busy with the synchronous execution of a task assigned to it by an application. There are two reasons why the kernel has to access the address space of user applications:

❑ If a system call requires more than six different arguments, they can be passed only with the help of C structures that reside in process memory space. A pointer to the structures is passed to the system call by means of registers.

❑ Larger amounts of data generated as a side effect of a system call cannot be passed to the user process using the normal return mechanism. Instead, the data must be exchanged in defined memory areas. These must, of course, be located in userspace so that the user application is able to access them.

When the kernel accesses its own memory area, it can always be sure that there is a mapping between the virtual address and a physical memory page. The situation in userspace is different, as described in Chapter 3. Here, pages might be swapped out or not even be allocated.

The kernel may not therefore simply de-reference userspace pointers, but also must employ specific functions to ensure that the desired area resides in RAM. To make sure that the kernel complies with this convention, userspace pointers are labeled with the __user attribute to support automated checking by C check tools.[9]

Chapter 3 discusses the functions used to copy data between userspace and kernel space. In most cases, these will be copy_to_user and copy_from_user, but more variants are available.

13.3.3   System Call Tracing

The strace tool developed to trace the system calls of processes using the ptrace system call is described in Section 13.1.1.

Implementation of the sys_ptrace handler routine is architecture-specific and is defined in arch/arch/kernel/ptrace.c. Fortunately, there are only minor differences between the code of the individual versions. I therefore provide a generalized description of how the routine works without going into architecture-specific details.

Before examining the flow of the system call in detail, it should be noted that this call is needed because ptrace — essentially a tool for reading and modifying values in process address space — cannot be used directly to trace system calls. Only by extracting the desired information at the right places can trace processes draw conclusions on which system calls have been made. Even debuggers such as gdb are totally reliant on ptrace for their implementation. ptrace offers more options than are really needed to simply trace system calls.

ptrace requires four arguments as the definition in the kernel sources shows[10]:

<syscalls.h>
```
asmlinkage long sys_ptrace(long request, long pid, long addr, long data);
```

---

[9]Linus Torvalds himself designed the sparse tool to find direct userspace pointer de-referencings in the kernel.

[10]<syscalls.h> contains the prototypes for all architecture-independent system calls whose arguments are identical on all architectures.

❑   `pid` identifies the target process. The process identifier is interpreted with respect to the namespace of the caller. Even though the way in which `strace` is handled suggests that process tracing must be enabled right from the start, this is not true. The tracer program must "attach" itself to the target process by means of `ptrace` — and this can be done while the process is already running (not only when the process starts).

     `strace` is responsible for *attaching* to the process, usually immediately after the target program is started with `fork` and `exec`.

❑   `addr` and `data` pass a memory address and additional information to the kernel. Their meanings differ according to the operation selected.

❑   With the help of symbolic constants, `request` selects an operation to be performed by `ptrace`. A list of all possible values is given on the manual page `ptrace(2)` and in `<ptrace.h>` in the kernel sources. The available options are as follows:

     ❑   `PTRACE_ATTACH` issues a request to attach to a process and initiates tracing. `PTRACE_DETACH` detaches from the process and terminates tracing. A traced process is always terminated when a signal is pending. The options below enable `ptrace` to be stopped during a system call or after a single assembly language instruction.

         When a traced process is stopped, the tracer program is informed by means of a `SIGCHLD` signal that waiting can take place using the `wait` function discussed in Chapter 2.

         When tracing is installed, the `SIGSTOP` signal is sent to the traced process — this causes the tracer process to be interrupted for the first time. This is essential when system calls are traced, as demonstrated below by means of an example.

     ❑   `PEEKTEXT`, `PEEKDATA`, and `PEEKUSR` read data from the process address space. `PEEKUSR` reads the normal CPU registers and any other debug registers used[11] (of course, only the contents of a single register selected on the basis of its identifier are read — not the contents of the entire register set). `PEEKTEXT` and `PEEKDATA` read any words from the text or data segment of the process.

     ❑   `POKETEXT`, `POKEDATA`, and `PEEKUSR` write values to the three specified areas of the monitored process and therefore manipulate the process address space contents; this can be very important when debugging programs interactively.

         Because `PTRACE_POKEUSR` manipulates the debug registers of the CPU, this option supports the use of advanced debugging techniques; for example, monitoring of events that halt program execution at a particular point when certain conditions are satisfied.

     ❑   `PTRACE_SETREGS` and `PTRACE_GETREGS` set and read values in the privileged register set of the CPU.

     ❑   `PTRACE_SETFPREGS` and `PTRACE_GETFPREGS` set and read registers used for floating-point computations. These operations are also very useful when testing and debugging applications interactively.

     ❑   System call tracing is based on `PTRACE_SYSCALL`. If `ptrace` is activated with this option, the kernel starts process execution until a system call is invoked. Once the traced process has been stopped, `wait` informs the tracer process, which then analyzes the process address

---

[11]Because a process other than the traced process is running when the `ptrace` system call is invoked, the physical registers of the CPU naturally hold the values of the tracer program and not those of the traced process. This is why the data of the `pt_regs` instance discussed in Chapter 14 are used; these data are copied into the register set when the process is activated after a task switch. Manipulating the data of this structure is tantamount to manipulating the registers themselves.

space using the above `ptrace` operations to gather relevant information on the system call. The traced process is stopped for a second time after completion of the system call to allow the tracer process to check whether the call was successful.

Because the system call mechanism differs according to platform, trace programs such as `strace` must implement the reading of data separately for each architecture; this is a tedious task that quickly renders source code for portable programs unreadable (the `strace` sources are overburdened with pre-processor conditionals and are no pleasure to read).

❑ `PTRACE_SINGLESTEP` places the processor in single-step mode during execution of the traced process. In this mode, the tracer process is able to access the traced process after *each* assembly language instruction. Again, this is a very popular application debugging technique, particularly when attempting to track down compiler errors or other such subtleties.

Implementation of the single-step function is strongly dependent on the CPU used — after all, the kernel is operating on a machine-oriented level at this point. Nevertheless, a uniform interface is available to the tracer process on all platforms. After execution of the assembler function, a `SIGCHLD` signal is sent to the tracer, which gathers detailed information on the process state using further `ptrace` options. This cycle is constantly repeated — the next assembler instruction is executed after invoking `ptrace` with the `PTRACE_SINGLESTEP` argument, the process is put to sleep, the tracer is informed accordingly by means of `SIGCHLD`, and so on.

❑ `PTRACE_KILL` closes the traced process by sending a `KILL` signal.

❑ `PTRACE_TRACEME` starts tracing the *current* process. The parent of the current process automatically assumes the role of tracer and must be prepared to receive tracing information from its child.

❑ `PTRACE_CONT` resumes execution of a traced process without specifying special conditions for stopping the process — the traced application next stops when it receives a signal.

System Call Tracing

The following short sample program illustrates the use of `ptrace`. `ptrace` attaches itself to a process and checks system call usage; as such, it is a minimal replacement for `strace`.

```
/* Simple replacement for strace(1) */

#include<stdio.h>
#include<stdlib.h>
#include<signal.h>
#include<unistd.h>
#include<sys/ptrace.h>
#include<sys/wait.h>
#include<asm/ptrace.h>      /* for ORIG_EAX */

static long pid;

int upeek(int pid, long off, long *res) {
  long val;

  val = ptrace(PTRACE_PEEKUSER, pid, off, 0);
```

```
    if (val == -1) {
      return -1;
    }

    *res = val;
    return 0;
}

void trace_syscall() {
  long res;

  res = ptrace(PTRACE_SYSCALL, pid, (char*) 1, 0);
  if (res < 0) {
    printf("Failed to execute until next syscall: %d\n", res);
  }
}

void sigchld_handler (int signum) {
  long scno;
  int res;

  /* Find out the system call (system-dependent)...*/
  if (upeek(pid, 4*ORIG_EAX, &scno) < 0) {
    return;
  }

  /* ... and output the information */
  if (scno != 0) {
    printf("System call: %u\n", scno);
  }

  /* Activate tracing until the next system call */
  trace_syscall();
}

int main(int argc, char** argv) {
  int res;

  /* Check the number of arguments */
  if (argc != 2) {
    printf("Usage: ptrace <pid>\n");
    exit(-1);
  }

  /* Read the desired pid from the command-line parameters */
  pid = strtol(argv[1], NULL, 10);
  if (pid <= 0) {
    printf("No valid pid specified\n");
    exit(-1);
  } else {
    printf("Tracing requested for PID %u\n", pid);
  }

  /* Install handler for SIGCHLD */
```

```
struct sigaction sigact;
sigact.sa_handler = sigchld_handler;
sigaction(SIGCHLD, &sigact, NULL);

/* Attach to the desired process */
res = ptrace(PTRACE_ATTACH, pid, 0, 0);
if (res < 0) {
  printf("Failed to attach: %d\n", res);
  exit(-1);
} else {
  printf("Attached to %u\n", pid);
}

for (;;) {
  wait(&res);
  if (res == 0) {
    exit(1);
  }
}
}
```

The program structure is roughly as follows:

❑ The PID of the traced program is read from the command line, and the usual checks are carried out.

❑ A handler for the CHLD signal is installed because the kernel sends this signal to the tracer process each time the traced program is interrupted.

❑ The tracer process attaches itself to the target application by means of the ptrace request PTRACE_ATTACH.

❑ The main part of the tracer program consists of a simple endless loop that repeatedly invokes the wait command to wait for the arrival of new CHLD signals.

This structure is not dependent on a particular processor type and can be used for all systems supported by Linux. However, the method by which the number of the system call invoked is determined is very architecture-specific. The method shown works only on IA-32 systems because they keep the number at a specific offset in the saved register set. This offset is held in the ORIG_EAX constant defined in asm/ptrace.h. Its value can be read using PTRACE_PEEKUSER and must be multiplied by the factor of 4 because the registers on this architecture are 4 bytes wide.

Of course, the above would be implemented differently on other architectures. For details, see the system call-relevant code in the kernel sources and the sources of the standard strace tool.

Our main goal is to illustrate how ptrace calls are used to check monitored processes. Once process tracing has been started by means of PTRACE_ATTACH, the bulk of the work is delegated to the handler function of the CHLD signal implemented in sigchld_handler. This function is responsible for peforming the following tasks:

❑ Helping to find the number of the system call invoked using platform-dependent means.

The information found is output if the result is a system call number not equal to 0. Testing for 0 is necessary to ensure that only requests for system calls are logged but not the signals sent to the traced process.

❏   Helping to resume program flow. The kernel must, of course, be informed that execution will be stopped at the next system call; this is done using the `ptrace` request `PTRACE_SYSCALL`.

Program flow is obvious once the ball is rolling. A system call requested by the traced process triggers the `ptrace` mechanism in the kernel, which sends a `CHLD` signal to the tracer process. The handler of the tracer process reads the required information — the number of the system call — and outputs it, again using the `ptrace` mechanism. Execution of the traced process is resumed and interrupted again when a system call is invoked.

But how is the ball set rolling? Somehow or other the handler function must be invoked for the first time in order to log system call tracing. As noted above, the kernel also sends `SIGCHLD` signals to the tracer process when a signal is sent to the *traced* process — in doing so, it invokes the same handler function activated when a system call occurs. The fact that the kernel automatically sends a `STOP` signal to the traced process when tracing is initiated ensures that the handler function is invoked when tracing starts — even if the process receives no other signals. This sets the ball — that is, system call tracing — rolling.

Kernel-Side Implementation

As expected, the handler function for the `ptrace` system call is called `sys_ptrace`. The architecture-independent part of the implementation that is used for all except a handful of architectures can be found in `kernel/ptrace.c`. The architecture-dependent part, that is, the function `arch_ptrace`, is located in `arch/`*arch*`/kernel/ptrace.c`. Figure 13-2 shows the code flow diagram.

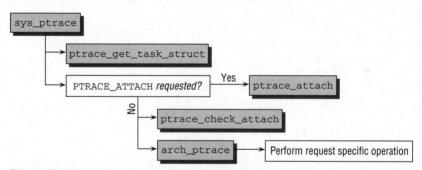

Figure 13-2: Code flow diagram for `sys_ptrace`.

The `ptrace` system call is dominated by its `request` parameter — this is immediately apparent in the structure of its code. Preliminary work is carried out, primarily to determine the `task_struct` instance of the passed PID using `ptrace_get_task_struct`. This basically uses `find_task_by_vpid` to find the required instance of `task_struct`, but also prevents tracing of the `init` process — the ptrace operation is aborted if a value of 1 is passed for `pid`.

Starting Tracing

Process task structures include several `ptrace`-specific elements that are needed below.

<sched.h>
```
struct task_struct {
...
```

```
        unsigned int ptrace;
...
        /* ptrace_list/ptrace_children forms the list of my children
         * that were stolen by a ptracer. */
        struct list_head ptrace_children;
        struct list_head ptrace_list;
...
        struct task_struct *real_parent; /* real parent process (when being debugged) */
...
};
```

If PTRACE_ATTACH is set, ptrace_attach establishes a link between the tracer process and the target process. When this is done,

❑ The ptrace element of the target process is set to PT_TRACED.

❑ The tracer process becomes the parent process of the target process (the real parent process is held in real_parent).

❑ The traced process is added to the ptrace_children list of the tracer using the ptrace_list task structure element.

❑ A STOP signal is sent to the traced process.

If a different action from PTRACE_ATTACH was requested, ptrace_check_attach first checks whether a tracer is attached to the process, and the code splits depending on the particular ptrace operation. This is handled in arch_ptrace; the function is defined by every architecture and cannot be provided by the generic code. However, this is not entirely true: Some requests can, in fact, be handled by architecture-independent code, and they are handled in ptrace_request (from kernel/ptrace.c) called by arch_ptrace. Only very simple requests are processed by this function. For example, PTRACE_DETACH to detach a tracer from a process is one of them.

Usually, a large case structure that deals separately with each case (depending on the request parameter) is employed for this purpose. I discuss only some important cases: PTRACE_ATTACH and PTRACE_DETACH, PTRACE_SYSCALL, PTRACE_CONT as well as PTRACE_PEEKDATA and PTRACE_POKEDATA. The implementation of the remaining requests follows a similar pattern.

All further tracing actions performed by the kernel are present in the signal handler code discussed in Chapter 5. When a signal is delivered, the kernel checks whether the PT_TRACED flag is set in the ptrace field of task_struct. If it is, the state of the process is set to TASK_STOPPED (in get_signal_to_deliver in kernel/signal.c) in order to interrupt execution. notify_parent with the CHLD signal is then used to inform the tracer process. (The tracer process is woken up if it happens to be sleeping.) The tracer process then performs the desired checks on the target process as specified by the remaining ptrace options.

Implementation of **PTRACE_CONT** and **_SYSCALL**

PTRACE_CONT resumes a traced process after it was suspended owing to delivery of a signal. The kernel-side implementation of this function is strongly associated with PTRACE_SYSCALL (which suspends a traced process not only after the arrival of a signal but also before and after system calls are invoked).

Both are discussed in the same section because their code differs only slightly:

❑ When PTRACE_SYSCALL is used, the TIF_SYSCALL_TRACE flag is set in the task structure of the monitored process.

❑ When PTRACE_CONT is used, the flag is removed using clear_tsk_thread_flag.

Both flag routines set the corresponding bit in the flags field of the thread_info instance of the process.

Once the flag has been set or removed, the kernel need only wake the traced process using wake_up_process before resuming its normal work.

What are the effects of the TIF_SYSCALL_TRACE flag? Because invoking system calls is very hardware-related, the effects of the flag extend into the assembly language source code of entry.s. If the flag is set, the C function do_syscall_trace is invoked on system call completion — but only on IA-32, PPC, and PPC64 systems. Other architectures use other mechanisms not described here.

Nevertheless, the effects of the flag are the same on all supported platforms. Before and after the execution of a system call by the monitored process, the process state is set to TASK_STOPPED, and the tracer is informed accordingly by means of a CHLD signal. Required information can then be extracted from the contents of registers or specific memory areas.

Stopping Tracing

Tracing is disabled using PTRACE_DETACH, which causes the central ptrace handler to delegate this task to the ptrace_detach function in kernel/ptrace.c. The task itself comprises the following steps:

1. The architecture-specific hook ptrace_disable allows for performing any required low-level operations to stop tracing.

2. The flag TIF_SYSCALL_TRACE is removed from the child's thread flags.

3. The ptrace element of the task_struct instance is reset to 0, and the target process is removed from the ptrace_children list of the tracer process.

4. The parent process is reset to the original task by overwriting task_struct->parent with the value stored in real_parent.

The traced process is woken up with wake_up_process so that it can resume its work.

Reading and Modifying Target Process Data

PTRACE_PEEKDATA reads information from the data segment.[12] The ptrace call requires two parameters for the request:

❑ addr specifies the address to be read in the data segment.

❑ data accepts the associated result.

---

[12]Because memory management does not differentiate between text and data segments — both begin at different addresses but are accessed in the same way — the information provided applies equally for PTRACE_PEEKTEXT.

The read operation is delegated to the `access_process_vm` function that is implemented in `mm/memory.c`. (It used to be located in `kernel/ptrace.c`, but the new location is clearly a better choice.)

This function uses `get_user_pages` to find the page matching the desired address in userspace memory. A temporary memory location in the kernel is used to buffer the required data. After some clean-up work, control is returned to the dispatcher.

Because the required data are still in kernel space, `put_user` must be used to copy the result to the userspace location specified by the `addr` parameter.

The traced process is manipulated in a similar way by `PTRACE_POKEDATA`. (`PTRACE_POKETEXT` is used in exactly the same way because again there is no difference between the two segments of virtual address space.) `access_process_vm` finds the memory page with the required address. `access_process_vm` is directly responsible for replacing existing data with the new values passed in the system call.[13]

13.4 Summary

One possible way to view the kernel is as a comprehensive library of things it can do for userland applications. System calls are the interface between an application and this library. By invoking a system call, an application can request a service that the kernel then fulfills. This chapter first introduced you to the basics of system programming, which led to how system calls are implemented within the kernel. In contrast to regular functions, invoking system calls requires more effort because a switch between the kernel and user modes of the CPU must be performed. Since the kernel lives in a different portion of the virtual address space from userland, you have also seen that some care is required when the kernel transfers data from or to an application. Finally, you have seen how system call tracing allows for tracking the behavior of programs and serves as an indispensable debugging tool in userspace.

System calls are a synchronous mechanism to change from user into kernel mode. The next chapter introduces you to interrupts that require asynchronously changing between the modes.

---

[13]A Boolean parameter can be selected to specify whether data are read only (PTRACE_POKETEXT or PTRACE_POKEDATA) or are to be replaced with a new value *en passant*.

14

Kernel Activities

Chapter 13 demonstrated that system execution time can be split into two large and different parts: kernel mode and user mode. In this chapter, we investigate the various kernel activities and reach the conclusion that a finer-grained differentiation is required.

System calls are not the only way of switching between user and system mode. As is evident from the preceding chapters, all platforms supported by Linux employ the concept of *interrupts* to introduce periodic interruptions for a variety of reasons. Two types of interrupt are distinguished:

❑ **Hardware Interrupts** — Are produced automatically by the system and connected peripherals. They support more efficient implementation of device drivers, but are also needed by the processor itself to draw attention to exceptions or errors that require interaction with the kernel code.

❑ **SoftIRQs** — Are used to effectively implement deferred activities in the kernel itself.

In contrast to other parts of the kernel, the code for handling interrupts and system call-specific segments contains very strong interweaving between assembly language and C code to resolve several subtle problems that C could not reasonably handle on its own. This is not a Linux-specific problem. Regardless of their individual approach, most operating system developers try to hide the low-level handling of such points as deeply as possible in the kernel sources to make them invisible to the remaining code. Because of technical circumstances, this is not always possible, but the interrupt handling layer has evolved over time to a state where high-level code and low-level hardware interaction are separated as well and cleanly as possible.

Frequently, the kernel needs mechanisms to defer activities until a certain time in the future or to place them in a queue for later processing when time is available. You have come across a number of uses for such mechanisms in earlier chapters. In this section, we take a closer look at their implementation.

14.1 Interrupts

Until kernel 2.4, the only commonality in the implementation of interrupts on the diverse platforms supported by the Linux kernel used to be that they exist at all — but that's where the similarity came to an end. Lots of code (and lots of duplicated functionality) was spread across architecture-specific components. The situation was improved considerably during the development of kernel 2.6 because a generic framework for interrupts and IRQs was introduced. Individual platforms are now only responsible to interact with the hardware on the lowest levels. Everything else is provided by generic code.

Let's start our discussion by introducing the most common types of system interrupts as our starting point before focusing on how they function, what they do, and what problems they cause.

14.1.1 Interrupt Types

Generally, interrupt types can be grouped into two categories:

❑ **Synchronous Interrupts** and **Exceptions** — Are produced by the CPU itself and are directed at the program currently executing. Exceptions may be triggered for a variety of reasons: because of a programming error that occurred at run time (a classical example is division by zero), or because — as the name suggests — an exceptional situation or an anomalous condition has arisen and the processor needs "external" help to deal with it.

In the first case, the kernel must inform the application that an exception has arisen. It can use, for example, the signaling mechanism described in Chapter 5. This gives the application an opportunity to correct the error, issue an appropriate error message, or simply terminate.

An anomalous condition may not necessarily be caused directly by the process but must be repaired with the help of the kernel. A possible example of this is a page fault that always occurs when a process attempts to access a page of virtual address space that is not held in RAM. As discussed in Chapter 4, the kernel must then interact with the CPU to ensure that the desired data are fetched into RAM. The process can then resume at the point at which the exception occurred. It does not even notice that there has been a page error because the kernel recovered the situation automatically.

❑ **Asynchronous interrupts** — Are the classical interrupt type generated by peripheral devices and occur at arbitrary times. Unlike synchronous interrupts, asynchronous interrupts are not associated with a particular process. They can happen at any time, regardless of the activities the system is currently performing.[1]

Network cards report the arrival of new packages by issuing an associated interrupt. Because the data reach the system at an arbitrary moment in time, it is highly likely that some process or other that has nothing to do with the data is currently executing. So as not to disadvantage this process, the kernel must ensure that the interrupt is processed as quickly as possible by "buffering" data so that CPU time can be returned to the process. This is why the kernel needs mechanisms to defer activities; these are also discussed in this chapter.

What are the common features of the two types of interrupt? If the CPU is not already in kernel mode, it initiates a switch from user to kernel mode. There it executes a special routine called an *interrupt service*

---

[1]Because, as you will learn shortly, interrupts can be disabled, this statement is not totally correct. The system can at least influence when interrupts do *not* occur.

routine (*ISR* for short) or an *interrupt handler*. The purpose of this routine is to handle exception conditions or anomalous situations — after all, the specific goal of an interrupt is to draw the attention of the kernel to such changes.

A simple distinction between synchronous and asynchronous interrupts is not sufficient to fully describe the features of these two types of interrupt. A further aspect needs to be considered. Many interrupts can be disabled, but a few cannot. The latter category includes, for example, interrupts issued as a result of hardware faults or other system-critical events.

Wherever possible, the kernel tries to avoid disabling interrupts because they are obviously detrimental to system performance. However, there are occasions when it is *essential* to disable them to prevent the kernel itself from getting into serious trouble. As you will see when we take a closer look at interrupt handlers, major problems may arise in the kernel if a second interrupt occurs *while* a first interrupt is being handled. If the kernel is interrupted while processing what is already critical code, the synchronization problems discussed in Chapter 5 may arise. In the worst case scenario, this can provoke a kernel deadlock that renders the entire system unusable.

If the kernel allows itself too much time to process an ISR when interrupts are disabled, it can (and will) happen that interrupts are lost although they are essential for correct system operation. The kernel resolves this problem by enabling interrupt handlers to be divided into two parts — a performance-critical *top half* that executes with disabled interrupts, and a less important *bottom half* used later to perform all less important actions. Earlier kernel versions included a mechanism of the same name for deferring activities to a later time. However, this has been replaced by more efficient mechanisms, discussed below.

Each interrupt has a number. If interrupt number n is assigned to a network card and $m \neq n$ is assigned to the SCSI controller, the kernel is able to differentiate between the two devices and call the corresponding ISR to perform a device-specific action. Of course, the same principle also applies for exceptions where different numbers designate different exceptions. Unfortunately, owing to specific (and usually historical) design "features"(the IA-32 architecture is a particular case in point), the situation is not always as simple as just described. Because only very few numbers are available for hardware interrupts, they must be shared by several devices. On IA-32 processors, the maximum number is usually 15, not a particularly generous figure — especially considering that some interrupts are already permanently assigned to standard system components (keyboard, timers, etc.), thus restricting still further the number available for other peripheral devices.

This procedure is known as *interrupt sharing*.[2] However, both hardware support and kernel support are needed to use this technique because it is necessary to identify the device from which an interrupt originates. This is covered in greater detail in this chapter.

14.1.2 Hardware IRQs

The term *interrupt* has been used carelessly in the past to denote interrupts issued by the CPU as well as by external hardware. Savvy readers will certainly have noticed that this is not quite correct. Interrupts cannot be raised directly by processor-external peripherals but must be requested with the help of a standard component known as an *interrupt controller* that is present in every system.

---

[2]Naturally, bus systems with a sophisticated *overall design* are able to dispense with this option. They provide so many interrupts for hardware devices that there is no need for sharing.

From the peripheral devices (or their slots) electronic lines lead to the component used to send interrupt requests to the interrupt controller. After performing various electro-technical tasks, which are of no further interest to us here, the controller forwards such requests to the interrupt inputs of the CPU. Because peripheral devices cannot directly force interrupts but must request them via the above component, such requests are known more correctly as IRQs, or *interrupt requests*.

Because, in terms of software, the difference between IRQs and interrupts is not all that great, the two terms are often used interchangeably. This is not a problem as long as it is clear what is meant.

However, one important point concerning the numbering of IRQs and interrupts should not be overlooked as it has an impact on software. Most CPUs make only a small extract from the whole range of available interrupt numbers available for processing hardware interrupts. This range is usually in the middle of the number sequence; for example, IA-32 CPUs provide a total of 16 numbers from 32 to 47.

As any reader who has configured an I/O card on an IA-32 system or has studied the contents of `/proc/interrupts` knows, IRQ numbering of expansion cards starts at 0 and finishes at 15, provided the classical interrupt controller 8256A is used. This means that there are also 16 different options but with different numerical values. As well as being responsible for the electrical handling of the IRQ signals, the interrupt controller also performs a "conversion" between IRQ number and interrupt number; with the IA-32 system, this is the equivalent of simply adding 32. If a device issues IRQ 9, the CPU produces interrupt 41; this must be taken into account when installing interrupt handlers. Other architectures use other mappings between interrupt and IRQ numbers, but I will not deal with these in detail.

14.1.3 Processing Interrupts

Once the CPU has been informed of an interrupt, it delegates further handling to a software routine that corrects the fault, provides special handling, or informs a user process of an external event. Because each interrupt and each exception has a unique number, the kernel uses an array containing pointers to handler functions. The associated interrupt number is found by referring to the array position, as shown in Figure 14-1.

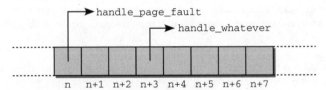

Figure 14-1: Managing interrupt handlers.

Entry and Exit Tasks

As Figure 14-2 shows, interrupt handling is divided into three parts. First, a suitable environment in which the handler function can execute must be set up; then the handler itself is called, and finally the system is restored (in the view of the current program) to its exact state *prior* to the interrupt. The parts that precede and follow invocation of the interrupt handler are known as the *entry* and *exit path*.

The entry and exit tasks are also responsible for ensuring that the processor switches from user mode to kernel mode. A key task of the entry path is to make the switch from the user mode stack to the kernel mode stack. However, this alone is not sufficient. Because the kernel also uses CPU resources to execute its code, the entry path must save the current register status of the user application in order to restore it upon termination of interrupt activities. This is the same mechanism used for context switching during scheduling. When kernel mode is entered, only part of the complete register set is saved. The kernel does not use all available registers. Because, for example, no floating point operations are used in kernel code (only integer calculations are made), there is no need to save the floating point registers.[3] Their value does not change when kernel code is executed. The platform-specific data structure pt_regs that lists all registers modified in kernel mode is defined to take account of the differences between the various CPUs (Section 14.1.7 takes a closer look at this). Low-level routines coded in assembly language are responsible for filling the structure.

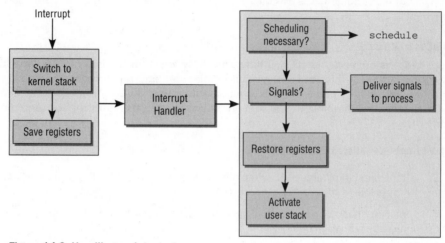

Figure 14-2: Handling an interrupt.

In the exit path the kernel checks whether

❑   the scheduler should select a new process to replace the old process.

❑   there are signals that must be delivered to the process.

Only when these two questions have been answered can the kernel devote itself to completing its regular tasks after returning from an interrupt; that is, restoring the register set, switching to the user mode stack, switching to an appropriate processor mode for user applications, or switching to a different protection ring.[4]

Because interaction between C and assembly language code is required, particular care must be taken to correctly design data exchange between the assembly language level and C level. The corresponding code is located in arch/*arch*/kernel/entry.S and makes thorough use of the specific characteristics of the individual processors. For this reason, the contents of this file should be modified as seldom as possible — and then only with great care.

---

[3]Some architectures (e.g., IA-64) do not adhere to this rule but use a few registers from the floating comma set and save them each time kernel mode is entered. The bulk of the floating point registers remain "untouched" by the kernel, and no explicit floating point operations are used.

[4]Some processors make this switch automatically without being requested explicitly to do so by the kernel.

> Work in the entry and exit path of an interrupt is made even more difficult by the fact that the processor may be in either user mode or kernel mode when an interrupt arrives. This requires several additional technical modifications that, for reasons of clarity, are not shown in Figure 14.2. (There is no need to switch between kernel mode stack and user mode stack, and there is no need to check whether it is necessary to call the scheduler or deliver signals.)

The term *interrupt handler* is used ambiguously. It is used to designate invocation of an ISR call by the CPU, and combines the entry/exit path and the ISR itself. Of course, it would be more correct to refer only to the routine that is executed *between* the entry path and the exit path and that is implemented in C.

Interrupt Handlers

Interrupt handlers can encounter difficulties particularly when further interrupts occur while they are executing. Although this can be prevented by disabling interrupts during processing by a handler, this creates other problems such as missing important interrupts. *Masking* (the term used to denote the selective disabling of one or more interrupts) can therefore only be used for short periods.

ISRs must therefore satisfy two requirements:

1. Implementation (above all, when other interrupts are disabled) must consist of as little code as possible to support rapid processing.

2. Interrupt handler routines that can be invoked during the processing of other ISRs must not interfere with each other.

Whereas the latter requirement can be satisfied by intelligent programming and clever ISR design, it is rather more difficult to fulfill the former. Depending on the specific interrupt, a fixed program *must* be run to satisfy the minimum requirements for remedying the situation. Code size cannot therefore be reduced arbitrarily.

How does the kernel resolve this dilemma? Not every part of an ISR is equally important. Generally, each handler routine can be divided into three parts of differing significance:

1. *Critical* actions must be executed immediately following an interrupt. Otherwise, system stability or correct operation of the computer cannot be maintained. Other interrupts must be disabled when such actions are performed.

2. *Noncritical* actions should also be performed as quickly as possible but with enabled interrupts (they may therefore be interrupted by other system events).

3. *Deferrable* actions are not particularly important and need not be implemented in the interrupt handler. The kernel can delay these actions and perform them when it has nothing better to do.

The kernel makes *tasklets* available to perform deferrable actions at a later time. I deal with tasklets in more detail in Section 14.3.

14.1.4 Data Structures

There are two facets to the technical implementation of interrupts — assembly language code, which is highly processor-dependent and is used to process the relevant lower-level details on the particular platform; and an abstracted interface, which is required by device drivers and other kernel code to install and manage IRQ handlers. I focus on the second aspect. The countless details needed to describe the functioning of the assembly language part are best left to books and manuals on processor architecture.

To respond to the IRQs of peripheral devices, the kernel must provide a function for each potential IRQ. This function must be able to register and de-register itself dynamically. A static table organization is not sufficient because modules may also be written for devices that interact with the rest of the system by means of interrupts.

The central point at which information on IRQs is managed is a global array with an entry for each IRQ number. Because array position and interrupt number are identical, it is easy to locate the entry associated with a specific IRQ: IRQ 0 is at position 0, IRQ 15 at position 15, and so on; to which processor interrupt the IRQs are ultimately mapped is of no relevance here.

The array is defined as follows:

kernel/irq/handle.c
```
struct irq_desc irq_desc[NR_IRQS] __cacheline_aligned_in_smp = {
        [0 ... NR_IRQS-1] = {
                .status = IRQ_DISABLED,
                .chip = &no_irq_chip,
                .handle_irq = handle_bad_irq,
                .depth = 1,
  ...
        }
};
```

Although an architecture-*in*dependent data type is used for the individual entries, the maximum possible number of IRQs is specified by a platform-dependent constant: NR_IRQS. This constant is for most architectures defined in the processor-specific header file include/asm-*arch*/irq.h.[5] Its value varies widely not only between the different processors but also within processor families depending on which auxiliary chip is used to help the CPU manage IRQs. Alpha computers support between 32 interrupts on "smaller" systems and a fabulous 2,048 interrupts on Wildfire boards; IA-64 processors always have 256 interrupts. IA-32 systems, in conjunction with the classical 8256A controller, provide a meager 16 IRQs. This number can be increased to 224 using the IO-APIC (advanced programmable interrupt controller) expansion that is found on all multiprocessor systems but that can also be deployed on UP machines. Initially, all interrupt slots use handle_bad_irq as a handler function that just acknowledges interrupts for which no specific handler function is installed.

More interesting than the maximum number of IRQs is the data type used for the array entries (in contrast to the simple example above, it is not merely a pointer to a function). Before I get into the technical details, I need to present an overview of the kernel's IRQ-handling subsystem.

---

[5]The IA-32 architecture, however, uses /include/asm-x86/mach-type/irq_vectors_limits.h.

The early versions of kernel 2.6 contained much platform-specific code to handle IRQs that was identical in many points. Thus, a new, generic IRQ subsystem was introduced during further development of kernel 2.6. It is able to handle different interrupt controllers and different types of interrupts in a unified way. Basically, it consists of three abstraction layers as visualized in Figure 14-3:

1. **High-Level Interrupt Service Routines (ISRs)** — Perform all necessary work caused by the interrupt on the device driver's (or some other kernel component's) side. If, for instance, a device uses an interrupt to signal that some data have arrived, then the job of the high-level ISR could be to copy the data to an appropriate place.

2. **Interrupt Flow Handling** — Takes care of handling the various differences between different interrupt flow types like edge- and level triggering.

   Edge-triggering means that hardware detects an interrupt by sensing a difference in potential on the line. In *level-triggered* systems, interrupts are detected when the potential has a specific value — the change in potential is not relevant.

   From the kernel viewpoint, level-triggering is more complicated because, after each interrupt, the line must be explicitly set to the potential that indicates "no interrupt."

3. **Chip-Level Hardware Encapsulation** — Needs to communicate directly with the underlying hardware that is responsible to generate interrupts at the electronic level. This layer can be seen as some sort of "device driver" for interrupt controllers.

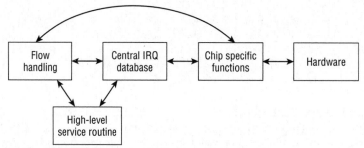

Figure 14-3: Various types of interrupt handlers and how they are connected.

Let's return to the technical side of the problem. The structure used to represent an IRQ descriptor is (slightly simplified) defined as follows[6]:

```
<irq.h>
struct irq_desc {
        irq_flow_handler_t        handle_irq;
        struct irq_chip           *chip;
```

---

[6] Among some technical elements, support for message signaled interrupts (MSIs) has also been omitted. MSIs are an optional extension to the PCI standard and a required component of PCI express. They allow for sending an interrupt without using a physical pin on some piece of hardware, but via a "message" on the PCI bus. Because the number of available pins on modern processors is not unlimited, but pins are required for many purposes, they are a scarce resource. Hardware designers are thus looking for alternative methods to send interrupts, and the MSI mechanism is one of them. It will gain increased importance in the future. `Documentation/MSI-HOWTO.txt` in the kernel source tree contains some more information about this mechanism.

```
        void                    *handler_data;
        void                    *chip_data;
        struct irqaction        *action;          /* IRQ action list */
        unsigned int            status;           /* IRQ status */

        unsigned int            depth;            /* nested irq disables */
        unsigned int            irq_count;        /* For detecting broken IRQs */
        unsigned int            irqs_unhandled;
  ...
        const char              *name;
} ____cacheline_internodealigned_in_smp;
```

In the view of the high-level code in the kernel, each IRQ is fully described by this structure. The three abstraction layers introduced above are represented in the structure as follows:

❑ The flow-level ISR is provided by handle_irq. handler_data may point to some arbitrary, IRQ, and handler function-specific data. handle_irq is called by the architecture-specific code whenever an interrupt occurs. The function is then responsible to use the controller-specific methods provided in chip to perform the necessary low-level actions required to process the interrupt. Default functions for various interrupt types are provided by the kernel. Examples for such handler functions are discussed in Section 14.1.5.

❑ action provides a chain of actions that need to be executed when the interrupt occurs. This is the place where device drivers for devices that are notified by the interrupt can place their specific handler functions. A special data structure is used to represent these actions, discussed in Section 14.1.4.

❑ Flow handling and chip-specific operations are encapsulated in chip. A special data structure is introduced for this purpose, covered in a moment. chip_data points to arbitrary data that may be associated with chip.

❑ name specifies a name for the flow handler that is displayed in /proc/interrupts. This line is usually either "edge" for edge-, or " level" for level-triggered interrupts.

There are some more elements in the structure that need to be described. depth has two tasks. It can be used to determine whether an IRQ line is enabled or disabled. A positive value indicates that the latter is true, whereas 0 indicates an enabled line. Why are positive values used for *disabled* IRQs? Because this allows the kernel to differentiate between enabled and disabled lines and also to repeatedly disable one and the same interrupt. Each time code from the remaining part of the kernel disables an interrupt, the counter is incremented by 1; each time the interrupt is enabled again, the counter is decremented accordingly. Only when depth has returned to 0 may the IRQ be freed again by the hardware. This approach supports the correct handling of nested disabling of interrupts.

An IRQ can change its status not only during handler installation but also at run time: status describes the current status. The <irq.h> file defines various constants that describe the current IRQ line status. Each constant stands for a set bit in a bit string, and several values can be set at the same time, providing that they do not contradict each other.

❑ IRQ_DISABLED is used for an IRQ line disabled by a device driver. It instructs the kernel not to enter the handler.

❑ During execution of an IRQ handler the state is set to IRQ_INPROGRESS. As with IRQ_DISABLED, this prohibits the remaining kernel code from executing the handler.

- ❏ IRQ_PENDING is active when the CPU has noticed an interrupt but has not yet executed the corresponding handler.

- ❏ IRQ_MASKED is required to properly handle interrupts that occur during interrupt processing; see Section 14.1.4.

- ❏ IRQ_PER_CPU is set when an IRQ can occur on a single CPU only. (On SMP systems this renders several protection mechanisms against concurrent accesses superfluous.)

- ❏ IRQ_LEVEL is used on Alpha and PowerPC to differentiate level-triggered and edge-triggered IRQs.

- ❏ IRQ_REPLAY means that the IRQ has been disabled but a previous interrupt has not yet been acknowledged.

- ❏ IRQ_AUTODETECT and IRQ_WAITING are used for the automatic detection and configuration of IRQs. I will not discuss this in more detail, but mention that the respective code is located in kernel/irq/autoprobe.c.

- ❏ IRQ_NOREQUEST is set if the IRQ can be shared between devices and must thus not be exclusively requested by a single device.

Using the current contents of status, it is easy for the kernel to query the status of a certain IRQ without having to know the hardware-specific features of the underlying implementation. Of course, just *setting* the corresponding flags does not produce the desired effect. Disabling an interrupt by setting the IRQ_DISABLED flag is not possible. The underlying hardware must also be informed of the new state. Consequently, the flags may be set only by controller-specific functions that are simultaneously responsible for making the required low-level hardware settings. In many cases, this mandates the use of assembly language code or the writing of magic numbers to magic addresses by means of out commands.

Finally, the fields irq_count and irq_unhandled of irq_desc provide some statistics that can be used to detect stalled and unhandled, but permanently occurring interrupts. The latter ones are usually called *spurious interrupts*. I will not discuss how this is done in more detail.[7]

IRQ Controller Abstraction

handler is an instance of the hw_irq_controller data type that abstracts the specific characteristics of an IRQ controller for the architecture-independent part of the kernel. The functions it provides are used to change the status of an IRQ, which is why they are also responsible for setting flag:

```
<irq.h>
struct irq_chip {
        const char      *name;
        unsigned int    (*startup)(unsigned int irq);
        void            (*shutdown)(unsigned int irq);
        void            (*enable)(unsigned int irq);
        void            (*disable)(unsigned int irq);

        void            (*ack)(unsigned int irq);
        void            (*mask)(unsigned int irq);
        void            (*mask_ack)(unsigned int irq);
        void            (*unmask)(unsigned int irq);
        void            (*eoi)(unsigned int irq);
```

---

[7]If you are interested in how this detection is performed, see the function note_interrupt in kernel/irq/spurious.c.

```
    void            (*end)(unsigned int irq);
    void            (*set_affinity)(unsigned int irq, cpumask_t dest);
...
    int             (*set_type)(unsigned int irq, unsigned int flow_type);
...
```

The structure needs to account for all peculiarities of the different IRQ implementations that appear in the kernel. Thus, a particular instance of the structure usually only defines a subset of all possible methods.

name holds a short string to identify the hardware controller. Possible values on IA-32 systems are "XT-PIC" and "IO-APIC," and the latter one is also used for most interrupts on AMD64 systems. On other systems there is a colorful mix of values because many different controller types are available and in widespread use.

The function pointers have the following meaning:

❑   startup refers to a function for the first-time initialization of an IRQ. In most cases, initialization is limited to enabling the IRQ. As a result, the startup function is just a means of forwarding to enable.

❑   enable activates an IRQ; in other words, it performs a transition from the disabled to the enabled state. To this end, hardware-specific numbers must be written to hardware-specific points in I/O memory or in the I/O ports.

❑   disable is the counterpart to enable and is used to deactivate an IRQ. shutdown completely closes down an interrupt source. If this is not explicitly possible, the function is an alias for disable.

❑   ack is closely linked with the hardware of the interrupt controller. In some models, the arrival of an IRQ request (and therefore of the corresponding interrupt at the processor) must be explicitly acknowledged so that subsequent requests can be serviced. If a chipset does not issue this request, the pointer can be supplied with a dummy function or a null pointer. ack_and_mask acknowledges an interrupt, but masks it in addition afterward.

❑   end is called to mark the end of interrupt processing at the flow level. If an interrupt was disabled during interrupt processing, it is the responsibility of this handler to re-enable it again.

❑   Modern interrupt controllers do not need much flow control from the kernel, but manage nearly everything themselves out of the box. A single callback to the hardware is required when interrupts are processed, and this callback is provided in eoi — *end of interrupt*.

❑   In multiprocessor systems, set_affinity can be used to declare the affinity of a CPU for specified IRQs. This allows IRQs to be distributed to certain CPUs (typically, IRQs on SMP systems are spread evenly across all processors). This method has no relevance on single-processor systems and is therefore supplied with a null pointer.

❑   set_type allows for setting the IRQ flow type. This is mostly required on ARM, PowerPC, and SuperH machines; other systems can do without and set set_type to NULL.

The auxiliary function set_irq_type(irq, type) is a convenience function to set the IRQ type for irq. The types IRQ_TYPE_RISING and IRQ_TYPE_FALLING specify edge-triggered interrupts that use the rising of falling flank, while IRQ_TYPE_EDGE_BOTH works for both flank types. Level-triggered interrupts are denoted by IRQ_TYPE_LEVEL_HIGH and IRQ_TYPE_LEVEL_LOW — you will have guessed that low and high signal levels are distinguished. IRQ_TYPE_NONE, finally, sets an unspecified type.

One particular example for an interrupt controller chip implementation is the IO-APIC on AMD64 systems. It is given by the following definition:

arch/x86/kernel/io_apic_64.c
```
static struct irq_chip ioapic_chip __read_mostly = {
        .name           = "IO-APIC",
        .startup        = startup_ioapic_irq,
        .mask           = mask_IO_APIC_irq,
        .unmask         = unmask_IO_APIC_irq,
        .ack            = ack_apic_edge,
        .eoi            = ack_apic_level,
#ifdef CONFIG_SMP
        .set_affinity   = set_ioapic_affinity_irq,
#endif
};
```

Note that the kernel defines the alias `hw_interrupt_type` for `irq_chip`; this is for compatibility with previous versions of the IRQ subsystem. The name is, for instance, still in use on Alpha systems that define the chip level operations for the i8259A standard interrupt controller as follows[8]:

arch/alpha/kernel/i8529.c
```
struct hw_interrupt_type i8259a_irq_type = {
        .typename       = "XT-PIC",
        .startup        = i8259a_startup_irq,
        .shutdown       = i8259a_disable_irq,
        .enable         = i8259a_enable_irq,
        .disable        = i8259a_disable_irq,
        .ack            = i8259a_mask_and_ack_irq,
        .end            = i8259a_end_irq,
};
```

As the code shows, only a subset of all possible handler functions are neecsssary to operate the device.

i8259A chips are also still present in many IA-32 systems. Support for this chipset has, however, already been converted to the more modern `irq_chip` representation. The interrupt controller type used (and the allocation of all system IRQs) can be seen in `/proc/interrupts`. The following example is from a (rather unchallenged) quad-core AMD64 box:

```
wolfgang@meitner> cat /proc/interrupts
          CPU0       CPU1       CPU2       CPU3
  0:        48          1          0          0   IO-APIC-edge      timer
  1:         1          0          1          0   IO-APIC-edge      i8042
  4:         3          0          0          3   IO-APIC-edge
  8:         0          0          0          1   IO-APIC-edge      rtc
  9:         0          0          0          0   IO-APIC-fasteoi   acpi
 16:        48         48      96720      50082   IO-APIC-fasteoi   libata, uhci_hcd:usb1
 18:         1          0          2          0   IO-APIC-fasteoi   uhci_hcd:usb3, uhci_hcd:usb6,
                                                                   ehci_hcd:usb7
 19:         0          0          0          0   IO-APIC-fasteoi   uhci_hcd:usb5
 21:         0          0          0          0   IO-APIC-fasteoi   uhci_hcd:usb2
 22:    407287     370858       1164       1166   IO-APIC-fasteoi   libata, libata, HDA Intel
```

---

[8]Using typename instead of name is also obsolete by now, but still supported for compatibility reasons.

23:	0	0	0	0	IO-APIC-fasteoi uhci_hcd:usb4, ehci_hcd:usb8
NMI:	0	0	0	0	Non-maskable interrupts
LOC:	2307075	2266433	2220704	2208597	Local timer interrupts
RES:	22037	18253	33530	35156	Rescheduling interrupts
CAL:	363	373	394	184	function call interrupts
TLB:	3355	3729	1919	1630	TLB shootdowns
TRM:	0	0	0	0	Thermal event interrupts
THR:	0	0	0	0	Threshold APIC interrupts
SPU:	0	0	0	0	Spurious interrupts
ERR:	0				

Note that the chip name is concatenated with the flow handler name, which results, for instance, in "IO-APIC-edge." Besides listing all registered IRQs, the file also provides some statistics at the bottom.

Handler Function Representation

An instance of the irqaction structure defined as follows exists for each handler function:

<interrupt.h>
```
struct irqaction {
        irq_handler_t handler;
        unsigned long flags;
        const char *name;
        void *dev_id;
        struct irqaction *next;
}
```

The most important element in the structure is the handler function itself, which takes the form of the handler pointer and is located at the beginning of the structure. The handler function is invoked by the kernel when a device has requested a system interrupt and the interrupt controller has forwarded this to the processor by raising an interrupt. We will look more closely at the meaning of the arguments when we consider how to register handler functions. Note, however, that the type irq_handler_t clearly distinguishes this handler type from flow handlers that are of type irq_flow_handler_t!

name and dev_id uniquely identify an interrupt handler. While name is a short string used to identify the device (e.g., "e100," "ncr53c8xx," etc.), dev_id is a pointer to any data structure that uniquely identifies the device among all kernel data structures — for example, the net_device instance of a network card. This information is needed when removing a handler function if several devices share an IRQ and the IRQ number alone is not sufficient to identify the device.

flags is a flag variable that describes some features of the IRQ (and associated interrupt) with the help of a bitmap whose individual elements can, as usual, be accessed via predefined constants. The following constants are defined in <interrupt.h>:

❑ IRQF_SHARED is set for *shared IRQs* and signals that more than one device is using an IRQ line.

❑ IRQF_SAMPLE_RANDOM is set when the IRQ contributes to the kernel entropy pool.[9]

❑ IRQF_DISABLED indicates that the IRQ handler must be executed with interrupts *disabled*.

❑ IRQF_TIMER denotes a timer interrupt.

---

[9]This information is used to generate relatively secure random numbers for /dev/random and /dev/urandom.

next is used to implement shared IRQ handlers. Several irqaction instances are grouped into a linked list. All elements of a linked list must handle the same IRQ number (instances for different numbers are located at various positions in the irq_desc array). As discussed in Section 14.1.7, the kernel scans the list when a shared interrupt is issued to find out for which device the interrupt is actually intended. Particularly on laptops that integrate many different devices (network, USB, FireWire, sound card, etc.) on a single chip (with just one interrupt), handler chains of this kind can consist of about five elements. However, the desirable situation is that only a single device is registered for each IRQ.

Figure 14-4 shows an overview of the data structures described to illustrate how they interact. Because one type of interrupt controller normally dominates on a system (there is nothing preventing the coexistence of multiple handlers, though), the handler elements of all irq_desc entries point to the same instance of irq_chip.

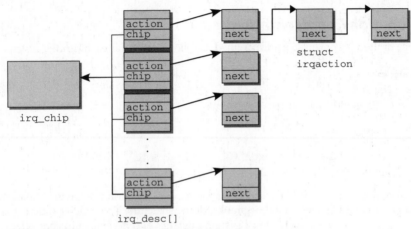

Figure 14-4: Data structures in IRQ management.

14.1.5 Interrupt Flow Handling

Now let's examine how flow handling is implemented. The situation in this area was quite painful before the interrupt rework in 2.6, and architecture-specific code was heavily involved in flow handling. Thankfully, the situation is now much improved, and a generic framework that accounts for nearly all available hardware with only very few exceptions is available.

Setting Controller Hardware

First of all, I need to mention some standard functions that are provided by the kernel to register irq_chips and set flow handlers:

```
<irq.h>
int set_irq_chip(unsigned int irq, struct irq_chip *chip);
void set_irq_handler(unsigned int irq, irq_flow_handler_t handle);
void set_irq_chained_handler(unsigned int irq, irq_flow_handler_t handle)
void set_irq_chip_and_handler(unsigned int irq, struct irq_chip *chip,
                              irq_flow_handler_t handle);
void set_irq_chip_and_handler_name(unsigned int irq, struct irq_chip *chip,
                                   irq_flow_handler_t handle, const char
                                   *name);
```

❑   `set_irq_chip` associates an IRQ chip in the form of an `irq_chip` instance with a specific interrupt. Besides picking the proper element from `irq_desc` and setting the `chip` pointer, the function also inserts default handler functions if no chip-specific implementation is supplied.

If a `NULL` pointer is given for the chip, then the generic "no controller" variant `no_irq_chip`, which provides only no-op operations, is used.

❑   `set_irq_handler` and `set_irq_chained_handler` set the flow handler function for a given IRQ number. The second variant is required to signal that the handler must deal with shared interrupts. This enables the flags `IRQ_NOREQUEST` and `IRQ_NOPROBE` in `irq_desc[irq]->status`: the first one because shared interrupts cannot be reserved for exclusive use, and the second one because it is obviously a bad idea to use interrupt probing on lines where multiple devices are present.

Both functions use `__set_irq_handler` internally, which performs some sanity checks and sets `irq_desc[irq]->handle_irq`.

❑   `set_chip_and_handler` is a convenient shortcut used instead of calling the functions discussed above one after another. The _name variant works identically, but allows for specifying a name for the flow handler that is stored in `irq_desc[irq]->name`.

Flow Handling

Before discussing how flow handlers are implemented, we need to introduce the type used for them. `irq_flow_handler_t` specifies the signature of IRQ flow handler functions:

<irq.h>
```
typedef void fastcall (*irq_flow_handler_t)(unsigned int irq,
                                            struct irq_desc *desc);
```

Flow handlers get both the IRQ number and a pointer to the `irq_handler` instance that is responsible for the interrupt. This information can then be used to implement proper flow handling.

Recall that different hardware requires different approaches to flow handling — edge- and level-triggering need to be dealt with differently, for instance. The kernel provides several default flow handlers for various types. They have one thing in common: Every flow handler is responsible to call the high-level ISRs once its work is finished. `handle_IRQ_event` is responsible to activate the high-level handlers; this is discussed this in Section 14.1.7. For now, let us examine how flow handling is performed.

Edge-Triggered Interrupts

Edge-triggered interrupts are most common on the majority of today's hardware, so I consider this type first. The default handler is implemented in `handle_edge_irq`. The code flow diagram is shown in Figure 14-5.

Edge-triggered IRQs are not masked when they are processed — in contrast to level-triggered IRQs, there is no need to do so. This has one important implication for SMP systems: When an IRQ is handled on one CPU, another IRQ with the same number can appear on another CPU that we denote as the *second CPU*. This implies that the flow handler will be called once more while it is still running on the CPU that triggered the first IRQ. But why should two CPUs be engaged with running the same IRQ handler simultaneously? The kernel wants to avoid this situation: The handler should only be processed on a single CPU. The initial portion of `handle_edge_irq` has to deal with this case. If the `IRQ_INPROGRESS` flag is set, the IRQ is already being processed on another CPU. By setting the `IRQ_PENDING` flag, the kernel remembers that another IRQ needs to be served later. After masking the IRQ and sending an acknowledgment to the controller via mask_ack_irq, processing can be aborted. The second CPU can thus go back to work as usual, while the first CPU will handle the IRQ later.

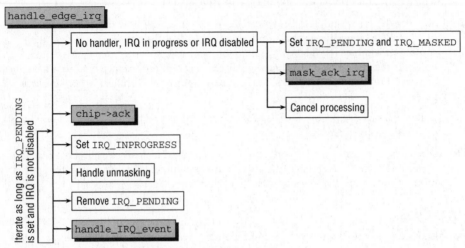

Figure 14-5: Code flow diagram for `handle_edge_irq`.

Note that processing is also aborted if no ISR handler is available for the IRQ or if it is disabled. (Faulty hardware might nevertheless generate the IRQ, so this case needs to be taken into account by the kernel.)

Now the proper work to handle the IRQ starts. After sending an acknowledgment to the interrupt controller with the chip-specific function chip->ack, the kernel sets the IRQ_INPROGRESS flag. This signals that the IRQ is being processed and can be used to avoid the same handler executing on multiple CPUs.

Let us assume that only a single IRQ needs to be processed. In this case, the high-level ISR handlers are activated by calling handle_IRQ_event, and the IRQ_INPROGRESS flag can be removed afterward. However, the situation is more complicated in reality, as the source code shows:

kernel/irq/chip.c
```
void fastcall
handle_edge_irq(unsigned int irq, struct irq_desc *desc)
{
...
        desc->status |= IRQ_INPROGRESS;

        do {
                struct irqaction *action = desc->action;
                irqreturn_t action_ret;

...
                /*
                 * When another irq arrived while we were handling
                 * one, we could have masked the irq.
                 * Renable it, if it was not disabled in meantime.
```

```
        */
    if (unlikely((desc->status &
                (IRQ_PENDING | IRQ_MASKED | IRQ_DISABLED)) ==
                (IRQ_PENDING | IRQ_MASKED))) {
            desc->chip->unmask(irq);
            desc->status &= ~IRQ_MASKED;
    }

    desc->status &= ~IRQ_PENDING;
    action_ret = handle_IRQ_event(irq, action);
} while ((desc->status & (IRQ_PENDING | IRQ_DISABLED)) == IRQ_PENDING);
```

Processing the IRQ runs in a loop. Suppose we are at the point right beneath the call to `handle_IRQ_event`. While the ISR handlers for the first IRQ were running, a second IRQ could have appeared as shown before. This is indicated by `IRQ_PENDING`. If the flag is set (and the IRQ has not been disabled in the meantime), another IRQ is waiting to be processed, and the loop is started again from the beginning.

In this case, however, the IRQ will have been masked. The IRQ must thus be unmasked with `chip->unmask` and the `IRQ_MASKED` flag be removed. This guarantees that only one interrupt can occur during the execution of `handle_IRQ_event`.

After removing the `IRQ_PENDING` flag — technically, one IRQ is still pending right now, but it is going to be processed immediately — `handle_IRQ_event` can also serve the second IRQ.

Level-Triggered Interrupts

Level-triggered interrupts are a little easier to process than their edge-triggered relatives. This is also reflected in the code flow diagram of the flow handler `handle_level_irq`, which is depicted in Figure 14-6.

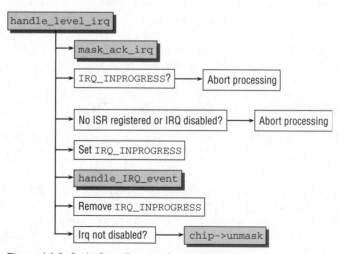

Figure 14-6: Code flow diagram for `handle_level_irq`.

Note that level-triggered interrupts must be masked when they are processed, so the first thing that needs to be done is to call `mask_ack_irq`. This auxiliary function masks and acknowledges the IRQ by either calling `chip->mask_ack` or, if this is not available, `chip->mask` and `chip->ack` consecutively. On multiprocessor systems, a race condition might occur such that `handle_edge_irq` is called although the IRQ is already processed on another CPU. This can be detected by checking for the `IRQ_INPROGRESS` flag, and the routine can immediately be left — the IRQ is already being processed on another CPU, in this case.

If no handler is registered for the IRQ, processing can also be aborted — there is nothing to do. One more reason to abort processing is when `IRQ_DISABLED` is set. Despite being disabled, broken hardware could nevertheless issue the IRQ, but it can be ignored.

Then the proper processing starts. `IRQ_INPROGRESS` is set to signal that the IRQ is being processed, and the actual work is delegated to `handle_IRQ_event`. This triggers the high-level ISRs, as discussed below. The `IRQ_INPROGRESS` can be removed after the ISRs are finished.

Finally, the IRQ needs to be unmasked. However, the kernel needs to consider that an ISR could have disabled the interrupt, and in this case, it needs to remain masked. Otherwise, the chip-specific unmask function `chip->unmask` is used.

Other Types of Interrupts

Besides edge- and level-triggered IRQs, some more less common flow types are also possible. The kernel also provides default handlers for them.

- ❏ Modern IRQ hardware requires only very little flow handling. Only one chip-specific function needs to be called after IRQ processing is finished: `chip->eoi`. The default handler for this type is `handle_fasteoi_irq`. It is basically identical with `handle_level_irq`, except that interaction with the controller chip is only required at the very end.

- ❏ Really simple interrupts that require no flow control at all are managed by `handle_simple_irq`. The function can also be used if a caller wants to handle the flow itself.

- ❏ Per-CPU IRQs, that is, IRQs that can only happen on one specific CPU of a multiprocessor system, are handled by `handle_percpu_irq`. The function acknowledges the IRQ after reception and calls the EOI routine after processing. The implementation is very simple because no locking is required — the code can by definition only run on a single CPU.

14.1.6 Initializing and Reserving IRQs

In this section, we will turn our attention to how IRQs are registered and initialized.

Registering IRQs

Dynamic registration of an ISR by a device driver can be performed very simply using the data structures described. The function had been implemented by platform-specific code before the interrupt rework in 2.6. Naturally, the prototype was identical on all architectures as this is an absolute prerequisite for programming platform-independent drivers. Nowadays, the function is implemented by common code:

kernel/irq/manage.c
```
int request_irq(unsigned int irq,
                irqreturn_t handler,
                unsigned long irqflags, const char *devname, void *dev_id)
```

Figure 14-7 shows the code flow diagram for `request_irq`.

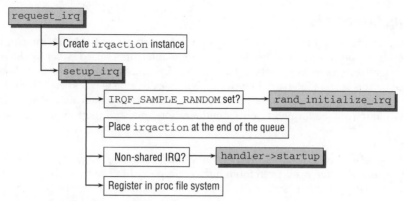

Figure 14-7: Code flow diagram for `request_irq`.

The kernel first generates a new instance of `irqaction` that is then supplied with the function parameters. Of special importance is, of course, the handler function `handler`. All further work is delegated to the `setup_irq` function that performs the following steps:

1. If `IRQF_SAMPLE_RANDOM` is set, the interrupt contributes to the kernel entropy source used for the random number generator in `/dev/random`. `rand_initialize_irq` adds the IRQ to the corresponding data structures.

2. The `irqaction` instance generated by `request_irq` is added to the end of the list of routines for a specific IRQ number; this list is headed by `irq_desc[NUM]->action`. This is how the kernel ensures that — in the case of shared interrupts — handlers are invoked in the same sequence in which they were registered when an interrupt occurs.

3. If the installed handler is the first in the list for the IRQ number, the `handler->startup` initialization function is invoked.[10] This is not necessary if handlers for the IRQ have already been installed.

4. `register_irq_proc` generates the directory `/proc/irq/NUM` in the `proc` filesystem. `register_handler_proc` generates `proc/irq/NUM/name`. The system is then able to see that the corresponding IRQ channel is in use.

Freeing IRQs

The reverse scheme is adopted in order to free interrupts. First, the interrupt controller is informed that the IRQ has been removed by means of a hardware-specific (`chip->shutdown`) function,[11] and then the relevant entries are removed from the general data structures of the kernel. The auxiliary function `free_irq` assumes these tasks. While it has been an architecture-dependent function before the genirq rework, it can today be found in `kernel/irq/manage.c`.

When an IRQ handler is required to remove a shared interrupt, the number alone is not sufficient to identify the IRQ. In this case, it is necessary to also use the `dev_id` discussed above for purposes of

---

[10]If no explicit `startup` function is available, the IRQ is simply enabled by calling `chip->enable` instead.
[11]If no explicit `shutdown` function is available, the interrupt is simply disabled by `chip->disable` instead.

unique identification. The kernel scans the list of all registered handlers until it finds a matching element (with a matching `dev_id`). Only then can the entry be removed.

Registering Interrupts

The mechanisms discussed above are effective only for interrupts raised by an interrupt request from a system peripheral. But the kernel must also take care of interrupts raised either by the processor itself or by software mechanisms in an executing user process. In contrast to IRQs, the kernel need not provide an interface for this kind of interrupt in order to dynamically register handlers. This is because the numbers used are made known at initialization time and do not change thereafter. Registering of interrupts, exceptions, and traps is performed at kernel initialization time, and their reservations do not change at run time.

The platform-specific kernel sources have very few commonalities, not surprising in view of the sometimes large technical differences. Even though the concepts behind some variants may be similar, their concrete implementation differs strongly from platform to platform. This is because implementation must walk a fine line between C and assembly language code in order to do justice to the specific features of a system.

The greatest similarity between the various platforms is a filename. `arch/`arch`/kernel/traps.c` contains the system-specific implementation for registering interrupt handlers.

The outcome of all implementations is that a handler function is invoked automatically when an interrupt occurs. Because interrupt sharing is not supported for system interrupts, all that need be done is to establish a link between the interrupt number and function pointer.

Generally, the kernel responds to interrupts in one of two ways.

❑ A signal is sent to the current user process to inform it that an error has occurred. On IA-32 and AMD64 systems, for example, a division by 0 is signaled by interrupt 0. The automatically invoked assembly language routine `divide_error` sends the `SIGPFE` signal to the user process.

❑ The kernel corrects the error situation invisibly to the user process. This is the case on, for example, IA-32 systems, where interrupt 14 is used to signal a page fault, which the kernel can then correct by employing the methods described in Chapter 18.

14.1.7 Servicing IRQs

Once an IRQ handler has been registered, the handler routine is executed each time an interrupt occurs. The problem again arises as to how to reconcile the differences between the various platforms. Owing to the nature of things, the differences are not restricted to various C functions with platform-specific implementations but start deep down in the domain of the manually optimized assembly language code used for low-level processing.

Fortunately, several structural similarities between the individual platforms can be identified. For example, the interrupt action on each platform comprises three parts, as discussed earlier. The entry path switches from user mode to kernel mode, then the actual handler routine executes, and finally the kernel switches back to user mode. Even though much assembly language code is involved, there are at least some C fragments that are similar on all platforms. These are discussed below.

Switching to Kernel Mode

The switch to kernel mode is based on assembly language code executed by the processor automatically after every interrupt. The tasks of this code are described above. Its implementation can be found in `arch/arch/kernel/entry.S`,[12] which usually defines various entry points at which the processor sets the flow of control when an interrupt occurs.

Only the most necessary actions are executed directly in assembly language code. The kernel attempts to return to regular C code as quickly as possible because it is far easier to handle. To this end, an environment must be created that is compatible with the expectations of the C compiler.

Functions are called in C by placing the required data — return address and parameters — on the stack in a certain order. When switching between user mode and kernel mode, it is also necessary to save the most important registers on the stack so that they can be restored later. These two actions are performed by platform-dependent assembly language code. On most platforms, control flow is then passed to the C function `do_IRQ`,[13] whose implementation is also platform-dependent, but which greatly simplifies the situation. Depending on the platform, the function receives as its parameter either the processor register

arch/arch/kernel/irq.c
```
fastcall unsigned int do_IRQ(struct pt_regs regs)
```

or the number of the interrupt together with a pointer to the processor register

arch/arch/kernel/irq.c
```
unsigned int do_IRQ(int irq, struct pt_regs *regs)
```

`pt_regs` is used to save the registers used by the kernel. The values are pushed one after another onto the stack (by assembly language code) and are left there before the C function is invoked.

`pt_regs` is defined to ensure that the register entries on the stack coincide with the elements of the structure. The values are not only saved for later, but can also be read by the C code. Figure 14-8 illustrates this.

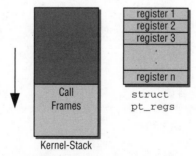

Figure 14-8: Stack layout after entry into kernel mode.

---

[12]The unified x86 architecture distinguishes between `entry_32` for IA-32 and `entry_64` for AMD64 systems.
[13]Exceptions are Sparc, Sparc64, and Alpha.

Alternatively, the registers can also be copied to a location in address space that is not identical to the stack. In this case, do_IRQ receives as its parameter a pointer to pt_regs, which does not change the fact that the register contents have been saved and can be read by the C code.

The definition of struct pt_regs is platform-dependent because different processors provide different register sets. The registers used by the kernel are held in pt_regs. Registers not listed here may be used by user mode applications only. On IA-32 systems, pt_regs is typically defined as follows:

include/asm-x86/ptrace.h
```
struct pt_regs {
        long ebx;
        long ecx;
        long edx;
        long esi;
        long edi;
        long ebp;
        long eax;
        int  xds;
        int  xes;
        long orig_eax;
        long eip;
        int  xcs;
        long eflags;
        long esp;
        int  xss;
};
```

PA-Risc processors, for instance, use a totally different set of registers:

include/asm-parisc/ptrace.h
```
struct pt_regs {
        unsigned long gr[32];    /* PSW is in gr[0] */
         __u64 fr[32];
        unsigned long sr[ 8];
        unsigned long iasq[2];
        unsigned long iaoq[2];
        unsigned long cr27;
        unsigned long pad0;      /* available for other uses */
        unsigned long orig_r28;
        unsigned long ksp;
        unsigned long kpc;
        unsigned long sar;       /* CR11 */
        unsigned long iir;       /* CR19 */
        unsigned long isr;       /* CR20 */
        unsigned long ior;       /* CR21 */
        unsigned long ipsw;      /* CR22 */
};
```

The general trend in 64-bit architectures is to provide more and more registers, with the result that pt_regs definitions are becoming larger and larger. IA-64 has, for example, almost 50 entries in pt_regs, reason enough not to include the definition here.

On IA-32 systems, the number of the raised interrupt is saved in the most significant 8 bits of `orig_eax`. Other architectures use other locations. As mentioned above, some platforms even adopt the approach of placing the interrupt number on the stack as a direct argument.

IRQ Stacks

The situation described above is only valid if the kernel uses the kernel stack to process IRQs. This need not always be the case. The IA-32 architecture provides the configuration option `CONFIG_4KSTACKS`.[14] If it is activated, the size of the kernel stack is reduced from 8 KiB to 4 KiB. Since the page size is 4 KiB on this machine, the number of pages necessary to implement the kernel stack is reduced from two to one. This makes life easier for the VM subsystem when a huge number of processes (or threads) is active on the system because single pages are easier to find than two consecutive ones as required before. Unfortunately, 4 KiB might not always be enough for the regular kernel work *and* the space required by IRQ processing routines, so two more stacks come into play:

❑ A stack for hardware IRQ processing.

❑ A stack for software IRQ processing.

In contrast to the regular kernel stack that is allocated *per process*, the two additional stacks are allocated *per CPU*. Whenever a hardware interrupt occurs (or a softIRQ is processed), the kernel needs to switch to the appropriate stack.

Pointers to the additional stacks are provided in the following array:

arch/x86/kernel/irq_32.c
```
static union irq_ctx *hardirq_ctx[NR_CPUS] __read_mostly;
static union irq_ctx *softirq_ctx[NR_CPUS] __read_mostly;
```

Note that the attribute `__read_mostly` does *not* refer to the stack itself, but to the pointer that points to the appropriate place in memory. This is only manipulated when the stacks are initially allocated, but no more during the system's lifetime.

The data structure used for the stacks is not too complicated:

arch/x86/kernel/irq_32.c
```
union irq_ctx {
        struct thread_info      tinfo;
        u32                     stack[THREAD_SIZE/sizeof(u32)];
};
```

`tinfo` is used to store information about the thread that was running before the interruption occurred (see Chapter 2 for more details). `stack` provides the stack space itself. `STACK_SIZE` is defined to 4,096 if 4-KiB stacks are enabled, so this guarantees the desired stack size. Note that since a `union` is used to combine `tinfo` and `stack[]`, the data structure fits into exactly one page frame. This also implies that the thread information contained in `tinfo` is always available on the stack.

---

[14]The PowerPC and SuperH architectures provide the configuration option `CONFIG_IRQSTACKS` to enable separate stacks for IRQ processing. Since the mechanism used there is similar, these cases are not discussed separately.

Calling the Flow Handler Routine

How the flow handler routines are called differs from architecture to architecture; in the following, how this is done is discussed for AMD64 and IA-32. Additionally, we also examine the old handler mechanism that was the default before the IRQ subsystem rewrite, and is still used in some places.

Processing on AMD64 Systems

Let us first turn our attention to how do_IRQ is implemented on AMD64 systems. This variant is simpler as compared to IA-32, and many other modern architectures use a similar approach. The code flow diagram is shown in Figure 14-9.

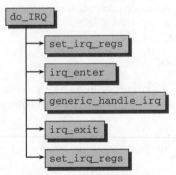

Figure 14-9: Code flow diagram
for **do_IRQ.** on AMD64 systems.

The prototype of the function is as follows:

arch/x86/kernel/irq_64.c
```
asmlinkage unsigned int do_IRQ(struct pt_regs *regs)
```

The low-level assembler code is responsible to pass the current state of the register set to the function, and the first task of do_IRQ is to save a pointer to them in a global per-CPU variable using set_irq_regs (the old pointer that was active before the interrupt occurred is preserved for later). Interrupt handlers that require access to the register set can access them from there.

irq_enter is then responsible to update some statistics; for systems with dynamic ticks, the global jiffies time-keeping variable is updated if the system has been in a tickless state for some time (more about dynamic ticks follows in Section 15.5.). Calling the ISRs registered for the IRQ in question is then delegated to the architecture-*independent* function generic_handle_irq, which calls irq_desc[irq]->handle_irq to activate the flow control handler.

irq_exit is then responsible for some statistics bookkeeping, but also calls (assuming the kernel is not still in interrupt mode because it is processing a nested interrupt) do_softirq to service any pending software IRQs. This mechanism is discussed in more detail in Section 14.2. Finally, another call to set_irq_regs restores the pointer to struct regs to the setting that was active before the call. This ensures that nested handlers work correctly.

Processing on IA-32 Systems

IA-32 requires slightly more work in do_IRQ, as the code flow diagram in Figure 14-10 shows. We first suppose that a single page frame is used for the kernel stack, that is, 4 KiB are available per process for the kernel. This is configured if CONFIG_4KSTACKS is set. Recall that in this case a separate stack is used to handle IRQ processing.

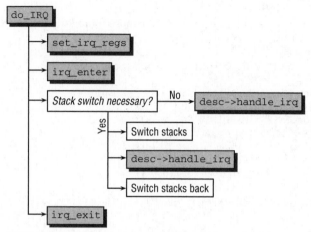

Figure 14-10: Code flow diagram for do_IRQ on IA-32 systems.

As in the AMD64 case, the functions set_irq_regs and irq_enter are called with the same purpose as before. The kernel must switch to the IRQ stack. The current stack can be obtained by calling the auxiliary function current_thread_info, which delivers a pointer to the thread_info instance currently in use. Recall from above that this information is in a union with the current stack. A pointer to the appropriate IRQ-stack can be obtained from hardirq_ctx as discussed above.

Two cases are possible:

1. The process is already using the IRQ stack because nested IRQs are processed. In this case, the kernel can be lazy — nothing needs to be done because everything is already set up. irq_desc[irq]->handle_irq can be called to activate the ISR stored in the IRQ database.

2. The current stack is not the IRQ stack (curctx != irqctx), and a switch between both is required. In this case, the kernel performs the required low-level assembler operations to switch between the stacks, calls irq_desc[irq]->handle_irq, and switches the stacks back.

Note that in both cases the ISR is called directly and not via a detour over generic_handle_irq as on AMD64 systems.

The remaining work is done in the same way as on AMD64 systems. irq_exit handles some accounting and activates SoftIRQs, and set_irq_regs restores the register pointer to the state before the IRQ happened.

When stacks with 8-KiB size, that is, two page frames, are used, IRQ handling is simplified because a potential stack switch does not need to be taken into account and `irq_desc[irq]->handle_irq` can be called immediately in any case.

Old-Style Processing

In the discussion of how AMD64 calls the flow control handler, it was mentioned that the code ends up in `generic_handle_irq`, which selects and activates the proper `handle_irq` function from the IRQ database `irq_desc`. However, `generic_handle_irq` is a little more complicated in practice:

```
<irq.h>
static inline void generic_handle_irq(unsigned int irq)
{
        struct irq_desc *desc = irq_desc + irq;

#ifdef CONFIG_GENERIC_HARDIRQS_NO__DO_IRQ
        desc->handle_irq(irq, desc);
#else
        if (likely(desc->handle_irq))
                desc->handle_irq(irq, desc);
        else
                __do_IRQ(irq);
#endif
}
```

Before the generic IRQ rework, the kernel used a colorful mixture of architecture-*dependent* approaches to IRQ handling. Most important, there was no separation between flow handling and ISR handling: Both tasks were performed simultaneously in a single architecture-specific routine usually called `__do_IRQ`.

Modern code should activate the configuration option `GENRIC_HARDIRQS_NO__DO_IRQ` and implement flow handling as shown in the preceding discussions. In this case, `generic_handle_irq` really boils down to just calling `irq_desc[irq]->handle_irq`.

What if this option is not set? The kernel provides a default implementation of `__do_IRQ` that combines flow handling for all interrupt types, and also calls the required ISRs.[15] Basically, there are three possibilities of how to use this function and implement flow handling:

1. Use generic flow handlers for some IRQs, and leave the handlers for others undefined. For these, `__do_IRQ` is employed to handle both flow and high-level processing. It is required to call `generic_handle_IRQ` from `do_IRQ` in this case.

2. Call `__do_IRQ` directly from `do_IRQ`. This bypasses the flow separation completely. Some off-mainstream architectures like M32R, H8300, SuperH, and Cris still use this approach.

3. Handle IRQs in a completely architecture-dependent way without reusing any of the existing frameworks. Clearly, this is not the brightest idea — to say the least.

Since it is needless to say that the long-term goal for all architectures is to convert to the generic IRQ framework, `__do_IRQ` is not discussed in detail.

---

[15]The implementation is based on the version used on IA-32 systems before the generic IRQ framework was introduced.

Calling the High-level ISR

Recall from above that the various flow handler routines all have one thing in common: They employ `handle_IRQ_event` to activate the high-level ISRs associated with a particular IRQ. The time has come to examine this function a little more closly. The function requires the IRQ number and the action chain to be passed as parameters:

kernel/irq/handle.c
```
irqreturn_t handle_IRQ_event(unsigned int irq, struct irqaction *action);
```

`handle_IRQ_event` performs various actions:

❏ If `IRQF_DISABLED` was *not* set in the first handler function, the interrupts (for the current CPU) are enabled with `local_irq_enable_in_hardirq`; in other words, the handlers can be interrupted by other IRQs. However, depending on the flow type, it is possible that the IRQ just processed is always masked out.

❏ The `action` functions of the registered IRQ handlers are invoked one after the other.

❏ If `IRQF_SAMPLE_RANDOM` is set for the IRQ, `add_interrupt_randomness` is called in order to use the time of the event as a source for the entropy pool (interrupts are an ideal source if they occur randomly).

❏ `local_irq_disable` disables the interrupts. Because enabling and disabling of interrupts is not nested, it is irrelevant whether they were enabled or not at the start of processing. `handle_IRQ_event` was called with interrupts disabled, and is also expected to leave again with interrupts disabled.

With shared IRQs the kernel has no way of finding out which device raised the request. This is left entirely to the handler routines that use device-specific registers or other hardware characteristics to find the source. Routines not affected also recognize that the interrupt was not intended for them and return control as quickly as possible. Neither is there any way that a handler routine can report to higher-level code that the interrupt was intended for it or not. The kernel always executes *all* handler routines in turn, regardless of whether the first or the last leads to success.

Nevertheless, the kernel can check whether *any* handler was found to be responsible for the IRQ. `irqreturn_t` is defined as the return type of handler functions and boils down to a simple integer variable. It accepts the value `IRQ_NONE` or `IRQ_HANDLED`, depending on whether the IRQ was serviced by the handler routine or not.

During servicing of all handler routines, the kernel combines the results with a logical "or" operation. This is how it is finally able to determine whether the IRQ was serviced or not.

kernel/irq/handle.c
```
irqreturn_t handle_IRQ_event(unsigned int irq, struct irqaction *action)
{
...
        do {
                ret = action->handler(irq, action->dev_id);
                if (ret == IRQ_HANDLED)
                        status |= action->flags;
                retval |= ret;
                action = action->next;
```

```
        } while (action);
...
        return retval;
}
```

Implementing Handler Routines

Some important points must be noted when implementing handler routines. These greatly influence not only the speed but also the stability of the system.

Restrictions

The main problem when implementing ISRs is that they execute in what is known as the *interrupt context*. Kernel code can sometimes run both in the regular context and in the interrupt context. To distinguish between these two variants and to design code accordingly, the kernel provides the in_interrupt function to indicate whether or not an interrupt is currently being serviced.

The interrupt context differs in three important points from the normal context in which the kernel otherwise executes:

1. Interrupts are executed asynchronously; in other words, they can occur at any time. As a result, the handler routine is not executed in a clearly defined environment with respect to the reservation of userspace. This prohibits access to userspace and prevents above all the copying of memory contents into and out of the userspace addresses.

   For network drivers, for example, it is therefore not possible to forward data received directly to the waiting application. After all, it is not certain that the application waiting for the data is running at the time (this is, in fact, extremely unlikely).

2. The scheduler may not be invoked in the interrupt context. It is therefore impossible to surrender control voluntarily.

3. The handler routine may not go to sleep. Sleep states can only be broken when an external event causes a state change and wakes the process. However, because interrupts are not allowed in the interrupt context, the sleeping process would wait forever for the relieving news. As the scheduler may also not be invoked, no other process can be selected to replace the current sleeping process.

   It is not, of course, enough simply to make sure that only the direct code of a handler routine is free of possible sleeping instructions. All invoked procedures and functions (and procedures and functions invoked by these, in turn) must be free of expressions that could go to sleep. Checking that this is the case is not always trivial and must be done very carefully, particularly if control paths have numerous branches.

Implementing Handlers

Recall that the prototype of ISR functions is specified by irq_handler_t. I have not shown the actual definition of this typedef, but do so now:

<interrupt.h>
```
typedef irqreturn_t (*irq_handler_t)(int, void *);
```

irq specifies the IRQ number, and dev_id is the device ID passed when the handler is registered. irqreturn_t is another typedef to a simple integer.

Note that the prototype of ISRs was changed during the development of 2.6.19! Before, the arguments of the handler routine also included a pointer to the saved registers:

<interrupt.h>
```
irqreturn_t (*handler)(int irq, void *dev_id, struct pt_regs *regs);
```

Interrupt handlers are obviously hot code paths, and time is very critical. Although most handlers do not need the register state, time and stack space is required to pass a pointer to it to every ISR. Removing this pointer from the prototype is thus a good idea.[16]

Handlers that need the register set can still access it. The kernel defines a global per-CPU array that stores the registers, and `get_irq_regs` from >include/asm-generic/irq_regs.h> can be used to retrieve a pointer to the `pt_regs` instance. This instance contains the register setting that was active when the switch to kernel mode was made. The information is not used by normal device drivers but sometimes comes in useful when debugging kernel problems.

Again we emphasize that interrupt handlers can only use two return values: `IRQ_HANDLED` if the IRQ was handled correctly, or `IRQ_NONE` if the ISR did not feel responsible for the IRQ.

What are the tasks of a handler routine? To service a shared interrupt, the routine must first check whether the IRQ is intended for it. If the peripheral device is of a more modern design, the hardware offers a simple method of performing this check, usually by means of a special device register. If the device has caused an interrupt, register value is set to 1. In this case, the handler routine must restore the value to its default (usually 0) and then start normal servicing of the interrupt. If it finds the value 0, it can be sure that the managed device is not the source of the interrupt, and control can be returned to the higher-level code.

If a device does not have a state register of this kind, the option of manual polling still remains. Each time an interrupt occurs, the handler checks whether data are available for the device. If so, the data are processed. If not, the routine is terminated.

A handler routine can, of course, be responsible for several devices at the same time, for example, two network cards of the same type. If an IRQ is received, the same code is executed on both cards because both handler functions point to the same position in the kernel code. If the two devices use different IRQ numbers, the handler routine can differentiate between them. If they share a common IRQ, reference can still be made to the device-specific `dev_id` field to uniquely identify each card.

14.2 Software Interrupts

Software interrupts enable the kernel to defer tasks. Because they function in a similar way to the interrupts described above but are implemented fully in the software, they are logically enough known as *software interrupts* or *softIRQs*.

The kernel is informed of an anomalous condition by means of a software interrupt, and the situation is resolved at some later time by special handler routines. As already noted, the kernel services all pending software interrupts at the end of `do_IRQ` so that regular activation is ensured.

---

[16]Since the patch that introduced the change had to change every ISR, it might well be the one to touch most files at a single blow in the kernel history.

From a more abstract view, software interrupts can therefore be described as a form of kernel activity that is deferred to a later point in time. However, despite the clear similarities between hardware and software interrupts, they are not always comparable.

The central component of the softIRQ mechanism is a table with 32 entries to hold elements of the `softirq_action` type. This data type has a very simple structure and consists of two elements only:

```
<interrupt.h>
struct softirq_action
{
        void    (*action)(struct softirq_action *);
        void    *data;
};
```

Whereas `action` is a pointer to the handler routine executed by the kernel when a software interrupt occurs, `data` accepts a nonspecified pointer to private data of the handler function.

The definition of the data structure is architecture-independent, as is the complete implementation of the softIRQ mechanism. With the exception of processing activation, no processor-specific functions or features are deployed; this is in clear contrast to normal interrupts.

Software interrupts must be registered before the kernel can execute them. The `open_softirq` function is provided for this purpose. It writes the new softIRQ at the desired position in the `softirq_vec` table:

```
kernel/softirq.c
void open_softirq(int nr, void (*action)(struct softirq_action*), void *data)
{
        softirq_vec[nr].data = data;
        softirq_vec[nr].action = action;
}
```

`data` is used as a parameter each time the `action` softIRQ handler is called.

The fact that each softIRQ has a unique number immediately suggests that softIRQs are relatively scarce resources that may not be used randomly by all manner of device drivers and kernel parts but must be used judiciously. By default, only 32 softIRQs may be used on a system. However, this limit is not too restrictive because softIRQs act as a basis for implementing other mechanisms that also defer work and are better adapted to the needs of device drivers. The corresponding techniques (tasklets, work queues, and kernel timers) are discussed below.

Only the central kernel code uses software interrupts. SoftIRQs are used at a few points only, but these are all the more important:

```
<interrupt.h>
enum
{
        HI_SOFTIRQ=0,
        TIMER_SOFTIRQ,
        NET_TX_SOFTIRQ,
        NET_RX_SOFTIRQ,
        BLOCK_SOFTIRQ,
```

```
        TASKLET_SOFTIRQ
        SCHED_SOFTIRQ,
#ifdef CONFIG_HIGH_RES_TIMERS
        HRTIMER_SOFTIRQ,
#endif
};

};
```

Two serve to implement tasklets (`HI_SOFTIRQ` and `TASKLET_SOFTIRQ`), two are used for send and receive operations in networks (`NET_TX_SOFTIRQ` and `NET_RX_SOFTIRQ`, the source of the softIRQ mechanism and its most important application), one is used by the block layer to implement asynchronous request completions (`BLOCK_SOFTIRQ`), and one is used by the scheduler (`SCHED_SOFTIRQ`) to implement periodic load balancing on SMP systems. When high-resolution timers are enabled, they also require a softIRQ (`HRTIMER_SOFTIRQ`).

Numbering of the softIRQs produces a priority sequence, which does not affect the frequency of execution of individual handler routines or their priority with respect to other system activities, but does define the sequence in which the routines are executed if several are marked as active or pending at the same time.

`raise_softirq(int nr)` is used to raise a software interrupt (similarly to a normal interrupt). The number of the desired softIRQ is passed as a parameter.

This function sets the corresponding bit in the per-CPU variable `irq_stat[smp_processor_id].__softirq_pending`. This marks the softIRQ for execution but defers execution. By using a processor-specific bitmap, the kernel ensures that several softIRQs — even identical ones — can be executed on different CPUs at the same time.

Providing `raise_softirq` was not called in the interrupt context, `wakeup_softirqd` is called to wake the softIRQ daemon; this is one of the two alternative ways of launching the processing of softIRQs. The daemon is discussed in more detail in Section 14.2.2.

14.2.1 Starting SoftIRQ Processing

There are several ways of starting softIRQ processing, but all come down to invoking the `do_softirq` function. For this reason, let's take a closer look at this function. Figure 14-11 shows the corresponding code flow diagram that presents the essential steps.

The function first ensures that it is *not* in the interrupt context (meaning, of course, that a hardware interrupt is involved). If it is, it terminates immediately. Because softIRQs are used to execute time-uncritical parts of ISRs, the code itself must not be called within an interrupt handler.

With the help of `local_softirq_pending`, the bitmap of all softIRQs set on the current CPU is determined. If any softIRQ is waiting to be processed, then `__do_softirq` is called.

This function resets the original bitmap to 0; in other words, all softIRQs are deleted. Both actions take place (on the current processor) with disabled interrupts to prevent modification of the bitmap as a result of interference by other processes. Subsequent code, on the other hand, executes with interrupts enabled. This allows the original bitmap to be modified at any time during processing of the softIRQ handlers.

The `action` functions in `softirq_vec` are invoked in a `while` loop for each enabled softIRQ.

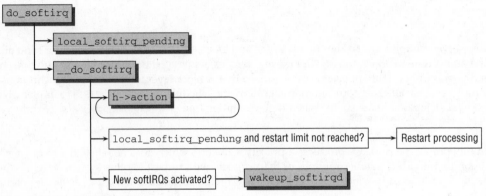

Figure 14-11: Code flow diagram for `do_softirq`.

Once all marked softIRQs have been serviced, the kernel checks whether new softIRQs have been marked in the original bitmap in the meantime. At least one softIRQ not serviced in the previous cycle must remain, and the number of restarts must not exceed `MAX_SOFTIRQ_RESTART` (usually set to 10). If this is the case, the marked softIRQs are again processed in sequence. This operation is repeated until no new unprocessed softIRQs remain after execution of all handlers.

Should softIRQs still remain after the `MAX_SOFTIRQ_RESTART` time of restarting the processing, `wakeup_softirqd` is called to wake up the softIRQ daemon:

14.2.2 The SoftIRQ Daemon

The task of the softIRQ daemon is to execute softIRQs asynchronously to remaining kernel code. To this end, each system processor is allocated its own daemon named `ksoftirqd`.

`wakeup_softirqd` is invoked at two points in the kernel to wake up the daemon:

❑ In `do_softirq`, as just mentioned.

❑ At the end of `raise_softirq_irqoff`. This funtion is called by `raise_softirq` internally, and can also be used directly if the kernel has interrupts turned off at the moment.

The wake-up function itself can be dealt with in a few lines. A pointer to the `task_struct` of the softIRQ daemon is read from a per-CPU variable by means of a few macros. If the current task state is not already `TASK_RUNNING`, it is put back in the list of processes ready to run by means of `wake_up_process` (see Chapter 2). Although this does not immediately start servicing of all pending software interrupts, the daemon (which runs with priority 19) is selected as soon as the scheduler has nothing better to do.

The softIRQ daemons of the system are generated shortly after init is called at system startup using the initcall mechanism described in Appendix D. After initialization, each daemon executes the following endless loop[17]:

kernel/softirq.c
```
static int ksoftirqd(void * __bind_cpu)
...
        while (!kthread_should_stop()) {
                if (!local_softirq_pending()) {
                        schedule();
                }

                __set_current_state(TASK_RUNNING);

                while (local_softirq_pending()) {
                        do_softirq();
                        cond_resched();
                }
                set_current_state(TASK_INTERRUPTIBLE);
        }

...
}
```

Each time it is awakened, the daemon first checks whether marked softIRQs are pending, as otherwise control can be passed to another process by explicitly invoking the scheduler.

If there are marked softIRQs, the daemon gets on with servicing them. In a while loop the two functions do_softirq and cond_resched are invoked repeatedly until no marked softIRQS remain. cond_resched ensures that the scheduler is called if the TIF_NEED_RESCHED flag was set for the current process (see Chapter 2). This is possible because all functions execute with enabled hardware interrupts.

14.3   Tasklets

Software interrupts are the most effective way of deferring the performance of activities to a future point in time. However, this deferral mechanism is very complicated to handle. Because softIRQs can be serviced simultaneously and independently on several processors, the handler routine of one and the same softIRQ can run on several CPUs at the same time. This represents a key contribution to the effectiveness of the concept — network implementation is a clear winner on multiprocessor systems. However, the handler routines must be designed to be fully reentrant and thread-safe. Alternatively, critical areas must be protected with spinlocks (or with other IPC mechanisms; see Chapter 5), and this requires a great deal of careful thought.

Tasklets and work queues are mechanisms for the deferred execution of work; their implementation is based on softIRQs, but they are easier to use and therefore more suitable for device drivers (and also for other general kernel code).

---

[17]kthread_should_stop() returns a true value if the softIRQ daemon is stopped explicitly. Since this happens only when a CPU is removed from the system, I will not discuss this case. I also omit preemption handling for the sake of clarity.

Before going into the technical details, a word of caution on the terminology used: For historical reasons, the term *bottom half* is often used to mean two different things; first, it refers to the lower half of the code of an ISR that performs no time-critical actions. Unfortunately, the mechanisms used in earlier kernel versions to defer the execution of actions was also referred to as the bottom half, with the result that the term is often used ambiguously. In the meantime, bottom halves no longer exist as a kernel mechanism. They were discarded during the development of 2.5 and replaced with tasklets, a far better substitute.

Tasklets are "small tasks" that perform mini jobs that would be wasted on full processes.

14.3.1 Generating Tasklets

Not surprisingly, the central data structure of each tasklet is called `tasklet_struct` and is defined as follows:

```
<interrupt.h>
struct tasklet_struct
{
        struct tasklet_struct *next;
        unsigned long state;
        atomic_t count;
        void (*func)(unsigned long);
        unsigned long data;
};
```

From the perspective of a device driver, the most important element is `func`. It points to the address of a function whose execution is to be deferred. `data` is passed as a parameter when the function is executed.

`next` is a pointer used to build a linked list of `tasklet_struct` instances. This allows several tasks to be queued for execution.

`state` indicates the current state of the task — as for a genuine task. However, only two options are available, each represented by a separate bit in `state`, which is why they can be set and removed independently of each other:

❑ `TASKLET_STATE_SCHED` is set when the tasklet is registered in the kernel and scheduled for execution.

❑ `TASKLET_STATE_RUN` indicates that a tasklet is currently being executed.

The second state is only of relevance on SMP systems. It is used to protect tasklets against concurrent execution on several processors.

The atomic counter `count` is used to disable tasklets already scheduled. If its value is not equal to 0, the corresponding tasklet is simply ignored when all pending tasklets are next executed.

14.3.2 Registering Tasklets

`tasklet_schedule` registers a tasklet in the system:

```
<interrupt.h>
static inline void tasklet_schedule(struct tasklet_struct *t);
```

If the TASKLET_STATE_SCHED bit is set, registration is terminated because the tasklet is already registered. Otherwise, the tasklet is placed at the start of a list whose list header is the CPU-specific variable tasklet_vec. This list contains all registered tasklets and uses the next element for linking purposes.

The tasklet list is marked for processing once a tasklet has been registered.

14.3.3 Executing Tasklets

The most important part in the life of a tasklet is its execution. Because tasklets are implemented on top of softIRQs, they are always executed when software interrupts are handled.

Tasklets are linked with the TASKLET_SOFTIRQ softIRQ. Consequently, it is sufficient to invoke raise_softirq(TASKLET_SOFTIRQ) to execute the tasklets of the current processor at the next opportunity. The kernel uses tasklet_action as the action function of the softIRQ.

The function first determines the CPU-specific list in which the tasklets marked for execution are linked. It then redirects the list header to a local element, and thus removes all entries from the public list. They are then processed one after the other in the following loop:

kernel/softirq.c
```
static void tasklet_action(struct softirq_action *a)
...
        while (list) {
                struct tasklet_struct *t = list;
                list = list->next;

                if (tasklet_trylock(t)) {
                        if (!atomic_read(&t->count)) {
                                if (!test_and_clear_bit(TASKLET_STATE_SCHED, &t->state))
                                        BUG();
                                t->func(t->data);
                                tasklet_unlock(t);
                                continue;
                        }
                        tasklet_unlock(t);
                }
                ...
        }
...
}
```

Executing tasklets in a while loop is similar to the mechanism used when handling softIRQs.

Because a tasklet can be executed on only one processor at a time, but other tasklets may run in parallel, tasklet-specific locking is required. The state state is used as the locking variable. Before the handler function of a tasklet is executed, the kernel uses tasklet_trylock to check whether the state of the tasklet is TASKLET_STATE_RUN; in other words, whether it is already running on another processor of the system:

<interrupt.h>
```
static inline int tasklet_trylock(struct tasklet_struct *t)
{
        return !test_and_set_bit(TASKLET_STATE_RUN, &(t)->state);
}
```

If the corresponding bit has not yet been set, it is set now.

If the count element is not equal to 0, the tasklet is regarded as deactivated. In this case, the code is not executed.

Once both checks have been passed successfully, the kernel executes the handler function of the tasklet with the corresponding function parameters by invoking t->func(t->data). Finally, the TASKLET_SCHED_RUN bit of the tasklet is deleted using tasklet_unlock.

If new tasklets were queued for the current processor during execution of the tasklets, the softIRQ TASKLET_SOFTIRQ is raised to execute the new tasklets as soon as possible. (Because the code needed to do this is not particularly interesting, it is not included above.)

In addition to normal tasklets, the kernel uses a second kind of tasklet of a "higher" priority. Its implementation is absolutely identical to that of normal tasklets except for the following modifications:

❑   HI_SOFTIRQ is used as a softIRQ instead of TASKLET_SOFTIRQ; its associated action function is tasklet_hi_action.

❑   The registered tasklets are queued in the CPU-specific variable tasklet_hi_vec. This is done using tasklet_hi_schedule.

In this context, "higher priority" means that the softIRQ handler HI_SOFTIRQ is executed *before* all other handlers — particularly before network handlers that account for the main part of software interrupt activity.

Currently, mostly sound card drivers make use of this alternative because deferring actions too long can impair the sound quality of audio output. But also network cards for high-speed transmission lines can profit from this mechanism.

14.4   Wait Queues and Completions

Wait queues are used to enable processes to wait for a particular event to occur without the need for constant polling. Processes sleep during wait time and are woken up automatically by the kernel when the event takes place. *Completions* are mechanisms that build on wait queues and are used by the kernel to wait for the end of an action. Both mechanisms are frequently used, primarily by device drivers, as shown in Chapter 6.

14.4.1   Wait Queues

Data Structures

Each wait queue has a head represented by the following data structure:

```
<wait.h>
struct __wait_queue_head {
        spinlock_t lock;
        struct list_head task_list;
};
typedef struct __wait_queue_head wait_queue_head_t;
```

Because wait queues can also be modified in interrupts, a spinlock named `lock` must be acquired before the queue is manipulated (see Chapter 5). `task_list` is a doubly linked list used to implement what it's best at: queues.

The elements in the queue are instances of the following data structure:

```
<wait.h>
struct __wait_queue {
        unsigned int flags;
        void *private;
        wait_queue_func_t func;
        struct list_head task_list;
};

typedef struct __wait_queue wait_queue_t;
```

❑ `flags` has the value `WQ_FLAG_EXCLUSIVE` or it does not — other flags are not defined at the moment. A set `WQ_FLAG_EXCLUSIVE` flag indicates that the waiting process would like to be woken up exclusively (this is discussed in more detail shortly).

❑ `private` is a pointer to the task structure of the waiting process. The variable can basically point to some arbitrary private data, but this is only seldom used in the kernel, so I will not discuss these cases any further.

❑ `func` is invoked to wake the element.

❑ `task_list` is used as a list element to position `wait_queue_t` instances in a wait queue.

Wait queue use is divided into two parts:

1. To put the current process to sleep in a wait queue, it is necessary to invoke the `wait_event` function (or one of its equivalents, discussed below). The process goes to sleep and relinquishes control to the scheduler.

The kernel invokes this function typically after it has issued a request to a block device to transfer data. Because transfer does not take place immediately and there is nothing else to do in the meantime, the process can sleep and therefore make CPU time available to other processes in the system.

2. At another point in the kernel — in our example, after data have arrived from the block device — the `wake_up` function (or one of its equivalents, discussed below) must be invoked to wake the sleeping processes in the wait queue.

> When processes are put to sleep using `wait_event`, you must always ensure that there is a corresponding `wake_up` call at another point in the kernel.

Putting Processes to Sleep

The `add_wait_queue` function is used to add a task to a wait queue; this function delegates its work to `__add_wait_queue` once the necessary spinlock has been acquired:

```
<wait.h>
static inline void __add_wait_queue(wait_queue_head_t *head, wait_queue_t *new)
{
```

```
       list_add(&new->task_list, &head->task_list);
}
```

Nothing more need be done than to add the new task to the wait list using the standard `list_add` list function.

`add_wait_queue_exclusive` is also available. It works in the same way as `add_wait_queue` but inserts the process at the queue tail and also sets its flag to `WQ_EXCLUSIVE` (what is behind this flag is discussed below).

Another method to put a process to sleep on a wait queue is `prepare_to_wait`. In addition to the parameters required by `add_wait_queue`, a task state is required as well:

kernel/wait.c
```
void fastcall
prepare_to_wait(wait_queue_head_t *q, wait_queue_t *wait, int state)
{
       unsigned long flags;

       wait->flags &= ~WQ_FLAG_EXCLUSIVE;
       spin_lock_irqsave(&q->lock, flags);
       if (list_empty(&wait->task_list))
               __add_wait_queue(q, wait);
...
       set_current_state(state);
       spin_unlock_irqrestore(&q->lock, flags);
}
```

After calling `__add_wait_queue` as discussed above, the kernel sets the current state of the process to the state passed to `prepare_to_wait`.

`prepare_to_wait_exclusive` is a variant that sets the `WQ_FLAG_EXCLUSIVE` flag and appends the wait queue element to the queue tail.

Two standard methods are available to initialize a wait queue entry:

1. `init_waitqueue_entry` initializes a dynamically allocated instance of `wait_queue_t`:

   <wait.h>
   ```
   static inline void init_waitqueue_entry(wait_queue_t *q,
                                           struct task_struct *p)
   {
          q->flags = 0;
          q->private = p;
          q->func = default_wake_function;
   }
   ```

   `default_wake_function` is just a parameter conversion front end that attempts to wake the process using the `try_to_wake_up` function described in Chapter 2.

2. `DEFINE_WAIT` allows for creating a static instance of `wait_queue_t` that is automatically initialized:

\<wait.h\>
```
#define DEFINE_WAIT(name) \
        wait_queue_t name = { \
                .private          = current, \
                .func             = autoremove_wake_function, \
                .task_list        = LIST_HEAD_INIT((name).task_list), \
        }
```

`autoremove_wake_function` is now used to wake the process. The function not only calls `default_wake_function`, but also removes the wait queue element from the wait queue.

`add_wait_queue` is normally not used directly. It is more common to use `wait_event`. This is a macro that requires two parameters:

1. A wait queue to wait on.

2. A condition in the form of a C expression of the event to wait for.

All the macro needs to do is to ensure that the condition is not yet already fulfilled; in this case, processing can be immediately stopped because there is nothing to wait for. The hard work is delegated to `__wait_event`:

\<wait.h\>
```
#define __wait_event(wq, condition)                                      \
do {                                                                     \
        DEFINE_WAIT(__wait);                                             \
                                                                         \
        for (;;) {                                                       \
                prepare_to_wait(&wq, &__wait, TASK_UNINTERRUPTIBLE);     \
                if (condition)                                           \
                        break;                                           \
                schedule();                                              \
        }                                                                \
        finish_wait(&wq, &__wait);                                       \
} while (0)
```

After setting up the wait queue element with `DEFINE_WAIT`, the macro produces an endless loop. The process is put to sleep on the wait queue using `prepare_to_wait`. Every time it is woken up, the kernel checks if the specified condition is fulfilled, and exits the endless loop if this is so. Otherwise, control is given to the scheduler, and the task is put to sleep again.

It is essential that both `wait_event` and `__wait_event` are implemented as macros — this allows for specifying conditions given by standard C expressions! Since C does not support any nifty features like higher-order functions, this behavior would be impossible (or at least very clumsy) to achieve using regular procedures.

When the condition if fulfilled, `finish_wait` sets the task state back to `TASK_RUNNING` and removes the entry from the wait queue list.[18]

In addition to `wait_event`, the kernel defines several other functions to place the current process in a wait queue. Their implementation is practically identical to that of `sleep_on`:

<wait.h>
```
#define wait_event_interruptible(wq, condition)
#define wait_event_timeout(wq, condition, timeout) { ... }
#define wait_event_interruptible_timeout(wq, condition, timeout)
```

❏   `wait_event_interruptible` uses the `TASK_INTERRUPTIBLE` task state. The sleeping process can therefore be woken up by receiving a signal.

❏   `wait_event_timeout` waits for the specified condition to be fulfilled, but stops waiting after a time-out specified in jiffies. This prevents a process from sleeping for ever.

❏   `wait_event_interruptible_timeout` puts the process to sleep so that it can be woken up by receiving a signal. It also registers a time-out. Kernel nomenclature is usually not a place for surprises!

Additionally the kernel defines a number of deprecated functions (`sleep_on`, `sleep_on_timeout`, `interruptible_sleep_on`, and `interruptible_sleep_on_timeout`) that are deprecated and not supposed to be used in new code anymore. They still sit around for compatibility purposes.

Waking Processes

The kernel defines a series of macros that are used to wake the processes in a wait queue. They are all based on the same function:

<wait.h>
```
#define wake_up(x)                   __wake_up(x, TASK_UNINTERRUPTIBLE | TASK_INTERRUPTIBLE, 1, NULL)
#define wake_up_nr(x, nr)            __wake_up(x, TASK_UNINTERRUPTIBLE | TASK_INTERRUPTIBLE, nr, NULL)
#define wake_up_all(x)               __wake_up(x, TASK_UNINTERRUPTIBLE | TASK_INTERRUPTIBLE, 0, NULL)
#define wake_up_interruptible(x)        __wake_up(x, TASK_INTERRUPTIBLE, 1, NULL)
#define wake_up_interruptible_nr(x, nr) __wake_up(x, TASK_INTERRUPTIBLE, nr, NULL)
#define wake_up_interruptible_all(x)    __wake_up(x, TASK_INTERRUPTIBLE, 0, NULL)
```

`__wake_up` delegates work to `__wake_up_common` after acquiring the necessary lock of the wait queue head.

kernel/sched.c
```
static void __wake_up_common(wait_queue_head_t *q, unsigned int mode,
                             int nr_exclusive, int sync, void *key)
{
        wait_queue_t *curr, *next;
...
```

---

[18]However, some care is required when doing this because `finished_wait` is invoked from many places and the task could have been removed by the wake-up function. However, the kernel manages to get everything right by careful manipulation of the list elements.

q selects the desired wait queue and mode specifies what state processes may have in order to be woken up. nr_exclusive indicates how many tasks with a set WQ_FLAG_EXCLUSIVE are to be woken up.

The kernel then iterates through the sleeping tasks and invokes their wake-up function func:

kernel/sched.c
```
        list_for_each_safe(curr, next, &q->task_list, task_list) {
                unsigned flags = curr->flags;

                if (curr->func(curr, mode, sync, key) &&
                                (flags & WQ_FLAG_EXCLUSIVE) && !--nr_exclusive)
                        break;
        }
}
```

The list is scanned repeatedly until there are either no further tasks or until the number of exclusive tasks specified by nr_exclusive has been woken up. This restriction is used to avoid a problem known as the *thundering herd*. If several processes are waiting for exclusive access to a resource, it makes no sense to wake all waiting processes because all but one will have to be put back to sleep. nr_exclusive generalizes this restriction.

The most frequently used wake_up function sets nr_exclusive to 1 and thus makes sure that only one exclusive task is woken up.

Recall from above that WQ_FLAG_EXCLUSIVE tasks are added to the end of the wait queue. This implementation ensures that in mixed queues all normal tasks are woken up first, and only then is the restriction for exclusive tasks taken into consideration.

It is useful to wake all processes in a wait queue if the processes are waiting for a data transfer to terminate. This is because the data of several processes can be read at the same time without mutual interference.

14.4.2 Completions

Completions resemble the semaphores discussed in Chapter 5 but are implemented on the basis of wait queues. What interests us is the completions interface. Two actors are present on the stage: One is waiting for something to be completed, and the other declares when this completion has happened. Actually, this is a simplification: An arbitrary number of processes can wait for a completion. To represent the "something" that the processes wait for to be completed, the kernel uses the following data structure:

<completion.h>
```
struct completion {
        unsigned int done;
        wait_queue_head_t wait;
};
```

done allows for handling the situation in which an event is completed *before* some other process waits for its completion. This is discussed below. wait is a standard wait queue on which waiting processes are put to sleep.

init_completion initializes a completion instance that was dynamically allocated, while DECLARE_COMPLETION is the macro of choice to set up a static instance of the data structure.

Processes can be added to the list using wait_for_completion, where they wait (in exclusive sleep state) until their request is processed by some part of the kernel. The function requires a completion instance as a parameter:

<completion.h>
```
void wait_for_completion(struct completion *);
int wait_for_completion_interruptible(struct completion *x);
unsigned long wait_for_completion_timeout(struct completion *x,
                                          unsigned long timeout);
unsigned long wait_for_completion_interruptible_timeout(
                struct completion *x, unsigned long timeout);
```

Several refined variants are additionally available:

❑ Normally processes that wait for completion of an event are in an uninterruptible state, but this can be changed if wait_for_completion_interruptible is used. The function returns -ERESTARTSYS if the process was interrupted, and 0 otherwise.

❑ wait_for_completion_timeout waits for a completion event to occur, but provides an additional time-out in jiffies that cancels waiting after a defined time. This helps to prevent waiting for an event indefinitely. If the completion is finished before the time-out occurs, then the remaining time is returned as result, otherwise 0.

❑ wait_for_completion_interruptible_timeout is a combination of both variants.

Once the request has been processed by another part of the kernel, either complete or complete_all must be invoked from there to wake the waiting processes. Because only one process can be removed from the completions list at each invocation, the function must be invoked exactly *n* times for *n* waiting processes. complete_all, on the other hand, wakes up all processing waiting for the completion. complete_and_exit is a small wrapper that first applies complete and then calls do_exit to finish the kernel thread.

<completion.h>
```
void complete(struct completion *);
void complete_all(struct completion *);
```

kernel/exit.c
```
NORET_TYPE void complete_and_exit(struct completion *comp, long code);
```

complete, complete_all, and complete_and_exit require a pointer to an instance of struct completion as a parameter that identifies the completion in question.

Now what is the meaning of done in struct completion? Each time complete is called, the counter is incremented by 1, and the wait_for functions only puts the caller to sleep if done is not equal to 0. Effectively, this means that processes do not wait for events that are already completed. complete_all works similarly, but sets the counter to the largest possible value (UINT_MAX/2 — half of the maximal value of an unsigned integer because the counter can also assume negative values) such that processes that call wait_ after the event has completed will never go to sleep.

14.4.3 Work Queues

Work queues are a further means of deferring actions until later. Because they are executed in the user context by means of daemons, the functions can sleep as long as they like — it does not matter at all to the kernel. During the development of 2.5, work queues were designed as a replacement for the keventd mechanism formerly used.

Each work queue has an array with as many entries as there are processors in the system. Each entry lists tasks to be performed at a later time.

For each work queue, the kernel generates a new kernel daemon in whose context the deferred tasks are performed using the wait queue mechanism just described.

A new wait queue is generated by invoking one of the functions create_workqueue or create_workqueue_singlethread. While the first one creates a worker thread on all CPUs, the latter one just creates a single thread on the first CPU of the system. Both functions use __create_workqueue_key internally[19]:

kernel/workqueue.c
```
struct workqueue_struct *__create_workqueue(const char *name,
                                            int singlethread)
```

The name argument indicates the name under which the generated daemon is shown in the process list. If singlethread is set to 0, a thread is created on every CPU of the system, otherwise just on the first one.

All tasks pushed onto wait queues must be packed into instances of the work_struct structure in which the following elements are important in the view of the work queue user:

<workqueue.h>
```
struct work_struct;
typedef void (*work_func_t)(struct work_struct *work);

struct work_struct {
        atomic_long_t data;
        struct list_head entry;
        work_func_t func;
}
```

entry is used as usual to group several work_struct instances in a linked list. func is a pointer to the function to be deferred. It is supplied with a pointer to the instance of work_struct that was used to submit the work. This allows the worker function to obtain the data element that can point to arbitrary data associated with the work_struct.

---

[19] Another variant, create_freezable_workqueue, is available to create work queues that are friendly toward system hibernation. Since I do not discuss any mechanisms related to power management, I will also not discuss this alternative any further. Also note that the prototype of __create_workqueue is simplified and does not contain parameters related to lock depth management and power management.

Why does the kernel use `atomic_long_t` as the data type for a pointer to some arbitrary data, and not `void *` as usual? In fact, former kernel versions defined `work_struct` as follows:

<workqueue.h>
```
struct work_struct {
...
        void (*func)(void *);
        void *data;
...
};
```

`data` was represented by a pointer as expected. However, the kernel does use a little trick — which is fairly on the edge of being dirty — to squeeze more information into the structure without spending more memory. Because pointers are aligned on 4-byte boundaries on all supported architectures, the first 2 bits are guaranteed to be zero. They are therefore abused to contain flag bits. The remaining bits hold the pointer information as usual. The following macros allow masking out the flag bits:

<workqueue.h>
```
#define WORK_STRUCT_FLAG_MASK (3UL)
#define WORK_STRUCT_WQ_DATA_MASK (~WORK_STRUCT_FLAG_MASK)
```

Currently only a single flag is defined: `WORK_STRUCT_PENDING` allows for finding out whether a delayable work item is currently pending (if the bit is set) or not. The auxiliary macro `work_pending(work)` allows for checking for the bit. Note that the atomic data type of `data` ensures that the bit can be modified without concurrency problems.

To simplify declaring and filling a static instance of this structure, the kernel provides the `INIT_WORK(work, func)` macro, which supplies an existing instance of `work_struct` with a delayed function. If a data argument is required, it must be set afterward.

There are two ways of adding a `work_queue` instance to a work queue — `queue_work` and `queue_work_delayed`. The first alternative has the following prototype:

kernel/workqueue.c
```
int fastcall queue_work(struct workqueue_struct *wq, struct work_struct *work)
```

It adds `work` to the work queue `wq`; the work itself is performed at an undefined time (when the scheduler selects the daemon).

To ensure that work queued will be executed *after* a specified time interval has passed since submission, the `work_struct` needs to be extended with a timer. The solution is as obvious as can be:

<workqueue.h>
```
struct delayed_work {
        struct work_struct work;
        struct timer_list timer;
};
```

`queue_delayed_work` is used to submit instances of `delayed_work` to a work queue. It ensure that *at least* one time interval specified (in jiffies) by `delay` elapses before the deferred work is performed.

kernel/workqueue.c
```
int fastcall queue_delayed_work(struct workqueue_struct *wq,
                    struct delayed_work *dwork, unsigned long delay)
```

This function first generates a kernel timer whose time-out occurs in `delayed` jiffies. The associated handler function then uses `queue_work` to add the work to the work queue in the normal way.

The kernel generates a standard wait queue named `events`. This queue can be used by all parts of the kernel for which it is not worthwhile creating a separate work queue. The two functions below, whose implementation I need not discuss in detail, must be used to place new work in this standard queue:

kernel/workqueue.c
```
int schedule_work(struct work_struct *work)
int schedule_delayed_work(struct delay_work *dwork, unsigned long delay)
```

14.5 Summary

The kernel can be activated synchronously or asynchronously. While the preceeding chapter discussed how system calls are employed for synchronous activation, you have seen in this chapter that there is a second, asynchronous activation method triggered from the hardware using interrupts.

Interrupts are used when the hardware wants to notify the kernel of some condition, and there are various ways that interrupts can be implemented physically. After discussing the different possibilities, we have analyzed the generic data structures of the kernel that are employed to manage interrupts, and have seen how to implement flow handling for various IRQ types. The kernel has to provide service routines for IRQs, and some care is required to implement them properly. Most important, it is necessary to make these handlers as fast as possible, and the work is therefore often distributed into a quick top half and a slower bottom half that runs outside the interrupt context.

The kernel offers some means to defer actions until a later point in time, and I have discussed the corresponding possibilities in this chapter: SoftIRQs are the software equivalent to hardware IRQs, and tasklets are built on this mechanism. While they enable the kernel to postpone work until later, they are not allowed to go to sleep. This is, however, possible with wait queues and work queues, also examined in this chapter.

15

Time Management

All the methods of deferring work to a future point in time discussed in this book so far do not cover one specific area — the *time-based deferral of tasks*. The different variants that have been discussed do, of course, give some indication of when a deferred task will be executed (e.g., tasklets when handling softIRQs), but it is not possible to specify an exact time or a time interval after which a deferred activity will be performed by the kernel. The simplest kind of usage in this respect is obviously the implementation of time-outs where the kernel on behalf of a userland process waits a specific period of time for the arrival of an event — for example, 10 seconds for a user to press a key as a last opportunity to cancel before an important operation is carried out. Other usages are widespread in user applications.

The kernel itself also uses timers for various tasks, for example, when devices communicate with associated hardware, often using protocols with chronologically defined sequences. A large number of timers are used to specify wait timeouts in TCP implementation.

Depending on the job that needs to be performed, timers need to provide different characteristics, especially with respect to the maximal possible resolution. This chapter discusses the alternatives provided by the Linux kernel.

15.1 Overview

First of all, an overview of the subsystem that we are about to inspect in detail is presented.

15.1.1 Types of Timers

The timing subsystem of the kernel has grown tremendously during the development of 2.6. For the initial releases, the timer subsystem consisted solely of what are now known as low-resolution timers. Essentially, low-resolution timers are centered around a periodic tick which happens at regular intervals. Events can be scheduled to be activated at one of these intervals. Pressure to extend this comparatively simple framework came predominantly from two sources:

❑ Devices with limited power (i.e., laptops, embedded systems, etc.) need to use as little energy as possible when there is nothing to do. If a periodic clock is running, there is, however, nearly always something to do — the tick must be provided. But if no users for the tick are present, it would basically not need to run. Nevertheless, the system needs to be brought from a low-power state into a state with higher power consumption just to implement the periodic tick.

❑ Multimedia-oriented applications need very precise timekeeping, for instance, to avoid frame skips in videos, or jumps during audio playback. This necessitated increasing the available resolution.

Finding a good solution agreeable to all developers (and users!) who come into contact with time management — and there is quite a large number of them — took many years and a good many proposed patches. The current state is rather unusual because two rather distinct types of timers are supported by the kernel:

❑ *Classical timers* have been available since the initial versions of the kernel. Their implementation is located in `kernel/timer.c`. A resolution of typically 4 milliseconds is provided, but the value depends on the frequency with which the machine's timer interrupt is operated. These classical timers are called *low-resolution* or *timer wheel* timers.

❑ For many applications, especially media-oriented ones, a timer resolution of several milliseconds is not good enough. Indeed, recent hardware provides means of much more precise timing, which can achieve resolutions in the nanosecond range formally. During the development of kernel 2.6, an additional timer subsystem was added allowing the use of such timer sources. The timers provided by the new subsystem are conventionally referred to as *high-resolution timers*.

Some code for high-resolution timers is always compiled into the kernel, but the implementation will only perform better than low-resolution timers if the configuration option `HIGH_RES_TIMERS` is set. The framework introduced by high-resolution timers is reused by low-resolution timers (in fact, low-resolution timers are implemented on top of the high-resolution mechanism).

Classical timers are bound by a fixed raster, while high-resolution clock events can essentially happen at arbitrary times; see Figure 15-1. Unless the dynamic ticks feature is active, it can also happen that ticks occur when no event expires. High-resolution events, in contrast, only occur when some event is due.

Figure 15-1: Comparison between low- and high-resolution timers.

Why did the developers not choose the seemingly obvious path and improve the already existing timer subsystem, but instead added a completely new one? Indeed, some people tried to pursue this strategy, but the mature and robust structure of the old timer subsystem did not make it particularly easy to improve while still being efficient — and without creating new problems. Some more thoughts on this problem can be found in `Documentation/hrtimers.txt`.

Independent of the resolution, the kernel nomenclature distinguishes two types of timers:

❑ **Time-outs** — Represent events that are bound to happen after some time, but can and usually will be canceled before. For example, consider that the network subsystem waits for an incoming packet that is bound to arrive within a certain period of time. To handle this situation, a timer is set that will expire after the time is over. Since packets usually arrive on time, chances are that the timer will be removed before it will actually go off. Besides resolution is not very critical for these types of timers. When the kernel allows an acknowledgment to a packet to be sent within 10 seconds, it does not really matter if the time-out occurs after 10 or 10.001 seconds.

❑ **Timers** — Are used to implement temporal sequences. For instance, a sound card driver could want to issue some data to a sound card in small, periodic time intervals. Timers of this sort will usually expire and require much better resolution than time-outs.

An overview of the building blocks employed to implement the timing subsystem is given in Figure 15-2. Owing to the nature of an overview, it is not too precise, but gives a quick glance at what is involved in timekeeping, and how the components interact with each other. Many details are left to the following discussion.

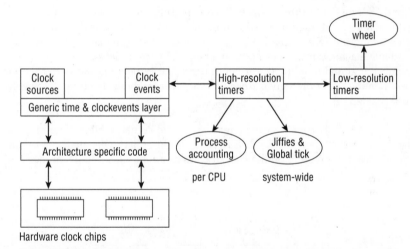

Figure 15-2: Overview of the components that build up the timing subsystem.

The raw hardware sits at the very bottom. Every typical system has several devices, usually implemented by clock chips, that provide timing functionality and can serve as clocks. Which hardware is available depends on the particular architecture. IA-32 and AMD64 systems, for instance, have a *programmable interrupt timer* (PIT, implemented by the 8253 chip) as a classical clock source that has only a very modest resolution and stability. CPU-local APICs (*advanced programmable interrupt controllers*), which were already mentioned in the context of IRQ handling, provide much better resolution and stability. They are suitable as high-resolution time sources, whereas the PIT is only good enough for low-resolution timers.

Hardware naturally needs to be programmed by architecture-specific code, but the *clock source* abstraction provides a generic interface to all hardware clock chips. Essentially, read access to the current value of the running counter provided by a clock chip is granted.

Periodic events do not comply with a free running counter very well, thus another abstraction is required. *Clock events* are the foundation of periodic events. Clock events can, however, be more powerful. Some time devices can provide events at arbitrary, irregular points in time. In contrast to periodic event devices, they are called *one-shot* devices.

The high-resolution timer mechanism is based on clock events, whereas the low-resolution timer mechanism utilizes periodic events that can either come directly from a low-resolution clock or from the high-resolution subsystem. Two important tasks for which low-resolution timers assume responsibility are

1. Handle the global `jiffies` counter. The value is incremented periodically (or at least it *looks* periodical to most parts of the kernel) and represents a particularly simple form of time reference.[1]

2. Perform per-process accounting. This also includes handling classical low-resolution timers, which can be associated with any process.

15.1.2 Configuration Options

Not only are there two distinct (but nevertheless related) timing subsystems in the kernel, but the situation is additionally complicated by the dynamic ticks feature. Traditionally, the periodic tick is active during the entire lifetime of the kernel. This can be wasteful in systems where power is scarce, with laptops and portable machines prime examples. If a periodic event is active, the system will never be able to go into power-saving modes for long intervals of time. The kernel thus allows to configure *dynamic ticks*,[2] which do not require a periodic signal. Since this complicates timer handling, assume for now that this feature is not enabled.

Four different timekeeping scenarios can be realized by the kernel. While the number may not sound too large, understanding the time-related code is not exactly simplified when many tasks can be implemented in four different ways depending on the chosen configuration. Figure 15-3 summarizes the possible choices.

High-res Dynamic ticks	High-res Periodic ticks
Low-res Dynamic ticks	Low-res Periodic ticks

Figure 15-3: Possible timekeeping configurations that arise because of high- and low-resolution timers and dynamic/periodic ticks.

Computing all four possible combinations from two sets with two elements is certainly not complicated. Nevertheless, it is important to realize that all combinations of low/high res and dynamic/periodic ticks are valid and need to be accounted for by the kernel.

---

[1]Updating the jiffies value is not easy to categorize between low- and high-resolution frameworks because it can be performed by both, depending on the kernel configuration. The fine details of jiffie updating are discussed in the course of this chapter.

[2]It is also customary to refer to a system with this configuration option enabled as a *tickless* system.

15.2 Implementation of Low-Resolution Timers

Since low-resolution timers have been around in the kernel for many years and are used in hundreds of places, their implementation is covered first. In the following, assume that the kernel is defined to work with periodic ticks. The situation is more involved if dynamic ticks are in use, but that case is discussed in Section 15.5.

15.2.1 Timer Activation and Process Accounting

As the time base for timers, the kernel uses the timer interrupt of the processor or any other suitable periodic source. On IA-32 and AMD64 systems, the programmable interrupt timer (PIT) or the High Precision Event Timer (HPET) can be employed for this purpose. Nearly all modestly modern systems of this type are equipped with an HPET, and if one is available, it is preferred to the PIT.[3] The interrupt occurs at regular intervals — exactly HZ times per second. HZ is defined by an architecture-specific preprocessor symbol in <asm-arch/param.h>. The assigned value can be configured at compile time via the configuration option CONFIG_HZ.

HZ=250 is used as the default value for most machine types, especially on the ubiquitous IA-32 and AMD64 architectures.

> The HZ frequency is also defined (and used) when dynamic ticks are enabled because it is the fundamental quantity for many timekeeping tasks. On a busy system where something nontrivial (unlike the idle task) is always available to be done, there is superficially no difference between dynamic and periodic ticks. Differences only arise when there is little to do and some timer interrupts can be skipped.

Higher HZ values will, in general, lead to better interactivity and responsiveness of the system, particularly because the scheduler is called at each timer tick. As a drawback, more system work needs to be done because the timer routines are called more often; thus the general kernel overhead will increase with increasing HZ settings. This makes large HZ values preferable for desktop and multimedia systems, whereas lower HZ values are better for servers and batch machines where interactivity is not much of a concern.

Early kernels in the 2.6 series directly hooked into the timer interrupt to start timer activation and process accounting, but this has been somewhat complicated by the introduction of the generic clock framework. Figure 15-4 provides an overview of the situation on IA-32 and AMD64 machines.

The details differ for other architectures, but the principle is nevertheless the same. (How a particular architecture proceeds is usually set up in time_init which is called at boot time to initialize the fundamental low-resolution timekeeping.) The periodic clock is set up to operate at HZ ticks per second. IA-32 registers timer_interrupt as the interrupt handler, whereas AMD64 uses timer_event_interrupt. Both functions notify the generic, architecture-independent time processing layers of the kernel by calling the event handler of the so-called global clock (see Section 15.3). Different handler functions are employed

---

[3]Using the HPET can be disabled with the kernel command-line option hpet=disable, though.

depending on which timekeeping model is used. In any case, the handler will set the ball rolling for periodic low-resolution timekeeping by calling the following two functions:

❏ do_time is responsible for system-wide, global tasks: Update the jiffies value, and handle process accounting. On a multiprocessor system, one particular CPU is selected to perform both tasks, and all other CPUs are not concerned with them.

❏ update_process_times needs to be performed by every CPU on SMP systems. Besides process accounting, it activates and expires all registered classical low-resolution timers and provides the scheduler with a sense of time. Since these topics merit a discussion of their own (and are not so much related to the rest of this section), they are inspected in detail in Section 15.8. Here we are only concerned with timer activation and expiration, which is triggered by calling run_local_timers. The function, in turn, raises the softIRQ TIMER_SOFTIRQ, and the handler function is responsible to run the low-resolution timers.

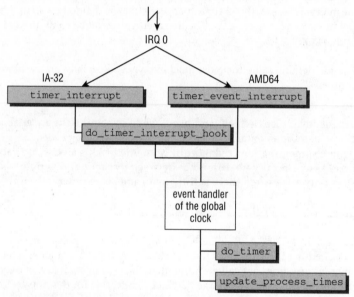

Figure 15-4: Overview of periodic low-resolution timer interrupts on IA-32 and AMD64 machines.

First, consider do_time. The function performs as shown in Figure 15-5.

The global variable jiffies_64 (an integer variable with 64 bits on all architectures)[4] is incremented by 1. All that this means is that jiffies_64 specifies the exact number of timer interrupts since the system started. Its value is increased with constant regularity when dynamic ticks are disabled. If dynamic ticks are active, more than one tick period can have passed since the last update.

---

[4]This is achieved on 32-bit processors by combining two 32-bit variables.

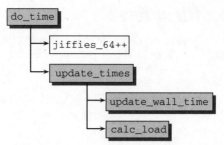

Figure 15-5: Code flow diagram for do_time.

For historical reasons, the kernel sources also include another time base. `jiffies` is a variable of the `unsigned long` type and is therefore only 4 bytes long on 32-bit processors, and this corresponds to 32 and not 64 bits. This causes a problem. After a longer system uptime, the counter reaches its maximum value and must be reset to 0. Given a timer frequency of 100 Hz, this situation would arise after just less than 500 days, and correspondingly earlier for higher `HZ` settings.[5] When a 64-bit data type is used, the problem never occurs because uptimes of 10^{12} days are a little utopian, even for a very stable kernel such as Linux.

The kernel uses a trick to prevent efficiency losses when converting between the two different time bases. `jiffies` and `jiffies_64` match in their less significant bits and therefore point to the same memory location or the same register. To achieve this, the two variables are declared separately, but the linker script used to bind the final kernel binary specifies that `jiffies` equates to the 4 less significant bytes of `jiffies_64`, where either the first or last 4 bytes must be used depending on the endianness of the underlying architecture. The two variables are synonymous on 64-bit machines.

Caution: Times specified by jiffies and the `jiffies` variable itself require some special attention. The peculiarities are discussed in Section 15.2.2 immediately below.

The remaining actions that must be performed at each timer interrupt are delegated by `update_times`:

❑   `update_wall_time` updates the wall time that specifies how long the system has already been up and running. While this information is also roughly provided by the jiffies mechanism, the wall clock reads the time from the current time source and updates the wall clock accordingly. In contrast to the jiffies mechanism, the wall clock uses a human readable format (nanoseconds) to represent the current time.

❑   `calc_load` updates the system load statistics that specify how many tasks have on average been waiting on the run queue in a ready-to-run state during the last 1, 5, and, 15 minutes. This status can be output using, for example, the `w` command.

---

[5]Most computers do not, of course, run uninterruptedly for so long, which is why the problem might appear to be somewhat marginal at first glance. However, there are some applications — for instance, servers in embedded systems — in which uptimes of this magnitude can easily be achieved. In such situations it must be ensured that the time base functions reliably.
During the development of 2.5, a patch was integrated to cause the jiffies value to wrap around 5 minutes after system boot. Potential problems can, therefore, be found quickly without waiting for years for wraparound to occur.

15.2.2 Working with Jiffies

Jiffies provide a simple form of low-resolution time management in the kernel. Although the concept is simple, some caveats apply when the variable is read or when times specified in jiffies need to be compared.

Since `jiffies_64` can be a composed variable on 32-bit systems, it must not be read directly, but may only be accessed with the auxiliary function `get_jiffies_64`. This ensures that the correct value is returned on all systems.

Comparing Times

To compare the temporal relation of events, the kernel provides several auxiliary functions that prevent off-by-one errors if they are used instead of a home-grown comparisons (a, b, and c denote jiffie time values for some events):

❏ `timer_after(a,b)` returns true if time a is after time b. `time_before(a,b)` will be true if time a is before time b, as you will have guessed.

❏ `time_after_eq(a,b)` works like `time_after`, but also returns true if both times are identical. `time_before_eq(a,b)` is the inverse variant.

❏ `time_in_range(a,b,c)` checks if time a is contained in the time interval denoted by $[b, c]$. The boundaries are included in the range, so a may be identical to b or c.

Using these functions ensures that wraparounds of the jiffies counter are handled correctly. As a general rule, kernel code should therefore never compare time values directly, but always use these functions.

Although there are fewer problems when 64-bit times as given by `jiffies_64` are compared, the kernel also provides the functions shown above for 64-bit times. Save for `time_in_range`, just append `_64` to the respective function name to obtain a variant that works with 64-bit time values.

Time Conversion

When it comes to time intervals, jiffies might not be the unit of choice in the minds of most programmers. It is more conventional to think in milliseconds or microseconds for short time intervals. The kernel thus provides some auxiliary functions to convert back and forth between these units and jiffies:

```
<jiffies.h>
unsigned int jiffies_to_msecs(const unsigned long j);
unsigned int jiffies_to_usecs(const unsigned long j);
unsigned long msecs_to_jiffies(const unsigned int m);
unsigned long usecs_to_jiffies(const unsigned int u);
```

The functions are self-explanatory. However, Section 15.2.3 shows that conversion functions between jiffies and `struct timeval` and `struct timespec`, respectively, are also available.

15.2.3 Data Structures

Let us now turn our attention to how low-resolution timers are implemented. You have already seen that processing is initiated by `run_local_timers`, but before this function is discussed, some prerequisites in the form of data structures must be introduced.

Timers are organized on lists, and the following data structure represents a timer on a list:

\<timer.h\>
```
struct timer_list {
        struct list_head entry;
        unsigned long expires;

        void (*function)(unsigned long);
        unsigned long data;

        struct tvec_t_base_s *base;
};
```

As usual, a doubly linked list is used to link registered timers with each other. `entry` is the list head. The other structure items have the following meaning:

- ❑   `function` saves a pointer to the callback function invoked upon time-out.

- ❑   `data` is an argument for the callback function.

- ❑   `expires` specifies the time, in jiffies, at which the timer expires.

- ❑   `base` is a pointer to a base element in which the timers are sorted on their expiry time (discussed in more detail shortly). There is a base element for each processor of the system; consequently, the CPU upon which the timer runs can be determined using `base`.

The macro `DEFINE_TIMER(_name, _function, _expires, _data)` is provided to declare a static `timer_list` instance.

Times are given in two formats in the kernel — as offsets or as absolute values. Both make use of `jiffies`. While offsets are used when a new timer is installed, all kernel data structures use absolute values because they can easily be compared with the current `jiffies` time. The `expires` element of `timer_list` also uses absolute times and not offsets.

Because programmers tend to think in seconds rather than in HZ units when defining time intervals, the kernel provides a matching data structure plus the option of converting into `jiffies` (and, of course, vice versa):

\<time.h\>
```
struct timeval {
        time_t          tv_sec;         /* seconds */
        suseconds_t     tv_usec;        /* microseconds */
};
```

The elements are self-explanatory. The complete time interval is calculated by adding the specified second and microsecond values. The `timeval_to_jiffies` and `jiffies_to_timeval` functions are used to convert between this representation and a `jiffies` value. These functions are implemented in \<timer.h\>.

Another possibility to specify times includes nanoseconds instead of microseconds:

\<time.h\>
```
struct timespec {
        time_t tv_sec; /* seconds */
        long tv_nsec; /* nanoseconds */
};
```

Again auxiliary functions convert back and forth between jiffies and `timespecs`: `timespec_to_jiffies` and `jiffies_to_timespec`.

15.2.4   Dynamic Timers

The kernel needs data structures to manage *all* timers registered in the system (these may be assigned to a process or to the kernel itself). The structures must permit rapid and efficient checking for expired timers so as not to consume too much CPU time. After all, such checks must be performed at each timer interrupt.[6]

Mode of Operation

Before taking a closer look at the existing data structures and the implementation of the algorithms, let's illustrate the principle of timer management by reference to a simplified example, since the algorithm used by the kernel is more complicated than might be expected at first glance. (This complexity brings its rewards in the form of greater performance that could not be achieved with simpler algorithms and structures.) Not only must the data structure hold all the information needed to manage timers,[7] but it must also be capable of being scanned easily at periodic intervals so that expired timers can execute and then be removed. Figure 15-6 shows how timers are managed by the kernel.

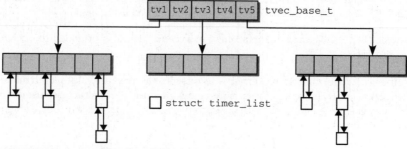

Figure 15-6: Data structures for managing timers.

The main difficulty lies in scanning the list for timers that are about to expire and that have just expired. Because simply stringing together all `timer_list` instances is not satisfactory, the kernel creates different groups into which timers are classified according to their expiry time. The basis for grouping is the main array with five entries whose elements are again made up of arrays. The five positions of the main array sort the existing timers roughly according to expiry times. The first group is a collection of all timers whose expiry time is between 0 and 255 (or 2^8) ticks. The second group includes all timers with an expiry time between 256 and $2^{8+6} - 1 = 2^{14} - 1$ ticks. The range for the third group is from 2^{14} to $2^{8+2\times6} - 1$, and so on. The entries in the main table are known as *groups* and are sometimes referred to as *buckets*. Table 15-1 lists the intervals of the individual timer groups. I have used the bucket sizes for regular systems as the basis of our calculations. The intervals differ on small systems with little memory.

Each group itself comprises an array in which the timers are sorted again. The array of the first group consists of 256 elements, each position standing for a possible `expires` value between 0 and 256. If there

---

[6]Although the chosen data structure is well suited for the intended purpose, it is nevertheless too inefficient for high-resolution timers that require even better organization.

[7]For the moment, ignore the additional data required for process-specific interval timers.

are several timers in the system with the same `expires` value, they are linked by means of a doubly linked standard list (and via the `entry` element of `timer_list`).

Table 15-1: Interval Lengths for Timers

Group	Interval
`tv1`	$0-255$
`tv2`	$2^8 = 256 - 2^{14} - 1$
`tv3`	$2^{14} - 2^{20} - 1$
`tv4`	$2^{20} - 2^{26} - 1$
`tv5`	$2^{26} - 2^{32} - 1$

The remaining groups also consist of arrays but with fewer entries, namely, 64. The array entries also accept `timer_list` instances linked in a doubly linked list. However, each array entry no longer holds just one possible value of `expires` but an entire interval. The length of the interval depends on the group. While the second group permits $256 = 2^8$ consecutive time values per array element, this figure is 2^{14} in the third group, 2^{20} in the fourth, and 2^{26} in the fifth and final group. Why these interval sizes make sense will become clear when we consider how timers are executed in the course of time and how the associated data structure is changed.

How are timers executed? The kernel is responsible primarily for looking after the first of the above groups because this includes all timers due to expire shortly. For simplicity's sake, let us assume that each group has a counter that stores the number of an array position (actual kernel implementation is the same in functional terms but is far less clearly structured as you will see shortly).

The index entry of the first group points to the array element that holds the `timer_list` instances of the timers shortly due to be executed. The kernel scans this list every time there is a timer interrupt, executes all timer functions, and increments the index position by 1. The timers just executed are removed from the data structure. The next time a timer interrupt occurs, the timers at the new array position are executed and deleted from the data structure, and the index is again incremented by 1, and so on. Once all entries have been processed, the value of the index is 255. Because addition is modulo 256, the index reverts to its initial position (position 0).

Because the contents of the first group are exhausted after at most 256 ticks, timers of the higher groups must be pushed forward successively in order to replenish the first group. Once the index position of the first group has reverted to its initial position, the group is replenished with all timers of a *single* array entry of the second group. This explains the interval size selection in the individual groups. Because 256 different expiry times per array element are possible in the first group, the data of a *single* entry in the second group are sufficient to replenish the complete array of the first group. The same applies for higher groups. The data in an array element of the third group are sufficient to replenish the entire second group; an element of the fourth group is sufficient for the entire third group, and an element of the fifth group is sufficient for the entire fourth group.

The array positions of the higher groups are not, of course, selected randomly — the index entry again has a role to play. However, the index entry value is no longer incremented by 1 after each timer tick but only after each 256^{i-1} tick, where i stands for the number of the group.

Let's examine this behavior by reference to a concrete example: 256 jiffies have expired since processing of the first group was started, which is why the index is reset to 0. At the same time, the contents of the first array element of the second group are used to replenish the data of the first group. Let us assume that the jiffies system timer has the value 10,000 at the time of reset. In the first element of the second group, there is a linked list of timers due to expire at 10,001, 10,015, 10,015, and 10,254 ticks. These are distributed over array positions 1, 15, and 254 of the first group, and a linked list made up of two pointers is created at position 15 — after all, both expire at the same time. Once copying is complete, the index position of the second group is incremented by 1.

The cycle then starts afresh. The timers of the first group are processed one after the other until index position 255 is reached. All timers in the second array element of the second group are used to replenish the first group. When the index position of the *second* group has reached 63 (from the second group onward the groups contain only 64 entries), the contents of the first element of the *third* group are used to replenish the data of the second group. Finally, when the index of the third group has reached its maximum value, data are fetched from the fourth group; the same applies for the transfer of data between the fifth and the fourth groups.

To determine which timers have expired, the kernel need not scan through an enormous list of timers but can limit itself to checking a *single* array position in the first group. Because this position is usually empty or contains only a single timer, this check can be performed very quickly. Even the occasional copying of timers from the higher groups requires little CPU time, because copying can be carried out efficiently by means of pointer manipulation (the kernel is not required to copy memory blocks but need only supply pointers with new values as is usually the case in standard list functions).

Data Structures

The contents of the above groups are generated by two simple data structures that differ minimally:

kernel/timer.c
```
typedef struct tvec_s {
        struct list_head vec[TVN_SIZE];
} tvec_t;

typedef struct tvec_root_s {
        struct list_head vec[TVR_SIZE];
} tvec_root_t;
```

While tvec_root_t corresponds to the first group, tvec_t represents higher groups. The two structures differ only in the size of the array elements; for the first group, TVR_SIZE is defined as 256. All other groups use TVN_SIZE entries with a default value of 64. Systems where memory is scarce set the configuration option BASE_SMALL; in this case, 64 entries are reserved for the first and 16 for all other groups.

Each processor in the system has its own data structures for managing timers that run on it. A per-CPU instance of the following data structure is used as the root element:

kernel/timer.c
```
struct tvec_t_base_s {
...
        unsigned long timer_jiffies;
        tvec_root_t tv1;
        tvec_t tv2;
        tvec_t tv3;
        tvec_t tv4;
        tvec_t tv5;
} ____cacheline_aligned_in_smp;
```

The elements `tv1` to `tv5` represent the individual groups; their function should be clear from the above description. Of particular interest is the `timer_jiffies` element. It records the time (in jiffies) by which all timers of the structure were executed. If, for example, the value of this variable is 10,500, the kernel knows that all timers up to the jiffies value 10,499 have been executed. Usually, `timer_jiffies` is equal to or 1 less than `jiffies`. The difference may be a little greater (with very high loading) if the kernel is not able to execute timers for a certain period.

Implementing Timer Handling

Handling of all timers is initiated in `update_process_times` by invoking the `run_local_timers` function. This limits itself to using `raise_softirq(TIMER_SOFTIRQ)` to activate the timer management softIRQ, which is executed at the next opportunity.[8] `run_timer_softirq` is used as the handler function of the softIRQ; it selects the CPU-specific instance of `struct tvec_t_base_s` and invokes `__run_timers`.

`__run_timers` implements the algorithm described above. However, nowhere in the data structures shown is the urgently required index position for the individual rough categories to be found! The kernel does not require an explicit variable because all necessary information is contained in the `timer_jiffies` member of `base`. The following macros are defined for this purpose:

kernel/timer.c
```
#define TVN_BITS (CONFIG_BASE_SMALL ? 4 : 6)
#define TVR_BITS (CONFIG_BASE_SMALL ? 6 : 8)
#define TVN_SIZE (1 << TVN_BITS)
#define TVR_SIZE (1 << TVR_BITS)
#define TVN_MASK (TVN_SIZE - 1)
#define TVR_MASK (TVR_SIZE - 1)
```

kernel/timer.c
```
#define INDEX(N) ((base->timer_jiffies >> (TVR_BITS + (N) * TVN_BITS)) & TVN_MASK)
```

The configuration option `BASE_SMALL` can be defined on small, usually embedded systems to save some space by using a smaller number of slots than in the regular case. The timer implementation is otherwise unaffected by this choice.

---

[8]Because softIRQs cannot be handled directly, it can happen that the kernel does not perform any timer handling for a few jiffies. Timers can, therefore, sometimes be activated too late but can never be activated too early.

The index position of the first group can be computed by masking the value of `base->timer_jiffies` with `TVR_MASK`.

```
int index = base->timer_jiffies & TVR_MASK;
```

Generally, the following macro can be used to compute the current index position in group `N`:

```
#define INDEX(N) (base->timer_jiffies >> (TVR_BITS + N * TVN_BITS)) & TVN_MASK
```

Doubting Thomases can easily convince themselves of the correctness of the bit operations by means of a short Perl script.

The implementation produces exactly the results described above using the following code (`__run_timers` is called by the abovementioned `run_timer_softirq`):

kernel/timer.c
```
static inline void __run_timers(tvec_base_t *base)
{

        while (time_after_eq(jiffies, base->timer_jiffies)) {
                struct list_head work_list;
                struct list_head *head = &work_list;
                int index = base->timer_jiffies & TVR_MASK;
...
```

If the kernel has missed a number of timers in the past, they are dealt with now by processing all pointers that expired between the last execution point (`base->timer_jiffies`) and the current time (`jiffies`):

kernel/timer.c
```
                if (!index &&
                        (!cascade(base, &base->tv2, INDEX(0))) &&
                                (!cascade(base, &base->tv3, INDEX(1))) &&
                                        !cascade(base, &base->tv4, INDEX(2)))
                        cascade(base, &base->tv5, INDEX(3));
...
```

The `cascade` function is used to replenish the timer lists with timers from higher groups (although its implementation is not discussed here, suffice it to say that it uses the mechanism described above).

kernel/timer.c
```
                ++base->timer_jiffies;
                list_replace_init(base->tv1.vec + index, &work_list);
...
```

All timers located in the first group at the corresponding position for the `timer_jiffies` value (which is incremented by 1 for the next cycle) are copied into a temporary list and therefore removed from the original data structures.

All that need then be done is to execute the individual handler routines:

kernel/timer.c
```
                while (!list_empty(head)) {
                        void (*fn)(unsigned long);
```

```
                               unsigned long data;

                               timer = list_entry(head->next,struct timer_list,entry);
                               fn = timer->function;
                               data = timer->data;

                               detach_timer(timer, 1);
                               fn(data);
                        }
                }
        ...
        }
```

Activating Timers

When new timers are installed, a distinction must be made as to whether they are required by the kernel itself or by applications in userspace. First, let's discuss the mechanism for kernel timers because user timers also build on this mechanism.

add_timer is used to insert a fully supplied instance of timer_list into the structures just described above:

<timer.h>
```
static inline void add_timer(struct timer_list *timer);
```

After checking several safety conditions (e.g., the same timer may not be added twice), work is delegated to the internal_add_timer function whose task is to place the new timer at the right position in the data structures.

The kernel must first compute the number of ticks after which time-out of the new timer will occur because an absolute time-out value is specified in the data structure of new drivers. To compensate for any missed timer handling calls, expires - base->timer_jiffies is used to compute the offset.

The group and the position within the group can be determined on the basis of this value. All that now need be done is to add the new timer to the linked list. Because it is placed at the *end* of the list and because the run_timer_list is processed from the beginning, a first-in, first-out mechanism is implemented.

15.3 Generic Time Subsystem

Low-resolution timers are useful for a wide range of situations and deal well with many possible use cases. This broadness, however, complicates support for timers with high resolution. Years of development have shown that it is very hard to integrate them into the existing framework. The kernel therefore supports a second timing mechanism.

While low-resolution timers are based on jiffies as fundamental units of time, high-resolution timers use human time units, namely, nanoseconds. This is reasonable because high precision timers are mostly required for userland applications, and the natural way for programmers to think about time is in human units. And, most important, 1 nanosecond is a precisely defined time interval, whereas the length of one jiffy tick depends on the kernel configuration.

High-resolution timers place more requirements on the architecture-specific code of the individual architectures than classical timers. The generic time framework provides the foundations for high-resolution timers. Before getting into the details of high-resolution timers, let's take a look into how high-precision timekeeping is achieved in the kernel.

The core of the second timer subsystem of the kernel can be found in `kernel/time/hrtimer.c`. The generic timekeeping code that forms the basis for high-resolution timers is located in several files in `kernel/time`. After providing an overview of the mechanisms used, the new API that comes with high-resolution timers is introduced, and then their implementation is examined in detail.

15.3.1 Overview

Figure 15-7 provides an overview of the generic time system that provides the foundation of high-resolution timers.

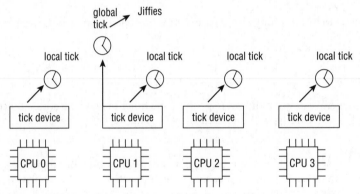

Figure 15-7: Overview of the generic time subsystem.

First, let's discuss the available components and data structures, the details of which will be covered in the course of this chapter. Three mechanisms form the foundation of any time-related task in the kernel:

1. **Clock Sources** (defined by `struct clocksource`) — Form the backbone of time management. Essentially each clock source provides a monotonically increasing counter with Read Only access for the generic kernel parts. The accurateness of different clock sources varies depending on the capabilities of the underlying hardware.

2. **Clock event devices** (defined by `struct clock_event_device`) — Add the possibility of equipping clocks with events that occur at a certain time in the future. Note that it is also common to refer to such devices as *clock event sources* for historical reasons.

3. **Tick Devices** (defined `struct tick_device`) — Extend clock event sources to provide a continuous stream of tick events that happen at regular time intervals. The dynamic tick mechanism allows for stopping the periodic tick during certain time intervals, though.

The kernel distinguishes between two types of clocks:

1. A **global clock** is responsible to provide the periodic tick that is mainly used to update the jiffies values. In former versions of the kernel, this type of clock was realized by the programmable interrupt timer (PIT) on IA-32 systems, and on similar chips on other architectures.

2. One **local clock** per CPU allows for performing process accounting, profiling, and last but not least, high-resolution timers.

The role of the global clock is assumed by one specifically selected local clock. Note that high-resolution timers only work on systems that provide per-CPU clock sources. The extensive communication required between processors would otherwise degrade system performance too much as compared to the benefit of having high-resolution timers.

The overall concept is complicated by problems that unfortunately arise on the two most widespread platforms: AMD64 and IA-32 (the MIPS platform is also affected). Local clocks on SMP systems are based on APIC chips. Unfortunately, these clocks only work properly dependent on the power-saving mode they are in. For low-power modes (ACPI mode C3, to be precise), the local APIC timers are stopped, and thus become useless as clock sources. A system-global clock that still works at this power management state is then used to periodically activate signals that look as if they would originate from the original clock sources. The workaround is known as the *broadcasting mechanism*; more about this follow in Section 15.6.

> Since broadcasting requires communication between the CPUs, the solution is slower and less accurate than proper local time sources; the kernel will automatically switch back high-resolution to low-resolution mode.

15.3.2 Configuration Options

Timer implementation is influenced by several configuration symbols. Two choices are possible at compile time:

1. The kernel can be built with or without support for dynamic ticks. If dynamic ticks are enabled, the pre-processor constant CONFIG_NO_HZ is set.

2. High-resolution support can be enabled or disabled. The pre-processor symbol CONFIG_HIGH_RES_TIMERS is enabled if support for them is compiled in.

Both are important in the following discussion of timer implementation. Recall that both choices are independent of each other; this leads to four different configurations of the time and timer subsystems.

Additionally, each architecture is required to make some configuration choices. They cannot be influenced by the user.

❑ GENERIC_TIME signals that the architecture supports the generic time framework. GENERIC_CLOCKEVENTS states that the same holds for generic clock events. Since both are necessary requirements for dynamic ticks and high-resolution timers, only architectures that provide both are considered.[9] Actually most widespread architectures have been updated to support both options, even if some (for instance SuperH) do this only for certain time models.

❏ CONFIG_TICK_ONESHOT builds support for the one-shot mode of clock event devices. This is automatically selected if high-resolution timers or dynamic ticks are enabled.

❏ GENERIC_CLOCKEVENTS_BROADCAST must be defined if the architecture suffers from problems that require broadcasting. Currently only IA-32, AMD64, and MIPS are affected.

15.3.3 Time Representation

The generic time framework uses the data type ktime_t to represent time values. Irregardless of the underlying architecture, the type always resolves to a 64-bit quantity. This makes the structure convenient to work with on 64-bit architectures as only simple integer operations are required for time-related operations.

To reduce the effort on 32-bit machines, the definition ensures that the two 32-bit values are ordered such that they can be directly interpreted as a 64-bit quantity without further ado — clearly this requires sorting the fields differently depending on the processor's endianness:

```
<ktime.h>
typedef union {
        s64       tv64;
#if BITS_PER_LONG != 64 && !defined(CONFIG_KTIME_SCALAR)
        struct {
# ifdef __BIG_ENDIAN
        s32       sec, nsec;
# else
        s32       nsec, sec;
# endif
        } tv;
#endif
} ktime_t;
```

If a 32-bit architecture provides functions that handle 64-bit quantities efficiently, it can set the configuration option KTIME_SCALAR — IA-32 is the only architecture that makes use of this possibility at the moment. A separation into two 32-bit values is not performed in this case, but the representation of kernel times as direct 64-bit quantities is used.

Several auxiliary functions to handle ktime_t objects are defined by the kernel. Among them are the following:

❏ ktime_sub and ktime_add are used to subtract and add ktime_ts, respectively.

❏ ktime_add_ns adds a given number of nanoseconds to a ktime_t. ktime_add_us is another variant for microseconds. ktime_sub_ns and ktime_sub_us are also available.

❏ ktime_set produces a ktime_t from a given number of seconds and nanoseconds.

❏ Various functions of the type x_to_y convert between representation x and y, where the types ktime_t, timeval, clock_t, and timespec are possible.

---

[9]Architectures that are currently migrating to the generic clock event framework can set GENERIC_CLOCKEVENTS_MIGR. This will build the code, but not use it at run time.

Note that a direct interpretation of a ktime_t as a number of nanoseconds would be possible on 64-bit machines, but can lead to problems on 32-bit machines. Thus, the function ktime_to_ns is provided to perform the conversion properly. The auxiliary function ktime_equal is provided to decide if two ktime_ts are identical.

To provide exchangeability with other time formats used in the kernel, some conversion functions are available:

<ktime.h>
```
ktime_t timespec_to_ktime(const struct timespec ts)
ktime_t timeval_to_ktime(const struct timeval tv)
struct timespec ktime_to_timespec(const ktime_t kt)
struct timeval ktime_to_timeval(const ktime_t kt)
s64 ktime_to_ns(const ktime_t kt)
s64 ktime_to_us(const ktime_t kt)
```

The function names specify which quantity is converted into which, so there's no need to add anything further.

15.3.4 Objects for Time Management

Recall from the overview that three objects manage timekeeping in the kernel: clock sources, clock event devices, and tick devices. Each of them is represented by a special data structure discussed in the following.

Clock Sources

First of all, consider how time values are acquired from the various sources present in a machine. The kernel defines the abstraction of a clock source for this purpose:

<clocksource.h>
```
struct clocksource {
        char *name;
        struct list_head list;
        int rating;
        cycle_t (*read)(void);
        cycle_t mask;
        u32 mult;
        u32 shift;
        unsigned long flags;
    ...
};
```

A human-readable name for the source is given in name, and list is a standard list element that connect all available clock sources on a standard kernel list.

Not all clocks are of the same quality, and the kernel obviously wants to select the best possible one. Thus, every clock has to (honestly) specify its own quality in rating. The following intervals are possible:

❑   A rating between 1 and 99 denotes a very bad clock that can only be used as a last resort or during boot up, that is, when no better clock is available.

❑   The range 100–199 describes a clock that is fit for real use, but not really desirable if something better can be found.

❑ Clocks with a rating between 300 and 399 are reasonably fast and accurate.

❑ Perfect clocks that are the ideal source get a rating between 400 and 499.

The best clock sources can currently be found on the PowerPC architecture where two clocks with a rating of 400 are available. The time stamp counter (TSC) on IA-32 and AMD64 machines — usually the most accurate device on these architectures — has a rating of 300. The best clocks on most architectures have similar ratings. The developers do not exaggerate the performance of the devices and leave plenty of space for improvement on the hardware side.

It does not come as a surprise that read is used to read the current cycle value of the clock. Note that the value returned does not use any fixed timing basis for all clocks, but needs to be converted into a nanosecond value individually. For this purpose, the field members mult and shift are used to multiply or divide, respectively, the cycles value as follows:

```
<clocksource.h>
static inline s64 cyc2ns(struct clocksource *cs, cycle_t cycles)
{
        u64 ret = (u64)cycles;
        ret = (ret * cs->mult) >> cs->shift;
        return ret;
}
```

Note that cycle_t is defined as an unsigned integer with 64 bits independent of the underlying platform.

If a clock does not provide time values with 64 bits, then mask specifies a bitmask to select the appropriate bits. The macro CLOCKSOURCE_MASK(bits) constructs the proper mask for a given number of bits.

Finally, the field flags of struct clocksource specifies — you will have guessed it — a number of flags. Only one flag is relevant for our purposes. CLOCK_SOURCE_CONTINUOUS represents a continuous clock, although the meaning is not quite the mathematical sense of of "continuous." Instead, it describes that the clock is free-running if set to 1 and thus cannot skip. If it is set to 0, then some cycles might be lost; that is, if the last cycle value was n, then the next value does not necessarily need to be $n+1$ even if it was read at the next possible moment. A clock must exhibit this flag to be usable for high-resolution timers.

For booting purposes and if nothing really better is available on the machine (which should never be the case after bootup), the kernel provides a jiffies-based clock[10]:

```
kernel/time/jiffies.c
#define NSEC_PER_JIFFY  ((u32)((((u64)NSEC_PER_SEC)<<8)/ACTHZ))

struct clocksource clocksource_jiffies = {
        .name = "jiffies",
        .rating = 1, /* lowest valid rating*/
        .read = jiffies_read,
        .mask = 0xffffffff, /*32bits*/
        .mult = NSEC_PER_JIFFY << JIFFIES_SHIFT, /* details above */
        .shift = JIFFIES_SHIFT,
};
```

---

[10]Note that if the jiffy clock were used as the main clock source, then the kernel would be responsible to update the jiffies value by some apt means, for instance, directly from the timer interrupt. Usually, architectures don't do this. It, therefore, does not really make sense to use this clock for tickless systems that emulate the jiffies layer via clock sources. In fact, using the jiffies clock source is a nice way to crash dynamic tick systems, at least on kernel 2.6.24 ...

At a first glance, it might not make much sense to first multiply by JIFFIES_SHIFT and then again divide by the same value. Nevertheless, this bogosity is required because the NTP code does not work with zero shifts.[11] Also note that the jiffies clock has a rating of 1, which makes it definitely the worst clock in the whole system.

The read routine for the jiffies clock is particularly simple: No hardware interaction is required. It suffices to return the current jiffies value.

The time-stamp counter usually provides the best clock found on IA-32 and AMD64 machines:

arch/x86/kernel/tsc_64.c
```
static struct clocksource clocksource_tsc = {
        .name = "tsc",
        .rating = 300,
        .read = read_tsc,
        .mask = CLOCKSOURCE_MASK(64),
        .shift = 22,
        .flags = CLOCK_SOURCE_IS_CONTINUOUS |
                 CLOCK_SOURCE_MUST_VERIFY,
};
```

read_tsc uses some assembler code to read out the current counter value from hardware.

Working with Clock Sources

How can a clock be used? First of all, it must be registered with the kernel. The function clocksource_register is responsible for this. The source is only added to the global clocksource_list (defined in kernel/time/clocksource.c), which sorts all available clock sources by their rating. select_clocksource is called to select the best clock source. Normally this will pick the clock with the best rating, but it is also possible to specify a preference from userland via /sys/devices/system/clocksource/clocksource0/current_clocksource, which is used by the kernel instead. Two global variables are provided for this purpose:

1. current_clocksource points to the clock source that is currently the best one.

2. next_clocksource points to an instance of struct clocksource that is better than the one used at the moment. The kernel automatically switches to the best clock source when a new best clock source is registered.

To read the clock, the kernel provides the following functions:

❑ __get_realtime_clock_ts takes a pointer to an instance of struct timespec as argument, reads the current clock, converts the result, and stores in the timespec instance.

❑ getnstimeofday is a front-end for __get_realtime_clock_ts, but also works if no high-resolution clocks are available in the system. In this case, getnstimeofday as defined in kernel/time.c (instead of kernel/time/timekeeping.c) is used to provide a timespec that fulfills only low-resolution requirements.

---

[11]The definition of NSEC_PER_JIFFY contains the pre-processor symbol ACTHZ. While HZ denotes the base low-resolution frequency that can be selected at compile time, the frequency that the system actually provides will differ slightly because of hardware limitations. ACTHZ stores the frequency at which the clock is actually running.

Clock Event Devices

Clock event devices are defined by the following data structure:

<clockchips.h>
```
struct clock_event_device {
        const char *name;
        unsigned int features;
        unsigned long max_delta_ns;
        unsigned long min_delta_ns;
        unsigned long mult;
        int shift;
        int rating;
        int irq;
        cpumask_t cpumask;
        int (*set_next_event)(unsigned long evt,
                              struct clock_event_device *);
        void (*set_mode)(enum clock_event_mode mode,
                         struct clock_event_device *);
        void (*event_handler)(struct clock_event_device *);
        void (*broadcast)(cpumask_t mask);
        struct list_head list;
        enum clock_event_mode mode;
        ktime_t next_event;
};
```

Recall that clock event devices allow for registering an *event* that is going to happen at a defined point of time in the future. In comparison to a full-blown timer implementation, however, only a single event can be stored. The key elements of every `clock_event_device` are `set_next_event` because it allows for setting the time at which the event is going to take place, and `event_handler`, which is called when the event actually happens.

Besides, the elements of `clock_event_device` have the following purpose:

❑   `name` is a human-readable representation for the event device. It shows up in `/proc/timerlist`.

❑   `max_delta_ns` and `min_delta_ns` specify the maximum or minimum, respectively, difference between the current time and the time for the next event. Clocks work with individual frequencies at which device cycles occur, but the generic time subsystem expects a nanosecond value when the event shall take place. The auxiliary function `clockevent_delta2ns` helps to convert one representation into the other.

Consider, for instance, that the current time is 20, `min_delta_ns` is 2, and `max_delta_ns` is 40 (of course, the exemplary values do not represent any situation possible in reality). Then the next event can take place during the time interval [22, 60] where the boundaries are included.

❑   `mult` and `shift` are a multiplier and a divider, respectively, used to convert between clock cycles and nanosecond values.

❑   The function pointed to by `event_handler` is called by the hardware interface code (which usually is architecture-specific) to pass clock events on to the generic layers.

❑ irq specifies the number of the IRQ that is used by the event device. Note that this is only required for global devices. Per-CPU local devices use different hardware mechanisms to emit signals and set irq to −1.

❑ cpumask specifies for which CPUs the event device works. A simple bitmask is employed for this purpose. Local devices are usually only responsible for a single CPU.

❑ broadcast is required for the broadcasting implementation that provides a workaround for non-functional local APICs on IA-32 and AMD64 in power-saving mode. See Section 15.6 for more details.

❑ rating allows — in analogy to the mechanism described for clock devices — comparison of clock event devices by explicitly rating their accuracy.

❑ All instances of struct clock_event_device are kept on the global list clockevent_devices, and list is the list head required for this purpose.

The auxiliary function clockevents_register_device is used to register a new clock event device. This places the device on the global list.

❑ ktime_t stores the absolute time of the next event.

Each event device is characterized by several features stored as a bit string in features. A number of constants in <**clockchips.h**> define possible features. For our purposes, two are of interest[12]:

❑ Clock event devices that support periodic events (i.e., events that are repeated over and over again without the need to explicitly activate them by reprogramming the device) are identified by CLOCK_EVT_FEAT_PERIODIC.

❑ CLOCK_EVT_FEAT_ONESHOT marks a clock capable of issuing one-shot events that happen exactly once. Basically, this is the opposite of periodic events.

set_mode points to a function that allows for toggling the desired mode of operation between periodic and one-shot mode. mode designates the current mode of operation. A clock can only be in *either* periodic *or* one-shot mode at a time, but it can nevertheless provide the ability to work in both modes — actually, most clocks allow both possibilities.

Generic code does not need to call set_next_event directly because the kernel provides the following auxiliary function for this task:

kernel/time/clockevents.c
```
int clockevents_program_event(struct clock_event_device *dev, ktime_t expires,
                              ktime_t now)
```

The (absolute) expiration time for the device dev is given in expires, while now denotes the current time. Usually the caller will directly pass the result of ktime_get() for this parameter.

On IA-32 and AMD64 systems, the role of the global clock event device is initially assumed by the PIT. The HPET takes over this duty once it has been initialized. To keep track of which device is used

---

[12]Recall that local APICs on IA-32 and AMD64 systems expose a problem: They stop working at certain power save levels. This problem is reported to the kernel by setting the "feature" CLOCK_EVT_FEAT_C3STOP, which should rather be named a *mis-feature*.

to handle global clock events on x86 systems, the global variable `global_clock_event` as defined in `arch/x86/kernel/i8253.c` is employed. It points to the `clock_event_device` instance for the global clock device that is currently in use.

Clock devices and clock event device are formally unconnected at the data structure level. However, one particular hardware chip in the system provides capabilities that allow fulfillment of the requirements for both interfaces, so the kernel usually registers a clock device and a clock event device per time hardware chip. Consider, for instance, the HPET device on IA-32 and AMD64 systems. The capabilities as clock source are collected in `clocksource_hpet`, while `hpet_clockevent` is an instance of `clock_event_device`. Both are defined in `arch/x86/kernel/hpet.c`. `hpet_init` first registers the clock source and then the clock event device. This adds two time-management objects to the kernel, but only a single piece of hardware is required.

Tick Devices

One particular important use of clock event devices is to provide periodic ticks — recall from Section 15.2 that ticks are, for instance, required to operate the classical timer wheel. A tick device is an extension of a clock event device:

```
<tick.h>
struct tick_device {
        struct clock_event_device *evtdev;
        enum tick_device_mode mode;
}

enum tick_device_mode {
        TICKDEV_MODE_PERIODIC,
        TICKDEV_MODE_ONESHOT,
};
```

A `tick_device` is just a wrapper around `struct clock_event_device` with an additional field that specifies which mode the device is in. This can either be periodic or one-shot. The distinction will be important when tickless systems are considered; this is discussed further in Section 15.5. For now, it suffices to see a tick device as mechanism to provides a continuous stream of tick events. These form the basis for the scheduler, the classical timer wheel, and related components of the kernel.

Again, the kernel distinguishes global and local (per-CPU) tick devices. The local devices are collected in `tick_cpu_device` (defined in `kernel/time/tick-internal.h`). Note that the kernel automatically creates a tick device when a new clock event device is registered.

Several global variables are additionally defined in `include/time/tick-internal.h`:

❑   `tick_cpu_device` is a per-CPU list containing one instance of `struct tick_device` for each CPU in the system.

❑   `tick_next_period` specifies the time (in nanoseconds) when the next global tick event will happen.

❑   `tick_do_timer_cpu` contains the CPU number whose tick device assumes the role of the global tick device.

❑   `tick_period` stores the interval between ticks in nanoseconds. It is the counterpart to `HZ` that denotes the frequency at which ticks occur.

To set up a tick device, the kernel provides the function `tick_setup_device`. The prototype is as follows, and the code flow diagram is depicted in Figure 15-8[13]:

kernel/time/tick-common.c
```
static void tick_setup_device(struct tick_device *td,
                              struct clock_event_device *newdev, int cpu,
                              cpumask_t cpumask);
```

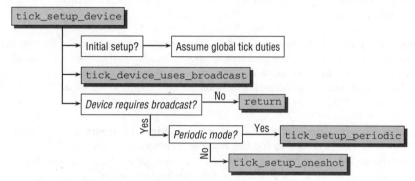

Figure 15-8: Code flow diagram for `tick_setup_device`.

The parameter `td` specifies the `tick_device` instance that is going to be set up. It is about to be equipped with the clock event device `newdev`. `cpu` denotes the processor to which the device is associated, and `cpumask` is a bitmask that allows for restricting the tick device to specific CPUs.

When the device is set up for the first time (i.e., if no clock event device is associated with the tick device), the kernel performs two actions:

1. If no tick device has been chosen to assume the role as global tick device yet, then the current device is selected, and `tick_do_timer_cpu` is set to the processor number to which the current device belongs. `tick_period`, that is, the interval between ticks in nanoseconds, is computed based on the value of `HZ`.

2. The tick device is set to work in periodic mode.

After assigning the event device to the tick device, the function is finished if broadcasting mode is active (recall that this is used if the system is in a power-saving state where the local clocks don't work; see Section 15.6 for more details). Otherwise, the kernel needs to establish a periodic tick. How this is done depends on whether the tick device runs in periodic or oneshot mode, and the work is correspondingly delegated either to `tick_setup_periodic` or `tick_setup_oneshot`.

> The fact that the tick device is in one-shot mode does not automatically mean that dynamic ticks are enabled! Ticks in high-resolution mode are, for instance, always implemented on top of one-shot timers.

---

[13]The function is automatically called if a new clock event device is registered that allows for creating a better tick device than the previously available ones. Devices with a higher quality are favored, but not if the new and more accurate device does not support one-shot mode, while the old device does provide this support.

Before discussing these functions, let us therefore consider which situations are faced by the kernel depending on the selected configuration:

- ❏ A low-resolution system without dynamic ticks always uses a periodic tick. Support for one-shot operations is not included in the kernel at all.

- ❏ Low-resolution systems with dynamic ticks use the tick device in one-shot mode.

- ❏ High-resolution systems always use one-shot mode independent of whether they work with dynamic ticks or not.

All systems initially work in low-resolution mode and without dynamic ticks; they switch to a different combination only later when the required hardware is initialized. I therefore focus on the low-resolution, periodic tick case here. The more advanced options are discussed in Sections 15.4.5 (high-resolution timers) and 15.5 (dynamic ticks). Some corrections are also required for broadcast mode; Section 15.6 covers them in more detail.

Before examining the low-resolution case without dynamic ticks, I would like to point out that Figure 15-9 provides an overview of the tick handler functions that are used for the various possible combinations. Note that which broadcast function is chosen for a system without dynamic ticks depends on the mode of the underlying tick device. The details are given below.

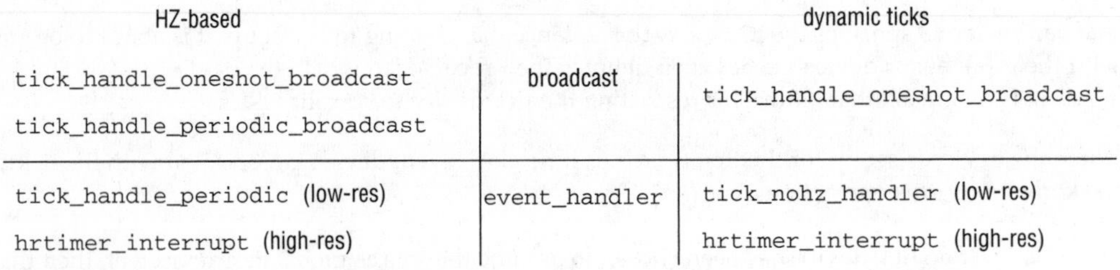

HZ-based		dynamic ticks
`tick_handle_oneshot_broadcast` `tick_handle_periodic_broadcast`	broadcast	`tick_handle_oneshot_broadcast`
`tick_handle_periodic` (low-res) `hrtimer_interrupt` (high-res)	event_handler	`tick_nohz_handler` (low-res) `hrtimer_interrupt` (high-res)

Figure 15-9: Tick event and broadcast handler functions for all possible combinations of low- and high-resolution mode, and with/without dynamic ticks.

Let us finally turn our attention to `tick_setup_periodic`. The code flow diagram is shown in Figure 15-10.

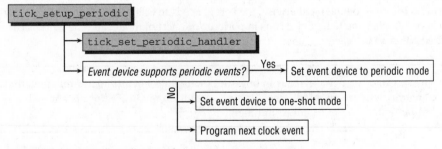

Figure 15-10: Code flow diagram for `tick_setup_periodic`.

Actually, the task is quite simple if the clock event device supports periodic events. In this case, `tick_set_periodic_handler` installs `tick_handle_periodic` as handler function, and `clockevents_set_mode` ensures that the clock event device runs in periodic mode.

If the event device does not support periodic events, then the kernel must make do with one-shot events. `clockevents_set_mode` sets the event device to this mode, but additionally, the next event needs to be programmed in manually using `clockevents_program_event`.

In both cases, the handler function `tick_handle_periodic` is called on the next event of the tick device. (Recall that we focus on the low-res case without dynamic ticks here; other settings will use different handler functions!) Before discussing the handler function, I need to introduce the auxiliary function `tick_periodic`. It is responsible for handling the periodic tick on a given CPU required as an argument:

kernel/time/tick_common.c
```
static void tick_periodic(int cpu);
```

Figure 15-11 shows what is going on inside the function.

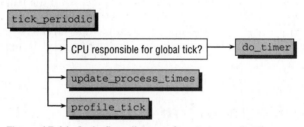

Figure 15-11: Code flow diagram for `tick_periodic`.

If the current tick device is responsible for the global tick, then `do_timer` is called. Recall that this function is discussed in Section 15.2.1. Nevertheless, remember that `do_timer` is responsible to update the global `jiffies` value that is used as the coarse-grained time base in many parts of the kernel.

`update_process_times` is called by every tick handler, as well as `profile_tick`. The first function is discussed in Section 15.2.1. `profile_tick` is responsible for profiling, but the details are not discussed here.

Let's go back to the handler function. Things are again easier here if periodic events are in use:

kernel/tick/tick-common.c
```
void tick_handle_periodic(struct clock_event_device *dev)
{
        int cpu = smp_processor_id();
        ktime_t next;
        tick_periodic(cpu);
        if (dev->mode != CLOCK_EVT_MODE_ONESHOT)
                return;
...
```

All the kernel needs to do is call `tick_periodic`. If the clock event device operates in one-shot mode, the next tick event needs to be programmed:

kernel/tick/tick-common.c

```
...
          /*
           * Setup the next period for devices, which do not have
           * periodic mode:
           */
          next = ktime_add(dev->next_event, tick_period);
          for (;;) {
                  if (!clockevents_program_event(dev, next, ktime_get()))
                          return;
                  tick_periodic(cpu);
                  next = ktime_add(next, tick_period);
          }
}
```

Since `tick_device->next_event` contains the time of the *current* tick event, the time for the next event can easily be computed by incrementing the value with the length of the interval as specified in `tick_period`. Programming this event is then usually just a matter of calling `clockevents_program_event`. Should this fail[14] because the time for the next clock event lies already in the past, then the kernel calls `tick_periodic` manually and tries again to reprogram the event until it succeeds.

15.4 High-Resolution Timers

After having discussed the generic time framework, we are now ready to take the next step and dive into the implementation of high-resolution timers. Two fundamental differences distinguish these timers from low-resolution timers:

1. High-resolution (high-res) timers are time-ordered on a red-black tree.

2. They are independent of periodic ticks. They do not use a time specification based on jiffies, but employ nanosecond time stamps.

Merging the high-resolution timer mechanism into the kernel was an interesting process in itself. After the usual development and testing phase, kernel 2.6.16 contained the basic framework that provided most of the implementation except one thing: support for high-resolution timers . . . . The classical implementation of low-resolution timers had, however, been replaced with a new foundation in this release. It was based on the high-resolution timer framework, although the supported resolution was not any better than before. Following kernel releases then added support for another class of timers that did actually provide high-resolution capabilities.

This merge strategy is not only of historical interest: Since low-resolution timers are implemented on top of the high-resolution mechanism, (partial) support for high-resolution timers will also be built into the kernel even if support for them is not explicitly enabled! Nevertheless, the system will only be able to provide timers with low-resolution capabilities.

---

[14]Note that 0 is returned on success, so `!clockevents_program_event(...)` checks for failure.

Components of the high-resolution timer framework that are not universally applicable, but do really provide actual high-resolution capabilites are bracketed by the pre-processor symbol CONFIG_HIGH_RES_TIMERS, and are only compiled in if high-resolution support is selected at compile time. The generic part of the framework is always added to the kernel.

> **This means that even kernels that only support low resolution contain parts of the high-resolution framework, which can sometimes lead to confusion.**

15.4.1 Data Structures

High-resolution timers can be based on two different types of clocks (which are referred to as *clock bases*). The monotonic clock starts at 0 when the system is booted (CLOCK_MONOTONIC). The other clock (CLOCK_REALTIME) represents the real time of the system. The latter clock may exhibit skips if, for instance, the system time is changed, but the monotonic clock runs, well, monotonously all the time.

For each CPU in the system, a data structure with both clock bases is available. Each clock base is equipped with a red-black tree that sorts all pending high-resolution timers. Figure 15-12 summarizes the situation graphically. Two clock bases (monotonic and real time) are available per CPU. All timers are sorted by expiration time on a red-black tree, and expired timers whose callback handlers still need to be executed are moved from the red-black tree to a linked list.

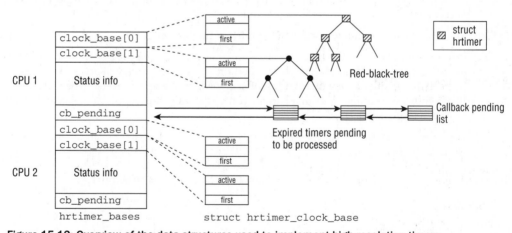

Figure 15-12: Overview of the data structures used to implement high-resolution timers.

A clock base is given by the following data structure:

<hrtimer.h>
```
struct hrtimer_clock_base {
        struct hrtimer_cpu_base *cpu_base;
        clockid_t               index;
        struct                  rb_root active;
        struct                  rb_node *first;
        ktime_t                 resolution;
        ktime_t                 (*get_time)(void);
```

```
              ktime_t                    (*get_softirq_time)(void);
              ktime_t                    softirq_time;
#ifdef CONFIG_HIGH_RES_TIMERS
              ktime_t                    offset;
              int                        (*reprogram)(struct hrtimer *t,
                                              struct hrtimer_clock_base *b,
                                              ktime_t n);

#endif
};
```

The meaning of the fields is as follows:

❑   hrtimer_cpu_base points to the per-CPU basis to which the clock base belongs.

❑   index distinguishes between CLOCK_MONOTONIC and CLOCK_REALTIME.

❑   rb_root is the root of a red-black tree on which all active timers are sorted.

❑   first points to the timer that will expire first.

❑   Processing high-res timers is initiated from the high-resolution timer softIRQ HRTIMER_SOFTIRQ
     as described in the next section. softirq_time stores the time at which the softIRQ was issued,
     and get_softirq_time is a function to obtain this time. If high-resolution mode is not active,
     then the stored time will be coarse-grained.

❑   get_time reads the fine-grained time. This is simple for the monotonic clock (the value delivered
     by the current clock source can be directly used), but some straightforward arithmetic is required
     to convert the value into the real system time.

❑   resolution denotes the resolution of the timer in nanoseconds.

❑   When the real-time clock is adjusted, a discrepancy between the expiration values of timers
     stored on the CLOCK_REALTIME clock base and the current real time will arise. The offset field
     helps to fix the situation by denoting an offset by which the timers needs to be corrected. Since
     this is only a temporary effect that happens only seldomly, the complications need not be dis-
     cussed in more detail.

❑   reprogram is a function that allows for reprogramming a given timer event, that is, changing the
     expiration time.

Two clock bases are established for each CPU using the following data structure:

<hrtimer.h>
```
struct hrtimer_cpu_base {
        struct hrtimer_clock_base        clock_base[HRTIMER_MAX_CLOCK_BASES];
#ifdef CONFIG_HIGH_RES_TIMERS
        ktime_t                          expires_next;
        int                              hres_active;
        struct list_head                 cb_pending;
        unsigned long                    nr_events;
#endif
};
```

HRTIMER_MAX_CLOCK_BASES is currently set to 2 because a monotonic and a real-time clock exist as discussed above. Note that the clock bases are directly embedded into hrtimer_cpu_base and not referenced
via pointers! The remaining fields of the structure are used as follows:

❏ expires_next contains the absolute time of the next event that is due for expiration.

❏ hres_active is used as a Boolean variable to signal if high-resolution mode is active, or if only low-resolution is available.

❏ When a timer expires, it is moved from the red-black tree to a list headed by cb_pending.[15] Note that the timers on this list still need to be processed. This will take place in the softIRQ handler.

❏ nr_events keeps track of the total number of timer interrupts.

he global per-CPU variable hrtimer_cpu_base contains an instance of struct hrtimer_base_cpu for each processor in the system. Initially it is equipped with the following contents:

kernel/hrtimer.c
```
DEFINE_PER_CPU(struct hrtimer_cpu_base, hrtimer_bases) =
{

        .clock_base =
        {
                {
                        .index = CLOCK_REALTIME,
                        .get_time = &ktime_get_real,
                        .resolution = KTIME_LOW_RES,
                },
                {

                        .index = CLOCK_MONOTONIC,
                        .get_time = &ktime_get,
                        .resolution = KTIME_LOW_RES,
                },
        }
};
```

Since the system is initialized in low-resolution mode, the achievable resolution is only KTIME_LOW_RES. The pre-processor constant denotes the timer interval between periodic ticks with frequency HZ in nanoseconds. ktime_get and ktime_get_real both obtain the current time by using getnstimeofday, discussed in Section 15.3.

A very important component is still missing. How is a timer itself specified? The kernel provides the following data structure for this purpose:

\<hrtimer.h\>
```
struct hrtimer {
        struct rb_node          node;
        ktime_t                 expires;
        int                     (*function)(struct hrtimer *);
        struct hrtimer_base     *base;
        unsigned long           state;
#ifdef CONFIG_HIGH_RES_TIMERS
        enum hrtimer_cb_mode    cb_mode;
        struct list_head        cb_entry;
#endif
};
```

---

[15]This requires that the timer is allowed to be executed in softIRQ context. Alternatively, timers are expired directly in the clock hardware IRQ without involving the detour via the expiration list.

node is used to keep the timer on the red-black tree as mentioned above, and base points to the timer base. The fields that are interesting for the timer's user are function and expires. While the latter denotes the expiration time, function is the callback employed when the timer expires. cb_entry is the list element that allows for keeping the timer on the callback list headed by hrtimer_cpu_base->cb_pending. Each timer may specify conditions under which it may or must be run. The following choices are possible:

```
<hrtimer.h>
/*
 * hrtimer callback modes:
 *
 * HRTIMER_CB_SOFTIRQ:              Callback must run in softirq context
 * HRTIMER_CB_IRQSAFE:             Callback may run in hardirq context
 * HRTIMER_CB_IRQSAFE_NO_RESTART:  Callback may run in hardirq context and
 *              does not restart the timer
 * HRTIMER_CB_IRQSAFE_NO_SOFTIRQ:  Callback must run in hardirq context
 *              Special mode for tick emultation
 */
enum hrtimer_cb_mode {
        HRTIMER_CB_SOFTIRQ,
        HRTIMER_CB_IRQSAFE,
        HRTIMER_CB_IRQSAFE_NO_RESTART,
        HRTIMER_CB_IRQSAFE_NO_SOFTIRQ,
};
```

The comment explains the meaning of the individual constants well, and nothing need be added. The current state of a timer is kept in state. The following values are possible[16]:

❑ HRTIMER_STATE_INACTIVE denotes an inactive timer.

❑ A timer that is enqueued on a clock base and waiting for expiration is in state HRTIMER_STATE_ENQUEUED.

❑ HRTIMER_STATE_CALLBACK states that the callback is currently executing.

❑ When the timer has expired and is waiting on the callback list to be executed, the state is HRTIMER_STATE_PENDING.

The callback function deserves some special consideration. Two return values are possible:

```
<hrtimer.h>
enum hrtimer_restart {
        HRTIMER_NORESTART, /* Timer is not restarted */
        HRTIMER_RESTART, /* Timer must be restarted */
};
```

Usually, the callback will return HRTIMER_NORESTART when it has finished executing. In this case, the timer will simply disappear from the system. However, the timer can also choose to be restarted. This requires two steps from the callback:

1. The result of the callback must be HRTIMER_RESTART.

---

[16]In a rare corner case, it is also possible that a timer is both in the states HRTIMER_STATE_ENQUEUED *and* HRTIMER_STATE_CALLBACK. See the commentary in <hrtimer.h> for more information.

2. The expiration of the timer must be set to a future point in time. The callback function can perform this manipulation because it gets a pointer to the `hrtimer` instance for the currently running timer as function parameter. To simplify matters, the kernel provides an auxiliary function to forward the expiration time of a timer:

<hrtimer.h>
```
unsigned long
hrtimer_forward(struct hrtimer *timer, ktime_t now, ktime_t interval);
```

This resets the `timer` so that it expires after `now` [usually `now` is set to the value returned by `hrtimer_clock_base->get_time()`]. The exact expiration time is determined by taking the old expiration time of the timer and adding `interval` so often that the new expiration time lies past `now`. The function returns the number of times that `interval` had to be added to the expiration time to exceed `now`.

Let us illustrate the behavior by an example. If the old expiration time is 5, `now` is 12, and `interval` is 2, then the new expiration time will be 13. The return value is 4 because $13 = 5 + 4 \times 2$.

A common application for high-resolution timers is to put a task to sleep for a specified, short amount of time. The kernel provides another data structure for this purpose:

<hrtimer.h>
```
struct hrtimer_sleeper {
        struct hrtimer timer;
        struct task_struct *task;
};
```

An `hrtimer` instance is bundled with a pointer to the task in question. The kernel uses `hrtimer_wakeup` as the expiration function for sleepers. When the timer expires, the `hrtimer_sleeper` can be derived from the `hrtimer` using the `container_of` mechanism (note that the timer is embedded in `struct hrtimer_sleeper`), and the associated task can be woken up.

15.4.2 Setting Timers

Setting a new timer is a two-step process:

1. `hrtimer_init` is used to initialize a `hrtimer` instance.

   <hrtimer.h>
   ```
   void hrtimer_init(struct hrtimer *timer, clockid_t which_clock,
                     enum hrtimer_mode mode);
   ```

   `timer` denotes the affected high-resolution timer, `clock` is the clock to bind the timer to, and `mode` specifies if absolute or relative time values (relative to the current time) are used. Two constants are available for selection:

   <hrtimer.h>
   ```
   enum hrtimer_mode {
           HRTIMER_MODE_ABS,      /* Time value is absolute */
           HRTIMER_MODE_REL,      /* Time value is relative to now */
   };
   ```

2. `hrtimer_start` sets the expiration time of a timer and starts it.

The implementation of both functions is purely technical and not very interesting, their code need not be discussed in detail.

To cancel a scheduled timer, the kernel offers `hrtimer_cancel` and `hrtimer_try_to_cancel`. The difference between both functions is that `hrtimer_try_to_cancel` provides the extra return value −1 if the timer if currently executing and thus cannot be stopped anymore. `hrtimer_cancel` waits until the handler has executed in this case. Besides, both functions return 0 if the timer was not active, and 1 if it was active, that is, if its status is either `HRTIMER_STATE_ENQUEUED` or `HRTIMER_STATE_PENDING`.

Restarting a canceled timer is done with `hrtimer_restart`:

```
<hrtimer.h>
int hrtimer_cancel(struct hrtimer *timer)
int hrtimer_try_to_cancel(struct hrtimer *timer)
int hrtimer_restart(struct hrtimer *timer)
```

15.4.3 Implementation

After having introduced all required data structures and components, let's fill in the last missing pieces by discussing the mechanisms of how high-resolution timers are expired and their callback function run.

Recall that parts of the high-resolution timer framework are also compiled into the kernel even if explicit support for them is disabled. Expiring high-resolution timers is in this case driven by a clock with low-resolution. This avoids code duplication because users of high-resolution timers need not supply an extra version of their timing-related code for systems that do not have high-resolution capabilities. The high-resolution framework is employed as usual, but operates with only low resolution.

Even if high-resolution support is compiled into the kernel, only low resolution will be available at boot time, so the situation is identical to the one described above. Therefore, we need to take two possibilities into account for how high-resolution timers are run: based on a proper clock with high-resolution capabilities, and based on a low-resolution clock.

High-Resolution Timers in High-Resolution Mode

Let us first assume that a high-resolution clock is up and running, and that the transition to high-resolution mode is completely finished. The general situation is depicted in Figure 15-13.

When the clock event device responsible for high-resolution timers raises an interrupt, `hrtimer_interrupt` is called as event handler. The function is responsible to select all timers that have expired and either move them to the expiration list (if they may be processed in softIRQ context) or call the handler function directly. After reprogramming the clock event device so that an interrupt is raised when the next pending timer expires, the softIRQ `HRTIMER_SOFTIRQ` is raised. When the softIRQ executes, `run_hrtimer_softirq` takes care of executing the handler functions of all timers on the expiration list.

Let's discuss the code responsible to implement all this. First, consider the interrupt handler `hrtimer_interrupt`. Some initialization work is necessary in the beginning:

```
kernel/hrtimer.c
void hrtimer_interrupt(struct clock_event_device *dev)
{
        struct hrtimer_cpu_base *cpu_base = &__get_cpu_var(hrtimer_bases);
```

```
        struct hrtimer_clock_base *base;
        ktime_t expires_next, now;
...
retry:
        now = ktime_get();

        expires_next.tv64 = KTIME_MAX;
        base = cpu_base->clock_base;
...
```

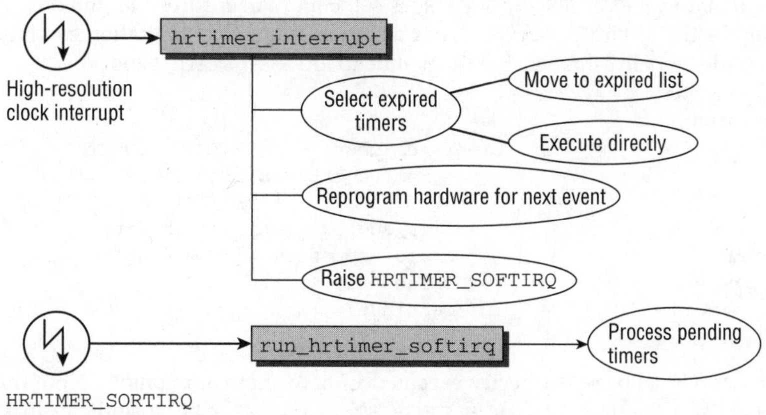

Figure 15-13: Overview of expiration of high-resolution timers with high-resolution clocks.

The expiration time of the timer that is due next is stored in expires_next. Setting this to KTIME_MAX initially is another way of saying that no next timer is available. The main work is to iterate over all clock bases (monotonic and real-time).

kernel/hrtimer.c
```
for (i = 0; i < HRTIMER_MAX_CLOCK_BASES; i++) {
        ktime_t basenow;
        struct rb_node *node;
        basenow = ktime_add(now, base->offset);
```

Essentially, basenow denotes the current time. base->offset is only non-zero when the real-time clock has been readjusted, so this will never affect the monotonic clock base. Starting from base->first, the expired nodes of the red-black tree can be obtained:

kernel/hrtimer.c
```
while ((node = base->first)) {
        struct hrtimer *timer;

        timer = rb_entry(node, struct hrtimer, node);
        if (basenow.tv64 < timer->expires.tv64) {
                ktime_t expires;

                expires = ktime_sub(timer->expires,
                base->offset);
```

```
                              if (expires.tv64 < expires_next.tv64)
                                    expires_next = expires;
                        break;
                }
```

If the next timer's expiration time lies in the future, processing can be stopped by leaving the while loop. The time of expiration is, however, remembered because it is later required to reprogram the clock event device.

If the current timer has expired, it is moved to the callback list for later processing in the softIRQ if this is allowed, that is, if HRTIMER_CB_SOFTIRQ is set. continue ensures that the code moves to the next timer. Erasing the timer with __remove_timer also selects the next expiration candidate by updating base->first. Additionally, this sets the timer state to HRTIMER_STATE_PENDING:

kernel/hrtimer.c
```
                if (timer->cb_mode == HRTIMER_CB_SOFTIRQ) {
                        __remove_hrtimer(timer, base,
                                        HRTIMER_STATE_PENDING, 0);
                        list_add_tail(&timer->cb_entry,
                        &base->cpu_base->cb_pending);
                        raise = 1;
                        continue;
                }
```

Otherwise, the timer callback is directly executed in hard interrupt context. Note that this time __remove_timer sets the timer state to HRTIMER_STATE_CALLBACK because the callback handler is executed immediately afterward:

kernel/hrtimer.c
```
                __remove_hrtimer(timer, base,
                                HRTIMER_STATE_CALLBACK, 0);

  . . .

                if (timer->function(timer) != HRTIMER_NORESTART) {
                        enqueue_hrtimer(timer, base, 0);
                }
                timer->state &= ~HRTIMER_STATE_CALLBACK;
        }
        base++;
}
```

The callback handler is executed by timer->function(timer). If the handler requests to be restarted by returning HRTIMER_RESTART, then enqueue_hrtimer fulfills this request. The HRTIMER_STATE_CALLBACK flag can be removed once the handler has been executed.

When the pending timers of all clock bases have been selected, the kernel needs to reprogram the event device to raise an interrupt when the next timer is due. Additionally, the HRTIMER_SOFTIRQ must be raised if any timers are waiting on the callback list:

kernel/hrtimer.c
```
        cpu_base->expires_next = expires_next;

        /* Reprogramming necessary ? */
        if (expires_next.tv64 != KTIME_MAX) {
                if (tick_program_event(expires_next, 0))
```

```
                    goto retry;
        }

        /* Raise softirq ? */
        if (raise)
                raise_softirq(HRTIMER_SOFTIRQ);
}
```

Note that reprogramming fails if the next expiration date is already in the past — this can happen if timer processing took too long. In this case, the whole processing sequence is restarted by jumping to the `retry` label at the beginning of the function.

One more final step is necessary to complete one round of high-resolution timer handling: Run the softIRQ to execute the pending callbacks. The softIRQ handler is `run_hrtimer_softirq`, and Figure 15-14 shows the code flow diagram.[17]

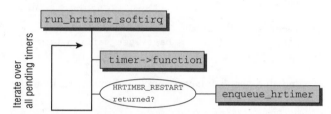

Figure 15-14: Code flow diagram for `run_hrtimer_softirq`.

Essentially, the function iterates over the list of all pending timers. For each timer, the callback handler is executed. If the timer requests to be restarted, then `enqueue_hrtimer` does the required mechanics.

High-Resolution Timers in Low-Resolution Mode

What if no high-resolution clocks are available? In this case, expiring high resolution timers is initiated from the `hrtimer_run_queues`, which is called by the high-resolution timer softIRQ `HRTIMER_SOFTIRQ` (since softIRQ processing is based on low-resolution timers in this case, the mechanism does not provide any high-resolution capabilities naturally). The code flow diagram is depicted in Figure 15-15. Note that this is a simplified version. In reality, the function is more involved because switching from low- to high-resolution mode is started from this place. However, these problems will not bother us now; the required extensions are discussed in Section 15.4.5.

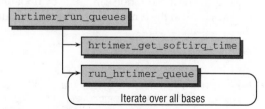

Figure 15-15: Code flow diagram for
`hrtimer_run_queues`.

---

[17]The corner case that a timer is rearmed on another CPU after the callback has been executed is omitted. This possibly requires reprogramming the clock event device to the new expiration time if the timer is the first on the tree to expire.

The mechanism is not particularly complicated: After the coarse time is stored in the timer base by `hrtimer_get_softirq_time`, the code loops over all clock bases (the monotonic and real-time clocks) and processes the entries in each queue with `run_hrtimer_queue`.

First of all, the function checks if any timers must be processed (if `hrtimer_cpu_base` is a NULL pointer, then no first timer exists, and thus nothing needs to be done):

kernel/hrtimer.c
```
static inline void run_hrtimer_queue(struct hrtimer_cpu_base *cpu_base,
                                     int index)
{
        struct rb_node *node;
        struct hrtimer_clock_base *base = &cpu_base->clock_base[index];

        if (!base->first)
                return;

        if (base->get_softirq_time)
                base->softirq_time = base->get_softirq_time();
...
```

Now the kernel has to find all timers that have expired and must be activated:

kernel/hrtimer.c
```
        while ((node = base->first)) {
                struct hrtimer *timer;
                enum hrtimer_restart (*fn)(struct hrtimer *);
                int restart;

                timer = rb_entry(node, struct hrtimer, node);
                if (base->softirq_time.tv64 <= timer->expires.tv64)
                        break;
...
                fn = timer->function;
                __remove_hrtimer(timer, base, HRTIMER_STATE_CALLBACK, 0);
...
```

Starting from the timer that is the first expiration candidate (`base->first`), the kernel checks if the timer has already expired and calls the timer's expiration function if this is the case. Recall that erasing the timer with `__remove_timer` also selects the next expiration candidate by updating `base->first`. Additionally, the flag `HRTIMER_STATE_CALLBACK` is set in the timer because the callback function is about to be executed:

kernel/hrtimer.c
```
                restart = fn(timer);

                timer->state &= ~HRTIMER_STATE_CALLBACK;
                if (restart != HRTIMER_NORESTART) {
                        enqueue_hrtimer(timer, base, 0);
                }
        }
}
```

When the handler has finished, the `HRTIMER_STATE_CALLBACK` flag can be removed again. If the timer requested to be put back into the queue, then `enqueue_hrtimer` fulfills this request.

15.4.4 Periodic Tick Emulation

The clock event handler in high-resolution mode is `hrtimer_interrupt`. This implies that `tick_handle_periodic` does not provide the periodic tick anymore. An equivalent functionality thus needs be made available based on high-resolution timers. The implementation is (nearly) identical between the situations with and without dynamic ticks. The generic framework for dynamic ticks is discussed in Section 15.5; the required components are covered here only cursorily.

Essentially, `tick_sched` is a special data structure to manage all relevant information about periodic ticks, and one instance per CPU is provided by the global variable `tick_cpu_sched`.

`tick_setup_sched_timer` is called to activate the tick emulation layer when the kernel switches to high-resolution mode. One high-resolution timer is installed per CPU. The required instance of `struct hrtimer` is kept in the per-CPU variable `tick_sched`:

```
<tick.h>
struct tick_sched {
        struct hrtimer sched_timer;
...
}
```

The function `tick_sched_timer` is used as the callback handler. To avoid a situation in which all CPUs are engaged in running the periodic tick handlers at the same time, the kernel distributes the acceleration time as shown in Figure 15-16. Recall that the length of a tick period (in nanoseconds) is `tick_period`. The ticks are spread across the first half of this period. Assume that the first tick starts at time 0. If the system contains N CPUs, the remaining periodic ticks are started at times $\Delta, 2\Delta, 3\Delta, \ldots$ The offset Δ is given by `tick_period/(2N)`.

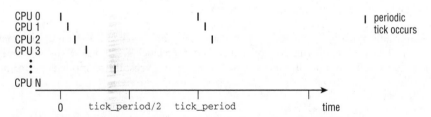

Figure 15-16: Distributing periodic tick handlers in high-resolution mode.

The tick timer is registered like every other regular high-resolution timer. The function displays some similarities to `tick_periodic`, but is slightly more complicated. The code flow diagram is shown in Figure 15-17.

If the CPU that is currently executing the timer is responsible to provide the global tick (recall that this duty has already been distributed in low-resolution mode at boot time), then `tick_do_update_jiffies64` computes the number of jiffies that have passed since the last update — in our case, this will always be

1 because I do not consider dynamic tick mode for now. The previously discussed function `do_timer` is used to handle all duties of the global timer. Recall that this includes updating the global `jiffies64` variable.

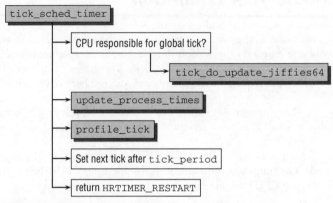

Figure 15-17: Code flow diagram for `tick_sched_timer`.

When the per-CPU periodic tick tasks have been performed in `update_process_times` (see Section 15.8) and `profile_tick`, the time for the next event is computed, and `hrtimer_forward` programs the timer accordingly. By returning `HRTIMER_RESTART`, the timer is automatically re-queued and activated when the next tick is due.

15.4.5 Switching to High-Resolution Timers

High-resolution timers are not enabled from the very beginning, but can only be activated when suitable high-resolution clock sources have been initialized and added to the generic clock framework. Low-resolution ticks, however, are provided (nearly) from the very beginning. In the following, I discuss how the kernel switches from low- to high-resolution mode.

The high-resolution queue is processed by `hrtimer_run_queue` when low-resolution timers are active. Before the queues are run, the function provides checks if a clock event device suitable for high resolution timers is present in the system. In this case, the switch to high resolution mode is performed:

kernel/hrtimer.c
```
void hrtimer_run_queues(void)
{
...
        if (tick_check_oneshot_change(!hrtimer_is_hres_enabled()))
            if (hrtimer_switch_to_hres())
                    return;
...
}
```

`tick_check_oneshot_change` signalizes that high-resolution timers can be used if a clock that supports one-shot mode and fulfills the resolution requirements for high-res timers, that is, if the flag `CLOCK_SOURCE_VALID_FOR_HRES` is set. `hrtimer_switch_to_hres` performs the actual switch. The required steps are summarized in Figure 15-18.

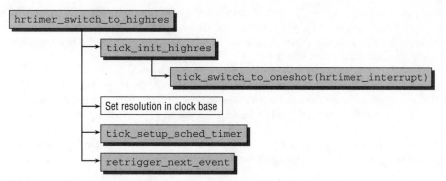

Figure 15-18: Code flow diagram for `hrtimer_switch_to_hires`.

`tick_init_switch_to_highres` is a wrapper function using `tick_switch_to_oneshot` to set the clock event device to one-shot mode. Additionally, `hrtimer_interrupt` is installed as event handler. Afterward the periodic tick emulation is activated with `tick_init_highres` as discussed above. Since the resolution is now improved, this also needs to be reflected in the data structures:

kernel/hrtimer.c
```
static int hrtimer_switch_to_hres(void)
{
...
        base->hres_active = 1;
        base->clock_base[CLOCK_REALTIME].resolution = KTIME_HIGH_RES;
        base->clock_base[CLOCK_MONOTONIC].resolution = KTIME_HIGH_RES;
...
}
```

Finally, `retrigger_next_event` reprograms the clock event device to set the ball rolling. High-resolution support is now active!

15.5 Dynamic Ticks

Periodic ticks have provided a notion of time to the Linux kernel for many of years. The approach is simple and effective, but shows one particular deficiency on systems where power consumption does matter: The periodic tick requires that the system is in an active state at a certain frequency. Longer periods of rest are impossible because of this.

Dynamic ticks mend this problem. The periodic tick is only activated when some tasks actually do need to be performed. Otherwise, it is temporarily disabled. Support for this technique can be selected at compile time, and the resulting system is also referred to as a *tickless system*. However, this name is not entirely accurate because the fundamental frequency HZ at which the periodic tick operates when it is functional still provides a raster for time flow. Since the tick can be activated and deactivated according to the current needs, the term *dynamic ticks* fits very well.

How can the kernel decide if the system has nothing to do? Recall from Chapter 2 that if no active tasks are on the run queue, the kernel picks a special task — the idle task — to run. At this point, the dynamic tick mechanism enters the game. Whenever the idle task is selected to run, the periodic tick is disabled until the next timer will expire. The tick is re-enabled again after this time span, or when an interrupt occurs. In the meantime, the CPU can enjoy a well-deserved sleep. Note that only classical timers need to be considered for this purpose. High-resolution timers are not bound by the tick frequency, and are also not implemented on top of periodic ticks.

Before discussing the dynamic tick implementation, let us note that one-shot clocks are a prerequisite for them. Since a key feature of dynamic ticks is that the tick mechanism can be stopped and restarted as necessary, purely periodic timers will fundamentally not suit the mechanism.

In the following, *periodic ticks* mean a tick implementation that does *not* use dynamic ticks. This must not be confused with clock event devices that work in periodic mode.

15.5.1   Data Structures

Dynamic ticks need to be implemented differently depending on whether high- or low-resolution timers are used. In both cases, the implementation is centered around the following data structure:

<tick.h>
```
struct tick_sched {
        struct hrtimer sched_timer;
        enum tick_nohz_mode nohz_mode;
        ktime_t idle_tick;
        int tick_stopped;
        unsigned long idle_jiffies;
        unsigned long idle_calls;
        unsigned long idle_sleeps;
        ktime_t idle_entrytime;
        ktime_t idle_sleeptime;
        ktime_t sleep_length;
        unsigned long last_jiffies;
        unsigned long next_jiffies;
        ktime_t idle_expires;
};
```

The individual elements are used as follows:

❑   `sched_timer` represents the timer used to implement the ticks.

❑   The current mode of operation is stored in `nohz_mode`. There are three possibilities:

<tick.h>
```
enum tick_nohz_mode {
        NOHZ_MODE_INACTIVE,
        NOHZ_MODE_LOWRES,
        NOHZ_MODE_HIGHRES,
};
```

`NOHZ_MOD_INACTIVE` is used if periodic ticks are active, while the other two constants indicate that dynamic ticks are used based on low- and high-resolution timers, respectively.

❑   `idle_tick` stores the expiration time of the last tick before ticks are disabled. This is important to know when ticks are enabled again because the next tick must appear at exactly the same time as if ticks had never been disabled. The proper point in time can be computed by using the value stored in `idle_tick` as basis. A sufficient number of tick intervals are added to obtain the expiration time for the next tick.

❑   `tick_stopped` is 1 if periodic ticks are stopped, that is, if there is nothing tick-based currently to do. Otherwise, the value is 0.

The remaining fields are used for bookkeeping:

❑   `idle_jiffies` stores the value of jiffies when periodic ticks were disabled.

❑   `idle_calls` counts how often the kernel has tried to deactivate periodic ticks. `idle_sleeps` counts how often this actually succeeded. The values differ because the kernel does not deactivate ticks if the next tick is only one jiffy away.

❑   `idle_sleeptime` stores the exact time (with the best current resolution) when periodic ticks were last disabled.

❑   `sleep_length` stores how long the periodic tick will remain disabled, that is, the difference between the time the tick was disabled and when the next tick is scheduled to happen.

❑   `idle_sleeptime` accumulates the total time spent with ticks deactivated.

❑   `next_jiffies` stores the jiffy value at which the next timer will expire.

❑   `idle_expires` stores when the next classical timer is due to expire. In contrast to the value above, the resolution of the value is as good as possible and not in jiffies.

The statistical information gathered in `tick_sched` is exported to userland via `/proc/timer_list`.

`tick_cpu_sched` is a global per-CPU variable that provides an instance of `struct tick_sched`. This is required because disabling ticks naturally works per CPU, not globally for the whole system.

15.5.2   Dynamic Ticks for Low-Resolution Systems

Consider the situation in which the kernel does not use high-resolution timers and provides only low resolution. How are dynamic ticks implemented in this scenario? Recall from above that the timer softIRQ calls `hrtimer_run_queues` to process the high-resolution timer queue, even if only low resolution is available in the underlying clock event device. Again, I emphasize that this does not provide better resolution for timers, but makes it possible to use the existing framework independent of the clock resolution.

Switching to Dynamic Ticks

`hrtimer_run_queues` calls `tick_check_oneshot_change` to decide if high-resolution timers can be activated. Additionally, the function checks if dynamic ticks can be enabled on low-resolution systems. This is possible under two conditions:

1.   A clock event device that supports one-shot mode is available.

2.   high-resolution is not enabled.

If both are fulfilled, then `tick_nohz_switch_to_nohz` is called to activate dynamic ticks. However, this does not ultimately enable dynamic ticks. If support for tickless systems was disabled at compile time, the function is just an empty dummy function, and the kernel will remain in periodic tick mode. Otherwise, the kernel proceeds as shown in Figure 15-19.

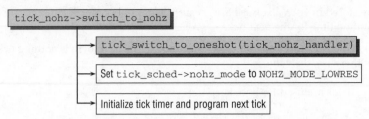

Figure 15-19: Code flow diagram for `tick_nohz_switch_to_nohz`.

The most important change required for the transition to dynamic ticks is to set the clock event device to one-shot mode, and to install an appropriate tick handler. This is done by calling `tick_switch_to_oneshot`. The new handler is `tick_nohz_handler`, examined below.

Since the dynamic tick mode is now active, the `nohz_mode` field of the per-CPU instance of `struct tick_sched` is changed to `NOHZ_MODE_LOWRES`. To get things going, the kernel finally needs to activate the first periodic tick by setting the timer to expire at the point in time when the next periodic tick would have been due.

The Dynamic Tick Handler

The new tick handler `tick_nohz_handler` needs to assume two responsibilities:

1. Perform all actions required for the tick mechanism.

2. Reprogram the tick device such that the next tick expires at the right time.

The code to satisfy these requirements looks as follows. Some initialization work is required to obtain the per-CPU instance of `struct tick_sched` and the current time:

kernel/time/tick-sched.c
```
static void tick_nohz_handler(struct clock_event_device *dev)
{
        struct tick_sched *ts = &__get_cpu_var(tick_cpu_sched);
        struct pt_regs *regs = get_irq_regs();
        int cpu = smp_processor_id();
        ktime_t now = ktime_get();

        dev->next_event.tv64 = KTIME_MAX;
```

The role of the global tick device is as before assumed by one particular CPU, and the handler needs to check if the current CPU is the responsible one. However, the situation is a bit more complicated with dynamic ticks. If a CPU goes into a long sleep, then it cannot be responsible for the global tick anymore, and drops the duty. If this is the case, the next CPU whose tick handler is called must assume the duty[18]:

kernel/time/tick-sched.c
```
        if (unlikely(tick_do_timer_cpu == -1))
                tick_do_timer_cpu = cpu;
```

---

[18]The case in which all processors sleep for longer than one jiffy is also possible. The kernel needs to consider this case as the discussion of `tick_do_updates_jiffies64` shows below.

```
        /* Check, if the jiffies need an update */
        if (tick_do_timer_cpu == cpu)
                tick_do_update_jiffies64(now);

        update_process_times(user_mode(regs));
        profile_tick(CPU_PROFILING);
```

If the CPU is responsible to provide the global tick, it is sufficient to call `tick_do_update_jiffies64`, which takes care of everything required — details will follow in a moment. `update_process_times` and `profile_tick` take over the duties of the local tick as you have seen several times before.

The crucial part is to reprogram the tick device. If the tick mechanism is stopped on the current CPU, this is not necessary, and the CPU will go into a complete sleep. (Note that setting `next_event.tv64` = `KTIME_MAX` ensures that the event device will not expire anytime soon, or never for practical purposes.)

If ticks are active, then `tick_nohz_reprogram` sets the tick timer to expire at the next jiffy. The `while` loop ensures that reprogramming is repeated until it succeeds if the processing should have taken too long and the next tick lies already in the past:

kernel/time/tick-sched.c
```
        /* Do not restart, when we are in the idle loop */
        if (ts->tick_stopped)
                return;

        while (tick_nohz_reprogram(ts, now)) {
                now = ktime_get();
                tick_do_update_jiffies64(now);
        }
}
```

Updating Jiffies

The global tick device calls `tick_do_update_jiffies64` to update the global `jiffies_64` variable, the basis of low-resolution timer handling. When periodic ticks are in use, this is comparatively simple because the function is called whenever a jiffy has passed. When dynamic ticks are enabled, the situation can arise in which all CPUs of the system are idle and none provides global ticks. This needs to be taken into account by `tick_do_update_jiffies64`. Let's go directly to the code to see how:

kernel/time/tick-sched.c
```
static void tick_do_update_jiffies64(ktime_t now)
{
unsigned long ticks = 0;
ktime_t delta;

delta = ktime_sub(now, last_jiffies_update);
```

Since the function needs to decide if more than a single jiffy has passed since the last update, the difference between the current time and `last_jiffies_update` must be computed.

Updating the jiffies value is naturally only required if the last update is more than one tick period ago:

kernel/time/tick-sched.c
```
        if (delta.tv64 >= tick_period.tv64) {

                delta = ktime_sub(delta, tick_period);
                last_jiffies_update = ktime_add(last_jiffies_update,
                                                tick_period);
```

The most common case is that one tick period has passed since the last jiffy update, and the code shown above handles this situation by increasing `last_jiffies_update` correspondingly. This accounts for the present tick.

However, it is also possible that the last update was more than one jiffy ago. Some more effort is required in this case:

kernel/time/tick-sched.c
```
                /* Slow path for long timeouts */
                if (unlikely(delta.tv64 >= tick_period.tv64)) {
                        s64 incr = ktime_to_ns(tick_period);

                        ticks = ktime_divns(delta, incr);

                        last_jiffies_update = ktime_add_ns(last_jiffies_update,
                                                           incr * ticks);
                }
```

The computation of `ticks` computes one tick less than the number of ticks that have been skipped, and `last_jiffies_updates` is updated accordingly. Note that the offset by one is necessary because one tick period was already added to `last_jiffies_update` at the very beginning. This way, the usual case (i.e., one tick period since the last update) runs fast, while more effort is required for the unusual case where more than one tick period has passed since the last update.

Finally, `do_timer` is called to update the global jiffies value as discussed in Section 15.2.1:

kernel/time/tick-sched.c
```
                do_timer(++ticks);
        }
}
```

15.5.3 Dynamic Ticks for High-Resolution Systems

Since clock event devices run in one-shot mode anyway if the kernel uses high timer resolution, support for dynamic ticks is much easier to implement than in the low-resolution case. Recall that the periodic tick is emulated by `tick_sched_timer` as discussed above. The function is also used to implement dynamic ticks. In the discussion in Section 15.4.4, I omitted two elements required for dynamic ticks:

1. Since CPUs can drop global tick duties, the handler needs to check if this has been the case, and assume the duties:

   kernel/time/tick-sched.c
   ```
   #ifdef CONFIG_NO_HZ
           if (unlikely(tick_do_timer_cpu == -1))
                   tick_do_timer_cpu = cpu;
   #endif
   ```

This code is run at the very beginning of `tick_sched_timer`.

2. When the handler is finished, it is usually required to reprogram the tick device such that the next tick will happen at the right time. If ticks are stopped, this is not necessary:

kernel/time/tick-sched.c
```
        /* Do not restart, when we are in the idle loop */
        if (ts->tick_stopped)
                return HRTIMER_NORESTART;
```

Only a single change to the existing code is required to initialize dynamic tick mode in a high-resolution regime. Recall that `tick_setup_sched_timer` is used to initialize the tick emulation layer for high-resolution systems. If dynamic ticks are enabled at compile time, a short piece of code is added to the function:

kernel/time/tick-sched.c
```
void tick_setup_sched_timer(void)
{
...
#ifdef CONFIG_NO_HZ
        if (tick_nohz_enabled)
                ts->nohz_mode = NOHZ_MODE_HIGHRES;
#endif
}
```

This announces officially that dynamic ticks are in use with high-resolution timers.

15.5.4   Stopping and Starting Periodic Ticks

Dynamic ticks provide the framework to defer periodic ticks for a while. What the kernel still needs to decide is *when* ticks are supposed to be stopped and restarted.

A natural possibility to stop ticks is when the idle task is scheduled: This proves that a processor really does not have anything better to do. `tick_nohz_stop_sched_tick` is provided by the dynamic tick framework to stop ticks. Note that the same function is used independent of low and high resolution. If dynamic ticks are disabled at compile time, the function is replaced by an empty dummy.

The idle task is implemented in an architecture-specific way, and not all architectures have been updated to support disabling the periodic tick yet. At the time of writing, ARM, MIPS, PowerPC, SuperH, Sparc64, IA-32, and AMD64[19] turn off ticks in the idle task.

Integrating `tick_nohz_stop_sched_tick` is rather straightforward. Consider, for instance, the implementation of `cpu_idle` (which is run in the idle task) on ARM systems:

arch/arm/kernel/process.c
```
void cpu_idle(void)
{
...
        /* endless idle loop with no priority at all */
```

---

[19] And user-mode Linux if you want to count that as a separate architecture.

```
              while (1) {
    ...
                      tick_nohz_stop_sched_tick();
                      while (!need_resched())
                              idle();
    ...
                      tick_nohz_restart_sched_tick();
    ...
              }
      }
```

Other architectures differ in some details, but the general principle is the same. After calling `tick_nohz_stop_sched_tick` to turn off ticks, the system goes into an endless loop that ends when a process is available to be scheduled on the processor. Ticks are then necessary again, and are reactivated by `tick_nohz_restart_sched_tick`.

Recall that a sleeping process waits for some condition to be fulfilled such that it switches into a runnable state. A change of this condition is signaled by an interrupt — just suppose that the process has been waiting for some data to arrive, and the interrupt notifies the system that the data are now available. Since interrupts occur at random times from the kernel's point of view, it can well happen that one is raised during an idle period with ticks turned off. Two conditions can thus require restarting ticks:

1. An external interrupt make a process runnable, which requires the tick mechanism to work.[20] In this case, ticks need to be resumed earlier than initially planned.

2. The next tick event is due, and the clock interrupt signals that the time for this has come. In this case, the tick mechanism is resumed as planned before.

Stopping Ticks

Essentially, `tick_nohz_stop_sched_tick` needs to perform three tasks:

1. Check if the next timer wheel event is more than one tick away.

2. If this is the case, reprogram the tick device to omit the next tick only when it is necessary again. This automatically omits all ticks that are not required.

3. Update the statistical information in `tick_sched`.

Since many details require much attention to corner cases, the actual implementation of `tick_nohz_stop_sched_tick` is rather bulky, so I consider a simplified version below.

First of all, the kernel needs to obtain the tick device and the `tick_sched` instance for the current CPU:

kernel/time/tick-sched.c
```
void tick_nohz_stop_sched_tick(void)
{
```

---

[20]To simplify matters, I ignore that `tick_nohz_stop_sched_tick` is also called from `irq_exit` if an interrupt has disturbed a tickless interval, but did not change the state of the system such that any process became runnable. This also simplifies the discussion of `tick_nohz_stop_sched_tick` because multiple subsequent invocations of the function need not be taken into account. Additionally, I do not discuss that the jiffies value needs to be updated in `irq_enter` because interrupt handlers would otherwise assume a wrong value. The function in charge for this is `tick_nohz_update_jiffies`.

```
unsigned long seq, last_jiffies, next_jiffies, delta_jiffies, flags;
struct tick_sched *ts;
ktime_t last_update, expires, now, delta;
struct clock_event_device *dev = __get_cpu_var(tick_cpu_device).evtdev;
int cpu;

cpu = smp_processor_id();
ts = &per_cpu(tick_cpu_sched, cpu);
```

Some statistical information is updated. Recall that the meaning of these fields has already been described in Section 15.5.1. The last jiffy update and the current jiffy value are stored in local variables:

kernel/time/tick-sched.c
```
now = ktime_get();

ts->idle_entrytime = now;
ts->idle_calls++;

last_update = last_jiffies_update;
last_jiffies = jiffies;
```

It only makes sense to deactivate ticks if the next periodic event is more than one tick away. The auxiliary function `get_next_timer_interrupt` analyzes the timer wheel and discovers the jiffy value at which the next event is due. `delta_wheel` then denotes how many jiffies away the next event is:

kernel/time/tick_sched.c
```
/* Get the next timer wheel timer */
next_jiffies = get_next_timer_interrupt(last_jiffies);
delta_jiffies = next_jiffies - last_jiffies;
```

If the next tick is at least one jiffy away (note that it can also be possible that some event is due in the current jiffy), the tick device needs to be reprogrammed accordingly:

kernel/timer/tick-sched.c
```
/* Schedule the tick, if we are at least one jiffie off */
if ((long)delta_jiffies >= 1) {

        ts->idle_tick = ts->sched_timer.expires;
        ts->tick_stopped = 1;
        ts->idle_jiffies = last_jiffies;
```

The meaning of the modified `tick_sched` fields has been discussed before.

If the current CPU had to provide the global tick, the task must be handed to another CPU. This is simply achieved by setting `tick_do_timer_cpu` to −1. The next tick handler that will be activated on another CPU then automatically takes the duties of the global tick source:

kernel/time/tick-sched.c
```
        if (cpu == tick_do_timer_cpu)
                tick_do_timer_cpu = -1;

        ts->idle_sleeps++;
```

Finally, the tick device is reprogrammed to provide the next event at the proper point in time. While the method to set the timer differs between high- and low-resolution mode, the code jumps to the label `out` if programming is successful in both cases:

kernel/time/tick-sched.c

```
                expires = ktime_add_ns(last_update, tick_period.tv64 *
                                       delta_jiffies);
                ts->idle_expires = expires;

                if (ts->nohz_mode == NOHZ_MODE_HIGHRES) {
                        hrtimer_start(&ts->sched_timer, expires,
                                       HRTIMER_MODE_ABS);
                        /* Check, if the timer was already in the past */
                        if (hrtimer_active(&ts->sched_timer))
                                goto out;
                } else if(!tick_program_event(expires, 0))
                                goto out;

                tick_do_update_jiffies64(ktime_get());
        }
        raise_softirq_irqoff(TIMER_SOFTIRQ);
out:
        ts->next_jiffies = next_jiffies;
        ts->last_jiffies = last_jiffies;
        ts->sleep_length = ktime_sub(dev->next_event, now);

}
```

If reprogramming failed, then too much time was spent in processing, and the expiration date already lies in the past. In this case, `tick_do_update_jiffies_64` updates jiffies to the correct value, and the timer softIRQ `TIMER_SOFTIRQ` is raised to process any pending timer-wheel timers. Note that the softIRQ is also raised if some events are due in the current jiffy period.

Restarting Ticks

`tick_nohz_restart_sched_tick` is used to restart ticks. The code flow diagram is given by Figure 15-20.

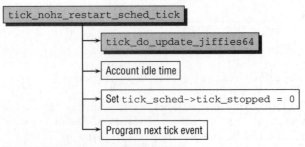

Figure 15-20: Code flow diagram for
`tick_nohz_restart_sched_tick`.

Again, the implementation is complicated by various technical details, but the general principle is rather simple. Our old acquaintance `tick_do_updates_jiffies64` is called first. After correctly accounting the idle time, `tick_sched->tick_stopped` is set to 0 because the tick is now active again. Finally, the next tick event needs to be programmed. This is necessary because the idle time might have ended before the expected time because of an external interrupt.

15.6 Broadcast Mode

On some architectures, clock event devices will go to sleep when certain power-saving modes are active. Thankfully, systems do not have only a single clock event device, so another device that still works can replace the stopped devices. The global variable `tick_broadcast_device` defined in `kernel/tick/tick-broadcast.c` contains the `tick_device` instance for the broadcast device.

An overview of broadcast mode is given in Figure 15-21.

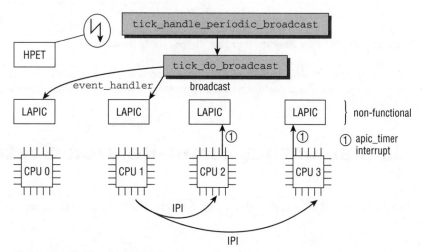

Figure 15-21: Overview of the situation when broadcasting replaces nonfunctional tick devices.

The APIC devices are not functional, but the broadcast event device still is. `tick_handle_periodic_broadcast` is used as the event handler. It deals with both periodic and one-shot modes of the broadcast device, so this need not concern us any further. The handler will be activated after each `tick_period`.

The broadcast handler uses `tick_do_periodic_broadcast`. The code flow diagram is shown in Figure 15-22. The function invokes the `event_handler` method of the nonfunctional device on the current CPU. The handler cannot distinguish if it was invoked from a clock interrupt or from the broadcast device, and is thus executed as if the underlying event device were functional.

If there are more nonfunctional local tick devices, then `tick_do_broadcast` employs the `broadcast` method of the first device in the list.[21] For local APICs, the broadcast method is `lapic_timer_broadcast`. It is responsible to send the inter-processor interrupt (IPI) LOCAL_TIMER_VECTOR to all CPUs that are associated with nonfunctional tick devices. The vector has been set up by the kernel to call

---

[21] This is possible because at the moment the same broadcast handler is installed on all devices that can become nonfunctional.

`apic_timer_interrupt`. The result is that the clock event device cannot distinguish between IPIs and real interrupts, so the effect is the same as if the device were still functional.

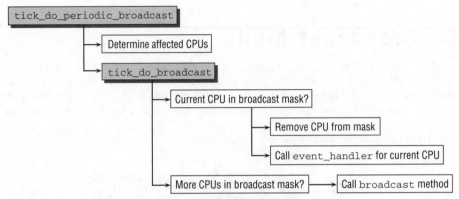

Figure 15-22: Code flow diagram for `tick_do_periodic_broadcast`.

Inter-processor interrupts are slow, and thus the required accuracy and resolution for high-resolution timers will not be available. The kernel therefore always switches to low-resolution mode if broadcasting is required.

15.7 Implementing Timer-Related System Calls

The kernel provides several system calls that involve timers; the most important ones are considered in the following:

15.7.1 Time Bases

When timers are used, there are three options to distinguish how elapsed time is counted or in which time base[22] the timer resides. The kernel features the following variants that draw attention to themselves by various signals when a time-out occurs:

❑ ITIMER_REAL measures the actual elapsed time between activation of the timer and time-out in order to trigger the signal. In this case, the timer continues to tick regardless of whether the system is in kernel mode or user mode or whether the application using the timer is currently running or not. A signal of the SIGALRM type is sent when the timer times out.

❑ ITIMER_VIRTUAL runs only during the time spent by the owner process of the timer in user mode. In this case, time spent in kernel mode (or when the processor is busy with another application) is ignored. Time-out is indicated by the SIGVTALRM signal.

❑ ITIMER_PROF calculates the time spent by the process both in user and kernel mode — time continues to elapse when a system call is executed on behalf of the task. Other processes of the system are ignored. The signal sent at time-out is SIGPROF.

---

[22]Often also referred to as *time domain*.

As already suggested by its name, the primary use of this timer is in the *profiling* of applications in which a search is made for the most compute-intensive fragments of a program so that these can be optimized accordingly. This is an important consideration, particularly in scientific or operating system-related applications.

The timer type — and the periodic interval length — must be specified when an interval timer is installed. In our example, TTIMER_REAL is used for a real-time timer.

The behavior of alarm timers can be simulated with interval timers by selecting ITIMER_REAL as the timer type and deinstalling the timer after the first time-out. Interval timers are therefore a generalized form of alarm timers.

15.7.2 The alarm and setitimer System Calls

alarm installs timers of the ITIMER_REAL type (real-time timers), while setitimer is used to install not only real-time, but also virtual and profiling timers. The system calls all end up in do_setitimer. The implementation of both system calls rests on a common mechanism that is defined in kernel/itimer.c. The implementation is centered around struct hrtimer, so if high-resolution support is available, the corresponding advantages are automatically transferred into userland and not only available to the kernel. Note that since alarm uses a timer of type ITIMER_REAL, the system calls can interfere with each other.

The starting points of the system calls are, as usual, the two functions sys_alarm and sys_setitimer. Both functions use the auxiliary function do_setitimer to actually implement the timer:

kernel/itimer.c
```
int do_setitimer(int which, struct itimerval *value, struct itimerval *ovalue)
```

Three parameters are required. which specifies the timer type, and can be ITIMER_REAL, ITIMER_VIRTUAL, or ITIMER_PROF. value contains all relevant information about the new timer. If the timer replaces an already existing one, then ovalue is employed to return the previously active timer description.

Specifying timer properties is simple:

<time.h>
```
struct itimerval {
        struct timeval it_interval; /* timer interval */
        struct timeval it_value; /* current value */
};
```

Essentially, timeval denotes the length of the periodic interval after which the timer expires. it_value denotes the amount of time remaining until the timer expires next. All details are documented in the manual page setitimer(2).

Extensions to the Task Structure

The task structure of each process contains a pointer to an instance of struct signal_struct that includes several elements to accommodate information required for timers:

<sched.h>
```
struct signal_struct {
...
        /* ITIMER_REAL timer for the process */
```

```
        struct hrtimer real_timer;
        struct task_struct *tsk;
        ktime_t it_real_incr;

        /* ITIMER_PROF and ITIMER_VIRTUAL timers for the process */
        cputime_t it_prof_expires, it_virt_expires;
        cputime_t it_prof_incr, it_virt_incr;
    ...
    }
```

Two fields are reserved for profiling and virtual timer type:

1. The time at which the next time-out is to occur (`it_prof_expires` and `it_virt_expires`).

2. The interval after which the timer is called (`it_prof_incr` and `it_virt_incr`).

`real_timer` is an instance of `hrtimer` (*not* a pointer to it) that is inserted in the other data structures of the kernel and is used to implement real-time timers. The other two types of timer (virtual and profiling) manage without this entry. `tsk` points to the task structure of the process for which the timers are set. The interval for real timers is specified in `it_real_incr`.

It is therefore possible to have just three different timers of *different* kinds per process — given the existing data structures, the kernel cannot manage more with the `setitimer` and `alarm` mechanism. For example, a process can execute a virtual and a real-time timer at the same time, but not two real-time timers.

POSIX timers that are implemented in `kernel/posix-timers.c` provide an extension to this scheme that allow more timers, but need not be discussed any further. Virtual and profiling timers are also implemented on top of this framework.

Real-Time Timers

When installing a real-time (`ITIMER_REAL`) timer, it is first necessary to preserve the properties of a possibly existing old timer (they will be returned to userland once the new timer has been installed) and cancel the timer with `hrtimer_try_to_cancel`. Installing a timer "overwrites" previous values.

The timer period is stored in the task-specific `signal_struct->it_real_incr` field (if this field is zero, then the timer is not periodic, but only activated once), and `hrtimer_start` starts a timer that expires at the desired time.

No handler routine is executed in userspace when a dynamic timer expires. Instead, a signal is generated that results in the invocation of a signal handler and thus indirectly to the invocation of a callback function. How does the kernel ensure that the signal is sent, and how is the timer made periodic?

The kernel uses the callback handler `it_real_fn`, which is executed for all userspace real-time timers. This function sends the `SIGALRM` signal to the process that installed the timer, but does *not* reinstall the signal handler to make the signal periodic.

Instead, the timer is reinstalled when the signal is delivered in process context (in `dequeue_signal`, to be precise). After forwarding the expiration time with `hrtimer_forward`, the timer is restarted with `hrtimer_restart`.

What keeps the kernel from reactivating the timer immediately after it has expired? Earlier kernel versions did, in fact, choose this approach, but problems arise if high-resolution timers are active. A process can choose a very short repetition interval that would cause timers to expire over and over — resulting in excessive time spent in the timer code. Put less politely, one could also call this a denial-of-service attack, and the current approach avoids this.

15.7.3 Getting the Current Time

The current time of the system needs to be known for two reasons: First, many operations rely on time stamps — for instance, the kernel needs to record when a file was last changed or when some log information was produced. Second, the absolute time — that is, the real time of the outside world — of the system is needed to inform the user with a clock, for example.

While absolute accuracy is not too important for the first purpose as long as the time flow is continuous (i.e., the time stamps of successive operations should follow their order), it is more essential for the second purpose. Hardware clocks are notorious for being either fast, slow, or a random combination of both. There are various methods to solve this problem, with the most common one in the age of networked computers being synchronization with a reliable time source (e.g., an atomic clock) via NTP. Since this is purely a userland issue, I won't discuss it any further.

Two means are provided to obtain timing information:

1. The system call `adjtimex`. A small utility program of the same name can be used to quickly display the exported information. The system call allows for reading the current kernel internal time. Other possibilities are documented in the associated manual page 2 (`adjtimex`).

2. The device special file `/dev/rtc`. This source can be operated in various modes, but one of them delivers the current date and time to the caller.

I focus on `adjtimex` in the following. The entry point is as usual `sys_adjtimex`, but after some preparations, the real work is delegated to `do_adjtimex`. The function is rather lengthy, but the portion required for our purposes is quite compact:

kernel/time.c
```
int do_adjtimex(struct timex *txc)
{
...
        do_gettimeofday(&txc->time);
...
}
```

The call to `do_gettimeofday` obtains the kernel's internal time in the best possible resolution. The best time source that was selected by the kernel as described in Section 15.4 is used for this purpose.

15.8 Managing Process Times

The task structure contains two elements related to process times that are important in our context:

<sched.h>
```
struct task_struct {
...
        cputime_t utime, stime;
...
}
```

`update_process_times` is used to manage process-specific time elements and is invoked from the local tick.

As the code flow diagram in Figure 15-23 shows, four things need to be done:

1. `account_process_tick` uses either `account_user_time` or `account_sys_time` to update the values for user or system CPU time consumed in the task structure (`utime` or `stime`, respectively). The `SIGXCPU` signal is also sent at intervals of 1 second if the process has exceeded its CPU limits specified by Rlimit.

2. `run_local_timers` activates and expires low-resolution timers. Recall that this was discussed in detail in Section 15.2.

3. `scheduler_tick` is a helper for the CPU scheduler as discussed in Chapter 2.

4. `run_posix_cpu_timers` initiates that the currently registered POSIX timers are run. This includes running the abovementioned interval timers since their implementation is based on POSIX CPU timers. Since these timers are otherwise not very interesting, their implementation is not covered in detail.

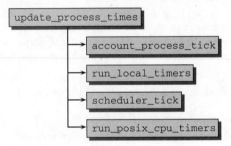

Figure 15-23: Code flow diagram for
`update_process_times`.

15.9 Summary

The kernel needs to keep track of time for various purposes, and there are also a good many aspects that must be considered to solve the problem. In this chapter, first you were introduced to the general concept of timekeeping and the difference between timers and time-outs. You have seen that the implementation of timers and time-outs is based on hardware that can manage the time. Typically, each system contains more than one component for this purpose, and you were introduced to the data structures that allow for representing these components and sorting them by quality. Traditionally, the kernel relied on low-resolution timers, but recent hardware progress and a rework of the timing subsystem have allowed the introduction of a new class of *high-resolution timers*.

After a discussion of the implementation of high- and low-resolution timers, you were introduced to the concept of *dynamic ticks*. Traditionally, a periodic timer tick was issued with HZ frequency, but this is suboptimal for machines where power is scarce: When a system is idle and has nothing to do, the tick is superfluous and can be temporarily disabled to allow components to enter deeper sleep states without being woken up at periodic intervals. The dynamic tick mode allows for achieving exactly this.

Time is also relevant for userspace processes, and thus I finally discussed various system calls that are available in this area.

16

Page and Buffer Cache

Performance and efficiency are two factors to which great importance is attached during kernel development. The kernel relies not only on a sophisticated overall concept of interaction between its individual components, but also on an extensive framework of buffers and caches designed to boost system speed.

Buffering and caching make use of parts of system RAM to ensure that the most important and the most frequently used data of block devices can be manipulated not on the slow devices themselves but in main memory. RAM memory is also used to store the data read in from block devices so that the data can be subsequently accessed directly in fast RAM when it is needed again rather than fetching it from external devices.

Of course, this is done transparently so that the applications do not and cannot notice any difference as to from where the data originate.

Data are not written back after each change but after a specific interval whose length depends on a variety of factors such as the free RAM capacity, the frequency of usage of the data held in RAM, and so on. Individual write requests are bundled and collectively take less time to perform. Consequently, delaying write operations improves system performance as a whole.

However, caching has its downside and must be employed judiciously by the kernel:

❑ Usually there is far less RAM capacity than block device capacity so that only carefully selected data may be cached.

❑ The memory areas used for caching are not exclusively reserved for "normal" application data. This reduces the RAM capacity that is effectively available.

❑ If the system crashes (owing to a power outage, e.g.), the caches may contain data that have not been written back to the underlying block device. Such data are irretrievably lost.

However, the advantages of caching outweigh the disadvantages to such an extent that caches are permanently integrated into the kernel structures.

Caching is a kind of "reverse" swapping or paging operation (the latter are discussed in Chapter 18). Whereas fast RAM is sacrificed for caching (so that there is no need for slow operations on block devices), RAM memory is replaced virtually with slow block devices to implement swapping. The kernel must therefore do its best to cater to both mechanisms to ensure that the advantages of the one method are not canceled out by the disadvantages of the other — no easy feat.

Previous chapters discussed some of the means provided by the kernel for caching specific structures. The slab cache is a memory-to-memory cache whose purpose is not to accelerate operations on slower devices but to make simpler and more effective use of existing resources. The dentry cache is also used to dispense with the need to access slow block devices but cannot be put to general use since it is specialized to handle a single data type.

The kernel features two general caching options for block devices:

1. The **page cache** is intended for all operations in units of a page — and takes into account the page size on the specific architecture. A prime example is the memory-mapping technique discussed in many chapters. As other types of file access are also implemented on the basis of this technique in the kernel, the page cache is responsible for most caching work for block devices.

2. The **buffer cache** operates with blocks. When I/O operations are performed, the access units used are the individual blocks of a device and not whole pages. Whereas the page size is the same with all filesystems, the block size varies depending on the particular filesystem or its settings. The buffer cache must therefore be able to handle blocks of different sizes.

   While buffers used to be the traditional method to perform I/O operations with block devices, they are nowadays in this area only supported for very small read operations where the advanced methods are too bulky. The standard data structure used for block transfers has become `struct bio`, which is discussed in Chapter 6. It is much more efficient to perform block transfers this way because it allows for merging subsequent blocks in a request together that speeds things up.

   Nevertheless, buffers are still the method of choice to represent I/O operations on individual blocks, even if the underlying I/O is performed with `bios`. Especially systems often have to read metadata blockwise, and buffers are much easier to handle for this task than other more powerful structures. All in all, buffers still have their own identity and are not around solely for compatibility reasons.

In many scenarios, page and buffer caches are used in combination. For example, a cached page is divided into various buffers during write operations so that the modified parts of the page can be more finely grained. This has advantages when the data are written back because only the modified part of the page and not the whole page need be transferred back to the underlying block device.

16.1 Structure of the Page Cache

As its name suggests, the *page cache* deals with memory pages that divide virtual memory and RAM memory into small segments. This not only makes it easier for the kernel to manipulate the large address space, but also supports a whole series of functions such as paging, demand loading, memory mapping, and the like. The task of the page cache is to obtain some of the available physical page frames to speed up the operations performed on block devices on a page basis. Of course, the way the page cache behaves is transparent to user applications as they do not know whether they are interacting directly with a block device or with a copy of their data held in memory — the read and write system calls return identical results in both cases.

Naturally, the situation is somewhat different for the kernel. In order to support the use of cached pages, anchors must be positioned at the various points in the code that interact with the page cache. The operation required by the user process must always be performed regardless of whether the desired page resides in the cache or not. When a cache hit occurs, the appropriate action is performed quickly (this is the very purpose of the cache). In the event of a cache miss, the required page must first be read from the underlying block device, and this takes longer. Once the page has been read, it is inserted in the cache and is, therefore, quickly available for subsequent access.

The time spent searching for a page in the page cache must be minimized to ensure that cache misses are as cheap as possible — if a miss occurs, the compute time needed to perform the search is (more or less) wasted. The efficient organization of the cached pages is, therefore, a key aspect of page cache design.

16.1.1 Managing and Finding Cached Pages

The problem of quickly fetching individual elements (pages) from a large data set (page cache) is not specific to the Linux kernel. It has long been common to all areas of information technology and has spawned many sophisticated data structures that have stood the test of time. Tree data structures of various kinds are very popular, and Linux also opts for such a structure — known as a radix tree — to manage the pages held in page caches.

Appendix C provides a more detailed description of this data structure. This chapter gives a brief overview of how the individual pages are organized in the structure.

Figure 16-1 shows a radix tree in which various instances of a data structure (represented by squares) are interlinked.[1]

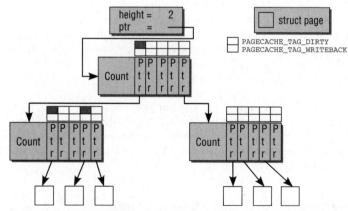

Figure 16-1: Example of a radix tree.

---

[1]The structure shown is simplified because the kernel makes use of additional tags in each node to hold specific information on the pages organized in the node. This has no effect on the basic architecture of the tree.

The structure does not correspond to that of the binary or ternary search trees in general use. Neither are radix trees balanced; in other words, there may be any number of height differences between the branches of the tree. The tree itself consists of two different data structures and a further data structure to represent the leaves and hold the useful data. Because memory pages must be organized, the leaves are instances of the page structure in this case, a fact that is of no further importance in the implementation of the tree. (The kernel sources do not define a particular data type but use a void pointer; this means that radix trees could also be used for other purposes, although this is not done at present.)

The root of the tree is represented by a simple data structure that holds the height of the tree (the maximum number of levels to accommodate the nodes) and a pointer to the first node data structure of which the tree is comprised.

The nodes are basically arrays. For the sake of simplicity, the nodes are shown with four elements in the figure, but in the kernel sources, they actually have $2^{\text{RADIX\_TREE\_MAP\_SHIFT}}$ entries. Since RADIX_TREE_MAP_SHIFT is typically defined as 6, each array has 64 elements — considerably more than are shown in the figure. Small systems use a RADIX_TREE_MAP_SHIFT setting of 4 to save precious memory.

The elements of the tree are addressed by means of a unique key consisting of a simple integer. The details of the algorithm used to find elements by reference to their key are not discussed here. A description of the relevant code is given in Appendix C.

Enlarging the tree and deleting tree elements are kernel operations that require little effort, so minimum time is lost in performing cache management operations. Their implementation is also described in greater detail in Appendix C.

Observe from Figure 16-1 that the tree is equipped with two *search tags*. They allow for specifying if a given page is dirty (i.e., the page contents are not identical with the data in the backing store) or if it is currently being written back to the underlying block device. It is important that the tags are not only set in the leaf elements, but also all the way up to the root element. If at least one pointer in level $n + 1$ has a tag set, then the pointer on level n will also acquire the tag.

This allows the kernel to decide that one or more pages in a range have a tag bit set. The figure provides an example: Since the dirty tag bit on the leftmost pointer in the first level is set, the kernel knows that one or more of the pages associated with the corresponding second-level node have the dirty tag bit set. If, on the other hand, a tag is *not* set for a pointer in the higher levels, then the kernel can be sure that none of the pages in the lower levels has the tag.

Recall from Chapter 3 that each page as represented by an instance of struct page is equipped with a set of flags. These also include dirty and writeback flags. The information in the radix tree tags therefore only augments kernel knowledge. Page cache tags are useful to quickly determine if at least one page in a region is dirty or under writeback without scanning all pages in the whole region. They are, however, no replacement for the direct page flags.

16.1.2 Writing Back Modified Data

Thanks to the page cache, write operations are not performed directly on the underlying block device but are carried out in memory where the modified data are first collected for subsequent transfer to the lower kernel layer, where the write operations can be further optimized — as discussed in Chapter 6 — to fully exploit the specific capabilities of the individual devices. Here we are interested only in the situation as seen by the page cache, which is primarily concerned with one specific question: *at which point in time* should the data be written back? This automatically includes the question as to *how often* should writeback take place.

Understandably, there is no universally valid answer to this question as different systems with different load conditions give rise to very different scenarios. For example, a server running overnight receives very few requests to modify data so that the services of the kernel are seldom required. The same scenario applies on personal computers when users take a break from work. However, the situation can change suddenly when the server launches a huge FTP transfer or the PC user starts a lengthy compiler run to process and produce large volumes of data. In both scenarios, the caches initially have very little to write back, but then, from one moment to the next, they are required to frequently synchronize with the underlying storage medium.

For these reasons, the kernel provides several parallel synchronization alternatives:

❑ Several special kernel daemons called `pdflush` run in the background and are activated periodically — regardless of the current situation in the page cache. They scan the pages in the cache and write back the data that have not been synchronized with the underlying block device for a specific period.

Earlier kernel versions employed a userspace daemon named `kudpated` for this purpose, and this name is still commonly used to describe this mechanism.

❑ A second operating mode of `pdflush` is activated by the kernel if the number of modified data items in a cache has increased substantially within a short period.

❑ System calls are available to users and applications to instruct the kernel to write back all non-synchronized data. The best known is the `sync` call because there is also a userspace tool of the same name that builds on it.

The various mechanisms used to write back dirty data from the caches are discussed in Chapter 17.

To manage the various target objects that can be processed and cached in whole pages, the kernel uses an abstraction of the "address space" that associates the pages in memory with a specific block device (or any other system unit or part of a system unit).

> This type of address space must not be confused with the virtual and physical address spaces provided by the system or processor. It is a separate abstraction of the Linux kernel that unfortunately bears the same name.

Initially, we are interested in only one aspect. Each address space has a "host" from which it obtains its data. In most cases, these are inodes that represent just one file.[2] Because all existing inodes are linked with their superblock (as discussed in Chapter 8), all the kernel need do is scan a list of all superblocks and follow their associated inodes to obtain a list of cached pages.

Usually, modifications to files or other objects cached in pages change only part and not the whole of the page contents. This gives rise to a problem when data are synchronized; it doesn't make sense to write

---

[2]Since the majority of cached pages result from file accesses, most host objects, indeed, represent a regular file. It is, however, also possible that an inode host object stems from the pseudo-block device filesystem. In this case, the address space is not associated with a single file, but with a whole block device or a partition thereof.

the entire page back to the block device because most of the page data in memory are still synchronized with the data on the block device. To save time, the kernel divides each page in the cache into smaller units known as *buffers* during write operations. When data are synchronized, the kernel is able to restrict writeback to the smaller units that have actually been modified. As a result, the basically sound idea of page caching is not compromised in any way.

16.2 Structure of the Buffer Cache

A page-oriented method has not always been used in the Linux kernel to bear the main caching burden. Earlier versions included only the buffer cache to speed file operations and to enhance system performance. This was a legacy of other UNIX look-alikes with the same structure. Blocks from the underlying block devices were kept in main memory buffers to make read and write operations faster. The implementation is contained in `fs/buffers.c`.

In contrast to pages in memory, blocks are not only (mostly) smaller but vary in size depending on the block device in use (or on the filesystem, as demonstrated in Chapter 9).

As a result of the ever increasing trend toward generic file access methods implemented by means of page-based operations, the buffer cache has lost much of its importance as a central system cache, and the main caching burden is now placed firmly on the page cache. Additionally, the standard data structure for block-based I/O is not a buffer anymore, but `struct bio` as discussed in Chapter 6.

Buffers are kept for small I/O transfers with block size granularity. This is often required by filesystems to handle their metadata. Transfer of raw data is done in a page-centric fashion, and the implementation of buffers is also on top of the page cache.[3]

The buffer cache consists of two structural units:

1. A *buffer head* holds all management data relating to the state of the buffer including information on block number, block size, access counter, and so on, discussed below. These data are *not* stored directly after the buffer head but in a separate area of RAM memory indicated by a corresponding pointer in the buffer head structure.

2. The useful data are held in specially reserved pages that may also reside in the page cache. This further subdivides the page cache as illustrated in Figure 16-2; in our example, the page is split into four identically sized parts, each of which is described by its own buffer head. The buffer heads are held in memory areas unrelated to the areas where the useful data are stored.

    This enables the page to be subdivided into smaller sections because no gaps arise as a result of prefixing the buffer data with header data. As a buffer consists of at least 512 bytes, there may be up to a maximum of MAX_BUF_PER_PAGE buffers per page; the constant is defined as a function of the page size:

    <buffer_head.h>
    ```
    #define MAX_BUF_PER_PAGE (PAGE_CACHE_SIZE / 512)
    ```

---

[3]This contrasts kernels before and including the 2.2 series that used separate caches for buffers and pages. Having two distinct caching possibilities requires enormous efforts to synchronize both, so the kernel developers chose to unify the caching scheme many years ago.

If one of the buffers is modified, this has an immediate effect on the contents of the page (and vice versa) so that there is no need for explicit synchronization of the two caches — after all, both share identical data.

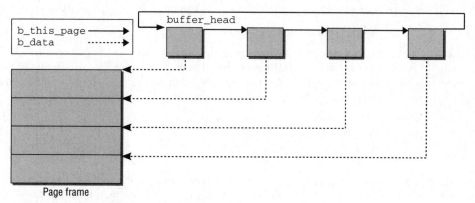

Page frame

Figure 16-2: Link between pages and buffers.

There are, of course, applications that access block devices using blocks rather than pages — reading the superblock of a filesystem is one such example. A separate buffer cache is used to speed access of this kind. The buffer cache operates independently of the page cache, not in addition to it. To this end, buffer heads — the data structure is the same in buffer caches and page caches — are grouped together in an array of constant size whose individual entries are managed on a least recently used basis. After an entry has been used, it is placed at position 0 and the other entries are moved down accordingly; this means that the entries most frequently used are located at the beginning of the array and those less frequently used are pushed further back until they finally "drop" off the array if they have not been used for a lengthy period.

As the size of the array and therefore the number of entries in the LRU list are restricted to a fixed value that does not change during kernel run time, the kernel need not execute separate threads to trim the cache size to reasonable values. Instead, all it need do is remove the associated buffer from the cache when an entry drops off the array in order to release memory for other purposes.

Section 16.5 discusses in detail the technical details of buffer implementation. Before this, it is necessary to discuss the concept of address spaces because these are key to the implementation of cache functionality.

16.3   Address Spaces

Not only have caches progressed from a buffer orientation to a page orientation during the course of Linux development, but also the way in which cached data are linked with their sources has been replaced with a more general schema as compared to previous Linux versions. Whereas in the early days of Linux and other UNIX derivatives, inodes were the only objects that acted as the starting point for obtaining data from cache contents, the kernel now uses much more general *address spaces* that establish the link between cached data and the objects and devices required to obtain the data. Although file contents still account for much of the data in caches, the interfaces are so generalized that the caches are also able to hold data from other sources in order to speed access.

How do address spaces fit into the structures of the page cache? They implement a translation mechanism between two units:

1. Pages in main memory are allocated to each address space. The contents of these pages can be manipulated by user processes or by the kernel itself using a variety of methods.

   These data represent the contents of the cache.

2. The *backing store* specifies the sources from which the address space pages are filled. Address spaces relate to the virtual address space of the processor and are a mapping of the segment managed by the processor in virtual memory and the corresponding positions on a source device (using a block device).

   If a position in virtual memory that is not associated with a physical page in memory is accessed, the kernel can refer to the address space structure to discover from where the data must be read.

To support data transfer, each address space provides a set of operations (in the form of function pointers) to permit interaction between the two sides of address space — for instance, to read a page from a block device or filesystem, or to write back a modified page. The following section takes a close look at the data structures used before examining the implementation of address space operations.

Address spaces are one of the most crucial data structures in the kernel. Their management has evolved to one of the central issues faced by the kernel. Numerous subsystems (filesystems, swapping, synchronization, caching) are centered around the concept of an address space. They can therefore be regarded as one of the fundamental abstraction mechanisms of the kernel, and range in importance among the traditional abstractions like processes and files.

16.3.1 Data Structures

The basis of an address space is the `address_space` structure, which is in slightly simplified form defined as follows:

<fs.h>
```
struct address_space {
        struct inode            *host;          /* owner: inode, block_device */
        struct radix_tree_root  page_tree;      /* radix tree of all pages */
        unsigned int            i_mmap_writable;/* count VM_SHARED mappings */
        struct prio_tree_root   i_mmap;         /* tree of private and shared mappings */
        struct list_head        i_mmap_nonlinear;/*list VM_NONLINEAR mappings */
        unsigned long           nrpages;        /* number of total pages */
        pgoff_t                 writeback_index;/* writeback starts here */
        struct address_space_operations *a_ops; /* methods */
        unsigned long           flags;          /* error bits/gfp mask */
        struct backing_dev_info *backing_dev_info; /* device readahead, etc */
        struct list_head        private_list;   /* ditto */
        struct address_space    *assoc_mapping; /* ditto */
} __attribute__((aligned(sizeof(long))));
```

❑ The link with the areas managed by an address space is established by means of a pointer to an inode instance (of type `struct inode`) to specify the backing store and a root radix tree (`page_tree`) with a list of all physical memory pages in the address space.

❑ The total number of cached pages is held in the `nrpages` counter variable.

❑ `address_space_operations` is a pointer to a structure that contains a list of function pointers to specific operations for handling address spaces. Its definition is discussed below.

❑ `i_mmap` is the root element of a tree that holds all normal memory mappings of the inode (normal in the sense that they were not created using the nonlinear mapping mechanism). The task of the tree is to support finding all memory regions that include at least one page in a given interval, and the auxiliary macro `vma_prio_tree_foreach` is provided for this purpose. Recall that the purpose of the tree is discussed in Section 4.4.3. The details of tree implementation are of no relevance to us at the moment — it is sufficient to know that all pages of the mapping can be found on the tree and that the structure can be manipulated easily.

❑ Two further elements are concerned with the management of memory mappings: `i_mmap_writeable` counts all mappings created with a set `VM_SHARED` attribute so that they can be shared by several users at the same time. `i_mmap_nonlinear` is used to set up a list of all pages included in nonlinear mappings (reminder: nonlinear mappings are generated by skillful manipulation of the page tables under the control of the `remap_file_pages` system call).

❑ `backing_dev_info` is a pointer to a further structure that holds information on the associated *backing store*.

   Backing store is the name used for the peripheral device that serves as a "backbone" for the information present in the address space. It is typically a block device:

   \<backing-dev.h\>
   ```
   struct backing_dev_info {
           unsigned long ra_pages; /* max readahead in PAGE_CACHE_SIZE units */
           unsigned long state;    /* Always use atomic bitops on this */
           unsigned int capabilities; /* Device capabilities */
   ...
   };
   ```

   `ra_pages` specifies the maximum number of pages to be read in anticipation (readahead). The state of the backing store is stored in `state`. `capabilities` holds information on the backing store — for example, whether the data in the store can be executed directly as is necessary in ROM-based filesystems. However, the most important information in `capabilities` is whether pages can be written back. This can always be done with genuine block devices but is not possible with memory-based devices such as RAM disks because there would be little point in writing back data from memory to memory.

   If `BDI_CAP_NO_WRITEBACK` is set, then synchronization is not required; otherwise, it is. Chapter 17 discusses the mechanisms used for this purpose in detail.

❑ `private_list` is used to interlink `buffer_head` instances which hold filesystem metadata (usually indirection blocks). `assoc_mapping` is a pointer to the associated address space.

❑ The flag set in `flags` is used primarily to hold information on the GFP memory area from which the mapped pages originate. It can also hold errors that occur during asynchronous input/output and that cannot therefore be propagated directly. `AS_EIO` stands for a general I/O error, and `AS_ENOSPC` indicates that there is no longer sufficient space for an asynchronous write operation.

Figure 16-3 sketches how address spaces are connected with various other parts of the kernel. Only the most important links are shown in this overview; more details will be discussed in the remainder of this chapter.

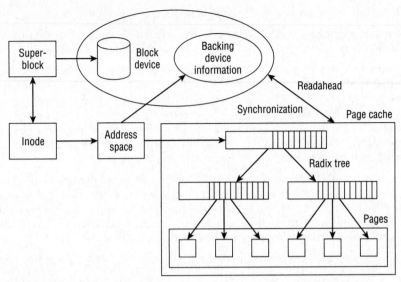

Figure 16-3: Address spaces and their connection with central kernel data structures and subsystems.

16.3.2 Page Trees

The kernel uses radix trees to manage all pages associated with an address space at least possible cost. A general overview of trees of this kind was provided above; now the corresponding data structures in the kernel are focused on.

As is clear from the layout of `address_space`, the `radix_tree_root` structure is the root element of every radix tree:

```
<radix_tree_root.h>
struct radix_tree_root {
        unsigned int            height;
        gfp_t                   gfp_mask;
        struct radix_tree_node  *rnode;
};
```

❏   `height` specifies the height of the tree, that is, the number of levels below the root. On the basis of this information and the number of entries per node, the kernel is able to calculate quickly the maximum number of elements in a given tree and to expand the tree accordingly if there is insufficient capacity to accept new data.

❏   `gfp_mask` specifies the zone from which memory is to be allocated.

❏   `rnode` is a pointer to the first node element of the tree. The `radix_tree_node` date type discussed below is used for this node.

Implementation

The nodes of a radix tree are essentially represented by the following data structure:

```
<lib/radix_tree.c>
#define RADIX_TREE_TAGS          2
#define RADIX_TREE_MAP_SHIFT     (CONFIG_BASE_SMALL ? 4 : 6)
#define RADIX_TREE_MAP_SIZE      (1UL << RADIX_TREE_MAP_SHIFT)
#define RADIX_TREE_TAG_LONGS     \
        ((RADIX_TREE_MAP_SIZE + BITS_PER_LONG - 1) / BITS_PER_LONG)

struct radix_tree_node {
        unsigned int    height;          /* Height from the bottom */
        unsigned int    count;
        struct rcu_head rcu_head;
        void            *slots[RADIX_TREE_MAP_SIZE];
        unsigned long   tags[RADIX_TREE_TAGS][RADIX_TREE_TAG_LONGS];
};
```

The layout of this data structure is also very simple. `slots` is an array of `void` pointers that — depending on the level in which the node is located — point to either data elements or further nodes. `count` holds the number of used array entries in the node. The array is filled with entries starting at the top, and unused entries have null pointers.

Each tree node can point to 64 further nodes (or leaves) as indicated in the definition of the `slot` array in `radix_tree_node`. The direct consequence of this definition is that each node may have only an array size that is a power of two. Also, the size of *all* radix elements may only be defined at compilation time (of course, the maximum number of elements in a tree can change at run time). This behavior is rewarded by speed gains.

Tagging

The information discussed so far — the address space and the page tree — does not, however, allow the kernel to make a direct distinction between the clean and dirty pages of a mapping. This distinction is essential when, for example, pages are to be written back to store changes permanently on the underlying block device. Earlier kernel versions provided additional lists of dirty and clean pages in `address_space`. In principle, the kernel could, of course, scan the entire tree and filter out the pages with the appropriate state, but this is obviously very time-consuming. For this reason, each node of the radix tree includes additional tagging information that specifies whether each page in the node has the property specified in the tag. For example, the kernel uses a tag to label nodes with dirty pages. Nodes without this tag can therefore be skipped during a scan for dirty pages. This approach is a compromise between simple, unified data structures (no explicit lists are needed to hold pages with different states) and the option of performing a quick search for pages with specific properties. Currently, two tags are supported:

1. `PAGECACHE_TAG_DIRTY` specifies whether a page is dirty.
2. `PAGECACHE_TAG_WRITEBACK` indicates that the page is being written back at the moment.

The tagging information is stored in a two-dimensional array (tags) that is a part of radix_tree_node. The first array dimension distinguishes between the possible tags, and the second contains a sufficient number of elements of unsigned longs so that there is a bit for each page that can be organized in the node.

radix_tree_tag_set is used to set a flag for a specific page:

<radix-tree.h>
```
void *radix_tree_tag_set(struct radix_tree_root *root,
                         unsigned long index, unsigned int tag);
```

The kernel searches for the corresponding positions in the bit list and sets the bit to 1. When this is done, the tree is scanned from top to bottom to update the information in all nodes.

In order to find all pages with a certain tag, the kernel still has to scan the entire tree, but this operation can be accelerated by first filtering out all subtrees that contain *at least one* page for which the flag is set. Again, this can be speeded up because the kernel does not check each bit one after the other but simply checks whether at least one of the unsigned long variables in which the bits are stored is greater than 1:

lib/radix-tree.c
```
int radix_tree_tagged(struct radix_tree_root *root, int tag)
{
        int idx;

        if (!root->rnode)
                return 0;
        for (idx = 0; idx < RADIX_TREE_TAG_LONGS; idx++) {
                if (root->rnode->tags[tag][idx])
                        return 1;
        }
        return 0;
}
```

Accessing Radix Tree Elements

The kernel also provides the following functions to process radix trees (they are all implemented in lib/radix_tree.c):

<radix-tree.h>
```
int    radix_tree_insert(struct radix_tree_root *, unsigned long, void *);
void *radix_tree_lookup(struct radix_tree_root *, unsigned long);
void *radix_tree_delete(struct radix_tree_root *, unsigned long);

int    radix_tree_tag_get(struct radix_tree_root *root,
                          unsigned long index, unsigned int tag);
void *radix_tree_tag_clear(struct radix_tree_root *root,
                           unsigned long index, unsigned int tag);
```

❑ radix_tree_insert adds a new element to a radix tree by means of a void pointer. The tree is automatically expanded if too little capacity is available.

❑ radix_tree_lookup finds a radix tree element whose key — an integer — was passed to the function as argument. The value returned is a void pointer that must be converted to the appropriate target data type.

❏ `radix_tree_delete` removes a tree element selected by means of its integer key. A pointer to the deleted object is returned if deletion was successful.

❏ `radix_tree_tag_get` checks if a tag is present on a radix tree node. If the tag is set, the function returns 1; otherwise, 0.

❏ `radix_tree_tag_clear` deletes a tag in a radix tree node. The change is propagated upward in the tree; that is, if all elements on one level have no tags, then the bit is also removed in the next higher level, and so on. The address of the tagged item is returned upon success.

These functions are implemented largely by shifting numbers as described in Appendix C.

To ensure that radix trees are manipulated very quickly, the kernel uses a separate slab cache that holds instances of `radix_tree_node` for rapid allocation.

> **Caution: The slab cache stores only the data structures needed to create the tree. This has nothing to do with the memory used for the cached pages, which is allocated and managed independently.**

Each radix tree also has a per-CPU pool of pre-allocated node elements to further speed the insertion of new elements into the tree. `radix_tree_preload` is a container that ensures that at least one element resides in this cache. The function is always invoked before an individual element is added to the radix tree using `radix_tree_insert` (this is ignored in the following sections).[4]

Locking

Radix trees do not provide any form of protection against concurrent access in general. As usual in the kernel, it is the responsibility of each subsystem that deploys radix trees to care for correction locking or any other synchronization primitive, as discussed in Chapter 5. However, an exception is made for several important read functions. This includes `radix_tree_lookup` to perform a lookup operation, `radix_tree_tag_get` to obtain a tag on a radix tree node, and `radix_tree_tagged` to test whether any items in the tree are tagged.

The first two functions can be called without subsystem-specific locking if they are embraced by `rcu_read_lock()` ... `rcu_read_unlock()`, while the third function does not require any lock at all.

`rcu_head` provides the required connection between radix tree nodes and the RCU implementation. Notice that `<radix-tree.h>` contains more advice on how to implement proper synchronization for radix trees, so I will not discuss the problem in more detail here.

16.3.3 Operations on Address Spaces

Address spaces connect backing stores with memory segments. Not only data structures but also functions are needed to perform the transfer operations between the two. Because address spaces can be used in various combinations, the requisite functions are not defined statically but must be determined according to the particular mapping with the help of a special structure that holds function pointers to the appropriate implementation.

---

[4]To be more accurate, the insert operations are embedded between `radix_tree_preload()` ... and `radix_tree_preload_end()`. The use of per-CPU variables means that kernel preemption (see Chapter 2) must be disabled and then enabled again upon completion of the operation. This is currently the only task of `radix_tree_preload_end`.

As demonstrated when discussing `struct address_space`, each address space contains a pointer to an `address_space_operations` instance that holds the above function list:

<fs.h>
```
struct address_space_operations {
        int (*writepage)(struct page *page, struct writeback_control *wbc);
        int (*readpage)(struct file *, struct page *);
        int (*sync_page)(struct page *);

        /* Write back some dirty pages from this mapping. */
        int (*writepages)(struct address_space *, struct writeback_control *);

        /* Set a page dirty */
        int (*set_page_dirty)(struct page *page);

        int (*readpages)(struct file *filp, struct address_space *mapping,
                        struct list_head *pages, unsigned nr_pages);


        /*
         * ext3 requires that a successful prepare_write() call be followed
         * by a commit_write() call - they must be balanced
         */
        int (*prepare_write)(struct file *, struct page *, unsigned, unsigned);
        int (*commit_write)(struct file *, struct page *, unsigned, unsigned);

        int (*write_begin)(struct file *, struct address_space *mapping,
                                loff_t pos, unsigned len, unsigned flags,
                                struct page **pagep, void **fsdata);
        int (*write_end)(struct file *, struct address_space *mapping,
                                loff_t pos, unsigned len, unsigned copied,
                                struct page *page, void *fsdata);

        /* Unfortunately this kludge is needed for FIBMAP. Don't use it */
        sector_t (*bmap)(struct address_space *, sector_t);
        int (*invalidatepage) (struct page *, unsigned long);
        int (*releasepage) (struct page *, gfp_t);
        ssize_t (*direct_IO)(int, struct kiocb *, const struct iovec *iov,
                        loff_t offset, unsigned long nr_segs);
        struct page* (*get_xip_page)(struct address_space *, sector_t,
                        int);
        int (*migratepage) (struct address_space *,
                                struct page *, struct page *);
        int (*launder_page) (struct page *);
};
```

❏   `writepage` and `writepages` write one or more pages of the address space back to the underlying block device. This is done by delegating a corresponding request to the block layer.

The kernel makes a number of standard functions available for this purpose [`block_write_full_page` and `mpage_readpage(s)`]; these are typically used instead of a manual implementation. Section 16.4.4 discusses the functions of the `mpage_` family.

❏   `readpage` and `readpages` read one or more consecutive pages from the backing store into a page frame. `readpage` and `readpages` are likewise not usually implemented manually but are executed by standard functions of the kernel (`mpage_readpage` and `mpage_readpages`) that can be used for most purposes.

Notice that the `file` argument of `readpage` is not required if the standard functions are used to implement the desired functionality because the inode associated with the desired page can be determined via `page->mapping->host`.

❏ `sync_page` performs synchronization of data that have not yet been written back to the backing store. Unlike `writepage`, the function operates on block layer level and attempts to perform pending write requests still held in buffers in this layer. In contrast, `writepage` operates on the address space layer and simply forwards the data to the block layer without bothering about active buffering there.

The kernel provides the standard function `block_sync_page`, which obtains the address space mapping that belongs to the `page` in question and unplugs the block device queue to start I/O.

❏ `set_page_dirty` allows an address space to provide a specific method of marking a page as dirty. However, this option is rarely used. In this case, the kernel automatically uses ccode__set_page_dirty_buffers to simultaneously mark the page as dirty on the buffer level and to add it to the `dirty_pages` list of the current mapping.

❏ `prepare_write` and `commit_write` perform write operations triggered by the `write` system call. To cater to the special features of journaling filesystems, this operation must be split into two parts: `prepare_write` stores the transaction data in the journal, and `commit_write` performs the actual write operation by sending the appropriate commands to the block layer.

When data are written, the kernel must ensure that the two functions are always invoked in pairs and in the correct sequence as otherwise the journal mechanism serves no purpose.

It has by now become common practice that even non-journaling filesystems (like Ext2) split writing into two parts.

> Unlike `writepage`, `prepare_` and `commit_write` do not directly initiate I/O operations (in other words, they do not forward corresponding commands to the block layer) but, in the standard implementation, make do with marking whole pages or parts thereof as dirty; the write operation itself is triggered by a kernel daemon that is provided for this purpose and that periodically checks the existing pages.

❏ `write_begin` and `write_end` are replacements for `prepare_write` and `commit_write`. While the intention of the functions is identical, the required parameters and especially the way in which locking of involved objects is handled have changed. Since `Documentation/filesystems/vfs.txt` provides a detailed description of how the functions operate, nothing more needs to be added here.

❏ `bmap` maps a logical block offset within an address space to a physical block number. This is usually straightforward for block devices, but since files are in general not represented by a linear number of blocks on a device, the required information cannot be determined otherwise.

`bmap` is required by the swap code (see Section 18.3.3), the `FIBMAP` file ioctl, and internally by some filesystems.

❑ `releasepage` prepares page release in journaling filesystems.

❑ `invalidatepage` is called if a page is going to be removed from the address space and buffers are associated with it as signalized by the `PG_Private` flag.

❑ `direct_IO` is used to implement direct read and write access. This bypasses buffering in the block layer and allows an application to communicate very directly with a block device. Large databases make frequent use of this feature as they are better able to forecast future input and output than the generic mechanisms of the kernel and can therefore achieve better results by implementing their own caching mechanisms.

❑ `get_xip_page` is used for the execute-in-place mechanism that can launch executable code without having to first load it into the page cache. This is useful on, for example, memory-based filesystems such as a RAM disk or on small systems with little memory that can address ROM areas containing filesystems directly via the CPU. As this mechanism is seldom used, it need not be discussed at length.

❑ `migrate_page` is used if the kernel wants to relocate a page, that is, move contents of one page onto another page. Since pages are often equipped with private data, it is not just sufficient to copy the raw information from the old to the new page. Moving pages is, for instance, required to support memory hotplugging.

❑ `launder_page` offers a last chance to write back a dirty page before it is freed.

Most address spaces do not implement all functions and therefore assign null pointers to some. In many cases, the kernel's default routines are invoked instead of the specific implementation of the individual address spaces. Below a few of the kernel's `address_space_operations` are examined to give an overview of the options available.

The Third Extended Filesystem defines the `ext3_writeback_aops` global variable, which is a filled instance of `address_space_operations`. It contains the functions used in writeback mode:

fs/ext3/inode.c
```
static const struct address_space_operations ext3_writeback_aops = {
        .readpage        = ext3_readpage,
        .readpages       = ext3_readpages,
        .writepage       = ext3_writeback_writepage,
        .sync_page       = block_sync_page,
        .write_begin     = ext3_write_begin,
        .write_end       = ext3_writeback_write_end,
        .bmap            = ext3_bmap,
        .invalidatepage  = ext3_invalidatepage,
        .releasepage     = ext3_releasepage,
        .direct_IO       = ext3_direct_IO,
        .migratepage     = buffer_migrate_page,
};
```

The pointers that are not explicitly set are automatically initialized with NULL by the compiler.

At first sight, Ext3 appears to set a rather large number of function pointers to use its own implementations. However, this supposition is quickly disproved by looking at the definitions of `ext2_`... in the kernel sources. Many functions consist of few lines and delegate work to the generic helper functions of the kernel:

Function	Standard implementation
ext3_readpage	mpage_readpage
ext3_readpages	mpage_readpages
ext3_writeback_writepage	block_write_full_page
ext3_write_begin	block_write_begin
ext3_writeback_write_end	block_write_end
ext3_direct_IO	blockdev_direct_IO

The functions of the `address_space_operations` structure and the generic helpers of the kernel use other arguments so that a brief wrapper function is needed for purposes of parameter conversion. Otherwise, in most cases, the pointers could point directly to the helper functions mentioned.

Other filesystems also use assignments of the `address_space_operations` instances that make direct or indirect use of kernel standard functions.

The structure of the `address_space_operations` instance of the shared-memory filesystem is particularly simple since only two fields need to be filled with non-NULL pointers:

mm/shmem.c
```
static struct address_space_operations shmem_aops = {
        .writepage      = shmem_writepage,
        .set_page_dirty = __set_page_dirty_no_writeback,
        .migratepage    = migrate_page,
};
```

All that need be implemented is the marking of the page as dirty, page writeback, and page migration. The other operations are not used to provide shared memory.[5] With which backing store does the kernel operate in this case? Memory from the shared-memory filesystem is totally independent of a specific block device because all files of the filesystem are generated dynamically (e.g., by copying the contents of a file from another filesystem, or by writing calculated data into a new file) and do not reside on any original block device.

Memory shortage can, of course, also apply to pages that belong to this filesystem so that it is then necessary to write the pages back to the backing store. Because there is no backing store in the real sense, the swap area is used in its stead. Whereas normal files are written back to their filesystem on the hard disk (or on any other block device) in order to free the used page frame, files of the shared-memory filesystem must be stored in the swap area.

Since access to block devices need not always be made by way of filesystems but may also apply to raw devices, there are address space operations to support the direct manipulation of the contents of block devices (this kind of access is required, e.g., when creating filesystems from within userspace):

fs/block_dev.c
```
struct address_space_operations def_blk_aops = {
        .readpage       = blkdev_readpage,
        .writepage      = blkdev_writepage,
```

---

[5]If `tmpfs`, which is implemented on top of shared memory, is enabled, then `readpage`, `write_begin`, and `write_end` are also implemented.

```
        .sync_page      = block_sync_page,
        .write_begin    = blkdev_write_begin,
        .write_end      = blkdev_write_end,
        .writepages     = generic_writepages,
        .direct_IO      = blkdev_direct_IO,
};
```

Again, it is clear that a large number of special functions are used to implement the requirements, but they quickly lead to the kernel's standard functions:

Block layer	Standard function
blkdev_readpage	block_read_full_page
blkdev_writepage	block_write_full_page
blkdev_write_begin	block_write_begin
blkdev_write_end	block_write_end
blkdev_direct_IO	__blockdev_direct_IO

The implementation of the address space operations for filesystems and raw access to block devices have much in common in the kernel since both share the same helper functions.

16.4 Implementation of the Page Cache

The page cache is implemented on top of radix trees. Although the cache belongs to the most performance-critical parts of the kernel and is widely used across all subsystems, the implementation is astonishingly simple. Well-designed data structures are an essential ingredient for this.

16.4.1 Allocating Pages

page_cache_alloc is used to reserve the data structure of a new page to be added to the page cache. The variant postfixed by _cold works identically, but tries to obtain a cache cold page:

<pagemap.h>
```
struct page *page_cache_alloc(struct address_space *x)
struct page *page_cache_alloc_cold(struct address_space *x)
```

Initially, the radix tree is left untouched because work is delegated to alloc_pages, which takes a page frame from the buddy system (described in Chapter 3). However, the address space argument is required to infer from which memory region that page must come.

Adding the new page to the page cache is a little more complicated and falls under the responsibility of add_to_page_cache. Here, radix_tree_insert inserts the page instance associated with the page into the radix tree of the address space involved:

mm/filemap.c
```
int add_to_page_cache(struct page *page, struct address_space *mapping,
            pgoff_t offset, gfp_t gfp_mask)
{
...
        error = radix_tree_insert(&mapping->page_tree, offset, page);
```

```
        if (!error) {
                page_cache_get(page);
                SetPageLocked(page);
                page->mapping = mapping;
                page->index = offset;
                mapping->nrpages++;
        }
...
        return error;
}
```

The index in the page cache and the pointer to the address space of the page are held in the corresponding elements of `struct page` (`mapping` and `index`). Finally, the address space page count (`nrpages`) is incremented by 1 because there is now one more page in the cache.

An alternative function named `add_to_page_cache_lru` with identical prototype is also available. This first invokes `add_to_page_cache` to add a page to the address space-specific page cache before also adding the page to the system's LRU cache using the `lru_cache_add` function.

16.4.2 Finding Pages

Keeping all cached pages in a radix tree data structure is especially beneficial when the kernel needs to decide if a given page is cached or not. `find_get_page` is provided for this purpose:

mm/filemap.c
```
struct page * find_get_page(struct address_space *mapping, pgoff_t offset)
{
        struct page *page;

        page = radix_tree_lookup(&mapping->page_tree, offset);
        if (page)
                page_cache_get(page);
        return page;
}
```

Life is easy for the page cache because all the hard work is done by the radix tree implementation: `radix_tree_lookup` finds the desired page at a given `offset`, and `page_cache_get` increments the page's reference count if one was found.

However, pages will very often belong to a file. Unfortunately, positions in a file are specified as byte offsets, not as offsets within the page cache. How can a file offset be converted into a page cache offset?

Currently, the granularity of the page cache is a single page; that is, the leaf elements of the page cache radix tree are single pages. Future kernels might, however, increase the granularity, so assuming a page size granularity is not valid. Instead, the macro `PAGE_CACHE_SHIFT` is provided. The object size for a page cache element can be computed by $2^{\text{PAGE\_CACHE\_SHIFT}}$.

Converting between byte offsets in a file and page cache offsets is then a simple matter of dividing the index by `PAGE_CACHE_SHIFT`:

```
index = ppos >> PAGE_CACHE_SHIFT;
```

ppos is a byte offset into a file, and `index` contains the corresponding page cache offset.

Two auxiliary functions are provided for convenience:

<pagemap.h>
```
struct page * find_or_create_page(struct address_space *mapping,
                                  pgoff_t index, gfp_t gfp_mask);
struct page * find_lock_page(struct address_space *mapping,
                             pgoff_t index);
```

`find_or_create_page` does what the name promises — it looks up a page in the page cache and allocates a fresh one if it is not there. The page is inserted into the cache and the LRU list by calling `add_to_page_cache_lru`.

`find_lock_page` works like `find_get_page`, but locks the page.

Caution: If the page is already locked from some other part of the kernel, the function can sleep until the page is unlocked.

It is also possible to search for more than one page. Here are the prototypes of the responsible auxiliary functions:

<pagemap.h>
```
unsigned find_get_pages(struct address_space *mapping, pgoff_t start,
                        unsigned int nr_pages, struct page **pages);
unsigned find_get_pages_contig(struct address_space *mapping, pgoff_t start,
                               unsigned int nr_pages, struct page **pages);
unsigned find_get_pages_tag(struct address_space *mapping, pgoff_t *index,
                            int tag, unsigned int nr_pages, struct page **pages);
```

❏ `find_get_pages` returns up to `nr_pages` pages in the mapping starting from the page cache off-set `start`. Pointers to the pages are placed on the array `pages`. The function does not guarantee to return a continuous range of pages — there can be holes for non-present pages. The return value is the number of pages that were found.

❏ `find_get_pages_contig` works similarly to `find_get_pages`, but the selected page range is guaranteed to be continuous. The function stops to add pages to the `page` array when the first hole is discovered.

❏ `find_get_pages_tag` operates like `find_pages`, but only selects pages that have a specific `tag` set. Additionally, the `index` parameter points to the page cache index of the page that immediately follows the last page in the resulting page array.

16.4.3 Waiting on Pages

The kernel often needs to wait on pages until their status has changed to some desired value. The synchronization implementation, for instance, sometimes wants to ensure that writing back a page has been finished and the contents in memory are identical with the data on the underlying block device. Pages under writeback have the `PG_writeback` bit set.

The function `wait_on_page_writeback` is provided to wait until the bit disappears:

<pagemap.h>
```
static inline void wait_on_page_writeback(struct page *page)
{
        if (PageWriteback(page))
                wait_on_page_bit(page, PG_writeback);
}
```

`wait_on_page_bit` installs a wait queue on which the process can sleep until the `PG_writeback` bit is removed from the page flags.

Likewise, the need to wait for a page to become unlocked can arise. `wait_on_page_locked` is responsible to handle this case.

16.4.4   Operations with Whole Pages

Modern block devices can — despite their name — transfer not just individual blocks but much larger units of data in a single operation, thus boosting system performance. This is reflected by a strong kernel focus on algorithms and structures that use pages as the elementary units of transfer between block devices and memory. Buffer-by-buffer transfer acts as a substantial brake on performance when handling complete pages. In the course of redesign of the block layer, BIOs were introduced during the development of 2.5 as a replacement for buffers to handle transfers with block devices. Four new functions were added to the kernel to support the reading and writing of one or more pages:

<mpage.h>
```
int mpage_readpages(struct address_space *mapping, struct list_head *pages,
                            unsigned nr_pages, get_block_t get_block);
int mpage_readpage(struct page *page, get_block_t get_block);
int mpage_writepages(struct address_space *mapping,
                struct writeback_control *wbc, get_block_t get_block);
int mpage_writepage(struct page *page, get_block_t *get_block,
                struct writeback_control *wbc);
```

The meaning of the parameters is evident from the preceding sections, the only exception being `writeback_control`. As discussed in Chapter 17, this is an option for fine control of the writeback operation.

Since the implementations of the four functions share much in common (their goal is always to construct a suitable `bio` instance for transfer to the block layer), this discussion will be confined to examining just the one specimen — `mpage_readpages`. The function expects `nr_pages` page instances as parameters passed in a linked list. `mapping` is the associated address space, and `get_block` is, as usual, invoked to find the matching block addresses.

The function iterates in a loop over all `page` instances:

fs/mpage.c
```
int
mpage_readpages(struct address_space *mapping, struct list_head *pages,
                        unsigned nr_pages, get_block_t get_block)
```

```
    {
                struct bio *bio = NULL;
                unsigned page_idx;
                sector_t last_block_in_bio = 0;
                struct buffer_head map_bh;
                struct pagevec lru_pvec;

                clear_buffer_mapped(&map_bh);
                for (page_idx = 0; page_idx < nr_pages; page_idx++) {
                        struct page *page = list_entry(pages->prev, struct page, lru);
```

Each loop pass first adds the page to the address space-specific cache before a `bio` request is created to read the desired data for the block layer:

fs/mpage.c

```
                    list_del(&page->lru);
                    if (!add_to_page_cache_lru(page, mapping,
                                            page->index, GFP_KERNEL)) {
                            bio = do_mpage_readpage(bio, page,
                                            nr_pages - page_idx,
                                            &last_block_in_bio, &map_bh,
                                            &first_logical_block,
                                            get_block);
                    } else {
                            page_cache_release(page);
                    }
            }
```

The pages are installed both in the page cache and in the kernel's LRU list using `add_to_page_cache_lru`.

When `do_mpage_readpage` builds the `bio` request, the BIO data of the preceding pages are also included so that a combined request can be constructed. If several successive pages are to be read from the block device, this can be done in a single request rather than submitting an individual request for each page. Notice that the `buffer_head` passed to `do_mpage_readpage` is usually not required. However, if an unusual situation is encountered (e.g., a page that contains buffers), then it falls back to using the old-fashioned, blockwise read routines.

If, at the end of the loop, a BIO request is left unprocessed by `do_mpage_readpage`, it is now submitted:

fs/mpage.c

```
        if (bio)
                mpage_bio_submit(READ, bio);
        return 0;
    }
```

16.4.5 Page Cache Readahead

Predicting the future is generally accepted to be a rather hard problem, but from time to time, the kernel cannot resist making a try nevertheless. Actually, there are situations where it is not too hard to say what will happen next, namely, when a process is reading data from a file.

Usually pages are read sequentially — this is also an assumption made by most filesystems. Recall from Chapter 9 that the extended filesystem family makes great effort to allocate adjacent blocks for a file such that the head of a block device only needs to move as little as possible when data are read and written.

Consider the situation in which a process has read a file linearly from position A to position B. Then this practice will usually continue for a while. It therefore makes sense to read ahead of B (say, until position C) such that when requests for pages between B and C are issued from the process, the data are already contained in the page cache.

Naturally readahead cannot be tackled by the page cache alone, but support by the VFS and memory management layers is required. In fact, the read-ahead mechanism was discussed in Sections 8.5.2 and 8.5.1. Recall that readahead is controlled from three places as far as the kernel is directly concerned[6]:

1.   do_generic_mapping_read, a generic read routine in which most filesystems that rely on the standard routines of the kernel to read data end up at some point.

2.   The page fault handler filemap_fault, which is responsible to read missing pages for memory mappings.

3.   __generic_file_splice_read, a routine invoked to support the splice system call that allows for passing data between two file descriptors directly in kernel space, without the need to involve userspace.[7]

The temporal flow of readahead routines on the source code level were discussed in Chapter 8, but it is also instructive to observe the behavior from a higher level. Such a viewpoint is provided in Figure 16-4. For the sake of simplicity, I restrict my consideration to do_generic_mapping_read in the following.

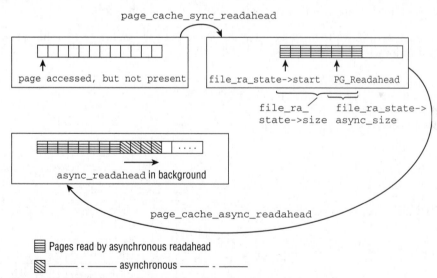

Figure 16-4: Overview of the readahead mechanism and the required interplay between VFS and page cache.

Suppose that a process has opened a file and wants to read in the first page. The page is not yet contained in the page cache. Since typical users will not only read in a single page, but multiple sequential

---

[6]These are at least the places covered in this book. Readahead can also be influenced from userland with the madvise, fadvice, and readahead system calls, but I will not discuss them any further.

[7]I do not discuss this system call anywhere in more detail, but refer you to the manual page splice(2) for more information.

pages, the kernel employs `page_cache_sync_readahead` to read in 8 pages in a row — the number is just an example that does not comply with reality. The first page is immediately available for `do_generic_mapping_read`.[8] Pages selected to be read in before they are actually required are said to be in a *readahead* window.

The process now continues to read in pages and behaves linearly as expected. When the sixth page is accessed (notice that the page was already contained in the page cache before the process issued a corresponding request), `do_generic_mapping_read` notices that the page was equipped with the `PG_Readahead` bit in the synchronous read pass.[9] This triggers an *asynchronous* operation that reads in a number of pages *in the background*. Since two more pages are left in the page cache, there is no need to hurry; thus a synchronous operation is not required. However, the I/O performed in the background will ensure that the pages are present when the process makes further progress in the file. If the kernel would not adopt this scheme, then readahead could only start after a process has experienced a page fault. While the required page (and some more pages for readahead) could be then brought into the page cache synchronously, this would introduce delays, which are clearly undesired.

This scheme is now repeated further. Since `page_cache_async_read` — which is responsible to issue the asynchronous read request — has again marked a page in the readahead window with the `PG_Readahead` bit, the kernel will start asynchronous readahead again when the process comes to this page, and so on.

So much for `do_generic_readahead`. The differences in how `filemap_fault` handles things are twofold: Asynchronous, adaptive readahead is only performed if a sequential read hint is set. If no readahead hint is given, then `do_page_cache_readahead` does a single-shot readahead without setting `PG_Readahead`, and also without updating the file's readahead state tracking information.

Several functions are used to implement the readahead mechanism. Figure 16-5 shows how they are connected with each other.

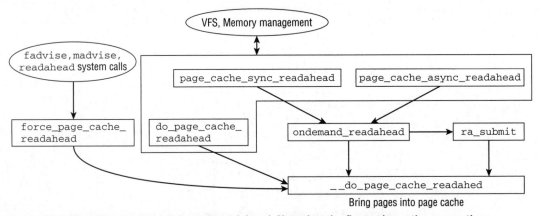

Figure 16-5: Functions used to implement readahead. Note that the figure shows the connections between the functions, but is not a proper code flow diagram.

---

[8]Actually, the term *synchronous* as adopted by the kernel is a bit misleading here. No effort is made to wait on completion of the read operation submitted by `page_cache_sync_readhead`, so it is not synchronous in the usual sense of the word. However, since reading in one page is fast, chances are very good that the page will usually have arrived when `page_cache_sync_readahead` returns to the caller. Nevertheless, the caller has to make precautions for the case in which the page is not yet available.

[9]Since the readahead state for each file is separately tracked, the kernel would essentially not require this special flag because the corresponding information could also be obtained otherwise. However, it is required when multiple concurrent readers act on a file.

Reading pages into the page cache before they are actually required is simple from a technical point of view and can easily be achieved with the framework introduced so far in this chapter. The challenge lies in predicting the optimal size of the readahead window. For this purpose, the kernel keeps track of the last setting for each file. The following data structure is associated with every `file` instance:

```
<fs.h>
struct file_ra_state {
        pgoff_t start;          /* where readahead started */
        unsigned int size;      /* # of readahead pages */
        unsigned int async_size; /* do asynchronous readahead when
                                    there are only # of pages ahead */
        unsigned int ra_pages;  /* Maximum readahead window */
...
        loff_t prev_pos;        /* Cache last read() position */
};
```

`start` denotes the position in the page cache where readahead was started, and `size` gives the size of the readahead window. `async_size` represents the least number of remaining readahead pages. If only this many pages are still available in the readahead window, then asynchronous readahead is initiated to bring more pages into the page cache. The meaning of these values is also illustrated in Figure 16-4.

`ra_pages` denotes the maximum size of the readahead window. The kernel can decide to read in fewer pages than specified by this value, but it will never read in more. Finally, `prev_pos` denotes the position that was last visited in previous reads.

> The offset is given as a byte offset into the file, *not* as a page offset into the page cache! This allows filesystem code that does not know anything about page cache offsets to aid the readahead mechanism.

The most important providers of this value are, however, `do_generic_mapping_read` and `filemap_fault`.

The routine `ondemand_readahead` is responsible to implement readahead policy, that is, decide how many pages will be read in before they are actually required. As Figure 16-5 shows, both `page_cache_sync_readahead` and `page_cache_async_readahead` rely on this function. After deciding on the size of the readahead window, `ra_submit` is called to delegate the technical aspects to `__do_page_cache_readahead`. Here pages are allocated in the page cache and subsequently filled from the block layer.

Before discussing `ondemand_readahead`, two helper functions must be introduced: `get_init_ra_size` determines the initial readahead window size for a file, and `get_next_ra_size` computes the window for subsequent reads, that is, when a previous readahead window exists. `get_init_ra_size` determines the window size based on the number of pages requested from the process, and `get_next_ra_size` bases the computation on the size of the previous readahead window. Both functions ensure that the size of the readahead window does not exceed a file-specific upper limit. While the limit can be modified with the `fadvise` system call, it is usually set to `VM_MAX_READAHEAD * 1024 / PAGE_CACHE_SIZE`, which equates to 32 pages on systems with a page size of 4 KiB. The results of both functions are shown in Figure 16-6. The graph shows how the size of the initial readahead scales with request size, and also demonstrates how the size of subsequent readahead operations scales depending on the size of the previous readahead window. Mathematically speaking, the maximal readahead size is a fixed point of both functions. In practical terms, this means that the readahead window can never grow beyond the maximally allowed value, in this case, 32 pages.

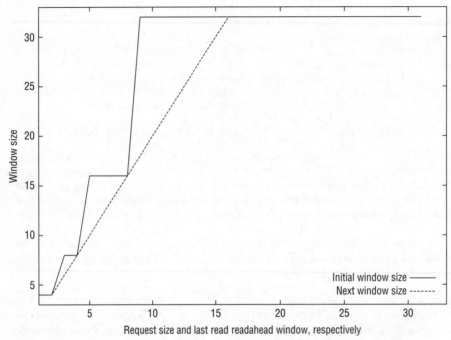

Figure 16-6: How the kernel determines the readahead window depending on the request size.

Let's go back to `ondemand_readahead`, which has to set the readahead window with the help of these auxiliary functions. Three cases are most essential:

1. The current offset is either at the end of the previous readahead window or at the end of the interval that was synchronously read in. In both cases, the kernel assumes sequential read access, and uses `get_next_ra_size` to compute the new window size as discussed.

2. If the readahead marker was hit, but the previous readahead state does not predict this, then most likely two or more concurrent streams perform interleaved reads on the file — and invalidate each other's readahead state in the process. The kernel constructs a new readahead window that suits all readers.

3. If (among others) first read access on a file is performed or a cache miss has happened, a new readahead window is set up with `get_init_ra_size`.

16.5 Implementation of the Buffer Cache

The buffer cache is used not only as an add-on to the page cache but also as an independent cache for objects that are not handled in pages but in blocks.

16.5.1 Data Structures

Fortunately, the data structures for both types of cache — the independent buffer cache and the elements used to support the page cache — are identical, and this greatly simplifies implementation. The principal elements of the buffer cache are the buffer heads, whose basic characteristics are discussed above. The buffer head definition in the kernel sources is as follows:

<buffer_head.h>
```
struct buffer_head {
        unsigned long b_state;          /* buffer state bitmap (see above) */
        struct buffer_head *b_this_page;/* circular list of page's buffers */
        struct page *b_page;            /* the page this bh is mapped to */

        sector_t b_blocknr;             /* start block number */
        size_t b_size;                  /* size of mapping */
        char *b_data;                   /* pointer to data within the page */

        struct block_device *b_bdev;
        bh_end_io_t *b_end_io;          /* I/O completion */
        void *b_private;                /* reserved for b_end_io */
...
        atomic_t b_count;               /* users using this buffer_head */
};
```

Buffers, like pages, can have many states. The current state of a buffer head is held in the b_state element that accepts the following selection of values (the full list of values is available as an enum called bh_state_bits in include/linux/buffer_heads.h):

❏ The state is BH_Uptodate if the current data in the buffer match the data in the backing store.

❏ Buffers are labeled as BH_Dirty if their data have been modified and no longer match the data in the backing store.

❏ BH_Lock indicates that the buffer is locked for further access. Buffers are explicitly locked during I/O operations to prevent several threads from handling the buffers concurrently and thus interfering with each other.

❏ BH_Mapped means that there is a mapping of the buffer contents on a secondary storage device, as is the case with all buffers that originate from filesystems or from direct accesses to block devices.

❏ BH_New marks newly created buffers as new.

> **b_state is interpreted as a bitmap. Every possible constant stands for a position in the bitmap. As a result, several values (BK_Lock and BH_Mapped, e.g.) can be active at the same time — as also at many other points in the kernel.**

> **BH_Uptodate and BH_Dirty can also be active *at the same time*, and this is often the case. Whereas BH_Uptodate is set after a buffer has been filled with data from the block device, the kernel uses BH_Dirty to indicate that the data in memory have been modified but not yet been written back. This may appear to be confusing but must be remembered when considering the information below.**

Besides the above constants, a few additional values are defined in enum bh_state_bits. They are ignored because they are either of little importance or are simply no longer used. They are retained in the kernel sources for historical reasons and will disappear sooner or later.

The kernel defines the set_buffer_foo and get_buffer_foo functions to set and read the buffer state bits for BH_Foo.

The buffer_head structure also includes further elements whose meanings are given below:

❑ b_count implements the usual access counter to prevent the kernel from freeing buffer heads that are still in active use.

❑ b_page holds a pointer to a page instance with which the buffer head is associated when used in conjunction with the page cache. If the buffer is independent, b_page contains a null pointer.

❑ As discussed above, several buffers are used to split the contents of a page into smaller units. All buffer heads belonging to these units are kept on a singly linked, circular list using b_this_page (the entry for the last buffer points to the entry for the first buffer to create a circular structure).

❑ b_blocknr holds the number of the block on the underlying block device, and b_size specifies the size of the block. b_bdev is a pointer to the block_device instance of the block device. This information uniquely identifies the source of the data.

❑ The pointer to the data in memory is held in b_data (the end position can be calculated from b_size; there is therefore no need for an explicit pointer to this position, although a pointer was used above for the sake of simplicity).

❑ b_end_io points to a routine that is automatically invoked by the kernel when an I/O operation involving the buffer is completed (it is required by the BIO routines described in Chapter 6). This enables the kernel to postpone further buffer handling until a desired input or output operation has, in fact, been completed.

❑ b_private is a pointer reserved for private use by b_end_io. It is used primarily by journaling filesystems. It is usually set to NULL if it is not needed.

16.5.2 Operations

The kernel must provide a set of operations so that the rest of the code can easily and efficiently exploit the functionality of buffers. This section describes the mechanisms for creating and managing new buffer heads.

Caution: These mechanisms make no contribution to the actual caching of data in memory, discussed in later sections.

Before buffers can be used, the kernel must first create an instance of the buffer_head structure on which the remaining functions act. As the new generation of new buffer heads is a frequently recurring task, it should be performed as quickly as possible. This is a classical situation for the use of a slab cache as described in Chapter 3.

> **Caution: When a slab cache is used, memory is allocated only for the buffer head. The actual data are ignored when the buffer head is created and must be stored elsewhere.**

The kernel sources do, of course, provide functions that can be used as front ends to create and destroy buffer heads. `alloc_buffer_head` generates a new buffer head, and `free_buffer_head` destroys an existing head. Both functions are defined in `fs/buffer.c`. As you might expect, they essentially consist of straightforward gymnastics with memory management functions and statistics accounting and need not be discussed here.

16.5.3 Interaction of Page and Buffer Cache

Buffer heads become much more interesting when used in conjunction with the useful data that they are to hold in memory. This section examines the link between pages and buffer heads.

Linking of Pages and Buffer Heads

How are buffers and pages interlinked? Recall that this approach was briefly discussed above. A page is split into several data units (the actual number varies between architectures depending on page and block size), but the buffer heads are held in a separate memory area that has nothing to do with the actual data. The page contents are *not* modified by the interaction with buffers, as the latter simply provide a new view of the page data.

The `private` element of `struct page` is required to support interaction between a page and buffers. It is of type `unsigned long` and can therefore be used as a pointer to any positions in virtual address space (the exact definition of `page` is given in Chapter 3):

```
<mm.h>
struct page {
        ...
        unsigned long private;              /* Mapping-private opaque data */
        ...
}
```

The `private` element can also be used for various other purposes that, depending on page use, need have nothing to do with buffers.[10] However, its predominant use is to link buffers and pages. In this case, `private` points to the first buffer head used to split the page into smaller units. The various buffer heads are linked in a cyclic list by means of `b_this_page`. In this list, each pointer points to the next buffer, and the `b_this_page` element of the last buffer head points to the first buffer. This enables the kernel to easily scan all `buffer_head` instances associated with the page, starting from the `page` structure.

How is the association between the `page` and the `buffer_head` structures established? The kernel provides the `create_empty_buffers` and `link_dev_buffers` functions for this purpose, both of which are implemented in `fs/buffer.c`. The latter serves to associate an existing set of buffer heads with a page, whereas `create_empty_buffers` generates a completely new set of buffers for association with the page. For example, `create_empty_buffers` is invoked when reading and writing complete pages with `block_read_full_page` and `__block_write_full_page`.

`create_empty_buffers` first invokes `alloc_page_buffers` to create the required number of buffer heads (this number varies according to page and block size). It returns a pointer to the first element of a singly

---

[10]If the page resides in the swap cache, an instance of `swp_entry_t` is also stored in the cache. If the page is not in use, the element holds the order in the buddy system.

linked list in which each `b_this_page` element points to the next buffer. The only exception is the last buffer, where `b_this_page` holds a null pointer:

fs/buffer.c
```
void create_empty_buffers(struct page *page,
                        unsigned long blocksize, unsigned long b_state)
{
        struct buffer_head *bh, *head, *tail;

        head = alloc_page_buffers(page, blocksize, 1);
...
```

The function then iterates over all buffer heads to set their state and generate a cyclic list:

fs/buffer.c
```
        do {
                bh->b_state |= b_state;
                tail = bh;
                bh = bh->b_this_page;
        } while (bh);
        tail->b_this_page = head;
...
```

The state of the buffers depends on the state of the data in the page in memory:

fs/buffer.c
```
        if (PageUptodate(page) || PageDirty(page)) {
                bh = head;
                do {
                        if (PageDirty(page))
                                set_buffer_dirty(bh);
                        if (PageUptodate(page))
                                set_buffer_uptodate(bh);
                        bh = bh->b_this_page;
                } while (bh != head);
        }
        attach_page_buffers(page, head);
}
```

`set_buffer_dirty` and `set_buffer_uptodate` set the corresponding flags `BH_Dirty` and `BH_Uptodate`, respectively, in the buffer head.

The concluding invocation of `attach_page_buffers` associates the buffer with the page in two separate steps:

1. The `PG_private` bit is set in the page flags to inform the rest of the kernel code that the `private` element of the `page` instance is in use.

2. The `private` element of the page is equipped with a pointer to the first buffer head in the cyclic list.

At first sight, setting the `PG_Private` flag would not appear to be a far-reaching action. However, it is important because it is the only way that the kernel is able to detect whether a page has attached buffers. Before the kernel launches any operations to modify or process buffers associated with a page, it must first check whether buffers are actually present — this is not always the case. It provides `page_has_buffers(page)` to do this by checking whether the flag is set. This function is called at very large number of places in the kernel sources and is therefore worthy of mention.

Interaction

Setting up a link between pages and buffers serves little purpose if there are no benefits for other parts of the kernel. As already noted, some transfer operations to and from block devices may need to be performed in units whose size depends on the block size of the underlying devices, whereas many parts of the kernel prefer to carry out I/O operations with page granularity as this makes things much easier — especially in terms of memory management.[11] In this scenario, buffers act as intermediaries between the two worlds.

Reading Whole Pages in Buffers

Let us first look at the approach adopted by the kernel when it reads whole pages from a block device, as is the case in `block_read_full_page`. Let's discuss the sections of interest as seen by buffer implementation. Figure 16-7 shows the buffer-related function calls that make up `block_read_full_page`.

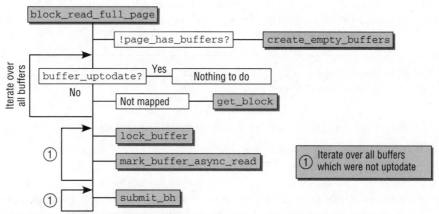

Figure 16-7: Code flow diagram for the buffer-related operations of `block_read_full_page`.

`block_read_full_page` reads a full page in three steps:

1. The buffers are set up and their state is checked.
2. The buffers are locked to rule out interference by other kernel threads in the next step.
3. The data are transferred to the buffers.

The first step involves checking whether buffers are already attached to the page as this is not always the case. If not, buffers are created using the `create_empty_buffers` function discussed a few sections

---

[11]I/O operations are usually more efficient if data are read or written in pages. This was the main reason for introducing the BIO layer that has replaced the old concept based on buffer heads.

back. Thereafter, the buffers — whether just created or already in existence — are identified using `page_buffers` before they are handled as described below. `page_buffers` simply translates the `private` element of the page into a `buffer_head` pointer by means of pointer conversion because, by convention, `private` points to the first buffer if buffers are attached to a page.

The main work of the kernel is to find out which buffers are current (their data match that on the block device or may even be more up-to-date) and therefore need not be read, and which buffers hold invalid data. To do this, the kernel makes use of the `BH_Mapping` and `BH_Uptodate` state bits, both of which may be set or unset.

It iterates over all buffers attached to the page and performs the following checks:

1. If the buffer contents are up-to-date (this can be checked with `buffer_uptodate`), the kernel continues to process the next buffer. In this case, the data in the page cache and on the block device match, and an additional read operation is not required.

2. If there is *no* mapping (`BH_Mapping` is not set), `get_block` is invoked to determine the position of the block on the block storage medium.

    `ext2_get_block` and `ext3_get_block`, respectively, are used for this purpose on Ext2/Ext3 filesystems. Other filesystems use functions with similar names. Common to all alternatives is that the `buffer_head` structure is modified so that it can be used to locate the desired block in the filesystem. Essentially, this involves setting the `b_bdev` and `b_blocknr` fields because they identify the desired block.

> The actual reading of data from the block device is performed *not* by **get_block** but later during the course of **block_read_full_page**.

    After execution of `get_block`, the state of the buffer is `BH_Mapped` but not `BH_Uptodate`[12].

3. A third situation is also possible. The buffer already has a mapping but is not up-to-date. The kernel then need perform no other actions.

4. Once the individual combinations of `BH_Uptodate` and `BH_Mapped` have been distinguished, the buffer is placed in a temporary array if it has a mapping but is not up-to-date. Processing then continues with the page's next buffer until no further buffers are available.

If *all* buffers attached to the page are up-to-date, the whole page can be set to this state using `SetPageUptodate`. The function then terminates because all the data on the whole page now reside in memory.

However, there are usually still buffers that have a mapping but do not reflect the current contents of the block device. Reminder: Buffers of this kind are collected in an array that is used for the second and third phases of `block_read_full_page`.

In the second phase, all buffers to be read are locked using `lock_buffer`. This prevents two kernel threads from reading the same buffer at the same time and therefore interfering with each other.

---

[12]There is one other state in which a buffer is up-to-date but is not mapped. This state occurs when a file with gaps is read (as can occur with the Second Extended Filesystem, e.g.). In this case, the buffer is filled with null bytes, but I shall ignore this scenario.

`mark_buffer_async_read` is also invoked to set `end_buffer_async_read` for `b_end_io` — this function is invoked automatically when data transfer ends.

Actual I/O is triggered in the third phase in which `submit_bh` forwards all buffers to be read to the block or BIO layer where the read operation is started. The function stored in `b_end_io` (`end_buffer_async_read` in this case) is called when the read operation terminates. It iterates over all the page's buffers, checks their state, and sets the state of the entire page to up-to-date assuming *all* buffers have this state.

As can be seen, the advantage of `block_read_full_page` is that it is necessary to read only those parts of the page that are not up-to-date. However, if it is certain that the entire page is not up-to-date, `mpage_readpage` is the better alternative as the buffer overhead is then superfluous.

Writing Whole Pages into Buffers

Not only reading but also writing of full pages can be divided into smaller buffer units. Only those parts of a page that have actually been modified need be written back, not the whole page contents. Unfortunately, from the buffer viewpoint, the implementation of write operations is much more complicated than the read operations described above. I ignore the minor details of the (somewhat simplified) write operations and focus on the key actions required of the kernel in my discussion below.

Figure 16-8 shows the code flow diagram for the error-free performance of the buffer-related operations needed to write back dirty pages in the `__block_write_full_page` function (to simplify matters, I also omit some seldom required corner cases that must be dealt with in reality).

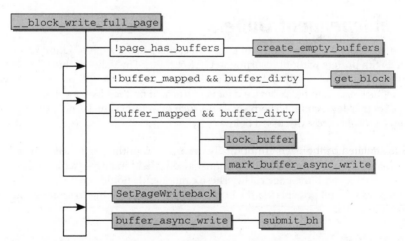

**Figure 16-8: Code flow diagram for the buffer-related operations of
`__block_write_full_page`.**

The writeback process is split into several parts, each of which repeatedly iterates over the singly linked list of buffers attached to a page.

As usual, it is first necessary to check that buffers are actually attached to the page — this cannot be taken for granted. As when a page is read, `page_has_buffers` is invoked to check whether buffers are present. If not, they are created using `create_empty_buffers`.

The kernel then iterates a total of three times over the list of buffers, as shown in the code flow diagram:

1. The purpose of the first iteration is to create a mapping between the buffer and the block device for all unmapped but dirty buffers. The function held in the `get_block` function pointer is invoked to find the matching block of the block device for the buffer.

2. In the second iteration, all dirty buffers are filtered out; this can be checked by `test_clear_buffer_dirty` — if the flag was set, it is deleted when the function is invoked because the buffer contents are due to be written back immediately.[13] `mark_buffer_async_write` sets the `BH_Async_Write` state bit and assigns `end_buffer_async_write` as the BIO completion handler to `b_end_io`.

   At the end of this iteration, `set_page_writeback` sets the `PG_writeback` flag for the full page.

3. In the third and final iteration, all buffers marked with `BH_Async_Write` in the previous pass are forwarded to the block layer that performs the actual write operation by invoking `submit_bh`, which submits a corresponding request to the block layer (by means of BIOs; see Chapter 6).

When the write operation for a buffer terminates, `end_buffer_async_write` is invoked automatically to check whether this also applies for all other buffers of the page. If so, all processes that are sleeping on the queue associated with the page and that are waiting for this event are woken.

16.5.4 Independent Buffers

Buffers are used not only in the context of pages. In earlier versions of the Linux kernel, all caching was implemented with buffers without resorting to page caching. The value of this approach has diminished in successive versions, and nearly all importance has been attached to full pages. However, there are still situations in which access to block device data is performed on the block level and not on the page level in the view of higher-level code. To help speed up such operations, the kernel provides yet another cache known as an *LRU buffer cache* discussed below.

This cache for independent buffers is not totally divorced from the page cache. Since RAM memory is always managed in pages, buffered blocks must also be held in pages, with the result that there are some points of contact with the page cache. These cannot and should not be ignored — after all, access to individual blocks is still possible via the buffer cache without having to worry about the organization of the blocks into pages.

Mode of Operation

Why LRU? As we know, this abbreviation stands for *least recently used* and refers to a general method in which the elements of a set that are most frequently used can be managed efficiently. If an element is frequently accessed, the likelihood is that it resides in RAM (and is therefore cached). Less frequently or seldom used elements drop out of the cache automatically with time.

---

[13] At this point, the kernel must also call `buffer_mapped` to ensure that there is a mapping for the buffer. This is not the case if there are holes in files, but then there is nothing to write back.

To make lookup operations faster, the kernel first scans the cache entries from top to bottom to find an independent buffer each time a request is made. If an element contains the required data, the instance in the cache can be used. If not, the kernel must submit a low-level request to the block device to get the desired data.

The element last used is automatically placed at the first position by the kernel. If the element was already in the cache, only the positions of the individual elements change. If the element was read from the block device, the last element of the array "drops out" of the cache and can therefore be removed from memory.

The algorithm is very simple but nevertheless effective. The time needed to look up frequently used elements is reduced because the element is automatically located at one of the top array positions. At the same time, less used elements automatically drop out of the cache if they are not accessed for a certain period. The only disadvantage of this approach is the fact that almost the full contents of the array need to be repositioned after each lookup operation. This is time-consuming and can be implemented for small caches only. Consequently, buffer caches have only a low capacity.

Implementation

Let us examine how the kernel implements the algorithm just described for the LRU cache.

Data Structures

As the algorithm is not complicated, it requires only relatively simple data structures. The starting point of the implementation is the `bh_lru` structure which is defined as follows:

fs/buffer.c
```
#define BH_LRU_SIZE     8

struct bh_lru {
        struct buffer_head *bhs[BH_LRU_SIZE];
};

static DEFINE_PER_CPU(struct bh_lru, bh_lrus) = {{ NULL }};
```

It is defined in a C file and not in a header file — as usual, an indication for the rest of the kernel code that the cache data structures should (and, besides, can!) not be addressed directly but by means of the dedicated helper functions discussed below.

`bhs` is an array of pointers to buffer heads and is used as a basis for implementing the LRU algorithm (eight entries are used as the pre-processor definition shows). The kernel uses `DEFINE_PER_CPU` to instantiate an instance for each CPU of the system to improve utilization of the CPU caches.

The cache is managed and utilized by two public functions provided by the kernel: `lookup_bh_lru` checks whether a required entry is present in the cache, and `bh_lru_install` adds new buffer heads to the cache.

The function implementations hold no surprises since they merely implement the algorithm described above.[14] All they need do is select the corresponding array for the current CPU at the start of the action using

---

[14]Or as aptly put by a comment in the kernel code: `The LRU management algorithm is dopey-but-simple. Sorry.`

fs/buffer.c
```
lru = &__get_cpu_var(bh_lrus);
```

Caution: If `lookup_bh_lru` *fails, the desired buffer is not automatically read from the block device. This is done by the following interface functions.*

Interface Functions

Normal kernel code does not generally come into contact with either `bh_lookup_lru` or `bh_lru_install` because these functions are encapsulated. The kernel provides generic routines for accessing individual blocks, and these automatically cover the buffer cache, thus rendering explicit interaction with the cache unnecessary. These routines include `__getblk` and `__bread`, which are implemented in `fs/buffer.c`.

Before discussing their implementation, it is best to describe not only what the two functions have in common, but also how they differ. First, they both require the same parameters:

fs/buffer.c
```
struct buffer_head *
__getblk(struct block_device *bdev, sector_t block, int size)
{
...
}

struct buffer_head *
__bread(struct block_device *bdev, sector_t block, int size)
{
...
}
```

A data block is uniquely identified by the `block_device` instance of the desired block device, the sector number (of type `sector_t`), and the block size.

The differences relate to the goals of the two functions. `__bread` *guarantees* that an up-to-date buffer is returned; this entails, if necessary, read access to the underlying block device.

Invocations of `__getblk` always return a non-NULL pointer (i.e., a buffer head).[15] If the data of the desired buffer already reside in memory, the data are returned, but there is no guarantee as to what their state will be — in contrast to `__bread`, it need not be up-to-date. In the second possible scenario, the buffer does not yet exist in memory. In this case, `__getblk` ensures that the memory space required for the data are reserved and that the buffer head is inserted in the LRU cache.

> `__getblk` *always* returns a buffer head with the result that even senseless requests — for non-existent sector addresses — are processed.

---

[15] There is one exception. The function returns a NULL pointer if the desired block size is less than 512 bytes, larger than a page, or not a multiple of the hardware sector size of the underlying block device. However, a stack dump is also output at the same time because an invalid block size is interpreted as a kernel bug.

The function __getblk

Figure 16-9 shows the code flow diagram for __getblk (this function is discussed first because it is invoked by __bread).

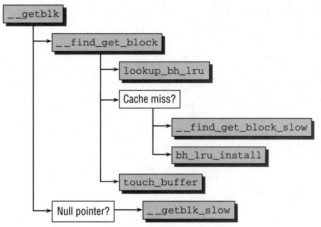

Figure 16-9: Code flow diagram for __getblk.

As the code flow diagram shows, there are two possible options when __getblk executes. __find_get_block is invoked to find the desired buffer using the method described below. A buffer_head instance is returned if the search is successful. Otherwise, the task is delegated to __getblk_slow. As the name suggest, __getblk_slow yields the desired buffer but takes longer than __find_get_block. However, this function is able to guarantee that a suitable buffer_head instance will always be returned and that the space needed for the data will be reserved.

> As already noted, the fact that a buffer head is returned does *not* mean that the contents of the data area are correct. But because the buffer head itself is correct, it is inserted in the buffer cache at the end of the function by means of **bh_lru_install**, and **touch_buffer** calls the **mark_page_accessed** method (see Chapter 18) for the page associated with the buffer.

The key issue is obviously the difference between __find_get_block and __getblk_slow, where the main work of __getblk takes place.

The familiar lookup_bh_lru function is invoked at the start of __find_get_block to check whether the required block is already present in the LRU cache.

If not, other means must be applied to continue the search. __find_get_block_slow attempts to find the data in the page cache, and this can produce two different results:

❑ A null pointer is returned if the data are *not* in the page cache, if it is in the page cache but the page does *not* have any attached buffers.

❑ The pointer to the desired buffer head is returned if the data are in the page cache and the page also has attached buffers.

If a buffer head is found, __find_get_block invokes the bh_lru_install function to add it to the cache. The kernel returns to __getblk after touch_buffer has been invoked to mark the page associated with the buffer using mark_page_accessed (see Chapter 18).

The second code path implemented in __getblk_slow must be entered if __find_get_block returns a null pointer. This path guarantees that at least the space required for the buffer head and data element is reserved. Its implementation is relatively short:

fs/buffer.c
```
static struct buffer_head *
__getblk_slow(struct block_device *bdev, sector_t block, int size)
{
        ...
        for (;;) {
                struct buffer_head * bh;
                int ret;

                bh = __find_get_block(bdev, block, size);
                if (bh)
                        return bh;

                ret = grow_buffers(bdev, block, size);
                if (ret < 0)
                        return NULL;
                if (ret == 0)
                        free_more_memory();
        }
}
```

Surprisingly, the first thing __getblk_slow does is to invoke __find_get_block — the function that has just failed. If a buffer head is found, it is returned by the function. Of course, the function only succeeds if another CPU has installed the desired buffer and created the corresponding data structures in memory in the meantime. Although this is admittedly not very likely, it still has to be checked.

This rather strange behavior becomes clear when we examine the exact course of the function. It is, in fact, an endless loop that repeatedly tries to read the buffer using __find_get_block. Obviously, the code doesn't content itself with doing nothing if the function fails. The kernel uses grow_buffers to try to reserve memory for the buffer head and buffer data and to add this space to the kernel data structures:

1. If this is successful, __find_get_block is invoked again, and this returns the desired buffer_head.

2. If the call to grow_buffers returns a negative result, this means that the block lies outside the possible maximum addressable page cache range, and the loop is aborted because the desired block does not physically exist.

3. If grow_buffers returns 0, then not enough memory was available to grow the buffers, and the subsequent call to free_more_memory tries to fix this condition by trying to release more RAM as described in Chapters 17 and 18.

This is why the functions are packed into an endless loop — the kernel tries again and again to create the data structures in memory until it finally succeeds.

The implementation of `grow_buffers` is not especially lengthy. A few correctness checks are carried out before work is delegated to the `grow_dev_page` function whose code flow diagram is shown in Figure 16-10.

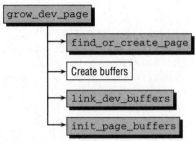

Figure 16-10: Code flow diagram for grow_dev_page.

The function first invokes `find_or_create_page` to a suitable page or generates a new page to hold the buffer data.

> *Of course, this and other allocation operations will fail if insufficient memory is available. In this case, the function returns a null pointer, thus causing the complete cycle to be repeated in `__getblk_slow` until sufficient memory is available. This also applies for the other functions that are invoked so there is no need to mention them explicitly.*

If the page is already associated with a buffer of the correct size, the remaining buffer data (`b_bdev` and `b_blocknr`) are modified by `init_page_buffers`. `grow_dev_page` then has nothing else to do and can be exited.

Otherwise, `alloc_page_buffers` generates a new set of buffers that can be attached to the page using the familiar `link_dev_buffers` function. `init_page_buffers` is invoked to fill the status (`b_status`)and the management data (`b_bdev`, `b_blocknr`) of the buffer heads.

The function `__bread`

In contrast to the methods just described, `__bread` ensures that an up-to-date buffer is returned. The function is not difficult to implement as it builds on `__getblk`:

fs/buffer.c
```
__bread(struct block_device *bdev, sector_t block, int size)
{
        struct buffer_head *bh = __getblk(bdev, block, size);

        if (likely(bh) && !buffer_uptodate(bh))
                bh = __bread_slow(bh);
        return bh;
}
```

The first action is to invoke the `__getblk` routine to make sure that memory is present for the buffer head and data contents. A pointer to the buffer is returned if the buffer is already up-to-date.

If the buffer data are not up-to-date, the rest of the work is delegated to __bread_slow — in other words, to the slow path, as the name indicates. Essentially, this submits a request to the block layer to physically read the data, and waits for the operation to complete. The buffer — which is now guaranteed to be filled and current — is then returned.

Use in the Filesystem

When is it necessary to read individual blocks? There are not too many points in the kernel where this must be done, but these are nevertheless of great importance. Filesystems in particular make use of the routines described above when reading superblocks or management blocks.

The kernel defines two functions to simplify the work of filesystems with individual blocks:

```
<buffer_head.h>
static inline struct buffer_head *
sb_bread(struct super_block *sb, sector_t block)
{
        return __bread(sb->s_bdev, block, sb->s_blocksize);
}

static inline struct buffer_head *
sb_getblk(struct super_block *sb, sector_t block)
{
        return __getblk(sb->s_bdev, block, sb->s_blocksize);
}
```

As the code shows, the routines are used to read specific filesystem blocks found using a superblock, a block number, and a block size.

16.6 Summary

Reading data from external storage devices like hard disks is much slower than reading data from RAM, so Linux uses caching mechanisms to keep data in RAM once they have been read in, and accesses them from there. Page frames are the natural units on which the page cache operates, and I have discussed in this chapter how the kernel keeps track of which portions of a block device are cached in RAM. You have been introduced to the concept of address spaces which allow for linking cached data with their source, and how address spaces are manipulated and queried. Following that, I have examined the algorithms employed by Linux to handle the technical details of bringing content into the page cache.

Traditionally, Unix caches used smaller units than complete pages, and this technique survived until today in the form of the buffer cache. While the main caching load is handled by the page cache, there are still some users of the buffer cache, and you have therefore also been introduced to the corresponding mechanisms.

Using RAM to cache data read from a disk is one aspect of the interaction between RAM and disks, but there's also another side to the story: The kernel must also take care of synchronizing modified data in RAM back to the persistent storage on disk; the next chapter will introduce you to the corresponding mechanisms.

17

Data Synchronization

RAM memory and hard disk space are mutually interchangeable to a good extent. If a large amount of RAM is free, the kernel uses part of it to buffer block device data. Conversely, disk space is used to swap data out from memory if too little RAM is available. Both have one thing in common — data are always manipulated in RAM before being written back (or flushed) to disk at some random time to make changes persistent. In this context, block storage devices are often referred to as RAM *backing store*.

Linux provides a variety of caching methods as discussed extensively in Chapter 16. However, what was not discussed in that chapter is how data are written back from cache. Again, the kernel provides several options that are grouped into two categories:

1. Background threads repeatedly check the state of system memory and write data back at periodic intervals.

2. Explicit flushing is performed when there are too many dirty pages in system caches and the kernel needs clean pages.

This chapter discusses these techniques.

17.1 Overview

There is a clear relationship between *flushing*, *swapping*, and *releasing* pages. Not only the state of memory pages but also the size of free memory needs checking regularly. When this is done, unused or seldom used pages are swapped out automatically but not before the data they hold have been synchronized with the backing store to prevent data loss. In the case of dynamically generated pages, the system swap areas act as the backing stores. The swap areas for pages mapped from files are the corresponding sections in the underlying filesystems. If there is an acute scarcity of memory, flushing of dirty data must be enforced in order to obtain clean pages.

Synchronization between memory/cache and backing store is split into two conceptually different parts:

❑ *Policy* routines control *when* data are exchanged. System administrators can set various parameters to help the kernel decide when to exchange data as a function of system load.

❑ The technical implementation deals with the hardware-related details of synchronization between cache and backing store and ensures that the instructions issued by the policy routines are carried out.

> *Synchronization* and *swapping* must not be confused with each other. Whereas *synchronization* simply aligns the data held in RAM and in the backing store, *swapping* results in the flushing of data from RAM to free space for higher-priority items. Before data are cleared from RAM, they are synchronized with the data in the associated backing store.

The mechanisms for flushing data are triggered for different reasons and at different times:

❑ Periodic kernel threads scan the lists of dirty pages and pick some to be written back based on the time at which they became dirty. If the system is not too busy with write operations, there is an acceptable ratio between the number of dirty pages and the load imposed on the system by the hard disk access operations needed to flush the pages.

❑ If there are too many dirty pages in the system as a result, for example, of a massive write operation, the kernel triggers further mechanisms to synchronize pages with the backing store until the number of dirty pages returns to an acceptable level. What is meant by "too many dirty pages" and "acceptable level" is a moot point, discussed below.

❑ Various components of the kernel require that data must be synchronized when a special event has happened, for instance, when a filesystem is re-mounted.

The first two mechanisms are implemented by means of the kernel thread `pdflush` which executes the synchronization code, while the third alternative can be triggered from many points in the kernel.

Since the implementation of data synchronization consists of an unusually large number of interconnected functions, an overview of what lies ahead of us precedes a detailed discussion of everything in detail. Figure 17-1 show the dependence among the functions that constitute the implementation. The figure is not a proper code flow diagram, but just shows how the functions are related to each other and which code paths are possible. The diagram concentrates on synchronization operations originating from the `pdflush` thread, system calls, and explicit requests from filesystem-related kernel components.

The kernel can start to synchronize data from various different places, but all paths save one end up in `sync_sb_inodes`. The function is responsible to synchronize all dirty inodes belonging to a given superblock, and `writeback_single_inode` is used for each inode. Both the `sync` system call and numerous generic kernel layers (like the partition code or the block layer) make use of this possibility.

On the other hand, the need to synchronize the dirty inodes of *all* superblocks in the system can also arise. This is especially required for periodic and forced writeback. When dirtying data in filesystem code, the kernel additionally ensures that the number of dirty pages does not get out of hand by starting synchronization before this happens.

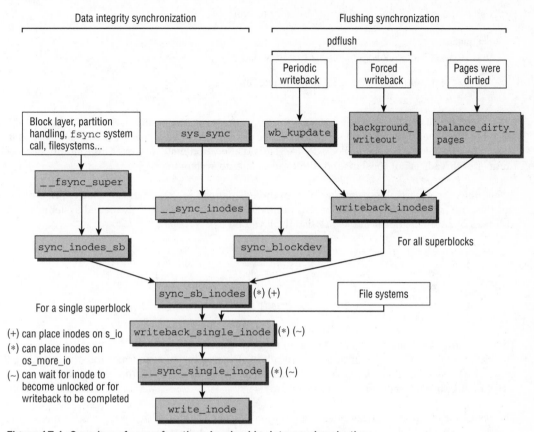

Figure 17-1: Overview of some functions involved in data synchronization.

Synchronizing all dirty inodes of a superblock is often much too coarse grained for filesystems. They often require synchronizing a single dirty inode and thus use `writeback_single_inode` directly.

Even if the synchronization implementation is centered around inodes, this does not imply that the mechanisms just work for data contained in mounted filesystems. Recall that raw block devices are represented by inodes via the bdev pseudo-filesystem as discussed in Section 10.2.4. The synchronization methods therefore also affect raw block devices in the same way as regular filesystem objects — good news for everyone who wants to access data directly.

One remark on terminology: When I talk about inode synchronization in the following, I always mean synchronization of both the inode metadata and the raw data managed by the inode. For regular files, this means that the synchronization code's aim is to both transfer time stamps, attributes, and the like, as well as the contents of the file to the underlying block device.

17.2 The `pdflush` Mechanism

The `pdflush` mechanism is implemented in a single file: `mm/pdflush.c`. This contrasts with the fragmented implementation of the synchronization mechanisms in earlier versions.

pdflush is started with the usual kernel thread mechanisms:

mm/pdflush.c
```
static void start_one_pdflush_thread(void)
{
        kthread_run(pdflush, NULL, "pdflush");
}
```

start_one_pdflush starts a single pdflush thread — however, the kernel uses several threads at the same time in general, as you will see below. It should be noted that a specific pdflush thread is *not* always responsible for the same block device. Thread allocation may vary over time simply because the number of threads is not constant and differs according to system load.

In fact, the kernel starts the specific number of threads defined in MIN_PDFLUSH_THREADS when it initializes the pdflush subsystem. Typically, this number is 2 so that in a normally loaded system, two active instances of pdflush appear in the task list displayed by ps:

```
wolfgang@meitner> ps fax
    2 ?        S<     0:00 [kthreadd]
...
  206 ?        S      0:00 _ [pdflush]
  207 ?        S      0:00 _ [pdflush]
...
```

There is a lower and an upper limit to the number of threads. MAX_PDFLUSH_THREADS specifies the maximum number of pdflush instances, typically 8. The number of concurrent threads is held in the nr_pdflush_threads global variable, but no distinction is made as to whether the threads are currently active or sleeping. The current value is visible to userspace in /proc/sys/vm/nr_pdflush_threads.

The policy for when to create and destroy pdflush threads is simple. The kernel creates a new thread if no idle thread has been available for 1 second. In contrast, a thread is destroyed if it has been idle for more than 1 second. The upper and lower limits on the number of concurrent pdflush threads defined in MIN_PDFLUSH_THREADS (2) and MAX_PDFLUSH_THREADS (8) are always obeyed.

Why is more than one thread required? Modern systems will be typically equipped with more than one block device. If many dirty pages exist in the system, it is the kernel's job to keep these devices as busy as possible with writing back data. Queues of different block devices are independent of each other, so data can be written in parallel. Data transfer rates are mainly limited by I/O bandwidth, not CPU power on current hardware. The connection between pdflush threads and writeback queues is summarized in Figure 17-2. The figure shows that a dynamically varying number of pdflush threads feeds the block devices with data that must be synchronized with the underlying block devices. Notice that a block device may have more than one queue that can transfer data, and that a pdflush thread may either serve all queues or just a specific one.

Former kernel versions only employed a single flushing daemon (which was then called bdflush), but this led to a performance problem: If one block device queue was congested because too many writeback operations were pending, other queues for *different* devices could not be fed with new data anymore. They remained idle, which can be a good thing on a summer vacation, but certainly not for block devices if there is work to do. This problem is solved by the dynamical creation and destruction of pdflush kernel threads, which allows for keeping many queues busy in parallel.

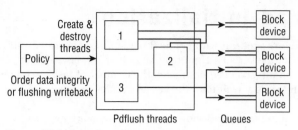

Figure 17-2: Overview of the `pdflush` mechanism.

17.3 Starting a New Thread

The pdflush mechanism consists of two central components — a data structure to describe the work of the thread and a strategy routine to help perform the work.

The data structure is defined as follows:

mm/pdflush.c
```
struct pdflush_work {
        struct task_struct *who;        /* The thread */
        void (*fn)(unsigned long);      /* A callback function */
        unsigned long arg0;             /* An argument to the callback */
        struct list_head list;          /* On pdflush_list, when idle */
        unsigned long when_i_went_to_sleep;
};
```

As usual, the fact that the data structure is defined in a C header file instead of a header file indicates to the kernel that the structure may be used only by internal code. Generic code uses other mechanisms to access the kernel synchronization capabilities that are examined below:

- ❏ who is a pointer to the kernel thread task_struct instance used to represent the specific pdflush instance in the process table.

- ❏ Several instances of pdflush_work can be grouped together in a doubly linked standard list using the list list head. The kernel uses the global variable pdflush_list (defined in mm/pdflush.c) to draw up a list of the work still to be done.

- ❏ The extraordinarily long when_i_went_to_sleep element stores the time in jiffies when the thread last went to sleep. This value is used to remove superfluous pdflush threads from the system (i.e., threads that are still in memory but have been idle for a longer period).

- ❏ The fn function pointer (in conjunction with arg0) is the backbone of the structure. It holds the function in which the actual work to be done is implemented. arg0 is passed as an argument when the function is invoked.

    By using different function pointers for fn, the kernel is able to incorporate a variety of synchronization routines in the pdflush framework so that the right routine can be selected for the job in hand.

17.4 Thread Initialization

pdflush is used as a work procedure for kernel threads. Once generated, pdflush threads go to sleep and wait until other parts of the kernel assign them tasks that are described in pdflush_work. Consequently, the number of pdflush threads need not match the number of tasks to be performed. The generated threads are on call and simply wait until the kernel decides to give them work to do.

The code flow diagram in Figure 17-3 shows how pdflush works.

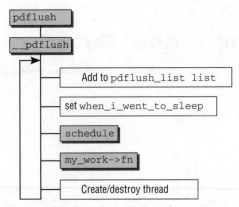

Figure 17-3: Code flow diagram for **pdflush**.

The start routine for generating a new pdflush thread is pdflush, but control flow is passed immediately to __pdflush.[1]

In __pdflush, the worker function of the pdflush_work instance is set to NULL because the thread has not been given a particular job to do. The global counter (nr_pdflush_threads) must also be incremented by 1 because a new pdflush thread has now been added to the system.

The thread then goes into an endless loop in which the following actions are performed:

❑   The pdflush_work instance of the thread is added to the global list pdflush_list (reminder: the kernel is able to identify the thread by means of the who element).

❑   when_i_went_to_sleep is set to the current system time in jiffies to remember when the thread started sleeping.

❑   schedule is invoked — this is the most important action. Because the status of the thread was previously set to TASK_INTERRUPTIBLE, the thread now goes to sleep until woken by an external event.

If the kernel requires a worker thread, it sets the worker function of a pdflush_work instance in the global list and wakes the corresponding thread, which resumes work immediately after schedule — but now with the fn worker function.

---

[1] All that happens in pdflush is that an instance of pdflush_work is generated; a pointer to it is passed to __pdflush_work as a parameter. This is to stop the compiler from performing unfortunate optimizations on this variable. Additionally, the process priority is set to 0, and the allowed CPUs are limited to the ones granted for the parent kthreadd.

❏ The worker function is invoked with the stored argument so that it can set about its task.

❏ Upon termination of the worker function, the kernel checks whether there are too many or too few worker threads. If no idle worker thread was available for longer than 1 second,[2] start_one_pdflush_thread generates a new thread. If the sleepiest thread (which is at the end of the pdflush_list list) has been asleep for more than 1 second, the *current* thread is removed from the system by exiting the endless loop. In this case, the only clean-up action required besides handling locking is to decrement nr_pdflush_threads — one pdflush thread less is available.

17.5 Performing Actual Work

pdflush_operation assigns a worker function to a pdflush thread and wakes it up. If no thread is available, −1 is returned; otherwise, a thread is removed from the list and woken. To simplify matters, we have omitted the required locking in the code:

mm/pdflush.c
```
int pdflush_operation(void (*fn)(unsigned long), unsigned long arg0)
{
        unsigned long flags;
        int ret = 0;

        if (list_empty(&pdflush_list)) {
                ret = -1;
        } else {
                struct pdflush_work *pdf;

                pdf = list_entry(pdflush_list.next, struct pdflush_work, list);
                list_del_init(&pdf->list);
                if (list_empty(&pdflush_list))
                        last_empty_jifs = jiffies;
                pdf->fn = fn;
                pdf->arg0 = arg0;
                wake_up_process(pdf->who);
        }
        return ret;
}
```

pdflush_operation accepts two arguments that specify the worker function and its argument.

If the list pdflush_list is empty and thus no pdflush daemon can be awoken, an error code is returned. If a sleeping pdflush instance is in the queue, it is removed and is no longer available to any other part of the kernel. The values for the worker function and argument are assigned to the corresponding fields of pdflush_work, and immediately thereafter the thread is woken with wake_up_process. Thanks to the who element in pdflush_work, the kernel knows which process is meant.

To ensure that there are always enough worker threads, the kernel checks whether the pdflush_list list is empty after removing the current instance, but before waking the thread. If it is, last_empty_jifs is set to the current system time. When a thread terminates, the kernel uses this information to check the period during which no surplus threads were available — it can then start a new thread as described above.

---

[2]The time the pdflush_list list was last empty is noted in the global variable last_empty_jifs.

17.6 Periodic Flushing

Now that you are familiar with the framework in which the `pdflush` mechanism operates, let's move on to describe the routines responsible for the actual synchronization of cache contents with the associated backing store. Recall that two alternatives are available, one periodic and one enforced. First, let's discuss the periodic writeback mechanism.

In earlier kernel versions, a user mode application was used to perform periodic write operations. This application was started at kernel initialization time and invoked a system call at regular intervals to write back dirty pages. In the meantime, this not particularly elegant procedure was replaced with a more modern alternative that does not take the long route via user mode and is therefore not only more efficient but also more aesthetic.

What's left of the earlier method is the name *kupdate*. The name appears as a component of some functions and is often used to describe the flushing mechanism.

Two things are needed to periodically flush dirty cache data: the worker function that is executed with the help of the `pdflush` mechanism, and code to regularly activate the mechanism.

17.7 Associated Data Structures

The `wb_kupdate` function in `mm/page-writeback.c` is responsible for the technical aspects of flushing. It is based on the address space concept (discussed in Chapter 4) that establishes the relationship among RAM, files or inodes, and the underlying block devices.

17.7.1 Page Status

`wb_kupdate` is based on two data structures that control how it functions. One of these structures is the global array `vm_stat`, which enables the status of all system memory pages to be queried:

mm/vmstat.c
```
atomic_long_t vm_stat[NR_VM_ZONE_STAT_ITEMS];
```

The array holds a comprehensive collection of statistical information to describe the status of the memory pages *of each CPU*; consequently, there is an instance of the structure for each CPU in the system. The individual instances are grouped together in an array to simplify access.

> **The structure elements are simple, elementary numbers and therefore indicate only**
> *how many* **pages have a specific status. Other means must be devised to find out**
> *which* **pages these are. This issue is discussed below.**

The following statistics are collected in `vm_stat`:

<mmzone.h>
```
enum zone_stat_item {
        /* First 128 byte cacheline (assuming 64 bit words) */
        NR_FREE_PAGES,
        NR_INACTIVE,
        NR_ACTIVE,
        NR_ANON_PAGES,  /* Mapped anonymous pages */
```

```
                NR_FILE_MAPPED,  /* pagecache pages mapped into pagetables.
                                    only modified from process context */
                NR_FILE_PAGES,
                NR_FILE_DIRTY,
                NR_WRITEBACK,
                /* Second 128 byte cacheline */
                NR_SLAB_RECLAIMABLE,
                NR_SLAB_UNRECLAIMABLE,
                NR_PAGETABLE,            /* used for pagetables */
                NR_UNSTABLE_NFS,         /* NFS unstable pages */
                NR_BOUNCE,
                NR_VMSCAN_WRITE,
#ifdef CONFIG_NUMA
                /* Omitted: NUMA-specific statistics */
#endif
NR_VM_ZONE_STAT_ITEMS };
```

The meanings of the entries are easy to guess from their names. NR_FILE_DIRTY specifies the number of file-based dirty pages, and NR_WRITEBACK indicates how many are currently being written back. NR_PAGETABLE stores the number of pages used to hold the page tables, and NR_FILE_MAPPED specifies how many pages are mapped by the page table mechanism (only the file-based pages are accounted for; direct kernel mappings are not included). Finally, NR_SLAB_RECLAIMABLE and NR_SLAB_UNRECLAIMABLE indicate how many pages are used for the slab cache described in Chapter 3 (despite their name, the constants work also for the slub cache). The remaining entries consider special cases that are not interesting for our purposes.

Note that the kernel not only keeps a global array to collect page statistics, but also provides the same information resolved by memory zone:

<mmzone.h>
```
struct zone {
...
        /* Zone statistics */
        atomic_long_t            vm_stat[NR_VM_ZONE_STAT_ITEMS];
...
}
```

It is the job of memory management to keep the global and zone-specific arrays up-to-date. Of prime interest at this point is how the information is used. To gain a status overview of the entire system, it is necessary to combine the information in the array entries to obtain not only CPU-specific data but the data of the overall system. The kernel provides the auxiliary function global_page_state, which delivers the current value of a particular field of vm_stat:

<vmstat.h>
```
unsigned long global_page_state(enum zone_stat_item item)
```

> Because the **vm_stat** arrays and their entries are not protected by a locking mechanism, it may happen that the data change while **global_page_state** is running. The result returned is not exact but an approximation. This is not a problem because the figures are simply a general indication of how effectively work is distributed. Minor differences between real data and returned data are acceptable.

17.7.2 Writeback Control

A second data structure holds the various parameters that control writeback of dirty pages. Upper layers use it to pass information about how writeback is to be performed to the lower layers (top to bottom in Figure 17-1). However, the structure also allows for propagating status information in the reverse direction (bottom to top):

\<writeback.h\>
```
/* A control structure which tells the writeback code what to do. */
struct writeback_control {
        struct backing_dev_info *bdi;   /* If !NULL, only write back this
                                           queue */
        enum writeback_sync_modes sync_mode;
        unsigned long *older_than_this; /* If !NULL, only write back inodes
                                           older than this */
        long nr_to_write;               /* Write this many pages, and decrement
                                           this for each page written */
        long pages_skipped;             /* Pages which were not written */

        loff_t range_start;
        loff_t range_end;

        unsigned nonblocking:1;            /* Don't get stuck on request queues */
        unsigned encountered_congestion:1; /* An output: a queue is full */
        unsigned for_kupdate:1;            /* A kupdate writeback */
        unsigned for_reclaim:1;            /* Invoked from the page allocator */
        unsigned for_writepages:1;         /* This is a writepages() call */
        unsigned range_cyclic:1;           /* range_start is cyclic */
};
```

The meanings of the structure elements are as follows:

❑ bdi points to a structure of type backing_dev_info, which summarizes information on the underlying storage medium. This structure is discussed briefly in Chapter 16. Two things interest us here. First, the structure provides a variable to hold the status of the writeback queue (this means, e.g., that congestion can be signaled if there are too many write requests), and second, it allows RAM-based filesystems that do not have a (block device) backing store to be labeled — writeback operations to systems of this kind make no sense.

❑ sync_mode distinguishes between three different synchronization modes:

\<writeback.h\>
```
enum writeback_sync_modes {
        WB_SYNC_NONE,   /* Don't wait on anything */
        WB_SYNC_ALL,    /* Wait on every mapping */
        WB_SYNC_HOLD,   /* Hold the inode on sb_dirty for sys_sync() */
};
```

To synchronize data, the kernel needs to pass a corresponding write request to the underlying block device. Requests to block devices are asynchronous by nature. If the kernel wants to ensure that the data have safely reached the device, it needs to wait for completion after the request has been issued. This behavior is mandated with WB_SYNC_ALL. Waiting for writeback to complete is performed in __sync_single_inode discussed below; recall from Figure 17-1 that it sits at the bottom of the mechanism, where it is responsible to delegate synchronization of a single inode to the filesystem-specific methods. All functions that wait on inodes because WB_SYNC_ALL is set are marked in Figure 17-1.

Notice that writeback with WB_SYNC_ALL set is referred to as *data integrity writeback*. If a system crash happens immediately after writeback in this mode has been finished, no data are lost because everything is synchronized with the underlying block devices.

If WB_SYNC_NONE is used, the kernel will send the request, but continue with the remaining synchronization work immediately afterward. This mode is also referred to as *flushing writeback*.

WB_SYNC_HOLD is a special form used for the sync system call that works similarly to WB_SYNC_NONE. The exact differences are subtle and are discussed in Section 17.15.

❑   When the kernel performs writeback, it must decide which dirty cache data need to be synchronized with the backing store. It uses the older_than_this and nr_to_write elements for this purpose. Data are written back if they have been dirty for longer than specified by older_than_this.

> **older_than_this is defined as a pointer type, which is unusual for a single long value. Its numeric value, which can be obtained by appropriate de-referencing, is of interest. If the pointer is NULL, then age checking is not performed, and all objects are synchronized irrespective of when they became dirty. Setting nr_to_write to 0 likewise disables any upper limit on the number of pages that are supposed to be written back.**

❑   nr_to_write can restrict the maximal number of pages that should be written back. The upper bound for this is given by MAX_WRITEBACK_PAGES, which is usually set to 1,024.

❑   If pages were selected to be written back, functions from lower layers perform the required operations. However, they can fail for various reasons, for instance, because the page is locked from some other part of the kernel. The number of skipped pages can be reported to higher layers via the counter pages_skipped.

❑   The nonblocking flag specifies whether writeback queues block or not in the event of congestion (more pending write operations than can be effectively satisfied). If they are blocked, the kernel waits until the queue is free. If not, it relinquishes control. The write operation is then resumed later.

❑   encountered_congestion is also a flag to signal to higher layers that congestion has occurred during data writeback. It is a Boolean variable and accepts the values 1 or 0.

❑   for_kupdated is set to 1 if the write request was issued by the periodic mechanism. Otherwise, its value is 0. for_reclaim and for_writepages are used in a similar manner: They are set if the writeback operation was initiated from memory reclaim from the do_writepages function, respectively.

❑   If range_cyclic is set to 0, the writeback mechanism is restricted to operate on the range given by range_start and range_end. The limits refer to the mapping for which the writeback was initiated.

If range_cyclic is set to 1, the kernel may iterate many times over the pages associated with a mapping, thus the name of the element.

17.7.3 Adjustable Parameters

The kernel supports the fine-tuning of synchronization by means of parameters. These can be set by the administrator to help the kernel assess system usage and loading. The sysctl mechanism described in Chapter 10 is used for this purpose, which means that the proc filesystem is the natural interface to manipulate the parameters — they are located in /proc/sys/vm/. Four parameters can be set, all of which are defined in mm/page-writeback.c[3]:

❏ dirty_background_ratio specifies the percentage of dirty pages at which pdflush starts periodic flushing in the background. The default value is 10 so that the update mechanism kicks in when more than 10 percent of the pages have changed as compared to the backing store.

❏ vm_dirty_ratio (the corresponding sysctl is dirty_ratio) specifies the percentage of dirty pages (with respect to non-HIGHMEM memory) at which data flushing will be started. The default value is 40.

Why is high memory excluded from the percentage? Older kernel versions before 2.6.20 did not, in fact, distinguish between high and normal memory. However, if the ratio between high memory and low memory is too large (i.e., if main memory is much more than 4 GiB on 32-bit processors), the default settings for dirty_background_ratio and dirty_ratio were required to be scaled back slightly when the writeback mechanism was initialized.

Retaining the default values would have necessitated an excessively large number of buffer_head instances, and these would have had to be held in valuable low memory. By excluding high memory from the calculation, the kernel does not deal with scaling anymore, which simplifies matters somewhat.

❏ The interval between two invocations of the periodic flushing routine is defined in dirty_writeback_interval (the corresponding sysctl is dirty_writeback_centisecs). The interval is specified in hundredths of a second (also called *centiseconds* in the sources). The default is 500, which equates to an interval of 5 seconds between invocations.

On systems where a very large number of write operations are performed, lowering this value can have a positive effect, but increasing the value on systems with very few write operations delivers only small performance gains.

❏ The maximum period during which a page may remain dirty is specified in dirty_expire_interval (the sysctl is dirty_expire_centisecs). Again, the period is expressed is hundredths of a second. The default value is 3,000, which means that a page may remain dirty for a maximum of 30 seconds before it is written back at the next opportunity.

17.8 Central Control

The key periodic flushing component is the wb_kupdate procedure defined in mm/page-writeback.c. It is responsible for dispatching lower-level routines to find the dirty pages in memory and synchronize them with the underlying block device. As usual, our description is based on a code flow diagram as shown in Figure 17-4.

The superblocks are synchronized right at the start of the function because this is essential to ensure filesystem integrity. Incorrect superblock data result in consistency errors throughout the filesystem

---

[3]The name of the sysctls differs with the variables names for historical reasons.

and, in most cases, lead to loss of at least part of the data. This is why `sync_supers`, whose purpose is described in more detail in Section 17.9, is invoked first.

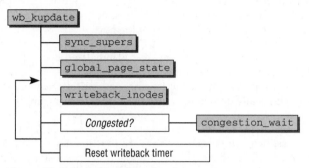

Figure 17-4: Code flow diagram of `wb_kupdate`.

Thereafter, "normal" dirty data are written back from the page cache. The kernel invokes the `global_page_state` function to get a picture of the current status of all system pages in a `page_state` instance. The key item of information is the number of dirty pages held in the `NR_FILE_DIRTY` element of the `vm_stats` array.

This function then goes into a loop whose code is repeatedly executed until there are no dirty pages in the system. After a `writeback_control` instance has been started to initiate non-blocking writeback of `MAX_WRITEBACK_PAGES` pages (normally 1,024), `writeback_inodes` writes back the data that can be reached via the inodes. This is quite a lengthy function so it is discussed separately in greater detail in Section 17.10, but a couple of salient points are listed below:

❑ Not *all* dirty pages are written back — in fact, the number is restricted to `MAX_WRITEBACK_PAGES`. Because inodes are locked during writeback, smaller groups of dirty pages are processed to prevent overly long blocking of an inode that adversely affects system performance.

❑ The number of pages actually written back is transferred between `wb_kupdate` and `writeback_inodes` by subtracting the number of pages written back — which are therefore no longer dirty — from the `nr_to_write` element of the `writeback_control` instance after each `writeback_inodes` call.

When `writeback_inodes` terminates, the kernel repeats the loop until there are no more dirty pages in the system.

The `congestion_wait` function is invoked if queue congestion occurs (the kernel detects this by means of the set `encountered_congestion` element of the writeback instance). The function waits until congestion has eased and then continues the loop as normal. Section 17.10 takes a closer look at how the kernel defines congestion.

Once the loop has finished, `wb_kupdate` makes sure that the kernel invokes it again after the interval defined by `dirty_writeback_interval` in order to guarantee periodic background flushing. Low-resolution kernel timers as discussed in Chapter 15 are used for this purpose — in this particular case, the timer is implemented by means of the global timer list `wb_timer` (defined in `mm/page_writeback.c`).

Usually, the interval between two calls of the `wb_kupdate` function is the value specified in `dirty_writeback_centisecs`. However, a special situation arises if `wb_kupdate` takes *longer* than the time specified in `dirty_writeback_centisecs`. In this case, the time of the next `wb_kupdate` call is postponed until 1 second after the *end* of the current `wb_kupdate` call. This also differs from the normal situation because the interval is not calculated as the time between the start of two successive calls but as the time between the end of one call and the start of the next.

The ball is set rolling when the synchronization layer is initialized in `page_writeback_init`, where the kernel first starts the timer. Initial values for the `wb_timer` variable — primarily the `wb_timer_fn` callback function that is invoked when the timer expires — are set statically when the variable is declared in `mm/page-writeback.c`. Logically, the timer expiry time changes over time and is reset at the end of each `wb_kupdate` call, as just described.

The structure of the periodically invoked `wb_timer_fn` function is very simple as it consists only of a `pdflush_operation` call by `wb_kupdate`. At this point, it is *not* necessary to reinitialize the timer because this is done in `wb_kupdate`. The timer must be reset in one situation only — if no `pdflush` thread is available, the next `wb_timer_fn` call is postponed by 1 second by the function itself. This ensures that `wb_kupdate` is invoked regularly to synchronize cache data with block device data, even if the `pdflush` subsystem is heavily loaded.

17.9 Superblock Synchronization

Superblock data are synchronized by a dedicated function called `sync_supers` to differentiate it from normal synchronization operations. This and other functions relevant to superblocks are defined in `fs/super.c`. Its code flow diagram is shown in Figure 17-5.

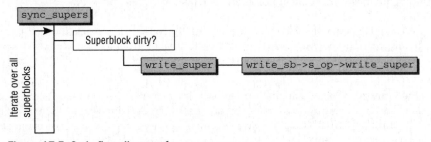

Figure 17-5: Code flow diagram for `sync_supers`.

Recall from Chapter 8 that the kernel provides the global list `super_blocks` to hold the `super_block` instances of all mounted filesystems. As the code flow diagram shows, the initial task of `sync_supers` is to iterate over all superblocks and to check whether they are dirty using the `s_dirt` element of the superblock structure. If they are, the superblock data contents are written to the data medium by `write_super`.

The `write_super` method included in the superblock-specific `super_operations` structure does the actual writing. If the pointer is not set, superblock synchronization is not needed for the filesystem (this is the case with virtual and RAM-based filesystems). For instance, the `proc` filesystem uses a null pointer. Of course, normal filesystems on block devices, such as Ext3 or Reiserfs, provide appropriate methods (e.g., `ext3_write_super`) to communicate with the block layer and write back relevant data.

17.10   Inode Synchronization

`writeback_inodes` writes back installed mappings by walking through the system inodes (for the sake of simplicity, this is called *inode writeback*, but in fact not the inode but the dirty data associated with it are written back). The function shoulders the main burden of synchronization because most system data are provided in the form of address space mappings that make use of inodes. Figure 17-6 illustrates the code flow diagram for `writeback_inodes`. The function is slightly more complicated in reality because some more details and corner cases need to be handled properly. We consider a simplified variant that nevertheless contains everything that is essential when inodes are written back.

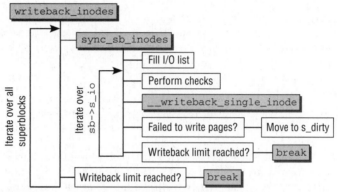

Figure 17-6: Code flow diagram for `writeback_inodes`.

The function uses the data structures discussed in Chapter 8 to establish a link among superblocks, inodes, and associated data.

17.10.1   Walking the Superblocks

When mappings are written back inode-by-inode, the initial path taken is via all system superblock instances that represent the mounted filesystems. `sync_sb_inodes` is invoked for each instance in order to write back the superblock inode data, as shown in the code flow diagram in Figure 17-6. Walking the superblock list can be terminated by two different conditions:

1.   All superblock instances have been scanned sequentially. The kernel has reached the end of the list, and its work is therefore done.

2.   The maximum number of writeback pages specified by the `writeback_control` instance has been reached. Since writeback requires obtaining various important locks, the system should not be disturbed for too long to make the inodes available for other parts of the kernel again.

17.10.2   Examining Superblock Inodes

Once it has been established with the help of the superblock structure that the filesystem contains inodes with dirty data, the kernel hands over to `sync_sb_inodes`, which synchronizes the dirty superblock inodes. The code flow diagram is in Figure 17-6.

Great effort would be needed if the kernel were to run through the *complete* list of filesystem inodes each time in order to differentiate between clean and dirty inodes. The kernel therefore implements a far less costly option by placing all dirty inodes on the superblock-specific list super_block->s_dirty. Notice that inodes on the list are reverse time-ordered. The later an inode was dirtied, the closer it is to the tail of the list.

Two more list heads are additionally required to perform the synchronization of these inodes. The relevant portion of the super_block structure is as follows:

```
<fs.h>
struct super_block {
...
        struct list_head        s_dirty;        /* dirty inodes */
        struct list_head        s_io;           /* parked for writeback */
        struct list_head        s_more_io;      /* parked for more writeback */
...
}
```

All dirty inodes of the superblock are held in the s_dirty list — and are practically served up on a platter to the synchronization mechanism. This list is updated automatically by the relevant code of the VFS layer. s_io keeps all inodes that are currently under consideration of the synchronization code.

s_more_io contains inodes that have been selected for synchronization and were placed on s_io, but could not be processed in one go. It would seem to be the simplest solution that the kernel puts such inodes back to s_io, but this could starve newly dirtied inodes or lead to locking problems, so a second list is introduced. All functions that place inodes on s_io or s_more_io are indicated in Figure 17-1.

The first task of sync_sb_inodes is to fill the s_io list. Two cases must be distinguished:

1. If the synchronization request did *not* originate from the periodic mechanism, then all inodes on the dirty list are put onto the s_io list. If inodes are present on the more_io list, they are placed at the end of the i_io list. The auxiliary function queue_io is provided to perform both list operations. The behavior ensures that inodes from previous synchronization passes still get consideration, but more recently dirtied inodes are preferred. This way, large dirtied files cannot starve smaller files that were dirtied afterward.

2. If the periodic mechanism wb_kupdate has triggered synchronization, the s_io list is only replenished with additional dirty inodes if it is completely empty. Otherwise, the kernel waits until all members of s_io have been written back. There is no particular pressure for the periodic mechanism to write back as many inodes as possible in the shortest amount of time. Instead, it is more important to slowly but surely write out a constant stream of inodes.

If the writeback control parameter specifies an older_than_this criterion, only inodes marked dirty within a specified minimum period into the past are included in the synchronization process. If the time stored in this element is *before* the time held in the dirtied_when element of the mapping, the requisite condition is not satisfied and the kernel does not move the inode from the dirty to the s_io list.

After the members of the s_io list have been selected, the kernel starts to iterate over the individual elements.

Some checks ascertain that the inode is suitable for synchronization before actual writeback is performed:

❑ Purely memory-based filesystems like RAM disks or pseudo-filesystems or purely virtual filesystems, respectively, do not require synchronization with an underlying block device. This is signaled by setting `BDI_CAP_NO_WRITEBACK` in the `backing_dev_info` instance that belongs to the filesystem's mapping. If an inode of this type is encountered, processing can be aborted immediately.

   However, there is one filesystem whose metadata are purely memory-based and without physical backing store, but that cannot be skipped: the block device pseudo-filesystem `bdev`. Recall from Chapter 10 that `bdev` is used to handle access to raw block devices or partitions thereof. An inode is provided for each partition, and access to the raw device is handled via this inode. While the inode metadata are important in memory, it does not make sense to store them anywhere permanently since they are just used to implement a uniform abstraction mechanism. This, however, does not imply that the contents of the block device do not require synchronization: Quite the opposite is true. Access to the raw device is as usual buffered by the page cache, and any changes are reflected in the radix tree data structures. When modifications are made on the contents of a block device, they go through the page cache. The pages must therefore be synchronized like all other pages in the page cache with the underlying hardware from time to time.

   The block device pseudo-filesystem `bdev` thus does *not* set `BDI_CAP_NO_WRITEBACK`. However, no `write_inode` method is contained in the associated `super_operations`, so metadata synchronization is not performed. Data synchronization, on the other hand, runs as for any other filesystem.

❑ If the synchronization queue is congested (the `BDI_write_congested` bit is set in the status field of the `backing_dev_info` instance) and non-blocking writeback was selected in `writeback_control`, the congestion needs to be reported to the higher layers. This is done by setting the `encountered_congestion` field in the `writeback_control` instance to 1.

   If the current inode belongs to a block device, then the auxiliary function `requeue_io` is used to move the inode from `s_io` to `more_io`. It is possible that different inodes of a block device are backed by different queues, for instance, if multiple physical devices are combined into a single logical device. The kernel therefore continues to process the other inodes on the `s_io` list in the hope that they belong to different queues that are not congested.

   If the current inode, however, stems from a regular filesystem, it can be assumed that all other inodes are backed by the same queue. Since this queue is already congested, it does not make sense to synchronize the other inodes, so the loop iteration is aborted. The unprocessed inodes remain in the `s_io` list and are dealt with the next time `sync_sb_inodes` is called.

❑ `pdflush` can be instructed via `writeback_control` to focus on a single queue. If a regular filesystem inode that uses a different queue is encountered, processing can be aborted. If the inode represents a block device, processing skips forward to the next inode on the `s_io` list for the same reason as in the write congestion case.

❑ The current system time in jiffies is held in a local variable at the start of `sync_sb_inodes`. The kernel now checks whether the time when the inode just processed was marked as dirty is after the start time of `sync_sb_inodes`. If so, synchronization is aborted in its entirety. The unprocessed inodes are again left on `s_io`.

❑ A further situation leads to termination of sync_sb_inodes. If a pdflush thread is already in the process of writing back the processed queue (this is indicated by the BDI_pdflush bit of the status element of backing_dev_info), the current thread lets the running pdflush thread process the queue on its own.

Inode writeback may not be initiated until the kernel has ensured that the above conditions are satisfied. As the code flow diagram in Figure 17-6 shows, the inode is written back using __writeback_single_inode, examined below. It can happen that writing back pages does not succeed for all pages that should be written back, for instance, because a page might be locked from another part of the kernel, or connections for network filesystems might be unavailable. In this case, the inode is moved back to the s_dirty list again, possibly updating the dirtied_when field unless the inode has been re-dirtied while it was written out. The kernel will automatically retry to synchronize the data in one of the next synchronization runs. Additionally, the kernel needs to make sure that the inverse time ordering of all inodes on s_dirty is preserved. The auxiliary function redirty_tail takes care of this.

The process is repeated until one of the two conditions below is fulfilled:

1. All dirty inodes of the superblock have been written back.

2. The maximum number of page synchronizations (specified in nr_to_write) has been reached. This is necessary to support the unit-by-unit synchronization described above.

   The remaining inodes in s_io are processed the next time sync_sb_inodes is invoked.

17.10.3 Writing Back Single Inodes

As noted above, the kernel delegates synchronization of the data associated with an inode to __writeback_single_inode. The corresponding code flow diagram is shown in Figure 17-7.

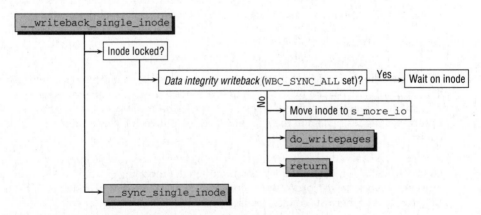

Figure 17-7: Code flow diagram for __writeback_single_inode.

The function is essentially a dispatcher for __sync_single_inode, but is charged with the important task of distinguishing whether a data integrity (WB_SYNC_ALL) or regular writeback is performed. This influences how locked inodes are handled.

A set `I_LOCK` bit in the `state` element of the inode data structure indicates that the element is already being synchronized by another part of the kernel — and therefore cannot be modified at the moment in the current path. If a regular writeback is active, this is not much of a problem: The kernel can simply skip the inode and place it on the `s_more_io` list, which guarantees that it will be reconsidered some time later. Before returning to the caller, `do_writepages` is used to write out some of the data associated with the inode since this can do no harm.[4]

The situation is more involved if a data integrity writeback is performed though. In this case, the kernel does *not* skip the inode but sets up a wait queue (see Chapter 14) to wait until the inode is available again, that is, until the `I_SYNC` bit is cleared. Notice that it is not sufficient to know that another part of the kernel is already synchronizing the inode. This could be a regular writeback that does not guarantee that the dirty data are actually written to disk. This is not what `WB_SYNC_ALL` is about: When the synchronization pass completes, the kernel has to guarantee that all data have been synchronized, and waiting on the inode is therefore essential.

Once the inode is available, the job is passed on to `__sync_single_inode`. This extensive function writes back the data associated with the inode and also the inode metadata. Figure 17-8 shows the code flow diagram.

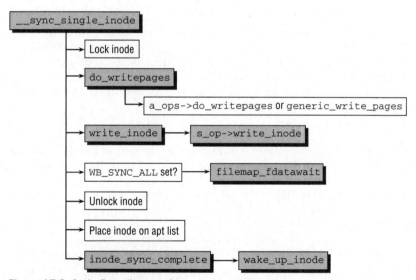

Figure 17-8: Code flow diagram for **`__sync_single_inode`**.

1. First of all, the inode must be locked by setting the `I_LOCK` bit in the inode structure status field. This prevents other kernel threads from processing the inode.

2. Synchronization of an inode consists of two parts: Synchronizing the data and synchronizing the metadata.

---

[4] Actually, the call also does not have any benefit and will be removed in kernel 2.6.25, which was still under development when this book was written. Since `do_writepages` is also called in `__sync_single_inodes`, the call is superfluous.

The actual write operation for the data is initiated in `do_writepages`. This function invokes the `writepages` method of the corresponding `address_space_operations` structure if the method exists and is not assigned a null pointer; for example, the `ext3_writepages` method is invoked for the Ext3 filesystem.

If no method exists, the kernel invokes the `generic_writepages` function, which finds all dirty pages of the mapping and sequentially writes them back using `writepage` from the address space operations (note that in contrast to `writepages`, there is no *s* at the end of the name) or `mpage_writepage` if the former does not exist.

3. `write_inode` writes back the metadata needed to manage the inode itself. The function is not complicated; it simply checks whether the superblock operations associated with the inode instance include the `write_inode` method (the block device filesystem does not provide one, e.g.). If it exists, it is invoked to find the relevant data and write it back via the block layer.

> **Filesystems often choose to perform no actual writes to a block device, but just submit a dirty buffer to the generic code. This needs to be dealt with in the sync system call discussed below.**

Note that calling `write_inode` is skipped if `I_DIRTY_SYNC` of `I_DIRTY_DATASYNC` is set because this signals that only data, but not the metadata, require to be written back.

4. If the current synchronization aims at data integrity, that is, if `WB_SYNC_ALL` is set, then `filemap_fdatawait` is used to wait until all pending write operations (which are usually processed asynchronously) are performed. The function waits for write operations to complete on a page-by-page basis. Pages currently written to their backing store have the `PG_writeback` status bit set, which is automatically removed by the responsible block layer code when the operation is complete. Therefore, the synchronization code just needs to wait until the bit goes away.

The above steps complete inode synchronization, at least in the view of the filesystem (naturally, the block layer still has a few things to do if `filemap_fdatawait` has not been called to await the results before), but the layer structure of the kernel means that this is of no further relevance to us). The inode now needs to be put back into the correct list, and the kernel must update the inode status if it has changed as a result of synchronization. There are four different lists in which the inode can be inserted:

1. If the inode data have become dirty again in the meantime (i.e., if the `I_DIRTY` bit is set in the status element), the inode is added to the `s_dirty` list of the superblock.

    It is also placed in this list if not all dirty data of the mapping were written back — because, for example, the number of pages specified by writeback control was too small to allow all dirty pages to be processed in one go. In this case, the inode status is set to `I_DIRTY_PAGES` so that synchronization of the metadata is skipped the next time `__sync_single_inode` is invoked — these data have just been written back and are still intact.

2. If not all data of the mapping were written back, but `pdflush` was called from `wb_kupdate`, the inode is placed on `s_more_io` and will be dealt with in later synchronization runs.

    If not all data were written back and `pdflush` was *not* called from `wb_kupdate`, then the inode is placed back on the dirty list. This avoids that one large dirty file that cannot be written properly suspends other pending files for a long time or indefinitely. `redirty_tail` is responsible to keep the inverse time ordering on `s_dirty` intact.

3. If the inode access counter (`i_count`) has a value greater than 1, the kernel inserts the inode in the global `inode_in_use` list because it is still in use.

4. When the access counter drops to 0, the inode can be placed in the global list of unused inode instances (`inode_unused`).

The `i_list` element of the inode is used as a list element in all the above situations.

The final step is to invoke `wake_up_inode` via the dispatcher `inode_sync_complete`. This function wakes processes that were placed on the queue of inodes waiting to be written back but whose `I_LOCK` bit is set. Because the inode is no longer needed by the current thread (and is therefore no longer locked), the scheduler selects one of these processes to handle the inode. If the data have already been fully synchronized, this process has nothing else to do. If dirty pages still need to be synchronized, the process goes ahead and synchronizes them.

17.11   Congestion

I have used the term *congestion* a few times without precisely defining what it means. On an intuitive level it is not difficult to understand — when a kernel block device queue is overloaded with read or write operations, it doesn't make sense to add further requests for communication with the block device. It is best to wait until a certain number of requests have been processed and the queue is shorter before submitting new read or write requests.

Below I examine how the kernel implements this definition on a technical level.

17.11.1   Data Structures

A double wait queue is needed to implement the *congestion* method. The definition is as follows:

mm/backing-dev.c
```
static wait_queue_head_t congestion_wqh[2] = {
                __WAIT_QUEUE_HEAD_INITIALIZER(congestion_wqh[0]),
                __WAIT_QUEUE_HEAD_INITIALIZER(congestion_wqh[1])
        };
```

The kernel provides two queues, one for input and one for output. Two pre-processor constants (`READ` and `WRITE`) are defined in `<fs.h>` to allow access to the array elements and to clearly differentiate between the two queues without the direct use of numbers.

> The kernel makes a distinction between the *directions* in which data are transmitted to the queue — in other words, between input and output. The data structure does *not* differentiate between the various devices in the system. As you will see shortly, the data structures of the block layer contain queue-specific information on possible congestion.

Notice that the queues are not supposed to be manipulated directly with standard wait queue methods. Instead, a number of auxiliary functions declared in `<backing-dev.h>` are provided by the kernel; they are covered in the following discussion.

17.11.2 Thresholds

When does the kernel regard a queue as being congested and when does it give the "all clear"? The answer is surprisingly easy — a simple check is made to ascertain whether certain minimum and maximum limit values (or thresholds) for requests have been exceeded in a specific queue.

The kernel does *not* use fixed constants to do this. Instead, it defines the limit values in relation to the system's main memory because the number of block `requests` is scaled accordingly.

Recall from Chapter 6 that each block device is equipped with a request queue defined by `struct request`. The fields that are interesting for our purposes are reproduced below:

```
<blkdev.h>
struct request_queue
{
...
        unsigned long nr_requests;          /* Max # of requests */
        unsigned int nr_congestion_on;
        unsigned int nr_congestion_off;
        unsigned int nr_batching;
...
}
```

The `nr_requests` element is used to define the number of request structures per queue. Typically, this number is set to `BLKDEV_MAX_RQ`, which equates to 128 but can be changed using `/sys/block/<device>/queue/nr_requests`. A lower bound on the number of requests is given by `BLKDEV_MIN_RQ`, which equates to 4.

❑ `nr_congestion_on` denotes the limit value at which a queue is regarded as congested. There must be fewer free `request` structures than specified by the value for this state to occur.

❑ `nr_congestion_off` (note the "off") also specifies a limit value at which a queue is regarded as *no longer* congested. When there are more free `requests` than indicated by this number, the kernel regards the queue as free.

The functions `queue_congestion_on_threshold` and `queue_congestion_off_threshold` are provided to read the current threshold values. Although the functions are trivial, they must be used instead of reading the values directly. Should the implementation change in future kernel versions, the user will nevertheless be able to enjoy the same interface and will not require modifications.

The congestion thresholds are computed by `blk_congestion_threshold`:

block/ll_rw_blk.c
```
static void blk_queue_congestion_threshold(struct request_queue *q)
```

Figure 17-9 displays the congestion thresholds that are computed for a request queue with a given length. The values for `congestion_on` and `congestion_off` differ slightly. This minor difference (known as *hysteresis* in the kernel sources, a term borrowed from physics) prevents queues from switching constantly between both states when the number of requests is close to the congestion threshold.

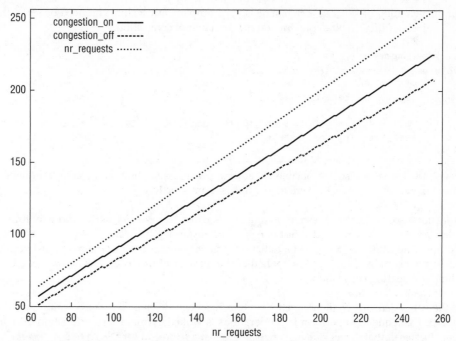

Figure 17-9: Thresholds for the number of requests that turn congestion on and off, respectively. The thresholds are obviously always smaller than the number of requests that can maximally be queued.

17.11.3 Setting and Clearing the Congested State

The kernel provides two standard functions (declared in `<blkdev.h>`) to set queues to the congested state and to clear this state: `blk_set_queue_congested` and `blk_clear_queue_congested`, respectively. Both obtain the `backing_dev_info` for the queue under consideration and hand over the real work to `set_bdi_congested` or `clear_bdi_congested`, respectively, in `mm/backing-dev.c`.

Two data structures are manipulated to change the state. First, the request queue of the block device must be modified (you are familiar with the associated `request_queue` data structure from Chapter 6), and second, note must be taken of the global congestion array (`congestion_wqh`).

`blk_set_queue_congested` is used to mark a queue as congested. Remarkably, it is invoked at only a single point in the kernel — by `get_request`.[5] As discussed in Chapter 6, the purpose of `get_request` is to allocate a `request` instance for a queue or to fetch one from the appropriate cache. This is the ideal place to check for congestion. If the number of `request` instances falls below the threshold, `set_queue_congested` informs the remaining code that congestion has occurred.

---

[5]This is not entirely precise: It is also called from `queue_request_store`. But since this code path is only activated if the system administrator changes the `nr_requests` field of a request queue via sysfs, I do not bother to discuss this possibility any further.

The implementation of `set_bdi_congested` is very simple. Only a single bit need be set in the request queue — albeit a different bit depending on the direction of congestion:

block/backing-dev.c
```
void set_bdi_congested(struct backing_dev_info *bdi, int rw)
{
        enum bdi_state bit;

        bit = (rw == WRITE) ? BDI_write_congested : BDI_read_congested;
        set_bit(bit, &bdi->state);
}
```

However, the kernel is also responsible for adding processes waiting on a congested queue to the `congestion_wqh` wait queue. I describe how this is done shortly.

The function used to clear congestion on a queue is `clear_queue_congested` and is not much more complicated. Again, it is invoked at just one point in the kernel[6] by `_freed_request`, which is in the code path originating from `blk_put_request` that returns `request` instances no longer needed to the kernel cache. At this point, it is easy to check whether the number of free `requests` has exceeded the above threshold for clearing congestion.

Once the congested bit for the desired direction has been deleted, a process waiting on the `congestion_wqh` queue to perform I/O operations is woken by the `wake_up` function described in Chapter 14. Recall that `clear_queue_congested` is just a front end for `clear_bdi_congested`:

block/ll_rw_blk.c
```
void clear_bdi_congested(struct backing_dev_info *bdi, int rw)
{
        enum bdi_state bit;
        wait_queue_head_t *wqh = &congestion_wqh[rw];

        bit = (rw == WRITE) ? BDI_write_congested : BDI_read_congested;
        clear_bit(bit, &bdi->state);

        if (waitqueue_active(wqh))
                wake_up(wqh);
}
```

17.11.4 Waiting on Congested Queues

Of course, it's no use marking queues as congested and clearing them when the situation improves — the kernel must also be able to wait until a queue is free again. You have already seen that a wait queue is employed for this purpose, so it remains to discuss how processes are added to the wait queue.

The kernel uses the `congestion_wait` function for this purpose. It adds a process to the `congestion_wqh` wait queue when congestion occurs. The function requires two parameters — the direction of data flow (read or write operation) and a time out after which the process is always woken, even if the queue is still congested. The time out is used to prevent excessively long periods of inactivity — after all, a queue may be congested for quite some time.

---

[6]This again ignores the possibility that the system administrator fiddles with `nr_requests` of the queue.

mm/backing-dev.c
```
long congestion_wait(int rw, long timeout)
{
        long ret;
        DEFINE_WAIT(wait);
        wait_queue_head_t *wqh = &congestion_wqh[rw];

        prepare_to_wait(wqh, &wait, TASK_UNINTERRUPTIBLE);
        ret = io_schedule_timeout(timeout);
        finish_wait(wqh, &wait);
        return ret;
}
```

congestion_wait invokes some functions once the requisite data structures have been initialized:

❑ prepare_to_wait is used in conjunction with a time out to implement waiting for clearance of congested queues. It puts the process in the TASK_UNINTERRUPTIBLE state and places it on the appropriate wait queue.

❑ io_schedule_timeout implements the desired time out using the resources described in Chapter 15. Control is passed to other processes until the time out expires.

Upon expiry of the time out (1 second is used for background synchronization), finish_wait is invoked to remove the process from the wait queue so that work can continue.

17.12 Forced Writeback

The above mechanisms for writing back pages as a background activity function very well when system load is not too high. The kernel is able to ensure that the number of dirty pages never gets out of hand and that there is an adequate exchange of data between RAM and the underlying block devices. However, this situation changes when the cached data of one or two processes quickly become dirty, thus necessitating more synchronization operations than can be handled by normal methods.

When the kernel receives an urgent request for memory and cannot satisfy it because of the very large number of dirty pages, it must try to transfer the page contents to the block device as quickly as possible to free RAM for other purposes. The same methods are used as for flushing data in the background, but in this case, synchronization is not initiated by periodic processes but is triggered explicitly by the kernel — in other words, writeback is "forced."

The request for immediate synchronization may originate not only from the kernel but also from userspace. The familiar sync command (and the corresponding sync system call) instructs the kernel to flush all dirty data to the block devices. Other system calls also provided by the kernel for this purpose are described in Section 17.14.

Synchronization is based on wakeup_pdflush, which is implemented in mm/page-writeback.c. The number of pages to be flushed is passed as a parameter:

mm/page-writeback.c
```
int wakeup_pdflush(long nr_pages)
{
        if (nr_pages == 0)
```

```
        nr_pages = global_page_state(NR_FILE_DIRTY) +
                       global_page_state(NR_UNSTABLE_NFS);
    return pdflush_operation(background_writeout, nr_pages);
}
```

If the number of writeback pages is not explicitly restricted by passing the parameter 0, the kernel invokes `global_page_state` to determine the system-wide number of (file-based) dirty pages in the system. A `pdflush` thread is then activated but this time using the `background_writeout` function and *not* `wb_kupdate`. Although the name of the former includes the word background, it is *not* used to perform background synchronization in the intuitive sense; this is done by `wb_kupdate`. However, `background_writeout` does not explicitly wait on pages to be written to the backing store, but just initiates a corresponding request, so the background term is justified. When, in contrast, data integrity synchronization is performed (as is the case when the requests originate from a system call), the kernel does explicitly wait until an issued write request is completed. This then definitely cannot be called background synchronization anymore.

As already stated, as far as the *technical* aspects of synchronization are concerned, it is basically irrelevant whether synchronization is initiated from the periodic mechanism or is requested explicitly. There are only the following minor differences in detail between `background_writepages` and `wb_kupdate`:

❏ `background_writepages` does not require pages to have been dirty for any minimum period of time before they can be written back. The technical implications are that the value of the `older_than_this` element of writeback control is set to NULL.

❏ The superblocks are not synchronized in `background_writepages` because the corresponding `sync_supers` call is missing.

❏ No timer is set to periodically restart the writeback mechanism.

More important are the places in the kernel at which flushing is initiated. Interestingly, `wakeup_pdflush` is invoked with a non-zero argument at only two places in the kernel sources:

1. In `free_more_memory`, which is always used when there is insufficient memory to generate page caches. In this case, the argument used is the fixed value of 1,024.

2. In `try_to_free_pages`, the *page reclaim* discussed in Chapter 18, which employs the `wakeup_pdflush` method to write back dirty data in pages regarded as superfluous when the caches were scanned. (When laptop mode is in use, `try_to_free_pages` also calls `wakeup_pdflush` with a zero argument; see Section 17.13.)

All other calls write back all dirty pages; that is, there is no limit on the maximum number of pages.

Understandably, writeback of all dirty pages is a very costly and time-consuming action and should therefore be used only with extreme care and at very few points in the kernel as indicated below:

❏ When synchronization of dirty data was requested explicitly by the `sync` system call.

❏ When emergency synchronization or an emergency remount was requested using the magic system request key.

❏ `balance_dirty_pages` also instructs `background_writeout` to write as many pages as possible. The function is called by the VFS layer when filesystems (or any other part of the kernel) have created dirty pages on a mapping. If the number of dirty pages in the system becomes too large, then `background_writeout` is used to start synchronizing. In contrast to all cases discussed above, the `pdflush` thread may not operate on all queues of the system. Only the queue of the backing device to which the dirtied page belongs is considered.

17.13 Laptop Mode

Laptop users have a natural tendency to reduce power consumption of their machines as much as possible — this is because laptop batteries, on the other side, have a natural tendency to provide power for n time units when $n + k$ time units (with $k > 0$) are required to finish some really important work far away from any power outlet. There are some points where `pdflush` can contribute. Hard disks are, with today's hardware, implemented by *disks* in the true sense of the word — alternatives in the form of solid-state devices have started to appear on the horizon, but are still far from being widespread. A hard disk needs to spin in order to be operational. This consumes power, and spinning down the hard disk when it is not needed thus helps to decrease power consumption.

What is still worse than a spinning hard disk is, however, a hard disk that accelerates. This requires more energy than a disk running at constant speed. The optimization goals of the kernel are therefore twofold:

1. Keep the disk spun down as long as possible. This can be satisfied by deferring write requests longer than usual.

2. When accelerating the disk cannot be avoided, perform all pending write operations even if these would still be delayed under normal circumstances.[7] This helps to prevent the disk from spinning up and down.

    Essentially, disk operations need to be performed in bursts: If data must be read in from the device, then all pending write operations can be performed since the device is now active anyway.

To achieve these goals, the kernel offers a *laptop mode* that can be activated via `/proc/sys/vm/laptop_mode`. The global variable `laptop_mode` acts as a Boolean indicator if laptop mode is currently active. Userland daemons can, for instance, use this file to enable and disable laptop mode depending on whether the device operates from a battery or a power supply. Notice that some documentation about this technique is available in `Documentation/laptop-mode.txt`.

Laptop mode requires astonishingly few changes in the synchronization code:

❑　A new `pdflush` worker routine is used: `laptop_flush` just calls `sys_sync` to synchronize all dirty data present in the system (the effect is identical to calling the `sync` system call). Since this will generate a whole lot of disk I/O, it is essential to activate the thread only when it is known that the disk is up and running.

　　When requests are processed, block devices use the standard function `end_that_request_last` to signal that the last request in a series has been submitted. Since this ensures that a disk is up and running, the function calls `laptop_io_completion`, which installs a timer on `laptop_mode_wb_timer` that executes `laptop_timer_fn` 1 second from now.

---

[7]Read operations require spinning up the disk anyway, so there's little that can be done here except to avoid useless reads.

> laptop_timer_fn starts pdflush with laptop_flush as the worker function. This causes a full synchronization to be performed.

❑ Recall from above that balance_dirty_pages activates a pdflush thread if the ratio of dirty pages in memory becomes too high. In laptop mode, however, pdflush is started as soon as some data have been written.

❑ try_to_free_pages is also slightly modified. If the routine decides to use a pdflush thread, then the number of pages that may be written back is not limited. This makes sense because if the disk needs to be spun up, then as much I/O as possible should be triggered.

Notice finally that laptop mode benefits from setting the values in /proc/sys/vm/dirty_writeback_centisec /proc/sys/vm/dirty_expire_centisec to large values. This will delay write operations longer than usual. When a write operation finally takes place, then the changes in laptop mode as described above automatically ensure that the spinning disk is brought to good use.

17.14 System Calls for Synchronization Control

The kernel synchronization mechanisms can be enabled from within userspace by various system calls to ensure full or partial data integrity between memory and block devices. Three basic options are available:

1. The *entire* cache contents can be flushed using the sync system call; in certain circumstances, this can be very time-consuming.

2. The contents of individual files (as well as the associated metadata of the inode) can be transferred to the underlying block device. The kernel provides the fsync and fdatasync system calls for this purpose. Whereas sync is normally used in conjunction with the sync system tool mentioned above, fsync and fdatasync are reserved for particular applications because the files to be flushed are selected by means of the process-specific file descriptors introduced in Chapter 8. There are therefore no generic userspace tools for writing back specific files.

3. msync is used to synchronize memory mappings.

17.15 Full Synchronization

As per kernel convention, the sync system call is implemented in sys_sync. Its code is held in fs/buffer.c, and the associated code flow diagram is shown in Figure 17-10.

The routine is very simply structured and consists of a chain of function calls (via do_sync) starting with wakeup_pdflush, which is invoked with the parameter 0. As described above, this triggers writeback of *all* dirty pages in the system.

The next step is synchronization of the inode metadata by means of sync_inodes. This is the first time we have come across this procedure that ensures that all inodes are written back. We take a closer look at it below.

sync_supers iterates over all superblocks in the super_blocks list and calls super_block->write_super if the routine exists. This triggers writing the superblock-specific information for each filesystem.

`sync_filesystems` synchronizes the mounted filesystems by iterating once more over the `super_blocks` list and invoking the `sync_fs` superblock operations routine for each filesystem that is mounted in Read/Write mode and provides a `sync_fs` method. The method is only called when explicit synchronization via a system call is requested and gives individual filesystems the ability to hook into the process. The Ext3 filesystem, for instance, uses the opportunity to start a commit of all currently running transactions.

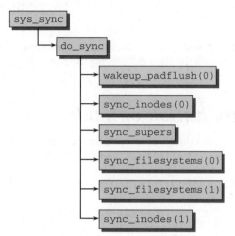

Figure 17-10: Code flow diagram for `sys_sync`.

As the code flow diagram shows, `sync_inodes` and `sync_filesystems` are invoked *twice*, first with the parameter 0 and then 1. The parameter specifies whether the functions are to wait until the write operations are finished (1) or whether they are to execute asynchronously (0). Splitting the operation into two passes allows the write operations to be initiated in the first pass. This triggers the synchronization of dirty pages associated with inodes, and also uses `write_inode` to synchronize the metadata. However, a filesystem implementation may choose just to dirty the buffers or pages that contain the metadata, but not send an actual write request to the block device. Since `sync_inodes` iterates over all dirty inodes, the small contributions from the individual metadata changes will pile up to a comparatively large amount of dirty data.

The second pass is therefore required for two reasons:

1. The dirtied pages resulting from the calls to `write_inode` are written to disk (synchronization of raw block devices ensures this). Since metadata changes need not be processed on a piece-by-piece basis, the approach improves write performance.

2. The kernel now explicitly waits for all write operations to complete that have been triggered — this is ensured because `WB_SYNC_ALL` is set in the second pass.

The two-pass behavior requires one change to `sync_sb_inodes` that I have not discussed yet. The second pass wants to wait for all pages that have been submitted. This includes the pages submitted during the first pass. Recall from our previous considerations (the overview in Figure 17-1 might be helpful here) that the corresponding wait operations are issued in `__sync_single_inode`. However, the function only sees inodes that have been present on one of the lists `s_dirty`, `s_io`, or `s_more_io` of the superblock when `sync_sb_inodes` is called. If `sync_sb_inodes` were called with `WB_SYNC_NONE` in the first pass, then the inodes would not be on any of these lists anymore, and waiting could not be performed!

For this purpose, the special writeback mode `WB_SYNC_HOLD` is introduced. It is nearly identical with `WB_SYNC_NONE`. The important difference is that inodes that have been synchronized are not removed from `s_io` in `sync_sb_inodes`, but are placed back onto the `s_dirty` list. Thus they are still visible in the second pass and can be waited for. The block layer can, nevertheless, start to write out data in between the passes.

The additional CPU time consumed by the redundant invocation of functions during the `sync` system call is negligible compared to the time needed for the slow I/O operations and is therefore totally acceptable.

17.15.1 Synchronization of Inodes

`sync_inodes` synchronizes all dirty inodes. Its code flow diagram is shown in Figure 17-11.

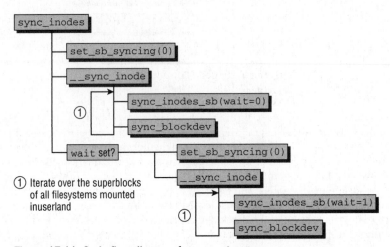

Figure 17-11: Code flow diagram for `sync_inodes`.

`sys_sync` is a *front end* that directs the real synchronization performed in `__sync_inodes`. Before `__sync_inodes` is called, the kernel uses `set_sb_syncing` to set the `s_syncing` element of `struct super_block` to 0 for all superblocks. This helps to avoid synchronization of superblocks from multiple places.

The `__sync_inodes` function iterates over all superblocks and invokes several methods for each block. The function has one parameter:

fs/fs-writeback.c
```
static void __sync_inodes(int wait)
```

`wait` is a Boolean variable that decides if the kernel should wait for write operations to finish or not. Recall from above that this behavior is essential for the `sync` system call.

This is what __sync_inodes does:

❏ If the superblock is currently being synchronized from another part of the kernel (i.e., if s_syncing of struct super_block is set), it is skipped. Otherwise, s_syncing is set to 1 to signal that this superblock is being synchronized to other places in the kernel.

❏ sync_inodes_sb synchronizes all dirty inodes associated with the superblock. The current page state is queried with get_page_state, and then the function creates an instance of writeback_control. There, the value of nr_to_write (maximum number of pages to be written) is set as follows:

fs/fs-writeback.c
```
unsigned long nr_dirty = global_page_state(NR_FILE_DIRTY);
unsigned long nr_unstable = global_page_state(NR_UNSTABLE_NFS);

wbc.nr_to_write = nr_dirty + nr_unstable +
(inodes_stat.nr_inodes - inodes_stat.nr_unused) +
nr_dirty + nr_unstable;
wbc.nr_to_write += wbc.nr_to_write / 2; /* Bit more for luck */
```

The computed value should usually suffice to cover all dirty pages of the system, but 50 percent more is added. This ensures that absolutely all dirty pages of the inode are written back, but avoids some concurrency problems that can appear if no limit is set on the number of pages that may be written.

Thereafter, the familiar sync_sb_inodes function is invoked to call the low-level synchronization routines of the various filesystems.

❏ The low-level synchronization routines of most filesystems simply mark buffers or pages as dirty but do not perform actual writeback. For this reason, the kernel then invokes sync_blockdev to synchronize all mappings of the block device on which the filesystem resides (in this step, the kernel is *not* restricted to a specific filesystem). This ensures that the data are actually written back.

17.15.2 *Synchronization of Individual Files*

The contents of individual files can be synchronized without the need to synchronize all the data in the system. This option is used by applications that must ensure that the data they modify in memory are always written back to the appropriate block device. Because normal write access operations first land in cache, this option provides added safety for really important data (of course, another alternative would be to use direct I/O operations that bypass the cache).

As already noted, several different system calls are available for this purpose:

1. fsync synchronizes the contents of a file and also writes the metadata associated with the file's inode back to the block device.

2. fdatasync writes back only the data contents and ignores the metadata.

3. sync_file_range is a comparatively new system call that was introduced in kernel 2.6.16. It allows for controlling synchronization for precisely defined parts of open files. Essentially, the implementation selects the desired pages for writeback and possibly awaits the result. Since this is not too different from the methods employed for the above system calls, I will not bother to discuss sync_file_range in detail.

The implementation of `fsync` and `fdatasync` differs only at a single point (to be more accurate, in a single character):

fs/sync.c
```
asmlinkage long sys_fsync(unsigned int fd)
{
        return __do_fsync(fd, 0);
}

asmlinkage long sys_fdatasync(unsigned int fd)
{
        return __do_fsync(fd, 1);
}
```

The code flow diagram for the common function __do_fsync is shown in Figure 17-12.

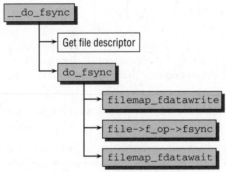

Figure 17-12: Code flow diagram for __do_sync.

Synchronization of a single file is relatively straightforward. `fget` is used to find the appropriate `file` instance by reference to the file descriptor, and then work is delegated to three functions:

1. `filemap_fdatawrite` (via a detour over `__filemap_fdatawrite` and `__filemap_fdatawrite_range`) first generates a `writeback_control` instance whose `nr_to_write` value (maximum number of pages to be flushed) is set to double the number of pages of the mapping to ensure that all pages are written back. Afterward, the familiar `do_writepages` method invokes the low-level write routines of the filesystem in which the file is located.

2. The filesystem-dependent `fsync` function found using the `file_operations` structure of the file is then invoked to write back the cached file data. This is where `fsync` and `fdatasync` differ — `fsync` has a parameter to specify whether metadata are also to be flushed as well as the regular caches. The parameter is set to 0 for `fsync` and to 1 for `fdatasync`.

3. Synchronization is then concluded by invoking `filemap_fdatawait` to wait for the end of the write operation initiated in `filemap_fdatawrite`. This ensures that the asynchronous write operations appear as synchronous to the user application because the system call does not return control to userspace until writeback of the desired data has been completed in the view of both the block layer and the filesystem layer.

The methods provided for `file_operations->fsync` are very similar for most filesystems. Figure 17-13 shows the code flow diagram for a generalized method.

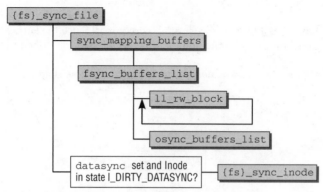

Figure 17-13: Code flow diagram for `f_op->fsync`.

The code performs two tasks:

1. `sync_mapping_buffers` writes back all private inode buffers in the `private_list` of the `mapping` instance. These normally hold indirection blocks or other internal filesystem data that are *not* part of the inode management data but are used to manage the data themselves.

   This function delegates work to `fsync_mapping_buffers`, which iterates over all buffers. The buffer data are written to the block layer by the `ll_rw_block` function with which you are familiar from Chapter 6. With the help of `osync_buffers_list`, the kernel then waits until the write operations have been completed (the block layer also buffers write accesses) and then ensures that synchronization of the associated metadata outside `sync_buffers_list` appears as a synchronous operation.

2. `fs_sync_inode` writes back the inode management data (i.e., the data held directly in the filesystem-specific inode structure). Note that the `datasync` argument of `fsync` must be set to (0) to invoke the method. This is the one and only difference between `fdatasync` and `fsync`.

Since writeback of inode management data is filesystem-specific, see Chapter 9.

17.15.3 Synchronization of Memory Mappings

The kernel provides the `msync` system call implemented in `sys_msync` to synchronize memory mappings in part or in total:

mm/msync.c
```
asmlinkage long sys_msync(unsigned long start, size_t len, int flags)
```

`start` and `len` select an area in the user address space of a process whose mapped data are to be synchronized with the underlying file.

The implementation of the system call is remarkably simple. As documented in the manual page msync(2), the system call essentially distinguishes two modes. If MS_SYNC is set in the flags, then dirty pages are written to disk synchronously, while MS_ASYNC is supposed to schedule dirty data for later writeback.

The good news is that for MS_ASYNC, no work at all is required! Since the kernel tracks the state of dirty pages, they will be synchronized at some point by the mechanisms described in this chapter anyway.

With MS_SYNC set, a little more work is necessary, and the code flow diagram in Figure 17-14 considers this case solely.

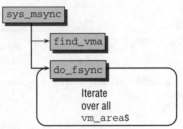

Figure 17-14: Code flow diagram for sys_msync with the flag MS_SYNC set.

find_vma finds the first vm_area instance in the selected area. vm_area->vm_file holds a pointer to the file instance from which the mapped data originate (this is discussed in Chapter 4). Therefore, do_fsync can be used to synchronize the file as described above.

The method is repeated for all intervals in the desired area. This is possible because the intervals are linked by means of vm_area->next, as discussed in Chapter 4.

17.16 Summary

Data are persistently stored on block devices but modified in RAM. This makes it necessary to synchronize the contents of both from time to time, and this chapter has introduced you to the corresponding methods. There are several system calls that allow for explicitly requesting that some portions of memory are written back to disk. Additionally, the kernel uses threads that perform the same job periodically to ensure that not too much modified data exist in RAM. While it is a good thing to keep disks busy, the kernel needs to ensure that not more information than the disk can handle is scheduled to be written back, and this chapter has discussed the techniques used to avoid congestion of the block layer. Additionally, some corrections are necessary for systems where power is scarce, and the policy changes in laptop mode have also been examined.

You have been introduced to all technical aspects of how data are shuffled back and forth between block devices and RAM by now. What is still lacking is the decision of *which* pages are supposed to be synchronized or discarded from RAM once the kernel gets short on memory, which is the subject of the next chapter.

18

Page Reclaim
and Swapping

The available RAM memory in a computer is never enough to meet user needs or to always satisfy memory-intensive applications. The kernel therefore enables seldom-used parts of memory to be swapped out to block devices, effectively providing more main memory. This mechanism, which is referred to as *swapping* or *paging*, is implemented transparently by the kernel for application processes that automatically profit from it. Swapping, however, is not the only mechanism to evict pages from memory. If a seldom-used page is backed by a block device (e.g., memory mappings of files) then the modified pages need not be swapped out, but can be directly *synchronized* with the block device. The page frame can be reused, and if the data are required again, it can be reconstructed from the source. If a page is backed by a file but cannot be modified in memory (e.g., binary executable data), then it can be *discarded* if it is currently not required. All three techniques, together with the selection of policy for pages that experience little activity, go by the name of *page reclaim*. Notice that pages allocated for the core kernel (i.e., not for caches) cannot be reclaimed because this would complicate things more than it would benefit them.

Page reclaim is the cornerstone to one of the kernel's fundamental decisions with respect to caching. The size of caches is never fixed, and they can grow as necessary. The rationale behind this is simple: RAM that is not used for something is simply wasted, so it should *always* be used to cache something. If, however, some important task requires memory that is filled by the caches, the kernel can *reclaim* memory to support these needs. This Chapter describes how swapping and page reclaim are implemented.

18.1 Overview

Synchronization of data with the underlying block device as described in the previous chapter makes the situation easier for the kernel when the available RAM memory limit has been reached. Writing back cached data allows some memory pages to be released in order to make RAM available for more important functions. Since the data involved can be read in again from the block device as and when required, this does take time, but no information is lost.

Naturally, this procedure also has its limits. At some time the point is reached where the caches and buffers can no longer be shrunk. Furthermore, it does not work for pages whose content is generated dynamically and that have no backing store.

As in typical systems (with the exception of some embedded or handheld PCs) considerably more hard disk capacity is generally available than RAM memory space, the kernel — in conjunction with the capability of the processor to manage virtual address spaces that are larger than the existing RAM memory — can "commandeer" parts of the disk in order to use them as memory expansions. Since hard disks are considerably slower than RAM memory, swapping is purely an emergency solution that keeps the system running but at considerably reduced speed.

The term *swapping* originally referred to the swapping-out of an entire process — with all its data, program code, and the like — and *not* to the page-by-page, selective exporting of process data to secondary expanded RAM memory. While this strategy was adopted in *very* early versions of UNIX, where it was perhaps sometimes appropriate, such behavior is now inconceivable. The resultant latency times during context switching would make interactive working not just sluggish but intolerably slow. However, a distinction is not made between swapping and paging below. Both stand for the fine-grained swapping-out of process data. This is now established usage of the terms not just amongst experts but also (and above all) in the kernel sources.

Two questions must be answered when considering how to implement swapping and page reclaim in the kernel:

1. According to what scheme should pages be reclaimed; that is, how does the kernel decide which pages it should reclaim in order to ensure maximum possible benefit and least possible disadvantage?

2. How are pages that have been swapped out organized in the swap area, and how does the kernel write pages to the swap area and read them in again later? How does it synchronize pages with their backing device?

The question as to which memory pages are swapped out and which ones remain in RAM is crucial to system performance. If the kernel selects a frequently used page, a page in memory is then briefly freed for other purposes. However, because the original data are soon needed again, another page must be swapped out to create a free page to hold the data that have just been swapped out and are now required again. This is obviously not very efficient and must therefore be prevented.

18.1.1 Swappable Pages

Only a few kinds of pages may be swapped out to a swap area — all others have an alternative backing storage on a block device that is used instead:

❑ Pages of the MAP_ANONYMOUS category that are not associated with a file (or are a mapping of /dev/zero); for example, a process stack or memory area mapped anonymously using mmap. (The reference manual on the GNU C standard library or the customary standard reference works on system programming provide further information on mappings of this kind.)

❑ Private mappings of a process used to map files in which changes are *not* written to the underlying block device, as would normally be the case. As the file is no longer available as a backing store in this case, the pages must be swapped out to the swap area if RAM memory becomes scarce since the contents can no longer be restored from the file. The kernel (and therefore the C standard library) uses the MAP_PRIVATE flag to create mappings of this type.

❑   All pages that belong to the process heap and were reserved using `malloc` (and consequently using the `brk` system call or ultimately an anonymous mapping); see Chapter 3

❑   Pages that are used to implement one of the interprocess communication mechanisms. These include, for instance, shared memory pages that are used to exchange data between processes.

Memory pages used by the kernel itself are *never* swapped out. The reasons are obvious. The complexity of the kernel code would increase dramatically. Since the kernel does not require very much memory as compared to other user applications, the potential gain is too low to justify the additional effort.

Naturally, pages used to map peripherals to memory space cannot be swapped out either. This would make no sense, especially as the pages are used only as a means of communication between the application and the device and not for actually storing data persistently.

> **Even though it is not possible to swap out all page types, the kernel's swapping page reclaim must still cater to page types that are based on other backing stores. The most frequent page types of this kind relate to data from files that are mapped into memory. Ultimately, it is irrelevant which pages from *which* category are written from RAM memory to backing store because the effect is always the same — a page frame is freed to make space for more important data that must reside in the RAM.**

18.1.2   Page Thrashing

A further problem that may occur when performing swapping operations is *page thrashing*. As the term implies, this involves intensive transfers between swap space and RAM memory; this boils down to nothing more than the repeated backward and forward swapping of pages. This phenomenon tends to increase as the number of system processes increases. It occurs when important data are swapped out and are needed again very soon afterward.

The main problem that the kernel must address to prevent page thrashing is to determine the *working set* of a process (in other words, the pages that are needed most frequently) as accurately as possible so that the least important pages can be moved to the swap area or some other backing store and the really important data can be kept in memory.

To do this, the kernel needs an appropriate algorithm to evaluate the importance of pages to the overall system. On the one hand, pages must be evaluated as fairly as possible so that processes are not unduly favored or disadvantaged. On the other hand, the algorithm must be implemented simply and efficiently to ensure that not too much processing time is needed to select the pages to be swapped out.

The many CPU types provide different methods of supporting the kernel in this task that vary in their level of sophistication. However, Linux is not able to use all methods as they are not always available on simpler CPUs and may also be difficult to emulate. As usual, the lowest common denominator must be found upon which the kernel can build its hardware-independent layers.

One particularly simple, but important trick that is completely independent of the processor's abilities is to keep a *swap token* in the system that is given to one single process that swaps in pages. The kernel tries to avoid swapping out pages from this process, thus alleviating its situation by giving it some time to, hopefully, finish a task. After some time, the swap token is passed to some other process that also undergoes swapping and requires memory more exigent than the current token holder.

18.1.3 Page-Swapping Algorithms

Over the last few decades, a whole host of algorithms has been developed for purposes of page swapping, each of which has its own specific advantages and disadvantages. The general literature on operating systems includes detailed descriptions and analyses. Below, two techniques on which the Linux swapping implementation is based are described.

Second Chance

Second chance is an algorithm that is extremely simple to implement and that features a minor modification to a classical FIFO algorithm. A system's pages are managed in a linked list. When a page fault occurs, the newly referenced page is placed at the beginning of the list; this automatically moves the existing pages back by one position. Since only a finite number of positions are available in the FIFO queue, the system must reach its capacity limit at some point or other. When it does, the pages at the end of the queue "drop off" the list and are swapped out. When they are needed again, the processor triggers a page fault that causes the kernel to read the page data in again and to place the page at the start of the list.

For obvious reasons, this procedure is not particularly smart. When pages are swapped out, no account is taken of whether the pages are used frequently or rarely. After a given number of page faults (determined by how many places there are in the queue), the page is written into the swap area. If it is required frequently, it is read in again immediately — not to the benefit of system performance.

This situation can be improved by offering a page a *second chance* before it is swapped out. Each page is assigned a special field containing a bit that is controlled by the hardware. When the page is accessed, the bit is automatically set to 1. The software (kernel) is responsible for un-setting the bit.

When a page reaches the end of the list, the kernel does not immediately swap it out but first checks whether the aforementioned bit is set. If it is, it is unset and the page is moved to the start of the FIFO queue; in other words, it is treated like a new page that has been added to the system. If the bit is not set, the page is swapped out.

Thanks to this extension, the algorithm does take minimum account of whether pages are used frequently or not, but does not deliver the performance expected of state-of-the-art memory management. Nevertheless, the second chance algorithm is a good starting point when combined with other techniques.

LRU Algorithm

LRU is short for *least recently used* and refers to various algorithms that attempt to find least used pages according to a similar scheme. This reverse approach avoids the need for more complex searching for most used pages.

Clearly, pages frequently used over a short period in the recent past are likely to be used in the (near) future. The LRU algorithm is based on the converse assumption that pages not used recently will not be needed frequently in the immediate future. Such pages are therefore likely candidates for swap-out when memory is scarce.

The fundamental LRU principle may be simple, but it is difficult to implement it appropriately. How can the kernel mark or sort pages as simply as possible in order to estimate access frequency without requiring an inordinate amount of time to organize data structures? The simplest LRU variant uses a (doubly) linked list with all the pages in the system. This list is resorted each time memory is accessed. The page in question is found and moved to the start of the list. In the course of time, this results in a kind of "equilibrium" in which frequently used pages are at the beginning of the list and least used pages are right at the end (a similar algorithm is used to manage the buffer caches discussed in Chapter 16).

The algorithm works beautifully but can only be implemented effectively for a small number of elements. This means that it cannot be used in its unadulterated form for memory management as this would be far too costly in terms of system performance. Simpler implementations that consume less CPU time are therefore required.

Special support by the processor makes implementation of the LRU algorithm significantly less costly. Unfortunately, this support is available on few architectures and cannot be used by Linux; after all, memory management should not be tailored to a specific processor type. A counter is then incremented by 1 in each CPU period. After each page access, a further counter field for the page is set to the value of the system counter. The processor itself must perform this action to ensure sufficient speed. If a page fault occurs because a required page is no longer available, the operating system need only compare the counters of all pages to ascertain which page was accessed the longest time ago. This technique still necessitates searching through the list of all memory pages every time a page fault occurs but does not require lengthy list operations after each memory access.

18.2 Page Reclaim and Swapping in the Linux Kernel

This section summarizes the design decisions of the Linux page reclaim subsystem before considering the technical aspects of implementation and examining how requirements are met.

Swapping out pages and all related actions do not appear to be very complicated when the situation is viewed from the high ground without taking development details into consideration. Unfortunately, the very opposite is the case. Hardly any part of the kernel entails as many technical difficulties as the virtual memory subsystem, of which the implementation of swapping is a part. Not only a host of minor hardware details but above all numerous interconnections in the kernel must be taken into account if implementation is to succeed. Speed also plays a crucial role since system performance ultimately depends on memory management performance. Not without reason is memory management one of the hottest kernel development topics, which has given rise to countless discussions, flame wars, and rival implementations.

When discussing the design of the swap subsystem, certain aspects come to mind as characterized by the following questions:

❑   How should swap areas on block storage media be organized to ensure not only that pages swapped out can be uniquely identified, but also that memory space is used as effectively as possible to permit read and write operations at maximum speed?

❑   Which methods are available to enable the kernel to check when and how many pages need to be swapped out in order to achieve the best possible balance between the provision of free page frames for upcoming needs and minimization of the time needed to perform swap operations?

❑ According to which criteria should the pages be selected for swapping? In other words, which page replacement algorithm should be used?

❑ How are page faults handled as effectively and quickly as possible, and how are pages returned from a swap area to system RAM?

❑ Which data can be removed from the various system caches (from the inode or dentry cache, e.g.) *without* a backing store because it can be reconstructed indirectly? This question is not, in fact, directly related to the execution of swapping operations but concerns both the cache and swap subsystems. However, as cache shrinking is initiated by the swap subsystem, this question is addressed below in this chapter.

As I have demonstrated, not only are the technical details of paramount importance in achieving an efficient and powerful implementation of the swap system, but the design of the overall system must also support the best possible interaction between the various components to ensure that actions are performed smoothly and harmoniously.

18.2.1 Organization of the Swap Area

Swapped-out pages are held either on a dedicated partition without a filesystem or in a file of fixed size in an existing filesystem. As every system administrator knows, several such areas can be used in parallel. It is also possible to assign priorities based on the speed of the various swap areas. These priorities can then be adopted by the kernel when it uses the swap areas.

Each swap area is subdivided into a number of continuous *slots*, each of which is precisely the size of one page frame in the system. On most processors this is still 4 KiB. However, larger pages are commonly used on newer systems.

Basically, any page in the system can be accommodated in any slot of a swap area. However, the kernel also uses a structuring method referred to as *clustering* to handle accesses to swap areas as quickly as possible. Consecutive pages in the memory area of a process (or at least pages that are swapped out consecutively) are written to the hard disk one after the other, with a particular cluster size — normally 256 pages. If no further memory space is available in the swap area for clusters of this size, the kernel adds the pages at any positions that are currently free.

If several swap areas with the same priority are used, the kernel uses a round robin process to ensure that they are utilized as uniformly as possible. If the swap areas have different priorities, the kernel fills the ones with higher priority first before gradually moving on to the ones with lower priority.

To keep track of which pages are where in which swap partition, the kernel must retain some data structures that hold this information in memory. The most important structure element is a bitmap that tracks the used and free state of the slots in a swap area. Other elements yield data to support selection of the slot to be used next and to help implement clustering.

Two userspace tools are available to create and enable swap areas; these are `mkswap` (for "formatting" a swap partition/file) and `swapon` (for enabling a swap area). As these programs are crucial to a functioning swap subsystem, they are described (and the system call for `swapon`) below.

18.2.2 Checking Memory Utilization

Prior to swapping out pages, the kernel checks memory utilization to identify whether capacity is low. As when synchronizing pages, the kernel uses a combination of two mechanisms:

1. A periodic daemon (kswapd) runs in the background and repeatedly checks current memory utilization in order to initiate page swap-out when a particular threshold value is reached. This method ensures that no swap storms occur in which a very large number of pages suddenly need to be swapped out; this would result in long wait times and must be prevented on all accounts.

2. Nevertheless, the kernel must expect acute memory shortage whenever, for example, a large memory area is allocated by the buddy system or when buffers are generated. If insufficient RAM is available to satisfy the request for memory, the kernel must attempt to free space by swapping out pages as quickly as possible. Swap-out in the event of an acute emergency is part of *direct reclaim*.

The VM subsystem has only one option if a kernel request for memory cannot be satisfied even after pages have been swapped out — the targeted termination of a process by means of the OOM (out of memory) killer. Even if this sometimes entails severe losses, it is still better than a complete system crash, which would otherwise result.

18.2.3 Selecting Pages to Be Swapped Out

The key question faced by the swapping subsystem is always the same. Which pages can be swapped out to ensure maximum benefits at minimum cost to the system? The kernel uses a mixture of the ideas discussed earlier and implements a rough-grained LRU method that makes use of only one hardware feature — the setting of an accessed bit following a page access — because this function is available on all supported architectures and can be emulated with little effort.

In contrast to the general algorithms, the LRU implementation of the kernel is based on *two* linked lists that are referred to as the *active* and the *inactive* list (separate lists exist for each memory zone in the system). As the two names imply, all the pages in active use are on the one list, while all inactive pages that may be mapped into one or more processes but are not very frequently used are held on the other. To distribute the pages between the lists, the kernel performs a regular balancing operation that determines — by means of the above accessed bit — whether a page is regarded as active or inactive, in other words, whether or not it is frequently accessed by the applications in the system. Transfers between the two lists are possible in both directions. Pages can be transferred from active to inactive and vice versa. However, transfer does *not* take place after every single page access but at longer intervals.

In the course of time, the least frequently used pages collect at the end of the *inactive* list. When there is a memory shortage, the kernel selects these pages for swap-out. Since these pages have been little used so far, the LRU principle dictates that this will prove least disruptive to system operation.

18.2.4 Handling Page Faults

All architectures on which Linux runs support the concept of page faults that are triggered when a page in virtual address space is accessed but is not present in physical memory. The page fault instructs the kernel to read the missing data from the swap area or from another backing store, possibly by first deleting other pages to make space for the new data.

Page fault handling is in two parts. First, strongly processor-dependent (assembler) code must be used to intercept the page fault and query the associated data. Second, a system-independent part of code is responsible for the further handling of the situation. Because of optimizations used by the kernel when managing processes, it is not sufficient to simply search for the relevant page in the backing store and load it into the RAM memory because the page fault may have been triggered for other reasons (see Chapter 4). For example, copy-on-write pages may be involved; these are copied only when a write access is executed after a process has `forked`. Page faults also occur with demand paging, where the pages of a mapping are loaded only when actually needed. I ignore these problems here, however, and focus on the situation in which a swapped-out page must be reloaded into memory.

Once again, there's more to be done than just finding the page in the swap area. As access to the hard disk is even slower than usual if the read head has to move to a new position (disk seek), the kernel uses a readahead mechanism to guess which pages will be needed next and also includes these in the read operation. Thanks to the clustering method mentioned above, the Read/Write head ideally only moves forward and does not have to jump backward and forward when reading consecutive pages.

18.2.5 Shrinking Kernel Caches

Swapping out pages that belong to userspace applications is not the kernel's only way of freeing memory space. Shrinking numerous caches often results in good gains. Here, too, the kernel must naturally weigh up the pros and cons by deciding which data are to be removed from caches and how far the memory space available for this data may be shrunk without impairing system performance too much. As kernel caches are generally not particularly huge, the kernel begins to shrink them only as a last resort.

As explained in previous chapters, the kernel provides various caches in numerous different areas. This makes it very difficult to define a general scheme according to which caches can be shrunk because it is difficult to asses the importance of the data they contain. For this reason, earlier kernel versions featured numerous caches-specific functions to perform this task for the individual caches.

The methods of shrinking the various caches are still implemented separately today since the structures of the individual variants differ too greatly to allow the adoption of a generally applicable shrinking algorithm. However, a general framework is now available to manage the cache-shrinking methods. Functions written to shrink caches are referred to as *shrinkers* in the kernel and can be registered dynamically. When memory is scarce, the kernel invokes all registered shrinkers to obtain fresh memory.

18.3 Managing Swap Areas

Linux is relatively flexible in its support for swap areas. As we have already explained, it is possible to manage several areas with different priorities, and these may be located both on local partitions and in files of a predefined size. Swap partitions can also be added and removed dynamically in an active system without the need for rebooting.

The technical differences between the various approaches are made as transparent as possible to userspace. The modular structure of the kernel also means that the algorithms associated with swapping can be of a generalized design where the differences between the approaches need only be addressed on the lower technical levels.

18.3.1 Data Structures

As usual, the description begins with a presentation of the central data structures that form the backbone of implementation and hold all the information and data needed by the kernel. The cornerstone of swap area management is the `swap_info` array defined in `mm/swap-info.c;` its entries store information on the individual swap areas in the system[1]:

mm/swapfile.c
```
struct swap_info_struct swap_info[MAX_SWAPFILES];
```

The number of elements is defined statically in `MAX_SWAPFILES` at compilation time. The constant is normally defined as $2^5 = 32$.

> The kernel uses the term *swap file* to refer not only to swap files but also to swap partitions; the array therefore includes both types. As normally only one swap file is used, the limitation to a specific number is of no relevance. Neither does this number impose any kind of restriction on numerical calculations or other memory-intensive programs because, depending on architecture, swap areas may now have sizes in the gigabyte range. The restriction to 128 MiB in older versions no longer applies.

Characterization of Swap Areas

struct `swap_info_struct` describes a swap area and is defined as follows:

<swap.h>
```
struct swap_info_struct {
        unsigned int flags;
        int prio;                          /* swap priority */
        struct file *swap_file;
        struct block_device *bdev;
        struct list_head extent_list;
        struct swap_extent *curr_swap_extent;
        unsigned short * swap_map;
        unsigned int lowest_bit;
        unsigned int highest_bit;
        unsigned int cluster_next;
        unsigned int cluster_nr;
        unsigned int pages;
        unsigned int max;
        unsigned int inuse_pages;
        int next;                          /* next entry on swap list */
};
```

The main data on the swap state can be quickly queried with the help of the `proc` filesystem:

```
wolfgang@meitner> cat /proc/swaps
Filename                           Type       Size    Used   Priority
/dev/hda5                          partition  136512  96164  1
/mnt/swap1                         file       65556   6432   0
/tmp/swap2                         file       65556   6432   0
```

---

[1]During the development of kernel 2.6.18, the ability to migrate pages physically between NUMA nodes while keeping their virtual addresses has been added. This requires using two `swap_info` entries to handle pages that are currently under migration, so the number of possible swap files is reduced. The configuration option `MIGRATION` is required to include the page migration code. This is, for instance, helpful on NUMA systems, where pages can be moved nearer to processors using them, or for memory hot remove. Page migration, however, is not considered in detail in this book.

A dedicated partition and two files are used to accommodate the swap areas in this example. The swap partition has the highest priority and is therefore used preferentially by the kernel. Both files have priority 0 and are used on the basis of a round robin process when no more space is available on the partition with priority 0. (How it can nevertheless occur that there are data in the swap files although the swap partition is not completely full, as indicated by the `proc` output, is explained below.)

What is the meaning of the various elements in the `swap_info_struct` structure? The first entries are used to hold the classical management data required for swap areas:

❏ The state of the swap area can be described with various flags stored in the `flags` element. `SWP_USED` specifies that the entry in the swap array is used. Since the array is otherwise filled with zeros, a distinction can easily be made between used and unused elements. `SWP_WRITEOK` specifies that the swap area may be written to. Both flags are set after a swap area has been inserted into the kernel; the abbreviation for this state is `SWP_ACTIVE`.

❏ `swap_file` points to the `file` structure associated with the swap area (the layout and contents of the structure are discussed in Chapter 8). With swap partitions, there is a pointer to the device file of the partition on the block device (in our example, `/dev/hda5`). With swap files, this pointer is to the `file` instance of the relevant file, that is, `/mnt/swap1` or `/tmp/swap2` in our example.

❏ `bdev` points to the `block_device` structure of the underlying block device.

> *Even if all swap areas in our example are located on the same block device (`/dev/hda`), all three entries point to different instances of the data structure. This is because the two files are on different partitions of the hard disk and the swap partition is a separate partition anyway. Since, in structural terms, the kernel manages partitions essentially as if they were autonomous block devices, this results in three different pointers to the three swap areas, although all are located on the same disk.*

❏ The relative priority of a swap area is held in the `prio` element. Since this is a signed data type, both positive and negative priorities are possible. As already noted, the higher a swap partition's priority is, the more important the swap partition is.

❏ The total number of usable page slots, each of which can store a complete memory page, is held in `pages`. For example, the swap partition in our sample mapping has space for 34,128 pages, which, given a page size of 4 KiB in the IA-32 system used for the mapping, corresponds to a memory volume of $\approx$ 128 MiB.

❏ `max` yields the total number of page slots that the swap area contains. In contrast to `pages`, not just usable pages but *all* pages are counted here — including those that (owing to block device faults, e.g.) are defective or are used for management purposes. Because defective blocks are extremely rare on state-of-the-art hard disks (and swap partitions need not necessarily be created in such an area), `max` is typically only 1 greater than `pages`, as is the case with all three swap areas in the example above. There are two reasons for this one-page difference. First, the very first page of a swap area is used by the kernel for identification purposes (after all, totally random parts of the disk should not be overwritten with swap data). Second, the kernel also uses the first slot to store state information, such as the size of the area and a list of defective section, and this information must be permanently retained.

❏ `swap_map` is a pointer to an array of short integers (which is unsurprisingly referred to as *swap map* in the following) that contains as many elements as there are page slots in the swap area. It is used as an access counter for the individual slots to indicate the number of processes that share the swapped-out pages.

❏ The kernel uses a somewhat unusual method to link the various elements in the swap list according to priority. Since the data of the various areas are arranged in the elements of a linear array, the next variable is defined to create a relative order between the areas despite the fixed array positions. next is used as an index for swap_info[]. This enables the kernel to track the individual entries according to their priority.

But how is it possible to determine which swap area is to be used *first*? Since this area is not necessarily located at the first array position, the kernel also defines the global variable swap_list in mm/swapfile.c. It is an instance of the swap_list_t data type defined specifically for the purpose of finding the first swap area:

<swap.h>
```
struct swap_list_t {
        int head;       /* head of priority-ordered swapfile list */
        int next;       /* swapfile to be used next */
};
```

head is an index into the swap_info[] array and is used to select the swap area with the highest priority. The kernel works its way through the list to the swap areas with low priorities using the next elements. next is used to implement a round robin process to uniformly fill multiple swap areas with pages if the areas have the same priority. I return to this variable below when I examine how the kernel selects swap pages.

Let us take a close look at the system's mode of operation by reference to the example above. The entry point is the first array entry that contains the swap area with the highest priority. The value of head is therefore 0.

next specifies which swap area is used next. This need not always be the swap area with the highest priority. If the latter is already full, next points to another swap area.

❏   In order to reduce search times when the complete swap area is scanned for a free slot, the kernel manages the upper and lower limits of the search zone with the aid of the lowest_bit and highest_bit elements. There are no free pages above or below these positions so it would be pointless to search this area.

> Although the names of the two variables end with _bit, they are *not* bit fields but absolutely normal integers that are interpreted as indexes with regard to the linearly arranged pages of a swap area.

❏   The kernel also provides two elements — cluster_next and cluster_nr — to implement the cluster technique mentioned briefly above. The former specifies which slot of an existing cluster in the swap area is to be used next, and cluster_nr indicates how many pages are still available for use in the current cluster before it is necessary to start a new cluster, or (if not enough free pages are available for a new cluster) that recourse is made to fine-grained allocation.

Extents for Implementing Non-Contiguous Swap Areas

The kernel uses the extent_list and curr_swap_extent elements to implement *extents*, which create mappings between the swap slots that are assumed to be contiguous and the disk blocks of the swap file. This is not necessary if partitions are used as the basis for swap space because the kernel can then rely on the fact that the blocks on the disk are arranged linearly. Mapping between page slots and disk blocks is therefore very simple. Starting from the position of the first block, it is only necessary to multiply a constant offset by the required page number in order to obtain the required address, as illustrated in Figure 18-1. In this case, just one swap_extent instance is needed. (Actually, this could also be dispensed with, but its existence makes things easier for the kernel as it narrows the differences between partition swap areas and file swap areas.)

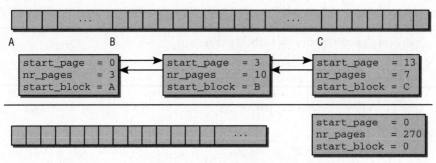

Figure 18-1: Extents for managing non-contiguous swap areas.

The situation is more complicated when files are used as the basis for swap memory because there is then no guarantee that all blocks of the file are located sequentially on disk. Consequently, mapping between page slots and disk blocks is more complex. Figure 18-1 illustrates this by means of an example.

A file consists of multiple sections located anywhere on the block device. (The lesser disk fragmentation there is, the smaller the number of sections — after all, it is best if file data are kept as close together as possible, as discussed in Chapter 9.) The `extent_list` list has the task of associating the scattered blocks of the file with the linear page slots. In doing so, it should ensure two things — that as little memory space as possible is used, and that search time is kept to a minimum.

It is not necessary to associate the page slot and block number for *every* page slot. It is sufficient to associate the first block of a contiguous block group with the corresponding page slot and to note how many blocks there are after the first block so that the file structure can be reproduced in a very compact manner.

Let us illustrate the procedure using the example above. As the figure shows, the first three contiguous block groups consist of 3, 10, and 7 blocks. What happens when the kernel wants to read the data of the sixth page slot? These data are not in the first block group as this block contains only slots 0 through 2. The search terminates successfully at the second group, which contains slots 3 through 12 and logically slot 6. The kernel must therefore determine the start block of the second group (using the extent list). The group's third member (which corresponds to the sixth page slot) can be found easily by twice adding the page size to the start address as the offset.

The extent structure `struct extent_list` is defined to serve exactly this purpose:

```
<swap.h>
struct swap_extent {
        struct list_head list;
        pgoff_t start_page;
        pgoff_t nr_pages;
        sector_t start_block;
};
```

`list` is used to manage the members of the extent list on a doubly linked standard list. The other members describe the data of a single, contiguous block group:

❑   The number of the first page slot in a block group is held in `start_page`.

❑   `nr_pages` specifies the number of pages that fit into the block group.

❑   `start_block` is the block number of the first block of the group on the hard disk.

These lists can become extremely long. The two sample swap areas in files that each contain around 16,000 pages consist of, for example, 37 or even 76 block groups. The second extent mechanism requirement — high search speed — is not always met by doubly linked lists since they may well comprise hundreds of entries. It is, of course, extremely time-consuming to scan through such lists each time the swap area is accessed.

The solution is relatively simple. An additional element called `curr_swap_extent` in `swap_info_struct` is used to hold a pointer to the last element accessed in the extent list. Each new search starts from this element. As access is often made to consecutive page slots, the searched block is generally found in this or the next extent element.[2]

If the search by the kernel is not immediately successful, the entire extent list must be scanned element-by-element until the entry for the required block is found.

18.3.2 Creating a Swap Area

New swap partitions are not created directly by the kernel itself. This task is delegated to a userspace tool (`mkswap`) whose sources are in the `util-linux-ng` tool collection. Since creating a swap area is a mandatory step that must be performed before swap memory can be used, let's briefly analyze the mode of operation of this utility.

The kernel need not provide any new system calls to support the creation of swap areas — after all, it also does not provide any system calls to create regular filesystems, and this is clearly not a kernel problem. The existing call variants for direct communication with block devices (or, in the case of a swap file, with a file on a block device) are quite sufficient to organize the swap area in accordance with kernel requirements.

`mkswap` requires just one argument — the name of the device file of the partition or file in which the swap area is to be created.[3] The following actions are performed:

❑ The size of the required swap area is divided by the page size of the machine concerned in order to determine how many page frames can be accommodated.

❑ The blocks of the swap area are checked individually for read or write errors in order to find defective areas. As the machine's page size is used as the block size for swap areas, a defective block always means that the swap area's capacity is reduced by one page.

❑ A list with the addresses of all defective blocks is written to the first page of the swap area.

---

[2]A comment in the kernel sources notes that measurements have demonstrated that on average only 0.3 list operations are, in fact, needed to create a mapping between a page slot and a block number.

[3]Other parameters such as the explicit size of the swap area or the page size can be specified. However, in most cases, this is pointless because these data can be calculated automatically and reliably. The authors of `mkswap` do not have a high opinion of users who make their own explicit specifications, as the source code shows:

```
if (block_count) {
/* this silly user specified the number of blocks explicitly */
...
}
```

❑ To identify the swap area as such to the kernel (after all, it could simply be a normal partition with filesystem data which, of course, may not be inadvertently overwritten if the administrator uses an invalid swap area), the SWAPSPACE2 label is set to the end of the first page.[4]

❑ The number of available pages is also stored in the header of the swap area. This figure is calculated by subtracting the number of defective pages from the total number of available pages. 1 must also be subtracted from this number since the first page is used for state information and for the list of defective blocks.

> Although it may seem very important to deal with defective blocks when a swap area is created, this activity can simply be skipped. In this case, mkswap does not check the data area for errors and consequently does not write any data into the list of defective blocks. Since the quality of today's hardware means that very few errors occur on block devices, an explicit check is normally not needed.

18.3.3 Activating a Swap Area

Interaction with userspace is required in order to notify the kernel that an area initialized with mkswap is to be used as RAM expansion. The kernel provides the swapon system call for this purpose. As usual, it is implemented in sys_swapon whose code resides in mm/swapfile.c.

Although sys_swapon is one of the kernel's longer functions, it is not particularly complex. It performs the following actions.

❑ In a first step, the kernel searches for a free element in the swap_info array. Initial values are then assigned to the entry. If a block device partition provides the swap area, the associated block_device instance is claimed with bd_claim. Recall from Chapter 6.5.2 that the function claims a block device for a specific holder (in this case the swap implementation) and signalizes to other parts of the kernel that the device is already attached to it.

❑ After the swap file (or swap partition) has been opened, the first page containing information on bad blocks and the area size is read in.

❑ setup_swap_extents initializes the extent list. We examine this function in more detail below.

❑ As the last step, the new area is added to the swap list according to its priority. As described above, the swap list is defined using the next elements of the swap_info_struct entries. Two global variables are also updated:

  ❑ nr_swap_pages specifies the total number of swap pages currently available; it is incremented by the relevant number of pages provided by the newly activated swap area since the new pages are still completely unused.

  ❑ total_swap_pages yields the *total* number of swap pages, regardless of how many are used and how many are still free. This value is also incremented by the number of swap pages in the new swap area.

If no explicit priority is specified for the new area when the system call is invoked, the kernel uses the lowest existing priority minus 1. According to this scheme, new swap areas are included in descending priority unless the administrator intervenes manually.

---

[4]Earlier versions of the kernel used a different swap area format labeled SWAP-SPACE. This had certain disadvantages — above all, the maximum size limits of 128 or 512 MiB depending on CPU type — and is now no longer supported by the kernel.

Reading the Swap Area Characteristics

The characteristics of a swap area are held in the first page slot of the area. The kernel uses the following structure to interpret these data:

```
<swap.h>
union swap_header {
        struct
        {
                char reserved[PAGE_SIZE - 10];
                char magic[10];                 /* SWAP-SPACE or SWAPSPACE2 */
        } magic;
        struct
        {
                char            bootbits[1024];  /* Space for disklabel etc. */
                __u32           version;
                __u32           last_page;
                __u32           nr_badpages;
                unsigned char   sws_uuid[16];
                unsigned char   sws_volume[16];
                __u32           padding[117];
                __u32           badpages[1];
        } info;
};
```

The `union` allows *identical* data to be interpreted in different ways, as illustrated in Figure 18-2.

❑ The first 1,024 bytes are left free to create space for boot loaders that on some architectures must be present at defined places on the hard disk. This enables swap areas to be positioned right at the start of a disk on such architectures even though boot loader code is also located there.

❑ Details of the swap area version (`version`) then follow, plus the number of the last page (`nr_lastpage`) and the number of unusable pages (`nr_badpages`). A list with the number of unusable blocks follows after 117 integer filler entries, which can be used for additional information in any new versions of the swap format. Even if formally this list has only one element in the data structure, it has in reality `nr_badpages` members.

`label` and `uuid` allow associating a label and a UUID (Universally Unique Identifier) with a swap partition. The kernel does not use these fields, but they are required by some userland tools (the manual page `blkid8` provides more information about the rationale behind these identifiers).

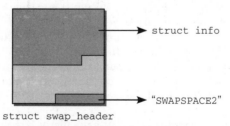

struct swap_header

Figure 18-2: Layout of the swap header.

The reason why two data structures are used to analyze this information is historical (new information is created only in areas that were not used by the old format — in other words, between the 1,024 reserved bytes at the start of the partition and the signature at the end), but is also partly because the kernel must be able to handle different page sizes, and this is simpler if different structures are used. Since information is located at the start *and* at the end of the first swap page, the space between must be filled with a suitable number of empty filler elements — at least from the data structure's viewpoint. However, access to the swap signature at the bottom end of the page is easier if the fill space required is calculated by simply deducting the length of the signature (10 characters) from the page size — which is specified by PAGE_SIZE on all architectures. This yields the required position. When the upper elements are accessed, it is only necessary to specify the definition of the upper part. From the viewpoint of the data structure, the data that then follow are of no interest since they merely contain the list of bad blocks whose array position addresses can be calculated very easily.

Creating the Extent List

setup_swap_extents is used to create the extent list. The associated code flow diagram is shown in Figure 18-3.

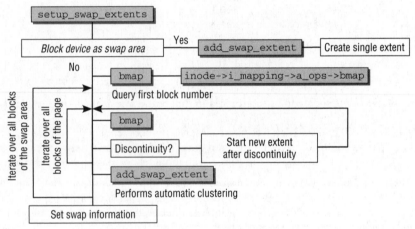

Figure 18-3: Code flow diagram for setup_swap_extents.

The task of the procedure is simple when a swap partition rather than a swap file is used. It is then guaranteed that all sectors are contained in a contiguous list; consequently, only a single entry is required in the extent list. This entry is created using add_swap_extent and includes all blocks in the partition.

If the swap area is a file, the kernel is required to do a little more work since the blocks of the file must be scanned individually to determine how blocks are assigned to sectors. The bmap function is used for this purpose. It is part of the virtual filesystem and invokes the bmap function in the address space operations of the specific filesystem. The various filesystem-specific implementations are of no interest to us here since they all yield the same result — a sector number that specifies which hard disk sector belongs to a given block number. The logical blocks of a file can be regarded as contiguous by the remainder of the kernel. However, this is not the case for the associated sectors on the disk, as discussed in Chapter 9.

The algorithm for creating the mapping list is not particularly complicated. As swap areas are rarely activated, the kernel need not concern itself with speed issues, which means that implementation is very straightforward. The first step is to determine the sector address of the first block in the swap area by means of bmap. This address serves as the starting point for further examination of the area.

The kernel must then find and compare the sector addresses of *all* blocks in the area to ascertain whether the blocks are contiguous. Discontinuity is established if this is not the case. The kernel first performs the operation for the number of blocks that constitute a page. If their sector addresses are consecutive, a linear area equivalent to one page is found on the disk. `add_swap_extent` inserts this information in the extent data structure.

This whole operation is then repeated, this time starting at the address of the next file block whose sector address had not yet been checked. Once the kernel has ascertained that the sectors of the blocks on this page are also consecutive on the disk, `add_swap_extent` is again invoked to add this information to the extent list.

If `add_swap_extent` were to add a new list element to the extent list each time it is invoked, it would not be possible to merge contiguous areas larger than a single page. Consequently, `add_swap_extent` automatically attempts to keep the list as compact as possible. When a new entry is added and its start sector is immediately after the final sector of the last entry (or, expressed differently, when the sum of the `start_block` and `nr_pages` elements of the last `swap_extent` element is equal to the start sector of the new entry), *one* combined entry is automatically created to merge the data of both elements. This ensures that the list comprises as few entries as possible.

But what happens when the kernel encounters a discontinuity? Since `setup_swap_extents` only checks areas that are the size of one page, the current area can be completely discarded. It serves no purpose because the minimum swapping unit is a full page. When a discontinuity is detected in the sectors, the kernel restarts the search starting at the sector address of the next file block. This is repeated until the next page is found that is mapped contiguously on the hard disk. If a new entry is then added to the extent list using `add_swap_extent`, the end address of the old sector and the start address of the new sector no longer match. This means that the two entries can no longer be merged and the kernel must create a new list element.

The above procedure is repeated until all blocks in the swap area have been processed. Once this has been done, the final step is to enter the number of usable pages in the relevant `swap_info` element.

18.4 The Swap Cache

Now that I have described the layout of the swap subsystem by reference to its data structures, let us turn our focus in the following sections on the techniques employed by the kernel to write pages from memory into a swap area and to read pages from the swap area back into memory.

The kernel makes use of a further cache, known as a *swap cache*, that acts as a liaison between the operation to select the pages to be swapped out and the mechanism that actually performs swapping. At first sight, this seems a little peculiar. What's the use of another swapping cache and *what* exactly needs to be cached? The answers are given below.

Figure 18-4 shows how the swap cache interacts with the other components of the swap subsystem.

The swap cache is an agent between the page selection policy and the mechanism for transferring data between memory and swap areas. These two parts interact via the swap cache. Input in one part triggers corresponding actions in the other. Notice that the policy routines can, nevertheless, directly interact with the writeback routines for pages that need not be swapped out, but can be synchronized.

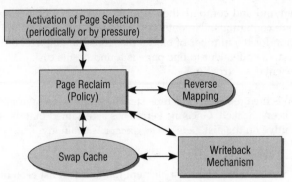

Figure 18-4: Interaction between the swap cache and the other components of the swap subsystem.

Which data are kept in the swap cache? As the swap cache is simply another page cache built using the structures discussed in Chapter 3, the answer is simple — memory pages. However, in contrast to the other page caches in the system, its purpose is not to keep pages in RAM for performance reasons although the associated data could also always be obtained from a block storage medium (this would run totally counter to the swapping principle). Instead, the swap cache is used for the following, depending on the "direction" of the swapping request (read or write):

❑ When pages are swapped out, the selection logic first selects a suitable seldom-used page frame. This is buffered in the page cache, from where it is transferred to the page cache.

❑ If a page used simultaneously by several processes is swapped out, the kernel must set the page entry in the directories of the process to point to the relevant position in the swap-out file. When one of the processes accesses the data on the page, the page is swapped in again, and the page table entry for *this single* process is set to the current memory address at which the page is now located. However, this causes a problem. The entries of all other processes still point to the entry in the swap-out file because, although it is possible to determine the number of processes that share a page, it is not possible to identify *which* processes these are.

When shared pages are swapped in, they are therefore retained in the swap cache until *all* processes have requested the page from the swap area and are all thus aware of the new position of the page in memory. This situation is illustrated in Figure 18-5.

Without the aid of the swap cache, the kernel is not able to determine whether or not a shared memory page has already been swapped back in, and this would inevitably result in redundant reading of data.

The importance of the swap cache is not the same in both directions. It is far more important when pages are swapped in than when they are swapped out. This asymmetry came about during the development of 2.5 when the *reverse mapping* scheme (rmap) described in Chapter 4 was introduced. Recall that the rmap mechanism finds all processes that share a page.[5]

---

[5]In earlier versions, shared memory pages could only be swapped out using the swap cache. Once the page had been removed from the page tables of a *single* process, the kernel had to wait until the page had also been removed from the page tables of all other processes before it could remove the data from memory; this required the systematic scanning of all system page tables. The pages were kept in the swap cache in the meantime.

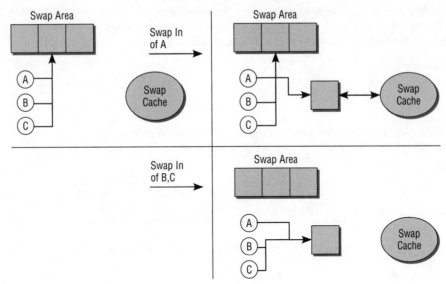

Figure 18-5: Swapping a page in via the swap cache.

When a shared page is swapped out, rmap finds all processes that reference the data in the page. Consequently, the relevant page table entries of *all* processes that reference the page can be updated to indicate the new position in the swap area. This means that the page data can be swapped out immediately without having to retain in the swap cache for a lengthy period.

18.4.1 Identifying Swapped-Out Pages

As discussed in Chapter 4, a memory page is identified on the basis of a virtual address using a system of page tables to find the address of the associated page frame in RAM. This only works if the data are actually present in memory; otherwise, there is no page table entry. It must also be possible to correctly identify swapped-out pages; in other words, it must be possible to find the address of a memory page in a swap area by reference to a given virtual address.

Swapped-out pages are marked in the page table by means of a special entry whose format depends on the processor architecture used. Each system uses special coding to satisfy the particular requirements.

Common to all CPUs is that the following information is stored in the page table entry of a swapped-out page:

❑   An indicator that the page has been swapped out.

❑   The *number of the swap area* in which the page is located.

❑   An *offset* that specifies the relevant page slot is also required to enable the page to be found within the swap area.

The kernel defines an architecture-independent format that can be derived (by the processor-specific code) from the architecture-dependent data and is used to identify pages in the swap area. The advantage of this approach is clearly that all swapping algorithms can be implemented regardless of the hardware used and need not be rewritten for each processor type. The only interface to the actual hardware are the functions for converting between architecture-specific and architecture-independent representation.

In the architecture-independent representation, the kernel must store both the identification (also referred to as *type*) of the swap partition and an offset within this area in order to be able to uniquely identify a page. This information is kept in a special data type called swap_entry_t, which is defined as follows:

<swap.h>
```
typedef struct {
        unsigned long val;
} swp_entry_t;
```

Only one variable is used, although two different information items must be stored. The components of the variable can be filtered out by selecting different areas, as illustrated in Figure 18-6.

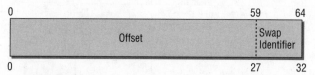

Figure 18-6: Components of an architecture-independent swap identifier.

Why is just a single unsigned long variable used to formally store both items of information? First, all systems supported so far are happily able to make do with the information provided in this way. And second, the value held in the variable is also used as a search key for the radix tree that lists all swap cache pages. Since the swap cache is merely a page cache that uses longs as a key, a swapped-out page can be uniquely identified in this way.

As this situation may change in the future, the unsigned long value is not used directly but is hidden in a structure. As the contents of a swap_entry_t value may only be accessed by special functions, the internal representation may be modified in future versions without having to rewrite significant parts of the swap implementation.

To ensure access to both information items in swap_entry_t, the kernel defines two constants for the bit arrangement shown in Figure 18-6:

<swapops.h>
```
#define SWP_TYPE_SHIFT(e)        (sizeof(e.val) * 8 - MAX_SWAPFILES_SHIFT)
#define SWP_OFFSET_MASK(e)       ((1UL << SWP_TYPE_SHIFT(e)) - 1)
```

MAX_SWAPFILES_SHIFT has the value 5, regardless of platform. The length of unsigned long on 32-bit architectures is 4; on 64-bit platforms, it is 8 bytes.

This special arrangement is relatively uninteresting for the rest of the kernel code. Much more important are the functions that extract the individual components from the structure:

<swapops.h>
```
static inline unsigned swp_type(swp_entry_t entry)
{
        return (entry.val >> SWP_TYPE_SHIFT(entry));
}

static inline pgoff_t swp_offset(swp_entry_t entry)
{
        return entry.val & SWP_OFFSET_MASK(entry);
}
```

Since `swap_entry_t` instances may never be manipulated directly, the kernel must provide a function that generates a `swap_entry_t` from a given type/offset pair:

<swapops.h>
```
static inline swp_entry_t swp_entry(unsigned long type, pgoff_t offset)
{
        swp_entry_t ret;

        ret.val = (type << SWP_TYPE_SHIFT(ret)) |
                        (offset & SWP_OFFSET_MASK(ret));
        return ret;
}
```

A few bit operations are used to pack the parameters in an `unsigned long` variable that is returned as the content of a new `swap_entry_t`.

The kernel requires the ability to switch between the architecture-*dependent* and architecture-*independent* representations, so the `pte_to_swp_entry` function is provided for this purpose:

<swapops.h>
```
static inline swp_entry_t pte_to_swp_entry(pte_t pte)
{
        swp_entry_t arch_entry;

        arch_entry = __pte_to_swp_entry(pte);
        return swp_entry(__swp_type(arch_entry), __swp_offset(arch_entry));
}
```

Conversion is performed in two steps. Starting with a page table entry that — as explained in Chapter 4 — is represented by an instance of data type `pte_t`, the data it contains are converted to an architecture-*dependent* `swap_entry_t`.

> **Even if the same data type is used in the processor-specific representation and in the architecture-*independent* memory model, the way in which the bits are distributed generally differs in the two variants.**

`__pte_to_swp_entry` is an architecture-dependent function that is defined in the CPU-specific include file `<asm-arch/pgtable.h>`. It gives the kernel the opportunity to extract the processor-specific information in the page table. On many architectures, this can be achieved by means of a simple typecast that does not change the content of the page table entry — just for a change, even the Sparc processors, which are otherwise somewhat eccentric in this respect, do not call for anything special here.

In the second step, the information contained in the newly created `swap_entry_t` instance is converted to the architecture-independent format, where usually a number of bits are devoted to management tasks, for instance, to mark the identifier as swap entry in contrast to regular page table entries. The kernel is again reliant on the help of the processor-specific code. All systems must feature the `__swp_type` and `__swp_offset` functions (note the leading underscores that are absent in the architecture-independent versions) that extract the type and offset from the machine-specific format and return the information in the general format, which is then put together by `swp_entry` to create a new `swap_entry_t`.

The number of bits used to address swap space locations in the architecture-independent format of a swap entry will in general be larger than in the architecture-specific format. Because architectures are not required to define the number of bits used for a swap offset in a constant visible to the public, the kernel needs to employ a little trick to find the maximally addressable swap offset:

```
maxpages = swp_offset(pte_to_swp_entry(swp_entry_to_pte(swp_entry(0,~0UL)))) - 1;
```

`swp_entry(0, 0UL)` specifies a swap offset with all bits set. The conversion to a page table entry and then back to an architecture-independent format guarantees that only valid bits survive. The largest addressable swap page number is obtained by picking the swap offset from the result.

18.4.2 Structure of the Cache

In terms of its data structures, the swap cache is nothing more than a page cache, as described in Chapter 3. At the heart of its implementation is the `swapper_space` object, which groups together the internal functions and list structures associated with the cache:

mm/swap_state.c
```
struct address_space swapper_space = {
        .page_tree       = RADIX_TREE_INIT(GFP_ATOMIC|__GFP_NOWARN),
        .tree_lock       = RW_LOCK_UNLOCKED(swapper_space.tree_lock),
        .a_ops           = &swap_aops,
        .i_mmap_nonlinear = LIST_HEAD_INIT(swapper_space.i_mmap_nonlinear),
        .backing_dev_info = &swap_backing_dev_info,
};
```

> Although each system may have several swap areas, there is just one variable via which the remaining kernel code accesses the swap cache. The pages are not organized into different areas until the data are actually written back. In the view of that part of the kernel that determines which pages are to be swapped out, there is only *one* swap cache to which the appropriate instructions must be forwarded, and this cache is represented by the `swapper_space` object mentioned above.

Since most of the fields are lists, they are initialized to their (empty) basic settings using suitable macros. The meaning of the entries is discussed in Chapter 4.

The kernel provides a set of swap cache access functions that can be used by any kernel code involved with memory management. They allow, for example, pages to be added to the swap cache or a search to be made for pages in the cache. They constitute the interface between the swap cache and the page replacement logic and are therefore used to issue commands to swap pages in or out without having to worry about the technical details of how the data are subsequently transferred.

A set of functions is also provided to handle with the address space made available by the swap cache. As is common with address spaces and therefore with page caches, these functions are grouped into an `address_space_operations` instance that is associated with `swapper_space` by means of the `aops` element. The functions constitute the "downward" interface of the swap cache; in other words, to the data transfer implementation between the system's swap areas and RAM memory. In contrast to the function set mentioned earlier, these routines are not concerned with which pages are swapped out or in or when this is done, but are responsible for the technical aspects of data transfer for the selected pages.

`swap_aops` is defined as follows:

mm/page_io.c
```
static struct address_space_operations swap_aops = {
        .writepage     = swap_writepage,
        .sync_page     = block_sync_page,
        .set_page_dirty = __set_page_dirty_nobuffers,
};
```

We will look at the significance and implementation of these functions more closely later on. Initially, it is sufficient to outline what they do:

1. `swap_writepage` synchronizes dirty pages with the underlying block device. This is not done to maintain consistency between RAM memory and the block device, as is the case for all other page caches. Its purpose is to *remove* pages from the swap cache and to transfer their data to a swap area. The function is therefore responsible for implementing data transfer between RAM memory and the swap area on the disk.

2. Pages must be marked as "dirty" in the swap cache without having to allocate new memory — a resource that is scarce enough anyway when swap-out mechanisms are used. As discussed in Chapter 16, one possible procedure to mark pages as dirty is to create buffers that enable the data to be written back chunk-by-chunk. However, additional memory is needed to hold the `buffer_head` instances that store the required management data. This is pointless as only complete pages in the swap cache are written back anyway. The `__set_page_dirty_nobuffers` function is therefore used to mark pages as dirty; it sets the `PG_dirty` flag but does not create buffers.

3. As with most other page caches, the standard implementation of the kernel (`block_sync_page`) is used to synchronize pages in the swap area. This function does nothing more than unplug to corresponding block queues. As far as the swap cache is concerned, this means that all data transfer requests forwarded to the block layer are then executed.

All "static" elements of the swap cache have been introduced, and the fundamentals upon which the swapping implementation rests are in place. Before discussing how they are brought to use in live action, let us briefly survey the functions that we will encounter in due course — there is a considerable number of them. Figure 18-7 shows the most important ones and how they are connected.

The figure resembles the rough overview from Figure 18-4, but provides many more details. The general structure introduced there can be immediately recognized. The individual functions that realize this structure are discussed in the remainder of this chapter.

18.4.3 Adding New Pages

Adding new pages to the swap cache is a very simple matter because the appropriate page cache mechanisms are used. The standard methods reduce the requisite effort to invoking the `add_to_page_cache` function described in Chapter 16. This function inserts the data structure of a given page into the corresponding lists and trees of the `swapper_space` address space.

However, this does not constitute the whole of the task. The page is not only added to the swap cache, but also requires space in one of the swap areas. Even though the data are not yet copied to hard disk at this point, the kernel must nevertheless consider which area it wants to select for the page and into which slot it will be inserted. This decision must then be saved in the data structures of the swap cache.

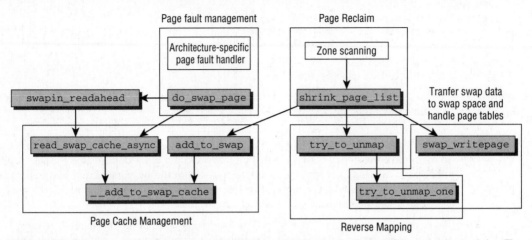

Figure 18-7: Overview of the most important functions that implement swapping and page reclaim. The figure is not a proper code flow diagram and skips some intermediate functions.

Two kernel methods add pages to the swap cache but serve different purposes:

1. add_to_swap is invoked when the kernel wants to swap out a page *actively*; that is, when the policy algorithm has determined that insufficient memory is available. The routine not only adds the page to the swap cache (where it remains until its data are written to disk), but also reserves a slot in one of the swap areas.

2. When a page shared by several processes (this can be determined by referring to the usage counter in the swap area) is read in from the swap area, the page is retained in both the swap area and the swap cache until it is either swapped out again or until it is swapped in by all the processes that share it. The kernel implements this behavior by means of the add_to_swap_cache function, which adds a page to the swap cache *without* performing operations on the swap areas themselves.

Reserving Page Slots

Before dealing with the implementation details of these two functions, we should examine how page slots are reserved in swap areas. The kernel delegates this task to get_swap_page, which — when called without parameters — returns the number of the page slot to be used next.

The function must first ensure that the system does, in fact, have swap areas — if so, the global variable nr_swap_pages has a value greater than 0.

swap_list.next always yields the number of the swap area currently in use (if there is only one swap area, it obviously always returns the same number). Logically, the kernel begins the search for a free page slot in this area. scan_swap_map scans the page bitmap, making use of swap clustering — a technique examined below.

If *no* free slot is found in the current swap area, the kernel checks the alternate slots. To do this, it runs through the list of all swap areas until it finds a free slot. Naturally, searching is performed in line with the priorities defined for each individual area by means of the next element of each swap_info[] entry.

When the area with the lowest priority is reached, the kernel starts searching again from the beginning (i.e., in the area with the highest priority). The search is terminated if no free entry is found after *all* swap areas in the system have been traversed. The kernel is then not able to swap out the page, and this fact is reported by returning the page number 0 to the calling code.

How are the slot bitmaps of the individual swap areas scanned? Empty entries are recognized because their usage counters equal 0. `scan_swap_map` therefore scans the `swap_map` array of the relevant swap partition for such entries, but this is made a little more difficult by swap clustering. A cluster consists of `SWAPFILE_CLUSTER` contiguous entries into which pages are written sequentially. The kernel first deals with the situation in which there is *no* free entry in the cluster. Since this is rarely the case, I postpone a discussion of the appropriate code until later.[6]

mm/swapfile.c

```
static inline unsigned long scan_swap_map(struct swap_info_struct *si)
{
        unsigned long offset, last_in_cluster;
...
        if (unlikely(!si->cluster_nr)) {
            /* Find new cluster*/
        }
```

We assume that `si->cluster_nr` is greater than 0, indicating that the current cluster still has free slots (recall that `cluster_nr` specifies the number of free slots in the current cluster). Once the kernel has ensured that the current offset does not exceed the limit set by `swap_info->highest_bit`, it checks whether the swap counter of the entry is 0 at the proposed position, indicating that the entry is available for use:

mm/swapfile.c

```
...
        si->cluster_nr--;
cluster:
        offset = si->cluster_next;
        if (offset > si->highest_bit)
lowest:         offset = si->lowest_bit;
        if (!si->highest_bit)
                goto no_page;
        if (!si->swap_map[offset]) {
                if (offset == si->lowest_bit)
                        si->lowest_bit++;
                if (offset == si->highest_bit)
                        si->highest_bit--;
                si->inuse_pages++;
                if (si->inuse_pages == si->pages) {
                        si->lowest_bit = si->max;
                        si->highest_bit = 0;
                }
                si->swap_map[offset] = 1;
                si->cluster_next = offset + 1;
...
                return offset;
        }
...
```

---

[6]The implementation still includes a few explicit scheduler calls, not reproduced here. They are executed to minimize kernel latency times when the kernel spends too long searching for a free swap slot.

Once the entries for the lower and upper limits have been updated (if necessary), the kernel increments the offset for the next search by 1 and uses the offset of the position just found.

If the proposed page is not free, the kernel iterates over the positions until it finds the first one that is free:

mm/swapfile.c

```
...
        while (++offset <= si->highest_bit) {
                if (!si->swap_map[offset]) {
                        goto checks;
                }
        }
...
        goto lowest;

no_page:
        return 0;
}
```

If this also fails, the kernel jumps to the lowest label, thus restarting the search at the lower limit of the free area. This does not produce an endless loop because highest_bit is set to 0 when the last available page is allocated. As the previous code section shows, this is an abort condition for the search.

We must now examine what happens if there is no current cluster. In this case, the kernel attempts to open a new cluster. This presupposes that an empty section consisting of at least SWAPFILE_CLUSTER empty slots is present in the swap area. As clusters do not require any particular alignment of their starting position, the kernel starts searching from the lowest position as of which there are free entries and which is defined by lowest_bit (the code shown is at the position of the /* Find new cluster */ comment inserted above):

mm/swapfile.c

```
                si->cluster_nr = SWAPFILE_CLUSTER - 1;
                if (si->pages - si->inuse_pages < SWAPFILE_CLUSTER)
                        goto lowest;

                offset = si->lowest_bit;
                last_in_cluster = offset + SWAPFILE_CLUSTER - 1;

                /* Locate the first empty (unaligned) cluster */
                for (; last_in_cluster <= si->highest_bit; offset++) {
                        if (si->swap_map[offset])
                                last_in_cluster = offset + SWAPFILE_CLUSTER;
                        else if (offset == last_in_cluster) {
                                si->cluster_next = offset-SWAPFILE_CLUSTER-1;
                                goto cluster;
                        }
                }
                goto lowest;
```

When there are not enough free slots to create a new cluster, the kernel branches to the lowest label and starts an entry-by-entry search there.

Starting at the current position, the kernel checks whether all subsequent slots — SWAPFILE_CLUSTER in number — are free; this check is performed by the for loop within the if query. If the kernel finds an allocated entry whose swap_map entry is greater than 0, the search for a free cluster is resumed at the next slot position. This is repeated until a position is finally reached at which there is insufficient space to create a cluster.

If the kernel is successful in its search for a new cluster, it jumps to the lowest label, as above.

Allocating Swap Space

After the policy routine has decided that a particular page needs to be swapped out, add_to_swap from mm/filemap.c comes into play. This function accepts a struct page instance as parameter and forwards the swap-out request to the technical part of swapping implementation.

As the code flow diagram in Figure 18-8 shows, this is not a very difficult task and consists basically of three steps. After the get_swap_page routine mentioned above has reserved a page slot in one of the swap areas, all that needs to be done is move the page into the swap area. This is the responsibility of the __add_to_swap_cache function, which is very similar to the standard add_to_page_cache function described in Chapter 16. The primary difference is that the PG_swapcache flag is set and the swap identifier swp_entry_t is stored in the private element of the page — it will be required to construct an architecture-dependent page table entry when the page is actually swapped out. Additionally, the global variable total_swapcache_pages is incremented to update the statistics. Nevertheless, as we would expect of add_to_page_cache, the page is inserted in the radix tree set up by swapper_space.

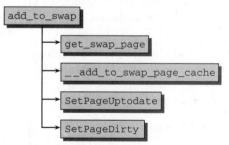

Figure 18-8: Code flow diagram for add_to_swap.

Finally, SetPageUpdate and SetPageDirty modify the page flags appropriately. Dirtying the page is essential because the contents of the page are not yet contained in the swap area. Recall from Chapter 17 that pages in the page cache are synchronized with their underlying block device when they are dirty. For a swap page, the underlying block device *is* the swap space, and synchronization is therefore (nearly) equivalent to swapping the page out! What remains to be done after the page has been written to a swap slot is updating the page table to reflect this.

But, otherwise, that's it. Nothing more is required of the policy routines when pages are swapped out. The rest of the work — particularly the transferring of data from memory to the swap area — is performed by the address-space-specific operations associated with swapper_space. The implementation of the routines is discussed below — as far as the policy is concerned, it is enough to know that the kernel actually writes the data to the swap area and thus releases a page after add_to_swap has been invoked. More details follow in the discussion of the shrink_page_list function.

Caching Swap Pages

In contrast to `add_to_swap`, `add_to_swap_cache` adds a page to the swap cache, but requires that a page slot has already been allocated for the page.

If a page already has a swap cache entry, why is it added to the swap cache? This is required when pages are *swapped in*. Suppose that a page that was shared among many processes has been swapped out. When the page is swapped in again, it is necessary to retain the data in the cache after the first page-in until *all* processes have successfully reclaimed the page. Only then can the page be deleted from the swap cache because all user processes are then informed of the page's new position in memory. The swap cache is also used in this way when readahead is performed for swap pages; in this case, the pages read in have not yet been requested because of a page fault but will most likely be shortly.

`add_to_swap_cache` is simple as the code flow diagram in Figure 18-9 shows. The basic task is to invoke `__add_to_swap_cache`, which adds the pages to the swap cache in the same way as `add_to_swap`. However, `swap_duplicate` must be called beforehand to ensure that the page already has a swap entry. The swap map count is also incremented by `swap_duplicate`; this signals that the page was swapped out from more than one place.

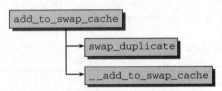

**Figure 18-9: Code flow diagram of
`add_to_swap_cache`.**

The main difference between `add_to_swap` and `add_to_swap_cache` is that the latter sets neither of the page flags `PG_uptodate` nor `PG_dirty`. Essentially, this means that the kernel does not need to write the page into the swap area — the contents of both are currently synchronized.[7]

18.4.4   Searching for a Page

`lookup_swap_cache` checks whether a page is located in the swap cache. Its implementation requires only a few lines[8]:

mm/swap_state.c
```
struct page * lookup_swap_cache(swp_entry_t entry)
{
        struct page *page;

        page = find_get_page(&swapper_space, entry.val);

        return page;
}
```

---

[7]Notice that kernel 2.6.25, which was under development when this book was written, will reshuffle the function names discussed here slightly. `add_to_swap_cache` will be merged into its only caller `read_swap_cache_async`, and will not exist anymore. `__add_to_swap_cache`, however, will take its place and will be renamed to `add_to_swap_cache`. The callers are updated accordingly.

[8]Like many other swapping functions described in this chapter, the original function in the kernel sources includes a few short calls to update the key statistics of the swapping subsystem. I will not include such calls in our discussion because they essentially deal with simple manipulation of counters, which is not very interesting.

This function yields the required page by reference to a `swp_entry_t` instance by scanning the `swapper_space` address space using the familiar `find_get_page` function discussed in Chapter 16. As for many other address space related tasks, all the hard work is done by the radix tree implementation! Note that if the page is not found, the code returns a null pointer. The kernel must then fetch the data from the hard disk.

18.5 Writing Data Back

Another part of the swapping implementation is the "downward" interface that is used to write page data to a selected reserved position in the swap area (or, to be precise, that issues the appropriate request to the block layer). As you have seen, this is done from the swap cache using the `writepage` address space operation, which points to `swap_writepage`. Figure 18-10 shows the code flow diagram of the function defined in `mm/page_io.c`.

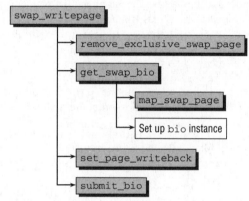

Figure 18-10: Code flow diagram for
`swap_writepage`.

As most of the work has been done by the above mechanisms, there is little left for `swap_writepage` to do. The very first thing the kernel does is to invoke `remove_exclusive_swap_page` to check that the relevant page is used by the swap cache but not by any other parts of the kernel. If this is true, the page is no longer needed and can be removed from memory.

Before the kernel can write the page data, it requires a correctly filled instance of `struct bio` with all the parameters needed for the block layer — as discussed in Chapter 6. This task is delegated to `get_swap_bio`, which returns a finished `bio` instance.

Not only the destination block device and the length of the data to be written back, but more particularly, the sector number, are required when the `bio` structure is filled. As discussed above in Section 18.3.1, it is not always certain that a swap area is located in a contiguous area on disk. Consequently, extents are used to create a mapping between the page slots and the available blocks. This extent list must now be searched:

```
mm/page_io.c
sector_t map_swap_page(struct swap_info_struct *sis, pgoff_t offset)
{
        struct swap_extent *se = sis->curr_swap_extent;
        struct swap_extent *start_se = se;
```

```
        for ( ; ; ) {
                struct list_head *lh;

                if (se->start_page <= offset &&
                                offset < (se->start_page + se->nr_pages)) {
                        return se->start_block + (offset - se->start_page);
                }
                lh = se->list.next;
                if (lh == &sis->extent_list)
                        lh = lh->next;
                se = list_entry(lh, struct swap_extent, list);
                sis->curr_swap_extent = se;
        }
}
```

The search does not begin at the start of the list but at the list element last used. This is stored in curr_swap_extent since in most cases, access is made to slots that are next to or at least close to each other. The address can be calculated with the help of the same extent list element.

A page slot is held in a list element when the offset number — that is, the number of the searched page slot — is equal to or greater than se->start_page but less than se->start_page + se->nr_pages. If this does not apply, the list is searched sequentially until the matching element is found. As a matching element *must* exist, the search can be performed in an endless loop that is terminated when the sector number is returned.

Once the bio instance has been filled with the appropriate data, the PG_writeback flag must be set for the page using SetPageWriteback before the write request is forwarded to the block layer by means of bio_submit.

When the write request has been executed, the block layer invokes the end_swap_bio_write function (which is based on the standard function end_page_writeback) to remove the PG_writeback flag from the page structure.

Notice that writing the contents of a page to the page slot in the swap area is *not* sufficient to fully swap out a page! Before a page can be considered to be completely removed from RAM, the page tables need to be updated. The page table entry needs, on the one hand, to specify that the page is not in memory and must, on the other hand, point to the location in the swap space. Since the change must be performed for all current users of the page, this is an involved task discussed in Section 18.6.7.

18.6 Page Reclaim

Now that I have explained the technical details of writeback, let's turn our attention to the second major aspect of the swapping subsystem — the *swap policy* adopted to determine which pages can be swapped out of RAM memory without seriously degrading the kernel's performance. Since page frames are freed by this and new memory is available for urgent needs, the technique is also called *page reclaim*.

> **In contrast to the previous sections concerning pages in the swap address space, this section focuses on pages in any address space. The principles of the swap policy apply for all pages without a backing store, regardless of whether their data are read from a file or are generated dynamically. The only difference is the location to which the data are written out when the kernel decides that the pages are to be**

> removed from memory. This issue has no effect on whether a page is swapped out or not. Some pages have a permanent backing store into which they can be brought, while others must be put into the swap area (recall that Section 18.1.1 contains a more refined characterization of pages that can be swapped out).

Implementation of the swap policy algorithm is one of the more complex parts of the kernel. This is due not only to the latent question of maximum speed, but also and primarily to the multitude of special situations that must be addressed. In the examples below, I concentrate on the most frequent situations that account for the overwhelming share of the swapping subsystem's work. For the sake of brevity, I shall not discuss rare phenomena that are due largely to the interplay among the various processors on SMP systems or to random coincidences on uniprocessor systems. A general overview of the interaction between the individual components involved in swapping is much more important (and is complicated enough on its own) than the detailed minutia of every swapping operation.

18.6.1 Overview

The general approach to implementation of the swap policy algorithms has been discussed above. The following sections focus on the interaction of the swap policy functions and procedures and describe their implementation in detail. Figure 18-11 shows a code flow diagram listing the most important methods and illustrating how they are interlinked.

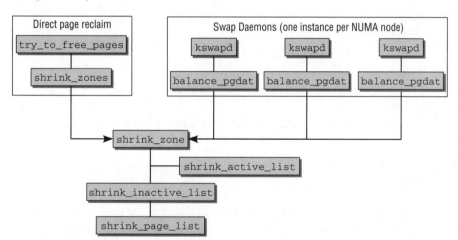

Figure 18-11: "Big picture" of the page reclaim implementation. Note that the figure is not a proper code flow diagram but just displays the most important functions.

The diagram is another refinement of the overview shown in Figure 18-7. *Page reclaim* is triggered at two points, as shown in the figure:

1. `try_to_free_pages` is invoked if the kernel detects an acute shortage of memory during an operation. It checks all pages in the current memory zone and frees those least frequently needed.

2. A background daemon named *kswapd* checks memory utilization at regular intervals and detects impending memory shortage. It can be used to swap out pages as a preventive measure before the kernel discovers in the course of another operation that it does not have enough memory.

> On NUMA machines, which do not share memory uniformly over all processors (see Chapter 3), there is a separate kswapd daemon for each NUMA zone. Each daemon is responsible for all memory zones in a NUMA zone.
>
> On non-NUMA systems, there is just one instance of kswapd, which is responsible for all main memory zones (*non*-NUMA zones). Recall that, for instance, IA-32 can have up to three zones — ISA-DMA, normal memory, and high memory.

The paths of the two versions merge very quickly in the shrink_zone function. The remaining code of the page reclaim subsystem is identical for both options.

Once the number of pages to be swapped out in order to provide the system with fresh memory has been determined — using algorithms designed to deal with acute memory shortage in try_to_free_pages and to regularly check memory utilization in the kswap daemon — the kernel must still decide which specific pages are to be swapped out (and ultimately pass these from the policy part of the code to the kernel routines responsible for writing the pages back to their backing store and adapting the page table entries).

Recall from Chapter 3.2.1 that the kernel tries to categorize pages into two LRU lists: one for active pages, and one for inactive pages. These lists are managed per memory zone:

```
<mmzone.h>
struct zone {
...
        struct list_head active_list;
        struct list_head inactive_list;
...
}
```

It is an essential job of the kernel to decide to which category a given page belongs, and a good proportion of this chapter is devoted to answering this question.

The decision about how many pages and which pages are to be reclaimed is performed in the following steps:

1. shrink_zone is the entry point for removing rarely used pages from memory and is called from within the periodical kswapd mechanism. This method is responsible for two things: It attempts to maintain a balance between the number of active and inactive pages in a zone by moving pages between the active and inactive lists (using shrink_active_list). It also controls the release of a selectable number of pages by means of shrink_cache. shrink_zone acts as a go-between between the logic that defines *how many* pages of a zone are to be swapped out and the decision as to *which* pages these are.

2. shrink_active_list is a comprehensive helper function used by the kernel to transfer pages between the active and inactive page lists. The function is informed of the number of pages to be transferred between the lists and then attempts to select the active pages least used.

    shrink_active_list is therefore essentially responsible for deciding which pages are subsequently swapped out and which are not. In other words, this is where the policy part of page selection is implemented.

3. `shrink_inactive_list` removes a selectable number of inactive pages from the `inactive` list of a given zone and transfers them to `shrink_page_list`, which then reclaims the selected pages by issuing requests to the various backing stores to write data back in order to free space in RAM.

If, for any reason, pages cannot be written back (some programs can explicitly prevent write-back), `shrink_inactive_list` must put them back on the list of active or inactive pages.

18.6.2 Data Structures

Before analyzing these functions in detail, we need to discuss a few of the data structures used by the kernel. They include page vectors, which — with the help of an array — can hold a specific number of pages on which the same operation is performed. This is best done in "batch mode," which is much quicker than performing the same operation separately on each page. I also examine the LRU cache used to place pages on the `active` or `inactive` list of a zone.

Page Vectors

The following structure is defined in the kernel to group several pages in a small array:

<pagevec.h>
```
struct pagevec {
        unsigned nr;
        int cold;
        struct page *pages[PAGEVEC_SIZE];
};
```

This is simply an array with pointers to `page` instances that also allow the number of elements they contain to be queried using the `nr` element. The `page` array itself provides space for `PAGEVEC_SIZE` pointers to pages (the default value is 14).

The `cold` element is an addition that helps the kernel distinguish between *hot* and *cold* pages. Pages whose data are held in one of the CPU caches are described as *hot* because their data can be accessed very quickly. Pages not held in the cache are therefore *cold*. For the sake of simplicity, this property of memory pages is ignored in the following descriptions.

Page vectors enable operations to be performed on a whole list of `page` structures; this is sometimes quicker than performing operations on individual pages. Currently, the kernel provides functions that are primarily concerned with releasing pages:

❑ `pagevec_release` decrements the usage counter of all pages in the vector batchwise. Pages whose usage counter value reaches 0 — these are therefore no longer in use — are automatically returned to the buddy system. If the page was on an LRU list of the system, it is removed from the list, regardless of the value of its usage counter.

❑ `pagevec_free` returns the memory space occupied by a collection of pages to the buddy system. The caller is responsible for ensuring that the usage counter is 0 — which indicates that the pages are not in use anywhere else — and that they are not included on any LRU list.

❑ `pagevec_release_nonlru` is a further function for releasing pages that decrements the usage counter of all pages of a given collection by 1. When the counter reaches 0, the memory occupied by the page is returned to the buddy system. In contrast to `pagevec_release`, this function assumes that all pages in the vector are not on any LRU list.

All these functions expect a `pagevec` structure containing the pages to be processed as parameter. If the vector is empty, all the functions return to the caller immediately.

There are also versions of the same functions with two preceding underscores (e.g., `__pagevec_release`). These do *not* test whether the vector passed contains pages or not.

What is still lacking is a function to add pages to a page vector:

```
<pagevec.h>
static inline unsigned pagevec_add(struct pagevec *pvec, struct page *page)
```

`pagevec_add` adds a new page `page` to a given page vector `pvec`.

The implementation of the function is not considered in detail here as it is very straightforward and reveals little of interest.

The LRU Cache

The kernel provides a further cache known as the *LRU cache* to speed up the addition of pages to the system's LRU lists. It makes use of page vectors to collect `page` instances and place them block-by-block on the system's `active` and `inactive` lists. The list is a hotspot in the kernel, but must be protected by a spinlock. To keep lock contention low, new pages are not immediately added to the list, but are first buffered on a per-CPU list:

```
mm/swap.c
static DEFINE_PER_CPU(struct pagevec, lru_add_pvecs) = { 0, };
```

The function to add new elements via this buffer is `lru_cache_add`. It provides a way of deferring the addition of pages to the system's LRU lists until a certain number of pages specified by `PAGEVEC_SIZE` is reached:

```
mm/swap.c
void fastcall lru_cache_add(struct page *page)
{
        struct pagevec *pvec = &get_cpu_var(lru_add_pvecs);

        page_cache_get(page);
        if (!pagevec_add(pvec, page))
                __pagevec_lru_add(pvec);
        put_cpu_var(lru_add_pvecs);
}
```

Since the function accesses a CPU-specific data structure, it must prevent the kernel from interrupting execution and resuming later on another CPU. This form of protection is enabled implicitly by invoking `get_cpu_var`, which not only disables preemption, but also returns the per-CPU variable.

`lru_cache_add` first increments the `count` usage counter of the `page` instance as the page is now in the page cache (and this is interpreted as usage). The page is then added to the CPU-specific page vector using `pagevec_add`.

pagevec_add returns the number of elements that are still free *after* the new page has been added. __pagevec_lru_add is invoked if NULL is returned, which indicates that the page vector is now completely full after addition of the last element. This function places all pages in the page vector on the inactive lists of the zone to which the individual pages belong (the pages may all be associated with different zones). The PG_lru bit is set for each page because they are now contained on an LRU list. The contents of the page vector are then deleted to make space for new pages in the cache.

If there are still free elements in the per-CPU list after pagevec_add added a page, the page instance is in the page vector, but *not yet* on one of the system's LRU lists.

lru_cache_add_active works in exactly the same way as lru_add_cache but is used for active rather than inactive pages. It uses lru_add_pvecs_active as a buffer. When pages are transferred from the buffer to the active list, not just the PG_lru bit, but additionally the PG_active bit, is set.

lru_cache_add is required only in add_to_page_cache_lru from mm/filemap.c and adds a page to both the page cache and the LRU cache. This is, however, the standard function to introduce a new page both into the page cache and the LRU list. Most importantly, it is used by mpage_readpages and do_generic_mapping_read, the standard functions in which the block layer ends up when reading data from a file or mapping.

Usually a page is first regarded as inactive and has to earn its merits to be considered active. However, a selected number of procedures have a high opinion of their pages and invoke lru_cache_add_active to place pages directly on the zone's active list[9]:

❑ read_swap_cache_async from mm/swap_state.c; this reads pages from the swap cache.

❑ The page fault handlers __do_fault, do_anonymous_page, do_wp_page, and do_no_page; these are implemented in mm/memory.c.

Understanding what is required to be promoted from an inactive to an active page is the subject of the next section. This is directly related to operations that move pages from the active to the inactive list and vice versa. Before these operations can be performed, it is necessary that the kernel transfer all pages from the per-CPU LRU caches to the global lists; otherwise, pages could be missed by the page-moving logics. The auxiliary function lru_add_drain is provided for this purpose.

Finally, Figure 18-12 summarizes the movements between the different lists graphically.

18.6.3 Determining Page Activity

The kernel must track not only whether a page is actually used by one or more processes, but also *how often* it is accessed in order to assess its importance. As only very few architectures support a direct access counter for memory pages, the kernel must resort to other means and has therefore introduced two page flags named *referenced* and *active*. The corresponding bit values are PG_referenced and PG_active, and the usual set of macros as discussed in Section 3.2.2 is available to set or receive the state. Recall that, for instance, PageReferenced checks the PG_referenced bit, while SetPageActive sets the PG_active bit.

Why are two flags used for the page state? Suppose that only a single flag were used to determine page activity — PG_active would lend itself to that rather well. When the page is accessed, the flag is

---

[9]The page migration code for NUMA systems, which is otherwise not covered in this book, is also a user of the function.

set, but when is it going to be removed again? Either the kernel does not remove it automatically, but then the page would remain in the active state forever even if it would only be used very little, or not at all anymore. To remove the flag automatically after some specific time-out would require a huge number of kernel timers because appropriate hardware support is not available on all CPUs supported by Linux. Considering the large number of pages that are present in a typical system, this approach is also doomed to fail.

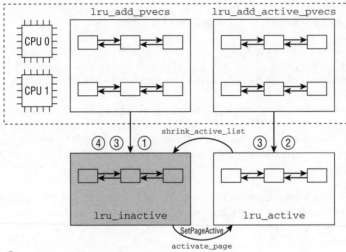

① __pagevec_lru_add
② __pagevec_lru_add_active
③ SetPageLRU
④ SetPageActive

Figure 18-12: Page movements between the per-CPU page lists and the global LRU lists. To simplify matters, only a single zone is used as the basis of the global lists. Only the most important functions that move pages between the active and inactive lists are shown.

Having two flags allows for implementing a more sophisticated approach to determining page activity. The core idea is to use one flag to denote the current activity rating, and another one that signals if the page has been recently referenced. Both bits need to be set in close cooperation. Figure 18-13 illustrates the corresponding algorithm. Essentially the following steps are necessary:

1. If the page is deemed active, the PG_active flag is set; otherwise, not. The flag directly corresponds to the LRU list the page is on, namely, the (zone-specific) inactive or active list.

2. Each time the page is accessed, the flag PG_referenced is set. The function responsible for this is mark_page_accessed, and the kernel must make sure to call it appropriately.

3. The PG_referenced flag and information provided by reverse mapping are used to determine page activity. The crucial point is that the PG_referenced flag is *removed* each time an activity check is performed. page_referenced is the function that implements this behavior.

4. Enter mark_page_accessed again. When it finds that the PG_accessed bit is already set when it checks the page, this means that *no* check was performed by page_referenced. The calls

to mark_page_accessed have thus been more frequent than the calls to page_referenced, which implies that the page is often accessed. If the page is currently on the inactive list, it is moved to the active list. Additionally, the PG_active bit is set, and PG_referenced is *removed*.

5. A downward promotion is also possible. If the page is on the active list and receives much attention, then PG_referenced is usually set. Once the page starts to experience less activity, then *two* calls of page_referenced are required without intervention of mark_page_accessed before it is put on the inactive list.

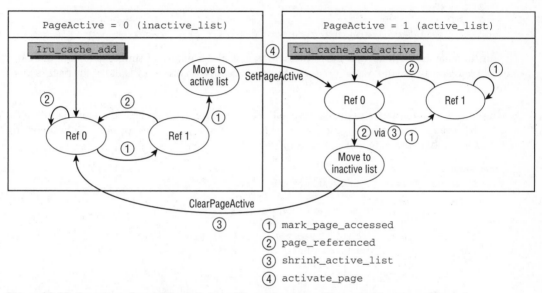

Figure 18-13: Overview of possible state transitions of a page with respect to PG_active and PG_referenced, and the corresponding placement of the page on the active and inactive lists.

If a page is steadily accessed, then the calls of mark_page_accessed and page_referenced will essentially average out, so the page remains on its current list.

A page that is not often accessed (and thus inactive) has *none* of the bits PG_active and PG_referenced set. This means that *two* subsequent activity markings with mark_page_accessed (and without the interference of page_referenced in between) are required to move it from the inactive to the active list. The same holds vice versa: A highly active page has *both* PG_active and PG_referenced set.

All in all, the solution ensures that pages do not bounce between the active and inactive lists too fast, which would clearly be undesirable for a reliable estimation of the page's activity level. The method is a variation of the "second chance" approach discussed at the beginning of this chapter: Highly active pages get a second chance before they are down-promoted to an inactive page, and highly inactive pages require a second proof before they become active pages. This is combined with a "least recently used" method (or at least an approximation, because no exact usage count is available for the pages) to realize page reclaim policy.

Note that while Figure 18-13 illustrates the most important state and list transitions, some more are still possible. This is caused, on the one hand, by code not covered in this book (e.g., the page migration code). On the other hand, some changes are necessary to handle special cases, (e.g., the lumpy page reclaim technique). These exceptions are discussed in the course of this chapter.

Several auxiliary functions are provided by the kernel to support moving pages between both LRU lists:

<mm_inline.h>
```
void add_page_to_active_list(struct zone *zone, struct page *page)
void add_page_to_inactive_list(struct zone *zone, struct page *page)

void del_page_from_active_list(struct zone *zone, struct page *page)
void del_page_from_inactive_list(struct zone *zone, struct page *page)

void del_page_from_lru(struct zone *zone, struct page *page)
```

The function names say it all, and the implementation is also a matter of simple list manipulation. The only thing to note is that del_page_from_lru must be used if the current LRU list of the page is unknown to the caller.

Moving pages from the active to the inactive list does, however, require more than just handling the list entries. To promote an inactive page to the active list, activate_page is responsible. Without locking and statistics accounting, the code looks as follows:

mm/swap.c
```
void fastcall activate_page(struct page *page)
{
        struct zone *zone = page_zone(page);

        if (PageLRU(page) && !PageActive(page)) {
                del_page_from_inactive_list(zone, page);
                SetPageActive(page);
                add_page_to_active_list(zone, page);
        }
}
```

This implements exactly the transition as discussed above.

Moving a page from the active to the inactive list is hidden within a larger function that is also responsible to handle shrinking of caches in a wider context, shrink_active_list, discussed in Section 18.6.6. Internally, the function relies on page_referenced. Besides handling the PG_referenced bit in the way described above, the function is responsible to query how often the page is referenced from the page table. This is mainly an application of the reverse mapping mechanism. page_referenced requires the parameter is_locked, which declares whether the page under consideration is locked by the caller:

mm/rmap.c
```
int page_referenced(struct page *page, int is_locked)
{
        int referenced = 0;
...
        if (TestClearPageReferenced(page))
                referenced++;

        if (page_mapped(page) && page->mapping) {
                if (PageAnon(page))
                        referenced += page_referenced_anon(page);
```

```
                        else if (is_locked)
                                referenced += page_referenced_file(page);
                        else if (TestSetPageLocked(page))
                                referenced++;
                        else {
                                if (page->mapping)
                                        referenced += page_referenced_file(page);
                                unlock_page(page);
                        }
                }
                return referenced;
        }
```

The function sums up the number of references the page has received lately. If PG_referenced bit is set, this is clearly a reference and counted accordingly. Note as per the previous discussion the bit is removed if it was set.

If the page is mapped into some process address space, the references to the page must be determined via the hardware-specific bits in the page table. Recall from Section 4.8 that page_referenced_anon computes the number of accesses to a page in an anonymous mapping, while page_referenced_file does the same for file-based mappings. On IA-32 and AMD64, for instance, this amounts to summing the number of page table entries that point to the page in question and have the _PAGE_BIT_ACCESSED bit set, which is automatically updated by the hardware.

page_referenced_file requires that the page is locked (to protect, e.g., against truncations that would erase the mapping while the kernel is operating on it). If an unlocked page is passed to page_referenced, the page is locked. Notice that the *last* else branch will be executed for an initially unlocked page because TestSetPageLocked will return the value of the PG_locked bit before changing it to one. Should the page have been locked from some other part of the kernel in the meantime, then does not make sense to wait until the lock is released. Instead, the reference counter is just incremented by 1 because at least the process that initiated locking the page has accessed the page.

Note that page_referenced will (via page_referenced_one, employed by both page_referenced_file and page_referenced_anon) also mark a page as referenced if the system currently undergoes swapping and the page belongs to a particular process that holds the swap token — even if it has not been accessed from somewhere. This prevents pages from this process from being reclaimed, and will increase performance in situations with heavy swapping. See the details of this mechanism in Section 18.7.

Finally, there's mark_page_accessed to consider. The implementation is straightforward:

mm/swap.c
```
void fastcall mark_page_accessed(struct page *page)
{
        if (!PageActive(page) && PageReferenced(page) && PageLRU(page)) {
                activate_page(page);
                ClearPageReferenced(page);
        } else if (!PageReferenced(page)) {
                SetPageReferenced(page);
        }
}
```

This implements the state transitions illustrated in Figure 18-13. They are additionally summarized in Table 18-1.

Table 18-1: Swap Page States

Initial state	Target state
Inactive, unreferenced	Inactive, *referenced*
Inactive, referenced	*Active, unreferenced*
Active, unreferenced	*Active, referenced*

18.6.4 Shrinking Zones

The routines for shrinking zones are (among others) supplied with the following information by the other parts of the kernel:

❑ The NUMA section and the memory zones it contains that are to be processed.

❑ The number of pages to be swapped out.

❑ The maximum number of pages that may be examined to find out if they are suitable for swapping out before the operation is aborted.

❑ The priority assigned to the attempt to free pages. This is not a process priority in the classical UNIX sense, as this would make little sense in kernel mode anyway, but an integer that specifies how urgently the kernel needs fresh memory. When pages are swapped out in the background as a preventive measure, this need is not as immediate as when, for example, the kernel has detected an acute memory shortage and urgently needs fresh memory to execute or complete an action.

Page selection begins in shrink_zone. However, some more infrastructure must be introduced before we can discuss the code.

Controlling Scanning

A special data structure that holds the parameters is used to control the scan operation. Notice that the structure is not only used to pass instructions on how to proceed from the higher level functions to the lower level ones, but is also used to propagate results in the inverse direction. This informs the caller on how successful an operation was:

mm/vmscan.c
```
struct scan_control {
        /* Incremented by the number of inactive pages that were scanned */
        unsigned long nr_scanned;
        /* This context's GFP mask */
        gfp_t gfp_mask;
        int may_writepage;
        /* Can pages be swapped as part of reclaim? */
        int may_swap;
...

        int swappiness;
        int all_unreclaimable;
        int order;
};
```

The meanings of the elements are closely reflected in their variable names:

❑ nr_scanned reports to the caller how many inactive pages have been scanned and is used to communicate between the various kernel functions involved in page reclaim.

❑ gfp_mask specifies allocation flags that are valid for the context in which the reclaim function is invoked. This is important because it is sometimes necessary to allocate fresh memory during page reclaim. If the context from which reclaim is initiated is not allowed to sleep, this constraint must, of course, be forwarded to all functions called; this is precisely what gfp_mask is designed to do.

❑ may_writepage selects whether the kernel is allowed to write out pages to the backing store. Disabling this opportunity is required sometimes when the kernel runs in laptop mode, as discussed in Chapter 17.13.

❑ may_swap decides if swapping is allowed as part of the page reclaim endeavors. Swapping is only forbidden in two cases: if page reclaim runs on behalf of the software suspend mechanism, and if a NUMA zone explicitly disables swapping. These possibilities are not considered any further in this book.

❑ swap_cluster_max is not actually related to swapping, but gives a threshold for the number of pages per LRU list that are at least scanned in one page reclaim step. Usually, this is set to SWAP_CLUSTER_MAX, defined to 32 per default.

❑ swappiness controls how aggressively the kernel tries to swap out pages; the value can range between 0 and 100. Per default, vm_swappiness is used. The standard setting is 60, but this can be tuned via /proc/sys/vm/swappiness. See the discussion in Section 18.6.6 for more details on how this parameter is used.

❑ all_unreclaimable is used to report the unfortunate situation in which memory in all zones is currently completely unreclaimable. This can happen, for example, if all pages are pinned by the mlock system call.

❑ The kernel can actively try to reclaim page clusters of a given page order. The order denotes that 2^{order} contiguous pages are supposed to be reclaimed.

Higher-order allocations consisting of more than a single page are complicated to reclaim especially when the system has been up and running for some time. The kernel uses the *lumpy reclaim* trick — which could also well be called a dirty trick — to nevertheless satisfy such requests, as discussed below.

Before discussing the page-reclaiming code, recall that struct zone as introduced a long time ago in Chapter 3.2.2 contains numerous fields that will be required in the following:

<mmzone.h>
```
struct zone {
...
        unsigned long nr_scan_active;
        unsigned long nr_scan_inactive;
        unsigned long pages_scanned;
...
        /* Zone statistics */
        atomic_long_t vm_stat[NR_VM_ZONE_STAT_ITEMS];
...
}
```

The kernel needs to scan the active and inactive lists to find pages that can be moved between the lists, or that can be reclaimed from the inactive list. However, the complete lists are not scanned in each pass, but only `nr_scan_active` elements on the active, and `nr_scan_inactive` on the inactive list. Since the kernel uses an LRU scheme, the number is counted from the tail of the list. `pages_scanned` remembers how many pages were scanned in the previous reclaim pass, and `vm_stat` provides statistical information about the zone, for instance, the number of currently active and inactive pages. Recall that the statistical elements can be accessed with the auxiliary function `zone_page_state`.

Implementation

After having introduced the required auxiliary data structures, let's discuss how zone shrinking is initiated. `shrink_zone` expects an instance of `scan_control` as a parameter. This instance must be filled with the appropriate values by the caller. Initially, the function is concerned with determining how many active and inactive pages are to be scanned; it does this by referring to the current state of the processed zone and to the passed `scan_control` instance:

mm/vmscan.c
```
static unsigned long shrink_zone(int priority, struct zone *zone,
struct scan_control *sc)
{
        unsigned long nr_active;
        unsigned long nr_inactive;
        unsigned long nr_to_scan;
        unsigned long nr_reclaimed = 0;

        /*
         * Add one to 'nr_to_scan' just to make sure that the kernel will
         * slowly sift through the active list.
         */
        zone->nr_scan_active +=
                (zone_page_state(zone, NR_ACTIVE) >> priority) + 1;
        nr_active = zone->nr_scan_active;
        if (nr_active >= sc->swap_cluster_max)
                zone->nr_scan_active = 0;
        else
                nr_active = 0;

        zone->nr_scan_inactive +=
                (zone_page_state(zone, NR_INACTIVE) >> priority) + 1;
        nr_inactive = zone->nr_scan_inactive;
        if (nr_inactive >= sc->swap_cluster_max)
                zone->nr_scan_inactive = 0;
        else
                nr_inactive = 0;
```

Each time `shrink_zone` is called, the number of active and inactive pages that are to be scanned in this pass is incremented by the value of `nr_scan_active` or `nr_scan_inactive`, which is scaled with the current priority by means of a right shift, that is, approximately an integer division by $2^{priority}$. 1 is always added to ensure that the counter is also incremented even if the bit-shift operation results in 0 over a lengthy period; this can happen with certain load situations. Adding 1 also ensures that, in this situation too, the inactive zone is filled or the caches are shrunk at some time or other.

If one of the values is greater than or equal to the maximum page number in a current swap cluster, the value of the zone element is reset to 0, and the value of the local variable nr_active or nr_inactive is retained; otherwise, the zone value remains the same, and the local variables are set to 0.

This behavior ensures that the kernel does not start further actions unless the number of active and inactive pages to be scanned is greater than the threshold value specified by sc->swap_cluster_max, as the next part of the function shows:

mm/vmscan.c
```
        while (nr_active || nr_inactive) {
                if (nr_active) {
                        sc->nr_to_scan = min(nr_active,
                                        (unsigned long)sc->swap_cluster_max);
                        nr_active -= sc->nr_to_scan;
                        shrink_active_list(nr_to_scan, zone, sc, priority);
                }

                if (nr_inactive) {
                        sc->nr_to_scan = min(nr_inactive,
                                        (unsigned long)sc->swap_cluster_max);
                        nr_inactive -= sc->nr_to_scan;
                        nr_reclaimed += shrink_inactive_list(nr_to_scan, zone,
                                                        sc);
                }
        }
...
        return nr_reclaimed;
}
```

The loop is not executed unless the threshold is exceeded for nr_active or nr_inactive. In the loop, the kernel makes a distinction as to whether inactive, pages, active pages, or both are to be scanned:

❑   If active pages are to be scanned, the kernel uses shrink_active_list to move pages from the active to the inactive LRU list. Naturally, the least used of the active pages are moved.

❑   Inactive pages can be removed directly from the caches by means of shrink_active_list. The function tries to take the required number of pages to be reclaimed from the inactive list. The number of pages for which this actually succeeded is returned.

The loop is terminated when sufficient pages of both categories have been scanned and the local counters have reached 0.

Shrinking the LRU lists in shrink_active_list and shrink_inactive_list requires a means to select pages from these lists, so an auxiliary function to perform this job must be introduced before we can discuss them.

18.6.5   Isolating LRU Pages and Lumpy Reclaim

Both the active and inactive pages of a zone are kept on lists that need to be protected by a spinlock, to be precise: by zone->lru_lock. To simplify matters, I have ignored this lock until now because it was not essential for our purposes. Now we need to consider it, though. When operations with the LRU lists are performed, they need to be locked, and one problem arises: The page reclaim code belongs to the hottest and most important paths in the kernel for many workloads, and lock contention is rather high. Therefore, the kernel need to work outside the lock as often as possible.

One optimization is to place all pages that are about to be analyzed in shrink_active_list and shrink_inactive_list on a local list, drop the lock, and proceed with the pages on the local list. Since they are not present on any global zone-specific list anymore, no other part of the kernel except the owner of the local list can touch them — the pages will not be affected by subsequent operations on the zone lists. Taking the zone list lock to work with the *local* list of pages is therefore not required.

The function isolate_lru_pages is responsible for selecting a given number of pages from either the active, or the inactive list. This is not very difficult: Starting from the end of the list — which is very important because the oldest pages must be scanned first in an LRU algorithm! — a loop iterates over the list, takes off one page in each step, and moves it to the local list until the desired number of pages is reached. For each page, the PG_lru bit is removed because the page is now not on an LRU list anymore.[10]

So far for the simplest case. Reality, however, is slightly more involved because isolate_lru_pages also implements the *lumpy reclaim algorithm*. What is the purpose of lumpy reclaim? It can be difficult to fulfill higher-order allocation requests that require a continuous interval of physical RAM that consists of more than one page — the more pages, the harder is the problem. When a system has been running for some time, physical memory tends to become fragmented more and more. How can this problem be solved? Consider Figure 18-14, which illustrates the kernel's approach.[11]

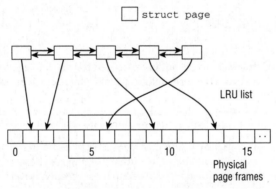

Figure 18-14: The lumpy reclaim technique helps the kernel reclaim larger continuous intervals of physical RAM.

Assume that the kernel requires four page frames in a row. Unfortunately, the page frames belonging to the pages that are currently on the LRU list are scattered in memory, and the largest continuous region consists of two pages. To escape this situation, lumpy reclaim simply takes page frames that surround a page frame belonging to one of the pages on the LRU list, the tag page. Not only the tag page, but also the surrounding pages, are selected for reclaim. This way, four continuous page frames in a row can be attempted to be freed. This does not yet guarantee that a block with four free pages will result because

---

[10]Besides, the function needs to acquire a reference on the page and also ensure that the reference count was zero before. Usually, pages with zero reference count are in the buddy system, as discussed in Chapter 3.5. However, concurrency allows pages with zero page count to live on the LRU list for a short amount of time.

[11]While lumpy reclaim is not exactly what computer science likes to teach, it works well in practice, and is above all very simple — which is sometimes much more important to the kernel than looking good and elegant on paper.

the selected page frames could very well be unreclaimable. However, an attempt has been made, and the probability of reclaiming higher-order allocations is drastically increased with lumpy reclaim as compared to the situation without this technique.

Naturally, there are some complications in practice, but these are best discussed directly with the source code. The first part of `isolate_lru_pages` is not very interesting. As described above, a single page is isolated from the LRU list under consideration:

mm/vmscan.c
```
static unsigned long isolate_lru_pages(unsigned long nr_to_scan,
                struct list_head *src, struct list_head *dst,
                unsigned long *scanned, int order, int mode)
{
        unsigned long nr_taken = 0;
        unsigned long scan;

        for (scan = 0; scan < nr_to_scan && !list_empty(src); scan++) {
                struct page *page;
                unsigned long pfn;
                unsigned long end_pfn;
                unsigned long page_pfn;
                int zone_id;

                /* Isolate a single LRU page */
                ...

        if (!order)
                continue;
```

The `for` loop iterates until the desired number of pages has been scanned. If no desired allocation order is given in `order`, each loop pass continues after isolating a single page from the LRU list.

However, more work is required for lumpy page reclaim. Recall that `page_to_pfn` and `pfn_to_page` allow converting between instances of `struct page` and the corresponding page frame number, and vice versa:

mm/vmscan.c
```
                zone_id = page_zone_id(page);
                page_pfn = page_to_pfn(page);
                pfn = page_pfn & ~((1 << order) - 1);
                end_pfn = pfn + (1 << order);
                for (; pfn < end_pfn; pfn++) {
                        struct page *cursor_page;
```

Since it is desirable for the buddy system that higher allocation orders are order-aligned, the kernel computes the appropriate page frame interval into which the page frame of the current tag page falls. Consider, as in the example, that the tag page has page frame 6. The allocation order-aligned intervals for second-order allocations are $[0,3]$, $[4,7]$, $[8,11]$, and so on. The kernel therefore needs to scan the page frames 4 to 7, inclusive:

mm/vmscan.c
```
                        /* The target page is in the block, ignore it. */
                        if (unlikely(pfn == page_pfn))
                                continue;
```

```
              /* Avoid holes within the zone. */
              if (unlikely(!pfn_valid_within(pfn)))
                      break;

              cursor_page = pfn_to_page(pfn);
              /* Check that we have not crossed a zone boundary. */
              if (unlikely(page_zone_id(cursor_page) != zone_id))
                      continue;
              switch (__isolate_lru_page(cursor_page, mode)) {
              case 0:
                      list_move(&cursor_page->lru, dst);
                      nr_taken++;
                      scan++;
              break;

...
              default:
                      break;
              }
      }

      *scanned = scan;
      return nr_taken;
}
```

The kernel must ignore the target page — it is already contained in the set of selected pages. Processing must be aborted if the computed interval crosses a memory zone boundary because mixed allocations (e.g., mixing DMA memory with normal memory) are not allowed.

Notice that __isolate_lru_page has an extra parameter that allows for controlling the activity state of pages that compose the new cluster. Three choices are possible:

mm/vmscan.c
```
#define ISOLATE_INACTIVE 0    /* Isolate inactive pages. */
#define ISOLATE_ACTIVE 1      /* Isolate active pages. */
#define ISOLATE_BOTH 2        /* Isolate both active and inactive pages. */
```

The comments say it all — __isolate_lru_pages can be instructed to take only pages in an active state, inactive state, or either of the two states. Since the pages are directly selected via their page frame number and not via an LRU list, all possibilities can arise. Note, however, that unused pages that are not part of any LRU list are not accepted — the page flag PG_lru *must* be set. Otherwise, __lru_isolate_page returns the error code -EINVAL. This is handled in the default branch of case, and page selection can be aborted because the kernel cannot hope for a larger continuous interval because of the resulting hole anymore.

18.6.6 *Shrinking the List of Active Pages*

Moving pages from the inactive list to the active list is one of the key actions in the implementation of the policy algorithm for page reclaim because this is where the importance of the various pages in the system (or, to be more precise, in the zone) is assessed. It therefore comes as no surprise that `refill_inactive_zone` is among the longer functions in the kernel. It performs the following principal steps:

1. It copies the required number of pages defined by `nr_pages` from the `active` list to a temporary, local list using `isolate_lru_pages`.

2. It distributes the pages over the active and inactive lists according to their activity level.

3. It frees unimportant pages in bundles.

Figure 18-15 shows the code flow diagram for the first `refill_inactive_zone` step.

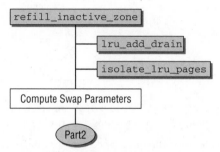

**Figure 18-15: Code flow diagram for
`refill_inactive_zone` (Part 1).**

First of all, the kernel calculates a few parameters to define the aggressiveness and the behavior of the page reclaim algorithm. Some statistical data are analyzed:

mm/vmscan.c

```
      . . .
           distress = 100 >> min(zone->prev_priority, priority);
           mapped_ratio = ((global_page_state(NR_FILE_MAPPED) +
                           global_page_state(NR_ANON_PAGES)) * 100) /
                           vm_total_pages;
           mapped_ratio = (sc->nr_mapped * 100) / total_memory;
           swap_tendency = mapped_ratio / 2 + distress + sc->swappiness;

           imbalance = zone_page_state(zone, NR_ACTIVE);
           imbalance /= zone_page_state(zone, NR_INACTIVE) + 1;
           imbalance *= (vm_swappiness + 1);
           imbalance /= 100;
           imbalance *= mapped_ratio;
           imbalance /= 100;

           swap_tendency += imbalance;
           if (swap_tendency >= 100)
                   reclaim_mapped = 1;
      . . .
```

Four values, whose meanings are given below, are calculated[12]:

❑ distress is the key indicator as to how urgently the kernel needs fresh memory. It is calculated using the prev_priority value for right-shifting the fixed value 100. prev_priority specifies the priority with which the zone had to be scanned during the last try_to_free_pages run until the required number of pages was freed. Notice that the lower prev_priority is, the higher the priority. The shift operations produce the following distress values for various priorities:

Priority	Distress
7	0
6	1
5	3
4	6
3	12
2	25
1	50
0	100

All priority values greater than 7 yield a distress factor of 0. While 0 ensures the kernel that there is no problem at all, 100 indicates massive trouble.

❑ mapped_ratio indicates the ratio of mapped memory pages (not only used to cache data but also explicitly requested by processes to store data) to the total available memory. The ratio is calculated by dividing the current number of mapped pages by the total number of pages available at system start. The result is scaled to a percentage value by multiplying by 100.

❑ mapped_ratio is used only to calculate a further value that is called swap_tendency and — as its name suggests — indicates the swap tendency of the system. You are already familiar with the first two calculation variables. sc_swappiness is an additional kernel parameter that is usually based on the setting in /proc/sys/vm/swappiness.

❑ If there is a large imbalance between the lengths of the active and inactive lists, the kernel allows swapping and page reclaim to happen more easily than usual to balance the situation. However, some effort is made that large imbalances do not have much influence at low swappiness values.

❑ The kernel now reduces all the information calculated so far to a truth value that answers the following question: Are mapped pages to be swapped out or not?

If swap_tendency is greater than or equal to 100, mapped pages are also swapped out, and reclaim_mapped is set to 1. Otherwise, the variable retains its default value of 0 so that pages are only reclaimed from the page cache.

As vm_swappiness is added to swap_tendency, the administrator can enable the swapping of mapped pages at any time regardless of the other system parameters by assigning the value of 100 to the variable.

The lru_add_drain procedure, which is invoked after the parameters have been calculated, distributes the data currently held in the LRU cache to the system's LRU lists. In contrast to lru_cache_add, touched upon in Section 18.6.2, copying is performed when the temporary caches contain at least one element, not only when they are completely filled.

---

[12]The individual formulas were derived heuristically and are designed to guarantee good performance in many different situations.

Ultimately, the task of `shrink_active_list` is to move a specific number of pages in the list of active pages in a zone back to the list of active or inactive pages in a zone. Three local lists, on which `page` instances can be buffered, are created to enable the pages to be scanned:

❑   `l_active` and `l_inactive` hold pages that are to be put back on the list of active or inactive pages of the zone at the end of the function.

❑   `l_hold` stores pages still to be scanned before it is decided to which list they are returned.

This task is delegated to `isolate_lru_pages` discussed just above. Recall that the function reads the LRU list from tail to head, but arranges the pages in opposite order on the temporary local list. This is a key point when implementing the LRU algorithm for page replacement. The seldom-used pages on the `active` list automatically move to the rear. As a result, the kernel finds it very easy to scan the least-used pages because they are located at the beginning of the `l_hold` list.

The second section of `refill_inactive_list` begins once the parameters have been calculated. In this section, the individual pages are distributed to the `l_active` and `l_inactive` lists of the zone. Instead of using a code flow diagram to show how this is done, let's reproduce and discuss the relevant code:

mm/vmscan.c

```
. . .
        while (!list_empty(&l_hold)) {
                cond_resched();
                page = lru_to_page(&l_hold);
                list_del(&page->lru);
                if (page_mapped(page)) {
                        if (!reclaim_mapped ||
                                (total_swap_pages == 0 && PageAnon(page)) ||
                                page_referenced(page, 0)) {
                                list_add(&page->lru, &l_active);
                                continue;
                        }
                }
                list_add(&page->lru, &l_inactive);
        }
. . .
```

The code becomes more complex since we are getting to the very heart of page reclaim. The basic action is represented by a loop that iterates over all elements of the `l_hold` list, which in the previous section was filled with pages regarded as active. These pages must now be reclassified and placed on the `l_active` and `l_inactive` lists.

`page_mapped` first checks whether the page is embedded in the pages tables of any process. This is easy to do using the reverse mapping data structures. Recall from Chapter 4 that the information as to whether the page is mapped in page tables is held in the `_mapcount` element of each `page` instance. If the page is mapped by a single process, the counter value is 0; for non-mapped pages, it is −1. Logically, `page_mapped` must therefore check whether `page->_mapping` is greater than or *equal to* 0.

If there is no mapping, the page is immediately placed on the list of inactive pages.

If `page_mapped` returns a true value indicating that the page is associated with at least one process, it is a little more difficult to decide whether the page is important for the system. One of the following three conditions must apply before the page can be moved back to the start of the list of active pages:

1. As discussed in Chapter 4.8.3, the reverse mapping mechanism provides the `page_referenced` function to check the number of processes that have used a page since the last check. This is done by referring to corresponding status bits of the hardware that are held in the individual page table entries. Although the function returns the number of processes, it is only necessary to know whether at least one process has accessed the page, that is, whether the value returned is greater than 0. The condition is satisfied if this is the case.

2. `reclaim_mapped` is equal to 0; that is, mapped pages are not to be reclaimed.

3. The system has no swap area and the page just examined is registered as an anonymous page (in this case, there is nowhere to swap the page out).

Recall that Section 18.6.3 discussed how the call to `page_referenced` and possibly moving the page to the inactivity list afterward fit into the big picture of deeming a page active or inactive.

The kernel enters the third and final phase of `refill_inactive_zone` once all pages have been redistributed from the zone-specific `active` list to the temporary local `l_active` and `l_inactive` lists. Again there is no need for a separate code flow diagram.

The last step entails not only copying the data in the temporary lists to the corresponding LRU lists of the processed zone, but also checking whether there are pages that are no longer used (their usage counters are equal to 0) and can be returned to the buddy system.

To do this, the kernel iterates sequentially over all the pages that have accumulated in the local `l_active` and `l_inactive` lists. It handles all the individual pages in the same way:

❑ Pages taken from the tail of the local lists `zone->active_list` or `inactive_list` are added to the head of the zone-specific active or inactive LRU lists, respectively.

❑ The `page` instance is added to a page vector. When this is full, all its pages are transferred collectively to `__pagevec_release`, which first decrements the usage counter by 1 and then returns the memory space to the buddy system when the counter reaches 0.

All the kernel need do after placing the processed pages back on the zone-specific lists is update a few variables relating to memory management statistics.

18.6.7 Reclaiming Inactive Pages

Up to now, the pages in a zone have been redistributed on LRU lists to find good candidates for reclaim. However, their memory space has not been released. This final step is performed by the `shrink_inactive_list` and `shrink_page_list` functions, which work hand-in-hand. `shrink_inactive_lists` groups pages from `zone->inactive_list` into chunks, which benefits swap clustering, while `shrink_page_list` passes the members on the resulting list downward and sends the page to the associated backing store (which means the page is synchronized, swapped out, or discarded). This apparently simple task, however, gives rise to a few problems, as you will see below.

Besides a list of pages and the usual shrink control parameter, `shrink_page_list` accepts another parameter that allows two modes of operations: `PAGEOUT_IO_ASYNC` for asynchronous and `PAGEOUT_IO_SYNC` for synchronous writeout. In the first case, writeout requests are handed to the block layer without further ado, while in the second case, the kernel waits for the write operations to complete after issuing a corresponding request.

Shrinking the Inactive List

As shrink_inactive_list is responsible only for removing pages from the zone->inactive_list chunk-by-chunk, its implementation is not particularly complicated, as the code flow diagram in Figure 18-16 shows.

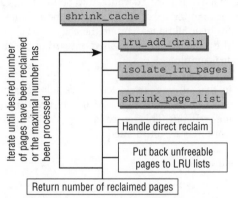

Figure 18-16: Code flow diagram for shrink_cache.

The first step is to invoke the familiar lru_add_drain function to distribute the current content of the LRU cache to the lists of active and inactive pages in the various zones. This is necessary to cover *all* inactive pages currently present in the system.

A loop is then repeatedly executed until either the maximum permissible number of pages has been scanned or the required number of pages has been written back. Both numbers are passed to the procedure as a parameter.

Within the loop, the isolate_lru_pages function, as discussed in Section 18.6.5, is invoked to remove a bundle of pages from the back of the list of inactive pages so that the most inactive pages are swapped out by preference. The kernel essentially passes the finished list to shrink_page_list, which initiates writing back the pages on the list. However, things are slightly complicated by lumpy writeback:

mm/vmscan.c
```
nr_taken = isolate_lru_pages(sc->swap_cluster_max,
                &zone->inactive_list,
                &page_list, &nr_scan, sc->order,
                (sc->order > PAGE_ALLOC_COSTLY_ORDER)?
                            ISOLATE_BOTH : ISOLATE_INACTIVE);
nr_active = clear_active_flags(&page_list);
...
/* Handle page accounting */
...
nr_freed = shrink_page_list(&page_list, sc, PAGEOUT_IO_ASYNC);
```

Recall that `isolate_lru_pages` also picks pages adjacent to the page frame of a page on the free list if lumpy reclaim is used. If the allocation order of the request that led to the current reclaim pass is larger than the threshold order specified in `PAGE_ALLOC_COSTLY_ORDER`, lumpy reclaim is allowed to use both active and inactive pages when picking pages surrounding the tag page. For small allocation orders, only inactive pages may be used. The reason behind this is that larger allocations usually cannot be satisfied if the kernel is restricted to inactive pages — the chance that an active page is contained in large intervals is simply too big on a busy kernel. `PAGE_ALLOC_COSTLY_ORDER` is per default set to 3, which means that the kernel considers allocations of 8 and more continuous pages as *complicated*.

Although all pages on the inactive list are guaranteed to be inactive, lumpy reclaim can lead to active pages on the result list of `isolate_lru_pages`. To account these pages properly, the auxiliary function `clear_active_flags` iterates over all pages, counts the active ones, and clears the page flag `PG_active` from any of them. Finally, the page list can be pushed onward to `shrink_page_list` for writeout. Notice that the asynchronous mode is employed.

Notice that it is not certain that all pages selected for reclaim can actually be reclaimed. `shrink_page_list` leaves such pages on the passed list and returns the number of pages for which it succeeded to initiate writeout. This figure must be added to the total number of swapped-out pages to determine when work may be terminated.

Direct reclaim requires one more step:

mm/vmscan.c
```
if (nr_freed < nr_taken && !current_is_kswapd() &&
                       sc->order > PAGE_ALLOC_COSTLY_ORDER) {
        congestion_wait(WRITE, HZ/10);
...
        nr_freed += shrink_page_list(&page_list, sc,
                                  PAGEOUT_IO_SYNC);
}
```

If not all pages that were supposed to be reclaimed could have been reclaimed, that is, if `nr_freed` < `nr_taken`, some pages on the list have been locked and could not be written out in asynchronous mode.[13] If the kernel is performing the current reclaim pass in direct reclaim mode, that is, was not called from the swapping daemon `kswapd`, and reclaims to fulfill a high-order allocation, then it first waits for any congestion on the block devices to settle. Afterward, another writeout pass is performed in synchronous mode. This has the drawback that higher-order allocations are somewhat delayed, but since they do not happen so often, this is not an issue. Allocations smaller than `PAGE_ALLOC_COSTLY_ORDER` that arise much more frequently are not disturbed.

Finally, the non-reclaimable pages must be returned to the LRU lists. Lumpy reclaim and failed writeout attempts might have led to active pages on the local list, so both the active and the inactive LRU lists are possible destinations. To preserve the LRU order, the kernel iterates over the local list from tail to head. Depending on whether the page is active or not, it is returned to the start of the appropriate LRU list using either `add_page_to_active_list` or `add_page_to_inactive_list`. Once again, the usage counter of each page must be decremented by 1 because it was incremented accordingly at the start of the procedure. The now familiar page vectors are used to ensure that this is done as quickly as possible because they perform processing block-by-block.

---

[13]There can also be other reasons for this, for instance, a failed writeout, but the reason mentioned is the essential cause.

Performing Page Reclaim

`shrink_page_list` takes a list of pages selected for reclaim and attempts to write back to the appropriate backing store. This is the last step performed by the policy algorithm — everything else is the responsibility of the technical part of swapping. The `shrink_page_list` function forms the interface between the kernel's two subsystems. The associated code flow diagram is shown in Figure 18-17. Some of the many corner cases this function has to deal with are ignored so that inessential details do not obstruct the view on the essential principles of operation.

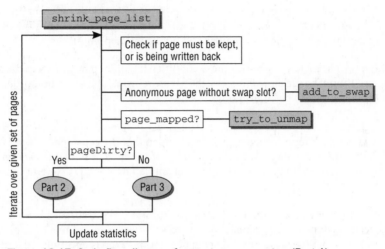

Figure 18-17: Code flow diagram for `shrink_page_list` (Part 1)

Here, too, the basic framework of the function is a loop that iterates over the various elements of the page list until there are none left. As the pages are either passed permanently to the lower layers of the swapping subsystem or are put on a second list if they cannot be reclaimed, it is certain that the loop will be finished at some time or other and will not continue to run endlessly.

In each loop iteration, a page is selected from the page list (the list is processed from head to tail again). First of all, the kernel must decide if the page must be kept. This can happen for the following reasons:

❑ The page is locked by some other part of the kernel. If this is the case, the page is not reclaimed; otherwise, it is locked by the current path and will be reclaimed.

❑ The second condition is more complicated. The following code snippet shows the conditions under which a page is *not* reclaimed, but returned to the *active* LRU list:

mm/vmscan.c
```
referenced = page_referenced(page, 1);
/* In active use or really unfreeable? Activate it. */
if (sc->order <= PAGE_ALLOC_COSTLY_ORDER &&
                    referenced && page_mapping_inuse(page))
       /* Set PG_active flag and keep page */
```

`page_referenced` checks (as discussed above) if the page was recently referenced by any of its users. This alone, however, is not sufficient to prevent reclaiming the page. Additionally,

the allocation order for which the current reclaim pass works must be below or equal to
PAGE_ALLOC_COSTLY_ORDER, that is, less than or equal to eight pages. Besides, the page must
fulfill one of the following conditions:

❑ The page is mapped into a page table as checked by page_mapped — see Section 4.8.3 —
or is used in a user-mode virtual address space.

❑ The page is contained in the swap cache.

❑ The page is contained in an anonymous mapping.

❑ The page is mapped into userland via a file mapping. This case is not checked with the help
of page tables, but by mapping->i_mmap and mapping_i_map_nonlinear, which contain the
mapping information for regular and nonlinear mappings.

page_mapping_in_use checks for these conditions. Fulfilling any of them does not mean that
the page cannot be reclaimed at all — the pressure from high allocation orders that wait to be
fulfilled just needs to be large enough.

Recall that shrink_inactive_list can call shrink_page_list twice: first in asynchronous and then
in synchronous writeback mode. Therefore, it can happen that the considered page is currently under
writeback as indicated by the page flag PG_writeback. If the current pass requests synchronous writeback, then wait_on_page_writeback is used to wait until all pending I/O operations on the page have
been finished.

If the page currently being considered by shrink_page_list is not associated with a backing store, then
the page has been generated anonymously by a process. When pages of this type must be reclaimed,
their data are written into the swap area. When a page of this type is encountered and no swap slot has
been reserved yet, add_to_swap is invoked to reserve a slot and add the page to the swap cache. At the
same time, the relevant page instance is provided with swapper_space (see Section 18.4.2) as a mapping
so that it can be handled in the same way as all other pages that already have a mapping.

If the page is mapped into the address tables of one or more processes (as before, checked using
page_mapped), the page table entries that point to the page must be removed from the page tables
of *all* processes that reference it. The rmap subsystem provides the try_to_unmap function for this
purpose; it unmaps the page from *all* processes that use it (we do not examine this function in detail
because its implementation is not particularly interesting). In addition, the architecture-specific
page table entries are replaced with a reference indicating where the data can now be found. This
is done in try_to_unmap_one. The necessary information is obtained from the page's address space
structure, which contains all backing store data. It is important that two bits are *not* set in the new page
table entry:

❑ A missing _PAGE_PRESENT bit indicates that the page has been swapped out. This is important
when a process accesses the page: A page fault is generated, and the kernel needs to detect that
the page has been swapped out.

❑ A missing _PAGE_FILE bit indicates that the page is in the swap cache. Recall from Section 4.7.3
that page table entries used for nonlinear mappings also lack _PAGE_PRESENT, but can be distinguished from swap pages by a *set* _PAGE_FILE bit.

Clearing the page table entry with ptep_clear_flush delivers a copy of the previous page
table entry (PTE). If it contains the dirty bit, then the page was modified by some user during
the reverse mapping process. It needs to be synchronized with the backing store (in this case

the swap space) in `shrink_page_list` afterward. Therefore the dirty bit is transferred from the PTE to the *page* bit `PG_dirty`.

Let's turn our attention back to `shrink_page_list`. What now follows is a series of queries that, depending on page state, trigger all the operations needed to reclaim the page.

`PageDirty` checks whether the page is dirty and must therefore be synchronized with the underlying storage medium. This also includes pages that live in the swap address space. If the page is dirty, this requires a few actions that are represented by Part 2 in Figure 18-17. They are better discussed by looking at the code itself.

❏   The kernel ensures that the data are written back by invoking the `writepage` address space routine (which is called by the `pageout` helper function that supplies all the required arguments). If the data were mapped from a file in the filesystem, a filesystem-specific routine handles the appropriate synchronization, and swap pages are inserted in their assigned page slot using `swap_writepage`.

❏   Depending on the result of `pageout`, different actions are required:

mm/vmscan.c
```
/* Page is dirty, try to write it out here */
switch (pageout(page, mapping, sync_writeback)) {
case PAGE_KEEP:
        goto keep_locked;
case PAGE_ACTIVATE:
        goto activate_locked;
case PAGE_SUCCESS:
        if (PageWriteback(page) || PageDirty(page))
                goto keep;
...
case PAGE_CLEAN:
        ; /* try to free the page below */
}
```

The `sync_writeback` parameter to `pageout` denotes the writeback mode in which `shrink_page_list` is operating.

The most desirable return code is `PAGE_CLEAN`: The data are synchronized with the backing store and the memory can be reclaimed — this happens in Part 3 of the code flow diagram.

If a write request was successfully issued to the block layer, then `PAGE_SUCCESS` is returned. In asynchronous writeback mode, the page will usually still be under writeback when `pageout` returns, and jumping to the label `keep` just keeps the page on the local page list, which is returned to the `shrink_list` — they will be returned to the LRU lists there. Once the write operation has been performed, the page contents are synchronized with the backing store so that the page is no longer dirty the next time `shrink_list` is invoked and can therefore be swapped out.

If the write operation was already finished when `pageout` returned, the data have been written back, and the kernel can continue with Step 3.

If an error has occurred during writeback, the result is either `PAGE_KEEP` or `PAGE_KEEP_ACTIVATE`. Both make the function keep the page on the aforementioned return list, but `PAGE_KEEP_ACTIVATE` additionally sets the page state to `PG_active` (this can, e.g., happen if the page's address space does not provide a `writeback` method, which makes trying to synchronize the page useless).

Figure 18-18 shows the code flow diagram for the case that the page is *not* dirty. Keep in mind that the kernel can also reach this path coming from Step 2.

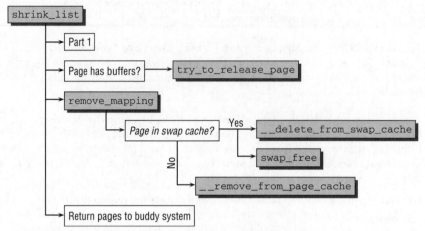

Figure 18-18: Code flow diagram for `shrink_list` (Part 3).

❑ `try_to_release` is invoked if the page has private data and buffers are therefore associated with the page (this is typically the case with pages that contain filesystem metadata). This function attempts either to release the page using the `releasepage` operation in the address space structure or, if there is no mapping, to free the data using `try_to_free_buffers`.

❑ The kernel then detaches the page from its address space. The auxiliary function `remove_mapping` is provided for this purpose.

If the page is held in the swap cache, it is certain that the data are by now present *both* in the swap space and in the swap cache. Since the page has been swapped out, the swap cache has fulfilled its duty, and the page can be removed from there with `__delete_from_swap_cache`. The kernel additionally uses `swap_free` to decrement the usage counter of the page in the swap area. This is necessary to reflect the fact that there is no longer a reference to the page in the swap cache.

❑ If the page is *not* in the swap cache, it is removed from the general page cache using `__remove_from_page_cache`.

It is now guaranteed that the processed page is not present in the kernel's data structures. Nevertheless, the main issue has not been resolved — the RAM memory occupied by the page has not yet been freed. The kernel does this in chunks using page vectors. The page to be freed is inserted in the local `freed_pvec` page vector using `pagevec_add`. When this vector is full, all its elements are released collectively by means of `__pagevec_release_nonlru`. As discussed in Section 18.6.2, the function returns the memory space occupied by the pages to the buddy system. The memory reclaimed in this way can be used for more important tasks — and this is precisely the purpose of swapping and page reclaim.

A few trivial points need to be cleared up once `shrink_list` has iterated over all the pages passed:

❑ The kernel's swapping statistics are updated.

❑ The number of freed pages is returned as an integer result.

18.7 The Swap Token

One of the methods to avoid page thrashing is the swap token, as briefly discussed in Section 18.1.2. The method is simple but effective. When multiple processes swap pages concurrently, it can occur that most of the time is spent writing the pages to disk and reading them in again, only to swap them out again after a short interval. This way much of the available time is spent writing pages back and forth to disk, but little progress is achieved. Clearly, this is a rare situation, but nevertheless a very frustrating one if an interactive user sits on his chair and watches the activity on the hard disk, while nothing is actually being achieved.

To prevent this situation, the kernel makes one and only one of the processes that currently swap in pages the owner of the so-called swap token. The benefit of having the swap token is that pages of the holder will not be reclaimed — or will, at least, be exempted from reclaim as well as possible. This allows any swapped-in pages to remain in memory, and increases the chance that work is going to be finished.

Essentially, the swap token implements a sort of "superordinate scheduling" for processes that swap in pages. (However, the results of the CPU scheduler are not modified at all!) As with every scheduler, fairness between processes must be ensured, so the kernel guarantees that the swap token will be taken away from one process after some time and passed on to another one. The original swap token proposal (see Appendix F) uses a time-out after which the token is passed to the next process, and this strategy was employed in kernel 2.6.9 when the swap token approach was first integrated. During the development of kernel 2.6.20, a new scheme to preempt the swap token was introduced; how this works is discussed below. It is interesting that the swap token implementation is very simple and consists of only roughly 100 lines — this proves once more that good ideas need not be complicated.

The swap token is implemented by a global pointer to the `mm_struct` of the process that is currently owning the token[14]:

mm/thrash.h
```
struct mm_struct *swap_token_mm;
static unsigned int global_faults;
```

The global variable `global_faults` counts the number of calls to `do_swap_page`. Every time a page is swapped in, this function is called (more about this in the next section), and the counter is increased. This provides a possibility for deciding how often a process has tried to grab the swap token in contrast to other processes in the system. Three fields in `struct mm_struct` are used to answer this question:

<mm_types.h>
```
struct mm_struct {
...
        unsigned int faultstamp;
        unsigned int token_priority;
        unsigned int last_interval;
...
}
```

---

[14]Actually, the memory region could be shared among several processes, and the swap token is associated with a specific memory region, not a specific process. The swap token could therefore belong to more than one process at a time in this sense. In reality, it belongs to the specific memory region. To simplify matters, however, assume that just one single process is associated with the memory region of the swap token.

faultstamp contains the value of `global_faults` when the kernel tried to grab the token last. `token_priority` is a swap-token-related scheduling priority that regulates access to the swap token, and `last_interval` denotes the length of the interval (again in units of `global_faults`) during which the process was waiting for the swap token.

The swap token is grabbed by calling `grab_swap_token`, and the meaning of the aforementioned values will become clearer by inspecting the source code:

mm/thrash.c
```
void grab_swap_token(void)
{
        int current_interval;
        global_faults++;
        current_interval = global_faults - current->mm->faultstamp;
...
        /* First come first served */
        if (swap_token_mm == NULL) {
                current->mm->token_priority = current->mm->token_priority + 2;
                swap_token_mm = current->mm;
                goto out;
        }
...
}
```

If the swap token is not assigned to any process yet, it can be grabbed without problems. Jumping to the label `out` will just update the settings for `faultstamp` and `last_interval` as you will see below.

Naturally, things are slightly more involved if the swap token is currently held by some process. In this case, the kernel has to decide if the new process should preempt the old one:

mm/thrash.c
```
        if (current->mm != swap_token_mm) {
                if (current_interval < current->mm->last_interval)
                        current->mm->token_priority++;
                else {
                        if (likely(current->mm->token_priority > 0))
                                current->mm->token_priority--;
                }
                /* Check if we deserve the token */
                if (current->mm->token_priority >
                                swap_token_mm->token_priority) {
                        current->mm->token_priority += 2;
                        swap_token_mm = current->mm;
                }
        } else {
                /* Token holder came in again! */
                current->mm->token_priority += 2;
        }
...
```

Consider the simple case first: If the process requesting the swap token already *has* the token (the second `else` branch), this means that it swaps in a lot of pages. Accordingly, the token priority is increased because it is badly required.

If a different process holds the token, then the current task's token priority is increased if it has been waiting longer for the token than the holder had to, or decreased otherwise. Should the current token priority exceed the priority of the holder, then the token is taken from the holder and given to the requesting process.

Finally, the token time stamps of the current process need to be updated:

mm/thrash.c
```
out:
        current->mm->faultstamp = global_faults;
        current->mm->last_interval = current_interval;
        return;
}
```

Notice that if a process *cannot* obtain the swap token, it still can swap in pages as required but will *not* be protected from memory reclaim.

grab_swap_token is only called from a single place, namely, at the beginning of do_swap_page, which is responsible for swapping-in pages. The token is grabbed if the requested page cannot be found in the swap cache and needs to be read in from the swap area:

mm/memory.c
```
static int do_swap_page(struct mm_struct *mm, struct vm_area_struct *vma,
unsigned long address, pte_t *page_table, pmd_t *pmd,
int write_access, pte_t orig_pte)
{
...
        page = lookup_swap_cache(entry);
        if (!page) {
                grab_swap_token(); /* Contend for token _before_ read-in */
...
                /* Read the page in */
...
        }
...
}
```

put_swap_token must be employed to release the swap token for the current process when the mm_struct of the current swap token is not required anymore. disable_token takes the token away forcefully. This is necessary when swapping out is really necessary, and you will encounter the corresponding cases below.

The key to the swap token implementation lies in the places where the kernel checks if the current process is the owner of the swap token, and the consequences for the process if it has the swap token. has_swap_token tests if a process has the swap token. The check is, however, only performed at a single place in the kernel: when it checks if a page has been referenced (recall that this is one of the essential ingredients to decide if a page is going to be reclaimed, and that page_referenced_one is a subfunction of page_referenced, which is only called from there):

mm/rmap.c
```
static int page_referenced_one(struct page *page,
        struct vm_area_struct *vma, unsigned int *mapcount)
{
...
        /* Pretend the page is referenced if the task has the
           swap token and is in the middle of a page fault. */
```

```
        if (mm != current->mm && has_swap_token(mm) &&
                        rwsem_is_locked(&mm->mmap_sem))
                referenced++;
    ...
}
```

Two situations must be distinguished:

1. The memory region in which the page in question is located belongs to the task on whose behalf the kernel is currently operating, and this task holds the swap token. Since the owner of the swap token is allowed to do what it wants with its pages, `page_referenced_one` ignores the effect of the swap token.

   This means that the current holder of the swap token is not prevented from reclaiming pages — if it wants to do so, then the page is really not necessary and can be reclaimed without hindering its work.

2. The kernel operates on behalf of a process that does not hold the swap token, but operates on a page that belongs to the address space of the swap token holder. In this case, the page is marked as referenced and is therefore protected from being moved to the inactive list from being reclaimed, respectively.

   However, one more thing needs to be considered: While the swap token has a beneficial effect on highly loaded systems, it affects loads with little swapping adversely. The kernel therefore adds another check before it marks the page referenced, namely, if a certain semaphore is held. The original swap token proposal requires enforcing the effect of the swap token at the moment when a page fault is handled. Since this is not so easy to detect in the kernel, the behavior is approximated by checking if the `mmap_sem` semaphore is held. While this can happen for several reasons, it also happens in the page fault code, and this is good enough as an approximation.

   The probability is low that a page fault happens when the system requires only little or no swapping. However, the probability increases if the corresponding swap pressure gets higher. All in all, this means that the swap token mechanism is gradually being enforced the more page faults there are in the system. This removes the negative impact of the swap token on systems with little swapping activity but retains the positive effect on highly loaded systems.

18.8   Handling Swap-Page Faults

While swapping pages out of RAM memory is a relatively complicated undertaking, swapping them in is much simpler. As discussed in Chapter 4, the processor triggers a page fault when an attempt is made to access a page that is registered in the virtual address space of the process but is not mapped into RAM memory. This does not necessarily mean that a swapped-out page has been accessed. It is also possible, for example, that an application has tried to access an address that is not reserved for it, or that a nonlinear mapping is involved. The kernel must therefore first find out whether it is really necessary to swap in a page; it invokes the architecture-specific function `handle_pte_fault`, as discussed in Section 4.11 to do this by examining the memory management data structures.

> Although the kernel *reclaims* all pages in the same way regardless of their backing store, this does not apply for the opposite direction. The method described here is only for anonymously mapped data that are read from one of the system's swap areas. When a page belonging to a file mapping is not present, the mechanisms discussed in Chapter 8 are responsible for providing the data.

18.8.1 Swapping Pages in

You already know from Chapter 4 that page faults as a result of accessing a swapped-out page are handled by `do_swap_page` from `mm/memory.c`. As the associated code flow diagram in Figure 18-19 shows, it is much easier to swap a page in than to swap it out, but it still involves more than just a simple read operation.

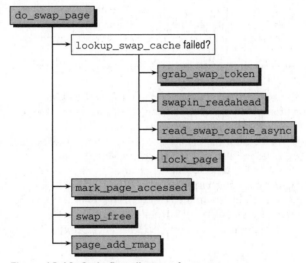

Figure 18-19: Code flow diagram for `do_swap_page`.

The kernel must not only check whether the requested page is still or already in the swap cache, but it also uses a simple readahead method to read several pages from the swap area in a chunk to anticipate future possible page faults.

As discussed in Section 18.4.1, the swap area and slot of a swapped-out page are held in the page table entry (the actual representation differs from machine to machine). To obtain general values, the kernel first invokes the familiar `pte_to_swp_entry` function to a `swp_entry_t` instance with machine-independent values that uniquely identify the page.

On the basis of these data, `lookup_swap_cache` checks whether the required page is in the swap cache. This applies if either the data have not yet been written or the data are shared and have already been read earlier by another process.

If the page is not in the swap cache, the kernel must not only cause the page to be read, but must also initiate a *readahead* operation to read a few pages in anticipation:

❑ `grab_swap_token` grabs the swap token as described before.

❑ `swapin_readahead` is responsible to perform the readahead. As a result, read requests are issued not only for the desired page but also for a few pages in the adjacent slots. This requires relatively little effort but speeds things up considerably because processes very often access the data they need from memory sequentially. When this happens, the corresponding pages will have already been read into memory by the readahead mechanism.

❑ `read_swap_cache_async` is called once more for the presently required page. As the function name indicates, the read operation is asynchronous. However, the kernel uses a trick to ensure that the required data have been read in before further work is commenced. `read_swap_cache_async` locks the page before a read request is submitted to the block layer. When the block layer has finished the data transfer, the page is unlocked. Therefore, it is sufficient to call `lock_page` in `do_swap_page` to lock the page — the operation will have to wait until the block layer unlocks the page. Unlocking the page from the block layer's side is, however, a confirmation that the read request has been completed.

I take a look at the implementation of these two actions below.

Once the page has been swapped in (if necessary), the following points must be addressed regardless of whether the page came from the page cache or had to be read from a block device.

The page is first marked with `mark_page_accessed` so that the kernel regards it as accessed — recall the state diagram in Figure 18-13 in this context. It is then inserted in the page tables of the process, and the corresponding caches are flushed if necessary. Thereafter, `page_add_anon_rmap` is invoked to include the page in the reverse mapping mechanism discussed in Chapter 4. The familiar `swap_free` function then checks whether the slot in the swap area can be freed. This also ensures that the usage counter in the swap data structure is decremented by 1. If the slot is no longer needed, the routine modifies the `lowest_bit` or `highest_bit` fields of the `swap_info` instance provided the swap page is at one of its two ends.

If the page is accessed in Read/Write mode, the kernel must conclude the operation by invoking `do_wp_page`. This creates a copy of the page, adds it to the page tables of the process that caused the fault, and decrements the usage counter on the original page by 1. These are the same steps performed by the copy-on-write mechanism discussed in Chapter 4.

18.8.2 Reading the Data

Two functions read data from swap space into system RAM. `read_swap_cache_async` creates the necessary preconditions and performs additional management tasks, and `swap_readpage` is responsible for submitting the actual read request to the block layer. Figure 18-20 shows the code flow diagram for `read_swap_cache_async` (assume that no errors occur during page allocation or because of race conditions when reading in swapped-out pages).

`find_get_page` is first invoked to check whether the page is in the swap cache. This can be the case because the readahead operations could have already provided the page. It's good if the page is already here because this simplifies things: The desired page can immediately be returned.

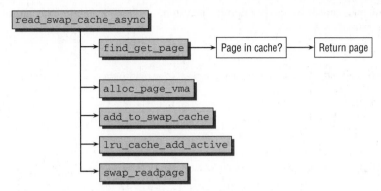

Figure 18-20: Code flow diagram for `read_swap_cache_async`.

If the page is not found, `page_alloc_vma` (which ultimately reduces to `alloc_page` on non-NUMA systems) must be called to allocate a fresh memory page to hold the data from the swap area. Requests for memory made with `alloc_pages` enjoy high priority. For instance, the kernel attempts to swap out other pages to provide fresh memory if not enough free space is available. Failure of this function — indicated by the return of a `NULL` pointer — is *very* serious and results in immediate abortion of swap-in. In this situation, the higher-level code instructs the OOM killer to close the least-important process in the system that has a comparatively large number of memory pages in order to obtain free memory.

If the page is successfully reserved (and this is usually the case because only very few users manage to inadvertently load the system to such an extent that the OOM killer must be deployed), the kernel adds the `page` instance to the swap cache using `add_to_swap_cache` and to the LRU cache (of the active pages) using `lru_cache_add_active`. The page data are then transferred from the swap area to RAM memory by means of `swap_readpage`.

`swap_readpage` initiates data transfer from hard disk to RAM memory once the necessary preconditions have been satisfied. This is done in two short steps. `get_swap_bio` generates an appropriate BIO request to the block layer, and `submit_bio` sends the request.

Two things require special attention:

- ❑   `add_page_to_swap_cache` automatically locks the page.

- ❑   `swap_readpage` instructs the block layer to call `end_swap_bio_read` when the page has been completely read in. This sets the `PG_uptodate` flag if everything went well, and additionally unlocks the page. This is important because the read operation is asynchronous. However, the kernel can be sure that the page is filled with the required data when it is marked up-to-date and unlocked.

18.8.3 Swap Readahead

As when reading files, the kernel also uses a readahead mechanism to read data from swap areas. This ensures that data are read in anticipation so that future page-in requests can be satisfied quickly, thus improving system performance. In contrast to the rather complicated file readahead method, the corresponding mechanism for the swapping subsystem mechanism is relatively simple, as the following code demonstrates:

mm/memory.c

```
void swapin_readahead(swp_entry_t entry, unsigned long addr,struct vm_area_struct *vma)
{
        int i, num;
        struct page *new_page;
        unsigned long offset;

        /*
         * Get the number of handles we should do readahead io to.
         */
        num = valid_swaphandles(entry, &offset);
        for (i = 0; i < num; offset++, i++) {
                /* Ok, do the async read-ahead now */
                new_page = read_swap_cache_async(swp_entry(swp_type(entry),
                                                 offset), vma, addr);
                if (!new_page)
                        break;
                page_cache_release(new_page);
        }
        lru_add_drain();        /* Push any new pages onto the LRU now */
}
```

The kernel invokes `valid_swaphandles` to calculate the number of readahead pages. Typically, $2^{page\_cluster}$ pages are read, where `page_cluster` is a global variable that is set to 2 for systems with less than 16 MiB of memory and to 3 for all others. This produces a readahead window of four or eight pages (`/proc/sys/vm/page-cluster` allows for tuning the variable from userspace, and to disable swap-in readahead by setting it to zero). However, the value calculated by `valid_swaphandles` must be reduced in the following situations:

❏   If the requested page is near the end of the swap area, the number of readahead pages must be reduced to prevent reading beyond the area boundary.

❏   If the readahead window includes free or unused pages, the kernel reads only the valid data *before* these pages.

`read_swap_cache_async` successively submits read requests for the selected pages to the block layer. If the function returns a `NULL` pointer because no memory page could be allocated, the kernel aborts swap-in because clearly no memory is available for further pages and the readahead mechanism is therefore less important than the memory shortage prevailing in the system.

18.9   Initiating Memory Reclaim

In the implementation overview at the beginning of this chapter, I demonstrated that the page selection and swap-out routines discussed so far are controlled by a further layer that decides *when* and *how many* pages are reclaimed. This decision is redirected to two places — first to the `kswapd` daemon that attempts to maintain optimal memory balance in the system when no too-memory-intensive applications are running; and second to an emergency mechanism that kicks in when the kernel thinks it is nearly totally out of memory.

18.9.1 Periodic Reclaim with `kswapd`

`kswapd` is a kernel daemon that is activated by `kswap_init` each time the system is started and continues to execute for as long as the machine is running:

mm/vmscan.c
```
int kswapd_run(int nid)
{
        pg_data_t *pgdat = NODE_DATA(nid);
        int ret = 0;
...
        pgdat->kswapd = kthread_run(kswapd, pgdat, "kswapd%d", nid);
...
        return ret;
}

static int __init kswapd_init(void)
{
        pg_data_t *pgdat;

        swap_setup();
        for_each_node_state(nid, N_HIGH_MEMORY)
                kswapd_run(nid);

        return 0;
}
```

The code shows that a separate instance of `kswapd` is activated for each NUMA zone. On some machines, this serves to enhance system performance as different speeds of access to various memory areas are compensated. Non-NUMA systems use only a single `kswapd`, though.

More interesting is the execution of the `kswapd` daemon implemented in `kswapd` from `mm/vmscan.c`. Once the necessary initialization work has been completed,[15] the following endless loop is executed:

mm/vmscan.c
```
static int kswapd(void *p)
{
        unsigned long order;
        pg_data_t *pgdat = (pg_data_t*)p;
        struct task_struct *tsk = current;
        DEFINE_WAIT(wait);
...
        current->reclaim_state = &reclaim_state;

        tsk->flags |= PF_MEMALLOC | PF_SWAPWRITE | PF_KSWAPD;
...
        order = 0;
        for ( ; ; ) {
                unsigned long new_order;

                prepare_to_wait(&pgdat->kswapd_wait, &wait, TASK_INTERRUPTIBLE);
                new_order = pgdat->kswapd_max_order;
                pgdat->kswapd_max_order = 0;
```

[15]On NUMA systems, set_cpus_allowed restricts execution of the daemon to processors associated with the memory zone.

```
                    if (order < new_order) {
                            /*
                             * Don't sleep if someone wants a larger 'order'
                             * allocation
                             */
                            order = new_order;
                    } else {
                            schedule();
                            order = pgdat->kswapd_max_order;
                    }
                    finish_wait(&pgdat->kswapd_wait, &wait);
...
                    balance_pgdat(pgdat, 0, order);
            }
            return 0;
    }
```

❑   prepare_wait places the task on a NUMA-zone-specific wait queue that is passed as parameter to the daemon.

❑   The function keeps a record of the last allocation order for which node balancing was performed. If the allocation order specified in kswapd_max_order is greater than the last value, balance_pgdat is invoked to rebalance the node (I discuss this shortly). Otherwise, the kernel transfers control to another function or to userspace by means of schedule.

     If the kernel thinks it necessary to invoke the daemon out of sequence, it does so by means of wake_up_interruptible.

     As described in Chapter 14, finish_wait performs the necessary clean-up work after the task has been woken.

❑   Following wakeup and after schedule, the kernel first rebalances the node and then the process starts afresh. If the current allocation order is greater than that for which balancing was last performed, balance_pgdat is invoked again with the larger parameter; otherwise the daemon goes to sleep.

Figure 18-21 shows the code flow diagram for the balance_pgdat function defined in mm/vmscan.c. In this function, the kernel decides how many memory pages are to be freed and forwards this information to the shrink_zone function discussed above.

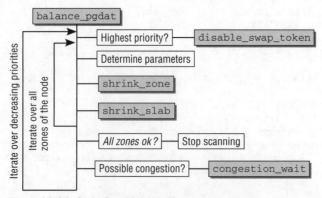

Figure 18-21: Code flow diagram for balance_pgdat.

Once the kernel has finished all the required management work at the beginning of balance_pgdat (the prime task is to create a swap_control instance), two nested loops are executed. The outer loop runs backward through the integer variable priority starting at DEF_PRIORITY (typically declared as 12 in mm/vmscan.c). This generates a priority for shrink_zone. A *higher* number corresponds to a *lower* priority; this has a corresponding impact on calculation of page selection behavior in refill_inactive_zone. By applying descending priorities, the kernel attempts to achieve its goal with the minimum of effort and therefore with the minimum of system disruption. The inner loop iterates over all zones of the NUMA node.

Before the inner loop is entered, the kernel must determine the zone (starting at ZONE_DMA) up to which scanning is to be performed. To this end, the zones are traversed in descending order and their state is checked using zone_watermark_ok (this function is discussed in detail in Chapter 3). If scanning is performed with highest priority (i.e., priority 0), the swap token is disabled because preventing pages from being swapped out to accelerate tasks is not desirable in situations that are desperate for memory:

mm/vmscan.c
```
static unsigned long balance_pgdat(pg_data_t *pgdat, unsigned long nr_pages,
                                   int order)
{
...
        for (priority = DEF_PRIORITY; priority >= 0; priority--) {
                int end_zone = 0;          /* Inclusive.  0 = ZONE_DMA */
                unsigned long lru_pages = 0;

                /* The swap token gets in the way of swapout... */
                if (!priority)
                        disable_swap_token();

                all_zones_ok = 1;

                /*
                 * Scan in the highmem->dma direction for the highest
                 * zone which needs scanning
                 */
                for (i = pgdat->nr_zones - 1; i >= 0; i--) {
                        struct zone *zone = pgdat->node_zones + i;

                        if (!populated_zone(zone))
                                continue;

                        if (zone_is_all_unreclaimable(zone) &&
                            priority != DEF_PRIORITY)
                                continue;

                        if (!zone_watermark_ok(zone, order, zone->pages_high,
                                               0, 0)) {
                                end_zone = i;
                                break;
                        }
                }
                if (i < 0)
                        goto out;
```

zone is the `struct zone` instance used to define the characteristic data of the memory zone. The layout and meaning of the structure are discussed in Chapter 3. Three auxiliary functions are employed to find a suitable zone:

❑ `zone_is_all_unreclaimable` checks for the flag `ZONE_ALL_UNRECLAIMABLE`. This is set if the zone is full of pinned pages because, for instance, all have been locked with the system call `mlock`. In this case, the zone need not be considered for page reclaim. The flag is automatically removed when at least one page in the zone is returned to the buddy system layer.

❑ `populated_zone` checks if any pages are present in the zone at all.

❑ `zone_watermark_ok` checks if memory can still be taken from a zone. See Section 3.5.4, where I have discussed this function.

> `zone->pages_high` *is the targeted value for the ideal number of free pages (low and minimum values are defined by* `pages_low` *and* `pages_min`).

As soon as a zone with an unacceptable status is found, the kernel branches to the `scan` label and starts scanning. However, it may well be that all zones are in order, in which case the kernel need do nothing and immediately jumps to the end of `balance_pgdat`.

All LRU pages in the zones to be scanned are determined before scanning starts:

mm/vmalloc.c

```
        for (i = 0; i <= end_zone; i++) {
                struct zone *zone = pgdat->node_zones + i;
                lru_pages += zone_page_state(zone, NR_ACTIVE)
                                + zone_page_state(zone, NR_INACTIVE);
        }
    . . .
```

As the code flow diagram shows, the kernel iterates over all zones. The direction goes from highmem to DMA. Two functions must be invoked for each zone (zones that are unpopulated or where all pages that are pinned are skipped):

❑ `shrink_zone` starts the mechanism for selecting and reclaiming RAM pages that was discussed in Section 18.6.4.

❑ `shrink_slab` is invoked by the kernel to shrink caches for various data structures allocated with the help of the slab system. Section 18.10 discusses this function. Although the page cache accounts for the lion's share of memory utilization, shrinking other caches — such as the dentry or inode cache — can also achieve tangible effects.

If the kernel iterates over the zones and finds that they are all in an acceptable status, the outer loop that iterates over all priorities can be terminated. Otherwise, the `congestion_wait` function discussed in Chapter 17 is called if pages have been scanned and the scan priority is below `DEF_PRIORITY - 2`. This prevents congestion of the block layer as a result of too many requests.

18.9.2   Swap-out in the Event of Acute Memory Shortage

The `try_to_free_pages` routine is invoked for rapid, unscheduled memory reclaim. Figure 18-22 shows the code flow diagram for the function.

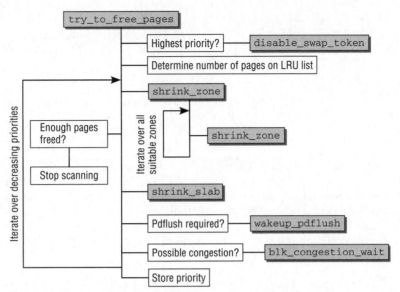

Figure 18-22: Code flow diagram for `try_to_free_pages`.

It is first necessary to determine the number of pages in the LRU cache as this information is required as the parameter for subsequent functions. The kernel acquires this information as before in `balance_pgdat`. Again, similar to before, the main part of `try_to_free_pages` is a large loop that runs through all priorities from `DEF_PRIORITY` to 0. If the kernel operates with highest priority, then the swap token is disabled.

The decision as to *how many* pages are to be freed is delegated to `shrink_zones` implemented in `mm/vmscan.c`.

> The `shrink_zones` function is not the same as the `shrink_zone` function discussed above — note the "s" at the end.

As in the `kswapd` mechanism, `shrink_zones` iterates over all zones of the current NUMA node and invokes `shrink_zone` if this is possible. The kernel dispenses with the call if there are no pages in a zone, if all pages in the zone are pinned, or if the current CPU is not permitted to act on the zone; but this is very rare.

After the slab caches have been shrunk with `shrink_slab` — more on this in the next section — the kernel must decide whether enough pages have been freed. If so, `try_to_free_pages` can be terminated since the target has been reached (the kernel then jumps to the `out` label at the end of the function). In the code excerpt below, `nr_reclaimed` indicates how many pages have been freed so far:

mm/vmscan.c
```
for (priority = DEF_PRIORITY; priority >= 0; priority--) {
        ......
        total_scanned += sc.nr_scanned;
        if (nr_reclaimed >= sc.swap_cluster_max) {
                ret = 1;
                goto out;
        }
```

```
        ...
                            if (total_scanned > sc.swap_cluster_max +
                                            sc.swap_cluster_max / 2) {
                                wakeup_pdflush(laptop_mode ? 0 : total_scanned);
                                sc.may_writepage = 1;
                            }

                            /* Take a nap, wait for some writeback to complete */
                            if (sc.nr_scanned && priority < DEF_PRIORITY - 2)
                                congestion_wait(WRITE, HZ/10);
            }
```

Depending on the number of pages freed, the kernel wakes the pdflush daemon to enable the periodic writeback mechanism. Notice that the number of pages to be flushed is usually restricted to the number of pages that were scanned. In laptop mode, however, the number of pages is unrestricted. As discussed in Section 17.13, if the hard disk must be spun up from a power-saving state, then it is supposed to do as much work as possible before it goes into a power-saving state again. congestion_wait is also invoked to prevent congestion in the block layer by waiting until a few flushing operations have completed successfully.

Finally, the priority of the successful pass is stored in the prev_priority element of the zone data structure as refill_inactive_zone uses this information to calculate the swap pressure.

18.10   Shrinking Other Caches

In addition to the page cache, the kernel manages other caches that are generally based on the slab (or *slub* or *slob*, but we'll use the term *slab* for all of them in the following) mechanism discussed in Chapter 3.

> *Slabs manage frequently required data structures to ensure that memory managed page-by-page by the buddy system is used more efficiently and that instances of the data types can be allocated quickly and easily as a result of caching.*

Kernel subsystems that use their own caches of this type are able to register *shrinker* functions dynamically with the kernel; these are called when memory is low to free some memory space already in use (technically, there is no fixed association between slabs and shrinker functions, but currently there are no other cache types for which shrinkers are used).

In addition to routines for registering and removing shrinker functions, the kernel must also provide methods to initiate cache shrinking. These are closely examined in the following sections.

18.10.1   Data Structures

The kernel defines its own data structure to describe the characteristics of shrinker functions:

mm/vmscan.c
```
struct shrinker {
        int (*shrink)(int nr_to_scan, gfp_t gfp_mask);
        int                     seeks;  /* seeks to recreate an obj */

        /* These are for internal use */
        struct list_head        list;
        long                    nr;     /* objs pending delete */
};
```

❏ shrink is a pointer to the function invoked to shrink a cache. Every shrinker function must accept two parameters — the number of memory pages to be examined and the memory type — and return an integer number that indicates *how many* objects are still in the cache.

> **This differs from the kernel's normal practice of returning the number of released objects/pages.**

If −1 is returned, the function could not perform any shrinking.

When the kernel wants to query the size of the cache, it passes 0 as `nr_to_scan` argument.

❏ seeks is a factor to adjust the cache weight in relation to the page cache. I examine this in more detail when I discuss how caches are shrunk.

❏ All registered shrinkers are kept in a doubly linked standard list. `list` serves as the list element.

❏ nr is the number of elements to be freed by the shrinker function. The kernel uses this value to enable the batch processing of objects for performance reasons.

18.10.2 Registering and Removing Shrinkers

`register_shrinker` is used to register a new shrinker:

mm/vmscan.c
```
void register_shrinker(struct shrinker *shrinker)
```

The function expects a `shrinker` instance where `seek` and `shrink` are set appropriately. Besides, the function only ensures that `shrinker` is added to the global list `shrinker_list`.

At present, only a small number of shrinkers are present in the kernel. This includes the following:

❏ `shrink_icache_memory` shrinks the inode cache discussed in Chapter 8 and also manages struct Inode objects.

❏ `shrink_dcache_memory` is responsible for the dentry cache also discussed in Chapter 8.

❏ `mb_cache_shrink_fn` shrinks a general cache for filesystem metadata (currently used to implement enhanced attributes in the Ext2 and Ext3 filesystems).

The `remove_shrinker` function removes shrinkers from the global list by reference to their `shrinker` instance:

mm/vmscan.c
```
void remove_shrinker(struct shrinker *shrinker)
```

18.10.3 Shrinking Caches

`shrink_slab` is invoked to shrink all caches registered as *shrinkable*. The allocation mask that specifies the required memory type and the number of pages scanned during page reclaim are passed to the function. Essentially, it iterates over all shrinkers in `shrinker_list`:

mm/vmscan.c
```
static int shrink_slab(long scanned, unsigned int gfp_mask)
{
```

```
        struct shrinker *shrinker;
        unsigned long ret = 0;
...
        list_for_each_entry(shrinker, &shrinker_list, list) {
...
```

To achieve an even balance between page cache and shrinker cache shrinking, the number of cache elements to be removed is calculated on the basis of the scanned value, which, in turn, is weighted with the seek factor of the cache and the maximum number of elements that can be freed by the current shrinker:

mm/vmscan.c

```
        unsigned long long delta;
        unsigned long total_scan;
        unsigned long max_pass = (*shrinker->shrinker)(0, gfp_mask);

        delta = (4 * scanned) / shrinker->seeks;
        delta *= max_pass;
        do_div(delta, lru_pages + 1);
        shrinker->nr += delta;

        if (shrinker->nr > max_pass * 2)
                shrinker->nr = max_pass * 2;
```

By convention, invoking the shrinker function with 0 as argument returns the number of objects in the cache. The kernel also ensures that never more than half the entries in the cache are freed so that no endless loop occurs.

The calculated number of objects to be freed is cumulated in shrinker->nr. Shrinking is triggered as long as this value exceeds the SHRINK_BATCH threshold value (typically defined as 128):

mm/vmscan.c

```
        total_scan = shrinker->nr;
        shrinker->nr = 0;
        while (total_scan >= SHRINK_BATCH) {
                long this_scan = SHRINK_BATCH;
                int shrink_ret;
                int nr_before;

                nr_before = (*shrinker->shrink)(0, gfp_mask);
                shrink_ret = (*shrinker->shrink)(this_scan, gfp_mask);
                if (shrink_ret == -1)
                        break;
                if (shrink_ret < nr_before)
                        ret += nr_before - shrink_ret;
                mod_page_state(slabs_scanned, this_scan);
                total_scan -= this_scan;

                cond_resched();
        }

        shrinker->nr += total_scan;
}
...
}
```

Objects are freed in chunks of 128 to ensure that the system is not blocked for too long. Between each invocation of the shrinker function, `cond_resched` gives the kernel the opportunity to perform scheduling so that latency does not become too high during cache shrinking.

18.11 Summary

One of the fundamental design decisions of the Linux kernel is that caches are usually never fixed in size, but can grow dynamically until all available RAM is used. You have seen in this chapter that filling RAM with information is a good thing because unused memory is a wasted resource, but that the kernel needs to use a mechanism that allows for shrinking caches if memory is required for more urgent tasks. You have been introduced to the mechanisms employed to judge whether pages are actively used or not. This allows for evicting rarely used pages from memory, and depending on how the pages are used, they can be discarded, synchronized, or swapped out. The last point implements the inverse of caching: A block device can be used to extend the effectively available amount of memory at the cost of access speed.

The kernel uses two mechanisms to reclaim memory: A periodic daemon consistently monitors memory usage and tries to keep the most active pages in RAM, but there are also routines that handle acute memory pressure.

While page reclaim and swapping work on page-sized objects, the kernel also provides mechanisms to shrink caches with smaller objects, and you have been introduced to the corresponding routines at the end of this chapter.

19

Auditing

Developers working on the kernel often have a natural interest to watch and inspect what is going on inside the code. But they are not the only ones who would like to know what the kernel does. System administrators, for instance, might want to observe which decisions the kernel has taken and which actions were performed. This can be beneficial for a number of reasons, ranging from increased security to postmortem forensic investigation of things that went wrong. It could, for instance, be very interesting to not only observe that a wrong security decision caused by some misconfiguration was made by the kernel, but also to know which process or users took advantage of this. This chapter describes the methods provided by the kernel for this purpose.

19.1 Overview

Obviously, the surveillance needs of administrators differ considerably from those of developers. While programmers are usually interested in comparatively low-level information, administrators will tend to need a higher-level view: Which processes have opened network connections? Which users have started programs? When did the kernel grant or refuse certain privileges?[1] To answer such questions, the kernel provides the audit subsystem.

While programmers will run their experiments on machines solely devoted to development, administrators face a different problem: The machines they have to monitor usually serve as production machines. This places two crucial constraints on the audit mechanism:

❑   It must be possible to dynamically change the criteria that select the types of events to be logged. In particular reboots or insertion and removal of kernel modules must not be required.

❑   System performance must not degrade by a significant amount when auditing is in use. Disabling the audit mechanism should also leave no negative impact on system performance.

---

[1]This includes the ability to check if (and which) users were nosy enough to try peeking into files that they shouldn't have access to.

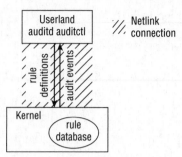

Figure 19-1: Overview of the audit subsystem.

A sketch of the overall design of the audit subsystem is depicted in Figure 19-1. The kernel contains a database with rules to specify the events that must be recorded. The database is filled from userland by means of the `auditctl` tool. If a certain event happens and the kernel decides per the database that it must be audited, a message is sent to the `auditd` daemon. The daemon can store the message in a log file for further inspection. Communication between userland and the kernel (rule manipulation and message transmission) is performed with the aid of a netlink socket (this connection mechanism was discussed in Chapter 12). The kernel and userland parts of the audit mechanism are mutually dependent on each other. Because the impact of audit on the kernel is minimal if only events are logged that appear with comparatively low frequency, the implementation is also referred to as the *lightweight auditing framework*.

To further decrease the impact on system performance, the audit mechanism distinguishes between two types of audit events, as follows:

❏ System call auditing allows recording whenever the kernel enters or leaves a system call. Although additional constraints can be specified to limit the number of logged events (for example, a restriction to a certain UID), system calls still happen with a rather high frequency, so a certain impact on system performance is unavoidable if system call auditing is employed.

❏ All other types of events that are not directly connected with system calls are handled separately. It is possible to disable auditing of system calls and to record only events of this type. This will affect the system load only very little.

It is important to understand the difference (and relationship) between auditing and more canonical techniques like system call tracing. If an audited process creates new children by forking, attributes relevant to auditing are inherited. This allows *audit trails* to be generated, which are important to observe the behavior of an application as a whole, or to track the actions of a certain user. In general, the audit mechanism allows (trusted) applications to be traced in a more task-oriented manner (i.e., from a higher-level point of view) than pure system call tracing (as implemented by `ptrace`) would allow. Various hooks that produce audit events are distributed across the kernel, but nearly all parts of the kernel could be extended with code to send specific audit messages.

Although audit is a fairly general mechanism, SELinux and AppArmor (a competitor to SELinux that is not included in the official kernel source, but is, for instance, employed by OpenSUSE) are the most notable users of the auditing features.

19.2 Audit Rules

How is it possible to place constraints on the types of events for which an audit log record can be generated? This is done with the help of audit rules, and this chapter discusses their format and purpose. However, you should also consult the manual pages that accompany the audit framework — especially 8(auditctl) — for more information. In general, an audit rule consists of the following components:

❑ The basic information is given by a *filter*/*value* pair. The *filter* denotes the kind of event to which the rule belongs. Examples for possible values are entry for system call entrance or task for task creation auditing.

❑ The *value* can either be NEVER or ALWAYS. Although the latter choice enables a rule, the first one is used to suppress generation of audit events. This is meaningful because all rules for a given filter type are stored in a list, and the first rule that matches is applied. By placing a NEVER rule in front, this allows you to (temporarily) disable processing of rules that would normally generate audit events.

The filters partition the set of auditable events into smaller classes, but these are nevertheless still very broad. More constraints are required to select practicable subsets of events. This is possible by specifying a number of *field*/*comparator*/*value* pairs. A *field* is a quantity that can be observed by the kernel. This can, for instance, be a certain UID, a process identifier, a device number, or an argument to a system call. *comparator* and *value* allow specifying conditions for the field. If these conditions are fulfilled, an audit log event is issued; otherwise, it is not. The usual comparison operators (less than, less or equal, and so on) can be employed. The method to feed new rules to the kernel is via the auditctl tool, which is in general called as follows:

```
root@meitner # auditctl -a filter,action -F field=value
```

Observe, for instance, how it is possible to audit all events where the root user has created a new process:

```
root@meitner # auditctl -a task,always -F euid=0
```

When system calls are being audited, it is also possible (and highly advisable!) to restrict record generation to specific system calls. The following example instructs the kernel to log all events when the user with UID 1000 fails to open a file:

```
root@meitner # auditctl -a exit,always -S open -F success=0 -F auid=1000
```

If the user tries to open /etc/shadow, but fails to provide the required credentials, the following log record will be generated:

```
root@meitner # cat /etc/audit/audit.log
...
type=SYSCALL msg=audit(1201369614.531:1518950): arch=c000003e syscall=2
    success=no exit=-13 a0=71ac78 a1=0 a2=1b6 a3=0 items=1 ppid=3900 pid=8358
    auid=4294967295 uid=1000 gid=100 euid=1000 suid=1000 fsuid=1000 egid=100
    sgid=100 fsgid=100 tty=pts0 comm="cat" exe="/usr/bin/cat" key=(null)

...
```

19.3   Implementation

The audit implementation belongs to the very core of the kernel (the source is located directly in `kernel/`). This stresses how much emphasis the kernel developers place on the framework. As with every code in the core kernel directory, much care was taken to make it as compact, efficient, and clean as possible. The code is basically distributed across three files:

❏   `kernel/audit.c` provides the core audit mechanism.

❏   `kernel/auditsc.c` implements system call auditing.

❏   `kernel/auditfilter.c` contains means to filter audit events.

Another file, `kernel/audit_tree.c`, contains data structures and routines that allow auditing of complete directory trees. Since a rather large amount of code is required to implement this comparatively small benefit, for simplicity's sake this chapter does not discuss this possibility any further.

Detailed documentation of the log format used, usage descriptions for the associated tools, and so on can be found on the developer's website `http://people.redhat.com/peterm/audit`, and in the corresponding manual pages. With this in mind, you can dive directly into the details of implementation in this section!

As is the case for most parts of the kernel, understanding the data structures of the audit framework is a big step toward understanding the implementation.

19.3.1   Data Structures

The audit mechanism uses data structures that fall into three main categories. First, processes need to be instrumented with a per-task data structure that is especially important for system call auditing. Second, audit events, filtering rules and so on need to be represented within the kernel. Third, a communication mechanism with the userland utilities needs to be established.

Figure 19-2 illustrates the connection of the different data structures that form the core of the auditing mechanism. The task structure is extended with an audit context that allows storing all data relevant for a system call, and a database that contains all audit rules is established. The data structures used to transfer audit data between kernel and userspace are not too interesting in this context, so they are not included in the figure.

Extensions to `task_struct`

Every process in the system is represented by an instance of `struct task_struct`, as discussed in Chapter 2. A pointer member of the structure is used to equip a process with an audit context as follows:

```
<sched.h>
struct task_struct {
...
        struct audit_context *audit_context;
...
}
```

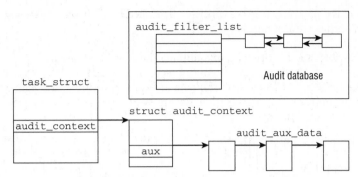

Figure 19-2: Data structures used by the audit mechanism.

Note that audit_context may well be a NULL pointer. This is because an instance of audit_context is allocated only if system call auditing is requested for a specific process. If no auditing is to be performed, it is unnecessary to expend memory on a superfluous data structure. The definition of struct audit_context is as follows:

kernel/auditsc.c
```
/* The per-task audit context. */
struct audit_context {
        int              in_syscall; /* 1 if task is in a syscall */
        enum audit_state state;
        unsigned int     serial;     /* serial number for record */
        struct timespec  ctime;      /* time of syscall entry */
        uid_t            loginuid;   /* login uid (identity) */
        int              major;      /* syscall number */
        unsigned long    argv[4];    /* syscall arguments */
        int              return_valid; /* return code is valid */
        long             return_code;/* syscall return code */
        int              auditable;  /* 1 if record should be written */
        int              name_count;
        struct audit_names names[AUDIT_NAMES];
        char * filterkey; /* key for rule that triggered record */
        struct dentry *   pwd;
        struct vfsmount * pwdmnt;
        struct audit_context *previous; /* For nested syscalls */
        struct audit_aux_data *aux;
        struct audit_aux_data *aux_pids;

                         /* Save things to print about task_struct */
        pid_t            pid;
        uid_t            uid, euid, suid, fsuid;
        gid_t            gid, egid, sgid, fsgid;
        unsigned long    personality;
        int              arch;
    ...
};
```

Most elements of the data structure are concisely described by their accompanying comments, and the undocumented entries are as follows:

❑   state denotes the activity level of auditing. The possible states are given by audit_state, namely: AUDIT_DISABLED (no system call recording), AUDIT_BUILD_CONTEXT (create an audit context and always fill in system call data at system call entry), and AUDIT_RECORD_CONTEXT (create an audit context, always fill in data at system call entry, and always write the audit record at system call exit).[2]

AUDIT_DISABLED only makes sense when system call auditing was active at some time, but has been stopped. If no auditing has been performed yet, then no audit_context is allocated and no state is required.

❑   names enables you to store the data of up to AUDIT_NAMES (usually set to 20) filesystem objects (the precise contents of this structure will be defined in a moment). name_count records how many of the available slots are presently in use.

❑   audit_aux_data allows for storing auxiliary data in addition to the audit context (the associated data structure is also described in a moment.) Although aux is for general use, aux_pids is employed to register the PIDs of processes that received a signal from a system call that was audited.

Fields like pid, sgid, personality, and so on that are defined at the end of the structure reflect their counterparts in task_struct. They are used to copy values from a given instance of task_struct so that they are available without needing to hold a reference to the task_struct.

The need to store information about filesystem objects arises when system calls are being audited. The following data structure provides a means to store this information:

kernel/auditsc.c
```
struct audit_names {
        const char      *name;
        int             name_len;       /* number of name's characters to log */
        unsigned long   ino;
        dev_t           dev;
        umode_t         mode;
        uid_t           uid;
        gid_t           gid;
        dev_t           rdev;
        u32             osid;
};
```

The members describe the usual properties of filesystem objects, so this section does not bother with the details. The array names from struct audit_context allows up to AUDIT_NAMES (usually set to 20) to be stored.

The current audit state of a process is stored in the state field of audit_context. The kernel defines audit rules that facilitate switching between different audit modes. The names of the actions, however, differ from the constants used for state. The following excerpt from the rule processing state machine

---

[2]Another alternative (AUDIT_SETUP_CONTEXT) can also be found in the definition of enum audit_state, but it is currently unused.

describes the relationship between them (refer to Section 19.3.1 for more information on how to transmit audit rules to the kernel):

kernel/auditsc.c
```
switch (rule->action) {
case AUDIT_NEVER:   *state = AUDIT_DISABLED;        break;
case AUDIT_ALWAYS:  *state = AUDIT_RECORD_CONTEXT; break;
}
```

Auxiliary data can be attached to an `audit_context` instance with the help of `audit_context->aux`. The kernel employs the following data structure:

kernel/auditsc.c
```
struct audit_aux_data {
        struct audit_aux_data   *next;
        int                     type;
};
```

`next` implements a single linked list of `aux_data` instances, and `type` denotes the type of auxiliary data. The purpose of `audit_aux_data` is to be embedded into a higher-level data structure that provides the actual data. To illustrate this with an example, the following excerpt shows how audit information for IPC objects is stored:

kernel/auditsc.c
```
struct audit_aux_data_ipcctl {
        struct audit_aux_data   d;
        struct ipc_perm         p;
        unsigned long           qbytes;
        uid_t                   uid;
        gid_t                   gid;
        mode_t                  mode;
        u32 osid;
};
```

Note that a `struct audit_aux_data` is located at the very beginning of `audit_aux_data_ipc`; the real payload follows afterward. This allows for using generic methods for list traversal and manipulation. Typecasts to the specific data type reveal the proper information.

Currently, the kernel defines auxiliary data structures for numerous object types:

❏   `audit_aux_data_ipcctl` (for auxiliary objects of type `AUDIT_IPC` and `AUDIT_IPC_SET_PERM`)

❏   `audit_aux_data_socketcall` (type `AUDIT_SOCKETCALL`)

❏   `audit_aux_data_sockaddr` (type `AUDIT_SOCKADDR`)

❏   `audit_aux_data_datapath` (type `AUDIT_AVC_PATH`)

❏   `audit_aux_data_data_execve` (type `AUDIT_EXECVE`)

❏   `audit_aux_data_mq_{open,sendrewcv,notify,getsetattr}` (types `AUDIT_MQ_{OPEN,SENDRECV,NOTIFY,GETSETATTR})`)

❏   `audit_aux_data_fd_pair` (type `AUDIT_FD_PAIR`)

Since the general structure of all other auxiliary audit data structures is similar, this section doesn't bother with showing them explicitly. You can refer to `kernel/auditsc.c` for their definitions.

Records, Rules and Filtering

The fundamental data structure to format an audit record is defined as follows:

kernel/audit.c
```
struct audit_buffer {
        struct list_head      list;
        struct sk_buff        *skb;        /* formatted skb ready to send */
        struct audit_context *ctx;         /* NULL or associated context */
        gfp_t                 gfp_mask;
};
```

`list` is a list element that allows for storing the buffer on various lists. Since netlink sockets are used to communicate between kernel and userland, a socket buffer of type `sk_buff` is used to encapsulate messages. The connection with the audit context is realized by `ctx` (which may also be a `NULL` pointer if no context exists because system call auditing is disabled), and `gfp_mask` finally determines from which memory pool allocations are supposed to be satisfied.

Since audit buffers are frequently used, the kernel keeps a number of pre-allocated instances of `audit_buffer` ready for use. `audit_buffer_alloc` and `audit_buffer_free` are responsible for allocating and initializing new buffers respectively freeing them — handling the audit buffer cache is implicitly performed by these functions. Their implementation is straightforward, so they are not discussed any further here.

An audit rule that is transferred from userspace into the kernel is represented by the following data structure[3]:

<audit.h>
```
struct audit_rule_data {
        __u32 flags; /* AUDIT_PER_{TASK,CALL}, AUDIT_PREPEND */
        __u32 action; /* AUDIT_NEVER, AUDIT_POSSIBLE, AUDIT_ALWAYS */
        __u32 field_count;
        __u32 mask[AUDIT_BITMASK_SIZE]; /* syscall(s) affected */
        __u32 fields[AUDIT_MAX_FIELDS];
        __u32 values[AUDIT_MAX_FIELDS];
        __u32 fieldflags[AUDIT_MAX_FIELDS];
        __u32 buflen; /* total length of string fields */
        char buf[0]; /* string fields buffer */
};
```

First, `flags` denotes when the rule is supposed to be activated. The following choices are possible:

<audit.h>
```
#define AUDIT_FILTER_USER    0x00  /* Apply rule to user-generated messages */
#define AUDIT_FILTER_TASK    0x01  /* Apply rule at task creation (not syscall) */
#define AUDIT_FILTER_ENTRY   0x02  /* Apply rule at syscall entry */
```

---

[3]Previous kernel versions employed the slightly simpler `struct audit_rule`, which did not allow for non-integer or variable-length string data fields. The structure still exists in the kernel to provide backward-compatibility with userspace, but must not be used by new code.

```
#define AUDIT_FILTER_WATCH  0x03  /* Apply rule to file system watches */
#define AUDIT_FILTER_EXIT   0x04  /* Apply rule at syscall exit */
#define AUDIT_FILTER_TYPE   0x05  /* Apply rule at audit_log_start */
```

When a rule matches, two actions (as denoted by `action`) can be performed. `AUDIT_NEVER` simply does nothing, and `AUDIT_ALWAYS` generates an audit record.[4]

If system calls are audited, `mask` specifies with a bit field which system calls to include.

Field/value pairs are employed to specify conditions under which an audit rule applies. The field denotes some quantity that identifies an object within the kernel, such as a process ID. The value argument, together with some comparison operators (e.g., "less than," "greater than," and so on), specifies which set of values the field is allowed to possess to trigger an audit event. One particular example could be "create an audit log for all events where a process with PID 0 opens a message queue." The `fields` and `values` arrays represent such pairs, and the operator flags are kept in `fieldflags`. `field_count` denotes how many pairs are included in a rule. The possible `fields` values are listed in `<audit.h>`. There are quite a few of them, so this section does not document them all in detail — the documentation that accompanies the audit userland tools provides a much better reference. Usually, the constant names are self-explanatory, as the following example demonstrates:

<audit.h>
```
#define AUDIT_PID 0
#define AUDIT_UID 1
#define AUDIT_EUID 2
#define AUDIT_SUID 3
...
```

The `values` array is only used for specifying numerical values, but this is not sufficient to create rules that are restricted to filenames and other non-numerical quantities. A string argument can therefore be appended behind `struct audit_rule_data`. It is accessible via the pseudo-array `buf`, and the string length is denoted by `buflen`.

While `struct audit_rule_data` is employed to transmit rules from userspace to the kernel, two more data structures are used to represent rules within the kernel itself. They are defined as follows:

kernel/audit.h
```
struct audit_field {
        u32 type;
        u32 val;
        u32 op;
...
};

struct audit_krule {
        int vers_ops;
        u32 flags;
        u32 listnr;
        u32 action;
        u32 mask[AUDIT_BITMASK_SIZE];
        u32 buflen; /* for data alloc on list rules */
```

---

[4]`AUDIT_POSSIBLE` is still listed as another alternative, but it's deprecated and not supposed to be used any more.

```
                 u32 field_count;
                 char *filterkey; /* ties events to rules */
                 struct audit_field *fields;
    ...
    };
```

The contents are similar to `struct audit_rule_data`, except that the data types employed can be manipulated and traversed in a more convenient fashion. All rules are contained in an array pointed at by `fields`, and each rule is represented by an instance of `struct audit_field`.

To convert between both audit rule representations, the kernel provides the auxiliary function `audit_rule_to_entry`. Since the transformation is a somewhat mechanical process that does not provide any special insights into how rules work, this section doesn't bother to discuss the code in detail. All you need to know here is that the routine takes an instance of `struct audit_rule` and converts it into an instance of `struct audit_entry`, which is a container for `audit_krule`.

kernel/audit.h
```
struct audit_entry {
        struct list_head list;
        struct rcu_head rcu;
        struct audit_krule rule;
};
```

This container allows for storing rules in filter lists. Six different filter lists are provided by `audit_filter_list`.

kernel/auditsc.c
```
static struct list_head audit_filter_list[AUDIT_NR_FILTERS] = {
        LIST_HEAD_INIT(audit_filter_list[0]),
    ...
        LIST_HEAD_INIT(audit_filter_list[5]),
};
```

Each list keeps all rules that are to be applied at one of the opportunities defined by the `AUDIT_FILTER_` macros.

Note that new rules are added with `audit_add_rule` that is called when an appropriate request is sent from the `auditd` daemon to the kernel. Since this routine is likewise rather technical and mostly uninteresting, this section does not cover it in detail.

19.3.2 Initialization

Initialization of the audit subsystem is performed by `audit_init`. In addition to setting up data structures, the function creates a netlink socket used for communication with the userland as follows:

kernel/audit.c
```
static int __init audit_init(void)
{
...
audit_sock = netlink_kernel_create(&init_net, NETLINK_AUDIT, 0,
                                   audit_receive, NULL, THIS_MODULE);
...
}
```

The code snippet reveals that `audit_receive` is responsible for processing any received packets. It implements a dispatcher that is discussed later.

Note that there is a kernel command line parameter (`audit`) that can be set to either 0 or 1. The value is stored in the global variable `enable_audit` during initialization. If it is set to 0, auditing is completely disabled. When it is set to 1, auditing is enabled, but since no rules are supplied by default, no audit events will be generated unless appropriate rules are given to the kernel.

There is also a kernel thread for the audit mechanism. Instead of starting the thread during subsystem initialization, a slightly unconventional way has been chosen: As soon as the userspace daemon `auditd` sends the first message, the kernel thread `kaudit_task` is started. The function executed by the thread is `kauditd_thread`, which is responsible for sending already prepared messages from the kernel to the userspace daemon. Note that this daemon is necessary because an audit event may end within an interrupt handler, and since the netlink functions cannot be called from here, the finished audit records are put on a queue and processed later by the kernel daemon that sends them back to userspace. Sending and receiving is performed with a simple netlink operation and standard queue processing, as discussed in Chapter 12.

19.3.3 Processing Requests

Userspace applications may (dependent on the usual security checks) issue requests to the audit subsystem. Since the implementations of routines to satisfy such requests are rather similar, this section discusses only the dispatching mechanism and an exemplary case.

`audit_receive` is called by the network subsystem whenever a new request arrives over the netlink socket. The code flow diagram for the function can be found in Figure 19-3.

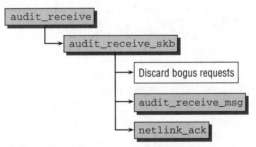

Figure 19-3: Code flow diagram for
`audit_receive`.

`audit_receive` handles the required locking and delegates the real work to `audit_skb_receive`. This function iterates over the queue as long as there are outstanding requests. Requests with a bogus size are discarded without further notice. Proper ones are forwarded to `audit_receive_msg`. An acknowledgment is sent with `netlink_ack` if this is either explicitly requested (as indicated by thge `NLM_F_ACK` flag) or if processing the request failed.

Observe from the code flow diagram in Figure 19-4 that `audit_receive_message` first uses `audit_netlink_ok` to verify that the sender is allowed to perform the request. If the request was authorized, the function verifies that the kernel daemon is already running. Should this not be the case because no request has been sent before, `kauditd` is launched.

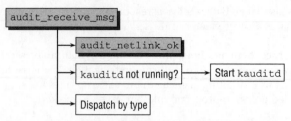

Figure 19-4: Code flow diagram for `audit_receive_msg`.

The remainder of the function is a dispatcher that calls specific processing functions selected by request type after the required information has been extracted from the netlink message. As usual, the dispatcher is implemented with a large case statement.

Let us focus our attention on one particular example of how to handle a request, namely how the kernel adds new audit rules to the rule database. For requests of type AUDIT_ADD_RULE, the dispatcher delegates further processing to audit_receive_filter, where the following piece of code is responsible for dealing with the request:

kernel/auditfilter.c
```
switch (type) {
..
        case AUDIT_ADD:
        case AUDIT_ADD_RULE:
                if (type == AUDIT_ADD)
                        entry = audit_rule_to_entry(data);
                else
                        entry = audit_data_to_entry(data, datasz);
                if (IS_ERR(entry))
                        return PTR_ERR(entry);

                err = audit_add_rule(entry,
                                        &audit_filter_list[entry->rule.listnr]);
                audit_log_rule_change(loginuid, sid, "add", &entry->rule, !err);
...
        break;
}
```

The request type AUDIT_ADD is supported only for backward compatibility, so it is not important in this context. audit_data_to_entry was mentioned before: It takes an instance of struct audit_rule_data that comes from userspace, and converts it into an instance of struct audit_krule — the kernel internal representation of an audit rule. audit_add_rule, in turn, is responsible for placing the newly constructed object on the appropriate audit rule list in audit_filter_list. Since adding audit rules is a decision worth remembering, audit_log_rule_change prepares a corresponding audit log message that is sent to the userland audit daemon.

19.3.4 Logging Events

With all the infrastructure in place, you can now take a look at how the actual auditing is implemented. The process is split into three phases. First, the logging process needs to be started via audit_log_start.

Afterwards, a log message is formatted with `audit_log_format`, and finally the audit log is closed with `audit_log_end` and the message is queued for transmission to the audit daemon.

Audit Start

To start auditing, `audit_log_start` needs to be called. The associated code flow diagram can be seen in Figure 19-5.

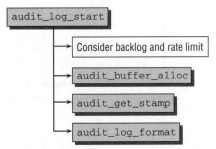

Figure 19-5: Code flow diagram for `audit_log_start`.

Basically, the job of `audit_log_start` is to set up an instance of `audit_buffer` and return it to the caller; but before this, the backlog limit and rate limit need to be considered.

The maximal length of the backlog queue (i.e., the queue where the finished audit records are stored) is given by the global variable `audit_backlog_limit`. If this number is surpassed,[5] `audit_log_start` schedules a timeout and retries the operation afterward, hoping that the backlog has been reduced in the meantime. Additionally, a rate check ensures that not more than a certain number of messages are sent per second. The global variable `audit_rate_limit`) determines the maximal frequency. If this frequency is surpassed, a message that indicates this condition is sent to the daemon and allocation is aborted. These measures are necessary to avoid denial-of-service attacks, and to provide protection against audit events that occur with too-high frequency.

If backlog and rate limits allow the creation of new audit buffers, `audit_buffer_alloc` is used to do what its name says — allocate an `audit_buffer` instance. Before the buffer is returned to the caller, `audit_get_stamp` provides a unique serial number, and an initial log message that contains the creation time and the serial number is written to the buffer.

Writing Log Messages

`audit_log_format` is used to write a log message into a given audit buffer. The prototype of the function is as follows:

kernel/audit.c
```
void audit_log_format(struct audit_buffer *ab, const char *fmt, ...)
```

As the prototype suggests, `audit_log_format` is — more or less — a variant of `printk`. The format string given in `fmt` is evaluated and filled in with the parameters given by the `va_args` list, and the resulting string is written into the data space of the socket buffer associated with the audit buffer.

---

[5]Note that audit records that are allocated *without* the `__GFP_WAIT` flag are considered more urgent. The backlog length threshold at which they are prevented from being created is higher than for other allocation types.

Closing the Audit Log

After all necessary log messages have been written to an audit buffer, `audit_log_end` needs to be called to ensure that the audit log is sent to the userspace daemon. The code flow diagram for the function can be found in Figure 19-6.

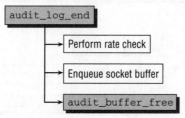

Figure 19-6: Code flow diagram for
`audit_log_end`.

After performing another rate check (if messages have been submitted too frequently, then the present message is lost and a "rate limit exceeded" message is sent to the daemon instead), the socket buffer associated with the audit buffer is put on a queue for later processing by kauditd:

kernel/audit.c
```
void audit_log_end(struct audit_buffer *ab)
{
...
            struct nlmsghdr *nlh = (struct nlmsghdr *)ab->skb->data;
            nlh->nlmsg_len = ab->skb->len - NLMSG_SPACE(0);
            skb_queue_tail(&audit_skb_queue, ab->skb);
            ab->skb = NULL;
            wake_up_interruptible(&kauditd_wait);
...
}
```

Note that the kernel provides the convenience function `audit_log`, which can be used as an abbreviation for the three aforementioned tasks (starting an audit log, writing messages, and ending the log). It has the following prototype:

<audit.h>
```
struct audit_buffer *audit_log_start(struct audit_context *ctx,
                        gfp_t gfp_mask, int type,
                        const char *fmt, ...);
```

19.3.5 System Call Auditing

By now, all data structures and mechanisms required for system call auditing have been described, so this section continues the description of the implementation. System call auditing is different from the basic audit mechanism because it relies on an extension of the task structure with an *audit context* that was introduced in a previous section.

Audit Context Allocation

First of all, you need to consider under which circumstances such contexts are allocated. Since this is an expensive operation, it is only performed if system call auditing was explicitly enabled.

If this is the case, `copy_process` (i.e., originating from the `fork` system call) is the place where `audit_alloc` is called to allocate a new instance of `struct audit_context`. Figure 19-7 shows the code flow diagram for `audit_context`.

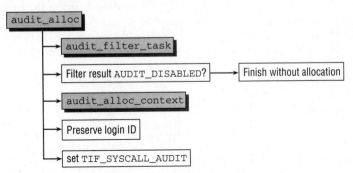

Figure 19-7: Code flow diagram for `audit_context`.

First, `audit_filter_task` determines if system call auditing needs to be activated for the present task. If the audit system is disabled completely, not even this needs to take place, so `audit_alloc` is left immediately. The function applies the registered filters of type `AUDIT_FILTER_TASK`. If the verdict is `AUDIT_DISABLED`, `audit_alloc` can return immediately without allocating an instance of `audit_context` because no system call auditing is required (the rest of the audit code can check this easily — the `audit_context` element of `task_struct` remains a `NULL` pointer in this case).

If system call auditing is desired, `audit_alloc_context` allocates a new instance of `audit_context`. The routine prepares the instance with `state` set to the state given by the filter operation.

Finally, the kernel preserves the login UID of the currently running task (this is necessary to create audit trails where the login UID is preserved over `fork`s), as follows:

kernel/auditsc.c
```
int audit_alloc(struct task_struct *tsk)
{
...
                                    /* Preserve login uid */
        context->loginuid = -1;
        if (current->audit_context)
                context->loginuid = current->audit_context->loginuid;

        tsk->audit_context  = context;
        set_tsk_thread_flag(tsk, TIF_SYSCALL_AUDIT);
        return 0;
}
```

Additionally, the `TIF_SYSCALL_AUDIT` flag is set in the instance of `task_struct` that belongs to the process. This is necessary for the low-level interrupt processing code to call the auditing functions at interrupt entry and exit — otherwise, this step will be skipped for performance reasons.

Note that the call to `audit_alloc` originates from processing `fork` system calls, so the decision about whether system call auditing needs to be enabled or not is made whenever a process creates a duplicate of itself. This ensures that the check is performed for every task in the system.

System Call Events

The audit subsystem is involved when a system call is entered and when a system call is finished — `audit_syscall_entry` is called in the first case, and `audit_syscall_exit` is called in the second case. To make this possible, support by the low-level, architecture-specific interrupt processing code is required. This support is integrated into `do_syscall_trace`, which is called by the low-level interrupt processing code whenever an interrupt occurs or when interrupt processing is finished.[6] For the IA-32 architecture, the implementation is done as follows:

arch/x86/kernel/ptrace_32.c
```
__attribute__((regparm(3)))
int do_syscall_trace(struct pt_regs *regs, int entryexit)
{
...
        if (unlikely(current->audit_context) && !entryexit)
                audit_syscall_entry(current, AUDIT_ARCH_I386, regs->orig_eax,
                                    regs->ebx, regs->ecx, regs->edx, regs->esi);
...
        if (unlikely(current->audit_context))
                audit_syscall_exit(current, AUDITSC_RESULT(regs->eax),
                                   regs->eax);
...
}
```

The code flow diagram for `audit_syscall_entry` is presented in Figure 19-8.

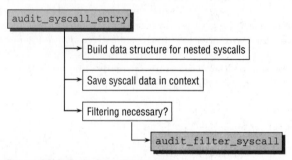

Figure 19-8: Code flow diagram for `audit_syscall_entry`.

If the actual system call happened during another system call that was audited, the possibility of linking multiple audit contexts needs to be utilized by allocating a new audit context, connecting the previous one with it, and using the freshly allocated context as previous one.

The system call number, the arguments passed to the system call (denoted by a1 ... a4), and the system architecture (such as `AUDIT_ARCH_i386` for IA-32, or constants for other architectures defined in `<audit.h>`) are stored in the audit context as follows:

kernel/auditsc.c
```
void audit_syscall_entry(struct task_struct *tsk, int arch, int major,
                         unsigned long a1, unsigned long a2,
                         unsigned long a3, unsigned long a4)
```

---

[6]Additionally, the flag `TIF_SYSCALL_AUDIT` needs to be set for this. It is enabled in `audit_alloc` if the audit filter determines that system call auditing needs to be activated for a task.

```
{
...
        context->arch       = arch;
        context->major      = major;
        context->argv[0]    = a1;
        context->argv[1]    = a2;
        context->argv[2]    = a3;
        context->argv[3]    = a4;
...
}
```

Depending on the audit mode of the process, filtering needs to be applied by using `audit_filter_list`, which applies all appropriate filters registered in the kernel as follows:

kernel/auditsc.c

```
    state = context->state;
    if (!context->dummy && (state == AUDIT_SETUP_CONTEXT || state == AUDIT_BUILD_CONTEXT))
        state = audit_filter_syscall(tsk, context, &audit_filter_list[AUDIT_FILTER_ENTRY]);
    if (likely(state == AUDIT_DISABLED))
        return;

    context->serial     = 0;
    context->ctime      = CURRENT_TIME;
    context->in_syscall = 1;
    context->auditable  = !!(state == AUDIT_RECORD_CONTEXT);
}
```

Note that `context->dummy` is set if auditing is enabled, but no audit rules are defined. In this case, filtering is obviously unnecessary.

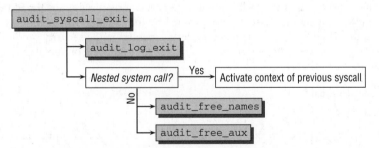

Figure 19-9: Code flow diagram for `audit_syscall_exit`.

Let us now turn our attention to how system call exits are handled. The code flow diagram for `audit_syscall_exit` is shown in Figure 19-9. The most important part is the call to `audit_log_exit`, which (among other things) creates an audit record for the information contained in the audit context as follows:

kernel/auditsc.c

```
static void audit_log_exit(struct audit_context *context, struct task_struct *tsk)
# {
        audit_log_format(ab, "arch=%x syscall=%d",
                    context->arch, context->major);
...
        if (context->return_valid)
```

```
                 audit_log_format(ab, " success=%s exit=%ld",
                            (context->return_valid==AUDITSC_SUCCESS)?"yes":"no",
                            context->return_code);
...
        audit_log_format(ab,
                " a0=%lx a1=%lx a2=%lx a3=%lx items=%d"
                " pid=%d auid=%u uid=%u gid=%u"
                " euid=%u suid=%u fsuid=%u"
                " egid=%u sgid=%u fsgid=%u",
                context->argv[0],
                context->argv[1],
                context->argv[2],
                context->argv[3],
                context->name_count,
                context->pid,
                context->loginuid,
                context->uid,
                context->gid,
                context->euid, context->suid, context->fsuid,
                context->egid, context->sgid, context->fsgid);
...
}
```

The system call number, the system call return code, and some generic information about the process are logged by the preceding code. Afterwards, `audit_syscall_exit` has to make sure that the previous audit context (should one exist) is restored as the active context; additionally, several now-unused resources need to be deallocated.

Access Vector Cache Auditing

A very prominent example where auditing is a rather crucial requirement is the SELinux access vector cache. Granting or denying permissions is performed by the function `avc_audit`, which is called from `avc_has_perm`, that is, whenever a permission query is passed to the security server. First, the function needs to check if auditing is required for the current case (i.e., granting or denial is supposed to be audited or not) as follows:

security/selinux/avc.c
```
void avc_audit(u32 ssid, u32 tsid,
            u16 tclass, u32 requested,
            struct av_decision *avd, int result, struct avc_audit_data *a)
{
        struct task_struct *tsk = current;
        struct inode *inode = NULL;
        u32 denied, audited;
        struct audit_buffer *ab;

        denied = requested & ~avd->allowed;
        if (denied) {
                audited = denied;
                if (!(audited & avd->auditdeny))
                        return;
        } else if (result) {
                audited = denied = requested;
```

```
        } else {
                audited = requested;
                if (!(audited & avd->auditallow))
                        return;
        }
    ...
```

If an audit message needs to be created, the basic information (granting or denial, the access vector in question, and the task's PID) is generated as follows:

security/selinux/avc.c
```
        ab = audit_log_start(current->audit_context, GFP_ATOMIC, AUDIT_AVC);
        if (!ab)
                return;          /* audit_panic has been called */
        audit_log_format(ab, "avc:  %s ", denied ? "denied" : "granted");
        avc_dump_av(ab, tclass,audited);
        audit_log_format(ab, " for ");
        if (a && a->tsk)
                tsk = a->tsk;
        if (tsk && tsk->pid) {
                audit_log_format(ab, " pid=%d comm=", tsk->pid);
                audit_log_untrustedstring(ab, tsk->comm);
        }
    ...
```

avc_dump_av is used to display an access vector in human-readable form (this is a purely cosmetic conversion). If auxiliary data are associated with the query, it is also put into the audit record. Afterwards the record can be closed.

security/selinux/avc.c
```
        if (a) {
                switch (a->type) {
                case AVC_AUDIT_DATA_IPC:
                        audit_log_format(ab, " key=%d", a->u.ipc_id);
                        break;
                case AVC_AUDIT_DATA_CAP:
                        audit_log_format(ab, " capability=%d", a->u.cap);
                        break;
    ...
                case AVC_AUDIT_DATA_NET:
                        /* Audit networking related information */
    ...
                }
        }
        audit_log_format(ab, " ");
        avc_dump_query(ab, ssid, tsid, tclass);
        audit_log_end(ab);
    }
```

Standard Hooks

Although it is sufficient to record only entry and exit for most system calls, some can provide more information to the audit subsystem. Section 19.3.1 mentioned that the audit context provides the capability to store auxiliary data — this is used by several system calls. Since the method to realize this is nearly identical for all cases, only `sys_socketcall` is shown as an example here. The following hook function is used to allocate and fill in the auxiliary data:

kernel/auditsc.c
```
int audit_socketcall(int nargs, unsigned long *args)
{
        struct audit_aux_data_socketcall *ax;
        struct audit_context *context = current->audit_context;

        if (likely(!context || context->dummy))
                return 0;

        ax = kmalloc(sizeof(*ax) + nargs * sizeof(unsigned long), GFP_KERNEL);
...

        ax->nargs = nargs;
        memcpy(ax->args, args, nargs * sizeof(unsigned long));

        ax->d.type = AUDIT_SOCKETCALL;
        ax->d.next = context->aux;
        context->aux = (void *)ax;
        return 0;
}
```

If auditing system calls is disabled, then no audit context is allocated, so the routine can exit immediately. Otherwise, an auxiliary context is added to the audit context.

Every time `sys_socketcall` is invoked, it calls `audit_socketcall` as follows:

net/socket.c
```
asmlinkage long sys_socketcall(int call, unsigned long __user *args)
{
...
        err = audit_socketcall(nargs[call]/sizeof(unsigned long), a);
...
}
```

The remaining parts of `sys_socketcall` can use the auxiliary context to store specific socket-related information that will be passed to the audit userspace tools.

19.4 Summary

Observing what is going on inside a system is interesting for a number of reasons, and this chapter introduced you to one particular solution provided by the kernel for this purpose: Auditing is a low-overhead mechanism that can be employed on stable production systems to obtain a comprehensive set of information without impacting system performance too much. After introducing audit rules that allow you to specify which information is interesting, the chapter discussed how the kernel gathers the corresponding data and forwards it to userland.

Architecture Specifics

One of the key benefits of the kernel is the fact that it is mostly architecture-*independent*. Because the majority of the sources are written in C, the implemented algorithms are not tied to a particular CPU or computer family but can, in principle, be ported to on any platform with modest effort — assuming that a suitable C compiler is available. Inevitably, the kernel must provide interfaces to the underlying hardware, perform various system-specific tasks that involve countless details, and exploit the special functions of the processors used. These must generally be written in an assembly language. However, there are also some architecture specific data structures that are defined in C, so architecture-specific does not necessarily equate to assembler-specific. This appendix describes some hardware-specific aspects of important Linux ports.

A.1 Overview

To facilitate extensibility on new architectures, the kernel strictly segregates architecture-*dependent* and architecture-*independent* code. The `include/asm-arch/` directory holds header files that contain the definitions and prototypes for processor-specific elements of the kernel, whereas C and assembler source codes that implement the machine-specific part of the kernel reside in `arch/arch/`. Together these occupy on average between 1 and 3 MiB in the kernel sources of each architecture. Although this represents a fair amount of code, it is nevertheless relatively compact for a complete abstraction layer.

There are basically two categories of architecture-specific code:

❑ Components that are used and invoked exclusively by the architecture-specific parts of the kernel. As far as the rest of the code is concerned, the location of this code and the functions that are called are irrelevant.

❑ Interface functions that *must* be defined by every architecture as they are invoked by architecture-independent code. For example, each port must provide a `switch_to` function to take care of hardware-control details when switching between two processes. The scheduler makes use of this function by deciding — *regardless* of the architecture — which task runs next and then delegating the actual task switch to processor-specific code.

Memory management also employs a variety of interface functions and definitions — to specify page size or to update caches, for instance.

This chapter is designed to give a brief summary of how various system-specific tasks are performed on the most popular architectures supported by the kernel. This is based on the fact that the kernel must exploit a very large number of hardware features that differ from processor to processor and require in-depth knowledge of the individual architectures. Considering that each processor family is typically accompanied by a reference manual of a thousand pages or more to describe architectural subtleties and oddities, this book cannot even begin to examine every little detail of importance to the kernel. Instead, this chapter sketches out the rough structure that supports the Linux port to a specific architecture. This book also describes various special features of some of the ports.

The build system takes into account the need to resort to architecture-specific defined mechanisms at various points in the generic code. All processor-specific header files are located in `include/asm-arch`. Once the kernel has been configured for a specific architecture, a symbolic link (named `include/asm`) to the appropriate machine-specific directory is created; for example, this link would be `include/asm -> include/asm-alpha` on an Alpha AXP system. This enables the kernel to link in architecture-specific headers by means of `#include<asm/file.h>`.

This book gives only a brief overview of the standard headers that must be made available by the individual ports and of the functions and definitions these headers must declare (and also implement). It would require another entire book to cover the details of each architecture supported.

A.2 Data Types

The kernel makes a basic distinction between the following three elementary data types:

❑ Standard data types as used in every C program; for example, `unsigned long`, `void *`, and `char`. The number of bits that these types have is not fixed by the C standard. Only various inequalities are guaranteed; for instance, `unsigned long` has at least as many if not more bits than `int`.

In terms of portability, it should be noted that the bit size of standard data types can differ between architectures.

❑ Data types with a fixed number of bits. The kernel provides special integer data types with names like `u32` and `s16` for unsigned (`u`) and signed (`s`) integers with a predefined number of bits. The individual architectures must define the abbreviations in such a way that they can be mapped (using `typedef`) to corresponding elementary data types.

❑ Subsystem-specific types that are never manipulated directly but always by specially written functions. Converting the data type definition is easy, because all subsystems that use any of these data types are never able to manipulate them directly but must delegate this task to the specific subsystem. Only the standard manipulation functions need to be modified; the remaining kernel parts remain unchanged.

Examples of subsystem-specific data types are `pid_t` for managing pids and `sector_t` for identifying sector numbers.

The data types with a fixed number of bits are defined in `<asm-arch/types.h>`.

> The pre-processor constant **__KERNEL__** must always be defined before the file is linked into the kernel sources; otherwise, only data type names prefixed with a double underscore are defined (for example, __u32) to prevent overlaps with definitions in the userspace namespace.

A.3   Alignment

The alignment of data on certain memory addresses is necessary to make the best possible use of processor caches and to boost performance. Some architectures *mandate* that data types of a particular length have a specific alignment. Even architectures that are able to handle random alignment can read and write certain alignments faster than when access is unaligned. Alignment is typically on byte addresses that are divisible without remainder by the byte length of the data type. In certain situations, the required alignment may be a little larger. Relevant information is given in the architecture documentation of the processor in question. The alignment of a data type on its own length is referred to as *natural alignment*.

It may be necessary to access non-aligned data types at some points in the kernel. The various architectures must therefore define two macros for this purpose (in <asm-*arch*/unaligned.h>):

❑   get_unaligned(ptr) de-references a pointer at an unaligned memory location.

❑   put_unaligned(val, ptr) writes val to a memory location specified by ptr that is unaligned (and not suitable for direct access).

These support access by, for example, copying the value to another memory location and accessing it there. When the GCC organizes memory for structs or unions, it automatically selects the appropriate alignment so that the programmer is not required to do this.

A.4   Memory Pages

Memory pages are 4 KiB in size on many but not all architectures. More modern processors also support sizes up to several MiB. The following macros must be defined in the architecture-specific file asm-arch/page.h to indicate the page size used:

❑   PAGE_SHIFT specifies the binary logarithm of the page size. (The kernel implicitly assumes that the page size can be represented as a power of 2, as is true on all architectures supported.)

❑   PAGE_SIZE specifies the size of a memory page in bytes.

❑   PAGE_ALIGN(addr) aligns any address on the page boundary.

Two standard operations on pages must also be implemented, generally by means of optimized assembler commands:

❑   clear_page(start) deletes the page beginning at start by filling it with null bytes.

❑   copy_page(to, from) copies the page data at position from to position to.

The PAGE_OFFSET macro specifies the position in virtual address space where the physical pages are to be mapped. On most architectures, this implicitly defines the size of the user address space or the division of the entire address space into a kernel address space and a user address space. However, this does not apply on all architectures. (Sparc is one such exception, because it has two separate address spaces for the kernel and userspace. AMD64 is another exception, because its virtual address space has a non-addressable hole in the middle.) As a result, the `TASK_SIZE` constant defined in `asm-arch/process.h` must be used instead of `PAGE_OFFSET` to determine the size of userspace.

A.5 System Calls

The mechanism for issuing system calls to perform a controlled switch from userspace to kernel space differs on all supported platforms. However, a standard file named `<asm-arch/unistd.h>` is responsible for the following two aspects relevant to system calls:

❑ It defines pre-processor constants to link the descriptors of all system calls with symbolic constants. The constants have names such as `__NR_chdir` and `__NR_send`. Because the individual architectures do their best to remain compatible with the descriptors of the specific native operating system (for example, OSF/1 on Alpha, or Solaris on Sparc), the numeric values differ from architecture to architecture.

❑ It defines functions to invoke system calls from within the kernel itself. Generally, a pre-processor mechanism is used for this purpose together with an inline assembler for automatic generation.

A.6 String Processing

Operations on strings are performed at various points in the kernel and are therefore particularly time-critical. Because many architectures provide special assembler commands to carry out the requisite tasks, or because manually optimized assembler code executes faster than compiler-generated code, all architectures may define various string operations of their own in `<asm-arch/string.h>`:

❑ `int strcmp(const char * cs, const char * ct)` compares two strings, character by character.

❑ `int strncmp(const char * cs, const char * ct, size_t count)` is similar to `strcmp` but compares a maximum of `count` characters.

❑ `int strnicmp(const char *s1, const char *s2, size_t len)` is similar to `strncmp` but compares the individual characters regardless of case.

❑ `char * strcpy(char * dest, const char *src)` copies a null-terminated string from `src` to `dest`.

❑ `char * strncpy(char * dest, const char *src, size_t count)` is similar to `strcpy` but restricts the maximum copy length to `count` bytes or characters.

❑ `size_t strlcpy(char *dest, const char *src, size_t size)` is similar to `strncpy`, but the destination string is also null-terminated if the source string has more than `size` characters.

❑ `char * strcat(char * dest, const char * src)` adds `src` to `dest`.

❑ `char * strncat(char *dest, const char *src, size_t count)` is similar to `strcat`, but restricts the operation to a maximum of `count` copied bytes.

❑ `size_t strlcat(char *dest, const char *src, size_t count)` is similar to `strncat`, but restricts the length of the result (and not the number of copy operations) to `count` bytes.

- ❏ `char * strchr(const char * s, int c)` finds the first position in the string `s` at which the character `c` occurs.

- ❏ `char * strrchr(const char * s, int c)` finds the last position in the string `s` at which the character `c` occurs.

- ❏ `size_t strlen(const char * s)` determines the length of a null-terminated string.

- ❏ `size_t strnlen(const char * s, size_t count)` is similar to `strlen` but restricts the operation to a maximum length of `count`.

- ❏ `size_t strspn(const char *s, const char *accept)` calculates the length of the substring of `s` which, consists entirely of characters in `accept`.

- ❏ `size_t strcspn(const char *s, const char *reject)` is similar to `strspn`, but calculates the length of the substring of `s` that consists entirely of characters *not* in `reject`.

- ❏ `char * strstr(const char * s1, const char * s2)` searches `s1` for the substring `s2`.

- ❏ `char * strpbrk(const char * cs, const char * ct)` searches for the first occurrence of a member of the string (`ct`) in another string (`cs`).

- ❏ `char * strsep(char **s, const char *ct)` splits a string into tokens separated by `ct`.

The following operations act on general memory areas and not on strings:

- ❏ `void * memset(void * s, int c, size_t count)` fills `count` bytes with the value specified by `c` starting at address `s`.

- ❏ `memset_io` does the same for I/O memory areas.

- ❏ `char * bcopy(const char * src, char * dest, int count)` copies an area of size `count` from `src` to `dest`.

- ❏ `memcpy_fromio` does the same to copy an area of I/O address space to normal address space.

- ❏ `void * memcpy(void * dest, const void *src, size_t count)` is similar to `bcopy` but uses `void` pointers as arguments to define the areas involved.

- ❏ `void * memmove(void * dest, const void *src, size_t count)` is similar to `memcpy` but also functions with overlapping source and destination areas.

- ❏ `int memcmp(const void * cs, const void * ct, size_t count)` compares two areas of memory, byte-by-byte.

- ❏ `void * memscan(void * addr, int c, size_t size)` scans the area specified by `addr` and `size` to find the first occurrence of character `c`.

- ❏ `void *memchr(const void *s, int c, size_t n)` is similar to `memscan` but returns a null pointer (and not a pointer to the first byte after the scanned area) if the desired element is not found.

All operations are replacement routines for the C standard library member of the same name that are employed by userspace programs to perform the same tasks as in the kernel.

The `__HAVE_ARCH_OPERATION` macro must be set for each string operation that is defined as optimized by an architecture; for instance, `__HAVE_ARCH_MEMCPY` must be set for `memcpy`. All nonimplemented functions are replaced with architecture-independent standard operations that are implemented in `lib/string.c`.

A.7   Thread Representation

The state of a running process is defined primarily by the contents of the processor registers. Processes that are not currently running must keep this data in corresponding data structures from which the data can be read and moved to the appropriate registers when the process is next activated by the scheduler. The structures needed to do this are defined in the following files:

❑   <asm-arch/ptrace.h> provides the pt_regs structure to hold all registers that are placed on the kernel stack when the process switches from user mode to space mode as a result of a system call, an interrupt, or any other mechanism. The file also defines the sequence of the registers on the stack by means of pre-processor constants. This is necessary when tracing a process in order to read register values from the stack.

❑   <asm-arch/processor.h> accommodates the thread_struct structure used to describe all other registers and all other task state information. This structure is typically split into further processor-specific components.

❑   <asm-arch/thread.h> defines the thread_info structure (not to be confused with thread_struct), which contains all task structure elements that the assembler code must access to implement kernel entry and exit.

The definitions of pt_regs and thread_struct as they apply on the most popular architectures are reproduced in the following sections to provide an overview of their register sets.

A.7.1   IA-32

The IA-32 architecture suffers permanent register shortage, so there is not much to save when kernel mode is entered, as the following definition of pt_regs shows:

include/asm-x86/ptrace.h
```
struct pt_regs {
        long ebx;
        long ecx;
        long edx;
        long esi;
        long edi;
        long ebp;
        long eax;
        int  xds;
        int  xes;
        long orig_eax;
        long eip;
        int  xcs;
        long eflags;
        long esp;
        int  xss;
};
```

What's conspicuous here is that the orig_eax field contains an extra value in addition to the register values. Its purpose is to store the system call number passed in the eax register when kernel mode is entered. Because this register is also used to transfer the result into userspace, it must be modified during the course of the system call. Nevertheless, it is still possible to determine the number of the system call via orig_eax (if, for example, the process is traced using ptrace).

Newer versions of the architecture use a much larger register set, which the kernel saves only as needed. Consequently, the corresponding elements are held in the thread_struct structure, as shown here:

include/asm-x86/processor_32.h
```
struct thread_struct {
/* cached TLS descriptors. */
        struct desc_struct tls_array[GDT_ENTRY_TLS_ENTRIES];
        unsigned long    esp0;
        unsigned long    sysenter_cs;
        unsigned long    eip;
        unsigned long    esp;
        unsigned long    fs;
        unsigned long    gs;
/* Hardware debugging registers */
        unsigned long    debugreg[8];   /* %%db0-7 debug registers */
/* fault info */
        unsigned long    cr2, trap_no, error_code;
/* floating point info */
        union i387_union        i387;
/* virtual 86 mode info */
        struct vm86_struct __user * vm86_info;
        unsigned long            screen_bitmap;
        unsigned long            v86flags, v86mask, saved_esp0;
        unsigned int             saved_fs, saved_gs;
/* IO permissions */
        unsigned long    *io_bitmap_ptr;
        unsigned long    iopl;
/* max allowed port in the bitmap, in bytes: */
        unsigned long    io_bitmap_max;
};
```

Depending on the processor version, the coprocessor provides various register sets as specified in i387_union:[1]

include/asm-x86/processor_32.h
```
union i387_union {
        struct i387_fsave_struct        fsave;
        struct i387_fxsave_struct       fxsave;
        struct i387_soft_struct soft;
};
```

Old 80386 and 80486SX processors that do not have a hardware-based coprocessor employ kernel-side software emulation whose state is held in i387_soft_struct. Machines whose coprocessors support only the classic registers (that is, eight 10-byte-wide floating-point registers) store their data in i387_fsave_struct. Because most registers are never used alone but are always read or written to block-by-block, the kernel puts them in a contiguous memory area provided in the structure by an array of suitable size:

include/asm-x86/processor_32.h
```
struct i387_fsave_struct {
        long    cwd;
        long    swd;
```

---

[1]Coincidentally, the definition of i387_union for kernel 2.6.17 is located in line 387.

```
        long    twd;
        long    fip;
        long    fcs;
        long    foo;
        long    fos;
        long    st_space[20];   /* 8*10 bytes for each FP-reg = 80 bytes */
        long    status;         /* software status information */
};
```

More recent processor versions use slightly wider registers and also support a second set of registers known as XMM.

include/asm-x86/processor_32.h
```
struct i387_fxsave_struct {
        u16     cwd;
        u16     swd;
        u16     twd;
        u16     fop;
        u64     rip;
        u64     rdp;
        u32     mxcsr;
        u32     mxcsr_mask;
        u32     st_space[32];   /* 8*16 bytes for each FP-reg = 128 bytes */
        u32     xmm_space[64];  /* 16*16 bytes for each XMM-reg = 128 bytes */
        u32     padding[24];
} __attribute__ ((aligned (16)));
```

A.7.2 IA-64

In the design of IA-64, the designated successor of the aging IA-32 architecture, Intel has kept abreast of the times and has given the processor a much bigger register set (with a more systematic name).

include/asm-ia64/processor.h
```
struct pt_regs {
        /* The following registers are saved by SAVE_MIN: */
        unsigned long b6;               /* scratch */
        unsigned long b7;               /* scratch */

        unsigned long ar_csd;           /* used by cmp8xchg16 (scratch) */
        unsigned long ar_ssd;           /* reserved for future use (scratch) */

        unsigned long r8;               /* scratch (return value register 0) */
        unsigned long r9;               /* scratch (return value register 1) */
        unsigned long r10;              /* scratch (return value register 2) */
        unsigned long r11;              /* scratch (return value register 3) */

        unsigned long cr_ipsr;          /* interrupted task's psr */
        unsigned long cr_iip;           /* interrupted task's instruction pointer */
        /*
         * interrupted task's function state; if bit 63 is cleared, it
         * contains syscall's ar.pfs.pfm:
         */
        unsigned long cr_ifs;
```

```
        unsigned long ar_unat;          /* interrupted task's NaT register (preserved) */
        unsigned long ar_pfs;           /* prev function state  */
        unsigned long ar_rsc;           /* RSE configuration */
        /* The following two are valid only if cr_ipsr.cpl > 0 || ti->flags & _TIF_MCA_INIT */
        unsigned long ar_rnat;          /* RSE NaT */
        unsigned long ar_bspstore;      /* RSE bspstore */

        unsigned long pr;               /* 64 predicate registers (1 bit each) */
        unsigned long b0;               /* return pointer (bp) */
        unsigned long loadrs;           /* size of dirty partition << 16 */

        unsigned long r1;               /* the gp pointer */
        unsigned long r12;              /* interrupted task's memory stack pointer */
        unsigned long r13;              /* thread pointer */

        unsigned long ar_fpsr;          /* floating point status (preserved) */
        unsigned long r15;              /* scratch */

        /* The remaining registers are NOT saved for system calls.  */

        unsigned long r14;              /* scratch */
        unsigned long r2;               /* scratch */
        unsigned long r3;               /* scratch */

        /* The following registers are saved by SAVE_REST: */
        unsigned long r16;              /* scratch */
        unsigned long r17;              /* scratch */
        unsigned long r18;              /* scratch */
        unsigned long r19;              /* scratch */
        unsigned long r20;              /* scratch */
        unsigned long r21;              /* scratch */
        unsigned long r22;              /* scratch */
        unsigned long r23;              /* scratch */
        unsigned long r24;              /* scratch */
        unsigned long r25;              /* scratch */
        unsigned long r26;              /* scratch */
        unsigned long r27;              /* scratch */
        unsigned long r28;              /* scratch */
        unsigned long r29;              /* scratch */
        unsigned long r30;              /* scratch */
        unsigned long r31;              /* scratch */

        unsigned long ar_ccv;           /* compare/exchange value (scratch) */

        /*
         * Floating point registers that the kernel considers scratch:
         */
        struct ia64_fpreg f6;           /* scratch */
        struct ia64_fpreg f7;           /* scratch */
        struct ia64_fpreg f8;           /* scratch */
        struct ia64_fpreg f9;           /* scratch */
        struct ia64_fpreg f10;          /* scratch */
        struct ia64_fpreg f11;          /* scratch */
};
```

The thread data strucure holds not only debug (`dbr` and `ibr`) and floating-point registers (`fph`), but, additionally, kernel also stores information required for IA-32 emulation if this option is available in the kernel configuration, as shown here:

include/asm-ia64/processor.h

```
struct thread_struct {
        __u32 flags;                    /* various thread flags (see IA64_THREAD_*) */
        /* writing on_ustack is performance-critical, so it's worth spending 8 bits on it... */
        __u8 on_ustack;                 /* executing on user-stacks? */
        __u8 pad[3];
        __u64 ksp;                      /* kernel stack pointer */
        __u64 map_base;                 /* base address for get_unmapped_area() */
        __u64 task_size;                /* limit for task size */
        __u64 rbs_bot;                  /* the base address for the RBS */
        int last_fph_cpu;               /* CPU that may hold the contents of f32-f127 */

#ifdef CONFIG_IA32_SUPPORT
        __u64 eflag;                    /* IA32 EFLAGS reg */
        __u64 fsr;                      /* IA32 floating pt status reg */
        __u64 fcr;                      /* IA32 floating pt control reg */
        __u64 fir;                      /* IA32 fp except. instr. reg */
        __u64 fdr;                      /* IA32 fp except. data reg */
        __u64 old_k1;                   /* old value of ar.k1 */
        __u64 old_iob;                  /* old IOBase value */
        struct partial_page_list *ppl;  /* partial page list for 4K page size issue */
        /* cached TLS descriptors. */
        struct desc_struct tls_array[GDT_ENTRY_TLS_ENTRIES];
#endif /* CONFIG_IA32_SUPPORT */
#ifdef CONFIG_PERFMON
        __u64 pmcs[IA64_NUM_PMC_REGS];
        __u64 pmds[IA64_NUM_PMD_REGS];
        void *pfm_context;              /* pointer to detailed PMU context */
        unsigned long pfm_needs_checking;  /* when >0, pending perfmon work on kernel exit */
#endif
        __u64 dbr[IA64_NUM_DBG_REGS];
        __u64 ibr[IA64_NUM_DBG_REGS];
        struct ia64_fpreg fph[96];      /* saved/loaded on demand */
};
```

IA-64 also features a *performance monitoring* subsystem. Additional registers must be saved if the kernel is configured to interoperate with this subsystem.

A.7.3 ARM

ARM systems come in two versions because the processor is designed with 26-bit and 32-bit word lengths. Because all of the more recent systems operate with 32 bits, only the corresponding definitions for this machine type are included in this appendix.

The following definition of the `pt_regs` structure consists simply of an array to hold the values of all registers manipulated in kernel mode:

include/asm-arm/ptrace.h

```
struct pt_regs {
        long uregs[18];
};
```

The symbolic names of the registers and their positions within the array are defined by means of pre-processor constants:

include/asm-arm/ptrace.h

```
#define ARM_cpsr        uregs[16]
#define ARM_pc          uregs[15]
#define ARM_lr          uregs[14]
#define ARM_sp          uregs[13]
#define ARM_ip          uregs[12]
#define ARM_fp          uregs[11]
#define ARM_r10         uregs[10]
#define ARM_r9          uregs[9]
#define ARM_r8          uregs[8]
#define ARM_r7          uregs[7]
#define ARM_r6          uregs[6]
#define ARM_r5          uregs[5]
#define ARM_r4          uregs[4]
#define ARM_r3          uregs[3]
#define ARM_r2          uregs[2]
#define ARM_r1          uregs[1]
#define ARM_r0          uregs[0]
#define ARM_ORIG_r0     uregs[17]
```

It is not necessary to save any floating-point registers because ARM processors provide only software support for floating-point operations:

include/asm-arm/processor.h

```
struct thread_struct {
                                                        /* fault info    */
        unsigned long           address;
        unsigned long           trap_no;
        unsigned long           error_code;
                                                        /* debugging     */
        struct debug_info       debug;
};
```

However, machine instructions (in the form of their opcode) can be saved together with a memory address for debugging purposes, as shown here:

include/asm-arm/processor.h

```
union debug_insn {
        u32     arm;
        u16     thumb;
};

struct debug_entry {
        u32                     address;
        union debug_insn        insn;
};

struct debug_info {
        int                     nsaved;
        struct debug_entry      bp[2];
};
```

A.7.4 Sparc64

Sparc64 processors also make use of an array in the `pt_regs` structure to provide memory space for the individual registers. The registers are named and space is allocated by means of pre-processor constants, as follows:

include/asm-sparc64/ptrace.h

```
struct pt_regs {
        unsigned long u_regs[16]; /* globals and ins */
        unsigned long tstate;
        unsigned long tpc;
        unsigned long tnpc;
        unsigned int y;
        unsigned int fprs;
};

#define UREG_G0         0
#define UREG_G1         1
#define UREG_G2         2
#define UREG_G3         3
#define UREG_G4         4
#define UREG_G5         5
#define UREG_G6         6
#define UREG_G7         7
#define UREG_I0         8
#define UREG_I1         9
#define UREG_I2         10
#define UREG_I3         11
#define UREG_I4         12
#define UREG_I5         13
#define UREG_I6         14
#define UREG_I7         15
#define UREG_FP         UREG_I6
#define UREG_RETPC      UREG_I7
```

In contrast to other architectures, Sparc64 tries to store the registers that are not always saved in `thread_info` instead of in `thread_struct`. As usual, the platform must be able to differentiate itself from the other ports. If the kernel is not compiled with the spinlock debugging option, the structure could be empty. However, owing to an (earlier) GCC error (that the authors of the Sparc port do not greatly appreciate, as suggested by the following source code comment), the structure contains a dummy element:

include/asm-sparc64/processor.h

```
/* The Sparc processor specific thread struct. */
/* XXX This should die, everything can go into thread_info now. */
struct thread_struct {
#ifdef CONFIG_DEBUG_SPINLOCK
        /* How many spinlocks held by this thread.
         * Used with spin lock debugging to catch tasks
         * sleeping illegally with locks held.
         */
        int smp_lock_count;
        unsigned int smp_lock_pc;
```

```
#else
        int dummy; /* f'in gcc bug... */
#endif
};
```

The memory location for saving the floating-point registers and the *lazy state* are held in `thread_info` as shown here:

include/asm-sparc64/thread_info.h

```
struct thread_info {
        /* D$ line 1 */
        struct task_struct      *task;
        unsigned long           flags;
        __u8                    cpu;
        __u8                    fpsaved[7];
        unsigned long           ksp;

        /* D$ line 2 */
        unsigned long           fault_address;
        struct pt_regs          *kregs;
        struct exec_domain      *exec_domain;
        int                     preempt_count;
         __u8                    new_child;
        __u8                    syscall_noerror;
        __u16                   __pad;

        unsigned long           *utraps;

        struct reg_window       reg_window[NSWINS];
        unsigned long           rwbuf_stkptrs[NSWINS];

        unsigned long           gsr[7];
        unsigned long           xfsr[7];

        __u64                   __user *user_cntd0;
        __u64                   __user *user_cntd1;
        __u64                   kernel_cntd0, kernel_cntd1;
        __u64                   pcr_reg;

        __u64                   cee_stuff;

        struct restart_block    restart_block;

        struct pt_regs          *kern_una_regs;
        unsigned int            kern_una_insn;

        unsigned long           fpregs[0] __attribute__ ((aligned(64)));
};
```

A.7.5 Alpha

As classic RISC machines, Alpha CPUs employ a large register set whose members are identified mainly by numbers according to an orderly principle. As already noted, the Alpha architecture uses the PAL (*privileged architecture level*) code to perform system tasks. This code is also used in the implementation of system calls. The C or assembler code of the kernel need not save all registers listed in `pt_regs` because some of them are automatically placed on the stack by PAL code routines. Those that need be are the following:

include/asm-alpha/ptrace.h
```
struct pt_regs {
        unsigned long r0;
        unsigned long r1;
        unsigned long r2;
        unsigned long r3;
        unsigned long r4;
        unsigned long r5;
        unsigned long r6;
        unsigned long r7;
        unsigned long r8;
        unsigned long r19;
        unsigned long r20;
        unsigned long r21;
        unsigned long r22;
        unsigned long r23;
        unsigned long r24;
        unsigned long r25;
        unsigned long r26;
        unsigned long r27;
        unsigned long r28;
        unsigned long hae;
/* JRP - These are the values provided to a0-a2 by PALcode */
        unsigned long trap_a0;
        unsigned long trap_a1;
        unsigned long trap_a2;
/* These are saved by PAL-code: */
        unsigned long ps;
        unsigned long pc;
        unsigned long gp;
        unsigned long r16;
        unsigned long r17;
        unsigned long r18;
};
```

This architecture likewise makes use of an empty `thread_struct` structure:

include/asm-alpha/processor.h
```
/* This is dead.  Everything has been moved to thread_info.  */
struct thread_struct { };
```

The contents of floating-point registers `f0` to `f31` are not held in `thread_info`, but instead are held on the stack using the following structure (a few integer registers are saved as well as the floating-point registers; normally, the former are not needed by the kernel):

include/asm-alpha/ptrace.h
```
struct switch_stack {
        unsigned long r9;
        unsigned long r10;
        unsigned long r11;
```

```
            unsigned long r12;
            unsigned long r13;
            unsigned long r14;
            unsigned long r15;
            unsigned long r26;
            unsigned long fp[32];    /* fp[31] is fpcr */
    };
```

The kernel defines the following structure to identify the position of the individual registers on the stack:

arch/alpha/kernel/ptrace.c
```
#define PT_REG(reg) \
  (PAGE_SIZE*2 - sizeof(struct pt_regs) + offsetof(struct pt_regs, reg))

#define SW_REG(reg) \
  (PAGE_SIZE*2 - sizeof(struct pt_regs) - sizeof(struct switch_stack) \
  + offsetof(struct switch_stack, reg))

static int regoff[] = {
        PT_REG(    r0), PT_REG(    r1), PT_REG(    r2), PT_REG(    r3),
        PT_REG(    r4), PT_REG(    r5), PT_REG(    r6), PT_REG(    r7),
        PT_REG(    r8), SW_REG(    r9), SW_REG(   r10), SW_REG(  r11),
        SW_REG(   r12), SW_REG(   r13), SW_REG(   r14), SW_REG(  r15),
        PT_REG(   r16), PT_REG(   r17), PT_REG(   r18), PT_REG(  r19),
        PT_REG(   r20), PT_REG(   r21), PT_REG(   r22), PT_REG(  r23),
        PT_REG(   r24), PT_REG(   r25), PT_REG(   r26), PT_REG(  r27),
        PT_REG(   r28), PT_REG(    gp),             -1,           -1,
        SW_REG(fp[ 0]), SW_REG(fp[ 1]), SW_REG(fp[ 2]), SW_REG(fp[ 3]),
        SW_REG(fp[ 4]), SW_REG(fp[ 5]), SW_REG(fp[ 6]), SW_REG(fp[ 7]),
        SW_REG(fp[ 8]), SW_REG(fp[ 9]), SW_REG(fp[10]), SW_REG(fp[11]),
        SW_REG(fp[12]), SW_REG(fp[13]), SW_REG(fp[14]), SW_REG(fp[15]),
        SW_REG(fp[16]), SW_REG(fp[17]), SW_REG(fp[18]), SW_REG(fp[19]),
        SW_REG(fp[20]), SW_REG(fp[21]), SW_REG(fp[22]), SW_REG(fp[23]),
        SW_REG(fp[24]), SW_REG(fp[25]), SW_REG(fp[26]), SW_REG(fp[27]),
        SW_REG(fp[28]), SW_REG(fp[29]), SW_REG(fp[30]), SW_REG(fp[31]),
        PT_REG(    pc)
    };
```

A.7.6 Mips

Mips processors use an array entry in pt_regs to store the main processor registers, as shown in the following code. The 32-bit and 64-bit versions of the processor use practically the same structure:

include/asm-mips/ptrace.h
```
struct pt_regs {
#ifdef CONFIG_32BIT
        /* Pad bytes for argument save space on the stack. */
        unsigned long pad0[6];
#endif

        /* Saved main processor registers. */
        unsigned long regs[32];

        /* Saved special registers. */
```

```
            unsigned long cp0_status;
            unsigned long hi;
            unsigned long lo;
            unsigned long cp0_badvaddr;
            unsigned long cp0_cause;
            unsigned long cp0_epc;
    };
```

Because Mips processors do not necessarily have a numeric coprocessor, no floating-point registers may need to be saved — just the status of the software emulation, as shown here:

include/asm-mips/processor.h
```
struct thread_struct {
            /* Saved main processor registers. */
            unsigned long reg16;
            unsigned long reg17, reg18, reg19, reg20, reg21, reg22, reg23;
            unsigned long reg29, reg30, reg31;

            /* Saved cp0 stuff. */
            unsigned long cp0_status;

            /* Saved fpu/fpu emulator stuff. */
            union mips_fpu_union fpu;

            /* Saved state of the DSP ASE, if available. */
            struct mips_dsp_state dsp;

            /* Other stuff associated with the thread. */
            unsigned long cp0_badvaddr;      /* Last user fault */
            unsigned long cp0_baduaddr;      /* Last kernel fault accessing USEG */
            unsigned long error_code;
            unsigned long trap_no;
            unsigned long mflags;
            unsigned long irix_trampoline;  /* Wheee... */
            unsigned long irix_oldctx;
            struct mips_abi *abi;
    };
```

A.7.7 PowerPC

PowerPCs save most registers in an array held in `pt_regs`:

include/asm-powerpc/ptrace.h
```
struct pt_regs {
            unsigned long gpr[32];
            unsigned long nip;
            unsigned long msr;
            unsigned long orig_gpr3;        /* Used for restarting system calls */
            unsigned long ctr;
            unsigned long link;
            unsigned long xer;
            unsigned long ccr;
#ifdef __powerpc64__
            unsigned long softe;            /* Soft enabled/disabled */
```

```
#else
        unsigned long mq;                  /* 601 only (not used at present) */
                                           /* Used on APUS to hold IPL value. */
#endif
        unsigned long trap;                /* Reason for being here */
        /* N.B. for critical exceptions on 4xx, the dar and dsisr
           fields are overloaded to hold srr0 and srr1. */
        unsigned long dar;                 /* Fault registers */
        unsigned long dsisr;               /* on 4xx/Book-E used for ESR */
        unsigned long result;              /* Result of a system call */
};
```

Depending on the processor type, it may be necessary to consider whether the AltiVec extension (and therefore an additional register set) is present when floating-point registers are saved. Debug registers must also be saved on some system types:

include/asm-powerpc/processor.h
```
struct thread_struct {
        unsigned long   ksp;               /* Kernel stack pointer */
#ifdef CONFIG_PPC64
        unsigned long   ksp_vsid;
#endif
        struct pt_regs  *regs;             /* Pointer to saved register state */
        mm_segment_t    fs;                /* for get_fs() validation */
#ifdef CONFIG_PPC32
        void            *pgdir;            /* root of page-table tree */
        signed long     last_syscall;
#endif
#if defined(CONFIG_4xx) || defined (CONFIG_BOOKE)
        unsigned long   dbcr0;             /* debug control register values */
        unsigned long   dbcr1;
#endif
        double          fpr[32];           /* Complete floating point set */
        struct {                           /* fpr ... fpscr must be contiguous */

                unsigned int pad;
                unsigned int val;          /* Floating point status */
        } fpscr;
        int             fpexc_mode;        /* floating-point exception mode */
#ifdef CONFIG_PPC64
        unsigned long   start_tb;          /* Start purr when proc switched in */
        unsigned long   accum_tb;          /* Total accumiled purr for process */
#endif
        unsigned long   vdso_base;         /* base of the vDSO library */
        unsigned long   dabr;              /* Data address breakpoint register */
#ifdef CONFIG_ALTIVEC
        /* Complete AltiVec register set */
        vector128       vr[32] __attribute((aligned(16)));
        /* AltiVec status */
        vector128       vscr __attribute((aligned(16)));
        unsigned long   vrsave;
        int             used_vr;           /* set if process has used altivec */
#endif /* CONFIG_ALTIVEC */
};
```

A.7.8 AMD64

Even though the AMD64 architecture is very similar to its IA32 predecessor, a number of registers have been added so that there are some differences as concerns the registers that must be saved during system calls:

include/asm-x86/ptrace.h
```
struct pt_regs {
        unsigned long r15;
        unsigned long r14;
        unsigned long r13;
        unsigned long r12;
        unsigned long rbp;
        unsigned long rbx;
/* arguments: non interrupts/non tracing syscalls only save upto here*/
        unsigned long r11;
        unsigned long r10;
        unsigned long r9;
        unsigned long r8;
        unsigned long rax;
        unsigned long rcx;
        unsigned long rdx;
        unsigned long rsi;
        unsigned long rdi;
        unsigned long orig_rax;
/* end of arguments */
/* cpu exception frame or undefined */
        unsigned long rip;
        unsigned long cs;
        unsigned long eflags;
        unsigned long rsp;
        unsigned long ss;
/* top of stack page */
};
```

The close ties between the two architectures are very apparent in the following `thread_struct` structure which has almost exactly the same layout as in IA32:

include/asm-x86_64/processor.h
```
struct thread_struct {
        unsigned long    rsp0;
        unsigned long    rsp;
        unsigned long    userrsp;        /* Copy from PDA */
        unsigned long    fs;
        unsigned long    gs;
        unsigned short   es, ds, fsindex, gsindex;
/* Hardware debugging registers */
        unsigned long    debugreg0;
        unsigned long    debugreg1;
        unsigned long    debugreg2;
        unsigned long    debugreg3;
        unsigned long    debugreg6;
        unsigned long    debugreg7;
/* fault info */
```

```
        unsigned long   cr2, trap_no, error_code;
/* floating point info */
        union i387_union        i387 __attribute__((aligned(16)));
/* IO permissions. the bitmap could be moved into the GDT, that would make
   switch faster for a limited number of ioperm using tasks. -AK */
        int             ioperm;
        unsigned long   *io_bitmap_ptr;
        unsigned io_bitmap_max;
/* cached TLS descriptors. */
        u64 tls_array[GDT_ENTRY_TLS_ENTRIES];
} __attribute__((aligned(16)));
```

include/adm-x86/processor_64.h
```
union i387_union {
        struct i387_fxsave_struct        fxsave;
};
```

Formally, the i387_union *used to save the floating-point registers has the same name as in IA32. However, because AMD64 processors always have a math coprocessor, no software emulation needs to be included.*

A.8   Bit Operations and Endianness

The kernel frequently works with bit fields; for instance, when searching for a free slot in an allocation bitmap. This section describes the facilities provided for bit operations. It also describes how endianness questions are settled.

A.8.1   *Manipulation of Bit Chains*

Although some of the functions needed for bit manipulation are implemented in C, the kernel prefers optimized assembler functions that are able to exploit the special features of the individual processors. Because some operations are atomic, they cannot be implemented in assembler code. The architecture-specific parts of the kernel must define the following functions in <asm-arch/bitops.h>:

- ❑   void set_bit(int nr, volatile unsigned long * addr) sets the bit at position nr; counting begins at addr.

- ❑   int test_bit(int nr, const volatile unsigned long * addr) checks whether the specified bit is set.

- ❑   void clear_bit(int nr, volatile unsigned long * addr) deletes the bit at position nr (counting begins at addr).

- ❑   void change_bit(int nr, volatile unsigned long * addr) reverses the bit value at position nr (counting begins at addr); in other words, a set bit is unset and vice versa.

- ❑   int test_and_set_bit(int nr, volatile unsigned long * addr) sets a bit and returns its former value.

- ❑   int test_and_clear_bit(int nr, volatile unsigned long * addr) deletes a bit and returns its former value.

- ❑   int test_and_change_bit(int nr, volatile unsigned long* addr) reverses a bit value and returns its former value.

All of these functions are executed atomically, because lock statements are integrated in the assembler code. There are also non-atomic versions of these functions, which are prefixed with a double underscore (for example, __set_bit).

A.8.2 Conversion between Byte Orders

Architectures supported by the kernel use one of two byte orders — little endian or big endian. Some architectures are able to handle both, but one must be configured. The kernel must therefore provide functions to convert data between both orders. For device drivers, it is particularly important that function versions are available to convert a specific byte order to the format used by the host without the need for numerous #ifdef pre-processor statements. The kernel provides the <byteorder/little_endian.h> and <byteorder/big_endian.h> files. The version for the current processor is linked into <asm-arch/byteorder.h>.[2]

In order to implement the functions for converting between byte orders, the kernel needs efficient ways of swapping bytes that can be optimized for each specific processor. C default functions are defined in <byteoorder/swab.h>, but they can be overwritten by a processor-specific implementation. __arch__swab16, __arch__swab32, and __arch__swab64 swap the bytes between the representations, and therefore convert big endian to little endian and vice versa. __swab16p, __arch__swab32p, and __arch__swab64p do the same for pointer variables. swab stands for *swap bytes*.

The __arch__operation pre-processor constant (__arch__swab16p, for example) must be set if an architecture provides an optimized version of one of these functions.

The following functions implement the conversion routines for little endian hosts as follows (note that the conversion routines perform a null operation if they are executed on a number already in the relevant format):

<byteorder/little_endian.h>
```
#define __constant_htonl(x) ((__force __be32)___constant_swab32((x)))
#define __constant_ntohl(x) ___constant_swab32((__force __be32)(x))
#define __constant_htons(x) ((__force __be16)___constant_swab16((x)))
#define __constant_ntohs(x) ___constant_swab16((__force __be16)(x))
#define __constant_cpu_to_le64(x) ((__force __le64)(__u64)(x))
#define __constant_le64_to_cpu(x) ((__force __u64)(__le64)(x))
#define __constant_cpu_to_le32(x) ((__force __le32)(__u32)(x))
#define __constant_le32_to_cpu(x) ((__force __u32)(__le32)(x))
#define __constant_cpu_to_le16(x) ((__force __le16)(__u16)(x))
#define __constant_le16_to_cpu(x) ((__force __u16)(__le16)(x))
#define __constant_cpu_to_be64(x) ((__force __be64)___constant_swab64((x)))
#define __constant_be64_to_cpu(x) ___constant_swab64((__force __u64)(__be64)(x))
#define __constant_cpu_to_be32(x) ((__force __be32)___constant_swab32((x)))
#define __constant_be32_to_cpu(x) ___constant_swab32((__force __u32)(__be32)(x))
#define __constant_cpu_to_be16(x) ((__force __be16)___constant_swab16((x)))
#define __constant_be16_to_cpu(x) ___constant_swab16((__force __u16)(__be16)(x))
#define __cpu_to_le64(x) ((__force __le64)(__u64)(x))
#define __le64_to_cpu(x) ((__force __u64)(__le64)(x))
#define __cpu_to_le32(x) ((__force __le32)(__u32)(x))
```

---

[2]The byte order for VAX systems used to be declared as 3412 in <byteorder/pdp_endian.h>. However, because the architecture is not supported by the kernel, this was somewhat pointless, so the file was removed during the development of kernel 2.6.21.

```
#define __le32_to_cpu(x) ((__force __u32)(__le32)(x))
#define __cpu_to_le16(x) ((__force __le16)(__u16)(x))
#define __le16_to_cpu(x) ((__force __u16)(__le16)(x))
#define __cpu_to_be64(x) ((__force __be64)__swab64((x)))
#define __be64_to_cpu(x) __swab64((__force __u64)(__be64)(x))
#define __cpu_to_be32(x) ((__force __be32)__swab32((x)))
#define __be32_to_cpu(x) __swab32((__force __u32)(__be32)(x))
#define __cpu_to_be16(x) ((__force __be16)__swab16((x)))
#define __be16_to_cpu(x) __swab16((__force __u16)(__be16)(x))
```

The names of the functions indicate their purpose. For example, __be32_to_cpus converts a 32-bit big endian value to the CPU-specific format, and __cpu_to_le64 converts the CPU-specific format to little endian for a 64-bit value.

The functions for big endian hosts are implemented using the same means (only the conversions made are different).

A.9 Page Tables

To simplify memory management and to provide a memory model that abstracts the differences between the various architectures, the ports must offer functions to manipulate page tables and their entries. These are declared in <asm-arch/pgtable.h>. Chapter 3 discusses the most interesting definitions in this file, so there's no need to repeat them here.

A.10 Miscellaneous

This section covers three additional architecture-specific topics, which don't fit into any of the previous categories.

A.10.1 Checksum Calculation

Calculating checksums for packets is a key aspect of communication via IP networks and takes considerable time. If possible, each architecture should therefore employ manually optimized assembler code to calculate the checksums. The code needed to do this is declared in <asm-arch/checksum.h>. Two functions are of prime importance:

❏ unsigned short ip_fast_csum calculates the requisite checksum based on the IP header and the header length.

❏ csum_partial calculates the checksum for a packet from the fragments that are received one by one.

A.10.2 Context Switch

The hardware-dependent part of context switching takes place once the scheduler has decided to instruct the current process to relinquish the CPU so that another process can run. For this purpose, all architectures must provide the switch_to function or a corresponding macro with the following prototype in <asm-arch/system.h>:

<asm-arch/system.h>
```
void switch_to(struct task_struct *prev, struct task_struct *next,
               struct task_struct *last)
```

The function performs a context switch by saving the state of the process specified by prev and activating the process designated by next.

Although the last parameter may initially appear to be superfluous, it is used to find the process that was running immediately prior to the function *return*. Note that switch_to is not a function in the usual sense because the system state can change in any number of ways between the start and end of the function.

This can be best understood via an example in which the kernel switches from process A to process B. prev points to A and next to B. Both are local variables in context A.

After process B has executed, the kernel switches to other processes and finally arrives at process X; when this process ends, the kernel reverts to process A. Because process A was exited in the middle of switch_to, execution resumes in the second half of the process. The local variables are retained (the process is not allowed to notice that the scheduler has reclaimed the CPU in the meantime), so prev points to A and next to B. However, this information is not sufficient to enable the kernel to establish which process was running immediately prior to activation of A — although it is important to know this at various points in the kernel. This is where the last variable comes in. The low-level assembler code to implement context switching must ensure that last points to the task structure of the process that ran last so that this information is still available to the kernel after a switch has been made to process A.

A.10.3 Finding the Current Process

The purpose of the current macro is to find a pointer to the task structure of the currently running process. It must be declared by each architecture in <asm-arch/current.h>. The pointer is held in a separate processor register that can be queried directly or indirectly using current. The registers reserved by the individual architectures are listed in Table A-1.

Table A-1: Registers Holding Pointers to the Current task_struct **or** thread_info **Instance**

Architecture	Register	Contents
IA-32	esp	thread_info
IA-64	r13	task_struct
ARM	sp	thread_info
Sparc and Sparc64	g6	thread_info
Alpha	r8	thread_info
Mips	r28	thread_info

Note that the register is used for different purposes, depending on architecture. Some architectures use it to store a pointer to the current task_struct instance, but most use it to hold a pointer to the currently valid thread_info instance. Since, on the latter architectures, thread_info contains a pointer to the `task_struct` associated with the process, `current` can be implemented in a roundabout way as demonstrated below for the Arm architecture:

include/asm-arm/current.h
```
static __always_inline struct task_struct * get_current(void)
{
        return current_thread_info()->task;
}

#define current get_current()
```

The pointer to the current `thread_info` instance found using `current_thread_info` is stored in register sp, as shown here:

include/asm-arm/thread_info.h
```
static inline struct thread_info *current_thread_info(void)
{
        register unsigned long sp asm ("sp");
        return (struct thread_info *)(sp & ~(THREAD_SIZE - 1));
}
```

The AMD64 and IA-32 architectures are not included in Table A-1 because they adopt their own method of finding the current process. Each CPU in the system has a per-processor private data area which holds various interesting items of information. For AMD64, it is defined as follows:

include/asm-x86/pda.h
```
struct x8664_pda {
        struct task_struct *pcurrent;    /* 0 Current process */
        unsigned long data_offset;       /* 8 Per cpu data offset from linker
                                              address */
        unsigned long kernelstack; /* 16 top of kernel stack for current */
...
        unsigned irq_call_count;
        unsigned irq_tlb_count;
        unsigned irq_thermal_count;
        unsigned irq_threshold_count;
        unsigned irq_spurious_count;
} ____cacheline_aligned_in_smp;
```

The segment selector register gs always points to the data structure, and elements of it can therefore be simply addressed as offsets to the segment. This structure includes the `pcurrent` pointer that points to the `task_struct` instance of the current process.

A.11 Summary

The largest part of the Linux kernel is written in architecture-independent C, and this is one of the prerequisites that enables Linux to be ported to a huge number of platforms. However, a small core of hardware-specific data structures and functions must be provided by every platform. This appendix explored some examples of definitions for a number of important architectures, and described the generic mechanisms provided by the kernel to bridge differences between various platforms.

B

Working with the Source Code

Over the years, Linux has grown from a minor hacker project to a gigantic system that effortlessly competes with the largest and most complex software systems. As a result, developers must deal with more than just the technical problems relating to how the kernel functions. The organization and structure of the sources are also key issues whose importance should be not underestimated. This appendix addresses the two most interesting questions in this context. How can the kernel be configured so that the corresponding parts of the source can be selected not only for a given architecture but also for a specific computer configuration? And how is the compilation process controlled? The second question is of particular importance when the kernel is repeatedly compiled for different configurations. Parts not involved in a configuration change obviously need not be recompiled, and this can save a great deal of time.

Everyone concerned with the kernel sources is impressed by their sheer size. Because the prime purpose of this book is to promote an understanding of the sources, this appendix examines various methods that are best suited to browsing and analyzing the source code. These include predominantly hypertext systems. This appendix also describes the options available to debug running kernels and to provide an insight into their structures — both are useful aids to understanding. The appendix delves into User-Mode Linux (UML), a kernel port that runs as a user process on a Linux system and was incorporated into the official sources during the development of version 2.5. It also discusses the debugging facilities available to analyze a kernel running on a real system — with all the benefits of modern debuggers, including single-stepping through assembler statements.

B.1 Organization of the Kernel Sources

The source files are spread over a widely ramified network of directories to help keep track of related kernel components. This is no easy task because it is not always clear to which category a particular file belongs.

Appendix B: Working with the Source Code

The main kernel directory contains a number of subdirectories to roughly classify their contents. The key kernel components reside in the following directories:

❑ The `kernel` directory contains the code for the components at the heart of the kernel. It accommodates only about 120 files, with a total of approximately 80,000 lines of code — a surprisingly small number for a project of this size. Developers stress how important it is to not add to the contents of this directory unless absolutely necessary — patches that modify the files in the directory are handled with extreme care and are very often the subject of long and controversial discussions before final acceptance.

❑ High-level memory management resides in `mm/`. The memory management subsystem comprises around 45,000 lines of code and is about the same size as the kernel itself.

❑ The code needed to initialize the kernel is held in `init/`. It is discussed in AppendixD.

❑ The implementation of the System V IPC mechanism resides in `ipc/`, which was discussed in Chapter 5.

❑ `sound/` contains the drivers for sound cards. Because there are devices for many of the supported buses, the directory includes bus-specific subdirectories with the corresponding driver sources. Although they are kept in their own directory, the sound card drivers are not much different from other device drivers.

❑ `fs/` holds the source code for all filesystem implementations and takes up approximately 25 MiB of space in the kernel sources.

❑ `net/` contains the network implementation, which is split into a core section and a section to implement the individual protocols. The network subsystem is 15 MiB in size and is one of the largest kernel components.

❑ `lib/` contains generic library routines that can be employed by all parts of the kernel, including data structures to implement various trees and data compression routines.

❑ `drivers/` occupies the lion's share (130 MiB) of the space devoted to the sources. However, only a few of its elements are found in the compiled kernel because, although Linux now supports a huge number of drivers, only a few are needed for each system. The directory is further subdivided in accordance with varying strategies. It includes bus-specific subdirectories (such as `drivers/pci/`) that group all drivers for accessory cards used with a specific bus type — the drivers for the bus itself are also held in this directory. There are also a few category-specific subdirectories, such as `media/` and `isdn/`, that contain cards of the same category but for different buses.

❑ `include/` contains all header files with publicly exported functions. (If functions are only used privately by a subsystem or are used in a single file only, the kernel inserts an include file in the same directory as the C source code.) A distinction is made between two types of include files — processor-dependent information is given in the subdirectory named `include/arch-arch/`, and general architecture-*independent* definitions are provided in `include/linux/`. A symbolic link (`include/asm`) to the directory appropriate to the architecture is created when the kernel is configured. When the kernel sources are compiled, the header search path of the C compiler is set so that files from `include/linux` can be linked in by means of `#include<file.h>` — normally, this is only possible for the standard include files in `/usr/include/`.

❑ crypto/ contains the files of the crypto layer (which is not discussed in this book). It includes implementations of various ciphers that are needed primarily to support IPSec (encrypted IP connection).

❑ The security/ directory is used for security frameworks and key management for cryptography. For kernel 2.6.24, it contains only the SELinux security framework,[1] but kernel 2.6.25, which was still under development at the time of this writing, will also contain the SMACK framework.

❑ Documentation/ contains numerous text files to document various aspects of the kernel. However, some of this information is very old (documenting software is not the favorite pastime of kernel developers).

❑ arch/ holds all architecture-specific files, both include files and C and Assembler sources. There is a separate subdirectory for each processor architecture supported by the kernel. The architecture-specific directories differ only slightly and are similar to the top-level directory of the kernel in that they include subdirectories such as arch/mm/, arch/kernel, and so on.

❑ scripts/ contains all scripts and utilities needed to compile the kernel or to perform other useful tasks.

The source size distribution among the various kernel components is illustrated in Figure B-1.

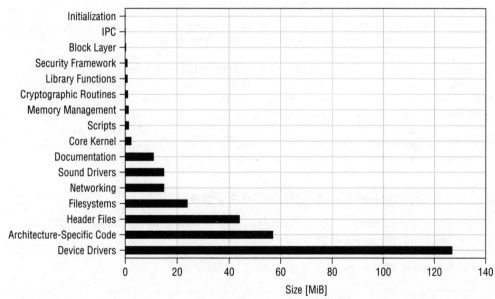

Figure B-1: Distribution of code sizes among components found in the top-level directory of kernel 2.6.24.

---

[1]SELinux extends the classic DAC (*discretionary access control*) rights model of the kernel to include role-based access control options, MAC (*mandatory access control*) and MLS (multilevel security). These special topics aren't discussed here because their implementation is lengthy, the underlying concept is complex, and the options are available in only a small number of Linux distributions.

B.2 Configuration with Kconfig

As you know, the kernel must be configured prior to compilation. By referring to a list of options, users can decide which functions they want to include in the kernel, which they want to compile as modules, and which they want to leave out. With this in mind, developers must provide a system that indicates which features are available. To this end, the kernel employs a configuration language known as *Kconfig*, which is discussed throughout the remainder of this section.

The configuration language must address the following issues:

❑ Components can be permanently compiled into the kernel, compiled as modules, or simply ignored (because it may not be possible to compile some components as modules in certain circumstances).

❑ There may be mutual dependencies between configuration options. In other words, some options can be selected only in combination with one or more other options.

❑ It must be possible to show a list of alternative options from which users may select one. There are also situations in which users are prompted to enter numbers (or similar values).

❑ It must be possible to arrange the configuration options hierarchically (in a tree structure).

❑ The configuration options differ from architecture to architecture.

❑ The configuration language should not be over-complicated because writing configuration scripts is not exactly what most kernel programmers prefer to do.

The configuration information is spread throughout the entire source tree so that there is no need for a gigantic, central configuration file that would be difficult to patch. There must be a configuration file in each subdirectory whose code contains configurable options. The following subsection uses an example to illustrate the proper syntax of a configuration file.

The following discussion deals only with the way in which the configuration options are specified. How the options are implemented in the kernel sources is not important at the moment.

B.2.1 A Sample Configuration File

The syntax of the configuration files is not especially complicated as the following (slightly modified) example taken from the USB subsystem shows:

drivers/usb/Kconfig
```
#
# USB device configuration
#

menuconfig "USB support"
        bool "USB support"
        depends on HAS_IOMEM
        default y
        ---help---
          This option adds core support for Universal Serial Bus (USB).
          You will also need drivers from the following menu to make use of it.
```

```
if USB_SUPPORT

config USB_ARCH_HAS_HCD
        boolean
        default y if USB_ARCH_HAS_OHCI
        ...
        default PCI

config USB_ARCH_HAS_OHCI
        boolean
        # ARM:
        default y if SA1111
        default y if ARCH_OMAP
        # PPC:
        default y if STB03xxx
        default y if PPC_MPC52xx
        # MIPS:
        default y if SOC_AU1X00
        # more:
        default PCI

config USB
        tristate "Support for USB"
        depends on USB_ARCH_HAS_HCD
        ---help---
          Universal Serial Bus (USB) is a specification for a serial bus
          subsystem which offers higher speeds and more features than the
          traditional PC serial port.  The bus supplies power to peripherals
          ...

source "drivers/usb/core/Kconfig"
source "drivers/usb/host/Kconfig"
...
source "drivers/usb/net/Kconfig"

comment "USB port drivers"
        depends on USB

config USB_USS720
        tristate "USS720 parport driver"
        depends on USB && PARPORT
        ---help---
          This driver is for USB parallel port adapters that use the Lucent
          Technologies USS-720 chip. These cables are plugged into your USB
          port and provide USB compatibility to peripherals designed with
          parallel port interfaces.
          ...

source "drivers/usb/gadget/Kconfig"

endif  # USB_SUPPORT
```

Figure B-2 illustrates how the defined tree structure is displayed on screen to enable users to select the options they want.

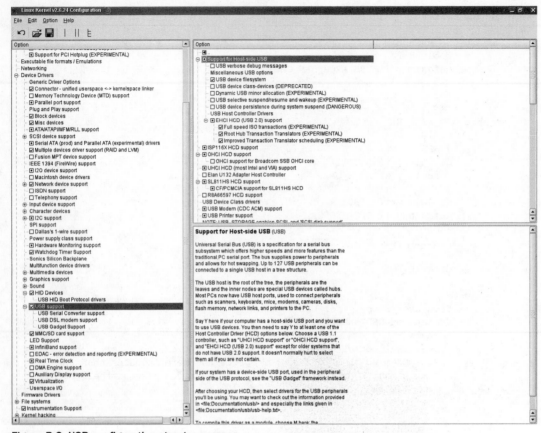

Figure B-2: USB configuration structure screen.

`menuconfig` generates a menu item whose heading is given as a string — in this case `USB support`. When users configure the kernel with `make menuconfig` or the graphical equivalent `make xconfig` or `make gconfig`, this item appears as the root of a new subtree. The choice is stored in a variable, in this case `USB_SUPPORT`, and two values are possible because the choice is Boolean, as indicated by `bool`. If `USB_SUPPORT` is deselected, then no further customization options will appear in the configuration tree, which is ensured by the `if` clause.

`source` enables further configuration files to be linked in (by convention, they are all named `Kconfig`). Their contents are interpreted as if the text they contain were held in the configuration file into which they are linked.

`comment` creates a comment in the list of configuration options. The comment text is displayed, but users cannot make a selection.

The actual configuration options are specified with `config`. There is just one entry of this kind for each option. The string following `config` is known as a *configuration symbol* and accepts the user selection. Each option requires a type to define the kind of selection that users can make. In this case, the selection type is `tristate`; that is, one of three options can be selected — "compiled in," "modular," or "do not compile." Depending on the choice made, the configuration symbol is assigned the value y, m, or n. In addition to tristate, the kernel provides other selection types, which are discussed later in this section.

Configuration option dependencies are specified by depends on. Other configuration symbols are passed to the statement as parameters, and they can be linked using the logical operators used in C (&& = "and", || = "or", and ! = "logical negation"). The menu item is not displayed unless the specified precondition is satisfied.

The --help--[2] entry indicates that the text after it is help text that users can display if they are not sure of the meaning of the configuration entry. The end of the help text is indicated by a change in indentation so that the kernel knows it is again dealing with normal configuration statements.

Two configuration options are shown in the example. The first defines the USB configuration symbol on which all other configuration entries depend. However, this choice is not displayed unless a host controller for USB can be presented. This is dependent on the USB_ARCH_HAS_HCD configuration option that may be either true or false. There are different ways of assigning a true value to the option — the following two are shown in the example:

❏ Direct support is available for a host controller chipset (OHCI in the example).

❏ The PCI bus is supported (the PCI symbol has a true value).

Support for the OHCI chipset is available if USB_ARCH_HAS_OHCI is set. This is always the case when the PCI bus is supported. However, various systems use the chipset *without* PCI support. These are explicitly listed and include, for example, ARM-based machines and some PPC-based models.

The second configuration option (USS720) is dependent on two things. Support must be available not only for USB, but also for the parallel port. Otherwise, the driver option is not even displayed.

As the example shows, there may be dependencies between comments as well as between configuration options. The USB Port drivers entry is not displayed unless USB support is selected.

Generation of the configuration tree starts at arch/arch/Kconfig, which must first be read by the configuration files. All other Kconfig files are linked in recursively from there by means of source.

B.2.2 Language Elements of Kconfig

The previous example does not make full use of all options of the Kconfig language. This section provides a systematic overview of all language features based on the documentation in the kernel sources.[3]

Menus

Menus are specified using the following command:

```
menu "string"
     <attributes>

<configuration options>

endmenu
```

---

[2]The minus signs can be omitted; help is sufficient as a separator.

[3]This documentation can be found in Documentation/kbuild/kconfig-language.txt.

where `string` is the name of the menu. All entries between `menu` and `endmenu` are interpreted as subitems of the menu and automatically inherit the dependencies of the menu item (these are added to the existing dependencies of the subitems).

The keyword `menuconfig` is used to define a configuration symbol and a submenu together. Instead of writing this:

```
menu "Bit bucket compression support"

        config BIT_BUCKET_ZLIB
            tristate "Bit bucket compression support"
```

you can also specify the shorter form as follows:

```
menuconfig BIT_BUCKET_ZLIB
        tristate "Bit bucket compression support"
```

Another keyword, `mainmenu`, may occur only at the top of the configuration hierarchy (and then once only) to specify a title for the entire hierarchy. The entry is therefore used only in `arch/arch/Kconfig` because these files represent the starting point of the configuration hierarchy. For example, the version for Sparc64 processors includes the following entry:

```
mainmenu "Linux/UltraSPARC Kernel Configuration"
```

Configuration Options

Configuration options are introduced by the keyword `config` that must be followed by a configuration symbol.

```
config <symbol>
    <type-name> "Description"
    <attributes>
```

The type name indicates the option type. As mentioned earlier, the tristate type has one of the following states: y, n, or m. Additional option types include the following:

❑   `bool` permits a Boolean query that returns either y or n — in other words, the entry may be selected or not.

❑   `string` queries a string.

❑   `hex` and `integer` read hexadecimal and decimal numbers respectively.

The following syntax can be used instead of the type name:

```
config <symbol>
    <type-name>
    prompt "Description"
```

In functional terms, this is identical to the previous, shorter alternative.

The `choice` element must be used with the following syntax if users are required to select *one* of a group of options:

```
choice
    <attributes>

config <symbol_1>
    <type-name>
    <attributes>

...

config <symbol_n>
    <type-name>
    <attributes>

endchoice
```

Each configuration option has its own configuration symbol that has the value `y` if the option is selected or `n` if not. `choice` selections are usually indicated by radio buttons in the configuration front ends, as illustrated in Figure B-3.

The source code for the CPU selection shown in the figure looks like this (the help texts have been omitted to improve readability):

```
choice
        prompt "Processor family"
        default M686 if X86_32

config M386
        bool "386"
        depends on X86_32 && !UML
        ---help---
          This is the processor type of your CPU. This information is used for
          optimizing purposes. In order to compile a kernel that can run on
          all x86 CPU types (albeit not optimally fast), you can specify
          "386" here.
          ...

config M486
        bool "486"

config M586
        bool "586/K5/5x86/6x86/6x86MX"

config M586TSC
        bool "Pentium-Classic"

config M586MMX
        bool "Pentium-MMX"

config M686
        bool "Pentium-Pro"
```

```
config MPENTIUMII
        bool "Pentium-II/Celeron(pre-Coppermine)"

...

config MGEODE_LX
        bool "Geode GX/LX"

config MCYRIXIII
        bool "CyrixIII/VIA-C3"

config MVIAC3_2
        bool "VIA C3-2 (Nehemiah)"

...

endchoice
```

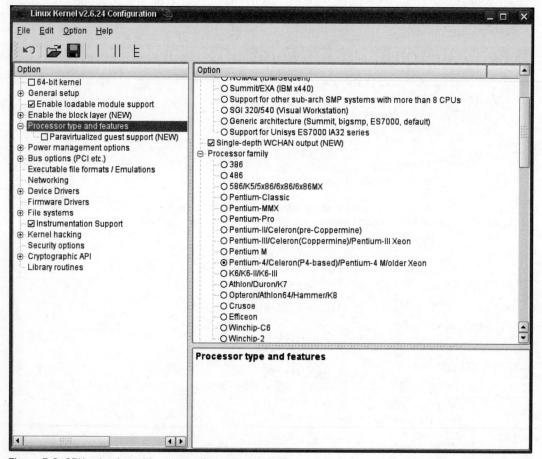

Figure B-3: CPU selection with `choice` elements on IA-32.

Attributes

Attributes are used to more precisely specify the effect of configuration options. The following excerpt from the kernel sources makes use of attributes:

```
config SWAP
        bool "Support for paging of anonymous memory (swap)"
        depends on MMU & BLOCK
        default y
```

depends on specifies that SWAP may be chosen only if the kernel is compiled for a system with MMU, and if the block layer is compiled in. default indicates that y is selected by default — if users do not change the setting, this value is automatically assigned to the SWAP symbol.

Before moving on to deal with how the dependency specification is used (described in the next subsection), take a look at the following attributes:

❑   default specifies the default setting for the config entry. For bool queries, the possible defaults are y or n. m is a third alternative for tristate. Modified defaults must be specified for the other option types: strings for string, and numbers for integer and hex.

❑   range limits the possible value range for numeric options. The first argument specifies the lower limit; the second argument specifies the upper limit.

❑   select is used to automatically select other configuration options if the entry is selected using the select statement. This *reverse dependency* mechanism can be used only with tristates and bool.

❑   help and --help-- introduce help text, as demonstrated previously.

All these attributes may also be followed by an if clause, which specifies the conditions in which the attribute applies. As with depends on, this is done by linking the symbols on which the attribute depends by means of logical operators, as shown in the following (fictitious) example:

```
config ENABLE_ACCEL
   bool "Enable device acceleration"
   default n

...

config HYPERCARD_SPEEDUP
   integer "HyperCard Speedup"
   default 20 if ENABLE_ACCEL
   range 1 20
```

Dependencies

As previously explained, entry dependencies can be specified in the form of logical clauses based on a syntax similar to C. A dependency specification must be structured as follows:

```
depends [on] <expr>
<expr> ::= <Symbol>
           <Symbol> '=' <Symbol>
           <Symbol> '!=' <Symbol>
```

```
'(' <expr> ')'
'!' <expr>
<expr> '&&' <expr>
<expr> '||' <expr>
```

The possible expressions are listed in the order in which they are interpreted. In other words, the expressions listed first have a higher priority than those that follow.

The meaning of the operations is the same as in the C syntax: $y = 2$, $n = 0$, and $m = 1$. A menu item is not visible unless the result of the dependency calculation is not 0.

A particular dependency is specified by "EXPERIMENTAL." Drivers still in the experimental stage must be labeled with this dependency (as a && logical operation if the driver has other dependencies of its own). Because the kernel provides a configuration option in init/Kconfig to allow users to set the symbol to y or n (Prompt for development and/or incomplete code/drivers), it is easy to remove drivers of this kind from the configuration options for those users who crave stability. The string "(Experimental)" should appear at the end to indicate that the driver code is in fact experimental.

B.2.3   *Processing Configuration Information*

The configuration information is processed in following steps:

1. The kernel is first configured by the user. This presupposes that a list of all possible options has been prepared and presented in text or graphical form (the available configurations are already limited by the choice of architecture without the user having to intervene).

2. The user selection is then stored in a separate file to ensure that the information is retained until the next (re)configuration and to make it available to the tools employed.

3. The selected configuration symbols must be present, both for the build system implemented by a series of Makefiles and for pre-processor statements in the kernel sources.

There are various make destinations (make *dest*config) to initiate kernel configuration. Each serves a different purpose.

❑   menuconfig provides a console-driven front end, while xconfig and gconfig feature a graphical user interface that builds on various X11 toolkits (Qt or GTK).

❑   oldconfig analyzes configuration options already stored in .config and issues prompts that may have been added after a kernel update and have not yet been assigned to a selection.

❑   defconfig applies the default configuration defined by the architecture maintainer (the relevant information is held in arch/*arch*/defconfig).

❑   allyesconfig creates a new configuration file in which all selections are set to y (where this is supported). allmodconfig also sets all selections to y but uses m if this is a possible alternative. allnoconfig generates a minimum configuration from which additional options not needed to compile the key kernel components have been removed.

These three targets are used for test purposes when new kernel releases are being created. Normally, they cannot be sensibly used by end users.

All configuration options must analyze the configuration information in the diverse Kconfig files. The resulting configuration must also be saved. The kernel sources provide the `libkconfig` library for this purpose. It holds the routines needed to perform the appropriate tasks. (This appendix does not discuss the implementation of the parser that employs the Bison and Flex parser and scanner generators. For that, refer to the relevant sources in `scripts/kconfig/zconf.y` and `zconf.l`.)

The user-defined configuration options are held in `.config`, as shown in this example:

```
wolfgang@meitner> cat .config
#
# Automatically generated make config: don't edit
# Linux kernel version: 2.6.24
# Thu Mar 20 00:09:15 2008
#
CONFIG_64BIT=y
# CONFIG_X86_32 is not set
CONFIG_X86_64=y
CONFIG_X86=y
CONFIG_GENERIC_TIME=y
...
#
# General setup
#
CONFIG_EXPERIMENTAL=y
CONFIG_LOCK_KERNEL=y
CONFIG_INIT_ENV_ARG_LIMIT=32
CONFIG_LOCALVERSION="-default"
CONFIG_LOCALVERSION_AUTO is not set
...
CONFIG_PLIST=y
CONFIG_HAS_IOMEM=y
CONFIG_HAS_IOPORT=y
CONFIG_HAS_DMA=y
CONFIG_CHECK_SIGNATURE=y
```

All configuration symbols are prefixed with the `CONFIG_` string. =y or =n is appended if the entry is set. Options that are not set are commented out using a number sign (#).

The `<config.h>` file must be linked in to make the selected configuration visible in the kernel sources. In turn, this file incorporates `<autoconf.h>` into the source text. The latter contains configuration information in a form that the pre-processor can easily digest, as shown here:

\<autoconf.h\>
```
/*
 * Automatically generated C config: don't edit
 * Linux kernel version: 2.6.24
 * Thu Mar 20 00:09:26 2008
 */
#define AUTOCONF_INCLUDED
#define CONFIG_USB_SISUSBVGA_MODULE 1
#define CONFIG_USB_PHIDGETMOTORCONTROL_MODULE 1
#define CONFIG_VIDEO_V4L1_COMPAT 1
```

1153

```
#define CONFIG_PCMCIA_FMVJ18X_MODULE 1
...
#define CONFIG_USB_SERIAL_SIERRAWIRELESS_MODULE 1
#define CONFIG_VIDEO_SAA711X_MODULE 1
#define CONFIG_SATA_INIC162X_MODULE 1
#define CONFIG_AIC79XX_RESET_DELAY_MS 15000
#define CONFIG_NET_ACT_GACT_MODULE 1
...
#define CONFIG_USB_BELKIN 1
#define CONFIG_NF_CT_NETLINK_MODULE 1
#define CONFIG_NCPFS_PACKET_SIGNING 1
#define CONFIG_SND_USB_AUDIO_MODULE 1
#define CONFIG_I2C_I810_MODULE 1
#define CONFIG_I2C_I801_MODULE 1
```

The configuration symbols are again prefixed with CONFIG_. Each option selected is defined as 1. Module options (m) are likewise defined as 1, but the _MODULE string is also appended to the pre-processor symbol. Configuration entries that are not selected are explicitly marked as undefined with undef. Numeric values and character strings are replaced with the value selected by the user.

This enables queries (as they appear throughout this book) to be inserted in the source text. For example:

```
#ifdef CONFIG_SYMBOL
/* Code if SYMBOL is set */
#else
/* Code if SYMBOL is not set */
#endif
```

B.3   Compiling the Kernel with Kbuild

After the kernel has been configured, the sources must be compiled to generate the kernel image and to obtain the module binaries. The kernel uses GNU Make to do this. It employs a complex system of Makefiles to satisfy special requirements that arise when building kernels but not when building normal applications. Deep insight into the box of make tricks is needed to fully understand how this mechanism works, so this appendix doesn't go into detail but simply examines system use from the viewpoint of end users and kernel programmers (not from the viewpoint of Kbuild developers). Documentation/kbuild/makefiles.txt contains the detailed system documentation on which this section is partly based.

B.3.1   Using the Kbuild System

The help target was introduced during the development of 2.5 to display all make targets available to users. It outputs a list of targets in which a distinction is made between architecture-dependent and architecture-independent variants. On UltraSparc systems, for example, it displays the following list:

```
wolfgang@ultrameitner> make help
Cleaning targets:
  clean            - Remove most generated files but keep the config and
                     enough build support to build external modules
  mrproper         - Remove all generated files + config + various backup files
```

```
    distclean        - mrproper + remove editor backup and patch files

Configuration targets:
    config           - Update current config utilising a line-oriented program
    menuconfig       - Update current config utilising a menu based program
    xconfig          - Update current config utilising a QT based front-end
    gconfig          - Update current config utilising a GTK based front-end
    oldconfig        - Update current config utilising a provided .config as base
    silentoldconfig  - Same as oldconfig, but quietly
    randconfig       - New config with random answer to all options
    defconfig        - New config with default answer to all options
    allmodconfig     - New config selecting modules when possible
    allyesconfig     - New config where all options are accepted with yes
    allnoconfig      - New config where all options are answered with no

Other generic targets:
    all              - Build all targets marked with [*]
  * vmlinux          - Build the bare kernel
  * modules          - Build all modules
    modules_install  - Install all modules to INSTALL_MOD_PATH (default: /)
    dir/             - Build all files in dir and below
    dir/file.[ois]   - Build specified target only
    dir/file.ko      - Build module including final link
    rpm              - Build a kernel as an RPM package
    tags/TAGS        - Generate tags file for editors
    cscope           - Generate cscope index
    kernelrelease    - Output the release version string
    kernelversion    - Output the version stored in Makefile
    headers_install  - Install sanitised kernel headers to INSTALL_HDR_PATH
                       (default: /home/wolfgang/linux-2.6.24/usr)
Static analysers
    checkstack       - Generate a list of stack hogs
    namespacecheck   - Name space analysis on compiled kernel
    export_report    - List the usages of all exported symbols
    headers_check    - Sanity check on exported headers

Kernel packaging:
    rpm-pkg          - Build the kernel as an RPM package
    binrpm-pkg       - Build an rpm package containing the compiled kernel
                       and modules
    deb-pkg          - Build the kernel as an deb package
    tar-pkg          - Build the kernel as an uncompressed tarball
    targz-pkg        - Build the kernel as a gzip compressed tarball
    tarbz2-pkg       - Build the kernel as a bzip2 compressed tarball

Documentation targets:
 Linux kernel internal documentation in different formats:
    htmldocs         - HTML
    installmandocs   - install man pages generated by mandocs
    mandocs          - man pages
    pdfdocs          - PDF
    psdocs           - Postscript
    xmldocs          - XML DocBook
```

```
Architecture specific targets (sparc64):
* vmlinux        - Standard sparc64 kernel
  vmlinux.aout   - a.out kernel for sparc64
  tftpboot.img   - Image prepared for tftp

  make V=0|1 [targets] 0 => quiet build (default), 1 => verbose build
  make V=2   [targets] 2 => give reason for rebuild of target
  make O=dir [targets] Locate all output files in "dir", including .config
  make C=1   [targets] Check all c source with $CHECK (sparse by default)
  make C=2   [targets] Force check of all c source with $CHECK

Execute "make" or "make all" to build all targets marked with [*]
For further info see the ./README file
```

IA-32 and AMD64 systems provide different architecture-specific targets.

```
wolfgang@meitner> make help
Architecture specific targets (x86):
* bzImage           - Compressed kernel image (arch/x86/boot/bzImage)
  install           - Install kernel using
                        (your) ~/bin/installkernel or
                        (distribution) /sbin/installkernel or
                        install to $(INSTALL_PATH) and run lilo
  bzdisk            - Create a boot floppy in /dev/fd0
  fdimage           - Create a boot floppy image
  isoimage          - Create a boot CD-ROM image

  i386_defconfig        - Build for i386
  x86_64_defconfig      - Build for x86_64
```

As the help text explains, all targets marked with * are compiled if make is invoked without arguments.

B.3.2   Structure of the Makefiles

The Kbuild mechanism makes use of the following components in addition to the .config file:

❑   The main Makefile (/path/to/src/Makefile) that generates the kernel itself and the modules by recursively compiling the subdirectories in accordance with the configuration and by merging the compilation results into the final product.

❑   The architecture-specific Makefile in arch/arch/Makefile that is responsible for the processor-specific subtleties that must be observed during compilation — special compiler optimization options, for instance. This file also implements all make targets specified in the architecture-specific help discussed previously.

❑   scripts/Makefile.* that contain make rules relating to general compilation, module production, the compilation of various utilities, and the removal of object files and temporary files from the kernel tree.

❑   Various kernel source subdirectories that contain Makefiles that cater to the specific needs of a driver or subsystem (and employ a standardized syntax).

The Main Makefile

The main Makefile is key to kernel compilation. It defines the call paths for the C compiler, linker, and so on. The following distinction must be made between two toolchain alternatives:

❑   A toolchain to generate *local* programs that execute on the host that compiles the kernel. Examples of such programs are the menuconfig binaries or tools for analyzing module symbols.

❑   A toolchain to generate the kernel itself.

The toolchains are usually identical. Differences arise only when a kernel is cross-compiled; in other words, when a specific architecture is used to compile a kernel for a different architecture. This method is applied if the target computer is either an embedded system with few resources (e.g., an ARM or MIPS handheld device) or a very old and slow computer (a classic Sparc or m68 Mac). In this case, a cross-compiler (and appropriate cross-binutils) must be available for the toolchain responsible for creating the kernel so that the desired code can be generated.

The local tools are defined as follows:

```
wolfgang@meitner> cat Makefile
...
HOSTCC          = gcc
HOSTCXX         = g++
HOSTCFLAGS      = -Wall -Wstrict-prototypes -O2 -fomit-frame-pointer
HOSTCXXFLAGS    = -O2
...
```

The kernel tools are defined as follows:

```
wolfgang@meitner> cat Makefile
...
CROSS_COMPILE=

AS              = $(CROSS_COMPILE)as
LD              = $(CROSS_COMPILE)ld
CC              = $(CROSS_COMPILE)gcc
CPP             = $(CC) -E
AR              = $(CROSS_COMPILE)ar
NM              = $(CROSS_COMPILE)nm
STRIP           = $(CROSS_COMPILE)strip
OBJCOPY         = $(CROSS_COMPILE)objcopy
OBJDUMP         = $(CROSS_COMPILE)objdump
AWK             = awk
GENKSYMS        = scripts/genksyms/genksyms
DEPMOD          = /sbin/depmod
KALLSYMS        = scripts/kallsyms
PERL            = perl
CHECK           = sparse

CHECKFLAGS      := -D__linux__ -Dlinux -D__STDC__ -Dunix -D__unix__ -Wbitwise $(CF)
MODFLAGS        = -DMODULE
```

```
CFLAGS_MODULE    = $(MODFLAGS)
AFLAGS_MODULE    = $(MODFLAGS)
LDFLAGS_MODULE   = -r
CFLAGS_KERNEL    =
AFLAGS_KERNEL    =
...
```

The CROSS_COMPILE prefix that precedes a definition is normally left blank. It must be assigned an appropriate value (ia64-linux-, for example) if the kernel is to be compiled for a different architecture.[4] As a result, two different toolsets are used for the host and the target.

All other Makefiles may *never* use the names of the tools directly, but must always employ the variables defined here.

The main Makefile declares the ARCH variable to indicate the architecture for which the kernel is compiled. It contains a value that is automatically detected and that is compatible with the directory names in arch/. For example, ARCH is set to i386 for IA-32 because the architecture-specific files reside in arch/i386/.

If the kernel is to be cross-compiled, ARCH must be modified accordingly. For example, the following calls are required to configure and compile the kernel for ARM systems (assuming that the appropriate toolchain is available):

```
make ARCH=arm menuconfig
make ARCH=arm CROSS_COMPILE=arm-linux-
```

In addition to these definitions, the Makefile includes the statements needed to descend recursively into the individual subdirectories and to compile the files they contain with the help of the local Makefile. This appendix doesn't go into the implementation details of this mechanism because it involves a large number of make subtleties.

Driver and Subsystem Makefiles

The Makefiles in the driver and subsystem directories are used to compile the correct files — in accordance with the configuration in .config — and to direct the compilation flow to the required subdirectories. The Kbuild framework makes the creation of such Makefiles relatively easy. Only the following line is needed to generate an object file for permanent compilation into the kernel (regardless of the configuration):

```
obj-y = file.o
```

By reference to the filename, Kbuild automatically detects that the source file is file.c and invokes the C compiler with the appropriate options to generate the binary object file if it is not already present or if the source file has been modified after generation of an old version of the object file. The generated file is also automatically included when the kernel is linked by the linker.

This approach can also be adopted if there are several object files. The specified files must then be separated by blanks.

---

[4]This can be set explicitly in the Makefile, specified by means of a shell variable in the environment, or passed as a parameter for make.

If there is a choice of linking in kernel components or not (in other words, if configuration is controlled by a bool query), the Makefile must react accordingly to the user's selection. The configuration symbol in the Makefile can be used for this purpose, as the following example taken from the Makefile in the kernel/ directory illustrates:

```
obj-y = sched.o fork.o exec_domain.o panic.o printk.o profile.o \
        exit.o itimer.o time.o softirq.o resource.o \
        sysctl.o capability.o ptrace.o timer.o user.o user_namespace.o \
        signal.o sys.o kmod.o workqueue.o pid.o \
        rcupdate.o extable.o params.o posix-timers.o \
        kthread.o wait.o kfifo.o sys_ni.o posix-cpu-timers.o mutex.o \
        hrtimer.o rwsem.o latency.o nsproxy.o srcu.o \
        utsname.o notifier.o

obj-$(CONFIG_SYSCTL) += sysctl_check.o
obj-$(CONFIG_STACKTRACE) += stacktrace.o
obj-y += time/
...
obj-$(CONFIG_GENERIC_ISA_DMA) += dma.o
obj-$(CONFIG_SMP) += cpu.o spinlock.o
obj-$(CONFIG_DEBUG_SPINLOCK) += spinlock.o
...
obj-$(CONFIG_MODULES) += module.o
obj-$(CONFIG_KALLSYMS) += kallsyms.o
obj-$(CONFIG_PM) += power/
...
obj-$(CONFIG_SYSCTL) += utsname_sysctl.o
obj-$(CONFIG_TASK_DELAY_ACCT) += delayacct.o
obj-$(CONFIG_TASKSTATS) += taskstats.o tsacct.o
obj-$(CONFIG_MARKERS) += marker.o
```

The files that are *always* compiled are at the top of the list. The files below them are not compiled by Kbuild unless their configuration symbol is set to y. For example, if module support is configured, the corresponding line expands to the following:

```
obj-y += module.o
```

Note the use of += instead of a normal equal sign (=), which causes the object to be added to the target obj-y.

If module support is not configured, the line expands as follows:

```
obj-n += module.o
```

All files of the target obj-n are ignored by the Kbuild system and are therefore not compiled.

The following line for power management is particularly interesting:

```
obj-$(CONFIG_PM) += power/
```

Here the target is not a file but a directory. If CONFIG_PM is set, Kbuild switches to the kernel/power/ file during compilation and processes the Makefile that it contains.

Kbuild links all the object files of a directory that are contained in the target obj-y into an overall object file built-in.o, which is subsequently linked into the finished kernel.[5]

Modules fit seamlessly into this mechanism, as the following Ext3 Makefile example demonstrates:

```
#
# Makefile for the linux ext3-filesystem routines.
#

obj-$(CONFIG_EXT3_FS) += ext3.o

ext3-y := balloc.o bitmap.o dir.o file.o fsync.o ialloc.o inode.o \
ioctl.o namei.o super.o symlink.o hash.o resize.o ext3_jbd.o

ext3-$(CONFIG_EXT3_FS_XATTR) += xattr.o xattr_user.o xattr_trusted.o
ext3-$(CONFIG_EXT3_FS_POSIX_ACL) += acl.o
ext3-$(CONFIG_EXT3_FS_SECURITY) += xattr_security.o
```

If the Ext3 filesystem is compiled as a module and CONFIG_EXT3_FS therefore expands to m, the standard target obj-m stipulates that a file named ext3.o must be generated. The contents of this object file are defined by a further explicit target called ext3-y.

The kernel employs indirect specification of the source files rather than direct specification in obj-m so that additional features (whether enabled or not) can be taken into account. (The corresponding configuration symbols in the Kconfig mechanism are described by a bool selection, and a tristate is used for the main symbol CONFIG_EXT3_FS.)

If, for example, extended attributes are to be used, CONFIG_EXT3_FS_XATTR expands to y, and this produces the following line in the Makefile:

```
ext3-y      += xattr.o xattr_user.o xattr_trusted.o
```

This links the additionally required object files into the object file and clearly indicates why the indirect target ext3-y is used. If the following had been used, there would be two targets (obj-y and obj-m):

```
obj-$(CONFIG_EXT3_FS)} += xattr.o xattr_user.o xattr_trusted.o
```

As a result, the additional files would not be included in the standard Ext3 object.

Of course, the indirect approach also works when Ext3 is permanently compiled into the kernel.

B.4 Useful Tools

Many excellent tools are available to help programmers manage major software projects and keep track of sources. They also render very good services in the Linux sector. This section describes some of the helpers that facilitate work with the kernel. The selection of tools presented here is purely subjective — they are my personal preferences, but countless alternatives are available on the Internet.

---

[5]If the object files use initcalls (as discussed in Appendix D), the sequence in which the files are specified in obj-y is the order in which the initcalls of the same category are invoked because the link sequence is identical to the sequence in obj-y.

B.4.1 LXR

LXR is a cross-referencing tool. It analyzes the kernel sources and generates a hypertext representation in HTML for viewing in a browser. LXR lets users search on variables, functions, and other symbols, and supports branching to their definitions in the source code as well as listing all points at which they are used. This is useful when tracing code flow paths in the kernel. Figure B-4 shows how the source text is displayed in the web browser.

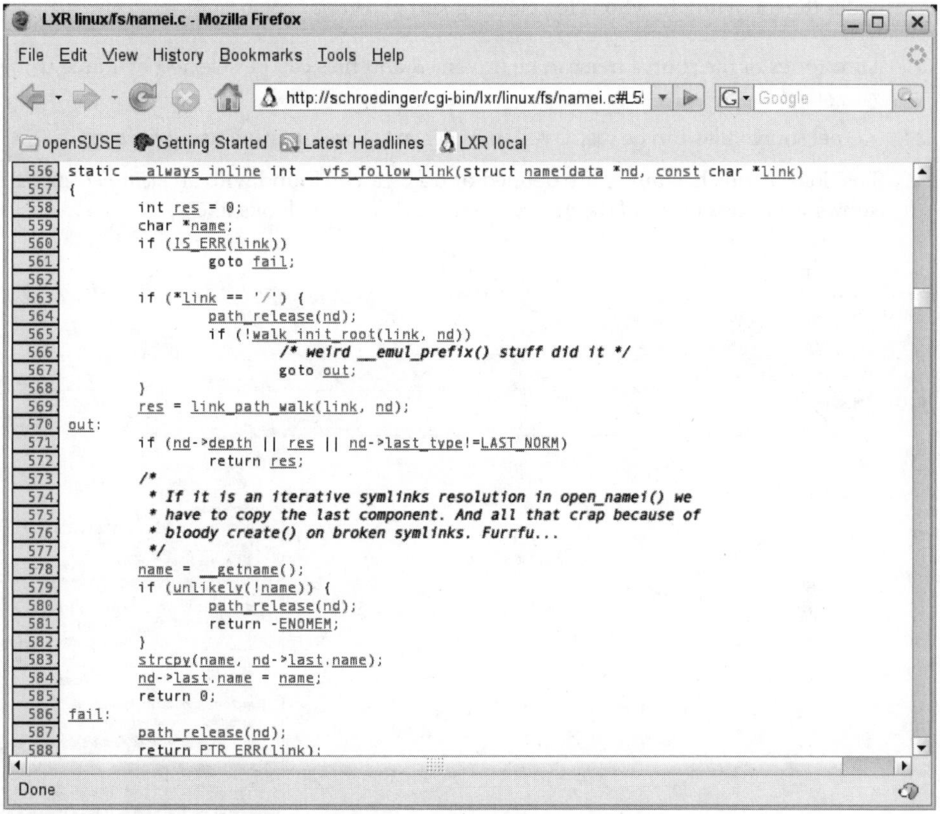

Figure B-4: Linux source text as LXR-generated hypertext.

A web browser and a web server, preferably Apache, are needed to use LXR locally. The `glimpse` search engine is also required to search the sources for random strings.

The canonical version of LXR can be downloaded from `sourceforge.net/projects/lxr`. Unfortunately, this version has not seen any development for a number of years, and although the code works just fine, it misses a number of features present in modern web applications.

Appendix B: Working with the Source Code

A more experimental version of LXR that is actively maintained is available from the git repository `git://lxr.linux.no/git/lxrng.git`. It provides more features than the variant described previously, and can, for instance, employ proper databases like PostgreSQL to store the generated information about the source code. The installation method for this experimental version is still in a constant flux, so this appendix does not discuss how to install the software — for information about this version, refer to the accompanying documentation.

Working with LXR

LXR provides the following functions for viewing kernel components:

- ❑ Directories of the source tree can be traversed and files can be selected by name using *source navigation*.

- ❑ Kernel source files can be displayed in hypertext representation using *file view*.

- ❑ Positions at which symbols are defined or used can be found with an *identifier search*. Figure B-5 shows what the output of the `vfs_follow_link` function looks like.

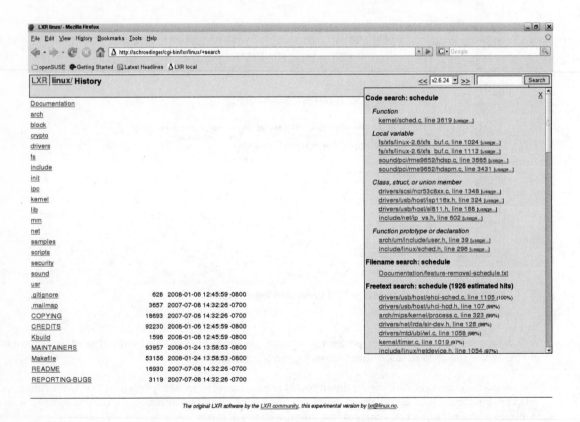

Figure B-5: View of the information on `schedule`.

❑ The kernel source text can be scanned for any string using *freetext search*.

❑ *File search* enables users to search for files by name if they don't know where those files are located in the sources.

B.4.2 Patch and Diff

Kernel patches were the only way of tracking ongoing kernel development in the early days of Linux. Patches still have an important role to play because git builds implicitly on diffs and patches, and patches are the required form when changes are communicated to a mailing list.

patch and diff are complementary tools. Whereas diff analyzes the differences between two files or a set of files, patch applies the differences held in a file generated by diff to an existing source text.

Unified Context Diffs

The following example illustrates the format used by diff to record the differences between two versions of a file. It reflects a change made to the scheduler during the development of kernel 2.6.24.

```
diff -up a/include/linux/sched.h b/include/linux/sched.h
--- a/include/linux/sched.h
+++ b/include/linux/sched.h
@@ -908,6 +908,7 @@ struct sched_entity {
  u64 sum_exec_runtime;
  u64 vruntime;
  u64 prev_sum_exec_runtime;
+ u64 last_min_vruntime;

 #ifdef CONFIG_SCHEDSTATS
  u64 wait_start;
diff -up a/kernel/sched.c b/kernel/sched.c
--- a/kernel/sched.c
+++ b/kernel/sched.c
@@ -1615,6 +1615,7 @@ static void __sched_fork(struct task_struct *p)
  p->se.exec_start = 0;
  p->se.sum_exec_runtime = 0;
  p->se.prev_sum_exec_runtime = 0;
+ p->se.last_min_vruntime = 0;

 #ifdef CONFIG_SCHEDSTATS
  p->se.wait_start = 0;
@@ -6495,6 +6496,7 @@ static inline void init_cfs_rq(struct cfs_rq *cfs_rq, struct rq *rq)
 #ifdef CONFIG_FAIR_GROUP_SCHED
  cfs_rq->rq = rq;
 #endif
+ cfs_rq->min_vruntime = (u64)(-(1LL << 20));
 }

 void __init sched_init(void)
diff -up a/kernel/sched_fair.c b/kernel/sched_fair.c
--- a/kernel/sched_fair.c
+++ b/kernel/sched_fair.c
@@ -243,6 +243,15 @@ static u64 sched_slice(struct cfs_rq *cfs_rq, struct sched_entity *se)
  return period;
```

```
 }

+static u64 __sched_vslice(unsigned long nr_running)
+{
+ u64 period = __sched_period(nr_running);
+
+ do_div(period, nr_running);
+
+ return period;
+}
+
 /*
  * Update the current task's runtime statistics. Skip current tasks that
  * are not in our scheduling class.
```

The first three lines of a `diff` contain the header information. This indicates which files were handled and includes the time stamps of both files as a comparison criterion. The second line gives the name of the old file version, and the third line, the name of the new file version. The first line lists the options with which the `diff` utility was invoked. Here, the `-up` option is particularly important because it generates diffs in the easy-to-read *unified context format*, which also includes the C function name to which the change applies — all other formats are deprecated in the Linux kernel community.

`diff` compares two files line by line to find the differences between them. Isolated sections of the file where differences are found are referred to as *hunks*. The preceding example consists of three hunks, each of which is introduced by two symbols.[6]

Each hunk has a header to indicate the position in both files at which the difference occurs. The format of the header is as follows:

```
@@ start_old,count_old start_new,count_new @@ C function
```

`start_old` specifies the line number in the old file to which the `diff` refers. `count_old` specifies the number of lines over which the differences extend. `start_new` and `count_new` have the same meanings but relate to the source file. The C function in which the code is contained is also recorded.

The lines following the hunk header indicate what has changed in the file. Lines prefixed with a plus sign (+) are not present in the old file, and lines prefixed with a minus sign are destined for removal from the old file. Lines without either sign are identical in both the new file and the old file. They are used by `patch` as a context to move the patch up or down if the file to be patched does not fully match the original file for which the patch was created. This is useful when, for example, another otherwise orthogonal patch[7] inserts new code at the start of a file and the patch position is therefore moved down.

Applying Patches

A *patch* is a collection of diffs that reside in a common file. For example, patches that contain the differences between two kernel versions are made available at `www.kernel.org` for updating purposes. It is then no longer necessary to download the entire source tree, thus saving time and bandwidth.

---

[6]If two files are totally different, `diff` creates a single large hunk that covers the whole file.

[7]Patches are referred to as *orthogonal* if they do not mutually influence each other; that is, if a patch changes only code segments that do not affect other segments.

Patches are applied with the help of the `patch` tool, which is not especially difficult to handle. The following statement updates the kernel sources in `/home/wolfgang/linux-2.6.23` from version 2.6.23 to version 2.6.24:

```
wolfgang@meitner> cd /home/wolfgang
wolfgang@meitner> bzcat patch-2.6.24.bz2 | patch -p0
```

`patch` can not only apply patches but also *remove* them. This is an extremely useful feature when troubleshooting because modifications can be selectively removed from the sources until a particular error no longer occurs. This at least isolates the modification that gave rise to the error.[8] The `-R` option must be specified to "reverse" the patch. The following example reverses the kernel sources of version 2.6.24 back to version 2.6.23 by removing the preceding patch:

```
wolfgang@meitner> bzcat patch-2.6.24.bz2 | patch -R -p0
```

`patch` provides many other options, which are documented in detail on the `patch(1)` man page.

B.4.3 Git

Git is a relatively novel version control system on which the Linux kernel development model is based. A large group of developers spread throughout the world are cooperating on a software product although they are not in direct personal contact. They are working not with a central repository, on which classical systems such as CVS build, but with a large number of subtrees that are synchronized with each other at intervals in order to swap changes.

The first proper version control system employed by the kernel community was BitKeeper. However, Linus Torvalds himself launched the development of an alternative tool because it was no longer possible to continue using BitKeeper due to various conflicts between BitMover (the company responsible for BitKeeper), and sections of the kernel community. The conflicts revolve around the fact that BitKeeper is not an open-source product (and is in no way free software in the GPL sense) but is sold under proprietary license. BitKeeper could be used free of charge for noncommercial purposes, but this right has been revoked by BitMover, so the kernel community had to come up with a different solution — and indeed it did.

The solution is a completely new version control system which goes by the name *git*. Git is designed as a content tracker — it makes a kind of database layer available to enable changes to files to be archived. Great importance is attached to the fact that necessary operations can be performed directly in the filesystem with the help of regular files — no direct database back end is needed.

Git used to have a front end by the name of cogito. It was required for early versions of git to provide the standard features of a version control system, and was easier to use than pure git. However, the former deficiencies of git have by now been resolved, so cogito is not actively being developed anymore, and it's no longer required because git provides everything directly.

`qgit` and `gitk` are graphical front ends to handle git repositories. It greatly simplifies work for those who do not use git regularly and are therefore not familiar with the numerous commands. The following sections describe the shell commands and the graphical user interface.

---

[8]Notice that git also offers possibilities to automatize the search for erroneous patches via the `git-bisect` tool.

Git does not rank behind BitKeeper in terms of kernel developer productivity. Because it is a very useful tool to track kernel development history, investigate errors, and carry out programming work, the focus here is on its most important characteristics. However, if you are interested in detailed information on the capabilities of git, refer to the documentation that comes with the product.

When working with git, it is very useful to create a *clone* of Linus Torvalds's repository as it contains the "official" kernel versions. The repository of developer version 2.6 is available at git://git.kernel.org/pub/scm/linux/kernel/git/torvalds/linux-2.6.git. It can be cloned using the following command:

```
wolfgang@meitner> git clone git://git.kernel.org/pub/scm/linux/kernel/git-torvalds/linux-2.6.git
```

Depending on the network connection, a file transfer initiated by this command takes between a few minutes and several hours (with extremely slow modems).

The following sections deal with several important commands used to track kernel development history, although these represent only part of the git functionality. Further information can be obtained by invoking the online help with git help. The help system provides an overview of available commands. A detailed description of the individual commands can be requested by entering git help *command*.

Tracking Development History

Git employs *commits* to group development steps. When a new feature that requires modification of several files is added to the kernel, the changes to all the files are concentrated in a commit that is applied as a whole to a repository. Each commit includes a comment to indicate the purpose of the change. An individual comment may also be added to each file in a commit.

Displaying Commits

The git log command displays all commits applied to a repository. For example:

```
wolfgang@meitner> git log
commit f1d39b291e2263f5e2f2ec5d4061802f76d8ae67
tree 29c33d63b3679103459932d43b8818abdcc7d3d5
parent fd60ae404f104f12369e654af9cf03b1f1047661
author Unicorn Chang <uchang@tw.ibm.com> Tue, 01 Aug 2006 12:18:07 +0800
committer Jeff Garzik <jeff@garzik.org> Thu, 03 Aug 2006 17:34:52 -0400

    [PATCH] ahci: skip protocol test altogether in spurious interrupt code

    Skip protocol test altogether in spurious interrupt code. If PIOS is receive
    when it shouldn't, ahci will raise protocol violation.

    Signed-off-by: Unicorn Chang <uchang@tw.ibm.com>
    Signed-off-by: Jeff Garzik <jeff@garzik.org>

commit c54772e751c0262073e85a7aa87f093fc0dd44f1
tree 5b6ef64c20ac5c2027f73a59bc7a6b4b21f0b63e
parent e454358ace657af953b5b289f49cf733973f41e4
author Brice Goglin <brice@myri.com> Sun, 30 Jul 2006 00:14:15 -0400
committer Jeff Garzik <jeff@garzik.org> Thu, 03 Aug 2006 17:31:10 -0400

    [PATCH] myri10ge - Fix spurious invokations of the watchdog reset handler
```

```
        Fix spurious invocations of the watchdog reset handler.

            Signed-off-by: Brice Goglin <brice@myri.com>
            Signed-off-by: Jeff Garzik <jeff@garzik.org>

    commit e454358ace657af953b5b289f49cf733973f41e4
    tree 62ab274bead7523e8402e7ee9d15a55e10a0914a
    parent 817acf5ebd9ea21f134fc90064b0f6686c5b169d
    author Brice Goglin <brice@myri.com> Sun, 30 Jul 2006 00:14:09 -0400
    committer Jeff Garzik <jeff@garzik.org> Thu, 03 Aug 2006 17:31:10 -0400

        [PATCH] myri10ge - Write the firmware in 256-bytes chunks

        When writing the firmware to the NIC, the FIFO is 256-bytes long,
        so we use 256-bytes chunks and a read to wait until the previous
        write is done.

            Signed-off-by: Brice Goglin <brice@myri.com>
            Signed-off-by: Jeff Garzik <jeff@garzik.org>
    ...
```

Tracking the Development History of a Single File

The `git log` command also enables the development history of a specific file to be tracked across several commits. It is invoked with a filename as its argument (if the filename is omitted, the development history of the entire project is displayed). Instead of using the text listing, it is much more convenient, however, to observe the history in a graphical front end. Figure B-6 shows the screen display generated by QGit, a QT-based graphical to git.

It is also possible to inspect all changes that were introduced with a specific commit, as illustrated in Figure B-7. This includes the affected files on the right, a description of the patch in the center, and the patch itself below that.

The `git fetch` command transfers changes made in the parent repository to the local repository. It also enables changes in other repositories to be transferred provided they originate from the same parent repository as the local repository.

Developers with a particular interest in the progress of a specific part of the kernel for which development is performed in an own git repository can integrate all changes that have not found their way into the Torvalds sources in their local repository. For example:

```
    wolfgang@meitner> git fetch git://foobar.frobnicate.org/exult.git
```

The main repository that serves as a template for the local clone is used if `git fetch` is invoked without a repository name.

Incorporating Modifications

This section briefly describes a few other commands that are needed to make modifications to repositories. Before you make any changes, you should create a copy of the local repository for subsequent synchronization with the upstream sources. Because git is able to use hard links to copy repositories (providing that the copy and the original are located on the same filesystem), not much space or time is needed to generate a development copy of a repository. Changes made to the copy are not transferred automatically to the original unless explicitly initiated.

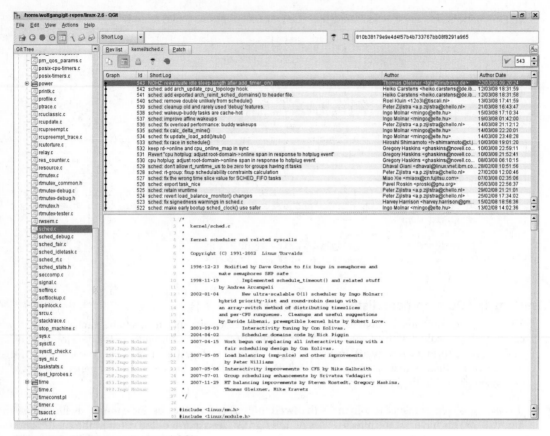

Figure B-6: File history displayed QGit.

The following input is required to clone the repository:

```
wolfgang@meitner> git clone /home/wolfgang/git-repos/linux-2.6 /home/wolfgang/linux-work
```

After you are done making your changes to the files, you can add comments and group them into a commit using `git commit`. Note that `git gui` provides a graphical front end to create commits, which can be used intuitively and does not require much explanation.

Exporting

Git features the `git archive` command to export the status of the complete repository at a given time.

Tags are important when a specific revision is exported from the repository. These tags are specially marked points along the development time axis. In the Linux context, these points in time represent the published versions of the kernel. For example, the tag for version `2.6.24` is `v2.6.24`. This symbolic identifier can be used as an abbreviation for the usual combination of digits because it is much easier to remember. The use of tags to identify releases is a Linus Torvalds convention for the Linux sources. Tags can, of course, be used for many other purposes; for example, to mark the beginning or end of far-reaching changes, or to identify interim versions.

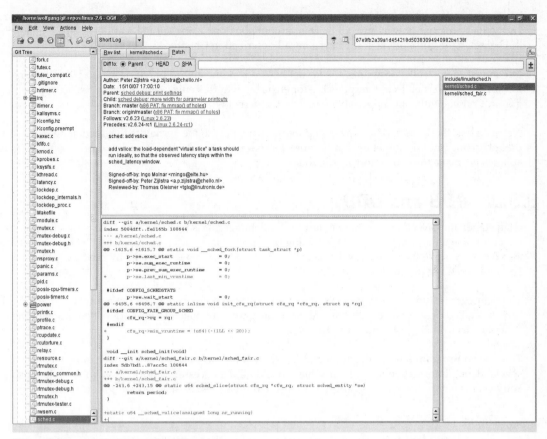

Figure B-7: Inspecting commits with `qgit`.

The following input is necessary to export the entire source code of the named version into a separate directory:

```
wolfgang@meitner> git archive --format=tar --prefix=linux-2.6.24/ v2.6.24
```

Because this will write the resulting tarball to the standard output, you might want to redirect the result to a file.

`git archive` can also be used to generate different types of archives. A filename with the suffix `.tar.gz`, `.tgz`, or `.tar.bz2` must be used instead of the tar file shown here.

B.5   Debugging and Analyzing the Kernel

To gain an insight into what happens in the kernel, it is often practical not only to read the static source code but also to take a close look at the kernel while it is running in order to track its dynamic processes. Programmers are familiar with how this is done for normal C programs. Using debugging information generated by the compiler and an external debugger, it is possible to step through program execution line by line (or, if desired, assembler statement by assembler statement) to view and modify data structures, and to halt program flow at any point. This can only be done using special features made available by the kernel in the guise of the `ptrace` system call described in Chapter 13.

In contrast to normal C programs, the kernel has no runtime environment provided by an external instance — the kernel itself is responsible for ensuring that this environment exists for user-space programs. Consequently, it is impossible to debug the kernel with classical means.

Nevertheless, there are various ways of applying debuggers to the kernel, as this section describes. Even though debugging the kernel is slightly more complicated than debugging normal programs, the valuable results make the extra effort worthwhile.

B.5.1   GDB and DDD

GDB stands for *GNU debugger*, the default Linux debugger. It is included with every distribution as a ready-made binary that can be loaded using the appropriate packet mechanism. Of course, you are also free to compile the sources available at www.gnu.org (or on one of the many mirrors), although this appendix does not discuss how this is done.

The debugger features very extensive options, and this appendix provides only a brief overview of their use. A detailed description of GDB is available in the guide (in makeinfo format) that comes with the tool; it can be viewed using `info gdb`, for example.

To debug a program (and in this respect, the kernel is no exception), the compiler must incorporate special debug information in the binary file to yield all the necessary information on the relationship between the binary file and the sourcecode. The `-g` option must be selected for `gcc`, as follows:

```
wolfgang@meitner> gcc -g test.c -o test
```

The size of the executable file grows considerably as a result of the debug symbols it contains.

`-g` must also be activated during compilation. In earlier versions the option had to be entered under `CFLAGS_KERNEL` in the main `Makefile`. However, during development of 2.5, a separate option, `Kernel hacking->Compile the kernel with debug info`,was built into the kernel configuration to do this automatically. The `Compile the kernel with frame pointers` option included in the same menu should also be selected at the same time because it enables the limit for activation records or stack frames (see Appendix C) and therefore supplies the debugger with useful information.

GDB is able to do the following:

❑   Trace program execution line by line, in procedures and functions steps or in individual assembler statements.

❑   Determine the type of all symbols used in the program.

❑   Display or manipulate the current values of symbols.

❑   De-reference pointers or access random memory locations of the program and read or modify their values.

❑ Set breakpoints that halt the program when it reaches a given position in the source code and then enable the debugger.

❑ Set watchpoints that halt the program when a given condition is satisfied — for example, when the value of a variable is set to a predefined value.

The specific kernel debugging options that are available depend on the method used.

The command syntax for performing these operations is simple to learn and remember because it is based on C. It is excellently explained in the GDB documentation.

Like most UNIX tools, GDB is text-based. This has its benefits but also its downsides, particularly the fact that it is not possible to visualize the relationship between data structures by means of graphical pointers. Similarly, the GDB view on source text is not always ideal because only very short sections are displayed.

DDD — the *Data Display Debugger* — was developed to rectify these deficiencies and is now included in all popular distributions. As a graphical tool for X11, it remedies the known disadvantages of GDB. DDD is a user interface to GDB and therefore supports all features of the debugger. Because it is possible to type in GDB commands directly, all options are available — not just those integrated into the graphical user interface.

The DDD package comes with a very good guide, so this appendix doesn't explain how to use it, particularly because the user interface is very intuitive.

B.5.2 Local Kernel

The proc filesystem includes a file named kcore that contains an image of the current state of the kernel in ELF core format (see Appendix E). Because GDB core files can be read and processed, they can be used in conjunction with a kernel and its debug symbols to visualize data structures and read their internal state. (GDB core files are typically used for postmortem analyses of userspace programs to find out why they have crashed.)

DDD must be invoked with the name of the kernel image (including the debug symbols) and of the kcore file as parameters:

```
wolfgang@meitner> ddd /home/wolfgang/linux-2.6.24/vmlinux /proc/kcore
```

This must be done as root user or the access permission to /proc/kcore must be changed to allow the file to be read by the specific user. (There is a security risk if the access rights to /proc/kcore are not sufficiently restrictive because it enables the user to modify the kernel memory.)

Even though, for obvious reasons, no breakpoints or similar items can be set for the running kernel, the DDD is ideally suited to examine the data structures of the system, as Figure B-8 shows.

The starting points for such an examination are instances of data structures that are defined as global variables of the kernel. Entering graph display proc_root instructs DDD to display the instance of type proc_dir_entry declared in fs/proc_root.c. The other instances associated with the data structure by means of pointers are opened by double-clicking.

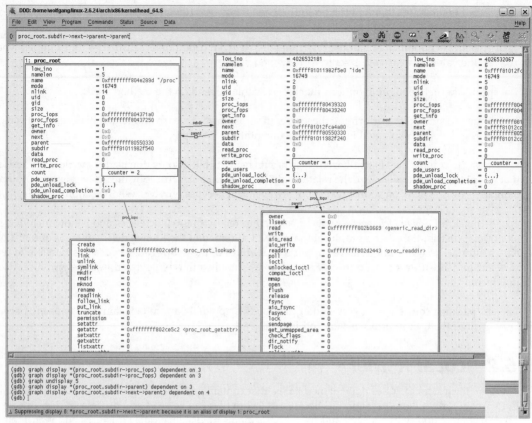

Figure B-8: Examining data structures of the local kernel.

If no type information is present for a pointer (this is, frequently the case in doubly linked standard lists), C-style typecasts can be specified in the GDB input field.

The Data->Detect Aliases option must be enabled to instruct DDD to detect pointers to the same memory area and to redirect the arrows to an existing representation of the structure rather than inserting a new graphic representation. This is the case in the previous example, as indicated by the parent pointers that all (correctly) point to the same element. Note however that DDD is much slower than usual when it operates in this mode.

The core files are not normally modified when they are processed by a debugger, so GDB does not notice if any change is made to a value in kernel memory — changes are propagated via the kcore file. If the memory contents that are relevant to a user change, the user must explicitly reload the core file with core /proc/kcore. DDD automatically displays values that have changed against a yellow background so that they are easy to recognize.

B.5.3 KGDB

Two machines connected via a network or a serial cable provide a better debugging setup with practically all the same options as are available when debugging normal applications. The *KGDB* patch installs a short stub code in the kernel to provide an interface to a debugger running on a second system. Because GDB supports remote debugging, the kernel can make use of this form of debugging, which features breakpoints, single-step processing, and the like.

KGDB is not included in kernel 2.6.24, but after long years of struggle, it will have been included in kernel 2.6.26 by the time you are reading this. Patches are also available for older kernel versions in case you need KGDB support for them.

Once you have obtained a kernel with KGDB support, the configuration includes the new menu item `Kernel hacking->KGDB: kernel debugging with remote gdb` that must be enabled. If the serial interface is used for data transfer, the correct settings must be made for the particular hardware. Debug symbols should, of course, also be included in the kernel binary.

Because KGDB is evolving rather dynamically at the time of this writing, you should refer to `Documentation/DocBook/kgdb.html` (which can be generated with `make htmldocs`) for information on how to connect `gdb` to a running kernel.

B.6   User-Mode Linux

UML (*User-Mode Linux*) is a port of Linux to Linux itself. The kernel runs on a Linux box as a userspace process — a setup that is not without a certain beauty.

This facilitates many applications that would be difficult or impossible to implement with a classic Linux kernel on genuine hardware, above all the ability to successively test new kernel features without the need for dozens of time-consuming restarts.

UML also supports the use of debuggers, either of the built-in, console-based type or as external programs. This section briefly describes how DDD can be used in conjunction with UML to provide versatile options for analyzing the kernel and its data structures. As with KGDB, breakpoints can be set and variables can be changed in memory; however, only a single system is needed.

`ARCH=um` must be specified in the command line to indicate that the kernel is to be generated for UML and not for the local processor (`CROSS_COMPILE` need not be set as would otherwise be necessary for genuine cross-compilation.) For example:

```
wolfgang@meitner> make menuconfig ARCH=um
wolfgang@meitner> make linux ARCH=um
```

To compile UML on an AMD64 architecture, you also need to add `SUBARCH=i386`. The default configuration of UML is a reasonable setup for most purposes and need not be modified.

The compilation result is an executable file called `linux` that is located in the main directory of the kernel sources. This file contains Linux as a user process.

You can debug UML in the same way as a normal Linux process. As Figure B-9 shows, it is also possible to set breakpoints.

UML offers many other options; for example, shared use of a filesystem with the host for ease of data exchange, or a setup of network connections between the host and UML (and even between several UML processes). Refer to the UML documentation for a detailed description of these options. Also notice that the designer of UML has written a book solely devoted to this topic[Dik06].

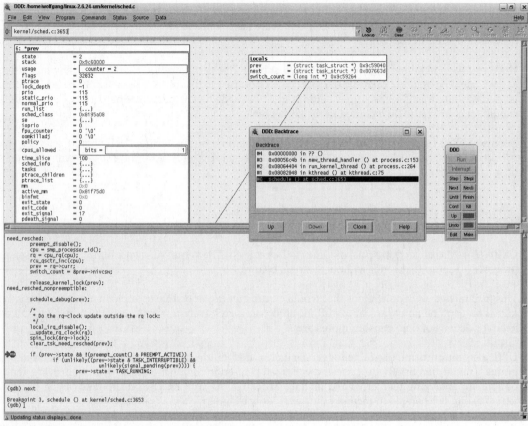

Figure B-9: Breakpoint in a running UML kernel.

B.7 Summary

The Linux kernel is a huge project, and in addition to improving the software, managing the comprehensive code base is a challenging undertaking for its developers. This appendix introduced you to how the kernel sources are organized, and which tools are employed to build a customized kernel binary (and the associated modules) according to the user's needs. In addition, this appendix described a selection of useful tools that aid you in understanding the complex code base, allow for tracking the ongoing development of the kernel, and help in finding and correcting errors using advanced debugging schemes.

C

Notes on C

For more than 25 years, C has been the preferred programming language for implementing operating systems of all kinds — including Linux. The major part of the kernel — with the exception of a few assembly language segments — is programmed in C. Therefore, it is not possible to understand the kernel without a mastery of C. This book assumes that you have already gained sufficient experience with C in userspace programming. This appendix discusses little-used and very specific aspects of C in kernel programming.

The kernel sources are especially designed for compilation with the GNU C compiler.[1] This compiler is available for many architectures (far more than are supported by the kernel) and also features numerous enhancements used by the kernel, as discussed in this appendix.

C.1 How the GNU C Compiler Works

In addition to using GNU enhancements to the C language, the kernel also relies on a number of optimizations performed by the compiler when it generates assembler code from the C sources. Because very close cooperation between the sources and the compiler is necessary at some points in the kernel, this section provides a brief overview of the actions performed by the GNU Compiler Collection (GCC) when it compiles a program and of the various techniques used. The following information is, of course, of a summary nature. For detailed information, refer to the *GCC Internals* manual provided with the compiler sources and available online at gcc.gnu.org.

---

[1]On IA-32 platforms, the proprietary compiler of Intel can also be used. It produces slightly better assembler code and makes the kernel a fraction faster but does not provide the prime benefit of architecture independence. Because the Intel compiler supports all GNU C enhancements used by the kernel, you do not need to modify the kernel code to support compilation with the Intel compiler.

C.1.1 *From Source Code to Machine Program*

The work of compilers can be divided into several phases, as the following overview demonstrates:

❑ **Preprocessing** — All pre-processor actions are performed in this phase. Depending on the compiler version, this phase is supported by an external utility (cpp) or by special library functions — both are initiated automatically by the compiler. On completion of preprocessing, there is only one (large) input file generated from the source file and all header files are included using the #include directive. The compiler itself is then no longer required to take account of the distributed structure of C programs over several files.

❑ **Scanning and Parsing** — The syntax of a programming language can be described by means of grammatical rules that are similar to those of a natural language such as English but that must understandably be much more restrictive. (Although the existence of several alternatives to represent one and the same fact contribute greatly to the appeal and subtlety of a language, ambiguity must be avoided at all costs in programming languages.) This phase usually comprises two closely linked tasks. The *scanner* analyzes the source text character-by-character and looks for keywords of the programming language. The *parser* takes the input stream supplied by the scanner and already abstracted from source text representation and checks that the structures it detects are correct in terms of the grammar rules of the language. It also creates data structures in computer memory that are a further abstraction of the source code and are designed for processing by a computer (in contrast to the actual source code of the program that should be as easy as possible to read and manipulate by human beings).

❑ **Intermediate Code Generation** — A further step along the path toward the final machine code converts the *parse tree* (i.e., the data structure created in memory) set up by the scanner and parser into another language known as the *register transfer language* (RTL). This is a kind of assembly language for a hypothetical machine. This language can be optimized — independently of the target processor for the most part. However, this does not mean that the RTL code generated in this phase of the compilation process is the same for all target processors. Depending on the architecture, a range of assembler statements are available — and this fact must be taken into account during RTL generation.

The individual statements of the RTL are already on a very low level and are a step away from the high-level C language on the path to the assembly language. Their main task is to manipulate register values to support execution of the compiled program. There are, of course, also conditional statements and other mechanisms to control program flow. However, this intermediate code still includes various elements and structures common to higher-level programming languages (these are *not* specific to a particular language such as C, Pascal, etc.) that do not appear in a pure assembly language.

❑ **Optimization** — The most compute-intensive phase of program compilation is optimization of the intermediate code in the RTL language. The reasons why programs are optimized are clear. But how is this done by the compiler? Because the mechanisms used are generally not only complex but also sophisticated and even devious (subtle details must always be taken into account), it would not be difficult to write a long tome on optimization techniques alone, and a further one on their usage in the GCC. Nevertheless, this appendix illustrates at least some of the techniques employed. All optimization options are based on ideas that initially appear to be relatively simple. However, in practice (and in theory) they are difficult to implement. Such options include, above all, the simplification of arithmetic expressions (algebraic rewriting of terms into expressions that can be computed more efficiently and/or with a less-intensive use of memory), elimination of dead code (parts of code that cannot be reached by the program flow), merging of repeated expressions and items of code in a program, rewriting of program flow into a more efficient form, and so on — these are covered as individual topics in this appendix.

❑ **Code generation** — The last phase is concerned exclusively with the generation of the actual assembler code for the target processor. However, this does *not yet* produce an executable binary file, but instead, it produces a text file with assembler instructions that is converted into binary machine code by further external programs (assemblers and possibly linkers). In principle, the assembler code has the same form as the code of the final program but can still be read by humans (not by machines) even if the power of the individual commands has reached machine level.

To provide you with a general overview of the various compiler steps involved, this appendix uses a classical example — the "Hello, World" program.

```
#include<stdio.h>

int main() {
  printf("Hello, World!\n");
  return 0;
}
```

The program does nothing more than output the line Hello, World! and is typically the first program discussed in any C textbook. On IA-32 systems, the following assembler code is generated for further processing by the assembler and linker:

```
        .file   "hello.c"
        .section        .rodata
.LC0:
        .string "Hello, World!\n"
        .text
.globl main
        .type   main,@function
main:
        pushl   %ebp
        movl    %esp, %ebp
        subl    $8, %esp
        andl    $-16, %esp
        movl    $0, %eax
        subl    %eax, %esp
        movl    $.LC0, (%esp)
        call    printf
        movl    $0, %eax
        leave
        ret
.Lfe1:
        .size   main,.Lfe1-main
        .ident  "GCC: (GNU) 3.2.1"
```

If you are already familiar with assembler programming, you may be surprised by the somewhat strange form of the code. The GNU assembler employs the AT&T syntax instead of the more-widespread and therefore better-known Intel/Microsoft variant. Of course, both alternatives implement the same functionality but use different arrangements of source and destination registers and different forms of constant addressing. Section C.1.7 provides a brief description of these syntax elements.

Appendix C: Notes on C

The exact meaning of the individual assembler commands is of no concern here, because it is beyond the scope of this appendix to provide a full introduction to assembler programming. Indeed, a separate book would be needed for each architecture supported by the kernel. Of more importance is the structure of the code generated. Constant strings are held in a separate section from which they are loaded when they are passed to a function (`printf` in this case) or when they are generally needed. In assembler code, functions (only `main` is used here) retain the same name as in C code.

The same initial code generates totally different assembler code on IA-64 systems (because the architecture is completely different), but the ultimate *effect* is identical to that of the code generated on IA-32 systems.

```
            .file    "hello.c"
            .pred.safe_across_calls p1-p5,p16-p63
            .section          .rodata
            .align 8
    .LC0:
            stringz "Hello, World!\n"
            .text
            .align 16
            .global main#
            .proc main#
    main:
            .prologue 14, 33
            .save ar.pfs, r34
            alloc r34 = ar.pfs, 0, 4, 1, 0
            .vframe r35
            mov r35 = r12
            .save rp, r33
            mov r33 = b0
            .body
            addl r14 = @ltoff(.LC0), gp
            ;;
            ld8 r36 = [r14]
            mov r32 = r1
            br.call.sptk.many b0 = printf#
            ;;
            mov r1 = r32
            mov r14 = r0
            ;;
            mov r8 = r14
            mov ar.pfs = r34
            mov b0 = r33
            .restore sp
            mov r12 = r35
            br.ret.sptk.many b0
            ;;
            .endp main#
            .ident   "GCC: (GNU) 3.1"
```

To give you an example of how this is handled by a non-Intel architecture, the following is the code generated by the ARM variant:

```
            .file    "hello.c"
            .section          .rodata
            .align  2
```

```
.LC0:
        .ascii   "Hello, World!\n\000"
        .text
        .align   2
        .global  main
        .type    main,function
main:
        @ args = 0, pretend = 0, frame = 0
        @ frame_needed = 1, uses_anonymous_args = 0
        mov      ip, sp
        stmfd    sp!, {fp, ip, lr, pc}
        sub      fp, ip, #4
        ldr      r0, .L2
        bl       printf
        mov      r3, #0
        mov      r0, r3
        ldmea    fp, {fp, sp, pc}
.L3:
        .align   2
.L2:
        .word    .LC0
.Lfe1:
        .size    main,.Lfe1-main
        .ident   "GCC: (GNU) 3.2.1"
```

How does the GCC obtain information on the capabilities and command options of the target processor? The answer is that a *machine description* is present for each target architecture supported. This consists of two parts and provides the desired information.

First, there is a file with *instruction patterns* whose structure is a mixture of LISP and RTL syntax.[2] Some parts of this pattern can be supplied with values by the compiler when RTL code is generated. Restrictions can be placed on the possible values by defining various conditions or other prerequisites. Generation of the actual code is performed by the output patterns that represent the possible assembler instructions and are associated with the instruction patterns. The source files that hold the instruction patterns for the individual systems are a very important part of the compiler and are therefore correspondingly large. The statement list for IA-32 processors is about 14,000 lines long; the Alpha variant is 6,000 lines long; and approximately 10,000 lines are needed for the Sparc family.

The *instruction patterns* are supplemented by C header files and macro definitions in which processor-specific special situations that do not fit into the instruction patterns can be handled.[3] It is necessary to use C code, even if the target instruction cannot be implemented with a fixed string or simple macro substitutions.

---

[2]LISP is a programming language whose origins lie in artificial intelligence. It is often used as a dynamic extension language for application programs. Large parts of emacs are programmed in a LISP dialect, and the GIMP image manipulation program uses the Scheme extension language (a simplified LISP variant). GUILE, a library developed by the GNU project, features simple options for providing programs with a Scheme interpreter as an extension language.

[3]An explicit goal when developing the GCC was to rank performance higher than theoretic elegance. It would be possible to describe processors solely with the help of the instruction pattern files, but this would entail a loss of performance and flexibility. The additional macro definitions do not contribute to the elegance of the overall system, but are a useful enhancement to help accomodate the special features of the individual CPU types.

The size of the additional macro and C files is similar to that of the actual instruction patterns (IA-32: 12,000 lines; Alpha: 9,000 lines; and Sparc: 12,000 lines). They constitute an important part of the CPU definition and are essential for the generation of efficient code.

C.1.2 Assembly and Linking

At the end of the actual compilation process, the original C program has been translated into assembler code, and the final steps along the path to binary code require little compiler effort because the assembler and linker (often referred to as the "binder") do the rest of the work.

As compared to the task of the compiler, the work of the assembler is very simple. The individual assembler statements (and their arguments) are translated into a special binary format that differs according to processor type (each assembler command has its own binary code notation; on some systems, such as IA-32, different binary forms may be available for a command depending on the argument types used). A further task of the assembler is to accommodate constant data (such as fixed strings or numeric constants) in the binary code. Usually the ELF format (described at length in Appendix E) is employed to arrange the program and data in a binary file.

The linker must (among other things) adjust the branch addresses in the assembler code. Although the assembler source text can still reference symbolic names (for example, the preceding assembler code uses calls to the `printf` function defined in the standard library), the binary variant must specify *relative* or *absolute* branch addresses; for instance, "skip the next 5 bytes" or "branch to position x").

C.1.3 Procedure Calls

An interesting aspect in C not specifically associated with the use of the GNU compiler[4] is the implementation of procedure and function calls. Because, at certain points, the kernel is responsible for ensuring the interoperability of assembler and C code (in other words, C functions are called from within assembler code), it is important to know the mechanisms behind function calls. This section describes these mechanisms by reference to the IA-32 architecture, although the approach is generally similar on other architectures.[5]

Let's discuss the basic terms involved in procedure calls by reference to Figure C-1. The system stack is a memory area at the end of the address space of a process. It grows from top to bottom when elements are pushed on to it — this is contrary to the expected direction associated with the word "grow". It is used to provide memory for the local variables of the function. It also supports parameter-passing when functions are invoked. If nested procedures are called, the stack grows from top to bottom and accepts new *activation records* that hold all data needed for *one* procedure. The activation record of the procedure currently executing is delimited at the top by the *frame pointer* and at the bottom by the *stack pointer*. While the upper boundary stays the same throughout procedure execution, the lower boundary can be extended downward if necessary in order to create more space.

---

[4]The call conventions of other compilers may differ in their details, but the underlying principle is always the same.

[5]A major exception is the IA-64 architecture, which adopts the concept of *register windows* to persuade programs that the size of the register set is unlimited, a fact that can be exploited when implementing function calls. The resulting mechanism differs substantially from the variant discussed here. Detailed information can be found in the processor-specific documentation on IA-64.

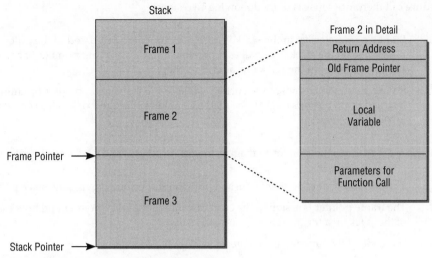

Figure C-1: Activation records on the stack.

Figure C-1 also shows an enlargement of the second stack frame indicating its constituent parts, as follows:

❑ At the top of the stack are the return address and the stored frame pointer value. While the return address specifies the point in memory at which code flow resumes at the end of the procedure, the stored frame pointer holds the value of the frame pointer for the *previous* activation record. After completion of the local procedure, this value can be used to reconstruct the stack area available to the calling procedure — this is important when attempting to debug a stack trace.

❑ The main part of the activation record is the memory space reserved for local variables of the procedure. In C, these variables are also referred to as *automatic* variables.

❑ Values to be passed as parameters to another function when the function is invoked are stored at the bottom of the stack.

All common architectures provide the following two stack manipulation commands:

❑ push places a value on the stack and *decrements* the stack pointer by the number of bytes in memory required by the value. The end of the stack is moved down to lower addresses.

❑ pop removes a value from the stack and *increments* the value of the stack pointer accordingly — in other words, the end of the stack is moved up.

The following two commands are also provided to invoke and exit functions (with automatic return to the calling procedure) — they also automatically manipulate the stack:

❑ call pushes the current value of the instruction pointer onto the stack and branches to the start address of the function to be called.

❑ return pops the bottom value from the stack and branches to the specified address. Procedures must be implemented so that return is the last command and the address placed on the stack by call is at the bottom.

A procedure call therefore consists of the following two steps:

1. Build a parameter list in the stack. The *first* argument to be passed to the called function is placed *last* on the stack; this makes it possible to pass a varying number of arguments that can be `popped` from the stack one after the other.

2. Invoke `call`, which causes the current value of the instruction pointer (pointing to the instruction that *follows* `call`) to be pushed onto the stack and delegates code flow to the invoked function.

The procedure called is responsible for managing the frame pointer and performs the following steps:

1. The previous frame pointer is pushed onto the stack, thus moving the stack pointer down.

2. The frame pointer is assigned the current value of the stack pointer and now marks the start of the stack area for the function to be executed.

3. The code of the function is executed.

4. When the function terminates, the stored frame pointer is at the bottom of the stack. Its value is `popped` from the stack and saved in the frame pointer that now again points to the start of the stack area of the previous function. The return address saved when the function was called is now located at the bottom end of the stack.

5. Invoking `return` causes the return address to be `popped` from the stack. The processor branches to the return address, thus returning the code flow to the calling function.

At first glance, this approach may seem a little confusing. To dispel any confusion, let's consider the following simple C example:

```
#include<stdio.h>

int add (int a, int b) {
        return a+b;
}

int main() {
        int a,b;
        a = 3;
        b = 4;
        int ret = add(a,b);
        printf("Result: %u\n", ret);

        exit(0);
}
```

The following assembler code is generated on IA-32 systems — albeit with compiler optimization switched off (which would produce much improved code but complicate the explanation). This example uses Intel representation because it is easier to read and explain than the AT&T variant preferred by the GCC. Line numbers are not usually included in assembler syntax, but they have been added here to simplify the code explanation.

```
<main>:
1:   push    ebp
2:   mov     ebp,esp
3:   sub     esp,0x18
4:   mov     eax,0x0

5:   mov     DWORD PTR [ebp-4],0x3
6:   mov     DWORD PTR [ebp-8],0x4
7:   mov     eax,DWORD PTR [ebp-8]
8:   mov     DWORD PTR [esp+4],eax
9:   mov     eax,DWORD PTR [ebp-4]
10:  mov     DWORD PTR [esp],eax
11:  call    <add>
12:  mov     DWORD PTR [ebp-12],eax
13:  mov     eax,DWORD PTR [ebp-12]

14:  mov     DWORD PTR [esp+4],eax
15:  mov     DWORD PTR [esp],0x0
16:  call    <printf>
17:  mov     DWORD PTR [esp],0x0
18:  call    <exit>

<add>:
19:  push    ebp
20:  mov     ebp,esp

21:  mov     eax,DWORD PTR [ebp+12]
22:  add     eax,DWORD PTR [ebp+8]

23:  pop     ebp
24:  ret
```

main begins with the standard operations described previously to save the frame pointer that, on IA-32 systems, is held in the ebp register. The value is pushed onto the lowest position in the stack, and this causes the stack pointer to be moved down automatically by 4 bytes — simply because 4 bytes are needed to represent a pointer on IA-32 systems. The value of the stack pointer is then stored in the frame pointer register using the mov statement. mov a, b copies the value in register b to register a. Line 2 therefore causes the current value of the stack pointer to be copied into the frame pointer.

Line 3 subtracts 0x18 bytes from the stack pointer and moves it down, thus increasing the size of the stack by 0x18 = 24. Line 4 initializes eax, a general-purpose register, with the value 0.

The local variables must now be placed on the stack. As the C code indicates, there are two variables, a and b, for main. They are both integer variables and therefore each needs 4 bytes of memory. Because the first 4 bytes of the stack hold the old value of the frame pointer, the compiler reserves the two 4-byte areas below for the variables.

To assign the initial values to the reserved memory space, the compiler makes use of the pointer dereferencing option of the processor. The DWORD PTR [ebp-4] statement in line 5 instructs the compiler to reference the position in memory to which the value "frame pointers minus 4" points. The value 3 is written to this position using mov. The compiler proceeds in the same way with the second local variable, which is lower in the stack and is given the value 4.

The local variables a and b must be used as arguments for the add procedure to be called. The compiler builds the parameter list by placing the appropriate values at the end of the local stack — the first parameter is at the bottom, as already mentioned. The stack pointer is used to find the end of the stack. The corresponding position in memory is determined by means of pointer de-referencing. This position is supplied with the value in the eax register that was previously filled for both parameters with the value of the local variables on the stack. Lines 7 and 8 set the second parameter (b), and lines 9 and 10 are responsible for the first parameter (a). When reading the source code, it is important not to confuse the very similar names esp and ebp.

Figure C-2 shows the status of the stack once the preceding operations have been carried out.

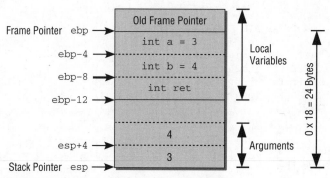

Figure C-2: Frame status prior to calling add.

add can now be invoked using the call command. (In a real program, an address would be given for the function instead of the <add> placeholder on completion of relocation.) The command pushes the previous value of the instruction pointer onto the stack and resumes the code flow at the beginning of the add routine.

In accordance with convention, the routine starts by pushing the previous value of the frame pointer onto the stack and assigning the value of the stack pointer to the frame pointer. This results in the stack situation illustrated in Figure C-3 (only the parts relevant for add are shown).

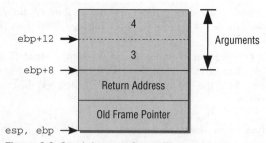

Figure C-3: Stack layout after calling add.

The procedure parameters are found by reference to the frame pointer. The compiler knows that they are located directly at the end of the activation record of the calling function and that two 4-byte values are stored at the beginning of the active activation record. The variables are therefore accessed by de-referencing ebp+8 and ebp+12. add is used to add both values, and the eax register is used as the workspace. The value is left in the register so that the result can be passed to the calling function.

The following two actions are needed to return to the calling function:

❑ The stored frame pointer value is removed from the stack using pop and is written to the ebp register. The top end of the stack is therefore reconstructed for main.

❑ ret pops the return address from the stack and goes there.

Because a further local variable (ret), in which the return value of add is stored, was created in main, the value in the eax register must still be copied to the appropriate position in the stack.

The rest of the assembler code (lines 14 through 24) is concerned with calling the printf and exit library functions in the usual way.

The use of frame pointers is not mandatory. They can just as easily be omitted, because functionally equivalent code can be generated without them. This is the purpose of the gcc option -omit-frame-pointer. Because each procedure then has two fewer assembler operations, the resulting code is a little bit faster — this is why the kernel normally dispenses with frame pointers.

However, the downside is that it is no longer possible to create stack backtraces to reconstruct the call sequence of functions. Because backtraces yield very useful information when debugging or decoding kernel oopses (i.e., the emergency message generated when the kernel encounters a serious problem), the option of adding frame pointers to code was introduced when 2.5 was developed. It is advisable to enable this option unless maximum system performance is required.

C.1.4 Optimization

Optimization is an important functionality of compilers that enables fast code to be generated without modifying the effect of the program. It frees programmers of the burden of performing micro-optimization on their programs. Instead, they are able to concentrate on writing informative, easy-to-read C code, which the compiler then automatically translates into the best possible assembler code. Unfortunately, optimization is a very complex topic that requires not only a great deal of programming skill in C and Assembler, but also a profound knowledge of mathematics and formal logics. For this reason, the following sections give only a brief overview of the optimization features of the GCC.

Constant Simplification

Constant simplification is one of the most basic optimization techniques — which is why much faster and much more compact code should not be expected. The name itself suggests the direction that optimization takes, but what does simplification actually achieve? The best way to answer this is by examining a short C example in which values are supplied to a number of variables.

```
int x,y;
x = 10;
y = x + 42;
const int z = y * 23;
printf("x, y, z: %d, %d, %d\n", x,y,z);
```

Non-optimized assembler output looks like this:

```
            .file    "calc.c"
            .section         .rodata
    .LC0:
            .string "x, y, z: %d, %d, %d\n"
            .text
    .globl main
            .type    main,@function
    main:
            pushl    %ebp
            movl     %esp, %ebp
            subl     $40, %esp
            andl     $-16, %esp
            movl     $0, %eax
            subl     %eax, %esp
            movl     $10, -4(%ebp)
            movl     -4(%ebp), %eax
            addl     $42, %eax
            movl     %eax, -8(%ebp)
            movl     -8(%ebp), %edx
            movl     %edx, %eax
            addl     %eax, %eax
            addl     %edx, %eax
            sall     $3, %eax
            subl     %edx, %eax
            movl     %eax, -12(%ebp)
            movl     -12(%ebp), %eax
            movl     %eax, 12(%esp)
            movl     -8(%ebp), %eax
            movl     %eax, 8(%esp)
            movl     -4(%ebp), %eax
            movl     %eax, 4(%esp)
            movl     $.LC0, (%esp)
            call     printf
            leave
            ret
    .Lfe1:
            .size    main,.Lfe1-main
            .ident   "GCC: (GNU) 3.2.1"
```

The value of the individual assignments is not clear at the outset but must first be computed (by means of addition and multiplication). The results achieved in the various program runs do not differ because the same initial values are always used. If optimization is switched off, the C code is compiled into assembler code in a relative straightforward way. Two computations are performed and three variables are supplied with values. If optimization is switched on, an additional constant appears in the assembler output: the exact result of the computation (which in this case is 1196).

The optimized assembler code looks like this:

```
            .file    "calc.c"
            .section         .rodata.str1.1,"aMS",@progbits,1
    .LC0:
            .string "x, y, z: %d, %d, %d\n"
```

```
        .text
        .p2align 4,,15
.globl main
        .type   main,@function
main:
        pushl   %ebp
        movl    %esp, %ebp
        subl    $24, %esp
        andl    $-16, %esp
        movl    $1196, 12(%esp)
        movl    $52, 8(%esp)
        movl    $10, 4(%esp)
        movl    $.LC0, (%esp)
        call    printf
        movl    %ebp, %esp
        popl    %ebp
        ret
.Lfe1:
        .size   main,.Lfe1-main
        .ident  "GCC: (GNU) 3.2.1"
```

The computation is no longer made at runtime because the results are already known. However, faster program execution[6] is not the only benefit produced by this optimization step. The resulting code now uses only one variable (z) because the two temporary variables (x and y) are superfluous. This not only shortens execution time, but also saves storage space — a major consideration in large programs with a large number of variables.

Loop Optimization

Code in loops may be executed repeatedly and therefore merits thorough optimization because speed gains are particularly noticeable. If a loop is iterated 1,000 times and the runtime of the loop body is shortened by one thousandth of a second as a result of optimization, total program runtime is one second shorter. One second may not seem to be much. However, the benefits are best assessed by considering very time-critical kernel actions such as task switching or long-running programs such as physical simulation. While execution time in the latter case may differ by hours or even days, savings of fractions of a second are a desirable goal in the former case — after all, task switches are performed at short intervals (which are beyond human perception) to give the illusion of parallel program execution.

This optimization feature is not difficult to understand and, in technical terms, appears to be relatively simple. This feature can be illustrated via the following short sample program:

```
int count;

for (count = 0; count < 3; count++) {
  printf("Pass: %d\n", count);
}
```

The loop is iterated three times in succession and outputs the number of the current pass (0, 1, or 2). What can be optimized here? The loop is implemented in assembler code by incrementing the count

---

[6]Note that compilation naturally takes longer when results are computed at compilation time. This is a common aspect of all optimization efforts — execution speed is boosted at the expense of compilation speed. However, this is acceptable because compilation is performed once only and execution takes place regularly.

status variable at the end of the loop body and then checking its value. If it is less than 3, the loop is restarted (a branch is made to the beginning of the loop body); otherwise, the code following the loop is executed. Without optimization, the generated assembler code looks like this:

```
                .file    "loop.c"
                .section           .rodata
        .LC0:
                .string "Pass: %d\n"
                .text
        .globl main
                .type    main,@function
        main:
                pushl    %ebp
                movl     %esp, %ebp
                subl     $24, %esp
                andl     $-16, %esp
                movl     $0, %eax
                subl     %eax, %esp
                movl     $0, -4(%ebp)
        .L2:
                cmpl     $2, -4(%ebp)
                jle      .L5
                jmp      .L3
        .L5:
                movl     -4(%ebp), %eax
                movl     %eax, 4(%esp)
                movl     $.LC0, (%esp)
                call     printf
                leal     -4(%ebp), %eax
                incl     (%eax)
                jmp      .L2
        .L3:
                leave
                ret
        .Lfe1:
                .size    main,.Lfe1-main
                .ident   "GCC: (GNU) 3.2.1"
```

If the number of loop passes is small, the code is often executed more quickly if the assembler code of the loop body is written to the output file *several times in succession*. There is then no need to compare the status variable with the end value, and the conditional branch can be dispensed with. If optimized *loop unrolling* is used, the GCC generates the following code:

```
                .file    "loop.c"
                .section           .rodata.str1.1,"aMS",@progbits,1
        .LC0:
                .string "Pass: %d\n"
                .text
                .p2align 4,,15
        .globl main
                .type    main,@function
        main:
                pushl    %ebp
                movl     %esp, %ebp
```

```
        subl    $8, %esp
        andl    $-16, %esp
        movl    $0, 4(%esp)
        movl    $.LC0, (%esp)
        call    printf
        movl    $1, 4(%esp)
        movl    $.LC0, (%esp)
        call    printf
        movl    $2, 4(%esp)
        movl    $.LC0, (%esp)
        call    printf
        movl    %ebp, %esp
        popl    %ebp
        ret
.Lfe1:
        .size   main,.Lfe1-main
        .ident  "GCC: (GNU) 3.2.1"
```

It should be noted that if this method is used, the size of the program code generated can increase drastically. The technical difficulty associated with this method is actually *deciding* whether to apply optimization or not. The optimal number of loop passes for which an improvement is achieved depends not only on the code in the loop body, but also on the processor type. The definition of corresponding heuristics in the compiler is therefore difficult, although the result they produce is easy to understand.

Common Subexpression Elimination

This optimization feature involves enhancing recurring algebraic expressions in a program. However, these are no longer static expressions that can be simplified by various manipulations. In this case, the compiler searches for recurring *subexpressions* in a program section. If the variables used for computation purposes are unchanged, explicit recomputation can be skipped by reusing the result of the first computation. In other words, this technique necessitates a search for frequently used or common subexpressions, some of which can be eliminated in order to optimize program code. Not surprisingly, the technique is known as *common subexpression elimination*.[7] The technique is best illustrated by reference to the following short example:

```
int p,x,y,z;
scanf("%u", &x);
y = 42;

p = x*y;

if (x > 23) {
   z = x*y;
}
else {
   z = 61*x*y;
}
```

The recurring *expression* is obviously x*y. An analysis of program execution (usually referred to as program flow analysis in technical documents and research papers) reveals that this expression must be evaluated at least twice. The scanf statement reads the value for x from the console — that is, users

---

[7]To be strictly accurate, there are two different versions of this elimination technique. Which is used depends on whether the goal of optimization is to shorten execution time or to reduce code size — each option employs different algorithms.

can type in any value they want. The reason for using this unwieldy method instead of just assigning a specific value to the x variable is simple. If the value of x is fixed, a further optimization feature can be applied (called dead code elimination, as described in the next section). This would change the code so that the optimization feature discussed here would no longer be needed.

When a value is assigned to z, the program distinguishes two cases that depend on the size of the value stored in x. What is common to both cases is that the expression x*y is used in the assignment and, as can be confirmed easily by humans, but with extreme difficulty by compilers, the variables used in both branches of program flow do not change. The value previously computed as the assignment value for p can therefore be reused. Again, the difficulty with this optimization feature lies not in the actual technical replacement but in finding expressions that remain unchanged in *all possible execution variants*.

Dead Code Elimination

On first reading, the term "dead code elimination" sounds quite violent. On second reading, it seems to be somewhat contradictory. After all, how can code that is already dead be eliminated? Only when the term is examined for a third time does it become apparent that it refers to an optimization feature in which program sections that can never execute are eliminated from code generation to reduce the size of the assembler code.

How does dead code accumulate in a program? It would be normal to expect programmers to give some thought as to how their programs should run. And why should they waste their time writing superfluous program fragments? This is indeed true for *simple* programs, but the situation may well be different for larger chunks of code that define a range of constants for specific program purposes. Elimination of dead code is one of several important aspects when compiling C code for the architecture-independent memory model discussed in detail in Chapter 3 (this model provides a uniform interface to the various processors supported by the kernel). To understand how this optimization works take a look at the following short example:

```
int x;
x=23;

if (x < 10) {
   printf("x is less than 10!\n");
}
else {
   printf("x is greater than or equal to 10!\n");
}
```

Without optimization, the following assembler code would be generated:

```
        .file   "dead.c"
        .section        .rodata
.LC0:
        .string "x is less than 10!\n"
        .align 32
.LC1:
        .string "x is greater than or equal to 10!\n"
        .text
.globl main
        .type   main,@function
main:
        pushl   %ebp
```

```
        movl    %esp, %ebp
        subl    $8, %esp
        andl    $-16, %esp
        movl    $0, %eax
        subl    %eax, %esp
        movl    $23, -4(%ebp)
        cmpl    $9, -4(%ebp)
        jg      .L2
        movl    $.LC0, (%esp)
        call    printf
        jmp     .L3
.L2:
        movl    $.LC1, (%esp)
        call    printf
.L3:
        leave
        ret
.Lfe1:
        .size   main,.Lfe1-main
        .ident  "GCC: (GNU) 3.2.1"
```

Because the value of 23 assigned to x cannot change prior to the if query, the result of the query is obvious — the second program branch (the else clause) always executes, and this renders explicit computation to determine whether x is less than or greater than 23 superfluous. The code for the first query is therefore a dead program section because it can never be reached. Therefore, the compiler need not compile the corresponding statements. But there is also a further benefit because the string constant is less than 10! no longer needs to be stored in the object file. In addition to speeding program execution, optimization also reduces the size of the generated code. Omission of the character string from the object file is a relatively new optimization feature only supported by GCC Version 3 and higher.

The optimized assembler code looks like this:

```
        .file   "dead.c"
        .section        .rodata.str1.32,"aMS",@progbits,1
        .align 32
.LC1:
        .string "x is greater than or equal to 10!"
        .text
        .p2align 4,,15
.globl main
        .type   main,@function
main:
        pushl   %ebp
        movl    %esp, %ebp
        subl    $8, %esp
        andl    $-16, %esp
        movl    $.LC1, (%esp)
        call    puts
        movl    %ebp, %esp
        popl    %ebp
        ret
.Lfe1:
        .size   main,.Lfe1-main
        .ident  "GCC: (GNU) 3.2.1"
```

Once you understand this optimization feature, the use of scanf to read the x variable in the previous example becomes clearer. If the value of x cannot change prior to the if query, dead code elimination is also applied to this program. Alternatively, it would have been possible to declare the variable as volatile. This informs the compiler that the value of the variable can be modified by uncontrollable side effects (such as interrupts), and this suppresses some kinds of optimization — including dead code elimination.

C.1.5 Inline Functions

Compared with other programming languages, function calls in C carry relatively little overhead but still require a certain amount of CPU time that may be crucial in the case of *very* frequently used code sections (or extremely time-critical segments such as interrupt handlers). To avoid having to split the code into small sections and having to work with long functions, an earlier, widely adopted solution to the problem is to employ macros. A function is replaced by a macro that the pre-processor automatically copies into the ''calling'' function. The aesthetics of this approach are, of course, dubious, and the absence of type checking for the procedure arguments (apart from a few unpleasant characteristics of the pre-processor that must be noted when writing code) means that macros are not necessarily the method of choice.

Inline functions implemented by the GCC offer an elegant alternative. The keyword inline is added to a function. This causes the compiler to copy the code — such as a macro — to the position at which the function is called. Type checking at compilation time is retained, as is done in regular function calls. Functions can be transformed into inline functions simply by prefixing them with the keyword inline like this:

```
inline int add (int a, int b) {
    ...
}
```

If the arguments are constant when an inline function is called, the compiler may be able to apply other optimization options (e.g., dead code elimination or CSE) — these would not be possible with normal function calls.

Of course, there is always a reverse side to the coin. If longer, frequently used chunks of code are declared inline, the size of the generated binary code grows enormously, and this can give rise to problems, particularly in low-resource embedded systems.

In the meantime, inline functions have been included in the C99 standard, so they can now be translated by other compilers. However, there are a number of small differences between the standard implementation and the GCC implementation, which are described in the GCC manual.

C.1.6 Attributes

Attributes supply compilers with more detailed information on the use of functions or variables. This enables them to apply more precise optimization options in order to generate better code, or permits formulations that would not be possible in normal C. A range of code output details can also be influenced.

GCC supports dozens of attributes for all possible purposes. These are described in the GCC documentation. This section describes the attributes used by the kernel.

Attributes are specified by prefixing the declaration of a variable or function with the keyword `__attribute__((list))` as follows:

```
int add (int a, int b) __attribute__((regparam(3)));
struct xyy { } __attribute((__aligned__(SMP_CACHE_BYTES))
```

The following attributes are used in the kernel sources:

❏ `noreturn` is specified if a function does not return to the caller. Optimization contributes to slightly better code (however, because functions that do not return usually cause programs to abort, the fact that the code is better is of little relevance). This attribute is used primarily to prevent compiler warnings about non-initialized variables that can occur in corresponding code.

In the kernel, this keyword is appropriate for functions that trigger a panic or stop the machine once it has been shut down normally.

❏ `regparam` is an IA-32–specific directive that specifies that function arguments are to be passed in registers and not on the stack as they usually would be. It requires a parameter to indicate the *maximum* number of arguments that can be passed in this way — provided there are enough free registers. Given the scarcity of registers in this architecture, this is never certain. The `eax`, `edx`, and `ecx` registers are used for this purpose.

The kernel defines the following macros that use the attribute:

include/asm-x86/linkage_32.h
```
#define asmlinkage CPP_ASMLINKAGE __attribute__((regparm(0)))
#define FASTCALL(x)     x __attribute__((regparm(3)))
#define fastcall __attribute__((regparm(3)))
```

`FASTCALL` is used — as the name clearly suggests — to invoke a function quickly.

`asmlinkage` identifies functions to be called from within assembler code. Because parameter passing must be coded manually in this case (and are therefore not accessible to the compiler), there must be no surprises as to how many parameters are to be passed in registers and how many are to be passed on the stack — this is why the option of passing parameters in registers must be explicitly disabled. The `CPP_ASMLINKAGE` keyword usually expands to an empty string (the `extern C` keyword is inserted only if a C++ compiler is used to compile the kernel), which instructs the compiler to use the C calling convention (the first argument is last on the stack) instead of the C++ calling convention (the first argument is first on the stack).

On all architectures other than IA-32, the macros shown above are defined to expand to an empty string.

❏ `section` allows the compiler to place variables and functions in other sections of the binary file than would usually be the case (refer to Appendix E for a more detailed description of the binary format). This is important when implementing the init and exit calls mentioned throughout this book. The name of the section where the material is to be placed must be passed to the attribute as a string parameter.

To define init calls, the compiler uses, for example, the following macro to place the functions in sections named `.initcall0.init` and so on:

<init.h>
```
#define __define_initcall(level,fn,id) \
        static initcall_t __initcall_##fn##id __attribute_used__ \
        __attribute__((__section__(".initcall" level ".init"))) = fn
```

❑ align specifies the minimum alignment of data — in other words, their alignment in memory. The attribute requires an integer argument that must be divisible by the memory address (at which the data are held) without a remainder. The unit used is bytes.

This attribute is important for the kernel because it allows maximum use to be made of CPU caches by placing the key parts of a structure at the best place in memory.

The ____cacheline_aligned macro, for example, is defined as follows:

\<cache.h\>
```
#define __cacheline_aligned
    __attribute__((__aligned__(SMP_CACHE_BYTES), \
                    __section__(".data.cacheline_aligned")))
```

Its purpose is to align data on the L1 cache of the processor even if the constant used suggests that alignment is achieved only on multiprocessor systems. The preceding code implements a generic version of the keyword, but individual architectures are free to provide their own definitions:

A slightly stricter version of the macro looks like this:

\<cache.h\>
```
#define INTERNODE_CACHE_SHIFT L1_CACHE_SHIFT
#define ____cacheline_internodealigned_in_smp \
        __attribute__((__aligned__(1 << (INTERNODE_CACHE_SHIFT))))
```

Alignment is based on the maximum possible L1 cache size for the underlying architecture — regardless of whether the processor actually has an L1 cache of this size. This means that the defined alignment yields maximum cache benefits but wastes more space, which is why its use should be carefully considered.

C.1.7 Inline Assembler

When short assembler segments are to be inserted in C code, it is unpractical and cumbersome to create a separate assembler file, translate it into binary code, and link it with the generated object code of the C compiler. Therefore, GCC features a special option to integrate assembler code directly in C with the help of special statements — the compiler assumes responsibility for joint code generation. Not only does this method require less technical effort from the programmer, it has the added advantage that the machine code generated from C code can be refined to interoperate with the assembler segment because the compiler has more information about its structure than is the case when an assembler object file is linked. The programmer does not need to guess in which register or at which point in memory any required input parameters are held — this can be defined unambiguously by means of the interface between C and the inline assembler.

Of course, inserting assembler code is a platform-specific affair, because the opcodes and registers used differ between the individual processor architectures. Nevertheless, the mechanism that integrates the statements in the C code is platform-independent.

The asm statement is employed to specify the assembler code itself and the registers used. Its syntax is as follows (the equivalent __asm__ keyword may also be used instead of asm):

```
asm ("Assembler code";
        : Output operand specification
        : Input operand specification
```

```
        : Modified registers
    );
```

On IA-32 systems, the assembler code itself must be given in AT&T notation (on all other platforms, the preferred notation of the particular architecture is used). Input and output register specifications establish which input parameters are supplied in registers (or in memory) and which registers or memory positions are used to output values. To be more accurate, they define the various conditions for the registers involved and therefore represent the interface to the C implementation that supplies the input data and further processes the output data. By specifying all *modified register*s that are changed in the assembler statements (although they are not part of the input and output specification), the compiler is provided with additional information. For example, prior to execution of the assembler code, modified registers may not be used by the compiler to store values that it needs to access later. Notice that the original GCC documentation refers to "modified registers" as *clobbered registers*.

For the purposes of this appendix, it is sufficient to summarize the AT&T assembler syntax into the following five rules:

❑   Registers are referenced by prefixing their name with a percent symbol. For example, to use register eax, %eax must appear in the assembler code.

> ***Two* percent symbols must be specified in C source code in order to generate *one* percent symbol in output that is forwarded to the assembler program.**

❑   The source register is always specified before the destination register. For example, in mov statements, this means that mov a, b copies the contents of register a into register b.

❑   The operand size is given by a suffix after the assembler statement. b stands for *byte*, l for *long*, and w for *word*. To move a long value from register eax to register ebx on IA-32 systems, it is therefore necessary to specify movl %eax, %ebx.

❑   Indirect memory references (de-referencing of pointers) are possible by including a register in parentheses. For example, movl (%eax), %ebx moves the long value at the address in memory pointed to by the value of register eax to the register ebx.

❑   offset(register) specifies that the register value is to be used together with an offset that is added to its actual value. For example, 8(%eax) specifies that eax + 8 is to be used as an operand. This notation is used primarily for memory access — for example, to specify offsets from the stack or frame pointer in order to access certain local variables.

The following example illustrates the meaning of the input and output specifications:

```
int move() {
  int a = 5;
  int b;

  asm ("movl %1, %%eax;
        movl %%eax, %0;"
       : "=r"(b)    /* Output register */
       : "r" (a)    /* Input register */
       : "%eax");   /* Modified registers */

  printf("b: %u\n", b);
}
```

This code copies the value in a to b — not a very demanding task. This could also have been formulated as b = a to enable the compiler to generate equivalent or better code. The code makes use of an input register, an output register, and a temporary register. While the input and output register are selected by the compiler and are denoted as %1 and %0 in the assembler code (all the code does is to define the conditions applied to the registers), the name of the temporary register must be specified explicitly. This example uses eax. Recall that two percent symbols must be entered in the source code in order to produce one percent symbol in the compiler output, which is why the register is given as %%eax.

The example generates the following assembler output in AT&T syntax (only the relevant part of the output is shown here.)

```
        movl -4(%ebp), %edx
#APP
        movl %edx, %eax;
        movl %eax, %edx;
#NO_APP
        movl %edx, %eax
        movl %eax, -8(%ebp)
```

The assembler code generated by the asm statement is embedded between #APP and #NO_APP in the compiler output.

The effect of the code is as anticipated. The compiler first copies the value of the local variable a held at position ebp - 4 in the local activation record into a register (edx). The assembler code is executed and copies the value (pointlessly) into register eax; it then copies the value of eax into output register edx. The subsequent code is again generated by the compiler — it copies the result value of the assembler code (via register eax) into the local target variable b located at position ebp - 8 in the activation record.

Neither the assembler code nor the output generated by the compiler is particularly intelligent in this example. If the GCC is requested to produce optimized code, it generates the following assembler output:

```
        movl $5, %edx
#APP
        movl %edx, %eax;
        movl %eax, %ecx;
#NO_APP
```

The local variables are now no longer stored on the stack (they are not needed there) but are held in registers. edx is used for a and is initialized directly with the constant 5. b is held in register ecx. Both registers can be used in user-specified assembler code and this dispenses with the need for unwieldy copy operations between registers and the stack.

> GCC cannot check whether correct assembler instructions for the specific platform are used in the code part of asm, or whether the registers used are really suitable for the particular application. This is the sole responsibility of the programmer.

The input and output registers used are defined by means of *constraints*, which take the following form:

```
"constraint" (variable)
```

The previous example employs two constraints:

❑ `"r"` specifies that a register is to be used to represent the value of the given variable (a or b) in the assembler code. Which register is used is left to the compiler and is not known to the programmer when the assembler code is written, which is why `%0`, `%1`, and so on are used to work with the registers.

❑ `"=r"` specifies that an output operand in the form of a register is involved.

In general, constraints are used to indicate whether a value is located in memory or in a register, which kinds of registers may be used, and so on. GCC supports a wide range of constraints, some of which are architecture-dependent and some are not. For a full description, refer to the compiler documentation. This section describes only the features relevant to the kernel.

The following architecture-independent constraints are used in the kernel:

❑ `r` indicates that a general-purpose register is used.

❑ `m` specifies that an address in memory is used.

❑ `I` and `J` define a constant within the range 0–31 or 0–64 on IA-32 systems. This can be used for shift operations.

These constraints can be refined by using the following *modifiers* prefixed to the actual constraint:

❑ `=` specifies that the operand may only be written. The previous value is discarded and replaced with the output value of the operation.

❑ `+` specifies that an operand may be read and written.

The next two examples demonstrate how the facilities of the inline assembler are used in the kernel. First, the atomic setting of a bit in a `unsigned long` variable is performed by the following code:

include/asm-x86/bitops_32.h
```
static inline void set_bit(int nr, volatile unsigned long * addr)
{
        __asm__ __volatile__( LOCK_PREFIX
                "btsl %1,%0"
                :"+m" (ADDR)
                :"Ir" (nr));
}
```

`bts` stands for the assembler statement "bit test and set," which queries the value of a given bit in a long value, stores the value in the CF flag of the processor, and then sets the bit to one. Because long values comprise 32 bits, the bit position can be specified by means of a constant in the range 0..31, which is why the constraint type `I` is used. The position must also be specified in a register as required by the architecture — in this case, the `r` constraint is used.

Because the processed data resides in memory and is modified by a write access, the constraint `+m` must be used for the long value.

The pre-processor constant LOCK_PREFIX is used to make the operation atomic. On single-processor systems, this constant is empty because a single assembly statement that cannot be interrupted is used to set the bit. On SMP systems, the constant expands to lock. This is a separate assembler statement, known as a *lock prefix*, which prevents all other processors of the system from interfering with the following statement, and thus makes it atomic.

Naturally, not only individual assembler statements are used in inline code. For example, atomic incrementing of an integer variable is a complex operation on Alpha CPUs as shown here:

include/asm-alpha/atomic.h
```
static __inline__ void atomic_add(int i, atomic_t * v)
{
        unsigned long temp;
        __asm__ __volatile__(
        "1:     ldl_l %0,%1\n"
        "       addl %0,%2,%0\n"
        "       stl_c %0,%1\n"
        "       beq %0,2f\n"
        ".subsection 2\n"
        "2:     br 1b\n"
        ".previous"
        :"=&r" (temp), "=m" (v->counter)
        :"Ir" (i), "m" (v->counter));
}
```

This appendix does not discuss why so much code is needed because that would necessitate an excursion into the characteristics of Alpha processors. The sole aim of the example is to demonstrate that comparatively complicated operations that do not just use single assembler statements can be implemented in inline assembler.

C.1.8   __builtin *Functions*

__builtin functions provide the compiler with additional options to perform more manipulations on programs than would normally be possible in C without having to resort to the inline assembler.

Each architecture defines its own set of __builtin functions, which are described in detail in the GCC documentation. A number of __builtin variants are common to all architectures and two of these are used by the kernel.

❑   __builtin_return_address(0) yields the return address to which code flow is positioned at the end of a function. As described previously, this information can also be extracted from the activation record. This is actually an architecture-specific task but the preceding __builtin function makes a universal front-end available for it.

   The argument specifies how many levels the function should work upward in the activation records. 0 delivers the return address to which the function currently running will return, 1 yields the address to which the function that called the current function will return, and so on.

> On some architectures (IA-64, for instance), there are basic difficulties in determining activation records. For this reason, the function always returns the value 0 for arguments larger than 0.

❏   `__builtin_expect(long exp, long c)` helps the compiler optimize branch predictions. `exp` specifies the result value of an expression that is computed, whereas `c` returns the expected result — 0 or 1. As an example, take a look at the following `if` query:

```
if (expression) {
   /* Yes */
}
else {
   /* No */
}
```

If this is to be optimized, and it is expected that the condition will return the value 1 in most cases, the `__builtin_expect` function can be used as follows:

```
if (__builtin_expect(expression, 1)) {
   /* Yes */
}
else {
   /* No */
}
```

The compiler influences the branch predictions of the processor in such a way that, by preference, the first branch is computed in advance.

The kernel defines the following two macros to identify likely and unlikely branches in the code:

<compiler.h>
```
#define likely(x)      __builtin_expect(!!(x), 1)
#define unlikely(x)    __builtin_expect(!!(x), 0)
```

The double negation `!!` is used for two reasons:

❏   It enables the macros to be used with pointers that are implicitly converted into a truth value.

❏   Truth values greater than zero (explicitly allowed in C) are standardized to 1 as expected by `__builtin_expect`.

The macros are employed at many points in the kernel; for instance, in the implementation of the slab allocator as follows:

mm/slab.c
```
if (likely(ac->avail < ac->limit)) {
        STATS_INC_FREEHIT(cachep);
        ac_entry(ac)[ac->avail++] = objp;
        return;
} else {
        STATS_INC_FREEMISS(cachep);
        cache_flusharray(cachep, ac);
        ac_entry(ac)[ac->avail++] = objp;
}
```

The example shows that `__builtin_expect` can be used not only for simple values, but also for conditions that must first be evaluated.

C.1.9 Pointer Arithmetic

Normally, pointers may be used for computations in C only if they have an explicit type; for example, `int *` or `long *`. Otherwise, it is not possible to establish which increment steps are to be used. The GNU compiler circumnavigates this restriction and supports arithmetic with `void` pointers and function pointers — these are also used by the kernel at various points. In both cases, the increment step is 1 byte.

Interestingly, GCC had at least once support for a *bit-addressable* architecture — the Texas Instruments 34010 processor. Incrementing a pointer on this machine means that the memory position is advanced by one bit, not one byte — a feature that did not quite become ubiquitous. While the pure existence of the machine would most likely not be worth mentioning here, the fact that Andrew Morton — one of the key persons for the development of the 2.6 kernel series — once wrote a real-time kernel for this processor certainly does. You can download the source code from `www.zip.com.au/~akpm/`.

C.2 Standard Data Structures and Techniques of the Kernel

In its C sources, the kernel adopts a number of methods and approaches that are essential to the programming of operating systems but that are not normally used in C programs. This section discusses these techniques, as well as standard data structures that are needed time and time again and are therefore implemented as small, universal libraries.

C.2.1 Reference Counters

Instances of data structures required for a longer period are allocated by the kernel in its dynamic memory space. Once an instance is no longer needed, the allocated memory space can be returned to memory management, as in normal C programs. This is not a problem if only one kernel component in a control path is accessing the instance. In this case, it is easy to determine exactly when the memory space is no longer needed. Complications arise when several processes or kernel threads access the same instance, because they then share resources. The copy-on-write method and the shared usage of different process resources by cloning tasks are examples of situations in which an instance of a data structure is needed at several places. In this case, the kernel does not know when the data are no longer required and when it can return the associated memory space.

To solve this problem, the kernel employs a technique used in the implementation of hard links. Data structures are provided with a *usage* or *reference counter* which indicates at how many points in the kernel the resource is in use. The usage counter is an atomic integer variable that is embedded somewhere in the data structure and is usually named `count`, as in the following example:

```
struct shared {
...
        atomic_t count;
...
}
```

The allocation routine distinguishes two cases. If no suitable instance is present, a new instance is created and its usage counter is initialized to 1. If a suitable instance is present (which can be checked with the help of a hash table in which all existing instances are arranged), a pointer to the instance is returned after the usage counter has been incremented.

The instance is not returned by simply freeing the memory space. Instead, this task is delegated to a function that first checks whether the usage counter is greater than 1. If it is, the instance is still required in other parts of the kernel, and the counter is decremented by 1. Only when the counter is decremented to 0 (it is 1 when the function is started) can the memory space occupied by the data structure be returned to memory management because the instance is no longer in use.

C.2.2 Pointer Type Conversions

A frequent source of error in the programming of portable C applications is the false assumption that integer and pointer sizes can be typecast by means of type conversions, as in the following example:

```
int var;
void *ptr = &var;

printf("ptr before typecast:  %p\n", ptr);

var = (int)ptr;
ptr = (void*)var;

printf("ptr after typecast: %p\n", ptr);
```

The program would seem to work if the same value is returned in both outputs. However, the perfidious aspect of this example is that it functions correctly on 32-bit machines although it is actually incorrect. C does not guarantee that pointer and integer variables have the same bit length, but it happens to be the case on 32-bit systems where both integer and pointer variables require 4 bytes.

This no longer applies on 64-bit platforms where pointers require 8 bytes and integer variables still need only 4 bytes. On IA-64 systems, the sample program would produce the following output:

```
wolfgang@64meitner> ./ptr
ptr before typecast:  0x9ffffffffffff930
ptr after typecast: 0xfffffffffffff930
```

The values cannot be typecast without loss. Because of careless 32-bit practice, this is a source of frequent errors when converting programs to run on 64-bit architectures. The kernel source code must, of course, be 64-bit clean if it is to execute on architectures of both word lengths.

According to the C standard, programs again cannot assume that pointers and unsigned long variables can be typecast. However, because this is possible on all existing architectures, the kernel makes this assumption a prerequisite and explicitly allows type conversion as shown here:

```
unsigned long var;
void* ptr;

var = (unsigned long)ptr;
ptr = (void*)var;
```

Because unsigned long variables are sometimes easier to handle than void pointers, they may be typecast. This is beneficial when, for example, it is necessary to examine parts of a compound data type. With normal pointer arithmetic, `var++` would cause the value to be increased by `sizeof(data type)`. If the variable is cast into the `unsigned long` data type beforehand, the structure can be analyzed byte-by-byte or its contents can be traversed (this can be very useful when extracting embedded substructures).

C.2.3   Alignment Issues

Let us now turn our attention to alignment issues.

Natural Alignment

Most modern RISC machines mandate that memory accesses are *naturally* aligned: The address at which an elementary datum is stored must be divisible by the width of the data type. Consider, for instance, a pointer that is 8 bytes wide on 64-bit architectures. Consequently these pointers must be stored at addresses that are divisible by 8, so 24, 32, 800, and so on are valid addresses, whereas 30 and 25 are not. This is not a problem for all "regular" operations because when memory is allocated in the kernel, it will be allocated properly. The compiler additionally ensures that structures are *padded* to enforce natural alignment, but if memory access on arbitrary, non-aligned locations is required, the following two auxiliary functions must be employed:

❏   `get_unaligned(ptr)`, which allows for reading an unaligned pointer.

❏   `put_unaligned(val, ptr)`, which writes `val` to the unaligned memory location denoted by `ptr`.

Older architectures such as IA-32 handle unaligned access transparently, but most RISC machines do not, so the functions must be used on all unaligned accesses to ensure portability.

Consider the following structure:

```
struct align {
        char *ptr1;
        char c;
        char *ptr2;
};
```

On 64-bit systems, a pointer requires 8 bytes, while a `char` variable needs 1 byte. Although only 17 bytes are stored in the structure, the size of this definition as reported by `sizeof` will be 24. This is because the compiler ensures that the second pointer, `ptr2`, is correctly aligned by placing 7 fill bytes — which are unused — after `c`. This is illustrated in Figure C-4.

0   ptr1   7 c 8   Padding   15   ptr2   23

Figure C-4: The compiler automatically inserts padding space into structures to make them fulfill alignment requirements.

The padded bytes in the structure lend themselves naturally to be filled with *useful* information, so you should try to arrange your structures accordingly.

If padding must be avoided because, for instance, a data structure is employed to exchange data with a peripheral device that must receive a data structure exactly as it was defined, the attribute `__packed` can be specified in the structure definition to prevent the compiler from introducing pad bytes. Naturally, the possibly unaligned components of this structure must then be accessed using the aforementioned functions.

Bytes are always aligned by definition — their width is 1 byte, and every address is divisible by one.

Generic Alignment

Sometimes, it is necessary to fulfill additional alignment criteria besides natural alignment — such as when a data structure must be aligned along cache lines, but there are numerous other applications in the memory management implementation. The kernel provides the macro ALIGN(x,y) for this purpose: It returns the minimum alignment required to align the datum x on y byte boundaries. Some examples of how to use this macro were previously presented in Table 3-9.

C.2.4 Bit Arithmetic

Bit operations are part of the standard kernel repertoire and are frequently used in all subsystems. In the past, operations of this kind were often employed in userspace programs because some things could be done faster than with standard C resources. Now that the optimization mechanisms of compilers have become more sophisticated, bit operations are hardly ever needed. However, as an extremely performance-critical program, the kernel is an exception. Similarly, bit operations are able to achieve certain effects that are not possible using other statements.

int numbers can be held in memory as a bit string with 32 entries. Similarly, unsigned long values can be regarded as bit strings with 32 or 64 positions — depending on the word length of the processor. However, by default, C provides no facilities for accessing the individual bits of a variable. This is why the kernel has to resort to a number of tricks.

Two basic operations with integers are left and right shift, represented by the << and >> operators. The argument specifies how many positions all bits in the string are to be moved left or right. For example, a = a >> 3 moves all bits of a three positions to the right.

Because the n-th bit in a bit string has the value 2^n and a shift operation moves all bit positions one to the left or one to the right, the value of a bit changes to $2^{n\pm 1}$. This is the equivalent of dividing or multiplying the expression by 2. Likewise, an n-fold shift is the same as a division or multiplication by 2^n because this equates to n consecutive shift operations. Multiplication and division by the power of two can therefore be replaced with bit shifts for integer numbers as the following example demonstrates (like all other arithmetic operators, shift operators can also be used in the form <<= or >>= to link the shift with assignment of a new value to the old variable):

```c
int main() {
  unsigned int val = 1;
  unsigned int count;

  for (count = 0; count <= 10; count++) {
    printf("count, val: %u, %u\n", count, val);
    val <<= 1;
  }
}
```

The program generates the following output:

```
wolfgang@meitner> ./shift
count, val: 0, 1
count, val: 1, 2
count, val: 2, 4
count, val: 3, 8
count, val: 4, 16
count, val: 5, 32
count, val: 6, 64
count, val: 7, 128
count, val: 8, 256
count, val: 9, 512
count, val: 10, 1024
```

C provides a range of bitwise operators to link two numbers, which are listed in Table C-1. The ~ operator is also available to apply bitwise NOT to the individual bits of a number.

Table C-1: Operations for Bitwise Linking of Two Numbers

Operator	Meaning
&	Bitwise "AND"
|	Bitwise "OR"
^	Bitwise "Exclusive OR" (XOR)

These operations can be used to query and manipulate the individual bits of a bit string without recourse to special assembler commands of the processor. However, such commands are occasionally used by Linux to manipulate a bit string quickly or atomically. The general concept includes using a mask to select a specific bit. In this mask, all bits are set to 0 and only the bit to be selected has the value 1. The desired bit is selected by "ANDing" the mask with the actual number. The following example builds a mask to help test the fifth bit of a bit string:

```
int main() {
  int val1 = 33;
  int val2 = 18;

  int mask = 1;
  mask <<= 4;

  if (val1 & mask) {
    printf("Bit 5 in val1 is set\n");
  }

  if (val2 & mask) {
    printf("Bit 5 in val2 is set\n");
  }
}
```

As expected, the program produces the following output:

```
wolfgang@meitner> ./bitmask
Bit 5 in val2 is set
```

It is, of course, possible to mask out not just one but several bits of a number by designing an appropriate mask. If, for example, the last 5 bits of a number are to be analyzed, a mask can be designed in which the first bit is moved to position 6 and then 1 is subtracted from the resulting number.

Bit position numbering begins at 0 as usual. The bits at positions 0 to 5 are equal to 1 as a result of subtraction, while the bits at positions 6 to 31 are equal to 0.

The desired bits in a bit string can be selected by ANDing as shown here:

```
int main() {
  unsigned int val = 49;
  unsigned int res;

  unsigned int mask = 1;
  mask <<= 5;
  mask -= 1; printf("mask: %u\n", mask);

  res = val & mask;
  printf("val, res: %u, %u\n", val, res);
}
```

The program generates the following output:

```
wolfgang@meitner> ./maskfive
mask: 31
val, res: 49, 17
```

A common programming error occurs when the operators && (logical AND) and & (bitwise AND) are confused. Because the former checks only whether both arguments are greater than 0 and the latter performs a bitwise comparison, they return different results.

The following example illustrates the difference between both operations:

```
int main() {
  int val1 = 4;
  int val2 = 8;

  if (val1 & val2) {
    printf("And\n");
  }

  if (val1 && val2) {
    printf("And and\n");
  }
}
```

The program produces the following output:

```
wolfgang@meitner> and
And and
```

Because both numbers have no matching bit values at any bit position, bitwise AND returns 0 as its result.

If 4 and 5 are used as input instead, both operators return a true value because the bits at position 2 in both numbers are equal to 1 — in any case, both are greater than 0 (for `&&`).

The moral of the story (and please excuse the word play) is that AND and AND AND[8] are not always the same.

Finally, notice that the kernel defines the auxiliary function `DECLARE_BITMAP` to create a bitmap with sufficient space to store the number of bits given by the `bits` parameter:

<types.h>
```
#define DECLARE_BITMAP(name,bits) \
        unsigned long name[BITS_TO_LONGS(bits)]
```

The macro automatically computes the required number of `longs` in the array such that sufficient space for all bits is available.

C.2.5 Pre-Processor Tricks

Most programmers are familiar with the pre-processor. However, the kernel uses two constructions that are not usually needed and are therefore worthy of discussion.

Macro arguments that occur within strings are normally not replaced. If a string is to be generated from a parameter, it is necessary to use a special pre-processor function known as *stringification*. Arguments within strings that are to be replaced with their macro parameters must be prefixed by a hash mark, as in the following example:

```
#define warning(text)\
    printf("Warning: " #text "\n")
```

If the macro is used as follows:

```
warning(foobar not found);
```

the pre-processor generates the following output:

```
printf("Warning: " "foobar not found" "\n");
```

If functions (whose names are to be specified in part by macro parameters) are defined with the help of the pre-processor, it is necessary to make use of the (*concatenation*) capability of the pre-processor. This is illustrated by the following example used in the kernel to define functions for port IO with various data types. Two hash marks are used to merge two consecutive tokens into a compound token once all pre-processor replacements have been carried out.

---

[8]Which reminds of the PL/I construct IF IF = THEN THEN THEN = ELSE ELSE ELSE = IF;.

include/asm-x86/io_32.h
```
#define BUILDIO(bwl,bw,type) \
static inline void out##bwl##_local(unsigned type value, int port) { \
        __asm__ __volatile__("out" #bwl " %" #bw "0, %w1" : : "a"(value), "Nd"(port)); \
}
```

bwl accepts one of the three values b, 1, or w depending on the data type for which the function is defined. type specifies the corresponding C data type. The macro is called as follows to define char operations or byte operations:

```
BUILDIO(b,b,char)
```

After processing by the pre-processor, the C file contains the following code (extra line breaks have been added to improve readability):

```
static inline void outb_local(unsigned char value, int port) { _
    _asm__ __volatile__("out" "b" " %" "b" "0, %w1"
                            :
                            : "a"(value), "Nd"(port));
}
```

C.2.6   Miscellaneous

There are three further items that do not fit into any of the previous categories.

Macros in the kernel very often include constructions of the following kind:

drivers/block/ataflop.c
```
#define FDC_WRITE(reg,val)                      \
    do {                                        \
        dma_wd.dma_mode_status = 0x80 | (reg);  \
        udelay(25);                             \
        dma_wd.fdc_acces_seccount = (val);      \
        MFPDELAY();                             \
    } while(0)
```

The do statement formally ensures that the code is executed just once when the macro is "called" and does not alter the semantics as compared to a variant without an enclosing do loop. The advantage of this construction becomes clear when the macro is used in if queries or similar language elements as shown here:

```
if (condition)
    FDC_WRITE(a,b);
```

At first reading, the code appears to be correct because single-line if bodies can — and in the kernel usually are — used without braces. However, after macro expansion there would be a problem if the enclosing do construction were not present:

```
if (condition)
        dma_wd.dma_mode_status = 0x80 | (reg);
        udelay(25);
        dma_wd.fdc_acces_seccount = (val);
        MFPDELAY();
```

Only the first line is included in the `if` body. The remaining lines are executed regardless of `condition` and this is not, of course, what was intended. Because structurally the `do` construction counts as a statement, it ensures that *all* statements included in the macro are placed within the `if` body.

Further elements that cause some confusion when reading kernel sources are the C statements `break` and `continue`. The following chunks of code can easily be confused:

```
unsigned int count;
for (count = 0; count < 5; count++) {
  if (count == 2) {
    continue;
  }
  printf("count: %u\n", count);
}
```

The code produces the following output when executed:

```
wolfgang@meitner> ./continue
count: 0
count: 1
count: 3
count: 4
```

The third loop pass is exited prematurely because of the `continue` statement. Nevertheless, the subsequent loop passes are still executed.

If `continue` is replaced with a `break` statement as shown in the following code, program behavior is modified:

```
unsigned int count;
for (count = 0; count < 5; count++) {
  if (count == 2) {
    break;
  }
  printf("count: %u\n", count);
}
```

Program output is now as follows:

```
wolfgang@meitner> ./break
count: 0
count: 1
```

Again, the third loop pass is terminated. However, loop processing is not resumed, and the subsequent code is executed. In other words, `break` completely terminates the loop.

A further stumbling block in C are the semantics of `select` queries, as the following example shows:

```
int var = 3;
switch (var) {
case 1:
```

```
    printf("one\n"); break;
case 2:
    printf("two\n"); break;
case 3:
    printf("three\n");
default:
    printf("default\n");
}
```

The code generates the following output:

```
wolfgang@meitner> ./switch
three
default
```

Because the case statement for 3 does *not* include a break statement, code flow descends to the default label, which under normal circumstances would not have been selected. Generally, switch statements can be exited only by means of break statements (or at the end of the statement itself). Once a suitable statement is found, the code descends until it reaches a corresponding statement — regardless of whether it comes across further labels or not.

C.2.7 Doubly Linked Lists

Doubly linked lists appear in practically every larger data structure of the kernel. A number of general functions and structures are therefore provided to implement such lists for a wide range of purposes. Chapter 1 discussed the API needed to work with lists. This section describes its implementation, which involves some interesting aspects of generic programming in C.

The starting point for linked lists is the following data structure that can be embedded in other data structures:

```
<list.h>
struct list_head {
        struct list_head *next, *prev;
};
```

The meaning of the elements is clear. next points to the next element, and prev points to the previous element. The list is also organized cyclically — in other words, the predecessor of the first list element is the last entry, and the successor of the last list element is the first entry.

Implementation of list functions is made more difficult by the following conditions:

❑   The list elements need not be at the beginning of a structure, but may be located anywhere in the structure. Because list processing is supposed to function with any data types, this causes problems if a selected element is to be typecast into the target data type.

❑   Several list elements can be used jointly in a structure so that they can be held in various lists.

List function implementation is based on a *container* mechanism provided by the kernel to embed objects in other objects. If structure A contains a substructure B, as in the following example, A is referred to as the container of B:

```
struct A {
...
    struct B {
    } element;
...
} container;
```

When new elements are inserted in a list, the container property is not yet needed, as the following code of list_add shows:

<list.h>
```
/*
 * Insert a new entry between two known consecutive entries.
 *
 * This is only for internal list manipulation where we know
 * the prev/next entries already!
 */
static inline void __list_add(struct list_head *new,
                              struct list_head *prev,
                              struct list_head *next)
{
        next->prev = new;
        new->next = next;
        new->prev = prev;
        prev->next = new;
}


/**
 * list_add - add a new entry
 * @new: new entry to be added
 * @head: list head to add it after
 *
 * Insert a new entry after the specified head.
 * This is good for implementing stacks.
 */
static inline void list_add(struct list_head *new, struct list_head *head)
{
        __list_add(new, head, head->next);
}
```

Elements are also deleted in the classical textbook style:

<list.h>
```
#define LIST_POISON1  ((void *) 0x00100100)
#define LIST_POISON2  ((void *) 0x00200200)


/*
 * Delete a list entry by making the prev/next entries
 * point to each other.
 *
 * This is only for internal list manipulation where we know
```

```
 * the prev/next entries already!
 */
static inline void __list_del(struct list_head * prev, struct list_head * next)
{
        next->prev = prev;
        prev->next = next;
}

/**
 * list_del - deletes entry from list.
 * @entry: the element to delete from the list.
 * Note: list_empty on entry does not return true after this, the entry is
 * in an undefined state.
 */
static inline void list_del(struct list_head *entry)
{
        __list_del(entry->prev, entry->next);
        entry->next = LIST_POISON1;
        entry->prev = LIST_POISON2;
}
```

The two `LIST_POISON` values in the `next` and `prev` pointers of the deleted entry are used for debugging purposes in order to detect removed list elements in memory.

The most interesting aspects of list implementation are revealed by two questions: How is it possible to iterate over the list elements, and how are entries removed from the list? In other words, how is their data extracted, and how is the full structure that was saved — not only the list element — reconstructed? Note this is *not* talking about *deleting* elements from the list.

The kernel provides the following macro to iterate over a list:

<list.h>
```
/**
 * list_for_each_entry  -        iterate over list of given type
 * @pos:        the type * to use as a loop cursor.
 * @head:       the head for your list.
 * @member:     the name of the list_struct within the struct.
 */
#define list_for_each_entry(pos, head, member)                      \
        for (pos = list_entry((head)->next, typeof(*pos), member);  \
                prefetch(pos->member.next), &pos->member != (head); \
                pos = list_entry(pos->member.next, typeof(*pos), member))
```

All the preceding code resides in the loop head of the `for` *loop. The body is not added until the macro is used. The purpose of the list is to save, one after the other, pointers to all list elements of the* `typeof(*pos)` *type in* `pos`, *and to make these available to the loop body.*

A sample use of this routine is to iterate over all files (represented by `struct file`) that are associated with a superblock (`struct super_block`) and are therefore included in a doubly linked list starting at the superblock, as shown here:

```
struct super_block *sb = get_some_sb();
struct file *f;
```

```
list_for_each_entry(f, &sb->s_files, f_list) {
        /* Code for processing the elements in f */
}
```

To illustrate the work of `list_for_each_entry`, an overview of the essential elements of the `file` and `super_block` structures involved is needed. Their important elements are as follows:

<fs.h>
```
struct file {
        struct list_head        f_list;
        ...
};
```

<fs.h>
```
struct super_block {
        ...
        struct list_head        s_files;
        ...
```

`super_block->s_files` serves as the starting point of a list in which elements of the `file` type are stored. `file->f_list` is used as a list element to establish the link between the individual entries.

Iteration over the elements is split into the following two phases:

1. Finding the `list_head` instance of the next entry. This is not dependent on the concrete data structure in the list. The kernel performs this task by de-referencing the `next` element of the current entry and thus finding the position of the next list element.

   The inserted `prefetch` statements supply information to the compiler on which elements are to be transferred by preference from memory into one of the processor caches. When iterating over a list, this is particularly useful for the `next` elements.

2. Finding the container element of the list elements. This contains the useful data and is found by means of the `list_entry` macro, discussed below.

As a result of the cyclic nature of the list, the kernel easily detects when it has iterated over all elements. The `next` element of the current entry then points to the start of the list specified by `head`.

`list_entry` is defined as follows:

<list.h>
```
#define list_entry(ptr, type, member) \
        container_of(ptr, type, member)
```

`ptr` is a pointer to the list element, `type` specifies the type of the container element (`struct file` in the example), and `member` defines which element of the container accepts the list elements (this element is `f_list` in the example, because the list elements are stored in `file->f_list`).

`list_entry` is implemented by means of the previously mentioned container mechanism. The following definition of `container_of` may first appear to be somewhat confusing:

\<kernel.h\>
```
#define offsetof(TYPE, MEMBER) ((size_t) &((TYPE *)0)->MEMBER)

/**
 * container_of - cast a member of a structure out to the containing structure
 * @ptr:        the pointer to the member.
 * @type:       the type of the container struct this is embedded in.
 * @member:     the name of the member within the struct.
 *
 */
#define container_of(ptr, type, member) ({                      \
        const typeof( ((type *)0)->member ) *__mptr = (ptr);    \
        (type *)( (char *)__mptr - offsetof(type,member) );})
```

In this example, the `offsetof` macro expands as follows (some brackets have been omitted to improve readability):

```
(size_t) &((struct file *)0)->f_list
```

The null "pointer" 0 is converted to a pointer to `struct file` by means of a typecast. This is allowed because it does not de-reference the pointer. Consecutive execution of `->` and the address-of operator `&` (C operator precedence!) computes the offset that must be added to a pointer to an instance of the `struct file` type in order to get to the `f_list` element. In the example, the element is directly at the beginning of the structure, so the value 0 is returned. If the list head is at any other point in the data structure, the function returns a positive offset. This is demonstrated in the following example:

```
struct test {
  int a;
  int b;
  struct list_head *f_list;
  int c;
};

long diff = (long)&((struct test*)0)->f_list;
printf("Offset: %ld\n", diff);
```

The program yields an offset of 8 bytes because the two integer variables, each of 4 bytes, must be skipped to get to `f_list`.

If the following variant is used instead of the previous definition of `struct test`, the program returns an offset of 0 as expected:

```
struct test {
  struct list_head *f_list;
  int a;
  int b;
  int c;
};
```

Armed with this information, the `container_of` macro is able to set about extraction of the container data structure. In the example, the code expands as follows:

```
const (struct file*) __mptr = (ptr);
(struct file *)( (char *)__mptr - offset;
```

`ptr` points to the `list_head` instance in the container element. The kernel first creates a pointer `__mptr` with the same value whose type is a pointer to the desired target data type — in this case, `struct file`. Then the offset information previously computed is used to move `__mptr` so that it no longer points to the list element but to the container element. To make sure that the requisite pointer arithmetic is performed byte-by-byte, `__mptr` is converted into a `char*` pointer. However, this change is reversed during final assignment after computation.

C.2.8   Hash Lists

The kernel also provides an adapted version of doubly linked lists that is especially suitable to implement overflow lists in hash tables. In this case, the list elements are also embedded into other data structures, but there is an asymmetry between the list head and the list elements:

```
<list.h>
struct hlist_head {
        struct hlist_node *first;
};

struct hlist_node {
   struct hlist_node *next, **pprev;
};
```

The list elements themselves are still doubly linked, but the list head is connected with the list by a single pointer. The end of the list cannot be accessed in constant time any more, but this is usually never required for hash lists anyway. Instead, the containing data structure becomes slightly smaller because only one pointer instead of two is required. To manipulate hash lists, essentially the same API can be used as for regular lists. The only difference is that `list` must be replaced by `hlist` — so `list_add_head` will become `hlist_add_head`; `list_del` will become `hlist_del`. It's all quite logical.

As for lists, it is possible to use the RCU mechanism to provide protection against concurrent access. If this is desired, the hash list operations must be postfixed with `_rcu` — for instance, `hlist_del_rcu` to delete a list element. See Chapter 5 for a description of the protection that the RCU mechanism offers.

C.2.9   Red-Black Trees

Red-black trees (RB trees) are used when implementing memory management in order to organize sorted elements in a tree. RB trees are frequently used data structures in computer science because they offer a good mix of speed and implementation complexity. This section describes some general properties of RB trees and the data structures used in the kernel without discussing the implementation of the possible tree operations. (which are covered in the classical textbooks on algorithms).

Red-black trees are binary trees characterized by the following properties:

❑   Each node is either red or black.

❑   Each leaf (or node at the edge of the tree) is black.

❑ If a node is red, both children must be black. It therefore follows that there may be no two consecutive red nodes on any path from the root of the tree to any leaf, but there may be any number of black nodes.

❑ The number of black nodes on a simple path from a node to a leaf is the same for all leaves.

One advantage of red-black trees is that all important tree operations (inserting, deleting, and searching for elements) can be performed in $\mathcal{O}(\log n)$ steps, where n is the number of elements in the tree.

To represent the nodes of an RB tree, the data structure needs not only pointers to the children and a field to hold the useful data, but also an element to hold color information. The kernel implements this by means of the following definition:

\<rbtree.h\>
```
#define RB_RED          0
#define RB_BLACK        1

struct rb_node
{
        unsigned long rb_parent_color;
        int rb_color;
        struct rb_node *rb_right;
        struct rb_node *rb_left;
} __attribute__((aligned(sizeof(long))));
```

Although this is not directly visible in the definition, the kernel maintains an additional pointer to the parent node. It is hidden in `rb_parent_color`: Only one bit is needed to represent two colors, and this information is contained in the lowest bit of `rb_parent_color`. The rest of the variable is used to hold the parent pointer. This is possible because pointers are on all architectures at least aligned on 4-byte boundaries, so the two lowest-valued bits are guaranteed to be 0. It is, however, essential that the kernel masks out the color information before de-referencing the pointer as follows:

\<rbtree.h\>
```
#define rb_parent(r) ((struct rb_node *)((r)->rb_parent_color & ~3))
```

The color information must also be obtained with a special macro as shown here:

\<rbtree.h\>
```
#define rb_color(r)   ((r)->rb_parent_color & 1)
```

Additionally, the kernel provides convenience functions that distinguish red and black nodes and allow to set the node color as follows:

\<rbtree.h\>
```
#define rb_is_red(r)    (!rb_color(r))
#define rb_is_black(r) rb_color(r)
#define rb_set_red(r) do { (r)->rb_parent_color &= ~1; } while (0)
#define rb_set_black(r) do { (r)->rb_parent_color |= 1; } while (0)
```

The useful data associated with a node is not linked to it by means of a further element — instead, the kernel uses the container mechanism (which you've seen in the context of list implementation) to implement the node as part of the useful data. The following macro is provided to get to the useful data starting at a node:

\<rbtree.h\>
```
#define rb_entry(ptr, type, member) container_of(ptr, type, member)
```

To ensure that RB tree implementation is generally available and is not restricted to memory management, the kernel provides only general standard functions for manipulating trees (rotation operations, for example) — these are implemented in `lib/rbtree.c`.

For example, the Ext3 filesystem uses RB trees to sort directory entries in RAM. As already described, data items are implemented as containers of the nodes.

fs/ext3/dir.c
```
struct fname {
        __u32           hash;
        __u32           minor_hash;
        struct rb_node  rb_hash;
        struct fname    *next;
        __u32           inode;
        __u8            name_len;
        __u8            file_type;
        char            name[0];
};
```

Search and insert operations must be provided by all subsystems that use red-black trees. Searching is performed in the same way as normal searches in an organized binary tree and can therefore be implemented very easily. The insertion routine must place new elements in the tree as red leaves (`rb_link_node` can be used to do this). The `rb_insert_color` standard function must then be invoked to rebalance the tree so that it still complies with the previously described rules. \<rbtree.h\> includes examples on which the functions to be provided can be based.

C.2.10 Radix Trees

The second tree implementation provided in library form in the kernel makes use of radix trees to organize data in memory. Radix trees differ from other trees because it is not necessary to compare the entire key at every branch, but only part of the key with the stored value of the node when performing search operations. This results in slightly different worst-case and average-case behavior than in other implementations, which are described in detail in the corresponding textbooks on algorithms. Also, radix trees are not particularly difficult to implement, which adds to their attraction.

The node data structure is defined as follows in the kernel sources:

lib/radix-tree.c
```
#define RADIX_TREE_MAP_SHIFT  (CONFIG_BASE_SMALL ? 4 : 6)
#define RADIX_TREE_MAP_SIZE   (1UL << RADIX_TREE_MAP_SHIFT)
#define RADIX_TREE_MAP_MASK   (RADIX_TREE_MAP_SIZE-1)

struct radix_tree_node {
        unsigned int    height; /* Height from the bottom */
        unsigned int    count;
        struct rcu_head rcu_head;
```

```
        void            *slots[RADIX_TREE_MAP_SIZE];
        unsigned long   tags[RADIX_TREE_MAX_TAGS][RADIX_TREE_TAG_LONGS];
};
```

`slots` is an array of pointers that, according to their position in the tree (i.e., the level on which the node is located), point either to other nodes or to data elements. `count` indicates the number of occupied array positions. The macros defined in the code segment specify statically how many array positions there are in each node. By default, the kernel uses $2^6 = 64$. Empty slots are given a null pointer.

Every tree node can be associated with *tags* that correspond to a set or an unset bit. Per node, a maximum of `RADIX_TREE_MAX_TAGS` different tags are possible, the default setting is a meager 2. This is, however sufficient for the page cache.

The RCU mechanism (described in Chapter 5) is used to allow lock-free radix tree lookups.

An array of `unsigned longs` is used to represent the tags, and `RADIX_TREE_TAG_LONGS` is computed by the kernel such that sufficient storage space is available to hold the tags. A `long` array with `RADIX_TREE_MAX_TAGS*RADIX_TREE_TAG_LONGS` contains enough bits to attach `RADIX_TREE_MAX_TAGS` tags to each slot. The functions `radix_tree_tag_set` and `radix_tree_tag_clear` are provided to set and clear tag bits, respectively. Notice that a tag is not only set in the leaf entry, but in every entry from root to bottom.

The tree root is defined by the following data structure (notice that this definition is in a public visible header file, in contrast to the definition of tree nodes):

<radix-tree.h>
```
struct radix_tree_root {
        unsigned int            height;
        gfp_t                   gfp_mask;
        struct radix_tree_node  *rnode;
};
```

`height` specifies the current height of the tree, and `rnode` points to the first node. `gfp_mask` specifies the memory area from which the required data structure instances of the tree are to be taken.

The maximum number of elements that can be stored in a tree can be derived directly from the tree height — that is, from the number of node levels. The kernel provides the following function to compute the height:

lib/radix-tree.c
```
static inline unsigned long radix_tree_maxindex(unsigned int height)
{
        return height_to_maxindex[height];
}
```

`height_to_maxindex` is an array that stores the maximum number of elements for different tree heights. The number is computed when the system is initialized as shown here:

lib/radix-tree.c
```
#define RADIX_TREE_INDEX_BITS  (8 /* CHAR_BIT */ * sizeof(unsigned long))
#define RADIX_TREE_MAX_PATH (DIV_ROUND_UP(RADIX_TREE_INDEX_BITS, \
                                    RADIX_TREE_MAP_SHIFT))
```

lib/radix-tree.c
```
static __init unsigned long __maxindex(unsigned int height)
{
        unsigned int width = height * RADIX_TREE_MAP_SHIFT;
        int shift = RADIX_TREE_INDEX_BITS - width;

        if (shift < 0)
                return ~0UL;
        if (shift >= BITS_PER_LONG)
                return 0UL;
        return ~0UL >> shift;
}

static __init void radix_tree_init_maxindex(void)
{
        unsigned int i;

        for (i = 0; i < ARRAY_SIZE(height_to_maxindex); i++)
                height_to_maxindex[i] = __maxindex(i);
}
```

At runtime, only simple array lookup is needed, and this can be done very quickly. This is important because the maximum number of elements for a given tree height needs to be computed frequently.

The elements contained in the tree are characterized by a descriptor that accepts continuous values from 0 up to the maximum number of elements that can currently be stored in the tree as follows:

radix_tree_insert is used to insert a new element in a radix tree as follows:

lib/radix-tree.c
```
static inline void *radix_tree_indirect_to_ptr(void *ptr)
{
        return (void *)((unsigned long)ptr & ~RADIX_TREE_INDIRECT_PTR);
}

int radix_tree_insert(struct radix_tree_root *root,
                        unsigned long index, void *item)
{
        struct radix_tree_node *node = NULL, *slot;
        unsigned int height, shift;
        int offset;
        int error;

        /* Make sure the tree is high enough.  */
        if (index > radix_tree_maxindex(root->height)) {
                error = radix_tree_extend(root, index);
                if (error)
                        return error;
        }

        slot = radix_tree_indirect_to_ptr(root->rnode)

        height = root->height;
        shift = (height-1) * RADIX_TREE_MAP_SHIFT;
```

```
        offset = 0;                          /* uninitialised var warning */
while (height > 0) {
        if (slot == NULL) {
                /* Have to add a child node.  */
                if (!(slot = radix_tree_node_alloc(root)))
                        return -ENOMEM;
                if (node) {
                        rcu_assign_pointer(node->slots[offset], slot);
                        node->count++;
                } else
                        rcu_assign_pointer(root->rnode,
                                radix_tree_ptr_to_indirect(slot));
        }

        /* Go a level down */
        offset = (index >> shift) & RADIX_TREE_MAP_MASK;
        node = slot;
        slot = node->slots[offset];
        shift -= RADIX_TREE_MAP_SHIFT;
        height--;
}

if (slot != NULL)
        return -EEXIST;

if (node) {
        node->count++;
        rcu_assign_pointer(node->slots[offset], item)
} else {
        rcu_assign_pointer(root->rnode, item);
}

return 0;
}
```

If the descriptor of the element is larger than the current number of elements that can be processed, the tree must be enlarged; this is described later in this section.

The code traverses the tree from top to bottom starting at the root, and the path is defined solely by the key being searched. Depending on the position in the tree, certain parts of the key are selected to find the matching entry in the slot array that leads to the next lower tree level. This corresponds exactly to the characteristics of radix trees. The tree is traversed in order to allocate tree branches not yet present. When this is done, the tree height does *not* change, because the tree can grow only in its width. The new entry is inserted in the matching slot once the code has reached level 0. Since the tree is protected by the RCU mechanism, the data pointers must not be assigned directly, but only via rcu_assign_pointer as discussed in Chapter 5.

The height of the tree is modified by radix_tree_extend — which is called, if needed, at the start of the function. It is defined as follows in the kernel sources:

lib/radix-tree.c
```
static int radix_tree_extend(struct radix_tree_root *root, unsigned long index)
{
```

```
            struct radix_tree_node *node;
            unsigned int height;
            int tag;

            /* Figure out what the height should be.  */
            height = root->height + 1;
            while (index > radix_tree_maxindex(height))
                    height++;

            if (root->rnode == NULL) {
                    root->height = height;
                    goto out;
            }

            do {
                    if (!(node = radix_tree_node_alloc(root)))
                            return -ENOMEM;

                    /* Increase the height. */
                    node->slots[0] = radix_tree_indirect_to_ptr(root->rnode)


                    /* Propagate the aggregated tag info into the new root */
                    for (tag = 0; tag < RADIX_TREE_MAX_TAGS; tag++) {
                            if (root_tag_get(root, tag))
                                    tag_set(node, tag, 0);
                    }

                    newheight = root->height+1;
                    node->height = newheight;
                    node->count = 1;
                    node = radix_tree_ptr_to_indirect(node);
                    rcu_assign_pointer(root->rnode, node);
                    root->height = newheight;
            } while (height > root->height);
    out:
            return 0;
    }
```

Depending on the new maximum index, it may be necessary to add more than one level to the tree.

The tree is expanded from the top because there is then no need to copy elements. An additional node is inserted between the root and the previous top node for each new level. Because node branches are allocated automatically when new elements are inserted, the kernel need not concern itself with this task.

The kernel provides the `radix_tree_lookup` function to find an element in a radix tree by reference to its key as shown here:

lib/radix-tree.c
```
void *radix_tree_lookup(struct radix_tree_root *root, unsigned long index)
{
        unsigned int height, shift;
        struct radix_tree_node *node, **slot;
```

```
        node = rcu_dereference(root->rnode);
        if (node == NULL)
                return NULL;

                if (!radix_tree_is_indirect_ptr(node)) {
                        if (index > 0)
                                return NULL;
                        return node;
                }
                node = radix_tree_indirect_to_ptr(node);

                height = node->height;
                if (index > radix_tree_maxindex(height))
                        return NULL;

                shift = (height-1) * RADIX_TREE_MAP_SHIFT;

                do {
                        slot = (struct radix_tree_node **)
                            (node->slots + ((index>>shift) & RADIX_TREE_MAP_MASK));
                        node = rcu_dereference(*slot);
                        if (node == NULL)
                                return NULL;

                        shift -= RADIX_TREE_MAP_SHIFT;
                        height--;
                } while (height > 0);

        return node;
}
```

Logically, the algorithm for traversing the tree is identical to the one described previously for inserting new elements. However, searching is a simple operation because the kernel need not concern itself with allocating new branches. If a slot at any height in the tree has a null pointer and is therefore not present, the element being searched is not in the tree. Consequently, work can be terminated immediately and a null pointer can be returned.

C.3 Summary

C is a Spartan language, and one might be tempted at first glance to equate this with simplicity. However, it is quite the opposite: Despite being frugal, C allows for many tricks of the trade that can be used for good, but can likewise be abused to create unreadable and unmaintainable code. This chapter described some of the more off-standard features of C that are required in kernel development to squeeze the last percents of performance out of hardware. It also briefly introduced you to the internals of the GNU C compiler, and showed you some optimization techniques. Additionally, the chapter described some extensions to the C language that are heavily employed in kernel development.

Finally, this chapter covered some standard data structures that are used all over the kernel sources, and that therefore must be implemented as generically as possible — which again requires you to utilize some of the finer points of C.

System Startup

Like any other program, the kernel goes through a load and initialization phase before performing its normal tasks. Although this phase is not particularly interesting in the case of normal applications, the kernel — as the central system layer — has to address a number of specific problems. The boot phase is split into the following three parts:

❑ Kernel loading into RAM and the creation of a minimal runtime environment.

❑ Branching to the (platform-*dependent*) machine code of the kernel and system-specific initialization of the elementary system functions written in assembly language.

❑ Branching to the (platform-*independent*) part of the initialization code written in C, and complete initialization of all subsystems with a subsequent switch to normal operation.

As usual, a boot loader is responsible for the first phase. Its tasks depend largely on what the particular architecture is required to do. Because in-depth knowledge of specific processor features and problems is needed to understand all details of the first phase, the architecture-specific reference manual is a good source of information. The second phase is also very hardware-dependent. Consequently, this appendix describes only some key areas of the IA-32 architecture.

In the third, system-independent phase, the kernel is already resident in memory and (on some architectures) the processor has switched from boot mode to execution mode in which the kernel then runs. On IA-32 machines, it is necessary to switch the processor from 8086 emulation, which is immediately active at boot time, to *protected mode* to make the system 32-bit capable. Setup work is also required on other architectures — for instance, it is often necessary to activate paging explicitly, and central system components must be placed in a defined initial state so that work can begin. All these tasks must be coded in assembly language and therefore are not the most inviting parts of the kernel.

Concentrating on the third phase of startup allows for dispensing with many architecture-specific trifles and has the added advantage that, generally speaking, the remaining sequence of operations is independent of the particular platform on which the kernel runs.

D.1 Architecture-Specific Setup on IA-32 Systems

Once the kernel has been loaded into physical memory using the bootloader (LILO, GRUB, etc.), the setup assembler "function" in `arch/x86/boot/header.S` is invoked by switching the control flow to the appropriate point in memory by means of a jump statement. This is possible because the setup function is always at the same place in the object file.

The code performs the following tasks, which require a great deal of assembly code:

1. It checks whether the kernel was loaded to the correct position in memory. To do this, it uses a 4-byte signature that is integrated in the kernel image and that must be located, unchanged, at the correct position in RAM.

2. It determines how big system memory is.

3. It initializes the graphics card.

4. It moves the kernel image to a position in memory where it does not get in its own way during subsequent decompression.

5. It switches the CPU to protected mode.

On completion of these tasks, the code branches to the startup_32 function (in `arch/x86/boot/compressed/head_32.S`), which does the following:

1. It creates a provisional kernel stack.

2. It fills uninitialized kernel data with null bytes. The relevant area is between the _edata and _end constants. When the kernel is linked, these constants are automatically supplied with the correct values as generated for the kernel binary.

3. It calls the C routine decompress_kernel in `arch/x86/boot/compressed/misc_32.c`. This decompresses the kernel and writes the uncompressed machine code to position 0x100000,[1] directly after the first MiB of memory. Uncompressing is the first operation performed by the kernel, as indicated by the screen messages Uncompressing Linux... and Ok, booting the kernel.

The final part of processor-specific initialization is started by redirecting control flow to startup_32 in `arch/x86/kernel/head_32.S`.

> This is a *different* routine from the previously described **startup_32** function and is defined in a different file. The kernel need not concern itself with the fact that both "functions" have the same label because it branches directly to the appropriate address, which is patched in by the assembler and is not associated with the symbolic labels used in the source code.

---

[1]The address can differ if the kernel was built as a relocatable kernel, but this scenario is not relevant here.

This boot section is responsible for the following steps:

1. Activating paging mode and setting up a final kernel stack.

2. Filling the .bss segment located between __bss_start and __bss_stop with null bytes.

3. Initializing the interrupt descriptor table. However, the ignore_int dummy routine is entered for all interrupts — the actual handlers are installed later.

4. Detecting the processor type. The cpuid statement can be used to recognize recent models. It returns information on the processor type and capabilities, but it does not distinguish between 80386 and 80486 processors — this is done by means of various assembler tricks that are neither important nor interesting.

Platform-specific initialization is now complete and the code branches to the start_kernel function. Unlike the code described previously, this function is implemented as a normal C function and is therefore much easier to handle.

D.2 High-Level Initialization

start_kernel acts as a dispatcher function to perform both platform-independent and platform-dependent tasks, all of which are implemented in C. It is responsible for invoking the high-level initialization routines of almost all kernel subsystems. Users can recognize when the kernel enters this initialization phase because one of the first things the function does is display the Linux banner on screen. For example, the following message is displayed on one of the author's systems:

```
Linux version 2.6.24-default (wolfgang@schroedinger) (gcc version 4.2.1 (SUSE
Linux)) #1 SMP PREEMPT Thu Mar 20 00:17:06 CET 2008
```

> **The message is generated early on in the boot operation but is not displayed on-screen until the console system has been initialized. It is buffered in the intervening period.**

The number of screen outputs increases dramatically during the subsequent steps because the subsystems being initialized display a wide range of status information on the console. This information is very useful, particularly for troubleshooting.

The following sections deal extensively with start_kernel and cast light on the kernel startup process after completion of the architecture-dependent phase.

D.2.1 Subsystem Initialization

Figure D-1 shows a code flow diagram to briefly illustrate the function's tasks and goals.

The first step is to output the version message. The message text is held in the linux_banner global variable defined in init/version.c. This is followed by a further architecture-specific initialization step, which no longer deals with lower-level processor details but is written in C and which, on most systems, has the primary task of setting the framework for initialization of high-level memory management. The bulk of the initialization work — setting up the central data structures of the various kernel subsystems — is performed in `start_kernel` once the command-line arguments passed to the kernel at startup have been interpreted. This is a very comprehensive task because it involves practically all subsystems. It is therefore broken down into a large number of short procedures, which are described in the subsequent sections. The final step is to generate the idle process that the kernel calls when it has absolutely nothing else to do. The `init` process is also started with PID 1 — this runs the initialization routines of various subsystems and then starts `/sbin/init` as the first user space process. This concludes kernel-side initialization.

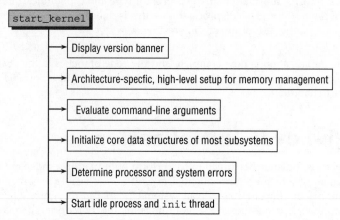

Figure D-1: Code flow diagram for `start_kernel`.

Architecture-Specific Setup

As its name clearly suggests, `setup_arch` is an architecture-specific function. It performs setup tasks written in C and concerns itself primarily with the initialization of various aspects of memory management. For example, on most systems, it finalizes enabling of paging and sets up suitable data structures for kernel mode. On some architectures with several variants (IA-64 and Alpha, for example), variant-specific setup is performed at this point.

For simplicity's sake, this section examines only the implementation of `setup_arch` for IA-32 systems as touched upon briefly in Chapter 3. Figure D-2 shows the corresponding code flow diagram.

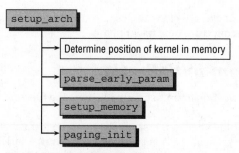

Figure D-2: Code flow diagram for `setup_arch` on IA-32 systems.

First, the location of the kernel in physical and virtual memory is noted. This is done using constants inserted by the linker when the kernel was compiled. These constants specify the start and end addresses of the various segments as shown here (see also Appendix E):

arch/x86/kernel/setup_32.c
```
init_mm.start_code = (unsigned long) _text;
init_mm.end_code = (unsigned long) _etext;
init_mm.end_data = (unsigned long) _edata;
init_mm.brk = init_pg_tables_end + PAGE_OFFSET;

code_resource.start = virt_to_phys(_text);
code_resource.end = virt_to_phys(_etext)-1;
data_resource.start = virt_to_phys(_etext);
data_resource.end = virt_to_phys(_edata)-1;
bss_resource.start = virt_to_phys(&__bss_start);
bss_resource.end = virt_to_phys(&__bss_stop)-1;
```

parse_early_param performs partial interpretation of the command-line parameters. It does this only for arguments relating to memory management setup; for example, the total size of available physical memory, or the position of specific ACPI and BIOS memory areas. Users can overwrite values that the kernel has detected incorrectly. Armed with this information, setup_memory detects the number of physical memory pages in the low-memory and high-memory areas. It also initializes the bootmem allocator.

paging_init then sets up the kernel's reference page table. This is used not only to map physical memory but also to manage the vmalloc areas, as discussed in Chapter 3. The new page table is enabled by inserting the address of swapper_pg_dir — the variable in which the page table data structures are saved — into the CR3 register of the processor.

The build_all_zonelists function (which was discussed in Chapter 3 and which is responsible for creating the memory management zone lists) is invoked by start_kernel to complete memory management initialization and to put the bootmem allocator in control of the rest of the boot procedure.

Interpreting Command-Line Arguments

parse_args is invoked by parse_early_param in start_kernel and assumes responsibility for interpreting the command-line parameters passed to the kernel at boot time. The same inherent problem is encountered as in userspace — a string containing key/value pairs in the form key1=val1 key2=val2 must be broken down into its constituent parts. The options set must be saved in the kernel or specific responses must be triggered.

The kernel is faced with this parameter problem not only at boot time but also when modules are inserted. It therefore makes good sense to use the same mechanism to solve the problem in order to avoid the unnecessary duplication of code.

The binary file contains an instance of kernel_param for each kernel parameter — both in dynamically loaded modules and in the static kernel binary. This instance is structured as follows:

<moduleparam.h>
```
/* Returns 0, or -errno.  arg is in kp->arg. */
typedef int (*param_set_fn)(const char *val, struct kernel_param *kp);
/* Returns length written or -errno.  Buffer is 4k (ie. be short!) */
```

```
typedef int (*param_get_fn)(char *buffer, struct kernel_param *kp);

struct kernel_param {
        const char *name;
        param_set_fn set;
        param_get_fn get;
        union {
                void *arg;
                const struct kparam_string *str;
                const struct kparam_array *arr;
        };
};
```

name gives the name of the parameter, and the set and get functions set and read the parameter value. arg is an (optional) argument that is also passed to the preceding functions. As expected, it allows the same function to be used for different parameters. The pointer can also be specifically interpreted as a string or an array.

Parameters are registered with the kernel by the following macros: module_param, module_param_named, and so on. They fill an instance of kernel_param with the appropriate values and write them to the __param section of the binary file.

This greatly simplifies parameter interpretation at boot time. All that is needed is a loop that performs the following actions until all parameters have been processed:

1. next_arg extracts the next name/value pair from the command line provided by the kernel in the form of a text string.

2. parse_one runs through the list of all registered parameters, compares the value passed with the name element of the kernel_param instances, and invokes the set function when a match is found.

Initializing Central Data Structures and Caches

As a quick glance at the following kernel sources shows, the most substantial task of start_kernel is to invoke subroutines to initialize almost all important kernel subsystems:

init/main.c
```
asmlinkage void __init start_kernel(void)
{
...
        trap_init();
        rcu_init();
        init_IRQ();
        pidhash_init();
        sched_init();
        init_timers();
        hrtimers_init();
        softirq_init();
        timekeeping_init();
        time_init();
        profile_init();
...
```

1228

```
        early_boot_irqs_on();
        local_irq_enable();

...

        /*
         * HACK ALERT! This is early. We're enabling the console before
         * we've done PCI setups etc, and console_init() must be aware of
         * this. But we do want output early, in case something goes wrong.
         */
        console_init();

...

        mem_init();
        kmem_cache_init();

...

        calibrate_delay();
        pidmap_init();
        pgtable_cache_init();

...

        vfs_caches_init(num_physpages);
        radix_tree_init();
        signals_init();
        /* rootfs populating might need page-writeback */
        page_writeback_init();
#ifdef CONFIG_PROC_FS
        proc_root_init();
#endif
...
```

However, most functions are of little interest because all they do is call on the bootmem allocator to reserve memory for data structure instantiation. The most important functions were covered in detail in the subsystem-specific chapters, so the following simply summarizes the meaning of the individual actions:

❑ trap_init and init_IRQ set the handlers for traps and IRQs — this is an architecture-specific task. For instance, the following code is used on IA-32 systems to register trap handlers for error messages returned by the processor:

arch/x86/kernel/traps_32.c

```
void __init trap_init(void)
{
        set_trap_gate(0,&divide_error);
        set_intr_gate(1,&debug);
        set_intr_gate(2,&nmi);
        set_system_gate(4,&overflow);
        set_system_gate(5,&bounds);
        set_trap_gate(6,&invalid_op);
        set_trap_gate(7,&device_not_available);
        set_task_gate(8,GDT_ENTRY_DOUBLEFAULT_TSS);
        set_trap_gate(9,&coprocessor_segment_overrun);
        set_trap_gate(10,&invalid_TSS);
        set_trap_gate(11,&segment_not_present);
        set_trap_gate(12,&stack_segment);
        set_trap_gate(13,&general_protection);
        set_intr_gate(14,&page_fault);
        set_trap_gate(15,&spurious_interrupt_bug);
```

```
        set_trap_gate(16,&coprocessor_error);
        set_trap_gate(17,&alignment_check);
        set_trap_gate(19,&simd_coprocessor_error);
    ...
        set_system_gate(SYSCALL_VECTOR,&system_call);
    ...
    }
```

As the code shows, this is also where the interrupt used for system calls is defined as a system gate (`SYSCALL_VECTOR` is set to `0x80`).

The IRQ handlers are initialized similarly.

❑ `sched_init` initializes the data structures of the scheduler (for the main processor in this case) and run queues are created.

❑ `pidhash_init` allocates the hash tables used by the PID allocator to manage free and assigned PIDs.

❑ `softirq_init` registers the softIRQ queues for tasklets with normal and high priority (`TASKLET_SOFTIRQ` and `HI_SOFTIRQ`).

❑ `time_init` reads the system time from the hardware clock. This is a processor-specific function because different architectures use different mechanisms to read the clock.

❑ `init_console` initializes the system consoles. The *early printk* mechanism is also disabled on systems that provide this facility to allow messages to be output to the console before it has been fully initialized (on other systems, messages are buffered until the console is activated).

❑ `page_address_init` sets up the hash table that the Persistent Kernel Map (PKMap) mechanism uses to determine the physical page address of a permanent kernel mapping by reference to a given virtual address.

❑ `mem_init` disables the bootmem allocator (and performs a number of minor architecture-specific actions that are of no concern), and `kmem_cache_init` initializes the slab allocator in a multistage process described in detail in Chapter 3.

❑ `calibrate_delay` calculates the BogoMIPS value, which specifies how many empty loops the CPU can run through per jiffy. The kernel requires this value to estimate the time needed for some tasks that are performed with polling or busy waiting. The following code yields a good approximation of the number of loops per jiffy and stores the result in `loops_per_jiffy`[2]:

init/calibrate.c
```
void __init calibrate_delay(void)
{
        unsigned long ticks, loopbit;
        int lps_precision = LPS_PREC;

        loops_per_jiffy = (1<<12);

        printk("Calibrating delay loop... ");
        while (loops_per_jiffy <<= 1) {
                /* wait for "start of" clock tick */
```

---

[2]It is also possible to preset the BogoMIPS value, but this prevents the kernel from doing one of the most important operations ever, which would clearly be boring.

```
                ticks = jiffies;
                while (ticks == jiffies)
                        /* nothing */;
                /* Go .. */
                ticks = jiffies;
                __delay(loops_per_jiffy);
                ticks = jiffies - ticks;
                if (ticks)
                        break;
        }


        /*
         * Do a binary approximation to get loops_per_jiffy set to
         * equal one clock (up to lps_precision bits)
         */
        loops_per_jiffy >>= 1;
        loopbit = loops_per_jiffy;
        while ( lps_precision-- && (loopbit >>= 1) ) {
                loops_per_jiffy |= loopbit;
                ticks = jiffies;
                while (ticks == jiffies)
                        /* nothing */;
                ticks = jiffies;
                __delay(loops_per_jiffy);
                if (jiffies != ticks)   /* longer than 1 tick */
                        loops_per_jiffy &= ~loopbit;
        }


        /* Round the value and print it */
        printk("%lu.%02lu BogoMIPS (lpj=%lu)\n",
                loops_per_jiffy/(500000/HZ),
                (loops_per_jiffy/(5000/HZ)) % 100,
                loops_per_jiffy);
        }
}
```

The following construction is particularly interesting (although in C, it would not normally make sense or would produce an endless loop):

init/main.c

```
ticks = jiffies;
while (ticks == jiffies)
        /* nothing */;
```

However, the loop does terminate at some point because the value of `jiffies` is incremented by 1 in the interrupt handler routine at each tick of the system clock (which sleeps with the frequency HZ). As a result, the condition in the `while` loops produces an incorrect value after a certain time, thus causing the loop to terminate.

❏   `pidmap_init` allocates the array in which the free positions of the PID allocator are saved. It also reserves the (unused) PID 0 for all PID types.

❏   `fork_init` allocates the `task_struct` slab cache (providing there is no architecture-specific mechanism to generate and cache `task_struct` instances) and calculates the maximum number of threads that can be generated.

❑ proc_caches_init initiates slab caches for the remaining data structures involved in the process description. The following structures are considered: sighand, signal, files, fs, fs_struct, and mm_struct.

❑ buffer_init generates a cache for buffer_heads and calculates the value of the max_buffer_heads variable so that the buffer heads never use more than 10 percent of the memory in ZONE_NORMAL.

❑ vfs_caches_init creates caches for various data structures needed by the virtual filesystem (VFS) layer.

❑ radix_tree_init creates a slab cache for radix_tree_node instances needed by memory management.

❑ page_writeback_init initializes the flushing mechanism and, more specifically, defines the limit value for dirty pages after which the mechanism comes into effect.

❑ proc_root_init initializes the inode cache of the proc filesystem, registers the process filesystem (procfs) in the kernel, and generates the central filesystem entries — for example, /proc/meminfo, /proc/uptime, /proc/version, and so on.

Searching for Known System Errors

Software is not the only thing that has bugs — mishaps also occur when implementing processors and, as a result, chips do not function as they should. Fortunately, most error situations can be remedied with workarounds. However, before workarounds can be put in place, the kernel needs to know whether a particular processor does, in fact, have any bugs. This can be established using the architecture-specific check_bugs function.

For instance, the following code is available for IA-32 systems:

arch/x86/kernel/cpu/bugs.c

```
static void __init check_bugs(void)
{
        identify_boot_cpu();

        check_config();
        check_fpu();
        check_hlt();
        check_popad();
        init_utsname()->machine[1] = '0' + (boot_cpu_data.x86 > 6 ? 6 : boot_cpu_data.x86);
        alternative_instructions();
}
```

The last statement (alternative_instructions) also invokes a function that replaces certain assembler instructions — depending on processor type — with faster, more modern alternatives. This enables distributors to create kernel images that are capable of running on a wide variety of machines without having to forgo more recent features.

For comparison of the CPU quality, here is the check_bugs routine of S390, Alpha, Extensa, H8300, v850, FRV, Blackfin, Cris, PA-RISC, and PPC64:

```
static void check_bugs(void)
```

The S390 kernel is among the most confident ones, as you can see in the following code:

include/asm-s390/bugs.h
```
static inline void check_bugs(void)
{
    /* s390 has no bugs ... */
}
```

Idle and `init` Thread

The last two actions of `start_kernel` are as follows:

1. `rest_init` starts a new thread that, after performing a few more initialization operations as described the next step, ultimately calls the userspace initialization program `/sbin/init`.

2. The first, and formerly only, kernel thread becomes the idle thread that is called when the system has nothing else to do.

`rest_init` is essentially implemented in just a few lines of code:

init/main.c
```
static void rest_init(void)
{
        kernel_thread(kernel_init, NULL, CLONE_FS | CLONE_SIGHAND);
        pid = kernel_thread(kthreadd, NULL, CLONE_FS | CLONE_FILES);
        kthreadd_task = find_task_by_pid(pid);
        unlock_kernel();
...
        schedule();
        cpu_idle();
}
```

Once a new kernel thread named `init` (which will start the init task) and another thread named `kthreadd` (which will be used by the kernel to start kernel daemons) have been started, the kernel invokes `unlock_kernel` to unlock the big kernel lock and makes the existing thread the idle thread by calling `cpu_idle`. Prior to this, `schedule` must be called at least once to activate the other thread.

The idle thread uses as little system power as possible (this is very important in embedded systems) and relinquishes the CPU to runnable processes as quickly as possible. In addition, it handles turning off the periodic tick completely if the CPU is idle and the kernel is compiled with support for dynamic ticks as discussed in Chapter 15.

The `init` thread, whose code flow diagram is shown in Figure D-3, is in parallel existence with the idle thread and `kthreadd`.

First, the current task needs to be registered as `child_reaper` for the global PID namespace. The kernel makes it very clear what its intentions are:

init/main.c
```
static int __init kernel_init(void * unused)
{
...
```

```
        /*
         * Tell the world that we're going to be the grim
         * reaper of innocent orphaned children.
         */
        init_pid_ns.child_reaper = current;
    ...
}
```

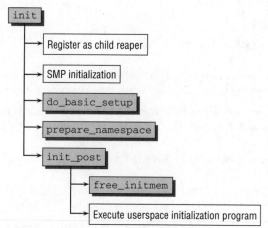

Figure D-3: Code flow diagram for `init`.

Up to now, the kernel has used just one of the several CPUs on multiprocessor systems, so it's time to activate the others. This is done in the following three steps:

1. `smp_prepare_cpus` ensures that the remaining CPUs are activated by executing their architecture-specific boot sequences. However, the CPUs are not yet linked into the kernel scheduling mechanism and are therefore still not available for use.

2. `do_pre_smp_initcalls` is — despite its name — a mix of symmetric multiprocessing and uniprocessor initialization routines. On SMP systems, its primary task is to initialize the migration queue used to move processes between CPUs as discussed in Chapter 2. It also starts the softIRQ daemons.[3]

3. `smp_init` enables the remaining CPUs in the kernel so that they are available for use.

Driver Setup

The next `init` step is to start general initialization of drivers and subsystems using the `do_basic_setup` function whose code flow diagram is shown in Figure D-4.

Some of the functions are quite extensive but not very interesting. They simply initialize further kernel data structures already discussed in the chapters on the specific subsystems. `driver_init` sets up the data structures of the general driver model, and `init_irq_proc` registers entries with information about IRQs

---

[3]To be precise, the kernel invokes a callback function that starts the daemons when a CPU is activated by the kernel. Suffice it to say that ultimately an instance of the daemon is started for each CPU.

in the `proc` filesystem. `init_workqueues` generates the `events` work queue, and `usermodehelper_init` creates the `khelper` work queue.

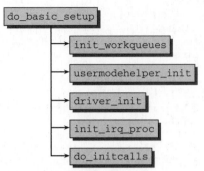

Figure D-4: Code flow diagram for do_basic_setup.

Much more interesting is `do_initcalls`, which is responsible for invoking the driver-specific initialization functions. Because the kernel can be custom configured, a facility must be provided to determine the functions to be invoked and to define the sequence in which they are executed. This facility is known as the *initcall mechanism* and is discussed in detail later in this section.

The kernel defines the following macros to detect the initialization routines and to define their sequence or priority:

```
<init.h>
#define __define_initcall(level,fn,id) \
        static initcall_t __initcall_##fn##id __attribute_used__ \
        __attribute__((__section__(".initcall" level ".init"))) = fn

#define pure_initcall(fn)            __define_initcall("0",fn,0)

#define core_initcall(fn)           __define_initcall("1",fn,1)
#define postcore_initcall(fn)       __define_initcall("2",fn,2)
#define arch_initcall(fn)           __define_initcall("3",fn,3)
#define subsys_initcall(fn)         __define_initcall("4",fn,4)
#define fs_initcall(fn)             __define_initcall("5",fn,5)
#define rootfs_initcall(fn)         __define_initcall("rootfs",fn,rootfs)
#define device_initcall(fn)         __define_initcall("6",fn,6)
#define late_initcall(fn)           __define_initcall("7",fn,7)
```

The names of the functions are passed to the macros as parameters, as shown in the examples for `device_initcall(time_init_device)` and `subsys_initcall(pcibios_init)`. This generates an entry in the `.initcalllevel.init` section. The `initcall_t` entry type is used and is defined as follows:

```
<init.h>
typedef int (*initcall_t)(void);
```

This is a pointer to functions that do not expect an argument and return an integer to indicate their status.

The linker places initcall sections one after the other in the correct sequence in the binary file. The order is defined in the architecture-*independent* file `<include/asm-generic/vmlinux.lds.h>`, as shown here:

<asm-generic/vmlinux.lds.h>
```
#define INITCALLS                               \
        *(.initcall0.init)                      \
        *(.initcall1.init)                      \
        *(.initcall2.init)                      \
        *(.initcall3.init)                      \
        *(.initcall4.init)                      \
        *(.initcall5.init)                      \
        *(.initcallrootfs.init)                 \
        *(.initcall6.init)                      \
        *(.initcall7.init)                      \
```

This is how a linker file employs the specification (the linker script for Alpha processors is shown here, but the procedure is practically the same on all other systems):

arch/alpha/kernel/vmlinux.lds.S
```
        .initcall.init : {
                __initcall_start = .;
                INITCALLS
                __initcall_end = .;
        }
...
```

The linker holds the start and end of the initcall range in the __initcall_start and __initcall_end variables, which are visible in the kernel and whose benefits are described shortly.

> **The mechanism described defines only the call sequence of the different initcall *categories*. The call sequence of the functions in the individual categories is defined implicitly by the position of the specified binary file in the link process and cannot be modified manually from within the C code.**

Because the compiler and linker do the preliminary work, the task of `do_initcalls` is not all that complicated as the following glance at the kernel sources shows:

init/main.c
```
static void __init do_initcalls(void)
{
        initcall_t *call;
        int count = preempt_count();

        for (call = __initcall_start; call < __initcall_end; call++) {
...
                char *msg;
                int result;

                if (initcall_debug) {
                        printk("calling initcall 0x%p\n", *call);
...
```

```
        }

            result = (*call)();
...
    }

        /* Make sure there is no pending stuff from the initcall sequence */
        flush_scheduled_work();
}
```

Basically, the code iterates through all entries in the `.initcall` section whose boundaries are indicated by the variables defined automatically by the linker. The addresses of the functions are extracted, and the functions are invoked. Once all initcalls have been executed, the kernel uses `flush_scheduled_work` to flush any remaining `keventd` work queue entries that may have been created by the routines.

Removing Initialization Data

Functions to initialize data structures and devices are normally needed only when the kernel is booted and are never invoked again. To indicate this explicitly, the kernel defines the __init attribute, which is prefixed to the function declaration as shown previously in the kernel source sections. The attribute is defined as follows:

<init.h>
```
#define __init          __attribute__ ((__section__ (".init.text"))) __cold
#define __initdata      __attribute__ ((__section__ (".init.data")))
```

The kernel also enables data to be declared as initialization data by means of the __initdata attribute.

The linker writes functions labeled with __init or __initdata to a specific section of the binary file as follows (linker scripts on other architectures are almost identical to the Alpha version shown here):

arch/alpha/kernel/vmlinux.lds.S
```
        /* Will be freed after init */
        . = ALIGN(PAGE_SIZE);
        /* Init code and data */
        __init_begin = .;
        .init.text : {
                _sinittext = .;
                *(.init.text)
                _einittext = .;
        }
        .init.data : {
                *(.init.data)
        }

        . = ALIGN(16);
        .init.setup : {
                __setup_start = .;
                *(.init.setup)
                __setup_end = .;
        }

        . = ALIGN(8);
        .initcall.init : {
```

```
                    __initcall_start = .;
                    INITCALLS
                    __initcall_end = .;
            }
    ...

        . = ALIGN(2 * PAGE_SIZE);
        __init_end = .;
        /* Freed after init ends here */
```

A few other sections are also added to the initialization section that includes, for example, the initcalls discussed previously. However, for the sake of clarity, this appendix does not describe all data and function types removed from memory by the kernel on completion of booting.

`free_initmem` is one of the last actions invoked by `init` to free kernel memory between `__init_begin` and `__init_end`. The value of the variable is set automatically by the linker as follows:

arch/i386/mm/init.c
```
void free_init_pages(char *what, unsigned long begin, unsigned long end)
{
        unsigned long addr;

        for (addr = begin; addr < end; addr += PAGE_SIZE) {
                ClearPageReserved(virt_to_page(addr));
                init_page_count(virt_to_page(addr));
                memset((void *)addr, POISON_FREE_INITMEM, PAGE_SIZE);
                free_page(addr);
                totalram_pages++;
        }
        printk(KERN_INFO "Freeing %s: %luk freed\n", what, (end - begin) >> 10);
}

void free_initmem(void)
{
        free_init_pages("unused kernel memory",
                        (unsigned long)(&__init_begin),
                        (unsigned long)(&__init_end));
}
```

Although this is an architecture-specific function, its definition is virtually identical on all supported architectures. For brevity's sake, only the IA-32 version is described. The code iterates through the individual pages reserved by the initialization data and returns them to the buddy system using `free_page`. A message is then output indicating how much memory was freed, usually around 200 KiB.

Starting Userspace Initialization

As its final action, `init` invokes `init_post` — which, in turn, launches a program that continues initialization in userspace in order to provide users with a system on which they can work. Under UNIX and Linux, this task is traditionally delegated to `/sbin/init`. If this program is not available, the kernel tries a number of alternatives. The name of an alternative program can be passed to the kernel by `init=program` in the command line. An attempt is then made to start this program before the default options (the name is held in `execute_command` when the command line is parsed). If none of the options functions, a kernel panic is triggered because the system is unusable, as shown here:

init/main.c
```
static int noinline init_post(void)
{
        if (execute_command) {
                run_init_process(execute_command);
                printk(KERN_WARNING "Failed to execute %s. Attempting "
                "defaults...\n", execute_command);
        }
        run_init_process("/sbin/init");
        run_init_process("/etc/init");
        run_init_process("/bin/init");
        run_init_process("/bin/sh");

        panic("No init found. Try passing init= option to kernel.");
}
```

`run_init_post` sets up a minimal environment for the `init` process as follows:

init/main.c
```
static char * argv_init[MAX_INIT_ARGS+2] = { "init", NULL, };
char * envp_init[MAX_INIT_ENVS+2] = { "HOME=/", "TERM=linux", NULL, };

static void run_init_process(char *init_filename)
{
        argv_init[0] = init_filename;
        kernel_execve(init_filename, argv_init, envp_init);
}
```

`kernel_execve` is a wrapper for the `sys_execve` system call, which must be provided by each architecture.

D.3   Summary

Booting the Linux kernel is a highly architecture-specific process, at least for the initial stages. This chapter introduced you to some of the intricacies to get a kernel up and running on IA-32 systems. Additionally, this chapter discussed the higher-level startup process in which the kernel sets up the hardware step-by-step until it can finally invoke the first userland process (usually /sbin/init) and can commence its regular execution.

The ELF Binary Format

ELF stands for *Executable and Linkable Format*. It is the file format used for executable files, object files, and libraries. It has long established itself as the standard format under Linux and has replaced the a.out format of the early years. The particular benefit of ELF is that the same file format can be used on practically all architectures supported by the kernel. This simplifies not only the creation of userspace tools, but also programming of the kernel itself — for example, when it is necessary to generate load routines for executable files. However, the fact that the file *format* is the same does *not* mean that binary compatibility exists between the programs of different systems — between FreeBSD and Linux, for instance, both of which use ELF as their binary format. Although both *organize* the data in their files in the same way, there are still differences in the system call mechanism and in the semantics of the system calls. This is the reason why FreeBSD programs cannot run under Linux without an intermediate emulation layer (the reverse is naturally also true). Understandably, binary programs cannot be swapped between different architectures (for example, Linux binaries compiled for Alpha CPUs cannot execute on Sparc Linux), because the underlying architectures are totally different. However, thanks to ELF, the way in which information on programs and their components is coded in the binary file is the same in all cases.

Linux employs ELF not only for userspace applications and libraries, but also to build modules. The kernel itself is also generated in ELF.

ELF is an open format whose specification is freely available (also on the Web site associated with this book). This appendix is structured in the same way as the specification and summarizes information that is relevant.

E.1 Layout and Structure

As Figure E-1 shows, ELF files consist of various parts. Note that in this context, a distinction must be made between link objects and executable files:

❑ In addition to a few bytes that identify the file as an ELF file, the ELF header holds information on the file type and size or on the entry point at which program execution starts when the file is loaded.

Appendix E: The ELF Binary Format

❑ The program header table provides the system with information on how the data of an executable file is to be arranged in the virtual address space of a process. It also indicates how many sections the file may contain, where they are located, and what purpose they serve.

❑ The individual sections hold the various forms of data associated with a file; for example, the symbol table, the actual binary code or fixed values such as strings, or numeric constants used by the program.

❑ The section header table contains additional information on the individual sections.

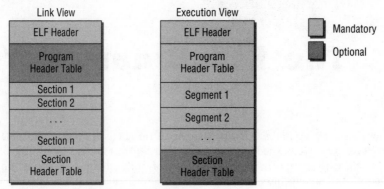

Figure E-1: Basic layout of ELF files.

readelf is a useful tool for analyzing the structure of ELF files, as demonstrated in the following simple program.

```c
#include<stdio.h>

int add (int a, int b) {
  printf("Numbers are added together\n");
  return a+b;
}

int main() {
  int a,b;
  a = 3;
  b = 4;
  int ret = add(a,b);
  printf("Result: %u\n");
  exit(0);
}
```

Of course, this program is not necessarily the most useful of its kind, but it serves as a good example to illustrate how an executable file and an object file are generated:

```
wolfgang@meitner> gcc test.c -o test
wolfgang@meitner> gcc test.c -c -o test.o
```

file shows that the compiler has generated two ELF files — an executable file and a relocatable object file.

```
wolfgang@meitner> file test
filetest: ELF 32-bit LSB executable, Intel 80386, version 1, dynamically linked
(uses shared libs), not stripped
wolfgang@meitner> file test.o
test.o: ELF 32-bit LSB relocatable, Intel 80386, version 1, not stripped
```

E.1.1 ELF Header

Ths section uses readelf to examine the constituent elements of both files.[1] First, consider the ELF header:

```
wolfgang@meitner> readelf test
ELF Header:
  Magic:    7f 45 4c 46 01 01 01 00 00 00 00 00 00 00 00 00
  Class:                             ELF32
  Data:                              2's complement, little endian
  Version:                           1 (current)
  OS/ABI:                            UNIX - System V
  ABI Version:                       0
  Type:                              EXEC (Executable file)
  Machine:                           Intel 80386
  Version:                           0x1
  Entry point address:               0x80482d0
  Start of program headers:          52 (bytes into file)
  Start of section headers:          10148 (bytes into file)
  Flags:                             0x0
  Size of this header:               52 (bytes)
  Size of program headers:           32 (bytes)
  Number of program headers:         6
  Size of section headers:           40 (bytes)
  Number of section headers:         29
  Section header string table index: 26
```

There are four identification bytes at the top of the file. An ASCII code 0x7f character is followed by the ASCII values of the characters E (0x45), L (0x4c), and F (0x46). This enables all ELF processing tools to recognize that the file is of the desired format. There is also some information on the specific architecture — in this case, a Pentium III system that is IA32-compatible. The class information (ELF32) correctly indicates that this is a 32-bit machine (on Alphas, IA-64, Sparc64, and other 64-bit platforms, the value in this field would be ELF64).

The file type is EXEC, meaning that the file is executable. The version field enables a distinction to be made between the various revisions of the ELF standard. However, because version 1 is still current, this feature is not needed at the moment. Also included is information on the size and index positions of various constituents of the ELF file (discussed in more detail later). Because the size of the sections may vary from program to program, the corresponding data must be supplied in the header.

---

[1]The program has more command-line options than those shown here. They are documented on the manual page readelf(1) and can be displayed using readelf-help.

Which fields differ if you look at an object file instead of an executable file? For the sake of simplicity, this appendix deals only with the following fields displayed by `readelf`:

```
wolfgang@meitner> readelf -h test.o
...
   Type:                              REL (Relocatable file)
...
   Start of program headers:          0 (bytes into file)
...
   Size of program headers:           0 (bytes)
   Number of program headers:         0
...
```

The file type is shown as REL. In other words it is a relocatable file whose code can be moved to any position.[2] The file has no program header table because this is not needed for link objects — for this reason, all sizes are set to 0:

E.1.2   Program Header Table

The following is the program header table in an executable file (object files have no such table):

```
wolfgang@meitner> readelf -l test

Elf file type is EXEC (Executable file)
Entry point 0x80482d0
There are 6 program headers, starting at offset 52

Program Headers:
   Type         Offset   VirtAddr   PhysAddr   FileSiz MemSiz  Flg Align
   PHDR         0x000034 0x08048034 0x08048034 0x000c0 0x000c0 R E 0x4
   INTERP       0x0000f4 0x080480f4 0x080480f4 0x00013 0x00013 R   0x1
      [Requesting program interpreter: /lib/ld-linux.so.2]
   LOAD         0x000000 0x08048000 0x08048000 0x0046d 0x0046d R E 0x1000
   LOAD         0x000470 0x08049470 0x08049470 0x00108 0x0010c RW  0x1000
   DYNAMIC      0x000480 0x08049480 0x08049480 0x000c8 0x000c8 RW  0x4
   NOTE         0x000108 0x08048108 0x08048108 0x00020 0x00020 R   0x4

 Section to Segment mapping:
  Segment Sections...
   00
   01     .interp
   02     .interp .note.ABI-tag .hash .dynsym .dynstr .gnu.version
          .gnu.version_r .rel.dyn .rel.plt .init .plt .text .fini .rodata
   03     .data .eh_frame .dynamic .ctors .dtors .jcr .got .bss
   04     .dynamic
   05     .note.ABI-tag
```

Six sections are listed under `Program Headers` — these constitute the final program in memory. Information on size and position in virtual and physical address space,[3] flags, access authorizations, and

---

[2]In particular, this means that relative branch addresses must be used instead of absolute addresses in assembly language code.

[3]The physical address information is ignored because this information is allocated dynamically by the kernel depending on which physical page frames are mapped onto the corresponding positions in virtual address space. This information is of relevance only on systems that have no MMU and therefore no virtual memory — on small embedded processors, for instance.

alignment is provided for each section. A type is also specified to describe the section more precisely. The sample program includes five different types with the following meanings:

- ❏ PHDR holds the program header table in memory.

- ❏ INTERP specifies which interpreter must be called once the program has been mapped from the executable file into memory. In this context, interpreter does *not* mean that the contents of the binary file must be interpreted by a further program, as is the case with Java byte code and with the Java Virtual Machine (JVM). It refers to a program that satisfies unresolved references by linking additional libraries.

  Normally, /lib/ld-linux.so.2, /lib/ld-linux-ia-64.so.2 and so on, is used to insert the required dynamic libraries in virtual address space. The C standard library libc.so must be mapped for almost all programs, and various libraries are added to is, such as GTK, the mathematical library, libjpeg, and many more.

- ❏ LOAD denotes a section that is mapped from the binary file into virtual address space. It holds constant data (such as strings), the object code of the program, and so on.

- ❏ DYNAMIC sections hold information used by the dynamic linker (i.e., by the interpreter specified in INTERP).

- ❏ NOTE holds proprietary information, which is not relevant to the current topic.

The various segments in virtual address space are filled with the data of specific sections in the ELF file. The second part of the readelf output therefore specifies which sections are loaded into which segment (Section to Segment Mapping).

> These are not segments as used in IA32 processors to implement different isolated ranges of virtual address space but are simply address space areas.

Other platforms adopt basically the same approach, but different sections are mapped into the individual areas depending on the particular architecture, as the following IA-64 example shows:

```
wolfgang@meitner> readelf -l test_ia64
Elf file type is EXEC (Executable file)
Entry point 0x40000000000004e0
There are 7 program headers, starting at offset 64

Program Headers:
  Type           Offset             VirtAddr           PhysAddr
                 FileSiz            MemSiz              Flags  Align
  PHDR           0x0000000000000040 0x4000000000000040 0x4000000000000040
                 0x0000000000000188 0x0000000000000188  R E    8
  INTERP         0x00000000000001c8 0x40000000000001c8 0x40000000000001c8
                 0x0000000000000018 0x0000000000000018  R      1
      [Requesting program interpreter: /lib/ld-linux-ia64.so.2]
  LOAD           0x0000000000000000 0x4000000000000000 0x4000000000000000
                 0x00000000000009f0 0x00000000000009f0  R E    10000
  LOAD           0x00000000000009f0 0x60000000000009f0 0x60000000000009f0
                 0x0000000000000270 0x0000000000000280  RW     10000
  DYNAMIC        0x00000000000009f8 0x60000000000009f8 0x60000000000009f8
```

```
                      0x00000000000001a0 0x00000000000001a0  RW     8
    NOTE              0x00000000000001e0 0x40000000000001e0 0x40000000000001e0
                      0x0000000000000020 0x0000000000000020  R      4
IA_64_UNWIND          0x0000000000000009a8 0x40000000000009a8 0x40000000000009a8
                      0x0000000000000048 0x0000000000000048  R      8
```

```
Section to Segment mapping:
 Segment Sections...
  00
  01     .interp
  02     .interp .note.ABI-tag .hash .dynsym .dynstr .gnu.version .gnu.version_r
         .rela.IA_64.pltoff .init .plt .text .fini .rodata .opd
         .IA_64.unwind_info .IA_64.unwind
  03     .data .dynamic .ctors .dtors .jcr .got .IA_64.pltoff .sdata .sbss .bss
  04     .dynamic
  05     .note.ABI-tag
  06     .IA_64.unwind
```

Notwithstanding the fact that 64-bit addresses are used, it is also apparent that a further section of the IA_64_UNWIND type has been added. This section stores *unwind information* that is used to analyze stack frames (if, for example, a backtrace is to be generated) because, for architecture-specific reasons, this cannot be done on IA-64 systems by simply analyzing the stack contents.[4] The exact meanings of the various sections are discussed next.

> The segments can overlap, as the `readelf` output for IA-32 shows. Segment 02 of type **LOAD** extends from 0x08048000 to 0x8048000 + 0x0046d = 0x0804846d. It contains the `.note.ABI-tag` segment. However, the same area in virtual address space is used to implement segment 06 (of the **NOTE** type) that extends from 0x08048108 to 0x08048108 + 0x00020 = 0x08048128 and therefore lies *within* segment 02. This behavior is explicitly allowed by the standard.

E.1.3 Sections

The contents of segments are described by specifying the sections whose data are to be copied into the segments. A further table known as a *section header table* is used to manage the sections of a file, as shown in Figure E-1. Again, `readelf` can be used to display the sections of a file, like this:

```
wolfgang@meitner> readelf -S test.o
There are 10 section headers, starting at offset 0x114:

Section Headers:
  [Nr] Name              Type            Addr     Off    Size   ES Flg Lk Inf Al
  [ 0]                   NULL            00000000 000000 000000 00     0   0   0
  [ 1] .text             PROGBITS        00000000 000034 000065 00  AX 0   0   4
  [ 2] .rel.text         REL             00000000 000374 000030 08     8   1   4
```

---

[4]IA-64 uses *register stacks* to store the local variables of a procedure. The processor automatically reserves a window in the comprehensive processor register set for this purpose. Depending on requirements, parts of these registers can be swapped out into memory transparently to the program. Because the size of the register stacks is different for each procedure and different registers may be swapped out depending on the call chain, a backtrace can no longer be generated by simply running backward through the stack frames by means of the frame pointers, as is possible in most other architectures. IA-64 machines require the saved unwind information.

```
[ 3] .data        PROGBITS    00000000 00009c 000000 00  WA  0   0  4
[ 4] .bss         NOBITS      00000000 00009c 000000 00  WA  0   0  4
[ 5] .rodata      PROGBITS    00000000 00009c 000025 00   A  0   0  1
[ 6] .comment     PROGBITS    00000000 0000c1 000012 00       0   0  1
[ 7] .shstrtab    STRTAB      00000000 0000d3 000041 00       0   0  1
[ 8] .symtab      SYMTAB      00000000 0002a4 0000b0 10       9   7  4
[ 9] .strtab      STRTAB      00000000 000354 00001d 00       0   0  1
Key to Flags:
  W (write), A (alloc), X (execute), M (merge), S (strings)
  I (info), L (link order), G (group), x (unknown)
  O (extra OS processing required) o (OS specific), p (processor specific)
```

The specified offset (in this case, 0x114) refers to the binary file. The section information need not be copied into the final process image created in virtual address space for executable files. Nevertheless, the information is always present in the binary file.

Each section is assigned a type that defines the semantics of the section data. The most important values in the example are PROGBITS (information that the program must interpret; binary code, for example[5]), SYMTAB (symbol table), and REL (relocation information). STRTAB is used to store strings relevant to the ELF format but not directly linked with the program; for example, symbolic names of sections such as .text or .comment.

The section size and its offset within the binary file are specified for each section. The address field can be used to specify at which position in virtual space the section is to be loaded. However, because the example deals with a link object, the destination address is not defined and is therefore represented by the value 0. Flags indicate how the individual sections may be accessed or how they are to be handled. The A flag is of particular interest because it governs whether section data are to be copied into virtual address space when the file is loaded.

Although the names of sections are freely selectable,[6] Linux (and all other UNIX look-alikes that use ELF) features a number of standard sections, some of which are mandatory. There is always a section named .text that holds the binary code, and therefore the program information linked with the file. .rel.text holds relocation information (which is discussed later in this appendix) for the text section.

Executable files contain additional information, as shown here:

```
wolfgang@meitner> readelf -S test
There are 29 section headers, starting at offset 0x27a4:

Section Headers:
  [Nr] Name          Type      Addr     Off    Size   ES Flg Lk Inf Al
  [ 0]               NULL      00000000 000000 000000 00      0   0  0
  [ 1] .interp       PROGBITS  080480f4 0000f4 000013 00  A   0   0  1
  [ 2] .note.ABI-tag NOTE      08048108 000108 000020 00  A   0   0  4
  [ 3] .hash         HASH      08048128 000128 000030 04  A   4   0  4
  [ 4] .dynsym       DYNSYM    08048158 000158 000070 10  A   5   1  4
  [ 5] .dynstr       STRTAB    080481c8 0001c8 00005e 00  A   0   0  1
  [ 6] .gnu.version  VERSYM    08048226 000226 00000e 02  A   4   0  2
```

---

[5]The binary code of a program is often referred to as *text* but what is meant is, of course, binary information as used for machine code.

[6]Sections whose names begin with a dot are used by the system itself. If an application wants to define its own sections, they should not start with a dot so that conflicts with system section names are avoided.

[7]	.gnu.version_r	VERNEED	08048234	000234	000020	00	A	5	1	4
[8]	.rel.dyn	REL	08048254	000254	000008	08	A	4	0	4
[9]	.rel.plt	REL	0804825c	00025c	000018	08	A	4	b	4
[10]	.init	PROGBITS	08048274	000274	000018	00	AX	0	0	4
[11]	.plt	PROGBITS	0804828c	00028c	000040	04	AX	0	0	4
[12]	.text	PROGBITS	080482d0	0002d0	000150	00	AX	0	0	16
[13]	.fini	PROGBITS	08048420	000420	00001e	00	AX	0	0	4
[14]	.rodata	PROGBITS	08048440	000440	00002d	00	A	0	0	4
[15]	.data	PROGBITS	08049470	000470	00000c	00	WA	0	0	4
[16]	.eh_frame	PROGBITS	0804947c	00047c	000004	00	WA	0	0	4
[17]	.dynamic	DYNAMIC	08049480	000480	0000c8	08	WA	5	0	4
[18]	.ctors	PROGBITS	08049548	000548	000008	00	WA	0	0	4
[19]	.dtors	PROGBITS	08049550	000550	000008	00	WA	0	0	4
[20]	.jcr	PROGBITS	08049558	000558	000004	00	WA	0	0	4
[21]	.got	PROGBITS	0804955c	00055c	00001c	04	WA	0	0	4
[22]	.bss	NOBITS	08049578	000578	000004	00	WA	0	0	4
[23]	.stab	PROGBITS	00000000	000578	0007b0	0c		24	0	4
[24]	.stabstr	STRTAB	00000000	000d28	001933	00		0	0	1
[25]	.comment	PROGBITS	00000000	00265b	00006c	00		0	0	1
[26]	.shstrtab	STRTAB	00000000	0026c7	0000dd	00		0	0	1
[27]	.symtab	SYMTAB	00000000	002c2c	000450	10		28	31	4
[28]	.strtab	STRTAB	00000000	00307c	0001dd	00		0	0	1

Key to Flags:
W (write), A (alloc), X (execute), M (merge), S (strings)
I (info), L (link order), G (group), x (unknown)
O (extra OS processing required) o (OS specific), p (processor specific)

In contrast to the 10 sections of object files, executable files have 29 sections, not all of which are relevant to the topic at hand. The following sections are of particular relevance:

❏ .interp holds the filename of the interpreter as an ASCII string.

❏ .data holds initialized data that is part of the normal program data and can be modified at program run time (for example, pre-initialized structures).

❏ .rodata holds *read-only* data that can be read but not modified. For example, the compiler packs all static strings that occur in printf statements into this section.

❏ .init and .fini hold code for process initialization and termination. These sections are usually added automatically by the compiler and are not checked by the application programmer.

❏ .hash is a hash table that permits rapid access to all symbol table entries without performing a linear search across all table elements.

The address fields of the sections (for executable files) hold valid values because the code must be mapped to certain defined positions in virtual address space. (Under Linux, the memory area above 0x08000000 is used for applications.)

E.1.4 Symbol Table

The symbol table is an important part of each ELF file, because it holds all (global) variables and functions implemented or used by a program. Symbols are referred to as *undefined* if a program references a symbol that is not defined in its own code (in the example, the printf function that is included in the C standard library). References of this kind must be resolved during static linking with other object modules or libraries or by means of dynamic linking at load time (using `ld-linux.so`). The nm tool generates a list of all symbols defined and used by a program, as shown here:

```
wolfgang@meitner> nm test.o
00000000 T add
         U exit
0000001a T main
         U printf
```

The left column shows the symbol value — the object file position at which the symbol definition is located. The example includes two different symbol types — functions defined in the text segment (as indicated by the abbreviation T) and undefined references indicated by a U. Logically, the undefined references do not have a symbol value.

Many more symbols appear in executable files. However, because most are generated automatically by the compiler and are used for internal purposes of the runtime system, the following example shows only the elements that also appeared in the object file:

```
wolfgang@meitner> nm test
08048388 T add
         U exit@@GLIBC_2.0
080483a2 T main
         U printf@@GLIBC_2.0
```

`exit` and `printf` remain undefined, but in the meantime, information has been added indicating the earliest version of the GNU standard library from which the functions must be taken (in the example, no version earlier than 2.0 may be used, which means that the program does not function with Libc5 and Libc4[7]). The add and main symbols defined by the program have been moved to fixed positions in virtual address space (their code was mapped to these positions when the file was loaded).

How is the symbol table mechanism implemented in ELF? The following three sections are used to accept the relevant data:

❑   `.symtab` establishes the link between the name of a symbol and its value. However, the symbol name is not coded directly as a string but indirectly as a number that is used as an index into a string array.

❑   `.strtab` holds the string array.

❑   `.hash` holds a hash table that helps find symbols quickly.

Expressed in simple terms, each entry in the `.symtab` section consists of two elements — the position of the name in the string table and the associated value. (As you will see next, the real situation is a little more complicated, because more information needs to be considered for each entry.)

E.1.5 String Tables

Figure E-2 shows how string tables are implemented to manage strings for ELF files.

---

[7]The version numbering seems rather strange but is correct. Libc4 and Libc5 were special C standard libraries for Linux — Glibc 2.0 was the first cross-system variant of the library that replaced the old versions.

Figure E-2: String table for ELF files.

The first byte of the table is a null byte, followed by strings separated by null bytes.

To reference a string, a position must be specified that is an index into the array. This selects all characters before the next null byte (if the position of a null byte is used as an index, this corresponds to an empty string). This supports the (very limited) use of substrings by allowing not just the start position but any position in the middle of a string to be selected as an index.

.strtab is not the only string table found by default in an ELF file. .shstrtab is used to hold the text names of the individual sections (.text, for example) in the file.

E.2 Data Structures in the Kernel

The ELF file format is used at two points in the kernel. First, it is used to handle executable files and libraries, and then to implement modules. Different code is used at each of these points to read and manipulate data, but both instances make use of the data structres introduced in this section. The basis is the header file <elf.h>, in which the specifications of the standard are implemented virtually unchanged.

E.2.1 Data Types

Because ELF is a processor- and architecture-independent format, it cannot rely on a specific word length or data alignment (little or big endian) — at least not for elements of the file that need to be read and understood on all systems. (Machine code, as occurs in the .text segment, is stored as a representation of the host system so that no unwieldy conversion operations are needed.) For this reason the kernel defines a number of data types that have the same bit number on all architectures, as shown here:

```
<elf.h>
/* 32-bit ELF base types. */
typedef __u32   Elf32_Addr;
typedef __u16   Elf32_Half;
typedef __u32   Elf32_Off;
typedef __s32   Elf32_Sword;
typedef __u32   Elf32_Word;

/* 64-bit ELF base types. */
typedef __u64   Elf64_Addr;
typedef __u16   Elf64_Half;
typedef __s16   Elf64_SHalf;
typedef __u64   Elf64_Off;
typedef __s32   Elf64_Sword;
typedef __u32   Elf64_Word;
typedef __u64   Elf64_Xword;
typedef __s64   Elf64_Sxword;
```

Because the architecture-specific code must always clearly define integer data types with their sign and bit number, the data types required by the ELF standard can be implemented as direct typedefs with little effort.

E.2.2 Headers

A separate data structure for 32-bit and 64-bit systems is available for the various headers in ELF format:

ELF Header

On 32-bit architectures, the identification header is represented by the following data structure:

<elf.h>
```
typedef struct elf32_hdr{
  unsigned char e_ident[EI_NIDENT];
  Elf32_Half    e_type;
  Elf32_Half    e_machine;
  Elf32_Word    e_version;
  Elf32_Addr    e_entry;  /* Entry point */
  Elf32_Off     e_phoff;
  Elf32_Off     e_shoff;
  Elf32_Word    e_flags;
  Elf32_Half    e_ehsize;
  Elf32_Half    e_phentsize;
  Elf32_Half    e_phnum;
  Elf32_Half    e_shentsize;
  Elf32_Half    e_shnum;
  Elf32_Half    e_shstrndx;
} Elf32_Ehdr;
```

The entries have the following meanings:

❏ e_ident accepts 16 (EI_NIDENT) bytes represented by the char data type on all architectures. The first four bytes hold a null byte and the letters E, L, and F, as discussed previously. A number of other bit positions have specific meanings.

> ❏ EI_CLASS (4) identifies the class of the file to distinguish between 32-bit and 64-bit files. Currently, defined values are therefore ELFCLASS32 and ELFCLASS64.[8]

> ❏ EI_DATA (5) specifies which endian the format uses. ELFDATA2LSB stands for *least significant byte* (and therefore, little endian), and ELFDATA2MSB stands for *most significant byte* (and therefore, big endian).

> ❏ EI_VERSION (6) indicates the file version of the ELF header (this version is potentially independent of the data section version). Currently, only EV_CURRENT — which corresponds to the first version — is permitted.

> ❏ As of EI_PAD (7), the identification part of the header is padded with null bytes because the remaining positions are not needed (at the moment).

❏ e_type distinguishes between the various ELF file types listed in Table E-1.

---

[8]In this case, and many other cases, the ELF standard defines constants that stand for "undefined" or "invalid." For the sake of simplicity, they are not included in this description.

Appendix E: The ELF Binary Format

Table E-1: ELF File Types

Value	Meaning
ET_REL	Relocatable file (object file)
ET_EXEC	Executable file
ET_DYN	Dynamic library
ET_CORE	Core dump

❑   e_machine specifies the required architecture for the file. Table E-2 lists the various options available and supported by Linux. Note that every architecture needs to define the function elf_check_arch, which is used by the generic code to ensure that the ELF file that is loaded is indeed the right one for the architecture.

❑   e_version holds version information to distinguish between ELF variants. However, at the moment only version 1 of the specification is defined. It is represented by EV_CURRENT.

❑   e_entry gives the entry point in virtual memory. This is where execution begins once the program has been loaded and mapped into memory.

❑   e_phoff holds the offset at which the program header table is located in the binary file.

❑   e_shoff holds the offset at which the section header table is located.

❑   e_flags can hold processor-specific flags. Currently, these are not used by the kernel.

❑   e_ehsize specifies the header size in bytes.

❑   e_phentsize specifies the size, in bytes, of an entry in the program header table (all entries are the same size).

❑   e_phnum specifies the number of entries in the program header table.

❑   e_shentsize specifies the size, in bytes, of an entry in the section header table (all entries are the same size).

❑   e_shnum specifies the number of entries in the section header table.

❑   e_shstrndx holds the index position of the string table containing the section names in the header table.

A 64-bit data structure is defined in the same way. The only difference is that the corresponding 64-bit data types are used in place of their 32-bit equivalents, thus making the header a little larger. However, the first 16 bytes are identical in both variants. Both architecture types are able to recognize ELF files for machines with different word lengths by reference to these bytes, as shown here:

```
<elf.h>
typedef struct elf64_hdr {
  unsigned char e_ident[16];            /* ELF "magic number" */
  Elf64_Half e_type;
  Elf64_Half e_machine;
  Elf64_Word e_version;
  Elf64_Addr e_entry;            /* Entry point virtual address */
  Elf64_Off e_phoff;            /* Program header table file offset */
```

```
        Elf64_Off  e_shoff;              /* Section header table file offset */
        Elf64_Word e_flags;
        Elf64_Half e_ehsize;
        Elf64_Half e_phentsize;
        Elf64_Half e_phnum;
        Elf64_Half e_shentsize;
        Elf64_Half e_shnum;
        Elf64_Half e_shstrndx;
    } Elf64_Ehdr;
```

Table E-2: Architectures Supported by ELF

Value	Architecture
EM_SPARC	32-bit Sparc
EM_SPARC32PLUS	32-bit Sparc ("v8 Plus")
EM_SPARCV9	64-bit Sparc
EM_386 and ELF_486	IA-32
EM_IA_64	IA-64
EM_X86_64	AMD64
EM_68K	Motorola 68k
EM_MIPS	Mips
EM_PARISC	Hewlet-Packard PA-Risc
EM_PPC	PowerPC
EM_PPC64	PowerPC 64
EM_SH	Hitachi SuperH
EM_S390	IBM S/390
EM_S390_OLD	Former interim value for S390
EM_CRIS	Axis Communications Cris
EM_V850	NEC v850
EM_H8_300H	Hitachi H8/300H
EM_ALPHA	Alpha AXP
EM_M32R	Renseas M32R
EM_H8_300	Renseas H8/300
EM_FRV	Fujitsu FR-V

Program Header

The program header table consists of several entries that are handled in the same way as the entries of an array (the number of entries is specified by e_phnum in the ELF header). A separate structure is defined as a data type for the entries. On 32-bit systems, it has the following contents:

<elf.h>
```
typedef struct elf32_phdr{
   Elf32_Word    p_type;
   Elf32_Off     p_offset;
   Elf32_Addr    p_vaddr;
   Elf32_Addr    p_paddr;
   Elf32_Word    p_filesz;
   Elf32_Word    p_memsz;
   Elf32_Word    p_flags;
   Elf32_Word    p_align;
} Elf32_Phdr;
```

The meaning of the elements is as follows:

❑ p_type indicates what kind of segment the current entry describes. The following constants are defined for this purpose:

  ❑ PT_NULL indicates an unused segment.

  ❑ PT_LOAD is used for loadable segments that are mapped from the binary file into memory before the program can be executed.

  ❑ PT_DYNAMIC indicates that the segment contains information for the dynamic linker (discussed in Section E.2.6).

  ❑ PT_INTERP indicates that the current segment specifies the program interpreter used for dynamic linking. Usually, this is ld-linux.so as previously mentioned.

  ❑ PT_NOTE specifies a segment that may contain additional proprietary compiler information.

Two further variants (PT_LOPROC and PT_HIGHPROC) are defined for processor-specific purposes but are not used by the kernel.

❑ p_offset gives the offset (in bytes from the beginning of the binary file) at which the data of the segment described resides.

❑ p_vaddr gives the position in virtual address space to which the data of the segment is mapped (for segments of the PT_LOAD type). Systems that support physical but not virtual addressing use the information stored in p_paddr instead.

❑ p_filesz specifies the size (in bytes) of the segment in the binary file.

❑ p_memsz specifies the size (in bytes) of the segment in virtual address space. Size differences as compared with the physical segments are compensated by truncating data or padding with null bytes.

❑ p_flags holds flags to define access permissions to the segment. PF_R gives read permission, PF_W gives write permission, and PF_X gives execute permission.

❑ p_align specifies how the segment is to be aligned in memory and in the binary file (the p_vaddr and p_offset addresses must be modulo p_align). A p_align value of $0x1000 = 4096$ means, for example, that the segment must be aligned on 4 KiB pages.

As you can see in the following code, a similar data structure is defined for 64-bit architectures. The only difference as compared to the 32-bit variant is that other data types are used. Nevertheless, the meaning of the entries is the same:

<elf.h>

```
typedef struct elf64_phdr {
  Elf64_Word p_type;
  Elf64_Word p_flags;
  Elf64_Off p_offset;                /* Segment file offset */
  Elf64_Addr p_vaddr;                /* Segment virtual address */
  Elf64_Addr p_paddr;                /* Segment physical address */
  Elf64_Xword p_filesz;              /* Segment size in file */
  Elf64_Xword p_memsz;               /* Segment size in memory */
  Elf64_Xword p_align;               /* Segment alignment, file & memory */
} Elf64_Phdr;
```

Section Header

The section header table is implemented by means of an array in which each entry contains a section. The individual sections form the contents of the segments defined in the program header table. The following data structure represents a section:

<elf.h>

```
typedef struct {
  Elf32_Word    sh_name;
  Elf32_Word    sh_type;
  Elf32_Word    sh_flags;
  Elf32_Addr    sh_addr;
  Elf32_Off     sh_offset;
  Elf32_Word    sh_size;
  Elf32_Word    sh_link;
  Elf32_Word    sh_info;
  Elf32_Word    sh_addralign;
  Elf32_Word    sh_entsize;
} Elf32_Shdr;
```

The elements have the following meanings:

❑ sh_name specifies the name of the section. Its value is not the string itself but an index into the section header string table.

❑ sh_type specifies the section type. The following section types are available:

  ❑ SH_NULL indicates that the section is not used. Its data are ignored.

  ❑ SH_PROGBITS holds program-specific information whose format is undefined and is irrelevant to this discussion.

  ❑ SH_SYMTAB holds a symbol table whose structure is discussed in Section E.2.4. SH_DYNSYM also holds a symbol table. The difference between these two types is discussed later in this appendix.

  ❑ SH_STRTAB indicates a section that contains a string table.

  ❑ SH_RELA and SHT_RELA hold relocation sections whose structure is discussed in Section E.2.5.

❏   SH_HASH defines a section that holds a hash table so that entries in symbol tables can be found more quickly (as mentioned previously).

❏   SH_DYNAMIC holds information on dynamic linking, as discussed in Section E.2.6.

The type values SHT_HIPROC, SHT_LOPROC, SHT_HIUSER, and SHT_LOUSER also exist. They are reserved for processor- and application-specific purposes and are of no further interest here.

❏   sh_flags indicate the following: whether the section can be written to (SHF_WRITE), whether virtual memory is to be reserved (SHF_ALLOC), and whether the section contains executable machine code (SHF_EXECINSTR).

❏   sh_addr specifies the position in virtual address space to which the section is to be mapped.

❏   sh_offset specifies the position in the file at which the section begins.

❏   sh_size specifies the size of the section in bytes.

❏   sh_link references another section header table entry that is interpreted differently according to section type. This is discussed in more detail in the next bulleted list.

❏   sh_info is used in conjunction with sh_link. Again, its exact meaning is discussed in the next bulleted list.

❏   sh_addralign specifies how the section data are to be aligned in memory.

❏   sh_entsize specifies the size, in bytes, of the entries of the section if they are all of the same size — such as in a symbol table.

sh_link and sh_info are used with different meanings depending on section type, as described here:

❏   Sections of the SHT_DYMAMIC type use sh_link to reference the string table employed by the section data. sh_info is not used and is therefore set to 0.

❏   Hash tables (sections of the SHT_HASH type) use sh_link to reference the symbol table whose entries are hashed. sh_info is not used.

❏   Relocation sections of the SHT_REL and SHT_RELA type use sh_link to reference the associated symbol table. sh_info holds the index of the section in the section header table to which the relocations refer.

❏   sh_link specifies which string table is used for symbol tables (SHT_SYMTAB and SHT_DYNSYM), and sh_info indicates the index position in the symbol table immediately after the last local symbol (of the STB_LOCAL type).

As usual, there is a separate data structure for 64-bit systems but its contents do not differ from those of the 32-bit variant, as you can see here:

<elf.h>
```
typedef struct elf64_shdr {
  Elf64_Word sh_name;          /* Section name, index in string tbl */
  Elf64_Word sh_type;          /* Type of section */
  Elf64_Xword sh_flags;        /* Miscellaneous section attributes */
  Elf64_Addr sh_addr;          /* Section virtual addr at execution */
  Elf64_Off sh_offset;         /* Section file offset */
  Elf64_Xword sh_size;         /* Size of section in bytes */
  Elf64_Word sh_link;          /* Index of another section */
```

```
    Elf64_Word sh_info;            /* Additional section information */
    Elf64_Xword sh_addralign;      /* Section alignment */
    Elf64_Xword sh_entsize;        /* Entry size if section holds table */
} Elf64_Shdr;
```

The ELF standard defines a number of sections with fixed names. These are used to perform standard tasks needed in most object files. All names begin with a dot to distinguish them from user-defined or non-standard sections. The most important standard sections are as follows:

❑   .bss holds uninitialized data sections of the program that are padded with null bytes before the program begins to run.

❑   .data contains initialized program data — for instance, pre-initialized structures that were filled with static data at compilation time. These data can be changed during program run time.

❑   .rodata holds read-only data that is used by the program but cannot be modified — strings, for example.

❑   .dynamic and .dynstr hold the dynamic information discussed at the end of this appendix.

❑   .interp holds the name of the program interpreter in the form of a string.

❑   .shstrtab contains a string table that defines section names.

❑   .strtab holds a string table that contains primarily the strings required for the symbol table.

❑   .symtab holds the symbol table of the binary file.

❑   .init and .fini hold machine instructions that are executed to initialize or terminate the program. The contents of these sections are usually generated automatically by the compiler and its auxiliary tools in order to create a suitable runtime environment.

❑   .text holds the main machine instructions that make up the actual program.

E.2.3   String Tables

The format of string tables was discussed previously in Section E.1.5. Because their format is very dynamic, the kernel is not able to provide a fixed data structure but must analyze the existing data "manually."

E.2.4   Symbol Tables

Symbol tables hold all the information needed to find program symbols, assign values to them, and relocate them. As already noted, a special section type holds symbol tables. The tables themselves consist of entries whose format is defined by the following data structure:

<elf.h>
```
typedef struct elf32_sym{
  Elf32_Word    st_name;
  Elf32_Addr    st_value;
  Elf32_Word    st_size;
  unsigned char st_info;
  unsigned char st_other;
  Elf32_Half    st_shndx;
} Elf32_Sym;
```

The primary task of a symbol is to associate a string with a value. For example, the `printf` symbol represents the address of the `printf` function in virtual address space where the function machine code resides. Symbols may also have absolute values that are interpreted, for example, as numeric constants.

The exact purpose of a symbol is defined by `st_info`, which is divided into two parts (how the bits are divided between the two parts is not relevant to this discussion). The following information is defined:

❏ The *binding* of the symbol. This determines the visibility of a symbol and allows the following three different settings:

❏ *Local symbols* (`STB_LOCAL`), which are visible only within the object file and are not visible to other parts of the program when combined. There is no problem if several object files of a program define symbols with the same names. As long as they are all local symbols, they do not interfere with each other.

❏ *Global symbols* (`STB_GLOBAL`), which are visible within the object file in which they are defined and can also be referenced by all other object files that make up the program. Each global symbol may be defined only once within a program; otherwise, the linker would report an error.

Undefined references that point to a global symbol are supplied with the symbol position during relocation. If undefined references to global symbols cannot be satisfied, program execution or static binding is rejected.

❏ *Weak symbols* (`STB_WEAK`), which are also visible to the entire program, but can have multiple definitions. If a global symbol and a local symbol have the same name in a program, the global symbol is automatically given precedence.

Programs are statically or dynamically linked even if a weak symbol remains undefined — in this case, the value 0 is assigned.

❏ The symbol *type* is selected from a number of alternatives, of which only the following three are relevant to the current topic (a description of the other alternatives is provided in the ELF standard):

❏ `STT_OBJECT` indicates that the symbol is associated with a data object such as a variable, an array, or a pointer.

❏ `STT_FUNC` is used when the symbol is associated with a function or a procedure.

❏ `STT_NOTYPE` means that the symbol type is not specified. It is used for undefined references.

The `Elf32_Sym` structure includes other elements in addition to `st_name`, `st_value`, and `st_info`. Their meanings are as follows:

❏ `st_size` specifies the size of the object; for example, the length of a pointer or the number of bytes contained in a `struct` object. Its value can be set to 0 if the size is not known.

❏ `st_other` is not used in the current version of the standard.

❏ `st_shndx` holds the index of a section (in the section header table) with which the symbol is bound — it is usually defined in the code of this section. However, the following two values have special meanings:

❑ SHN_ABS specifies that the symbol has an absolute value that will not change because of relocation.

❑ SHN_UNDEF identifies undefined symbols that must be resolved by external sources (such as other object files or libraries).

As expected, there is a 64-bit variant of the symbol table that — with the exception of the data types used — has the same contents as its 32-bit counterpart, as you can see here:

<elf.h>

```
typedef struct elf64_sym {
  Elf64_Word st_name;            /* Symbol name, index in string tbl */
  unsigned char st_info;         /* Type and binding attributes */
  unsigned char st_other;        /* No defined meaning, 0 */
  Elf64_Half st_shndx;           /* Associated section index */
  Elf64_Addr st_value;           /* Value of the symbol */
  Elf64_Xword st_size;           /* Associated symbol size */
} Elf64_Sym;
```

readelf can also be used to find all symbols in the symbol table of a program. The following five entries are especially important for the test.o object file (the other elements are generated automatically by the compiler and are not relevant to this discussion):

```
wolfgang@meitner> readelf -s test.o
   Num:    Value  Size Type    Bind   Vis      Ndx Name
...
     1: 00000000     0 FILE    LOCAL  DEFAULT  ABS test.c
...
     7: 00000000    26 FUNC    GLOBAL DEFAULT    1 add
     8: 00000000     0 NOTYPE  GLOBAL DEFAULT  UND printf
     9: 0000001a    75 FUNC    GLOBAL DEFAULT    1 main
    10: 00000000     0 NOTYPE  GLOBAL DEFAULT  UND exit
```

The name of the source file is stored as an absolute value — it is constant and is not changed by relocations. The local symbol uses the STT_FILE type to link an object file with the name of its source file.

The two functions defined in the file — main and add — are stored as global symbols of the STT_FUNC type. Both symbols refer to segment 1, which is the file text segment that holds the machine code of the two functions.

The printf and exit symbols are undefined references with index UND. Therefore, they must be associated with functions in the standard library (or in some other library that defines symbols with this name) when the program is linked. Because the compiler does not know which type of symbol is involved, the symbol type is STT_NOTYPE.

E.2.5 Relocation Entries

Relocation is the process by which undefined symbols in ELF files are associated with valid values. In the standard example (test.o), this means that undefined references to printf and add must be replaced with the addresses at which the appropriate machine code is located in the virtual address space of the process. Replacement must be performed at all points in the object file where one of the symbols is used.

The kernel is not involved in symbol replacement in userspace programs because all replacement operations are carried out fully by external tools. The situation is different for kernel modules, as demonstrated in Chapter 7. Because the kernel receives the raw data of a module in the exact same form as it is stored in the binary file, the kernel itself is responsible for relocation.

A special table with relocation entries is present in each object file to identify where relocation must be performed. Each table entry holds the following information:

❑ An *offset* that specifies the position of the entry to be modified.

❑ A reference to the symbol (as an index into a symbol table) that supplies the data to be inserted in relocation positions.

To illustrate how relocation information is used, let's revisit the test.c test program described previously. First, all relocation entries in the file are displayed using readelf as follows:

```
wolfgang@meitner> readelf -r test.o
Relocation section '.rel.text' at offset 0x374 contains 6 entries:
 Offset     Info    Type        Sym.Value  Sym. Name
00000009  00000501 R_386_32       00000000   .rodata
0000000e  00000802 R_386_PC32     00000000   printf
00000046  00000702 R_386_PC32     00000000   add
00000050  00000501 R_386_32       00000000   .rodata
00000055  00000802 R_386_PC32     00000000   printf
00000061  00000a02 R_386_PC32     00000000   exit
```

The information in the *Offset* column is used when the machine code references functions or symbols whose position in virtual address space is not clear when the program is run or when test.o is linked to produce an executable file. The assembly language code of main has a number of function calls at the offsets 0x46 (add), 0xe and 0x55 (printf), and 0x61 (exit) — these can be rendered visible using the objdump tool. The relevant lines are shown in italics in the following output:

```
wolfgang@meitner> objdump  - disassemble test.o
...
0000001a <main>:
  1a:   55                      push   %ebp
  1b:   89 e5                   mov    %esp,%ebp
  1d:   83 ec 18                sub    $0x18,%esp
  20:   83 e4 f0                and    $0xfffffff0,%esp
  23:   b8 00 00 00 00          mov    $0x0,%eax
  28:   29 c4                   sub    %eax,%esp
  2a:   c7 45 fc 03 00 00 00    movl   $0x3,0xfffffffc(%ebp)
  31:   c7 45 f8 04 00 00 00    movl   $0x4,0xfffffff8(%ebp)
  38:   8b 45 f8                mov    0xfffffff8(%ebp),%eax
  3b:   89 44 24 04             mov    %eax,0x4(%esp,1)
  3f:   8b 45 fc                mov    0xfffffffc(%ebp),%eax
  42:   89 04 24                mov    %eax,(%esp,1)
  45:   e8 fc ff ff ff          call   46 <main+0x2c>
  4a:   89 45 f4                mov    %eax,0xfffffff4(%ebp)
  4d:   c7 04 24 17 00 00 00    movl   $0x17,(%esp,1)
  54:   e8 fc ff ff ff          call   55 <main+0x3b>
  59:   c7 04 24 00 00 00 00    movl   $0x0,(%esp,1)
  60:   e8 fc ff ff ff          call   61 <main+0x47>
```

Once the addresses of the `printf` and `add` functions have been determined, they must be inserted at the specified offsets in order to generate executable code that runs correctly.

Data Structures

For technical reasons, there are two different types of relocation information that are, unfortunately, represented by slightly different data structures. The first type refers to normal relocation. The relocation table entries in a `SHT_REL` type section are defined by the following data structure:

<elf.h>
```
typedef struct elf32_rel {
    Elf32_Addr     r_offset;
    Elf32_Word     r_info;
} Elf32_Rel;
```

While `r_offset` specifies the position of the entry to be relocated, `r_info` supplies not only a position in the symbol table but also additional information on the type of relocation (as described shortly). This is achieved by splitting the value into two parts (exactly how is not important here).

The alternative type — known as a relocation entry with a constant addend — may occur only in sections of the `SHT_RELA` type. The entries of such sections are defined by the following data structure:

<elf.h>
```
typedef struct elf32_rela{
    Elf32_Addr     r_offset;
    Elf32_Word     r_info;
    Elf32_Sword    r_addend;
} Elf32_Rela;
```

The `r_offset` and `r_info` fields of the first relocation type are supplemented by an `r_addend` element that holds a value known as an *addend*. When the relocation value is computed, this value is treated differently depending on relocation type.

> Notice that the addend value is also present when `elf32_rel` is used. Although it is not explicitly held in the data structure, the linker uses the value located at the memory position where the computed relocation size is to be inserted as the addend. The purpose of this value is illustrated in the following example.

There are functionally equivalent 64-bit data structures for both relocation types:

<elf.h>
```
typedef struct elf64_rel {
    Elf64_Addr r_offset;   /* Location at which to apply the action */
    Elf64_Xword r_info;    /* Index and type of relocation */
} Elf64_Rel;
```

<elf.h>
```
typedef struct elf64_rela {
    Elf64_Addr r_offset;   /* Location at which to apply the action */
    Elf64_Xword r_info;    /* Index and type of relocation */
    Elf64_Sxword r_addend;       /* Constant addend used to compute value */
} Elf64_Rela;
```

Since they are very similar to their 32-bit counterparts, they need no extra description.

Relocation Types

The ELF standard defines a large number of relocation types, and there is a separate set for each supported architecture. Most of the types are used when dynamic libraries or location-independent code are generated. On some platforms — particularly on IA-32 platforms — it is also necessary to compensate for many design errors or historical ballast. Fortunately, the kernel, which is interested only in the relocation of modules, makes do with just the following two relocation types:

❏   PC-relative relocation

❏   Absolute relocation

PC-relative relocation generates relocation entries that point to addresses in memory that are defined relative to the *program counter* (PC).[9] These are needed primarily for subroutine calls. The alternative form of relocation generates absolute addresses, as the name clearly suggests. Typically, these are used to refer to data in memory that is already known at compilation time — for instance, string constants.

On IA-32 systems the two relocation types are represented by the R_386_PC32 constant (PC-relative relocation) and the R_386_32 constant (absolute relocation). The relocation result is computed as follows:

$$\text{R\_386\_32} : Result = S + A$$

$$\text{R\_386\_PC32} : Result = S - P + A$$

A stands for the addend value that, on IA-32 architecture, is supplied implicitly by the memory contents of the relocation position. S is the value of the symbol held in the symbol table, and P stands for the relocation position offset — in other words, the position in the binary file to which the computed data are to be written. If the addend value is 0, absolute relocations simply insert the value of the symbol in the symbol table at the relocation position. In PC-relative relocations, however, the difference between symbol position and relocation position is computed — in other words, a computation is made to determine how many bytes the symbol is from the relocation position.

In both cases, the addend value is added and therefore produces a linear displacement of the result.

Example of Relative Displacements

The test file test.o includes the following call statement:

```
45:     e8 fc ff ff ff          call    46 <main+0x2c>
```

e8 is the opcode of the call statement and 0xfffffffc (little endian notation!) is the value passed to the statement as a parameter. Because IA-32 uses normal relocations instead of add relocations, this value is the addend value. Therefore, 0xfffffffc is not the final address, but must first run through the relocation process. In decimal terms, 0xfffffffc corresponds to the value −4, but it should be noted that 2's complement notation is used to represent signed integers.

---

[9]Reminder: The program counter is a special processor register that defines the position of the processor in the machine code during program execution.

> The `objdump` tool does not show the argument of the `call` statement on the right side, but it automatically recognizes that a relocation entry refers to the corresponding memory position (which is why this information is inserted).

As the relocation table shows, relocation position 46 is an `add` function call.

```
00000046  00000702 R_386_PC32         00000000   add
```

Because the sections of the binary file are moved to their final position in memory before relocation takes place, the position of `add` in memory is already known. For example, if `add` is positioned at 0x08048388, the `main` function should be at position 0x080483a2 — this means that the relocation position to which the relocation result is to be written is at 0x80483ce.

The relocation result is computed by applying the formula for PC-relative relocation:

$$Result = S - P + A$$
$$= 0x08048388 - 0x80483ce + (-4)$$
$$= 134513544 - 134513614 - 4$$
$$= -74$$

The result corresponds to the code in the executable file `test`, as can be confirmed using `objdump`.

```
80483cd:      e8 b6 ff ff ff       call   8048388 <add>
```

0xffffffb6 corresponds to the decimal number −74 (this can easily be checked, assuming that little endian notation and 2's complement notation are taken into account). The symbolic representation on the right side of the output of `objdump` does not show the relative branch address, but it converts the relative address into an absolute value to make it easier for programmers to find the corresponding position in the machine code.

At first glance, the result appears to be incorrect. As you have already seen, the machine code of the `add` statement is 70 bytes (0x46), not 74 bytes, *before* the relocation position. The displacement by 4 bytes is owing to the addend value. Why does the compiler set this value to -4 when generating the object file `test.o` instead of leaving it at 0? The reason has to do with the way in which IA-32 processors work. The program counter always points to the statement that *follows* the statement currently executing — and is therefore 4 bytes "too big"if the processor computes the absolute branch address from the relative address in the machine code. Consequently, the compiler must deduct 4 bytes from the relative branch address to obtain the correct position in the program.

Absolute relocations adopt the same scheme. However, computation is simpler because it is only necessary to combine the destination address of the desired symbol with the addend value.

E.2.6 Dynamic Linking

ELF files that must be linked dynamically with libraries in order to run are of little interest to the kernel. All references in modules can be resolved by means of relocations while dynamic linking of userspace programs is performed entirely by `ld.so` in userspace. Therefore, this appendix only touches upon the meaning of the dynamic sections.

Appendix E: The ELF Binary Format

The following two sections are used to hold data required by the dynamic linker:

❏ .dynsym holds a symbol table with all symbols resolved by means of external references.

❏ .dynamic holds an array with elements of the Elf32_Dyn type — these supply the data described in the following paragraphs.

The contents of .dynsym can be queried using readelf, as shown here:

```
wolfgang@meitner> readelf  - syms test
Symbol table '.dynsym' contains 7 entries:
   Num:    Value  Size Type    Bind   Vis      Ndx Name
     0: 00000000     0 NOTYPE  LOCAL  DEFAULT  UND
     1: 08049474     0 OBJECT  GLOBAL DEFAULT   15 __dso_handle
     2: 0804829c   206 FUNC    GLOBAL DEFAULT  UND __libc_start_main@GLIBC_2.0 (2)
     3: 080482ac    47 FUNC    GLOBAL DEFAULT  UND printf@GLIBC_2.0 (2)
     4: 080482bc   257 FUNC    GLOBAL DEFAULT  UND exit@GLIBC_2.0 (2)
     5: 08048444     4 OBJECT  GLOBAL DEFAULT   14 _IO_stdin_used
     6: 00000000     0 NOTYPE  WEAK   DEFAULT  UND __gmon_start__
   ...
```

The contents include not only a number of symbols added automatically when the executable file is generated, but also the print and exit functions used in the machine code. @GLIBC_2.0 specifies that *at least* version 2.0 of the GNU standard library must be used in order to resolve the references.

The data type of the array entries in the .dynamic section is defined in the kernel as follows, but is not used at all because the information is interpreted in userspace:

<elf.h>
```
typedef struct dynamic{
   Elf32_Sword d_tag;
   union{
    Elf32_Sword d_val;
    Elf32_Addr  d_ptr;
   } d_un;
 } Elf32_Dyn;
```

d_tag is used to distinguish between various tags that specify the type of information described by the entry. d_un holds either a virtual address or an integer that is interpreted differently depending on the particular tag.

The most important tags are as follows:

❏ DT_NEEDED specifies which dynamic libraries are needed to execute the program. d_un points to a string table entry with the name of the library.

Only the C standard library is required for the test.c test application, as the following readelf test shows:

```
wolfgang@meitner> readelf  - dynamic test
Dynamic segment at offset 0x480 contains 20 entries:
  Tag        Type                       Name/Value
 0x00000001 (NEEDED)                    Shared library: [libc.so.6]
  ...
```

1264

Real programs, such as the emacs editor, need a significantly larger number of dynamic libraries in order to run:

```
wolfgang@meitner> readelf  - dynamic /usr/bin/emacs
Dynamic segment at offset 0x1ea6ec contains 36 entries:
  Tag        Type                         Name/Value
 0x00000001 (NEEDED)                      Shared library: [libXaw3d.so.7]
 0x00000001 (NEEDED)                      Shared library: [libXmu.so.6]
 0x00000001 (NEEDED)                      Shared library: [libXt.so.6]
 0x00000001 (NEEDED)                      Shared library: [libSM.so.6]
 0x00000001 (NEEDED)                      Shared library: [libICE.so.6]
 0x00000001 (NEEDED)                      Shared library: [libXext.so.6]
 0x00000001 (NEEDED)                      Shared library: [libtiff.so.3]
 0x00000001 (NEEDED)                      Shared library: [libjpeg.so.62]
 0x00000001 (NEEDED)                      Shared library: [libpng.so.2]
 0x00000001 (NEEDED)                      Shared library: [libz.so.1]
 0x00000001 (NEEDED)                      Shared library: [libm.so.6]
 0x00000001 (NEEDED)                      Shared library: [libungif.so.4]
 0x00000001 (NEEDED)                      Shared library: [libXpm.so.4]
 0x00000001 (NEEDED)                      Shared library: [libX11.so.6]
 0x00000001 (NEEDED)                      Shared library: [libncurses.so.5]
 0x00000001 (NEEDED)                      Shared library: [libc.so.6]
 0x0000000f (RPATH)                       Library rpath: [/usr/X11R6/lib]
  ...
```

❑   DT_STRTAB holds the position of the string table in which the names of all dynamic libraries and symbols required for the dynamic section reside.

❑   DT_SYMTAB holds the position of the symbol table in which all information required for the dynamic section reside.

❑   DT_INIT and DT_FINI hold the addresses of the functions that are called to initialize and terminate the program.

E.3 Summary

The binary code in executable files is arranged according to the ELF standard on most architectures supported by Linux. This appendix has introduced you to the details of this layout. The format is important not only for userland applications, but also for kernel modules. After providing you with a general overview about ELF, this chapter discussed the in-kernel data structures that are required by the module loader, and that provide a convenient way to examine various features of the ELF file format.

The Kernel Development Process

This book has given you lots of information about concepts, algorithms, data structures, and code. Clearly these form the very core of Linux development, and that is what the kernel is all about. But there's another side of Linux that should not pass by unnoticed: the community that develops the kernel, the way it works, and how people interact. This aspect is interesting because the kernel is one of the largest and most complex open source projects in existence, and it's a role model for distributed, decentralized development on a gigantic scale. The purpose of this appendix is to provide an overview about numerous technical and social aspects of kernel development. Additionally, it talks about the relationship between the Linux kernel and academia.

F.1 Introduction

The kernel sources (in the main README file) describe the development community as a "loosely-knit team of hackers across the Net," and although both the number of people involved in kernel development and their professional affiliations have changed from the beginning until now, this statement has always been true. Openness is a direct outcome of this: Most communication among developers takes place on mailing lists and can be read by anyone who is interested in how an operating system evolves. One particularly important point is that developers from many companies that fiercely compete against each other in many aspects (the companies, not the developers …) closely cooperate in kernel development. Non-technical people, in particular, can often just stand by in amazement. And actually, this *is* quite a remarkable feat!

Not too much needs to be said about the essential principles of Linux kernel development nowadays. Although creating an open source operating system that could actually be used for something appeared to be a crazy idea only 15 years ago, at least most technical people got quite used to it. One essential difference between Linux kernel development in contrast to classical development models is that there are no fixed formal rules of how things have to work. There are established practices, but they are seldom formalized in documents. There is no development road map, and no single centralized repository. There are, however, *important* repositories and *important* developers. This can be an advantage in many cases, because development gets more dynamic and flexible than with fixed rigid structures, but it also makes things harder if you are new to the area.

Many of the topics discussed in this appendix are also addressed in the kernel source itself. A number of files in Documentation/ relate to the style and mechanics of the development process. Coverage there is quite comprehensive, so this appendix is just an overview of the essential ideas.

F.2 Kernel Trees and the Structure of Development

The Linux kernel is a very dynamic piece of software, and one of the most striking aspects of its development is that there is *no* development version! At least there's no explicit, long-term development version that's managed by Linus Torvalds.

This used to be different in former times. Traditionally, kernel development was split into two different branches. One branch contained stable kernel releases that were supposed to be used on production systems, and they were identified by an even minor release number. Kernel branches 2.0, 2.2, and 2.4 were stable branches (with 2.0.x, 2.2.x, and 2.4.x being individual releases within that series), while 2.1, 2.3, and 2.5 were development releases — again with 2.5.x and so on as individual versions. The basic idea of this approach was to allow new features and experimental patches to undergo a good deal of testing and improvement, and once enough new features had been added and things had stabilized and were perceived to be usable in practice, a new stable tree was opened. Ideally, distributors would then pick the kernels from this release branch and integrate it into their distributions.

Unfortunately, things have not quite worked this way. A development cycle required *years* before a new stable series could be opened, and this is a very large interval in the IT world. When a new piece of hardware comes out, buyers do not usually want to wait for several years before the kernel picks up support for it — or at least the kernel that most people use, the stable series. The same goes not just for device drivers, but also for most new features. Therefore, distributors did port new features from the development series back into their stable branch. And because every distribution has its own taste about what is necessary and required, a different selection of features was back-ported, which led to distribution kernels diverging more and more from each other.

Since kernel series 2.6, a new development policy has been employed. There is only a single kernel series, and the separation into stable and development trees does not exist anymore. Instead, a number of more experimentally oriented kernel trees are used to test new features initially, and after a stabilization and test period, they are directly merged into the main kernel series. The 2.6 tree is managed by Linus Torvalds, who — as you might have heard — was the initial creator of Linux and set the ball rolling. Kernels from this tree are usually referred to as *vanilla kernels*, to distinguish them from kernels adapted by distributions based on their needs, or various experimental trees. The kernel series is denoted as *mainline*.

Trees other than the main tree are conventionally identified by a postfix added to the version number. The most important tree besides mainline is 2.6-mm, which is managed by Andrew Morton, and most patches go through this tree before they are accepted into mainline 2.6. Many other subsystem-specific trees exist, and they usually focus on one particular aspect of the kernel: 2.6-net focuses on networking, and 2.6-rt contains work related to real-time issues and interactivity problems, to just name two examples. There's also a -stable release that is used to incorporate important bug fixes for problems that appear after a formal kernel release has taken place. Kernel trees come and go for various reasons: Developers might have lost their interest to maintain them, or the reason for the tree might have vanished because the problem it was concerned with has been solved by some means.

F.2.1 The Command Chain

All active components of the kernel have a *maintainer* who cares about development in a particular area. Many maintainers, especially for larger components, are employed by various Linux vendors, but some still work in their free time. A maintainer's responsibility can range from controlling a single device driver over some piece of infrastructure such as the kernel object mechanism to complete subsystems such as the whole networking code, the block layer, or all code in arch/ for a specific architecture. Maintainers are listed in the top-level MAINTAINERS file that comes with the kernel and contains several pieces of information, as you can see here:

```
MAINTAINERS
IA64 (Itanium) PLATFORM
P: Tony Luck
M: tony.luck@intel.com
L: linux-ia64@vger.kernel.org
W: http://www.ia64-linux.org/
T: git kernel.org:/pub/scm/linux/kernel/git/aegl/linux-2.6.git
S: Maintained
```

In addition to the name of the maintainer and his (or her, but usually the former — kernel development is not an actual hotbed of emancipation) e-mail contact, this file provides a mailing list on which development in the respective area is discussed. Usually it's much preferred to ask questions and discuss things on this mailing list than to directly interact with the maintainer. If the code is managed in a public-accessible version control repository, the location of the repository is specified — in this case, it's a git repository that is the preferred source code management system for many kernel developers (as discussed in Appendix 2). Finally, the entry may specify a web page that contains information about the subsystem, and the maintenance status. In principle, the entry can distinguish between paid and unpaid tending of subsystems with the states Supported and Maintained, but this can often be a philosophical question. More important is the distinction between actively maintained parts compared to code without a maintainer (Orphan), old and obsolete code (Obsolete), and parts that receive little attention but are not completely unmaintained (Odd Fixes).

Having maintainers for individual parts of the kernel that range from small portions such as drivers to complete subsystems creates a loose hierarchy among developers. But again, there is no formal authority that would determine this hierarchy — it all depends on the people who actually contribute code and how much they trust each other. When code gets into the kernel, the usual (but not the only) way is to traverse this hierarchy from bottom to top. A fix or new feature for a piece of code typically first goes to the device- or subsystem-specific mailing list or the respective maintainer, and then progresses to maintainers of higher levels, who pass it on to Andrew Morton's -mm tree,[1] from which it might finally be merged into the vanilla kernel tree. This process is often referred to as *merging upstream*. However, that's only one possibility, and rules are by no means fixed.

F.2.2 The Development Cycle

One of the foremost reasons why an explicit development kernel series was abandoned was the desire to accelerate the rate at which new features become available for production kernels

---

[1]To reduce the number of merge conflicts in the -mm tree that can arise when new code is incompatible with other new code, another development series named -next is supposed to sort such issues out before any new code gets into the -mm tree.

without having to be back-ported by distribution vendors. This goal has clearly been reached: The intervals between releases in the 2.6 series are roughly 70 to 110 days long, which means that a new kernel comes out every couple of months. Many aspects of how development works have been illuminated by a study published by the Linux Foundation [KHCM], and updates on that study appear loosely on www.lwn.net. One particularly interesting observation of this study is that progress in the vanilla kernel proceeds in *bursts*, which is intentional, but it took some time until everything worked out properly. Consider Figure F-1, which illustrates the temporal flow of changes to the kernel.

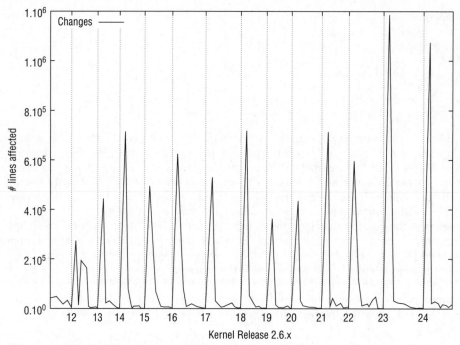

Figure F-1: Rate of change in the vanilla kernel. An open merge window leads to a rapid burst of changes, followed by a stabilization period with a considerably smaller change rate.

After a new kernel has been released, Linus Torvalds opens a *merge window* that is kept open during a short period, typically two weeks. New code is supposed to go in only during this period. Although there can be exceptions to the rule, this policy is usually enforced quite strictly. The rate of changes is rather drastic during this time. This period of fervent activity ends when the merge window is closed and release candidate kernels are prepared. Release candidates provide oppurtunities for testing how all changes interact as well as identifying and fixing bugs. The rate of changes declines rapidly, because fixes are often very short patches that are as important as the initial feature submission. Once things have stabilized, a new kernel version is released. The behavior is detailed in Figure F-2, which shows a close-up inspection of the development progress between kernel 2.6.21 and 2.6.24. Notice that a logarithmic scale is employed on the y axis. While the first release candidate contains one million changes(!), the number then drops to around 10,000 for the next releases, and even further until the final release.

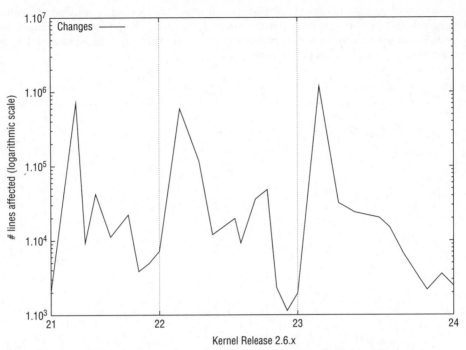

Figure F-2: Detailed inspection of the rate of change during the development of kernel version 2.6.22 to 2.6.24. Note that a logarithmic scale is employed on the _y_ axis.

Figure F-3 takes a slightly different look at the stabilization process by considering the changes made to individual kernel releases and release candidates cumulatively. The merge window is nicely visible by a rapid change in slope, followed by flat plateaus that mark the stabilization period.[2]

A word of warning: Measuring the productivity of software projects is always hard in terms of pure numbers, especially when these numbers are just based on added and removed lines of code. For example, it does not make much sense to first introduce vast amounts of code just to remove them later, although this would rate high in the approach chosen here. Nevertheless, the comparatively simple method presented here allows you to gain a good intuitive understanding of how the development process is organized. It should also be noted that such results can be obtained very easily because the full kernel development history is available in git repositories — it should not be difficult for you to analyze your own area of interest in the kernel sources with similar methods.

New features do not drop out of the blue sky — they have usually seen a long development history before they are considered for acceptance into the mainline kernel. How development happens in this phase strongly depends on the particular subsystem and the involved maintainers. Code that has been discussed for years before it is accepted into mainline is not uncommon. The Reiser filesystem, for instance, took a very long time before all issues that many developers had with it were resolved. Sometimes it takes a considerable amount of pushing to get work accepted into the vanilla kernel, but sometimes

---

[2]This way of presenting the data was inspired by Jonathan Corbet's _Kernel Report_ talk which you can enjoy during many Linux related conferences and similar occasions. Some conference web sites, such as linux.conf.au, offer a video of the talk.

things work much smoother. The Ext4 filesystem is, for instance, developed in close integration with the vanilla kernel, and the evolving code was present in the mainline from the very beginning to receive wide testing. Actually, the code base started out as a copy of Ext3 and was then successively modified to integrate many new ideas and improvements.

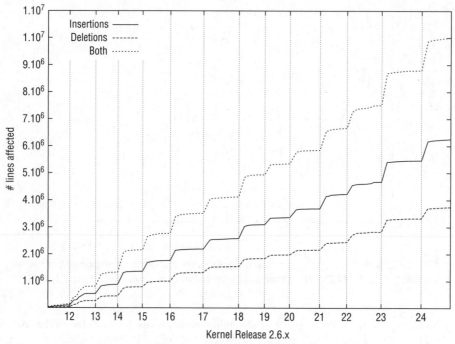

Figure F-3: Cumulative changes in the development of the Linux kernel. The effect of the merge window and the following stabilization period emerge very clearly.

F.2.3 Online Resources

There are numerous web sites devoted to Linux kernel development which provide useful information. Because of the web's rapidly changing structure, it does not really make sense to present a comprehensive survey here, since most links will tend to become outdated rather quickly. However, relying only on your favorite search engine to grab useful links about kernel development is also not the easiest path to success, especially when it comes to judging relevance and quality of the results. Therefore, the following list presents a selection of some fine links that are among the author's personal favorites (naturally, this selection is subjectively biased, but it's a good starting point):

❑ The current kernel source code as well as many essential userspace tools are available from www.kernel.org. Numerous git source code repositories are listed on git.kernel.org.

❑ www.lwn.net is *the* premier source for regular, weekly updates on the kernel development process. And these updates are not just for the kernel. Interesting news about all aspects of Linux development and related events in the IT community are collected on this site, and well-researched articles provide insightful updates on the state of the art of various projects.

Content is provided free of charge one week after it has been published initially, but the most current information is available to subscribers only. Since the fee is small, I highly recommend that you subscribe as soon as possible![3]

❑   Full-scale change logs of the kernel can easily take a number of megabytes in size. Although they meticulously register every commit that was accepted since the last release, it is practically not possible to get a broad overview of what has happened in kernel development. Thankfully, `www.linuxnewbies.net` provides less-detailed change logs that put more emphasis on the big picture than small individual details.

❑   The Linux Foundation provides a "weather forecast" service that tries to predict which patches and features are going to be accepted into future kernel versions. This is as close to a road map as the Linux kernel can get, and provides valuable information on the direction that development is heading in. The URL is `www.linux-foundation.org/en/Linux_Weather_Forecast`.

F.3   The Structure of Patches

Kernel developers expect that good patches fulfill certain fixed criteria. Although this puts more load onto the preparer of a patch, it makes things much easier for maintainers, reviewers, and testers because less time is required to understand individual changes if they all follow identical conventions. The kernel includes detailed instructions on how to prepare patches, which can be found in `Documentation/SubmittingPatches`. This section summarizes the essential points, but be sure to read the whole `SubmittingPatches` document before you send code to any maintainer or mailing list. Further advice is given in Andrew Morton's "The Perfect Patch" document, available on `www.zip.com.au/~akpm/linux/patches/stuff/tpp.txt`, and on the web site `linux.yyz.us/patch-format.html`.

First and foremost, it is essential to break larger changes into pieces that are easier to digest than a single patch that touches 10 million files across 50,000 subdirectories. A patch should do one logical change to the source code, even if that means that more than one patch in a patch series changes the same file. Ideally, patches should be *stackable* — that is, it should be possible to apply them independent of each other. However, owing to the nature of changes, this is not always possible, and in this case, the correct temporal ordering of the patches should be documented.

In principle, patch series can be created by hand using `diff` and `patch` as described in Appendix 2. This can become quite tedious after a while, but the `quilt` toolbox available on `http://savannah.nongnu.org/projects/quilt` provides some relief here by automating most of the process of managing patch stacks.

F.3.1   Technical Issues

As for the technical format of a patch, notice that a *unified* patch that includes information on the C functions being changed is required. Such a patch can be generated using `diff -up`. If the patch adds new files or concerns files in multiple subdirectories, then `diff -uprN` must be used to account for these cases. Appendix 2 discusses what the resulting patch looks like and which information it contains.

---

[3]And, no, I have no commercial interests nor any relation to LWN whatsoever. But the site is just awesome.

Coding Style

The kernel has some coding style requirements, which are defined in `Documentation/CodingStyle`. Although not all developers agree about each requirement in this file, many are very sensitive about coding-style violations. Having a common coding style is a good thing. The kernel contains vast amounts of code, and digging through patches and files that use all different conventions can become a real nuisance. Thankfully, the kernel displays less-religious zeal about coding style than other projects, but there is a clear opinion on what is not the ultimate fashionable style, as you can see in the following documentation snippet:

Documentation/CodingStyle
```
First off, I'd suggest printing out a copy of the GNU coding standards,
and NOT read it. Burn them, it's a great symbolic gesture.
```

But what do developers expect? The essential points are as follows:

❑ Different levels are always one tab apart, and one tab is always eight spaces long. This might seem quite excessive for programmers who've had much exposure to userland code before, but this is different in the kernel world. Naturally, code will tend to shift quickly to the right side of the screen after a few indentation levels, but this serves as a warning sign: Code that needs too many levels of indention should usually be replaced with something cleaner, or be split into functions, and then the problem will automatically go away.

Large indentations often cause strings and procedure arguments to exceed the 80-column boundary, and they must be sensibly broken into chunks. You have seen numerous examples of this all over the book.

In addition to the aforementioned reasons, many kernel developers tend to have rather unusual working practices, and long hacking sessions are not uncommon. After having written tons of beautiful code three days in a row without a break, vision tends to get blurred, and large indentations do definitely help in this situation (along with copious amounts of caffeinated beverages).

❑ Opening braces are put last on the line they are contained in, and closing braces are put first on their line. When a control statement is continued (as for `else` branches, or `while` conditionals in `do` loops), the continuation statement is not put on a new line, but after the closing brace. If a block contains only a single statement, no extra braces are necessary. In fact, they are even discouraged (just think of how much typing you will save over your whole life by this convention).

Functions follow a separate convention: The opening and closing brackets are both on separate lines.

The following code contains examples for the above rules:

kernel/sched.c
```
static void __update_rq_clock(struct rq *rq)
{
        u64 prev_raw = rq->prev_clock_raw;
        u64 now = sched_clock();
...
        if (unlikely(delta < 0)) {
                clock++;
                rq->clock_warps++;
        } else {
                /*
```

```
        * Catch too large forward jumps too:
        */
        if (unlikely(clock + delta > rq->tick_timestamp + TICK_NSEC)) {
                if (clock < rq->tick_timestamp + TICK_NSEC)
                        clock = rq->tick_timestamp + TICK_NSEC;
                else
                        clock++;
                rq->clock_overflows++;
        } else {
                if (unlikely(delta > rq->clock_max_delta))
                        rq->clock_max_delta = delta;
                clock += delta;
        }
    }

        rq->prev_clock_raw = now;
        rq->clock = clock;
}
```

❑ No surrounding space should be used inside parentheses, so if (condition) is frowned upon, while if (condition) will be universally loved. Keywords like if are followed by a space, whereas function definitions and functions calls are not. The preceding code excerpt also contains examples of these rules.

❑ Constants should be represented by macros or elements in enum enumerations, and their names should be in all capital letters.

❑ Functions should typically not be longer than one screen (i.e., 24 lines). Longer code should be broken into multiple functions, even if the resulting auxiliary functions will have only a single caller.

❑ Local variable names should be short (and firm), and not tell the story of a complete novel like OnceUponATimeThereWasACounterWhichMustBeIntializedWithZero. You can also use tmp, which also protects you from breaking your fingers during interaction with the keyboard.

   Global identifiers should tell a little more about themselves because they are visible in all contexts. prio_tree_remove is a fine name for a global function, whereas cur and ret are only apt for local variable names. Names composed of multiple expressions should use underscores to separate the constituents, and not employ mixed lower/uppercase letters.

❑ Typedefs are considered to be an incarnation of the devil because they hide the actual definition of an object, so they should usually not be employed. It might save the creator of a patch some typing, but will make reading harder for all other developers.

   However, sometimes it *is* necessary to hide the definition of a data type, such as when a quantity must be implemented differently depending on the underlying architecture, but common code should not notice this. For instance, consider the atomic_t type used for atomic counters, or the various page table elements like pte_t, pud_t, and so on. They must not be accessed and modified directly, but only via special auxiliary functions, so their definition *must not* be visible to generic code.

All these rules and more are discussed in depth in the coding style document Documentation/ CodingStyle, together with the rationale behind them (including the all-important rule number 17: Don't re-invent the wheel!) Accordingly, it does not make sense to repeat the information in the coding style here — the document comes with every kernel, so go and enjoy it there! Besides, when reading through the kernel sources, you will familiarize with the desired style very quickly.

The following two utilities can help to obey the desired coding style:

❑ Lindent, located in the kernel's scripts/ directory, feeds GNU indent with command-line options to re-indent a file according to the indentation settings preferred by the kernel.

❑ checkpatch.pl, likewise located in the scripts/ directory of the kernel source tree, scans a patch for violations of the coding style and can provide appropriate diagnostics.

Portability

The kernel runs across a wide range of architectures, and these differ widely in the various restrictions they impose on C code. One of the prerequisites for new code is that it is portable and will run on all supported architectures as far as this is possible in principle. This book has previously covered the differences between architectures and ways to circumvent those differences. Here is a reminder of some important issues that must be considered when code is written for the kernel:

❑ Use proper locking to ensure that your code runs safe in multiprocessor environments. Thanks to the preemptible kernel, this is also important on uniprocessor systems.

❑ Always write code that is neutral with respect to endianess. Your code must function on both little and big endian machines.

❑ Do not assume that page frames are 4 KiB in size, but employ PAGE_SIZE instead.

❑ Do not assume any specific bit widths for any data type. When a fixed number of bits is required, always use explicitly sized types like u16, s64, and so on. However, you can always assume that sizeof(long) == sizeof(void *).

❑ Do not use floating point calculations.

❑ Keep in mind that the stack size is fixed and limited.

Documenting Code

In addition to documenting patch submissions, it is also important to document your code — especially functions that can be called from other subsystems or drivers. The kernel uses the following special form of C comments for this purpose:

fs/char_dev.c
```
/**
 * register_chrdev() - Register a major number for character devices.
 * @major: major device number or 0 for dynamic allocation
 * @name: name of this range of devices
 * @fops: file operations associated with this devices
 *
 * If @major == 0 this functions will dynamically allocate a major and return
 * its number.
 *
 * If @major > 0 this function will attempt to reserve a device with the given
 * major number and will return zero on success.
 *
 * Returns a -ve errno on failure.
```

```
 *
 * The name of this device has nothing to do with the name of the device in
 * /dev. It only helps to keep track of the different owners of devices. If
 * your module name has only one type of devices it's ok to use, for example, the name
 * of the module here.
 *
 * This function registers a range of 256 minor numbers. The first minor number
 * is 0.
 */
int register_chrdev(unsigned int major, const char *name,
const struct file_operations *fops)
 ...
```

Notice that the comment line starts with *two* asterisks. This identifies the comment as a *kerneldoc* comment. Functions prefixed by such comments will be included in the API reference, which can be created with make htmldocs and similar commands. Variable names must be prefixed with the @ sign and will be formatted accordingly in the generated output. The comment should include the following:

❑ A description of the parameters that specifies *what* the function does (as opposed to *how* the function does this).

❑ The possible return codes and their meanings.

❑ Any limitations of the function, the range of valid parameters, and/or any special considerations that must be taken into account.

F.3.2   Submission and Review

This section describes two important social components of kernel development: Submitting patches to mailing lists, and the subsequent review process.

Preparing Patches for a Mailing List

Most patches are submitted to the mailing list of the respective subsystem before they are considered for inclusion into any kernel tree — unless you are a top-notch kernel contributor who submits patches directly to Linus or Andrew (in which case, you would probably not be reading this anyway . . .). Again, there are some conventions that should be obeyed as described here:

❑ Subject lines start with [PATCH], and the rest of the subject should give a concise description of what the patch is all about. A good subject is very important because it is not only used on the mailing list, but in the case of an acceptance, it will appear in the git change logs.

❑ If a patch is not supposed to be applied directly, or if it requires more discussion, it can be marked with an additional identifier such as [RFC].

❑ Larger changes should be split up into multiple patches with one logical change per patch. Likewise, you should send only one patch per e-mail. Each should be numbered as [PATCH m/N], where m is a counter and N is the total number of patches . [PATCH 0/N] should contain an overview about the follow-up patches.

❑ A more detailed description of each patch should be contained in the e-mail body. Again, this text will not get lost after the patch is integrated, but will find its way into the git repository where it serves to document the changes.

❑   The code itself should be directly present in the e-mail, without using any form of base64 encoding, compression, or other fancy tricks. Attachments are also not particularly favored, and the preferred way is to include the code directly. Any material that should be included in the description but is not supposed to go into the repository must be separated from the patch by three dashes on a single line.

Naturally, the code should not be line-wrapped by the e-mail client as there are rumors that compilers sometimes have a very hard time accepting randomly wrapped code. And after all that has been said, a remark that HTML e-mails are inappropriate is likely superfluous.

Below the e-mail subject lines of the submission of an experimental patch are shown. They obey all the conventions discussed before:

```
[PATCH 0/4] [RFC] Verification and debugging of memory initialisation Mel Gorman (Wed Apr 16 2008
- 09:51:19 EST)
    [PATCH 1/4] Add a basic debugging framework for memory initialisation Mel Gorman (Wed Apr 16
2008 - 09:51:32 EST)
    [PATCH 2/4] Verify the page links and memory model Mel Gorman (Wed Apr 16 2008 - 09:51:53 EST)
    [PATCH 3/4] Print out the zonelists on request for manual verification Mel Gorman (Wed Apr 16
2008 - 09:52:22 EST)
    [PATCH 4/4] Make defencive checks around PFN values registered for memory usage Mel Gorman (Wed
Apr 16 2008 - 09:52:37 EST)
```

Notice that the four messages containing the actual code have been posted as replies to the first, introductory message. This allows many mailer clients to group the posts, which makes it easier to recognize the patches as one entity.

Take a look at the contents of the first mail:

```
This patch creates a new file mm/mm_init.c which memory initialisation should
be moved to over time to avoid further polluting page_alloc.c. This patch
introduces a simple mminit_debug_printk() function and an (undocumented)
mminit_debug_level command-line parameter for setting the level of tracing
and verification that should be done.

Signed-off-by: Mel Gorman <mel@xxxxxxxxxx>
---

mm/Makefile    | 2 +-
mm/internal.h  | 9 +++++++++
mm/mm_init.c   | 40 ++++++++++++++++++++++++++++++++++++++++++
mm/page_alloc.c | 16 ++++++++++------
4 files changed, 60 insertions(+), 7 deletions(-)


(PATCH)
```

After an overview about the code, the diff statistics produced by diffstat are attached. These allow to quickly identify how many changes a patch introduces in terms of added and deleted lines, and where these changes are bound to happen. This statistical information is interesting for discussion of the code, but has no purpose in long-term changelogs (after all, the information can be generated from the patch), so it is placed after a three-dash line. This is followed by the patch as generated by diff, but as this is not relevant to this discussion, it is not reproduced here.

Origin of Patches

The description also contains a *signed-off* line, which identifies who wrote the patch, and serves as a bona fide statement that the author has the right to publish the code as open source, usually covered by the GNU General Public License (GPL), version 2.

Multiple persons can sign off a patch, even if they are not direct authors of the code. This signals that the signer has reviewed the patch, is intimately acquainted with the code, and believes to the best of his knowledge that it will work as announced and not cause data corruption, set your laptop on fire, or do other nasty things. It also tracks the path a patch has made through the developer hierarchy before it finally ended up in the vanilla kernel. Maintainers are heavily involved in signing off, because they have to review a fair amount of code that they have not written themselves for inclusion in their subsystems.

Only real names will be accepted for signed-off-lines — pseudonyms and fictitious names must not be used. Formally, signing off a patch means that the signer can certify the following:

Documentation/SubmittingPatches
```
Developer's Certificate of Origin 1.1

By making a contribution to this project, I certify that:

(a) The contribution was created in whole or in part by me and I
    have the right to submit it under the open source license
    indicated in the file; or

(b) The contribution is based upon previous work that, to the best
    of my knowledge, is covered under an appropriate open source
    license and I have the right under that license to submit that
    work with modifications, whether created in whole or in part
    by me, under the same open source license (unless I am
    permitted to submit under a different license), as indicated
    in the file; or

(c) The contribution was provided directly to me by some other
    person who certified (a), (b) or (c) and I have not modified
    it.

(d) I understand and agree that this project and the contribution
    are public and that a record of the contribution (including all
    personal information I submit with it, including my sign-off) is
    maintained indefinitely and may be redistributed consistent with
    this project or the open source license(s) involved.
```

Signing patches off was introduced to kernel development at a rather late stage, essentially as a reaction to a claim by a "three-letter company" that for various reasons assumed the impression that they would own all the code of the kernel, and therefore all Linux users should give them all their money. Naturally, some developers did not quite agree with this point of view, including Linus Torvalds himself:[4]

```
Some of you may have heard of this crazy company called SCO (aka "Smoking
Crack Organization") who seem to have a hard time believing that open
```

---

[4]Accusing people of smoking crack is, by the way, not completely uncommon on the Linux kernel mailing list, where conversations can sometimes be rough.

```
source works better than their five engineers do. They've apparently made
a couple of outlandish claims about where our source code comes from,
including claiming to own code that was clearly written by me over a
decade ago.
```

In fact, this case is mostly history now, and people (with the possible exception of the CEO of the afore-mentioned company) are universally convinced that a simple first-fit allocator whose copyright you *might* possibly own is not quite a complete UNIX kernel ... Nevertheless, thanks to Signed-off-by tags, it is now possible to precisely identify who wrote which patch.

There are also two weaker forms of marking patches:

❏ Acked-by means that a developer is not directly involved with the patch, but nevertheless deems it correct after some review.

> This does not necessarily imply that the ACK-ing developer has worked through the *complete* patch, but may just indicate compliance with the parts that touch the respective field of competence.
>
> If, for instance, an architecture maintainer acknowledges a patch that looks fine with respect to all changes performed in the arch/xyz directory, but that also contains code in fs/ that fries all strings composed of an odd number of chars in files that start with an M, you cannot blame the ACK-ing developer for this.
>
> However, it's highly unlikely that this will ever happen, because architecture maintainers are all very good at what they do, and would detect the subversive wickedness of the patch already by the smell of the file — this example just serves to explain the concept.

❏ CC is used to signify that a person has at least been informed about the patch, so he should theoretically be aware of the patch's existence, and had a chance to object.

During the development of kernel 2.6.25, a discussion arose, about the value of code review and how credit should be given to reviewers and one solution to which people agreed was to introduce the Reviewed-By patch tag. The tag states the following:

Documentation/SubmittingPatches
```
Reviewer's statement of oversight

By offering my Reviewed-by: tag, I state that:

    (a) I have carried out a technical review of this patch to
        evaluate its appropriateness and readiness for inclusion into
        the mainline kernel.

    (b) Any problems, concerns, or questions relating to the patch
        have been communicated back to the submitter.  I am satisfied
        with the submitter's response to my comments.

    (c) While there may be things that could be improved with this
        submission, I believe that it is, at this time, (1) a
        worthwhile modification to the kernel, and (2) free of known
        issues which would argue against its inclusion.
```

(d) While I have reviewed the patch and believe it to be sound, I
    do not (unless explicitly stated elsewhere) make any
    warranties or guarantees that it will achieve its stated
    purpose or function properly in any given situation.

Another new tag introduced in this context is `Tested-by`, which — you guessed it — states that the patch has been tested by the signer, and that the test has left enough of the machine to add a `Tested-by` tag to the patch.

F.4 Linux and Academia

Writing an operating system is not an easy task — as I'm sure you'll agree, it is one of the most involved challenges for software engineers. Many of the developers participating in the creation of the Linux kernel are among the most knowledgeable in their field, given that Linux is one of the best operating systems available. Academic degrees are not uncommon among developers, and computer science degrees are surely not underrepresented degrees.[5]

Operating systems are also the subject of active academic research. As with every other research field, there's a certain amount of theory that goes along with OS research, and this is just natural — you cannot tackle all problems in a practical way. In contrast to many other research areas that are concerned with fundamental problems, however, OS research works on inherently practical problems, and should therefore have an impact on practical things. What is OS research good for if it does not help to improve operating systems? And because an operating system is an inherently practical product (who, after all, would need a *theoretical* operating system? Hypothetical computers certainly have no use for an operating system, and even less do real computers require a theoretical OS), the outcome of OS research *has* to influence practice. People working on loop quantum gravity might be exempted from having to consider the practical impact of their work, but this is certainly not the case for OS research.

With this in mind, one could expect that Linux and the academic community are closely associated, but unfortunately, this is not the case. Quoting academic work in the kernel sources is a rare occurrence, and seeing the kernel being quoted in research papers is also not something that happens every day.

This is especially astonishing because the academic world used to have a close affiliation with UNIX, particularly with the Berkeley System Distribution (BSD) family. It's fair to say that BSD *is* the product of academic research, and for a long time, academia was the driving force behind this project.

A study published by the Linux Foundation [KHCM] has shown that contributions from academia account for 0.8 percent of all changes in recent kernel versions. Considering that a large number of ideas circulate in the academic community, this ratio is astonishingly low, and it would be worthwhile to improve the situation — for the benefit of both the kernel *and* academia. Open source is all about sharing things, and sharing good ideas is also a worthy goal.

Linux had a slightly bumpy start in its relations with academia. One of Linus Torvalds's initial motivations to write Linux was his dissatisfaction with Minix, a simple teaching operating system designed to educate students. This led to a famous debate between Torvalds and Andrew Tanenbaum, the creator of Minix. Tanenbaum suggested that Linux was obsolete because its design would not comply with

---

[5]Notice that I did not perform any quantitative analysis on this, but the curricula vitae of many developers are readily available on the Internet that support this suspicion (as does common sense.)

what the academic world envisioned to be suitable for future operating systems, and his arguments were collected in a Usenet newsgroup posting titled "Linux is obsolete." This, naturally, caused Linus Torvalds to reply, and one of his statements was the following:

```
Re 2: your job is being a professor and researcher: That's one hell of a
good excuse for some of the brain-damages of minix.
```

Although it was soon admitted that the message was a little rash, it reflects the attitude that is sometimes displayed by the kernel community toward academic research. Real-world operating systems and OS research are perceived as things that don't quite fit together.

This may indeed be true sometimes: Much academic research is not *supposed* to be integrated into real-world products, especially when it is concerned with fundamental issues. But as mentioned previously, there are also practical components of research, and these could often help to improve the kernel. Unfortunately, OS researchers and OS implementors have somewhat lost connection with each other, and Rob Pike, a member of the former UNIX team at Bell Labs, has gone so far as to make the pessimistic claim that systems software research is irrelevant.[6]

Contributing code to the kernel is hard for researchers for many reasons, one of which is that they have to take many different operating systems into account. It is already hard to keep up with the pace of Linux kernel development, but it is virtually impossible to chase all important operating systems in use today. Therefore, researchers usually cannot provide more than proof-of-concept implementations of their ideas. Integrating these into the kernel requires some effort from both communities. Consider, for instance, the integration of the swap token mechanism into the kernel. This was proposed in research as discussed in the next section, but has been implemented for the kernel by Rik van Riel, a kernel developer working in the area of memory management. The approach has proved to be quite successful, and could well serve as a role model for further collaboration.

Interaction between both communities is complicated by the following two aspects of kernel development:

❑ Many developers do not consider proposals without concrete code, and refuse to discuss the issue any further.

❑ Even if code is submitted to the mailing lists, a good part of the work will start only after the initial submission. Adaption of proposed code to a specific system is not highly credited in academia, so researchers have a natural tendency to avoid this step.

Ultimately, this leads to the conclusion that the interface between kernel development and academic research ideally requires one individual from each side collaborating with each other. If this is not possible, then it is a definitive advantage and surely worth the effort if researchers try to adapt to the culture of kernel development as much as possible.

F.4.1 Some Examples

This section presents some examples of when research results have been turned into kernel code and could help to improve particular aspects of Linux. Note that the presented selection is naturally not

---

[6]See www.cs.bell-labs.com/who/rob/utah2000.pdf. Since Pike also claims that the only progress in the operating system area comes from Microsoft, I certainly don't believe all his claims, but the talk nevertheless contains many noteworthy and valid ideas.

comprehensive, and the impact of academic research would be really negligible if it ever could be. It is primarily used to highlight that both worlds *can* benefit from each other.

❑ The swap token as discussed in Chapter 18 was first described in the paper "Token-Ordered LRU: An Effective Replacement Policy and its Implementation in Linux Systems" by S. Jiang and X. Zhang (Performance Evaluation, Vol. 60, Issue 1–4, 2005). Subsequently, it was implemented in kernel 2.6.9 by Rik van Riel. Interestingly, the paper extended kernel 2.2.14 to demonstrate the usefulness of the approach, but the corresponding code was never included in the mainline kernel.

❑ The slab allocator as discussed in Chapter 3 is directly based on a paper that describes the implementation of the slab system in Solaris: "The Slab Allocator: An Object-Caching Kernel Memory Allocator," Proceedings of the Summer 1994 USENIX Conference.

❑ The techniques of the anticipatory I/O scheduler (which was mentioned in Chapter 6, but not discussed in detail) were first presented in "Anticipatory Scheduling: A Disk Scheduling Framework to Overcome Deceptive Idleness in Synchronous I/O," 18th ACM Symposium on Operating Systems Principles, 2001.

❑ As discussed in Chapter 18, Linux employs a variant of the least-recently used technique to identify active pages and distinguish them from inactive pages. The paper "CLOCK-Pro: An Effective Improvement of the CLOCK Replacement" by S. Jiang, F. Chen, and X. Zhang (Proceedings of 2005 USENIX Annual Technical Conference) describes a page-replacement algorithm that not only prioritizes pages based on the time of their last access, but also incorporates the frequency with which pages are accessed. Patches have been designed by Rik van Riel and Peter Zijlstra, and the method has also been considered as a possible merge candidate (see www.lwn.net/Articles/147879/). The reason why you have read nothing about this technique in the preceeding chapters is simple: The patches have not yet made it into mainline. They are, however, examples of how Linux developers do sometimes actively try to integrate research results into the kernel.

The ideas presented in these papers have been directly integrated into the Linux kernel as direct extensions of existing code. Some examples of older papers that have had an indirect influence on the kernel include the following:

❑ The generic structure of the block layer that acts as a level of indirection between filesystems and disks is described in "The Logical Disk: A New Approach to Improving File Systems," by W. de Jonge, M. F. Kaashoeck, and W. C. Hsieh. Essentially, it describes techniques to decouple blocks on physical disks from logical disks as observed by the operating system, and this builds the fundament for the logical volume manager and the device mapper.

❑ Many key concepts of the extended filesystem family originate from other filesystems, and one particular example is the paper "A Fast File System for UNIX" by M. K. McKusick, W. N. Joy, S. J. Leffler, and R. S. Fabry (ACM Transactions on Computer Systems, 1984). It describes the use of multiple possible block sizes on disk, and introduces the idea of mapping a logical sequence of data to a sequential series of blocks on disk.

Tracking the indirect influence of older papers is naturally much harder than seeing ideas from research being directly integrated. The more generic an idea is, the more ubiquitous it will become if it prevails, and the harder it becomes to recognize the idea as such. At some point, it will have been absorbed into the field, and be indistinguishable from common knowledge. Or would you deem it necessary to quote any paper on the fact that computers tend to work with binary digits?

Essentially, most core ideas of the UNIX operating system are also present in Linux. Many of these ideas are today ubiquitous, but were new at the time UNIX was invented. This includes, for instance, the idea that nearly everything can be represented by a file as discussed in Chapter 8. Namespaces are another example for a technology that does indirectly stem from academic research: They were introduced as an integral part of Plan 9 — the successor to UNIX co-developed by some of the inventors of UNIX — many years before they were adopted into the mainline kernel.[7] The /proc filesystem is also modeled by the example of Plan 9.

Many other fundamental ideas of UNIX appear as integral parts of Linux without being recognized as research results, but this is not the direct concern of this section. However, it is interesting to observe where many concepts of Linux have their roots, such as in Vahalia's highly recommended technical discussion of UNIX internals for many flavors of the system [Vah96]. The account by Salus [Sal94] illuminates the history of UNIX, and allows for understanding why many things are designed the way they are.

F.4.2 Adopting Research

The preceding examples demonstrate that it *is* possible to integrate research results with the Linux kernel. But considering the magnitude of OS research, and the number of results integrated into the kernel, there seem to be some obstacles to transferring results from one world into another. One essential factor is that each community functions quite differently from each other. To my knowledge this point has not received the consideration it deserves (at least not in writing); therefore, this section highlights some of the essential differences.

Notice that the kernel sources contain some interesting information on how the kernel developers deal with project management issues in Documentation/ManagementStyle. The document also addresses some of the questions discussed here.

Different Communities

Software development and OS research seem to be dry and purely technical to many people, but both have an enormous social component: The acceptance of any work is based on its acceptance in the community, which is nothing else than acceptance by individual developers and researchers. This requires that individuals judge the contributions of other individuals, and as most readers will agree, this is always a difficult thing in a world of colorful, different, and sometimes complicated characters. In an ideal world, judgment would be solely based on objective criteria, but this is not the case in reality: People are only human, and sympathy, personal tastes, acquaintances, dislikes, bias, and the ability to communicate with each other play a crucial role.

One approach to this problem is to simply ignore it — pretend that we live in an ideal world where judgment *is* done on a purely technical and objective level, and all problems automatically disappear. This solution is adopted astonishingly often, especially in "official" statements.

---

[7]Notice that Plan 9 was not developed at a "classical" academic institution, but at the research division of Bell Labs, which is nowadays affiliated with Lucent Technologies. However, the methodology used is very similar to that of academic institutions: Papers are published about Plan 9, talks are held, and conferences are organized. Therefore, this appendix subsumes it under the same category as academia. The web site cm.bell-labs.com/plan9 contains more information about Plan 9.

But even if the problem is acknowledged, it is not easy to solve. Consider how decisions are often made in the research community to decide if a work is worthwhile (and should be credited by being admitted to a conference, or published in a paper) or not:

1. After research results have (hopefully) been obtained, they are written up in a paper and submitted to a journal (or conference, or similar, but this discussion will focus on publication for simplicity's sake).

2. The paper is submitted to one or more referees who have to evaluate the work. They have to judge correctness, validity, and scientific importance, and can point to weaknesses or things that should be improved. Usually reviewers are anonymous, and should not be directly related with the author personally or professionally.

3. Depending on the referee's appraisal, the editor can decide to reject or accept the paper. In the latter case, the editor may require the author to incorporate improvements suggested by the referees. Another round of peer review may take place after the improvements have been made.

Usually, the identity of authors is known to the referee, but not vice versa.

Work is considered worthwhile in the kernel community if it is included into some official tree. The way to achieve such an inclusion goes essentially along these lines:

❑   Code is submitted to an appropriate mailing list.

❑   Everyone on the mailing list can request changes to the code, and desired improvements are discussed in public.

❑   The code is adapted to the desires of the community. This can be tricky because there are often orthogonal opinions as to what constitutes an improvement and what will deteriorate the code.

❑   The code is re-submitted, and discussion starts anew.

❑   Once the code has achieved the desired form and a consensus is reached, it is integrated into official trees.

Notice that it is possible for people with high and long-standing reputations in their fields (which is, again, a social factor) to shortcut the process in both areas, but these cases are not of interest here.

There are similarities between the academic and kernel development communities, and both have their strengths and weaknesses. For example, there are some important differences between the review process in each community:

❑   Reviewing code for the kernel is not a formalized process, and there is no central authority to initiate code review. Review is performed completely voluntarily and uncoordinated — if no one is interested in the submitted code, the mailing lists can remain silent.

    Although review in the academic world is usually also performed voluntarily and without payment, it is impossible for submissions to be completely ignored. Papers are guaranteed to get *some* feedback, although it can be very superficial.

❑   The identities of the submitter and reviewer are known to each other in the kernel world, and both can interact directly. In the academic world, this is usually not the case, and conversation between the author and reviewer is mediated by the editor. Additionally, only a few rounds of exchanging arguments between the author and reviewers are possible before the editor decides to either accept or reject a submission.

❑ The result of a review is only known to the submitter, referees, and editor in the academic world. Usually the whole review process is public in the kernel world, and can be read by everyone.

In both worlds, reviewers can pass harsh criticism to the submitter. In the academic world, formulations in the inverse direction are usually chosen with much more care, while this depends on the identity of the submitter and reviewer in the kernel world.

Critique is certainly valuable and essential to improve the quality of any work, but *receiving* critique is a complicated matter. How this is handled is another important difference between kernel development and the academic world.

Harassing people verbally in various creative, and often insulting, ways has become a trademark of some kernel developers — and the corresponding statements are publically available on the Internet. This poses a serious problem, because nobody likes to be insulted in public, and developers can be driven away by this fairly quickly. This concern is shared by several leading Linux developers, but because all people on the mailing lists are grown-ups, it is not possible to solve this problem in any other form than appealing for more fairness, which is not always accepted.

Receiving a harsh critique by an anonymous referee in the academic world is certainly not particularly enjoyable, but it is much easier to be accused of having failed in private than in public.

As you can see from the following documentation excerpt, kernel developers do *not* strive for complete political correctness as a means of solving this problem:

Documentation/ManagementStyle
```
The option of being unfailingly polite really doesn't exist. Nobody will
trust somebody who is so clearly hiding his true character.
```

Pulling each other's legs *can* be a good thing, and is something of an intellectual challenge when properly employed. But it's also very easy to overdo it and end up with insulting accusations, which nobody likes to receive but unfortunately, everyone should be prepared for in the kernel world.

While the review process of the kernel world can be considerably more challenging socially than the academic counterpart, it also tends to be much more effective, taken that people are not driven away by the approach: Patches on the kernel mailing list usually go through many iterations before they are deemed to be acceptable, and in each iteration step remaining problems are identified by reviewers and can be changed by the authors. Because the goal of the kernel is to be the best in the world, it is important that only really good code is integrated. Such code is usually not created from the very beginning, but only after a period of improvement and refinement. The whole point of the review process is to generate the best possible code, and this often succeeds in practice.

The effect of review on academic papers is usually different. If a submission is rejected by one journal, it will certainly be revised by the authors to address the shortcomings. However, readers are invited to judge on their own how big the probability is that *really* substantial revisions are made considering that on the one hand, there is considerable pressure to publish as many papers as possible for gaining scientific reputation, and on the other hand, there are a large number of different (possibly less-renowned) journals to which the work can alternatively be submitted — and that these journals *rely* as their economic foundation on submissions by authors who pay(!) for being published. This is different with kernel code: Either you get code into the kernel, or a considerable amount of effort has been wasted.[8] This naturally provides a large incentive to put effort into improving the code.

Although the approaches employed by the academic and kernel communities to assess and ensure the quality of submissions are similar at first glance, there are numerous differences between them. Different cultures can be a considerable barrier for the exchange of ideas and code between both worlds, and should be taken into account when it comes to a collaboration between kernel and academia.

F.5 Summary

As one of the largest open source efforts in the world, the Linux kernel is not just interesting from a technological perspective, but also because a novel and unique way of distributed development across the whole world and between otherwise competing companies is employed. This appendix described how the process is organized, and what the requirements for contribution are. It also analyzed the connection between kernel development and academic research. In this appendix, you learned how the two worlds interact, how differences can arise from different "cultures," and how these are best bridged.

---

[8]It is surely possible to maintain code out-of-tree, and this has proven useful in many cases, but the final and most rewarding goal for developers (and their employers!) is nevertheless to get work into the mainline kernel.

References

[BBD+01] Michael Beck, Harald Böhme, Mirko Dziadzka, Ulrich Kunitz, Robert Magnus, and Dirk Verworrner. *Linux-Kernelprogrammierung*. Addison-Wesley, 2001.

[BC05] Daniel P. Bovet and Marco Cesati. *Understanding the Linux Kernel*. O'Reilly, 3rd edition, 2005.

[Ben05] Christian Benvenuti. *Understanding Linux Network Internals*. O'Reilly, 2005.

[BH01] Thomas Beierlein and Olaf Hagenbruch, editors. *Taschenbuch Mikroprozessortechnik*. Fachbuchverlag Leipzig, 2001.

[Bon94] Jeff Bonwick. The slab allocator: An object-caching kernel memory allocator. *Usenix proceedings*, 1994. Electronic document, available on `www.usenix.org/publications/library/proceedings/bos94/full_papers/bonwick.ps`.

[Cox96] Alan Cox. Network buffers and memory management. *Linux Journal*, 1996. Available on `www.linuxjournal.com/article.php?sid=1312`.

[CRKH05] Jonathan Corbet, Alessandro Rubini, and Greg Kroah-Hartman. *Linux Device Drivers*. O'Reilly, 3rd edition, 2005.

[CTT] Rémy Card, Theodore Ts'o, and Stephen Tweedie. *Design and Implementation of the Second Extended Filesystem*. Available on `e2fsprogs.sourceforge.net/ext2intro.html`.

[Dik06] Jeff Dike. *User Mode Linux*. Prentice Hall, 2006.

[Fri02] Æleen Frisch. *Essential System Administration*. O'Reilly, 2002.

[GC94] Benny Goodheart and James Cox. *The Magic Garden Explained*. Prentice Hall, 1994.

[Grü03] Andreas Grünbacher. *POSIX Access Control Lists on Linux*, Usenix 2003 technical conference, freenix track. Usenix, 2003. Available on `http://www.usenix.org/events/usenix03/tech/freenix03/full_papers/gruenbacher/gruenbacher.ps`.

References

[GWS94] Simson Garfinkel, Daniel Weise, and Steven Strassmann, editors. *The Unix-Haters Handbook*. IDG Books, Programmers Press, 1994. Available on `http://www.simson.net/ref/ugh.pdf`.

[Her03] Helmut Herold. *Linux-Unix-Systemprogrammierung*. Addison-Wesley, 2003.

[HP06] John L. Hennessy and David A. Patterson. *Computer Architecture*. Academic Press, 4th edition, 2006.

[KH07] Greg Kroah-Hartman. *Linux Kernel in a Nutshell*. O'Reilly, 2007.

[KHCM] Greg Kroah-Hartman, Jonathan Corbet, and Amanda McPherson. *Linux Kernel Development*. Electronic document available on `http://www.linux-foundation.org/publications/linuxkerneldevelopment.php`.

[Knu97] Donald E. Knuth. *Fundamental Algorithms*. Addison-Wesley, 3rd edition, 1997.

[KR88] Brian W. Kernighan and Dennis M. Ritchie. *C Programming Language*. Prentice Hall, 2nd edition, 1988.

[Lov05] Robert Love. *Linux Kernel Development*. Sams, 2005.

[Lov07] Robert Love. *Linux System Programming*. O'Reilly, 2007.

[LSM+01] Sandra Loosemore, Richard M. Stallman, Roland McGrath, Andrew Oram, and Ulrich Drepper. *The GNU C Library Reference Manual*. GNU Project, 2001.

[MBKQ96] Marshall Kirk McKusick, Keith Bostic, Michael J. Karels, and John S. Quarterman. *The Design and Implementation of the 4.4 BSD Operating System*. Addison-Wesley, 1996.

[MD03] Hans-Peter Messmer and Klaus Dembowski. *PC Hardwarebuch*. Addison-Wesley, 2003.

[ME02] David Mosberger and Stephane Eranian. *IA-64 Linux Kernel*. Prentice Hall, 2002.

[Mil] David S. Miller. *Cache and TLB Flushing under Linux*. Electronic document, available in the kernel sources as `Documentation/cachetlb.txt`.

[MM06] Richard McDougall and James Mauro. *Solaris Internals*. Prentice Hall, 2006.

[Moca] Patrick Mochel. *The kobject Infrastructure*. Available in the kernel sources as `Documentation/kobject.txt`.

[Mocb] Patrick Mochel. *The Linux Kernel Device Model*. Electronic document, available in the kernel sources in `Documentation/driver-model/`.

[Nut01] Gary J. Nutt. *Operating Systems: A Modern Perspective*. Addison-Wesley, 2001.

[PH07] David A. Patterson and John L. Hennessy. *Computer Organization and Design*. Morgan Kaufmann, 3rd edition, 2007.

[QK06] Jürgen Quade and Eva-Katharina Kunst. *Linux-Treiber entwickeln*. DPunkt Verlag, 2006.

[Sal94] Peter H. Salus. *A Quarter Century of UNIX*. Addison-Wesley, 1994.

[Sch94] Curt Schimmel. *UNIX Systems for Modern Architectures*. Addison-Wesley, 1994.

[SFS05]   Claudia Salzberg Rodriguez, Gordon Fischer, and Steven Smolski. *The Linux Kernel Primer*. Prentice Hall, 2005.

[SGG07]   Abraham Silberschatz, Peter Bear Galvin, and Peter Gagne. *Operating System Concepts*. John Wiley & Sons, 2007.

[Sin]   Amit Singh. *Max OS X Internals*. Addison-Wesley.

[SR05]   W. Richard Stevens and Stephen A. Rago. *Advanced Programming in the UNIX Environment*. Addison-Wesley, 2nd edition, 2005.

[Sta99]   William Stallings. *Computer Organization and Architecture*. Prentice Hall, 1999.

[Ste94]   W. Richard Stevens. *TCP/IP Illustrated I. The Protocols*. Addison-Wesley, 1994.

[Ste00]   W. Richard Stevens. *Programmieren von UNIX- Netzwerken*. Hanser, 2000.

[Swe06]   Dominic Sweetman. *See MIPS Run*. Morgan Kaufmann, 2006.

[Tan02]   Andrew S. Tanenbaum. *Computer Networks*. Prentice Hall, 2002.

[Tan07]   Andrew S. Tanenbaum. *Modern Operating Systems*. Prentice Hall, 2007.

[TW06]   Andrew S. Tanenbaum and Albert S. Woodhull. *Operating Systems: Design and Implementation*. Prentice Hall, 2006.

[Vah96]   Uresh Vahalia. *Unix Internals*. Prentice Hall, 1996.

[Ven08]   Sreekrishnan Venkateswaran. *Essential Linux Device Drivers*. Prentice Hall, 2008.

[WPR+01]   Klaus Wehrle, Frank Pählke, Hartmut Ritter, Daniel Müller, and Marc Bechler. *Linux Netzwerkarchitektur*. Addison-Wesley, 2001.

[WPR+04]   Klaus Wehrle, Frank Pahlke, Hartmut Ritter, Daniel Müller, and Marc Bechler. *Linux Networking Architecture*. Prentice Hall, 2004.

Index